THE INTERNATIONAL BIBLIOGRAPHY OF POLITICAL SCIENCE

This bibliography, with its sister publications, Anthropology, Economics and Sociology (known together as the *International Bibliography of the Social Sciences* (*IBSS*)) is an essential tool for librarians, academics and researchers wishing to keep up to date with the published literature in the social sciences.

IBSS lists journal articles and monographs from all over the world and in over 70 languages, all with English title translations where needed.

From 1991, users already familiar with the bibliography will notice major improvements in contents and currency. There is greater coverage of monographs as well as journals, with continued emphasis on international publications, especially those from the developing world and Eastern Europe. Indexing techniques have been refined: *IBSS* now offers more specific subject and geographical indexes together with an author index. A subject index in French continues to be provided.

Prepared until 1989 at the Fondation nationale des sciences politiques in Paris, *IBSS* is now compiled and edited by the British Library of Political and Economic Science at the London School of Economics. The International Committee for Social Science Information and Documentation and UNESCO continue to support the publication. The new *International Bibliography* not only maintains its traditional extensive coverage of periodical literature, but considerably extends its coverage of monographic material by incorporating most of that which would previously have been included in the *London Bibliography of the Social Sciences*, publication of which has now been discontinued.

Also available from Routledge

Copies of the *International Bibliography of the Social Sciences* for previous years.

Thematic Lists of Descriptors. Four subject volumes published in 1989, following the classification and index terms of the relevant volume of the *IBSS*.

Copies of the *London Bibliography of the Social Sciences* for previous years are available from Schmidt Periodicals, Dettendorf, D-8201 Bad Feilnbach 2, Germany.

INTERNATIONAL BIBLIOGRAPHY OF THE SOCIAL SCIENCES

BIBLIOGRAPHIE INTERNATIONALE DES SCIENCES SOCIALES

published annually in four parts since 1961: UNESCO, Paris
publiée chaque année en quatre parties depuis 1961 : UNESCO, Paris

International bibliography of sociology / Bibliographie internationale de sociologie
[red cover / couverture rouge] Vol.1:1951 (publ. 1952)

International bibliography of political science / Bibliographie internationale de science politique [grey cover / couverture grise] Vol.1:1952 (publ. 1954)

International bibliography of economics / Bibliographie internationale de sciences économiques
[yellow cover / couverture jaune] Vol.1:1952 (publ. 1955)

International bibliography of anthropology / Bibliographie internationale d'anthropologie
[green cover / couverture verte] Vol.1:1955 (publ. 1958)

Prepared by

THE BRITISH LIBRARY OF POLITICAL AND ECONOMIC SCIENCE

with the support of the International Committee for Social Science Information
and Documentation with the assistance of UNESCO

Editor
Jean Sykes
Librarian, British Library of Political and Economic Science

Editorial Manager
Rebecca Ursell

Assistant Editorial Manager
Thomas Carter

Database Design
Robert H. Browne

Editorial Assistants
Typhaine de Borne de Grandpre Julian Krause Luna Glucksberg
Marie Lagerwall Glenn Leihner-Guarin Dimitri Papadimitriou
Juana Schlenker Anne Schumann Jessica Tipton Monia Wadham

INTERNATIONAL BIBLIOGRAPHY OF THE SOCIAL SCIENCES

2005

INTERNATIONAL BIBLIOGRAPHY OF POLITICAL SCIENCE

VOLUME LIV

BIBLIOGRAPHIE INTERNATIONALE DES SCIENCES SOCIALES

BIBLIOGRAPHIE INTERNATIONALE DE SCIENCE POLITIQUE

International Bibliography
of the Social Sciences

Prepared with the support of the International Committee for Social Science Information and Documentation with the assistance of UNESCO

Établie avec le concours du Comité international pour l'information et la documentation en sciences sociales avec l'assistance de l'UNESCO

Routledge
Taylor & Francis Group

LONDON AND NEW YORK

First published in 2007 by
Routledge
(on behalf of the British Library of Political and Economic Science)

2 Park Square, Milton Park
Abingdon, Oxon OX14 4RN
&
270 Madison Ave.
New York NY 10016

Routledge is an imprint of the Taylor & Francis Group

© 2007 British Library of Political and Economic Science

Printed in Great Britain by
Cromwell Press, Trowbridge, Wiltshire

British Library Cataloguing in Publication Data

A CIP catalogue record for this book is available from the British Library.
ISBN 0-415-41717-1
ISSN 0085-2074

Editorial correspondence should be sent to:

International Bibliography of the Social Sciences
British Library of Political and Economic Science
London School of Economics
10 Portugal Street
London WC2A 2HD
United Kingdom

Telephone: (UK) 020-7955-7455
Fax: (UK) 020-7955-6923
email: ibss@lse.ac.uk
http://www.ibss.ac.uk

CONTENTS

INTERNATIONAL COMMITTEE FOR SOCIAL SCIENCE INFORMATION AND DOCUMENTATION

LE COMITÉ INTERNATIONAL POUR L'INFORMATION ET LA DOCUMENTATION EN SCIENCES SOCIALES

Krishna G. Tyagi, National Social Science Documentation Centre, New Delhi (President)

Arnaud Marks, SWIDOC/KNAW, Amsterdam (Secretary General)

ACKNOWLEDGEMENTS

The Editor would like to thank the members of the International Committee, and all those who have contributed to the production of these volumes, particularly: Bronisława Jaworska of the Centre for Ethnographic Documentation and Information, Polish Ethnological Society; Kaarlo Mäkelä of Eduskunnan Kirjasto, the Library of Parliament at Helsinki; Dr Csaba Nagy of the Library of the Hungarian Parliament, Budapest; Ekkehart Seusing of the Zentralbibliothek der Wirtschaftswissenschaften, Bibliothek des Instituts für Weltwirtschaft, Kiel; and Yusuke Iijima and the Database Committee of the Japan Sociological Society.

PREFACE

The **International Bibliography of the Social Sciences** is an annual four volume publication covering Economics, Political Science, Sociology and Social and Cultural Anthropology. It is compiled by the British Library of Political and Economic Science under the auspices of the International Committee for Social Science Information and Documentation. Until recently UNESCO gave financial support for the preparation of the IBSS volumes, but in consultation with the ICSSD it was decided that UNESCO's support should be transferred to the distribution of the IBSS volumes. This has greatly benefited a number of information and documentation centres in developing countries.

Some 100,000 articles (from over 2,700 journals) and 20,000 books are scanned each year in the process of compiling the **International Bibliography**. Coverage is international with publications in over 70 languages from more than 60 countries. Titles are given in their original language and in English translation.

The selection policy (criteria appear on page ix) is designed to provide a tool for retrospective search rather than current awareness. Each volume represents the most significant new material published in that discipline in a given year.

With the increase in interdisciplinary material published in the social sciences, some items will be listed in more than one of the four volumes. It is nonetheless advisable to check other disciplines in the series to avoid missing relevant items which may for some reason be cited in only one volume.

Production of the **International Bibliography** is computerized. The database from which it is extracted is also available online and on CD-ROM, providing access to a broader range of material than is cited in these volumes. Please contact IBSS for further details.

PRÉFACE

La **Bibliographie internationale des sciences sociales** est un ouvrage annuel en 4 volumes couvrant les sciences économiques, la science politique, la sociologie et l'anthropologie. Elle est préparée par la British Library of Political and Economic Science sous les auspices du Comité international pour l'information et la documentation en sciences sociales. Jusqu'à récemment, l'assistance financière de l'UNESCO fut consacrée à la préparation des volumes de la Bibliographie internationale des sciences sociales. Mais en consultation avec le CIDSS, il a été décidé de transférer cette assistance financière à la distribution de la BISS, ce dont bénéficient un certain nombre de centres d'information et de documentation dans les pays en voie de développement.

Chaque année, quelques 100 000 articles (provenant de 2 700 revues) et 20 000 livres sont analysés et indexés en vue de la préparation de la **Bibliographie internationale**. Il s'agit d'une bibliographie véritablement internationale puisqu'elle comprend des publications en plus de 70 langues, provenant de plus de 60 pays. Les titres sont présentés dans la langue originale avec une traduction en anglais.

La politique de sélection des références bibliographiques a été conçue pour fournir un instrument de recherche retrospective plutôt qu'un service d'information courante. Chaque volume présente les publications les plus pertinentes parues dans cette discipline au cours d'une année donnée.

Du fait du nombre croissant de publications de nature interdisciplinaire dans les sciences sociales, certaines références peuvent apparaître dans plus d'un des 4 volumes. Il est cependant conseillé de se reporter aux autres volumes de la série, dans le cas où des références importantes ne figureraient que dans un seul volume.

La préparation de la **Bibliographie internationale** est informatisée. La base de données dont elle est issue est aussi disponible en ligne et sur CD-ROM, donnant accès à une plus large sélection de publications que celles citées dans ces volumes. Veuillez contacter la BISS pour plus d'informations.

SELECTION CRITERIA

1. Subject.

Documents relevant to political science.

2. Nature and form.

Publications of known authorship and lasting significance to political science, whether in serial or monographic form, typically works with a theoretical component intending to communicate new knowledge, new ideas or making use of new materials.

Previously published materials in all formats are omitted, including most translations. Also excluded are textbooks, materials from newspapers or news magazines, popular or purely informative papers, presentations of predominantly primary data and legislative or judicial texts and items of parochial relevance only.

LIST OF PERIODICALS CONSULTED

LISTE DES PERIODIQUES CONSULTÉS

4 pages. (1251-8107). Noisy-le-Grand.

A contrario. Lausanne.

Abacus: Journal of accounting, finance and business studies. (0001-3072). Oxford.

Academy of Management executive. Ada OH.

Academy of Management journal. (0001-4273). Briarcliff Manor NJ.

Academy of Management review. (0363-7425). Ada OH.

Acadiensis: Journal of the history of the Atlantic Region. (0044-5851). Fredericton NJ.

ACCOMEX Actualités du commerce extérieur. (0753-4981). Paris.

Accounting and business research. (0001-4788). London.

Accounting horizons. (0888-7993). Sarasota FL.

Accounting review. (0001-4826). Sarasota FL.

Accounting, auditing and accountability journal. (0951-3574). Bradford.

Accounting, business and financial history. (0958-5206). Abingdon.

Accounting, organizations and society. (0361-3682). Oxford.

Acta asiatica. (0567-7254). Tokyo.

Acta ethnographica hungarica. (1216-9803). Budapest.

Acta geographica. Paris.

Acta Histriae. (1318-0185). Koper.

Acta humana. (0866-6628). Budapest.

Acta juridica hungarica. (1216-2574). Budapest.

Acta oeconomica. (0001-6373). Budapest.

Acta orientalia. (0001-6438). Copenhagen.

Acta politica. (0001-6810). Basingstoke.

Acta scansenologica. (0208-8053). Sanok.

Acta slavica iaponica. Hokkaido.

Acta sociologica [Mexico]. (0186-6028). Mexico City.

Acta sociologica [Norway]. (0001-6993). Oslo.

Acta Universitatis Łódziensis: Folia oeconomica. (0208-6018). Łódz.

Actes de la recherche en sciences sociales. (0335-5322). Paris.

Action nationale. (0001-7469). Montreal.

Action research. (1476-7503). London.

Actualité économique. (0001-771X). Montreal.

Actualité juridique: droit administratif. (0001-7728). Paris.

Actuel Marx. (0994-4524). Paris.

Addiction. (0965-2140). Abingdon.

Administration [Dublin]. (0001-8325). Dublin.

Administration [Paris]. (0223-5439). Paris.

Administration and society. (0095-3997). Thousand Oaks CA.

Administrative science quarterly. (0001-8392). Ithaca NY.

Affari sociali internazionali. (0390-1181). Milan.

Africa [Rome]. (0001-9747). Rome.

Africa development = Afrique & développement. (0850-3907). Dakar.

Africa insight. (0256-2804). Pretoria.
Africa quarterly. (0001-9828). New Delhi.
Africa: Journal of the International African Institute. (0001-9720). London.
African affairs. (0001-9909). Oxford.
African and Asian studies. (1569-2094). Leiden.
African arts. (0001-9933). Los Angeles CA.
African economic history. (0145-2258). Madison WI.
African finance journal. (1605-9786). Belleville.
African human rights law journal. (1609-073X). Pretoria.
African identities. (1472-5843). Abingdon.
African journal of international and comparative law = Revue africaine de droit international et
    comparé. (0954-8890). London.
African studies. (0002-0184). Witwatersrand.
African studies review. (0002-0206). New Brunswick NJ.
Africana. (0871-2336). Porto.
Africana marburgensia. (0174-5603). Berlin.
Afrika Spectrum. (0002-0397). Hamburg.
Afrika Zamani: An annual journal of African history. (0850-3079). Dakar.
Afrique 2000. (1017-0952). Brussels.
Afrique contemporaine. (0002-0478). Paris.
Afrique politique. Paris.
Ageing and society. (0144-686X). Cambridge.
Agenda. (1013-0950). Dalbridge.
Agir. Paris.
Agrekon. (0303-1853). Pretoria.
Agricultural history. (0002-1482). Berkeley CA.
AIDS care. (0954-0121). Abingdon.
Aim Explore. (0973-0001). Ghaziabad.
Akdeniz IIBF dergisi. (1302-9975). Antalya.
Al-Abhath. (0002-3973). Beirut.
Al-Qanṭara. (0211-3589). Madrid.
Aldea Mundo. (1316-6727). San Cristobal.
Aletheia. (1413-0394). Canoas.
Allemagne d'aujourd'hui. (0002-5712). Villeneuve d'Ascq.
Allgemeines statistisches Archiv. (0002-6018). Heidelberg.
Alternatives. (0304-3754). Boulder CO.
Alternatives économiques. (0247-3739). Dijon.
Alternatives internationales. Paris.
Alternatives non violentes. (0223-5498). Rouen.
Alternatives sud. Louvain-la-Neuve.
Ambiente & sociedade. (1414-753X). Campinas.
América indígena. (0002-7081). Mexico City.
American anthropologist. (0002-7294). Arlington VA.
American behavioral scientist. (0002-7642). Thousand Oaks CA.
American economic review. (0002-8282). Nashville TN.
American ethnologist. (0094-0496). Arlington VA.
American historical review. (0002-8762). Washington DC.
American journal of agricultural economics. (0002-9092). Ames IA.
American journal of comparative law. (0002-919X). Berkeley CA.
American journal of economics and sociology. (0002-9246). New York NY.
American journal of international law. (0002-9300). Washington DC.

American journal of Islamic social sciences. (0742-6763). Herndon VA.
American journal of orthopsychiatry. (0002-9432). New York NY.
American journal of physical anthropology. (0002-9483). New York NY.
American journal of political science. (0092-5853). Oxford.
American journal of primatology. (0275-2565). New York NY.
American journal of sociology. (0002-9602). Chicago IL.
American philosophical quarterly. (0003-0481). Bowling Green OH.
American political science review. (0003-0554). Washington DC.
American politics research. (1532-673X). Thousand Oaks CA.
American psychologist. (0003-066X). Washington DC.
American review of Canadian studies. (0272-2011). Washington DC.
American sociological review. (0003-1224). Washington DC.
American sociologist. (0003-1232). New Brunswick NJ.
Amerindia. (0221-8852). Paris.
Análise social. (0003-2573). Lisbon.
Analyse & Kritik: Zeitschrift für Sozialtheorie. (0171-5860). Stuttgart.
Analyse financière. Paris.
Analyses et documents économiques. (0755-3471). Montreuil.
Anarchist studies. (0967-3393). London.
Anatolian studies. (0066-1546). London.
Annales æquatoria. (0254-4296). Lovenjoel.
Annales d'économie et de statistique. (0769-489X). Paris.
Annales de droit de Louvain. (0770-6472). Louvain.
Annales de géographie. (0003-4010). Paris.
Annales de l'économie publique sociale et coopérative = Annals of public and cooperative economics.
    (1370-4788). Brussels.
Annales de la recherche urbaine. (0180-930X). Cachan.
Annales des mines: Gérer et comprendre. (0295-4397). Paris.
Annales internationales de criminologie = International annals of criminology = Anales internacionales
    de criminología. (0003-4452). Paris.
Annales: Histoire, sciences sociales. (0395-2649). Paris.
Annali della Fondazione Luigi Einaudi. (0531-9870). Turin.
Annali di scienze religiose. Milan.
Annali. Istituto Universitario Orientale. Naples.
Annals of family studies. Tokyo.
Annals of region and community studies. Tokyo.
Annals of regional science. (0570-1864). Berlin.
Annals of the American Academy of Political and Social Science. (0002-7162). Thousand Oaks CA.
Annals of the Association of American Geographers. (0004-5608). Washington DC.
Année sociale. (0066-2380). Brussels.
Année sociologique. (0066-2399). Paris.
Annuaire de l'Afrique du Nord. (0242-7540). Paris.
Annuaire de la Societe Japono-Francais de Sociologie. Tokyo.
Annuaire des pays de l'Ocean indien. (0247-400X). Paris.
Annuaire européen = European yearbook. (0071-3139). Dordrecht.
Annuaire français de droit international. (0066-3085). Paris.
Annuaire français de relations internationales. Paris.
Annual of the Department of Antiquities of Jordan. (0449-1564). Amman.
Annual review of anthropology. (0084-6570). Palo Alto CA.
Annual review of political science. (1094-2939). Palo Alto CA.
Annual review of sociology. (0360-0572). Palo Alto CA.

Anthropological forum. (0066-4677). Abingdon.
Anthropological linguistics. (0003-5483). Bloomington IN.
Anthropological notebooks. (1408-032X). Ljubljana.
Anthropological papers of the American Museum of Natural History. (0065-9452). New York NY.
Anthropological quarterly. (0003-5491). Washington DC.
Anthropological science. (0918-7960). Tokyo.
Anthropological theory. (1463-4996). London.
Anthropologie [Paris]. (0003-5521). Paris.
Anthropologie et sociétés. Quebec.
Anthropologist: International journal of contemporary and applied studies of man. (0972-0073). Delhi.
Anthropology & medicine. (1364-8470). Abingdon.
Anthropology and education quarterly. (0161-7761). Arlington VA.
Anthropology and humanism. (0193-5615). Arlington VA.
Anthropology Southern Africa. (0258-0144). Boordfontein.
Anthropology today. (0268-540X). London.
Anthropos [St. Augustin]. (0257-9774). Sankt Augustin.
Antipode. (0066-4812). Oxford.
Antiquity. (0003-598X). Cambridge.
Antropologia portuguesa. (0870-0990). Coimbra.
Anuario de estudios centroamericanos. (0377-7316). San José.
Anuario de eusko folklore. (0210-7732). San Sebastián.
Anuarul de istorie orală. (1454-4865). Cluj-Napoca.
Applied economics. (0003-6846). Abingdon.
Applied economics letters. (1350-4851). Abingdon.
Applied economics quarterly. (1611-6607). Berlin.
Applied financial economics. (0960-3107). Abingdon.
Applied linguistics. (0142-6001). Oxford.
Après-demain. (0003-7176). Paris
Apuntes. (0252-1865). Lima.
Arab law quarterly. (0268-0556). Leiden.
Arab studies journal. (1083-4753). Washington DC.
Arab world geographer. (1480-6800). Akron OH.
Arabica. (0570-5398). Leiden.
Archaeologia polona. (0066-5924). Warsaw.
Archaeological Dialogue. (1380-2038). Cambridge.
Archaeological papers of the AAA. Arlington VA.
Archaeology in Oceania. (0003-8121). Sydney.
Arche. (0518-2840). Paris.
Archeologia. (0066-605X). Warsaw.
Archeologia polski. (0003-8180). Warsaw.
Archipel. (0044-8613). Paris.
Archiv des öffentlichen Rechts. (0003-8911). Tübingen.
Archiv des Völkerrechts. (0003-892X). Tübingen.
Archiv für Rechts- und Sozialphilosophie = Archives de philosophie du droit et de philosophie sociale = Archives for philosophy of law and social philosophy = Archivo de filosofía jurídica y social. (0001-2343). Stuttgart.
Archiv für Sozialgeschichte. (0066-6505). Bonn.
Archív orientální. (0044-8699). Prague.
Archives de philosophie du droit. (0066-6564). Paris.
Archives de politique criminelle. (0242-5637). Montpellier.
Archives de sciences sociales des religions. (0335-5985). Meudon.

Archives européennes de sociologie = European journal of sociology = Europäisches Archiv für Soziologie. (0003-9756). Cambridge.
Archives of economic history. (1108-7005). Athens.
Archives of suicide research. (1381-1118). Dordrecht.
Archivist = Archiviste. (0705-2855). Ottawa.
Area. (0004-0894). London.
Arena journal. (1320-6567). Fitzroy.
Arena magazine. (1039-1010). Fitzroy.
Arès. (0181-009X). Grenoble.
Argumentation. (0920-427X). Dordrecht.
Armed forces and society. (0095-327X). New Brunswick NJ.
Artha vijñāna. (0971-586X). Pune.
Artibus asiae. (0004-3648). Ascona.
ASEAN economic bulletin. (0217-4472). Singapore.
Asia journal of theology. (0218-0812). Bangalore.
Asia major. (0004-4482). Princeton NJ.
Asia Pacific business review. (1360-2381). London.
Asia Pacific journal of anthropology. (1444-2213). Canberra.
Asia Pacific journal of environmental law. (1385-2140). Sydney.
Asia Pacific journal on environment and development. (1023-7895). Dhaka.
Asia Pacific review. (1343-9006). Tokyo.
Asia Pacific viewpoint. (1360-7456). Carlton South.
Asia-Pacific development journal. (1020-1246). Bangkok.
Asian and Pacific migration journal. (0117-1968). Quezon City.
Asian business and management. (1472-4782). Basingstoke.
Asian culture (Asian-Pacific culture) quarterly. (0378-8911). Taipei.
Asian development review. (0116-1105). Manila.
Asian economic review. (0004-4555). Hyderabad.
Asian ethnicity. (1463-1369). Abingdon.
Asian folklore studies. (0385-2342). Nagoya.
Asian journal of communication. (0129-2986). Singapore.
Asian journal of political science. (0218-5377). Singapore.
Asian journal of public administration. (0259-8272). Hong Kong.
Asian journal of social science. (1568-5314). Leiden.
Asian perspective [S. Korea]. (0258-9184). Seoul.
Asian perspectives [Hawaii]. (0066-8435). Honolulu HI.
Asian profile. (0304-8675). Hong Kong.
Asian studies review. (1035-7823). Sydney.
Asian survey. (0004-4687). Berkeley CA.
Asian thought and society. (0361-3968). New York NY.
Asian-Pacific economic literature. (0818-9935). Oxford.
Atlal: The journal of Saudi Arabian archaeology. Riyadh.
Atlantic studies. (1478-8810). Abingdon.
Aus der Südosteuropa-Forschung. Munich.
Aussenwirtschaft. (0004-8216). Zurich.
Australian Aboriginal studies. (0729-4352). Canberra.
Australian and New Zealand Journal of Criminology. (0004-8658). Bowen Hills.
Australian economic history review. (0004-8992). Oxford.
Australian economic papers. (0004-900X). Adelaide.
Australian economic review. (0004-9018). Oxford.
Australian feminist studies. (0816-4649). Basingstoke.

Australian geographer. (0004-9182). Gladesville.
Australian journal of agricultural and resource economics. (1364-985X). Carlton South.
Australian journal of anthropology. (1035-8811). Sydney.
Australian journal of Chinese affairs. (0156-7365). Canberra.
Australian journal of early childhood. (0312-5033). Canberra.
Australian journal of international affairs. (1035-7718). Canberra.
Australian journal of political science. (1036-1146). Oxford.
Australian journal of politics and history. (0004-9522). Queensland.
Australian journal of public administration. (0313-6647). Sydney.
Australian law journal. (0004-9611). North Ryde NSW.
AWR Bulletin. (0001-2947). Vienna.
Baessler-Archiv: Beiträge zur Völkerkunde. (0005-3856). Berlin.
Balkanologie. (1279-7952). Paris.
Banca Nazionale del Lavoro quarterly review. (0005-4607). Rome.
Bancaria. (0005-4623). Rome.
Bangladesh development studies. (0304-095X). Dhaka.
Bank of England quarterly bulletin. (0005-5166). London.
Banque & droit. (0992-3233). Paris.
Banque et marchés. (1167-4946). Paris.
Banque magazine. Paris
Banquet. (1164-7590). Paris.
BC studies. (0005-2949). Vancouver.
Beiträge zur Japanologie. (0522-6759). Vienna.
Belizean studies. (0250-6831). Belize City.
Benefits: a journal of social security research policy and practice. (0962-7898). Nottingham.
Berkeley journal of sociology. (0067-5830). Berkeley CA.
Berkeley technology law journal. (0885 2715). Berkeley CA.
Berliner indologische Studien. (0935-0004). Reinbek.
Berliner Journal für Soziologie. (0863-1808). Opladen.
Bevolking en gezin. (0772-764X). Brussels.
Biblioteka etnografii polskiej. (0067-7655). Warsaw.
Bijdragen tot de taal-, land- en volkenkunde. (0006-2294). Leiden.
Bilig. (1301-0549). Ankara.
Bioethics. (0269-9702). Oxford.
Biography. (0162-4962). Honolulu HI.
Biométrie humaine et anthropologie. (1279-7863). Paris.
BIOS: Zeitschrift für Biographieforschung, Oral History und Lebensverlaufsanalysen. (0933-5315).
    Wiesbaden.
Biuletyn stowarzyszenia muzeów na wolnym powietrzu w polsce. (1509-2453). Wdzydze.
Blätter der Wohlfahrtspflege: Deutsche Zeitschrift für Sozialarbeit. (0340-8574). Baden-Baden.
Body and society. (1357-034X). London.
Bohemia = Bohemia: Zeitschrift für Geschichte und Kultur der böhmischen Länder. (0523-8587).
    Kirchheim.
Boletim do Museu Paraense Emílio Goeldi: Série antropologia. (0522-7291). Belém.
Boletín de antropología americana. (0252-841X). Mexico City.
Boletin de la Academia Nacional de la Historia. (0325-0482). Buenos Aires.
Boletín. Centro de estudios monetarios latinoamericanos. (0186-7229). Mexico City.
Borneo research bulletin. (0006-7806). Phillips ME.
Borneo review. Sabah.
Botswana notes and records. (0525-5059). Gaborone.
Boundary and security bulletin. (0967-411X). Durham.

British accounting review. (0890-8389). London.
British educational research journal. (0141-1926). Abingdon.
British journal for the history of science. (0007-0874). Cambridge.
British journal of Canadian studies. (0269-9222). London.
British journal of clinical psychology. (0144-6657). Leicester.
British journal of criminology. (0007-0955). London.
British journal of developmental psychology. (0261-510X). Leicester.
British journal of educational studies. (0007-1005). Oxford.
British journal of industrial relations. (0007-1080). Oxford.
British journal of management. (1045-3172). Chichester.
British journal of Middle Eastern studies. (1353-0194). Durham.
British journal of political science. (0007-1234). Cambridge.
British journal of politics and international relations. (1369-1481). Oxford.
British journal of psychology. (0007-1269). Leicester.
British journal of social psychology. (0144-6665). Leicester.
British journal of social work. (0045-3102). Oxford.
British journal of sociology. (0007-1315). Oxford.
British journal of sociology of education. (0142-5692). Abingdon.
British year book of international law. (0068-2691). Oxford.
Brookings papers on economic activity. (0007-2303). Washington DC.
Bulgarska etnologiia. (1310-5213). Sofia.
Bulletin d'études indiennes. (0761-3156). Paris.
Bulletin de l'Association de géographes français. (0004-5322). Paris.
Bulletin de l'École française d'Extrême-Orient. (0336-1519). Paris.
Bulletin de l'Institut d'histoire du temps présent. (0247-0101). Paris.
Bulletin de l'Institut français d'études andines. Lima.
Bulletin de l'Institut Pierre Renouvin. (1276-8944).
Bulletin de la Société des études océaniennes. (0373-8957). Papeete.
Bulletin for international taxation. (0007-4624). Amsterdam.
Bulletin of comparative labour relations. Dordrecht.
Bulletin of economic research. (0307-3378). Oxford.
Bulletin of Indonesian economic studies. (0007-4918). Canberra.
Bulletin of Latin American research. (0261-3050). Amsterdam.
Bulletin of the American Schools of Oriental Research. (0003-097X). Baltimore MD.
Bulletin of the Indian Institute of History of Medicine. (0304-9558). New Delhi.
Bulletin of the International Committee on Urgent Anthropological and Ethnological Research. (0538-5865). Vienna.
Bulletin of the School of Oriental and African Studies. (0041-977X). London.
Bulletin of the World Health Organization: the international journal of public health. (0042-9686). Geneva.
Bulletin of Tibetology. (0525-1516). Gangtok.
Business economist. (0306-5049). Watford.
Business ethics quarterly. (1052-150X). Charlottesville VA.
Business ethics: a European review. (0962-8770). Oxford.
Business history. (0007-6791). Ilford.
Business history review. (0007-6805). Boston MA.
Business law international. (1467-632X). London.
Business strategy and the environment. (0964-4733). Chichester.
Cadres CFDT. (0398-3145).
Cahier d'histoire immédiate. Toulouse.
Cahiers africains = Afrika studies. (1021-9994). Tervuren.

Cahiers africains d'administration publique = African administrative studies. (0007-9588). Tangiers.
Cahiers d'économie et sociologie rurales. (0755-9208). Ivry.
Cahiers d'études africaines. (0008-0055). Paris.
Cahiers d'outre-mer. (0373-5834). Bordeaux.
Cahiers de droit européen. (0007-9758).
Cahiers de l'ISSP. Neuchâtel.
Cahiers de l'orient. (0767-6468). Paris.
Cahiers de la fonction publique et de l'administration. (0753-4418). Paris.
Cahiers de la Fondation. (0983-1851).
Cahiers de la Fondation Charles de Gaulle. (1266-2437).
Cahiers de sociologie économique et culturelle. (0761-9871). Le Havre.
Cahiers de sociologie et de démographie médicales. (0007-9995). Paris.
Cahiers de Tunisie. (0008-0012). Tunis.
Cahiers des Amériques latines. (1141-7161). Paris.
Cahiers du genre. (1298-6046). Paris.
Cahiers du Japon. (0388-113X). Tokyo.
Cahiers du journalisme. (1280-0082). Lille.
Cahiers du monde russe. (1252-6576). Paris.
Cahiers économiques de Bretagne. (0154-8557).
Cahiers français. (0008-0217).
Cahiers internationaux de sociologie. (0008-0276). Paris.
Cahiers pédagogiques. (0008-042X). Paris.
Cahiers québécois de démographie. (0380-1721). Montréal.
Caieţele tranziţiei. (1453-3561). Cluj-Napoca.
Cakalele: Maluku research journal. (1053-2285). Honolulu HI.
California management review. (0008-1256). Berkeley CA.
Cambridge anthropology. (0305-7674). Cambridge.
Cambridge archaeological journal. (0959-7743). Cambridge.
Cambridge journal of economics. (0309-166X). London.
Cambridge law journal. (0008-1973). Cambridge.
Cambridge review of international affairs. (0955-7571). Cambridge.
Canadian ethnic studies = Études ethniques au Canada. (0008-3496). Montréal.
Canadian geographer = Géographe canadien. (0008-3658). Montreal.
Canadian historical review. (0008-3755). Toronto.
Canadian journal of African studies = Revue canadienne des études africaines. (0008-3968). Toronto.
Canadian journal of agricultural economics = Revue canadienne d'économie rurale. (0008-3976). Ottawa.
Canadian journal of archaeology = Journal canadien d'archéologie. (0705-2006). Ottawa.
Canadian journal of criminology and criminal justice = Revue canadienne de criminologie et de justice pénale. (0704-9722). Ottawa.
Canadian journal of economics = Revue canadienne d'économique. (0008-4085). Downsview.
Canadian journal of Latin American and Caribbean studies. (0826-3663). Ontario.
Canadian journal of law and society = Revue canadienne droit et société. (0829-3201). Toronto.
Canadian journal of linguistics = Revue canadienne de linguistique. (0008-4131). Toronto.
Canadian journal of philosophy. (0045-5091). Calgary.
Canadian journal of political science = Revue canadienne de science politique. (0008-4239). Ottawa.
Canadian journal of sociology = Cahiers canadiens de sociologie. (0318-6431). Edmonton.
Canadian journal of statistics = Revue canadienne de statistiques. (0319-5724). Ottawa.
Canadian journal of women and the law = Revue femmes et droit. (0832-8781). Ontario.
Canadian journal on aging = Revue canadienne du vieillissement. (0714-9808). Ontario.
Canadian modern language review = Revue canadienne des langues vivantes. (0008-4506). Toronto.

Canadian public administration = Administration publique du Canada. (0008-4840). Toronto.
Canadian review of American studies. (0007-7720). Ottawa.
Canadian review of sociology and anthropology = Revue canadienne de sociologie et d'anthropologie. (0008-4948). Montréal.
Canadian review of studies in nationalism = Revue canadienne des études sur le nationalisme. (0317-7904). Charlottetown.
Canadian Slavonic papers. (0008-5006). Edmonton.
Canadian yearbook of international law = Annuaire canadien de droit international. (0069-0058). Vancouver.
Capital. (1162-6704). Paris.
Capital and class. (0309-8168). London.
Capitalism, nature, socialism. (1045-5752). Abingdon.
Caravelle. (1147-6753). Toulouse.
Caribbean studies = Estudios del Caribe = Études des Caraïbes. (0008-6533). Puerto Rico.
Časopis za suvremenu povijest. (0590-9597). Zagreb.
Catholica. (0295-2238). Paris.
Cato journal. (0273-3072). Washington DC.
CEMOTI: Cahiers d'études sur la Méditerranée orientale et le monde turco-iranien. (0764-9878). Paris.
Central Asia and the Caucasus: journal of social and political studies. (1404-6091). Luleå.
Central Asian survey. (0263-4937). Abingdon.
Central Asiatic journal. (0008-9192). Wiesbaden.
Central banking. (0960-6319). London.
Central Europe. (1479-0963). London.
Central European history. (0008-9389). Boston MA.
Central European political science review. (1586-4197). Budapest.
Centro: Journal of the Center of Puerto Rican Studies. (1538-6279). New York.
CEPAL review. (0251-2920). Santiago.
CESifo economic studies. (1610-241X). Munich.
Česko-slovenská historická ročenka. Brno.
Český lid: Etnologický časopis. (0009-0794). Prague.
Challenge. (0577-5132). Armonk NY.
Chelovek i trud. (0132-1552). Moscow.
Child care in practice. (1357-5279). Belfast.
Child development. (0009-3920). Chicago IL.
Child welfare. (0009-4021). Washington DC.
Childhood. (0907-5682). London.
Children and society. (0951-0605). London.
China city planning review. (1002-8447). Beijing.
China information. (0920-203X). Leiden.
China journal. (1324-9347). Canberra.
China quarterly. (0305-7410). London.
China report. (0009-4455). New Delhi.
China review international. (1069-5834). Honolulu HI.
China: an international journal. (0219-7472). Singapore.
Chinese economy. (0009-4552). Armonk NY.
Chinese sociology and anthropology. (0009-4625). Armonk NY.
Ching feng. (0009-4668). Hong Kong.
Chungara. (0717-7356). Arica.
Ciclos. (0327-4063). Buenos Aires.
Ciencia ergo sum: revista científica multidisciplinaria de la Universidad Autónoma del Estado de México. (1405-0269). Toluca.

CIRIEC-España: Revista de economía pública, social y cooperativa. (0213-8093). Valencia.
Cités: philosophie politique histoire. (1299-5495). Paris.
Cities. (0264-2751). London.
Citizenship studies. (1362-1025). Abingdon.
City. (1360-4813). London.
City & society. (0893-0465). Arlington VA.
Civil wars. (1369-8249). London.
Civilisations. (0009-8140). Brussels.
Climate policy. (1469-3062). London.
CM: Cahiers marxistes. (0591-0633). Brussels.
Cogniție, creier, comportament. (1224-8398). Cluj-Napoca.
Cognition. (0010-0277). Amsterdam.
Cognitive linguistics. (0936-5907). Berlin.
Cognitive science. (0364-0213). Norwood NJ.
Cold War history. (1468-2745). Ilford.
Collection. Purusartha. (0339-1744). Paris.
Collegium antropologicum. (0350-6134). Zagreb.
Colloquia: Journal of Central European history. (1223-5261). Cluj-Napoca.
Colombia internacional. (0121-5612). Bogota.
Colombian economic journal. (1692-3065). Bogotá.
Columbia journal of European law. (1076-6715). New York.
Columbia journal of transnational law. (0010-1931). New York NY.
Columbia law review. (0010-1958). New York NY.
Comercio exterior. (0185-0601). Mexico City.
Commentaire. (0180-8214). Paris.
Commonwealth and comparative politics. (1466-2043). Ilford.
Commonwealth: essays and studies. Dijon.
Communication et langages. (0336-1500). Ivry sur Seine.
Communication et organisation. (1168-5549). Talence.
Communication review. (1071-4421). New York NY.
Communication theory. (1050-3293). Cary NC.
Communications. (0751-3496). Paris.
Communications & stratégies. Montpellier.
Communisme. (2209-7007). Paris.
Communist and post-communist studies. (0967-067X). Exeter.
Community development journal. (0010-3802). Oxford.
Comparative and international law journal of Southern Africa. (0010-4051). Pretoria.
Comparative economic studies. (0888-7233). New York NY.
Comparative education. (0305-0068). Abingdon.
Comparative European politics. (1472-4790). Basingstoke.
Comparative political studies. (0010-4140). Thousand Oaks CA.
Comparative politics. (0010-4159). New York NY.
Comparative social research. (0195-6310). Greenwich CT.
Comparative studies in society and history. (0010-4175). New York NY.
Comparative studies of South Asia, Africa and the Middle East. (1089-201X). Durham NC.
Competition & change. (1024-5294). Abingdon.
Complutum. (1131-6993). Madrid.
Comprehensive urban studies. (0386-3506). Tokyo.
Comprendre: Revue de philosophie et de sciences sociales. (1626-4207). Paris.
Computational and mathematical organization theory. (1381-298X). Dordrecht.
Computational economics. (0927-7099). Dordrecht.

Comunicación y sociedad. (0214-0039). Navarre.
Comunicazioni sociali: Rivista di media, spettacolo e studi culturali. (0392-8667). Milan.
Comunità internazionale. (0010-5066). Padua.
Conflict resolution quarterly. (1536-5581). San Francisco CA.
Confluences en Méditerranée. (1148-2664). Paris.
Congo-Afrique. (0049-8513). Kinshasa.
Conjoncture. (0338-9162). Paris.
Conservation and management of archaeological sites. (1350-5033). London.
Constitutional political economy. (1043-4062). Dordrecht.
Consumption markets culture. (1025-3866). Abingdon.
Contemporary accounting research. (0823-9150). Toronto.
Contemporary British history. (1361-9462). Ilford.
Contemporary economic policy. (1074-3529). Oxford.
Contemporary economic problems. (0732-4308). Washington DC.
Contemporary justice review. (1028-2580). Abingdon.
Contemporary Pacific. (1043-898X). Honolulu HI.
Contemporary policy issues. (0735-0007). Huntington Beach CA.
Contemporary political theory. (1470-8914). Basingstoke.
Contemporary politics. (1356-9775). Abingdon.
Contemporary security policy. (1352-3260). Ilford.
Contemporary South Asia. (0958-4935). Abingdon.
Contemporary Southeast Asia: A journal of international and strategic affairs. (0129-797X). Singapore.
Continuity and change. (0268-4160). Cambridge.
Continuum: Journal of media & cultural studies. (1030-4312). Abingdon.
Contradictions. (0770-8521). Brussels.
Contretemps. (1633-597X). Paris.
Contributions to Indian sociology. (0069-9667). New Delhi.
Contributions to Nepalese studies. (0376-7574). Kirtipur.
Contributions to political economy. (0277-5921). London.
Convergencia: Revista de ciencias sociales. (1405-1435). Toluca.
Cooperation and conflict. (0010-8367). London.
Corporate governance: an international review. (0964-8410). Oxford.
Corporate ownership & control. (1727-9232). Sumy.
Cosmopolitiques. Paris.
Courrier des pays de l'Est. (0590-0239). Paris.
Courrier hebdomadaire du Centre de recherche et d'information sociopolitiques. (0009-0360). Brussels.
Coyuntura económica. (0120-3576). Bogota.
Coyuntura social. (0121-2532). Bogota.
Crime and delinquency. (0011-1287). Thousand Oaks CA.
Crime, law and social change. (0925-4994). Dordrecht.
Criminal justice studies. (1478-601X). Abingdon.
Criminologie. (0316-0041). Montréal.
Criminology. (0011-1384). Columbus OH.
Criminology and criminal justice: the international journal of policy and practice. (1748-8958). London.
Critica marxista. (0011-152X). Rome.
Critica sociologica. (0011-1546). Rome.
Critical Asian studies. (1467-2715). Abingdon.
Critical discourse studies. (1740-5904). Abingdon.
Critical perspectives on accounting. (1045-2354). London.
Critical review. (0891-3811). Chicago IL.
Critical social policy. (0261-0183). London.

Critical sociology. (0896-9205). Eugene OR.
Critical studies in media communication. (0739-3180). Abingdon.
Critique. Paris.
Critique internationale. Paris.
Critique of anthropology. (0308-275X). London.
Croatian economic survey. (1330-4860). Zagreb.
Cross-cultural research. (1069-3971). Thousand Oaks CA.
Crossings. (1327-0087). Queensland.
Crossroads. (0741-2037). DeKalb IL.
Cuadernos americanos. (0185-156X). Mexico City.
Cuadernos de administracion. (0120-3592). Bogota.
Cuadernos de economia [Bogotá]. (0121-4772). Bogotá.
Cuadernos de economia: Latin American journal of economics. (0717-6821). Santiago.
Cuadernos de nuestra América. Havana.
Cuestiones políticas. (0798-1406). Maracaibo.
Cultural anthropology. (0886-7356). Arlington VA.
Cultural critique. (0882-4371). Minneapolis.
Cultural dynamics. (0921-3740). London.
Cultural geographies. (1474-4740). London.
Cultural politics. (1743-2197). Oxford.
Cultural studies. (0950-2386). Abingdon.
Cultural studies - critical methodologies. (1532-7086). Thousand Oaks CA.
Culture & psychology. (1354-067X). London.
Culture and agriculture. (1048-4876). Arlington VA.
Culture and organization. (1475-9551). Abingdon.
Culture and religion. (1475-5610). Abingdon.
Culture, health and sexuality. (1369-1058). London.
Culture, medicine and psychiatry. (0165-005X). New York.
Culture, theory and critique. (1473-5784). Abingdon.
Current anthropology. (0011-3204). Washington DC.
Current history. (0011-3530). Philadelphia PA.
Current issues in language and society. (1352-0520). Clevedon.
Current politics and economics of Europe. (1057-2309). Huntington NY.
Current research on peace and violence. (0356-7893). Tampere.
Current sociology. (0011-3921). London.
Cyprus review. (1015-2881). Nicosia.
Czech sociological review. (1210-3861). Prague.
Człowiek i światopogląd. Łodz.
Dædalus. (0011-5266). Cambridge MA.
De Economist. (0013-063X). Dordrecht.
Débat. (0246-2346). Paris.
Debatte: Review of contemporary German affairs. (0965-156X). Abingdon.
Dedans dehors. Paris.
Defence and peace economics. (1024-2694). Abingdon.
Défense nationale. (0336-1489). Paris.
Dela. (0354-0596). Ljubljana.
Delhi law review. Delhi.
Democracy & nature. (1085-5661). Basingstoke.
Democratization. (1351-0347). Ilford.
Demográfia. (0011-8249). Budapest.
Demografie. (0011-8265). Prague.

Demography. (0070-3370). Washington DC.
Der Staat: Zeitschrift für Staatslehre und Verfassungsgeschichte, deutsches und europäisches öffentliches Recht. (0038-884X). Berlin.
Desafíos. (0124-4035). Bogotá.
Desarrollo económico. (0046-001X). Buenos Aires.
Desarrollo y sociedad. (0120-3584). Bogota.
Deutsche Zeitschrift für Kommunalwissenschaften. (1617-8203). Stuttgart.
Deutschland Archiv: Zeitschrift für das vereinigte Deutschland. (0012-1428). Opladen.
Developing economies. (0012-1533). Tokyo.
Developing world bioethics. (1471-8731). Oxford.
Development. (1011-6370). Rome.
Development & socio-economic progress. Cairo.
Development and change. (0012-155X). London.
Development and finance = Fejlesztés és finanszírozás: Quarterly Hungarian economic review. (1589-3820). Budapest.
Development bulletin. (1035-1132). Canberra.
Development dialogue. (0345-2328). Uppsala.
Development in practice. (0961-4524). Oxford.
Development policy review. (0950-6764). Oxford.
Development Southern Africa. (0376-835X). Halfway House.
Developmental psychology. (0012-1649). Washington DC.
Déviance et société. (0378-7931). Louvain-la-Neuve.
Dialectical anthropology. (0304-4092). Dordrecht.
Diaspora. (1044-2057). Toronto.
Die alte Stadt: Vierteljahreszeitschrift für Stadtgeschichte, Soziologie, Denkmalpflege und Stadtentwicklung. (0170-9364). Stuttgart.
Die Friedens-Warte: Journal of international peace and organization. (0340-0255). Berlin.
Die Verwaltung. (0042-4498). Berlin.
Die Welt des Islams. (0043-2539). Leiden.
Die Welt des Orients. (0043-2547). Göttingen.
Differences: a journal of feminist cultural studies. (1040-7391). Bloomington IN.
Diplomacy and statecraft. (0959-2296). Ilford.
Diplomatic history. (0145-2096). Wilmington, DE.
Dirasat: Administrative Sciences. (1026-373X). Amman.
Dirasat: Agricultural sciences. (1026-3764). Amman.
Dirasat: Educational Sciences. (1026-3713). Amman.
Dirasat: Human and Social Sciences. (1026-3721). Amman.
Dirasat: Shari'a and law sciences. (1026-3748). Amman.
Dirasat: Humanities. (0255-8033). Amman.
Disability and society. (0968-7599). Abingdon.
Disarmament forum = Forum du désarmement. (1020-7287). Geneva.
Disasters: Journal of disaster studies, policy and management. (0361-3666). Oxford.
Discourse & society. (0957-9265). London.
Discourse studies. (1461-4456). London.
Discourse: Journal for theoretical studies in media and culture. (1522-5321). Detroit MI.
Diskurs: Studien zu Kindheit, Jugend, Familie und Gesellschaft. (0937-9614). Wiesbaden.
Document numérique. (1279-5127). Paris.
Documents. (0151-0827). Paris.
Dokumente. (0012-5172). Bonn.
Dor ledor. Tel Aviv.
Dossiers du "Canard". Paris.

Dossiers solidarité et santé. Paris.
Droit social. (0012-6438). Paris.
Društvena Istraživanja. (1330-0288). Zagreb.
Dve domovini = Two homelands. (0353-6777). Ljubljana.
Dzieje Najnowsze. (0419-8824). Warsaw.
Early child development and care. (0300-4430). Abingdon.
East Asian review. Seoul.
East European Jewish affairs. (1350-1674). London.
East European politics and societies. (0888-3254). Berkeley CA.
East European quarterly. (0012-8449). Boulder CO.
Ebisu. (1253-8590). Tokyo.
Ecological economics. (0921-8009). Amsterdam.
Ecologie politique. (1166-3030). Paris.
Econometric reviews. (0747-4938). New York NY.
Econometric theory. (0266-4666). New York NY.
Econometrica. (0012-9682). Evanston IL.
Econometrics journal. (1368-4221). Oxford.
Economia & lavoro. (0012-978X). Rome.
Economia [Lisbon]. (0870-3531). Lisbon.
Economia chilena. (0717-3830). Santiago.
Economia e banca. (0393-9243). Trento.
Economia internazionale. (0012-981X). Genoa.
Economía y administración. (0716-0100). Concepción.
Economia y desarrollo. (0252-8584). Havana.
Economic affairs [Calcutta]. (0424-2513). Calcutta.
Economic and business review for Central and South-Eastern Europe. (1580-0466). Ljubljana.
Economic and industrial democracy. (0143-831X). London.
Economic and social review. (0012-9984). Dublin.
Economic bulletin. Norges bank. (0029-1676). Oslo.
Economic development and cultural change. (0013-0079). Chicago IL.
Economic development quarterly. (0891-2424). Thousand Oaks CA.
Economic geography. (0013-0095). Worcester MA.
Economic history review. (0013-0117). Oxford.
Economic inquiry. (0095-2583). Oxford.
Economic issues. (1363-7029). Stoke-on-Trent.
Economic journal. (0013-0133). Oxford.
Economic modelling. (0264-9993). Guildford.
Economic papers [Australia]. (0812-0439). East Hawthorn.
Economic papers. Bank of Korea. (1226-7589). Seoul.
Economic policy. (0266-4658). Oxford.
Economic record. (0013-0249). Sydney.
Economic roundup. Canberra.
Economic systems. (0939-3625). Heidelberg.
Economic systems research. (0953-5314). Abingdon.
Economic theory. (0938-2259). Berlin.
Economica [London]. (0013-0427). London.
Economics and philosophy. (0266-2671). New York NY.
Economics and politics. (0954-1985). Oxford.
Economics letters. (0165-1765). Amsterdam.
Economics of innovation & new technology. (1043-8599). Abingdon.
Economics of planning. (0013-0451). Dordrecht.

Economics of transition. (0967-0750). Oxford.
Économie & prévision. (0249-4744). Paris.
Économie appliquée. (0013-0494). Paris.
Économie et humanisme. (0245-9132). Lyon.
Économie et statistique. (0336-1454). Paris.
Économie internationale. (1240-8093). Paris.
Économies et sociétés. (0013-0567). Paris.
Economisch en sociaal tijdschrift. (0013-0575). Antwerp.
Economy and society. (0308-5147). Abingdon.
Education and urban society. (0013-1245). Thousand Oaks CA.
Education economics. (0964-5292). Abingdon.
Educational philosophy and theory. (0013-1857). Oxford.
Educational research. (0013-1881). Abingdon.
Educational review. (0013-1911). Abingdon.
Educational studies. (0305-5698). Abingdon.
Ekistics. (0013-2942). Athens.
Ekonomia. (1025-5508). Nicosia.
Ekonomika. (1392-1258). Vilnius.
Ekonomika Ukraïni. (0131-775X). Kiev.
Ekonomisk debatt. (0345-2646). Stockholm.
Ekonomist. (0869-4672). Moscow.
Ekonomista. (0013-3205). Warsaw.
Ekonomski pregled. (0424-7558). Zagreb.
Electoral studies. (0261-3794). Kidlington.
Electronic journal of contemporary Japanese studies. (1476-9158). Sheffield.
Electronic markets: The international journal of electronic commerce & business media. (1019-6781). Abingdon.
Emergences: journal for the study of media and composite cultures. (1045-7224). Basingstoke.
Empirica. (0340-8744). Dordrecht.
Empirical economics. (0377-7332). Heidelberg.
Encounters on education = Encuentros sobre educación = Rencontres sur l'éducation. (1494-4936). Kingston.
Energeia: Revista internacional de filosofia y epistemología de las ciencias económicas. (1666-5732). Buenos Aires.
Energy economics. (0140-9883). Oxford.
Energy policy. (0301-4215). Guildford.
Enfance. (0013-7545). Paris.
English world-wide. (0172-8865). Amsterdam.
Enjeux internationaux. (1379-4205). Brussels.
Enjeux les echos. (1167-2196). Paris.
Ensayos sobre política económica. (0120-4483). Bogota.
Enterprise & society: the international journal of business history. (1467-2227). Oxford.
Entrepreneurship & regional development. (0898-5626). London.
Entrepreneurship, innovation, and change. (1059-0137). New York NY.
Entrepreneurship: Theory and practice. (1042-2587). Waco TX.
Entreprises et histoire. (1161-2770). Paris.
Environment. (0013-9157). Washington DC.
Environment and behavior. (0013-9165). Thousand Oaks CA.
Environment and history. (0967-3407). Strond.
Environment and planning A. (0308-518X). London.
Environment and planning B: Planning and design. (0265-8135). London.

Environment and planning C: Government and policy. (0263-774X). London.
Environment and planning D: Society and space. (0263-7758). London.
Environment and urbanization. (0956-2478). London.
Environment, development and sustainability. (1387-585X). Dordrecht.
Environmental & resource economics. (0924-6460). Dordrecht.
Environmental impact assessment review. (0195-9255). New York NY.
Environmental law. (0046-2276). Portland OR.
Environmental politics. (0964-4016). Ilford.
Environmental values. (0963-2719). Strond.
Erziehungswissenschaft. (0938-5363). Wiesbaden.
Espace géographique. (0046-2497). Paris.
Espace populations sociétés. (0755-7809). Villeneuve d'Ascq.
Espoir. (0223-5994). Paris.
Esprit. (0014-0759). Paris.
Estudios de economía. (0304-2758). Santiago.
Estudios de sociolingüística. (1576-7418). Vigo.
Estudios demográficos y urbanos. (0186-7210). Mexico City.
Estudios económicos. Mexico City.
Estudios interdisciplinarios de América Latina y el Caribe. (0792-7061). Tel Aviv.
Estudios internacionales. (0716-0240). Santiago.
Estudios latinoamericanos. (0187-1811). Mexico City.
Estudios políticos. (0185-1616). Mexico City.
Estudios Políticos. (0121-5167). Medellin.
Estudios sociológicos. (0185-4186). Pedregal de Santa Teresa.
Estudios turísticos. (0423-5037). Madrid.
Estudos do Século XX. (1645-3530). Coimbra.
Estudos históricos. (0103-2186). Rio de Janeiro.
Estudos ibero-americanos. (0101-4064). Porto Alegre.
Etat de l'opinion. (0984-774X). Paris.
Ethical theory and moral practice. (1386-2820). Dordrecht.
Ethics. (0014-1704). Chicago IL.
Ethics and international affairs. (0892-6794). New York.
Ethics, place and environment. (1366-879X). Abingdon.
Ethnic and racial studies. (0141-9870). Abingdon.
Ethnicities. (1468-7968). London.
Ethnicity and Health. (1355-7858). Abingdon.
Ethnography. (1466-1381). London.
Ethnohistory. (0014-1801). Durham NC.
Ethnologia Balkanica: Journal for Southeast European anthropology. Sofia.
Ethnologia Polona. (0137-4079). Warsaw.
Ethnologie française. (0046-2616). Paris.
Ethnologies. (1481-5974). Quebec.
Ethnology. (0014-1828). Pittsburgh PA.
Ethnomusicology. (0014-1836). Bloomington IN.
Ethnomusicology forum. (1741-1912). London.
Ethnos. (0014-1844). Stockholm.
Ethos. (0091-2131). Arlington VA.
Etnografia polska. (0071-1861). Warsaw.
Etnograficheskoe obozrenie. Moscow.
Etnolingwistyka: problemy języka i kultury. (0860-8032). Lublin.
Etnološka tribina. (0351-1944). Zagreb.

Études. (0014-1941). Paris.
Études balkaniques. Sofia.
Études et documents. (0182-788X). Paris.
Études internationales. (0014-2123). Quebec.
Études inuit = Inuit studies. (0701-1008). Quebec.
Études maliennes. Bamako.
Études mongoles et sibériennes. (0766-507S). Nanterre.
Études normandes. (0014-2158). Mont-Saint-Aignan.
Études philosophiques. (0014-2166). Paris.
Études rurales. (0014-2182). Paris.
Études sociales. (0014-2204). Paris.
Eurasian studies. (1300-1612). Ankara.
Eurasian studies yearbook. (0042-0786). Bloomington IN.
Eure: Revista latinoamericana de estudios urbanos regionales. (0717-6236). Santiago.
Europa ethnica. (0014-2492). Vienna.
Európai Tükör. (1416-7484). Budapest.
Europarecht. (0531-2485). Baden-Baden.
Europe. (0014-2751). Paris.
Europe-Asia studies. (0966-8136). Abingdon.
European accounting review. (0963-8180). Abingdon.
European business organization law review. (1566-7529). The Hague.
European constitutional law review. (1574-0196). Cambridge.
European economic review. (0014-2921). Amsterdam.
European environment: the journal of European environmental policy. (0961-0405). Chichester.
European financial management. (1354-7798). Oxford.
European foreign affairs review. (1384-6299). The Hague.
European history quarterly. (0265-6914). London.
European journal for church and state research = Revue européenne des relations Églises-État. (1370-5954). Louvain.
European journal of archaeology. (1461-9571). London.
European journal of communication. (0267-3231). London.
European journal of comparative economics. (1824-2979). Castellanza.
European journal of crime, criminal law and criminal justice. (0928-9569). Dordrecht.
European journal of cultural studies. (1367-5494). London.
European journal of development research. (0957-8811). Ilford.
European journal of finance. (1351-847X). Abingdon.
European journal of housing policy. (1461-6718). Abingdon.
European journal of industrial relations. (0959-6801). London.
European journal of international relations. (1354-0661). London.
European journal of law and economics. (0929-1261). Dordrecht.
European journal of philosophy. (0966-8373). Oxford.
European journal of political economy. (0176-2680). Amsterdam.
European journal of political research. (0304-4130). Oxford.
European journal of political theory. (1474-8851). London.
European journal of population = Revue européenne de démographie. (0168-6577). Dordrecht.
European journal of social psychology. (0046-2772). Chichester.
European journal of social security. (1388-2627). Antwerp.
European journal of social theory. (1368-4310). London.
European journal of social work. (1369-1457). Oxford.
European journal of the history of economic thought. (0967-2567). Abingdon.
European journal of vocational training. (0378-5068). Thessaloniki.

European journal of women's studies. (1350-5068). London.
European journal on criminal policy and research. (0928-1371). Dordrecht.
European law journal. (1351-5993). Oxford.
European legacy: towards new paradigms. (1084-8770). Basingstoke.
European management journal. (0263-2373). London.
European political science. (1680-4333). Basingstoke.
European review of agricultural economics. (0165-1587). Oxford.
European review of economics and finance. Lisbon.
European review of history = Revue européenne d'histoire. (1350-7486). Abingdon.
European review of Latin American and Caribbean studies = Revista europea de estudios latinoamericanos y del Caribe. (0924-0608). Amsterdam.
European security. (0966-2839). Ilford.
European societies. (1461-6696). Abingdon.
European sociological review. (0266-7215). Oxford.
European Union politics. (1465-1165). London.
European urban and regional studies. (0969-7764). London.
Européens. Paris.
Evaluation. (1356-3890). London.
Evaluation review. (0193-841X). Thousand Oaks CA.
Evidence & policy. (1744-2648). Bristol.
Évkönyv. (1216-7851). Budapest.
Evolution and human behavior. (1090-5138). New York NY.
Evolutionary anthropology. (1060-1538). New York NY.
Experimental economics. (1386-4157). Dordrecht.
Explorations in economic history. (0014-4983). Duluth MN.
Extrême-orient, extrême-occident: Cahiers de recherches comparatives. (0754-5010). Paris.
Fabula. (0014-6242). Berlin.
Family and community history. (1463-1180). Leeds.
Family law. (0014-7281). Bristol.
Family relations: Interdisciplinary journal of applied family studies. (0197-6664). Minneapolis MN.
Far Eastern affairs: a Russian journal on China, Japan and Asia-Pacific. (0206-149X). Minneapolis MN.
Fasciculi archaeologiae historicae. (0860-0007). Warsaw.
Fashion theory: the journal of dress, body & culture. (1362-704X). Oxford.
Federalist. (0393-1358). Pavia.
Feminism & psychology. (0959-3535). London.
Feminist economics. (1354-5701). Abingdon.
Feminist legal studies. (0966-3622). Liverpool.
Feminist media studies. (1468-0777). Abingdon.
Feminist review. (0141-7789). Basingstoke.
Feminist studies. (0046-3663). College Park MD.
Feminist theory. (1464-7001). London.
Field methods. (1525-822X). Thousand Oaks CA.
Finance and stochastics. (0949-2984). Berlin.
Finance India. (0970-3772). Delhi.
Finances & développement. (0430-473X). Washington DC.
Financial analysts journal. (0015-198X). Charlottesville VA.
Financial history review. (0968-5650). Cambridge.
Financial management. (0046-3892). Tampa FL.
Financial markets, institutions and instruments. (0963-8008). Malden MA.
Finansi Ukraïni. Kiev.
Finanzarchiv. (0015-2218). Tübingen.

Finnish economic papers. (0784-5197). Helsinki.
Fiscal studies. (0143-5671). London.
Flux: Cahiers scientifiques internationaux réseaux et territoires. (1154-2721). Marne la Vallée.
FOCAAL: European journal of anthropology. (0920-1297). Utrecht.
FOCAS: forum on contemporary arts and society. (0219-5054). Singapore.
Folia primatologica. (0015-5713). Basle.
Folk. (0085-0756). Copenhagen.
Folk life: Journal of ethnological studies. (0430-8778). Leeds.
Folklore. (0015-587X). Abingdon.
Food and foodways. (0740-9710). New York NY.
Food policy. (0306-9192). Oxford.
Foreign affairs. (0015-7120). New York NY.
Foreign policy. (0015-7228). Washington DC.
Foreign trade review. New Delhi.
Formation emploi. (0759-6340). Paris.
Foro internacional. (0185-013X). Mexico City.
Foro interno. (1578-4576). Madrid.
Forschungsjournal neue soziale Bewegungen. (0933-9361). Wiesbaden.
Forum for development studies. (0803-9410). Oslo.
Francophonies d'Amérique. (1183-2487). Ottawa.
French cultural studies. (0957-1558). London.
French politics. (1476-3419). Basingstoke.
French politics, culture, and society. (0882-1267). Oxford.
French studies. (0016-1128). Belfast.
Fronteras de la historia. (0123-4676). Bogotá.
Futuribles. (0337-307X). Paris.
Games and economic behavior. (0899-8256). Orlando FL.
Garcia de Orta: série de antropobiologia. (0870-0168). Lisbon.
Gender and development. (1355-2074). Oxford.
Gender and education. (0954-0253). Abingdon.
Gender and history. (0953-5233). Oxford.
Gender and society. (0891-2432). Thousand Oaks CA.
Gender, place and culture: A journal of feminist geography. (0966-369X). Abingdon.
Gender, technology and development. (0971-8524). New Delhi.
Gender, work and organization. (0968-6673). Manchester.
Genèses. (1155-3219). France.
Geneva risk and insurance review. (1554-964X). Heidelberg.
Genre humain. (0293-0277). Paris.
Genus: An international journal of demography. (0016-6987). Rome.
Géocarrefour. (0035-113X). Lyon.
Géoéconomie. Paris.
Geoforum. (0016-7185). Oxford.
Geografiska annaler: Series B — Human geography. (0435-3684). Uppsala.
Geographia polonica. (0016-7282). Warsaw.
Geographical analysis. (0016-7363). Columbus OH.
Geographical journal. (0016-7398). London.
Geographical research. (1745-5863). Campbell.
Geographical review. (0016-7428). New York NY.
Geographical review of Japan. (0016-7444). Tokyo.
Géographie, économie, société. Cachan.
Geographische Rundschau. (0016-7460). Braunschweig.

Geographische Zeitschrift. (0016-7479). Stuttgart.
Geojournal. (0343-2521). Dordrecht.
Geopolitics. (1465-0045). Ilford.
Geopolitique. (0752-1693). Paris.
Géopolitique africaine. Saint Laurent.
Géopolitique de la faim. Paris.
George Washington international law review. (0748-4305). Washington DC.
Georgica [Netherlands]. (1385-3813). Amsterdam.
German history: the journal of the German History Society. (0266-3554). London.
German politics. (0964-4008). London.
German studies review. (0149-7952). Northfield MN.
Geschichte und Gesellschaft. (0340-613X). Göttingen.
Gesellschaft Wirtschaft Politik: Sozialwissenschaften für politische Bildung. (1619-6910). Wiesbaden.
Gewerkschaftliche Monatshefte. (0016-9447). Wiesbaden.
Gifted education international. (0261-4294). Bicester.
Giornale degli economisti e annali di economia. (0017-0097). Milan.
Glasnik Slovenskega Etnološkega Društva = Bulletin of the Slovene Ethnological Society. (0351-2908). Ljubljana.
Global change, peace and security. (1478-1158). Abingdon.
Global dialogue. (1450-0590). Nicosia.
Global economic review. Seoul.
Global environmental change: human and policy dimensions. (0959-3780). New York.
Global governance. (1075-2846). Boulder CO.
Global networks: a journal of transnational affairs. (1470-2266). Oxford.
Global public health. (1744-1692). Abingdon.
Global social policy: an interdisciplinary journal of public policy and social development. (1468-0181). London.
Global society. (1360-0826). Abingdon.
Globalisation, societies and education. (1476-7724). Abingdon.
Globe: Revue internationale d'études Québécoises. (1481-5869). Montreal.
GLQ: a journal of gay and lesbian studies. (1064-2684). Durham NC.
Golias. (1144-8814). Villeurbanne.
Gospodarka narodowa. (0867-0005). Warsaw.
Gosudarstvo i pravo. (0132-0769). Moscow.
Gothenburg studies in social anthropology. (0348-4076). Gothenburg.
Governance. (0952-1895). Oxford.
Government and opposition. (0017-257X). London.
Grassroots development. (0733-6608). Rosslyn VA.
Greener management international. (0966-9671). Sheffield.
Group & organization management: an international journal. (1059-6011). Thousand Oaks CA.
Group analysis: The journal of group analytic psychotherapy. (0533-3164). London.
Group decision and negotiation. (0926-2644). Dordrecht.
Group processes and intergroup relations. (1368-4302). London.
Groupwork. (0951-824X). London.
Growth and change. (0017-4815). Oxford.
Gruppendynamik und Organisationsberatung. (0046-6514). Wiesbaden.
Gruppenpsychotherapie und Gruppendynamik: Beiträge zur Sozialpsychologie und therapeutischen Praxis. (0017-4947). Göttingen.
GYAN: Journal of education. (0972-9992). Ghaziabad.
Habitat international. (0197-3975). Oxford.
Hacienda pública española: Revista de economía pública. (0210-1173). Madrid.

HAGAR: International Social Science Review. (1565-3323). Beer-Sheva.

Hallinnon tutkimus. (0359-6680). Tampere.

Hamburger Jahrbuch für Wirtschafts- und Gesellschaftspolitik. Tübingen.

Harvard journal of Asiatic studies. (0073-0548). Cambridge MA.

Harvard law review. (0017-811X). Cambridge MA.

Health & social work. (0360-7283). Washington DC.

Health and human rights. (1079-0969). Cambridge MA.

Health care analysis. (1065-3058). Dordrecht.

Health policy. (0168-8510). Shannon.

Health policy and planning: A journal on health in development. (0268-1080). Oxford.

Health sociology review. (1446-1242). Maleny.

Health transition review. (1036-4005). Canberra.

Health, risk & society. (1369-8575). Oxford.

Hebrew studies. (0146-4094). Madison WI.

Hedgehog review: Critical reflections on contemporary culture. (1527-9677). Charlottesville VA.

Hemispheres: studies on cultures and societies. (0239-8818). Warsaw.

Hérodote. (0338-487X). Issy-les-Moulineaux.

Hessische Blätter für Volks- und Kulturforschung. (1075-3479). Marburg.

Hevrah u-revahah = Society and welfare. Jerusalem.

High technology law journal. (0885-2715). Berkeley CA.

Higher education. (0018-1560). Dordrecht.

Higher education policy. (0952-8733). Basingstoke.

Hispanic American historical review. (0018-2168). Durham NC.

Histoire. (0182-2411). Paris.

Historia mexicana: Revista trimestral publicada por el Centro de estudios históricos de el Colegio de México. (0185-0172). Mexico City.

Historia: journal of the Historical Association of South Africa. (0018-229X). Pretoria.

Historiallinen Aikakauskirja. (0018-2362). Helsinki.

Historical archaeology. (0440-9213). Tucson AZ.

Historical journal. (0018-246X). Cambridge.

Historical social research = Historische Sozialforschung. (0172-6404). Cologne.

Historický časopis. (0018-2575). Bratislava.

Historie a vojenství. (0018-2583). Prague.

History. (0018-2648). London.

History and anthropology. (0275-7206). London.

History and technology. (0734-1512). Abingdon.

History and theory. (0018-2656). Middletown CT.

History in Africa. (0361-5413). New Brunswick NJ.

History of political economy. (0018-2702). Durham NC.

History of political thought. (0143-781X). Thorverton.

History of the family. (1081-602X). Greenwich CT.

History of the human sciences. (0952-6951). London.

Hitel. (0238-9908). Budapest.

Hitotsubashi journal of commerce and management. (0018-2796). Tokyo.

Hitotsubashi journal of economics. (0018-280X). Tokyo.

Hitotsubashi journal of law and politics. (0073-2796). Tokyo.

Hitotsubashi journal of social studies. (0073-280X). Tokyo.

Home cultures: the journal of dress, body & culture. (1740-6315). Oxford.

Homines. (0252-8908). Hato Rey.

Homme. (0439-4216). Paris.

Homme et la société. (0018-4306). Paris.

Hong Kong journal of social sciences. (1021-3619). Hong Kong.
Hong Kong journal of social work. (0219-2462). Hong Kong.
Horizons maghrebins. (0984-2616). Toulouse.
Horizontes antropológicos. (0104-7183). Porto Alegre.
Housing policy debate. (1051-1482). Washington DC.
Housing studies. (1466-1810). Abingdon.
Housing, theory and society. (1403-6096). Stockholm.
Howard journal of criminal justice. (0265-5527). Oxford.
Human biology: the international journal of population biology and genetics. (1534-6617). Detroit MI.
Human development. (0018-716X). Basle.
Human ecology: the CHEC journal. (0268-4918). London.
Human ethology bulletin. (0739-2036). Orono ME.
Human nature. (1045-6767). Hawthorne NY.
Human organization. (0018-7259). Temple Terrace FL.
Human relations. (0018-7267). London.
Human resource development international. (1367-8868). Abingdon.
Human rights quarterly. (0275-0392). Baltimore MD.
Human studies. (0163-8548). Dordrecht.
Humanitaire. (1624-4184). Paris.
Humor. (0933-1719). Berlin.
Hungarian quarterly. (0028 5390). Budapest.
Iberoamericana: América Latina - España - Portugal. (1577-3388). Madrid.
Identities: global studies in culture and power. (1070-289X). Newark NJ.
IDS bulletin. (0265-5012). Brighton.
IFRA: Les cahiers. Nairobi.
IGA: Zeitschrift für Klein- und Mittelunternehmen. (0020-9481). Berlin.
IMF staff papers. (1020-7635). Washington DC.
Immigrants and minorities. (0261-9288). Ilford.
Impact assessment and project appraisal. (1461-5517). Guildford.
Impacts. (0019-2899). Angers.
India quarterly. (0019-4220). New Delhi.
India review. (1473-6489). London.
Indian economic and social history review. (0019-4646). New Delhi.
Indian economic journal. (0019-4662). Bombay.
Indian economic review. (0019-4671). Delhi.
Indian journal of agricultural economics. (0019-5014). Bombay.
Indian journal of economics. (0019-5170). Allahabad.
Indian journal of gender studies. (0971-5215). New Delhi.
Indian journal of industrial relations. (0019-5286). New Delhi.
Indian journal of labour economics. (0971-7927). Patna.
Indian journal of physical anthropology and human genetics. Lucknow.
Indian journal of political science. (0019-5510). Madras.
Indian journal of public administration. (0019-5561). New Delhi.
Indian journal of regional science. (0046-9017). Calcutta.
Indian journal of social work. (0019-5634). Bombay.
Indian labour journal. (0019-5723). Shimla.
Indian psychological abstracts and reviews. (0971-524X). New Delhi.
Indian social science review. (0972-0731). New Delhi.
Indiana journal of global legal studies. (1080-0727). Bloomington IN.
Indicadores econômicos FEE. (0103-3905). Porto Alegre.
Indigenous affairs. (1024-3283). Copenhagen.

Indigenous world. (1024-0217). Copenhagen.
Indo-Iranian journal. (0019-7246). Dordrecht.
Indonesia. Ithaca NY.
Indonesia and the Malay world. (1363-9811). Oxford.
Industria: rivista di economia e politica industriale. (0019-7416). Bologna.
Industrial and corporate change. (0960-6491). Oxford.
Industrial and labor relations review. (0019-7939). Ithaca NY.
Industrial and social relations. (0258-7181). Bellville.
Industrial archaeology review. (0309-0728). Leicester.
Industrial law journal. (0395-9332). Oxford.
Industrial marketing management. (0019-8501). Amsterdam.
Industrial relations. (0019-8676). Oxford.
Industrial relations journal. (0019-8692). Oxford.
Industrielle Beziehungen. (0943-2779). Mering.
Industry & higher education. (0950-4222). London.
Industry and innovation. (1366-2716). Abingdon.
Información comercial española. (0019-977X). Madrid.
Information economics and policy. (0167-6245). Amsterdam.
Information géographique. (0020-0093). Paris.
Information technology & people. (0959-3845). Bradford.
Information, communication & society. (1369-118X). Abingdon.
Informationen zur Raumentwicklung. (0303-2493). Bonn.
Informations sociales. (0046-9459). Paris.
Inner Asia. (1464-8172). Strond.
Innovation: management, policy & practice. (1447-9338). Maleny.
Innovation: the European journal of social sciences. (1351-1610). Oxford.
Innowacje w edukacji akademickiej. (1643-6318). Łódz.
Inquiry. (0020-174X). Oslo.
Inroads: the Canadian journal of opinion. (1188-746X). Ontario.
Insight Turkey. (1302-177X). Ankara.
Insurance mathematics & economics. (0167-6687). Amsterdam.
Integración & comercio. (1026-0463). Buenos Aires.
Integración latinoamericana. (0325-1675). Buenos Aires.
Intelligence and national security. (0268-4527). Ilford.
Inter-Asia cultural studies. (1464-9373). Abingdon.
Interações: Revista internacional de desenvolvimento local. (1518-7012). Campo Grande.
Interchange. (0826-4805). Dordrecht.
Interfaces. (0092-2102). Linthicum MD.
Internasjonal politikk. (0020-577X). Oslo.
International affairs [London]. (0020-5850). London.
International affairs [Moscow]. (0130-9641). Minneapolis MN.
International and comparative law quarterly. (0020-5893). London.
International business and economics research journal. (1535-0754). Littleton CO.
International business review. (0969-5931). Amsterdam.
International communication gazette. (1748-0485). London.
International development planning review. (1474-6743). Liverpool.
International development policies: review of the activities of international organizations. (0964-699X). London.
International economic journal. (1016-8737). Abingdon.
International economic review. (0020-6598). Philadelphia PA.
International feminist journal of politics. (1461-6742). Abingdon.

International game theory review. (0219-1989). Singapore.
International history review. (0707-5332). Burnaby.
International journal. (0020-7020). Toronto.
International journal for philosophy of religion. (0020-7047). Dordrecht.
International journal of accounting. (0020-7063). Heidelberg.
International journal of adolescence and youth. (0267-3843). Bicester.
International journal of African historical studies. (0361-7882). Boston MA.
International journal of applied philosophy. (0739-098X). Charlottesville VA.
International journal of Asian studies. (1479-5914). Cambridge.
International journal of auditing. (1090-6738). Oxford.
International journal of children's rights. (0927-5568). Leiden.
International journal of comparative labour law and industrial relations. (0952-617X). The Hague.
International journal of comparative sociology. (0020-7152). Ontario.
International journal of constitutional law. (1474-2640). New York NY.
International journal of consumer studies. (1470-6423). Oxford.
International journal of critical psychology. (1471-4167). London.
International journal of cross cultural management. (1470-5958). London.
International journal of cultural policy. (1028-6632). Abingdon.
International journal of cultural studies. (1367-8779). London.
International journal of drug policy. (0955-3959). Amsterdam.
International journal of electronic government research. (1548-3886). Hershey PA.
International journal of entrepreneurship and innovation. (1465-7503). London.
International journal of game theory. (0020-7276). Heidelberg.
International journal of health services. (0020-7314). Amityville NY.
International journal of historical archaeology. (1092-7697). Dordrecht.
International journal of human resource management. (0958-5192). Abingdon.
International journal of industrial organization. (0167-7187). Amsterdam.
International journal of innovation and technology Management. (0219-8770). Singapore.
International journal of innovation management. (1363-9196). Singapore.
International journal of Japanese sociology. (0918-7545). Tokyo.
International journal of law and psychiatry. (0160-2527). Oxford.
International journal of law, policy, and the family. (1360-9939). Oxford.
International journal of Middle East studies. (0020-7438). New York NY.
International journal of philosophical studies. (0967-2559). Abingdon.
International journal of politics, culture and society. (0891-4486). New York NY.
International journal of primatology. (0164-0291). New York NY.
International journal of psychoanalysis. (0020-7578). London.
International journal of public opinion research. (0954-2892). Oxford.
International journal of social economics. (0306-8293). Bradford.
International journal of social psychiatry. (0020-7640). London.
International journal of social research methodology: theory & practice. (1364-5579). London.
International journal of sustainable development. (0960-1406). Geneva.
International journal of the economics of business. (1357-1516). Abingdon.
International journal of the history of sport. (0952-3367). Ilford.
International journal of the sociology of language. (0165-2516). Berlin.
International journal of the sociology of law. (0194-6595). London.
International journal of theoretical and applied finance. (0219-0249). Singapore.
International journal of transport economics. (0391-8440). Rome.
International journal of urban and regional research. (0309-1317). Oxford.
International journal on minority and group rights. (1385-4879). Leiden.
International labour review. (0020-7780). Geneva.

International migration = Migrations internationales = Migraciones internacionales. (0020-7985). Geneva.
International migration review. (0197-9183). New York NY.
International negotiation: a journal of theory and practice. (1382-340X). Leiden.
International organization. (0020-8183). Cambridge MA.
International peacekeeping. (1353-3312). Ilford.
International perspectives. (0381-4874). Ottawa.
International political science review = Revue internationale de science politique. (0192-5121). London.
International politics. (1384-5748). Basingstoke.
International regional science review. (0160-0176). Thousand Oaks CA.
International relations. (0047-1178). London.
International Relations of the Asia Pacific. (1470-482X). Oxford.
International review of administrative sciences. (0020-8523). London.
International review of applied economics. (0269-2171). Abingdon.
International review of applied linguistics in language teaching. (0019-042X). Berlin.
International review of education. (0020-8566). Dordrecht.
International review of law and economics. (0144-8188). New York NY.
International review of retail, distribution and consumer research. (0959-3969). Abingdon.
International review of social history. (0020-8590). Cambridge.
International review of sociology = Revue internationale de sociologie. (0390-6701). Abingdon.
International review of the Red Cross. (1560-7755). Geneva.
International review of victimology. (0269-7580). Bicester.
International security. (0162-2889). Cambridge MA.
International small business journal. (0266-2426). Macclesfield.
International social science journal. (0020-8701). Oxford.
International social work. (0020-8728). London.
International sociology. (0268-5809). London.
International spectator. (0393-2729). Rome.
International studies. (0020-8817). New Delhi.
International studies [Łódz]. (1641-4233). Łódz.
International studies in the philosophy of science. (0269-8595). Abingdon.
International studies of management & organization. (0020-8825). Armonk NY.
International studies quarterly. (0020-8833). Malden MA.
International studies review. (1521-9488). Malden MA.
International tax and public finance. (0927-5940). Dordrecht.
Internationale Politik. (1430-175X). Bielefeld.
Internationale Politik und Gesellschaft. (0945-2419). Bonn.
Internationales Asienforum. (0020-9449). Cologne.
Interventions: international journal of postcolonial studies. (1369-801X). Abingdon.
Investigaciones economicas. (0210-1521). Madrid.
Investigaciones y ensayos. (0539-242X). Buenos Aires.
Inžinernė Ekonomika = Engineering Economics. (1392-2785). Kaunas.
Iran and the Caucasus. (1609-8498). Leiden.
Iran nameh. Bethesda MD.
Iranian journal of international affairs. (1016-6130). Tehran.
Iranica antiqua. (0021-0870). Louvain.
Iraq. (0021-0889). London.
Irish banking review. (0021-1060). Dublin.
Irish journal of sociology. (0791-6035). Maynooth.
Irish political studies. (0790-7184). Limerick.
Irish review. (0790-7850). Cork.

Isis. (0021-1753). Chicago IL.

ISLA: Journal of Micronesian studies. Mangiloa.

Islam et sociétés au sud du Sahara. (0984-7685). Paris.

Islam: Zeitschrift für Geschichte und Kultur des islamischen Orients. (0021-1818). Berlin.

Islamic law and society. (0928-9380). Leiden.

Israel affairs. (1353-7121). Ilford.

Israel exploration journal. (0021-2059). Jerusalem.

Israel law review. (0021-2237). Jerusalem.

Israel oriental studies. (0334-4401). Winona Lake IN.

Israel yearbook on human rights. (0333-5925). Dordrecht.

Issues & studies. (1013-2511). Taipei.

Istina. (0021-2423). Boulogne-sur-Seine.

Istorija 20. veka. (0352-3160). Belgrade.

Italia contemporanea. (0392-3568). Milan.

IWK: Internationale wissenschaftliche Korrespondenz zur Geschichte der deutschen Arbeiterbewegung. (0046-8428). Berlin.

Iyunim bitkumat Israel. (0792-7169). Beer-Sheva.

Jahrbuch des öffentlichen Rechts der Gegenwart. (0075-2517). Tübingen.

Jahrbuch für Antisemitismusforschung. (0941-8563). Frankfurt.

Jahrbuch für christliche Sozialwissenschaften. (0075-2584). Münster.

Jahrbuch für Geschichte Lateinamerikas. (1438-4752). Cologne.

Jahrbuch für Kommunikationsgeschichte. (1438-4485). Stuttgart.

Jahrbuch für Soziologiegeschichte. (0939-6152). Opladen.

Jahrbuch für Wirtschaftsgeschichte. (0075-2800). Berlin.

Jahrbuch für Wirtschaftswissenschaften. (0948-5139). Göttingen.

Jahrbücher für Geschichte Osteuropas. (0021-4019). Stuttgart.

Jahrbücher für Nationalökonomie und Statistik. (0021-4027). Stuttgart.

Japan and the world economy. (0922-1425). Amsterdam.

Japan echo. (0388-0435). Tokyo.

Japan forum. (0955-5803). Abingdon.

Japan review of international affairs. (0913-8773). Tokyo.

Japanese annual of international law. (0448-8806). Tokyo.

Japanese economic review. (1352-4739). Tokyo.

Japanese Journal of Political Science. (1468-1099). Cambridge.

Japanese religions. (0448-8954). Kyoto City.

Javnost = Public. (1318-3222). Ljubljana.

Jazykovedný časopis. (0021-5597). Bratislava.

Jewish journal of sociology. (0021-6534). London.

Jewish social studies. (0021-6704). New York NY.

Jogtudományi közlöny. (0021-7166). Budapest.

Joint U.S.-Korea academic studies. (1054-6944). Washington DC.

Journal de la paix. (0021-7794). Paris.

Journal de la Société des Américanistes. (0037-9174). Paris.

Journal de la Société des Océanistes. (0300-953X). Paris.

Journal du droit international. (0021-8170). Paris.

Journal for cultural research. (1479-7585). Abingdon.

Journal for East European management studies. (0949-6181). Mering.

Journal for the scientific study of religion. (0021-8294). Provo UT.

Journal for the theory of social behaviour. (0021-8308). Oxford.

Journal für Entwicklungspolitik. (0258-2384). Frankfurt.

Journal für Psychologie: Theorie, Forschung, Praxis. (0942-2285). Göttingen.

Journal of accounting and economics. (0165-4101). Amsterdam.
Journal of accounting and public policy. (0278-4254). New York NY.
Journal of accounting research. (0021-8456). Chicago IL.
Journal of advertising. (0091-3367). Armonk NY.
Journal of African Archaeology. (1612-1651). Frankfurt am Main.
Journal of African economies. (0963-8024). Oxford.
Journal of African history. (0021-8537). Cambridge.
Journal of African law. (0221-8553). London.
Journal of agricultural economics. (0021-857X). Reading.
Journal of American studies. (0021-8758). Cambridge.
Journal of anthropological archaeology. (0278-4165). San Diego CA.
Journal of anthropological research. (0091-7710). Albuquerque NM.
Journal of applied business research. (0892-7626). Littleton CO.
Journal of applied econometrics. (0883-7252). Chichester.
Journal of applied economics. (1514-0326). Buenos Aires.
Journal of applied psychology. (0021-9010). Washington DC.
Journal of applied social psychology. (0021-9029). Columbia MD.
Journal of archaeological method and theory. (1072-5369). Dordrecht.
Journal of archaeological research. (1059-0161). Dordrecht.
Journal of Asian and African studies. (0021-9096). Thousand Oaks CA.
Journal of Asian business. (1068-0055). Ann Arbor MI.
Journal of Asian studies. (0021-9118). Ann Arbor MI.
Journal of Australian political economy. (0156-5826). Sydney.
Journal of Australian studies. (1444-3058). Queensland.
Journal of Baltic studies. (0162-9778). Portland OR.
Journal of banking and finance. (0378-4266). Amsterdam.
Journal of biosocial science. (0021-9320). Cambridge.
Journal of black psychology. (0095-7984). Thousand Oaks CA.
Journal of black studies. (0021-9347). Thousand Oaks CA.
Journal of British studies. (0021-9371). Chicago IL.
Journal of Burma Studies. (1094-799X). DeKalb IL.
Journal of business. (0021-9398). Chicago IL.
Journal of business and society. (1012-2591). Nicosia.
Journal of business ethics. (0167-4544). Dordrecht.
Journal of business finance and accounting. (0306-686X). Oxford.
Journal of business research. (0148-2963). Amsterdam.
Journal of Canadian studies = Revue d'études canadiennes. (0021-9495). Peterborough.
Journal of Central Asian studies. (0898-6827). Stillwater OK.
Journal of child and family studies. (1062-1024). New York NY.
Journal of children and poverty. (1079-6126). Abingdon.
Journal of Chinese economic and business studies. (1476-5284). Abingdon.
Journal of Chinese philosophy. (0301-8121). Malden MA.
Journal of church and state. (0021-969X). Waco TX.
Journal of civil liberties. (1362-3451). Newcastle.
Journal of classical sociology. (1468-795X). London.
Journal of cognition and culture. (1567-7095). Leiden.
Journal of cognitive and behavioral psychotherapies. (1584-7101). Cluj-Napoca.
Journal of Common Market studies. (0021-9886). Oxford.
Journal of communication. (0021-9916). New York NY.
Journal of communist studies and transition politics. (1352-3279). Ilford.
Journal of community and applied social psychology. (1052-9284). Chichester.

Journal of comparative economics. (0147-5967). Duluth MN.
Journal of comparative family studies. (0047-2328). Calgary.
Journal of comparative international management. (1481-0468). New Brunswick.
Journal of comparative policy analysis: research and practice. (1387-6988). Dordrecht.
Journal of conflict resolution. (0022-0027). Thousand Oaks CA.
Journal of conflict studies. (1198-8614). New Brunswick.
Journal of consulting and clinical psychology. (0022-006X). Washington DC.
Journal of consumer affairs. (0022-0078). Madison WI.
Journal of consumer behaviour. (1472-0817). Chichester.
Journal of consumer culture. (1469-5405). London.
Journal of consumer policy. (0168-7034). Dordrecht.
Journal of contemporary African studies. (0258-9001). Abingdon.
Journal of contemporary Asia. (0047-2336). Manila.
Journal of contemporary China. (1067-0564). Oxford.
Journal of contemporary ethnography. (0891-2416). Thousand Oaks CA.
Journal of contemporary history. (0022-0094). London.
Journal of cooperative studies. (0961-5784). Buxton.
Journal of corporate citizenship. (1470-5001). Sheffield.
Journal of cost management. (0899-5141). Boston MA.
Journal of criminal law. (0022-0183). London.
Journal of criminal law and criminology. (0091-4169). Chicago IL.
Journal of cross-cultural gerontology. (0169-3816). New York.
Journal of cultural economics. (0885-2545). Dordrecht.
Journal of cultural studies. (1595-0956). Lagos.
Journal of democracy. (1045-5736). Baltimore MD.
Journal of design history. (0952-4649). Oxford.
Journal of developing areas. (0022-037X). Macomb IL.
Journal of developing societies. (0169-796X). London.
Journal of development assistance. (1341-3953). Tokyo.
Journal of development economics. (0304-3878). Amsterdam.
Journal of development planning. (0085-2392). New York NY.
Journal of development studies. (0022-0388). Ilford.
Journal of e-government. New York.
Journal of East Asian affairs. (1010-1608). Seoul.
Journal of Eastern African research & development. (0251-0405). Nairobi.
Journal of Eastern Caribbean studies. (1028-8813). Bridgetown.
Journal of econometrics. (0304-4076). Amsterdam.
Journal of economic and social measurement. (0747-9662). Amsterdam.
Journal of economic behavior and organization. (0167-2681). Amsterdam.
Journal of economic cooperation among Islamic countries. (0252-953X). Ankara.
Journal of economic dynamics and control. (0165-1889). Amsterdam.
Journal of economic growth. (1381-4338). Dordrecht.
Journal of economic history. (0022-0507). New York NY.
Journal of economic issues. (0021-3624). Lewisburg PA.
Journal of economic literature. (0022-0515). Nashville TN.
Journal of economic methodology. (1350-178X). Abingdon.
Journal of economic perspectives. (0895-3309). Nashville TN.
Journal of economic psychology. (0167-4870). Amsterdam.
Journal of economic studies. (0144-3585). Bradford.
Journal of economic surveys. (0950-0804). Oxford.
Journal of economic theory. (0022-0531). Bruges.

Journal of economics & management strategy. (1058-6407). Cambridge MA.
Journal of economics [Austria] = Zeitschrift für Nationalökonomie. (0931-8658). Vienna.
Journal of education and work. (1469-9435). Abingdon.
Journal of education policy. (0268-0939). London.
Journal of elections, public opinion and parties. (1745-7289). Abingdon.
Journal of electronic commerce in organizations. (1539-2937). Hershey PA.
Journal of electronic commerce research. (1526-6133). Long Beach CA.
Journal of empirical finance. (0927-5398). Amsterdam.
Journal of energy & natural resources law. (0264-6811). London.
Journal of energy literature. (1359-3714). Oxford.
Journal of enterprising culture. (0218-4958). Singapore.
Journal of environment and development. (1070-4965). Thousand Oaks CA.
Journal of environmental assessment policy and management. (1464-3332). Singapore.
Journal of environmental economics and management. (0095-0696). Duluth MN.
Journal of environmental law. (0952-8873). Oxford.
Journal of environmental management. (0301-4797). London.
Journal of environmental planning and management. (0964-0568). Abingdon.
Journal of environmental policy and planning. (1523-908X). Abingdon.
Journal of ethnic and migration studies. (1369-183X). Abingdon.
Journal of ethnobiology. (0278-0771). Los Angeles CA.
Journal of European economic history. (0391-5115). Rome.
Journal of European integration. (0703-6337). Abingdon.
Journal of European integration history = Revue d'histoire de l'intégration européenne = Zeitschrift für
    Geschichte der europäischen Integration. (0947-9511). Baden-Baden.
Journal of European public policy. (1350-1763). Abingdon.
Journal of European social policy. (0958-9287). London.
Journal of evolutionary economics. (0936-9937). Berlin.
Journal of experimental child psychology. (0022-0965). Duluth MN.
Journal of experimental social psychology. (0022-1031). Duluth MN.
Journal of family and economic issues. (1058-0476). Dordrecht.
Journal of family history. (0363-1990). Thousand Oaks CA.
Journal of family therapy. (0163-4445). Oxford.
Journal of family violence. (0885-7482). New York NY.
Journal of finance. (0022-1082). New York NY.
Journal of financial and quantitative analysis. (0022-1090). Seattle WA.
Journal of financial economics. (0304-405X). Amsterdam.
Journal of financial intermediation. (1042-9573). Orlando FL.
Journal of financial services research. (0920-8550). Dordrecht.
Journal of folklore research. (0737-7037). Bloomington IN.
Journal of forecasting. (0277-6693). Chichester.
Journal of forensic psychiatry and psychology. (1478-9949). Abingdon.
Journal of futures markets. (0270-7314). New York NY.
Journal of gender studies. (0958-9236). Abingdon.
Journal of general management. (0306-3070). Henley-on-Thames.
Journal of genocide research. (1462-3528). Oxford.
Journal of GLBT family studies. (1550-428X). New York.
Journal of health communication. (1081-0730). London.
Journal of health economics. (0167-6296). Amsterdam.
Journal of health politics, policy and law. (0361-6878). Durham NC.
Journal of health psychology. (1359-1053). London.
Journal of historical sociology. (0952-1909). Oxford.

Journal of homosexuality. (0091-8369). Binghampton NY.
Journal of housing and the built environment. (1566-4910). Dordrecht.
Journal of housing economics. (1051-1377). Orlando FL.
Journal of housing research. (1052-7001). Washington DC.
Journal of human development. (1464-9888). Basingstoke.
Journal of human ecology. (0970-9274). Delhi.
Journal of human evolution. (0047-2484). London.
Journal of human resources. (0022-166X). Madison WI.
Journal of human rights. (1475-4835). London.
Journal of humanities and natural sciences. (0495-8012). Tokyo.
Journal of Imperial and Commonwealth history. (0308-6534). London.
Journal of income distribution. (0926-6437). Pistacataway NJ.
Journal of Indian philosophy. (0022-1791). Dordrecht.
Journal of Indo-European studies. (0092-2323). Washington DC.
Journal of industrial economics. (0022-1821). Oxford.
Journal of industrial history. (1463-6174). Lancaster.
Journal of industrial relations. (0022-1856). Sydney.
Journal of institutional and theoretical economics = Zeitschrift für die gesamte Staatswissenschaft.
    (0932-4569). Tübingen.
Journal of intercultural studies. (0725-6868). Abingdon.
Journal of interdisciplinary economics. (0260-1079). Bicester.
Journal of interdisciplinary history. (0022-1953). Cambridge MA.
Journal of intergenerational relationships: programs, policy, and research. (1535-0770). New York.
Journal of international accounting auditing and taxation. (1061-9518). Greenwich CT.
Journal of international affairs. (0022-197X). New York NY.
Journal of international agricultural and extension education. (1077-0755). College Station TX.
Journal of international and area studies. (1226-8550). Seoul.
Journal of international business studies. (0047-2506). New Orleans LA.
Journal of international development. (0954-1748). Chichester.
Journal of international economic law. (1369-3034). Oxford.
Journal of international economics. (0022-1996). Amsterdam.
Journal of international financial management and accounting. (0954-1314). Oxford.
Journal of international financial markets, institutions & money. (1042-4431). Binghampton NY.
Journal of international management. (1075-4253). Amsterdam.
Journal of international money and finance. (0261-5606). Guildford.
Journal of international relations and development. (1408-6980). Ljubljana.
Journal of international trade and economic development. (0963-8199). Abingdon.
Journal of Islamic studies. (0955-2340). Oxford.
Journal of Japanese studies. (0095-6848). Seattle WA.
Journal of Jewish studies. (0022-2097). Oxford.
Journal of Korean studies. Los Angeles CA.
Journal of labor economics. (0734-306X). Chicago IL.
Journal of labor research. (0195-3613). Fairfax VA.
Journal of language and social psychology. (0261-927X). London.
Journal of Latin American anthropology. Arlington VA.
Journal of Latin American studies. (0022-216X). Cambridge.
Journal of law and economics. (0022-2186). Chicago IL.
Journal of law and society. (0263-323X). Oxford.
Journal of law, economics, & organization. (8756-6222). Cary NC.
Journal of legal pluralism and unofficial law. (0732-9113). Münster.
Journal of legal studies. (0047-2530). Chicago IL.

Journal of legislative studies. (1357-2334). London.
Journal of libertarian studies. (0363-2873). Burlingame CA.
Journal of linguistic anthropology. (1055-1360). Arlington VA.
Journal of linguistics. (0022-2267). Cambridge.
Journal of macroeconomics. (0164-0704). Baton Rouge LA.
Journal of management and governance. (1385-3457). Dordrecht.
Journal of management studies. (0022-2380). Oxford.
Journal of marriage and the family. (0022-2445). Minneapolis MN.
Journal of material culture. (1359-1835). London.
Journal of mathematical economics. (0304-4068). Amsterdam.
Journal of mathematical sociology. (0022-250X). New York NY.
Journal of medicine and philosophy. (0360-5310). Lisse.
Journal of Mediterranean studies. (1016-3476). Msida.
Journal of modern African studies. (0022-278X). Cambridge.
Journal of modern history. (0022-2801). Chicago IL.
Journal of modern Italian studies. (1354-571X). Abingdon.
Journal of modern Korean studies. (8756-2235). Fredericksburg VA.
Journal of monetary economics. (0304-3932). Amsterdam.
Journal of money, credit and banking. (0022-2879). Columbus OH.
Journal of moral education. (0305-7240). Abingdon.
Journal of multilingual and multicultural development. (0143-4632). Clevedon.
Journal of multinational financial management. (1042-444X). Amsterdam.
Journal of Natal and Zulu history. Durban.
Journal of Near Eastern studies. (0022-2968). Chicago IL.
Journal of North African studies. (1362-9387). Ilford.
Journal of occupational and organizational psychology. (0963-1798). Leicester.
Journal of Pacific history. (0022-3344). Canberra.
Journal of Palestine studies. (0377-919X). Berkeley CA.
Journal of peace research. (0022-3433). London.
Journal of peacebuilding and development. (1542-3166). Washington DC.
Journal of peasant studies. (0306-6150). Ilford.
Journal of personality. (0022-3506). Malden MA.
Journal of personality and social psychology. (0022-3514). Washington DC.
Journal of philosophy. (0022-362X). New York NY.
Journal of pidgin and creole languages. (0920-9034). Amsterdam.
Journal of planning literature. (0885-4122). Thousand Oaks CA.
Journal of policy analysis and management. (0276-8739). New York NY.
Journal of policy history. (0898-0306). University Park PA.
Journal of policy modeling. (0161-8938). New York NY.
Journal of policy reform. (1384-1289). Abingdon.
Journal of political economy. (0022-3808). Chicago IL.
Journal of political ideologies. (1356-9317). Abingdon.
Journal of political philosophy. (0963-8016). Oxford.
Journal of politics. (0022-3816). Malden MA.
Journal of popular culture. (0022-3840). Bowling Green OH.
Journal of population economics. (0933-1433). Berlin.
Journal of population research. (1443-2447). Canberra.
Journal of post Keynesian economics. (0160-3477). Armonk NY.
Journal of pragmatics. (0378-2166). Amsterdam.
Journal of promotion management. (1049-6491). New York.
Journal of psychology. (0022-3980). Washington DC.

Journal of psychology in Africa. (1433-0237). Frankfurt am Main.
Journal of public administration. (0036-0767). Pretoria.
Journal of public administration research and theory. (1053-1858). Oxford.
Journal of public affairs. (1472-3891). Chichester.
Journal of public economics. (0047-2727). Amsterdam.
Journal of public policy. (0143-814X). Cambridge.
Journal of real estate finance and economics. (0895-5638). Dordrecht.
Journal of real estate literature. (0927-7544). Grand Forks ND.
Journal of real estate portfolio management. (1083-5547). Grand Forks ND.
Journal of real estate research. (0896-5803). Grand Forks ND.
Journal of refugee studies. (0951-6328). Oxford.
Journal of regional science. (0022-4146). Malden MA.
Journal of regulatory economics. (0922-680X). Dordrecht.
Journal of religion in Africa. (0022-4200). Leiden.
Journal of research in crime and delinquency. (0022-4278). Thousand Oaks CA.
Journal of risk and uncertainty. (0895-5646). Dordrecht.
Journal of risk research. (1366-9877). London.
Journal of ritual studies. (0890-1112). Pittsburgh PA.
Journal of rural cooperation. (0377-7480). Ramat Efal.
Journal of rural studies. (0743-0167). Oxford.
Journal of semantics. (0167-5133). Oxford.
Journal of sexual aggression. (1355-2600). Abingdon.
Journal of Slavic military studies. (1351-8046). Ilford.
Journal of social and clinical psychology. (0736-7236). New York NY.
Journal of social and evolutionary systems. (1061-7361). Stamford CT.
Journal of social and personal relationships. (0265-4075). London.
Journal of social archaeology. (1469-6053). London.
Journal of social development in Africa. (1012-1080). Harare.
Journal of social history. (0022-4529). Pittsburgh PA.
Journal of social issues. (0022-4537). Oxford.
Journal of social policy. (0047-2794). Cambridge.
Journal of social psychology. (0022-4545). Washington DC.
Journal of social sciences. (0971-8923). Delhi.
Journal of social welfare & family law. (0141-8033). Abingdon.
Journal of social work. (1468-0173). London.
Journal of social work practice. (0265-0533). Abingdon.
Journal of social, political and economic studies. (0193-5941). Washington DC.
Journal of sociology: journal of the Australian Sociological Association. (1440-7833). London.
Journal of Southeast Asian studies. (0022-4634). Cambridge.
Journal of Southeast European and Black Sea studies. (1468-3857). London.
Journal of Southern African studies. (0305-7070). Abingdon.
Journal of Southern Europe and the Balkans. (1461-3190). Oxford.
Journal of strategic studies. (0140-2390). Ilford.
Journal of studies in international education. (1028-3153). London.
Journal of the American Oriental Society. (0003-0279). Ann Arbor MI.
Journal of the American Statistical Association. (0162-1459). Alexandria VA.
Journal of the Anthropological Society of Oxford. (0044-8370). Oxford.
Journal of the Asia Pacific economy. (1354-7860). Abingdon.
Journal of the Asiatic Society of Bangladesh. Dhaka.
Journal of the British Archaeological Association. (0068-1288). Leeds.
Journal of the economic and social history of the Orient. (0022-4995). Leiden.

Journal of the European Economic Association. (1542-4766). Cambridge MA.
Journal of the history of economic thought. (1042-7716). Abingdon.
Journal of the history of ideas. (0022-5037). Baltimore MD.
Journal of the history of philosophy. (0022-5053). St. Louis MO.
Journal of the history of sexuality. (1043-4070). Chicago IL.
Journal of the history of the behavioral sciences. (0022-5061). New York NY.
Journal of the Japanese and international economies. (0889-1583). Duluth MN.
Journal of the Malaysian branch of the Royal Asiatic Society. (0126-7353). Kuala Lumpur.
Journal of the Oriental Institute. (0030-5324). Baroda.
Journal of the Pakistan Historical Society. (0030-9796). Karachi.
Journal of the Research Society of Pakistan. Lahore.
Journal of the Royal Anthropological Institute. (1359-0987). Oxford.
Journal of the Royal Asiatic Society. (1356-1863). Cambridge.
Journal of the Royal Asiatic Society (Sri Lanka branch). Colombo.
Journal of the Royal Australian Historical Society. (0035-8762). Sydney.
Journal of the Royal Statistical Society: Series A (Statistics in society). (0964-1998). London.
Journal of the Royal Statistical Society: Series B (Statistical methodology). (1369-7412). London.
Journal of the Royal Statistical Society: Series C (Applied statistics). (0035-9254). Oxford.
Journal of the Siam Society. (0857-7099). Bangkok.
Journal of the Third World spectrum. (1072-5040). Washington DC.
Journal of the Walter Roth Museum of Anthropology. (0256-4653). Georgetown DC.
Journal of theoretical politics. (0951-6298). London.
Journal of Third World studies. (8755-3449). Americus GA.
Journal of time series analysis. (0143-9782). Oxford.
Journal of Tokyo Keizai University. (1348-6411). Tokyo.
Journal of Transatlantic studies. (1479-4012). Edinburgh.
Journal of transport economics and policy. (0022-5258). Bath.
Journal of urban economics. (0094-1190). Duluth MN.
Journal of urban ethnology. (1429-0618). Warsaw.
Journal of urban history. (0096-1442). Thousand Oaks CA.
Journal of visual culture. (1470-4129). London.
Journal of women's history. (1042-7961). Bloomington IN.
Journal of women, politics and policy. (1554-477X). New York.
Journal of world business. (1090-9516). Stamford CT.
Journal of world history. (1045-6007). Honolulu HI.
Journal of world prehistory. (0892-7537). Dordrecht.
Journal of world trade. (1011-6702). London.
Journal officiel de la République française: Avis et rapports du Conseil. (0429-3541). Paris.
Journalism studies. (1461-670X). Abingdon.
Kailash: A journal of Himalayan studies. Kathmandu.
Kajian Malaysia. (0127-4082). Penang.
Kansai University review of law and politics. (0388-886X). Osaka.
Katedra: przestrzenie kobiecości. (1641-7046). Warsaw.
Keio economic studies. (0022-9709). Tokyo.
Kinovedcheskie zapiski. (0235-8212). Moscow.
Kisebbségkutatás: szemle a hazai és külföldi irodalomból. (1215-2684). Budapest.
Klio. St. Petersburg.
Knowledge, technology & policy. (0897-1986). Piscataway NJ.
Kobe economic and business review. (0075-6407). Kobe.
Kölner Zeitschrift für Soziologie und Sozialpsychologie. (0340-0425). Wiesbaden.
Konteksty: Polska sztuka ludowa. (1230-6142). Warsaw.

Kontext: Zeitschrift für Systemische Therapie und Familientherapie. (0720-1079). Göttingen.
Korea and world affairs. (0259-9686). Seoul.
Korea focus. (1225-8113). Seoul.
Korea journal. (0023-3900). Seoul.
Korea observer. (0023-3919). Seoul.
Korean social science journal. (1225-0368). Seoul.
Korean studies. (0145-840X). Honolulu HI.
Kosmopolis. (1236-1372). Tampere.
Közgazdasági szemle. (0023-4346). Budapest.
Kredit und Kapital. (0023-4591). Berlin.
Krisis. (0994-2440). Paris.
Kroeber Anthropological Society papers. (0023-4869). Berkeley CA.
Kultura i społeczeństwo. (0023-5172). Warsaw.
Kultura współczesna: Teoria interpretacje praktyka. Warsaw.
Kunapipi: Journal of post-colonial writing. (0106-5734). Wollongong.
Kunnallistieteellinen aikakauskirja. (0356-3669). Kuopio.
Kwartaalschrift economie. (1573-6202). Tilburg.
Kwartalnik filmowy. (0452-9502). Warsaw.
Kwartalnik historii kultury materialnej. (0023-5881). Warsaw.
Kwartalnik historyczny. (0023-5903). Warsaw.
Kwartalnik Opolski. (0023-592X). Opole.
Kyklos. (0023-5962). Basle.
Kyoto University economic review. (0023-6055). Kyoto.
L'Autre: cliniques, cultures et sociétés. Grenoble.
Labor history. (0023-656X). Abingdon.
Labour [Canada] = Travail. (0700-3862). St. John's.
Labour [Italy]: Review of Labour Economics and Industrial Relations. (1121-7081). Oxford.
Labour history. (0023-6942). Sydney.
Labour, capital and society = Travail, capital et société. (0706-1706). Montreal.
Labyrinthe. (1288-6289). Paris.
Land economics. (0023-7639). Madison WI.
Land reform, land settlement and cooperatives. (0251-1894). Rome.
Language. (0097-8507). Baltimore MD.
Language in society. (0047-4045). New York NY.
Language problems and language planning. (0272-2690). Amsterdam.
Lares. (0023-8503). Florence.
Lateinamerika Analysen. (1619-1684). Hamburg.
Latin American business review. (1097-8526). Binghamton NY.
Latin American perspectives. (0094-582X). Thousand Oaks CA.
Latin American politics and society. (1531-426X). Coral Gables FL.
Latin American research review. (0023-8791). Austin TX.
Latino studies. (1476-3435). London.
Latitudes noires. (1763-4245). Strasbourg.
Law and contemporary problems. (0023-9186). Durham NC.
Law and critique. (0957-8536). Liverpool.
Law and philosophy. (0167-5249). Dordrecht.
Law and policy. (0265-8240). Oxford.
Law and society review. (0023-9216). Amherst MA.
Ledelse og Erhvervsøkonomi. (0902-3704). Copenhagen.
Legicom. (1244-9288). Paris.
Legislative studies quarterly. (0362-9805). Iowa City IA.

Leiden journal of international law. (0922-1565). Cambridge.

Lendemains. Marburg.

Lětopis = Lětopis: Zeitschrift für sorbische Sprache, Geschichte und Kultur. (0943-2787). Bautzen.

Leviatán. (0210-6337). Madrid.

Liberté politique. (1288-0639). Levallois Perret.

Libyan studies. (0263-7189). London.

Lignes. (0246-6171). Paris.

Linguistic inquiry. (0024-3892). Cambridge MA.

Litaunistica. (0235-716X). Vilnius.

Literatura ludowa. (0024-4708). Wroclaw.

Lithuanian annual strategic review. (1648-8024). Vilnius.

Local economy. (0269-0942). Abingdon.

Local environment. (1354-9839). Abingdon.

Local government studies. (0300-3930). Ilford.

Łódzkie studia etnograficzne. (0076-0382). Łódz.

Loyola journal of social sciences. (0971-4960). Thiruvananthapuram.

Lud. (0076-1435). Wroclaw.

Lusotopie. Pessac.

Lutte contre le racisme et la xénophobie. (1263-0357). Paris.

Maastricht journal of European and comparative law. (1023-263X). Maastricht.

Maghreb review. (0309-457X). London.

Magyar jog. (0025-0147). Budapest.

Magyar közigazgatás. (0865-736X). Budapest.

Magyar tudomány. (0025-0325). Budapest.

Malaysian journal of tropical geography. (0127-1474). Kuala Lumpur.

Man in India. (0025-1569). Ranchi.

Management accounting research. (1044-5005). London.

Management international review. (0938-8249). Wiesbaden.

Management learning. (1350-5076). London.

Management revue. (0935-9915). Mering.

Management science. (0025-1909). Providence RI.

Managerial and decision economics. (0143-6570). Chichester.

Managing global transitions. (1581-6311). Koper.

Manchester School. (1463-6786). Oxford.

Mande studies. Madison WI.

Mankind quarterly. (0025-2344). Washington DC.

Marga. Colombo.

Marine policy. (0308-597X). Guildford.

Marketing letters. (0923-0645). Dordrecht.

Marketing science. (0732-2399). Linthicum MD.

Marvels & tales: Journal of fairy-tale studies. (1521-4281). Detroit MI.

Material religion. (1743-2200). Oxford.

Materiaux pour l'histoire de notre temps. (0769-3206).

Mathematical finance. (0960-1627). Oxford.

Mathematical social sciences. (0165-4896). Amsterdam.

Media culture and society. (0163-4437). London.

Media history. (1368-8804). Abingdon.

Media international Australia incorporating culture & policy. (1329-878X). St. Lucia.

Mediactive. (1740-8105). London.

Médiamorphoses. (1626-1429). Paris.

Medical anthropology. (0145-9740). London.

Medical anthropology quarterly. (0745-5194). Arlington VA.
Medicine, conflict and survival. (1362-3699). Ilford.
Medien & Kommunikationswissenschaft. (1615-634X). Baden-Baden.
Mediterranean politics. (1362-9395). Ilford.
Mediterranean quarterly: A journal of global issues. (1047-4552). Durham NC.
Medizin, Gesellschaft und Geschichte. (0939-351X). Stuttgart.
Medzinárodné otázky. (1210-1583). Bratislava.
Megamot: Behavioral sciences quarterly. (0025-8679). Jerusalem.
Men and masculinities. (1097-184X). Thousand Oaks CA.
Mens en maatschappij. (0025-9454). Houten.
Mesoamérica. (0252-9963). Guatemala.
Mesopotamia. (0076-6615). Florence.
Metroeconomica. (0026-1386). Oxford.
Mezinárodní vztahy. (0323-1844). Prague.
Middle East business and economic review. (1035-3704). Miranda.
Middle East journal. (0026-3141). Bloomington IN.
Middle East policy. (1061-1924). Washington DC.
Middle East quarterly. (1073-9467). Lawrence KS.
Middle East report. (0899-2851). Washington DC.
Middle East Studies Association bulletin. (0026-3184). Tucson AZ.
Middle Eastern studies. (0026-3206). Ilford.
Migracijske i etničke teme. (1333-2546). Zagreb.
Migration. (0721-2887). Berlin.
Migrations société. (0995-7367). Paris.
Milbank quarterly. (0887-378X). New York NY.
Millennium: journal of international studies. (0305-8298). London.
Millî folklor: International and quarterly journal of folklore. (1300-3984). Ankara.
Minerva. (0026-4695). Dordrecht.
Mir Rossii. Moscow.
Mirovaia ekonomika i mezhdunarodnye otnosheniia. (0131-2227). Moscow.
Mitologicas. (0326-5676). Buenos Aires.
Mitteilungen der Deutschen Orient-Gesellschaft zu Berlin. (0342-118X). Berlin.
Mittelweg 36: Zeitschrift des Hamburger Instituts fur Sozialforschung. (0941-6382). Hamburg.
Mobilization. (1086-671X). San Diego CA.
MOCI: Moniteur du commerce international. (0026-9719). Paris.
Modern & contemporary France. (0267-761X). Abingdon.
Modern Asian studies. (0026-749X). Cambridge.
Modern China. (0097-7004). Thousand Oaks CA.
Modern law review. (0026-7961). Oxford.
Monatsberichte der Deutschen Bundesbank. (0012-0006). Frankfurt am Main.
Monde arabe maghreb machrek. (1241-5294). Paris.
Monde chinois. (1767-3755). Paris.
Monde de l'éducation. (1297-2185). Paris.
Monde des religions. (1763-3346). Paris.
Mondes en développement. (0302-3052). Paris.
Moneta e credito. (0026-9611). Rome.
Monetaria. (0185-1136). Mexico City.
Money affairs. (0187-7615). Mexico City.
Mongolia survey. (1081-5082). Bloomington IN.
Mongolian studies. (0190-3667). Bloomington IN.
Monitoring obshchestvennogo mneniia. Moscow.

Monumenta nipponica. (0027-0741). Tokyo.
Monumenta serica. (0254-9948). Sankt Augustin.
Mots. (0243-6450). Lyon.
Mouseion = Mouseion: Journal of the Classical Association of Canada. (1496-9343). Calgary.
Mouvement social. (0027-2671). Paris.
Mouvements. (1291-6412). Paris.
Multilingua. (0167-8507). Berlin.
Multitudes. (0292-0107). Montigny le Bretonneux.
Museum anthropology. (0892-8339). Arlington VA.
NAPA bulletin. Arlington VA.
Naqd. (1111-4371). Alger.
Narodna umjetnost. (0547-2504). Zagreb.
National identities. (1460-8944). Abingdon.
National Institute economic review. (0027-9501). London.
National interest. (0884-9382). Washington DC.
National tax journal. (0028-0283). Columbus OH.
Nationalism and ethnic politics. (1353-7113). Ilford.
Nationalities papers. (0090-5992). Omaha NE.
Nations and nationalism. (1354-5078). Cambridge.
Natural resources forum. (0165-0203). Guildford.
Natural resources journal. (0028-0739). Albuquerque NM.
Negotiation journal. (0748-4526). New York NY.
NEHA-bulletin. (0920-9875). Amsterdam.
NEHA-jaarboek voor economische, bedrijfs- en techniekgeschiedenis. (1380-5517). Amsterdam.
Netherlands international law review. (0165-070X). The Hague.
Netherlands quarterly of human rights. (0169-3441). Utrecht.
Netherlands yearbook of international law. (0167-6768). The Hague.
Neue Gesellschaft / Frankfurter Hefte. (0177-6738). Bonn.
Neue politische literatur. (0028-3320). Frankfurt am Main.
Neue Zeitschrift für systematische Theologie und Religionsphilosophie. (0028-3517). Berlin.
New economy. (1070-3535). London.
New formations. (0950-2378). London.
New genetics and society. (1463-6778). Basingstoke.
New Left review. (0028-6060). London.
New media & society. (1461-4448). London.
New perspectives on Turkey. (0896-6346). Great Barrington MA.
New political economy. (1356-3467). Abingdon.
New political science. (0739-3148). Abingdon.
New politics. (0028-6494). Brooklyn NY.
New review of bioethics. (1740-0287). Abingdon.
New technology, work and employment. (0268-1072). Oxford.
New York University journal of international law and politics. (0028-7873). New York NY.
New Zealand international review. (0110-0262). Wellington.
New Zealand journal of history. (0028-8322). Auckland.
New Zealand sociology. (0112-921X). Wellington.
NIAS. (0904-597X). Copenhagen.
Nigerian field. (0029-0076). Ibadan.
Nigerian journal of economic and social studies. (0029-0092). Ibadan.
Nijmegen studies in development and cultural change. (0935-7173). Saarbrucken.
Nilo-Ethiopian studies. (1340-329X). Kyoto.
Nonprofit management and leadership. (1048-6682). San Francisco CA.

NORA: Nordic journal of women's studies. (0803-8740). Oslo.
Nord nytt. (0008-1345). Copenhagen.
Nordic journal of African studies. (1235-4481). Helsinki.
Nordicom review: Nordic research on media and communication. (0349-6244). Göteborg.
Nordiques. Paris.
Norois. Paris.
Norsk økonomisk tidsskrift. (0039-0720). Oslo.
Nouveaux dossiers de l'audiovisuel. (1769-101X). Bry-sur-Marne.
Nouveaux regards. (1262-0165). Paris.
Nouvelle alternative. (0764-7565). Paris.
Nouvelles de l'archéologie. (0242-7702). Paris.
Nouvelles pratiques sociales. (0843-4468). Montreal.
Nouvelles questions féministes. (0248-4951). Lausanne.
Nova economia: revista do Departamento de Ciências Econômicas da UFMG. (0103-6351). Belo Horizonte.
Numen. (0029-5973). Leiden.
Observatoire. (1165-2675). Paris.
Obshchestvennye nauki i sovremennost'. (0869-0499). Moscow.
Ocean development and international law. (0090-8320). London.
Oceania. (0029-8077). Sydney.
OECD economic studies. (0255-0822). Paris.
OPEC review. (0277-0180). Oxford.
Open economies review. (0923-7992). Dordrecht.
Opinião pública. (0104-6276). São Paulo.
Option de Confrontations Europe. Montreuil.
Oral history. (0143-0955). Colchester.
Orbis. (0030-4387). Philadelphia PA.
Ordo. (0048-2129). Stuttgart.
Organisationsberatung. Supervision. Coaching. (1618-808X). Wiesbaden.
Organization and environment. (1086-0266). Thousand Oaks CA.
Organization science. (1047-7039). Linthicum MD.
Organization studies. (0170-8406). Berlin.
Organization: the interdisciplinary journal of organization, theory and society. (1350-5084). London.
Organizational analysis. (1551-7470). Greenwich CT.
Organizational behavior and human decision processes. (0749-5978). Duluth MN.
Oriens Extremus: Zeitschrift für Sprache, Kunst und Kultur der Länder des Fernen Ostens. (0030-5197). Wiesbaden.
Orient. (0030-5227). Opladen.
Oriental anthropologist. (0972-558X). Delhi.
Orientalia. (0030-5367). Rome.
Orissa historical research journal. (0474-7267). Orissa.
Orita. (0030-5596). Ibadan.
Osaka economic papers. (0473-4548). Osaka.
Österreichische Zeitschrift für Politikwissenschaft. (1615-5548). Vienna.
Österreichische Zeitschrift für Soziologie. (1011-0070). Wiesbaden.
Osteuropa. (0030-6428). Stuttgart.
Osteuropa Wirtschaft. (0030-6460). Stuttgart.
Otemon economic studies. (0475-0756). Osaka.
Outlook on agriculture. (0030-7270). London.
Outre-mers: Revue d'histoire. (1631-0438). Paris.
Oxford bulletin of economics and statistics. (0305-9049). Oxford.

Oxford development studies. (1360-0818). Abingdon.
Oxford economic papers. (0030-7653). Oxford.
Oxford international review. (0966 0054). Oxford.
Oxford journal of archaeology. (0262-5253). Oxford.
Oxford journal of legal studies. (0143-6503). Oxford.
Oxford review of economic policy. (0266-903X). Oxford.
Oxford review of education. (0305-4985). Abingdon.
Pacific affairs. (0030-851X). Vancouver.
Pacific economic bulletin. (0817-8038). Canberra.
Pacific historical review. (0030-8684). Berkeley CA.
Pacific review. (0951-2748). Abingdon.
Pacific Rim law and policy journal. (1066-8632). Seattle WA.
Pacific studies. (0275-3596). Laie HI.
Pädagogische Rundschau. (0030-9273). Frankfurt.
Paideuma. (0078-7809). Stuttgart.
Pakistan development review. (0030-9729). Islamabad.
Pakistan economic and social review. (1011-002X). Lahore.
Pakistan horizon. (0030-980X). Karachi.
Pakistan journal of applied economics. (0254-9204). Karachi.
Palaeobulgarica. (0204-4021). Sofia.
Palaeoslavica: International journal for the study of Slavic medieval literature, history, language and
     ethnology. (1070-5465). Cambridge MA.
Palestine-Israel journal of politics, economics and culture. (0793-1395). Jerusalem.
Pan American journal of public health = Revista panamericana de salud pública. (1020-4989).
     Washington DC.
Państwo i prawo. (0031-0980). Warsaw.
Papeles de economía española. (0210-9107). Madrid.
Papeles de poblacíon. (1405-7425). Toluca.
Papers from the Institute of Archaeology, PIA. (0965-9315). London.
Papers in regional science. (1056-8190). Berlin.
Papers: revista de sociologia. (0210-2862). Barcelona.
Parallax. (1353-4645). Abingdon.
Parliamentary affairs. (0031-2290). Oxford.
Party politics. (1354-0688). London.
Passages. (0987-8505). Paris.
Passaggi: Rivista italiana di scienze transculturali. Rome.
Past and present. (0031-2746). Oxford.
Patterns of prejudice. (0031-322X). London.
Peace and conflict. (1078-1919). Mahwah NJ.
Penant. (0336-1551). Le Vésinet.
Péninsule. Paris.
Pensée. (0031-4773). Paris.
Pensée de midi. (1621-5338). Arles.
Pensiero politico. (0031-4846). Florence.
Pénzügyi szemle. (0031-496X). Budapest.
People and place. (1039-4788). Victoria.
Perfiles Latinoamericanos. (0188-7653). Mexico City.
Peripherie. (0173-184X). Berlin.
Personnel. (0223-5692).
Perspectiva económica. (0100-039X). São Leopoldo.
Perspectives chinoises. Hong Kong.

Perspectives in education. (0258-2236). Pretoria.
Perspectives on global development and technology. (1569-1500). Leiden.
Perspectives on politics. (1537-5927). Cambridge.
Pesquisa e planejamento econômico. (0100-0551). Rio de Janeiro.
Philippine quarterly of culture and society. (0115-0243). Cebu City.
Philippine studies. (0031-7837). Quezon City.
Philosophical quarterly. (0031-8094). Oxford.
Philosophoire. (1283-7091). Neuilly-sur-Seine.
Philosophy & public affairs. (0048-3915). Princeton NJ.
Philosophy & social criticism. (0191-4537). London.
Philosophy East and West. (0031-8221). Honolulu HI.
Philosophy in the contemporary world. (1077-1999). Charlottesville VA.
Philosophy of science. (0031-8248). Chicago IL.
Philosophy of the social sciences. (0048-3931). Thousand Oaks CA.
Planeación y desarrollo. (0034 8686). Bogota.
Planning practice and research. (0269-7459). London.
Planning theory & practice. (1464-9357). Abingdon.
PoLAR: political and legal anthropology. (1555-2934). Arlington VA.
Policing and society. (1043-9463). London.
Policy and politics. (0305-5736). Bristol.
Policy sciences. (0032-2687). Dordrecht.
Policy studies. (0144-2872). London.
Polis [Moscow]. (0321-2017). Moscow.
Polis [York]. (0412-257X). Thorverton.
Polish quarterly of international affairs. (1230-4999). Warsaw.
Política & sociedade. (1677-4140). Florianópolis.
Política internacional. (0873-6650). Lisbon.
Politica y cultura. (0188-7742). Mexico City.
Politica: tidsskrift for politisk videnskab. (0105-0710). Aarhus.
Political communication. (1058-4609). London.
Political economy journal of India. (0971-2097). Chandigarh.
Political geography. (0962-6298). Oxford.
Political psychology. (0162-895X). Malden MA.
Political quarterly. (0032-3179). Oxford.
Political research quarterly. (1065-9129). Salt Lake City UT.
Political science. (0032-3187). Wellington.
Political science and politics. (1049-0965). Washington DC.
Political science quarterly. (0032-3195). New York NY.
Political studies. (0032-3217). Oxford.
Political theory. (0090-5917). Thousand Oaks CA.
Politiche sociali e servizi. (1128-546X). Milan.
Politická ekonomie. (0032-3233). Prague.
Politička misao. (0032-3241). Zagreb.
Politics. (0263-3957). London.
Politics and society. (0032-3292). Thousand Oaks, CA.
Politics and the life sciences. (0730-9384). Lawrence KS.
Politics, philosophy & economics. (1470-594X). London.
Politiikka. (0032-3365). Tampere.
Politikatudományi szemle. (1216-1438). Budapest.
Politikon. (0258-9346). Stellenbosch.
Politique africaine. (0244-7827). Paris.

Politique et sociétés. (1203-9438). Montreal.
Politique étrangère. (0032-342X). Paris.
Politique internationale. (0221-2781). Paris.
Politiques d'éducation et de formation. (1377-3488). Brussels.
Politiques et management public. (0758-1726). Paris.
Politische Studien. (0032-3462). Munich.
Politische Vierteljahresschrift. (0032-3470). Wiesbaden.
Politisches Denken Jahrbuch. (0942-2307). Stuttgart.
Politix. (0295-2319). Paris.
Politologický časopis. (1211-3247). Brno.
Popular music & society. (0300-7766). Abingdon.
Population. (0032-4663). Paris.
Population and development review. (0098-7921). New York NY.
Population and environment. (0199-0039). New York NY.
Population et sociétés. (0184-7783). Paris.
Population research and policy review. (0167-5923). Dordrecht.
Population studies [London]. (0032-4728). London.
Population, space and place. (1544-8444). Chichester.
Portuguese economic journal. (1617-982X). Berlin.
Portuguese journal of social science. (1476-413X). Bristol.
Positions et médias. (1628-1888). Paris.
Post-communist economies. (1463-1377). Abingdon.
Post-Soviet affairs. (1060-586X). Columbia MD.
Postcolonial studies. (1368-8790). Abingdon.
Potchefstroomse Elektroniese Regsblad = Potchefstroom Electronic Law Journal. (1727-3781).
    Potchefstroom.
Pouvoirs. (0152-0768). Paris.
Pouvoirs locaux. (0998-8289). Paris.
Praca i zabezpieczenie społeczne. (0032-6186). Warsaw.
Prace i materialy Muzeum Archeologicznego i Etnograficznego w Lodzi. Seria Etnograficzna. (0076-
    0315). Łódz.
Practice. (0950-3153). Abingdon.
Practicing anthropology. (0999-4552). Oklahoma City OK.
Prague economic papers. (1210-0455). Prague.
Pratiques. (1161-3726). Montpellier.
Praxis der Kinderpsychologie und Kinderpsychiatrie. (0032-7034). Göttingen.
Présence africaine. (0032-7638). Paris.
Presidential studies quarterly. (0360-4918). New York NY.
Privredna kretanja i ekonomska politika. (1330-187X). Zagreb.
Problèmes d'Amérique latine. (0765-1333). Paris.
Problèmes économiques. (0032-9304). Paris.
Problèmes politiques et sociaux. (0015-9743). Paris.
Problems and perspectives in management. (1727-7051). Sumy.
Problems of economic transition. Armonk NY.
Prochoix. (1283-162X). Paris.
Professional geographer. (0033-0124). Oxford.
Progress in human geography. (0309-1325). Sevenoaks.
Progress in planning. (0305-9006). Oxford.
Projet. (0033-0884). Paris.
Prokla: Zeitschrift für kritische Sozialwissenschaft. (0342-8176). Berlin.
Prometheus. (0810-9028). Basingstoke.

Przegląd antropologiczny. (0033-2003). Poznan.
Przegląd archeologiczny. (0079-7138). Warsaw.
Przegląd Europejski. (1641-2478). Warsaw.
Przegląd historyczny. (0033-2186). Warsaw.
Przegląd orientalistyczny. (0033-2283). Warsaw.
Przegląd polonijny. (0137-303X). Wroclaw.
Przegląd Sejmowy. (1230-5502). Warsaw.
Przegląd socjologiczny. (0033-2356). Łódz.
Przegląd wschodni. Warsaw.
Psicologia & sociedade. (1807-0310). Porto Alegro.
Psicologia em estudo. (1413-7372). Maringa.
Psicologia teoria e prática. (1516-3687). Sao Paulo.
Psicologia USP. (1678-5177). Sao Paolo.
Psicologia: teoria e pesquisa. (1806-3446). Brasilia.
Psicoterapia e scienze umane. (0394-2864). Parma.
Psychiatrie de l'enfant. Paris.
Psychoanalytic review. (0033-2836). New York NY.
Psychoanalytic studies. (1460-8952). Oxford.
Psychological bulletin. (0033-2909). Washington DC.
Psychological review. (0033-295X). Washington DC.
Psychological science: a journal of the American Psychological Association. (0956-7976). Oxford.
Psychology and developing societies. (0971-3336). New Delhi.
Psychology of women quarterly. (0361-6843). New York NY.
Psychology, crime & law. (1068-316X). Abingdon.
Psychology, evolution & gender. (1461-6661). Abingdon.
Psychotherapie und Sozialwissenschaft. (1436-4638). Göttingen.
Public administration. (0033-3298). Oxford.
Public administration and development. (0271-2075). Chichester.
Public administration and policy. (1022-0275). Hong Kong.
Public administration review. (0033-3352). Washington DC.
Public affairs quarterly. (0887-0373). Bowling Green OH.
Public archaeology. (1465-5187). London.
Public choice. (0048-5829). Dordrecht.
Public culture. (0899-2363). Durham NC.
Public finance = Finances publiques. (0033-3476). Frankfurt am Main.
Public finance review. (1091-1421). Thousand Oaks CA.
Public interest. (0033-3557). Washington DC.
Public law. (0033-3565). London.
Public management review. (1471-9037). Abingdon.
Public money and management. (0954-0962). Oxford.
Public opinion quarterly. (0033-362X). Chicago IL.
Publius: the journal of federalism. (0048-5950). Easton PA.
Publizistik. (0033-4006). Konstanz.
Punishment & society. (1462-4745). London.
Pyramides. (1376-098X). Brussels.
Quaderni dell'osservatorio elettorale. (0392-6753). Florence.
Quaderni di sociologia. (0033-4952). Turin.
Quaderni di studi arabi. (1121-2306). Venice.
Quaderni storici. (0301-6307). Bologna.
Qualitative inquiry. (1077-8004). Thousand Oaks CA.
Qualitative research. (1468-7941). London.

Qualitative sociology. (0162-0436). Dordrecht.

Quality & quantity. (0033-5177). Dordrecht.

Quart monde. (0980-7764). Paris.

Quarterly journal of economics. (0033-5533). Cambridge MA.

Quarterly review of economics and finance. (0033-5797). Champaign IL.

Quest. (1011-226X). Groningen.

Questions internationales. (1761-7146). Paris.

Race and class. (0306-3968). London.

Race ethnicity and education. (1361-3324). Abingdon.

Radical history review. (0163-6545). New York NY.

Radical philosophy review. (1388-4441). Charlottesville VA.

Raison présente. (0033-9075). Paris.

Raison publique. (1767-0543). Paris.

Raisons politiques. Paris.

Rand journal of economics. (0741-6261). Santa Monica CA.

Rapport de recherche - Centre d'études de l'emploi. Noisy-le-Grand.

Rassegna economica. (0390-010X). Naples.

Rassegna italiana di sociologia. (0486-0349). Bologna.

Rassegna parlamentare. (0486-0373). Rome.

Rationality and society. (1043-4631). London.

Réalités industrielles. (1148-7941). Saint-Etienne.

Recherche. (0029-5671). Paris.

Recherche socialiste. (1283-7393). Paris.

Recherches économiques de Louvain. (0770-4518). Louvanin-la-Neuve.

Recherches sociographiques. (0034-1282). Quebec.

Recherches sociologiques. (0771-677X). Leuven.

Rechtstheorie. (0034-1398). Berlin.

Refractions. (1287-4086). Paris.

Refuge. (0229-5113). Toronto.

Regards sur l'actualité. (0337-7091). Paris.

Regards sur l'économie allemande. (1156-8992). Paris.

REGARDS: Rencontres enseignement gestion actions recherches dossiers sécurité sociale. (0988-6982). Paris.

Regio. (0865 557X). Budapest.

Region: Ekonomika i sotsiologiia. (0868-5169). Novosibirsk.

Regional and federal studies. (1359-7566). Ilford.

Regional science and urban economics. (0166-0462). Amsterdam.

Regional studies. (0034-3404). Abingdon.

Relaciones internacionales. (0185-0814). Mexico City.

Relações internacionais. (1645-9199). Lisbon.

Relations industrielles = Industrial relations. (0034-379X). Québec.

Relations internationales. (0335-2013). Paris.

Relazioni internazionali. (0034-3846). Milan.

Religion. (0048-721X). London.

Religion and theology. (1023-0807). Leiden.

Religion Staat Gesellschaft. (1438-955X). Berlin.

Religion, state and society. (0963-7494). Abingdon.

REM: Revue de l'économie meridionale. (0987-3813). Montpellier.

Renewal: The journal of Labour politics. (0968-252X). London.

Replika: Társadalomtudományi folyóirat. (0865-8188). Budapest.

Reproductive health matters. (0968-8080). London.

Res - Anthropology and aesthetics. (0277-1322). Cambridge MA.
Res publica [Brussels]. (0486-4700). Brussels.
Res publica [Creteil]. (1278-6209). Creteil.
Res publica [Liverpool]. (1356-4765). Liverpool.
Research in African literatures. (0034-5210). Bloomington IN.
Research in economic anthropology. (0190-1281). Greenwich CT.
Research in economics = Ricerche economiche. (1090-9443). Amsterdam.
Research in education. (0034-5237). Manchester.
Research in Melanesia. (0254-0665). Port Moresby.
Research in political economy. (0161-7230). Greenwich CT.
Research in social movements, conflicts and change. (0163-786X). Greenwich CT.
Research in social stratification and mobility. (0276-5624). Greenwich CT.
Research in the sociology of work. (0277-2833). Greenwich CT.
Research papers in education - policy and practice. (0267-1522). Abingdon.
Research policy. (0048-7333). Amsterdam.
Réseaux. (0751-7971). Cachan.
Reseaux - Ciephum. (0773-1213). Creteil.
Resources policy. (0301-4207). Oxford.
Rethinking Marxism. (0893-5696). New York NY.
Retraite et société. (1167-4687). Paris.
Review of African political economy. (0305-6244). Abingdon.
Review of Austrian economics. (0889-3047). Dordrecht.
Review of black political economy. (0034-6446). New Brunswick NJ.
Review of Central and East European law. (0925-9880). Leiden.
Review of economic conditions in Italy. (0034-6799). Rome.
Review of economic dynamics. (1094-2025). New York NY.
Review of economic studies. (0034-6527). Oxford.
Review of economics and statistics. (0034-6535). Cambridge.
Review of economies in transition. (1235-7405). Helsinki.
Review of education, pedagogy & cultural studies. (1071-4413). Philadelphia PA.
Review of financial studies. (0893-9454). Cary NC.
Review of income and wealth. (0034-6586). New York NY.
Review of Indonesian and Malaysian affairs. (0815-7251). Canberra.
Review of industrial organization. (0889-938X). Dordrecht.
Review of international economics. (0965-7576). Oxford.
Review of international political economy. (0969-2290). Abingdon.
Review of international studies. (0260-2105). Cambridge.
Review of Middle East economics and finance. (1475-3685). Abingdon.
Review of Pacific Basin financial markets and policies. (0219-0915). Singapore.
Review of political economy. (0953-8259). Abingdon.
Review of politics. (0034-6705). Notre Dame IN.
Review of population and social policy. (0918-788X). Tokyo.
Review of quantitative finance and accounting. (0924-865X). Dordrecht.
Review of radical political economics. (0486-6134). Thousand Oaks CA.
Review of social economy. (0034-6764). Abingdon.
Review of the economic situation of Mexico. (0187-3407). Mexico City.
Review of urban and regional development studies. (0917-0553). Tokyo.
Review of world economics. (1610-2878). Berlin.
Review. Federal Reserve Bank of St. Louis. (0014-9187). St. Louis MO.
Review. Fernand Braudel Center. (0147-9032). Binghamton NY.
Reviews in anthropology. (0093-8157). Newark NJ.

Revija za socijalnu politiku. (1330-2965). Zagreb.
Revista brasileira de ciências sociais. (0102-6909). São Paulo.
Revista brasileira de economia. (0034-7140). Rio de Janeiro.
Revista brasileira de estudos de população. (0102-3098). São Paulo.
Revista Colombiana de educación. (0120-3916). Bogotá.
Revista de administração de empresas. (0034-7590). Sao Paulo.
Revista de administração Mackenzie. (1518-6776). Sao Paulo.
Revista de administración pública. (0034-7639). Madrid.
Revista de ciencia política [Santiago]. (0718-090X). Santiago.
Revista de ciencias sociales. (0034-7817). Puerto Rico.
Revista de economía. (0797-5546). Montevideo.
Revista de economía del rosario. (0123-5362). Bogota.
Revista de economía institucional. (0124-5996). Bogota.
Revista de economia Mackenzie. (1678-5002). Sao Paulo.
Revista de economía y estadística. (0034-8066). Córdoba.
Revista de estudios políticos. (0048-7694). Madrid.
Revista de fomento social. (0015-6043). Madrid.
Revista de historia económica. (0212-6109). Madrid.
Revista de humanidades: tecnológico de Monterrey. (1405-4167). Monetrrey.
Revista de sociologia e política. (0104-4478). Curitiba.
Revista del Banco de la República. (0005-4828). Bogota.
Revista estudos feministas. (0104-026X). Florianópolis.
Revista gerencia y políticas de salud. (1657-7027). Bogotá.
Revista Iberoamericana de Ciencia, Tecnología y Sociedad. (1668-0030). Buenos Aires.
Revista internacional de lingüística Iberoamericana. (1579-9425). Madrid.
Revista Latinoamericana de administración. (1012-8255). Bogota.
Revista lusófona de educação. (1645-7250). Lisbon.
Revista mexicana de ciencias politicas y sociales. (0185-1918). Mexico City.
Revista paraguaya de sociología. (0035-0354). Asunción.
Revista transilvană de ştiinţe administrative = Transylvanian review of administrative sciences. (1454-1378). Cluj-Napoca.
Revista Universidad EAFIT. (0120-341X). Medellín.
Revista Uruguaya de Ciencia Política. (0797-9789). Montevideo.
Revue administrative. (0035-0672). Paris.
Revue algérienne des sciences juridiques économiques et politiques. (0035-0699). Algiers.
Revue archéologique. (0035-0737). Paris.
Revue belge de droit international = Belgian review of international law = Belgisch tijdschrift voor internationaal recht. (0035-0788). Brussels.
Revue belge de sécurité sociale. (0035-0834). Brussels.
Revue canadienne d'études de développement = Canadian journal of development studies. (0225-5189). Ottawa.
Revue critique de droit international privé. (0035-0958). The Hague.
Revue d'assyriologie et d'archéologie orientale. Paris.
Revue d'économie du développement. (1245-4060). Paris.
Revue d'économie financière. (0987-3368). Paris.
Revue d'économie politique. (0373-2630). Paris.
Revue d'économie régionale et urbaine. (0180-7307). Paris.
Revue d'études comparatives Est-Ouest. (0338-0599). Paris.
Revue d'études palestiniennes. (0252-8290). Paris.
Revue d'histoire diplomatique. (0035-2365). Paris.
Revue d'histoire moderne et contemporaine. (0048-8003). Paris.

Revue de droit des affaires de l'Université Paris II Panthéon-Assas. Paris.
Revue de droit international et de droit comparé. (0775-4663). Brussels.
Revue de droit international, de sciences diplomatiques et politiques. (0035-1091). Lausanne.
Revue de géographie alpine. (0035-1121). Grenoble.
Revue de l'Institut de sociologie. (0770-1055). Brussels.
Revue de l'integration et de la migration internationale = Journal of international migration and integration. (1488-3473). Edmonton.
Revue de l'IRES. (1145-1378). Noisy-le-Grand.
Revue de l'OFCE: Observations et diagnostics économiques. (1265-9576). Paris.
Revue de la Confédération française démocratique du travail. (1280-8180). Paris.
Revue de la recherche juridique, droit prospectif. (0249-8731). Aix-en-Provence.
Revue de métaphysique et de morale. (0035-1571). Paris.
Revue de science criminelle et de droit pénal comparé. (0035-1733). Paris.
Revue des deux mondes. (0750-9278). Paris.
Revue des études sud-est européennes. Bucharest.
Revue des sciences de gestion. (1160-7742). Epinay-sur-Orge.
Revue des sociétés, Journal des sociétés. (0242-5424).
Revue du droit de l'Union européenne. Paris.
Revue du droit public et de la science politique en France et à l'étranger. (0035-2578). Paris.
Revue du Marché commun et de l'Union européenne. (0035-2616). Paris.
Revue du monde musulman et de la Méditerranée. (0997-1327). Aix-en-Provence.
Revue du travail. (0035-2705). Brussels.
Revue du Trésor. (0035-2713). Paris.
Revue économique. (0035-2764). Paris.
Revue économique de l'OCDE. (0255-0830). Paris.
Revue économique et sociale. (0035-2772). Lausanne-Dorigny.
Revue européenne des migrations internationales. (0765-0752). Poitiers.
Revue européenne des sciences sociales: Cahiers Vilfredo Pareto. (0048-8046). Geneva.
Revue française d'administration publique. (0152-7401). Paris.
Revue française d'histoire des idées politiques. (1266-7862). Paris.
Revue française de civilisation britannique. (0248-9015). Paris.
Revue française de droit administratif. (0763-1219). Paris.
Revue française de finances publiques. (0294-0833).
Revue française de gestion. (0338-4551). Cachan.
Revue française de science politique. (0035-2950). Paris.
Revue française de sociologie. (0035-2969). Gap.
Revue française des affaires sociales. (0035-2985). Paris.
Revue générale de droit international public. (0035-3094). Paris.
Revue générale des collectivités territoriales. (1290-4473). Montreuil.
Revue Gestion 2000: Management et prospective. (0773-0543). Louvain.
Revue hellénique de droit international. (0035-3256). Athens.
Revue historique. (0035-3264). Paris.
Revue internationale de droit comparé. (0035-3337). Paris.
Revue internationale de droit économique. (1010-8831). Issy-les-Moulineaux.
Revue internationale de l'économie sociale: Recma. (0035-2020). Paris.
Revue internationale de sécurité sociale. (0379-0312). Pieterlen.
Revue internationale des sciences administratives. (0773-2961). Brussels.
Revue internationale et stratégique. (1287-1672). Paris.
Revue juridique de l'environnement. (0397-0299). Strasbourg.
Revue juridique et politique des Etats francophones. (1766-2516). Paris.
Revue juridique et politique, indépendance et coopération. (0035-3574).

Revue nouvelle. (0035-3809). Brussels.
Revue philosophique de la France et de l'étranger. (0035-3833). Paris.
Revue politique et parlementaire. (0035-385X). Paris.
Revue pratique de droit social. (0399-1148). Montreuil.
Revue socialiste. (1294-2529). Paris.
Revue trimestrielle de droit commercial et de droit économique. (0244-9358). Paris.
Revue trimestrielle de droit européen. (0035-4317). Paris.
Revue tunisienne des sciences sociales. (0035-4333). Tunis.
RIG: Kulturhistorisk tidskrift. (0035-5267). Stockholm.
Riron to hoho = Sociological theory and methods. (0913-1442). Sapporo.
Risk analysis = Risk An. (0272-4332). Oxford.
Risk, decision and policy. (1357-5309). Cambridge.
Risparmio. (0035-5615). Milan.
Rivista di diritto finanziario e scienza delle finanze. (0035-6131). Milan.
Rivista di economia agraria. (0035-6190). Bologna.
Rivista di politica economica. (0391-6170). Rome.
Rivista di storia economica. (0393-3415). Turin.
Rivista di studi politici internazionali. (0035-6611). Florence.
Rivista internazionale di scienze economiche e commerciali. (0035-6751). Padua.
Rivista internazionale di scienze sociali. (0035-676X). Milan.
Rivista italiana di politiche pubbliche. Rome.
Rivista italiana di scienza politica. (0048-8402). Bologna.
Rivista trimestrale di diritto pubblico. (0557-1464). Milan.
Roczniki socjologii rodziny. Studia socjologiczne oraz interdyscyplinarne. (0867-2059). Poznan.
Roma. Chandigarh.
Romani studies. (1528-0748). Cheverly MD.
Romanian journal of society and politics. (1582-5795). Bucharest.
Ronshu (Journal of Komatsu College). Komatsu.
Round table. (0035-8533). Abingdon.
Rozprawy i studia Uniwersytetu Szczecińskiego. (0860-2751). Szczecin.
Rural history: Economy, society, culture. (0956-7933). Cambridge.
Rural sociology. (0036-0112). College Station TX.
Russian politics and law. (1061-1940). Armonk NY.
Russian review. (0036-0341). Malden MA.
RWI-Mitteilungen: Zeitschrift für Wirtschaftsforschung. (0933-0089). Berlin.
Saeculum. (0080-5319). Freiburg.
SAHARA J. (1729-0376). Cape Town.
SAIS review. (0036-0775). Washington DC.
Sananjalka. (0558-4639). Turku.
Sangeet natak. New Delhi.
Santé publique. (0995-3914). Vandoeuvre-lès-Nancy.
Sarawak gazette. (0036-4762). Kuching.
Sarawak Museum journal. (0375-3050). Kuching.
Savanna. (0331-0523). Zaria.
Savings and development. (0393-4551). Milan.
Scandinavian economic history review. (0358-5522). Lund.
Scandinavian journal of development alternatives and area studies. (0280-2791). Stockholm.
Scandinavian journal of economics. (0347-0520). Oxford.
Scandinavian journal of history. (0346-8755). Oslo.
Scandinavian journal of social welfare. (0907-2055). Copenhagen.
Scandinavian journal of the Old Testament. (0901-8328). Aarhus.

Scandinavian political studies. (0080-6757). Oxford.

Schweizerische Zeitschrift für Soziologie = Revue suisse de sociologie = Swiss journal of sociology. (0379-3664). Zurich.

Schweizerische Zeitschrift für Volkswirtschaft und Statistik = Revue suisse d'économie et de statistique. (0303-9692). Basle.

Science and public policy. (0302-3427). Guildford.

Science and society. (0036-8237). New York NY.

Science as culture. (0950-5431). London.

Science, technology and society. (0971-7218). Thousand Oaks CA.

Science, technology, & human values. (0162-2439). Thousand Oaks CA.

Sciences de la société. (1168-1446). Toulouse.

Sciences humaines. (0996-6994). Auxerre.

Scottish geographical journal. (0036-9225). Glasgow.

Scottish journal of political economy. (0036-9292). Oxford.

Security dialogue. (0967-0106). London.

Security studies. (0963-6412). Ilford.

Sefarad. (0037-0894). Madrid.

Semaine juridique: Administrations et collectivités territoriales. (1637-5114). Paris.

Semaine juridique: Edition génerale. (0242-5777). Paris.

Semaine juridique: Entreprise et affaires. Paris.

Semaine juridique: Entreprise et affaires. Cahiers de droit de l'entreprise. Paris.

Semiotica. (0037-1998). Berlin.

Senri ethnological studies. Osaka.

Sens public. Paris.

Sève. (1765-8888). Paris.

Sexualities: studies in culture and society. (1363-4607). London.

Signs: Journal of women in culture and society. (0097-9740). Chicago IL.

Sikh review. (0037-5123). Calcutta.

Simulation and gaming. (1046-8781). Thousand Oaks CA.

Singapore economic review. (0217-5908). Singapore.

Sistema. (0210-0223). Madrid.

Slavic review. (0037-6779). Stanford CA.

Slavonic and East European review. (0037-6795). London.

Slovak foreign policy affairs. (1335-6259). Bratislava.

Slovanský přehled: Review for Central, Eastern and Southeastern European history. (0037-6922). Prague.

Slovensky národopis. (0037-7023). Bratislava.

Slovo. (0954-6839). London.

Small business economics. (0921-898X). Dordrecht.

Small enterprise development. (0957-1329). London.

Small wars and insurgencies. (0959-2318). Ilford.

Smithsonian contributions to anthropology. (0081-0223). Washington DC.

Social & cultural geography. (1464-9365). Abingdon.

Social action [New Delhi]. (0037-7627). New Delhi.

Social analysis [Adelaide]. (0155-977X). Adelaide.

Social and economic studies. (0037-7651). Kingston.

Social and legal studies. (0964-6639). London.

Social anthropology. (0964-0282). Cambridge.

Social biology. (0037-766X). New York NY.

Social choice and welfare. (0176-1714). Berlin.

Social cognition. (0278-016X). New York NY.

Social compass. (0037-7686). London.
Social development issues: Alternative approaches to global human needs. (0147-1473). Arlington TX.
Social dynamics. (0253-3952). Rondebosch.
Social forces. (0037-7732). Chapel Hill NC.
Social history. (0307-1022). Abingdon.
Social identities: journal for the study of race, nation and culture. (1350-4630). Abingdon.
Social indicators research. (0303-8300). Dordrecht.
Social justice. (0094-7571). San Francisco CA.
Social justice research. (0885-7466). Dordrecht.
Social movement studies. (1474-2837). Abingdon.
Social networks. (0378-8733). Amsterdam.
Social philosophy & policy. (0265-0525). Cambridge.
Social philosophy today. (1543-4044). Charlottesville VA.
Social policy. (0037-7783). New York NY.
Social policy and administration. (0144-5596). Oxford.
Social policy and society. (1474-7464). Cambridge.
Social politics: international studies in gender, state and society. (1072-4745). Cary NC.
Social problems. (0037-7791). Berkeley CA.
Social psychology quarterly. (0190-2725). Washington DC.
Social science & medicine. (0277-9536). Exeter.
Social science history. (0145-5532). Durham NC.
Social science information. (0539-0184). London.
Social science Japan. (1340-7155). Tokyo.
Social science Japan journal. (1369-1465). Oxford.
Social science quarterly. (0038-4941). Oxford.
Social science research. (0049-089X). Orlando FL.
Social sciences in China. (0252-9203). Beijing.
Social scientist. (0970-0293). New Delhi.
Social security: Journal of welfare and social security studies. (0334-231X). Jerusalem.
Social semiotics. (1035-0330). Queensland.
Social service review. (0037-7961). Chicago IL.
Social studies of science. (0306-3127). London.
Social theory and health. (1477-8211). Basingstoke.
Social work and social sciences review. (0953-5225). London.
Social work education. (0261-5479). London.
Socialism and democracy. (0885-4300). New York NY.
Socialist history. (0969-4331). London.
Socialno delo. (0352-7956). Ljubljana.
Sociétés contemporaines. (1150-1944). Paris.
Society. (0147-2011). New Brunswick NJ.
Society & animals. (1063-1119). Isle of Harris.
Socio-economic planning sciences. (0038-0121). Exeter.
Sociologia [Bratislava] = Sociology [Bratislava]. (0049-1225). Bratislava.
Sociologia [Rome]. (0038-0156). Rome.
Sociologia del lavoro. Milan.
Sociologia internationalis. (0038-0164). Berlin.
Sociologia ruralis. (0038-0199). Oxford.
Sociological bulletin. (0038-0229). New Delhi.
Sociological forum. (0884-8971). New York NY.
Sociological methodology. (0081-1750). Oxford.
Sociological methods and research. (0049-1241). Thousand Oaks CA.

Sociological perspectives. (0731-1214). Las Vegas NV.

Sociological quarterly. (0038-0253). Greenwich CT.

Sociological review. (0038-0261). London.

Sociological theory. (0735-2751). Malden MA.

Sociologický časopis. (0038-0288). Prague.

Sociologie du travail. (0038-0296). Paris.

Sociologie et sociétés. (0038-030X). Montréal.

Sociologija = Sociology [Belgrade]. Belgrade.

Sociologija: Mintis ir veiksmas. (1392-3358). Klaipeda.

Sociologische gids. (0038-0334). Meppel.

Sociologus. (0038-0377). Berlin.

Sociology [U.K.]. (0038-0385). Cambridge.

Sociology of health and illness. (0141-9889). Oxford.

Sociology of religion. (0038-0210). Holiday FL.

SOJOURN: Journal of social issues in Southeast Asia. (0217-9520). Singapore.

Šolsko polje. (1581-6036). Ljubljana.

Sosyal bilimler dergisi. (1303-0329). Sivas.

Sosyoloji Araştirmalari Dergisi = Journal of sociological research. (1302-4426). Ankara.

Sotahistoriallinen aikakauskirja. (0357-816X). Jyväskylä.

Sotsial'no-gumanitarnye znaniia. (0869-8120). Moscow.

Sotsiologicheski problemi. (0324-1572). Sofia.

Sotsiologicheskie issledovaniia (Sotsis). (0132-1625). Moscow.

Soudobé dějiny. (1210-7050). Prague.

Soundings: a journal of politics and culture. (1362-6620). London.

South African archaeological bulletin. (0038-1969). Vlaeberg.

South African geographical journal = Suid-Afrikaanse geografiese tydskrif. (0373-6245). Rondebosch.

South African historical journal = Suid-Afrikaanse historiese joernaal. (0258-2473). Rondebosch.

South African journal of African languages = Suid-Afrikaanse tydskrif vir Afrikatale. (0257-2117). Pretoria.

South African journal of economic history. (1011-3436). Pretoria.

South African journal of economics = Suid-Afrikaanse tydskrif vir ekonomie. (0038-2280). Pretoria.

South African journal of education. (0256-0100). Silver Lakes.

South African journal of international affairs. (1022-0461). Johannesburg.

South African journal on human rights. (0258-7203). Johannesburg.

South African law journal. (0258-2503). Kenwyn.

South Asia. (0085-6401). Armidale.

South Asia research. (0262-7280). New Delhi.

South Asian anthropologist. (0257-7348). Ranchi.

South Asian popular culture. (1474-6689). Abingdon.

South Asian studies. (0266-6030). London.

South Asian survey. (0971-5231). New Delhi.

South East Asia research. (0967-828X). London.

South East Asian review. Gaya.

South East Europe review for labour and social affairs. (1435-2869). Baden-Baden.

South European society & politics. (1360-8746). Ilford.

Southeast Asian affairs. (0377-5437). Singapore.

Southern economic journal. (0038-4038). Stillwater OK.

Sozial.Geschichte: Zeitchrift für historische Analyse des 20. und 21. Jahrhunderts. (1660-2870). Frankfurt.

Soziale systeme: Zeitschrift für soziologische theorie. (0948-423X). Stuttgart.

Soziale Welt. (0038-6073). Baden-Baden.

Sozialer Fortschritt: Unabhängige Zeitschrift für Sozialpolitik. Berlin.
Sozialersinn: Zeitschrift für hermeneutische Sozialforschung. (1439-9326). Wiesbaden.
Sozialwissenschaften und Berufspraxis. (0724-3464). Wiesbaden.
Soziologie: Forum der Deutschen Gesellschaft für Soziologie. (0340-918X). Opladen.
Soziologische Revue. (0343-4109). Munich.
Space & polity. (1356-2576). Abingdon.
Space and culture. (1206-3312). Thousand Oaks CA.
Spanish economic review. (1435-5469). Berlin.
Spanish journal of psychology. (1138-7416). Madrid.
Spoudai. (1105-8919). Piraeus.
Sprawozdania archeologiczne. (0081-3834). Warsaw.
Sprawy narodowościowe - Seria nowa. (1230-1698). Poznan.
State politics & policy quarterly. (1532-4400). Illinois.
Statisztikai szemle. (0039-0690). Budapest.
Statsvetenskaplig tidskrift. (0039-0747). Lund.
Statute law review. (0144-3593). Oxford.
Storia politica società. Turin.
Stosunki miedzynarodowe. (0209-0961). Warsaw.
Strategic management journal. (0143-2095). Chichester.
Strategic review for Southern Africa = Strategiese oorsig vir Suider-Afrika. (1013-1108). Pretoria.
Strategic studies. Islamabad.
Studi bresciani. (1121-6557). Brescia.
Studi di sociologia. Milan.
Studia africana. (1130-5703). Barcelona.
Studia choreologica. (1508-1354). Poznan.
Studia demograficzne. (0039-3134). Warsaw.
Studia diplomatica. (0770-2965). Brussels.
Studia etnologiczne i antropologiczne. (0208-6336). Katowice.
Studia fennica. (0085-6835). Helsinki.
Studia iranica. (0772-7852). Lésigny.
Studia orientalia. (0039-3282). Helsinki.
Studia prawno-ekonomiczne. (0081-6841). Łódz.
Studia rosenthaliana. (0039-3347). Amsterdam.
Studia Universitatis Babeş-Bolyai. Serie: Historia. (1220-0492). Cluj-Napoca.
Studia Universitatis Babeş-Bolyai. Serie: Iurisprudentia. (1220-045X). Cluj-Napoca.
Studia Universitatis Babeş-Bolyai. Serie: Oeconomica. (1220-0506). Cluj-Napoca.
Studia Universitatis Babeş-Bolyai. Serie: Philosophia. (1221-8138). Cluj-Napoca.
Studia Universitatis Babeş-Bolyai. Serie: Politica. (1224-8711). Cluj-Napoca.
Studia Universitatis Babeş-Bolyai. Serie: Psychologia-paedagogia. (1221-8111). Cluj-Napoca.
Studia Universitatis Babeş-Bolyai. Serie: Sociologia. (1224-8703). Cluj-Napoca.
Studia Universitatis Babeş-Bolyai. Serie: Studia Europaea. (1224-8746). Cluj-Napoca.
Studies and essays — behavioral sciences and philosophy. (1342-4262). Kanazawa.
Studies in American political development. (0898-588X). New York NY.
Studies in comparative international development. (0039-3606). New Brunswick NJ.
Studies in conflict and terrorism. (1057-610X). London.
Studies in East European thought. (0925-9392). Dordrecht.
Studies in family planning. (0039-3665). New York NY.
Studies in higher education. (0307-5079). Abingdon.
Studies in history. (0257-6430). New Delhi.
Studies in history and philosophy of modern physics. (1355-2198). Oxford.
Studies in history and philosophy of science. (0039-3681). Oxford.

Studies in philosophy and education. (0039-3746). Dordrecht.
Studies in political economy. (0707-8552). Ottawa.
Studies of tribes and tribals. (0972-639X). Delhi.
Südosteuropa Aktuell. Munich.
Südosteuropa Mitteilungen. (0340-174X). Munich.
Südosteuropa-Jahrbuch. Munich.
Südosteuropa-Studien. Munich.
Suomalais-Ugrilaisen Seuran Aikakauskirja. (0355-0214). Helsinki.
Suomalais-Ugrilaisen Seuran kansatieteellisiä julkaisuja. (0359-7679). Helsinki.
Survival. (0039-6338). Oxford.
Sustainable development. (0968-0802). Chichester.
Svobodnaia mysl'. (0869-4435). Moscow.
Swedish economic policy review. (1400-1829). Stockholm.
Swiss political science review. (1424-7755). Zurich.
Symbolic interaction. (0195-6086). Berkeley CA.
Symposium. (1480-2333). Ontario.
Syndicalisme et société. (1290-2896).
Systems research and behavioral science. (1092-7026). Chichester.
Századok. (0039-8098). Budapest.
Szkice humanistyczne. (1642-6363). Olsztyn.
Szociológiai szemle. (1216-2051). Budapest.
Tabula Rasa. (1794-2489). Bogotá.
Taiwan journal of anthropology. (1727-1878). Taipei.
Taiwan journal of democracy. (1815-7238). Taipei.
Tangent. (0219-4384). Singapore.
Tanzanian affairs. (0952-2948). London.
Tareas. (0494-7061). Panama City.
Társadalmi szemle. (0039-971X). Budapest.
Társadalomkutatás. (0580-4795). Budapest.
TDP. (1253-6032). Tours.
Technology analysis & strategic management. (0953-7325). London.
Technology and culture. (0040-165X). Baltimore MD.
Technology and development. (0914-918X). Tokyo.
Tel Aviv: Journal of the Institute of Archaeology of Tel Aviv University. (0334-4355). Tel Aviv.
Telecommunications policy. (0308-5961). Amsterdam.
Television & new media. (1527-4764). Thousand Oaks CA.
Telos. (0090-6514). New York NY.
Tempo social. (0103-2070). São Paulo.
Temps des médias. (1764-2507). Levallois-Perret.
Temps maudits. Bordeaux.
Temps modernes. (0040-3075). Paris.
Teología y vida. (0049-3449). Santiago.
Terrain. (0760-5668). Paris.
Territoires 2020. (1622-891X). Paris.
Territorios: revista de estudios regionales y urbanos. (0123-8418). Bogota.
Terrorism and political violence. (0954-6553). Ilford.
Text and talk: An interdisciplinary journal of language, discourse & communication studies. (1860-7330). Berlin.
Textile: the journal of cloth & culture. (1475-9756). Oxford.
Théologiques. (1188-7109). Montréal.
Theology and science. (1474-6719). Abingdon.

Theoria: a journal of social and political theory. (0040-5817). Pietermaritzburg.

Theory and decision. (0040-5833). Dordrecht.

Theory and psychology. (0959-3543). London.

Theory and research in education. (1477-8785). London.

Theory and society. (0304-2421). Dordrecht.

Theory culture and society. (0263-2764). London.

Thesis eleven. (0725-5136). London.

Third text: critical perspectives on contemporary art and culture. (0952-8822). Abingdon.

Third World quarterly. (0143-6597). Abingdon.

Tibet journal. (0970-5368). Dharamshala.

Tidsskriftet antropologi. (0906-3021). Copenhagen.

Tiers Monde. (0040-7356). Paris.

Tijdschrift voor economie en management. (0772-7664). Louvain.

Tijdschrift voor economische en sociale geografie = Journal of economic and social geography. (0040-747X). Oxford.

Tijdschrift voor sociale en economische geschiedenis. (1572-1701). Amsterdam.

Time & society. (0961-463X). London.

Tocqueville review. (0730-479X). Paris.

Tokovi istorije. (0354-6497). Belgrade.

TOPIA: Canadian journal of cultural studies. (1206-0143). Ontario.

Történelmi szemle. (0040-9634). Budapest.

Totalitarian movements and political religions. (1469-0764). Ilford.

Tourism economics. (1354-8166). London.

Tourism geographies. (1461-6688). Abingdon.

Tourism review international. (1544-2721). Elmsford NY.

Town planning review. (0041-0020). Liverpool.

Trabalho, educação e saúde. (1678-1007). Rio de Janeiro.

Trajets. Paris.

Transactions of the Institute of British Geographers: New series. (0020-2754). London.

Transfer: European review of labour and research. (1024-2589). Antwerp.

Transformation. (0258-7696). Durban.

Transformations in business & economics. (1648-4460). Kaunas.

Transit: Europäische Revue. (0938-2062). Frankfurt am Main.

Transitions & sociétés. Boulogne.

Transitions [Brussels]. (0779-3812). Brussels.

Transitions [Prague]. (1211-0205). Prague.

Transnational organized crime. (1357-7387). Ilford.

Transportation. (0049-4488). Dordrecht.

Transportation science. (0041-1655). Linthicum MD.

Travail et emploi. (0224-4365). Paris.

Travail humain. (0041-1868). Paris.

Travail, genre et sociétés. (1294-6303). Paris.

Trayectorias: revista de ciencias sociales. (1405-8928). Nuevo León.

Tribus. (0082-6413). Stuttgart.

Trimestre económico. (0041-3011). Mexico City.

Turkish review of Middle East studies. Istanbul.

Turkish studies. (1468-3849). Ilford.

Turkish yearbook of international relations = Milletlerarasi münasebetler Türk yilliği. (0544-1943). Ankara.

TV Diskurs: Verantwortung in audiovisuellen Medien. (1433-9439). Baden-Baden.

Twentieth century British history. (0955-2359). Oxford.

Tydskrif vir hedendaagse romeins-hollandse reg = Journal of contemporary Roman-Dutch law. (1682-4490). Durban.

Ufahamu. (0041-5715). Los Angeles CA.

Ukrainian economic review. (1080-725X). Philadelphia PA.

Ukrainian quarterly. (0041-6010). Clifton NJ.

Ulkopolitiikka. (0501-0659). Helsinki.

Uluslararasi hukuk & politika. (1305-5208). Ankara.

Uluslararasi ilişkiler. (1304-7310). Ankara.

Urban affairs annual reviews. (0083-4688). Thousand Oaks CA.

Urban affairs review. (1078-0874). Thousand Oaks CA.

Urban anthropology. (0894-6019). Brockport NY.

Urban design international. (1357-5317). Basingstoke.

Urban forum. (1015-3802). Pistcataway NJ.

Urban geography. (0272-3638). Columbia MD.

Urban policy and research. (0811-1146). Abingdon.

Urban public economics review = Revista de economía pública urbana. (1697-6223). Santiago de compostela.

Urban studies. (0042-0980). Abingdon.

Urbanisme. (0042-1014). Paris.

US-Japan women's journal. (1059-9770). Palo Alto CA.

Utilitas. (0953-8208). Edinburgh.

Utilities policy. (0957-1787). Oxford.

Vacarme. (1253-2479). Paris.

Valóság. (0324-7228). Budapest.

Venture capital. (1369-1066). London.

Verfassung und Recht in Übersee = Law and politics in Africa, Asia and Latin America. (0506-7286). Baden-Baden.

Vestnik Moskovskogo universiteta. Seriia 12 Politicheskie nauki. (0201-7385). Moscow.

Vestnik Moskovskogo universiteta. Seriia 6 Ekonomika. (0130-0105). Moscow.

Vestnik obshchestvennogo mneneiia. Moscow.

Vestnik Sankt-Peterburgskogo universiteta. Seriia 5 Ekonomika. (0233-755X). St. Petersburg.

Vestnik Sankt-Peterburgskogo universiteta. Seriia 6 Filosofiia, politologiia, sotsiologiia, psikhologiia, pravo, mezhdunarodnye otnosheniia. (0132-4624). Saint Petersburg.

Vestsi natsyianalnai akademii navuk Belarusi: Seryia gumanitarnykh navuk. (0321-1649). Minsk.

Vierteljahrschrift für Sozial- und Wirtschaftsgeschichte. (0340-8728). Stuttgart.

Vierteljahrshefte für Zeitgeschichte. (0042-5702). Kirchheim.

Vierteljahrshefte zur Wirtschaftsforschung. (0340-1707). Berlin.

Vietnam social sciences. (1013-4328). Hanoi.

Vietnamese studies. (0085-7823). Hanoi.

Vingtième siècle. (0294-1759). Paris.

Violence against women. (1077-8012). Thousand Oaks CA.

Virittäjä. (0042-6806). Helsinki.

Visual anthropology. (0894-9468). New York NY.

Visual anthropology review. (1058-7187). Arlington VA.

Visual communication. (1470-3572). London.

Visual studies. (1472-586X). London.

Volkskundig bulletin. (0166-0667). Amsterdam.

Voluntas. (0957-8765). New York.

Voprosy ekonomiki. (0042-8736). Moscow.

Vorgänge: Zeitschrift für Bürgerrechte und Gesellschaftspolitik. Wiesbaden.

Wadabagei: a journal of the Caribbean and its diaspora. (1091-5753). Lanham MD.

WAMP: West African Museums Programme bulletin. Dakar.
War studies journal. (1363-1225). London.
Waseda economic papers. (0511-1943). Tokyo.
Washington quarterly. (0163-660X). Cambridge MA.
Welt Trends: internationale Politik und vergleichende Studien. (0944-8101). Potsdam.
Weltwirtschaft. (0043-2652). Berlin.
West European politics. (0140-2382). Ilford.
WIFO Monatsberichte. Österreichisches Institut für Wirtschaftsforschung. (0029-9898). Vienna.
Wirtschaftsdienst. (0043-6275). Berlin.
Wirtschaftspolitische Blätter. (0043-6291). Vienna.
Women's studies. (0049-7878). Philadelphia PA.
Women's studies international forum. (0277-5395). Oxford.
Women: a cultural review. (0957-4042). Abingdon.
Work & stress. (1464-5335). Abingdon.
Work and occupations. (0730-8884). Thousand Oaks CA.
Work, employment and society. (0950-0170). Cambridge.
World archaeology. (0043-8243). Abingdon.
World Bank economic review. (0258-6770). Washington DC.
World Bank research observer. (0257-3032). Washington DC.
World development. (0305-750X). Oxford.
World economy. (0378-5920). Oxford.
World of music. (0043-8774). Bamberg.
World politics. (0043-8871). Baltimore MD.
World today. (0043-9134). London.
Wrocławskie studie wschodnie. (0239-6661). Wroclaw.
WSI Mitteilungen. (0342-300X). Frankfurt am Main.
Yagl-Ambu. (0254-0681). Papua New Guinea.
Yale journal on regulation. (0741-9457). New Haven CT.
Yale law journal. (0044-0094). New Haven CT.
Yapi kredi economic review. (1019-1232). Istanbul.
Yearbook of physical anthropology. (0096-848X). New York NY.
Young: Nordic journal of youth research. (1103-3088). London.
Youth & policy. (0262-9798). Leicester.
Zagreb journal of economics. (1331-4599). Zagreb.
Zeitschrift für Ausländerrecht und Ausländerpolitik. (0721-5746). Baden-Baden.
Zeitschrift für Balkanologie. (0044-2356). Wiesbaden.
Zeitschrift für Bevölkerungswissenschaft - Demographie. (0340-2398). Wiesbaden.
Zeitschrift für Ethnologie. (0044-2666). Berlin.
Zeitschrift für Evaluation. (1619-5515). Wiesbaden.
Zeitschrift für Familienforschung. (1437-2940). Wiesbaden.
Zeitschrift für internationale Beziehungen. (0946-7165). Baden-Baden.
Zeitschrift für öffentliche und gemeinwirtschaftliche Unternehmen = Journal for public and nonprofit
    services. Baden-Baden.
Zeitschrift für öffentliches Recht. (0948-4396). Vienna.
Zeitschrift für Ostmitteleuropa-Forschung. (0948-8294). Marburg.
Zeitschrift für Parlamentsfragen. (0340-1758). Wiesbaden.
Zeitschrift für Personalforschung. (0179-6437). Mering.
Zeitschrift für Politik. (0044-3360). Cologne.
Zeitschrift für Politikwissenschaft. (1430-6387). Wiesbaden.
Zeitschrift für Psychodrama und Soziometrie. (1619-5507). Wiesbaden.
Zeitschrift für qualitative Bildungs-, Beratungs- und Sozialforschung. (1438-8324). Wiesbaden.

Zeitschrift für Sexualforschung. (0932-8114). Stuttgart.
Zeitschrift für Soziologie. (0340-1804). Stuttgart.
Zeitschrift für Unternehmensgeschichte. (0342-2852). Munich.
Zeitschrift für vergleichende Rechtswissenschaft [Heidelberg]. (0044-3638). Heidelberg.
Zeitschrift für Verkehrswissenschaft. (0044-3670). Düsseldorf.
Zeitschrift für Weltgeschichte: Interdisziplinäre Perspektiven. (1615-2581). Frankfurt am Main.
Zeitschrift für Wirtschafts- und Unternehmensethik. (1439-880X). Mering.
Zeitschrift für Wirtschaftspolitik. (0721-3808). Stuttgart.
Zeszyty etnologii Wrocławskiej. Wroclaw.
Zeszyty naukowe uniwersytetu jagiellońskiego. Prace etnograficzne. Krakow.
Zeszyty naukowe Uniwersytetu Jagiellońskiego. Seria religiologica. (0137-2432). Krakow.
Zeszyty Wiejskie. (1506-6541). Łódz.
Zgodovinski časopis = Historical review. (0350-5774). Ljubljana.
Zhurnal issledovanii sotsial'noi politiki = Journal of social policy studies. (1727-0634). Saratov.

LIST OF ABBREVIATIONS USED

LISTE DES ABRÉVIATIONS UTILISÉES

A. Völk. Archiv des Völkerrechts. (0003-892X). J.C.B. Mohr (Paul Siebeck): Wilhelmstraße 18, Postfach 2040, D-72010 Tübingen, Germany.

ACCOMEX ACCOMEX Actualités du commerce extérieur. (0753-4981). Chambre de Commerce et d'Industrie de Paris: 27 avenue de Friedland, 75008 Paris, France.

Acta Geo. Acta geographica. Société de géographie: 184, boulevard Saint-Germain, 75006 Paris, France.

Acta Jur. Hun. Acta juridica hungarica. (1216-2574). Akadémiai Kiadó: Prielle Kornélia u. 19-35, H-1117 Budapest, Hungary, in association with Academiae Scientiarum Hungaricae.

Acta Pol. Acta politica. (0001-6810). Palgrave Macmillan: Brunel Road Building, Houndmills, Basingstoke, Hampshire, RG21 6XS, U.K., in association with The Dutch Political Science Association.

Action Nat. Action nationale. (0001-7469). L'Action nationale: 1215, rue de la Visitation, bureau 101, Montréal, Québec H2L 3B5, Canada.

Actual. Jurid. Actualité juridique: droit administratif. (0001-7728). Editions Dalloz: 31-35, rue Froidevaux, 75685 Paris Cedex 14, France.

Actuel Marx Actuel Marx. (0994-4524). Presses Universitaires de France: 6, avenue Reille, 75685 Paris Cedex 14.

Admin. Soc. Administration and society. (0095-3997). Sage Publications: 2455 Teller Road, Newbury Park, Thousand Oaks, CA 91320, U.S.A.

Administration [Dublin] Administration [Dublin]. (0001-8325). Institute of Public Administration of Ireland: 57-61 Lansdowne Road, Dublin 4, Ireland.

Afr. Affairs African affairs. (0001-9909). Oxford University Press: Great Clarendon Street, Oxford OX2 6DP, U.K., in association with Royal African Society: 18 Northumberland Avenue, London WC2N 5BJ, U.K.

Afr. Contemp. Afrique contemporaine. (0002-0478). Documentation Française: 29 quai Voltaire, Paris 7ème, France.

Afr. Dev. Africa development = Afrique & développement. (0850-3907). Council for the Development of Social Science Research in Africa / Conseil pour le développement de la recherche en sciences sociales en Afrique: Avenue Cheikh Anta Diop x Canal IV, BP 3304, CP 18524, Dakar, Senegal.

Afr. Q. Africa quarterly. (0001-9828). Indian Council for Cultural Relations: Azad Bhavan, Indraprastha Estate, New Delhi 110 002, India.

Africa Africa: Journal of the International African Institute. (0001-9720). International African Institute: School of Oriental and African Studies, Thornhaugh Street, Russell Square, London WC1 0XG, U.K.

Age. Soc. Ageing and society. (0144-686X). Cambridge University Press: The Edinburgh Building, Shaftesbury Road, Cambridge CB2 2RU, U.K., in association with Centre for Policy on Ageing / British Society of Gerontology.

Agir Agir. Société de Stratégie: 21, rue Henri Barbusse, 75005 Paris, France.

Akdeniz Akdeniz IIBF dergisi. (1302-9975). Akdeniz Universitesi Iktisadi ve Idari Bilimler Fakultesi: Dumlupinar Bulvari, Kampus, 07058, Antalya, Turkey.

Alle. Aujourd. Allemagne d'aujourd'hui. (0002-5712). Presses Universitaires du Septentrion: BP 199, Rue du Barreau 59654 Villeneuve d'Ascq.

Alt. Int. Alternatives internationales. Alternatives internationales: 28, rue du Sentier, 75002 Paris, France.

Alt. Sud Alternatives sud. Centre Tricontinental: Avenue Sainte Gertrude 5, B-1348 Louvain-la-Neuve, Belgium.

Alter. Econ. Alternatives économiques. (0247-3739). Alternatives Economiques: 28, rue du Sentier, 75002 Paris, France.

Alter. Non Viol. Alternatives non violentes. (0223-5498). ANV: Centre 308, 82 rue Jeanne d'Arc, 76000 Rouen, France.

Alternatives Alternatives. (0304-3754). Lynne Rienner Publishers: 1800 30th Street, Boulder, CO 80301, U.S.A.

Am. Behav. Sci. American behavioral scientist. (0002-7642). Sage Publications: 2455 Teller Road, Newbury Park, Thousand Oaks, CA 91320, U.S.A.

Am. Econ. R. American economic review. (0002-8282). American Economic Association: 2014 Broadway, Suite 305, Nashville, TN 37203, U.S.A.

Am. Hist. R. American historical review. (0002-8762). American Historical Association: 400 A Street S.E., Washington DC 20003, U.S.A.

Am. J. Agr. Econ. American journal of agricultural economics. (0002-9092). American Agricultural Economics Association: 415 South Duff Avenue, Suite C, Ames, IA 50011-6600, U.S.A.

Am. J. Comp. Law American journal of comparative law. (0002-919X). American Association for the Comparative Study of Law: University of California, School of Law (Boalt Hall), Berkeley, CA 94720, U.S.A.

Am. J. Int. Law American journal of international law. (0002-9300). American Society of International Law: 2223 Massachusetts Avenue N.W., Washington DC 20008-2864, U.S.A.

Am. J. Pol. Sci. American journal of political science. (0092-5853). Blackwell Publishing: 9600 Garsington Road, Oxford, OX4 2DQ, U.K., in association with Midwest Political Science Association.

Am. J. Sociol. American journal of sociology. (0002-9602). University of Chicago Press: 5720 S. Woodlawn Avenue, Chicago, IL 60637, U.S.A.

Am. Pol. Res. American politics research. (1532-673X). Sage Publications: 2455 Teller Road, Thousand Oaks, CA 91320, U.S.A.

Am. Pol. Sci. R. American political science review. (0003-0554). Cambridge University Press: The Edinburgh Building, Shaftesbury Road, Cambridge, CB2 2RU, UK, in association with American Political Science Association.

Am. R. Can. S. American review of Canadian studies. (0272-2011). Association for Canadian Studies in the United States: One Dupont Circle, Suite 620, Washington DC 20036, U.S.A.

Am. Sociol. R. American sociological review. (0003-1224). American Sociological Association: 1307 New York Avenue NW, Suite 700, Washington, DC 20005-4701, U.S.A.

Anál. Soc. Análise social. (0003-2573). Instituto de Ciências Sociais da Universidade de Lisboa: Avenida das Forças Armadas, Edificio I.S.C.T.E., Ala Sul, 1° andar, 1600 Lisbon, Portugal, in association with Junta Nacional de Investigação Científica e Tecnológia / Instituto Nacional de Investigação Científica.

Anarch. S. Anarchist studies. (0967-3393). Lawrence & Wishart: 99a Wallis Road, London, E9 9LN, U.K.

Ann. Am. Acad. Pol. Soc. Sci. Annals of the American Academy of Political and Social Science. (0002-7162). Sage Publications: 2455 Teller Road, Newbury Park, Thousand Oaks, CA 91320, U.S.A., in association with American Academy of Political and Social Science.

Ann. Droit Louvain Annales de droit de Louvain. (0770-6472). Bruylant: Rue de la Régence 67, B-1000 Bruxelles, Belgium, in association with Université Catholique de Louvain.

Ann. Fran. Rel. Int. Annuaire français de relations internationales. Ministère des affaires étrangéres: 244, boulevard Saint-Germain, 75303 Paris 07 SP, France.

Ann. Géog. Annales de géographie. (0003-4010). Armand Colin: 21, rue du Montparnasse, 75283 PARIS CEDEX 06, France.

Annales Annales: Histoire, sciences sociales. (0395-2649). Éditions de l'École des hautes études en sciences sociales: 54 boulevard Raspail, 75006 Paris, France.

Anthropos [St. Augustin] Anthropos [St. Augustin]. (0257-9774). Anthropos Institut: Arnold-Janssen-Str. 20, D-53754 Sankt Augustin, Germany.

Appl. Econ. Applied economics. (0003-6846). Routledge, Taylor & Francis Ltd: 2 Park Square, Milton Park, Abingdon, Oxfordshire, OX14 4RN.

Après-demain Après-demain. (0003-7176). Après-demain: BP 458 07, 75327 Paris Cedex 07, France.

Arab S. J. Arab studies journal. (1083-4753). Georgetown University, Center for Contemporary Arab Studies.

Arab World Geog. Arab world geographer. (1480-6800). Arab World Geographer: Department of Geography and Planning, University of Akron, Akron OH, 44325-5005, U.S.A.

Arc. Öffen. Recht Archiv des öffentlichen Rechts. (0003-8911). J.C.B. Mohr (Paul Siebeck): Wilhelmstraße 18, Postfach 2040, D-72010 Tübingen, Germany.

Arch. Recht. Soz.Philos. Archiv für Rechts- und Sozialphilosophie = Archives de philosophie du droit et de philosophie sociale = Archives for philosophy of law and social philosophy = Archivo de filosofía jurídica y social. (0001-2343). Franz Steiner Verlag: Birkenwaldstraße 44, Postfach 10 15 26, D-7000 Stuttgart 1, Germany, in association with Internationale Vereinigung für Rechts- und Sozialphilosophie.

Arche Arche. (0518-2840). L'Arche: 39, rue Broca, 75006 Paris, France.

Archipel Archipel. (0044-8613). Editions de l'École des hautes études en sciences sociales: 54 boulevard Raspail, 75006 Paris, France, in association with Association Archipel.

Archives Politique Crim. Archives de politique criminelle. (0242-5637). Equipe de recherche sur la politique criminelle: Faculté de droit, 39, rue de l'Université, 34000 Montpellier, France.

Arena J. Arena journal. (1320-6567). Arena Printing and Publishing: PO Box 18, North Carlton, Victoria, Australia 3054.

Arès Arès. (0181-009X). UPMF: Espace Europe, BP 47, 38040 Grenoble Cedex 9, France.

Argumentation Argumentation. (0920-427X). Springer: Van Godewijckstraat 30, P.O. Box 17, 3300 AA Dordrecht, Netherlands, in association with European Centre for the Study of Argumentation: Unversité Libre de Bruxelles, Institut de Philosophie, 143 avenue A.-Buyl, C.P. 188, B-1050 Brussels, Belgium.

Arm. Forces Soc. Armed forces and society. (0095-327X). Transaction Publishers: Rutgers University, New Brunswick, NJ 08903, U.S.A., in association with Inter-University Seminar on Armed Forces and Society: Box 46, 1126 East 59th Street, Chicago, IL 60637, U.S.A.

Asia Pac. J. Env. Law Asia Pacific journal of environmental law. (1385-2140). Australian Centre for Academic Law: University of Sydney, 173-175 Phillip St, Sydney 2000, Australia.

Asia Pac. R. Asia Pacific review. (1343-9006). Carfax Publishing, Taylor & Francis Ltd: P.O. Box 25, Abingdon, Oxfordshire OX14 3UE, U.K.

Asian Econ. R. Asian economic review. (0004-4555). Indian Institute of Economics: 11-6-841 Red Hills, Hyderabad-500 004, India.

Asian J. Communic. Asian journal of communication. (0129-2986). Routledge, Taylor & Francis Ltd: 240 MacPherson Road, 08-01 Pines Industrial Building, Singapore 348574, in association with Asian Media Information and Communication Centre/School of Communication Studies, Nanyang Technological University.

Asian J. Pol. Sci. Asian journal of political science. (0218-5377). Times Academic Press: Federal Publications (S) Pte Ltd, Times Centre, 1 New Industrial Road, Singapore 1953, Singapore.

Asian J. Publ. Admin. Asian journal of public administration. (0259-8272). University of Hong Kong, Department of Political Science: Pokfulam Road, Hong Kong.

Asian Persp. [S. Korea] Asian perspective [S. Korea]. (0258-9184). Kyungnam University, Institute for Far Eastern Studies: 28-42 Samchung-dong, Chongro-ku, Seoul 110-230, South Korea.

Asian Sur. Asian survey. (0004-4687). University of California Press Journals: 2120 Berkeley Way, Berkeley, CA 94720-5812, U.S.A.

Asian-Pac. Econ. Lit. Asian-Pacific economic literature. (0818-9935). Blackwell Publishing: 108 Cowley Road, Oxford OX4 1JF, U.K., in association with Australian National University, National Centre for Development Studies: G.P.O. Box 4, Canberra, ACT 2601, Australia.

Aussenwirtschaft Aussenwirtschaft. (0004-8216). Verlag Rüegger: Albisriederstr. 80a, Postfach 1470, CH-8040 Zürich, Switzerland, in association with Schweizerisches Institut für Aussenwirtschafts-Struktur- und Regionalforschung (SIASR): Dufourstrasse 48, CH-9000 St. Gallen, Switzerland.

Aust. Femin. S. Australian feminist studies. (0816-4649). Carfax Publishing, Taylor & Francis Ltd: Rankine Road, Basingstoke, Hants, RG24 8PR, UK.

Aust. Geog. S. Australian geographical studies. Blackwell Publishing: 108 Cowley Road, Oxford OX4 1JF, U.K., in association with Australian Defence Force Academy, Campbell, ACT 2600, Australia.

Aust. J. Int. Aff. Australian journal of international affairs. (1035-7718). Carfax Publishing, Taylor & Francis Ltd: 11 New Fetter Lane, London, EC4P 4EE, U.K.

Aust. J. Pol. Hist. Australian journal of politics and history. (0004-9522). Australian Journal of Politics and History: Department of Government, University of Queensland, St Lucia, Qld 4072 , Australia.

Aust. J. Pol. Sci. Australian journal of political science. (1036-1146). Carfax Publishing, Taylor & Francis Ltd: P.O. Box 25, Abingdon, Oxfordshire OX14 3UE, U.K., in association with Australasian Political Studies Association.

Aust. J. Publ. Admin. Australian journal of public administration. (0313-6647). Blackwell Publishing: 108 Cowley Road, Oxford, OX4 1JF, UK, in association with Institute of Public Administration, Australia.

Aust. Law J. Australian law journal. (0004-9611). The Law Book Company: 44-50 Waterloo Road, North Ryde, NSW 2113, Australia.

Autre L'Autre: cliniques, cultures et sociétés. La Pensée Sauvage: BP 141, 12 Place Notre-Dame, F-38002, Grenoble, France, in association with Service de psychopathologie - hopital avicenne.

AWR B. AWR Bulletin. (0001-2947). Wilhelm Braumüller: Servitengasse 5, A-1092, Vienna, Austria, in association with Association for the Study of the World Refugee Problem: FL-9490 Vaduz, P.O.B. 75, Liechtenstein.

B. Lat. Am. Res. Bulletin of Latin American research. (0261-3050). Blackwell Publishing: 9600 Garsington Road, Oxford OX4 2ZG, UK.

Banquet Banquet. (1164-7590). CERAP: 76 rue de Sèvres, 75007 Paris, France.

Belg. R. Int. Law Revue belge de droit international = Belgian review of international law = Belgisch tijdschrift voor internationaal recht. (0035-0788). Bruylant: rue de la Régence 67, 1000 Brussels, Belgium, in association with Société belge de droit internationale: avenue Jeanne 44 Johannlaan, 1050 Brussels, Belgium.

Benefits Benefits: a journal of social security research policy and practice. (0962-7898). Benefits Editorial Board: School of Social Studies, University of Nottingham, NG7 2RD, U.K..

Berkeley Techno. Law J. Berkeley technology law journal. (0885 2715). University of California Press Journals: 2120 Berkeley Way, Berkeley, CA 94720-5812, U.S.A.

Berl. J. Soziol. Berliner Journal für Soziologie. (0863-1808). VS Verlag für Sozialwissenschaften: Abraham-Lincoln-Straße 46, 65189 Wiesbaden, Germany, in association with Institut für Soziologie der Humbodt-Universität zu Berlin: Hans-Loch-Str. 349, O-1136 Berlin, Germany.

Bilig Bilig. (1301-0549). Foundation of Ahmet Yesevi University: Bilig Editörlügü, Ahmet Yesevi Üniversitesi, Mütevelli Heyet Baskanligi, Tashkent Caddesi, 10.sok. No:30, 06430 Bahçelievler, Anakara, Turkey.

Biography Biography. (0162-4962). University of Hawaii Press: 2840 Kolowalu Street, Honolulu, HI 96822-1888, U.S.A., in association with Center for Biographical Research: Varsity College, University of Hawaii, Honolulu, HI. 96822, U.S.A.

Br. J. Can. S. British journal of Canadian studies. (0269-9222). British Association for Canadian Studies: 21 George Square, Edinburgh EH8 9LD, U.K.

Br. J. Ind. Rel. British journal of industrial relations. (0007-1080). Blackwell Publishing: 108 Cowley Road, Oxford OX4 1JF, U.K., in association with London School of Economics: Houghton Street, London WC2A 2AE, U.K.

Br. J. Mid. East. S. British journal of Middle Eastern studies. (1353-0194). Centre for Middle Eastern and Islamic Studies: BRISMES Administraton Office, University of Durham, South Road, Durham, DH1 3TG, U.K.

Br. J. Pol. Int. Rel. British journal of politics and international relations. (1369-1481). Blackwell Publishing: 108 Cowley Road, Oxford OX4 1JF, U.K., in association with Political Studies Association.

Br. J. Pol. Sci. British journal of political science. (0007-1234). Cambridge University Press: The Edinburgh Building, Shaftesbury Road, Cambridge CB2 2RU, U.K.

Br. J. Sociol. Edu. British journal of sociology of education. (0142-5692). Carfax Publishing, Taylor & Francis Ltd: P.O. Box 25, Abingdon, Oxfordshire OX14 4RN, in association with School of Education, University of Sheffield.

Bull. Comp. Lab. Rel. Bulletin of comparative labour relations. Springer: Van Godewijckstraat 30, P.O. Box 17, 3300 AA Dordrecht, Netherlands.

Bus. Strat. Env. Business strategy and the environment. (0964-4733). John Wiley & Sons Ltd: The Atrium, Southern Gate, Chichester, West Sussex, PO19 8SQ, UK.

Cadres CFDT Cadres CFDT. (0398-3145).

Cah. Afr. Cahiers africains = Afrika studies. (1021-9994). Institut africain-CEDAF: Leuvensesteenweg 13, 3080 Tervuren, Belgium.

Cah. Afr. Admin. Publ. Cahiers africains d'administration publique = African administrative studies. (0007-9588). Centre Africain de Formation et de Recherche Administratives pour le Développement: P.O. Box 310, Tangiers 90001, Morocco.

Cah. CEVIPOF Cahiers du CEVIPOF. CEVIPOF: 98, rue de l'Université, 75007 Paris, France.

Cah. Econ. Bret. Cahiers économiques de Bretagne. (0154-8557).

Cah. Euro. Sorbonne Nouv. Cahiers europeens de la Sorbonne nouvelle.

Cah. Fonc. Publ. Admin. Cahiers de la fonction publique et de l'administration. (0753-4418). Berger-Levrault: 3, rue Ferrus, 75014 Paris, France.

Cah. Fondation Cahiers de la Fondation. (0983-1851).

Cah. Français Cahiers français. (0008-0217).

Cah. Hist. Immédiate Cahier d'histoire immédiate. Groupe de Recherche en Histoire Immédiate: Maison de le Recherche, 5 allées A. Machado, F. 31058 Toulouse cedex 9, France.

Cah. Japon Cahiers du Japon. (0388-113X). Japan Echo Inc.: Nippon Press Center Building, 2-2-1 Uchisaiwai-chô, Chiyoda-ku, Tokyo 100-0011, JAPAN, in association with Editions Sully, BP 171, 56005 Vannes Cedex, France.

Cah. Mars Cahiers de Mars. (1169-0402). Association MARS: BP 69-00445 ARMEES, France.

Cah. Marx. CM: Cahiers marxistes. (0591-0633). Cahiers Marxistes: Avenue Général Médecin Derache, 94 bte. 6, 1050 Bruxelles, Belgium.

Cah. Orient Cahiers de l'orient. (0767-6468). Le Monde Diplomatique: 60, rue des Cévennes, 75015 Paris.

Cah. Outre-Mer Cahiers d'outre-mer. (0373-5834). Institut de Géographie et d'Etudes Régionales, Université de Bordeaux III, France, in association with Institut d'Outre-Mer.

Camb. Law J. Cambridge law journal. (0008-1973). Cambridge University Press: The Edinburgh Building, Shaftesbury Road, Cambridge CB2 2RU, U.K., in association with University of Cambridge, Faculty of Law.

Can. J. Crimin. Canadian journal of criminology and criminal justice = Revue canadienne de criminologie et de justice pénale. (0704-9722). Canadian Criminology Association: 383 Parkdale Avenue, Suite 207, Ottawa, ON K1R 4R4, Canada, in association with University of Toronto Press.

Can. J. Law Soc. Canadian journal of law and society = Revue canadienne droit et société. (0829-3201). University of Toronto Press: Journals Division, 5201 Dufferin St., Toronto, ON, Canada M3H 5T8, in association with Faculté de science politique et de droit, Département des sciences juridiques: Université du Québec à Montréal, C.P. 8888, Succursale Centre-Ville, Montréal H3C 3P8 Canada.

Can. J. Philos. Canadian journal of philosophy. (0045-5091). University of Calgary Press: 2500 University Drive N.W., Calgary, Alberta T2N 1N4, Canada.

Can. J. Pol. Canadian journal of political science = Revue canadienne de science politique. (0008-4239). Wilfrid Laurier University Press: 75 University Avenue W., Waterloo, Ontario N2L 3C5, Canada, in association with Canadian Political Science Association = Association canadienne de science politique / Société québécoise de science politique: Suite 205, 1 Stewart Street, Ottawa, Ontario, Canada K1N 6H7 / Université du Québec à Montréal, Montreal, Quebec, Canada H3C 3PN.

Can. J. Wom. Law Canadian journal of women and the law = Revue femmes et droit. (0832-8781). University of Toronto Press: 5201 Dufferin Street Toronto, Ontario, Canada M3H 5T8, in association with Osgoode Hall Law School: York University, North York, Ontario, Canada M3J 1P3.

Can. Publ. Admin. Canadian public administration = Administration publique du Canada. (0008-4840). Institute of Public Administration of Canada: 1075 Bay Street Suite 401, Toronto, Ontario, Canada, M5S 2B1.

Can. R. S. Nation. Canadian review of studies in nationalism = Revue canadienne des études sur le nationalisme. (0317-7904). CRSN/RCEN: c/o Thomas Spira, University of Prince Edward Island, Charlottetown, Prince Edward Island C1A 4P3, Canada.

Can J. Lat. Am. Carib. S. Canadian journal of Latin American and Caribbean studies. (0826-3663). University of Western Ontario: London, ON Canada N6A 5B8.

Cap. Class Capital and class. (0309-8168). Conference of Socialist Economists: 25 Horsell Road, London N5 1XL, U.K.

Cap. Nat. Social. Capitalism, nature, socialism. (1045-5752). Routledge, Taylor & Francis Ltd.: 4 Park Square, Milton Park, Abingdon, Oxfordshire OX14 4RN.

Čas. Suvr. Povi. Časopis za suvremenu povijest. (0590-9597). Hrvatski Institut za Povijest: Opatička 10, Zagreb, Croatia.

CEMOTI CEMOTI: Cahiers d'études sur la Méditerranée orientale et le monde turco-iranien. (0764-9878). Association Française pour l'Étude de la Méditerranée Orientale et le Monde Turco-Iranien: 56 rue Jacob, 75006 Paris, France.

Cent. Asian Sur. Central Asian survey. (0263-4937). Carfax Publishing, Taylor & Francis Ltd: P.O. Box 25, Abingdon, Oxfordshire OX14 3UE, U.K., in association with Society for Central Asian Studies: Unit 8, 92 Lots Road, London SW10 4BQ, U.K.

Cent. Euro. Central Europe. (1479-0963). Maney Publishing: Hudson Road, Leeds, LS9 7DL, UK, in association with School of Slavonic and East European Studies.

Cent. Euro. Pol. Sci. R. Central European political science review. (1586-4197). Századvég Politikai Iskola: 1068 Budapest, Benczúr 33, HUNGARY, in association with Institute for Political Science, Hungarian Academy of Science.

Chi. J. China journal. (1324-9347). Contemporary China Centre: Australian National University, Research School of Pacific and Asian Studies, Canberra ACT 0200, Australia.

Chi. Q. China quarterly. (0305-7410). Cambridge University Press: The Edinburgh Building, Shaftesbury Road, Cambridge CB2 2RU, U.K., in association with School of Oriental and African Studies: Thornhaugh Street, Russell Square, London WC1H 0XG, U.K.

Chi. Rep. China report. (0009-4455). Sage Publications India: B-42 Panchsheel Enclave, Post Box 4109, New Delhi 110 017, India.

Childhood Childhood. (0907-5682). Sage Publications: 6 Bonhill Street, London EC2A 4PU, U.K., in association with Norwegian Centre for Child Research.

Chron. Int. IRES Chronique internationale de l'IRES. (1285-087X).

Cienc. Ergo Sum Ciencia ergo sum: revista científica multidisciplinaria de la Universidad Autónoma del Estado de México. (1405-0269). Autonomous University of the State of Mexico: A.V. Gomez Farias No. 200-2 Ote., Toluca, Mexico, 50000.

Citiz. S. Citizenship studies. (1362-1025). Carfax Publishing, Taylor & Francis Ltd: P.O. Box 25, Abingdon, Oxfordshire OX14 3UE, U.K.

Cold War Hist. Cold War history. (1468-2745). Frank Cass, Taylor & Francis Ltd: P.O. Box 25, Abingdon, Oxfordshire OX14 3UE, U.K.

Colom. Int. Colombia internacional. (0121-5612). Universidade de Los Andes: Departamento de Ciencia Politica, Carrera 1 Este No. 18A-10, Bogotá, Colombia.

Columb. J. Tr. Law Columbia journal of transnational law. (0010-1931). Columbia Journal of Transnational Law Association: Columbia University School of Law, Box D-25, New York, NY 10027, U.S.A.

Columb. Law R. Columbia law review. (0010-1958). Columbia Law Review Association: 435 West 116th Street, New York, NY 10027, U.S.A.

Columbia J. Euro. Law Columbia journal of European law. (1076-6715). Columbia Law School: 435 West 116th Street, New York NY 10027, U.S.A., in association with Institute for European Law of the Katholieke Universiteit in Leuven, Belgium and Parker School of Foreign and Comparative Law.

Com. Ex. Comercio exterior. (0185-0601). Bancomext: Camino a Santa Teresa 1679, octavo piso, Jardines del Pedregal, 01900, Mexico, Mexico City.

Communic. y. Soc. Comunicación y sociedad. (0214-0039). Ed. Ciencias Sociales: Facultad de Comunicación, Universidad de Navarra, Edificio de Ciencias Sociales, 31080 Pamplona, España.

Comm. Post-Comm. S. Communist and post-communist studies. (0967-067X). Elsevier Science: PO Box 211, 1000 AE Amsterdam, The Netherlands.

Commentaire Commentaire. (0180-8214). Commentaire: 116, rue du Bac, 75007 Paris, France.

Commonwealth Comp. Pol. Commonwealth and comparative politics. (1466-2043). Frank Cass, Taylor & Francis Ltd: P.O. Box 25, Abingdon, Oxfordshire OX14 3UE, U.K.

Comp. Econ. S. Comparative economic studies. (0888-7233). Palgrave Macmillan: Brunel Road Building, Houndmills, Basingstoke, Hampshire, RG21 6XS, U.K., in association with Association for Comparative Economic Studies.

Comp. Euro. Pol. Comparative European politics. (1472-4790). Palgrave Macmillan: Brunel Road Building, Houndmills, Basingstoke, Hampshire, RG21 6XS, U.K.

Comp. Int. Law J. Sth. Afr. Comparative and international law journal of Southern Africa. (0010-4051). University of South Africa, Institute of Foreign and Comparative Law: CILSA, P.O. Box 392, Pretoria 0003, South Africa.

Comp. Pol. Comparative politics. (0010-4159). Graduate Center, City University of New York: 365 Fifth Avenue, New York, NY 10016-4309, U.S.A.

Comp. Pol. S. Comparative political studies. (0010-4140). Sage Publications: 2455 Teller Road, Newbury Park, Thousand Oaks, CA 91320, U.S.A.

Comp. S. Soc. Hist. Comparative studies in society and history. (0010-4175). Cambridge University Press: 40 West 20th Street, New York, NY 10011-4211, U.S.A., in association with Society for the Comparative Study of Society and History.

Conf. Médit. Confluences en Méditerranée. (1148-2664). L'Harmattan: 16 rue des Ecoles, 75005 Paris, France.

Confl. Monde Conflits dans le monde. (1193-9230). Institut québécois des hautes études internationales: Bureau 5458, Pavillon Charles-De Koninck, Université Laval, Québec (Québec) G1K 7P4, Canada.

Consc. Liber. Conscience et liberté. (0251-3633).

Constit. Pol. Econ. Constitutional political economy. (1043-4062). Springer: Van Godewijckstraat 30, P.O. Box 17, 3300 AA Dordrecht, Netherlands, in association with Center for Study of Public Choice.

Cont. Pol. Contemporary politics. (1356-9775). Routledge, Taylor & Francis Ltd: 4 Park Square, Milton Park, Abingdon, Oxfordshire, OX14 4RN.

Contemp. Br. Hist. Contemporary British history. (1361-9462). Frank Cass, Taylor & Francis Ltd: P.O. Box 25, Abingdon, Oxfordshire OX14 3UE, U.K.

Contemp. Just. R. Contemporary justice review. (1028-2580). Routledge, Taylor & Francis Ltd: 11 New Fetter Lane, London London EC4P 4EE, U.K.

Contemp. Pac. Contemporary Pacific. (1043-898X). University of Hawaii Press: 2840 Kolowalu Street, Honolulu, HI 96822-1888, U.S.A., in association with Center for Pacific Islands Studies: University of Hawaii at Manoa, 1890 East-West Road, 215 Moore Hall, Honolulu, HI 96822, U.S.A.

Contemp. Sec. Policy Contemporary security policy. (1352-3260). Frank Cass, Taylor & Francis Ltd: P.O. Box 25, Abingdon, Oxfordshire OX14 3UE, U.K.

Contemp. Sth. Asia Contemporary South Asia. (0958-4935). Carfax Publishing, Taylor & Francis Ltd: 4 Park Square, Milton Park, Abingdon, Oxfordshire OX14 4RN, U.K., in association with University of Oxford.

Contemp. Sth.East Asia Contemporary Southeast Asia: A journal of international and strategic affairs. (0129-797X). Institute of Southeast Asian Studies: 30 Heng Mui Keng Terrace, Pasir Panjang, Singapore 119614, Singapore.

A Contrario A contrario. Revue interdisciplinaire de sciences sociales: Université de Lausanne, Internef, S.80.1, 1015 Lausanne, Switzerland.

Contretemps Contretemps. (1633-597X). Ed. Textuel: 48 rue Vivienne, 75002 Paris, France.

Contrib. Indian Sociol. Contributions to Indian sociology. (0069-9667). Sage Publications India: B-42 Panchsheel Enclave, Post Box 4109, New Delhi 110 017, India, in association with Institute of Economic Growth: University of Delhi, Delhi 110007, India.

Convergencia Convergencia: Revista de ciencias sociales. (1405-1435). Universidad Autónoma del Estado de México: Cerro de Coatepec s/n, Centro de Investigación en Ciencias Politicas y Administración Pública, Universidad Autónoma del Estado de México, Cludad Universitaria, C.P. 50100, Toluca, Estado de Mexico.

Coop. Confl. Cooperation and conflict. (0010-8367). Sage Publications: 6 Bonhill Street, London, EC2A 4PU, U.K., in association with Nordic Cooperation Committee for International Politics.

Cour. Hebdo. Courrier hebdomadaire du Centre de recherche et d'information sociopolitiques. (0009-0360). CRISP: Place Quetelet, 1A, 1210 Bruxelles, Belgium.

Cour. Pays Est Courrier des pays de l'Est. (0590-0239). Documentation Française: 29 quai Voltaire, Paris 7ème, France.

Coy. Econ. Coyuntura económica. (0120-3576). Fundación para la Educación Superior y el Desarrollo: Calle 78 no. 9-91, Apartado Aéreo 75074, Bogotá, Colombia.

Crim. Just. Criminal justice: the international journal of policy and practice. (1466-8025). Sage Publications: 6 Bonhill Street, London, EC2A 4PU, U.K.

Crit. Asian S. Critical Asian studies. (1467-2715). Routledge, Taylor & Francis Ltd: 2 Park Square, Milton Park, Abingdon, Oxfordshire OX14 4RN, U.K.

Crit. Int. Critique internationale. CERI: 56 rue Jacob, 75006 Paris, France.

Crit. R. Critical review. (0891-3811). Critical Review: P.O. Box 14528, Chicago, IL 60614, U.S.A., in association with Center for Independent Thought: 942 Howard Street, Room 109, San Francisco, CA 94103, U.S.A.

Crit. Soc. Policy Critical social policy. (0261-0183). Sage Publications: 6 Bonhill Street, London, EC2A 4PU, U.K.

Cuad. Am. Cuadernos americanos. (0185-156X). Universidad Nacional Autónoma de México, Facultad de Ciencias Políticas y Sociales: Ciudad Universitaria, Coyoacán, 04510 México D.F., Mexico.

Cuest. Pol. Cuestiones políticas. (0798-1406). Universidad del Zulia, Instituto de Estudios Políticos y Derecho Público, Facultad de Ciencias Jurídicas y Políticas: Maracaibo, Venezuela.

Cult. Pol. Cultural politics. (1743-2197). Berg Publishers: 1st Floor, Angel Court, 81 St Clements Street, Oxford OX4 1AW.

Cur. Pol. Econ. Euro. Current politics and economics of Europe. (1057-2309). Nova Science Publishers, Inc.: 227 Main Street, Suite 100, Huntington, NY 11743, U.S.A.

Curr. Hist. Current history. (0011-3530). Current History: Publications Office, 4225 Main Street, Philadelphia, PA 19127, U.S.A.

Dædalus Dædalus. (0011-5266). American Academy of Arts and Sciences: 136 Irving Street, Cambridge, MA 02138, U.S.A.

Débat Débat. (0246-2346). Éditions Gallimard: 5, rue Sébastien-Bottin, 75328 Paris, France.

Debatte Debatte: Review of contemporary German affairs. (0965-156X). Routledge, Taylor & Francis Ltd: 4 Park Square, Milton Park, Abingdon, Oxfordshire, OX14 4RN.

Dedans Dehors Dedans dehors. OIP: 31 rue des Lilas, 75019 Paris, France.

Def. Peace Econ. Defence and peace economics. (1024-2694). Carfax Publishing, Taylor & Francis Ltd: P.O. Box 25, Abingdon, Oxfordshire, OX14 3UE, U.K.

Défense Nat. Défense nationale. (0336-1489). Ecole militaire: 1 Place Joffre, B.P. 8607, 75325 Paris, Cedex 07, France.

Democratization Democratization. (1351-0347). Frank Cass, Taylor & Francis Ltd: P.O. Box 25, Abingdon, Oxfordshire OX14 3UE, U.K.

Desar. Econ. Desarrollo económico. (0046-001X). Instituto de Desarrollo Económico y Social: Aráoz 2838, 1425 Buenos Aires, Argentina.

Deutsch. Arch. Deutschland Archiv: Zeitschrift für das vereinigte Deutschland. (0012-1428). Leske + Budrich: Gerhart-Hauptmann-Straße 27, 51379 Leverkusen, Germany.

Deutsche Z. Kommunalwissenschaften Deutsche Zeitschrift für Kommunalwissenschaften. (1617-8203). Deutsches Institut für Urbanistik: Postfach 12 03 21, 10593 Berlin, Germany.

Dev. B. Development bulletin. (1035-1132). Development Studies Network Ltd: Research School of Social Sciences, Australian National University, Canberra ACT 0200, Australia.

Dev. Change Development and change. (0012-155X). Blackwell Publishing: 108 Cowley Road, Oxford OX4 1JF, U.K.

Dev. Policy R. Development policy review. (0950-6764). Blackwell Publishing: 108 Cowley Road, Oxford OX4 1JF, U.K., in association with Overseas Development Institute: Regent's College, Inner Circle, Regent's Park, London NW1 4NS, U.K.

Dev. Pract. Development in practice. (0961-4524). Carfax Publishing, Taylor & Francis Ltd: P.O. Box 25, Abingdon, Oxfordshire OX14 3UE, U.K., in association with Oxfam: 274 Banbury Road, Oxford OX2 7DZ, U.K.

Dev. Socio-econ. Prog. Development & socio-economic progress. Afro-Asian Peoples' Solidarity Organisation (AAPSO): 89 Abdel Aziz Al-Saoud Street, 11451-61 Manial El-Roda, Cairo, Egypt.

Dev. Sth. Afr. Development Southern Africa. (0376-835X). Carfax Publishing, Taylor & Francis Ltd: P.O. Box 25, Abingdon, Oxfordshire OX14 3UE, U.K.

Déviance Soc. Déviance et société. (0378-7931). UCL Département de criminologie et de droit pénal: Place Montesquieu 2, B-1348 Louvain-la-Neuve, Belgium.

Dipl. Hist. Diplomatic history. (0145-2096). Blackwell Publishing: 350 Main Street, Malden, MA 02148, U.S.A., in association with Society for Historians of American Foreign Relations.

Dipl. State. Diplomacy and statecraft. (0959-2296). Frank Cass, Taylor & Francis Ltd: P.O. Box 25, Abingdon, Oxfordshire OX14 3UE, U.K.

Dirasat Ad. Sci. Dirasat: Administrative Sciences. (1026-373X). Deanship of Academic Research: University of Jordan, Amman, Jordan.

Dirasat Hum. Soc. Sci. Dirasat: Human and Social Sciences. (1026-3721). Deanship of Academic Research: University of Jordan, Amman, Jordan.

Dirasat Sha. Law Dirasat: Shari'a and law sciences. (1026-3748). Deanship of Academic Research: University of Jordan, Amman, Jordan.

Disasters Disasters: Journal of disaster studies, policy and management. (0361-3666). Blackwell Publishing: 108 Cowley Road, Oxford OX4 1JF, U.K.

Disc. Soc. Discourse & society. (0957-9265). Sage Publications: 6 Bonhill Street, London EC2A 4PU, U.K.

Disk. Diskurs: Studien zu Kindheit, Jugend, Familie und Gesellschaft. (0937-9614). VS Verlag für Sozialwissenschaften: Abraham-Lincoln Strasse 46, 65189 Wiesbaden, Germany, in association with Deutsche Jugendinstitut.

Dokumente Dokumente. (0012-5172). Europa Union Verlag: Bachstraße 32, 53115 Bonn, Germany, in association with Gesellschaft für übernationale Zusammenarbeit: Bachstraße 32, 53005 Bonn, Germany.

Doss. Solid. Santé Dossiers solidarité et santé. La Documentation Française: 29, quai Voltaire, 75344 Paris Cedex 07, France.

East Euro. Pol. Soc. East European politics and societies. (0888-3254). University of California Press Journals: 2120 Berkeley Way, Berkeley, CA 94720-5812, U.S.A.

Ebisu Ebisu. (1253-8590). MFJ: 3-9-25 Ebisu, Shibuya-ku, Tokyo, Japan 150-0013.

Econ. Dev. Q. Economic development quarterly. (0891-2424). Sage Publications: 2455 Teller Road, Newbury Park, Thousand Oaks, CA 91320, U.S.A.

Econ. Hum. Economie et humanisme. (0245-9132). Economie & Humanisme: 14 rue Antoine Dumont, 69372 Lyon cedex 08, France.

Econ. Pol. Economics and politics. (0954-1985). Blackwell Publishing: 108 Cowley Road, Oxford OX4 1JF, U.K.

Econ. Policy Economic policy. (0266-4658). Blackwell Publishing: 108 Cowley Road, Oxford OX4 1JF, U.K., in association with Centre of Economic Policy Research / École des Hautes Études en Sciences Sociales.

Econ. Prévis. Economie & prévision. (0249-4744). SPMAE-DGTPE-MINEFI: Télédoc 624 Pièce B0082, 139 rue de Bercy, 75572 Paris, Cedex 12, France.

Econ. Soc. Economy and society. (0308-5147). Routledge, Taylor & Francis Ltd: 2 Park Square, Milton Park, Abingdon, Oxfordshire, OX14 4RN.

Econ. Soc. R. Economic and social review. (0012-9984). Economic and Social Review: 4 Burlington Road, Dublin 4, Ireland.

Écon. Sociét. Économies et sociétés. (0013-0567). Presses de l'Institut de Sciences Mathematiques et Économiques Appliquées: BP 22 - 75622 PARIS Cedex 13, France.

Edu. Ouvrière Education ouvrière. (0378-5572).

Electoral S. Electoral studies. (0261-3794). Elsevier Science: PO Box 211, 1000 AE Amsterdam, The Netherlands.

Empirica Empirica. (0340-8744). Springer: Van Godewijckstraat 30, P.O. Box 17, 3300 AA Dordrecht, Netherlands, in association with Austrian Institute of Economic Research: P.O. Box 91, A-1103 Vienna, Austria.

Energy Policy Energy policy. (0301-4215). Elsevier Science: PO Box 211, 1000 AE Amsterdam, The Netherlands.

Entr. Hist. Entreprises et histoire. (1161-2770). Éditions ESKA: 12, rue du Quatre-Septembre, 75002 Paris.

Entrepren. Theor. Prac. Entrepreneurship: Theory and practice. (1042-2587). Blackwell Publishing / Baylor University: Speight Avenue at 5th Street, Waco, TX 76798-8011, U.S.A.

Env. Imp. Assess. R. Environmental impact assessment review. (0195-9255). Elsevier Science: PO Box 211, 1000 AE Amsterdam, The Netherlands, in association with Department of Urban Studies and Planning, MIT.

Env. Law Environmental law. (0046-2276). Northwestern School of Law, Lewis and Clark College: 10015 S.W. Terwilliger Boulevard, Portland, OR 97219-7899, U.S.A.

Env. Plan. A Environment and planning A. (0308-518X). Pion: 207 Brondesbury Park, London NW2 5JN, U.K.

Env. Plan. C Environment and planning C: Government and policy. (0263-774X). Pion: 207 Brondesbury Park, London NW2 5JN, U.K.

Env. Plan. D Environment and planning D: Society and space. (0263-7758). Pion: 207 Brondesbury Park, London NW2 5JN, U.K.

Env. Pol. Environmental politics. (0964-4016). Frank Cass, Taylor & Francis Ltd: P.O. Box 25, Abingdon, Oxfordshire OX14 3UE, U.K.

Env. Resour. Econ. Environmental & resource economics. (0924-6460). Springer: Van Godewijckstraat 30, P.O. Box 17, 3300 AA Dordrecht, Netherlands.

Environment Environment. (0013-9157). Heldref Publications: 1319 Eighteenth Street N.W., Washington, DC 20036-1802, U.S.A.

Esprit Esprit. (0014-0759). Esprit: 212 rue Saint-Martin, 75003 Paris, France.

Est. Demog. Urb. Estudios demográficos y urbanos. (0186-7210). Colégio de México, Centro de Estudios Demográficos y de Desarrollo Urbano: Departamento de Publicaciones, Camino al Ajusco 20, 10740 México D.F., Mexico.

Est. Ib-Am. Estudos ibero-americanos. (0101-4064). Pontifícia Universidade Católica do Rio Grande do Sul: PUCRS/IFCH - PRÉDIO 5, Caixa postal 1429, 90619-900, Porto Alegre, RS, Brasil.

Est. Inter. Estudios internacionales. (0716-0240). Universidad de Chile, Instituto de Estudios Internacionales: Condell 249, Casilla 14187 Suc 21, Santiago 9, Chile.

Est. Sociol. Estudios sociológicos. (0185-4186). Colegio de México: Camino al Ajusco 20, Pedregal de Santa Teresa, 10740 México D.F., Mexico.

Ét. Int. Études internationales. (0014-2123). Institut Québécois des Hautes Études Internationales: Pavillon Charles-De Koninck, bureau 5458, Université Laval, Québec, Qué. G1K 7P4 Canada.

Ét. Philos. Études philosophiques. (0014-2166). Presses Universitaires de France: 6, avenue Reille, 75685 Paris Cedex 14, France.

Etat Opin. Etat de l'opinion. (0984-774X). Editions du Seuil: 27, rue Jacob, 75006 Paris, France.

Ethics Ethics. (0014-1704). University of Chicago Press: 5720 S. Woodlawn Avenue, Chicago, IL 60637, U.S.A.

Ethics Int. Aff. Ethics and international affairs. (0892-6794). Carnegie Council on Ethics and International Affairs: 170 East 64th Street, New York, NY 10021-7496.

Ethics Place Env. Ethics, place and environment. (1366-879X). Carfax Publishing, Taylor & Francis Ltd: P.O. Box 25, Abingdon, Oxfordshire OX14 3UE, U.K.

Ethn. Racial S. Ethnic and racial studies. (0141-9870). Routledge, Taylor & Francis Ltd: 2 Park Square, Milton Park, Abingdon, Oxfordshire OX14 4RN, U.K.

Ethnicities Ethnicities. (1468-7968). Sage Publications: 6 Bonhill Street, London EC2A 4PU, U.K.

Ethnohistory Ethnohistory. (0014-1801). Duke University Press: Box 90660, Durham, NC 27708-0660, U.S.A.

Etudes Etudes. (0014-1941). Ministère des affaires étrangéres: 14 rue d'Assas, 75006 Paris, France.

Euro. Constitutional Law R. European constitutional law review. (1574-0196). Cambridge University Press: Edinburgh Building, Shafetsbury Road, Cambridge CB2 2RU.

Euro. Env. European environment: the journal of European environmental policy. (0961-0405). John Wiley & Sons Ltd: The Atrium, Southern Gate, Chichester, West Sussex, PO19 8SQ, UK.

Euro. Ethn. Europa ethnica. (0014-2492). Wilhelm Braumüller: A-1092 Vienna, Servitengasse 5, Austria.

Euro. For. Aff. R. European foreign affairs review. (1384-6299). Kluwer Law International: P.O. Box 85889, 2508 CN The Hague, The Netherlands.

Euro. Hist. Q. European history quarterly. (0265-6914). Sage Publications: 6 Bonhill Street, London EC2A 4PU, U.K.

Euro. J. Communic. European journal of communication. (0267-3231). Sage Publications: 6 Bonhill Street, London EC2A 4PU, U.K.

Euro. J. Dev. Res. European journal of development research. (0957-8811). Frank Cass, Taylor & Francis Ltd: P.O. Box 25, Abingdon, Oxfordshire OX14 3UE, U.K.

Euro. J. Hist. Econ. Thou. European journal of the history of economic thought. (0967-2567). Routledge, Taylor & Francis Ltd: 2 Park Square, Milton Park, Abingdon, Oxfordshire, OX14 4RN.

Euro. J. Hous. Policy European journal of housing policy. (1461-6718). Routledge, Taylor & Francis Ltd: 2 Park Square, Milton Park, Abingdon, Oxfordshire, OX14 4RN.

Euro. J. Int. Rel. European journal of international relations. (1354-0661). Sage Publications: 6 Bonhill Street, London EC2A 4PU, U.K., in association with Standing Group on International Relations of the European Consortium for Political Research.

Euro. J. Law Econ. European journal of law and economics. (0929-1261). Springer: Van Godewijckstraat 30, P.O. Box 17, 3300 AA Dordrecht, Netherlands.

Euro. J. Philos. European journal of philosophy. (0966-8373). Blackwell Publishing: 108 Cowley Road, Oxford OX4 1JF, U.K.

Euro. J. Pol. Econ. European journal of political economy. (0176-2680). Elsevier Science Publishers: P.O. Box 1991, 1000 BZ Amsterdam, The Netherlands.

Euro. J. Pol. Res. European journal of political research. (0304-4130). Blackwell Publishing: 108 Cowley Road, Oxford OX4 1JF, in association with European Consortium for Political Research: University of Essex, Wivenhoe Park, Colchester CO4 3SQ, U.K.

Euro. J. Pol. Theory European journal of political theory. (1474-8851). Sage Publications: 6 Bonhill Street, London, EC2A 4PU, U.K.

Euro. J. Soc. Sec. European journal of social security. (1388-2627). Intersentia: Churchillaan 108, BE 2900 Schoten (Antwerp), Belgium.

Euro. J. Soc. Theory European journal of social theory. (1368-4310). Sage Publications: 6 Bonhill Street, London EC2A 4PU, U.K.

Euro. J. Sociol. Archives européennes de sociologie = European journal of sociology = Europäisches Archiv für Soziologie. (0003-9756). Cambridge University Press: The Edinburgh Building, Shaftesbury Road, Cambridge CB2 2RU, U.K.

Euro. Law J. European law journal. (1351-5993). Blackwell Publishing: 108 Cowley Road, Oxford OX4 1JF, U.K., in association with the European University Institute.

Euro. Leg. European legacy: towards new paradigms. (1084-8770). Carfax Publishing, Taylor & Francis Ltd: Rankine Road, Basingstoke, Hants, RG24 8PR, UK.

Euro. R. Lat. Am. Carib. S. European review of Latin American and Caribbean studies = Revista europea de estudios latinoamericanos y del Caribe. (0924-0608). Centre for Latin American Research and Documentation: Amsterdam Netherlands, in association with CEDLA (Interuniversitair Centrum voor Studie en Documentatie van Latijns Amerika) / RILA (Royal

Institute of Linguistics and Anthropology): Keizersgracht 395-397, 1016 Amsterdam, The Netherlands.

Euro. Sec. European security. (0966-2839). Frank Cass, Taylor & Francis Ltd: P.O. Box 25, Abingdon, Oxfordshire OX14 3UE, U.K.

Euro. Tükör Európai Tükör. (1416-7484). Stratégiai Elemzo Központ: Kossuth Lajos tér 4. H-1055 Budapest V, Hungary.

Euro. Uni. Pol. European Union politics. (1465-1165). Sage Publications: 6 Bonhill Street, London EC2A 4PU, U.K.

Euro.-Asia S. Europe-Asia studies. (0966-8136). Carfax Publishing, Taylor & Francis Ltd: P.O. Box 25, Abingdon, Oxfordshire OX14 3UE, U.K.

Europarecht Europarecht. (0531-2485). Nomos Verlagsgesellschaft: Waldseestr. 3-5 - D-76530 Baden-Baden, Germany.

Européens Européens. Fondation Robert Schuman: 29, boulevard Raspail, 75007 Paris, France.

Evaluation Evaluation. (1356-3890). Sage Publications: 6 Bonhill Street, London EC2A 4PU, U.K., in association with Tavistock Institute.

Evid. Policy Evidence & policy. (1744-2648). Policy Press, University of Bristol: 34 Tyndalls Park Road, Bristol BS8 1PY, U.K.

Expl. Econ. Hist. Explorations in economic history. (0014-4983). Academic Press: 1 East First Street, Duluth, MN 55802, U.S.A.

Fam. Law Family law. (0014-7281). Family Law: 21 St Thomas Street, Bristol, BS1 6JS, U.K.

Federalist Federalist. (0393-1358). EDIF: Via Porta Pertusi 6, 27100 Pavia, Italy, in association with Fondazione Europea Luciano Bolis.

Femin. Legal S. Feminist legal studies. (0966-3622). Kluwer Academic Publishers: P.O. Box 17, 3300 AA Dordrecht, The Netherlands, in association with Kent Law School: The University, Canterbury, Kent CT2 7NZ, U.K.

Fin. India Finance India. (0970-3772). India Institute of Finance: P.O. Box 8486, Ashok Vihar II, Delhi-110052 India.

Fis. Stud. Fiscal studies. (0143-5671). Institute for Fiscal Studies: 180/182 Tottenham Court Road, London W1P 9LE, U.K.

Food Policy Food policy. (0306-9192). Elsevier Science: PO Box 211, 1000 AE Amsterdam, The Netherlands.

Foreign Aff. Foreign affairs. (0015-7120). Council on Foreign Relations: 58 East 68th Street, New York, NY 10021, U.S.A.

Foro Int. Foro internacional. (0185-013X). El Colegio de México: Departamento de Publicaciones, Camino al Ajusco 20, Pedregal de Santa Teresa, 10740 México D.F., Mexico.

Forum Dev. S. Forum for development studies. (0803-9410). Norwegian Institute of International Affairs: Postboks 8159 Dep., 0033 Oslo 1, Norway.

Fre. Pol. French politics. (1476-3419). Palgrave Macmillan: Brunel Road Building, Houndmills, Basingstoke, Hampshire, RG21 6XS, U.K.

Fre. Pol. Cult. Soc. French politics, culture, and society. (0882-1267). Berghahn Books: 3, Newtec Place, Magdalen Road, Oxford OX4 1RE, U.K.

Futuribles Futuribles. (0337-307X). Futuribles: 55, rue de Varenne, 75341 Paris cedex 07, France.

Gazette Gazette: the international journal for communication studies. (0016-5492). Sage Publications: 6 Bonhill Street, London EC2A 4PU, U.K.

Gend. Place Cult. Gender, place and culture: A journal of feminist geography. (0966-369X). Carfax Publishing, Taylor & Francis Ltd: P.O. Box 25, Abingdon, Oxfordshire OX14 3UE, U.K.

Geoforum Geoforum. (0016-7185). Elsevier Science: PO Box 211, 1001 AE Amsterdam, The Netherlands.

Geojournal Geojournal. (0343-2521). Springer: Van Godewijckstraat 30, P.O. Box 17, 3300 AA Dordrecht, Netherlands.

Géopol. Afr. Géopolitique africaine. African Geopolitics: 2723 Denise Pelletier, Saint Laurent (Quebec), H4R 2T3 Canada.

Geopolitics Geopolitics. (1465-0045). Frank Cass, Taylor & Francis Ltd: P.O. Box 25, Abingdon, Oxfordshire OX14 3UE, U.K.

George Washington Int. Law R. George Washington international law review. (0748-4305). George Washington University, National Law Center: Washington DC 20052, U.S.A.

Ger. Pol. German politics. (0964-4008). Frank Cass, Taylor & Francis Ltd: P.O. Box 25, Abingdon, Oxfordshire OX14 3UE, U.K.

Gesell. Wirt. Pol. Gesellschaft Wirtschaft Politik: Sozialwissenschaften für politische Bildung. (1619-6910). VS Verlag für Sozialwissenschaften: Abraham-Lincoln-Straße 46, 65189 Wiesbaden, Germany.

Gifted Edu. Int. Gifted education international. (0261-4294). A.B. Academic Publishers: P.O. Box 42, Bicester, Oxon OX26 6NW, U.K.

Glo. Dial. Global dialogue. (1450-0590). Centre for World Dialogue: 39 Rega Fereou Street, CY-1087 Nicosia, Cyprus.

Glo. Econ. R. Global economic review. Institute of East and West Studies: Yonsei University, 134 Shinchondong, Seodaemoonku, Seoul 120-749, Korea.

Glo. Env. Chan. Global environmental change: human and policy dimensions. (0959-3780). Elsevier Science: PO Box 945, New York, NY 10010, U.S.A., in association with United Nations University.

Glo. Gov. Global governance. (1075-2846). Lynne Rienner Publishers: 1800 30th Street, Boulder, CO 80301, U.S.A.

Glo. Soc. Global society. (1360-0826). Carfax Publishing, Taylor & Francis Ltd: P.O. Box 25, Abingdon, Oxfordshire OX14 3UE, U.K., in association with University of Kent at Canterbury.

Glo. Soc. Policy Global social policy: an interdisciplinary journal of public policy and social development. (1468-0181). Sage Publications: 6 Bonhill Street, London EC2A 4PU, U.K.

Gos. Pravo Gosudarstvo i pravo. (0132-0769). MAIK Nauka/Interperiodika: 117997 Moscow, Profsoiuznaia ul. 90, Russia, in association with Rossiiskaia Akademiia Nauk.

Gov. Oppos. Government and opposition. (0017-257X). Government and Opposition Ltd.: Houghton Street, London WC2A 2AE, U.K.

Governance Governance. (0952-1895). Blackwell Publishing: 108 Cowley Road, Oxford OX4 1JF, U.K.

Grow. Chan. Growth and change. (0017-4815). Blackwell Publishing: 108 Cowley Road, Oxford OX4 1JF, U.K.

Hac. Públ. Esp. Hacienda pública española: Revista de economía pública. (0210-1173). Instituto de Estudios Fiscales: Ministerio de Hacienda, Avda. del Cardenal Herrera Oria, 378, 28035 Madrid.

Hall. Tut. Hallinnon tutkimus. (0359-6680). Hallinon Tutkimuksen Seura = Sällskapet för Förvaltningsforskning: Department of Administrative Sciences, University of Tampere, P.O.B. 607, 33101 Tampere, Finland.

Harv. Law R. Harvard law review. (0017-811X). Harvard Law Review Association: Gannett House, 1511 Massachusetts Avenue, Cambridge, MA 02138, U.S.A.

Health Care Anal. Health care analysis. (1065-3058). Springer: Van Godewijckstraat 30, P.O. Box 17, 3300 AA Dordrecht, Netherlands.

Health Hum. Rights Health and human rights. (1079-0969). Harvard School of Public Health: 8 Story Street, 5th Floor, Cambridge, MA 02138, U.S.A.

Health Policy Health policy. (0168-8510). Elsevier Science: PO Box 211, 1000 AE Amsterdam, The Netherlands.

Health Policy Plan. Health policy and planning: A journal on health in development. (0268-1080). Oxford University Press: Great Clarendon Street, Oxford OX2 6DP, U.K., in association with London School of Hygiene and Tropical Medicine: Keppel (Gower) Street, London WC1E 7HT, U.K.

Hedgehog R. Hedgehog review: Critical reflections on contemporary culture. (1527-9677). Institute for Advanced Studies in Culture: P.O. Box 400816, University of Virginia, Charlottesville, VA 22904-4816, U.S.A.

High. Edu. Higher education. (0018-1560). Springer: Van Godewijckstraat 30, P.O. Box 17, 3300 AA Dordrecht, Netherlands.

Hist. Čas. Historický časopis. (0018-2575). Slovak Academic Press: PO Box 57, Nám. Slobody 6, 810 05, Bratislava, Slovakia, in association with Slovenska Akademia Vied, Historického ústavu.

Hist. Hum. Sci. History of the human sciences. (0952-6951). Sage Publications: 6 Bonhill Street, London EC2A 4PU, U.K.

Hist. J. Historical journal. (0018-246X). Cambridge University Press: The Edinburgh Building, Shaftesbury Road, Cambridge CB2 2RU, U.K.

Hist. Pol. Thought History of political thought. (0143-781X). Imprint Academic: P.O. Box 1, Thorverton, Devon, EX5 5YX, U.K.

Hist. Techno. History and technology. (0734-1512). Routledge, Taylor & Francis Ltd: 11 New Fetter Lane, London EC4P 4EE, U.K.

Hist. Theory History and theory. (0018-2656). History and Theory, Wesleyan University: 287 High Street, Middletown, CT 06457-0507, U.S.A.

Histoire Histoire. (0182-2411). Société d'éditions scientifiques: 4, rue du Texel, 75014 Paris, France.

Historiens Géographes Historiens et géographes. (0046-757X).

History History. (0018-2648). Blackwell Publishing: 108 Cowley Road, Oxford, OX4 1JF, in association with Historical Association.

Hong Kong J. Soc. Sci. Hong Kong journal of social sciences. (1021-3619). City University of Hong Kong Press: Room B7518 Academic Building, City University of Hong Kong, 83 Tat Chee Avenue, Kowloon, Hong Kong.

Housing S. Housing studies. (1466-1810). Taylor & Francis: 4 Park Square, Milton Park, Abingdon, Oxfordshire, OX14 4RN.

Hum. Rights Q. Human rights quarterly. (0275-0392). Johns Hopkins University Press: 2715 North Charles Street, Baltimore, MD 21218-4363, U.S.A.

Iberoamericana Iberoamericana: América Latina - España - Portugal. (1577-3388). Iberoamericana Editorial / Vervuert: C/ Amor de Dios, 1 E-28014 Madrid, Spain, in association with Instituto Ibero-Americano, Berlin, Germany.

Ind. Econ. FEE Indicadores econômicos FEE. (0103-3905). Fundação de Economia e Estatística Siegfried Emanuel Heuser: Rua Duque de Caxias, 16591 - Porto Alegre, RS - CEP 90010-283.

Ind. High. Edu. Industry & higher education. (0950-4222). IP Publishing Ltd: Coleridge House, 4-5 Coleridge Gardens, London, NW6 3QH, U.K.

India Q. India quarterly. (0019-4220). Indian Council of World Affairs: Sapru House, Barakhamba Road, New Delhi 110001, India.

India R. India review. (1473-6489). Frank Cass, Taylor & Francis Ltd: P.O. Box 25, Abingdon, Oxfordshire OX14 3UE, U.K.

Indian Econ. R. Indian economic review. (0019-4671). Delhi School of Economics: University of Delhi, Delhi 110007, India.

Indian J. Pol. Sci. Indian journal of political science. (0019-5510). The Indian Journal of Political Science: Department of Political Science, Ch. Charan Singh University, Meerut, India.

Indian J. Publ. Admin. Indian journal of public administration. (0019-5561). Indian Institute of Public Administration: Indraprastha Estate, Ring Road East, New Delhi 110002, India.

Indian Soc. Sci. R. Indian social science review. (0972-0731). Indian Council of Social Science Research: Aruna Asaf Ali Road, New Delhi - 110 067, India.

Indiana J. Glob. Legal S. Indiana journal of global legal studies. (1080-0727). Indiana University Press: 601 N. Morton St., Bloomington, IN 47404, U.S.A., in association with Indiana University School of Law.

Indo. Malay. World Indonesia and the Malay world. (1363-9811). Carfax Publishing, Taylor & Francis Ltd: Rankine Road, Basingstoke, Hants RG24 8PR, UK, in association with School of Oriental and African Studies: Thornhaugh Street, Russell Square, London WC1H 0XG, U.K.

Info. Communic. Soc. Information, communication & society. (1369-118X). Routledge, Taylor & Francis Ltd: 2 Park Square, Milton Park, Abingdon, Oxfordshire OX14 4RN, U.K.

Info. Econ. Policy Information economics and policy. (0167-6245). Elsevier Science: PO Box 211, 1000 AE Amsterdam, The Netherlands, in association with International Telecommunications Society: c/o Professor R.G. Noll, Department of Economics, Stanford University, Stanford, CA 94305, U.S.A.

Info. Soc. Informations sociales. (0046-9459). Caisse Nationale des Allocations Familiales: 23 rue Daviel, 75634 Paris Cedex 13, France.

Info. Techno. People Information technology & people. (0959-3845). Emerald Group Publishing Ltd: 60/62 Toller Lane, Bradford, West Yorkshire, BD8 9BY.

Int. Aff. [London] International affairs [London]. (0020-5850). Blackwell Publishing: 108 Cowley Road, Oxford OX4 1JF, U.K., in association with Royal Institute of International Affairs: Chatham House, 10 St. James's Square, London SW1Y 4LE, U.K.

Int. Aff. [Moscow] International affairs [Moscow]. (0130-9641). East View Publications: 3020 Harbor Lane North, Minneapolis, MN 55447, U.S.A.

Int. Comp. Law Q. International and comparative law quarterly. (0020-5893). Oxford University Press: Great Clarendon Street, Oxford, OX2 6DP, U.K., in association with British Institute of International and Comparative Law: 17.

Int. Dev. Plan. R. International development planning review. (1474-6743). Liverpool University Press: 4 Cambridge Street, Liverpool L69 7ZU, U.K.

Int. Femin. J. Pol. International feminist journal of politics. (1461-6742). Routledge, Taylor & Francis Ltd: 2 Park Square, Milton Park, Abingdon, Oxfordshire, OX14 4RN.

Int. J. International journal. (0020-7020). Canadian Institute of International Affairs: 15 Kings College Circle, Toronto, Ontario, Canada M5S 2V9.

Int. J. Appl. Philos. International journal of applied philosophy. (0739-098X). Philosophy Documentation Center: PO Box 7147, Charlottesville, VA 22906-7147, U.S.A.

Int. J. Child. Rights International journal of children's rights. (0927-5568). Brill Academic Publishers: P.O. Box 9000, 2300 PA Leiden, The Netherlands.

Int. J. Comp. Lab. Law International journal of comparative labour law and industrial relations. (0952-617X). Kluwer Law International: P.O. Box 85889, 2508 CN The Hague, The Netherlands.

Int. J. Comp. Sociol. International journal of comparative sociology. (0020-7152). Sage Publications: 1 Oliver's Yard, 55 City Rd, London EC1Y 1SP.

Int. J. Const. Law International journal of constitutional law. (1474-2640). Oxford University Press: 200 Madison Avenue, New York, NY 10016, U.S.A., in association with New York University School of Law.

Int. J. Crit. Psychol. International journal of critical psychology. (1471-4167). Lawrence & Wishart: 99a Wallis Road, London E9 5LN, U.K.

Int. J. Cult. Policy International journal of cultural policy. (1028-6632). Routledge, Taylor & Francis Ltd: 2 Park Square, Milton Park, Abingdon, Oxfordshire, OX14 4RN.

Int. J. Health Serv. International journal of health services. (0020-7314). Baywood Publishing: 26 Austin Avenue, P.O. Box 337, Amityville, NY 11701, U.S.A.

Int. J. Hum. Res. Manag. International journal of human resource management. (0958-5192). Routledge, Taylor & Francis Ltd: 2 Park Square, Milton Park, Abingdon, Oxfordshire, OX14 4RN.

Int. J. Law Policy Fam. International journal of law, policy, and the family. (1360-9939). Oxford University Press: Great Clarendon Street, Oxford OX2 6DP, U.K.

Int. J. Law Psych. International journal of law and psychiatry. (0160-2527). Elsevier Science: PO Box 211, 1000 AE Amsterdam, The Netherlands.

Int. J. Mid. East S. International journal of Middle East studies. (0020-7438). Cambridge University Press: 40 West 20th Street, New York, NY 10011-4211, U.S.A., in association with Middle East Studies Association of North America: University of Arizona, 1232 North Cherry, Tuscon, AZ 85721, U.S.A.

Int. J. Publ. Opin. Res. International journal of public opinion research. (0954-2892). Oxford University Press: Great Clarendon Street, Oxford OX2 6DP, U.K., in association with World Association for Public Opinion Research.

Int. J. Trans. Econ. International journal of transport economics. (0391-8440). Gruppo Editoriale Internazionale: Via Ruggero Bonghi, 11/B, 00184 Rome, Italy.

Int. J. Urb. Reg. Res. International journal of urban and regional research. (0309-1317). Blackwell Publishing: 108 Cowley Road, Oxford, OX4 1JF, UK.

Int. Migr. R. International migration review. (0197-9183). Center for Migration Studies: 209 Flagg Place, Staten Island, NY 10304-1199, U.S.A.

Int. Negot. International negotiation: a journal of theory and practice. (1382-340X). Brill Academic Publishers: P.O. Box 9000, 2300 PA Leiden, The Netherlands.

Int. Org. International organization. (0020-8183). Cambridge University Press: 40 West 20th Street, New York, NY 10011-4211, U.S.A., in association with World Peace Foundation.

Int. Peace. International peacekeeping. (1353-3312). Frank Cass, Taylor & Francis Ltd: P.O. Box 25, Abingdon, Oxfordshire OX14 3UE, U.K.

Int. Pol. International politics. (1384-5748). Palgrave Macmillan: Brunel Road Building, Houndmills, Basingstoke, Hampshire, RG21 6XS, U.K.

Int. Pol. Gesell. Internationale Politik und Gesellschaft. (0945-2419). J.H.W. Dietz Nachf: In der Raste 2, D-53129 Bonn, Germany, in association with Friedrich-Ebert Stiftung: Godesberger Alle 149, D-53170 Bonn, Germany.

Int. Pol. Sci. R. International political science review = Revue internationale de science politique. (0192-5121). Sage Publications: 6 Bonhill Street, London EC2A 4PU, U.K., in association with International Political Science Association.

Int. Politik Internationale Politik. (1430-175X). W. Bertelsmann Verlag: Auf dem Esch 4, 33619 Bielefeld, Postfach 10 06 33, 33506 Bielefeld, in association with Deutsche Gesellschaft für Auswärtige Politik: Adenauerallee 131, D 5300 Bonn 1, Germany.

Int. R. Edu. International review of education. (0020-8566). Springer: Van Godewijckstraat 30, P.O. Box 17, 3300 AA Dordrecht, Netherlands.

Int. R. Law Econ. International review of law and economics. (0144-8188). Butterworth-Heinemann: Elsevier Science Inc, 655 Avenue of the Americas, New York, NY 10010, U.S.A.

Int. R. Red Cross International review of the Red Cross. (1560-7755). International Review of the Red Cross: 19 avenue de la Paix, 1202 Geneva, Switzerland, in association with International Committee of the Red Cross and Red Crescent Movement.

Int. R. Sociol. International review of sociology = Revue internationale de sociologie. (0390-6701). Carfax Publishing, Taylor & Francis Ltd: P.O. Box 25, Abingdon, Oxfordshire OX14 3UE, U.K.

Int. Rel. International relations. (0047-1178). Sage Publications: 6 Bonhill Street, London, EC2A 6HD, U.K., in association with David Davies Memorial Institute of International Studies.

Int. Rel. Asia Pacific International Relations of the Asia Pacific. (1470-482X). Oxford University Press: Great Clarendon St, Oxford, OX2 6DP.

Int. S. International studies. (0020-8817). Sage Publications India: B-42 Panchsheel Enclave, Post Box 4109, New Delhi 110 017, India.

Int. S. Q. International studies quarterly. (0020-8833). Blackwell Publishing: 350 Main Street, Malden, MA 02148, U.S.A., in association with International Studies Association: University of South Carolina, Columbia, SC 29208, U.S.A.

Int. S. R. International studies review. (1521-9488). Blackwell Publishing: 350 Main Street, Malden, MA 02148, U.S.A., in association with International Studies Association: University of South Carolina, Columbia, SC 29208, U.S.A.

Int. Secur. International security. (0162-2889). MIT Press: 55 Hayward Street, Cambridge, MA 02142, U.S.A., in association with Harvard University Center for Science and International Affairs: 79 John F. Kennedy Street, Cambridge, MA 02138, U.S.A.

Int. Soc. Work International social work. (0020-8728). Sage Publications: 6 Bonhill Street, London, EC2A 4PU, U.K., in association with International Association of Schools of Social Work.

Int. Sociol. International sociology. (0268-5809). Sage Publications: 6 Bonhill Street, London EC2A 4PU, U.K., in association with International Sociological Association: Consejo Superior de Investigaciones Cientificas. Pinar 25, 28006 Madrid, Spain.

Int. Spect. International spectator. (0393-2729). Istituto Affari Internazionali: Via Angelo Brunetti 9, 00186 Rome, Italy.

Integ. Lat.am. Integración latinoamericana. (0325-1675). Instituto para la Integración de América Latina: Esmeralda, Esmeralda 130, Pisos 16 y 17 (C1035ABD), Buenos Aires, Argentina.

Intel. Nat. Sec. Intelligence and national security. (0268-4527). Frank Cass, Taylor & Francis Ltd: P.O. Box 25, Abingdon, Oxfordshire OX14 3UE, U.K.

Internasjonal Pol. Internasjonal politikk. (0020-577X). Norwegian Institute of International Affairs: Postboks 8159 Dep., 0033 Oslo 1, Norway.

Interventions Interventions: international journal of postcolonial studies. (1369-801X). Routledge, Taylor & Francis Ltd: 11 New Fetter Lane, London, EC4P 4EE, U.K.

Islam. Law Soc. Islamic law and society. (0928-9380). Brill Academic Publishers: P.O. Box 9000, 2300 PA Leiden, The Netherlands.

Isr. Law R. Israel law review. (0021-2237). Israel Law Review Association, in association with c/o Faculty of Law, Hebrew University, Mt. Scopus, P.O.B. 24100, Jerusalem 91240, Israel.

Isr. Ybk Hum. Rig. Israel yearbook on human rights. (0333-5925). Martinus Nijhoff Publishers: P.O. Box 322, 3300 AH Dordrecht, The Netherlands, in association with Tel Aviv University, Faculty of Law.

Iss. Stud. Issues & studies. (1013-2511). National Chengchi University, Institute of International Relations: 64 Wan Shou Road, Wenshan 116, Taipei, Taiwan.

IWGIA New. Newsletter. IWGIA (International Work Group for Indigenous Affairs). (0105-6387). International Work Group for Indigenous Affairs: Fiolstraede 10, DK-1171 Copenhagen K, Denmark.

J. Afr. Econ. Journal of African economies. (0963-8024). Oxford University Press: Great Clarendon Street, Oxford OX2 6DP, U.K.

J. Afr. Law Journal of African law. (0221-8553). Cambridge University Press: The Edinburgh Building, Shaftesbury Road, Cambridge CB2 2RU, U.K., in association with School of Oriental and African Studies.

J. Agr. Econ. Journal of agricultural economics. (0021-857X). Agricultural Economics Society: Department of Agricultural and Food Economics, P.O. Box 237, University of Reading, Reading RG6 6AR, U.K.

J. Appl. Econ. Journal of applied economics. (1514-0326). Universidad del CEMA: Av. Córdoba 374 (1054), Buenos Aires, Argentina.

J. Asian Afr. S. Journal of Asian and African studies. (0021-9096). Sage Publications: 2455 Teller Road, Thousand Oaks, CA 91320, U.S.A.

J. Ayn Rand S. Journal of Ayn Rand studies. (1526-1018). Journal of Ayn Rand Studies Foundation: 1018 Walter Street, Suite 301, Port Townsend, WA 98668, U.S.A.

J. Baltic S. Journal of Baltic studies. (0162-9778). Association for the Advancement of Baltic Studies: 3465 East Burnside Street, Portland OR, 97214-2050, U.S.A., in association with Tartu University, Department of Political Science.

J. Bus. Res. Journal of business research. (0148-2963). Elsevier Science: PO Box 211, 1000 AE Amsterdam, The Netherlands.

J. Chur. State Journal of church and state. (0021-969X). J.M. Dawson Institute of Church-State Studies: Baylor University, P.O. Box 97308, Waco, TX 76798-7308, U.S.A.

J. Com. Mkt. S. Journal of Common Market studies. (0021-9886). Blackwell Publishing: 108 Cowley Road, Oxford OX4 1JF, U.K., in association with University Association for Contemporary European Studies.

J. Comm. S. Transit. Pol. Journal of communist studies and transition politics. (1352-3279). Frank Cass, Taylor & Francis Ltd: P.O. Box 25, Abingdon, Oxfordshire OX14 3UE, U.K.

J. Confl. Resol. Journal of conflict resolution. (0022-0027). Sage Publications: 2455 Teller Road, Newbury Park, Thousand Oaks, CA 91320, U.S.A., in association with Peace Science Society (International).

J. Confl. S. Journal of conflict studies. (1198-8614). University of New Brunswick: Fredericton, New Brunswick, E3B 5A3, Canada.

J. Cont. China Journal of contemporary China. (1067-0564). Carfax Publishing, Taylor & Francis Ltd: P.O. Box 25, Abingdon, Oxfordshire OX14 3UE, U.K.

J. Contemp. Afr. S. Journal of contemporary African studies. (0258-9001). Carfax Publishing, Taylor & Francis Ltd: P.O. Box 25, Abingdon, Oxfordshire OX14 3UE, U.K.

J. Contemp. Asia Journal of contemporary Asia. (0047-2336). Journal of Contemporary Asia Publishers: P.O. Box 592, Manila 1099, Philippines.

J. Contemp. Hist. Journal of contemporary history. (0022-0094). Sage Publications: 6 Bonhill Street, London EC2A 4PU, U.K.

J. Crim. Law Journal of criminal law. (0022-0183). Vathek Publishing: 5 Millennium Court, Derby Road, Douglas, Isle of Man, IM2 3EN, U.K.

J. Crim. Law Crimin. Journal of criminal law and criminology. (0091-4169). Northwestern University School of Law: 357 East Chicago Avenue, Chicago, IL 60611, U.S.A.

J. Cult. Econ. Journal of cultural economics. (0885-2545). Kluwer Academic Publishers: PO Box 17, 3300 AA Dordrecht, The Netherlands, in association with Association of Cultural Economics International.

J. Democ. Journal of democracy. (1045-5736). Johns Hopkins University Press: 2715 North Charles Street, Baltimore, MD 21218-4363, U.S.A.

J. Dev. Areas Journal of developing areas. (0022-037X). College of Business, Tennessee State University: Avon Williams Campus, 330 Tenth Avenue North, Nashville, TN 37203, U.S.A.

J. Dev. Econ. Journal of development economics. (0304-3878). Elsevier Science: P.O. Box 211, 1000 AE Amsterdam, Netherlands.

J. Dev. Soc. Journal of developing societies. (0169-796X). Sage Publications: 6 Bonhill Street, London EC2A 4PU, U.K.

J. Droit Int. Journal du droit international. (0021-8170). Editions du Juris-Classeur: 141, rue de Javel 75747 Paris, Cedex 15, France.

J. East Asian Aff. Journal of East Asian affairs. (1010-1608). Research Institute for International Affairs: Taewon Building 16th Floor, 143-40 Samsung-dong, Kangnam-gu, Seoul, Korea.

J. East Carib. S. Journal of Eastern Caribbean studies. (1028-8813). Sir Arthur Lewis Institute of Social and Economic Studies: University of the West Indies, P.O. Box 64, Bridgetown, Barbados.

J. Econ. Persp. Journal of economic perspectives. (0895-3309). American Economic Association: 2014 Broadway, Suite 305, Nashville, TN 37203, U.S.A.

J. Econ. Soc. Geog. Tijdschrift voor economische en sociale geografie = Journal of economic and social geography. (0040-747X). Blackwell Publishing: 108 Cowley Road, Oxford OX4 1JF, U.K., in association with Royal Dutch Geographical Society = Koninklijk Nederlands Aardrijkskundig Genootschap: Weteringschans 12, 1017 SG Amsterdam, Netherlands.

J. Edu. Policy Journal of education policy. (0268-0939). Taylor & Francis Ltd: 1 Gunpowder Square, London EC4A 3DE, U.K.

J. Edu. Work Journal of education and work. (1469-9435). Routledge, Taylor & Francis Ltd: 4 Park Square, Milton Park, Abingdon, Oxfordshire, OX14 4RN.

J. E-Gov. Journal of e-government. Haworth Press: 10 Alice Street, Binghampton NY, 13904-1580.

J. Ener. Nat. Resou. Law Journal of energy & natural resources law. (0264-6811). International Bar Association: 10th Floor, 1 Stephen Street, London W1T 1AT, UK, in association with Centre for Energy, Petroleum & Mineral Law & Policy, University of Dundee.

J. Entwick.pol. Journal für Entwicklungspolitik. (0258-2384). Südwind-Buchwelt Buchhandelsges.m.b.H: Baumgasse 79, A-1034 Wien, Austria, in association with Mattersburger Kreis für Entwicklungspolitik au den Österreichischen Universitäten: Weyrgasse 5, A-1030 Vienna, Austria.

J. Env. Econ. Manag. Journal of environmental economics and management. (0095-0696). Academic Press: 1 East First Street, Duluth, MN 55802, U.S.A., in association with Association of Environmental and Resource Economists: Resources for the Future, 1616 P. Street, N.W., Washington DC 20036, U.S.A.

J. Env. Law. Journal of environmental law. (0952-8873). Oxford University Press: Great Clarendon Street, Oxford OX2 6DP, U.K.

J. Env. Plan. Manag. Journal of environmental planning and management. (0964-0568). Carfax Publishing, Taylor & Francis Ltd: P.O. Box 25, Abingdon, Oxfordshire OX14 3UE, U.K.

J. Ethn. Migr. S. Journal of ethnic and migration studies. (1369-183X). Carfax Publishing, Taylor & Francis Ltd: P.O. Box 25, Abingdon, Oxfordshire OX14 3UE, U.K., in association with JEMS, CEMES: P.O. Box 4, Torpoint PL11 3YN, U.K.

J. Euro. Integ. Journal of European integration. (0703-6337). Routledge, Taylor & Francis Ltd: 4 Park Square, Milton Park, Abingdon, Oxfordshire, OX14 4RN.

J. Euro. Integ. Hist. Journal of European integration history = Revue d'histoire de l'intégration européenne = Zeitschrift für Geschichte der europäischen Integration. (0947-9511). Nomos Verlagsgesellschaft: Waldseestraße 3-5, 76530 Baden-Baden, Germany, in association with Group de liaison des professeurs d'histoire contemporaine auprès de la Commission européenne.

J. Euro. Publ. Policy Journal of European public policy. (1350-1763). Routledge, Taylor & Francis Ltd: 2 Park Square, Milton Park, Abingdon, Oxfordshire, OX14 4RN.

J. Euro. Soc. Policy Journal of European social policy. (0958-9287). Sage Publications: 6 Bonhill Street, London EC2A 4PU, U.K., in association with Journal of European Social Policy.

J. Genocide Res. Journal of genocide research. (1462-3528). Carfax Publishing, Taylor & Francis Ltd: P.O. Box 25, Abingdon, Oxfordshire OX14 3UE, U.K.

J. Health Pol. Policy Law Journal of health politics, policy and law. (0361-6878). Duke University Press: Box 90660, Durham, NC 27708-0660, U.S.A.

J. Homosexuality Journal of homosexuality. (0091-8369). Harrington Park Press, Inc: 10 Alice Street, Binghampton, NY 13904-1580, U.S.A.

J. Hum. Dev. Journal of human development. (1464-9888). Carfax Publishing, Taylor & Francis Ltd: Rankine Road, Basingstoke, Hants RG24 8PR, U.K., in association with United Nations Development Programme.

J. Hum. Res. Journal of human resources. (0022-166X). University of Wisconsin Press: 2537 Daniels Street, Madison, WI 53718-6772, U.S.A.

J. Imp. Commonw. Hist. Journal of Imperial and Commonwealth history. (0308-6534). Frank Cass, Taylor & Francis Ltd: P.O. Box 25, Abingdon, Oxfordshire OX14 3UE, U.K.

J. Inst. Theor. Econ. Journal of institutional and theoretical economics = Zeitschrift für die gesamte Staatswissenschaft. (0932-4569). J.C.B. Mohr (Paul Siebeck): Wilhelmstraße 18, Postfach 2040, D-72010 Tübingen, Germany.

J. Int. Aff. Journal of international affairs. (0022-197X). Columbia University, School of International Affairs: Box 4, International Affairs Building, Columbia University, New York, NY 10027, U.S.A.

J. Int. Econ. Law Journal of international economic law. (1369-3034). Oxford University Press: Great Clarendon Street, Oxford OX2 6DP, U.K.

J. Int. Rel. Dev. Journal of international relations and development. (1408-6980). University of Ljubljana, Faculty of Social Sciences, Centre of International Relations: PO Box 2547 SI-1001 Ljubljana Slovenia.

J. Lat. Am. S. Journal of Latin American studies. (0022-216X). Cambridge University Press: The Edinburgh Building, Shaftesbury Road, Cambridge CB2 2RU, U.K.

J. Law Econ. Journal of law and economics. (0022-2186). University of Chicago Press: 5720 S. Woodlawn Avenue, Chicago, IL 60637, U.S.A.

J. Law Soc. Journal of law and society. (0263-323X). Blackwell Publishing: 108 Cowley Road, Oxford OX4 1JF, U.K.

J. Legal S. Journal of legal studies. (0047-2530). University of Chicago Press: 5720 S. Woodlawn Avenue, Chicago, IL 60637, U.S.A.

J. Legis. St. Journal of legislative studies. (1357-2334). Frank Cass, Taylor & Francis Ltd: P.O. Box 25, Abingdon, Oxfordshire OX14 3UE, U.K., in association with Centre for Legislative Studies, University of Hull.

J. Libertarian S. Journal of libertarian studies. (0363-2873). Center for Libertarian Studies: P.O. Box 4091, Burlingame, CA 94011, U.S.A.

J. Mod. Afr. S. Journal of modern African studies. (0022-278X). Cambridge University Press: The Edinburgh Building, Shaftesbury Road, Cambridge CB2 2RU, U.K.

J. Mod. Ital. S. Journal of modern Italian studies. (1354-571X). Routledge, Taylor & Francis Ltd: 2 Park Square, Milton Park, Abingdon, Oxfordshire, OX14 4RN.

J. Nth. Afr. S. Journal of North African studies. (1362-9387). Frank Cass, Taylor & Francis Ltd: P.O. Box 25, Abingdon, Oxfordshire OX14 3UE, U.K.

J. Off. Repub. Fran. Journal officiel de la République française: Avis et rapports du Conseil. (0429-3541). Les éditions des journaux officiels: 26, rue Desaix, 75727 Paris Cedex 15, France.

J. Palestine S. Journal of Palestine studies. (0377-919X). University of California Press Journals: 2120 Berkeley Way, Berkeley, CA 94720-5812, U.S.A., in association with Institute for Palestine Studies: 3501 M Street NW, Washington DC 20007, U.S.A.

J. Peace Res. Journal of peace research. (0022-3433). Sage Publications: 6 Bonhill Street, London EC2A 4PU, U.K., in association with International Peace Research Institute, (PRIO): Fuglehauggata 11, 0260 Oslo 2, Norway.

J. Peacebuilding Dev. Journal of peacebuilding and development. (1542-3166). Center for Global Peace: 4400 Masachusets Avenue, N.W. , Washington DC, 20016-8123 U.S.A.

J. Peasant S. Journal of peasant studies. (0306-6150). Frank Cass, Taylor & Francis Ltd: P.O. Box 25, Abingdon, Oxfordshire OX14 3UE, U.K.

J. Pol. Journal of politics. (0022-3816). Blackwell Publishing: 108 Cowley Road, Oxford, OX4 1JF, U.K.

J. Pol. Econ. Journal of political economy. (0022-3808). University of Chicago Press: 5720 S. Woodlawn Avenue, Chicago, IL 60637, U.S.A.

J. Pol. Ideol. Journal of political ideologies. (1356-9317). Carfax Publishing, Taylor & Francis Ltd: P.O. Box 25, Abingdon, Oxfordshire OX14 3UE, U.K.

J. Pol. Philos. Journal of political philosophy. (0963-8016). Blackwell Publishing: 108 Cowley Road, Oxford OX4 1JF, U.K.

J. Policy Anal. Manag. Journal of policy analysis and management. (0276-8739). John Wiley & Sons: 605 Third Avenue, New York, NY 10158-0012, U.S.A., in association with Association for Public Policy Analysis and Management.

J. Policy Ref. Journal of policy reform. (1384-1289). Routledge, Taylor & Francis Ltd: 2 Park Square, Milton Park, Abingdon, Oxfordshire, OX14 4RN.

J. Publ. Admin. Res. Theory Journal of public administration research and theory. (1053-1858). Oxford University Press: Great Clarendon Street, Oxford OX2 6DP, UK, in association with Public Management Research Association.

J. Publ. Policy Journal of public policy. (0143-814X). Cambridge University Press: The Edinburgh Building, Shaftesbury Road, Cambridge CB2 2RU, U.K.

J. Refug. S. Journal of refugee studies. (0951-6328). Oxford University Press: Great Clarendon Street, Oxford OX2 6DP, U.K., in association with University of Oxford, Refugee Studies Programme: Queen Elizabeth House, 21 St. Giles, Oxford OX1 3LA, U.K.

J. Slav. Mil. S. Journal of Slavic military studies. (1351-8046). Frank Cass, Taylor & Francis Ltd: P.O. Box 25, Abingdon, Oxfordshire OX14 3UE, U.K.

J. Soc. Welf. Fam. Law Journal of social welfare & family law. (0141-8033). Routledge, Taylor & Francis Ltd: 4 Park Square, Milton Park, Abingdon, Oxfordshire, OX14 4RN.

J. Sth. Afr. S. Journal of Southern African studies. (0305-7070). Carfax Publishing, Taylor & Francis Ltd: P.O. Box 25, Abingdon, Oxfordshire OX14 3UE, U.K.

J. Sth. Euro. Balk. Journal of Southern Europe and the Balkans. (1461-3190). Carfax Publishing, Taylor & Francis Ltd: PO Box 25 Abingdon, Oxford OX14 3UE, U.K., in association with Association for the Study of Southern Europe and the Balkans.

J. Sth.East Euro. Black Sea S. Journal of Southeast European and Black Sea studies. (1468-3857). Frank Cass, Taylor & Francis Ltd: P.O. Box 25, Abingdon, Oxfordshire OX14 3UE, U.K.

J. Strategic S. Journal of strategic studies. (0140-2390). Frank Cass, Taylor & Francis Ltd: P.O. Box 25, Abingdon, Oxfordshire OX14 3UE, U.K.

J. Theor. Pol. Journal of theoretical politics. (0951-6298). Sage Publications: 6 Bonhill Street, London EC2A 4PU, U.K.

J. Transatlan. S. Journal of Transatlantic studies. (1479-4012). Edinburgh University Press: 22 George Square, Edinburgh, EH8 9LF.

J. Urb. Econ. Journal of urban economics. (0094-1190). Academic Press: 1 East First Street, Duluth, MN 55802, U.S.A.

J. World Tr. Journal of world trade. (1011-6702). Kluwer Law International: Sterling House, 66 Wilton Road, London SW1V 1DE.

Jahr. Öffent. Gegen. Jahrbuch des öffentlichen Rechts der Gegenwart. (0075-2517). J.C.B. Mohr (Paul Siebeck): Wilhelmstraße 18, Postfach 2040, D-72010 Tübingen, Germany.

Japanese J. Pol. Sci. Japanese Journal of Political Science. (1468-1099). Cambridge University Press: Edinburgh Building, Shaftesbury Road, Cambridge, CB2 2RU.

Javnost Javnost = Public. (1318-3222). European Institute for Communication and Culture: P.O. Box 2511, 1001 Ljubljana, Slovenia.

Jnl. Ele. Pub. Op. Par. Journal of elections, public opinion and parties. (1745-7289). Taylor & Francis: 4 Park Square, Milton Park, Abingdon, Oxfordshire OX14 4RN.

Jogtud. Köz. Jogtudományi közlöny. (0021-7166). Jogtudományi Közlöny: Országház u. 30, Budapest 1014, Hungary.

Journalism S. Journalism studies. (1461-670X). Routledge, Taylor & Francis Ltd: 4 Park Square, Milton Park, Abingdon, Oxfordshire, OX14 4RN.

Katedra Katedra: przestrzenie kobiecości. (1641-7046). Fundacja Res Publica: ul. Noakowskiego 26 m 40, 00-668 Warsaw, Poland, in association with Uniwersytet Warszawski, Instytut Stosowanych Nauk Społecznych.

Kor. Obs. Korea observer. (0023-3919). Institute of Korean Studies: C.P.O. Box 3410, Seoul 100-643, South Korea.

Kor. World Aff. Korea and world affairs. (0259-9686). Research Center for Peace and Unification of Korea: C.P.O. Box 6545, Seoul, South Korea.

Kosmopolis Kosmopolis. (1236-1372). Suomen rauhantutkimusyhdistys: Rauhan- ja konfliktintutkimuskeskus, TAPRI 33014, Tampereen yliopisto, Finland.

Kult. Społ. Kultura i społeczeństwo. (0023-5172). Instytut Studiów Politycznych: polkój 9, ul. Polna 18/20, 00-625 Warsaw, Poland, in association with Polska Akademia Nauk.

Kunnall. Aikak. Kunnallistieteellinen aikakauskirja. (0356-3669). Kuopion yliopisto: Sosiaaliteteiden laitos / TietoTeknia PL 1627, 70211 KUOPIO, Finland.

Labour [Canada] Labour [Canada] = Travail. (0700-3862). Committee on Canadian Labour History = Comité de l'histoire du travail du Canada: Department of History, Memorial University of Newfoundland, St. John's, Newfoundland. A1C 5S7, Canada.

Land Ref. Land Sett. Coop. Land reform, land settlement and cooperatives. (0251-1894). Food and Agriculture Organization: Viale delle Terme di Caracalla, 00100 Rome, Italy.

Lat. Am. Persp. Latin American perspectives. (0094-582X). Sage Publications: 2455 Teller Road, Newbury Park, Thousand Oaks, CA 91320, U.S.A.

Lat. Am. Pol. Soc. Latin American politics and society. (1531-426X). University of Miami: 1541 Brescia Avenue, P.O. Box 248123, Coral Gables, FL 33124-3010, U.S.A., in association with Institute of Interamerican Studies.

Lat. Am. Res. R. Latin American research review. (0023-8791). University of Texas Press: 2100 Comal, Austin, TX 78722-2550, U.S.A., in association with Latin American Studies Association.

Lat.Am. Anal. Lateinamerika Analysen. (1619-1684). Institut für Iberoamerika-Kunde: Alsterglacis 8, 20354 Hamburg.

Law Contemp. Prob. Law and contemporary problems. (0023-9186). Duke University, School of Law: Room 006, Durham, NC 27706, U.S.A.

Law Philos. Law and philosophy. (0167-5249). Springer: Van Godewijckstraat 30, P.O. Box 17, 3300 AA Dordrecht, Netherlands.

Legis. Stud. Q. Legislative studies quarterly. (0362-9805). Comparative Legislative Research Center: University of Iowa, 349 Schaeffer Hall, Iowa City, IA 52242, U.S.A.

Liberté Pol. Liberté politique. (1288-0639). Fondation de service politique: 23, rue Jean Jaurès, 92300 Levallois Perret, France.

Loc. Econ. Local economy. (0269-0942). Routledge, Taylor & Francis Ltd: 2 Park Square, Milton Park, Abingdon, Oxfordshire, OX14 4RN, in association with Local Economy Policy Unit: South Bank University, 103 Borough Road, London SE1 0AA, U.K.

Loc. Env. Local environment. (1354-9839). Carfax Publishing, Taylor & Francis Ltd: P.O. Box 25, Abingdon, Oxfordshire OX14 3UE, U.K.

Loc. Govt. S. Local government studies. (0300-3930). Frank Cass, Taylor & Francis Ltd: P.O. Box 25, Abingdon, Oxfordshire OX14 3UE, U.K.

Low Int. Confl. Law Enf. Low intensity conflict and law enforcement. (0966-2847). Frank Cass, Taylor & Francis Ltd: P.O. Box 25, Abingdon, Oxfordshire OX14 3UE, U.K.

Maastricht J. Euro. Comp. Law Maastricht journal of European and comparative law. (1023-263X). Maastricht University: METRO, PO Box 616, NL-6200 MD Maastricht, in association with Intersentia N.V.: Groenstraat 31 B-2640 Mortsel (Antwerpen), Belgium.

Mag. Köz. Magyar közigazgatás. (0865-736X).

Mag. Tud. Magyar tudomány. (0025-0325). Akadémiai Kiadó: P.O. Box 245, H-1519 Budapest, Hungary, in association with Magyar Tudományos Akadémia: Roosevelt-tér 9, 1051 Budapest, Hungary.

Manag. Sci. Management science. (0025-1909). Institute for Operations Research and the Management Sciences: 901 Elkridge Landing Road, Suite 400 Linthicum, MD 21090-2909, U.S.A.

Mankind Q. Mankind quarterly. (0025-2344). Council for Social and Economic Studies: Suite C-2, 1133 13th Street N.W., Washington DC 20005-4297, U.S.A.

Marine Policy Marine policy. (0308-597X). Pergamon, Elsevier Science Ltd: PO Box 211, 1000AE, Amsterdam, Netherlands.

Med. Confl. Surv. Medicine, conflict and survival. (1362-3699). Frank Cass, Taylor & Francis Ltd: P.O. Box 25, Abingdon, Oxfordshire OX14 3UE, U.K.

Med. Pol. Mediterranean politics. (1362-9395). Frank Cass, Taylor & Francis Ltd: P.O. Box 25, Abingdon, Oxfordshire OX14 3UE, U.K.

Media Cult. Soc. Media culture and society. (0163-4437). Sage Publications: 6 Bonhill Street, London EC2A 4PU, U.K.

Media Int. Aust. Media international Australia incorporating culture & policy. (1329-878X). University of Queensland: School of English, Media Studies & Art, St. Lucia QLD 4072 Australia, in association with Australia & New Zealand Communication Association.

Mediactive Mediactive. (1740-8105). Lawrence & Wishart: 99a Wallis Road, London, E9 5LN, in association with Barefoot Publications.

Medien Kommun.wissen. Medien & Kommunikationswissenschaft. (1615-634X). Nomos Verlagsgesellschaft: Waldseestr. 3-5 - D-76530 Baden-Baden, Germany.

Mediterr. Q. Mediterranean quarterly: A journal of global issues. (1047-4552). Duke University Press: Box 90660, Durham, NC 27708-0660, U.S.A.

Medz. Otázky Medzinárodné otázky. (1210-1583). Slovenský Inštitút Medzinárodných Štúdií: Drotárska Cesta 46, 811 02 Bratislava, Slovakia.

Metapolítica Metapolítica. (1405-4558). Centro de Estudios de Política Comparada: Playa Eréndira 19, Barrio Santiago Sur, México D.F. 08800, Mexico.

Mez. Vzt. Mezinárodní vztahy. (0323-1844). Ústav Mezinárodní Vztahu: Nerudova 3, 118 50 Prague 1, Czech Republic.

Mid. East J. Middle East journal. (0026-3141). Middle East Institute: 1761 N. Street N.W., Washington DC 20036-2882, U.S.A.

Mid. East Policy Middle East policy. (1061-1924). Middle East Policy Council: 1730 M. Street N.W., Suite 512, Washington DC, 20036-4505, U.S.A.

Mid. East Q. Middle East quarterly. (1073-9467). Allen Press Inc.,: AM&M, 810 East 10th Street, Lawrence, KS 66044-8897, U.S.A.

Mid. East Rep. Middle East report. (0899-2851). Middle East Research and Information Project (MERIP): Suite 119, 1500 Massachusetts Avenue N.W., Washington DC 20005, U.S.A.

Migrat. Soc. Migrations société. (0995-7367). CIEMI: 46, rue de Montreuil 75011 Paris, France.

Milbank Q. Milbank quarterly. (0887-378X). Blackwell Publishing: 108 Cowley Road, Oxford OX4 1JF, U.K., in association with Milbank Memorial Fund.

Mir. Ekon. Mezh. Ot. Mirovaia ekonomika i mezhdunarodnye otnosheniia. (0131-2227). MAIK Nauka/Interperiodika: 117997, Moscow, Profsoiuznaia ul. 90, Russia, in association with Rossiiskaia Akademiia Nauk.

Mir Rossii Mir Rossii. Vysshaia Shkola Ekonomiki: 101987 Moscow, ul. Vavilova 7a, kom. 314, Russia, in association with Institut ekonomicheskikh problem perekhodnogo perioda.

Mittelweg 36 Mittelweg 36: Zeitschrift des Hamburger Instituts fur Sozialforschung. (0941-6382). Hamburg Institut für Sozialforschung: Mittelweg 36 20148 Hamburg Germany.

Mobilization Mobilization. (1086-671X). San Diego State University, Department of Sociology: San Diego, CA 92182-4423, U.S.A.

Mod. Asian S. Modern Asian studies. (0026-749X). Cambridge University Press: The Edinburgh Building, Shaftesbury Road, Cambridge CB2 2RU, U.K.

Mod. Cont. France Modern & contemporary France. (0267-761X). Taylor & Francis: 4 Park Square, Milton Park, Abingdon, Oxon, OX14 4RN.

Mod. Law R. Modern law review. (0026-7961). Blackwell Publishing: 108 Cowley Road, Oxford OX4 1JF, U.K.

Mon. Dévelop. Mondes en développement. (0302-3052). ISMEA: avenue des Naïades 11, B-1170 Brussels, Belgium, in association with I.S.M.E.A.: rue Pierre et Marie Curie 11, Institut Henri Poincaré, F-75005 Paris, France.

Mon. Obshch. Mnen. Monitoring obshchestvennogo mneniia. VCIOM Press Ltd.: 103064, Moscow, ul. Kazakova 16, Russia, in association with Interdisciplinary Academic Centre for Social Sciences (InterCentre).

Monde Chin. Monde chinois. (1767-3755). L'Institut Choiseul: 16 rue de la Grange batelière, 75009 Paris, France.

Mouvements Mouvements. (1291-6412). La Decouverte: 9 bis, rue Abel-Hovelacque - 75013 Paris, France.

Multitudes Multitudes. (0292-0107). Multitudes: 24, place Étienne-Marcel, 78180 Montigny le Bretonneux, France.

Nat. Ethn. Pol. Nationalism and ethnic politics. (1353-7113). Frank Cass, Taylor & Francis Ltd: P.O. Box 25, Abingdon, Oxfordshire OX14 3UE, U.K.

Nat. Ident. National identities. (1460-8944). Carfax Publishing, Taylor & Francis Ltd: P.O. Box 25, Abingdon, Oxfordshire OX14 3UE, UK.

Nat. Interest National interest. (0884-9382). National Interest, Inc.: 1112 16th Street N.W., Suite 530, Washington DC 20036, U.S.A.

Nat. Nationalism Nations and nationalism. (1354-5078). Blackwell Publishing: 108 Cowley Road, Oxford OX4 1JF, UK, in association with Association for the Study of Ethnicity and Nationalism.

Nat. P. Nationalities papers. (0090-5992). Carfax Publishing, Taylor & Francis Ltd: P.O.Box 25, Abingdon, Oxfordshire OX14 3UE, U.K.

National Inst. Econ. R. National Institute economic review. (0027-9501). National Institute of Economic and Social Research: 2 Dean Trench Street, Smith Square, London SW1P 3HE, U.K.

Natur. Res. J. Natural resources journal. (0028-0739). University of New Mexico, School of Law: Albuquerque, NM 87131, U.S.A.

Neth. Int. Law R. Netherlands international law review. (0165-070X). T.M.C. Asser Press: P.O. Box 16163, 2500 BD, The Hague, The Netherlands.

Neth. Q. Hum. Rights Netherlands quarterly of human rights. (0169-3441). Intersentia: Churchilllaan 108, B2900 Schoten (Antwerp) Belgium.

Neue Pol. Liter. Neue politische literatur. (0028-3320). Peter Lang: Eschborner Landstraße 42-50, Postfach 940225, 6000 Frankfurt am Main, Germany.

New Gen. Soc. New genetics and society. (1463-6778). Carfax Publishing, Taylor & Francis Ltd: Rankine Road, Basingstoke, Hants, RG24 8PR, UK.

New Left R. New Left review. (0028-6060). New Left Review: 6 Meard Street, London W1V 3HR, U.K.

New Media Soc. New media & society. (1461-4448). Sage Publications: 6 Bonhill Street, London EC2A 4PU, U.K.

New Pol. New politics. (0028-6494). New Politics Associates: P.O. Box 98, Brooklyn, NY 11231, U.S.A.

New Pol. Econ. New political economy. (1356-3467). Carfax Publishing, Taylor & Francis Ltd: P.O. Box 25, Abingdon, Oxfordshire OX14 3UE, U.K.

New Pol. Sci. New political science. (0739-3148). Carfax Publishing, Taylor & Francis Ltd: P.O. Box 25, Abingdon, Oxfordshire OX14 3UE, U.K, in association with Caucus for a New Political Science.

New York Univ. J. Int. Law Pol. New York University journal of international law and politics. (0028-7873). New York University Law Publications: 110 West Third Street, New York, NY 10012, U.S.A.

Nonprof. Manag. Leader. Nonprofit management and leadership. (1048-6682). Jossey-Bass: 350 Sansome Street, 5th Floor, San Francisco, CA 94104, U.S.A.

Nord Ny. Nord nytt. (0008-1345). NEFA-Norden: Astrid Caspersen Institutfor Arkæologi og Etnologi, Københavns Universitetet Vandkunsten 5, DK-1470 Køvenhavn K.

Nordiques Nordiques. L'Instiut Choiseul: 16 rue de la Grange batalière, 75009 Paris, France.

Nouv. Alter. Nouvelle alternative. (0764-7565). La Nouvelle Alternative: 41 rue Bobillot, 75013 Paris, France.

Nouv. Prat. Soc. Nouvelles pratiques sociales. (0843-4468). Université du Québec à Montréal: Case postale 8888, succursale Centre-Ville, Montréal, Québec, Canada H3C 3P8.

Numen Numen. (0029-5973). Brill Academic Publishers: P.O. Box 9000, 2300 PA Leiden, The Netherlands, in association with International Association for the History of Religions.

Obshch. Nauki Sovrem. Obshchestvennye nauki i sovremennost'. (0869-0499). MAIK Nauka/Interperiodika: 117997 Moscow, Profsoiuznaia ul. 90, Russia, in association with Rossiiskaia Akademiia Nauk.

Ocean Dev. Int. Ocean development and international law. (0090-8320). Taylor & Francis Ltd: 11 New Fetter Lane, London EC4P 4EE, U.K.

OPEC R. OPEC review. (0277-0180). Blackwell Publishing: 108 Cowley Road, Oxford OX4 1JF, U.K.

Opin. Pub. Opinião pública. (0104-6276). Centro de estudios de opinião pública: Universidade Estadual de Campinas, Cidade Universitária "Zeferino Vaz", Caixa postal 6110, Campinas, São Paulo, Brazil.

Orbis Orbis. (0030-4387). Elsevier Science: PO Box 211, 1000 AE Amsterdam, The Netherlands, in association with Foreign Policy Research Institute.

Öster. Z. Pol.wissen. Österreichische Zeitschrift für Politikwissenschaft. (1615-5548). NOMOS Verlagsgesellschaft: Waldseestraße 3-5, PF 100310, D-76484 Baden-Baden, Germany, in association with Österreichische Gesellschaft für Politikwissenschaft.

Öster. Z. Soziol. Österreichische Zeitschrift für Soziologie. (1011-0070). VS Verlag für Sozialwissenschaften: Abraham-Lincoln-Straße 46, 65189 Wiesbaden, Germany.

Osteuro. Wirt. Osteuropa Wirtschaft. (0030-6460). Deutsche Verlags-Anstalt: Neckarstraße 121, Postfach 1060 12, D-70190 Stuttgart, Germany, in association with Deutsche Gesellschaft für Osteuropakunde: Schaperstraße 30, 1000 Berlin 15, Germany.

Osteuropa Osteuropa. (0030-6428). Deutsche Verlags-Anstalt: Neckarstraße 121, Postfach 1060 12, D70190 Stuttgart, Germany, in association with Deutsche Gesellschaft für Osteuropakunde: Schaperstraße 30, 1000 Berlin 15, Germany.

Outre-terre Outre-terre. Editions érès: BP 75278, 31152 Fenouillet Cedex, France.

Oxf. J. Leg. S. Oxford journal of legal studies. (0143-6503). Oxford University Press: Great Clarendon Street, Oxford, OX2 6DP, UK.

Oxf. R. Econ. Policy Oxford review of economic policy. (0266-903X). Oxford University Press: Great Clarendon Street, Oxford OX2 6DP, U.K.

Pac. Aff. Pacific affairs. (0030-851X). University of British Columbia: Vancouver BC, V6T 1Z2, Canada.

Pac. Econ. B. Pacific economic bulletin. (0817-8038). Australian National University, Research School of Pacific Studies: G.P.O. Box 4, Canberra ACT 2601, Australia.

Pac. Hist. R. Pacific historical review. (0030-8684). University of California Press Journals: 2120 Berkeley Way, Berkeley, CA 94720-5812, U.S.A., in association with American Historical Association, Pacific Coast Branch: 6339 Bunche Hall, Los Angeles, CA 90024, U.S.A.

Pac. R. Pacific review. (0951-2748). Routledge, Taylor & Francis Ltd: 2 Park Square, Milton Park, Abingdon, Oxfordshire, OX14 4RN.

Pak. Econ. Soc. R. Pakistan economic and social review. (1011-002X). University of the Punjab, Department of Economics: Quaid-i-Azam Campus, Lahore 54590, Pakistan.

Pakis. Horiz. Pakistan horizon. (0030-980X). Pakistan Institute of International Affairs: Awan-e-Sadar Road, P.O. Box 1447, Karachi 74200, Pakistan.

Palestine-Israel J. Pol. Econ. Cult. Palestine-Israel journal of politics, economics and culture. (0793-1395). Middle East Publications: 4 El Hariri Street, P.O.B. 19839 Jerusalem, Israel.

Pań. Prawo Państwo i prawo. (0031-0980). Dom Wydawniczy ABC: 01-231, Warszawa, ul Płocka 5a, Poland, in association with Polska Akademia Nauk, Komitet Nauk Prawnych.

Pap. Econ. Esp. Papeles de economía española. (0210-9107). Confederación Española de Cajas de Ahorros, Fondos para la Investigación Económica y Social: Juan HUrtado de Mendoza 19, 28036 Madrid, Spain.

Papers Papers: revista de sociologia. (0210-2862). Universitat Autònoma de Barcelona, Departament de Sociologia: Servei de Publicacions, Edifici A, 08193 Barcelona, Spain.

Parl. Aff. Parliamentary affairs. (0031-2290). Oxford University Press: Great Clarendon Street, Oxford OX2 6DP, U.K., in association with Hansard Society for Parliamentary Government.

Party Pol. Party politics. (1354-0688). Sage Publications: 6 Bonhill Street, London EC2A 4PU, U.K.

Patt. Prej. Patterns of prejudice. (0031-322X). Sage Publications: 6 Bonhill Street, London EC2A 4PU, U.K., in association with Institute of Jewish Affairs: 11 Hertford Street, London W1Y 7DX, U.K.

Penant Penant. (0336-1551). Édiéna: 17 rue Thiers, 78110 Le Vésinet, France.

Pens. Pol. Pensiero politico. (0031-4846). Leo S. Olschki editore: Viuzzo del Pozzetto 50126 Florence, Italy.

Pensée Pensée. (0031-4773). La Pensée, Espaces Marx: 64, Boulevard Auguste-Blanqui, 75013 Paris, France.

Pénz. Sz. Pénzügyi szemle. (0031-496X). Pénzügyminisztérium: Postafiók 481, 1369 Budapest, Hungary.

Peop. Place People and place. (1039-4788). Centre for Population and Urban Research: Monash University, PO Box 11A, Victoria, Australia 3800.

Pers. Gl. Dev. & Tech. Perspectives on global development and technology. (1569-1500). Brill Academic Publishers.

Persp. Chinoises Perspectives chinoises. Centre d'études français sur la Chine contemporaine: Room 304, Yu Yuet Lai Building, 43-55 Wyndham Street, Central, Hong Kong.

Philip. S. Philippine studies. (0031-7837). Ateneo de Manila University Press: P.O. Box 154, Manila 1099, Philippines.

Philos. Publ. Aff. Philosophy & public affairs. (0048-3915). Princeton University Press: 41 William Street, Princeton, NJ 08540, U.S.A.

Philos. Soc. Crit. Philosophy & social criticism. (0191-4537). Sage Publications: 6 Bonhill Street, London EC2A 4PU, U.K.

Plan. Desarr. Planeación y desarrollo. (0034 8686). Departamento Nacional de Planeación: Calle 26 No. 13-19 Piso 2º, Santafé de Bogota, Colombia.

Plan. Theory Pract. Planning theory & practice. (1464-9357). Routledge, Taylor & Francis Ltd: 11 New Fetter Lane, London, EC4P 4EE, U.K., in association with Royal Town Planning Institute, 26 Portland Place, London, W1N 4BE.

Pol. Afr. Politique africaine. (0244-7827). Éditions Karthala: 22-24 boulevard Arago, 75013 Paris, France, in association with Association des chercheurs de politique africaine.

Pol. Čas. Politologický časopis. (1211-3247). Masarykova univerzita v Brne: Udolni 53, 602 00 Brno, in association with Mezinárodní politologický ústav.

Pol. Communic. Political communication. (1058-4609). Taylor & Francis: 1 Gunpowder Square, London EC4A 3DE, U.K.

Pol. Cult. Politica y cultura. (0188-7742). Universidad Autónoma Metropolitana-Xochimilco: Czda. del Hueso 1100, Col. Villa Quietud, 04960 Mexico D.F., Mexico.

Pol. Den. Jahr. Politisches Denken Jahrbuch. (0942-2307). Schäffer-Poeschel Verlag für Wirtschaft Steuern Recht GmbH & Co. KG, Germany.

Pol. Econ. J. India Political economy journal of India. (0971-2097). Centre for Indian Development Studies: 206 Sector 9-C, Chandigarh-160017, India.

Pol. Ekon. Politická ekonomie. (0032-3233). University of Economics, Prague: 4 Winston Churchill Sq., CZ-130 67, Prague 3, Czech Republic.

Pol. et Soc. Politique et sociétés. (1203-9438). Société québécoise de science politique, Département de science politique: Université du Québec à Montréal, C.P. 8888, succ. A, Montreal, Quebec H3C 3P8, Canada.

Pol. Étran. Politique étrangère. (0032-342X). Institut Français des relations internationales: 27, rue de la Procession 75740 Paris Cedex 15 - France.

Pol. Manag. Publ. Politiques et management public. (0758-1726). Institut de management public: 111 boulevard Brune, BP 127, 75663 Paris Cedex 14.

Pol. Misao Politička misao. (0032-3241). Fakultet političkih znanosti u Zagrebu: 10000 Zagreb, Lepušićeva 6, Croatia.

Pol. Philos. Econ. Politics, philosophy & economics. (1470-594X). Sage Publications: 6 Bonhill Street, London EC2A 4PU, U.K., in association with Murphy Institute of Political Economy, Tulane University.

Pol. Psychol. Political psychology. (0162-895X). Blackwell Publishing: 350 Main Street, Malden, MA 02148, U.S.A., in association with International Society of Political Psychology.

Pol. Q. Political quarterly. (0032-3179). Blackwell Publishing: 108 Cowley Road, Oxford OX4 1JF, U.K.

Pol. S. Political studies. (0032-3217). Blackwell Publishing: 108 Cowley Road, Oxford OX4 1JF, U.K., in association with Political Studies Association of the United Kingdom: c/o Jack Hayward, Department of Politics, The University, Hull HU6 7RX, U.K.

Pol. Sci. Political science. (0032-3187). School of Political Science and International Relations: Victoria University of Wellington, P.O. Box 600, Wellington, New Zealand, in association with Victoria University of Wellington, School of Political Science and Public Administration: P.O.Box 600, Wellington 1, New Zealand.

Pol. Sci. Q. Political science quarterly. (0032-3195). Academy of Political Science: 475 Riverside Drive, Suite 1274, New York, NY 10115-1274, U.S.A.

Pol. Soc. Politics and society. (0032-3292). Sage Publications: 2455 Teller Road, Thousand Oaks, CA 91320, U.S.A.

Pol. Theory Political theory. (0090-5917). Sage Publications: 2455 Teller Road, Newbury Park, Thousand Oaks, CA 91320, U.S.A.

PoLAR PoLAR: political and legal anthropology. (1555-2934). American Anthropological Association: 4350 North Fairfax Drive, Suite 640, Arlington, VA 22203-1620, U.S.A., in association with University of California Press.

Pôle Sud Pôle Sud. (1262-1676).

Policing Soc. Policing and society. (1043-9463). Harwood Academic Publishers, Taylor & Francis Ltd: 11 New Fetter Lane, London, EC4P 4EE.

Policy Pol. Policy and politics. (0305-5736). Policy Press, University of Bristol: 34 Tyndalls Park Road, Bristol BS8 1PY, U.K.

Policy S. Policy studies. (0144-2872). Carfax Publishing, Taylor & Francis Ltd: P.O. Box 25, Abingdon, Oxfordshire OX14 3UE, U.K., in association with Policy Studies Institute.

Policy Sci. Policy sciences. (0032-2687). Springer: Van Godewijckstraat 30, P.O. Box 17, 3300 AA Dordrecht, Netherlands.

Polis [Moscow] Polis [Moscow]. (0321-2017). Polis: B.Yakimanka 35, str. 1, 119049 Moscow, Russia.

Pol. Int. Politique internationale. (0221-2781). Politique Internationale: 11 rue du Bois de Boulogne, 75116 Paris, France.

Pol. Viertel. Politische Vierteljahresschrift. (0032-3470). VS Verlag für Sozialwissenschaften: Abraham-Lincoln-Straße 46, 65189 Wiesbaden, Germany, in association with Deutsche Vereinigung für Politische Wissenschaft.

Politica Politica: tidsskrift for politisk videnskab. (0105-0710). Institut for Statskundskab, Aarhus Universitet: Bartholins Allé, Bygning 331, 8000 Århus C, Denmark.
Politiikka Politiikka. (0032-3365). Finnish Political Science Association: P.O.Box 54 (Unioninkatu 37) 00014 University of Helsinki.
Politik. Szem. Politikatudományi szemle. (1216-1438).
Politikon Politikon. (0258-9346). Carfax Publishing, Taylor & Francis Ltd: P.O. Box 25, Abingdon, Oxfordshire OX14 3UE, U.K., in association with South African Association of Political Studies.
Politische S. Politische Studien. (0032-3462). Hanns-Seidel-Stiftung Referat Presse- und Öffentlichkeitsarbeit,: Lazarettstr. 33, 80636 München.
Politix Politix. (0295-2319). HERMES Science Publications: 8, quai du Marché-Neuf, 75004 Paris, France.
Posit. Méd. Positions et médias. (1628-1888). SARL Cap Editions: 26, rue d'Artois, 75008 Paris, France.
Post-Comm. Econ. Post-communist economies. (1463-1377). Carfax Publishing, Taylor & Francis Ltd: P.O. Box 25, Abingdon, Oxfordshire OX14 3UE, U.K., in association with Centre for Research into Communist Economies: 57 Tufton Street, London SW1P 3QL, U.K.
Post-Sov. Aff. Post-Soviet affairs. (1060-586X). Bellwether Publishing Ltd: 8640 Guilford Road, #200, Columbia, MD 21046-3163, U.S.A., in association with Joint Committee on Soviet Studies of the American Council of Learned Societies and the Social Science Research Council.
Pouv. Loc. Pouvoirs locaux. (0998-8289).
Pouvoirs Pouvoirs. (0152-0768). Éditions du Seuil: 27 rue Jacob, 75006 Paris Cedex 06, France.
Practice Practice. (0950-3153). Carfax Publishing, Taylor & Francis Ltd: P.O. Box 25, Abingdon, Oxfordshire OX14 3UE, U.K., in association with British Association of Social Workers.
Pres. Stud. Q. Presidential studies quarterly. (0360-4918). Sage publications: 2455 Teller Road, Thousand Oaks, CA 91320.
Prob. Am. Lat. Problèmes d'Amérique latine. (0765-1333). Choiseul Editions: 16 rue de la Grange Batalière, 75009 Paris, France.
Prob. Pol. Soc. Problèmes politiques et sociaux. (0015-9743). Documentation Française: 29 Quai Voltaire, Paris, France.
Prochoix Prochoix. (1283-162X). ProChoix: 177, avenue Ledru-Rollin, 75011 Paris, France.
Prof. Geog. Professional geographer. (0033-0124). Blackwell Publishing: 108 Cowley Road, Oxford OX4 1JF, U.K., in association with Association of American Geographers.
Prog. Plan. Progress in planning. (0305-9006). Elsevier Science: PO Box 211, 1000 AE Amsterdam, The Netherlands.
Projet Projet. (0033-0884). Assas Éditions: 14, rue d'Assas, 75006 Paris, France.
Prokla Prokla: Zeitschrift für kritische Sozialwissenschaft. (0342-8176). Verlag Westfälisches Dampfboot: Dorotheenstrasse 26a, D-48145 Münster, Germany, in association with Vereinigung zur Kritik der politischen Ökonomie e.V.: Postfach 100 529, D-10565 Berlin, Germany.
Prometheus Prometheus. (0810-9028). Carfax Publishing, Taylor & Francis Ltd: Rankine Road, Basingstoke, Hants, RG24 8PR, UK.
Prz. Euro. Przegląd Europejski. (1641-2478). Dom Wydawniczy Elipsa: ul. Inflancka 15/198, 00-189 Warsaw, Poland, in association with Pracownia Instytucji Europejskich, Instytut Nauk Politycznych Uniwersytetu Warszawskiego.
Prz. Geog. Przegląd geograficzny. (0033-2143). Instytut Geografii i Przestrzennego Zagospodarowania: ul. Twarda 51/55, 00-818 Warsaw, Poland, in association with Polska Akademia Nauk.
Prz. Hist. Przegląd historyczny. (0033-2186). Wydawnictwo DiG: PL 01-524, Warszawa, al. Wojska Polskiego 4, Poland. E-mail: dig@dig.com.pl, in association with Towarzystwo Miłośników Historii.

Publ. Admin. Public administration. (0033-3298). Blackwell Publishing: 108 Cowley Road, Oxford OX4 1JF, U.K., in association with Royal Institute for Public Administration: 3 Birdcage Walk, London SW1H 9JH, U.K.

Publ. Admin. Dev. Public administration and development. (0271-2075). John Wiley & Sons Ltd: The Atrium, Southern Gate, Chichester, West Sussex, PO19 8SQ, UK, in association with Royal Institute of Public Administration: Regent's College, Inner Circle, Regent's Park, London NW1 4NS, U.K.

Publ. Admin. Policy Public administration and policy. (1022-0275). Hong Kong Public Administration Association, Department of Public and Social Administration, City University of Hong Kong: 83 Tat Chee Avenue, Kowloon, Hong Kong.

Publ. Admin. R. Public administration review. (0033-3352). Blackwell Publishing: 108 Cowley Road, Oxford, OX4 1JF, U.K., in association with American Society for Public Administration: 1120 G. Street N.W., Suite 500, Washington DC 20005, U.S.A.

Publ. Aff. Q. Public affairs quarterly. (0887-0373). University of Illinois Press: 1325 South Oak Street, Champaign, IL 61820-6903, U.S.A., in association with North American Philosophical Publications.

Publ. Choice Public choice. (0048-5829). Springer: Van Godewijckstraat 30, P.O. Box 17, 3300 AA Dordrecht, Netherlands.

Publ. Inter. Public interest. (0033-3557). National Affairs: 1112 16th Street N.W., Suite 530, Washington DC 20036, U.S.A.

Publ. Law Public law. (0033-3565). Sweet & Maxwell: South Quay Plaza, 183 Marsh Wall, London E14 9FT, U.K.

Publ. Manag. R. Public management review. (1471-9037). Routledge, Taylor & Francis Ltd: 11 New Fetter Lane, London, EC4P 4EE, U.K.

Publ. Mon. Manag. Public money and management. (0954-0962). Blackwell Publishing: 108 Cowley Road, Oxford OX4 1JF, U.K., in association with Public Management and Policy Association: 3 Robert Street, London WC2N 6RL, U.K.

Publ. Opin. Q. Public opinion quarterly. (0033-362X). University of Chicago Press: 5720 S. Woodlawn Avenue, Chicago, IL 60637, U.S.A., in association with American Association for Public Opinion Research.

Publius Publius: the journal of federalism. (0048-5950). Publius: the Journal of Federalism: Meyner Center for State and Local Government, 002 Kirby Hall of Civil Rights Lafayette College, Easton, PA 18042-1785, U.S.A.

Pyramides Pyramides. (1376-098X).

Q. J. Econ. Quarterly journal of economics. (0033-5533). MIT Press: 55 Hayward Street, Cambridge, MA 02142, U.S.A., in association with Harvard University.

Qual. Quan. Quality & quantity. (0033-5177). Springer: Van Godewijckstraat 30, P.O. Box 17, 3300 AA Dordrecht, Netherlands.

Quest. Int. Questions internationales. (1761-7146). La Documentation Française: 29, quai Voltaire 75007 Paris, France.

R. Admin. Públ. Revista de administración pública. (0034-7639). Centro de Estudios Constitucionales: Fuencarral 45-6, 28004 Madrid, Spain.

R. Afr. Pol. Econ. Review of African political economy. (0305-6244). Carfax Publishing, Taylor & Francis Ltd: P.O. Box 25, Abingdon, Oxfordshire OX14 3UE, U.K., in association with ROAPE: Regency House, 75-77 St. Mary's Road, Sheffield S2 4AN, U.K.

R. Belge Sécur. Soc. Revue belge de sécurité sociale. (0035-0834). Service public fédéral Sécurité Sociale: Eurostation II, Place Victor Horta 40, bte 20, 1060 Brussels, Belgium.

R. Black Pol. Econ. Review of black political economy. (0034-6446). Transaction Publishers: Rutgers University, New Brunswick, NJ 08903, U.S.A., in association with National Economic Association

/ Clark Atlanta University, Southern Center for Studies in Public Policy: 240 Brawley Drive S.W., Atlanta, GA 30314, U.S.A.

R. Bras. Econ. Revista brasileira de economia. (0034-7140). Fundação Getulio Vargas: Praia de Botafogo 190, Sala 1125, 22253 900 Rio de Janeiro, Brazil.

R. Cien. Pol. Revista de ciencia política [Santiago]. (0718-090X). Instituto de Ciencia Política, Facultad de Historia, Geografía y Ciencia Política: Avda. Vicuña Mackenna 4860, Casilla 114-D, Santiago de Chile.

R. Confédération française démocratique du travail Revue de la Confédération française démocratique du travail. (1280-8180). Confédération française démocratique du travail: 4, boulevard de la Villette, 75019 Paris, France.

R. Crit. Droit Int. Privé Revue critique de droit international privé. (0035-0958). Peace Palace Library: Carnegieplein 2, 2517 KJ, The Hague, Netherlands.

R. Deux Mondes Revue des deux mondes. (0750-9278). Revue des deux mondes: 97 Rue de Lille, 75007 Paris, France.

R. Droit Int. Comp. Revue de droit international et de droit comparé. (0775-4663). Bruylant: Rue de la Régence 67, B-1000 Brussels, Belgium.

R. Droit Int. Sci. Dip. Pol. Revue de droit international, de sciences diplomatiques et politiques. (0035-1091). United Nations: CP 151, CH 1000 Lausanne 13, Switzerland.

R. Droit Publ. Revue du droit public et de la science politique en France et à l'étranger. (0035-2578). Librairie Générale de Droit et de Jurisprudence: 31, rue Falguière, 75741 Paris cedex 15.

R. Droit Union Euro. Revue du droit de l'Union européenne. Clément Juglar: 62, avenue de Suffren, 75015 Paris, France.

R. Econ. Cond. It. Review of economic conditions in Italy. (0034-6799). Capitalia: Via dei Montecatini 17, 00187 Roma, Italy.

R. Econ. Inst. Revista de economía institucional. (0124-5996). Revista de Economía Institucional: Universidad Externado de Colombia, Facultad de Economía, Bloque A, Piso 3, Calle 12 No. 1 -17 este, Bogotá - Colombia.

R. Edu. Pedagogy Cult. S. Review of education, pedagogy & cultural studies. (1071-4413). Taylor & Francis, Inc.: 325 Chestnut St, Philadelphia PA, 19106 U.S.A.

R. Ét. Comp. Est-Ouest Revue d'études comparatives Est-Ouest. (0338-0599). Editions du Centre national de la recherche scientifique: 44 Rue de l'Amiral-Mouchez, 75014 Paris, France, in association with Institut de recherches juridiques comparatives du C.N.R.S., Centre d'études des pays socialistes / Économie et techniques de planification des pays de l'est.

R. Ét. Palest. Revue d'études palestiniennes. (0252-8290). Editions de Minuit: 7 rue Bernard-Palissy, 75006 Paris, France, in association with Institut des études palestiniennes / Fondation Diana Tamari Sabbagh.

R. Foment. Soc. Revista de fomento social. (0015-6043). CESI-JESPRE: Pablo Aranda 3, 28006 Madrid, Spain, in association with INSA-ETEA: Escritor Castilla Aguayo 4, Apartado 439, 14004 Cordoba, Spain.

R. Fran. Admin. Publ. Revue française d'administration publique. (0152-7401). Institut International d'Administration Publique: 2 avenue de l'Observatoire, 75006 Paris, France.

R. Fran. Civil. Brit. Revue française de civilisation britannique. (0248-9015). Presses de la Sorbonne nouvelle: 13, rue Santeuil, 75231 Paris Cedex 05, France.

R. Fran. Droit Admin. Revue française de droit administratif. (0763-1219). Editions Dalloz: 31-35, rue Froidevaux, Paris, France.

R. Fran. Hist. Id. Pol. Revue française d'histoire des idées politiques. (1266-7862). Picard Éditeur: 82 rue Bonaparte, 75006 Paris, France.

R. Fran. Ped. Revue française de pédagogie. (0556-7807).

R. Fran. Sci. Pol. Revue française de science politique. (0035-2950). Presses de Sciences Po: 44 Rue du Four, 75006 Paris, France.

R. Gén. Coll. Territ. Revue générale des collectivités territoriales. (1290-4473). Editions du Papyrus: 17, bd Rouget de Lisle, 93189 Montreuil cedex, France.

R. Gén. Droit Int. Publ. Revue générale de droit international public. (0035-3094). Editions A. Pedone: 13 rue Soufflot, Paris, France.

R. Hist. Dipl. Revue d'histoire diplomatique. (0035-2365). Editions A. Pedone: 13, rue Soufflot, Paris, France.

R. Hist. Mod. Contemp. Revue d'histoire moderne et contemporaine. (0048-8003). Société d'histoire moderne et contemporaine: c/o C.H.E.V.S., 44 rue du Four, 75006 Paris, France.

R. Iberoamer. Cienc. Tech. Soc. Revista Iberoamericana de Ciencia, Tecnología y Sociedad. (1668-0030). REDES - Centro de Estudios sobre Ciencia, Desarrollo y Educación Superior: Mansilla 2698, 2 piso, Buenos Aires, Argentina.

R. Int. Droit Comp. Revue internationale de droit comparé. (0035-3337). Société de legislation comparée: 28 Rue Saint-Guillaume, 75007 Paris, France, in association with Librairie Générale de Droit et de Jurisprudence.

R. Int. Pol. Comp. Revue internationale de politique comparée.

R. Int. Pol. Econ. Review of international political economy. (0969-2290). Routledge, Taylor & Francis Ltd: 2 Park Square, Milton Park, Abingdon, Oxfordshire, OX14 4RN.

R. Int. S. Review of international studies. (0260-2105). Cambridge University Press: The Edinburgh Building, Shaftesbury Road, Cambridge CB2 2RU, U.K., in association with British International Studies Association.

R. Int. Sci. Admin. Revue internationale des sciences administratives. (0773-2961). IISA: rue Defacqz 1, Bte 11, BE-1000 Bruxelles, Belgium.

R. Int. Sécur. Soc. Revue internationale de sécurité sociale. (0379-0312). Peter Lang SA: Editions scientifiques européennes, Moosstrasse 1, BP 350, CH-2542 Pieterlen, Switzerland.

R. Int. Stratég. Revue internationale et stratégique. (1287-1672). Institut de Relations Internationales et Stratégiques: 2 bis, rue Mercoeur - 75011 Paris, France.

R. Inter. Sc. Soc. Revue internationale des sciences sociales. UNESCO: 7-9 Place de Fontenoy, 75700 Paris, France.

R. Jurid. Envir. Revue juridique de l'environnement. (0397-0299). Société française pour le droit de l'environnement: 11, rue du Maréchal Juin - BP 68 - 67046 Strasbourg Cedex, France.

R. Jurid. Pol. Ind. Coop. Revue juridique et politique, indépendance et coopération. (0035-3574).

R. Mar. Comm. Revue du Marché commun et de l'Union européenne. (0035-2616). Éditions Techniques et Économiques: 3 rue Soufflot, 75005 Paris, France.

R. Mexicana Cien. Pol. Revista mexicana de ciencias politicas y sociales. (0185-1918). Universidad Nacional Autónoma de México, Facultad de Ciencias Políticas y Sociales: Ciudad Universitaria, Coyoacán, 04510 México D.F., Mexico.

R. Mon. Musul. Med. Revue du monde musulman et de la Méditerranée. (0997-1327). MMSH - IREMAM: 5 rue du Château de l'Horloge, BP 647, 13094 Aix-en-Provence Cedex 2, France, in association with Association pour l'étude des sciences humaines en Afrique du Nord et au Proche-Orient.

R. Nouvelle Revue nouvelle. (0035-3809). Association sans but lucratif: Boulevard Général Jacques 126, B-1050 Bruxelles, Belgium.

R. Pol. Review of politics. (0034-6705). University of Notre Dame: P.O. Box B, Notre Dame, IN 46556, U.S.A.

R. Pol. Parl. Revue politique et parlementaire. (0035-385X). Revue Politique et Parlementaire: 21 Rue de la Baume, 75008 Paris, France.

R. Prat. Droit Soc. Revue pratique de droit social. (0399-1148). Confédération Générale du Travail: 263, rue de Paris, 93 516 Montreuil, France.

R. Rech. Jurid. Droit Prosp. Revue de la recherche juridique, droit prospectif. (0249-8731). Éditions Presses Universitaires d'Aix-Marseille: 3 Avenue Robert Schumann 13628 Aix en Provence, France.

R. Sci. Crim. Revue de science criminelle et de droit pénal comparé. (0035-1733). Éditions Dalloz: 31-35 Rue Froidevaux, 75685 Paris Cedex 14, France, in association with Université Panthéon-Assas (Paris 2), Institut de Droit Comparé, Section de Science Criminelle.

R. Socialiste Revue socialiste. (1294-2529). Revue socialiste: 10, rue de Solférino, 75333 Paris Cedex 07, France.

R. Sociol. Pol. Revista de sociologia e política. (0104-4478). Universidade Federal do Paraná, Departamento de Ciências Sociais: Rua General Carneiro 460 sala 912, 80060-150, Curitiba PR, Brazil.

R. Trésor Revue du Trésor. (0035-2713). Revue du Trésor: 26, rue de Lille 75007 Paris, France.

R. Trim. Droit Euro. Revue trimestrielle de droit européen. (0035-4317). Éditions Dalloz: 31-35 Rue Froidevaux, 75685 Paris Cedex 14, France.

Race Class Race and class. (0306-3968). Sage Publications: 6 Bonhill Street, London EC2A 4PU, U.K., in association with Institute of Race Relations: 2-6 Leeke Street, King's Cross Road, London WC1X 9HS, U.K.

Race Ethnic. Edu. Race ethnicity and education. (1361-3324). Carfax Publishing, Taylor & Francis Ltd: 4 Park Square, Milton Park, Abingdon, Oxfordshire, OX14 4RN, UK.

Rapp. Rech. Centre d'études de l'emploi Rapport de recherche - Centre d'études de l'emploi. Le Descartes: 29, Promenade Michel Simon, 93166 Noisy-le-Grand, France.

Rass. Parl. Rassegna parlamentare. (0486-0373). Giuffrè Editore: Via Busto Arsizio 40, Milan 20151, Italy, in association with Istituto per la Documentazione e gli Studi Legislativi: Palazzo Grazioli, Via del Plebiscito 102, Rome, Italy.

Rech. Socialiste Recherche socialiste. (1283-7393). L'OURS: 86 rue de Lille 75007 Paris, France.

Rech. Sociogr. Recherches sociographiques. (0034-1282). Recherches sociographiques: Département de Sociologie, Université Laval, Québec G1K 7P4, Canada.

Rechtstheorie Rechtstheorie. (0034-1398). Duncker & Humblot: Carl-Heinrich-Becker-Weg 9, 12165 Berlin, Germany.

Recma Revue internationale de l'économie sociale: Recma. (0035-2020). Institut de l'économie sociale: Maison des sciences de l'homme, Bureau 05, 54 bd Raspail, 75006 Paris, in association with Coopérative d'information et d'édition mutualiste.

Reg. Fed. S. Regional and federal studies. (1359-7566). Frank Cass, Taylor & Francis Ltd: P.O. Box 25, Abingdon, Oxfordshire OX14 3UE, U.K.

Reg. S. Regional studies. (0034-3404). Carfax Publishing, Taylor & Francis Ltd: P.O. Box 25, Abingdon, Oxfordshire OX14 3UE, U.K., in association with Regional Studies Association.

Regar. Actual. Regards sur l'actualité. (0337-7091). Documentation Française: 29, Quai Voltaire, 75007 Paris, France.

Regio Regio. (0865 557X).

Region Region: Ekonomika i sotsiologiia. (0868-5169). Izdatel'stvo SO RAN: 630090, g. Novosibirsk, prosp. Akademika Lavrent'eva 17, IEiOPP, Komn. 338, Russia, in association with Institut ekonomiki i organizatsii promyshlennogo proizvodstva.

Relações Int. Relações internacionais. (1645-9199). Instituto Português de Relações Internacionais: UNL, Rua Dona Estefânia, 195-5°D, 1000-155 Lisboa, Portugal.

Relations Int. Relations internationales. (0335-2013). Société d'études historiques des relations internationales contemporaines: Université de Paris I, Institut Pierre-Renouvin, 11 cité Véron, F 75018 Paris, France, in association with Institut universitaire de hautes études internationales: Geneva, Switzerland.

Relig. Staat Gesell. Religion Staat Gesellschaft. (1438-955X). Duncker & Humblot: Carl-Heinrich-Becker-Weg 9, 12165 Berlin, Germany.

Relig. State Soc. Religion, state and society. (0963-7494). Carfax Publishing, Taylor & Francis Ltd: P.O. Box 25, Abingdon, Oxfordshire OX14 3UE, U.K., in association with Keston College: 33a Canal Street, Oxford OX2 6BQ, U.K.

Religion Religion. (0048-721X). Academic Press: 24-28 Oval Road, London NW1 7DX, U.K.

Renewal Renewal: The journal of Labour politics. (0968-252X). Lawrence & Wishart: 99a Wallis Road, London, E9 5LN.

Res. Policy Research policy. (0048-7333). Elsevier Science: PO Box 211, 1000 AE Amsterdam, The Netherlands.

Res Publica [Bruss.] Res publica [Brussels]. (0486-4700). Politologisch Instituut: Egmontstraat 11, B-1050 Brussels, Belgium.

Res Publica [Creteil] Res publica [Creteil]. (1278-6209). Res Publica: 1, Place Alphonse Deville, 75006 Paris, France.

Rev. Int. Sci. Econ. Com. Rivista internazionale di scienze economiche e commerciali. (0035-6751). Casa Editrice Dott. Antonio Milani (CEDAM S.p.A): Via Jappelli 5, 315121 Padua, Italy, in association with Università Commerciale Luigi Bocconi.

Revija Soc. Pol. Revija za socijalnu politiku. (1330-2965). Pravni fakultet Sveučilišta u Zagrebu: 10000 Zagreb, Croatia, Trg M. Tita 14, in association with Minstarstvo zdravstva i socijalne skrbi.

Riv. Dir. Finan. Sci. Fin. Rivista di diritto finanziario e scienza delle finanze. (0035-6131). Giuffrè Editore: Via Busto Arsizio 40, Milan 20151, Italy, in association with Dipartimento di Economia pubblica territoriale dell'Università / Camera di Commercio di Pavia / Università di Roma, Facoltà di Giurisprudenza, Istituto di diritto pubblico: Strada Nuova 65, 27100 Pavia, Italy.

Riv. Int. Sci. Soc. Rivista internazionale di scienze sociali. (0035-676X). Università Cattolica del Sacro Cuore: Vita e Pensiero, Largo A. Gemelli, 1-1 20123 Milan, Italy.

Riv. It. Pol. Pub. Rivista italiana di politiche pubbliche. Carocci editore: via Sardegna 50, 00187 Rome - Italy, in association with Universita' di Bologna, Dipartimento di organizzazione e sistema politico, Centro di analisi delle politiche pubbliche, Strada Maggiore 45, 40125 Bologna - Italy.

Riv. It. Sci. Pol. Rivista italiana di scienza politica. (0048-8402). il Mulino: Strada Maggiore 37, 40125 Bologna, Italy, in association with Facoltà di Sociologia, Trento.

Riv. S. Pol. Int. Rivista di studi politici internazionali. (0035-6611). Giuseppe Vedovato: 40 Lungarno del Tempio, 50121 Florence, Italy.

Riv. Trim. Pubbl. Rivista trimestrale di diritto pubblico. (0557-1464). Giuffrè Editore: Via Busto Arsizio 40, Milan 20151, Italy.

Round Tab. Round table. (0035-8533). Carfax Publishing, Taylor & Francis Ltd: P.O. Box 25, Abingdon, Oxfordshire OX14 3UE, U.K.

Rus. Pol. Law Russian politics and law. (1061-1940). M.E. Sharpe: 80 Business Park Drive, Armonk, NY 10504, U.S.A.

S. Afr. J. Human Rights South African journal on human rights. (0258-7203). Juta Law: P.O. Box 14373, Kenwyn 7790, South Africa, in association with Centre for Applied Legal Studies: University of the Witwatersrand, Wits 2050, South Africa.

S. Confl. Terror. Studies in conflict and terrorism. (1057-610X). Taylor & Francis Ltd: 11 New Fetter Lane, London EC4P 4EE, U.K.

S. Philos. Edu. Studies in philosophy and education. (0039-3746). Springer: Van Godewijckstraat 30, P.O. Box 17, 3300 AA Dordrecht, Netherlands.

S. Pol. Econ. Studies in political economy. (0707-8552). Studies in Political Economy: SR303, Carleton University, 1125 Colonel By Dr., Ottawa, Ontario K1S 5B6, Canada.

S. UBB: Pol. Studia Universitatis Babeş-Bolyai. Serie: Politica. (1224-8711). Cluj University Press: Str. Gh. Bilascu, nr. 24, 3400 Cluj-Napoca, Romania.

S. UBB: Stu. Eur. Studia Universitatis Babeş-Bolyai. Serie: Studia Europaea. (1224-8746). Cluj University Press: Str. Gh. Bilascu, nr. 24, 3400 Cluj-Napoca, Romania.

SAHARA J SAHARA J. (1729-0376). SAHARA: 10th Floor, Pleinpark Building, 69-83 Plein Park Street, Cape Town 8000, South Africa.

SAIS R. SAIS review. (0036-0775). Johns Hopkins University, Paul H. Nitze School of Advanced International Studies: 1619 Massachusetts Avenue N.W., Washington DC 20036, U.S.A.

Scand. Pol. S. Scandinavian political studies. (0080-6757). Blackwell Publishing: 108 Cowley Road, Oxford OX4 1JF, U.K., in association with Nordic Political Science Association.

Schweiz. Z. Soziol. Schweizerische Zeitschrift für Soziologie = Revue suisse de sociologie = Swiss journal of sociology. (0379-3664). Seismo Press: P.O. Box 313, CH-8028 Zürich, Switzerland, in association with Université de Genève.

Sci. Hum. Sciences humaines. (0996-6994). Sciences Humaines: 38, rue Rantheaume - BP 256, 89004 Auxerre Cedex, France.

Sci. Publ. Policy Science and public policy. (0302-3427). Beech Tree Publishing: 10 Watford Close, Guildford, Surrey GU1 2EP, U.K., in association with International Science Policy Foundation: 12 Whitehall, London SW1Y 2DY, U.K.

Sci. Soc. Science and society. (0036-8237). Guilford Publications: 72 Spring Street, New York, NY 10012, U.S.A.

Sci. Techno. Soc. Science, technology and society. (0971-7218). Sage India: B-42 Panchsheel Enclave, Post Box 4109, New Delhi, 110 017, India.

Secur. Dial. Security dialogue. (0967-0106). Sage Publications: 6 Bonhill Street, London EC2A 4PU, U.K.

Security S. Security studies. (0963-6412). Frank Cass, Taylor & Francis Ltd: P.O. Box 25, Abingdon, Oxfordshire OX14 3UE, U.K.

Sem. Jurid. Admin. Coll. Terr. Semaine juridique: Administrations et collectivités territoriales. (1637-5114). Lexis Nexis SA: 141, rue de Javel, 75747 Paris, France.

Sistema Sistema. (0210-0223). Fundación Sistema: Fuencarral 127, 1° 28010, Madrid, Spain.

Slavic R. Slavic review. (0037-6779). American Association for the Advancement of Slavic Studies: 128 Encina Commons, Stanford University, Stanford, CA 94305, U.S.A.

Slovo Slovo. (0954-6839). School of Slavonic and East European Studies: Senate House, Malet Street, London WC1E 7HU, U.K.

Sm. Wars Insurg. Small wars and insurgencies. (0959-2318). Frank Cass, Taylor & Francis Ltd: P.O. Box 25, Abingdon, Oxfordshire OX14 3UE, U.K.

Soc. Anal. [Adelaide] Social analysis [Adelaide]. (0155-977X). Berghahn Books Ltd: 3 Newtec Place, Magdalen Road, Oxford OX4 1RE, in association with University of Adelaide, Department of Anthropology: G.P.O. Box 498, Adelaide 5A 5001, Australia.

Soc. Compass Social compass. (0037-7686). Sage Publications: 6 Bonhill Street, London EC2A 4PU, U.K., in association with International Federation of Institutes for Social and Socio-Religious Research (FERES) / Centre de Recherches Socio-Religieuses: Université Catholique de Louvain, Belgium.

Soc. Contemp. Sociétés contemporaines. (1150-1944). L'Harmattan: 16 rue des Écoles, 75005 Paris, France, in association with Institut de Recherche sur les Sociétés Contemporaines (IRESCO), CNRS: 59/61 rue Pouchet, 75849 Paris Cedex 17, France.

Soc. Del. Socialno delo. (0352-7956). Facultet za socialno delo Univerze v Ljubljani: Topniška 31. 1000 Ljubljana.

Soc. Dem. Socialism and democracy. (0885-4300). Taylor & Francis: 4 Park Square, Milton Park, Abingdon, OX14 4RN.

Soc. Dev. Iss. Social development issues: Alternative approaches to global human needs. (0147-1473). School of Social Work, University of Texas at Arlington: Box 19129, Arlington, Texas 76019-0129, U.S.A., in association with Inter-University Consortium for International Social Development.

Soc. Econ. S. Social and economic studies. (0037-7651). University of the West Indies, Institute of Social and Economic Research: Mona, Kingston 7, Jamaica.

Soc. Just. Social justice. (0094-7571). Global Options: P.O. Box 40601, San Francisco, CA 94140, U.S.A.

Soc. Just. Res. Social justice research. (0885-7466). Springer: Van Godewijckstraat 30, P.O. Box 17, 3300 AA Dordrecht, Netherlands.

Soc. Legal S. Social and legal studies. (0964-6639). Sage Publications: 6 Bonhill Street, London EC2A 4PU, U.K.

Soc. Pol. Social politics: international studies in gender, state and society. (1072-4745). Oxford University Press: 2001 Evans Rd. Cary, NC 27513.

Soc. Policy Social policy. (0037-7783). Social Policy Corporation: 25 West 43rd Street, Room 620, New York, NY 10036, U.S.A.

Soc. Policy Admin. Social policy and administration. (0144-5596). Blackwell Publishing: 108 Cowley Road, Oxford OX4 1JF, U.K.

Soc. Policy Soc. Social policy and society. (1474-7464). Cambridge University Press: The Edinburgh Building, Shaftesbury Road, Cambridge CB2 2RU, U.K.

Soc. Prob. Social problems. (0037-7791). University of California Press Journals: 2120 Berkeley Way, Berkeley, CA 94720-5812, U.S.A., in association with Society for the Study of Social Problems.

Soc. S. Sci. Social studies of science. (0306-3127). Sage Publications: 6 Bonhill Street, London EC2A 4PU, U.K.

Soc. Sci. China Social sciences in China. (0252-9203). China Social Sciences Publishing House: Jia 158 Gulouxidajie, Beijing 100720, China, in association with Chinese Academy of Social Science.

Soc. Sci. Hist. Social science history. (0145-5532). Duke University Press: Box 90660, Durham, NC 27708-0660, U.S.A., in association with Social Science History Association.

Soc. Sci. Med. Social science & medicine. (0277-9536). Elsevier Science: PO Box 211, 1000 AE Amsterdam, The Netherlands.

Soc. Sci. Q. Social science quarterly. (0038-4941). Blackwell Publishing: 108 Cowley Road, Oxford, OX4 1JF, U.K., in association with Southwestern Social Science Association: W.C. Hogg Building, The University of Texas at Austin, Austin, TX 78713, U.S.A.

Soc. Serv. R. Social service review. (0037-7961). University of Chicago Press: 5720 S. Woodlawn Avenue, Chicago, IL 60637, U.S.A.

Socialist Hist. Socialist history. (0969-4331). Rivers Oram Press: 144 Hemingford Road, London, N1 1DE, U.K.

Society Society. (0147-2011). Transaction Publishers: Rutgers University, New Brunswick, NJ 08903, U.S.A.

Socio-econ. Plan. Sci. Socio-economic planning sciences. (0038-0121). Elsevier Science: PO Box 211, 1000 AE Amsterdam, The Netherlands.

Sociol. Q. Sociological quarterly. (0038-0253). Blackwell Publishing: 9600 Garsington Road, Oxford OX4 2ZG, UK.

Sociologia [Brat.] Sociologia [Bratislava] = Sociology [Bratislava]. (0049-1225). Redakcia Časopisu Sociológia: Klemensova 19, 813 64 Bratislava 1, Slovakia, in association with Slovak Academy of Sciences, Institute of Sociology.

Sociologia [Rome] Sociologia [Rome]. (0038-0156). Istituto Luigi Sturzo: Via delle Coppelle 35, 00186 Rome, Italy.

Sociology Sociology [U.K.]. (0038-0385). Sage Publications: 6 Bonhill Street, London EC2A 4PU, U.K.

Sots.Gum. Znan. Sotsial'no-gumanitarnye znaniia. (0869-8120). Sotsial'no-gumanitarnye znaniia: Komn. 307, D. 5, ul. B. Nikitskaia, Moscow 125009, Russia.

Soud. Děj. Soudobé dějiny. (1210-7050). Academia: Legerova 61, 120 00 Prague 2, Czech Republic, in association with Ústav pro soudobé dějiny AV ČR.

Soundings Soundings: a journal of politics and culture. (1362-6620). Lawrence & Wishart: 99a Wallis Road, London, E9 5LN.

Soz. Fort. Sozialer Fortschritt: Unabhängige Zeitschrift für Sozialpolitik. Duncker & Humblot: Carl-Heinrich-Becker-Weg 9, 12165 Berlin, Germany.

Sozialersinn Sozialersinn: Zeitschrift für hermeneutische Sozialforschung. (1439-9326). VS Verlag für Sozialwissenschaften: Abraham-Lincoln-Straße 46, 65189 Wiesbaden, Germany.

Space & Polity Space & polity. (1356-2576). Carfax Publishing, Taylor & Francis Ltd: P.O. Box 25, Abingdon, Oxfordshire OX14 3UE, U.K.

Der Staat Der Staat: Zeitschrift für Staatslehre und Verfassungsgeschichte, deutsches und europäisches öffentliches Recht. (0038-884X). Duncker & Humblot: Carl-Heinrich-Becker-Weg 9, 12165 Berlin, Germany.

Stat. Law R. Statute law review. (0144-3593). Oxford University Press: Great Clarendon Street, Oxford OX2 6DP, U.K., in association with Statute Law Society.

Stat. Szem. Statisztikai szemle. (0039-0690). A Központi Statisztikai Hivatal Folyóirata: H-1525 Budapest, P.O. Box 51 (Budapest II, Keleti Károly utca 5-7).

State Pol. Policy Q. State politics & policy quarterly. (1532-4400). State Politics and Policy Quarterly: Illinois Legislative Studies Center, PAC 466, PO Box 19243, Springfield, IL 62794-9243, U.S.A., in association with American Political Science Association.

Sth. Afr. Geog. J. South African geographical journal = Suid-Afrikaanse geografiese tydskrif. (0373-6245). South African Geographical Society = Suid-Afrikaanse Geografiese Vereniging: Department of Environmental and Geographical Science, University of Cape Town, Private Bag, Rondebosch 7700, South Africa.

Sth. Afr. J. Int. Aff. South African journal of international affairs. (1022-0461). South African Institute of International Affairs: P.O. Box 31596, Braamfontein, 2017 Johannesburg, South Africa.

Sth. Afr. Law. J. South African law journal. (0258-2503). Juta Law: P.O. Box 14373, Kenwyn 7790, South Africa.

Sth. Asia South Asia. (0085-6401). South Asian Studies Association of Australia: School of Historical Studies Monash University Victoria, 3800 Australia.

Sth. Asian Surv. South Asian survey. (0971-5231). Sage Publications India: B-42 Panchsheel Enclave, Post Box 4109, New Delhi 110 017, India, in association with Indian Council for South Asian Cooperation.

Sth. East Asia Res. South East Asia research. (0967-828X). IP Publishing Ltd: 4-5 Coleridge Gardens, London NW6 3QH, UK, in association with School of Oriental and African Studies.

Sth. Euro. Soc. Pol. South European society & politics. (1360-8746). Frank Cass, Taylor & Francis Ltd: P.O. Box 25, Abingdon, Oxfordshire OX14 3UE, U.K.

Strat. R. Sth. Afr. Strategic review for Southern Africa = Strategiese oorsig vir Suider-Afrika. (1013-1108). Institute for Strategic Studies: University of Pretoria, Pretoria 0002, South Africa.

Strat. S. Strategic studies. Institute of Strategic Studies: Sector F-5/2, Islamabad, Pakistan.

Stud. Dipl. Studia diplomatica. (0770-2965). Institut Royal des Relations Internationales = Koninklijk Instituut voor Internationale Betrekingen.

Südosteuro. Mitteil. Südosteuropa Mitteilungen. (0340-174X). Südosteuropa-Gesellschaft: Widenmayerstraße 49, 80538 Munich, Germany.

Survival Survival. (0039-6338). Oxford University Press: Great Clarendon Street, Oxford, OX2 6DP, U.K., in association with International Institute for Strategic Studies: 23 Tavistock Street, London WC2E 7NQ, U.K.

Svobod. Mysl' Svobodnaia mysl'. (0869-4435). Izdatel'stvo "Press": ul. Pravdy 24, 125865 Moscow, Russia.

Tangent Tangent. (0219-4384). World Scientific Publishing Co. Pte. Ltd.: 5 Toh Tuck Link, Singapore, 596224.

Társadalomkutatás Társadalomkutatás. (0580-4795). Akadémiai Kiadó: Prielle Kornélia utca 19-35, 1117 Budapest, Hungary, in association with Magyar Tudományos Akadémia.

TDP TDP. (1253-6032). Presses Universitaires FRancois Rabelais: 50, avenue Jean Portalis, BP0607, 37026 Tours, France.

Techno. Dev. Technology and development. (0914-918X). Institute for International Cooperation / Japan International Cooperation Agency: International Cooperation Center Building, 10-5 Ichigaya-Honmura-cho, Shinjuku-ku, Tokyo 162, Japan.

Telecom. Policy Telecommunications policy. (0308-5961). Elsevier Science: PO Box 211, 1000 AE Amsterdam, The Netherlands.

Telos Telos. (0090-6514). Telos Press: 431 E. 12th Street, New York, NY 10009, U.S.A.

Temps Mod. Temps modernes. (0040-3075). Gallimard: 5, rue Sébastien-Bottin, 75328 Paris cedex 07.

Terror. Pol. Viol. Terrorism and political violence. (0954-6553). Frank Cass, Taylor & Francis Ltd: P.O. Box 25, Abingdon, Oxfordshire OX14 3UE, U.K.

Theory Cult. Soc. Theory culture and society. (0263-2764). Sage Publications: 6 Bonhill Street, London EC2A 4PU, U.K.

Thes. Elev. Thesis eleven. (0725-5136). Sage Publications: 6 Bonhill Street, London EC2A 4PU, U.K.

Tiers Monde Tiers Monde. (0040-7356). Presses Universitaires de France: 6, avenue Reille, 75685, Paris, Cedex 14, in association with Université de Paris, Institut d'étude du développement économique et social: 58 boulevard Arago, 75013 Paris, France.

Tocqueville R. Tocqueville review. (0730-479X). Tocqueville Society: 69 quai d'Orsay, 75007 Paris, France.

Total. Mov. Pol. Relig. Totalitarian movements and political religions. (1469-0764). Frank Cass, Taylor & Francis Ltd: P.O. Box 25, Abingdon, Oxfordshire OX14 3UE, U.K.

Tour. Geog. Tourism geographies. (1461-6688). Routledge, Taylor & Francis Ltd: 2 Park Square, Milton Park, Abingdon, Oxfordshire, OX14 4RN.

Transformation Transformation. (0258-7696). Transformation: University of Natal, Economic History Department, King George V Avenue, 4001 Durban, South Africa.

Transit Transit: Europäische Revue. (0938-2062). Verlag Neue Kritik: Kettenhofweg 53, D-6000 Frankfurt am Main, Germany, in association with Institut für die Wissenschaften vom Menschen: Spittelauer Lände 3, A-1090, Vienna, Austria.

Trayectorias Trayectorias: revista de ciencias sociales. (1405-8928). Universidad Autonoma de Nuevo León: Biblioteca Universitaria, Avenida Alfonso Reyes 4000, Ala Oriente del Quinto Piso, Monterrey, Neuvo León, Mexico 64440.

Trim. Econ. Trimestre económico. (0041-3011). Fondo de Cultura Económica: Av Universidad 975, 03100 México D.F., Mexico.

Turkish S. Turkish studies. (1468-3849). Frank Cass, Taylor & Francis Ltd: P.O. Box 25, Abingdon, Oxfordshire OX14 3UE, U.K.

Uluslararasi Ilişkiler Uluslararasi Ilişkiler. (1304-7310). Uluslararasi Ilişkiler: Ataturk Bulvari, No 211/18, Kavaklidere, 06680, Ankara, Turkey.

Urb. Aff. R. Urban affairs review. (1078-0874). Sage Publications: 2455 Teller Road, Newbury Park, Thousand Oaks, CA 91320, U.S.A.

Urb. Policy Res. Urban policy and research. (0811-1146). Routledge, Taylor & Francis Ltd: 4 Park Square, Milton Park, Abingdon, Oxfordshire, OX14 4RN.

Urb. S. Urban studies. (0042-0980). Carfax Publishing, Taylor & Francis Ltd: P.O. Box 25, Abingdon, Oxfordshire OX14 3UE, U.K., in association with University of Glasgow, Centre for Urban and Regional Research: Adam Smith Building, University of Glasgow, Glasgow G12 8RT, U.K.

Utilitas Utilitas. (0953-8208). Edinburgh University Press: 22 George Square, Edinburgh EH8 9LF, U.K.

Valóság Valóság. (0324-7228). Hirlapkiadó Vállalat: Blaha Lujza ter 3, 1959 Budapest 8, Hungary, in association with Tudományos Ismeretterjesztő Társulat.

Verf. Recht Übersee Verfassung und Recht in Übersee = Law and politics in Africa, Asia and Latin America. (0506-7286). Nomos Verlagsgesellschaft: Waldseestraße 3-5, 76530 Baden-Baden, Germany, in association with Hamburger Gesellschaft für Völkerrecht und Auswärtige Politik: Rothenbaumchaussee 21-23, D-20148 Hamburg, Germany.

Verwalt. Die Verwaltung. (0042-4498). Duncker & Humblot: Carl-Heinrich-Becker-Weg 9, 12165 Berlin, Germany.

Vest. Mosk. Univ. 12 Pol. Vestnik Moskovskogo universiteta. Seriia 12 Politicheskie nauki. (0201-7385). Izdatelstvo Moskovskogo Universiteta: ul. B. Nikitskaia 5/7, 103009 Moscow, Russia.

Vest. Sankt-Peterburg. 5 Vestnik Sankt-Peterburgskogo universiteta. Seriia 5 Ekonomika. (0233-755X). Izdatel'stvo Sankt-Peterburgskogo Universiteta: Universitetskaia nab. 7/9, 199034 St. Petersburg, Russia.

Vest. Sankt-Peterburg. 6 Vestnik Sankt-Peterburgskogo universiteta. Seriia 6 Filosofiia, politologiia, sotsiologiia, psikhologiia, pravo, mezhdunarodnye otnosheniia. (0132-4624). Izdatel'stvo Sankt-Peterburgskogo Universiteta: Universiteta Nab. 7/9, 199034 St. Petersburg, Russia.

Vestnik Obshchestvennogo Mneniia Vestnik obshchestvennogo mneneiia. VTsIOM: Russia, Moscow, 103012, Ul. Nikols'kaia, 17.

Vier. Wirt.forsch. Vierteljahrshefte zur Wirtschaftsforschung. (0340-1707). Duncker & Humblot: Carl-Heinrich-Becker-Weg 9, 12165 Berlin, Germany, in association with Deutsches Institut für Wirtschaftsforschung: Königin-Luise-Straße 5, D-1000 Berlin 33, Germany.

Vingt. Sièc. Vingtième siècle. (0294-1759). Presses de Sciences Po: 117, boulevard Saint-Germain, 75006 Paris, France.

Voluntas Voluntas. (0957-8765). Springer: 233 Spring Street, New York, NY 10013-1578, U.S.A., in association with Charities Aid Foundation.

Vorgänge Vorgänge: Zeitschrift für Bürgerrechte und Gesellschaftspolitik. VS Verlag für Sozialwissenschaften: Abraham-Lincoln-Straße 46, 65189 Wiesbaden, Germany.

Washington Q. Washington quarterly. (0163-660X). MIT Press: 55 Hayward Street, Cambridge, MA 02142, U.S.A., in association with Center for Strategic and International Studies: 1800 K. Street N.W., Suite 400, Washington DC 20006, U.S.A.

Welt Trends Welt Trends: internationale Politik und vergleichende Studien. (0944-8101). Berliner Debatte Wissenschaftsverlag: PF 58 02 54, 10412 Berlin, Germany, in association with Universität Potsdam.

West Euro. Pol. West European politics. (0140-2382). Frank Cass, Taylor & Francis Ltd: P.O. Box 25, Abingdon, Oxfordshire OX14 3UE, U.K.

Wom. Pol. Women and politics. (0195-7732). Haworth Press: 10 Alice Street, Binghampton NY, 13904-1580.

Wom. S. Int. For. Women's studies international forum. (0277-5395). Elsevier Science: PO Box 211, 1000 AE Amsterdam, The Netherlands.

World Dev. World development. (0305-750X). Elsevier Science: PO Box 211, 1000 AE Amsterdam, The Netherlands.

World Pol. World politics. (0043-8871). Johns Hopkins University Press: 2715 North Charles Street, Baltimore, MD 21218-4363, U.S.A., in association with Princeton University, Center of International Studies: Bendheim Hall, Princeton, NJ 08544, U.S.A.

World Today World today. (0043-9134). Royal Institute of International Affairs: 10 St. James's Square, London SW1Y 4LE, U.K.

Y. Finnish For. Pol. Yearbook of Finnish foreign policy. (0355-0079). Finnish Institute of International Affairs: Pursimiehenkatu 8, SF 00150 Helsinki, Finland.

Yale Law J. Yale law journal. (0044-0094). Yale Law Journal Company: P.O. Box 208215, New Haven, CT 06520-8215, U.S.A.

Youth & Policy Youth & policy. (0262-9798). National Youth Agency: Eastgate Housetreet, Leicester, LE1 19-23 Humberstone Road, Leicester, LE5 3GJ.

Z. Eval. Zeitschrift für Evaluation. (1619-5515). VS Verlag für Sozialwissenschaften: Abraham-Lincoln-Straße 46, 65189 Wiesbaden, Germany.

Z. Int. Beziehung. Zeitschrift für internationale Beziehungen. (0946-7165). Nomos Verlagsgesellschaft: Waldseestr. 3-5 - D-76530 Baden-Baden, Germany.

Z. Öffent. Gemein. Unternehm. Zeitschrift für öffentliche und gemeinwirtschaftliche Unternehmen = Journal for public and nonprofit services. Nomos Verlagsgesellschaft: Waldseestr. 3-5 - D-76530 Baden-Baden, Germany.

Z. Öffent. Recht Zeitschrift für öffentliches Recht. (0948-4396). Springer-Verlag: Mölkerbastei 5, P.O. Box 367, A-1011 Vienna, Austria.

Z. Ostmit.euro.-Forsch. Zeitschrift für Ostmitteleuropa-Forschung. (0948-8294). Herder-Institut: Gisonenweg 5-7, 35037 Marburg, Germany.

Z. Parlament. Zeitschrift für Parlamentsfragen. (0340-1758). VS Verlag für Sozialwissenschaften: Abraham-Lincoln-Straße 46, 65189 Wiesbaden, Germany, in association with Deutsche Vereinigung für Parlamentsfragen.

Z. Pol. Zeitschrift für Politik. (0044-3360). Carl Heymanns Verlag: Luxemburger Straße 449, 5000 Cologne 41, Germany, in association with Hochschule für Politik München: Ludwigstraße 8, 8000 Munich, Germany.

Z. Pol.wissen. Zeitschrift für Politikwissenschaft. (1430-6387). VS Verlag für Sozialwissenschaften: Abraham-Lincoln-Straße 46, 65189 Wiesbaden, Germany.

Z. Soziol. Zeitschrift für Soziologie. (0340-1804). Lucius & Lucius Verlagsgesellschaft: Gerokstraße 51, D-70184, Stuttgart, Germany.

Z. Verkehr. Zeitschrift für Verkehrswissenschaft. (0044-3670). Verkehrs-Verlag J. Fischer: Paulusstraße 1, 40237 Düsseldorf, Germany.

Z. Wirt.pol. Zeitschrift für Wirtschaftspolitik. (0721-3808). Lucius & Lucius Verlagsgesellschaft: Gerokstraße 51, 70184 Stuttgart, Germany.

CLASSIFICATION SCHEME
PLAN DE CLASSIFICATION

A.   **General studies and methods / Études générales et méthodes.**

A.1.   Political science and the social sciences / Science politique et sciences sociales.

A.2.   Political science research / Recherche en science politique.

A.3.   Epistemology and historiography / Épistémologie et historiographie.

A.4.   Research methods and documentations / Méthodes de recherche et documentation.
Empirical and mathematical methods / Méthodes empiriques et mathématiques

B.   **Political thought / Pensée politique.**

B.1.   Political ideas / Idées politiques.

B.2.   History of political ideas / Histoire des idées politiques.
Ancient and medieval / Antiquité et Moyen Âge; 16th & 17th centuries / 16 ^{e} & 17 ^{e} siècles; 18th century / 18 ^{e} siècle; 19th century / 19 ^{e} siècle; 20th century / 20 ^{e} siècle

B.3.   Political doctrines and ideologies / Doctrines et idéologies politiques.
Liberalism / Libéralisme; Nationalism / Nationalisme; Socialism / Socialisme

C.   **Political systems / Systèmes politiques.**

C.1.   Political institutions / Institutions politiques.

C.1.1.   State and nation / État et nation.
Nation / Nation; State formation/ Construction de l'État ; State fragmentation / Fragmentation de l'État; State structure / Structure de l'État; State-society relations / Relations État-société

C.1.2.   Constitution / Constitution.

C.1.3.   Legislative power / Pouvoir législatif.

C.1.4.   Executive power / Pouvoir exécutif.

C.1.5.   Judiciary power / Pouvoir judiciaire.
Civil law / Droit civil; Criminal law / Droit pénal; Judicial process / Processus judiciaire; Legal systems / Systèmes juridiques; Public law / Droit public

C.1.6.   Relations between the powers / Relations entre les pouvoirs.

C.1.7.   Fundamental rights and freedoms / Droits et libertés fondamentaux.
Africa / Afrique; Americas / Amérique; Asia / Asie; Europe / Europe

C.2.   Public administration and management / Administration et gestion publique.
Public servants / Fonctionnaires

C.2.1.   Central government / Administration centrale.

C.2.2.   Sub-national government / Administration territoriale.
Administrative decentralization / Décentralisation administrative; Local government / Administration locale; Regional government / Administration régionale

C.2.3.   Colonial and post-colonial government / Administration coloniale et post-coloniale.

C.3.   Political systems performance / Fonctionnement des systèmes politiques.

C.3.1.   Political regimes / Régimes politiques.

C.3.2.   Political conditions / Conditions politiques.
Africa / Afrique; Americas / Amérique; Asia / Asie; Europe / Europe; Middle East / Moyen-Orient ; Oceania / Océanie

C.3.3.   Regime transition / Transition politique.

C.3.4.   Political opposition / Opposition politique.

C.3.5.   Civil order / Ordre public.
Civil-military relations / Relations civiles-militaires; Policing / Maintien de l'ordre

D. **Political life / Vie politique.**

D.1. Political actors / Acteurs politiques.

D.1.1. Politicians / Hommes politiques.
Political biography / Biographie politique; Political corruption / Corruption politique; Political elites / Élites politiques; Political leadership / Direction politique

D.1.2. Political forces / Forces politiques.

D.1.2.1. Political parties / Partis politiques.
Left-wing parties / Partis de gauche; Party systems / Systèmes de parti; Right-wing parties / Partis de droite

D.1.2.2. Political movements / Mouvements politiques.
Anti-capitalist movements / Mouvements anticapitalistes; Environmental movements / Mouvements écologiques; Nationalist and independence movements / Mouvements d'indépendance et nationalistes; Women's movements / Mouvements fémininistes

D.1.2.3. Interest groups / Groupes d'intérêt.

D.1.3. Social forces / Forces sociales.

D.1.3.1. Social system / Système social.

D.1.3.2. Geographic influences / Influences géographiques.

D.1.3.3. Race and ethnicity / Race et ethnicité.
Africa / Afrique; Americas / Amérique; Asia / Asie; Europe / Europe

D.1.3.4. Religion / Religion.
Christianity / Christianisme; Islam / Islam

D.1.3.5. Gender / Genre.

D.1.4. Economic forces / Forces économiques.

D.1.4.1. Business influences / Influences commerciales.

D.2. Political behaviour / Comportement politique.

D.2.1. Values / Valeurs.

D.2.2. Psychological factors / Facteurs psychologiques.

D.2.3. Opinion / Opinion.

D.2.4. Political culture / Culture politique.
Political socialization / Socialisation politique

D.2.5.   Elections / Élections.
> Electoral behaviour / Comportement électoral; Electoral campaigning / Campagne électorale; Electoral systems / Systèmes électoraux; Parliamentary elections / Élections parlementaires; Presidential elections / Élections présidentielles; Regional and local elections / Élections locales et régionales

D.2.6.   Information and media / Information et médias.
> Communications technology / Technologie des communications; Media and politics / Médias et politique

E.   Government policy / Politique gouvernementale.

E.1.   Public policy / Politique publique.
> Policy evaluation / Évaluation des politiques; Public sector / Secteur public

E.2.   Economic policy / Politique économique.
> Agricultural and fisheries policy / Politique agricole et de la pêche; Commercial policy / Politique commerciale; Development policy / Politique du développement; Energy policy / Politique énergétique; Transport policy / Politique des transports

E.3.   Financial policy / Politique financière.

E.4.   Social policy / Politique sociale.
> Health policy / Politique de la santé; Labour policy / Politique du travail; Migration policy / Politique migratoire; Population and family policies / Politique démographique et politique familiale; Rural and urban policies / Politiques urbaine et rurale; Welfare state / État providence

E.5.   Cultural, media and telecommunications policies / Politiques de la culture, des médias et des télécommunications.

E.6.   Education policy / Politique de l'éducation.

E.7.   Science policy / Politique scientifique.

E.8.   Environmental policy / Politique environnementale.
> Climate change / Changement climatique; Natural resources / Ressources naturelles; Pollution control / Contrôle de la pollution

F. **International life / Vie internationale.**

F.1. International law / Droit international.

F.1.1. International jurisdiction / Juridiction internationale.

F.1.2. International sovereignty / Souveraineté internationale.

F.1.3. International borders / Frontières internationales.
Seas and waterways / Mers et voies navigables

F.1.4. International agreements and conferences / Accords et conférences internationaux.

F.1.5. Refugees and international human rights / Réfugiés et droits de l'homme.
Human rights conventions / Conventions sur les droits de l'homme; Refugees / Réfugiés

F.2. International society / Société internationale.

F.2.1. International and regional integration / Intégration internationale et régionale.

F.2.2. European Union / Union européenne.
Enlargement and accession / Élargissement et adhésion; EU-member state relations / Relations U.E.-états membres; External policies / Politiques extérieures; Institutions and governance / Institutions et gouvernance; Internal policies / Politiques intérieures; Law and jurisdiction / Droit et juridiction; Treaties / Traités

F.2.3. International governmental organizations / Organisations gouvernementales internationales.
United Nations / Nations unies

F.2.4. International non-governmental organizations / Organisations non-gouvernementales internationales.

F.3. International relations / Relations internationales.

F.3.1. International relations theory / Théorie des relations internationales.
Conflict theory / Théorie des conflits; Globalization / Mondialisation; Realism, idealism and discourse / Réalisme, idéalisme et débats

F.3.2. Foreign policy / Politique étrangère.
Africa / Afrique; Americas / Amérique; Asia / Asie; Europe / Europe

F.3.3. National and international security / Sécurité nationale et internationale.
Armaments / Armements; Armaments industry and military expenditure / Industrie de l'armement et dépenses militaires; Armed forces / Forces armées; Arms limitation / Limitation des armements; Intelligence services

/ Services d'espionnage; NATO / OTAN; Regional security / Securité régionale; Terrorism / Terrorisme

F.3.4.   Foreign relations / Relations extérieures.

Americas / Amérique; Asia / Asie; Europe / Europe; Middle East / Moyen-Orient

F.3.5.   International political forces / Forces politiques internationales.

International political economy / Politique économique internationale; International religious influences / Influences religieuses internationales

F.3.6.   International aid / Aide internationale.

F.3.7.   International conflict and conflict resolution / Conflits internationaux et règlement des conflits.

Africa / Afrique; Asia / Asie; Europe / Europe; Middle East / Moyen-Orient

BIBLIOGRAPHY FOR 2005

BIBLIOGRAPHIE POUR 2005

A: GENERAL STUDIES AND METHODS
    ÉTUDES GÉNÉRALES ET MÉTHODES

A.1: **Political science and the social sciences**
      Science politique et sciences sociales

1   The disorder of political inquiry. Keith Lewis Topper. Cambridge MA: Harvard University Press, 2005. xi, 322p. *ISBN: 0674016785. Includes bibliographical references and index.*

2   Európa mesterelbeszélései a szabadságról. *[In Hungarian]*; (European master-narratives about freedom.) Ágnes Heller. **Mag. Tud.** 49:5 2005 pp.549-593.

3   Kulturwissenschaftliche Traditionslinien in der Politikwissenschaft: Eric Voegelin revisited. *[In German]*; [The tradition of cultural studies in political science: Eric Voegelin revisited]. Birgit Schwelling. **Z. Pol.** 52:1 3:2005 pp.3-24.

4   Mapping EU studies. John T.S. Keeler. **J. Com. Mkt. S.** 43:3 9:2005 pp.551-582.

5   Methods of negotiation research. James A. Wall, Jr.; David Matz; Ray Friedman; Ronald J. Fisher; Daniel Druckman; Jacob Bercovitch; Jonathan Wilkenfeld; Laurie R. Weingart; Mara Olekalns; Philip L. Smith; Aukje Nauta; Esther Kluwer; Xu Huang; Evert Van de Vliet; Bruce Barry; Ingrid Smithey Fulmer. **Int. Negot.** 9:3 2004 pp.345-502. *Collection of 11 articles.*

6   Musiikki ja identiteettipolitiikka : uutta vai vanhaa? *[In Finnish]*; [Music and identity politics: old or new?] *[Summary]*. Lauri Siisiäinen. **Kosmopolis** 34:1 2004 pp.25-46.

7   Political science on the cusp: recovering a discipline's past. John G. Gunnell. **Am. Pol. Sci. R.** 99:4 11:2005 pp.597-609.

8   Politicheskaia psikhologiia kak oblast' sovremennogo politologicheskogo znaniia: perspektivy i vektory razvitiia. *[In Russian]*; (Political psychology as a branch of modern political science: prospects and development trends.) E.B. Shestopal. **Vest. Mosk. Univ. 12 Pol.** 1 1-2:2005 pp.49-58.

9   A politikai tudás. *[In Hungarian]*; (Political knowledge.) *[Summary]*. András Lánczi. **Politik. Szem.** 13:1-2 2004 pp.5-30.

10 Politische Implikationen der kulturellen Evolution. *[In German]*; [Political implications of the cultural evolution]. Horst Feldmann. **Z. Pol.** 52:1 3:2005 pp.57-79.

11 Le retour du politique : politique de la finitude. *[In French]*; [The returns of politics: the politics of ends]. Frederic Treffel. Paris: L'Harmattan, 2004. 388p. *ISBN: 2747570452. Includes bibliographical references (p. [379]-383).*

12 Das Scheitern der Politikwissenschaft am Bündnis für Arbeit. Eine Kritik an der Problemlösungsliteratur über das Bündnis für Arbeit. *[In German]*; (The failure of political science to deal with the German Alliance for Jobs. Some critical remarks on the problem-solving literature about the German Alliance for Jobs.) *[Summary]*. Christine Trampusch. **Polit. Viertel.** 45:4 12:2004 pp.541-562.

13 Social mobility and political transitions. Bahar Leventoğlu. **J. Theor. Pol.** 17:4 10:2005 pp.465-496.

A.2:   Political science research
        Recherche en science politique

14   L'analyse comparative configurationnelle. *[In French]*; [Configurational comparative analysis]. Revue internationale de politique comparée. **R. Int. Pol. Comp.** 11:1 2004 pp.7-153.

15   Analysing political discourse: theory and practice. Paul Chilton. London: Routledge, 2004. xiv, 226p. *ISBN: 0415314712, 0415314720. Includes bibliographical references and index.*

16   Apologiia tsentra: o zabytom metodologicheskom resurse politicheskoi nauki. *[In Russian]*; (Apologia of the center: on the forgotten methodological resource that is political science.) *[Summary]*. S.I. Kaspe. **Polis [Moscow]** 1(84) 2005 pp.5-24.

17   Comparative politics in a globalizing world. Jeffrey Haynes. Cambridge, Malden MA: Polity, 2005. xi, 351p. *ISBN: 0745630936. Includes bibliographical references (p. [320]-344) and index.*

18   Context or conflict types: which determines the selection of communication mode. Katharina Holzinger. **Acta Pol.** 40:2 7:2005 pp.239-254.

19   Deliberation in formal arenas the deliberative dimensions of legislatures (Part II). André Bächtiger; Markus Spörndli; Marco R. Steenbergen; Jürg Steiner. **Acta Pol.** 40:2 7:2005 pp.225-238.

20   Demokratie-Audits. Zwischenbilanz zu einem neuen Instrument der empirischen Demokratieforschung. *[In German]*; [Democracy audits –evaluation of a new instrument for empirical democracy research]. André Kaiser; Eric Seils. **Polit. Viertel.** 46:1 3:2005 pp.133-143.

21   Elicited priors for Bayesian model specifications in political science research. Jeff Gill; Lee D. Walker. **J. Pol.** 67:3 8:2005 pp.841-872.

22   Empirical approaches to deliberative democracy. Michael Neblo; Robert E. Goodin; John S. Dryzek; Shawn Rosenberg; André Bächtiger; Markus Spörndli; Marco R. Steenbergen; Jürg Steiner; Katharina Holzinger; Simone Chambers. **Acta Pol.** 40:2 7:2005 pp.169-266. *Collection of 7 articles.*

23   The empirical study of deliberative democracy: setting a research agenda. Shawn Rosenberg. **Acta Pol.** 40:2 7:2005 pp.212-224.

24   O genezise, predmete i sovremennom sostoianii politicheskoi nauki v Rossii. *[In Russian]*; (The genesis, subject and contemporary situation of Russian political science.) Ia.A. Pliais. **Vest. Mosk. Univ. 12 Pol.** 1 1-2:2005 pp.9-32.

25   Government, knowledge and the business of policy making: the potential and limits of evidence-based policy. Geoff Mulgan. **Evid. Policy** 1:2 5:2005 pp.215-226.

26   If evidence-informed policy works in practice, does it matter if it doesn't work in theory? Iain Chalmers. **Evid. Policy** 1:2 5:2005 pp.227-242.

27   Integration and fragmentation in political science: exploring patterns of scholarly communication in a divided discipline. James C. Garand. **J. Pol.** 67:4 11:2005 pp.979-1005.

28   Is the evidence-based practice movement doing more harm than good? Reflections on Iain Chalmers' case for research-based policy making and practice; *[Summary in French]*; *[Summary in Spanish]*. Martyn Hammersley. **Evid. Policy** 1:1 1:2005 pp.85-100.

29   Is your evidence robust enough? Questions for policy makers and practitioners; *[Summary in French]*; *[Summary in Spanish]*. Louise Shaxson. **Evid. Policy** 1:1 1:2005 pp.101-111.

30   Khronopolitika: razvitie issledovatel'skoi programmy. *[In Russian]*; (Chronopolitics: development of a research program.) *[Summary]*. I.A. Chikharev. **Polis [Moscow]** 3(86) 2005 pp.21-33.

31   Linking research and policy on Capitol Hill: insights from research brokers. Elizabeth Rigby. **Evid. Policy** 1:2 5:2005 pp.195-213.

32   Measuring publicity's effect: reconciling empirical research and normative theory. Simone Chambers. **Acta Pol.** 40:2 7:2005 pp.255-266.

33   Obraz gosudarstva kak issledovatel'skaia zadacha sovremennoi politologii. *[In Russian]*;
      [The portrayal of the state as a research dilemma for modern political science]. A.V.
      Fediakin. **Vest. Mosk. Univ. 12 Pol.** 3 5-6:2005 pp.3-18.

34   Osnovnye napravleniia sovremennykh politicheskikh issledovanii. *[In Russian]*;
      [Fundamental directions of modern political research]. B.N. Korolev; A.H.A. Sultigov;
      A.A. Belov; A.S. Akhremenko. **Vest. Mosk. Univ. 12 Pol.** 6 11-12:2004 pp.5-75.
      Collection of 4 articles.

35   Poliittisesta aluetutkimuksesta konfliktinsäätelyteoriaan : radikalismi suomalaisen valtio-
      opin tutkimuskohteena 1950-luvulta 1970-luvulle. *[In Finnish]*; [From a political science
      of regions to conflict regulation theory: the study of radicalism in Finnish political science
      from the 1950s to the 1970s] *[Summary]*. Petri Koikkalainen. **Politiikka** 46:2 2004
      pp.103-120.

36   Politicheskaia nauka v SShA. *[In Russian]*; [Political science in the USA]. Iu.V. Irkhin.
      Sots.Gum. Znan. 6 2004 pp.260-277.

37   Razvitie politologicheskogo soobshchestva v postsovetskoi Rossii. *[In Russian]*;
      (Development of political science community in post-Soviet Russia.) *[Summary]*. D.M.
      Vorobev. **Polis [Moscow]** 6(83) 2004 pp.151-161.

38   Reviewing the evidence: reflections from experience. Clare L. Bambra. **Evid. Policy** 1:2
      5:2005 pp.243-255.

39   Sequencing deliberative moments. Robert E. Goodin. **Acta Pol.** 40:2 7:2005 pp.182-196.

40   A systemic view of deliberation thinking through democracy: between the theory and
      practice of deliberative politics (Part I). Michael Neblo. **Acta Pol.** 40:2 7:2005 pp.169-
      181.

41   What should the 'political' in political theory explore? Michael Freeden. **J. Pol. Philos.**
      13:2 6:2005 pp.113-134.

A.3:   **Epistemology and historiography**
            Épistémologie et historiographie

42   Den historiske drejning. *[In Danish]*; (The historical turn.) *[Summary]*. Mette Skak.
      Politica 37:1 2:2005 pp.5-20.

43   Le droit comparé en question(s) entre pragmatisme et outil épistémologique. *[In French]*;
      [Comparative law between pragmatism and epistemological tool] *[Summary]*; *[Summary
      in French]*. Marie Claire Ponthoreau. **R. Int. Droit Comp.** 57:1 1-3:2005 pp.7-27.

44   Az Európa fogalom történelmi változásairól. *[In Hungarian]*; (Historical changes in the
      notion of Europe.) *[Summary]*. John Lukács. **Euro. Tükör** 9:3 2004 pp.3-17.

45   Fenomen politicheskogo vremeni. *[In Russian]*; (The phenomenon of political time.)
      [Summary]. M.V. Il'in. **Polis [Moscow]** 3(86) 2005 pp.5-20.

46   La filosofía latinoamericana en perspectiva histórica. *[In Spanish]*; [Latin American
      philosophy in historical perspective]. Carmen L. Bohórquez. **Cuad. Am.** XVIII:6(108) 11-
      12:2004 pp.177-194.

47   Handle with care: the deadly hermeneutics of deliberative instrumentation. John S.
      Dryzek. **Acta Pol.** 40:2 7:2005 pp.197-211.

48   Die Internationalisierung der Lehre an deutschen Universitäten. Anforderungen an die
      politikwissenschaftliche Teildisziplin der Internationalen Beziehungen. *[In German]*; (The
      internationalization of teaching at German universities. Challenges for political science
      and international relations departments.) Volker Rittberger; Fariborz Zelli. **Z. Int.
      Beziehung.** 11:2 12:2004 pp.395-418.

49   Istoriia politicheskikh uchenii kak nauchnaia i obrazovatel'naia distsiplina v Rossii v XIX-
      nachale XX v. *[In Russian]*; (The history of political ideas as a scientific and academic
      subject in Russia in the 19th-20th centuries.) E.N. Moshchelkov. **Vest. Mosk. Univ. 12 Pol.**
      1 1-2:2005 pp.33-48.

50   Origins, modernity and resistance in the historiography of Stalinism. Daniel Beer. **J.
      Contemp. Hist.** 40:2 4:2005 pp.363-379.

51   Political reasonability. David Archard. **Can. J. Philos.** 35:1 3:2005 pp.1-25.

52   The politics of path dependency: political conflict in historical institutionalism. B. Guy Peters; Jon Pierre; Desmond S. King. **J. Pol.** 67:4 11:2005 pp.1275-1300.

53   Prostranstvo politicheskikh sobytii. *[In Russian]*; [The role of space in political events] *[Summary]*. A.F. Filippov. **Polis [Moscow]** 2(85) 2005 pp.6-25.

54   "Przedłużenie polityki środkami historycznymi" czy po prostu nauka? Badania nad historiografią polską, enerdowską i czechosłowacką drugiej połowy XX w. *[In Polish]*; ("Elongation of politics by means of history" or simply scholarship: studies on historiography in Poland, the German Democratic Republic and Czechoslovakia in the second half of the twentieth century.) *[Summary]*. M. Górny. **Prz. Hist.** XCV:1 2004 pp.53-72.

55   Rethinking agency: a phenomenological approach to embodiment and agentic capacities. Diana Coole. **Pol. S.** 53:1 3:2005 pp.124-142.

56   O slovenskej historiografii v Collegium Carolinum. *[In Slovak]*; (About Slovak historiography in Collegium Carolinum.) Dušan Kováč; Elena Mannová; Martina Winkler; Juraj Podoba; Peter Haslinger; Marína Zavacká; Ivan Kamenec; Peter Švorc; Éva Kovács; Eduard Nižňanský; Gabriela Dudeková; Pavla Vošahlíková; Peter Macho; Jan Rychlík; Ľubomír Lipták. **Hist. Čas.** 52:2 2004 pp.233-376. *Collection of 15 articles.*

57   Die Tradition einer multinationalen Reichsgeschichte in Mitteleuropa — Historiographische Konzepte gegenüber Altem Reich und Polen-Litauen sowie komparatistische Perspektiven. *[In German]*; [The tradition of multinational history in Central Europe –historiographical concepts for the Old Reich and Poland-Lithuania –comparative perspectives]. Hans-Jürgen Bömelburg. **Z. Ostmit.euro.-Forsch.** 53:3 2004 pp.318-350.

58   Tragedy as political theory: the self-destruction of Antigone's laws. J. Tralau. **Hist. Pol. Thought** XXVI:3 Autumn:2005 pp.377-396.

59   Die Wiederkehr des Raums — auch in der Osteuropakunde. *[In German]*; (The return of space, in East European studies and elsewhere.) Karl Schlögel. **Osteuropa** 55:3 3:2005 pp.5-16.

A.4:   **Research methods and documentations**
               Méthodes de recherche et documentation

60   Borges's encyclopedia and classification in presidential studies. Philip Abbott. **Pres. Stud. Q.** 34:4 12:2004 pp.709-731.

61   Counting the Seven Weeks War: dyads, disputes and balances of power; *[Summary in French]*. William Moul. **Can. J. Pol.** 38:1 3:2005 pp.153-174.

62   Facilitating transferable learning through cluster evaluation: new opportunities in the development partnerships of the EU 'EQUAL' programme; *[Summary in French]*. Philip Potter. **Evaluation** 11:2 4:2005 pp.189-205.

63   Formal theory and case-study methods in EU studies. Robert Pahre. **Euro. Uni. Pol.** 6:1 3:2005 pp.113-145.

64   Interpretation and its others. Mark Bevir; R.A.W. Rhodes. **Aust. J. Pol. Sci.** 40:2 6:2005 pp.169-187.

65   It's about time: catching method up to meaning — the usefulness of narrative inquiry in public administration research. Sonia M. Ospina; Jennifer Dodge. **Publ. Admin. R.** 65:2 3-4:2005 pp.143-157.

66   Kachestvennye metody v prikladnom politologicheskom issledovanii. *[In Russian]*; (Qualitative methods in applied political research.) M.V. Zherebtsov. **Vest. Mosk. Univ. 12 Pol.** 3 5-6:2005 pp.19-33.

67   Measuring political democracy: case expertise, data adequacy, and Central America. Kirk Bowman; Fabrice Lehouco; James Mahoney. **Comp. Pol. S.** 38:8 10:2005 pp.939-970.

68   Nested analysis as a mixed-method strategy for comparative research. Evan S. Lieberman. **Am. Pol. Sci. R.** 99:3 8:2005 pp.435-452.

69 One size doesn't fit all: selecting response scales for attitudes items. Robert Johns. **Jnl. Ele. Pub. Op. Par.** 15:2 9:2005 pp.237-264.

70 Politicians, public policy and poll following: conceptual difficulties and empirical realities. Murray Goot. **Aust. J. Pol. Sci.** 40:2 6:2005 pp.189-205.

71 The politics of evidence and methodology: lessons from the EPPI-centre; *[Summary in French]*; *[Summary in Spanish]*. Ann Oakley; David Gough; Sandy Oliver; James Thomas. **Evid. Policy** 1:1 1:2005 pp.5-31.

72 Problems and methods in the study of politics. Tarek E. Masoud [Ed.]; Ian. Shapiro [Ed.]; Rogers M. Smith [Ed.]. Cambridge: Cambridge University Press, 2004. xi, 419p. *ISBN: 0521539439, 0521831741. Conference papers on Problems and Methods in the Study of Politics, Yale, December 2001. Includes bibliographical references and index.*

73 O raznoobrazii form opisaniia institutov. *[In Russian]*; (Variety of descriptive forms of institutions.) V. Tambovtsev. **Obshch. Nauki Sovrem.** 2 2004 pp.107-118.

74 Theorising the evidence on discretionary decision making: alternative perspectives; *[Summary in French]*; *[Summary in Spanish]*. Elaine Campbell. **Evid. Policy** 1:1 1:2005 pp.33-60.

75 The vocation of political theory: principles, empirical inquiry and the politics of opportunity. Marc Stears. **Euro. J. Pol. Theory** 4:4 10:2005 pp.325-350.

76 When far apart becomes too far apart: evidence for a threshold effect in coalition formation. Paul V. Warwick. **Br. J. Pol. Sci.** 35:3 7:2005 pp.383-401.

Empirical and mathematical methods
Méthodes empiriques et mathématiques

77 An alternative approach to correcting response and nonresponse bias in election research. Robert J.J. Voogt. **Acta Pol.** 40:1 4:2005 pp.94-116.

78 Bargaining in less-democratic newly industrialized countries: model and evidence from South Korea, Taiwan, Singapore, and Malaysia. O. Fiona Yap. **J. Theor. Pol.** 17:3 7:2005 pp.283-309.

79 Do get-out-the-vote calls reduce turnout? The importance of statistical methods for field experiments. Kosuke Imai. **Am. Pol. Sci. R.** 99:2 5:2005 pp.283-300.

80 Dyadic effects of democratization on international disputes. Shuhei Kurizaki. **Int. Rel. Asia Pacific** 4:1 2004 pp.1-33.

81 An explanation of anomalous behavior in models of political participation. Jacob K. Goeree; Charles A. Holt. **Am. Pol. Sci. R.** 99:2 5:2005 pp.201-213.

82 How to measure constitutional rigidity: four concepts and two alternatives. Astrid Lorenz. **J. Theor. Pol.** 17:3 7:2005 pp.339-361.

83 The impossibility of a preference-based power index. Matthew Braham; Manfred J. Holler. **J. Theor. Pol.** 17:1 1:2005 pp.137-157.

84 Measuring regionalism: content analysis and the case of Rogaland in Norway. Rune Dahl Fitjar. **Reg. Fed. S.** 15:1 Spring:2005 pp.59-73.

85 Modeling the interaction of parties, activists and voters: why is the political center so empty? N. Schofield; I. Sened. **Euro. J. Pol. Res.** 44:3 5:2005 pp.355-390.

86 The possibility of a preference-based power index. Stefan Napel; Mika Widgrén. **J. Theor. Pol.** 17:3 7:2005 pp.377-387.

87 A prospect dynamic model of decision-making. Michael D. Kanner. **J. Theor. Pol.** 17:3 7:2005 pp.311-338.

88 Regime type and diffusion in comparative politics methodology; *[Summary in French]*. Stephen E. Hanson; Jeffrey S. Kopstein. **Can. J. Pol.** 38:1 3:2005 pp.69-99.

89 Rent-seeking for a risky rent: a model and experimental investigation. Ayse Öncüler; Rachel Croson. **J. Theor. Pol.** 17:4 10:2005 pp.403-429.

90 A valence model of political competition in Britain: 1992-1997. Norman Schofield. **Electoral S.** 24:3 9:2005 pp.347-370.

B.1: Political ideas
Idées politiques

91 Aonde vai a teoria política? *[In Portuguese]*; (Whither political theory?) *[Summary]*; *[Summary in French]*. Terence Ball. **R. Sociol. Pol.** 23 11:2004 pp.9-22.

92 Asian democracy in world history. Alan T. Wood. London: Routledge, 2004. 121p. *ISBN: 0415229421, 041522943X. Includes bibliographical references. (Series:* Themes in world history).

93 Capabilities versus opportunities for well-being. Peter Vallentyne. **J. Pol. Philos.** 13:3 9:2005 pp.359-371.

94 Choice, circumstance, and the value of equality. Samuel Scheffler. **Pol. Philos. Econ.** 4:1 2:2005 pp.5-28.

95 Citizenship, environment, economy. Andrew Dobson; Ángel Valencia Sáiz; Derek R. Bell; Simon Hailwood; Emilio Luque; Mojca Drevenšek; Joaquín Valdivielso; Neil Carter; Meg Huby; Graham Smith; Gill Seyfang. **Env. Pol.** 14:2 4:2005 pp.157-306. *Collection of 10 articles.*

96 Civilization and its contents. Bruce Mazlish. Stanford CA: Stanford University Press, 2004. xiv, 188p. *ISBN: 0804750823, 0804750831. Includes bibliographical references and index.*

97 Commons as counterhegemonic projects. James McCarthy. **Cap. Nat. Social.** 16:1 3:2005 pp.9-24.

98 Communitarianism v. individual rights in the West and the Islamic world. David Lea. **Mid. East Policy** XII:2 Summer:2005 pp.36-48.

99 The compatibility of effective self-ownership and joint world ownership. Magnus Jedenheim-Edling. **J. Pol. Philos.** 13:3 9:2005 pp.284-304.

100 Deliberation before the revolution: toward an ethics of deliberative democracy in an unjust world. Archon Fung. **Pol. Theory** 33:3 6:2005 pp.397-419.

101 Deliberative character. Paul Weithman. **J. Pol. Philos.** 13:3 9:2005 pp.263-283.

102 Democracy and justice. Joe Oppenheimer. **Soc. Just. Res.** 18:1 3:2005 pp.83-98.

103 Democracy and liberty: extending the paradigm. George Klosko. **R. Pol.** 67:1 Winter:2005 pp.135-152.

104 The dialectical context of Boghossian's memory argument. Sanford Goldberg. **Can. J. Philos.** 35:1 3:2005 pp.135-148.

105 Discourse and democracy. Todd Gitlin; David Brooks; James Davison Hunter; Karlyn Kohrs Campbell; John R. Searle; Christopher McKnight Nichols; Kathleen Hall Jamieson; Jennifer L. Geddes; David Franz. **Hedgehog R.** 6:3 Fall:2004 pp.7-92. *Collection of 7 articles.*

106 Does democracy preempt civil wars? M. Reynal-Querol. **Euro. J. Pol. Econ.** 21:2 6:2005 pp.445-465.

107 Does poststructuralist thought represent a challenge to the neoliberal project and actually existing capitalism? Richard Brosio. **S. Philos. Edu.** 24:1 1:2005 pp.63-78.

108 Equality and human rights. Allen Buchanan. **Pol. Philos. Econ.** 4:1 2:2005 pp.69-90.

109 Equality and opportunity: reconciling the irreconcilable. Timothy Macklem. **Mod. Law R.** 68:6 11:2005 pp.1016-1033.

110 Freedom with forgiveness. Marc Fleurbaey. **Pol. Philos. Econ.** 4:1 2:2005 pp.29-68.

111 Fünf soziologische Theorien der Demokratie. *[In German]*; [Five sociological theories of democracy] *[Summary]*. Hans-Joachim Schubert. **Euro. J. Sociol.** XLVI:1 2005 pp.3-44.

112 The future reach of the disembodied will. Eric Rakowski. **Pol. Philos. Econ.** 4:1 2:2005 pp.91-130.

113   'Good' and 'bad' democracies: how to conduct research into the quality of democracy. Leonardo Morlino. **J. Comm. S. Transit. Pol.** 20:1 3:2004 pp.5-27.

114   How to distinguish autonomy from integrity. Carolyn McLeod. **Can. J. Philos.** 35:1 3:2005 pp.107-133.

115   Az igazságosságelméletek megalapozás-problémája. *[In Hungarian]*; (On the foundation of the principles of justice.) *[Summary]*. István Balogh. **Társadalomkutatás** 22:4 2004 pp.379-426.

116   'Is not the power to punish essentially a power that pertains to the state?' The different foundations of the right to punish in early modern natural law doctrines. Dieter Hüning. **Pol. Den. Jahr.** 2004 pp.43-60.

117   Justice or freedom: Camus's aporia. Annabel Herzog. **Euro. J. Pol. Theory** 4:2 4:2005 pp.188-199.

118   Die Konstitution politischer Freiheit. Grundlagen, Probleme und Aktualität der politischen Theorie der Aufklärung. *[In German]*; [The constitution of political freedom. Foundations, problems and timeliness of enlightenment political thought]. Olaf Asbach. **Pol. Den. Jahr.** 2004 pp.77-105.

119   Kto dolzhen pravit': liudi ili zakony, massy ili lichnosti? (apologiia ekzistentsial'noi avtokratii). *[In Russian]*; (Who should rule: people or laws? The masses or individuals? (An apology for existential autocracy).) *[Summary]*. A.N. Fatenkov. **Polis [Moscow]** 2(85) 2005 pp.158-171.

120   Liberty: one concept too many? Eric Nelson. **Pol. Theory** 33:1 2:2005 pp.58-78.

121   The many moral particularisms. Sean McKeever; Michael Ridge. **Can. J. Philos.** 35:1 3:2005 pp.83-106.

122   The moral rights of creators of artistic and literary works. Charles R. Beitz. **J. Pol. Philos.** 13:3 9:2005 pp.330-358.

123   Morality and politics. Fred D. Miller [Ed.]; Ellen Frankel Paul [Ed.]; Jeffrey Paul [Ed.]. Cambridge: Cambridge University Press, 2004. xv, 354p. *ISBN: 0521542219. Includes bibliographical references and index.*

124   „Natürliches" Recht in „positivierter" Gestalt, das sich aus Pflichten herleitet? Von der Paradoxie der Menschenrechte. *[In German]*; ["Natural" right in a "positive" light –coming out of duty? On the paradox of human rights]. Lothar R. Waas. **Pol. Den. Jahr.** 2004 pp.107-123.

125   The paradox of transition in conflicted democracies. Fionnuala Ní Aoláin; Colm Campbell. **Hum. Rights Q.** 27:1 2:2005 pp.172-213.

126   Participatory democracy: prospects for democratizing democracy. C. George Benello [Ed.]; Dimitrios I. Roussopoulos [Ed.]. Montreal: Black Rose Books, 2005. xii, 347p. *ISBN: 1551642247, 1551642255. Includes bibliographical references and index.*

127   Politicheskie idei i ideologii postindustrial'noi tsivilizatsii. *[In Russian]*; (Political ideas and ideology of post-industrial civilization.) V. Borisiuk. **Mir. Ekon. Mezh. Ot.** 7 7:2004 pp.3-14.

128   Preferences and paternalism: on freedom and deliberative democracy. Christian F. Rostbøll. **Pol. Theory** 33:3 6:2005 pp.370-396.

129   The problem of global justice. Thomas Nagel. **Philos. Publ. Aff.** 33:2 Spring:2005 pp.113-147.

130   Recognition and redistribution: rethinking culture and the economic. Jacinda Swanson. **Theory Cult. Soc.** 22:4 8:2005 pp.87-118.

131   Reconstructing public reason. Eric MacGilvray. Cambridge MA: Harvard University Press, 2004. xiii, 247p. *ISBN: 0674015428. Includes bibliographical references and index.*

132   Self-ownership, abortion, and the rights of children: toward a more conservative libertarianism. Edward Feser. **J. Libertarian S.** 18:3 Summer:2004 pp.91-114.

133   Subjektphilosophie und Demokratiebegründung. *[In German]*; [Philosophy of the subject and reasons for democracy] *[Summary]*. Raphael Beer. **Arch. Recht. Soz.Philos.** 90:4 2004 pp.516-529.

134 Toleranz als politisches Problem in der pluralistischen Gesellschaft. *[In German]*; [Tolerance as a political problem in a pluralistic society] *[Summary]*. Stefan Huster. **Arch. Recht. Soz.Philos.** 91:1 2005 pp.20-35.

135 Transgenerational compensation. George Sher. **Philos. Publ. Aff.** 33:2 Spring:2005 pp.181-200.

136 Zukunft durch Verspätung. Helmuth Plessners Vision eines deutschen Beitrages zum politischen Humanismus Westeuropas. *[In German]*; [Helmuth Plessner's vision of a German contribution to the political humanism of western Europe]. Kai Haucke. **Pol. Den. Jahr.** 2004 pp.147-166.

B.2: **History of political ideas**
       Histoire des idées politiques

137 History of western political thought: a thematic introduction. John Morrow. Basingstoke, New York: Palgrave Macmillan, 2005. xvi, 416p. *ISBN: 1403935335, 1403935343. Includes bibliographical references (p. 390-406) and index.*

138 The holy history of mankind and other writings. Moses Hess; Shlomo Avineri. Cambridge, New York: Cambridge University Press, 2004. xxxv, 148p. *ISBN: 0521383471, 0521387566. Includes bibliographical references (p. xxxiv-xxxv) and index. (Series:* Cambridge texts in the history of political thought).

139 Participare politică și abilități civice: o scurtă istorie. *[In Romanian]*; [Political participation and citizens: a history] *[Summary]*. Marian Cosmin Gabriel. **S. UBB: Pol.** XLIX:1 2004 pp.77-87.

140 Passionarnyi aspekt ekonomicheskogo razvitiia. *[In Russian]*; [The emotional aspect of economic development]. M.A. Rumiantsev. **Vest. Sankt-Peterburg.** 5 3(21) 9:2004 pp.45-56.

141 Political philosophy across the Atlantic: a difficult relationship? Mario Ricciardi. **J. Mod. Ital. S.** 10:1 3:2005 pp.59-77.

142 Republicanism: a European inheritance? Joel Isaac. **Euro. J. Soc. Theory** 8:1 2:2005 pp.73-86.

Ancient and medieval
Antiquité et Moyen Âge

143 « Emplois pour philosophes » : l'art politique et l'étranger dans le politique à la lumière de Socrate et du philosophe dans le théétète. *[In French]*; ["Employment for philosophers": political art and the foreigner in the political]. Melissa S. Lane. **Ét. Philos.** 3 7:2005 pp.325-346.

144 Aristotle, Diderot, liberalism and the idea of 'middle class': a comparison of two contexts of emergence of a metaphorical formation. E. Adamovsky. **Hist. Pol. Thought** XXVI:2 Summer:2005 pp.303-333.

145 La division et l'unité du politique de Platon. *[In French]*; [The division and the unit of the Politics of Plato]. Dimitri El Murr. **Ét. Philos.** 3 7:2005 pp.295-324.

146 Die geteilte Seele. Zum Verhältnis von Anthropologie und Ethik bei Platon. *[In German]*; [The split soul –on the relations between anthropology and ethics in Plato]. Wolfgang H. Pleger. **Pol. Den. Jahr.** 2004 pp.11-23.

147 Grotius and Pufendorf on the right of necessity. J. Salter. **Hist. Pol. Thought** XXVI:2 Summer:2005 pp.284-302.

148 How the Sophists taught virtue: exhortation and association. D.D. Corey. **Hist. Pol. Thought** XXVI:1 Spring:2005 pp.1-20.

149 La juste mesure. Étude sur les rapports entre le politique et le philèbe. *[In French]*; [The right balance. Study on the relationship between Politics and the 6philèbe]. Sylvain Delcomminette. **Ét. Philos.** 3 7:2005 pp.347-366.

150 Justice, power and Athenian imperialism: an ideological moment in Thucydides' History. E. Podoksik. **Hist. Pol. Thought** XXVI:1 Spring:2005 pp.21-42.

151 « Il ne faut en rien être plus savant que les lois ». Loi et connaissance dans le politique. *[In French]*; ["One should not of anything be more erudite than the laws". Law and knowledge in Politics]. Fulcran Teisserenc. **Ét. Philos.** 3 7:2005 pp.367-384.

152 Nikolaus Cusanus und der Kampf um die Herrschaft in Kirche und Recht. *[In German]*; [Nikolaus Cusanus and the fight for the rule of church and law] *[Summary]*. Stefan Koslowski. **Arch. Recht. Soz.Philos.** 91:2 2005 pp.221-238.

153 Notas sobre la noción de mando político Aristóteles. *[In Spanish]*; [Notes on Aristotle's concept of political power] *[Summary]*. Sergio Raúl Castaño. **Arch. Recht. Soz.Philos.** 91:2 2005 pp.256-265.

154 On some aspects of the Roman concept of authority. Tamás Nótári. **Acta Jur. Hun.** 46:1-2 2005 pp.95-114.

155 Political disagreement and Socratic civic competence. Russell Bentley. **Pol. S.** 53:3 10:2005 pp.516-536.

156 Rumo ao estado moderno: as raízes medievais de alguns de seus elementos formadores. *[In Portuguese]*; (On route to the modern state: the medieval roots of some of its formative elements.) *[Summary]*; *[Summary in French]*. Raquel Kritsch. **R. Sociol. Pol.** 23 11:2004 pp.103-114.

157 Socratic citizenship: delphic oracle and divine sign. David D. Corey. **R. Pol.** 67:2 Spring:2005 pp.201-228.

158 Sokrat o blage i dobrodeteli. *[In Russian]*; [Socrates on welfare and virtue]. V.A. Vasil'ev. **Sots.Gum. Znan.** 1 2004 pp.276-290.

159 Le traitement des constitutions non idéales dans le politique. *[In French]*; [Treatment of the 'non-ideal' constitutions in Politics]. Christopher J. Rowe. **Ét. Philos.** 3 7:2005 pp.385-400.

160 Two cities and two loves: imitation in Augustine's moral psychology and political theory. J.M. Parrish. **Hist. Pol. Thought** XXVI:2 Summer:2005 pp.209-235.

161 The uses and abuses of philosophy: Aristotle's *Politics V* as an example. E. Garver. **Hist. Pol. Thought** XXVI:2 Summer:2005 pp.189-208.

162 Was Ptolemy of Lucca a civic humanist? Reflections on a newly-discovered manuscript of Hans Baron. J. La Salle; J.M. Blythe. **Hist. Pol. Thought** XXVI:2 Summer:2005 pp.236-265.

163 William of Malmesbury on kingship. Björn Weiler. **History** 90:297 1:2005 pp.3-22.

16ᵗʰ & 17ᵗʰ centuries
16ᵉ & 17ᵉ siècles

164 De la tolerancia, su contexto y una posible relación con el "nombre general" de propiedad en John Locke. *[In Spanish]*; [On tolerance, its context and likely relation to the 'general name' of property in John Locke]. Leonídas Montes. **R. Cien. Pol.** XXIV:2 2004 pp.142-158.

165 De l'exil et de l'histoire. *[In French]*; [On exile and history]. Nadia Manea. **S. UBB: Stu. Eur.** XLIX: 1-2 2004 pp.159-175.

166 Four seminal thinkers in international theory: Machiavelli, Grotius, Kant, and Mazzini. Martin Wight; Gabriele Wight [Ed.]; Brian Ernest Porter [Ed.]. Oxford, New York: Oxford University Press, 2005. lxiv, 166p. *ISBN: 0199273677. Includes bibliographical references (p. [129]-139) and index.*

167 Hobbes and the matter of self-consciousness. Samantha Frost. **Pol. Theory** 33:4 8:2005 pp.495-517.

168 Hobbes on representation. Quentin Skinner. **Euro. J. Philos.** 13:2 8:2005 pp.155-184.

169 John Locke's politics of moral consensus. Greg Forster. Cambridge, New York: Cambridge University Press, 2005. xi, 317p. *ISBN: 0521842182. Includes bibliographical references (p. 309-314) and index.*

170   Libertad y consentimiento en el pensamiento político de John Locke. *[In Spanish]*; [Freedom and consent in John Locke's thought] *[Summary]*. Óscar Godoy Arcaya. **R. Cien. Pol.** XXIV:2 2004 pp.159-182.

171   Liberty and Leviathan. Philip Pettit. **Pol. Philos. Econ.** 4:1 2:2005 pp.131-151.

172   Locke on language in (civil) society. H. Dawson. **Hist. Pol. Thought** XXVI:3 Autumn:2005 pp.397-425.

173   Locke y la adulación. *[In Spanish]*; [Locke and adulation] *[Summary]*. Tomás Chuaqui. **R. Cien. Pol.** XXIV:2 2004 pp.183-199.

174   Marriage in seventeenth-century English political thought. Belinda Roberts Peters. Basingstoke, New York: Palgrave Macmillan, 2004. ix, 243p. *ISBN: 1403920362. Includes bibliographical references (p. 204-231) and index.*

175   On the woman question in Machiavelli. Michelle Tolman Clarke. **R. Pol.** 67:2 Spring:2005 pp.229-255.

176   'Philosophy's gaudy dress': rhetoric and fantasy in the Lockean social contract. Linda M.G. Zerilli. **Euro. J. Pol. Theory** 4:2 4:2005 pp.146-163.

177   Poderes invisíveis versus poderes visíveis no Leviatã de Thomas Hobbes. *[In Portuguese]*; (Invisible versus visible powers in Thomas Hobbes' Leviathan.) *[Summary]*; *[Summary in French]*. Pedro Hermílio; Villas Bôas Castelo Branco. **R. Sociol. Pol.** 23 11:2004 pp.23-41.

178   Politics, patriotism, and language: Niccolo Machiavelli's "secular patria" and the creation of an Italian national identity. William J. Landon. New York: Peter Lang, 2005. xiv, 300p. *ISBN: 0820472751. Translated from the Italian. Includes bibliographical references (p. [281]-293) and index.* (Series: Studies in modern European history - vol. 57).

179   Pre-modern property and self-ownership before and after Locke: or, when did common decency become a private rather than a public virtue? Janet Coleman. **Euro. J. Pol. Theory** 4:2 4:2005 pp.125-145.

180   Prerogative and the rule of law in John Locke and the Lincoln presidency. Sean Mattie. **R. Pol.** 67:1 Winter:2005 pp.77-111.

181   Publishing the Prince: history, reading, & the birth of political criticism. Jacob Soll. Ann Arbor MI: University of Michigan Press, 2005. xii, 202p. *ISBN: 0472114735. Includes bibliographical references (p. 177-195) and index.*

182   Rationality in Leviathan: Hobbes and his game-theoretic admirers. Mark S. Peacock. **Euro. J. Hist. Econ. Thou.** 12:2 6:2005 pp.191-213.

183   The relevance of Locke's religious arguments for toleration. Micah Schwartzman. **Pol. Theory** 33:5 10:2005 pp.678-705.

184   Samuel Pufendorf — ein vergessener Klassiker des Naturrechts. *[In German]*; [Samuel Pufendorf — a forgotten classic of natural law]. Horst Denzer. **Pol. Den. Jahr.** 2004 pp.61-75.

185   Souveraineté, droit et gouvernementalité : lectures du politique moderne à partir de Bodin. *[In French]*; [Sovereignty, law and governance: lectures on modern policy since Bodin]. Thomas Berns. Paris: Scheer, 2005. 254p. *ISBN: 291528086X.*

186   Spinoza and republicanism. Raia Prokhovnik. Basingstoke, New York: Palgrave Macmillan, 2004. ix, 280p. *ISBN: 0333733908. Includes bibliographical references (p. 262-276) and index.*

187   Die „unzähmbare" Kraft des Leviathan. *[In German]*; [The untamable power of the Leviathan] *[Summary]*. Annekatrin Gebauer. **Arch. Recht. Soz.Philos.** 91:2 2005 pp.239-255.

188   What kind of democrat was Spinoza? Steven B. Smith. **Pol. Theory** 33:1 2:2005 pp.6-27.

189   Zwischen Widerstandsrecht und starkem Staat. Ein Beitrag zur deutschen Rezeptionsgeschichte von Hobbes. *[In German]*; [A contribution to the history of reading Hobbes in Germany]. Howard Williams; Mirko Wischke. **Pol. Den. Jahr.** 2004 pp.25-42.

18th century
18e siècle

190   Adam Ferguson: his social and political thought. David Kettler. New Brunswick NJ: Transaction Publishers, 2005. xvii, 371p. *ISBN: 1412804752. Includes bibliographical references and index.*

191   Condorcet and modernity. David Williams. Cambridge: Cambridge University Press, 2004. x, 306p. *ISBN: 0521841399. Includes bibliographical references and index.*

192   Edmund Burke's changing justification for intervention. Iain Hampsher-Monk. **Hist. J.** 48:1 3:2005 pp.65-100.

193   Enlightened histories: civilization, war and the Scottish Enlightenment. Bruce Buchan. **Euro. Leg.** 10:2 4:2005 pp.177-192.

194   Individualismo romântico e modernidade democrática: uma mútua configuração. *[In Portuguese]*; (Romantic individualism and democratic modernity: a mutual configuration.) *[Summary]; [Summary in French].* Rosmália Ferreira Santos. **R. Sociol. Pol.** 23 11:2004 pp.89-101.

195   J.S. Mill's doctrine of freedom of expression. Jonathan Riley. **Utilitas** 17:2 7:2005 pp.147-179.

196   Kant and property rights. Marcus Verhaegh. **J. Libertarian S.** 18:3 Summer:2004 pp.11-32.

197   Kantian personal autonomy. Robert S. Taylor. **Pol. Theory** 33:5 10:2005 pp.602-628.

198   Kantovski konstruktivizam u moralnoj teoriji. *[In Croatian]*; (Kantian constructivism in moral theory.) John Rawls; Ana Matan [Tr.]. **Pol. Misao** 41:3 2004 pp.3-48.

199   Le Mercier de La Rivière et les colonies d'Amérique. *[In French]*; [Le Mercier de La Rivière and the American colonies]. Florence Gauthier. **R. Fran. Hist. Id. Pol.** 20:2 2004 pp.261-283.

200   Le Mercier de La Rivière et l'établissement d'une hiérarchie normative. Entre droit naturel et droit positif. *[In French]*; [Le Mercier de La Rivière and the creation of a normative hierarchy. Between natural law and positive law]. Éric Gojosso. **R. Fran. Hist. Id. Pol.** 20:2 2004 pp.285-305.

201   Les physiocrates et la science politique de leur temps. *[In French]*; [Physiocrats and political science of their time]. Reinhard Bach. **R. Fran. Hist. Id. Pol.** 20:2 2004 pp.229-259.

202   The rhetoric of rebellion in Hume's constitutional thought. Thomas W. Merrill. **R. Pol.** 67:2 Spring:2005 pp.257-282.

203   Rousseau and imagined communities. Steven T. Engel. **R. Pol.** 67:3 Summer:2005 pp.515-537.

204   Il Rousseau di De Ruggiero. *[In Italian]*; [De Ruggiero's Rousseau]. M.L. Cicalese. **Pens. Pol.** XXXVII:2 2004 pp.206-230.

205   'The black, scabby Brazilian': some thoughts on race and early modern philosophy. Michael A. Rosenthal. **Philos. Soc. Crit.** 31:2 3:2005 pp.211-221.

206   Was Fichte an ethnic nationalist? On cultural nationalism and its double. A. Abizadeh. **Hist. Pol. Thought** XXVI:2 Summer:2005 pp.334-359.

207   What is enlightenment (oświecenie)? Some Polish answers, 1765-1820. Richard Butterwick. **Cent. Euro.** 3:1 5:2005 pp.19-38.

19th century
19e siècle

208   Affirmative action and Mill. Reginald M. Williams. **Publ. Aff. Q.** 19:1 1:2005 pp.65-80.

209   Apostles of the 'other Russia': Mikhail Bakunin and Eduard Limonov on paths of radical social transformation. Vladimir Sapon. **Rus. Pol. Law** 43:6 11-12:2005 pp.43-61.

210   Barbarian thoughts: imperialism in the philosophy of John Stuart Mill. Jahn Beate. **R. Int. S.** 31:3 7:2005 pp.599-618.

211 Contra Spooner. Colin Williams. **J. Libertarian S.** 18:3 Summer:2004 pp.1-10.

212 The dark side of Tocqueville: on war and empire. Roger Boesche. **R. Pol.** 67:4 Fall:2005 pp.737-752.

213 Elementos estáticos da teoria política de Augusto Comte: as pátrias e o poder temporal. *[In Portuguese]*; (Static elements of August Comte's political theory: fatherlands and temporal power.) *[Summary]*; *[Summary in French]*. Gustavo Biscaia de Lacerda. **R. Sociol. Pol.** 23 11:2004 pp.63-78.

214 « L'esprit légiste » chez Alexis de Tocqueville. *[In French]*; ['The spirit of law' in Tocqueville's works]. Charles Coutel. **Tocqueville R.** XXV:2 2004 pp.127-137.

215 Gladstone, religious freedom and practical reasoning. D.J. Lorenzo. **Hist. Pol. Thought** XXVI:1 Spring:2005 pp.90-119.

216 Hegel, Tocqueville, and 'individualism'. Dana Villa. **R. Pol.** 67:4 Fall:2005 pp.659-686.

217 Intervention and empire: John Stuart Mill and international relations. Carol A.L. Prager. **Pol. S.** 53:3 10:2005 pp.621-640.

218 James Madison: liberal, republican, democrat? Alan Gibson; Colleen A. Sheehan; Richard K. Matthews. **R. Pol.** 67:1 Winter:2005 pp.5-76. *Collection of 4 articles.*

219 Jean-Paul Marat's The Chains of Slavery in Britain and France, 1774-1833. Rachel Hammersley. **Hist. J.** 48:3 9:2005 pp.641-660.

220 Konzervativizmus versus szocializmus. Az egyenlőtlenség késő-viktoriánus prófétája, Mallcok. *[In Hungarian]*; (Conservatism versus socialism. The late-Victorian prophet of inequality, Mallock.) *[Summary]*. Gergely Egedy. **Társadalomkutatás** 22:1 2004 pp.147-162.

221 Kulturkritik und Demokratie bei Max Weber und Hannah Arendt. *[In German]*; [Cultural criticism and democracy in Max Weber and Hannah Arendt]. Winfried Thaa. **Z. Pol.** 52:1 3:2005 pp.25-56.

222 The liberal character of ethological governance. Melanie White. **Econ. Soc.** 34:3 8:2005 pp.474-494.

223 Lincoln and Tocqueville on democratic leadership and self-interest properly understood. Brian Danoff. **R. Pol.** 67:4 Fall:2005 pp.687-719.

224 Performing conscience: Thoreau, political action, and the plea for John Brown. Jack Turner. **Pol. Theory** 33:4 8:2005 pp.448-471.

225 'Plus ça change...': innovation and the spirit of enterprise in America. Christine Dunn Henderson. **R. Pol.** 67:4 Fall:2005 pp.753-774.

226 The power of silence and limits of discourse at Oliver Wendell Holmes's breakfast-table. Michael A. Weinstein. **R. Pol.** 67:1 Winter:2005 pp.113-133.

227 Principled pragmatism: Abraham Lincoln's method of political analysis. David J. Siemers. **Pres. Stud. Q.** 34:4 12:2004 pp.804-827.

228 Principles for developing youth policy: Kant's categorical imperative and developmental ethics. Judith Bessant. **Policy S.** 26:1 3:2005 pp.103-116.

229 Standing 'aloof' from the state: Thoreau on self-government. Ruth Lane. **R. Pol.** 67:2 Spring:2005 pp.283-310.

230 Thomas Paine and the literature of revolution. Edward Larkin. New York, Cambridge: Cambridge University Press, 2005. x, 205p. *ISBN: 0521841151. Includes bibliographical references (p. 195-201) and index.*

231 Tocqueville : un destin paradoxal. *[In French]*; [Tocqueville: a paradoxical destiny]. Jean-Louis Benoit. Paris: Bayard, 2005. 372p. *ISBN: 2227474297. Includes bibliographical references (p. 351-360).*

232 Tocqueville and Gobineau on the nature of modern politics. Aristide Tessitore. **R. Pol.** 67:4 Fall:2005 pp.631-657.

233 Tocqueville and local government: distinguishing democracy's second track. Robert T. Gannett, Jr. **R. Pol.** 67:4 Fall:2005 pp.721-736.

234 Tocqueville aujourd'hui. *[In French]*; [Tocqueville nowadays]. Raymond Boudon. Paris: Editions Odile Jacob, 2005. 301p. *ISBN: 2738115497. Includes bibliographical references (p. 281-[288]).*

235 Tocqueville et l'Algérie : le libéral et le colonial. *[In French]*; [Tocqueville and Algeria: the liberal and the colonizer]. Nourredine Saadi. **Tocqueville R.** XXV:2 2004 pp.111-125.

236 Tocqueville et l'esprit de la démocratie. *[In French]*; [Tocqueville and democracy's spirit]. Raymond Aron; Arthur Kaledin; François Bourricaud; François Furet; Olivier Zunz; Jean-Claude Lamberti; Franklin R. Ankersmit; Guillaume Bacot; Sonia Chabot; Claude Lefort; Agnès Antoine; Paul Thibaud; Françoise Mélonio; Daniel Jacques; Laurence Guellec; Daniel Bell; Melvin Richter; Mohamed Cherkaoui; Arthur Goldhammer. **Tocqueville R.** XXVI:1 2005 pp.25-531. *Collection of 19 articles.*

237 Tocqueville on Catholicism and democracy: views from Latin America. Claudio López-Guerra. **Tocqueville R.** XXV:2 2004 pp.141-162.

238 Tocqueville's brief encounter with Machiavelli: notes on the Florentine histories (1836). M. Richter. **Hist. Pol. Thought** XXVI:3 Autumn:2005 pp.426-442.

239 Tocqueville's paradoxical moderation. Aurelian Craiutu. **R. Pol.** 67:4 Fall:2005 pp.599-629.

240 Unity and difference: John Robert Seeley and the political theology of international relations. Duncan S.A. Bell. **R. Int. S.** 31:3 7:2005 pp.559-579.

241 Woman's eclipse: the silenced feminine in Nietzsche and Heidegger. Katrin Froese. **Philos. Soc. Crit.** 31:2 3:2005 pp.165-184.

20th century
20e siècle

242 Absolute adversity: Schmitt, Levinas, and the exceptionality of killing. Jesse Sims. **Philos. Soc. Crit.** 31:2 3:2005 pp.223-252.

243 Artful discussion: John Dewey's classroom as a model of deliberative association. Jason Kosnoski. **Pol. Theory** 33:5 10:2005 pp.654-677.

244 British idealism and the political philosophy of T.H. Green, Bernard Bosanquet, R.G. Collingwood and Michael Oakeshott. David Boucher; James Connelly; Stamatoula Panagakou; William Sweet; Colin Tyler. **Br. J. Pol. Int. Rel.** 7:1 2:2005 pp.97-125.

245 Carl Schmitts Klassiker-Interpretation und ihre verfassungsdogmatische Funktion. *[In German]*; [Carl Schmitt's interpretation of classical writers and constitutional law]. Ulrich Thiele. **Rechtstheorie** 35:2 2004 pp.232-246.

246 Carl Schmitts völkerrechtliches Großraumprinzip — Perspektiven einer neuen Weltordnung. *[In German]*; [Carl Schmitt's principle of common space based on human rights: a new world order]. Jean-Pierre Bussalb. **Rechtstheorie** 35:2 2004 pp.247-278.

247 Communicative action and rational choice. Cristina Lafont. **Philos. Soc. Crit.** 31:2 3:2005 pp.253-263.

248 Constructing justice for existing practice: Rawls and the status quo. Aaron James. **Philos. Publ. Aff.** 33:3 Summer:2005 pp.281-316.

249 The contribution and legacy of Edward Said. Colin Flint; Ghazi-Walid Falah; Nur Masalha; Muhammad A. Shuraydi; Khalil Barhoum; Timothy Brennan; Maria Dolors Garcia-Ramón; Andrew Kirby; Antoni Luna; Lluis Riudor; Perla Zusman; Audrey Kobayashi. **Arab World Geog.** 7:1-2 Spring-Summer:2004 pp.4-90. *Collection of 6 articles.*

250 Crooked timber or bent twig? Isaiah Berlin's nationalism. David Miller. **Pol. S.** 53:1 3:2005 pp.100-123.

251 Decent democratic centralism. Stephen C. Angle. **Pol. Theory** 33:4 8:2005 pp.518-546.

252 Defending Bosanquet's philosophical theory of the state: a reassessment of the 'Bosanquet-Hobhouse controversy'. Stamatoula Panagakou. **Br. J. Pol. Int. Rel.** 7:1 2:2005 pp.29-47.

253 A democracia do homem comum: resgatando a teoria política de John Dewey. *[In Portuguese]*; (The democracy of 'common man': reviving John Dewey's political theory.) *[Summary]*; *[Summary in French]*. Thamy Pogrebinschi. **R. Sociol. Pol.** 23 11:2004 pp.43-53.

254 Derrida's deconstruction of Marx(ism). Jules Townshend. **Cont. Pol.** 10:2 6:2004 pp.127-143.

255 Economic nationalism and the 'spirit of capitalism': civic collectivism and national wealth in the thought of John Fortescue. C. Nederman. **Hist. Pol. Thought** XXVI:2 Summer:2005 pp.266-283.

256 Az európai egyensúlytól a kölcsönös szolgáltatások társadalmáig. Bibó István a politikai gondolkodó. *[In Hungarian]*; (From the European equilibrium to the society of mutual performances. István Bibó the political philosopher.) Gábor Kovács. Budapest: Argumentum Kiadó, 2004. 494p. *ISBN: 9634462758. Includes bibliographical references (p. 473-485).*

257 European political thought since 1945. Noël OSullivan. Basingstoke: Palgrave Macmillan, 2004. xiv, 241p. *ISBN: 0333655591, 0333655605, 0333744403. Includes bibliographical references and index. (Series:* European culture and society).

258 The federal structure of a republic of reasons. Loren A. King. **Pol. Theory** 33:5 10:2005 pp.629-653.

259 Fichte and the idea of liberal socialism. Nedim Nomer. **J. Pol. Philos.** 13:1 3:2005 pp.53-73.

260 Freedom through political representation: Lefort, Gauchet and Rosanvallon on the relationship between state and society. Wim Weymans. **Euro. J. Pol. Theory** 4:3 7:2005 pp.263-282.

261 From order to justice. Russell Hardin. **Pol. Philos. Econ.** 4:2 6:2005 pp.175-194.

262 G.D.H. Cole on the general will: a socialist reflects on Rousseau. Peter Lamb. **Euro. J. Pol. Theory** 4:3 7:2005 pp.283-300.

263 Globality, plurality and freedom: the Arendtian perspective. Roland Axtmann. **R. Int. S.** 32:1 1:2005 pp.93-117.

264 Hannah Arendt: Zwischen deutscher Philosophie und jüdischer Politik. *[In German]*; [Hannah Arendt: between German philosophy and Jewish politics]. Annette Vowinckel. Berlin: Lukas, 2004. 139p. *ISBN: 3936872368.*

265 The headless republic: sacrificial violence in modern French thought. Jesse Goldhammer. Ithaca NY: Cornell University Press, 2005. x, 205p. *ISBN: 0801441501. Includes bibliographical references and index.*

266 Immanuel Wallerstein: sosyal bilimlere yeniden bakmak. *[In Turkish]*; (Immanuel Wallerstein: rethinking social sciences.) Elçin Aktoprak. **Uluslararasi Ilişkiler** 1:4 Winter:2004 pp.23-58.

267 Individuality, deliberation and welfare in Donald Winnicott. Gal Gerson. **Hist. Hum. Sci.** 18:1 2:2005 pp.107-126.

268 John Rawls' politischer Liberalismus und Kants langer Schatten. *[In German]*; (John Rawls' political liberalism and the long shadow of Kant.) Claus Dierksmeier. **Z. Pol.wissen.** 14:4 2004 pp.1297-1322.

269 Karl Jaspers: a biography. Navigations in truth. Suzanne Kirkbright. New Haven CT: Yale University Press, 2004. xxiii,360p. *ISBN: 0300102429. Includes bibliographical references (p. [344]-355) and index.*

270 Leo Strauss and Eric Voegelin on Machiavelli. Athanasios Moulakis. **Euro. J. Pol. Theory** 4:3 7:2005 pp.249-262.

271 Leo Strauss et George Bush. *[In French]*; [Leo Strauss and George Bush]. Corine Pelluchon. **Banquet** 19-20 1:2004 pp.281-292.

272 Marx et Foucault. *[In French]*; [Marx and Foucault]. Actuel Marx. **Actuel Marx** 36 7-12:2004 pp.13-121.

273 Michel Foucault: crises and problemizations. Alan Milchman; Alan Rosenberg. **R. Pol.** 67:2 Spring:2005 pp.335-351.

274 Milton's case for a free Commonwealth. Frank Lovett. **Am. J. Pol. Sci.** 49:3 7:2005 pp.466-478.

275 Mitä tekemistä identiteetillä on turvallisuuden kanssa? McSweeney vastaan Buzan ja Wæver. *[In Finnish]*; [What does identity have to do with security? McSweeney versus Buzan and Wæver] *[Summary]*. Jouko Huru. **Kosmopolis** 34:3 2004 pp.29-50.

14

276 National republican politics, intellectuals and the case of Pierre-André Taguieff. Christopher Flood. **Mod. Cont. France** 12:3 8:2004 pp.353-370.

277 Oakeshott, freedom and republicanism. David Boucher. **Br. J. Pol. Int. Rel.** 7:1 2:2005 pp.81-96.

278 Patrolling the boundaries of politics: Collingwood, political analysis and political action. James Connelly. **Br. J. Pol. Int. Rel.** 7:1 2:2005 pp.67-80.

279 'Perhaps the most important primary good': self-respect and Rawls's principles of justice. Nir Eyal. **Pol. Philos. Econ.** 4:2 6:2005 pp.195-219.

280 Political theorizing as a dimension of political life. Kari Palonen. **Euro. J. Pol. Theory** 4:4 10:2005 pp.351-366.

281 Pour une critique de la catégorie de totalitarisme. *[In French]*; [For a critique of the category of totalitarianism]. Domenico Losurdo. **Actuel Marx** 35 1-6:2004 pp.115-146.

282 Rawls — Kant. *[In Croatian]*; (Rawls v. Kant.) Zvonko Posavec. **Pol. Misao** 41:3 2004 pp.49-64.

283 Rawls's political ontology. Philip Pettit. **Pol. Philos. Econ.** 4:2 6:2005 pp.157-174.

284 Un regard japonais sur la modernité. La pensée politique de Maruyama. *[In French]*; [A Japanese look on modernity. Maruyama's political thought]. Bernard Stevens. **Esprit** 312 2:2005 pp.117-133.

285 Rol-Tanguy. *[In French]*; [Rol-Tanguy]. Roger Bourderon; Christine Levisse-Touze [Intro.]. Paris: Tallandier, 2004. 768p. *ISBN: 2847341498. Includes bibliographical references (p. [747]-753) and index.*

286 Rossiia i messianizm: k 'russkoi idee' N.A. Berdiaeva. *[In Russian]*; [Russia and messianism: towards the 'Russian idea' of N.A. Berdiaev]. Manuel Sarkisiants. St. Petersburg: Izdatelstvo Sankt Peterburgskogo Universiteta, 2005. 272p. *ISBN: 5288036012.*

287 Russkaia filosofiia v XX stoletii. *[In Russian]*; [Russian philosophy in the 20th century]. A.F. Zamaleev; V.S. Nikonenko; T.V. Chumakova; S.A. Vorob'eva; N.I. Bezlenkin; A.I. Brodskii; I.D. Osipov; A.G. Vlaskin; A.A. Ermichev; O.S. Klimkov; A.E. Rybas. **Vest. Sankt-Peterburg.** 6 2(6) 6:2004 pp.3-57. *Collection of 10 articles.*

288 Savage and modern liberty: Marcel Gauchet and the origins of new French thought. Samuel Moyn. **Euro. J. Pol. Theory** 4:2 4:2005 pp.164-187.

289 Sosiaaliset oikeudet ja sosiaalipolitiikka : T. H. Marshallin näkökulma hyvinvointivaltioon. *[In Finnish]*; [Social rights and social policy: T.H. Marshall's view of the welfare state] *[Summary]*. Tuomo Kokkonen. **Politiikka** 46:4 2004 pp.264-276.

290 Souveränität — Hürde oder Baustein der internationalen Beziehungen nach 1945? *[In German]*; [Sovereignty: obstacle or basis of international relations since 1945?] *[Summary]*. Markus Lang. **Mittelweg 36** 13:6 12-1:2004-2005 pp.24-40.

291 The substantive dimension of deliberative practical rationality. Pablo Gilabert. **Philos. Soc. Crit.** 31:2 3:2005 pp.185-210.

292 The theory of the partisan: Carl Schmitt's neglected legacy. G. Slomp. **Hist. Pol. Thought** XXVI:3 Autumn:2005 pp.502-519.

293 Transcending boundaries: Nishida Kitarō K'ang Yu-wei, and the politics of unity. C.S. Goto-Jones. **Mod. Asian S.** 39:4 10:2005 pp.793-816.

294 Vom Nutzen und Nachteil der Philosophie für die Politik —Laudatio auf Norberto Bobbio zur Verleihung des Hegel-Preises der Stadt Stuttgart. *[In German]*; [On the pros and cons of philosphy for politics]. Henning Ottmann. **Pol. Den. Jahr.** 2004 pp.191-195.

295 Vom Sinn einer philosophischen Theorie der Politik. Bemerkungen zum Theoriebegriff bei Hans Buchheim und Michael Oakeshott. *[In German]*; [On the meaning of a philosophical theory of politics]. Michael Henkel. **Pol. Den. Jahr.** 2004 pp.167-187.

296 Der Widerhall der Lehre von Hans Kelsen im Osten: Rezeption und Kritik im geschichtlichen Überblick am Beispiel von China. *[In German]*; [The reflection and critique of Hans Kelsen's thoughts in the East: the example of China]. Z. Liang. **Z. Öffent. Recht** 60:1 2005 pp.127-145.

B.3:   **Political doctrines and ideologies**
         Doctrines et idéologies politiques

297   Anarchy in political philosophy. Francis Dupuis-Déri. **Anarch. S.** 13:1 2005 pp.8-22.

298   The anatomy of fascism. Robert O. Paxton. London: Allen Lane, 2004. xii, 352p. *ISBN: 0713997206. Includes bibliographical references and index.*

299   Authoritarianism as a group phenomenon. Jost Stellmacher; Thomas Petzel. **Pol. Psychol.** 26:2 4:2005 pp.245-274.

300   Being feminist (politics of identity — VIII). Ruth Lister. **Gov. Oppos.** 40:3 Summer:2005 pp.442-463.

301   Between Geist and Zeitgeist: Martin Heidegger as ideologue of 'metapolitical fascism'. Matthew Feldman. **Total. Mov. Pol. Relig.** 6:2 9:2005 pp.175-198.

302   A critical cartography of feminist post-postmodernism. Rosi Braidotti. **Aust. Femin. S.** 20:47 7:2005 pp.169-180.

303   Des origines du totalitarisme aux apories des démocraties libérales : interprétations et usages de la pensée de Joseph de Maistre par Isaiah Berlin. *[In French]*; (The origins of totalitarianism: Isaiah Berlin on Joseph De Maistre.) *[Summary]*. Jean Zaganiaris. **R. Fran. Sci. Pol.** 54:6 12:2004 pp.981-1004.

304   Dictatorship in history and theory: Bonapartism, Caesarism and totalitarianism. Peter Baehr [Ed.]; Melvin Richter [Ed.]. Cambridge: Cambridge University Press, 2004. xi, 308p. *ISBN: 0521532701. Includes bibliographical references and index. (Series:* Publications of the German Historical Institute).

305   The emerging threat? South Africa's extreme right. Martin Schönteich. **Terror. Pol. Viol.** 16:4 Winter:2004 pp.757-776.

306   Exquisite rebel: the essays of Voltairine de Cleyre : feminist, anarchist, genius. Voltairine de Cleyre [Ed.]; Sharon Presley [Ed.]; Crispin Sartwell [Ed.]. Albany NY: State University of New York Press, 2005. xiv, 331p. *ISBN: 0791460932, 0791460940. Includes bibliographical references and index.*

307   A family of political concepts: tyranny, despotism, Bonapartism, Caesarism, dictatorship, 1750-1917. Melvin Richter. **Euro. J. Pol. Theory** 4:3 7:2005 pp.221-248.

308   Fascism as a political religion. Roger Griffin; Emilio Gentile; Richard Steigmann-Gall; Thomas Linehan; Radu Ioanid; Martin Durham; Chip Berlet; Martin Blinkhorn. **Total. Mov. Pol. Relig.** 5:3 Winter:2004 pp.291-526. *Collection of 8 articles.*

309   Faut-il supprimer l'Etat ? Vertiges anarchistes d'une certaine pensée libérale. *[In French]*; [Should the state be removed? Anarchism and libertarianism]. Drieu Godefridi. **Banquet** 21 10:2004 pp.273-292.

310   "Feministski-sotsialisticheskaia" kriticheskaia teoriia pozdnego kapitalizma N. Freizer. *[In Russian]*; (N. Fraser's 'feminist-socialist' critical theory of late capitalism.) *[Summary]*. V.N. Furs. **Polis [Moscow]** 6(83) 2004 pp.89-101.

311   'Forty acres and a mule' for women: Rawls and feminism. Susan Moller Okin. **Pol. Philos. Econ.** 4:2 6:2005 pp.233-248.

312   From anarchy to anarchism (300CE to 1939). Anarchism: a documentary history of libertarian ideas. Robert Graham [Ed.]. Montreal: Black Rose Books, 2005. xiv, 519p. *ISBN: 1551642506, 1551642514. Includes bibliographical references and index. Vol. 1.*

313   Future unknown. Gopal Balakrishnan. **New Left R.** 32 3-4:2005 pp.5-21.

314   Ideologies of globalization. Manfred B. Steger. **J. Pol. Ideol.** 10:1 2:2005 pp.11-30.

315   The indeterminacy of republican policy. Christopher McMahon. **Philos. Publ. Aff.** 33:1 Winter:2005 pp.67-93.

316   Inequality and the case for redistribution: Aristotle to Sen. Kirk White. **Rev. Int. Sci. Econ. Com.** LII:2 6:2005 pp.145-168.

317   Internalism and externalism in ethics applied to the liberal-communitarian debate. Maria Dimova-Cookson. **Br. J. Pol. Int. Rel.** 7:1 2:2005 pp.18-28.

318   Long live death! Fascism, resurrection, immortality. Mark Neocleous. **J. Pol. Ideol.** 10:1 2:2005 pp.31-49.

319   Monarchy and the consolidation of the constitutional state. Baldomero Oliver León. **Jahr. Öffent. Gegen.** 53 2005 pp.187-206.

320   Nationalsozialismus als Geschichte. Neuere Literatur zum Umgang mit der NS-Vergangenheit in Deutschland. *[In German]*; [Nazism as history. Latest literature on Germany's NS past]. Christoph Nonn. **Neue Pol. Liter.** XLIX:3 2004 pp.407-426.

321   'Nowhere at home', not even in theory: Emma Goldman, anarchism and political theory. Jim Jose. **Anarch. S.** 13:1 2005 pp.23-46.

322   The objects of ideology: historical transformations and the changing role of the analyst. G. Talshir. **Hist. Pol. Thought** XXVI:3 Autumn:2005 pp.520-549.

323   On anti-utopianism, more or less. Russell Jacoby. **Telos** 129 Fall-Winter:2004 pp.97-137.

324   Only a beginning: an anarchist anthology. Allan Antliff [Ed.]. Vancouver: Arsenal Pulp Press, 2004. 406p. *ISBN: 1551521679. Includes bibliographical references and index.*

325   Proudhon: from aesthetics to politics. Ali Nematollahy. **Anarch. S.** 13:1 2005 pp.47-60.

326   Reading the Earth Charter: cosmopolitan environmental citizenship or light green politics as usual? Sherilyn MacGregor. **Ethics Place Env.** 7:1-2 3-6:2004 pp.85-96.

327   Retooling collaboration: a vision for environmental change research. William Pike; Brent Yarnal; Alan M. MacEachren; Mark Gahegan; Chaoqing Yu. **Environment** 47:2 3:2005 pp.8-21.

328   Science and fascism: the case of Enrico Fermi. Spencer M. Di Scala. **Total. Mov. Pol. Relig.** 6:2 9:2005 pp.199-211.

329   The secular bias in ideology studies and the case of Islamism. Michaelle L. Browers. **J. Pol. Ideol.** 10:1 2:2005 pp.75-93.

330   Threat, authoritarianism, and selective exposure to information. Howard Lavine; Milton Lodge; Kate Freitas. **Pol. Psychol.** 26:2 4:2005 pp.219-244.

331   Totalitarian movements and political religions. Marina Cattaruzza; Emilio Gentile; Natalia Belozertseva [Tr.]; Roger Griffin; Hermann Lübbe; Renato Moro; Klaus Vondung; Klaus-Georg Riegel; Ulrich Schmid; Marius Turda. **Total. Mov. Pol. Relig.** 6:1 6:2005 pp.1-150. *Collection of 8 articles.*

332   Totalitarianism and political religions: concepts for the comparison of dictatorships. Hans Maier [Ed.]. London: Routledge, 2004. 406p. *ISBN: 0714685291, 0714656097. Includes index. (Series:* Totalitarian movements and political religions).

333   Understanding authoritarianism: psychological antecedents and ideological consequences. Bojan Todosijevic; Zsolt Enyedi. **Cent. Euro. Pol. Sci. R.** 5:15 Spring:2004 pp.35-51.

334   Violence, nonviolence, and the concept of revolution in anarchism. Andy Chan. **Anarch. S.** 12:2 2004 pp.103-123.

335   Wie viel Gemeinschaft benötigt eine Demokratie? Liberale und republikanische Positionen. *[In German]*; [How much community does a democracy need? Liberal and republican positions]. Gary S. Schaal. **Gesell. Wirt. Pol.** 53:4 2004 pp.425-436.

336   Winning the future: a 21st century contract with America. Newt Gingrich. Washington DC: Regnery Publishers, 2005. xxvii,243p. *ISBN: 0895260425. Includes bibliographical references and index.*

Liberalism
Libéralisme

337   Agrarian moral economies and neoliberalism in Brazil: competing worldviews and the state in the struggle for land. Wendy Wolford. **Env. Plan.** A 37:2 2:2005 pp.241-261.

338   Aristocratic liberalism in post-revolutionary France. Annelien de Dijn. **Hist. J.** 48:3 9:2005 pp.661-681.

339   Autonomy and the challenges of liberalism: new essays. John Philip Christman [Ed.]; Joel Anderson [Ed.]. Cambridge, New York: Cambridge University Press, 2005. xii, 383p. *ISBN: 0521839513.*

340   Capitalism and its economics: a critical history. Douglas Fitzgerald Dowd. London: Pluto Press, 2004. xv, 324p. *ISBN: 0745322808, 0745322794. Includes bibliographical references and index.*

341   Comparative topographies of neoliberalism in Mexico. Patricia M. Martin. **Env. Plan. A** 37:2 2:2005 pp.203-220.

342   Contenido y alcance de la educación liberal (segunda parte). *[In Spanish]*; [Liberal education (second part)]. John Stuart Mill. **R. Econ. Inst.** 7:12 2005 pp.241-270.

343   Covenants without swords: idealist liberalism and the spirit of empire. Jeanne Morefield. Princeton NJ: Princeton University Press, 2005. xii, 253p. *ISBN: 0691119929. Includes bibliographical references (p. 231-248) and index.*

344   Les deux principes du libéralisme. *[In French]*; [The two principles of liberalism]. Bertrand Binoche. **Actuel Marx** 36 7-12:2004 pp.123-150.

345   Do neoliberal policies deter political corruption? John Gerring; Strom C. Thacker. **Int. Org.** 59:1 Winter:2005 pp.233-254.

346   Equal treatment of cultures and the limits of postmodern liberalism. Jürgen Habermas. **J. Pol. Philos.** 13:1 3:2005 pp.1-28.

347   Hurley on egalitarianism and the luck-neutralizing aim. Kasper Lippert-Rasmussen. **Pol. Philos. Econ.** 4:2 6:2005 pp.249-265.

348   Is liberalism the only way toward democracy? Confucianism and democracy. Brooke A. Ackerly. **Pol. Theory** 33:4 8:2005 pp.547-576.

349   Liberal languages: ideological imaginations and twentieth-century progressive thought. Michael Freeden. Princeton NJ: Princeton University Press, 2005. x, 271p. *ISBN: 0691116776, 0691116784. Includes bibliographical references and index.*

350   Liberalism. Paul J. Kelly. Cambridge: Polity, 2005. ix, 183p. *ISBN: 0745632904, 0745632912. Includes bibliographical references and index. (Series: Key concepts).*

351   A liberalism of the common good: some recent studies of T. H. Green's Moral and political theory. Avital Simhony. **Br. J. Pol. Int. Rel.** 7:1 2:2005 pp.126-144.

352   Liberalism: the genius of American ideals. Marcus G Raskin. Lanham MD: Rowman & Littlefield, 2004. xviii, 323p. *ISBN: 0742515907, 0742515915. Includes bibliographical references (p. 297-306) and index.*

353   Liberalismus — metaphysisch und politisch. Anmerkungen zum Konzept eines freistehenden Liberalismus bei John Rawls. *[In German]*; [Liberalism –metaphysical and political. Comments on the concept of a free-standing liberalism in John Rawls] *[Summary]*. Kai Hauke. **Arch. Recht. Soz.Philos.** 91:1 2005 pp.49-60.

354   Liberalizm vzgliad iz literatury. *[In Russian]*; [Liberalism: a literal perspective] *[Summary]*. N.B. Ivanova [Ed.]. Moscow: Fond 'Liberal'naiia missiia', Ob'edinennoe gumanitarnoe izd-vo, 2005. 232p. *ISBN: 5983790242.* *Includes bibliographical references.*

355   Liberalizmden neoliberalizme güç olgusu ve sistemik bağımlılık. *[In Turkish]*; (Power and systemic dependence from liberalism to neoliberalism.) Yücel Bozdaglioglu; Çınar Özen. **Uluslararasi Ilişkiler** 1:4 Winter:2004 pp.59-79.

356   Libertarian natural rights. Siegfried Van Duffel. **Crit. R.** 16:4 Fall:2004 pp.353-375.

357   Mining mountains: neoliberalism, land tenure, livelihoods, and the new Peruvian mining industry in Cajamarca. Jeffrey Bury. **Env. Plan. A** 37:2 2:2005 pp.221-239.

358   Neoliberalism in (regional) theory and practice: the stronger communities action fund in New Zealand. Wendy Larner. **Aust. Geog. S.** 43:1 3:2005 pp.9-18.

359   Portrait politique de Nehru. L'idée libérale en Inde. *[In French]*; [Political portrait of Nehru. Liberal thought in India]. Sunil Khilnani. **Esprit** 312 2:2005 pp.101-116.

360   Putting liberalism in its place. Paul W. Kahn. Princeton NJ: Princeton University Press, 2005. 328p. *ISBN: 0691120242. Includes bibliographical references and index.*

361   Smoking, progressive liberalism, and the law. Ken I. Kersch. **Crit. R.** 16:4 Fall:2004 pp.405-429.

362   Une spiritualité libérale? Charles Taylor et Alasdair MacIntyre en conversation. *[In French]*; (A liberal spirituality? Charles Taylor and Alasdair MacIntyre.) *[Summary]*. Émile Perreau-Saussine. **R. Fran. Sci. Pol.** 55:2 4:2005 pp.299-315.

363   Why left-libertarianism is not incoherent, indeterminate, or irrelevant: a reply to Fried. Peter Vallentyne; Hillel Steiner; Michael Otsuka. **Philos. Publ. Aff.** 33:2 Spring:2005 pp.201-215.

Nationalism
Nationalisme

364   American nationalism and U.S. foreign policy from September 11 to the Iraq war. Paul T. McCartney. **Pol. Sci. Q.** 119:3 Fall:2004 pp.399-423.

365   The demonisation of pan-Arab nationalism. Ralph M. Coury. **Race Class** 46:4 3-6:2005 pp.1-19.

366   Hayden White, traumatic nationalism, and the public role of history. A. Dirk Moses. **Hist. Theory** 44:3 10:2005 pp.311-332.

367   Klassovoe kak etnicheskoe: ritorika russkogo radikal'no-natsionalisticheskogo dvizheniia. *[In Russian]*; (Class as ethnicity: the rhetoric behind Russia's extreme nationalist movement.) *[Summary]*. M.M. Sokolov. **Polis [Moscow]** 2(85) 2005 pp.127-137.

368   Nationalism and the mind. Liah Greenfeld. **Nat. Nationalism** 11:3 7:2005 pp.325-341.

369   Nationalism: distilling the cultural and the political. Ali Kemal Özcan. **Nat. Ethn. Pol.** 11:2 Summer:2005 pp.163-193.

370   The origins of Turkish republican citizenship: the birth of race. Bora Isyar. **Nat. Nationalism** 11:3 7:2005 pp.343-360.

371   Petliurovshchina. *[In Russian]*; (Petliurovshchina.) Sergei Shumov. Moscow: EKSMO, Algoritm, 2005. 249p. *ISBN: 5699091696.*

372   Politikai hisztériák Közép – és Kelet-Európában. Bibó István fasizmusról, nacionalizmusról, antiszemitizmusról. *[In Hungarian]*; (Political hysterias in Central and Eastern Europe. István Bibó on fascism, nationalism and anti-semitism.) Iván Balog. Budapest: Argumentum Kiadó, 2004. 289p. *ISBN: 9634462731. Includes bibliographical references (p. 271-284).*

373   Spanish nationalism: ethnic or civic? Diego Muro; Alejandro Quiroga. **Ethnicities** 5:1 3:2005 pp.9-29.

374   Theorizing nationalism. Graham Day; [Ed.]; Andrew Thompson. Basingstoke: Palgrave Macmillan, 2004. xii, 223p. *ISBN: 0333962648, 0333962656. Includes bibliographical references (p. 199-213) and index.*

375   Virtual sovereignty: nationalism, culture, and the Canadian question. Robert A. Wright. Toronto: Canadian Scholars' Press, 2004. 300p. *ISBN: 1551302586. Includes bibliographical references (p. 277-291) and index.*

376   What is national self-determination? Nationality and psychology during the apogee of nationalism. Glenda Sluga. **Nat. Nationalism** 11:1 1:2005 pp.1-20.

377   Zionism and the spirit of nations. Jacqueline Rose. **Soundings** 30 Summer:2005 pp.179-192.

Socialism
Socialisme

378   100 ans, 100 socialistes. *[In French]*; [100 years, 100 socialists]. Jean-Marc Binot; Denis Lefebvre; Pierre Serne. Paris: Bruno Leprince, 2005. 463p. *ISBN: 2909634949.*

379   The antinomies of Zizek. Geoff Boucher. **Telos** 129 Fall-Winter:2004 pp.151-172.

380   Communism, social democracy and the democracy gap. Stefan Berger. **Socialist Hist.** 27 2005 pp.1-20.

381   How the short course was created. Roy Medvedev. **Rus. Pol. Law** 43:3 5-6:2005 pp.69-95.

382   "Le trotskisme, une passion française". *[In French]*; ['Trotskyism, a French passion']. Marc Lazar. **Histoire** 285 3:2004 pp.75-85.

383   Permanence et métamorphoses du trotskisme. *[In French]*; [Permanence and metamorphoses of Trotskyism]. Jean-Pierre Le Goff. **Etudes** 400:1 2004 pp.43-55.

384   The postmodern prince: critical theory, left strategy, and the making of a new political subject. John Sanbonmatsu. New York: Monthly Review Press, 2004. 272p. *ISBN: 1583670904, 1583670890. Includes bibliographical references and index.*

385   Rothbard's time on the left. John Payne. **J. Libertarian S.** 19:1 Winter:2005 pp.7-24.

386   Sartre, Lukacs, Althusser: des marxistes en philosophie. *[In French]*; [Sartre, Lukacs, Althusser: philosophy's marxists]. Eustache Kouvelakis [Ed.]; Vincent Charbonnier [Ed.]; A. Chryssis [Contrib.]; M. Kail [Contrib.]; et al. Paris: Presses universitaires de France, 2005. 209p. *ISBN: 2130546765.*

387   Socialism and libertarianism. Peter McLaverty. **J. Pol. Ideol.** 10:2 6:2005 pp.185-198.

388   Le socialisme est-il soluble dans l'éthique ? *[In French]*; [Socialism and ethics]. Cahiers marxistes. 227 4-5:2004 pp.3-127.

389   Sovetskie ideologemy v russkom diskurse. *[In Russian]*; [Soviet ideologies in Russian discourse]. G.Ch. Guseinov. Moscow: Tri kvadrata, 2004. 269p. *ISBN: 594607024X. Includes bibliographical references (p. 947-[983]) and index.*

390   Strategies for the left: a symposium. Ed George; Rod Bush; Peter Hudis; Bertell Ollman; Steve Martinot; Joel Kovel; Ricardo Levins Morales; Aasim Sajjad Akhtar; Assata Zerai; Horace Campbell; Hamideh Sedghi; Stan Goff; Yusuf Nuruddin; Kevin Rashid Johnson; J.A. Shantz. **Soc. Dem.** 19:2 7:2005 pp.1-216. *Collection of 17 articles.*

391   The structure of Marx and Engels' considered account of utopian socialism. D. Leopold. **Hist. Pol. Thought** XXVI:3 Autumn:2005 pp.443-466.

392   A ticklish subject? Žižek and the future of left radicalism. Andrew Robinson; Simon Tormey. **Thes. Elev.** 80 2:2005 pp.94-107.

393   Vom Lügen — in Zeiten des Kommunismus. *[In German]*; [On lying –during communism]. Steffen Dietzsch. **Pol. Den. Jahr.** 2004 pp.125-145.

394   What is wrong with a free lunch? Legitimationsprobleme des Einkommensegalitarismus. *[In German]*; [Legitimacy problems of income egalitarianism]. Elmar Nass. **Z. Pol.** 51:4 12:2004 pp.456-469.

C.1: **Political institutions**
Institutions politiques

395 Les apprentissages mutuels de la Chine et de l'Inde. *[In French]*; [The mutual apprenticeships of China and India]. Amartya Sen. **Esprit** 312 2:2005 pp.88-100.

396 Bicameralism and policy performance: the effects of cameral structure in comparative perspective. Adrian Vatter. **J. Legis. St.** 11:2 Summer:2005 pp.194-215.

397 Bound for Canaan: the underground railroad and the war for the soul of America. Fergus M. Bordewich. New York: Amistad, 2005. xv,540p. *ISBN: 0060524308. Includes bibliographical references (p. 501-519) and index.*

398 Casualties and constituencies: democratic accountability, electoral institutions, and costly conflicts. Michael Koch; Scott Sigmund Gartner. **J. Confl. Resol.** 49:6 12:2005 pp.874-894.

399 Centripetal democratic governance: a theory and global inquiry. John Gerring; Strom C. Thacker; Carola Moreno. **Am. Pol. Sci. R.** 99:4 11:2005 pp.567-581.

400 La crisis de Argentina: reflexión sobre la representación política y la democracia. *[In Spanish]*; [Argentina' s crisis: reflection on political representation and democracy] *[Summary]*. Marina Larrondo; Nicolás Patrici. **Convergencia** 12:38 5-8:2005 pp.113-131.

401 Deliberative politics in action: analyzing parliamentary discourse. Jurg Steiner. et al; Cambridge: Cambridge University Press, 2004. vi, 199p. *ISBN: 0521828716, 0521535646. Includes bibliographical references (p. 180-193) and index. (Series:* Theories of institutional design).

402 A desconfiança nas instituições democráticas. *[In Portuguese]*; (The mistrust of democratic institutions.) *[Summary]*. José Álvaro Moisés. **Opin. Pub.** XI:1 3:2005 pp.33-63.

403 Erfolg und Versagen von Institutionen. *[In German]*; [Success and failure of institutions]. Thomas Apolte; Thomas Eger [Ed.]. Berlin: Duncker & Humblot, 2005. 220p. *ISBN: 342811731X.*

404 Institucionalni dizajn — najkonjunkturnija grana suvremene političke znanosti. *[In Croatian]*; (Institutional design — the most popular branch of contemporary political science.) *[Summary]*. Mirjana Kasapović. **Pol. Misao** 41:1 2004 pp.102-114.

405 Institutional dualism and international development a revisionist interpretation of good governance. Derick W. Brinkerhoff; Arthur A. Goldsmith. **Admin. Soc.** 37:2 5:2005 pp.199-224.

406 Les institutions politiques en danger. *[In French]*; (Political institutions at risk.) *[Summary]*. Marie Mendras. **Pouvoirs** 112 2004 pp.9-22.

407 Institutsional'nye lovushki: est' li vykhod? *[In Russian]*; (Institutional traps and ways out.) V. Polterovich. **Obshch. Nauki Sovrem.** 3 2004 pp.5-16.

408 Neo-liberalism and the decline of democratic governance in Australia: a problem of institutional design? Ian Marsh. **Pol. S.** 53:1 3:2005 pp.22-42.

409 Norms, interests and institutional change. Dionyssis G. Dimitrakopoulos. **Pol. S.** 53:4 12:2005 pp.676-693.

410 The political character of legal institutions and its conceptual significance. Mátyás Bódig. **Acta Jur. Hun.** 46:1-2 2005 pp.33-50.

411 Political institutions and economic policies: lessons from Africa. Macartan Humphreys; Robert Bates. **Br. J. Pol. Sci.** 35:3 7:2005 pp.403-428.

412 Political process and efficient institutional change. Yang Yao. **J. Inst. Theor. Econ.** 160:3 9:2004 pp.439-453.

413 Political time reconsidered: unbuilding and rebuilding the state under the Reagan administration. Daniel M. Cook; Andrew J. Polsky. **Am. Pol. Res.** 33:4 7:2005 pp.577-605.

414 Racism revised: courts, labor law, and the institutional construction of racial animus. Paul Frymer. **Am. Pol. Sci. R.** 99:3 8:2005 pp.373-388.

415 Real institutional responses to neoliberalism in Australia. Phillip O'Neill; Natalie Moore. **Aust. Geog. S.** 43:1 3:2005 pp.19-28.

416 The role of agency in cleavage formation. Z. Enyedi. **Écon. Sociét.** 44:5 8:2005 pp.697-720.

417 Sravnenie politicheskikh organov i konstitutsii Rossii i baltiiskikh stran: kul'turnaia obuslovlennost' i stechenie obstoiatel'stv. *[In Russian]*; (Comparison of political bodies and constitutions of Russia and the Baltic countries: cultural conditionality and concatenation of circumstances.) *[Summary]*. S. Nysten-Haarala. **Mir Rossii** XIII:3 2004 pp.131-160.

418 Vers une nouvelle gouvernance publique? La nouvelle loi budgétaire, la culture administrative et les pratiques décisionnelles. *[In French]*; [Towards a new public governance? The new budgetary law, administrative culture and decisional practices]. Bernard Perret; Sylvie Trosa. **Esprit** 312 2:2005 pp.65-87.

419 What are the political consequences of trust? A test of cultural and institutional theories in Russia. William Mishler; Richard Rose. **Comp. Pol. S.** 38:9 11:2005 pp.1050-1078.

420 What political institutions does large-scale democracy require? Robert A. Dahl. **Pol. Sci. Q.** 120:2 Summer:2005 pp.187-198.

421 Why the prime minister cannot be a president: comparing institutional imperatives in Britain and America. Richard Heffernan. **Parl. Aff.** 58:1 1:2005 pp.53-70.

C.1.1: **State and nation**
État et nation

422 Demokratische Staatlichkeit in Europa: Ein verblassendes Bild. *[In German]*; [Democratic states in Europe: a pale picture]. Helge Rossen-Stadtfeld. **Jahr. Öffent. Gegen.** 53 2005 pp.45-77.

423 From government to e-government: a transition model. Robert M. Davison; Christian Wagner; Louis C.K. Ma. **Info. Techno. People** 18:3 6:2005 pp.280-299.

424 Governance in contemporary Germany: the semisovereign state revisited. Simon Green [Ed.]; William E. Paterson [Ed.]. Cambridge, New York: Cambridge University Press, 2005. xii, 338p. *ISBN: 0521848814, 0521613167. Includes bibliographical references (p. 307-333) and index.*

425 The paradoxes of a regional construction [in Vojvodina]. Alpár Losoncz. **Regio** Supp 2004 pp.62-76.

426 El problema de gobernar. Hacia un nuevo diseño de gobernabilidad glocal postnacional. *[In Spanish]*; (The ruling issue towards a new design of post-national glocal governability.) *[Summary]*. José G. Vargas. **Trayectorias** 6:16 9-12:2004 pp.70-80.

427 Recognizing states and governments. Chris Naticchia. **Can. J. Philos.** 35:1 3:2005 pp.27-82.

428 Regional identities and meso-mega area dynamics in Slavic Eurasia: focused on Eastern Europe. Osamu Ieda. **Regio** Supp 2004 pp.3-22.

429 Restating the state? Andrew Gamble [Ed.]; Anthony Wright [Ed.]. Oxford: Blackwell Publishing Ltd., 2004. vi, 160p. *ISBN: 1405124547. Includes bibliographical references and index. The Political Quarterly.*

Nation
Nation

430   Anti-colonial nationalism and the West: toward a critique of recent, Western-based, anti-nationalist scholarship. Muhammed Noor Al-Abbood. **Dirasat Hum. Soc. Sci.** 32:1 2:2005 pp.213-231.

431   'Any place I hang my hat?' or: residence is the new nationality. Gareth Davies. **Euro. Law J.** 11:1 1:2005 pp.43-56.

432   Borroka — the legitimation of street violence in the political discourse of radical Basque nationalists. Hanspeter van den Broek. **Terror. Pol. Viol.** 16:4 Winter:2004 pp.714-736.

433   Brève psychanalyse de la France. *[In French]*; [A brief psychoanalysis of France]. Thierry Wolton. Paris: Plon, 2004. 265p. *ISBN: 2259199348. Includes bibliographical references.*

434   Building a new nation: collected articles on the Eritrean revolution (1983-2002). Dan Connell. Trenton NJ: Red Sea Press, 2004. *ISBN: 1569021988, 1569021996. Volume 2 of two volume series. Volume 1 "Taking on the superpowers". Includes bibliographical references and index.*

435   Competing institutions in national identity construction: the Croatian case. Mila Dragojević. **Nat. Ethn. Pol.** 11:1 Spring:2005 pp.61-87.

436   Contemporary Russian identity between East and West. Peter J.S. Duncan. **Hist. J.** 48:1 3:2005 pp.277-294.

437   La crisis del estado-nación en América Latina. *[In Spanish]*; [The nation state crisis in Latin America]. Michael Mann. **Desar. Econ.** 44:174 7-9:2004 pp.179-198.

438   The critical geopolitics of danger in Uzbekistan and Kyrgyzstan. Nick Megoran. **Env. Plan. D.** 23:4 8:2005 pp.555-580.

439   Dilemmas of autonomy and liberal pluralism: examples involving Hungarians in Central Europe. Stephen Deets; Sherrill Stroschein. **Nat. Nationalism** 11:2 4:2005 pp.285-305.

440   Disrespect and distrust: the external origins of contemporary Chinese nationalism. Jia Qingguo. **J. Cont. China** 14:42 2:2005 pp.11-22.

441   Do comparative and regional studies of nationalism intersect? Moshe Behar. **Int. J. Mid. East S.** 37:4 11:2005 pp.587-612.

442   Ethno-religious 'unmixing' of 'Turkey': 6-7 September riots as a case in Turkish nationalism. Ali Tuna Kuyucu. **Nat. Nationalism** 11:3 7:2005 pp.361-380.

443   Evolution of the Lithuanian national identity in the European context. Violetta Krakovska. **Slovo** 17:1 Spring:2005 pp.33-47.

444   The fate of the nation-state. Michel Seymour [Ed.]. Montreal: McGill-Queens University Press, 2004. vii, 441p. *ISBN: 0773526854, 0773526862. Includes bibliographical references and index.*

445   Globalisation, vulnerability and the role of the state: lessons for Ireland. Peadar Kirby. **Administration [Dublin]** 52:4 Winter:2004 pp.49-68.

446   The growth of English regionalism? Institutions and identity. Ross Bond; David McCrone. **Reg. Fed. S.** 14:1 Spring:2004 pp.1-25.

447   The hidden handshake: national identity and Europe in the post-communist world. Ales Debeljak; Rawley Grau [Tr.]. Lanham MD: Rowman & Littlefield, 2004. xiii, 123p. *ISBN: 0742517799, 0742517802. Includes bibliographical references (p. 111-114) and index.*

448   The Horn of Africa as common homeland: the state and self-determination in the era of heightened globalization. Leenco Lata. Waterloo: Wilfrid Laurier University Press, 2004. xi, 219p. *ISBN: 088920456X. Includes bibliographical references (p. 201-213) and index.*

449   Identifying Scotland and Wales: types of Scottish and Welsh national identities. Richard Haesly. **Nat. Nationalism** 11:2 4:2005 pp.243-263.

450   Imagining the Turkish nation through 'othering' Armenians. Ayla Göl. **Nat. Nationalism** 11:1 1:2005 pp.121-139.

451   Israeli identity in transition. Anita Shapira [Ed.]. Westport CT: Praeger Publishing, 2004. xii, 265p. *ISBN: 0275976602. (Series:* Jewish and Israeli studies).

452   Japan unbound: a volatile nation's quest for pride and purpose. John Nathan. Boston MA, New York: Houghton Mifflin, 2004. 271p. *ISBN: 0618138943. Includes bibliographical references and index.*

453   The liberty of strangers: making the American nation. Desmond S. King. New York: Oxford University Press, 2005. viii, 229p. *ISBN: 0195146387.*

454   Makedonische Identitäten und die Parameter Sprache, Ethnos und Nation. *[In German]*; [Macedonian identity and the parameters of language, ethnicity and nation]. Christian Voss. **Südosteuro. Mitteil.** 45:2 2005 pp.52-65.

455   Measuring gubernatorial ideology: a content analysis of state of the state speeches. Daniel Coffey. **State Pol. Policy Q.** 5:1 Spring:2005 pp.88-103.

456   The metaphysics of the national interest and the 'mysticism' of the nation-state. Véronique Pin-Fat. **R. Int. S.** 31:2 4:2005 pp.217-236.

457   Monténégro : démocratisation inachevée et débats autour de l'identité. *[In French]*; [Montenegro: uncompleted democratization and debates on identity] *[Summary]*. Florian Bieber. **Cour. Pays Est** 1043 5-6:2004 pp.76-89.

458   Narratives of nationalism in Eritrea: research and revisionism. Sara Rich Dorman. **Nat. Nationalism** 11:2 4:2005 pp.203-222.

459   Nationalism, ideology and China's 'Fourth generation' leadership. Ian Seckington. **J. Cont. China** 14:42 2:2005 pp.23-33.

460   Nationalism in New Caledonia. Alan B. Anderson; Kjell F. Anderson. **Can. R. S. Nation.** XXXI:1-2 2004 pp.91-106.

461   Nationalism in the French Basque country. Igor Ahedo Gurrutxaga. **Reg. Fed. S.** 15:1 Spring:2005 pp.75-91.

462   Nationalism, international factors and the 'Irish question' in the era of the First World War. Karen Stanbridge. **Nat. Nationalism** 11:1 1:2005 pp.21-42.

463   Nationalist idealisation and the state. Paul Howe. **Nat. Ident.** 7:1 3:2005 pp.79-102.

464   Nation-building through discourse theory. Claire Sutherland. **Nat. Nationalism** 11:2 4:2005 pp.185-202.

465   Les nations et leur destin : l'état-nation démocratique, seule communauté politique vivante aujourd'hui. *[In French]*; [Nations and their destiny: the democratic nation state as only living political community nowadays]. Pierre de Lauzun. Paris: Editions François-Xavier de Guibert, 2005. 217p. *ISBN: 286839714X.*

466   Patriotismus in Deutschland: Perspektiven für eine weltoffene Nation. *[In German]*; [Patriotism in Germany: perspectives of a cosmopolitan nation]. Volker Kronenberg. Wiesbaden: VS Verlag fur Sozialwissenschaften, 2005. 418p. *ISBN: 353114491X.*

467   Die Perspektive einer Perspektive Moldova und die Neue Nachbarschaftspolitik der EU. *[In German]*; (A perspective on a perspective: Moldova and the EU's new neighbourhood policy.) Anneli Ute Gabanyi. **Osteuropa** 55:2 2:2005 pp.24-39.

468   Politische Räume und nationale Identität. Der Mitteleuropadiskurs in der Tschechischen Republik. *[In German]*; (Political spaces and national identity. The discourse on Central Europe in the Czech Republic.) Steffi Franke. **Z. Int. Beziehung.** 11:2 12:2004 pp.203-238.

469   Post-Zionist perspectives on contemporary Israel. Jan Selby. **New Pol. Econ.** 10:1 3:2005 pp.107-120.

470   Problém integrace národních identit v procesu evropského sjednocování. *[In Czech]*; (The integration of national identities in the process of European unification.) *[Summary]*. Jan Pauer. **Soud. Děj.** XI:1-2 2004 pp.128-140.

471   Reframing sovereignty? Sub-state national societies and contemporary challenges to the nation-state. Stephen Tierney. **Int. Comp. Law Q.** 54:1 1:2005 pp.161-183.

472   Reinventing Korea. Eric J. Heikkila. **J. East Asian Aff.** XIX:1 Spring-Summer:2005 pp.27-45.

473   Rights to recognition: minority/indigenous politics in the emerging Taiwanese nationalism. Kun-hui Ku. **Soc. Anal. [Adelaide]** 49:2 Summer:2005 pp.99-121.

474   Rozhdenie natsii. *[In Russian]*; (The birth of a nation.) *[Summary]*. Valerii Solovei. **Svobod. Mysl'** 6 2005 pp.3-17.

475 Russia and the west: is there a values gap? Stephen White; Margot Light; Ian McAllister. **Int. Pol.** 42:3 9:2005 pp.314-333.

476 Russia's identity quest. Vladislav Martin Zubok. **Orbis** 49:1 Winter:2005 pp.183-193.

477 The shifting foundations of modern nation states: realignments of belonging. Frank Unger [Ed.]; Sima Godfrey [Ed.]. Toronto: University of Toronto Press, 2004. vi, 164p. *ISBN: 0802035019, 0802083943.* (*Series:* Green College thematic lecture).

478 Sobre la construcción y deconstrucción de Irak. *[In Spanish]*; [On Iraq's construction and deconstruction] *[Summary]*. Norberto Raúl Méndez. **Convergencia** 12:38 5-8:2005 pp.155-184.

479 State-building in Southern Iraq. Hilary Synnott. **Survival** 47:2 Summer:2005 pp.33-55.

480 Suverenost nacionalne države u eri globalizacije: teorijsko razmatranje. *[In Croatian]*; (Sovereignty of the nation-state in the era of globalization: a theory.) Abolade Adeniji. **Pol. Misao** 41:3 2004 pp.132-142.

481 'The tears of Portugal': empire, identity, 'race', and destiny in Portuguese geopolitical narratives. James D. Sidaway; Marcus Power. **Env. Plan. D.** 23:4 8:2005 pp.527-554.

482 True faith and allegiance: immigration and American civic nationalism. Noah M. Jedidiah Pickus. Princeton NJ: Princeton University Press, 2005. xiii, 257p. *ISBN: 0691121729. Includes bibliographical references and index.*

483 Unity in diversity: contending conceptions of the French nation and republic. Veronique Dimier. **West Euro. Pol.** 27:5 11:2004 pp.836-853.

484 War, rivalry, and state building in Latin America. Cameron G. Thies. **Am. J. Pol. Sci.** 49:3 7:2005 pp.451-465.

485 White Australia, settler nationalism and aboriginal assimilation. Anthony Moran. **Aust. J. Pol. Hist.** 51:2 6:2005 pp.168-193.

486 Wo wir uns finden: die Berliner Republik als Vaterland. *[In German]*; [Where we find ourselves: the Berlin Republic as fatherland]. Eckhard Fuhr. Berlin: Berlin Verlag, 2005. 156p. *ISBN: 3827005698.*

487 Zwischen nationaler Identität und Verfassungspatriotismus: Deutungsmuster der politischen Gemeinschaft in der Bundesrepublik Deutschland 1972-1989. *[In German]*; (Between national identity and constitutional patriotism: patterns of interpretation of political community in the Federal Republic of Germany 1972-1989.) Mateusz Stachura. **Polit. Viertel.** 46:2 6:2005 pp.288-312.

State formation
Construction de l'État

488 Den europæiske stats dannelse. *[In Danish]*; (The formation of the European state.) *[Summary]*. Gorm Harste. **Politica** 37:1 2:2005 pp.21-43.

489 El despliegue del estado en Buenos Aires: de Rosas a Mitre. *[In Spanish]*; [The deployment of state in Buenos Aires: From Rosas to Mitre] *[Summary]*. Juan Carlos Garavaglia. **Desar. Econ.** 44:175 10-12:2004 pp.415-445.

490 The early state, its alternatives and analogues. L.E. Grinin. Volgograd: Uchitel Publishing House, 2004. vi, 535p. *ISBN: 5705705476. Includes bibliographical references.*

491 Episteme, nation-builders and national identity: the re-construction of Irishness. Markus Kornprobst. **Nat. Nationalism** 11:3 7:2005 pp.403-421.

492 The instruction of great catastrophe: truth commissions, national history, and state formation in Argentina, Chile, and Guatemala. Greg Grandin. **Am. Hist. R.** 110:1 2:2005 pp.46-67.

493 Kazakhstan's kin state diaspora: settlement planning and the Oralman dilemma. Alexander C. Diener. **Euro.-Asia S.** 57:2 3:2005 pp.327-348.

494 Language and nation-building in Israel: Hebrew and its rivals. William Safran. **Nat. Nationalism** 11:1 1:2005 pp.43-63.

495 Die polnische Historiographie und der polnisch-litauische Staatsverband — multinationales Erbe und polnische Geschichtsschreibung. *[In German]*; [Polish

historiography and Polish-Lithuanian state formation –multinational region and Polish historiography]. Bogusław Dybaś. **Z. Ostmit.euro.-Forsch.** 53:3 2004 pp.351-362.

496   Timor Lorosa'e : naissance d'un nouvel état. *[In French]*; (The birth of Timor Loro'Sae, a new state.) *[Summary]*. Olivier Sevin. **Cah. Outre-Mer** 57:228 10-12:2004 pp.387-424.

497   Working with the warlords: designing an ethnofederal system for Afghanistan. Scott Radnitz. **Reg. Fed. S.** 14:4 Winter:2004 pp.513-537.

State fragmentation
Fragmentation de l'État

498   L'alienation corse. *[In French]*; [Corsican alienation]. Iviu Bourdiec. Paris: L'Harmattan, 2005. 141p. *ISBN: 2747591557.*

499   Bandits on the border: the last frontier in the search for Somali unity. Nene Mburu. Trenton NJ: Red Sea Press, 2005. xii, 263p. *ISBN: 1569022267, 1569022275. Includes bibliographical references and index.*

500   The cross-sectional determinants of secessionism in advanced democracies. Jason Sorens. **Comp. Pol. S.** 38:3 4:2005 pp.304-326.

501   Cultural determinism, Western hegemony and the efficacy of defective states. Tim Jacoby. **R. Afr. Pol. Econ.** 32:104-105 6-9:2005 pp.215-234.

502   Factionalism and secession in North Sulawesi province, Indonesia. Michael Jacobsen. **Asian J. Pol. Sci.** 12:1 6:2004 pp.65-94.

503   The next Yugoslavia? The fragmentation of Indonesia. David Armstrong. **Dipl. State.** 15:4 12:2004 pp.783-808.

504   Political fragmentation in Southeast Asia: alternative nations in the making. Vivenne Wee. New York, London: RoutledgeCurzon, 2004. 256p. *ISBN: 0415318610. (Series: RoutledgeCurzon/City University of Hong Kong South East Asia).*

505   A politics of sorrow: the disintegration of Yugoslavia. Davorka. Ljubisic. Montreal: Black Rose Books, 2004. xxviii, 194p. *ISBN: 1551642328, 1551642336. Includes bibliographical references (p. 184-188) and index.*

506   Povjesničari u potrazi za istinom o sukobima na prostoru bivše Jugoslavije u svojstvu vještaka pred ICTY-em. *[In Croatian]*; (The historians in search for truth about conflicts in the territory of former Yugoslavia as expert witness in front of the ICTY.) Ksenija Turković. **Čas. Suvr. Povi.** 36:1 2004 pp.15-70.

507   Vještački nalaz: o ratnim vezama Hrvatske i Bosne i Hercegovine (1991-1995). *[In Croatian]*; (Expert opinion: on the war connections of Croatia and Bosnia and Herzegovina (1991-1995).) Davor Marijan. **Čas. Suvr. Povi.** 36:1 2004 pp.211-292.

508   Yugoslavia: when ideals collide. Ann Lane. Basingstoke: Palgrave Macmillan, 2004. xii, 218p. *ISBN: 0333786629, 0333786637. Includes bibliographical references and index. (Series:* The making of the twentieth century).

State structure
Structure de l'État

509   Austria: a federation without federalism. Jan Erk. **Publius** 34:1 Winter:2004 pp.1-20.

510   Bosnien-Herzegowina zwischen Nachkrieg und Selbstverantwortung. *[In German]*; [Post-war Bosnia and Herzegovina and independence]. Roland Schönfeld. **Südosteuro. Mitteil.** 45:1 2005 pp.26-41.

511   Bremst der Föderalismus den Leviathan? Bundesstaat und Sozialstaat im internationalen Vergleich, 1880-2005. *[In German]*; (Reining in the Leviathan? Federalism and the welfare state, 1880-2005.) Francis G. Castles; Herbert Obinger; Stephan Leibfried. **Polit. Viertel.** 46:2 6:2005 pp.215-237.

512   The challenges of contracting and accountability across the federal system: from ambulances to space shuttles. Jocelyn M. Johnston; Barbara S. Romzek; Curtis H. Wood. **Publius** 34:3 Summer:2004 pp.155-182.

513   China as a normal state? Understanding China's unfinished transformation from state socialisation perspective. Zhongying Pang. **J. East Asian Aff.** XVIII:2 Fall-Winter:2004 pp.340-370.

514   Conceptions of political representation in Canada: an explanation of public opinion. Cameron D. Anderson; Elizabeth Goodyear-Grant. **Can. J. Pol.** 38:4 12:2005 pp.1029-1060.

515   Conservative perspectives on American federalism. Kimberly Hendrickson; Eric R. Claeys; Jeremy David Bailey; Jonathan H. Adler; John Kincaid; Craig Volden; Gerald J. Russello; Robert F. Nagel; G. Patrick Lynch. **Publius** 34:4 Fall:2004 pp.1-167. *Collection of 10 articles.*

516   Deadly ethnic: conflict and the imperative of power sharing: could a consociational federalism hold in Rwanda? Raphael Chijioke Njoku. **Commonwealth Comp. Pol.** 43:1 3:2005 pp.82-101.

517   Decentralization in the Czech Republic: the European Union, political parties, and the creation of regional assemblies. James T. LaPlant; Michael Baun; Jiri Lach; Dan Marek. **Publius** 34:1 Winter:2004 pp.35-52.

518   The dynamics of "real federalism": law, economic development, and indigenous communities in Russia and Canada. Peter H. Solomon [Ed.]. Toronto: University of Toronto Press, 2004. xi, 162p. *ISBN: 0969772394. Includes bibliographical references.*

519   An emerging cross-boundary metropolis in China: Hong Kong and Shenzhen under 'two systems'. Chun Yang. **Int. Dev. Plan. R.** 27:2 2005 pp.194-226.

520   Exploring the paradox of autonomy: federalism and secession in North America. Lawrence M. Anderson. **Reg. Fed. S.** 14:1 Spring:2004 pp.89-112.

521   Facial challenges and federalism. Gillian E. Metzger. **Columb. Law R.** 105:3 4:2005 pp.873-932.

522   Federalism and democracy in Moldova. Oleh Protsyk. **Post-Sov. Aff.** 21:1 1-3:2005 pp.72-90.

523   Federalism and the adjudication of constitutional issues: the Ethiopian experience. A. Fiseha. **Neth. Int. Law R.** LII:1 2005 pp.1-30.

524   Federalism and the evolving cross-border role of provincial, state, and municipal governments. Earl H. Fry. **Int. J.** LX:2 Spring:2005 pp.471-482.

525   Federalism within the Union: distribution of responsibilities in the Indian system. Akhtar Majeed [Ed.]; Jamia Hamdard, New Delhi. New Delhi: Manak Publications, 2004. 197p. *ISBN: 8178270927. Centre for Federal Studies, Hamdard University.*

526   Le fédéralisme renforcé : la jurisprudence de la Cour constitutionnelle fédérale allemande en 2004. *[In French]*; [Reinforced federalism: jurisprudence of the German Federal Constitutional Court in 2004]. Rainer Arnold. **R. Int. Droit Comp.** 56:4 10-12:2004 pp.917-927.

527   Federalismo e nazionalismo: il federalismo asimmetrico. *[In Italian]*; (Federalism and nationalism: asymmetric federalism.) Sofia Ventura. **Riv. It. Sci. Pol.** XXXIV:3 12:2004 pp.405-432.

528   Federalizm i regional'naia politika v Rossii v usloviiakh ukrepleniia vertikali vlasti. *[In Russian]*; (Federalism and regional policy under the strengthened power vertical.) *[Summary]*. V.E. Seliverstov. **Region** 1 2004 pp.26-56.

529   Federalizm kak sud'ba mnogonatsional'noi Rossii. *[In Russian]*; (Federalism as the appropriate state structure for Russia.) *[Summary]*. V.Iu. Zorin. **Region** 1 2004 pp.9-25.

530   Fiscal federalism in Russia: rules versus electoral politics. Vladimir Popov. **Comp. Econ. S.** 46:4 12:2004 pp.515-541.

531   Föderalismus: to be or not to be? Das Gebiet Sverdlovsk im Föderationsgefüge Rußlands. *[In German]*; (Federalism: to be or not to be? Sverdlovsk region in Russia's federal structure.) Hagen Ettner. **Osteuropa** 55:2 2:2005 pp.58-74.

532   Föderalismus und Wohlfahrtsstaat im historischen Kontext: Der Fall Kanada. *[In German]*; (Federalism and the welfare state in historical context: the case of Canada.) Jörg Broschek. **Polit. Viertel.** 46:2 6:2005 pp.238-262.

533   Fractured federalism: Nigeria's lessons for today's nation builders in Iraq. Adam M. Smith. **Round Tab.** 378 1:2005 pp.129-144.

534   Garantii gosudarstvennoi tselostnosti Rossiiskoi Federatsii: politicheskie i pravovye mekhanizmy. *[In Russian]*; [Integrity of the Russian state: political and legal aspects]. V.F. Kalina; V.B. Kudriavtsev. **Sots.Gum. Znan.** 1 2004 pp.49-63.

535   Government responsibility and electoral accountability in federations. Fred Cutler. **Publius** 34:2 Spring:2004 pp.19-38.

536   Guess what happened on the way to revolution? Precursors to the Supreme Court's federalism revolution. Cornell W. Clayton; J. Mitchell Pickerill. **Publius** 34:3 Summer:2004 pp.85-114.

537   Hinaus aus der Selbstblockade — Ziele und Wege zur Reform des Föderalismus. *[In German]*; [Out of self-inflicted blockade: the reform of the federalist state]. Rudolf Hrbek; Martin T.W. Rosenfeld; Gerhard Schick. **Z. Wirt.pol.** 54:2 2005 pp.177-208.

538   The institutional basis of secessionist politics: federalism and secession in the United States. Lawrence M. Anderson. **Publius** 34:2 Spring:2004 pp.1-18.

539   Inter-institutional relations in the devolved Great Britain: quiet diplomacy. Gerard W. Horgan. **Reg. Fed. S.** 14:1 Spring:2004 pp.113-135.

540   Making tradeoffs in federal block grant programs: understanding the interplay between SSBG and TANF. Kristina T. Lambright; Scott W. Allard. **Publius** 34:3 Summer:2004 pp.131-154.

541   Die modifizierte Senatslösung. Ein Vorschlag zur Verringerung von Reformblockaden im deutschen Föderalismus. *[In German]*; (The modified senate solution. How to reduce reform blockades in German federalism.) *[Summary]*. Uwe Wagschal; Maximilian Grasl. **Z. Parlament.** 35:4 12:2004 pp.732-752.

542   Moreno's multiple ethnoterritorial concurrence model: a re-formulation. André Lecours. **Reg. Fed. S.** 14:1 Spring:2004 pp.66-88.

543   The new federalism and the paradoxes of regional sovereignty in Russia. Donna Bahry. **Comp. Pol.** 37:2 1:2005 pp.127-146.

544   The new political economy of federal preservation: insights from Nigerian federal practice. John Boye Ejobowah. **Commonwealth Comp. Pol.** 43:2 7:2005 pp.178-193.

545   On the endogenous allocation of decision powers in federal structures. Oliver Lorz; Gerald Willmann. **J. Urb. Econ.** 57:2 3:2005 pp.242-257.

546   One continent, two federalisms: rediscovering the original meanings of Australian federal ideas. A.J. Brown. **Aust. J. Pol. Sci.** 39:3 11:2004 pp.485-504.

547   Ot federalisma k korporativnomu gosudarstvu. *[In Russian]*; (From federalism to a corporate state.) *[Summary]*. Nikolai Dobrynin. **Svobod. Mysl'** 6 2005 pp.22-32.

548   Rethinking the origins of federalism: puzzle, theory, and evidence from nineteenth-century Europe. Daniel Ziblatt. **World Pol.** 57:1 10:2004 pp.70-98.

549   The riddle of federalism: does federalism impact on democracy? Jan-Erik Lane; Svante Ersson. **Democratization** 12:2 4:2005 pp.163-182.

550   (The rise of regions and the clogging of "double-track politics" —Fei Xiaotong's reconstructing earthbound China reconsidered.); *[Text in Chinese]*. Xin He. **Hong Kong J. Soc. Sci.** 27 Spring-Summer:2004 pp.27-40.

551   Smeshannye formy pravleniia, ili 'kak maslo soediniaetsia s vodoi'. *[In Russian]*; (Mixed forms of government, or 'how oil will mix with water'.) *[Summary]*. O.I. Zaznaev. **Polis [Moscow]** 4(87) 2005 pp.158-171.

552   The state of American federalism, 2003-2004: polarized politics and federalist principles. Dale Krane. **Publius** 34:3 Summer:2004 pp.1-53.

553   Strengthening the political safeguards of federalism: the fate of recent federalism legislation in the U.S. Congress. John Dinan. **Publius** 34:3 Summer:2004 pp.55-83.

554   Surrogat imperii: o prirode i proiskhozhdenii federativnoi politicheskoi formy. *[In Russian]*; (Empire substitute: on the nature and origin of federative political form.) *[Summary]*. S.I. Kaspe. **Polis [Moscow]** 4(87) 2005 pp.5-29.

555   A theory of atomistic federalism for Melanesia. Philip T. Powell. **Pac. Econ. B.** 19:3 2004 pp.49-63.

556 William Riker on federalism: sometimes wrong but more right than anyone else? David McKay. **Reg. Fed. S.** 14:2 Summer:2004 pp.167-186.

State-society relations
Relations État-société

557 Arenas of citizenship: civil society, state and the global order. Alison M. Jaggar. **Int. Femin. J. Pol.** 7:1 2005 pp.3-25.

558 Between a rock and a hard place: African NGOs, donors and the state. Jim Igoe [Ed.]; Tim Kelsall [Ed.]. Durham NC: Carolina Academic Press, 2005. xvii, 309p. *ISBN: 1594600171. Includes bibliographical references and index.*

559 Caught in the headlights of history: Eritrea, the EPLF and the post-war nation-state. Richard Reid. **J. Mod. Afr. S.** 43:3 9:2005 pp.467-488.

560 Challenging traditional authority: the role of the state, the divine and the RSS. Peggy Froerer. **Contrib. Indian Sociol.** 39:1 1-4:2005 pp.39-74.

561 Citizenship and the biopolitics of post-nationalist Ireland. John A. Harrington. **J. Law Soc.** 32:3 9:2005 pp.424-449.

562 Citizenship for all. Barry Hindess. **Citiz. S.** 8:3 9:2004 pp.305-315.

563 Citizenship in a time of empire: the World Social Forum as a new public space. Janet Conway. **Citiz. S.** 8:4 12:2004 pp.367-381.

564 Civil society and federalism in Nigeria. Said Adejumobi. **Reg. Fed. S.** 14:2 Summer:2004 pp.211-231.

565 Civil society and public sector institutions: more than a zero-sum relationship. N. Uphoff; A. Krishna. **Publ. Admin. Dev.** 24:4 10:2004 pp.357-372.

566 Civil society in self-defense: the struggle against national security legislation in Hong Kong. Ngok Ma. **J. Cont. China** 14:44 8:2005 pp.465-482.

567 Civil society redefined. Sujit Lahiry. **Indian J. Pol. Sci.** LXVI:1 1-3:2005 pp.29-50.

568 Civilno društvo i demokracija. *[In Croatian]*; (Civil society and democracy.) Walter Reese-Schäfer. **Pol. Misao** 41:3 2004 pp.65-79.

569 Communicating global citizenship: multiple discourses beyond the academy. Hans Schattle. **Citiz. S.** 9:2 5:2005 pp.119-133.

570 Community consultation in public policy: the case of the Murray-Darling basin of Australia. Lin Crase; Brian Dollery; Joe Wallis. **Aust. J. Pol. Sci.** 40:2 6:2005 pp.221-237.

571 Deconstructing Balkan particularlism: the ambiguous social capital of Southeast Europe. Alina Mungiu-Pippidi. **J. Sth.East Euro. Black Sea S.** 5:1 1:2005 pp.49-68.

572 Deepening democracy or defending the nation? The europeanisation of minority rights and Greek citizenship. Dia Anagnostou. **West Euro. Pol.** 28:2 3:2005 pp.335-357.

573 Demokratiia i grazhdanskoe obshchestvo v Rossii. *[In Russian]*; [Democracy and civil society in Russia]. A.R. Tuzikov. **Sots.Gum. Znan.** 5 2004 pp.194-206.

574 "El mal samaritano": ni santo, ni genio, ni heroe (solidaridad y voluntariado). *[In Spanish]*; ['The bad Samaritan': neither saint, nor genius, or hero (solidarity and voluntary work)] *[Summary]*. Antonio Gutierrez Resa. **Sistema** 186 5:2005 pp.85-100.

575 Ethnic citizenship in the Slovenian state. Jelka Zorn. **Citiz. S.** 9:2 5:2005 pp.135-152.

576 Europäische Konvergenzen: Zur Restitution von Staatsangehörigkeit in Deutschland, Frankreich und Großbritannien. *[In German]*; (European convergences: towards restitution of nationality in Germany, France and Great Britain.) Christine Weinbach. **Berl. J. Soziol.** 15:2 2005 pp.199-218.

577 Evidence-based engagement in the voluntary sector: lessons from Canada. Rachel Laforest; Michael Orsini. **Soc. Policy Admin.** 39:5 10:2005 pp.481-497.

578 Expectations and practice in social citizenship: some insights from an attitude survey in a Chinese society. Chack-kie Wong; Ka-ying Wong. **Soc. Policy Admin.** 39:1 2:2005 pp.19-34.

579 Gewalt und Partizipation. Die Zivilgesellschaft im Zeitalter des Bellizismus. *[In German]*; [Violence and participation. The civil society in the age of war]. Jörn Leonhard. **Mittelweg 36** 14:4 7-9:2005 pp.49-69.

580 The idea of citizenship in the early civil rights movement. Michael Dennis. **Citiz. S.** 9:2 5:2005 pp.181-203.

581 Images revisited — postmodern perceptions of power and democracy: political empowerment in the Danish case. Niels Nørgaard Kristensen. **Scand. Pol. S.** 28:1 2005 pp.47-68.

582 Indian diaspora: projecting India's image. Fahmida Ashraf. **Strat. S.** XXV:1 Spring:2005 pp.33-48.

583 Interpreting e-government and development: efficiency, transparency or governance at a distance? Claudio Ciborra. **Info. Techno. People** 18:3 6:2005 pp.260-279.

584 Lula et la diversification de la société brésilienne. *[In French]*; [Lula and the diversification of Brazilian society]. Problèmes d'Amérique latine. **Prob. Am. Lat.** 52 Spring:2004 pp.7-98.

585 Managed participation in China. Yongshun Cai. **Pol. Sci. Q.** 119:3 Fall:2004 pp.425-451.

586 'Marshall-ing' social and political citizenship: towards a unified conception of citizenship. Michael Lister. **Gov. Oppos.** 40:4 Autumn:2005 pp.471-491.

587 Micro- and macrolevel models of the presidential expectations gap. Hank C. Jenkins-Smith; Carol L. Silva; Richard W. Waterman. **J. Pol.** 67:3 8:2005 pp.690-715.

588 Migration and citizenship. Gail Lewis; Sarah Neal; Rosemary Sales; Don Flynn; Alice Bloch; Liza Schuster; Nira Yuval-Davis; Floya Anthias; Eleonore Kofman; Anne-Marie Fortier. **Ethn. Racial S.** 28:3 5:2005 pp.423-578. *Collection of 7 articles.*

589 Neither seen nor heard: children's citizenship in contemporary democracies. Elizabeth F. Cohen. **Citiz. S.** 9:2 5:2005 pp.221-240.

590 The neurotic citizen. Engin F. Isin. **Citiz. S.** 8:3 9:2004 pp.217-236.

591 The new governance: practices and processes for stakeholder and citizen participation in the work of government. Lisa Blomgren Bingham; Tina Nabatchi; Rosemary O'Leary. **Publ. Admin. R.** 65:5 9-10:2005 pp.547-558.

592 New perspectives on politics and society. Steve Ellner; Miguel Tinker Salas. **Lat. Am. Persp.** 32:3(142) 5:2005 pp.3-7.

593 On the enchantment of the state; *[Summary in French]*; *[Summary in German]*. Sudipta Kaviraj. **Euro. J. Sociol.** XLVI:2 2005 pp.263-296.

594 Por uma outra justiça: direito penal, Estado e sociedade. *[In Portuguese]*; (Toward another justice: penal law, state and society.) *[Summary]*; *[Summary in French]*. Daniel dos Santos. **R. Sociol. Pol.** 23 11:2004 pp.127-139.

595 Por una nueva ciudadania. Una re-lectura y un punto de partida. *[In Spanish]*; [Towards a new citizenship] *[Summary]*. Jose Maria Seco Martinez; Rafael Rodriguez Prieto. **Sistema** 188 9:2005 pp.15-32.

596 The predicament of 'civil society' in Central Asia and the 'greater Middle East'. Olivier Roy. **Int. Aff. [London]** 81:5 10:2005 pp.1001-1012.

597 Protesting against citizenship. Nick Vaughan-Williams. **Citiz. S.** 9:2 5:2005 pp.167-179.

598 The quality of democracy in Belarus and Ukraine. Elena A. Korosteleva. **J. Comm. S. Transit. Pol.** 20:1 3:2004 pp.122-142.

599 Redefining community-state partnership in natural resource management: a case from India. Chetan Kumar; Umar Shankar Vashisht. **Dev. Pract.** 15:1 2:2005 pp.28-39.

600 Retreating state and common man. Hoshiar Singh. **Indian J. Pol. Sci.** 65:3 7-9:2004 pp.301-316.

601 The self-institution of society and representative government: can the circle be squared? Jean L. Cohen. **Thes. Elev.** 80 2:2005 pp.9-37.

602 The skeptical American: revisiting the meanings of trust in government and confidence in institutions. Timothy E. Cook; Paul Gronke. **J. Pol.** 67:3 8:2005 pp.784-803.

603 Social capital and democratic citizenship: the case of South Korea. Chong-Min Park; Doh Chull Shin. **Japanese J. Pol. Sci.** 6:1 4:2005 pp.63-86.

604 Social movements and state power: Argentina, Brazil, Bolivia, Ecuador. James F. Petras; Henry. Veltmeyer. London, Ann Arbor MI: Pluto Press, 2005. xi, 274p. *ISBN: 0745324231, 0745324223. Includes bibliographical references and index.*

605 Sociedad civil y sociedad política durante el primer peronismo. *[In Spanish]*; [Civil society and political society during Peronism]. Omar Acha. **Desar. Econ.** 44:174 7-9:2004 pp.199-230.

606 La société civile en question : pentecôtisme et démocratie. *[In French]*; (Pentecostalism and democracy: civil society revisited.) *[Summary]*. André Corten. **Tiers Monde** XLVI:181 1-3:2005 pp.167-183.

607 State and society in 21st century China: crisis, contention, and legitimation. Peter Hays Gries [Ed.]; Stanley Rosen [Ed.]. New York: Routledge, 2004. *ISBN: 0415332044, 0415332052.* (*Series:* Asia's transformations).

608 State and society in the Philippines. P. N. Abinales; Donna J. Amoroso. Lanham MD: Rowman & Littlefield, 2005. xxxiv, 351p. *ISBN: 0742510239, 0742510247.* (*Series:* State and society in East Asia).

609 Three theses on 'governance' and the political. Sergei Prozorov. **J. Int. Rel. Dev.** 7:3 10:2004 pp.267-293.

610 Tietoyhteiskunta identiteettiprojektina –demokraattinen kansalaisuus verkossa. *[In Finnish]*; [Knowledge society as an identity project –democratic citizenship on the net] *[Summary]*. Tapio Häyhtiö. **Politiikka** 46:4 2004 pp.277-291.

611 Ukotvljene i manjkave demokracije. *[In Croatian]*; (Embedded and defective democracies.) Wolfgang Merkel. **Pol. Misao** 41:3 2004 pp.80-104.

612 Uzbekistan: civil society in the heartland. Chris Seiple. **Orbis** 49:2 Spring:2005 pp.245-259.

613 Vladimir Putin i intelligentsiia. *[In Russian]*; [Vladimir Putin and intelligentsia]. O.I. Karpukhin; E.F. Makarevich. **Sots.Gum. Znan.** 4 2004 pp.36-49.

C.1.2: **Constitution**
Constitution

614 'A decent respect to the opinions of [human]kind': the value of a comparative perspective in constitutional adjudication. Ruth Bader Ginsburg. **Camb. Law J.** 64:3 11:2005 pp.575-592.

615 Afghanistan's constitution: success or sham? Carol Riphenburg. **Mid. East Policy** XII:1 Spring:2005 pp.31-43.

616 Against originalism: getting over the U.S. constitution. Austin Bramwell. **Crit. R.** 16:4 Fall:2004 pp.431-453.

617 The coherentism of Democracy and distrust. Michael C. Dorf. **Yale Law J.** 114:6 4:2005 pp.1237-1278.

618 Le conseil constitutionnel en questions. *[In French]*; [The constitutional council in questions]. Dominique Rousseau [Ed.]; Philippe Blachèr [Contrib.]; et al. Paris: L'Harmattan, 2004. 175p. *ISBN: 2747569470.*

619 Constitution as executive order: the administrative state and the political ontology of 'we the people'. Thomas J. Catlaw. **Admin. Soc.** 37:4 9:2005 pp.445-482.

620 The constitution of India: symbol of unity in diversity. Mahendra Pal Singh; Surya Deva. **Jahr. Öffent. Gegen.** 53 2005 pp.649-686.

621 The constitutional adjudication mosaic of Latin America. Patricio Navia; Julio Ríos-Figueroa. **Comp. Pol. S.** 38:2 3:2005 pp.189-217.

622 Constitutional odyssey: can Canadians become a sovereign people. Peter H. Russell. Toronto: University of Toronto Press, 2004. x, 364p. *ISBN: 0802039367, 0802037771. Includes bibliographical references and index.*

623 Constitutional theory: a 25th anniversary essay. Martin Loughlin. **Oxf. J. Leg. S.** 25:2 Summer:2005 pp.183-202.

624 Dialogues sur les origines, structures et changements constitutionnels dans les pays fédéraux. *[In French]*; [Dialogues on constitutional origins, structure and change in federal countries]. Raoul Blindenbacher [Ed.]; Abigail J. Ostien [Ed.]. Montreal: McGill-Queens University Press, 2005. ix, 77p. *ISBN: 0773529446. Translated from the English* Dialogues on constitutional origins, structure and change in federal countries. *Forum des fédérations. International Association of Centers for Federal Studies.*

625 Direkte Demokratie und Verfassungsgerichtsbarkeit. *[In German]*; [Direct democracy and constitutional jurisdiction]. Fabian Wittreck. **Jahr. Öffent. Gegen.** 53 2005 pp.111-185.

626 The dynamic constitution: an introduction to American constitutional law. Richard H. Fallon. Cambridge, New York: Cambridge University Press, 2004. xxi, 336p. *ISBN: 0521840945, 0521600782. Includes bibliographical references (p. 299-325) and index.*

627 Empire-building government in constitutional law. Daryl J. Levinson. **Harv. Law R.** 118:3 1:2005 pp.915-972.

628 Das erste Dutzend Jahre verfassungsrechtliche Entwicklung in Turkmenistan. *[In German]*; [The first 12 years of the development of constitutional rights in Turkmenistan]. Thietmar Bachmann. **Jahr. Öffent. Gegen.** 53 2005 pp.687-702.

629 The extra-territorial application of the South African constitution. Max du Plessis. **Sth. Afr. Law. J.** 121:4 2004 pp.797-819.

630 Författningsändring och problemlösning : en studie av kvalificerade majoriteter i 34 stater. *[In Swedish]*; [Constitutional amendment and problem-solving: supermajorities in 34 states] *[Summary]*. Dag Anckar. **Politiikka** 46:4 2004 pp.239-249.

631 From Linz to Tsebelis: three waves of presidential/parliamentary studies? Robert Elgie. **Democratization** 12:1 2:2005 pp.106-122.

632 Idee sulla costituzione, tra teoria delle fonti e teoria dell'interpretazione. *[In Italian]*; [Ideas on the constitution, between the theory of the sources and the theory of interpretation]. Antonio Ruggeri. **Rass. Parl.** XLVII:1 1-3:2005 pp.11-38.

633 Konstytucja RP a prawo wspólnotowe. *[In Polish]*; (The constitution of the Republic of Poland and community law.) Piotr Winczorek. **Pań. Prawo** LIX:II 11:2004 pp.3-17.

634 Legitimacy and the constitution. Jr. Fallon; H. Richard. **Harv. Law R.** 118:6 4:2005 pp.1789-1853.

635 Madison's opponents and constitutional design. David Brian Robertson. **Am. Pol. Sci. R.** 99:2 5:2005 pp.225-243.

636 Majoritarian democracy in Britain: New Labour and the constitution. Matthew Flinders. **West Euro. Pol.** 28:1 1:2005 pp.61-93.

637 Manifest der Hoffnung. Über die neue Verfassung Afghanistans. *[In German]*; [Document of hope: Afghanistan's new constitution]. Hajo Vergau. **Verf. Recht Übersee** 37:4 2004 pp.465-488.

638 Möglichkeiten und Grenzen der Zusammenarbeit nationaler Wissenschaftlergemeinschaften in Sachen Verfassungsstaat. *[In German]*; [Opportunities and limits of collaborations of national scientific communities regarding the constitutional state]. Peter Häberle. **Jahr. Öffent. Gegen.** 53 2005 pp.345-400.

639 Mosambik am Scheideweg — die Verfassung von 2004. *[In German]*; (Mozambique at crossroads — the constitution of 2004.) *[Summary]*. Dietrich Nelle. **Verf. Recht Übersee** 38:2 2005 pp.174-200.

640 None, one or several? Perspectives on the UK's constitution(s). David Feldman. **Camb. Law J.** 64:2 7:2005 pp.329-351.

641 Our unethical constitution. Candice E. Jackson. **J. Ayn Rand S.** 6:2 Spring:2005 pp.405-444.

642 Plebiszitäre Demokratie und Haushaltsgewalt. Zu den verfassungsrechtlichen Grenzen finanzwirksamer Volksgesetzgebung. *[In German]*; [Plebiscitarian democracy and budget control: on the constitutional limits of public finance laws]. Sebastian Müller-Franken. **Der Staat** 44:1 2005 pp.19-42.

643 Political learning: the neglected precondition of constitutional reform. Gerhard Wegner. **Constit. Pol. Econ.** 15:4 12:2004 pp.339-358.

644 Prime ministers and the constitution: Attlee to Blair. Kevin Theakston. **Parl. Aff.** 58:1 1:2005 pp.17-37.

645 Razgranichenie kompetentsii mezhdu urovniami vlasti: mirovoi opyt. *[In Russian]*; (Delimitation of competence among levels of authority: international experience.) R. Turovskii. **Mir. Ekon. Mezh. Ot.** 11 11:2004 pp.23-43.

646 Realising the constitutional vision: road blocks and road ahead. Nalin Kant Jha. **Indian J. Pol. Sci.** LXVI:1 1-3:2005 pp.9-28.

647 Regieren mit dem obligatorischen Verfassungsreferendum: Wirkung, Konterstrategie, Nutzungsversuche und Umgangsweise. *[In German]*; (Governing with mandatory constitutional referenda: effect, counter strategy, use and dealings with them.) Otmar Jung. **Z. Parlament.** 36:1 3:2005 pp.161-187.

648 Scandal: the sexual politics of the British constitution. Anna Clark. Princeton NJ: Princeton University Press, 2004. xii, 311p. *ISBN: 069111501X. Includes bibliographical references and index.*

649 Simón Bolívar (1783-1830) und die Verfassung der "Bolivarischen Republik Venezuela" von 1999: eine verfassungsgeschichtliche Bestandsaufnahme. *[In German]*; (Simón Bolívar (1783-1830) and the "Bolivarian Constitution of the V Republic" in Venezuela (1999).) *[Summary]*. Andreas Timmermann. **Verf. Recht Übersee** 38:1 2005 pp.78-104.

650 Sporting equality: title IX thirty years later. Rita James Simon [Ed.]. New Brunswick NJ: Transaction Publishers, 2005. 182p. *ISBN: 076580848X. Includes bibliographical references.*

651 Le traité établissant une Constitution pour l'Europe à l'épreuve de la Constitution française. *[In French]*; [The treaty establishing a European Constitution and the French Constitution]. Jérôme Roux. **R. Droit Publ.** 1 1-2:2005 pp.59-110.

652 Up the creek: fishing for a new constitutional order. Kiera L. Ladner. **Can. J. Pol.** 38:4 12:2005 pp.923-954.

653 Verfassung und Nation: Formen politischer Institutionalisierung in Deutschland und Frankreich. *[In German]*; [Constitution and nation: forms of political institutionalization in Germany and France]. Daniel Schulz. Wiesbaden: VS Verlag fur Sozialwissenschaften, 2004. 320p. *ISBN: 3531144103.*

654 Verfassungsschutz als Demokratiefürsorge? Zur Theorie eines Verfassungswächters bei Fichte, Sieyès und Constant. *[In German]*; [Protection of the constitution to preserve democracy? On the theories of Fichte, Sieyès and Constant]. Florian Weber. **Der Staat** 44:1 2005 pp.112-138.

655 Zur Verfassungsentwicklung der Republik Somalia: Frieden durch Verfassung? *[In German]*; [On the development of a constitution in the Republic of Somalia: peace through a constitution?] Jörg Luther. **Jahr. Öffent. Gegen.** 53 2005 pp.703-725.

656 Zwischen Kontinuität und Diskontinuität: Die Verfassungsänderung. *[In German]*; [Between continuity and discontinuity: the changes to the constitution]. Johannes Masing. **Der Staat** 44:1 2005 pp.1-17.

C.1.3: **Legislative power**
Pouvoir législatif

657 Assessing the electoral connection: evidence from the early United States. Jamie L. Carson; Erik J. Engstrom. **Am. J. Pol. Sci.** 49:4 10:2005 pp.746-757.

658 The behavioural consequences of institutional rules: republicans in the US house. Donald L. Davison; Michael Krassa; Daniel Reagan. **J. Legis. St.** 11:1 Spring:2005 pp.38-56.

659 Beyond collective representation: individual members of parliament and interest representation in the Netherlands. Jacques Thomassen; Rudy B. Andeweg. **J. Legis. St.** 10:4 Winter:2004 pp.47-69.

660 Bloc politics v. broad cooperation? The functioning of Danish minority parliamentarism. Christoffer Green-Pedersen; Lisbeth Hoffmann Thomsen. **J. Legis. St.** 11:2 Summer:2005 pp.153-169.

661   Breve crónica del proceso de incorporación de la institución jurídica de la responsabilidad patrimonial del Estado al orden constitucional y legal mexicano. *[In Spanish]*; [Brief chronicle on the process of incorporation of the patrimonial reponsability as legal institution in the state to the Mexican constitutional and legal order]. Alvaro Castro Estrada. **R. Admin. Públ.** 166 1-4:2005 pp.419-439.

662   Der Bundesrat: Vertretung der Länder oder Instrument der Parteien? *[In German]*; (The Bundesrat: representation of the Länder or party instrument?) *[Summary]*. Gerd Strohmeier. **Z. Parlament.** 35:4 12:2004 pp.717-731.

663   Casework, issues and voting in state legislative elections: a district analysis. George Serra; Neil Pinney. **J. Legis. St.** 10:4 Winter:2004 pp.32-46.

664   Clear, simple and precise legislative drafting: Australian guidelines explicated using an EC directive. Edwin Tanner. **Stat. Law R.** 25:3 2004 pp.223-250.

665   The common law power of the legislature: insurer conversions and charitable funds. Jill R. Horwitz; Marion R. Fremont-Smith. **Milbank Q.** 83:2 2005 pp.225-246.

666   Congressional authorization and the war on terrorism. Curtis A. Bradley; Jack L. Goldsmith. **Harv. Law R.** 118:7 5:2005 pp.2047-2133.

667   Congressional performance, incumbent behavior, and voting in Senate elections. Monika L. McDermott; David R. Jones. **Legis. Stud. Q.** XXX:2 5:2005 pp.235-257.

668   Determinants of congressional support for NAFTA and Clinton's economic package. Haroon A. Khan. **J. Dev. Areas** 38:2 Spring:2005 pp.143-154.

669   Do term limits make a difference? Ambition and motivations among U.S. state legislators. Rebekah Herrick; Sue Thomas. **Am. Pol. Res.** 33:5 9:2005 pp.726-747.

670   Exclusive committee assignments and party pressure in the U.S. House of Representatives. K. Kanthak. **Publ. Choice** 121:3-4 10:2004 pp.391-412.

671   Executing the treaty power. Nicholas Quinn Rosenkranz. **Harv. Law R.** 118:6 4:2005 pp.1867-1938.

672   Explaining the incidence and timing of congressional responses to the U.S. Supreme Court. Virginia A. Hettinger; Christopher Zorn. **Legis. Stud. Q.** XXX:1 2:2005 pp.5-28.

673   Extraterritorial application of Australian statutes proscribing misleading conduct. Justin Gleeson. **Aust. Law J.** 79:5 5:2005 pp.296-312.

674   Frogs, mice and mixed electoral institutions: party discipline in Italy's XIV chamber of deputies. Federico Ferrara. **J. Legis. St.** 10:4 Winter:2004 pp.10-31.

675   From the scrum to the chamber: social capital, public confidence, and the parliamentarian's dilemma. Jason Knauf. **Pol. Sci.** 57:1 6:2005 pp.21-38.

676   'From weird to wired': MPs, the internet and representative politics in the UK. Stephen Ward; Wainer Lusoli. **J. Legis. St.** 11:1 Spring:2005 pp.57-81.

677   House party switchers and committee assignments: who gets 'what, when, how?'.Antoine Yoshinaka. **Legis. Stud. Q.** XXX:3 8:2005 pp.391-406.

678   How Congress works and why you should care. Lee Hamilton. Bloomington IN: Indiana University Press, 2004. viii, 156p. *ISBN: 0253344255, 0253216958. Includes bibliographical references and index.*

679   How many bicameral legislatures are there? Philip Norton. **J. Legis. St.** 10:4 Winter:2004 pp.1-9.

680   Imposing a neo-liberal theory of representation on the Westminster model: a Canadian case. David Pond. **J. Legis. St.** 11:2 Summer:2005 pp.170-193.

681   Instiutsionalizatsiia Gosudarstvennoi Dumy i uchastie deputatov tret'ego sozyva v parlamentskikh vyborakh 2003 g. *[In Russian]*; (Institutionalization of the state Duma and the third convocation deputies' participation in the 2003 parliamentary elections.) *[Summary]*. Iu.D. Shevchenko. **Polis [Moscow]** 1(84) 2005 pp.120-134.

682   Issues and institutions: 'winnowing' in the U.S. Congress. Glen S. Krutz. **Am. J. Pol. Sci.** 49:2 4:2005 pp.313-326.

683   Konstitutsionno-pravovoi status deputata zakonodatel'nogo organa gosudarstvennoi vlasti v Rossiiskoi Federatsii. *[In Russian]*; [The legal constitutional status of the deputy of the legislative organ of state power in Russia] *[Summary]*. L.A. Nudnenko. St. Petersburg:

Iuridicheskii tsentr Press, 2004. 473p. *ISBN: 5942012849. Includes bibliographical references.*

684   The lawmaking process in Cuba: debating the bill on agricultural cooperatives. Peter Roman. **Soc. Dem.** 19:2 7:2005 pp.37-56.

685   Legislative bargaining under weighted voting. James M. Snyder, Jr.; Michael M. Ting; Stephen Ansolabehere. **Am. Econ. R.** 95:4 9:2005 pp.981-1004.

686   Legislative organization theory and committee preference outliers in state senates. David W. Prince; L. Marvin Overby. **State Pol. Policy Q.** 5:1 Spring:2005 pp.68-87.

687   Liaison legislature: the role of the national assembly in Senegal. Melissa A. Thomas; Oumar Sissokho. **J. Mod. Afr. S.** 43:1 3:2005 pp.97-117.

688   Minority rights and majority power: conditional party government and the motion to recommit in the House. Jason M. Roberts. **Legis. Stud. Q.** XXX:2 5:2005 pp.219-234.

689   Motywy bikameralizmu we współczesnej Europie. *[In Polish]*; (The premises of bicameralism in contemporary Europe.) *[Summary]*. Zbigniew Kiełmiński. **Prz. Euro.** 1(8) 2004 pp.26-42.

690   Old hacks or new blood? The effects of inter-party competition on PRI candidates for the Mexican chamber of deputies, 1997-2000. Christopher Diaz. **J. Legis. St.** 10:4 Winter:2004 pp.107-128.

691   Parlamentarische Gesetzgebung im „kooperativen Staat". *[In German]*; [Parliamentary legislation in the 'cooperative state']. Florian Becker. **Der Staat** 44:3 2005 pp.433-461.

692   Parlamentarische Informations – und Kontrollressourcen in 22 westlichen Demokratien. *[In German]*; (Parliamentary information and control resources in 22 Western democracies.) *[Summary]*. Kai-Uwe Schnapp; Philipp Harfst. **Z. Parlament.** 36:2 6:2005 pp.348-370.

693   Parlamentarismuskritik ohne Ende? Parteidissens und Repräsentationskonzepte, am Beispiel der Entparlamentarisierungs – und der Gewaltenteilungskritik. *[In German]*; (Endless criticism of parliamentary democracy? Party dissent and concepts of representation: the critique of deparliamentarization and the separation of powers.) Eberhard Schuett-Wetschky. **Z. Pol.wissen.** 15:1 2005 pp.3-34.

694   Party government in presidential democracies: extending cartel theory beyond the U.S. Congress. Mark P. Jones; Wonjae Hwang. **Am. J. Pol. Sci.** 49:2 4:2005 pp.267-282.

695   Peculiar institutions: slavery, sectionalism, and minority obstruction in the antebellum Senate. Gregory J. Wawro. **Legis. Stud. Q.** XXX:2 5:2005 pp.163-191.

696   Policy preference formation in legislative politics: structures, actors, and focal points. Nils Ringe. **Am. J. Pol. Sci.** 49:4 10:2005 pp.731-745.

697   Re-election and political career paths in the Uruguayan congress, 1985-99. David Altman; Daniel Chasquetti. **J. Legis. St.** 11:2 Summer:2005 pp.235-253.

698   Das Regulierungsrecht – Eine neue rechtswissenschaftliche Kategorie? *[In German]*; [Regulation legislation – a new legal discipline?] B. Kneihs. **Z. Öffent. Recht** 60:1 2005 pp.1-30.

699   Le riforme costituzionali nel Regno Unito: quale destino per la Camera dei Lords? *[In Italian]*; [Constitutional reforms in the UK: what future for the House of Lords?] Lara Trucco. **Rass. Parl.** XLVI:4 10-12:2004 pp.959-982.

700   Roger's revolution: Blitzkrieg in Kiwiland. Austin Mitchell. **J. Legis. St.** 11:1 Spring:2005 pp.1-15.

701   The role of the Belgian constitutional court in the legislative process. Patricia Popelier. **Stat. Law R.** 26:1 2005 pp.22-40.

702   Royal incapacity and constitutional continuity: the regent and counsellors of state. Rodney Brazier. **Camb. Law J.** 64:2 7:2005 pp.352-387.

703   The selection of committee leadership in the Brazilian chamber of deputies. Fabiano Santos; Lucio Rennó. **J. Legis. St.** 10:1 Spring:2004 pp.50-70.

704   El senado en las democracias contemporaneas: el caso mexicano desde una perspectiva comparada. *[In Spanish]*; [The Senate in contemporary democracies: the Mexican case from a comparative perspective]. Mijael Altamirano Santiago. Mexico City: Plaza y Valdés, 2004. 434p. *ISBN: 9707223006. Includes bibliographical references (p. 403-434).*

705 The Senatorial courtesy game: explaining the norm of informal vetoes in advice and consent nominations. Tonja Jacobi. **Legis. Stud. Q.** XXX:2 5:2005 pp.193-218.
706 State-building in Ukraine: the Ukrainian parliament, 1990-2003. Sarah Whitmore. London: Routledge, 2004. 222p. *ISBN: 0415331951.* (*Series:* Russian and East European studies).
707 Still a traditional political class? Patterns of parliamentary recruitment in Brazil (1946-2002); *[Summary in French]*. André Marenco Dos Santos. **Canadian J. Lat. Am. Caribbean S.** 30:60 2005 pp.13-40.
708 Testing the implications of incivility in the United States Congress, 1977-2000: the case of judicial confirmation delay. Scot Schraufnagel. **J. Legis. St.** 11:2 Summer:2005 pp.216-234.
709 The timing of cabinet reshuffles in five Westminster parliamentary systems. Christopher Kam; Indriði Indriðason. **Legis. Stud. Q.** XXX:3 8:2005 pp.327-363.
710 La trasposición de la directiva Marco de Aguas en España. *[In Spanish]*; [The transposition of the directive Marco de Aguas in Spain]. Francisco Delgado Piqueras. **R. Admin. Públ.** 165 9-12:2004 pp.181-213.
711 War and uncertainty. Lori Fisler Damrosch. **Yale Law J.** 114:6 4:2005 pp.1405-1417.

C.1.4: **Executive power**
Pouvoir exécutif

712 The central government of Russia: from Gorbachev to Putin. Iulia Shevchenko. Aldershot: Ashgate, 2004. 199p. *ISBN: 0754639827. Includes bibliographical references (p. [186]-192) and index.* (*Series:* Post-Soviet politics).
713 Les chefs d'État dans les PECO : pouvoirs constitutionnels et poids politique. *[In French]*; [Heads of state in Central and Eastern Europe: constitutional powers and political weight] *[Summary]*. François Frison-Roche. **Cour. Pays Est** 1043 5-6:2004 pp.52-66.
714 Considering the Bush presidency. Gary L Gregg [Ed.]; Mark J Rozell [Ed.]. New York: Oxford University Press, 2004. xi, 210p. *ISBN: 0195166817, 0195166809. Includes bibliographical references and index.*
715 Constitutional head of state without constitutional security: the governor and his removal. Priti Saxena. **Indian J. Publ. Admin.** LI:1 1-3:2005 pp.94-107.
716 Easy come, easy go: ministerial turnover in Russia, 1990-2004. Iulia Shevchenko. **Euro.-Asia S.** 57:3 5:2005 pp.399-428.
717 Executive prerogative and the 'good officer' in Thomas Jefferson's letter to John B. Colvin. Jeremy David Bailey. **Pres. Stud. Q.** 34:4 12:2004 pp.732-754.
718 The institutionalization of regulatory review: organizational stability and responsive competence at OIRA. William F. West. **Pres. Stud. Q.** 35:1 3:2005 pp.76-93.
719 The law: textbooks and the president's constitutional powers. David Gray Adler. **Pres. Stud. Q.** 35:2 6:2005 pp.376-388.
720 Political accountability in play: the Budd inquiry and David Blunkett's resignation. Nicholas Bamforth. **Publ. Law** Summer:2005 pp.229-238.
721 The president as reformer: when do presidents initiate administrative reform through legislation? Scott E. Robinson. **Pres. Stud. Q.** 34:4 12:2004 pp.793-803.
722 Presidential decision making. James P. Pfiffner; John P. Burke; Matthew J. Dickinson; Patrick J. Haney; Charles E. Walcott; Karen M. Hult; Timothy J. McKeown; Andrew Rudalevige. **Pres. Stud. Q.** 35:2 6:2005 pp.217-360. *Collection of 7 articles.*
723 Presidential powers. Harold J. Krent. New York: New York University Press, 2005. viii, 279p. *ISBN: 0814747825. Includes bibliographical references and index.*
724 'Presidentialization' in Japan? The prime minister, media and elections in Japan. Ellis S. Krauss; Benjamin Nyblade. **Br. J. Pol. Sci.** 35:2 4:2005 pp.357-368.
725 Prime ministers' identity in semi-presidential regimes: constitutional norms and cabinet formation outcomes. O. Protsyk. **Écon. Sociét.** 44:5 8:2005 pp.721-748.
726 Revisiting the two presidencies: the strategic use of executive orders. Bryan W. Marshall; Richard L. Pacelle. **Am. Pol. Res.** 33:1 1:2005 pp.81-105.

727 Rulers and servants of the state: the Blair style of government 1997-2004. Peter Hennessy. **Parl. Aff.** 58:1 1:2005 pp.6-16.
728 The secular decline in presidential domestic policy making: an organizational perspective. George A. Krause. **Pres. Stud. Q.** 34:4 12:2004 pp.779-792.
729 State secrets and executive power. William G. Weaver; Robert M. Pallitto. **Pol. Sci. Q.** 120:1 Spring:2005 pp.85-112.
730 Women ministers in Latin American government: when, where, and why? Maria Escobar-Lemmon; Michelle M. Taylor-Robinson. **Am. J. Pol. Sci.** 49:4 10:2005 pp.829-844.

C.1.5: **Judiciary power**
Pouvoir judiciaire

731 After government? On representing law without the state. Simon Roberts. **Mod. Law R.** 68:1 1:2005 pp.1-24.
732 The arguments from coherence: analysis and evaluation. Stefano Bertea. **Oxf. J. Leg. S.** 26:3 Autumn:2005 pp.369-391.
733 Beating the odds: the quest for justice by South African asbestos mining communities. Jock McCulloch. **R. Afr. Pol. Econ.** 32:103 3:2005 pp.63-77.
734 Certainty, reasonableness and argumentation in law. Stefano Bertea. **Argumentation** 18:4 2004 pp.465-478.
735 Christian Dahlman's reflections on the basic norm. Stanley Paulson. **Arch. Recht. Soz.Philos.** 91:1 2005 pp.96-108.
736 Civilized squatting. Oliver Radley-Gardner. **Oxf. J. Leg. S.** 25:4 Winter:2005 pp.727-747.
737 Conflict between the goals of social science and law: what can psychologists really contribute? Ralph Scott. **Mankind Q.** XLV:2 Winter:2004 pp.217-230.
738 Conflicts of interest: challenges and solutions in business, law, medicine, and public policy. Don A. Moore [Ed.]. Cambridge, New York: Cambridge University Press, 2005. xi, 300p. *ISBN: 0521844398. Includes bibliographical references and index.*
739 Contracting out war? Private military companies, law and regulation in the United Kingdom. Clive Walker; Dave Whyte. **Int. Comp. Law Q.** 54:3 7:2005 pp.651-690.
740 Critical legal theory (without modifiers) in the United States. Mark Tushnet. **J. Pol. Philos.** 13:1 3:2005 pp.99-112.
741 The difficulty of defining 'property'. Alexandra George. **Oxf. J. Leg. S.** 25:4 Winter:2005 pp.793-813.
742 Discourse and argument in instituting the governance of social law. Richard R. Weiner. **Cent. Euro. Pol. Sci. R.** 5:15 Spring:2004 pp.6-34.
743 Does obscenity cause moral harm? Andrew Koppelman. **Columb. Law R.** 105:5 6:2005 pp.1635-1679.
744 Farewell to the exclusive-inclusive debate. Danny Priel. **Oxf. J. Leg. S.** 25:4 Winter:2005 pp.675-696.
745 The gift of law: Greek euergetism and Ottoman waqf. Engin F. Isin; Alexandre Lefebvre. **Euro. J. Soc. Theory** 8:1 2:2005 pp.5-24.
746 Global concepts, local rules, practices of adjudication and Ronald Dworkin's law as integrity. Alan R. Madry. **Law Philos.** 24:3 5:2005 pp.211-238.
747 The 'Hart-phenomenon'. Csaba Varga. **Arch. Recht. Soz.Philos.** 91:1 2005 pp.83-95.
748 A hybrid theory of claim-rights. Gopal Sreenivasan. **Oxf. J. Leg. S.** 25:2 Summer:2005 pp.257-274.
749 Innocence in capital sentencing. Bradley R. Hall; Rob Warden; Jeffrey Fagan; Valerie West; Joshua Marquis; Samuel R. Gross; Kristen Jacoby; Daniel J. Matheson; Nicholas Montgomery; Sujata Patil; Joseph L. Hoffmann; Carol S. Steiker; Jordan M. Steiker; Ronald J. Allen; Amy Shavell. **J. Crim. Law Crimin.** 95:2 Winter:2005 pp.371-636. *Collection of 8 articles.*

750   Law, morality, and legal positivism. Kenneth Einar Himma [Ed.]. Stuttgart: Franz Steiner Verlag, 2004. 183p. *ISBN: 3515085130. Includes bibliographical references. (Series:* ARSP Beiheft - 98).

751   Legitimacy, rights and judicial review. Thomas Poole. **Oxf. J. Leg. S.** 25:4 Winter:2005 pp.697-725.

752   Lon Fuller and the moral value of the rule of law. Colleen Murphy. **Law Philos.** 24:3 5:2005 pp.239-262.

753   Majority norms, multiculturalism, and gender equality. Sarah Song. **Am. Pol. Sci. R.** 99:4 11:2005 pp.473-489.

754   Mandatory arbitration. David S. Schwartz; Linda J. Demaine; Deborah R. Hensler; Jean R. Sternlight; Elizabeth J. Jensen; Christopher R. Drahozal; Mark E. Budnitz; Stephen J. Ware; Paul D. Carrington; Paul Y. Castle; Lisa B. Bingham; Elizabeth G. Thornburg; Richard C. Reuben; Erica F. Schohn. **Law Contemp. Prob.** 67:1-2 Winter-Spring:2004 pp.5-336. *Collection of 11 articles.*

755   Means/ends reciprocity in the act of state doctrine. Patrick W. Pearsall. **Columb. J. Tr. Law** 43:3 2005 pp.999-1025.

756   Montesquieu's mistakes and the true meaning of separation. Laurence Claus. **Oxf. J. Leg. S.** 26:3 Autumn:2005 pp.419-452.

757   Moral paternalism. Gerald Dworkin. **Law Philos.** 24:3 5:2005 pp.305-319.

758   A neat trick if you can do it: legal interpretation as literary reading. Patrick Lenta. **Sth. Afr. Law. J.** 121:1 2004 pp.216-238.

759   The not so minimum content of natural law. Richard A. Epstein. **Oxf. J. Leg. S.** 25:2 Summer:2005 pp.219-255.

760   Le principe de laïcité : l'apaisement par le droit ? *[In French]*; [The principle of secularism: appeasement by law?] Jean-Pierre Camby. **R. Droit Publ.** 1 1-2:2005 pp.3-18.

761   Principle of legality and the clear statement principle. J.J. Spigelman. **Aust. Law J.** 79:12 12:2005 pp.769-782.

762   Proactive law enforcement, ambivalence, and autonomy. Paul M. Hughes. **Publ. Aff. Q.** 19:2 4:2005 pp.127-141.

763   Problemy zakonodatel'nogo obespecheniia gosudarstvennogo kontrolia. *[In Russian]*; (Problems of legislative enforcement of state control.) A.M. Tarasov. **Gos. Pravo** 10 10:2004 pp.15-25.

764   La prueba de razonabilidad y la estabilidad de las reglas de juego. *[In Spanish]*; (The test of reasonability and stable rules of the game.) María Mercedes Cuéllar. **R. Econ. Inst.** 7:12 2005 pp.13-42.

765   Religion on trial: how Supreme Court trends threaten freedom of conscience in America. Phillip E. Hammond; David W. Machacek; Eric Michael Mazur. Walnut Creek CA: AltaMira Press, 2004. xix, 177p. *ISBN: 0759106002, 0759106010. Includes bibliographical references (p. 165-170) and index.*

766   Revealing options. Lee Anne Fennell. **Harv. Law R.** 118:5 3:2005 pp.1399-1488.

767   Should plaintiffs win what defendants lose? Litigation stakes, litigation effort, and the benefits of decoupling. Albert Choi; Chris William Sanchirico. **J. Legal S.** 33:2 6:2004 pp.323-354.

768   Social science and diffusion of law. William Twining. **J. Law Soc.** 32:2 6:2005 pp.203-240.

769   The solution to the problem of outcome luck: why harm is just as punishable as the wrongful action that causes it. Ken Levy. **Law Philos.** 24:3 5:2005 pp.263-303.

770   Staatenloses Recht: Kelsens Konzeption und ihre Grenzen. *[In German]*; [Stateless law: Kelsen's conception and its limits] *[Summary]*. Alexander Somek. **Arch. Recht. Soz.Philos.** 91:1 2005 pp.61-82.

771   Sub'ekt prava v tsentre pravovoi sistemy. *[In Russian]*; (Subject of law at the centre of legal system.) S.I. Arkhipov. **Gos. Pravo** 7 7:2005 pp.13-23.

772   Three themes from Raz. Leslie Green. **Oxf. J. Leg. S.** 26:3 Autumn:2005 pp.503-523.

773 A tudomány igazsága kontra igazság tudománya. *[In Hungarian]*; (Justice of science v. science of justice. [Experts and evidence in litigation].) Mihály Makai. **Mag. Tud.** 49:7 2004 pp.678-697.

774 Über den Umgang mit biblischen und juristischen Quellen. *[In German]*; [On the treatment of Biblical and legal sources] *[Summary]*. Jörg Schneider; Gerson Trüg. **Arch. Recht. Soz.Philos.** 91:2 2005 pp.188-220.

775 War v. justice: terrorism cases, enemy combatants, and political justice in U.S. courts. Christiane Wilke. **Pol. Soc.** 33:4 12:2005 pp.637-669.

776 Was Bentham a utilitarian? *[Summary in French]*. Max Hocutt. **Can. J. Pol.** 38:3 9:2005 pp.697-717.

777 Western jurisprudence. Tim Murphy [Ed.]. Dublin: Round Hall, 2004. x, 530p. *ISBN: 1858003784.*

778 What is the greatest evil? Martha Minow. **Harv. Law R.** 118:7 5:2005 pp.2134-2169.

Civil law
Droit civil

779 Adapting adoption: a case of closet politics? Ian Dey. **Int. J. Law Policy Fam.** 19:3 12:2005 pp.289-309.

780 The African Union convention on combating corruption. Peter W. Schroth. **J. Afr. Law** 49:1 2005 pp.24-38.

781 L'animal dans nos sociétés. *[In French]*; [Animals in our societies]. Florence Burgat [Ed.]. **Prob. Pol. Soc.** 896 1:2004 pp.5-117.

782 Anti-discrimination rights without equality. Elisa Holmes. **Mod. Law R.** 68:2 3:2005 pp.175-194.

783 An Australian perspective on the evolution of the law in relation to the assessment of special contributions in 'big money' cases: never mind the law, feel the politics. Paul Guest. **Int. J. Law Policy Fam.** 19:2 8:2005 pp.148-162.

784 Benign segregation? A case study of the practice of gender separation in buses in the ultra-Orthodox community in Israel. Alon Harel. **S. Afr. J. Human Rights** 20:1 2004 pp.64-85.

785 The challenge of antisocial behaviour: new relationships between the state, children and parents. Alison Cleland; Kay Tisdall. **Int. J. Law Policy Fam.** 19:3 12:2005 pp.395-420.

786 Child brides, inegalitarianism, and the fundamentalist polygamous family in the United States. Eve D'Onofrio. **Int. J. Law Policy Fam.** 19:3 12:2005 pp.373-394.

787 Child marriage in India: socio-legal and human rights dimensions. Jaya Sagade. Delhi, Oxford: Oxford University Press, 2005. 250p. *ISBN: 0195668901.* Includes bibliographical references and index.

788 Contract law. Mindy Chen-Wishart. Oxford, New York: Oxford University Press, 2005. xiii, 680p. *ISBN: 0199268142. Includes bibliographical references and index.*

789 The courts and public discourse: the case of gay marriage. David W. Machacek; Adrienne Fulco. **J. Chur. State** 46:4 Autumn:2004 pp.767-785.

790 (The elements of the electronic damaging act in the Jordanian law.); *[Text in Arabic]*. Nael Ali Al-Masa'adeh. **Dirasat Sha. Law** 32:1 5:2005 pp.55-65.

791 (Elő-) kérdések tisztázása a Gt. konszernjogi fejezetének tervezett módosítására tekintettel. *[In Hungarian]*; (Clarification of assumptions regarding the planned amendment of Hungarian act on companies with respect to the formation of groups of companies.) *[Summary]*. Péter Nikolicza. **Jogtud. Köz.** 59:1 2004 pp.10-21.

792 Employment implications when universities merge. A.B. Leslie. **Sth. Afr. Law. J.** 121:4 2004 pp.841-857.

793 L'exténuation en sourdine de la souveraineté étatique : un diagnostic des contrats d'état du Congo. *[In French]*; [Exhaustion of state sovereignty: a diagnosis of the contracts of the state of Congo]. Bienvenu Bikoumou. **Penant** 847 4-6:2004 pp.170-187.

794 Family values in the classroom? Reconciling parental wishes and children's rights in state schools. Laura Lundy. **Int. J. Law Policy Fam.** 19:3 12:2005 pp.346-372.

795 For love and money: the political economy of commercial surrogacy. Debora L. Spar. **R. Int. Pol. Econ.** 12:2 5:2005 pp.287-309.

796 Giving money to children: the state's constitutional obligations to provide child support grants to child headed households. Beth Goldblatt; Sandra Liebenberg. **S. Afr. J. Human Rights** 20:1 2004 pp.151-164.

797 Grundrechtliche Einrichtungsgarantien. Die Figur der grundrechtlichen Einrichtungsgarantie, dargestellt am Beispiel des Grundrechts auf Ehe und Familie. *[In German]*; [Institutional guarantees at the example of marriage and family law] *[Summary]*. G. Baumgartner. **Z. Öffent. Recht** 59:4 2004 pp.321-349.

798 How do changes in welfare law affect domestic violence? An analysis of Connecticut towns, 1990-2000. Jennifer Nou; Christopher Timmins. **J. Legal S.** 34:2 6:2005 pp.445-470.

799 'I do' or 'we won't': legalising same-sex marriage in South Africa. Kerry Williams. **S. Afr. J. Human Rights** 20:1 2004 pp.32-63.

800 Indigenous peoples and family law: issues in Aotearoa/New Zealand. Jacinta Ruru. **Int. J. Law Policy Fam.** 19:3 12:2005 pp.327-345.

801 Industrial citizenship, human rights and the transformation of labour law: a critical assessment of Harry Arthur's legalization thesis; *[Summary in French]*. Michel Coutu. **Can. J. Law Soc.** 19:2 2004 pp.73-92.

802 Is better regulation smarter regulation? Robert Baldwin. **Publ. Law** Autumn:2005 pp.485-511.

803 Journalistic privilege: does it merit legal protection? Sanette Nel. **Comp. Int. Law J. Sth. Afr.** XXXVIII:1 3:2005 pp.99-112.

804 Juvenile curfews and the major confusion over minor rights. **Harv. Law R.** 118:7 5:2005 pp.2400-2421.

805 Une loi exemplaire sur la fin de vie. *[In French]*; [An exemplary law on the end of life]. Jacques Ricot. **Esprit** 315 6:2005 pp.119-129.

806 Lost in translation: corporate opportunities in comparative perspective. David Kershaw. **Oxf. J. Leg. S.** 25:4 Winter:2005 pp.603-628.

807 La mise en place de la justice des mineurs au Niger. *[In French]*; [The installation of children's rights in Niger]. Laurent Benkemoun. **Penant** 847 4-6:2004 pp.215-226.

808 Motherhood, fatherhood and law: child custody and visitation in Israel. Daphna Hacker. **Soc. Legal S.** 14:3 9:2005 pp.409-431.

809 New families, new property, new laws: the practical effects of the recognition of customary marriages act. Mothokoa Mamashela. **S. Afr. J. Human Rights** 20:4 2004 pp.616-641.

810 Not a drop to drink: disconnection of water services for non-payment and the right of access to water. Michael Kidd. **S. Afr. J. Human Rights** 20:1 2004 pp.119-137.

811 Observations comparatives sur la contestation de paternité. *[In French]*; [Comparative observations on paternity dispute] *[Summary]*; *[Summary in French]*. Rainer Franck. **R. Int. Droit Comp.** 57:1 1-3:2005 pp.85-102.

812 An outline of the law of contract. G. H. Treitel. London: Butterworth-Heinemann, 2004. lix, 455p. *ISBN: 0406972680*.

813 PACS — zarejestrowane związki partnerskie we Francji. *[In Polish]*; (PACS — registered partnership law in France.) *[Summary]*. Zuzanna Mitręga. **Katedra** 5 2004 pp.98-109.

814 The paradoxes of principle and pragmatism: ancillary relief in England and Wales. Rebecca Bailey-Harris. **Int. J. Law Policy Fam.** 19:2 8:2005 pp.229-241.

815 A peculiarly British protection of human rights? Alison L. Young. **Mod. Law R.** 68:5 9:2005 pp.858-872.

816 Principles of corporate insolvency law. Royston Miles Goode. London: Sweet & Maxwell, 2005. lxxxvi, 673p. *ISBN: 0421930209*.

817 The recasting of insolvency law. Vanessa Finch. **Mod. Law R.** 68:5 9:2005 pp.713-736.

818 Re-codification of the civil code? Conception for drafting the new civil code. Ildikó Basa. **Acta Jur. Hun.** 46:1-2 2005 pp.73-94.

819 Recognizing Aboriginal title: the Mabo case and indigenous resistance to English-settler colonialism. Peter H. Russell. Toronto: University of Toronto Press, 2005. xii, 470p. *ISBN: 0802038638. Includes bibliographical references (p. 425-450) and index.*

820 (Re)constructing the head teacher: legal narratives and the politics of school exclusions. Daniel Monk. **J. Law Soc.** 32:3 9:2005 pp.399-423.

821 Reproductive technology in Germany and the United States: an essay in comparative law and bioethics. John A. Robertson. **Columb. J. Tr. Law** 43:1 2004 pp.189-227.

822 Responsabilité civile et naissance d'un enfant. Aperçu comparatif. *[In French]*; [Civil responsibility and child birth. Comparative survey] *[Summary]*; *[Summary in French]*. Géraldine Demme; Romain Lorentz. **R. Int. Droit Comp.** 57:1 1-3:2005 pp.103-139.

823 Sex for sale: the prostitute as businesswoman. Elsje Bonthuys; Carla Monteiro. **Sth. Afr. Law. J.** 121:3 2004 pp.659-676.

824 Sex work from a feminist perspective: a visit to the Jordan case. Rósaan Krüger. **S. Afr. J. Human Rights** 20:1 2004 pp.138-150.

825 Sexisme et liberté d'expression: faut-il une loi. *[In French]*; [Sexism and freedom of speech: is there a need for a law]. Res publica. **Res Publica [Creteil]** 37 5:2004 pp.8-39.

826 A study of the system of spousal maintenance on divorce: a comparison between China and Russia. Chen Wei; Ran Qi-yu. **Int. J. Law Policy Fam.** 19:3 12:2005 pp.310-326.

827 Successor liability, mass tort, and mandatory-litigation class action. **Harv. Law R.** 118:7 5:2005 pp.2357-2377.

828 Technologies de l'information et de la communication et droits des salariés. *[In French]*; [Information and communication technologies and worker's rights]. Mélanie Carles. **R. Prat. Droit Soc.** 714 10:2004 pp.311-329.

829 The unity of the common law and the ending of appeals to the Privy Council. K.J. Keith. **Int. Comp. Law Q.** 54:1 1:2005 pp.197-210.

830 Die Verteilung der Finanzmittel aus dem zwischen der Bundesrepublik Deutschland und dem Zentralrat der Juden in Deutschland geschlossenen Staatsvertrag. *[In German]*; [The distribution of finances in the contract between the Federal Republic of Germany and the Central Council of Jews in Germany]. Kyrill-Alexander Schwarz. **Relig. Staat Gesell.** 6:1 2005 pp.123-164.

831 Der Vorrang des Kindeswohls. *[In German]*; [Children's rights] *[Summary]*. Erich Peter. **A. Völk.** 43:2 6:2005 pp.257-270.

832 Why financial orders on divorce should be unfair. Jonathan Herring. **Int. J. Law Policy Fam.** 19:2 8:2005 pp.218-228.

833 The yardstick of equality: assessing contributions in Australia and England. Patrick Parkinson. **Int. J. Law Policy Fam.** 19:2 8:2005 pp.163-175.

Criminal law
Droit pénal

834 The accusatorial system lost and regained: reforming criminal procedure in Italy. Ennio Amodio. **Am. J. Comp. Law** LII:2 Spring:2004 pp.489-500.

835 American prosecutors as democracy promoters: prosecuting corrupt foreign officials in U.S. courts. Matthew J. Spence. **Yale Law J.** 114:5 3:2005 pp.1185-1192.

836 Anarchist direct actions: a challenge for law enforcement. Randy Borum; Chuck Tilby. **S. Confl. Terror.** 28:3 5-6:2005 pp.201-223.

837 Carrots and sticks: the TRC and the South African amnesty process. Jeremy Sarkin-Hughes. Antwerp FL: Intersentia, 2004. xiii, 441p. *ISBN: 9050954006. Includes bibliographical references (p. 391-403) and index.*

838 Compulsory compassion: a critique of restorative justice. Annalise E. Acorn. Vancouver: UBC Press, 2004. xii, 207p. *ISBN: 0774809426. Includes bibliographical references (p. 192-201) and index. (Series: Law and society).*

839 Consent and the rules of the game: the interplay of civil and criminal liability for sporting injuries. Stefan Fafinski. **J. Crim. Law** 69:5 10:2005 pp.414-426.

840   Constructing victims rights: the Home Office, New Labour, and victims. Paul Elliott Rock. Oxford: Oxford University Press, 2004. xxv, 583p. *ISBN: 0199275491.*

841   Criminal defense advocacy in Russia under the 2001 criminal procedure code. Pamela A. Jordan. **Am. J. Comp. Law** LIII:1 Winter:2005 pp.157-187.

842   Death at the hands of the state. David Wilson. London: Howard League for Penal Reform, 2005. 143p. *ISBN: 0903683784.*

843   Dignity, criminal law, and the bill of rights. Shannon Hoctor. **Sth. Afr. Law. J.** 121:2 2004 pp.304-317.

844   Don't cache out your case: prosecuting child pornography possession laws based on images located in temporary internet files. Ty E. Howard. **Berkeley Techno. Law J.** 19:4 Fall:2004 pp.1227-1274.

845   Le droit pénal comme acte constituant. *[In French]*; [Criminal law as constitutive act]. Jean-Claude Paye. **Temps Mod.** 60:630-631 3-6:2005 pp.273-289.

846   Du prétendu homicide de l'enfant à naître. *[In French]*; [The so-called murder of the child to be born]. Jean Mouly. **R. Sci. Crim.** 1 1-3:2005 pp.47-57.

847   Electronic monitoring in England and Wales: evidence-based or not? George Mair. **Crim. Just.** 5:3 8:2005 pp.257-277.

848   L'européanisation de la science pénale. *[In French]*; [The Europeanisation of criminal science]. Alessandro Bernardi. **Archives Politique Crim.** 26 2004 pp.5-36.

849   Evaluating the crime reduction programme in England and Wales. Mike Maguire; Mike Hough; Nick Tilley; Elizabeth A. Stanko; Tim Hope; Peter Raynor. **Crim. Just.** 4:3 8:2004 pp.213-325. *Collection of 6 articles.*

850   'Evidence-based-policy' and the government of the criminal justice system — only if the evidence fits! Michael Naughton. **Crit. Soc. Policy** 25:1(82-85) 2:2005 pp.47-69.

851   Der Fall Jukos. *[In German]*; [The Yukos affair]. Otto Luchterhandt; Angelika Nußberger; Dmitrij Marenkov; Lev Gudkov; Boris Dubin; Julia Kusznir; S. Leutheusser-Schnarrenberger; Reinhold Vetter; Oleh Rybačuk; Ivo Bock; Stefan Plaggenborg; Franz Schindler; Karlheinz Kasper. **Osteuropa** 55:7 7:2005 pp.7-102. *Collection of 4 articles.*

852   Fixing the boundaries of the concept of crime: the challenge for human rights. Audrey Guinchard. **Int. Comp. Law Q.** 54:3 7:2005 pp.719-734.

853   Fourth amendment limitations on the execution of computer searches conducted pursuant to a warrant. David J.S. Ziff. **Columb. Law R.** 105:3 4:2005 pp.841-872.

854   German cures for English ailments? Appropriation versus taking away — significance and consequences of conceptual differences between the English and the German law of theft. Nils Weinrich. **J. Crim. Law** 69:5 10:2005 pp.427-441.

855   L'imputation des infractions en droit pénal du travail. *[In French]*; [The imputation of criminal work law offenses]. Emmanuel Dreyer. **R. Sci. Crim.** 4 10-12:2004 pp.813-826.

856   L'incitation à la réalisation de l'infraction : nouvelle catégorie juridique du droit pénal ivoirien ? *[In French]*; [Incitation to commit an offense: a new legal category in the criminal law of Côte d'Ivoire?] Siriki Fangnigue Soro. **Penant** 847 4-6:2004 pp.188-214.

857   Infractions contre les personnes. *[In French]*; [Offences against people]. Yves Mayaud. **R. Sci. Crim.** 1 1-3:2005 pp.71-80.

858   Instrumental arguments in criminal law: a mirage of tensions. Pamela-Jane Schwikkard. **Sth. Afr. Law. J.** 121:2 2004 pp.289-303.

859   L'interprétation des normes supralégislatives en matière pénale. *[In French]*; [The interpretation of supralegislative norms in penal law]. Frédéric Garron. **R. Sci. Crim.** 4 10-12:2004 pp.773-801.

860   "Justice as Fairness" — Ein Modell auch für das Strafverfahren? *[In German]*; ['Justice as fairness' –a model for criminal justice?] Tatjana Hörnle. **Rechtstheorie** 35:2 2004 pp.175-194.

861   O kriminologicheskoi klassifikatsii prestuplenii. *[In Russian]*; (On the criminological classification of crimes.) V.N. Kudriavtsev; V.V. Luneev. **Gos. Pravo** 6 6:2005 pp.54-66.

862   A la recherche de la preuve absolue : réflexions sur l'utilisation de l'ADN en procédure pénale et sur le développement des fichiers d'empreintes génétiques. *[In French]*; [In search of the absolute proof: reflections on the use of DNA in criminal procedures and on

the development of genetic imprints]. Yann Padova. **Archives Politique Crim.** 26 2004 pp.71-90.

863   The law of Duress and the economics of credible threats. Oren Bar-Gill; Omri Ben-Shahar. **J. Legal S.** 33:2 6:2004 pp.391-430.

864   Legal globalization: money laundering law and other cases. Heba Shams. London: British Institute of International and Comparative Law, 2004. xii, 249p. *ISBN: 0903067730. Includes bibliographical references. Dedman School of Law. Queen Mary and Westfield College. (Series:* International financial law. Sir Joseph Gold memorial - 5).

865   Lessons from the abolition of capital punishment in Hungary: a fortuitous constellation amidst and beyond democratic transition. Renáta Uitz. **Acta Jur. Hun.** 45:1-2 2004 pp.67-100.

866   Miranda: the story of America's right to remain silent. Gary L. Stuart. Tucson AZ: University of Arizona Press, 2004. xxii, 212p. *ISBN: 0816523134. Includes bibliographical references (p. [195]-204) and index.*

867   Nullum crimen, nulla poena sine lege: aspects and prospects. Aly Mokhtar. **Stat. Law R.** 26:1 2005 pp.41-55.

868   Ombres et lumières de la politique criminelle italienne dans l'ère de l'urgence perpétuelle. *[In French]*; [Italian criminal policy] *[Summary]*; *[Summary in German]*; *[Summary in Spanish]*. Alessandro Bernardi. **Déviance Soc.** 28:4 12:2004 pp.439-461.

869   Penalization and retreat: the changing face of Dutch criminal justice. Francis Pakes. **Crim. Just.** 5:2 5:2005 pp.145-161.

870   A penalty system to enforce policy measures under incomplete information. Alexander S. Kritikos. **Int. R. Law Econ.** 24:3 9:2004 pp.385-403.

871   Penitentsiarnaiia politika Rossii v XVIII-XX vv.: istoriko-pravovoi analiz tendentsii razvitiia. *[In Russian]*; [Russia's prison policy in the 18th-20th centuries: legal history analysis of development tendencies]. I.V. Uporov. St. Petersburg: Iuridicheskii tsentr Press; Colophon, 2004. 608p. *ISBN: 5942013403. Includes bibliographical references (p. [560]-608).*

872   Politics and state punitiveness in black and white. Jeff Yates; Richard Fording. **J. Pol.** 67:4 11:2005 pp.1099-1121.

873   Prawo administracyjno-karne, czy nowa dziedzina prawa? *[In Polish]*; (Penal administrative law — a new branch of law?) Dobrosława Szumiło-Kulczycka. **Pań. Prawo** LIX:9(703) 9:2004 pp.3-16.

874   La présomption d'innocence en Europe. *[In French]*; [The presumption of innocence in Europe]. Christine Lazerges. **Archives Politique Crim.** 26 2004 pp.127-138.

875   (Prosecuting evil cults: law and the limitation of freedom of religious beliefs in Mainland China.); *[Text in Chinese]*. Guobin Zhu. **Hong Kong J. Soc. Sci.** 27 Spring-Summer:2004 pp.1-26.

876   Prostitution debates in France. Gill Allwood. **Cont. Pol.** 10:2 6:2004 pp.145-157.

877   The public choice of elder abuse law. Margaret F. Brinig; Gerald Jogerst; Jeanette Daly; Gretchen Schmuch; Jeffrey Dawson. **J. Legal S.** 33:2 6:2004 pp.517-549.

878   Les représentations sociales de la justice pénale. *[In French]*; [Social representations of criminal justice]. Déviance et société. **Déviance Soc.** 28:2 2004 pp.139-194.

879   Restorative justice: deliberative democracy in action? John Parkinson; Declan Roche. **Aust. J. Pol. Sci.** 39:3 11:2004 pp.505-518.

880   (The right of the accused person to have a fair trial in the Jordanian law.); *[Text in Arabic]*. Mohammad Subhi Najm. **Dirasat Sha. Law** 32:1 5:2005 pp.122-139.

881   Sentencing guidelines for South Africa: lessons from elsewhere. S.S. Terblanche. **Sth. Afr. Law. J.** 121:4 2004 pp.858-882.

882   Shooting felons: law, practice, official culture, and perceptions of morality. A.W. Brian Simpson. **J. Law Soc.** 32:2 6:2005 pp.241-266.

883   Shoring up the weakest link: what lawmakers around the world need to consider in developing comprehensive laws to combat cybercrime. Richard W. Downing. **Columb. J. Tr. Law** 43:3 2005 pp.705-762.

884   Should the law of theft extend to information? Anna Louise Christie. **J. Crim. Law** 69:4 8:2005 pp.349-360.

885   Das Strafrecht in der Rechtsprechung der Landesverfassungsgerichte. *[In German]*; [Criminal law in the jurisdiction of the federal constitutional courts] *[Summary]*. Klaus Ferdinand Gärditz. **Arc. Öffen. Recht** 129:4 12:2004 pp.584-617.

886   Le système pénal OHADA ou l'uniformisation à mi-chemin. *[In French]*; [The OHADA penal system or halfway standardization]. Michel Mahouve. **Penant** 846 1-3:2004 pp.87-96.

887   Les transformations de l'administration de la preuve pénale. *[In French]*; [Transformations in the administration of criminal proof]. Archives de politique criminelle. **Archives Politique Crim.** 26 2004 pp.113-124.

888   Les transformations de l'administration de la preuve pénale : perspectives comparées (Allemagne, Belgique, Canada, Espagne, Etats-Unis, France, Italie, Portugal, Royaume-Uni). *[In French]*; [Transformations in the administration of criminal proof: comparative perspectives (Germany, Belgium, Canada, Spain, United States, France, Italy, Portugal, United Kingdom)]. Geneviève Giudicelli-Delage [Ed.]. **Archives Politique Crim.** 26 2004 pp.139-188.

889   Ugolovno-pravovye, kriminologicheskie i sotsial'no-psikhologicheskie osobennosti form souchastiia v presupleniiakh v sfere ekonomicheskoi deiatel'nosti. *[In Russian]*; [Criminal law, criminological and socio-psychological aspects of forms of complicity in financial crimes]. T.V. Dosiukova. **Gos. Pravo** 8 8:2005 pp.31-41.

890   Victims' rights in criminal trials: prospects for participation. Jonathan Doak. **J. Law Soc.** 32:2 6:2005 pp.294-316.

891   With malice aforethought: a study of the crime and punishment for homicide. Louis Jacques Blom-Cooper; Terence Morris. Oxford: Hart Publishing, 2004. xii, 204p. *ISBN: 1841134856.*

Judicial process
Processus judiciaire

892   Access to courts. Geoff Budlender. **Sth. Afr. Law. J.** 121:2 2004 pp.339-358.

893   Annahme nach Ermessen bei Verfassungsbeschwerden? *[In German]*; [The writ of certiorari-procedure of the US Supreme Court]. Wolfgang Graf Vitzthum. **Jahr. Öffent. Gegen.** 53 2005 pp.319-344.

894   Capacity, attitudes, and case attributes: the differential success of the states before the United States courts of appeals. Rorie Spill Solberg; Leonard Ray. **State Pol. Policy Q.** 5:2 Summer:2005 pp.147-167.

895   Choice of law in the American courts in 2004: eighteenth annual survey. Symeon C. Symeonides. **Am. J. Comp. Law** LII:4 Fall:2004 pp.919-993.

896   The consensual norm on the high court of Australia: 1904-2001; *[Summary in French]*. Paresh Kumar Narayan; Russell Smyth. **Int. Pol. Sci. R.** 26:2 4:2005 pp.147-168.

897   Consequences of the Rehnquist court's federalism decisions for congressional lawmaking. John Dinan. **Publius** 34:2 Spring:2004 pp.39-67.

898   Contractual discretion and administrative discretion: a unified analysis. Terence Daintith. **Mod. Law R.** 68:4 7:2005 pp.554-593.

899   Court decision making in police brutality cases, 1990-2000. Madhavi McCall. **Am. Pol. Res.** 33:1 1:2005 pp.56-80.

900   Courts and compliance in international regulatory regimes. Clifford J. Carrubba. **J. Pol.** 67:3 8:2005 pp.669-689.

901   De la composition pénale au plaider-coupable : le pouvoir de sanction du procureur. *[In French]*; [From penal composition to pleading guilty: the attorney's power to punish]. Claire Saas. **R. Sci. Crim.** 4 10-12:2004 pp.827-842.

902   Democracy, rights disagreements and judicial review. Patrick Lenta. **S. Afr. J. Human Rights** 20:1 2004 pp.1-31.

903   Does the appointment of judges increase the output of the judiciary? Michael Beenstock; Yoel Haitovsky. **Int. R. Law Econ.** 24:3 9:2004 pp.351-369.

904   The duty to defend. Barbara Allen Babcock. **Yale Law J.** 114:6 4:2005 pp.1489-1520.

905   La ejecución de sentencias de los tribunales contencioso-administrativos. *[In Spanish]*; [The execution of sentences from contentious-administrative courts]. Susana de la Sierra; Daniel Sarmiento. **R. Admin. Públ.** 166 1-4:2005 pp.441-475.

906   The elimination of hung juries: retrials and nonunanimous verdicts. William S. Neilson; Harold Winter. **Int. R. Law Econ.** 25:1 3:2005 pp.1-19.

907   An empire of light? Learning and lawmaking in the history of German law. Stefan Vogenauer. **Camb. Law J.** 64:2 7:2005 pp.481-500.

908   The empire strikes back: press judges and communication advisers in Dutch courts. Lieve Gies. **J. Law Soc.** 32:3 9:2005 pp.450-472.

909   Expert testimony in the dock. Adam Wilson. **J. Crim. Law** 69:4 8:2005 pp.330-348.

910   Female judges matter: gender and collegial decisionmaking in the federal appellate courts. Jennifer L. Peresie. **Yale Law J.** 114:7 5:2005 pp.1759-1790.

911   Fig leaves, fairy tales, and constitutional foundations: debating judicial review in Britain. Lori Ringhand. **Columb. J. Tr. Law** 43:3 2005 pp.865-904.

912   From ambiguity to legality: the future of English judicial review. Douglas E. Edlin. **Am. J. Comp. Law** LII:2 Spring:2004 pp.383-401.

913   Gideon in white/Gideon in black: race and identity in lawyering. Anthony V. Alfieri. **Yale Law J.** 114:6 4:2005 pp.1459-1488.

914   Government lawyers and non-judicial constitutional review in Estonia. Nancy Maveety; Vello Pettai. **Euro.-Asia S.** 57:1 1:2005 pp.93-115.

915   Les groupes d'intervention régionaux (GIR), un objet juridique désormais mieux identifié. *[In French]*; [Regional intervention groups (GIR), a juridical object now better identified]. Jean-Paul Jean. **R. Sci. Crim.** 1 1-3:2005 pp.59-64.

916   Intensity of judicial review in equal treatment cases. J.H. Gerards. **Neth. Int. Law R.** LI:2 2004 pp.135-184.

917   'Interpose your friendly hand': political supports for the exercise of judicial review by the United States Supreme Court. Keith E. Whittington. **Am. Pol. Sci. R.** 99:4 11:2005 pp.583-596.

918   John Hart Ely and the problem of gerrymandering: the lion in Winter. Pamela S. Karlan. **Yale Law J.** 114:6 4:2005 pp.1329-1351.

919   The judges' council. Thomas. **Publ. Law** Autumn:2005 pp.608-630.

920   Judicial restraint and overreach. Patrick Lenta. **S. Afr. J. Human Rights** 20:4 2004 pp.544-576.

921   Learning about judicial independence: institutional change in the state courts. F. Andrew Hanssen. **J. Legal S.** 33:2 6:2004 pp.431-474.

922   The lesson of Lopez: the political dynamics of federalism's political safeguards. **Harv. Law R.** 119:2 12:2005 pp.609-630.

923   Limiting coercive speech in class actions. Andrei Greenawalt. **Yale Law J.** 114:8 6:2005 pp.1953-1988.

924   Litigation, judicial path-dependence, and legal change. Vincy Fon; Francesco Parisi; Ben Depoorter. **Euro. J. Law Econ.** 20:1 7:2005 pp.43-56.

925   A multi-criteria modeling approach to jury selection. Marc J. Schniederjans; Ellen Hollcroft. **Socio-econ. Plan. Sci.** 39:1 3:2005 pp.81-102.

926   Pluralism and distrust: how courts can support democracy by lowering the stakes of politics. William N. Eskridge, Jr. **Yale Law J.** 114:6 4:2005 pp.1279-1328.

927   Politics and judiciary verdicts on vote-buying litigation in Taiwan. Chung-li Wu; Chi Huang. **Asian Sur.** XLIV:5 9-10:2004 pp.755-770.

928   Preclusion in class action litigation. Tobias Barrington Wolff. **Columb. Law R.** 105:3 4:2005 pp.717-808.

929   The problem of judicial control in Africa's neopatrimonial democracies: Malawi and Zambia. Peter VonDoepp. **Pol. Sci. Q.** 120:2 Summer:2005 pp.275-301.

930 Pro-poor court, anti-poor outcomes: explaining the performance of the South African land claims court. Theunis Roux. **S. Afr. J. Human Rights** 20:4 2004 pp.511-543.

931 Realizacja prawa do sądu a spory kompetencyjne w świetle nowych regulacji prawnych. *[In Polish]*; (Putting into effect the right to court and disputes about competences in the light of new regulations.) Renata Lewicka. **Pań. Prawo** LIX:II 11:2004 pp.62-72.

932 'Resettlements': revenue consequences of varying discretionary trusts. John Glover. **Aust. Law J.** 79:10 10:2005 pp.620-640.

933 The right to effective judicial protection in community law: intervention before community courts. Márton Varju. **Acta Jur. Hun.** 46:1-2 2005 pp.51-72.

934 'Salvage operations are ordinarily preferable to the wrecking ball': barring challenges to subject matter jurisdiction. Qian A. Gao. **Columb. Law R.** 105:8 12:2005 pp.2369-2408.

935 The scales of justice: balancing neutrality and efficiency in plea-bargaining encounters. Seung-hee Lee. **Disc. Soc.** 16:1 1:2005 pp.33-54.

936 Self-inflicted constraints on judicial government in Nigeria. Tunde I. Ogowewo. **J. Afr. Law** 49:1 2005 pp.39-53.

937 Shakedown: how corporations, government, and trial lawyers abuse the judicial process. Robert A. Levy. Washington DC: Cato Institute, 2004. ix, 325p. *ISBN: 1930865619. Includes bibliographical references and index.*

938 State power and unbalanced legal development in China. Yongshun Cai; Songcai Yang. **J. Cont. China** 14:42 2:2005 pp.117-134.

939 Strategic leadership and political change on the Canadian Supreme Court: analyzing the transition to chief justice; *[Summary in French]*. Matthew E. Wetstein; C.L. Ostberg. **Can. J. Pol.** 38:3 9:2005 pp.653-674.

940 Strony i uczestnicy postępowania sądowoadministracyjnego. *[In Polish]*; (Parties and participants in the judicial administrative proceedings.) Wojciech Chróścielewski. **Pań. Prawo** LIX:9(703) 9:2004 pp.32-45.

941 Supreme Court consensus and dissent: estimating the role of the selection screen. Brian Goff. **Publ. Choice** 122:3-4 3:2005 pp.483-499.

942 Taxpayers or governments? Default as determinant in Canadian and US Supreme Court tax decisions; *[Summary in French]*. Alexandra Flynn. **Can. J. Pol.** 38:3 9:2005 pp.605-626.

943 The tragedy of Dou E: issues relating to the question of evidence in the traditional administration of justice; *[Summary in Chinese]*. Su Li. **Soc. Sci. China** XXVI:3 Autumn:2005 pp.41-51.

944 Transformation de la philosophie et de la gestion pénales des femmes justiciables au Canada : trois cas de figure. *[In French]*; [The transformation of the philosophy and of the criminal management of women subject to trial in Canada: three types] *[Summary]*. Sylvie Frigon. **Can. J. Wom. Law** 16:2 2004 pp.353-418.

945 Trial by jury: still a lamp in the dark? Laura McGowan. **J. Crim. Law** 69:6 12:2005 pp.518-534.

946 The two discourses in Colombian constitutional jurisprudence: a new approach to modeling judicial behavior in Latin America. David Landau. **George Washington Int. Law R.** 37:3 2005 pp.687-744.

947 L'usage, fondement de la sentence rendue par le juge administratif camerounais. *[In French]*; (Practice as the basis of sentences passed by the administrative judge in Cameroon.) *[Summary]*. François-Narcisse Djame. **Verf. Recht Übersee** 38:2 2005 pp.154-173.

948 Wasted costs orders against lawyers in Australia. Bill Pincus; Linda Haller. **Aust. Law J.** 79:8 8:2005 pp.497-506.

949 Weak forms of judicial review — a solution to the 'mighty problem'? C. Lebeck. **Z. Öffent. Recht** 60:1 2005 pp.55-110.

950 What price justice(s)? Understanding campaign spending in state Supreme Court elections. Chris W. Bonneau. **State Pol. Policy Q.** 5:2 Summer:2005 pp.107-125.

951 When judges fail justice. Edwin Cameron. **Sth. Afr. Law. J.** 121:3 2004 pp.580-594.

952 Who will find the defendant if he stays with his sheep? Justice in rural China. Frank K. Upham. **Yale Law J.** 114:7 5:2005 pp.1675-1718.

953   Will the durational element endure? Only time will tell: temporary regulatory takings in the court of federal claims and federal circuit after Tahoe-Sierra. Heather G. Wight-Axling. **Natur. Res. J.** 45:1 Winter:2005 pp.201-237.

Legal systems
Systèmes juridiques

954   Abortion, gay rights and politics in Britain and America: a comparison. Martin Durham. **Parl. Aff.** 58:1 1:2005 pp.89-103.

955   Administration of justice in traditional African style: role of customary courts in Botswana. Keshav C. Sharma. **Indian J. Publ. Admin.** LI:1 1-3:2005 pp.108-124.

956   African women and participation in public life and governance: relevant laws and overview of recent experience. Kaniye S.A. Ebeku. **Verf. Recht Übersee** 38:1 2005 pp.56-77.

957   Against metaphysics in law: the historical background of American and Scandinavian legal realism compared. Heikki Pihlajamäki. **Am. J. Comp. Law** LII:2 Spring:2004 pp.469-488.

958   The application of South African law in the courts of Botswana. G. van Niekerk. **Comp. Int. Law J. Sth. Afr.** XXXVII:3 11:2004 pp.312-326.

959   Backlash against feminism: Canadian custody and access reform debates of the late twentieth century; *[Summary in French]*. Susan B. Boyd. **Can. J. Wom. Law** 16:2 2004 pp.255-290.

960   Börtön helyett egyezség? Mediáció és más alternatív szankciók Európában. *[In Hungarian]*; (Reconciliation instead of imprisonment. Mediation and other alternative sanctions in Europe.) Tünde Barabás A. Budapest: KJK-Kerszöv Kft, 2004. 243p. *ISBN: 9632246268. Includes bibliographical references (p. 195-205).*

961   Bremer's "Gordian knot": transitional justice and the US occupation of Iraq. Eric Stover; Hanny Megally; Hania Mufti. **Hum. Rights Q.** 27:3 8:2005 pp.830-857.

962   Canadian fundamental justice and U.S. due process: two models for a guarantee of basic adjudicative fairness. David M. Siegel. **George Washington Int. Law R.** 37:1 2005 pp.1-50.

963   The class action in common law legal systems: a comparative perspective. Rachael P. Mulheron. Oxford, Portland OR: Hart Publishing, 2004. lxxvi, 535p. *ISBN: 1841134368. Includes bibliographical references (p. [507]-526) and index.*

964   Codification in England: the need to move from an ideological to a functional approach — a bridge too far? Eva Steiner. **Stat. Law R.** 25:3 2004 pp.209-222.

965   Colonization and the rule of law: comparing the effectiveness of common law and civil law countries. Sandra F. Joireman. **Constit. Pol. Econ.** 15:4 12:2004 pp.315-338.

966   Comparative law as comparative jurisprudence — the comparability of legal systems. Catherine Valcke. **Am. J. Comp. Law** LII:3 Summer:2004 pp.713-740.

967   Compensation for personal injury in English, German and Italian law: a comparative outline. B.S. Markesinis; et al. Cambridge: Cambridge University Press, 2005. xxxvi, 238p. *ISBN: 0521846137. Includes bibliographical references and index.* (Series: Cambridge studies in international and comparative law).

968   Contrasting prisoners' rights: a comparative examination of Germany and England. Liora Lazarus. Oxford, New York: Oxford University Press, 2004. xliii, 289p. *ISBN: 0199259836. Includes bibliographical references (p. [255]-277) and index.*

969   A country I do not recognize: the legal assault on American values. Robert H. Bork [Ed.]. Stanford CA: Hoover Institution Press, 2005. xxxvi, 196p. *ISBN: 0817946020. Includes bibliographical references and index.* (Series: Hoover Institution Press publication - 535).

970   Delict, contract, and the bill of rights: a perspective from the United Kingdom. Hector L. MacQueen. **Sth. Afr. Law. J.** 121:2 2004 pp.359-394.

971   The dilemma of constitutional property in ethnic land regimes: Israel and South Africa compared. Aeyal M. Gross. **Sth. Afr. Law. J.** 121:2 2004 pp.448-465.

972   Discussion paper on variation and termination of trusts. Scottish Law Commission. Edinburgh: Stationery Office, 2005. vii, 77p. *ISBN: 010888175X. Includes bibliographical references.*

973   The economic ascent of the Middle East's religious minorities: the role of Islamic legal pluralism. Timur Kuran. **J. Legal S.** 33:2 6:2004 pp.475-515.

974   The effectiveness of the juvenile justice system. David J. Smith. **Crim. Just.** 5:2 5:2005 pp.181-195.

975   L'élection de droit : comparaison québéco-européenne. *[In French]*; [The law election: European-Quebec comparison] *[Summary]*; *[Summary in French].* Sylvette Guillemard. **R. Int. Droit Comp.** 57:1 1-3:2005 pp.49-83.

976   Em busca da judicialização da política no Brasil: apontamentos para uma nova abordagem. *[In Portuguese]*; (In search of judicialization of politics: notes for a new approach.) *[Summary]*; *[Summary in French].* Ernani Rodrigues de Carvalho. **R. Sociol. Pol.** 23 11:2004 pp.115-126.

977   From Lerotholi to Lando: some examples of comparative law methodology. Vernon Valentine Palmer. **Am. J. Comp. Law** LIII:1 Winter:2005 pp.261-290.

978   Gegenwärtige Lage und Entwicklungsrichtung des chinesischen Rechtssystems. Eine Skizze. *[In German]*; (Present situation and direction of development of the Chinese legal system.) *[Summary].* Robert Heuser. **Verf. Recht Übersee** 38:2 2005 pp.137-153.

979   Az igazságszolgáltatás reformja. 1987-1997. Rendszerváltozás a bíróságok igazgatásában. *[In Hungarian]*; (The reform of the justice. 1987-1997. Regime transition in the administration of the courts.) László Gatter. Budapest: KJK-Kerszöv Kft, 2004. 287p. *ISBN: 9632247922.*

980   Impediments to transnational cooperation in undercover policing: a comparative study of the United States and Italy. Jacqueline E. Ross. **Am. J. Comp. Law** LII:3 Summer:2004 pp.569-623.

981   The influence of law in the Supreme Court's search-and-seizure jurisprudence. Herbert M. Kritzer; Mark J. Richards. **Am. Pol. Res.** 33:1 1:2005 pp.33-55.

982   Institutionalizing collective memories of hate: law and law enforcement in Germany and the United States. Joachim J. Savelsberg; Ryan D. King. **Am. J. Sociol.** 111:2 9:2005 pp.579-616.

983   International treaties and British statutes. Franklin Berman. **Stat. Law R.** 26:1 2005 pp.1-12.

984   Introducción a los significados de la ordenación del territorio en Europa. *[In Spanish]*; [Introduction to the meaning of the arrangement of the territory in Europe]. Fernando López Ramón. **R. Admin. Públ.** 166 1-4:2005 pp.213-230.

985   (Irrevocable power of attorney in the Jordanian legislation.) *[Summary]*; *[Text in Arabic].* Ghazi Abu-Orabi. **Dirasat Sha. Law** 31:2 11:2004 pp.337-353.

986   Islamic law and gender equality: could there be a common ground? A study of divorce and polygamy in Sharia law and contemporary legislation in Tunisia and Egypt. Amira Mashhour. **Hum. Rights Q.** 27:2 5:2005 pp.562-596.

987   The Israeli constitutional revolution/evolution, models of constitutions, and a lesson from mistakes and achievements. Yoseph M. Edrey. **Am. J. Comp. Law** LIII:1 Winter:2005 pp.77-123.

988   Jogharmonizációs feladatok a csatlakozás után. *[In Hungarian]*; (Post-accession tasks of legal harmonisation.) *[Summary].* Judit Fazekas. **Euro. Tükör** 9:3 2004 pp.18-29.

989   Judicial activism in Australia. Ian Barker. **Aust. Law J.** 79:12 12:2005 pp.783-794.

990   Judicial independence in Bulgaria: a tale of splendour and misery. Bruno Schönfelder. **Euro.-Asia S.** 57:1 1:2005 pp.61-92.

991   The jurisprudential classification, evaluation and reform of evidentiary principles. C. Theophilopoulos. **Sth. Afr. Law. J.** 121:1 2004 pp.163-186.

992   Law, religion and secularism. Lama Abu-Odeh; Christina Jones-Pauly; Neamat Nojumi; Abdulmumini Adebayo Oba; Seval Yildirim. **Am. J. Comp. Law** LII:4 Fall:2004 pp.789-918. *Collection of 4 articles.*

993   Legal aid in South Africa: making justice reality. Hennie Van As. **J. Afr. Law** 49:1 2005 pp.54-72.

994   Legal infrastructure and governance reform in post-crisis Asia: the case of Indonesia. Tim Lindsey. **Asian-Pac. Econ. Lit.** 18:1 5:2004 pp.12-40.

995   (The methodologies of the scholars in the principles of Islamic jurisprudence in researching the issue of specifying the cause of legislating the rulings.); *[Text in Arabic].* M.S. Jaber; A.M. Al-Dabbagh. **Dirasat Sha. Law** 32:1 5:2005 pp.174-195.

996   Mexican law. Stephen Zamora. Oxford, New York: Oxford University Press, 2004. xxviii, 712p. *ISBN: 0198267770. Includes bibliographical references and index.*

997   Muslim laws, politics and society in modern nation states: dynamic legal pluralisms in England, Turkey, and Pakistan. Ihsan Yilmaz. Aldershot, Burlington VT: Ashgate, 2005. xxii, 248p. *ISBN: 0754643891. Includes bibliographical references (p. [183]-239) and index.*

998   The Norwegian supreme court and equitable considerations: problematic aspects of legal reasoning. Anne-Mette Magnussen. **Scand. Pol. S.** 28:1 2005 pp.69-89.

999   The origins and evolution of Islamic law. Wael B. Hallaq. Cambridge, New York: Cambridge University Press, 2005. ix, 234p. *ISBN: 0521803322, 0521005809. Includes bibliographical references and index. (Series:* Themes in Islamic law - 1).

1000   Racial bias and the English criminal trial jury. Gillian Daly; Rosemary Pattenden. **Camb. Law J.** 64:3 11:2005 pp.678-710.

1001   La reforma a la justicia en Colombia: un movimiento amplio de globalizaciones hegemónicas. *[In Spanish];* [The reform to justice in Colombia: a wide movement of hegemonic globalization] *[Summary].* Andrés Ucrós. **Colom. Int.** 59 2004 pp.162-176.

1002   La réforme de la justice en Mauritanie. *[In French];* [The reform of justice in Mauritania]. Haïmoud Ould Ramdan. **Penant** 846 1-3:2004 pp.5-71.

1003   Reforming the laws on public procurement in the developing world: the example of Kenya. Victor Mosoti. **Int. Comp. Law Q.** 54:3 7:2005 pp.621-650.

1004   The rule of law in the realm and the province of New York: prelude to the American revolution. Herbert A. Johnson. **History** 91:301 1:2005 pp.3-23.

1005   Stufung und "Entstufung" des Rechts. *[In German];* [Structural aspects of legal orders] *[Summary].* C. Jabloner. **Z. Öffent. Recht** 60:2 2005 pp.163-186.

1006   Symposium sentencing: what's at stake for the states? Gerard E. Lynch [Intro.]; William H. Pryor, Jr.; Nancy J. King; David A. Soulé; Sara Steen; Robert R. Weidner; Ronald F. Wright; Kyron Huigens; Kevin R. Reitz; Paul H. Robinson; Barbara A. Spellman; R.A. Duff; Richard S. Frase; Michael Tonry; Rachel E. Barkow; Frank O. Bowman, III; Marc L. Miller; Franklin E. Zimring. **Columb. Law R.** 105:4 5:2005 pp.933-1415. *Collection of 14 articles.*

1007   Towards a jurisprudence of legislators: a reflective look at contemporary jurisprudence against the backdrop of law transplantation. Shigong Jiang. **Soc. Sci. China** XXVI:2 Summer:2005 pp.61-72.

1008   The transition from socialist law and resurgence of traditional law. Marijan Pavčnik. **Acta Jur. Hun.** 46:1-2 2005 pp.13-31.

1009   Verfassungsreform und Systemtheorie: Aktuelle Wandlungen des spanischen Rechtssystems. *[In German];* [Constitutional reform and systems theory: current changes in the Spanish legal system]. Benito Aláez Corral. **Rechtstheorie** 36:1 2005 pp.68-90.

1010   Weighing and implementing the right to counsel. Stephen Ellmann. **Sth. Afr. Law. J.** 121:2 2004 pp.318-338.

1011   Why should Austria be different from Germany? The two recent nationality reforms in contrast. Alice Ludvig. **Ger. Pol.** 13:3 9:2004 pp.499-515.

1012   Worlds apart: Western and Central European judicial culture at the onset of the European enlargement. Zdeněk Kühn. **Am. J. Comp. Law** LII:3 Summer:2004 pp.531-567.

Public law
Droit public

1013   Aboriginal title, indigenous rights and the right to culture. Karin Lehmann. **S. Afr. J. Human Rights** 20:1 2004 pp.86-118.

1014   Alarmist or relaxed? Election expenditure limits and free speech. Jane Marriott. **Publ. Law** Winter:2005 pp.764-784.

1015   Alkotmánybírósági esetjog. *[In Hungarian]*; (Case law of the constitutional court.) Gábor Halmai [Ed.]. Budapest: INDOK, 2004. 462p. *ISBN: 963214726X.*

1016   L'attività normativa del governo nel periodo luglio-dicembre 2004. *[In Italian]*; [The government's normative activity in the period July-December 2004]. Lorenzo Casini; Martina Conticelli. **Riv. Trim. Pubbl.** 2 2005 pp.461-533.

1017   Breaking ground: some thoughts on the seismic shift in our administrative law. Kate O'Regan. **Sth. Afr. Law. J.** 121:2 2004 pp.424-437.

1018   Der Bundessicherheitsrat. *[In German]*; [The Federal Security Council]. Kai Zähle. **Der Staat** 44:3 2005 pp.462-482.

1019   Challenging warrantless inspections of abortion providers: a new constitutional strategy. Amalia W. Jorns. **Columb. Law R.** 105:5 6:2005 pp.1563-1596.

1020   China's administrative litigation in practice. Arthur K.C. Cheung. **Publ. Admin. Policy** 13:2 9:2004 pp.149-169.

1021   China's administrative litigation law. Arthur K.C. Cheung. **Publ. Law** Autumn:2005 pp.549-570.

1022   Chronique de jurisprudence administrative (2004). *[In French]*; [Chronicle on administrative jurisprudence 2004)]. Christophe Guettier. **R. Droit Publ.** 2 3-4:2005 pp.493-575.

1023   Código procesal administrativo. Modelo para Iberoamérica. *[In Spanish]*; [Contentious-administrative procedure act. A model for Latin America]. Jesús González Pérez. **R. Admin. Públ.** 165 9-12:2004 pp.381-405.

1024   Comentarios en torno a la ley del proceso contencioso-administrativo del Perú. *[In Spanish]*; [Comments on the contentious-administrative act in Peru]. Juan José Díez Sánchez. **R. Admin. Públ.** 165 9-12:2004 pp.327-351.

1025   La Constitution et l'Administration. *[In French]*; [Constitution and administration]. Francis Delpérée. **R. Int. Sci. Admin.** 70:4 12:2004 pp.641-651.

1026   The constitution: ultimate foundation of Australian law? W.M.C. Gummow. **Aust. Law J.** 79:3 3:2005 pp.167-181.

1027   Constitutional dialogue in Uganda. Erica Bussey. **J. Afr. Law** 49:1 2005 pp.1-23.

1028   Constitutional procedural law in Mexican state constitutions. Eduardo Ferrer Mac-Gregor. **Jahr. Öffent. Gegen.** 53 2005 pp.629-648.

1029   Constitutional reform and the rule of law in Greece. Pavlos Eleftheriadis. **West Euro. Pol.** 28:2 3:2005 pp.317-334.

1030   Constitutionalism in the age of rights – a prolegomenon. Lorraine E. Weinrib. **Sth. Afr. Law. J.** 121:2 2004 pp.278-288.

1031   Contracts in administrative law: life after formalism? Cora Hoexter. **Sth. Afr. Law. J.** 121:3 2004 pp.595-618.

1032   De la difficile adaptation du principe républicain de laïcité à l'évolution socio-culturelle française. *[In French]*; [From the difficult adaptation of the republican principle of secularism to the French sociocultural evolution]. Ludivine Delsenne. **R. Droit Publ.** 2 3-4:2005 pp.427-462.

1033   Il diritto amministrativo globale: una introduzione. *[In Italian]*; [Global administrative law: an introduction]. Sabino Cassese. **Riv. Trim. Pubbl.** 2 2005 pp.331-358.

1034   Droit de la fonction publique territoriale et management des ressources humaines. *[In French]*; [The law of territorial public administration and human resources management]. Jacques Fialaire. **R. Gén. Coll. Territ.** 31 11-12:2004 pp.847-859.

1035   La ejecución provisional de las sentencias contencioso-administrativas en Italia. *[In Spanish]*; [The provisional execution of contentious-administrative sentences in Italy]. Isaac Martín Delgado. **R. Admin. Públ.** 165 9-12:2004 pp.353-377.

1036   Fundamento constitucional del impuesto predial en Venezuela. *[In Spanish]*; (Constitutional bases for land taxation in Venezuela.) Rafael Romero Pirela. **Cuest. Pol.** 32 1-6:2004 pp.129-141.

1037   Geschäftsführung ohne Auftrag im Öffentlichen Recht. Entwicklung der Rechtsprechung im letzten Jahrzehnt. *[In German]*; [Managing business without mandate in public law. Legal developments of the past decade]. Friedrich Schoch. **Verwalt.** 38:1 2005 pp.91-110.

1038   Godność człowieka – aktualne kwestie sporne w niemieckim prawie państwowym. *[In Polish]*; (Human dignity – current controversial issues in German constitutional law.) Otto Luchterhandt; Roman Brüschke. **Pań. Prawo** LX:2(708) 2:2005 pp.34-48.

1039   Hochschulräte – Demokratieprinzip – Selbstverwaltung. *[In German]*; [University supervisory boards-democracy – self-government] *[Summary]*. Wolfgang Kahl. **Arc. Öffen. Recht** 130:2 6:2005 pp.225-262.

1040   I procedimenti comunitari composti: il caso delle telecomunicazioni. *[In Italian]*; [Communitarian composed procedures: the telecommunications case]. Lorenzo Saltari. **Riv. Trim. Pubbl.** 2 2005 pp.389-434.

1041   Indians 78, Washington State 0: stories about Indians and the law. Steven E. Aufrecht; David S. Case. **Publ. Admin. R.** 65:4 7-8:2005 pp.450-461.

1042   Interpreting the disability ground of the abortion act. Rosamund Scott. **Camb. Law J.** 64:2 7:2005 pp.388-412.

1043   Justiziabilität sozialer Grundrechte und Verfassungsaufträge. *[In German]*; [Justiciability of social basic rights and the constitution]. Gertrude Lübbe-Wolff. **Jahr. Öffent. Gegen.** 53 2005 pp.1-25.

1044   A Kanadai legfelsőbb bíróság Quebec secession reference ügyben hozott döntésének elemzése. *[In Hungarian]*; (The analysis of Canadian Supreme Court's decision in the Quebec secession reference case.) *[Summary]*. István János Molnár. **Jogtud. Köz.** 59:3 2004 pp.89-102.

1045   (Native) American exceptionalism in federal public law. Philip P. Frickey. **Harv. Law R.** 119:2 12:2005 pp.431-490.

1046   Organizzazioni internazionali e soggetti privati: verso un diritto amministrativo globale? *[In Italian]*; [International organizations and private subjects: towards a global administrative law?] Stefano Battini. **Riv. Trim. Pubbl.** 2 2005 pp.359-388.

1047   Popular? Constitutionalism? Larry Alexander; Lawrence B. Solum. **Harv. Law R.** 118:5 3:2005 pp.1594-1640.

1048   Por una nueva ley de expropiación forzosa y un nuevo sistema de determinación del justiprecio. *[In Spanish]*; [For a new law of forced expropriation and a new sistem of price determination]. Tomás-Ramón Fernández. **R. Admin. Públ.** 166 1-4:2005 pp.7-27.

1049   Pravovye normy v mekhanizme gosudarstvennogo upravleniia. *[In Russian]*; [Legal norms in public administration]. R.R. Aliullov. **Sots.Gum. Znan.** 6 2004 pp.308-318.

1050   Protección jurídico-administrativa del medio marino y transporte marítimo. Notas en torno al accidente del Prestige. *[In Spanish]*; [Legal-administrative protection of maritime areas and maritime transport. Notes regarding the accident of the Prestige]. María Zambonino Pulito. **R. Admin. Públ.** 165 9-12:2004 pp.215-235.

1051   Public law regulation of markets and fairs. Barry Hough. **Publ. Law** Autumn:2005 pp.586-607.

1052   The quest for equal treatment. Hale of Richmond [Baroness]. **Publ. Law** Autumn:2005 pp.571-585.

1053   The question of case selection in comparative constitutional law. Ran Hirschl. **Am. J. Comp. Law** LIII:1 Winter:2005 pp.125-155.

1054   Realising the right to food in South Africa: not by policy alone – a need for framework legislation. Sibonile Khoza. **S. Afr. J. Human Rights** 20:4 2004 pp.664-683.

1055   Das Regulierungsrecht im Spannungsfeld von öffentlichem und privatem Recht. *[In German]*; [Regulatory law in tension between public and private law] *[Summary]*. Franz Jürgen Säcker. **Arc. Öffen. Recht** 130:2 6:2005 pp.180-224.

1056   Le riforme amministrative in Italia. *[In Italian]*; [Administrative reforms in Italy]. Mario Savino. **Riv. Trim. Pubbl.** 2 2005 pp.435-460.

1057   Risiko – und Innovationsrecht im Verbund. *[In German]*; [Risk and innovation law bundled]. Wolfgang Hoffmann-Riem. **Verwalt.** 38:2 2005 pp.145-176.

1058   Sobre la responsabilidad patrimonial del Estado como autor de una ley declarada inconstitucional. *[In Spanish]*; [On the patrimonial responsibility of the state as author of a law declared un-constitutional]. Eduardo García de Enterría. **R. Admin. Públ.** 166 1-4:2005 pp.99-147.

1059   Sovershenstvovanie zakonodatel'nogo regulirovaniia instituta konstitutsionno-pravovoi otvetsvennosti sub"ektov Rossiiskoi Federatsii. *[In Russian]*; (Improvement in adjustment of constitutional responsibility of subjects of the Russian Federation.) A.V. Bezrukov; A.A. Kondrashev. **Gos. Pravo** 8 8:2004 pp.39-49.

1060   Staatliche Verantwortung für den Schutz privater Geheimnisse. Eine Rekonstruktion des Geheimnisschutzrechts. *[In German]*; [State responsibility for the protection of private secrets. Confidentiality law reconstructed]. Gernot Sydow. **Verwalt.** 38:1 2005 pp.35-64.

1061   La substitution de la loi à la jurisprudence administrative : la jurisprudence codifiée ou remise en cause par la loi. *[In French]*; [The substitution of law to administrative jurisprudence: jurisprudence codified or put into question by the law]. Sophie Théron. **R. Fran. Droit Admin.** 20:2 3-4:2004 pp.230-241.

1062   La théorie de l'apparence en droit administratif : vertus et risques de l'importation d'une tradition de common law. *[In French]*; [The theory of appearance in administrative law: virtues and risks of the importation of a common law tradition]. Stéphanie Gandreau. **R. Droit Publ.** 2 3-4:2005 pp.319-356.

1063   Theory and values in public law: an interpretation. Martin Loughlin. **Publ. Law** Spring:2005 pp.48-66.

1064   The theory of public law in Germany 1914-1945. Stanley L. Paulson. **Oxf. J. Leg. S.** 26:3 Autumn:2005 pp.525-545.

1065   Les tribunaux administratifs ont cinquante ans : état des lieux et perspectives. *[In French]*; [Administrative courts are fifty years old]. Actualité juridique. **Actual. Jurid.** 12 3:2004 pp.625-646.

1066   The use of government procurement as an instrument of policy. Phoebe Bolton. **Sth. Afr. Law. J.** 121:3 2004 pp.619-635.

1067   Verfassungsrevision und "Bewahrung" der Verfassung. *[In German]*; [Constitutional review] *[Summary]*. A. Gamper. **Z. Öffent. Recht** 60:2 2005 pp.187-216.

1068   Walter Bagehot: critic, constitutionalist, prophet? Ian Ward. **Publ. Law** Spring:2005 pp.67-82.

C.1.6:   **Relations between the powers**
            Relations entre les pouvoirs

1069   45 minutes of infamy? Hutton, Blair and the invasion of Iraq. Alan Doig. **Parl. Aff.** 58:1 1:2005 pp.109-123.

1070   Administrative law goes to war. Cass R. Sunstein. **Harv. Law R.** 118:8 6:2005 pp.2663-2672.

1071   Agency, truth and meaning: judging the Hutton report. Diana Coole. **Br. J. Pol. Sci.** 35:3 7:2005 pp.465-485.

1072   Americanization and the judicialization of Italian politics. James L. Newell. **J. Mod. Ital. S.** 10:1 3:2005 pp.27-42.

1073   Congressional oversight: vice president Richard B. Cheney's executive branch triumph. Bruce P. Montgomery. **Pol. Sci. Q.** 120:4 Winter:2005-2006 pp.581-617.

1074   Consolidación democrática y poder judicial: los riesgos de la judicialización de la policía. *[In Spanish]*; [Democratic consolidation and judiciary power: the risks of the judicialization of police] *[Summary]*. Javier Couso. **R. Cien. Pol.** XXIV:2 2004 pp.29-48.

1075   The constitutional reform act 2005: ministers, judges and constitutional change. Lord Windlesham. **Publ. Law** Winter:2005 pp.806-823.

1076   Controlling executive power in the war on terrorism. Mark Tushnet. **Harv. Law R.** 118:8 6:2005 pp.2673-2682.

1077   Der Deutsche Bundestag und die Auslandseinsätze der Bundeswehr. Zur Gratwanderung zwischen exekutiver Prärogative und legislativer Mitwirkung. *[In German]*; (The German Bundestag and the deployment of military forces abroad. The delicate balance between executive prerogative and legislative participation.) *[Summary]*. Rafael Biermann. **Z. Parlament.** 35:4 12:2004 pp.607-626.

1078   Divided power: the Presidency, Congress, and the formation of American foreign policy. Donald R. Kelley [Ed.]. Fayetteville AR: University of Arkansas Press, 2005. viii, 216p. *ISBN: 1557287988. Includes bibliographical references and index. (Series:* Fulbright Institute series on international affairs - 3).

1079   Divided we govern: party control, lawmaking, and investigations, 1946-2002. David R. Mayhew. New Haven CT, London: Yale University Press, 2005. 267p. *ISBN: 0300102887.*

1080   Do policy horizons structure the formation of parliamentary governments? The evidence from an expert survey. Paul V. Warwick. **Am. J. Pol. Sci.** 49:2 4:2005 pp.373-387.

1081   Evidence-based policy or policy-based evidence? Hutton and the government's use of secret intelligence. Anthony Glees. **Parl. Aff.** 58:1 1:2005 pp.138-155.

1082   Executive advisory opinions and the practice of judicial deference in foreign affairs cases. William R. Casto. **George Washington Int. Law R.** 37:2 2005 pp.501-510.

1083   Going public as a legislative weapon: measuring presidential appeals regarding specific legislation. Andrew W. Barrett. **Pres. Stud. Q.** 35:1 3:2005 pp.1-10.

1084   Hutton and Scott: a tale of two inquiries. Mark Phythian. **Parl. Aff.** 58:1 1:2005 pp.124-137.

1085   The impact of divided government on legislative production. J.R. Rogers. **Publ. Choice** 123:1-2 4:2005 pp.217-233.

1086   The judge in the Scottish Parliament Chamber. Barry K. Winetrobe. **Publ. Law** Spring:2005 pp.3-12.

1087   Judges and taxes: judicial review, judicial independence and the size of government. George Tridimas. **Constit. Pol. Econ.** 16:1 3:2005 pp.5-30.

1088   The law: when law and politics collide: presidents and the use of the twenty-fifth amendment. Nancy Kassop. **Pres. Stud. Q.** 35:1 3:2005 pp.147-165.

1089   Legislatures and executives: an investigation into the relationship at the heart of government. Graham P. Thomas; Kenneth O. Morgan; Anthony Seldon; Pranay Sanklecha; Peter D. Just; Jack Hayward; Ludger Helms; David Arter; John W. Schiemann; Petr Kopecký; Robert Elgie; John Stapleton; Paul Furlong; Lauren Cohen Bell; Jonathan Malloy; Peter Calvert; Robert H. Donaldson; Mikitaka Masuyama; Benjamin Nyblade; Emanuele Ottolenghi; Subhash C. Kashyap; Nicholas D.J. Baldwin. **J. Legis. St.** 10:2-3 Summer-Autumn:2004 pp.4-302. *Collection of 19 articles.*

1090   Locke on executive power and liberal constitutionalism; *[Summary in French]*. Lee Ward. **Can. J. Pol.** 38:3 9:2005 pp.719-744.

1091   Making policy, making law: an interbranch perspective. Mark C. Miller [Ed.]; Jeb Barnes [Ed.]. Washington DC: Georgetown University Press, 2004. xi, 244p. *ISBN: 1589010256. Includes bibliographical references (p. 209-230) and index. (Series:* American governance and public policy).

1092   'OfGov': a commissioner for government conduct? Robert P. Kaye. **Parl. Aff.** 58:1 1:2005 pp.171-188.

1093   Ombudsmanok Magyarországon. Az országgyűlés biztosai és az alkotmány védelme. *[In Hungarian]*; (Ombudsmen in Hungary. The parliamentary commissioners and the protection of the constitution.) András Varga Zs. Budapest: Rejtjel Kiadó, 2004. 199p. *ISBN: 9637255001. Includes bibliographical references (p. 189-199).*

1094   The origins of presidential conditional agenda-setting power in Latin America; *[Summary in Spanish]*. Eduardo Alemán; George Tsebelis. **Lat. Am. Res. R.** 40:2 2005 pp.3-26.

1095   Override propensity in the US Congress: veto challenge and override vote by the two chambers. Manabu Saeki. **J. Legis. St.** 10:4 Winter:2004 pp.70-83.

1096   Parrhesiastic accountability: investigatory commissions and executive power in an age of terror. Jonathan Simon. **Yale Law J.** 114:6 4:2005 pp.1419-1457.

1097   Party system change and parliamentary scrutiny of the executive in Italy. Paola Mattei. **J. Legis. St.** 11:1 Spring:2005 pp.16-37.

1098   The political logic of economic crisis in South Korea. Jung Kim. **Asian Sur.** XLV:3 5-6:2005 pp.453-474.

1099   Le pouvoir constituant à l'épreuve du Conseil constitutionnel. *[In French]*; [Executive power facing the constitutional council]. André Viola. **TDP** 8:15 1:2004 pp.91-100.

1100   Power: a radical view. Steven Lukes. New York: Palgrave Macmillan, 2005. viii, 192p. *ISBN: 0333420918, 0333420926. Includes bibliographical references (p. 169-187) and index.*

1101   Proving the potential of independent commissions: a critical review of the Richard commission on the powers and electoral arrangements of the national assembly for Wales. Laura McAllister. **Publ. Admin.** 83:2 2005 pp.493-512.

1102   Secret evidence in the war on terror. **Harv. Law R.** 118:6 4:2005 pp.1962-1984.

1103   State legislative influence over agency rulemaking: the utility of ex ante review. Brian J. Gerber; Cherie Maestas; Nelson C. Dometrius. **State Pol. Policy Q.** 5:1 Spring:2005 pp.24-46.

1104   The law: can you sue the White House? Opening the door for separation of powers immunity in Cheney v. District Court. Louis Klarevas. **Pres. Stud. Q.** 34:4 12:2004 pp.849-866.

1105   A theory of executive dominance of congressional politics: the committee system in the Brazilian chamber of deputies. Carlos Pereira; Bernardo Mueller. **J. Legis. St.** 10:1 Spring:2004 pp.9-49.

1106   Vzaimootnosheniia zakonodatel'nykh organov gosudarstvennoi vlasti respublik s vysshimi dolzhnostnymi litsami i ispolnitel'nymi organami respublik. *[In Russian]*; [Relations between the legislative bodies of Russian republics and civil servants and executive authorities of the republics]. M.M. Kurmanov. **Sots.Gum. Znan.** 2 2004 pp.59-71.

1107   The war on terrorism: international law, clear statement requirements, and constitutional design. Curtis A. Bradley; Jack L. Goldsmith. **Harv. Law R.** 118:8 6:2005 pp.2683-2697.

C.1.7:   **Fundamental rights and freedoms**
           Droits et libertés fondamentaux

1108   Die Bedeutung menschenrechtlicher Verträge für den Flüchtlingsschutz. Teil 1: Menschenrechte und ihre unterschiedlichen Begründungsansätze. *[In German]*; [The meaning of human rights contracts for refugee protection. Part 1: Differing rationales for human rights]. Simone Emmert. **AWR B.** 43(52):2 2005 pp.121-135.

1109   Children: rights and childhood. David Archard. London: Routledge, 2004. xiii, 247p. *ISBN: 0415305845, 0415305837. Includes bibliographical references and index.*

1110   Citizenship and childhood: the state of affairs in Israel. Asher Ben-Arieh; Yifat Boyer. **Childhood** 12:1 2:2005 pp.33-54.

1111   Demokracija i ljudska prava. *[In Croatian]*; (Democracy and human rights.) *[Summary]*. Georg Lohmann. **Pol. Misao** 41:1 2004 pp.115-125.

1112   Derrida's cities of refuge: toward a non-utopian utopia. Sean K. Kelly. **Contemp. Just. R.** 7:4 12:2004 pp.421-439.

1113   Desperately seeking democracy: unreflexive liberalism and the 'privacy bias' in journalism ethics. Jennifer Wilkinson. **Media Int. Aust.** 114 2:2005 pp.109-121.

1114 Les droits fondamentaux en pays arabo-musulmans. *[In French]*; [Fundamental rights in Arab-Muslim countries] *[Summary]*. Selim Jahel. **R. Int. Droit Comp.** 56:4 10-12:2004 pp.787-796.

1115 Elementos y obstáculos a tomar en cuenta en la conceptuación y apropiación de los derechos sexuales y reproductivos. *[In Spanish]*; (Elements and obstacles to be taken into account in the conceptualization and appropriation of sexual and reproductive rights.) *[Summary]*. Adriana Orztiz-Ortega. **Est. Demog. Urb.** 19:3 9-12:2004 pp.599-638.

1116 Az élet joga. Abortusz, eutanázia, művi megtermékenyítés. *[In Hungarian]*; (The right to life. Abortion, euthanasia, artificial insemination.) Gábor Jobbágyi. Budapest: Szent István Társulat, 2004. 303p. *ISBN: 9633615895. Includes bibliographical references (p. 303-304).*

1117 Les enjeux actuels de l'accès aux droits. Sens, portée, impact des politiques d'insertion. *[In French]*; [Access to rights. Meaning, scope and impact of integration policies]. Michel Borgetto. **Info. Soc.** 120 12:2004 pp.6-19.

1118 The future of women's rights: global visions and strategies. Joanna Kerr [Ed.]; Ellen Sprenger [Ed.]; Alison Symington [Ed.]. London: Zed Books, 2004. viii, 224p. *ISBN: 1842774581, 184277459X. Includes bibliographical references and index. Association for Women's Rights in Development. Mama Cash.*

1119 Gender, sexuality and human rights. Susan Millns; Harriet Samuels; Ralph Sandland; Sharon Cowan; Matthew Weait; Ruth Fletcher; Rebecca Probert; Joanne Conaghan. **Femin. Legal S.** 13:1 2005 pp.1-157. *Collection of 8 articles.*

1120 Health, human rights, and Islam: a focus on Yemen. Anthony Tirado Chase; Abdul Karim Alaug. **Health Hum. Rights** 8:1 2004 pp.115-138.

1121 The human rights-based approach to development: the right to water. Emilie Filmer-Wilson. **Neth. Q. Hum. Rights** 23:2 6:2005 pp.213-241.

1122 Indigenous rights and the quest for participatory democracy in Latin America. Priti Singh. **Int. S.** 42:1 2005 pp.61-76.

1123 Interpreting a bill of rights: the importance of legislative rights review. Janet L. Hiebert. **Br. J. Pol. Sci.** 35:2 4:2005 pp.235-255.

1124 Islam, authoritarianism, and female empowerment: what are the linkages? Daniela Donno; Bruce Russett. **World Pol.** 56:4 7:2004 pp.582-607.

1125 Laizismus und Religionsfreiheit im öffentlichen Raum. *[In German]*; [Freedom of religion in public spaces]. Juliane Kokott. **Der Staat** 44:3 2005 pp.343-366.

1126 Liberale Grundrechte im Zeltalter der neuen Informations-und Kommunikationstechnologien. *[In German]*; (Civil liberties in the age of information technology.) Markus M. Müller; Gary S. Schaal; Katharina Sophie Rürup; Nils Leopold; Dirk Günnewig; Doris Allhutter; Andreas Umland. **Öster. Z. Pol.wissen.** 33:4 2004 pp.363-436. *Collection of 6 articles.*

1127 Making the case for privacy rights. Maeve Cooke. **Philos. Soc. Crit.** 31:1 1:2005 pp.131-143.

1128 The mandatory reporting of torture by detention center officials: an original proposal. Henry Forbes Smith; Mark Freeman. **Hum. Rights Q.** 27:1 2:2005 pp.327-349.

1129 Negotiating the politics of gender and rights: some reflections on the status of women's human rights at 'Beijing plus ten'. Jill Steans; Vafa Ahmadi. **Glo. Soc.** 19:3 7:2005 pp.227-245.

1130 Occupied Palestinian territory: linking health to human rights. Angelo Stefanini; Hadas Ziv. **Health Hum. Rights** 8:1 2004 pp.161-178.

1131 Prawo do ochrony sfery intymności jednostki. *[In Polish]*; (The right to protection of the sphere of an individual's privacy.) Joanna Sieńczyło-Chlabicz. **Pań. Prawo** LIX:II 11:2004 pp.34-47.

1132 Protección, afirmación y sexualidad sin poder: un proyecto político y normativo para la construcción de los derechos sexuales. *[In Spanish]*; (Protection, affirmation and sexuality without power: a political and normative project for the construction of sexual rights.) *[Summary]*. Tracy Citeroni; Alejandro Cervantes-Carson. **Est. Demog. Urb.** 19:3 9-12:2004 pp.687-716.

1133   The protective environment: development support for child protection. Karin Landgren. **Hum. Rights Q.** 27:1 2:2005 pp.214-248.

1134   Religious human rights and a democratic state. James E. Wood, Jr. **J. Chur. State** 46:4 Autumn:2004 pp.739-765.

1135   The rights of indigenous peoples and the development process. Helen Quane. **Hum. Rights Q.** 27:2 5:2005 pp.652-682.

1136   A second look at the South African Human Rights Commission, access to information, and the promotion of socioeconomic rights. Jonathan Klaaren. **Hum. Rights Q.** 27:2 5:2005 pp.539-561.

1137   Selected papers from the fourth international conference on the capability approach. Amartya Sen; Martha C. Nussbaum; Frances Stewart; Siddiqur Rahman Osmani; Des Gasper; Jay Drydyk. **J. Hum. Dev.** 6:2 7:2005 pp.151-267. *Collection of 6 articles.*

1138   Sexuality and human rights: a global overview. Michael Kirby; Robert Reed; R. Douglas Elliott; Mary Bonauto; Helmut Graupner; Ronald Louw; Erick Laurent; Phillip Tahmindjis. **J. Homosexuality** 48:3-4 2005 pp.9-232. *Collection of 8 articles.*

1139   Svoboda mysli i vozmozhnost' vybora: politicheskaia i akademicheskaia demokratiia. *[In Russian]*; (Freedom of thought and choice: political and academic democracy.) V.N. Rastorguev. **Vest. Mosk. Univ. 12 Pol.** 1 1-2:2005 pp.58-79.

1140   Tres reflexiones sobre la sexualidad y los derechos humanos en el ámbito de la Iglesia católica. *[In Spanish]*; (Three reflections on sexuality and human rights in the sphere of the Catholic church.) *[Summary]*. Juan Guillermo Figueroa Perea. **Est. Demog. Urb.** 19:3 9-12:2004 pp.639-686.

1141   Universal (non)service? Water markets, household demand and the poor in urban Kenya. Sumila Gulyani; Debabrata Talukdar; R. Mukami Kariuki. **Urb. S.** 42:8 7:2005 pp.1247-1274.

1142   Women's rights and Islamic family law: perspectives on reform. Lynn Welchman [Ed.]. London: Zed Books, 2004. 300p. *ISBN: 1842770942, 1842770950. Includes bibliographical references and index.*

1143   Die Würde des Menschen: Giannozzo Manetti, Giovanni Pico della Mirandola, Albrecht Dürer und Avishai Margalit. *[In German]*; [The dignity of human beings: Giannozzo Manetti, Giovanni Pico della Mirandola, Albrecht Dürer and Avishai Margalit] *[Summary]*. Alexander Thumfart. **Z. Pol.** 51:4 12:2004 pp.434-455.

Africa
Afrique

1144   Children's rights in the Central Africa sub-region: poverty, conflicts and HIV/AIDS as context. Ndolamb Ngokwey. **Int. J. Child. Rights** 12:3 2004 pp.183-216.

1145   The development of social and economic rights in South Africa. R. Malherbe. **Z. Öffent. Recht** 60:1 2005 pp.111-125.

1146   Health and human rights: what can ten years of democracy in South Africa tell us? Leslie London. **Health Hum. Rights** 8:1 2004 pp.1-26.

1147   Human rights in Africa: from the OAU to the African Union. Rachel Murray. Cambridge: Cambridge University Press, 2004. viii, 349p. *ISBN: 0521839173. Includes bibliographical references and index.*

1148   Human rights law in Africa. Christof Heyns [Ed.]; Morne Van der Linde [Ed.]. : Martinus Nijhoff, 2004. *ISBN: 9004139338, 9004139346, 9004138811. Includes bibliographical references.*

1149   Is there a God of human rights? The complex relationship between human rights and religion: a South African case. J.A. van der Ven; J.S. Dreyer; H.J.C. Pieterse. Leiden MA, Boston MA: Brill, 2004. xx, 642p. *ISBN: 9004142096. Includes bibliographical references (p. [597]-625) and indexes. (Series: International studies in religion and society - 2).*

1150 Le Maroc des années de plomb : équité et réconciliation ? *[In French]*; (Morocco during the black years: fairness and reconciliation?) *[Summary]*. Frédéric Vairel. **Pol. Afr.** 96 12:2004 pp.181-195.

1151 Poverty, human rights law and socio-economic realities in South Africa. John C. Mubangizi; Betty C. Mubangizi. **Dev. Sth. Afr.** 22:2 6:2005 pp.277-290.

1152 Régimes politiques et droits humains au Maghreb. *[In French]*; [Political regimes and human rights in North Africa]. Lahouari Addi [Ed.]. **Conf. Médit.** 51 Fall:2004 pp.7-153.

1153 Taking fundamental rights seriously: the bill of rights and its implications for the development of contract law. Gerhard Lubbe. **Sth. Afr. Law. J.** 121:2 2004 pp.395-423.

1154 Testing the red lines: on the liberalization of speech in Morocco. Andrew R. Smith; Fadoua Loudiy. **Hum. Rights Q.** 27:3 8:2005 pp.1069-1119.

Americas
Amérique

1155 Casualty of war: the Bush administration's assault on a free press. David Dadge. Amherst NY: Prometheus Books, 2004. 349p. *ISBN: 1591021472. Includes bibliographical references (p. 295-328) and index.*

1156 Challenging U.S. human rights violations since 9/11. Ann Fagan Ginger [Ed.]. Amherst NY: Prometheus Books, 2005. 574p. *ISBN: 1591022797. Includes bibliographical references and index.*

1157 Civil peace and the quest for truth: the First Amendment freedoms in political philosophy and American constitutionalism. Murray Dry. Lanham MD: Lexington Books, 2004. x, 307p. *ISBN: 0739107461, 0739109316. Includes bibliographical references (p. 291-297) and index.*

1158 Human rights in the Commonwealth Caribbean: contemporary issues, instruments and institutions. Tushar Kant. **India Q.** LXI:1 1-3:2005 pp.161-183.

1159 Interdisciplinary approaches to human rights scholarship in Latin America. Paola Cesarini [Comments by]; Shareen Hertel [Comments by]. **J. Lat. Am. S.** 37:4 11:2005 pp.793-809.

1160 Internet surveillance after September 11: is the United States becoming Great Britain? A. James McAdams. **Comp. Pol.** 37:4 7:2005 pp.479-498.

1161 Last resorts and fundamental rights: the substantive due process implications of prohibitions on medical marijuana. **Harv. Law R.** 118:6 4:2005 pp.1985-2006.

1162 A little knowledge: privacy, security, and public information after September 11. John Podesta [Ed.]; Peter M. Shane [Ed.]; Richard C. Leone [Ed.]. New York: Century Foundation Press, 2004. 159p. *ISBN: 0870784870. Includes bibliographical references (p. 131-144) and index.*

1163 More secure, less free? Antiterrorism policy & civil liberties after September 11. Mark Sidel. Ann Arbor MI: University of Michigan Press, 2004. 218p. *ISBN: 047211428X. Includes bibliographical references and index.*

1164 Nouvelles perspectives pour la liberté religieuse en Amérique latine. *[In French]*; [New perspectives for religious freedom in Latin America]. Rosa María Martínez de Codes [Ed.]. **Consc. Liber.** 65 2004 pp.15-165.

1165 Los procesos de apropiación subjetiva de los derechos sexuales: notas para la discusión. *[In Spanish]*; (The process of subjectively appropriating sexual rights: notes for discussion.) *[Summary]*. Ana Amuchástegui Herrera; Marta Rivas Zivy. **Est. Demog. Urb.** 19:3 9-12:2004 pp.543-598.

1166 Securing access to transportation for the urban poor. Matthew A. Dombroski. **Columb. Law R.** 105:2 3:2005 pp.503-536.

1167 The struggle for indigenous rights in Latin America. Nancy Grey Postero [Ed.]; Leon Zamosc [Ed.]. Brighton, Portland OR: Sussex Academic Press, 2004. viii, 250p. *ISBN: 1845190068. Includes bibliographical references and index.*

1168 "The ticket to freedom": the NAACP and the struggle for black political integration. Manfred Berg; John David Smith [Foreword]. Gainesville FL: University Press of Florida,

2005. xx, 352p. *ISBN: 0813028329. Includes bibliographical references (p. 323-342) and index. (Series:* New perspectives on the history of the South).

1169   To address health disparities on the US-Mexico border — advance human rights. Delfi Mondragón; Jeffrey Brandon. **Health Hum. Rights** 8:1 2004 pp.179-195.

1170   The war on terror and the future of the United States. Franco Spoltore. **Federalist** XLVI:3 2004 pp.170-181.

Asia
Asie

1171   Kwangju and beyond: coping with past state atrocities in South Korea. In Sup Han. **Hum. Rights Q.** 27:3 8:2005 pp.998-1045.

1172   Media freedom in Malaysia. Mohd Azizuddin Mohd Sani. **J. Contemp. Asia** 35:3 2005 pp.341-367.

1173   Newspeak revisited: the lexical management of political discourse; *[Text in Chinese].* Alfian Sa'at. **Tangent** 4:2 2004 pp.100-115.

1174   On the closing down of the roundtable an email dialogue with Kevin Tan; *[Text in Chinese].* Kevin Tan; Chiu Wei Li. **Tangent** 4:2 2004 pp.89-98.

1175   To be a shoeshine boy in Hanoi: a different childhood narrative. Birgitta Rubenson; Dinh Phuong Hoa; Nguyen Van Chinh; Bengt Höjer; Eva Johansson. **Health Hum. Rights** 8:1 2004 pp.139-160.

1176   When human rights meet peace on the Korean peninsula: searching for a comprehensive approach. Bohyuk Suh. **Kor. World Aff.** 28:3 Fall:2004 pp.264-280.

Europe
Europe

1177   Against human rights. Slavoj Žižek. **New Left R.** 34 7-8:2005 pp.115-131.

1178   Belmarsh. Tom R. Hickman; Stephen Tierney; David Dyzenhaus; Janet L. Hiebert. **Mod. Law R.** 68:4 7:2005 pp.654-680. *Collection of 4 articles.*

1179   Die Bonn-Kopenhagener Erklärungen zu den Rechten der nationalen Minderheiten im deutsch-dänischen Grenzland 1955-2005. *[In German];* [The Bonn-Copenhagen declarations on the rights of national minorities in the German-Danish borderlands, 1955-2005]. Jørgen Kühl. **Euro. Ethn.** 62:1-2 2005 pp.39-54.

1180   Le commissaire aux droits de l'homme protecteur des droits des citoyens devant l'administration en Russie. *[In French];* [The human rights commissioner, citizens' rights protector before the Russian administration] *[Summary]; [Summary in French].* Mariane Viel. **R. Int. Droit Comp.** 57:1 1-3:2005 pp.171-194.

1181   Damage limitation: the courts and Human Rights Act damages. Richard Clayton. **Publ. Law** Autumn:2005 pp.429-439.

1182   Deformalizatsiia pravil: prichina ili sledstvie institsional'nykh lovushek? *[In Russian];* (Deformalization of rules: cause or consequence of institutional traps?) *[Summary].* A.D. Khlopin. **Polis [Moscow]** 6(83) 2004 pp.6-15.

1183   Dissidence at IMEMO. Petr Cherkasov. **Rus. Pol. Law** 43:2 3-4:2005 pp.31-69.

1184   Droits dedans : pour la reconnaissance des droits des détenus. *[In French];* [Rights inside: for the recognition of the rights of prisoners]. Dedans dehors. **Dedans Dehors** 44 7-8:2004 pp.9-21.

1185   Gendered citizenship: debating reproductive rights in Ireland. Siobhán Mullally. **Hum. Rights Q.** 27:1 2:2005 pp.78-104.

1186   Die grundrechtlichen Grenzen staatlicher Neutralität. *[In German];* [The limits of governmental neutrality]. Julian Krüper. **Jahr. Öffent. Gegen.** 53 2005 pp.79-110.

1187   HIV/AIDS and human rights in Hungary. Eszter Csernus [Ed.]. Budapest: Hungarian Civil Liberties Union, 2004. 183p. *ISBN: 9632125428. Includes bibliographical references.*

1188   Human rights culture: solidarity, diversity and the right to be different. Kate Nash. **Citiz. S.** 9:4 9:2005 pp.335-348.

1189   Hungarian Roma attitudes on minority rights: the symbolic violence of ethnic identification. Robert Koulish. **Euro.-Asia S.** 57:2 3:2005 pp.311-326.

1190   In the eye of the beholder? The foundations of subjective human rights conditions in East-Central Europe. Christopher J. Anderson; Aida Paskeviciute; Maria Elena Sandovici; Yuliya V. Tverdova. **Comp. Pol. S.** 38:7 9:2005 pp.771-798.

1191   Is Spain recovering its memory? Breaking the Pacto del Olvido. Madeleine Davis. **Hum. Rights Q.** 27:3 8:2005 pp.858-880.

1192   A leap to the realm of freedom. A brief essay on the most recent period in the history of contemporary Russian journalism. Vitalii Tret'iakov. **Rus. Pol. Law** 43:1 1-2:2005 pp.51-69.

1193   'Limited freedom' of the press a discussion. V.L. Inozemtsev [Discussant]; O.G. Dzhemal [Discussant]; A.V. Kiva [Discussant]; A.S. Salutskii [Discussant]; D.E. Furman [Discussant]. **Rus. Pol. Law** 43:3 5-6:2005 pp.51-66.

1194   O nadużyciu prawa do informacji publicznej. *[In Polish]*; (On abuse of the right to public information.) Agnieszka Knopkiewicz. **Pań. Prawo** LIX:10(704) 10:2004 pp.69-81.

1195   National and ethnic minorities in Poland — the legal problem of definition. Ewa Gdulewicz; Ewa Popławska. **Acta Jur. Hun.** 45:3-4 2004 pp.281-300.

1196   Neue Grundrechte in der Risikogesellschaft. *[In German]*; [New basic rights in the risk society]. Xenophon I. Contiades. **Jahr. Öffent. Gegen.** 53 2005 pp.27-44.

1197   Public authorities as 'victims' under the Human Rights Act. Howard Davis. **Camb. Law J.** 64:2 7:2005 pp.315-328.

1198   Should we be compelled to have identity cards? Justifications for the legal enforcement of obligations. Perri 6. **Pol. S.** 53:2 6:2005 pp.243-261.

1199   Taking the rights of parents and children seriously: confronting the welfare principle under the human rights act. Shazia Choudhry; Helen Fenwick. **Oxf. J. Leg. S.** 26:3 Autumn:2005 pp.453-492.

1200   Transitional road for traffic: analysing trafficking in women from and through Central and Eastern Europe. Chris Corrin. **Euro.-Asia S.** 57:4 6:2005 pp.543-560.

1201   Umstrittene Menschenrechte: Der Europarat, Russland und Tschetschenien. *[In German]*; [Controversial human rights: the Council of Europe, Russia and Chechnya]. Klaus Brummer. **Gesell. Wirt. Pol.** 53:4 2004 pp.437-447.

1202   Zum Grundrechtsschutz ausländischer juristischer Personen. *[In German]*; [The protection of the basic rights of foreigners]. Annette Guckelberger. **Arc. Öffen. Recht** 129:4 12:2004 pp.618-638.

C.2:   **Public administration and management**
       Administration et gestion publique

1203   Administrative reform in Germany: the new system of management as an application of new public management theory and the crisis of the welfare state. Hartmut Elsenhans; Roland Kulke; Christian Roschmann. **Indian J. Publ. Admin.** LI:1 1-3:2005 pp.15-33.

1204   Analysis of public management change processes: the case of local government accounting reforms in Germany. Hans-Gerd Ridder; Hans-Jürgen Bruns; Fabian Spier. **Publ. Admin.** 83:2 2005 pp.443-472.

1205   An assessment of public service reforms in Jamaica. Jimmy Kazaara Tindigarukayo. **Soc. Econ. S.** 53:3 9:2004 pp.81-109.

1206   Bürokratieabbau — richtige Ansätze unter falscher Flagge. *[In German]*; [Reducing bureaucracy —right approaches, wrong fundamentals]. Hans Peter Bull. **Verwalt.** 38:3 2005 pp.285-314.

1207   Challenges to state policy capacity: global trends and comparative perspectives. Martin Painter [Ed.]; Jon Pierre [Ed.]. Basingstoke: Palgrave Macmillan, 2005. ix, 287p. *ISBN: 1403935831, 1403935831.*

1208 Citizens, politicians, and providers: the Latin American experience with service delivery reform. Ariel Fiszbein [Ed.]. Washington DC: World Bank, 2005. ix, 67p. *ISBN: 0821360892. Includes bibliographical references (p. 63-67).*

1209 Civil service reform in post-communist Europe: the bumpy road to depoliticisation. Jan-Hinrik Meyer-Sahling. **West Euro. Pol.** 27:1 1:2004 pp.71-103.

1210 Classical pragmatism does not need an upgrade: lessons for public administration. Patricia M. Shields. **Admin. Soc.** 37:4 9:2005 pp.504-518.

1211 Contracts as reinvented institutions in the public sector: a cross-cultural comparison. Carsten Greve; Niels Ejersbo. Westport CT: Praeger, 2004. x, 148p. *ISBN: 1567205283. Includes bibliographical references (p. 141-146) and index.*

1212 Controlling modern government: variety, commonality, and change. Christopher Hood [Ed.]. Cheltenham: Edward Elgar Publishing, 2004. xiv, 220p. *ISBN: 1843766299.*

1213 Des services publics désorientés ? *[In French]*; [Disoriented public services?] Eric Nachtergaele [Ed.]. **Pyramides** 8 Spring:2004 pp.9-133.

1214 Diagnosis for organisational improvements: case study of a government agency. Richa Awasthy; Rajen K. Gupta. **Indian J. Publ. Admin.** 4:4 10-12:2004 pp.1134-1155.

1215 Does corruption grease or sand the wheels of growth? P.G. Méon; K. Sekkat. **Publ. Choice** 122:1-2 1:2005 pp.69-97.

1216 Ethics in public management. H. George. Frederickson [Ed.]; Richard K. Ghere [Ed.]. Armonk NY: M.E. Sharpe, 2005. viii, 390p. *ISBN: 076561460X, 0765614618. Includes bibliographical references and index.*

1217 Eticheskie aspekty regulirovaniia gosudarstvennoi sluzhby. *[In Russian]*; (Ethic aspects of regulation of state service.) A. Obolonskii. **Obshch. Nauki Sovrem.** 5 2004 pp.53-64.

1218 Explaining the adoption of innovation: an empirical analysis of public management reform. George A. Boyne; Julian S. Gould-Williams; Jennifer Law; Richard M. Walker. **Env. Plan. C.** 23:3 6:2005 pp.419-435.

1219 Exporting governance: Lithuania adapts a Canadian policy management model; *[Summary in French]*. G. Evans. **Can. Publ. Admin.** 48:1 Spring:2005 pp.4-34.

1220 From new public management to the new governance. James Radcliffe; Mike Dent; David Jary; Janet Newman; Bob McKee; Justin J. Waring. **Policy Pol.** 33:4 10:2005 pp.617-692. *Collection of 5 articles.*

1221 Une generation de reformes en management public : et après ? *[In French]*; [A generation of reforms in public management: and then?] Romain Laufer; Sylvie Trosa; Frédéric Marty; Arnaud Voisin; David Giauque; Daniel J. Caron; Lucie Rouillard; Jacques Bourgault; Mohamed Charih; Daniel Maltais; Valérie Merindol; Alice Teil; Antoine Richard; Éric Verdier; Amaury Legrain; Koen Verhoest. **Pol. Manag. Publ.** 22:3 9:2004 pp.1-191. *Collection of 6 articles.*

1222 La gestión de servicios públicos locales. *[In Spanish]*; [Management of local public services]. Ignacio del Guayo Castiella. **R. Admin. Públ.** 165 9-12:2004 pp.87-173.

1223 La gestion publique dans les pays en développement : quelques remarques concernant l'Erythrée. *[In French]*; [Public management in developing countries: a few remarks on Eritrea]. Joseph L. Soeters; Mussie Teclemichael Tessema. **R. Int. Sci. Admin.** 70:4 12:2004 pp.669-682.

1224 Gestion publique et autonomie organisationnelle : la validité persistante des connaissances passées significatives. *[In French]*; [Public management and organizational autonomy: the continued validity of significant past knowledge]. Ian Thynne; Roger Wettenhall. **R. Int. Sci. Admin.** 70:4 12:2004 pp.653-667.

1225 Getting the state right: think tanks and the dissemination of new public management ideas in Ghana. F.L.K. Ohemeng. **J. Mod. Afr. S.** 43:3 9:2005 pp.443-465.

1226 Good governance, moral economy, and the shift from secular state classes to cultural-identitarian political movements in developing countries. Hartmut Elsenhans. **Indian J. Pol. Sci.** LXV:4 10-12:2004 pp.469-498.

1227 Governance in the UK public sector: the involvement of the governing board. Catherine M. Farrell. **Publ. Admin.** 83:1 2005 pp.89-110.

1228   Ideas, reflexiones y propuestas del grupo de expertos para la reforma de la administración pública. *[In Spanish]*; [Ideas, reflections and proposals of the group of experts for the reform of the public administration]. Rafael Gómez-Ferrer Rincón. **R. Admin. Públ.** 165 9-12:2004 pp.275-295.

1229   Implementing the third way: modernizing government and public services in Quebec and the UK. David Clark. **Publ. Manag. R.** 6:4 12:2004 pp.493-510.

1230   Individual-level factors and organizational performance in government organizations. Sangmook Kim. **J. Publ. Admin. Res. Theory** 15:2 4:2005 pp.245-261.

1231   Informazione e comunicazione amministrativa. *[In Italian]*; [Information and administrative communication]. Bernardo Giorgio Mattarella. **Riv. Trim. Pubbl.** 1 2005 pp.1-21.

1232   Innovacion gubernamental: el paradigma de buen gobierno en la administracion del Presidente Vicente Fox. *[In Spanish]*; [Governmental innovation: good government paradigm in President Vicente Fox's administration]. Ramon Munoz Gutierrez. Mexico City: FCE, 2004. 465p. *ISBN: 9681673883, 968167412X*.

1233   Institutional capacity and choice in Australia's integrity systems. A.J. Brown; Brian Head. **Aust. J. Publ. Admin.** 64:2 6:2005 pp.84-95.

1234   Integrating rigor and relevance in public administration scholarship: the contribution of narrative inquiry. Jennifer Dodge; Sonia M. Ospina; Erica Gabrielle Foldy. **Publ. Admin. R.** 65:3 5-6:2005 pp.286-300.

1235   Integriertes E-Government auch im föderalen Staat? Herausforderungen auf dem Weg zu effizienten Verwaltungsverfahren. *[In German]*; [Integrated e-government also for the federal state? Challenges on the way to efficient administrative procedures]. Herbert Kubicek; Martin Wind. **Deutsche Z. Kommunalwissenschaften** 43:2 2004 pp.48-63.

1236   Inter-agency working and the delivery of family support services. Sinead Riordan. **Administration [Dublin]** 52:2 Summer:2004 pp.57-77.

1237   Les interdits dans la fonction publique. *[In French]*; [Prohitions in public administration]. Cahiers de la fonction publique et de l'administration. **Cah. Fonc. Publ. Admin.** 239 11:2004 pp.4-19.

1238   Je možné řídit efektivitu a výkonnost ministerstva zahraničních věcí? V Dánsku ano. *[In Czech]*; (Is it possible to manage the efficiency and performance of a Ministry of Foreign Affairs? In Denmark, the answer is yes.) *[Summary]*. Roman Holý. **Mez. Vzt.** 40:1 2005 pp.48-70.

1239   Kooperation statt Konfrontation. Möglichkeiten und Grenzen der Mediation bei Planfeststellungsverfahren. *[In German]*; [Cooperation instead of confrontation. The potential and limits of mediation in planning procedures]. Hermann Pünder. **Verwalt.** 38:1 2005 pp.1-34.

1240   Kuka tarvitsee arviointia, mihin? Arvioinnin ristiriitaiset pyrkimykset. *[In Finnish]*; [Who needs evaluation for what? Contradictory interests in evaluation] *[Summary]*. Hannu Kauppi. **Hall. Tut.** 23:2 2004 pp.73-85.

1241   Linking citizen satisfaction with e-government and trust in government. Eric W. Welch; Charles C. Hinnant; M. Jae Moon. **J. Publ. Admin. Res. Theory** 15:3 7:2005 pp.371-391.

1242   Managing the electronic government: from vision to practice. Kuno. Schedler; Lukas. Summermatter; Bernhard. Schmidt. Greenwich CT: Information Age Publishing, 2004. xv, 158p. *ISBN: 1593112459, 1593112440*. *Translated from the German. Includes bibliographical references (p. 145-158). (Series:* Research in public management*)*.

1243   Modernisierung der Verwaltung durch E-Government: Das Praxisbeispiel Bremen. *[In German]*; [Modernization of public administration through e-government: the example of Bremen]. Gisela Schwellach; Martin Hagen. **Deutsche Z. Kommunalwissenschaften** 43:2 2004 pp.114-128.

1244   The need for reflexivity in public administration. Ann L. Cunliffe; Jong S. Jun. **Admin. Soc.** 37:2 5:2005 pp.225-242.

1245   New public management in Austria: local variation on a global theme? Gerhard Hammerschmid; Renate E. Meyer. **Publ. Admin.** 83:3 2005 pp.709-733.

1246   Ohodnotenie výkonnosti verejnej správy: teoretické východiská a skúsenosti z experimentu v Slovenskej republike. *[In Czech]*; (Performance measurement in public administration: selected theory and experience from Slovakia.) *[Summary]*. Juraj Nemec; Jozef Medveď; Markéta Šumpíková. **Pol. Ekon.** 1 2005 pp.95-109.

1247   The politics of administrative reforms in Asia: paradigms and legacies, paths and diversities. Anthony B.L. Cheung. **Governance** 18:2 4:2005 pp.257-282.

1248   Public administrative science in Germany: problems and prospects of a composite discipline. Arthur Benz. **Publ. Admin.** 83:3 2005 pp.659-668.

1249   Public administrators' trust in citizens: a missing link in citizen involvement efforts. Kaifeng Yang. **Publ. Admin. R.** 65:3 5-6:2005 pp.273-285.

1250   Public management and departments: contemporary themes-future agendas. John Halligan. **Aust. J. Publ. Admin.** 64:1 3:2005 pp.25-34.

1251   Public management and the essential public health functions. P. Khaleghian; M. Das Gupta. **World Dev.** 33:7 7:2005 pp.1083-1099.

1252   Public sector reform: governance in South Africa. Karen Miller. Aldershot, Burlington VT: Ashgate, 2005. xi, 150p. *ISBN: 0754643158. Includes bibliographical references (p. [141]-146) and index.*

1253   Quangos: the debate of the 1970s in Britain. Michael Cole. **Contemp. Br. Hist.** 19:3 9:2005 pp.321-352.

1254   A question of genesis: an analysis of the determinants of public authorities. Carolyn Bourdeaux. **J. Publ. Admin. Res. Theory** 15:3 7:2005 pp.441-462.

1255   Rebuilding governance in failed states and post-conflict societies. D.W. Brinkerhoff; D.A. Rondinelli; J.D. Montgomery; N. Ball; S. Lister; A. Wilder; P. Jackson; J.B. Mayfield; P. Blunt; M. Turner. **Publ. Admin. Dev.** 25:1 2:2005 pp.1-87. *Collection of 8 articles.*

1256   The reform of public administration in Northern Ireland: from principles to practice. Paul Carmichael; Colin Knox. **Pol. S.** 53:4 12:2005 pp.772-792.

1257   La réforme administrative au gouvernement du Québec : étude du processus de changement sur la culture organisationnelle. *[In French]*; [The administrative reform of the government in Quebec: a study of the impact of change on the organizational structure] *[Summary]*. D. Proulx; S. Brière. **Can. Publ. Admin.** 48:1 Spring:2005 pp.53-72.

1258   The rhetoric of management control in Italian cities: constructing new meanings of public action. Fabrizio Battistelli; Giuseppe Ricotta. **Admin. Soc.** 36:6 1:2005 pp.661-687.

1259   'Running business like a government': management insights from the public sector. Patrick Butler; Neil Collins. **Administration [Dublin]** 52:4 Winter:2004 pp.69-83.

1260   Second generation reform in Latin America: reforming the public sector in Uruguay and Mexico. Francisco Panizza; George Philip. **J. Lat. Am. S.** 37:4 11:2005 pp.667-691.

1261   El service public francés y la daseinsvorsorge en Alemania. *[In Spanish]*; [The French service public and the German daseinsvorsorge]. Martin Bullinger. **R. Admin. Públ.** 166 1-4:2005 pp.29-49.

1262   Sifarish, sycophantes, pouvoir et collectivisme : la culture administrative au Pakistan. *[In French]*; ['Sifarish', informers, power and collectivism: administrative culture in Pakistan]. Nasir Islam. **R. Int. Sci. Admin.** 70:2 6:2004 pp.335-357.

1263   Some crucial issues and challenges of governance. C.P. Vithal. **Indian J. Publ. Admin.** 4:4 10-12:2004 pp.1025-1045.

1264   Testing how management matters in an era of government by performance management. Donald P. Moynihan; Sanjay K. Pandey. **J. Publ. Admin. Res. Theory** 15:3 7:2005 pp.421-439.

1265   The thinning of administrative institutions in the hollow state. Larry D. Terry. **Admin. Soc.** 37:4 9:2005 pp.426-444.

1266   Towards a new pattern of strategy formation in the public sector: first experiences with national strategies for sustainable development in Europe. Reinhard Steurer; André Martinuzzi. **Env. Plan. C.** 23:3 6:2005 pp.455-472.

1267   Towards mapping impact of governance reforms: the role of CAG in management of state finances. I. Ramabrahmam. **Indian J. Publ. Admin.** 4:4 10-12:2004 pp.1070-1081.

1268   Le traitement de la corruption : le cas du Kenya. *[In French]*; (Dealing with corruption: the case of Kenya.) *[Summary]*. Pierre Jacquemot. **Afr. Contemp.** 213 Winter:2005 pp.165-178.

1269   Trajectories of public administration and administrative history in Australia: rectifying 'a curious blight'? Joanne Scott; John Wanna. **Aust. J. Publ. Admin.** 64:1 3:2005 pp.11-24.

1270   Transformation der Verwaltung durch E-Government. *[In German]*; [Administrative transformation through e-government]. Hermann Hill. **Deutsche Z. Kommunalwissenschaften** 43:2 2004 pp.17-47.

1271   Transforming the administrative state: reform in Hong Kong and the future of the developmental state. Martin Painter. **Publ. Admin. R.** 65:3 5-6:2005 pp.335-346.

1272   La trasparenza, la advocacy democratica e l'amministrazione dello stato. *[In Italian]*; [Transparency, democratic advocacy and state administration] *[Summary]*. Bruce E. Cain. **Riv. It. Pol. Pub.** 1 4:2004 pp.5-22.

1273   Új tendenciák az európai közigazgatásban. *[In Hungarian]*; (New trends in European public administration.) *[Summary]*. Imre Forgács. **Euro. Tükör** 9:3 2004 pp.30-47.

1274   Verwaltungsreform in Deutschland: Das neue System des Managements als Anwendung der New-Public-Management-Theorie und die Krise des Wohlfahrtsstaats. *[In German]*; [Public administration reform and public management: the crisis of the welfare state]. Hartmut Elsenhans; Roland Kulke; Christian Roschmann. **Verwalt.** 38:3 2005 pp.315-337.

1275   Die wirtschaftliche Bewertung von E-Government: Eine richtige Weichenstellung? *[In German]*; [The economic evaluation of e-government: a correct strategic decision?] Andreas Engel. **Deutsche Z. Kommunalwissenschaften** 43:2 2004 pp.93-113.

1276   El zorro y el león: hacia una reforma del Estado más equilibrada para los países en desarrollo. *[In Spanish]*; (The lion and the fox: towards more balanced approaches in the reform of the state.) *[Summary]*. José Luis Méndez. **Foro Int.** XLV:2 4-6:2005 pp.165-195.

Public servants
Fonctionnaires

1277   Acting on values: an ethical dead end for public servants. J.W. Langford. **Can. Publ. Admin.** 47:4 Winter:2004 pp.429-450.

1278   Bureaucrats and revolutionary state-building in Ireland and Russia. Was Weber right? *[Summary in French]*. Stephen Velychenko. **Can. J. Pol.** 38:1 3:2005 pp.1-22.

1279   Case of generalists versus specialists in Indian bureaucracy and need for reforms. Mohan S. Kashikar. **Indian J. Pol. Sci.** LXV:4 10-12:2004 pp.543-555.

1280   Competency and higher civil servants. Patricia Wallace Ingraham; Heather Getha-Taylor; Christopher Hood; Martin Lodge; Marleen Brans; Annie Hondeghem; Frits M. Van Der Meer; Theo A.J. Toonen; Edward C. Page. **Publ. Admin.** 83:4 2005 pp.779-860. *Collection of 6 articles.*

1281   Domestic capital, civil servants and the state: Costa Rica and the Dominican Republic under globalisation. Diego Sánchez Ancochea. **J. Lat. Am. S.** 37:4 11:2005 pp.693-726.

1282   Federal and provincial overlap and civil servants: the case of occupational training in Quebec and Ontario; *[Summary in French]*. M. Marc. **Can. Publ. Admin.** 48:1 Spring:2005 pp.35-52.

1283   Los gerentes públicos pintados por sí mismos. *[In Spanish]*; [Public managers portrayed by themselves] *[Summary]*. Omar Guerrero Orozco. **Convergencia** 11:36 9-12:2004 pp.213-245.

1284   How financial managers deal with ethical stress. Gerald J. Miller; Samuel J. Yeager; W. Bartley Hildreth; Jack Rabin. **Publ. Admin. R.** 65:3 5-6:2005 pp.301-312.

1285   The implications for officers of new political management arrangements. Pam Fox. **Loc. Govt. S.** 30:3 Autumn:2004 pp.384-400.

1286   An impoverished neutrality? Public manager values in local government, Penang, Malaysia. Ali Haidar; Lim Hong Hai; Len Pullin. **Loc. Govt. S.** 30:1 Spring:2004 pp.88-107.

1287   Majority rule in consensual democracies: explaining political influence in Norwegian local councils. Pål E. Martinussen. **Loc. Govt. S.** 30:3 Autumn:2004 pp.303-330.

1288   Moderne Leibeigenschaft? Berufsbild und soziale Absicherung der persönlichen Mitarbeiter der Bundestagsabgeordneten. *[In German]*; (Modern serfdom? Job outline and social security of the personal assistants of members of the German Bundestag.) *[Summary]*. Volker Pilz. **Z. Parlament.** 35:4 12:2004 pp.667-681.

1289   The new political management in local government: public engagement or public indifference? John Fenwick; Howard Elcock. **Loc. Govt. S.** 30:4 Winter:2004 pp.519-537.

1290   Obrazovanje i usavršavanje javnih službenika u tranzicijskim zemljama. *[In Croatian]*; (Education and training of civil servants in the countries in transition.) *[Summary]*. Gordana Marčetić. **Revija Soc. Pol.** 12:2 4-6:2005 pp.133-156.

1291   Les personnes publiques face aux religions. *[In French]*; [Public servants and religions]. Cahiers de la fonction publique et de l'administration. **Cah. Fonc. Publ. Admin.** 233 4:2004 pp.4-18.

1292   The precarious position of embassy and consular employees in the United Kingdom. Richard Garnett. **Int. Comp. Law Q.** 54:3 7:2005 pp.705-718.

1293   La protection sociale des agents publics. *[In French]*; [Public servants' social security]. Cahiers de la fonction publique et de l'administration. **Cah. Fonc. Publ. Admin.** 236 7-8:2004 pp.4-16.

1294   Qui se présente dans la fonction publique et pourquoi ? Premiers résultats d'enquêtes spécifiques sur les candidats à différents concours de la fonction publique d'état. *[In French]*; (Who is interested in a civil service career and why? First results of surveys on candidates for various competitive examinations.) *[Summary]*. Dominique Meurs; Florence Audier. **R. Fran. Admin. Publ.** 111 2004 pp.547-566.

1295   Red tape and public employees: does perceived rule dysfunction alienate managers? Leisha DeHart-Davis; Sanjay K. Pandey. **J. Publ. Admin. Res. Theory** 15:1 1:2005 pp.133-148.

1296   'Reinvigorating the Australian survey'. Andrew Leigh. **Aust. J. Publ. Admin.** 64:1 3:2005 pp.3-7.

1297   (The relationship between the organizational trust and job satisfaction in Jordanian ministries (a field study).); *[Text in Arabic]*. M.A. Al-So'udi. **Dirasat Ad. Sci.** 32:1 1:2005 pp.100-114.

1298   Rozhodovací volnost úředníků veřejné a sociální politiky na státní a lokální úrovni. *[In Czech]*; (Discretion of officials in public and social policy at the central and local levels.) *[Summary]*. Pavel Horák. **Pol. Čas.** 1 2004 pp.35-51.

1299   Verantwortliche Amtsführung im demokratischen Verfassungsstaat. *[In German]*; [Responsible conduct in the democratic constitutional state] *[Summary]*. Wolfgang H. Lorig. **Z. Pol.** 51:4 12:2004 pp.384-400.

1300   A visit to New Zealand. David Tothill. **Dipl. State.** 15:1 3:2004 pp.163-194.

C.2.1:   **Central government**
            Administration centrale

1301   Central government responses to governance change in the English regions. Sarah Ayres; Graham Pearce. **Reg. Fed. S.** 14:2 Summer:2004 pp.255-280.

1302   From election to government: principal rules and deviant cases. Guy-Erik Isaksson. **Gov. Oppos.** 40:3 Summer:2005 pp.329-357.

1303   Government and democracy in Australia. Ian Cook. Victoria, Oxford: Oxford University Press, 2004. xxi, 322p. *ISBN: 019551405X. Includes bibliographical references (p. 308-317) and index.*

1304   Out with 'rainbow government' and in with 'Iraqgate': the Finnish general election of 2003. William M. Downs; Satu Riutta. **Gov. Oppos.** 40:3 Summer:2005 pp.424-441.

1305   The political significance of the George W. Bush administration. Joel D. Aberbach. **Soc. Policy Admin.** 39:2 4:2005 pp.130-149.

1306   Political succession and elite politics in twenty-first century China: toward a perspective of 'power balancing'. Zhiyue Bo. **Iss. Stud.** 41:1 3:2005 pp.162-189.

1307   Reconstructing the interagency process after Iraq. Donald R. Drechsler. **J. Strategic S.** 28:1 2:2005 pp.3-30.

1308   The rise of 'new' policy instruments in comparative perspective: has governance eclipsed government? Andrew Jordan; Rüdiger K.W. Wurzel; Anthony Zito. **Pol. S.** 53:3 10:2005 pp.477-496.

1309   Risk, uncertainty and government. Pat O'Malley. London: GlassHouse, 2004. iv, 211p. *ISBN: 1904385001. Includes bibliographical references and index.*

1310   Strateginen johtaminen valtioneuvostotason prosessina. *[In Finnish]*; [Strategic management in the Finnish government] *[Summary]*. Minna Tiili. **Hall. Tut.** 23:2 2004 pp.4-15.

1311   Survey research on New Zealand government: what next? Karen Baehler; et al. **Aust. J. Publ. Admin.** 64:1 3:2005 pp.43-61.

1312   Thaksin's model of government reform in Thailand: prime ministerialisation through 'a country is my company' approach. Bidhya Bowornwathana. **Asian J. Pol. Sci.** 12:1 6:2004 pp.135-153.

1313   Voting weights and formateur advantages in the formation of coalition governments. Stephen Ansolabehere; James M. Snyder, Jr.; Aaron B. Strauss; Michael M. Ting. **Am. J. Pol. Sci.** 49:3 7:2005 pp.550-563.

C.2.2:   **Sub-national government**
        Administration territoriale

1314   Auswirkungen der Dezentralisierung auf das Empowerment von Frauen. *[In German]*; [Decentralization effects on the empowerment of women] *[Summary]*. Julia Kloess. **J. Entwick.pol.** XX:1 2004 pp.70-84.

1315   Intergovernmental political competition in American federalism. Craig Volden. **Am. J. Pol. Sci.** 49:2 4:2005 pp.327-342.

1316   Local financial issues in Algeria. Zine M. Barka. **J. Nth. Afr. S.** 9:3 Autumn:2004 pp.40-59.

1317   New state spaces: urban governance and the rescaling of statehood. Neil Brenner. Oxford: Oxford University Press, 2004. xix, 351p. *ISBN: 0199270058, 0199270066. Includes bibliographical references and index.*

1318   Politics beyond the capital: the design of subnational institutions in South America. Kent Eaton. Stanford CA: Stanford University Press, 2004. xii, 267p. *ISBN: 0804749914. Includes bibliographical references and index.*

1319   The shequ experiment: grassroots political reform in urban China. James Derleth; Daniel R. Koldyk. **J. Cont. China** 13:41 12:2004 pp.747-777.

Administrative decentralization
Décentralisation administrative

1320   Análisis y evaluación de las consideraciones y perspectivas de los alcaldes venezolanos sobre la política de descentralización, la participación ciudadana y las Alcaldías. *[In Spanish]*; (Policy of decentralization and citizen participation at the mayors office level.) Zaira Reverón Escobar; Adolfo Enrique Vargas Cacique. **Cuest. Pol.** 32 1-6:2004 pp.31-63.

1321   L'autonomie corse face à l'indivisibilité de la République. *[In French]*; [The autonomy of Corsica and the indivisibility of the republic]. Elisabeth Vallet. **Fre. Pol. Cult. Soc.** 22:3 Fall:2004 pp.51-75.

1322   Autonomy, devolution and intergovernmental relations. Robert Agranoff. **Reg. Fed. S.** 14:1 Spring:2004 pp.26-65.

1323   Big bang localism: a rescue plan for British democracy. Simon Jenkins. London: Policy Exchange Limited, 2004. 136p. *ISBN: 0954752732.*

1324   Comparative decentralization lessons from Pakistan, Indonesia, and the Philippines. George M. Guess. **Publ. Admin. R.** 65:2 3-4:2005 pp.217-230.

1325   A decade of decentralisation? Assessing the role of the government offices for the English regions. Steven Musson; Adam Tickell; Peter John. **Env. Plan.** A 37:8 8:2005 pp.1395-1412.

1326   Décentralisation, " l'exception française ". *[In French]*; [Decentralization, the 'French exception']. Denis Fressoz. Paris: L'Harmattan, 2004. 116p. *ISBN: 2747574113.*

1327   La décentralisation au Pérou : de quelle participation parlons-nous. *[In French]*; [Decentralization in Peru: what kind of participation are we talking about?]; *[Summary in Spanish]*. Marguerite Bey. **Prob. Am. Lat.** 54 Fall:2004 pp.75-94.

1328   Décentralisation et développement local : un lien à repenser. *[In French]*; (Decentralization and local development: a link to reconsider.) *[Summary]*. Alain Dubresson [Ed.]; Yves-André Fauré [Ed.]. **Tiers Monde** XLVI:181 1-3:2005 pp.7-20.

1329   Décentralisation et développement local au Sénégal. Chronique d'un couple hypothétique. *[In French]*; (Decentralization and local development in Senegal. Chronicle of a hypothetical couple.) *[Summary]*. Alain Piveteau. **Tiers Monde** XLVI:181 1-3:2005 pp.71-93.

1330   Décentralisation et rééquilibrage en faveur des régions en Inde. L'exemple de l'Andhra Pradesh. *[In French]*; (Decentralization and balances in favour of India's regions. The example of Andhra Pradesh.) *[Summary]*. Loraine Kennedy. **Tiers Monde** XLVI:181 1-3:2005 pp.141-165.

1331   Décentralisation, État et territoires. *[In French]*; [Decentralization, state and territories]. Philippe Tronquoy [Ed.]. **Cah. Français** 318 1-2:2004 pp.1-87.

1332   Decentralization and intergovernmental fiscal relations: a review of past and recent trends. Piero Giarda. **Riv. Dir. Finan. Sci. Fin.** LXIII:4 12:2004 pp.527-561.

1333   Decentralizing government and decentering gender: lessons from local government reform in South Africa. Jo Beall. **Pol. Soc.** 33:2 6:2005 pp.253-276.

1334   Democratic deficit or the europeanisation of secession? Explaining the devolution referendums in Scotland. Paolo Dardanelli. **Pol. S.** 53:2 6:2005 pp.320-342.

1335   Démocratie territoriale : enjeux, défis, urgences. *[In French]*; [Territorial democracy: stakes, challenges and urgencies]. Pouvoirs locaux. **Pouv. Loc.** 62 9:2004 pp.25-176.

1336   Des politiques publiques décentralisées, entraves au développement local. Expériences brésiliennes. *[In French]*; (Decentralised public policies, blockages to local development. Brazilian experiences.) *[Summary]*. Yves-André Fauré. **Tiers Monde** XLVI:181 1-3:2005 pp.95-118.

1337   Devolution and development: governance prospects in decentralizing states. Mwangi S. Kimenyi [Ed.]; Patrick Meagher [Ed.]. Aldershot, Burlington VT: Ashgate, 2004. xxv, 349p. *ISBN: 0754639770. Includes bibliographical references and index.* (*Series:* Contemporary perspectives on developing societies).

1338   Devolution and economic governance. Martin Jones; Mark Goodwin; Rhys Jones; Andrés Rodríguez-Pose; Nicholas Gill; Mark Goodwin; Rhys Jones; Philip Cooke; Nick Clifton; Michael Keating; Martin Burch; Ricardo Gomez; Patricia Hogwood; Andrew Scott; Peter G. McGregor; Kim Swales; David Heald; Alasdair McLeod; Robert F. Elliott; David Bell; Anthony Scott; Ada Ma; Elizabeth Roberts; Kevin Cox; Alan Townsend. **Reg. S.** 39:4 6:2005 pp.397-553. *Collection of 10 articles.*

1339   Devolution and regional disparities in the Philippines: is there a connection? Joseph A. Silva. **Env. Plan. C.** 23:3 6:2005 pp.399-417.

1340   Dévolution des délégations de service public et sous-traitance. *[In French]*; [Devolution of public service delegations and subcontracting]. Laetitia Parisi. **Sem. Jurid. Admin. Coll. Terr.** 38 9:2004 pp.1167-1176.

1341   La devolution in Galles: verso il modello Scozzese? *[In Italian]*; (Devolution in Wales: towards the Scottish model?) Gianfranco Baldini. **Riv. It. Sci. Pol.** XXXIV:3 12:2004 pp.433-458.

1342   Devolution, Westminster and the English question. Brigid Hadfield. **Publ. Law** Summer:2005 pp.286-305.

1343   Les enjeux de la décentralisation en matière sociale : l'égalité, la solidarité. *[In French]*; [The social stakes of decentralization: equality and solidarity]. Michel Borgetto. **Info. Soc.** 121 1:2005 pp.6-16.

1344   'Filling in' the state: economic governance and the evolution of devolution in Wales. Rhys Jones; Mark Goodwin; Martin Jones; Kevin Pett. **Env. Plan. C.** 23:3 6:2005 pp.337-360.

1345   Forging a new political culture: plenary behaviour in the Scottish parliament. Ailsa Henderson. **J. Legis. St.** 11:2 Summer:2005 pp.275-301.

1346   From community government to communitarian partnership? Approaches to devolution in Birmingham. Howard Davis; Guy Daly. **Loc. Govt. S.** 30:2 Summer:2004 pp.182-195.

1347   Hastening slowly: the next phase of Welsh devolution. Richard Rawlings. **Publ. Law** Winter:2005 pp.824-852.

1348   If mayors are the answer then what was the question? Kevin Orr. **Loc. Govt. S.** 30:3 Autumn:2004 pp.331-344.

1349   The impact of the Scottish parliament in amending executive legislation. Mark Shephard; Paul Cairney. **Pol. S.** 53:2 6:2005 pp.303-319.

1350   The legislative future of Wales. Timothy H. Jones; Jane M. Williams. **Mod. Law R.** 68:4 7:2005 pp.642-654.

1351   Local e-government and devolution: electronic service delivery and the digital divide in Northern Ireland. Maeve Paris. **Loc. Govt. S.** 31:3 6:2005 pp.307-319.

1352   Métropolisation institutionnelle et spatialités économiques au Cap (Afrique du Sud). *[In French]*; (Institutional metropolitanism and economic spheres in the Cape (South Africa).) *[Summary]*. Alain Dubresson. **Tiers Monde** XLVI:181 1-3:2005 pp.21-44.

1353   Le pari de la décentralisation. *[In French]*; [The gamble of decentralization]. Alternatives économiques. **Alter. Econ.** 223 3:2004 pp.49-58.

1354   A sequential theory of decentralization: Latin American cases in comparative perspective. Tulia G. Falleti. **Am. Pol. Sci. R.** 99:3 8:2005 pp.327-346.

1355   Les services de l'Etat face à la décentralisation. *[In French]*; [State services and decentralization]. Cahiers de la fonction publique et de l'administration. **Cah. Fonc. Publ. Admin.** 231 2:2004 pp.4-15.

1356   Spatial diversity in local government revenue effort under decentralization: a neural-network approach. Mildred E. Warner; James E. Pratt. **Env. Plan. C.** 23:5 10:2005 pp.657-677.

1357   A step backwards or a step forwards? The politics and policies of decentralization under the goverments of the partido popular. Mireia Grau Creus. **Sth. Euro. Soc. Pol.** 10:2 7:2005 pp.263-279.

1358   Territorial administration and political control: decentralization in France. Jean-Claude Thoenig. **Publ. Admin.** 83:3 2005 pp.685-708.

Local government
Administration locale

1359   L'autonomie financière des collectivités locales : clarification et renforcement. *[In French]*; [Financial autonomy of local governments: clarification and strenghtening]. Jean-Luc Pissaloux. **R. Trésor** 7 7:2004 pp.674-681.

1360   Beyond Hanoi: local government in Vietnam. Benedict J. Kerkvliet [Ed.]; David G. Marr [Ed.]. Copenhagen: NIAS Publications, 2004. 359p. *ISBN: 8791114551. Includes index.*

1361   Comparative urban governance: uncovering complex causalities. Jon Pierre. **Urb. Aff. R.** 40:4 3:2005 pp.446-462.

1362   Comparing local governance: trends and developments. S.A.H. Denters [Ed.]; Lawrence E. Rose [Ed.]. Basingstoke: Palgrave Macmillan, 2005. xiv, 293p. *ISBN: 0333995554, 0333995562. Includes bibliographical references and index. (Series:* Government beyond the centre).

1363   Consultation in local government: a case study of practice at Devon county council. Michael Cole. **Loc. Govt. S.** 30:2 Summer:2004 pp.196-213.

1364   La democracia local: entre el espejismo neotocquevillista y la globalización. *[In Spanish]*; [Local democracy: between the neo-Tocquevillist mirage and globalization] *[Summary]*. Bernard Jouve. **R. Cien. Pol.** XXIV:2 2004 pp.116-132.

1365   Devolution and local government: evidence from Scotland. Mark McAteer; Michael Bennett. **Loc. Govt. S.** 31:3 6:2005 pp.285-306.

1366   La eficiencia en las administraciones locales ante diferentes especificaciones del output. *[In Spanish]*; (Local government efficiency and output specification.) *[Summary]*. María Teresa Balaguer Coll. **Hac. Públ. Esp.** 170 3:2004 pp.37-58.

1367   The emerging roles of county governments in metropolitan and nonmetropolitan areas: findings from a national survey. Linda Lobao; David S. Kraybill. **Econ. Dev. Q.** 19:3 8:2005 pp.245-259.

1368   Enhancing efficiency in Australian local government: an evaluation of alternative models of municipal governance. Brian Dollery; Andrew Johnson. **Urb. Policy Res.** 23:1 3:2005 pp.73-86.

1369   Environmental sustainability and management reform in local government: an empirical analysis; *[Summary in Spanish]*; *[Summary in French]*. Gareth Enticott; Richard M. Walker. **Policy Pol.** 33:2 4:2005 pp.297-322.

1370   Erfolgsfaktoren des kommunalen E-Government. *[In German]*; [Factors of success in communal e-government]. Busso Grabow; Helmut Drüke; Christine Siegfried. **Deutsche Z. Kommunalwissenschaften** 43:2 2004 pp.64-92.

1371   Ethics at the crossroads? Developments in the ethical framework for local government. Alan Lawton; Michael MacAulay. **Loc. Govt. S.** 30:4 Winter:2004 pp.624-638.

1372   Evaluating the extent of inter-organizational learning and change in local authorities through the English beacon council scheme. James Downe; Jean Hartley; Lyndsay Rashman. **Publ. Manag. R.** 6:4 12:2004 pp.531-553.

1373   Faktory i predposylki finansovoi avtonomiii mestnogo samoupravleniia. *[In Russian]*; (Factors and preconditions of local self-government's financial autonomy.) *[Summary]*. V.D. Nechaev. **Polis [Moscow]** 6(83) 2004 pp.36-54.

1374   Financing local government. Peter A. Watt. **Loc. Govt. S.** 30:4 Winter:2004 pp.609-623.

1375   Future shapers: children, young people, and planning in New Zealand local government. Claire Freeman; Elizabeth Aitken-Rose. **Env. Plan. C.** 23:2 4:2005 pp.227-246.

1376   Governance at community level: small towns in rural Victoria. Kevin O'Toole; Neil Burdess. **Aust. J. Pol. Sci.** 40:2 6:2005 pp.239-254.

1377   Governing the locals: local self-government and ethnic mobilization in Russia. Tomila Lankina. Lanham MD: Rowman & Littlefield, 2004. xvi, 212p. *ISBN: 0742530213. Includes bibliographical references (p. [187]-203) and index.*

1378   Intercommunalités et action sociale entre renouvellement et sédimentation. *[In French]*; [Local government and cooperation: social action between renewal and stagnation]. Éric Kerrouche. **Info. Soc.** 121 1:2005 pp.76-85.

1379   Kommunale Organisationshoheit unter Reformdruck. *[In German]*; [Communal government authorities under pressure to reform]. Utz Schliesky. **Verwalt.** 38:3 2005 pp.339-366.

1380   Local government initiatives in Thailand: cases and lessons learned. Weerasak Kruethep. **Asian J. Publ. Admin.** 26:2 12:2004 pp.217-239.

1381   Local government management development in Scotland: a study of public policy and its implementation, 1967-2002. Robert Mackie. **Loc. Govt. S.** 30:3 Autumn:2004 pp.345-359.

1382   Local government modernization and the views of chief financial officers. John Wilson. **Publ. Admin.** 83:1 2005 pp.221-232.

1383   Local government reforms in Great Britain, Sweden, Germany and France: between multi-function and single-purpose organisations. Hellmut Wollmann. **Loc. Govt. S.** 30:4 Winter:2004 pp.639-665.

1384   Local politics, central power: the future of representative local government in England. Andrew Coulson. **Loc. Govt. S.** 30:4 Winter:2004 pp.467-480.

1385   Mayors and the challenge of urban leadership. Richard M. Flanagan. Lanham MD: University Press of America, 2004. x, 217p. *ISBN: 0761828958. Includes bibliographical references and index.*

1386   Models of performance-measurement use in local governments: understanding budgeting, communication, and lasting effects. Julia Melkers; Katherine Willoughby. **Publ. Admin. R.** 65:2 3-4:2005 pp.180-190.

1387   The modernisation of local decision making: public participation and Scottish local government. Kevin Orr; Mark McAteer. **Loc. Govt. S.** 30:2 Summer:2004 pp.131-155.

1388   Modernisation or backward step? Women councillors and new decision-making structures in local government. Catherine Bochel; Hugh M. Bochel. **Loc. Govt. S.** 30:1 Spring:2004 pp.36-50.

1389   Municipal democratisation in rural Latin America: methodological insights from Ecuador. John D. Cameron. **B. Lat. Am. Res.** 24:3 7:2005 pp.367-390.

1390   Path dependency and the reform of English local government. Francesca Gains; Peter C. John; Gerry Stoker. **Publ. Admin.** 83:1 2005 pp.25-45.

1391   The privatisation of public space? The American experience of business improvement districts and their relationship to local governance. Mark Steel; Martin Symes. **Loc. Govt. S.** 31:3 6:2005 pp.321-334.

1392   Protecting the right of local self-government. Warren Magnusson. **Can. J. Pol.** 38:4 12:2005 pp.897-922.

1393   Qui nous gouverne au municipal : reproduction ou renouvellement? *[In French]*; [Who is ruling at the municipals: reproduction or renewal?] *[Summary]*; *[Summary in French]*. Carolle Simard. **Pol. et Soc.** 23:2-3 2004 pp.135-158.

1394   Relaciones intermunicipales y gobernabilidad urbana en zonas metropolitanas de México: el caso de la zona metropolitana de Xalapa. *[In Spanish]*; (Inter-municipal relations and urban governance in metropolitan zones of Mexico: the case of the metropolitan zone of Xalapa.) *[Summary]*. Juan Carlos Zentella Gómez. **Est. Demog. Urb.** 20:2 5-8:2005 pp.229-268.

1395   Seeing the bigger picture: delivering local sustainable development. Fay Blair; Bob Evans. York: Joseph Rowntree Foundation, 2004. 75p. *ISBN: 1859351573. (Series: Reconciling environmental and social concerns.)*

1396   Selbstevaluation durch Leistungsvergleiche in deutschen Kommunen. *[In German]*; (Self-evaluation by performance comparison in German local governments.) Sabine Kuhlmann. **Z. Eval.** 1 2005 pp.7-28.

1397   Strong politicians, small deficits: evidence from Norwegian local governments. L.E. Borge. **Euro. J. Pol. Econ.** 21:2 6:2005 pp.325-344.

1398   Why are local authorities reluctant to externalise (and do they have good reason)? Tom Entwistle. **Env. Plan. C.** 23:2 4:2005 pp.191-206.

Regional government
Administration régionale

1399   Choosing between impossible alternatives: creating a new constituency map for Wales, 2004. Ron Johnston; Iain McLean. **Pol. Q.** 76:1 1-3:2005 pp.67-81.

1400   Contracting out local government services: a comparative study of two New Zealand regional councils. Anne McLeod; Priya A. Kurian. **Asian J. Publ. Admin.** 26:2 12:2004 pp.115-133.

1401   Einfluss kleiner Parteien in Koalitionskonflikten: Das Beispiel der FDP beim Sturz des Ministerpräsidenten in Sachsen-Anhalt 1993. *[In German]*; (Influence of small parties in coalition conflicts: the example of the FDP during the resignation of the prime minister of Saxony-Anhalt in 1993.) Sebastian Putz. **Z. Parlament.** 36:1 3:2005 pp.120-141.

1402   Electoral success and federal-level influence of Russian regional executives. Peter J. Söderlund. **Euro.-Asia S.** 57:4 6:2005 pp.521-541.

1403   Le funzioni di province e comuni nella costituzione. *[In Italian]*; [Constitutional functions of provinces and commons]. Luca De Lucia. **Riv. Trim. Pubbl.** 1 2005 pp.23-82.

1404   Governing the mega-region: governance and networks across London and the South East of England. Peter John; Adam Tickell; Steven Musson. **New Pol. Econ.** 10:1 3:2005 pp.91-106.

1405   Haben die deutschen Landesparlamente noch eine Zukunft? *[In German]*; (Do the German state parliaments still have a future?) Joachim Linck. **Z. Pol.wissen.** 14:4 2004 pp.1215-1234.

1406   The limitations of central authority in the regions and the implications for the evolution of Russia's federal system. Elena A. Chebankova. **Euro.-Asia S.** 57:7 11:2005 pp.933-949.

1407   Old regionalism, new regionalism, and envision Utah: making regionalism work. **Harv. Law R.** 118:7 5:2005 pp.2291-2313.

1408   Politiques publiques de recherche et gouvernance régionale. *[In French]*; (Public research projects and regional governance.) *[Summary]*. Daniel Filâtre. **R. Fran. Admin. Publ.** 112 2004 pp.719-730.

1409   Public employment and regional redistribution in Spain; *[Summary in Spanish]*. José Manuel Marqués Sevillano; Joan Rosselló Villallonga. **Hac. Públ. Esp.** 170 3:2004 pp.59-80.

1410   Regional governance in unitary states: lessons from the Netherlands in comparative perspective. Rudie Hulst. **Loc. Govt. S.** 31:1 2:2005 pp.99-120.

1411   Regionalism in Galicia after regionalisation. Frans Schrijver. **J. Econ. Soc. Geog.** 96:3 2005 pp.275-286.

1412   The Russian subnational executives as institutional veto players. Peter J. Söderlund. **Reg. Fed. S.** 15:1 Spring:2005 pp.41-57.

1413   Serving different masters: regional executives and accountability in Ukraine and Russia. Andrew Konitzer-Smirnov. **Euro.-Asia S.** 57:1 1:2005 pp.3-33.

1414   State administration: development, finance and crime. Satya Prakash Dash. **Indian J. Pol. Sci.** 65:3 7-9:2004 pp.435-456.

1415   State and public policy in Kerala: an overview. J. Prabhash. **Indian J. Pol. Sci.** 65:3 7-9:2004 pp.403-418.

1416   A területi közigazgatás továbbfejlesztésének lehetőségei. *[In Hungarian]*; (Possibilities of further development of the regional administration.) Tibor Walter. Budapest: Gondolat Kiadó, 2004. 269p. *ISBN: 9639500534. Includes bibliographical references (p. 255-264).*

1417   Transformatsiia rossiiskoi regional'noi elity: vpered v nomenklaturnoe budushchee? *[In Russian]*; (Transformation of Russia's regional elite: looking at a 'nomenclature' future?) N. Lapina; A. Chirikova. **Mir. Ekon. Mezh. Ot.** 6 6:2005 pp.33-44.

1418   The value of independent commissions: an insider's perspective on the Richard Commission. Laura McAllister. **Parl. Aff.** 58:1 1:2005 pp.38-52.

C.2.3:   **Colonial and post-colonial government**
         Administration coloniale et post-coloniale

1419   Borders, nationalism, and the African state. Ricardo Rene Laremont [Ed.]. Boulder CO: Lynne Rienner Publishers, 2005. xvi, 351p. *ISBN: 1588263401. Includes bibliographical references (p. 327-340) and index.*

1420   By invitation only: Lord Mountbatten, Prince Philip, and the attempt to create a Commonwealth 'Bilderberg group', 1964-66. Philip Murphy. **J. Imp. Commonw. Hist.** 33:2 5:2005 pp.245-265.

1421   Coloniser, exterminer : sur la guerre et l'etat colonial. *[In French]*; [To colonise and to exterminate: on war and the colonial state]. Olivier Le Cour Grandmaison. Paris: Fayard, 2005. 365p. *ISBN: 2213623163*.

1422   Decolonization in France and Israel: a comparative approach. Lorenzo Veracini. **Arena J.** 23 2005 pp.37-52.

1423   Democratization, development, and the patrimonial state in the age of globalization. Eric N. Budd. Lanham MD: Lexington Books, 2004. x, 163p. *ISBN: 0739107143. Includes bibliographical references (p. 143-158) and index.*

1424   The impact of colonial bargaining on intergroup relations in Africa. Gilbert; Donald Rothchild; Owen J.M. Kalinga; Shaheen Mozaffar; Gilbert M. Khadiagala; Jacques Eric Roussellier. **Int. Negot.** 10:2 2005 pp.207-336. *Collection of 6 articles.*

1425   Liberation struggles in Southern Africa: case studies of Angola and South Africa from an Indian perspective. Rajen Harshe. **Afr. Q.** 44:1 5:2004 pp.33-48.

1426   The paradoxes of self-determination in the Cameroons under United Kingdom administration: the search for identity, well-being, and continuity. Bongfen Chem-Langhee. Lanham MD: University Press of America, 2004. xi, 238p. *ISBN: 0761825045. Includes bibliographical references and index.*

1427   The political economy of non-majoritarian institutions: constitutional implications for Hong Kong. Miron Mushkat; Roda Mushkat. **J. East Asian Aff.** XIX:1 Spring-Summer:2005 pp.143-164.

1428   Political reform in Hong Kong: the Principal Officials Accountability System. The first year (2002-2003). Christine Loh; Richard Cullen. **J. Cont. China** 14:42 2:2005 pp.153-176.

1429   Politiques indigènes en France et en Grande-Bretagne dans les années 1930 : aux origines coloniales des politiques de développement. *[In French]*; [Native policies in France and the United Kingdom in the 1930s: the colonial origins of development policies] *[Summary]*. Véronique Dimier. **Pol. et Soc.** 24:1 2005 pp.73-99.

1430   Post-imperial Australia. Graeme Davison; David Goldsworthy; John Chesterman; Jeppe Kristensen; Stuart Ward; Anne Pender; Andrew Hassam; Sara Wills; Jim Davidson; Nicholas Doumanis. **Aust. J. Pol. Hist.** 51:1 3:2005 pp.1-113. *Collection of 10 articles.*

1431   Que reste-t-il des révolutions du tiers monde? *[In French]*; [What is the legacy of revolutions in the third world?] Clifford Geertz. **Esprit** 315 6:2005 pp.46-65.

1432   Reparations for slavery: a reader. Ronald P. Salzberger [Ed.]; Mary C. Turck [Ed.]. Lanham MD: Rowman & Littlefield, 2004. xiii, 347p. *ISBN: 0742514757, 0742514765. Includes bibliographical references (p. 329-337) and index.*

1433   Strong executive, weak policy capacity: the changing environment of policy-making in Hong Kong. Anthony B.L. Cheung. **Asian J. Pol. Sci.** 12:1 6:2004 pp.1-30.

1434   Toward a viable independence? The Koniambo project and the political economy of mining in New Caledonia. Leah S. Horowitz. **Contemp. Pac.** 16:2 Fall:2004 pp.287-320.

1435   Von den Herero zum Holocaust? Einige Bemerkungen zur aktuellen Debatte. *[In German]*; [From the Herero to the Holocaust? Remarks on the current debate]. Birthe Kundrus. **Mittelweg 36** 14:4 7-9:2005 pp.82-91.

C.3:   **Political systems performance**
          Fonctionnement des systèmes politiques

C.3.1:   **Political regimes**
          Régimes politiques

1436   The accidental dictatorship of Alexander Lukashenko. Andrei Sannikov. **SAIS R.** XXV:1 Winter-Spring:2005 pp.75-88.

1437   The advantages of pure forms of parliamentary democracy over mixed forms. Charles B. Blankart; Dennis C. Mueller. **Publ. Choice** 121:3-4 10:2004 pp.431-453.

1438   Afghanistan : le lent retour du pouvoir central. *[In French]*; [Afghanistan: the slow return of central power]. Olivier Roy. **Polit. Int.** 105 Autumn:2004 pp.281-293.

1439   'Africanization' in the Pacific: blaming others for disorder in the periphery? David Chappell. **Comp. S. Soc. Hist.** 47:2 4:2005 pp.286-317.

1440   Algunas consideraciones sobre los actores políticos en la democracia venezolana desde una perspectiva sistémica. *[In Spanish]*; (Certain considerations as to political actors in Venezuelan democracy from a systemic perspective.) Miriam Rincón de Maldonado; María Alejandra Fernández G.; Hudilú T. Rodríguez S. **Cuest. Pol.** 32 1-6:2004 pp.64-102.

1441   Amerikanische und europäische Demokratie: Modelle für den Irak? *[In German]*; (American and European democracy: models for Iraq?); *[Summary in German]*. Roland Benedikter. **Int. Pol. Gesell.** 1 2005 pp.42-61.

1442   Authoritarian state building and the sources of regime competitiveness in the fourth wave: the cases of Belarus, Moldova, Russia, and Ukraine. Lucan A. Way. **World Pol.** 57:2 1:2005 pp.231-261.

1443   The Berlusconi anomaly: populism and patrimony in Italy's long transition. Phil Edwards. **Sth. Euro. Soc. Pol.** 10:2 7:2005 pp.225-244.

1444   Between development and the state: recasting South Korean dirigisme. Hun Joo Park. **Asian J. Pol. Sci.** 12:1 6:2004 pp.95-115.

1445   Beyond free and fair: monitoring elections and building democracy. Eric Bjornlund. Washington DC, Baltimore MA: Woodrow Wilson Center Press, Johns Hopkins University Press, 2004. xxiii, 383p. *ISBN: 0801880483, 0801880505. Includes bibliographical references and index.*

1446   Beyond the ballot: 57 democratic innovations from around the world. Graham Smith. London: Power Inquiry, 2005. 133p. *ISBN: 0955030307.*

1447   Bolivia: another uncompleted revolution. Robert R. Barr. **Lat. Am. Pol. Soc.** 47:3 Fall:2005 pp.69-90.

1448   Burma and U.S. sanctions: punishing an authoritarian regime. Donald M. Seekins. **Asian Sur.** XLV:3 5-6:2005 pp.437-452.

1449   Cambodia: getting away with authoritarianism? Duncan McCargo. **J. Democ.** 16:4 10:2005 pp.98-112.

1450   Changing facets of governance. Yogendra Narain. **Indian J. Publ. Admin.** 4:4 10-12:2004 pp.1017-1024.

1451   Complications of American democracy: elections are not enough. Demetrios James Caraley. **Pol. Sci. Q.** 120:3 Fall:2005 pp.379-405.

1452   The conservative consolidation in Iran. Ali Gheissari; Vali Nasr. **Survival** 47:2 Summer:2005 pp.175-190.

1453   Contentious collective action and the breakdown of authoritarian regimes. Jay Ulfelder. **Int. Pol. Sci. R.** 26:3 7:2005 pp.311-334.

1454   Corée du Nord : un goulag si discret... *[In French]*; [North Korea: such a discreet gulag...]. Pierre Rigoulot. **Polit. Int.** 105 Autumn:2004 pp.321-335.

1455   Democracy in the Arab countries and the West. Roberto Aliboni; Laura Guazzone. **Med. Pol.** 9:1 Spring:2004 pp.82-93.

1456   'Democracy' without a demos? The Bosnian constitutional experiment and the intentional construction of nonfunctioning states. Robert M. Hayden. **East Euro. Pol. Soc.** 19:2 Spring:2005 pp.226-259.

1457   Democratic governance is no panacea: the experience or India and South Asia. Dilip Halder. **Indian J. Publ. Admin.** 4:4 10-12:2004 pp.1046-1069.

1458   Democratic mobilisation through quotas: experiences in India and Germany. Brigitte Geissel; Evelin Hust. **Commonwealth Comp. Pol.** 43:2 7:2005 pp.222-244.

1459   Democratie, la panne. *[In French]*; [Democracy, the failure]. Jacques Capdevielle. Paris: Textuel, 2004. 187p. *ISBN: 2845971354. Includes bibliographical references.*

1460   Démocratie représentative, démocratie participative : les institutions représentatives à l'épreuve de la revendication citoyenne. *[In French]*; [Representative democracy, participative democracy: representative institutions and citizen demand]. Guy Putfin. **Rech. Socialiste** 29 12:2004 pp.31-46.

1461 Démocratie représentative et démocratie participative : les conditions d'une conciliation. *[In French]*; [Representative democracy and participative democracy: conditions of conciliation]. Bernard Rullier. **R. Socialiste** 17 9:2004 pp.116-126.

1462 Demokratiia – eto svobodnye vybory v svobodnom obschestve. *[In Russian]*; (Democracy means free elections in a free society.) Vladislav Inozemtsev [Interviewer]; Natan Shcharanskii. **Svobod. Mysl'** 8 2005 pp.30-43.

1463 Dictadores, instituciones y derechos de propiedad. *[In Spanish]*; (Parliaments in dictatorial regimes.) *[Summary]*. Abel Escribà Folch. **Foro Int.** XLV:2 4-6:2005 pp.220-248.

1464 The dimensionality of right-wing authoritarianism: lessons from the dilemma between theory and measurement. Friedrich Funke. **Pol. Psychol.** 26:2 4:2005 pp.195-218.

1465 Direkte Demokratie und repräsentative Demokratie: ein Vergleich Deutschland-Schweiz unter Berücksichtigung der Studie "Euromodul" des WZB. *[In German]*; [Direct democracy and representative democracy: a comparison between Germany and Switzerland considering the WZB 'Euromodul' study]. Christian Schulte; Ralph Warnke; Wissenschaftszentrum Berlin für Sozialforschung. Berlin: Logos, 2004. 141p. *ISBN: 3832505865.*

1466 Do political pacts freeze democracy? Spanish and South American lessons. Omar G. Encarnación. **West Euro. Pol.** 28:1 1:2005 pp.182-203.

1467 Du multipartisme vers le " one party democracy ". *[In French]*; [From the multiparty system towards the "one party democracy"]. Jacques Philippe Nguemegne. **Penant** 849 10-12:2004 pp.437-487.

1468 Dysfunctional elections and the political system in Hong Kong. Ian Scott; Joan Y.H. Leung. **Asian J. Pol. Sci.** 12:2 12:2004 pp.1-30.

1469 Empirical approaches to deliberative democracy (Part II). Pamela Johnston Conover; Donald D. Searing; James S. Fishkin; Robert C. Luskin; Hanspeter Kriesi; Davy Janssen; Raphaël Kies; Donatella della Porta; Cornelia Ulbert; Thomas Risse; Patrizia Nanz; Jens Steffek; Jürgen Habermas. **Acta Pol.** 40:3 9:2005 pp.269-394. *Collection of 8 articles.*

1470 The erosion of consent: Protestant disillusionment with the 1998 Northern Ireland agreement. Bernadette C. Hayes; Ian McAllister; Lizanne Dowds. **Jnl. Ele. Pub. Op. Par.** 15:2 9:2005 pp.147-167.

1471 Essai sur un despotisme post-moderne : le démo-despotisme. *[In French]*; [Essay on postmodern despotism: the demo-despotism]. Bernard Cubertafond. **Ann. Fran. Rel. Int.** 5 2004 pp.72-88.

1472 Ethno-religious politics, intra state conflict, and the future of democracy in Cote d'Ivoire. Dele Ogunmola; Isiaka Alani Badmus. **Dev. Socio-econ. Prog.** 28:88 5-8:2004 pp.31-49.

1473 Europe's last dictatorship: the roots and perspectives of authoritarianism in 'white Russia'. David R. Marples. **Euro.-Asia S.** 57:6 9:2005 pp.895-908.

1474 Examining democracy in Poland. Lucjan Miś; Alicja Miś. **Soc. Dev. Iss.** 27:1 Spring:2005 pp.73-87.

1475 Fragile democracy and schizophrenic liberalism: exit, voice, and loyalty in the Andes; *[Summary in French]*. Francisco Gutiérrez Sanín. **Int. Pol. Sci. R.** 26:1 1:2005 pp.125-139.

1476 A framework for the systematic study of election quality. Jørgen Elklit; Andrew Reynolds. **Democratization** 12:2 4:2005 pp.147-162.

1477 El franquismo y el estado de derecho. *[In Spanish]*; [The Franco period and the rule of law] *[Summary]*. Luis Aurelio Gonzalez Prieto. **Sistema** 187 7:2005 pp.3-33.

1478 From Argentina to Israel: escape, evacuation and exile. Mario Sznajder; Luis Roniger. **J. Lat. Am. S.** 37:2 5:2005 pp.351-377.

1479 From elections to democracy: building accountable government in Hungary and Poland. Susan Rose-Ackerman. Cambridge: Cambridge University Press, 2005. xii, 272p. *ISBN: 0521843839. Includes bibliographical references and index.*

1480 Getting Haiti right this time: the U.S. and the coup. Noam Chomsky; Paul Farmer; Amy Goodman. Monroe ME: Common Courage Press, 2004. 180p. *ISBN: 1567513190, 1567513182. (Series: Read & resist).*

1481   Global times once again: representative democracy and countervailing trends in Iberoamerica. Luis Roniger. **Iberoamericana** V:17 3:2005 pp.65-90.

1482   The ideals of democracy. B.L. Sah. **Indian J. Pol. Sci.** 65:3 7-9:2004 pp.421-434.

1483   Institutional quality and perceptions of representation in advanced industrial democracies. Robert Rohrschneider. **Comp. Pol. S.** 38:7 9:2005 pp.850-874.

1484   Is democracy the only game in town? Doh Chull Shin; Jason Wells. **J. Democ.** 16:2 4:2005 pp.88-101.

1485   The Italian first republic: 'degenerated consociationalism' in a polarised party system. Matthijs Bogaards. **West Euro. Pol.** 28:3 5:2005 pp.503-520.

1486   Joaquín Balaguer and contemporary Dominican politics and society. Emelio Betances. **Soc. Dem.** 19:1 3:2005 pp.33-47.

1487   Légitime violence? Enquêtes sur la réalité de l'état démocratique. *[In French]*; (The legitimation of violence? An inquiry into a democratic state.) *[Summary]*. Dominique Linhardt; Cédric Moreau de Bellaing. **R. Fran. Sci. Pol.** 55:2 4:2005 pp.269-298.

1488   Mbeki's South Africa. Jeffrey Herbst. **Foreign Aff.** 84:6 11-12:2005 pp.93-105.

1489   Mexican governance: from single-party rule to divided government. Armand B. Peschard-Sverdrup [Ed.]; Sara Rioff [Ed.]. Washington DC: Center for Strategic and International Studies, 2005. xviii, 317p. *ISBN: 0892064579. Includes bibliographical references and index.* (*Series:* Significant issues - 2).

1490   Mexico: la paradoja de su democracia. *[In Spanish]*; [Mexico: the paradox of democracy]. Manuel Alejandro Guerrero. : Universidad Iberoamericana; CEI Consulting Research, 2004. 210p. *ISBN: 9688595403. Includes bibliographical references (p. 189-210).*

1491   New conservatives or old liberals? Neocons and the republican internationalist revival. Saumyajit Ray. **India Q.** LXI:1 1-3:2005 pp.118-141.

1492   Un pais para todos: el sistema politico mexicano del siglo XXI. *[In Spanish]*; [A country for all: Mexican political system in the twenty first century]. Fernando Vazquez Rigada. Mexico City: Porrua, 2004. 279p. *ISBN: 9707015209. Includes bibliographical references (p. 273-279).*

1493   Participative democracy — some implications for the Irish polity. Tony Larkin. **Administration [Dublin]** 52:3 Autumn:2004 pp.43-56.

1494   Patterns of disagreement in democratic politics: comparing Germany, Japan, and the United States. Robert Huckfeldt; Ken'ichi Ikeda; Franz Urban Pappi. **Am. J. Pol. Sci.** 49:3 7:2005 pp.497-514.

1495   Politics of intraexecutive conflict in semipresidential regimes in Eastern Europe. Oleh Protsyk. **East Euro. Pol. Soc.** 19:2 Spring:2005 pp.135-160.

1496   Presidentialism and the effect of electoral law in postcommunist systems: regime type matters. Terry D. Clark; Jill N. Wittrock. **Comp. Pol. S.** 38:2 3:2005 pp.171-188.

1497   La 'presidenzializzazione' e l'erosione del governo di partito nei sistemi parlamentari: il caso del Regno Unito. *[In Italian]*; ('Presidential' rule and the erosion of party government in parliamentary systems: the case of the United Kingdom.) Paul Webb. **Riv. It. Sci. Pol.** XXXIV:3 12:2004 pp.347-378.

1498   The quality of democracies in Europe as measured by current indicators of democratization and good governance. Dirk Berg-Schlosser. **J. Comm. S. Transit. Pol.** 20:1 3:2004 pp.28-55.

1499   Quel avenir pour l'autoritarisme dans le monde arabe ? *[In French]*; (The future of authoritarianism in the Middle East.) *[Summary]*. Philippe Droz-Vincent. **R. Fran. Sci. Pol.** 54:6 12:2004 pp.945-979.

1500   La representación parlamentaria en México. *[In Spanish]*; [Parliamentary representation in Mexico]. Luisa Bejar Algazi; Gilda Waldman M. Mexico City: Ediciones Gernika, 2004. 247p. *ISBN: 9706371427.*

1501   Representative governance: exploring deficiencies. Snehlata Panda. **Indian J. Pol. Sci.** LXV:4 10-12:2004 pp.622-635.

1502   Restructuring Brazil: institutional reform, economic liberalism, and pluralism. Brian Wampler. **Lat. Am. Res. R.** 40:2 2005 pp.242-252.

1503   Rossiskaia demokratiia: koridor vozmozhnostei. *[In Russian]*; (Russian democracy: corridor of options.) *[Summary]*. Iu.A. Krasin. **Polis [Moscow]** 6(83) 2004 pp.125-135.

1504   The Russian predicament. Timothy J. Colton; Cindy Skach. **J. Democ.** 16:3 7:2005 pp.113-126.

1505   Semi-authoritarian incorporation and autocratic militarism in Turkey. Tim Jacoby. **Dev. Change** 36:4 7:2005 pp.641-665.

1506   The struggle against sultanism. Akbar Ganji. **J. Democ.** 16:4 10:2005 pp.38-51.

1507   Systemic vulnerability and the origins of developmental states: Northeast and Southeast Asia in comparative perspective. Richard F. Doner; Bryan K. Ritchie; Dan Slater. **Int. Org.** 59:2 Spring:2005 pp.327-361.

1508   Szorongás és remény. *[In Hungarian]*; (Anguish and hope.) László Lengyel. Budapest: Osiris Kiadó, 2004. 200p. *ISBN: 9633895820. Includes bibliographical references (p. 197-200).*

1509   A theory of coalitions and clientelism: coalition politics in Iceland, 1945-2000. I.H. Indridason. **Euro. J. Pol. Res.** 44:3 5:2005 pp.439-464.

1510   The transformation of access and veto points in Swiss federalism; (The transformation of access and veto points in Swiss federalism.) *[Summary]*. Adrian Vatter. **Reg. Fed. S.** 15:1 Spring:2005 pp.1-18.

1511   Turvallistaminen totalitaarisessa poliittisessa järjestelmässä : makrotason mallin ja mikrotason analyysin yhdistämisestä. *[In Finnish]*; [Securitization in a totalitarian regime: combining micro-level analysis with a macro-level model] *[Summary]*. Juha Vuori. **Kosmopolis** 34:3 2004 pp.4-28.

1512   The unraveling of representative democracy in Venezuela. Jennifer. McCoy [Ed.]; David J. Myers [Ed.]. Baltimore MD: Johns Hopkins University Press, 2004. xx, 342p. *ISBN: 0801879604. Includes bibliographical references (p. 311-326) and index.*

1513   Upravliaemyi pliuralizm: formiruiushchiisia rezhim V. Putina. *[In Russian]*; (Managed pluralism: Putin's political regime.) H. Balzer. **Obshch. Nauki Sovrem.** 2 2004 pp.46-59.

1514   Variations on a theme. Robert Elgie. **J. Democ.** 16:3 7:2005 pp.98-112.

1515   Venezuela: participatory democracy of government as usual? Gregory Wilpert. **Soc. Dem.** 19:1 3:2005 pp.7-32.

1516   What's wrong with democracy? From Athenian practice to American worship. Loren J. Samons. Berkeley CA: University of California Press, 2004. xx, 307p. *ISBN: 0520236602. Includes bibliographical references (p. 279-296) and index.*

1517   Why democracies collapse: the reasons for democratic failure and success. Abraham Diskin; Hanna Diskin; Reuven Y. Hazan. **Int. Pol. Sci. R.** 26:3 7:2005 pp.291-309.

C.3.2:   **Political conditions**
          Conditions politiques

Africa
Afrique

1518   Africa beyond the post-colonial: political and socio-cultural identities. Ola Uduku [Ed.]; Alfred B. Zack-Williams [Ed.]. Aldershot: Ashgate, 2004. xiv, 140p. *ISBN: 0754631710. Includes bibliographical references and index. (Series:* Interdisciplinary research series in ethnic, gender, and class relations).

1519   African power politics: a historical perspective. Godfrey N. Uzoigwe. **Orbis** 49:3 Summer:2005 pp.503-516.

1520   Algeria in transition: reforms and development prospects. John Keiger [Foreword]; Ahmed Aghrout [Ed.]; Mohamed Redha Bougherira [Ed.]. London, New York: RoutledgeCurzon, 2004. xx, 273p. *ISBN: 041534848X. Includes bibliographical references and index. (Series:* RoutledgeCurzon studies in Middle Eastern politics).

1521   Une alliance qui se délite? Contrôle partisan et dynamiques internes dans la Zanu-PF (1999-2003). *[In French]*; (A failing alliance? Partisan control and the internal dynamics of the Zanu-PF (1999-2003).) *[Summary]*. Adrienne LeBas. **Pol. Afr.** 93 3:2004 pp.105-124.

1522   The ANC's 'left turn' and South African sub-imperialism. Patrick Bond. **R. Afr. Pol. Econ.** 31:102 12:2004 pp.599-616.

1523   Angola: anatomy of an oil state. Tony. Hodges. Oxford; Bloomington IN: James Currey; Indiana University Press, 2004. xx, 236p. *ISBN: 0253339391, 0253214661, 0253216788, 0852558740. (Series:* African issues).

1524   Autour du lac Tchad : intégrations et désintégrations. *[In French]*; [Around Lake Chad: integration and disintegration]. Janet Roitman; Martin Zachary Njeuma; Olivier Pliez; Simon Tulipe; Saïbou Issa. **Pol. Afr.** 94 6:2004 pp.7-104. *Collection of 5 articles.*

1525   Background to the Liberia and Sierra Leone implosions. William R. Stanley. **Geojournal** 61:1 2004 pp.69-78.

1526   Between authoritarianism and post-democracy: agenda for reclaiming democracy in Africa. Samuel M. Makinda. **Afr. Q.** 44:1 5:2004 pp.17-32.

1527   Beyond clannishness and colonialism: understanding political disorder in Ethiopia's Somali region, 1991-2004. Tobias Hagmann. **J. Mod. Afr. S.** 43:4 12:2005 pp.509-536.

1528   Coups and conflict in West Africa, 1955-2004: part I, theoretical perspectives. Patrick J. McGowan. **Arm. Forces Soc.** 32:1 10:2005 pp.5-23.

1529   Crafting the new Nigeria: confronting the challenges. Robert I. Rotberg [Ed.]. Boulder CO: Lynne Rienner Publishers, 2004. viii, 273p. *ISBN: 1588262995. Includes bibliographical references (p. 255-260) and index.*

1530   A crisis of governance: Zimbabwe. Jacob W. Chikuhwa. New York: Algora Publishing, 2004. xiv, 353p. *ISBN: 0875862845, 0875862853, 0875862861. Includes bibliographical references (p. 337-341) and index.*

1531   A decade of freedom in South Africa. Nirode Bramdaw. **Afr. Q.** 44:1 5:2004 pp.1-16.

1532   Development denied: autocratic militarism in post-election Zimbabwe. Sarah Bracking. **R. Afr. Pol. Econ.** 32:104-105 6-9:2005 pp.341-357.

1533   Egyptian politics: the dynamics of authoritarian rule. Maye Kassem. Boulder CO: Lynne Rienner Publishers, 2004. x, 213p. *ISBN: 1588262227, 1588262472. Includes bibliographical references (p. 195-204) and index.*

1534   Ethiopia's extended transition. John W. Harbeson. **J. Democ.** 16:4 10:2005 pp.144-158.

1535   Islam, democracy and the state in Algeria: lessons for the Western Mediterranean and beyond. Luis Martinez; Ali Kouaouci; Azzedine Layachi; Clement M. Henry; William Quandt; Boutheina Cheriet; Abdelbaki Benziane; Kada Akacem; Fanny Colonna; Fulvio Attinà; Mohammed Akacem; Yahia H. Zoubir; Mark Tessler; John Entelis; I. William Zartman. **J. Nth. Afr. S.** 9:2 Summer:2004 pp.14-222. *Collection of 15 articles.*

1536   The legacies of transition governments: post-transition dynamics in Benin and Togo. Jennifer C. Seely. **Democratization** 12:3 6:2005 pp.357-377.

1537   Mandela's world: the international dimension of South Africa's political revolution 1990-1999. James Barber. Oxford: James Currey, 2004. 224p. *ISBN: 0852558775, 0852558767. Includes bibliographical references and index.*

1538   NEPAD and prospects for development in Africa. John Mukum Mbaku. **Int. S.** 41:4 10-12:2004 pp.387-409.

1539   Politics in southern Africa: state and society in transition. Gretchen Bauer; Scott D. Taylor. Boulder CO: Lynne Rienner Publishers, 2005. x, 404p. *ISBN: 1588263320, 1588263088. Includes bibliographical references (p. 363-383) and index.*

1540   Rwanda : les défis d'après la victoire. *[In French]*; [Rwanda: challenges following victory]. Colette Braeckman. **Géopol. Afr.** 13 Winter:2004 pp.189-201.

1541   Sénégal 2000-2004, l'alternance et ses contradictions. *[In French]*; [Senegal 2000-2004: political change and its contradictions]. Tarik Dahou; Vincent Foucher; Jean-François Havard; Leo Zeilig; Olivier Legros; Marie Brossier; Xavier Audrain. **Pol. Afr.** 96 12:2004 pp.5-118. *Collection of 6 articles.*

1542   Talk left, walk right: rhetoric and reality in the new South Africa. Patrick Bond. **Glo. Dial.** 6:3-4 Summer-Autumn:2004 pp.127-140.

1543   Talk left, walk right: South Africa's frustrated global reforms. Patrick Bond. London: Merlin Press, 2004. 266p. *ISBN: 0850365589. Includes bibliographical references and index.*

1544   To repair the irreparable: reparation and reconstruction in South Africa. Erik Doxtader [Ed.]; Charles Villa-Vicencio [Ed.]. Claremont: David Philip Publishers, 2004. xxii, 426p. *ISBN: 0864866186. Includes bibliographical references and index.*

1545   Zimbabwe : une tyrannie sans fin. *[In French]*; [Zimbabwe: an endless tyranny] *[Summary]*; *[Summary in Spanish]*. Daniel Compagnon. **Polit. Int.** 107 Spring:2005 pp.289-314.

Americas
Amérique

1546   Anatomy of a habit: America's unnecessary wars. John L. Harper. **Survival** 47:2 Summer:2005 pp.57-86.

1547   Argentinien nach dem Zusammenbruch des neoliberalen Modells. *[In German]*; (Argentina after the collapse of the neoliberal model.) *[Summary]*. Dieter Boris; Ingo Malcher. **Prokla** 35:1 3:2005 pp.131-148.

1548   The Caribbean: democracy adrift? Daniel P. Erikson; Adam Minson. **J. Democ.** 16:4 10:2005 pp.159-171.

1549   Charting Castro's possible successors. Daniel Erikson. **SAIS R.** XXV:1 Winter-Spring:2005 pp.89-103.

1550   Costa Rica: paradise in doubt. Fabrice Lehoucq. **J. Democ.** 16:3 7:2005 pp.140-154.

1551   Democracy and development in Latin America. George Philip. **Lat. Am. Res. R.** 40:2 2005 pp.207-220.

1552   De La Torre y la reforma política argentina: la cuestión electoral y los partidos políticos. *[In Spanish]*; [De la Torre and political reform in Argentina: the electoral question and political parties]. Jorge R. de Miguel. **Desar. Econ.** 44:175 10-12:2004 pp.447-468.

1553   Did 2004 transform US politics? Charles E. Cook, Jr. **Washington Q.** 28:2 Spring:2005 pp.173-186.

1554   The future of memory: children of the dictatorship in Argentina speak. Niki Johnson [Tr.]; Andres Jaroslavsky. London: Latin American Bureau, 2004. 234p. *ISBN: 1899365559.*

1555   Good government? Good citizens? Courts, politics, and markets in a changing Canada. W. A. Bogart. Vancouver: UBC Press, 2005. xiv, 248p. *ISBN: 0774811641. Includes bibliographical references and index. (Series:* Law and society).

1556   Haïti : l'impossible transition démocratique. *[In French]*; [Haiti: the impossible democratic transition]. Laurent Jalabert. **Cah. Hist. Immédiate** 25 Spring:2004 pp.101-119.

1557   Haiti: a slave revolution : 200 years after 1804. Pat Chin [Ed.]; Greg Dunkel; Kim Ives. New York: International Action Center, 2004. xiii, 223p. *ISBN: 097475210X. Includes bibliographical references (p. 219-220) and index.*

1558   Lula's Brazil at midterm. Wendy Hunter; Timothy J. Power. **J. Democ.** 16:3 7:2005 pp.127-139.

1559   Mexico en la region de America del Norte: problemas y perspectivas. *[In Spanish]*; [Mexico in North American region: problems and perspectives]. Gregorio Vidal; Victor M Soria. Mexico City: Universidad Autonoma Metropolitana; Miguel Angel Porrua, 2004. 325p. *ISBN: 970701489X. Includes bibliographical references.*

1560   On the Caribbean. R. Narayanan; Abdul Nafey; Priti Singh; Vishnu Priya; Satya R. Pattnayak; Raj Rajesh; R.L. Chawla; Aprajita Kashyap. **India Q.** 11:2004 pp.1-260. *Collection of 8 articles.*

1561   Un populista en 2006: retroceso o esperanza. Luis Pazos. Mexico City: Diana, 2004. 129p. *ISBN: 9681340361.*

1562   La présidence Bush : parenthèse ou changement structurel. *[In French]*; [The Bush presidency: parenthesis or structural change]. Politique étrangère. **Pol. Étran.** 69:3 Fall:2004 pp.515-573.

1563   Progressive Cuba-bashing. Richard Levins. **Soc. Dem.** 19:1 3:2005 pp.49-66.

1564   The referendum in Venezuela. One act in an unfinished drama. Jennifer McCoy. **J. Democ.** 16:1 1:2005 pp.109-123.

1565   Regime-Hybridität in Entwicklungsländern. Leistungen und Grenzen der neueren Transitionsforschung. *[In German]*; (Regime hybridity in developing countries. Achievements and limitations of new research on transitions.) Heidrun Zinecker. **Z. Int. Beziehung.** 11:2 12:2004 pp.239-272.

1566   Taking Lula's measure. Emir Sader. **New Left R.** 33 5-6:2005 pp.59-80.

1567   Transformation im Rückwärtsgang? Zur Krise der lateinamerikanischen Demokratie. *[In German]*; [Transformation in reverse gear? On the crisis of democracy in Latin America]. Dietmar Dirmoser. **Int. Pol. Gesell.** 2 2005 pp.116-129.

1568   Transformed by crisis: the presidency of George W. Bush and American politics. Jon Kraus [Ed.]; Kevin J. McMahon [Ed.]; David M. Rankin [Ed.]. New York, Basingstoke: Palgrave Macmillan, 2004. x, 216p. *ISBN: 1403965927. Includes bibliographical references and index.*

1569   Una reflexión en torno a Colombia, 1999-2002 ¿Negociación para la paz o proceso para la guerra? *[In Spanish]*; (Thoughts about Colombia, 1999-2002: peace negotiation or war process?) Juan Gabriel Tokatlian. **Foro Int.** XLIV:4 10-12:2004 pp.635-655.

1570   Venezuela mas allá de Chávez: crónicas sobre el "Proceso Bolivariano". *[In Spanish]*; [Venezuela beyond Chávez: chronicles on the 'Proceso Bolivariano']. Raul Zelikas. Barcelona: Virus Editorial, 2004. 198p. *ISBN: 8496044491.*

1571   Venezuelan exceptionalism revisited: the unraveling of Venezuela's model democracy. Edgardo Lander; Dick Parker; Steve Ellner; Jesús María Herrera Salas; Margarita López Maya; Luis Lander; María Pilar García-Guadilla; Marguerite Mayhall; Miguel Tinker Salas. **Lat. Am. Persp.** 32:2(141) 3:2005 pp.5-170. *Collection of 9 articles.*

1572   Venezuela's Bolivarian revolution: who are the Chavistas? Cristóbal Valencia Ramírez. **Lat. Am. Persp.** 32:3(142) 5:2005 pp.79-97.

1573   Venezuela's contemporary political crisis in historical context. Julia Buxton. **B. Lat. Am. Res.** 24:3 7:2005 pp.328-347.

Asia
Asie

1574   Afghanistan in 2004: electoral progress and an opium boom. Larry P. Goodson. **Asian Sur.** XLV:1 1-2:2005 pp.88-97.

1575   Analyse politico-stratégique du Japon. *[In French]*; [A political and strategical analysis of Japan]. Agir. **Agir** 17 3:2004 pp.5-78.

1576   Assessing the shifting qualities of democratic citizenship: the case of South Korea. Doh Chull Shin; Chong-min Park; Jiho Jang. **Democratization** 12:2 4:2005 pp.202-222.

1577   Candidate debates and equity news: international support for democratic deliberation in Cambodia. Caroline Hughes. **Pac. Aff.** 78:1 Spring:2005 pp.77-94.

1578   China in 2004: stability above all. Mary E. Gallagher. **Asian Sur.** XLV:1 1-2:2005 pp.21-32.

1579   La Chine. *[In French]*; [China]. François Jullien [Intro.]; Questions internationales. **Quest. Int.** 6 3-4:2004 pp.2-93.

1580   De la stabilité de l'État en Afghanistan. *[In French]*; (State stability in Afghanistan.) *[Summary]*. Olivier Roy. **Annales** 59:5-6 9-12:2004 pp.1183-1202.

1581   Democratic governance in the Philippines: analysing the sustainability issues. Samiul Hasan. **Publ. Admin. Policy** 13:2 9:2004 pp.73-96.

1582   La démocratie dans l'impasse à Hong Kong. *[In French]*; [Democracy in a dead-end in Hong Kong]. Ma Ngok. **Persp. Chinoises** 86 11-12:2004 pp.43-53.

1583   From external success to internal collapse: the case of democratic Russia. Geir Flikke. **Euro.-Asia S.** 56:8 12:2004 pp.1207-1234.

1584   India briefing: takeoff at last. Alyssa Ayres [Ed.]; Philip Oldenburg [Ed.]. Armonk NY: M.E. Sharpe, 2005. x, 285p. *ISBN: 0765615932. Includes bibliographical references and index.*

1585   India in 2004: regime change in a divided democracy. Baldev Raj Nayar. **Asian Sur.** XLV:1 1-2:2005 pp.71-82.

1586   Informelle Parteistrukturen und institutioneller Wandel: Japanische Erfahrungen nach den politischen Reformen des Jahres 1994. *[In German]*; (Informal party structures and institutional change: Japanese experiences after the political reforms of 1994.) *[Summary]*. Patrick Köllner. **Polit. Viertel.** 46:1 3:2005 pp.39-61.

1587   Japan in 2004: 'courageous' Koizumi carries on. Nobuhiro Hiwatari. **Asian Sur.** XLV:1 1-2:2005 pp.41-53.

1588   Kitai v nachale XXI veka. *[In Russian]*; (China at the beginning of the 21st century.) Iurii Galenovich. **Svobod. Mysl'** 8 2005 pp.16-29.

1589   The military occupation of Burma. Nancy Hudson-Rodd; Myo Hunt. **Geopolitics** 10:3 2005 pp.500-521.

1590   Nahzat-e-Nawin: modernization of the Badakhshani Isma'ili communities of Afghanistan. Hafizullah Emadi. **Loc. Govt. S.** 24:2 6:2005 pp.165-189.

1591   National identity and democratization in Taiwan. T.Y. Wang; John Fuh-sheng Hsieh; G. Andy Chang; Chi Huang; Lowell Dittmer; Emerson M.S. Niou; Ching-hsin Yu; Philip Paolino. **J. Asian Afr. S.** 40:1-2 2-4:2005 pp.5-147. *Collection of 8 articles.*

1592   Nepal: between dictatorship and anarchy. Sumit Ganguly; Brian Shoup. **J. Democ.** 16:4 10:2005 pp.129-143.

1593   Polet drakona. *[In Russian]*; (Flight of the dragon.) Vladimir Maliavin. **Svobod. Mysl'** 6 2005 pp.137-147.

1594   Political modernization: the concept, contours and dynamics. Mohammad Abid. **Indian J. Pol. Sci.** LXV:4 10-12:2004 pp.590-602.

1595   Politics in Indonesia: current state and future outlook. Shiraishi Takashi. **Asia Pac. R.** 12:1 5:2005 pp.25-39.

1596   Post-authoritarian Indonesia: a comparative Southeast Asian perspective. Ariel Heryanto; Vedi R. Hadiz. **Crit. Asian S.** 37:2 6:2005 pp.251-275.

1597   Prickly ambivalence: state, society and semidemocracy in Malaysia. Meredith Weiss. **Commonwealth Comp. Pol.** 43:1 3:2005 pp.61-81.

1598   Public health in Burma: anatomy of a crisis. Alfred Oehlers. **J. Contemp. Asia** 35:2 2005 pp.195-206.

1599   Un régime totalitaire en mutation. *[In French]*; [A mutating totalitarian regime]. Gilles Guiheux. **Quest. Int.** 6 3-4:2004 pp.8-22.

1600   Rethinking Japan's 'lost decade'. Hugo Dobson. **Glo. Soc.** 19:2 4:2005 pp.211-223.

1601   Role of ideas in the survival of the Chinese Communist Party. Waheed A. Khan. **Chi. Rep.** 41:2 4-6:2005 pp.131-148.

1602   El rumbo de la política interna y exterior de la federación Rusa a partir de marzo de 2004. ¿Se puede hablar de cambios en la política del Kremlin? *[In Spanish]*; (Current trends in domestic and foreign policies of the Russian Federation since March 2004. Can we talk of changes in Kremlin's politics?) *[Summary]*. Pablo Telman Sánchez Ramírez. **Foro Int.** XLV:2 4-6:2005 pp.196-219.

1603   Saviours of the nation or robber barons? Warlord politics in Tajikistan. Kirill Nourzhanov. **Loc. Govt. S.** 24:2 6:2005 pp.109-130.

1604   Studies of Taiwan politics. A.D. Marble; T.J. Cheng; Ching Ping Tang; Wei-chin Lee; Jih-wen Lin; Emile C.J. Sheng; Chen-yuan Tung; Philip Hsiaopong Liu; Deborah Brown; Chi Huang; Ming-chi Chen; Jieh-min Wu; Nien-hsuan Fang; Chien-san Feng; James A. Robinson; Robert Sutter; Allen S. Whiting; John F. Copper; Bruce J. Jacobs; Thomas B. Gold; Joseph Bosco; Shelley Rigger; Mikael Mattlin. **Iss. Stud.** 40:3-4 9-12:2004 pp.1-509. *Collection of 21 articles.*

1605   Taiwan's year of stress. Yun-han Chu. **J. Democ.** 16:2 4:2005 pp.43-57.

1606   A tale of two nationalisms. Wang Chaohua. **New Left R.** 32 3-4:2005 pp.83-103.

1607   La théorie du système successeur. Guide d'interprétation pour essayer de comprendre la Chine. *[In French]*; (Successor-system theory as an orienting device: trying to understand China.) David Schweickart. **Pensée** 341 1-3:2005 pp.11-26.

1608   La Transcaucasie est morte, vive le Caucase du Sud ? *[In French]*; [Trans-Caucasus is dead, long live South Caucasus?] Gaïdz Minassian. **Ann. Fran. Rel. Int.** 5 2004 pp.377-394.

1609   Turkmenistan in present scenario. Archana Srivastava. **India Q.** LX:3 7-9:2004 pp.82-119.

1610   The two South Koreas: a house divided. Hahm Chaibong. **Washington Q.** 28:3 Summer:2005 pp.57-72.

Europe
Europe

1611   After Thatcher. John Callaghan. **Soundings** 29 Spring:2005 pp.150-164.

1612   L'avenir européen des Balkans. *[In French]*; [The European futur of the Balkans]. Antoine Kuruneri-Millet [Ed.]. **Agir** 19 10:2004 pp.3-154.

1613   Biélorussie : un laboratoire pour le Kremlin. *[In French]*; [Belarus: a laboratory for the Kremlin] *[Summary]*; *[Summary in Spanish]*. Georges Mamoulia [Interviewer]; Alexandre Potoupa. **Polit. Int.** 107 Spring:2005 pp.49-71.

1614   Civic nationalism and ethnocultural justice in Turkey. Thomas W. Smith. **Hum. Rights Q.** 27:2 5:2005 pp.436-470.

1615   Civil wars, party politics and the consolidation of regimes in twentieth century Europe. Bill Kissane; Nick Sitter. **Democratization** 12:2 4:2005 pp.183-201.

1616   Communism, post-communism and democracy: a policy-outcomes perspective. Alexander J. Groth. **J. Comm. S. Transit. Pol.** 21:3 9:2005 pp.375-394.

1617   Concentrated orange: Fidesz and the remaking of the Hungarian centre-right, 1994-2002. Brigid Fowler. **J. Comm. S. Transit. Pol.** 20:3 9:2004 pp.80-114.

1618   Ein einig Volk von Träumern: Szenen der deutschen Krise. *[In German]*; [A united people of dreamers: scenes of the German crisis]. Sibylle Krause-Burger. Munich: Deutsche Verlags-Anstalt, 2005. 204p. *ISBN: 3421058741.*

1619   Elections in context. The Swiss elections of October 2003: two steps to system change? Clive H. Church. **West Euro. Pol.** 27:3 5:2004 pp.518-534.

1620   Emerging cleavages in new democracies: the case of Lithuania. Mindaugas Jurkynas. **J. Baltic S.** XXXV:3 Fall:2004 pp.278-296.

1621   Die Entstehung der modernen Ukraine — die westliche Dimension. *[In German]*; [The genesis of modern Ukraine]. Roman Szporluk. **Transit** 29 Summer:2005 pp.50-71.

1622   Europeanisation and internationalisation: the case of the Czech Republic. Bojan Petrovic; Etel Solingen. **New Pol. Econ.** 10:3 9:2005 pp.281-304.

1623   L'Europeizzazione della sfera pubblica in Italia: un processo "top-down"? *[In Italian]*; (The europeanization of the Italian public sphere: a "top-down" process?) Donatella della Porta; Manuela Caiani. **Riv. It. Sci. Pol.** XXXIV:3 12:2004 pp.459-490.

1624   External engagement: the Baltic experience. Ainius Lasas. **J. Baltic S.** XXXV:4 Winter:2004 pp.360-377.

1625   From Thatcherism to Blairism. Britain's long march to the market; *[Summary in German]*. Antonino Palumbo. **Öster. Z. Soziol.** 29:4 2004 pp.5-29.

1626   Germany at fifty-five: Berlin ist nicht Bonn. James Sperling [Ed.]. Manchester; New York: Manchester University Press; Palgrave Macmillan, 2004. xxvii, 563p. *ISBN: 0719064724, 0719064732. Includes bibliographical references (p. [523]-557) and index. (Series: Issues in German politics).*

1627   Getting the right right: redefining the centre-right in post-communist Europe. Seán Hanley. **J. Comm. S. Transit. Pol.** 20:3 9:2004 pp.9-27.

1628   Has Germany become a normal country again? N. Pavlov. **Int. Aff. [Moscow]** 51:6 2005 pp.10-20.

1629   How Russia is not ruled: reflections on Russian political development. Allen C Lynch. Cambridge: Cambridge University Press, 2005. xii, 276p. *ISBN: 0521840600, 0521549922. Includes bibliographical references (p. 257-268) and index.*

1630   The instrumental use of European Union conditionality: regionalization in the Czech Republic and Slovakia. Martin Brusis. **East Euro. Pol. Soc.** 19:2 Spring:2005 pp.291-316.

1631   Living under new labour: a local story. Steve Munby. **Soundings** 29 Spring:2005 pp.165-178.

1632   'Modernisation' and the structural constraints of Greek politics. Kevin Featherstone. **West Euro. Pol.** 28:2 3:2005 pp.223-241.

1633   Na puti k razvilke. *[In Russian]*; [At the crossroads]. Valerii Bushuev. **Svobod. Mysl'** 8 2005 pp.110-128.

1634   Norway: the transformation of a political system. Øyvind Østerud; Tom Christensen; Hilmar Rommetvedt; Harald Baldersheim; Anne Lise Fimreite; Kaare Strøm; Hanne Marthe Narud; Henry Valen; Knut Heidar; Ola Listhaug; Tommy Tranvik; Per Selle; Nina C. Raaum; Trygve Gulbrandsen; Fredrik Engelstad. **West Euro. Pol.** 28:4 9:2005 pp.705-918. *Collection of 10 articles.*

1635   Die Orange Revolution. *[In German]*; [The Orange Revolution]. Timothy Garton Ash; Timothy Snyder. **Transit** 29 Summer:2005 pp.14-30.

1636   Politics, paradigms, and intelligence failures: why so few predicted the collapse of the Soviet Union. Ofira Seliktar. Armonk NY: M.E. Sharpe, 2004. xiv, 281p. *ISBN: 0765614642, 0765614650. Includes bibliographical references (p. 226-262) and index.*

1637   Politiek jaarboek. *[In Flemish]*; Année politique. *[In French]*; (Political yearbook of Belgium.) Sam Depauw; Mark Deweerdt; Edith Drieskens; Bart Kerremans; William Fraeys; Bram Wauters; Karolien Weekers; Jean-Benoit Pilet. **Res Publica [Bruss.]** XLVI:2-3 2004 pp.145-406. *Collection of 6 articles.*

1638   Poutine : l'impasse autoritaire. *[In French]*; [Putin: the authoritarian deadlock]. Alternatives internationales. **Alt. Int.** 12 1-2:2004 pp.32-49.

1639   Power as end and means: Russia's two possible paths in past and present. Iurii Afanas'ev. **Rus. Pol. Law** 43:6 11-12:2005 pp.6-21.

1640   Preempting democracy: the case of Belarus. Vitali Silitski. **J. Democ.** 16:4 10:2005 pp.83-97.

1641   Putin's etatization project and limits to democratic reforms in Russia. S. Mohsin Hashim. **Comm. Post-Comm. S.** 38:1 3:2005 pp.25-48.

1642   Putin's Russia. Luisa Trumellini. **Federalist** XLVI:3 2004 pp.140-169.

1643   Re: Birth of Ukraine. *[In German]*; [The birth of Ukraine]. Yaroslav Hrytsak. **Transit** 29 Summer:2005 pp.31-49.

1644   Revolution in Orange: Analysen, Hintergründe, Prognosen. *[In German]*; [Revolution in orange: analysis, backgrounds and prognosis]. Mykola Rjabčuk; Gerhard Simon; Kerstin Zimmer; Winfried Schneider-Deters; Sabine Fischer; Astrid Sahm; Grigorij Pas'ko; Andrej Piontkovskij; Manfred Sapper [Tr.]; Birgit Menzel; Karlheinz Kasper. **Osteuropa** 55:1 1:2005 pp.4-90. *Collection of 6 articles.*

1645   Rootless Russia: Kaliningrad — status and identity. Romuald J. Misiunas. **Dipl. State.** 15:2 6:2004 pp.385-411.

1646   Russia in the year 2004. Timothy J. Colton; Marshall Goldman; Carol R. Saivetz; Roman Szporluk. **Post-Sov. Aff.** 21:1 1-3:2005 pp.1-25.

1647   Russland unter Putin. Kontinuität und Wandel. *[In German]*; (Russia under Putin. Continuity and change.) *[Summary]*. Hans-Georg Heinrich. **Osteuro. Wirt.** 49:4 12:2004 pp.303-316.

1648   Sailing towards the icebergs: New Labour's third term. Michael Rustin. **Soundings** 30 Summer:2005 pp.111-123.

1649   The sources and dynamics of competitive authoritarianism in Ukraine. Lucan A. Way. **J. Comm. S. Transit. Pol.** 20:1 3:2004 pp.143-161.

1650   Soviet nostalgia: an impediment to Russian democratization. Sarah E. Mendelson; Theodore P. Gerber. **Washington Q.** 29:1 Winter:2005-2006 pp.83-96.

1651   A Spanish spring? Carlos Prieto. **New Left R.** 31 1-2:2005 pp.43-70.

1652   Structural sources of post-communist market reform: economic structure, political culture, and war. Shale Horowitz. **Int. S. Q.** 48:4 12:2004 pp.755-778.
1653   Talking Turkey for democracy: fundamentalism, fascism and the EU. Surhan Cam. **Cap. Class** 85 Spring:2005 pp.1-12.
1654   Theft of a nation: Romania since communism. Tom Gallagher. London: Hurst, 2005. 428p. *ISBN: 1850657173, 1850657165. Includes bibliographical references.*
1655   UK 2004. Someone's responsible; no one's to blame. Stephen Ingle; Richard Kelly; Oonagh Gay; Isobel White; Andrew Gray; Bill Jenkins; Sue Prince; Philip Cowley; Mark Stuart; Andrew Hindmoor; Jonathan Bradbury; James Mitchell; David Baker; Philippa Sherrington; Steve Leach; Lawrence Pratchett; Paul Lambe; Colin Rallings; Michael Thrasher; Andrew Russell; Wyn Grant; Dominic Wring; Alan Doig; Andrew Blick; Iain Byrne; Stuart Weir. **Parl. Aff.** 58:2 4:2005 pp.199-423. *Collection of 15 articles.*
1656   Virtual politics: faking democracy in the post-Soviet world. Andrew Wilson. New Haven CT: Yale University Press, 2005. xviii, 332p. *ISBN: 0300095457. Includes bibliographical references and index.*
1657   Why not parties? Electoral markets, party substitutes, and stalled democratization in Russia. Henry E. Hale. **Comp. Pol.** 37:2 1:2005 pp.147-166.

Middle East
Moyen-Orient

1658   Arab unity and disunity: past and present. Fuad Baali. Lanham MD: University Press of America, 2004. ix, 61p. *ISBN: 0761829156. Includes bibliographical references (p. [51]-55) and index.*
1659   As reformas políticas das "petromonarquias" do Golfo. *[In Portuguese]*; (Political reform in the Gulf 'petromonarchies'.) *[Summary]*. Catarina Mendes Leal. **Relações Int.** 6 6:2005 pp.37-56.
1660   The bi-national idea in Israel/Palestine: past and present. Tamar Hermann. **Nat. Nationalism** 11:3 7:2005 pp.381-401.
1661   The conservative wave rolls on. Vali Nasr. **J. Democ.** 16:4 10:2005 pp.9-22.
1662   Democratic institutions and performance. Adeed Dawisha. **J. Democ.** 16:3 7:2005 pp.35-49.
1663   The interim Iraqi government and the ongoing political process. Satish Jacob. **India Q.** LX:4 10-12:2004 pp.35-72.
1664   Iran's clouded horizons. Kaveh Ehsani; Chris Toensing; Morad Saghafi; Farhad Khosrokhavar; Shiva Balaghi; Ziba Mir-Hosseini; Roschanack Shaery-Eisenlohr. **Mid. East Rep.** 34:4(233) Winter:2004 pp.10-43. *Collection of 6 articles.*
1665   O Iraque, tudo somado... (II). *[In Portuguese]*; (Iraq, all in all... (II).) *[Summary]*. Manuel de Lucena. **Relações Int.** 5 3:2005 pp.95-108.
1666   Losing peace in the Middle East: the Palestinian crisis. Beverley Milton-Edwards. **Int. Pol.** 12:2 6:2005 pp.246-263.
1667   Old challenges for new leaderships. The Palestinian elections in perspective. Margret Johannsen. **Int. Spect.** XL:1 1-3:2005 pp.107-117.
1668   Palestinian defiance. Éric Hazan [Interviewer]; Mustafa Barghouti. **New Left R.** 32 3-4:2005 pp.117-131.
1669   Structuring conflict in the Arab world: incumbents, opponents, and institutions. Ellen Lust-Okar. Cambridge, New York: Cambridge University Press, 2005. xvi, 279p. *ISBN: 0521838185. Includes bibliographical references (p. 243-267) and index.*
1670   Les surprises du nouvel Irak. *[In French]*; [Surprises of a new Iraq] *[Summary]*; *[Summary in Spanish]*. Pierre-Jean Luizard. **Polit. Int.** 107 Spring:2005 pp.225-240.
1671   The United Arab Emirates: a study in survival. Christopher M. Davidson. Boulder CO: Lynne Rienner Publishers, 2005. xi, 333p. *ISBN: 158826274X. Includes bibliographical references (p. 309-326) and index. (Series: The Middle East in the international system).*

1672   La vie politique dans le royaume : peut-on parler de coup d'arrêt à l'ouverture. *[In French]*; [Political life in the kingdom: can we speak of a set back to openness]. Jean-Christophe Augé. **Cah. Orient** 75 7-9:2004 pp.20-30.

Oceania
Océanie

1673   Beyond governance in Samoa: understanding Samoan political thought. Elise Huffer; Asofou So'o. **Contemp. Pac.** 17:2 2005 pp.311-333.

1674   Effective developement in Papua New Guinea: local initiatives and community innovation. R. Michael Bourke; Steven Pupune; Theresa Arek; Graeme Ross; Tingneo Mandan; Hartmut Holznecht; Sasa Zibe Kokino; Lorna Brew; John Vail; Elizabeth Cox; Isaac Wai; Paul Maia; Patrina Dikin; Paul Petrus; Pat Howley; Andre Kamane; Wayne Korarome; Nora Vagi Brash; Nancy Sullivan; Joseph Rainbubu; Nancy Warkia; Alun Beck; John Imbal; Gabriel Iso; Ila Geno; Stephen P. Mokis; Barbara Tomi; Nick Menzies; Naihuwo Ahai; Anthony J. Regan; David Kavanamur; Thomas Warr; Terry Murphy; Abby McLeod; Jane Strachan; Seman Dalesa. **Dev. B.** 67 4:2005 pp.6-123. *Collection of 34 articles.*

1675   The failure of the organic law on the integrity of political parties and candidates (OLIPPAC). Alphonse Gelu. **Pac. Econ. B.** 20:1 2005 pp.83-97.

1676   Indonesia's quest for accountable governance. Muhammad Qodari. **J. Democ.** 16:2 4:2005 pp.73-87.

1677   Indonésie 2004. Le chevalier caché et la fin d'un monde. *[In French]*; [Indonesia 2004. The hidden knight and the end of a world] *[Summary]*. François Raillon. **Archipel** 69 2005 pp.295-316.

1678   Papua New Guinea thirty years on. Michael Manning. **Pac. Econ. B.** 20:1 2005 pp.145-158.

1679   Political integrity in Papua New Guinea and the search for stability. Louise Baker. **Pac. Econ. B.** 20:1 2005 pp.98-117.

1680   Understanding reform in Papua New Guinea. David Kavanamur; Henry Okole; Michael Manning; Theodore Levantis. **Pac. Econ. B.** 20:1 2005 pp.118-133.

C.3.3:   **Regime transition**
         Transition politique

1681   After communism: critical perspectives on society and sociology. Carol Harrington [Ed.]; Ayman Salem [Ed.]; Tamara Zurabishvili [Ed.]. Oxford, New York: Peter Lang, 2004. 292p. *ISBN: 0820469513.*

1682   Anchors and democratic change. Leonardo Morlino. **Comp. Pol. S.** 38:7 9:2005 pp.743-770.

1683   Asian democratization at a crossroads: an update. Junhan Lee. **Kor. Obs.** 36:1 Spring:2005 pp.143-166.

1684   Between utopia and disillusionment: a narrative of the political transformation in Eastern Europe. Henri Vogt. New York: Berghahn Books, 2005. xii, 333p. *ISBN: 1571818952. Includes bibliographical references (p. 316-327) and index. (Series:* Studies in contemporary European history - 1).

1685   Building democracy after conflict. Marc F. Plattner; Larry Diamond; Larry Goodson; Gerald Knaus; Marcus Cox; Andrew Reynolds; Stephen D. Krasner; Francis Fukuyama. **J. Democ.** 16:1 1:2005 pp.5-88. *Collection of 7 articles.*

1686   Communist nostalgia and the consolidation of democracy in Central and Eastern Europe. Joakim Ekman; Jonas Linde. **J. Comm. S. Transit. Pol.** 21:3 9:2005 pp.354-374.

1687   Consolidated or defective democracy? Problems of regime change. Leonardo Morlino; Carsten Q. Schneider; Philippe C. Schmitter; Antoaneta Dimitrova; Geoffrey Pridham; Timm Beichelt; Karen Henderson; Hyug Baeg Im; Wolfgang Merkel; Aurel Croissant. **Democratization** 11:5 12:2004 pp.1-213. *Collection of 10 articles.*

1688   Constitutionalism on trial in South Korea. Hahm Chaihark; Sung Ho Kim. **J. Democ.** 16:2 4:2005 pp.28-42.
1689   Constructing an open model of transition: the case of North Africa. Francesco Cavatorta. **J. Nth. Afr. S.** 9:3 Autumn:2004 pp.1-18.
1690   Democracy: rising tide or mirage? Marina S. Ottaway; Jillian Schwedler; Shibley Telhami; Saad Eddin Ibrahim. **Mid. East Policy** XII:2 Summer:2005 pp.1-27.
1691   Democratic transition and political development in post-Soeharto Indonesia. Baladas Ghoshal. **Contemp. Sth.East Asia** 26:3 12:2004 pp.506-529.
1692   Democratic transitions: exploring the structural sources of the fourth wave. Renske Doorenspleet. Boulder CO: Lynne Rienner Publishers, 2005. xii, 203p. *ISBN: 1588263061. Includes bibliographical references (p. 185-195) and index.*
1693   Democratic transitions in East Africa. Paul J. Kaiser [Ed.]; F. Wafula Okumu [Ed.]. Aldershot: Ashgate, 2004. xiii, 229p. *ISBN: 075464278X. Includes bibliographical references and index.*
1694   Democratisation and the constitutional imperative. John Mukum Mbaku. **Glo. Dial.** 6:3-4 Summer-Autumn:2004 pp.48-61.
1695   Democratization and communication in Asia. Caroline Hughes; Gary Rawnsley; Ming-yeh Rawnsley; Graham Brown; Martin Gainsborough; William A. Callahan. **Pac. Aff.** 78:1 Spring:2005 pp.9-113. *Collection of 6 articles.*
1696   Democratization and communication in the Asia-Pacific region. Caroline Hughes. **Pac. Aff.** 78:1 Spring:2005 pp.9-22.
1697   Democratization and constitutional crises in presidential regimes: toward congressional supremacy? Aníbal Pérez-Liñán. **Comp. Pol. S.** 38:1 2:2005 pp.51-74.
1698   Democratization in Gulf monarchies: a new challenge to the GCC. Joseph A. Kéchichian. **Mid. East Policy** XI:4 Winter:2004 pp.37-57.
1699   Demokratisierung und Freiheitsstreben: Die Perspektive der Humanentwicklung. *[In German]*; (Liberty aspirations and democratization: the human development perspective.) *[Summary]*. Christian Welzel; Ronald Inglehart. **Polit. Viertel.** 46:1 3:2005 pp.62-85.
1700   Dimensions of disengagement in post-communist Russia. Stephen White; Ian McAllister. **J. Comm. S. Transit. Pol.** 20:1 3:2004 pp.81-97.
1701   Domestic and transnational perspectives on democratization. Hans Peter Schmitz. **Int. S. R.** 6:3 9:2004 pp.403-426.
1702   Du mauvais usage de la démocratie. *[In French]*; [On the poor use of democracy]. Christian Bouquet. **Géopol. Afr.** 14 Spring:2004 pp.237-253.
1703   A dynamic threesome: materialism, ideas, and leadership in the Soviet and Russian transition. Julie M. Newton. **J. Pol. Ideol.** 10:2 6:2005 pp.219-228.
1704   The economic costs of transition to democracy in the Maghreb: quantitative results for Algeria and Tunisia. Abdelaziz Testas. **J. Nth. Afr. S.** 10:1 3:2005 pp.43-60.
1705   The end of postcommunism in Romania. Peter Gross; Vladimir Tismaneanu. **J. Democ.** 16:2 4:2005 pp.146-162.
1706   Endogenizing social trust: democratization in East-Central Europe. Natalia Letki; Geoffrey Evans. **Br. J. Pol. Sci.** 35:3 7:2005 pp.515-529.
1707   L'évolution politique et institutionnelle récente au Mali : les leçons d'une expérience démocratique. *[In French]*; [Recent political and institutional evolution in Mali: lessons from a democratic experience]. Félix François Lissouck. **R. Jurid. Pol. Ind. Coop.** 58:1 1-3:2004 pp.21-42.
1708   Explaining lustration in Central Europe: a 'post-communist politics' approach. Kieran Williams; Brigid Fowler; Aleks Szczerbiak. **Democratization** 12:1 2:2005 pp.22-43.
1709   Facing the perils of presidentialism? Francis Fukuyama; Björn Dressel; Boo-seung Chang. **J. Democ.** 16:2 4:2005 pp.102-116.
1710   Frieden schaffen mit den Waffen der Demokratie? Theorie und Praxis von Demokratisierung als Friedensstrategie. *[In German]*; (Peace through democratic means? Democratization as peace strategy in theory and practice.) Solveig Richter. **Z. Int. Beziehung.** 12:1 6:2005 pp.77-116.

1711   Gauging Arab support for democracy. Mark Tessler; Eleanor Gao. **J. Democ.** 16:3 7:2005 pp.83-97.

1712   Hazar'a kıyıdaş Türkî cumhuriyetlerde devletin özgül gelişimi. *[In Turkish]*; (The unique evolution of the state in the Turkic republics of the Caspian sea.) Mert Bilgin. **Uluslararasi Ilişkiler** 1:4 Winter:2004 pp.141-163.

1713   History matters: past as prologue in building democracy in Iraq. Eric Davis. **Orbis** 49:2 Spring:2005 pp.229-244.

1714   Identity, culture and democratization: the case of Egypt. Nicola Pratt. **New Pol. Sci.** 27:1 3:2005 pp.69-86.

1715   Ignoring history: U.S. democratization in the Muslim world. James Kurth. **Orbis** 49:2 Spring:2005 pp.305-322.

1716   Interim imposition. Andrew Arato. **Ethics Int. Aff.** 18:3 2004 pp.25-50.

1717   International linkage and democratization. Steven Levitsky; Lucan A. Way. **J. Democ.** 16:3 7:2005 pp.20-34.

1718   Kuchma's failed authoritarianism. Lucan A. Way. **J. Democ.** 16:2 4:2005 pp.131-145.

1719   Le Mali, ou l'irrésistible " ancrage démocratique ". *[In French]*; [Mali, or the irresistible "democratic anchoring"]. Francis Laloupo. **Géopol. Afr.** 15-16 Summer-Fall:2004 pp.255-265.

1720   Model upravljanja i uspjeh tranzicije. *[In Croatian]*; (The model of governance and the transitional success.) Mirjana Dragičević. **Pol. Misao** 41:3 2004 pp.119-131.

1721   Namibia's transition to independence: case study of a successful UN mission. Brig Gurmeet Kanwal. **India Q.** LX:3 7-9:2004 pp.26-40.

1722   Náš hlavní problém: demokratizace myslí. *[In Slovak]*; (Our main problem: democratization of minds.) *[Summary]*. Jiří Pehe; Pavol Lukáč. **Medz. Otázky** XIII:1 2004 pp.118-124.

1723   Not yet democracy: West Africa's slow farewell to authoritarianism. Boubacar N'Diaye; Abdoulaye S. Saine; Mathurin C. Houngnikpo. Durham NC: Carolina Academic Press, 2005. xiii, 224p. *ISBN: 0890895333. Includes bibliographical references (p. 201-214) and index.*

1724   Party politics and different paths to democratic transitions: a comparison of Benin and Senegal. Lucy Creevey; Paul Ngomo; Richard Vengroff. **Party Pol.** 11:4 7:2005 pp.471-493.

1725   Politické riziko v tranzitivních ekonomikách a v Evropské unii. *[In Czech]*; (Political risk in transition economies and the European Union.) *[Summary]*. Milan Žák. **Pol. Ekon.** 1 2005 pp.3-30.

1726   Post-communist transition in Europe and its broader international implications. Mario Zucconi [Ed.]. Ravenna: Longo Editore, 2004. 245p. *ISBN: 8880634429. Includes bibliographical references. (Series:* Europe and the Balkans international network - 22).

1727   Postsovetskii politicheskii rezhim Kazakhstana. *[In Russian]*; [The post-Soviet political regime of Kazakhstan]. D. E. Furman. Moscow: Ogni, 2004. 103p. *ISBN: 5954800189. Includes bibliographical references.*

1728   Problems and prospects for democratic settlements: South Africa as a model for the Middle East and Northern Ireland? Courtney Jung; Ellen Lust-Okar; Ian Shapiro. **Pol. Soc.** 33:2 6:2005 pp.277-326.

1729   Promoting democracy abroad. Peter Burnell; Peter Calvert; James M. Scott; Carie A. Steele; Patrick Holden; Jeroen de Zeeuw; Krishna Kumar; Adam Fagan; Francesco Cavatorta; Julio Faundez. **Democratization** 12:4 8:2005 pp.433-586. *Collection of 8 articles.*

1730   Quinze ans de transition. *[In French]*; [15 years in transition]. Ion Iliescu; Mihnea Berindei [Interviewer]; Arielle Thédrel [Interviewer]. **Polit. Int.** 105(Supp.) Autumn:2004 pp.23-37.

1731   Le retour de la Libye dans le concert des nations ou l'émergence d'un nouveau régime "autoritaire libéral" au Maghreb. *[In French]*; [The return of Libya on the international scene or the emergence of a new 'liberal authoritarian' regime in North Africa]. Stéphane Papi. **Conf. Médit.** 50 Summer:2004 pp.151-165.

1732   Le réveil ukrainien. *[In French]*; [The Ukrainian awakening] *[Summary]*; *[Summary in Spanish]*. Galia Ackerman [Interviewer]; Viktor Iouchtchenko. **Polit. Int.** 107 Spring:2005 pp.15-32.

1733   Revisiting the crisis of representation thesis: the Indian context. Neera Chandhoke. **Democratization** 12:3 6:2005 pp.308-330.

1734   The rise of 'Muslim democracy'. Vali Nasr. **J. Democ.** 16:2 4:2005 pp.13-27.

1735   The role of ideas in post-communist politics: a reevaluation. Karen Dawisha; Venelin I. Ganev; Hilary Appel; Valerie Bunce. **East Euro. Pol. Soc.** 19:3 Summer:2005 pp.339-493. *Collection of 6 articles.*

1736   The search for Arab democracy: discourses and counter-discourses. Larbi Sadiki. New York: Columbia University Press, 2004. xxii, 457p. *ISBN: 0231125801, 023112581X. Includes bibliographical references (p. 410-434) and index.*

1737   Sindrom 'tsvetnykh revoliutsii'. *[In Russian]*; (The syndrome of 'coloured revolutions'.) Timur Poliannikov; Georgii Prokopov. **Svobod. Mysl'** 6 2005 pp.148-160.

1738   Single-member district electoral systems and democratic transition. Sarah Birch. **Electoral S.** 24:2 6:2005 pp.281-301.

1739   Sortir de la transition bloquée : Serbie-Monténégro. *[In French]*; [Get out of a locked transition: Serbia-Montenegro] *[Summary]*. Mirjana Morokvašic [Ed.]; Nebojsa Vukadinovic [Ed.]. **R. Ét. Comp. Est-Ouest** 35:1-2 3-6:2004 pp.5-373.

1740   Specyfika przeobrażeń politycznych: Litwa-Łotwa-Estonia. *[In Polish]*; (The specificity of political transformation: Lithuania, Latvia and Estonia.) *[Summary]*. Jacek Zieliński. **Prz. Euro.** 1(8) 2004 pp.43-54.

1741   'The president is coming to visit!' Dramas and the hijack of democratization in the Islamic Republic of Mauritania. Cédric Jourde. **Comp. Pol.** 37:4 7:2005 pp.421-440.

1742   Transforming Korean politics: democracy, reform, and culture. Young W. Kihl. Armonk NY: M.E. Sharpe, 2005. xv, 404p. *ISBN: 0765614278, 0765614286. Includes bibliographical references (p. 369-390) and index.*

1743   Transitions from postcommunism. Michael McFaul. **J. Democ.** 16:3 7:2005 pp.5-19.

1744   Ukraine: elections and democratisation. Robert S. Kravchuk; Victor Chudowsky; Taras Kuzio; Lucan A. Way; Robert K. Christensen; Edward R. Rakhimkulov; Charles R. Wise; Paul D'Anieri; Anna Makhorkina; Paul Kubicek. **Comm. Post-Comm. S.** 38:2 6:2005 pp.131-292. *Collection of 7 articles.*

1745   Understanding democratic survival and democratic failure in Africa: insights from divergent democratic experiments in Benin and Congo (Brazzaville). Bruce A. Magnusson; John F. Clark. **Comp. S. Soc. Hist.** 47:3 7:2005 pp.552-582.

1746   Understanding the Balkan democratization processes — a liberal approach. Albert Rakipi. **Südosteuro. Mitteil.** 44:4 2004 pp.78-93.

1747   Uroki ukrainskogo. *[In Russian]*; (Lessons of Ukrainian.) *[Summary]*. V.Ia. Gel'man. **Polis [Moscow]** 1(84) 2005 pp.36-49.

1748   Uzbekistan: a modernizing society. Laurence A. Jarvik. **Orbis** 49:2 Spring:2005 pp.261-274.

1749   Von Dynastien und Demokratien: Staatlichkeit im Postsozialismus. *[In German]*; [Of dynasties and democracies: statehood in post-socialism]. Stephan Hensell; Paul Georg Geiß; David Aphrasidze; Andrea Berg; Björn Opfer; Stephan Hensell; Jan Koehler; Christoph Zürcher. **Welt Trends** 45 Winter:2004 pp.11-96. *Collection of 7 articles.*

1750   Voraussetzungen der Demokratie in der postkommunistischen Systemtransformation: Tschechien, Belarus und die Ukraine. *[In German]*; (Prerequisites of democracy in post-communist system transformation: the Czech Republic, Belarus, and Ukraine.) *[Summary]*. Jerzy Maćków. **Z. Parlament.** 36:2 6:2005 pp.411-424.

1751   Der Wandel politischer Kontrolle in den parlamentarischen Demokratien Westeuropas. *[In German]*; (The change of political control in West European parliamentary democracies.) *[Summary]*. Ludger Helms. **Z. Parlament.** 36:2 6:2005 pp.390-410.

C.3.4: **Political opposition**
Opposition politique

1752   Anyone but Bush : contestation et dissidence aux Etats-Unis. *[In French]*; [Anyone but Bush: protest and dissidence in the United States]. Stéphane Spoiden; Olivier Blondeau; Yann Moulier Boutang. **Multitudes** 18 Fall:2004 pp.5-14.

1753   The elephant and the mice: election 2004 and the future of opposition politics in South Africa. James Hamill. **Round Tab.** 377 10:2004 pp.691-708.

1754   How can opposition support authoritarianism? Lessons from Egypt. Holger Albrecht. **Democratization** 12:3 6:2005 pp.378-397.

1755   The opposition's road to success. Taras Kuzio. **J. Democ.** 16:2 4:2005 pp.117-130.

1756   Pipelines of pork: Japanese politics and a model of local opposition party failure. Ethan Scheiner. **Comp. Pol. S.** 38:7 9:2005 pp.799-823.

1757   Political opposition in Russia: a dying species? Vladimir Gel'man. **Post-Sov. Aff.** 21:3 7-9:2005 pp.226-246.

1758   Sovereignty and its discontents: on the primacy of conflict and the structure of the political. William Rasch. London, Portland OR: Cavendish Publishing, 2004. 158p. *ISBN: 1859419844. Includes bibliographical references (p. [151]-156) and index.*

C.3.5: **Civil order**
Ordre public

1759   Analyzing bioterror response logistics: the case of anthrax. David L. Craft; Lawrence M. Wein; Alexander H. Wilkins. **Manag. Sci.** 51:5 5:2005 pp.679-694.

1760   As co-variatas políticas das mortes violentas. *[In Portuguese]*; (Political covariates of violent deaths.) *[Summary]*. Gláucio Ary Dillon Soares. **Opin. Pub.** XI:1 3:2005 pp.192-212.

1761   Causes of civil war in Asia and sub-Saharan Africa: a comparison. Volker Krause; Susumu Suzuki. **Soc. Sci. Q.** 86:1 3:2005 pp.160-177.

1762   Colombia's tipping point? Jorge A. Restrepo; Michael Spagat. **Survival** 47:2 Summer:2005 pp.131-152.

1763   Économies de la violence: or noir et espaces [in]gouvernables du Nigeria. *[In French]*; (Economies of violence: black gold and [in]governable spaces in Nigeria.) *[Summary]*. Michael Watts. **Pol. Afr.** 93 3:2004 pp.125-142.

1764   From political violence to negotiated settlement: the winding path to peace in twentieth-century Ireland. Maurice J. Bric [Ed.]; John Coakley [Ed.]. Dublin: University College Dublin Press, 2004. xiii, 257p. *ISBN: 1900621843. Includes bibliographical references and index.* (*Series:* Perspectives in British-Irish studies).

1765   Genocide in Rwanda: complicity of the churches. Carol Rittner [Ed.]; John K. Roth [Ed.]; Wendy Whitworth [Ed.]. St. Paul MN: Paragon House, 2004. xiii, 319p. *ISBN: 1557788375. Includes bibliographical references (p. 293-298) and index.*

1766   Greed, grievance, and mobilization in civil wars. Patrick M. Regan; Daniel Norton. **J. Confl. Resol.** 49:3 6:2005 pp.319-336.

1767   Guerrilla warfare, counterinsurgency and terrorism in the North Caucasus: the military dimension of the Russian — Chechen conflict. Mark Kramer. **Euro.-Asia S.** 57:2 3:2005 pp.209-290.

1768   How the street gangs took Central America. Ana Arana. **Foreign Aff.** 84:3 5-6:2005 pp.98-110.

1769   O legitimnosti sotsial'nogo poriadka v Rossii. *[In Russian]*; (The legitimacy of social order in Russia.) *[Summary]*. Lev Gudkov. **Vestnik Obshchestvennogo Mneniia** 2(70) 3-4:2004 pp.18-42.

1770   Nkrumah's legacy and Africa's triple heritage between globalization and counter terrorism. Ali A. Mazrui. Accra: Ghana Universities Press, 2004. 62p. *ISBN: 9964302967.*

1771   The Northern Ireland conflict: consociational engagements. John McGarry; Brendan O'Leary. Oxford, New York: Oxford University Press, 2004. xiii, 434p. *ISBN: 0199266573. Includes bibliographical references and index.*

1772   Notizen aus Amerika: Von der "elektronischen Fessel" und Fox News zur Garnisonsgesellschaft. *[In German]*; [A note from the U.S.A.: from "electronic chains" and Fox News to the garrison society]. Barbara Franz. **AWR B.** 43(52):2 2005 pp.110-120.

1773   Organizovaný zločin v postkomunistických zemích střední Evropy podobné problémy při budování bezpečnosti, podobné závazky po vstupu do EU. *[In Czech]*; (Organised crime in states of the post-communist Central Europe similar problems security building, similar duties after joining the EU.) *[Summary]*. Miroslav Nožina. **Mez. Vzt.** 39:4 2004 pp.61-75.

1774   Paradigm in distress? Primary commodities and civil war. James Ron; Thad Dunning; James D. Fearon; Macartan Humphreys; Päivi Lujala; Nils Petter Gleditsch; Elisabeth Gilmore; Richard Snyder; Ravi Bhavnani; Jeremy M. Weinstein; Paul Collier; Anke Hoeffler. **J. Confl. Resol.** 49:4 8:2005 pp.443-633. *Collection of 8 articles.*

1775   Patterns of twentieth century genocides: the Armenian, Jewish, and Rwandan cases. Vahakn N. Dadrian. **J. Genocide Res.** 6:4 12:2004 pp.487-522.

1776   Le phénomène de la contrebande en Colombie au XIXème siècle. *[In French]*; [The phenomenon of smuggling in Colombia in the 19th century] *[Summary]*. Muriel Laurent. **Canadian J. Lat. Am. Caribbean S.** 30:59 2005 pp.131-160.

1777   The politics of rescue: peacekeeping and anti-trafficking programmes in Bosnia-Herzegovina and Kosovo. Carol Harrington. **Int. Femin. J. Pol.** 7:2 2005 pp.175-206.

1778   Popular contention and its impact in rural China. Kevin J. O'Brien; Lianjiang Li. **Comp. Pol. S.** 38:3 4:2005 pp.235-259.

1779   The privatisation and criminalisation of public space in the geopolitics of the Great Lakes region. Filip Reyntjens. **J. Mod. Afr. S.** 43:4 12:2005 pp.587-607.

1780   Pushing the boundaries in Northern Ireland: young people, violence and sectarianism. Sheena McGrellis. **Cont. Pol.** 11:1 3:2005 pp.53-71.

1781   Pyhää sotaa Herran nimeen? Pohjois-Ugandan sota konfliktintutkimuksen kohteena. *[In Finnish]*; [Holy war in the name of the Lord? War in Northern Uganda as a research subject of conflict studies] *[Summary]*. Mika Vehnämäki. **Kosmopolis** 34:4 2004 pp.7-33.

1782   Reconciliación en Guatemala: contra un muro del silencio. *[In Spanish]*; (Reconciliation in Guatemala: battling against a wall of silence.) *[Summary]*; *[Summary in German]*. Dirk Bornschein. **Lat.Am. Anal.** 11 6:2005 pp.131-154.

1783   States of contention: state-led political violence in post-socialist Romania. John Gledhill. **East Euro. Pol. Soc.** 19:1 Winter:2005 pp.76-104.

1784   The strategic impasse in low-intensity conflicts: the gap between Israeli counter-insurgency strategy and tactics during the Al-Aqsa intifada. Sergio Catignani. **J. Strategic S.** 28:1 2:2005 pp.57-76.

1785   To fight or to farm? Agrarian dimensions of the Mano River conflicts (Liberia and Sierra Leone). Paul Richards. **Afr. Affairs** 104:417 10:2005 pp.571-590.

1786   Troubled journey: Nigeria since the civil war. Levi Akalazu Nwachuku [Ed.]; G.N. Uzoigwe [Ed.]. Lanham MD: University Press of America, 2004. xxviii, 340p. *ISBN: 0761827129. Includes bibliographical references (p. 327-330) and index.*

1787   Urban riots and cricket in South Asia: a postscript to "Leveling Crowds". Stanley J. Tambiah. **Mod. Asian S.** 39:4 10:2005 pp.897-927.

1788   Violence and belonging: the quest for identity in post-colonial Africa. Vigdis Broch-Due [Ed.]. London: Routledge, 2005. x, 261p. *ISBN: 0415290074, 0415290066. Includes bibliographical references and index.*

1789   Violence and social order beyond the state: Somalia and Angola. Jutta Bakonyi; Kirsti Stuvøy. **R. Afr. Pol. Econ.** 32:104-105 6-9:2005 pp.359-382.

1790   Violence in the midst of peace negotiations: cases from Guatemala, Northern Ireland, South Africa and Sri Lanka. Kristine Hoglund. Uppsala: Uppsala University, 2004. 232p. *ISBN: 915061780X. (Series: Department of Peace and Conflict Research Report - 69).*

1791   Violencia estructural y masacre genocida en los pueblos indígenas de Chiapas (1997) y Oaxaca (2002). *[In Spanish]*; [Structural violence and genocide in the indigenous towns of

Chiapas (1997) and Oaxaca (2002)]. Natividad Gutiérrez. **Est. Sociol.** XXII:65 5-8:2004 pp.315-348.

1792   Die Weltgemeinschaft im Ausnahmezustand? *[In German]*; [The global community in a state of emergency?] *[Summary]*. Markus Kotzur. **A. Völk.** 42:4 12:2004 pp.353-388.

1793   What are we capable of? The motivations of perpetrators in South Africa during the apartheid era. Claire Bayntun. **Med. Confl. Surv.** 21:1 1-3:2005 pp.3-18.

Civil-military relations
Relations civiles-militaires

1794   Aufstieg und Wandel eines Gewaltakteurs: Die Befreiungsarmee des Kosovo (UÇK). *[In German]*; (Rise and change of a violent actor: the Kosovo Liberation Army (UÇK).) *[Summary]*. Cornelia Frank. **Welt Trends** 48 Autumn:2005 pp.147-158.

1795   Civil-military relations and the Maoist insurgency in Nepal. Prakash Nepali; Phanindra Subba. **Sm. Wars Insurg.** 16:1 3:2005 pp.83-110.

1796   Civil-military relations in Croatia: politicisation and politics of reform. Alex J. Bellamy; Timothy Edmunds. **Euro. Sec.** 14:1 3:2005 pp.71-93.

1797   Civil-military relations in postcommunist Europe: assessing the transition. Andrew Cottey [Intro.]; Timothy Edmunds [Intro.]; Anthony Forster [Intro.]. **Euro. Sec.** 14:1 3:2005 pp.1-16.

1798   Civil-military relations in Serbia-Montenegro: an army in search of a state. Timothy Edmunds. **Euro. Sec.** 14:1 3:2005 pp.115-135.

1799   The Condor years: how Pinochet and his allies brought terrorism to three continents. John Dinges. New York: New Press, 2004. xv, 322p. *ISBN: 1565847644, 1565849779. Includes bibliographical references and index.*

1800   Defence reform, Russian style: obstacles, options, opposition. Zoltan Barany. **Cont. Pol.** 11:1 3:2005 pp.33-51.

1801   The Guatemalan military since the peace accords: the fate of reform under Arzú and Portillo. J. Mark Ruhl. **Lat. Am. Pol. Soc.** 47:1 Spring:2005 pp.55-86.

1802   The military and politics in Africa: from engagement to democratic and constitutional control. George Klay Kieh [Ed.]; Pita Ogaba Agbese [Ed.]. Aldershot: Ashgate, 2004. xii, 221p. *ISBN: 0754618765. Includes bibliographical references and index. (Series:* Contemporary perspectives on developing societies).

1803   The myth of the military-nation: militarism, gender, and education in Turkey. Ayse Gul Altinay. New York, Basingstoke: Palgrave Macmillan, 2004. xi, 206p. *ISBN: 1403962812. Includes bibliographical references and index.*

1804   Not a 'real state'? Defence privatization in Canada. Christopher Spearin. **Int. J.** LX:4 Autumn:2005 pp.1093-1112.

1805   The perils of counterinsurgency: Russia's war in Chechnya. Mark Kramer. **Int. Secur.** 29:3 Winter:2004-2005 pp.5-63.

1806   Potemkin am Werk: Die Militärreform in Rußland. *[In German]*; (Potemkin at work: military reform in Russia.) *[Summary]*. Zoltán Barany. **Osteuropa** 54:11 11:2004 pp.16-31.

1807   The Thaksinization of Thailand. Duncan McCargo; Ukrist Pathmanand. Copenhagen: NIAS Publications, 2005. vi, 277p. *ISBN: 8791114454, 8791114462. Includes bibliographical references (p. [255]-264) and index. (Series:* Studies in contemporary Asian history).

1808   The transformation of postcommunist civil-military relations in Poland. Paul Latawski. **Euro. Sec.** 14:1 3:2005 pp.33-50.

1809   The transformation of Romanian civil-military relations: enabling force projection. Larry L. Watts. **Euro. Sec.** 14:1 3:2005 pp.95-114.

1810   Walking ghosts: murder and guerilla politics in Colombia. Steven S. Dudley. New York, London: Routledge, 2004. xviii, 253p. *ISBN: 041593303X. Includes bibliographical references and index.*

Policing
Maintien de l'ordre

1811   Dangers lurking in the deep: the transformative potential of the crime audit. Daniel Gilling; Adrian Barton. **Crim. Just.** 5:2 5:2005 pp.163-180.

1812   De la police administrative des activités culturelles. *[In French]*; [On administrative police of cultural activities]. Jean-Paul Pastorel. **R. Droit Publ.** 2 3-4:2005 pp.395-425.

1813   Une France sécuritaire ? *[In French]*; [Is France focused on security?] Après-demain. **Après-demain** 469 12:2004 pp.3-46.

1814   The home secretary and improved accountability of the police? Kiron Reid. **J. Crim. Law** 69:3 6:2005 pp.232-255.

1815   Human rights and police training in transitional societies: exporting the lessons of Northern Ireland. Mary O'Rawe. **Hum. Rights Q.** 27:3 8:2005 pp.943-968.

1816   La inevitable "mano dura": sociedad civil y violencia policial en Argentina y Chile. *[In Spanish]*; [The unavoidable 'heavy hand': civil society and political violence in Argentina and Chile] *[Summary]*. Claudio Fuentes. **R. Cien. Pol.** XXIV:2 2004 pp.3-28.

1817   KGB byl, est' i budet: FSB RF pri Barsukove (1995-1996). *[In Russian]*; [The KGB in the past, present and future: Russia's FSB under Barsukov (1995-96)]. Evgenii Strigin. Moscow: EKSMO, Algoritm, 2005. 602p. *ISBN: 5699082417.*

1818   Police efficiency in offences cleared: an analysis of English 'basic command units'. Leigh M. Drake; Richard Simper. **Int. R. Law Econ.** 25:2 6:2005 pp.186-208.

1819   Policing, crime and public health: lessons for Australia from the 'New York miracle'. David Dixon; Lisa Maher. **Crim. Just.** 5:2 5:2005 pp.115-143.

1820   Policing political protest after Seattle. John A. Noakes; Brian V. Klocke; Patrick F. Gillham; Mike King; David Waddington; Alex S. Vitale; Micael Björk; James Sheptycki; P.A.J. Waddington. **Policing Soc.** 15:3 9:2005 pp.235-375. *Collection of 6 articles.*

1821   The political economy of law-and-order policies: policing, class struggle, and neoliberal restructuring. Todd Gordon. **S. Pol. Econ.** 75 Spring:2005 pp.53-78.

1822   Procedural principles and safeguards for internment/administrative detention in armed conflict and other situations of violence. Jelena Pejic. **Int. R. Red Cross** 87:858 6:2005 pp.375-391.

1823   Prohibiting 'American concentration camps': repeal of the emergency detention act and the public historical memory of the Japanese American internment. Masumi Izumi. **Pac. Hist. R.** 74:2 5:2005 pp.165-193.

1824   A report from the field: Georgia's war against contraband and its struggle for territorial integrity. Theresa Freese. **SAIS R.** XXV:1 Winter-Spring:2005 pp.107-121.

1825   Rewarding policemen increases crime. Another surprising result from the inspection game. L. Andreozzi. **Publ. Choice** 121:1-2 10:2004 pp.69-82.

1826   Sovereignty and democratic exclusion in the new South Africa. Lars Buur. **R. Afr. Pol. Econ.** 32:104-105 6-9:2005 pp.253-268.

1827   Understanding covert repressive action: the case of the U.S. government against the Republic of New Africa. Christian Davenport. **J. Confl. Resol.** 49:1 2:2005 pp.120-140.

D: POLITICAL LIFE
VIE POLITIQUE

D.1: **Political actors**
Acteurs politiques

D.1.1: **Politicians**
Hommes politiques

1828   Clientélisme régional en Russie: les exemples de Briansk, Smolensk et Koursk. *[In French]*; (Regional patronage in Russia: Bryansk, Smolensk and Kursk.) *[Summary]*. Jean-Charles Lallemand. **Pouvoirs** 112 2004 pp.127-140.

1829   L'homme qui faisait trembler Saddam Hussein... *[In French]*; [The man who could make Saddam Hussein shake...] *[Summary]*; *[Summary in Spanish]*. Paul Wolfowitz; Alexis Debat [Interviewer]. **Polit. Int.** 107 Spring:2005 pp.209-222.

1830   National party efforts to recruit state legislators to run for the U.S. House. Cherie D. Maestas; L. Sandy Maisel; Walter J. Stone. **Legis. Stud. Q.** XXX:2 5:2005 pp.277-300.

1831   Party penetration of society in Hong Kong: the role of Mutual Aid Committees and political parties. Lo Shiu Hing. **Asian J. Pol. Sci.** 12:1 6:2004 pp.31-64.

1832   Reputational capital, opportunism, and self-policing in legislatures. Glenn R. Parker. **Publ. Choice** 122:3-4 3:2005 pp.333-354.

1833   Vlast' nasha: zametki polittekhnologa. *[In Russian]*; [Our power: a politechnologist's observations]. S.N. Egorov. Moscow: Kuchkovo pole, 2004. 160p. *ISBN: 5860900856.*

Political biography
Biographie politique

1834   Aleksey İvanoviç (Kutlu Muhammet) Tevkelev (şeceresi, İdil-yayık ve kazak tarihindeki rolü). *[In Turkish]*; (Aleksei İvanovich (Khutlu Mohammad) Tevkelev (his pedigree and his role in the history of the Khazakh and İtil-yayik area).) Osman Yorulmaz. **Bilig** 34 Summer:2005 pp.117-144.

1835   Anatolii Sobchak: tainy vkhozhdeniia vo vlast. *[In Russian]*; [Anatolii Sobchak: secrets of his rise to power]. Iurii Titovich Shutov. Moscow: Algoritm, 2005. 442p. *ISBN: 5926501725.*

1836   C'etait François Mitterrand. *[In French]*; [He was François Mitterrand]. Jacques Attali. Paris: Fayard, 2005. 446p. *ISBN: 2213627401. Includes index.*

1837   E.P. Thompson: history and commitment. David Renton. **New Pol.** X:3 Summer:2005 pp.96-109.

1838   Eugene Schuyler, the only diplomatist. Peter Bridges. **Dipl. State.** 16:1 3:2005 pp.13-22.

1839   Gennadii Ziuganov: "pravda" o vozhde. *[In Russian]*; [Gennadii Ziuganov: the 'truth' about the leader]. Aleksandr Alekseevich Il'in. Moscow: Algoritm, 2005. 510p. *ISBN: 5926501717.*

1840   Henri Frenay : premier resistant de France et rival du général de Gaulle. *[In French]*; [Henri Frenay: first resistant in France and rival of the general de Gaulle]. Pierre Giolitto. Paris: L'Harmattan, 2004. 647p. *ISBN: 2747577511. Includes bibliographical references (p. [621]-635).*

1841   Iurii Andropov: neizvestnoe ob izvestnom. *[In Russian]*; [Iurii Andropov: the unknown about the unknown]. Roy Aleksandrovich Medvedev. Moscow: Vremia, 2004. 484p. *ISBN: 5941171285. Includes bibliographical references.*

1842 Jack London, burning man: portrait of an American socialist. Jonah Raskin. **Soc. Dem.** 19:2 7:2005 pp.57-68.
1843 The Jeffords Switch and public support for divided government. Stephen P. Nicholson. **Br. J. Pol. Sci.** 35:2 4:2005 pp.343-356.
1844 Leonid Brezhnev: zolotaia epokha. *[In Russian]*; [Leonid Brezhnev: the golden epoch]. B.V. Sokolov. Moscow: ACT-PRESSKNIGA, 2004. 336p. *ISBN: 5813800034. Includes bibliographical references (p. [328-329]).*
1845 Looking back at LBJ: White House politics in a new light. Mitchell B. Lerner [Ed.]. Lawrence KS: University Press of Kansas, 2005. viii,303p. *ISBN: 0700613846. Includes bibliographical references and index.*
1846 Louise Michel. *[In French]*; [Louise Michel]. Franz van der Motte. Paris: L'Harmattan, 2004. 119p. *ISBN: 2747570444. Includes bibliographical references (p. 113-114).*
1847 Le monde comme je le vois. *[In French]*; [The world as I see it]. Lionel Jospin. Paris: Gallimard, 2005. 328p. *ISBN: 2070774430.*
1848 Moskovskaia model Iuriia Luzhkova. *[In Russian]*; [Iurii Luzhkov's plans for Moscow]. Roy Aleksandrovich Medvedev. Moscow: Vremia, 2005. 512p. *ISBN: 5969100110.*
1849 My times: an autobiography. J. B. Kripalani. New Delhi: Rupa & Co, 2004. xix, 986p. *ISBN: 817167917X. Includes index.*
1850 Myth, war memory, and popular music in Croatia: the case of Marko Perković Thompson. Catherine Baker. **Slovo** 17:1 Spring:2005 pp.19-32.
1851 [Patrice Lumumba, the political actor: from prison to the gates of power (July 1956 - February 1960)]; *[Text in French]*. Jean Omasombo; Benoît Verhaegen. **Cah. Afr.** 68-69-70 2005 pp.17-372. *Collection of 14 articles.*
1852 Pierre Mendes France au quotidien. *[In French]*; [Pierre Mendes France]. Simone Gros; Michel Mendès France [Foreword]. Paris: L'Harmattan, 2004. 160p. *ISBN: 2747569993.*
1853 Politik als Berufung: Hagiographischer Diskurs in der politischen Biographie von Franz-Josef Strauß. *[In German]*; (Politics as a vocation: hagiographic discourse in the political biography of Franz-Josef-Strauß.) *[Summary]*. Volker Fürst. **Sozialersinn** 2 2004 pp.227-246.
1854 Presidential address: George W. Bush's cowboy politics: an inquiry. Stanley A. Renshon. **Pol. Psychol.** 26:4 8:2005 pp.585-614.
1855 René Massigli (1888-1988), un grand du Quai d'Orsay. *[In French]*; (René Massigli (1888-1988), a great figure of the Quai d'Orsay.) Raphaële Ulrich-Pier. **Relations Int.** 122 4-6:2005 pp.3-16.
1856 Yasser Arafat: 1929-2004. Afif Safieh; Uri Avnery; Azzam Tawfiq Abu Saud; Danny Rubinstein; Mamdouh Nofal; Menachem Klein; Joseph Samaha. **Palestine-Israel J. Pol. Econ. Cult.** 11:3-4 2004-2005 pp.6-42. *Collection of 7 articles.*

Political corruption
Corruption politique

1857 African leaders and corruption. M.H. Khalil Timamy. **R. Afr. Pol. Econ.** 32:104-105 6-9:2005 pp.383-393.
1858 Anti-corruption agencies: rhetoric versus reality. Patrick Meagher. **J. Policy Ref.** 8:1 2005 pp.69-103.
1859 Anticorruption campaigns and the intensification of corruption in China. Andrew Wedeman. **J. Cont. China** 14:42 2:2005 pp.93-116.
1860 Can China learn from Hong Kong's experiences in fighting corruption? Shaomin Li. **Glo. Econ. R.** 33:1 2004 pp.1-19.
1861 Corruption: an alternative approach to its definition and measurement. Oskar Kurer. **Pol. S.** 53:1 3:2005 pp.222-239.
1862 Corruption and competition in bureaucracy: a cross-country analysis. Naved Ahmad. **Pak. Econ. Soc. R.** XVLII:1-2 2004 pp.61-86.

1863   Corruption, culture, and communism. Wayne Sandholtz; Rein Taagepera. **Int. R. Sociol.** 15:1 3:2005 pp.109-131.

1864   Corruption design: building clean government in mainland China and Hong Kong. Melanie Manion. Cambridge MA: Harvard University Press, 2004. x, 283p. *ISBN: 0674014863. Includes bibliographical references and index.*

1865   Corruption in India: an exercise in perpetuity. Vibhuti Singh Shekhawat. **Indian J. Pol. Sci.** LXVI:2 4-6:2005 pp.395-404.

1866   Crise politique en Lituanie : le Président Paksas frappé de destitution. *[In French]*; [President Paksas and the political crisis in Lithuania] *[Summary]*. Céline Bayou; Jaroslav Blaha. **Cour. Pays Est** 1042 3-4:2004 pp.72-81.

1867   Electoral incentives for political corruption under open-list proportional representation. Eric C.C. Chang. **J. Pol.** 67:3 8:2005 pp.716-730.

1868   État, bureaucratie et gouvernance en Afrique de l'Ouest francophone. *[In French]*; (State, bureaucracy, and governance in French-speaking West Africa. An empirical diagnostic, a historical perspective.) *[Summary]*. Jean-Pierre Olivier de Sardan. **Pol. Afr.** 96 12:2004 pp.139-162.

1869   International constitutional law and anti-corruption measures in the European Union's accession negotiations: Romania in comparative perspective. Peter W. Schroth; Ana Daniela Bostan. **Am. J. Comp. Law** LII:3 Summer:2004 pp.625-711.

1870   Korruption in Deutschland: Portrait einer Wachstumsbranche. *[In German]*; [Corruption in Germany: portrait of a growing industry]. Britta Bannenberg; Wolfgang J. Schaupensteiner. Munich: Beck, 2004. 227p. *ISBN: 3406510663. Includes bibliographical references (p. 216-227).*

1871   Money for our people? Decentralisation and corruption in Romania: the cases of the equalisation, infrastructure and pre-university education funds. S. Ioniță. **Publ. Admin. Dev.** 25:3 8:2005 pp.251-268.

1872   Oil and water? Elite politicians and corruption in France. John R. Heilbrunn. **Comp. Pol.** 37:3 4:2005 pp.277-296.

1873   Percepcija korupcije i erozija društvenog kapitala u Hrvatskoj 1995.-2003. *[In Croatian]*; (Perception of corruption and the erosion of social capital in Croatia, 1995-2003.) Aleksandar Štulhofer. **Pol. Misao** 41:3 2004 pp.156-169.

1874   Political and media liberalization and political corruption in Taiwan. Dafydd Fell. **Chi. Q.** 184 12:2005 pp.875-893.

1875   Proposal for a new measure of corruption, illustrated with Italian data. Miriam A. Golden; Lucio Picci. **Econ. Pol.** 17:1 3:2005 pp.37-75.

1876   Public sector integrity: a framework for assessment. Janos Bertok. Paris: OECD, 2005. 355p. *ISBN: 9264010599. Includes bibliographical references.*

Political elites
Élites politiques

1877   Guardians of the practitioners' virtue: diplomats at the warrior's den. Sasson Sofer. **Dipl. State.** 16:1 3:2005 pp.1-12.

1878   How's my driving? Abdullah's first year as Malaysian PM. William Case. **Pac. R.** 18:2 6:2005 pp.137-157.

1879   Inside the Putin court: a research note. Ol'ga Kryshtanovskaya; Stephen White. **Euro.-Asia S.** 57:7 11:2005 pp.1065-1075.

1880   Institutionalization and elite behavior in reform China. Xiaowei Zang. **Iss. Stud.** 41:1 3:2005 pp.204-219.

1881   Internacionalización de las elites chilenas. *[In Spanish]*; [Internationalization of Chilean elites]. Fanor Larraín V. **Est. Inter.** XXXVII:147 10-12:2004 pp.133-145.

1882   Iugoslavskii mif i rossiiskaia politicheskaia elita: konsensus ili rasshcheplennoe istoricheskoe soznanie? *[In Russian]*; (Yugoslav myth and Russian political elite.) S. Romanenko. **Obshch. Nauki Sovrem.** 4 2004 pp.120-133.

1883   Jeunes, jeunesse et intégration des élites politiques au Gabon : la place des trajectoires individuelles. *[In French]*; (The young, the youth and the integration of the political elite of Gabon: the role of personal social itineraries.) *[Summary]*Afr. **Contemp.** 213 Winter:2005 pp.197-216.

1884   Losing power in Russia. Ol'ga Kryshtanovskaya; Stephen White. **J. Comm. S. Transit. Pol.** 21:2 6:2005 pp.200-222.

1885   The new era in Chinese elite politics. Shiping Zheng. **Iss. Stud.** 41:1 3:2005 pp.190-203.

1886   The new Pearl Harbor: disturbing questions about the Bush administration and 9/11. David Ray Griffin. Northampton MA: Olive Branch Press, 2004. xxv, 214p. *ISBN: 1566565529.*

1887   Processus de démocratisation et rotation locale des élites au Cameroun. *[In French]*; (Democratization and rotation of local elites in Cameroon.) *[Summary]*; *[Summary in French]*. Ibrahim Mouiche. **Verf. Recht Übersee** 37:4 2004 pp.401-432.

1888   La route des Chapieux : la politique et la vie. *[In French]*; [The path of the Chapieux family: politics and life]. Herve Gaymard. Paris: Fayard, 2004. 258p. *ISBN: 2213621330.*

1889   Sovremennye kontseptsii politicheskoi elity i rossiiskaia praktika. *[In Russian]*; (Modern conceptions of political elite and Russian practice.) *[Summary]*. O. Kryshtanovskaia. **Mir Rossii** XIII:4 2004 pp.3-39.

1890   Symbolism as diplomacy: the United States and Britain's China policy during the first year of the Pacific war. Chan Lau Kit-ching. **Dipl. State.** 16:1 3:2005 pp.73-92.

1891   Vertrauen in Eliten und die politische Unterstützung der Demokratie. *[In German]*; (Trust in elites and political support of democracy.) *[Summary]*. Viktoria Kaina. **Polit. Viertel.** 45:4 12:2004 pp.519-540.

Political leadership
Direction politique

1892   Aftershocks: post war leadership survival, rivalry, and regime dynamics. Michael Colaresi. **Int. S. Q.** 48:4 12:2004 pp.713-727.

1893   De Gaulle : la grandeur et le neant: essai. *[In French]*; [De Gaulle: the greatness and the nothingness: essay]. Dominique Venner. Monaco: Rocher, 2004. 305p. *ISBN: 2268052028.*

1894   D'Iliescu à Iliescu... et après. *[In French]*; [From Iliescu to Iliescu... and afterwards]. Vladimir Tismaneanu. **Polit. Int.** 105(Supp.) Autumn:2004 pp.7-22.

1895   Eligio Ayala, el liderazgo moral transformador desde el gobierno. *[In Spanish]*; [Eligio Ayala, changing moral leadership from the government]. Beatriz González de Bosio. **Cuad. Am.** XVIII:6(108) 11-12:2004 pp.195-208.

1896   Finding a party and losing some friends: overcoming the weaknesses of the prime ministerial figure in Italy. Eoin O'Malley; Francesco Cavatorta. **Cont. Pol.** 10:3-4 9-12:2004 pp.271-286.

1897   First among equals: Abraham Lincoln's reputation during his administration. Hans Louis Trefousse. New York: Fordham University Press, 2005. xiv, 199p. *ISBN: 0823224686. Includes bibliographical references and index.*

1898   The founding fathers and the politics of character. Andrew S. Trees. Princeton NJ: Princeton University Press, 2004. xvi, 208p. *ISBN: 0691115524. Includes bibliographical references and index.*

1899   George W. Bush : le croisé de la démocratie. *[In French]*; [George W. Bush: the crusader for democracy] *[Summary]*; *[Summary in Spanish]*. Guillaume Parmentier. **Polit. Int.** 107 Spring:2005 pp.147-160.

1900   Helmut Kohl: Der Mythos vom Kanzler der Einheit. *[In German]*; [Helmut Kohl: the myth of the chancellor of reunification]. Karl Hugo Pruys. Berlin: Edition Q, 2004. 136p. *ISBN: 3861245868.*

1901   The implications of leadership change in the Arab world. Daniel L. Byman. **Pol. Sci. Q.** 120:1 Spring:2005 pp.59-83.

1902   In the public domain: presidents and the challenges of public leadership. Lori Cox Han [Ed.]; Diane J. Heith [Ed.]. Albany NY: State University of New York Press, 2005. xii,

293p. *ISBN: 0791465756. Includes bibliographical references and index. (Series:* SUNY series on the presidency).

1903   Jacques Chirac's balancing acts: the French right and Europe. Helen Drake. **Sth. Euro. Soc. Pol.** 10:2 7:2005 pp.297-314.

1904   Koizumi's coup. Gavan McCormack. **New Left R.** 35 9-10:2005 pp.5-16.

1905   Leadership and uncertainty in fiscal restructuring: Ralph Klein and Roy Romanow; *[Summary in French].* Cristine de Clercy. **Can. J. Pol.** 38:1 3:2005 pp.175-202.

1906   Leadership in New Zealand. Colin James; Simon Power; Tim Barnett; Seishi Gomibuchi; Stephen Levine; Nigel S. Roberts; Christine Cheyne; Damian Edwards; Rob Salmond; Keith Bolland; Jesse Nichols; Jon Johansson. **Pol. Sci.** 56:2 12:2004 pp.5-130. *Collection of 11 articles.*

1907   Malcolm X and African American self-consciousness. Magnus O. Bassey. Lewiston NY: Edwin Mellen Press, 2005. v, 216p. *ISBN: 0773462813. Includes bibliographical references (p. 175-185) and index. (Series:* Black studies - 26).

1908   The moral origin of Thailand's provincial strongman: the case of Banharn Silpa-archa. Yoshinori Nishizaki. **Sth. East Asia Res.** 13:2 7:2005 pp.184-234.

1909   On mosques and malls: understanding Khomeinism as a source of counter-hegemonic resistance to the spread of global consumer culture. Dan Webb. **J. Pol. Ideol.** 10:1 2:2005 pp.95-119.

1910   The operational codes of Fidel Castro and Kim Il Sung: the last cold warriors? Akan Malici; Johnna Malici. **Pol. Psychol.** 26:3 6:2005 pp.387-412.

1911   The Palestinians after Arafat. Graham Usher. **J. Palestine S.** XXXIV:3(135) Spring:2005 pp.42-56.

1912   Pas d'effet Falklands pour Tony Blair, mais pas de chrysanthèmes. *[In French]*; [No Falklands effect for Tony Blair, and no chrysanthemum]. Bruno Cautrès. **R. Pol. Parl.** 106:1031 7-9:2004 pp.76-86.

1913   Personifitsirovannaia legitimnost'. *[In Russian]*; (Personified legitimacy.) Alexandr Skiperskikh. **Svobod. Mysl'** 8 2005 pp.191-203.

1914   Political representation in leader democracy. András Körösényi. **Gov. Oppos.** 40:3 Summer:2005 pp.358-378.

1915   The Raffarin premiership: a case of failed political leadership. Raymond Kuhn. **Sth. Euro. Soc. Pol.** 10:2 7:2005 pp.245-261.

1916   Richard Nixon and the quest for a new majority. Robert Mason. Chapel Hill NC: University of North Carolina Press, 2004. 289p. *ISBN: 0807829056. Includes bibliographical references (p. 267-280) and index.*

1917   To run or not to run for office: explaining nascent political ambition. Richard L. Fox; Jennifer L. Lawless. **Am. J. Pol. Sci.** 49:3 7:2005 pp.642-659.

1918   The twilight of the Brezhnev era. Petr Cherkasov. **Rus. Pol. Law** 43:6 11-12:2005 pp.76-95.

1919   Unmasterly inactivity? Sir Julian Pauncefote, Lord Salisbury, and the Venezuela boundary dispute. Paul Gibb. **Dipl. State.** 16:1 3:2005 pp.23-55.

1920   What color is hegemony? Powell, Rice and the new global strategists. Clarence Lusane. **New Pol. Sci.** 27:1 3:2005 pp.23-41.

1921   Yasser Arafat : premiers bilans critiques. *[In French]*; [Yasser Arafat: first critical reviews]. Bilal al-Hassan; Shafiq al-Hout [Discussant]; Ahmad Khalifé [Interviewer]; Mamdouh Naufal; Saleh Abdel Jawad; Philippe Daumas; Mamdouh Adwân. **R. Ét. Palest.** 96 Summer:2005 pp.3-90. *Collection of 6 articles.*

1922   Yevgenii Primakov: "hard-liner" or casualty of the conventional wisdom? Jeffrey Surovell. **J. Comm. S. Transit. Pol.** 21:2 6:2005 pp.223-247.

D.1.2: Political forces
Forces politiques

D.1.2.1: Political parties
Partis politiques

1923   At the crossroads of ideological divides: cooperation between leftists and ultranationalists in Turkey. Filiz Başkan. **Turkish S.** 6:1 3:2005 pp.53-69.

1924   Les chants de guerre : par-dela droite et gauche, ou, Promethée delivré. *[In French]*; [War songs: beyond right and left or, Prometheus freed]. Eric. Delbecque; Alain-Gerard Slama [Foreword]. Monaco: Editions du Rocher, 2005. 290p. *ISBN: 2268052435.*

1925   Competition between unequals: the role of mainstream party strategy in niche party success. Bonnie M. Meguid. **Am. Pol. Sci. R.** 99:3 8:2005 pp.347-360.

1926   Conditional party government and the homogeneity of constituent interests. Jeffrey W. Ladewig. **J. Pol.** 67:4 11:2005 pp.1006-1029.

1927   Conservation of balance in the size of the parties. Rein Taagepera. **Party Pol.** 11:3 5:2005 pp.283-298.

1928   E-parties: Democratic and Republican state parties in 2000. Rick Farmer; Rich Fender. **Party Pol.** 11:1 1:2005 pp.47-58.

1929   From catch-all politics to cartelisation: the political economy of the cartel party. Mark Blyth; Richard S. Katz. **West Euro. Pol.** 28:1 1:2005 pp.33-60.

1930   The future of parties. Catherine Needham [Intro.]; Patrick Dunleavy; Philip Lynch; Robert Garner; Andrew Russell; Darren G. Lilleker; Judith Bara; Ben Rogers; Liam Byrne; Matthew Taylor; Ed Vaizey; Philip Parvin; Declan McHugh. **Parl. Aff.** 58:3 7:2005 pp.499-655. *Collection of 11 articles.*

1931   The heart and soul of the party: candidate selection in Ghana and Africa. Magnus Ohman. Uppsala: Uppsala University, 2004. 313p. *ISBN: 9155460046. Includes bibliographical references (p. [275]-313). (Series:* Acta Universitatis Upsaliensis. Skrifter utgivna av Statsvetenskapliga foreningen i Uppsala - 161).

1932   A history of the Liberal Party in the twentieth century. David Dutton; Charles Kennedy [Foreword]. Basingstoke: Palgrave Macmillan, 2004. xii, 347p. *ISBN: 0333746554, 0333746562. Includes bibliographical references and index.*

1933   Judaism and the ethics of war. Norman Solomon. **Int. R. Red Cross** 87:858 6:2005 pp.295-309.

1934   Lost property: what the third way lacks. Chris Pierson. **J. Pol. Ideol.** 10:2 6:2005 pp.145-163.

1935   Neue Rekrutierungs – und Professionalisierungsstrategien der Parteien: Fort – und Weiterbildung der Mitglieder. *[In German]*; (New recruitment and professionalization strategies of parties: advanced education of their members.) *[Summary]*. Christian Demuth. **Z. Parlament.** 35:4 12:2004 pp.700-716.

1936   Parteienfinanzierung in Slowenien und Kroatien. *[In German]*; [Party financing in Slovenia and Croatia] *[Summary]*. Jurij Toplak. **Südosteuro. Mitteil.** 44:5 2004 pp.14-35.

1937   Parteimitglieder neuen Typs? Sozialprofil und Bindungsmotive im Wandel. *[In German]*; (A new type of party member? Changing social profiles and motivations.) *[Summary]*. Heiko Biehl. **Z. Parlament.** 35:4 12:2004 pp.681-699.

1938   Parties, voters and policy priorities in the Netherlands, 1971-2002. Paul Pennings. **Party Pol.** 11:1 1:2005 pp.29-45.

1939   Partis politiques et changement de régime en Pologne : mobilisations autour de la restauration du parti paysan polonais PSL. *[In French]*; (The restoration of the Polish peasant party (PSL): political parties and changes in Poland.) *[Summary]*. Frédéric Zalewski. **R. Fran. Sci. Pol.** 54:6 12:2004 pp.911-944.

1940 Les partis régionalistes et nationalistes. *[In French]*; [Regionalist and nationalist parties] *[Summary]*. Margarita Gómez-Reino Cachafeiro [Ed.]; Romain Pasquier [Ed.]. **Pôle Sud** 20 5:2004 pp.3-164.

1941 Partisan politics: the impact of party in the confirmation of minority and female federal court nominees. Lisa A. Solowiej; Wendy L. Martinek; Thomas L. Brunell. **Party Pol.** 11:5 2005 pp.557-577.

1942 Party types, organisation and functions. Giovanni Sartori. **West Euro. Pol.** 28:1 1:2005 pp.5-32.

1943 Peronismo: evolución e identidad. Continuidades y rupturas en el imaginario político de tres generaciones. *[In Spanish]*; (Peronism: evolution and identity continuities and ruptures in the political imagery of three generations.) *[Summary]*. Ania Tizziani. **Trayectorias** 6:16 9-12:2004 pp.48-69.

1944 Political parties and political systems: the concept of linkage revisited. Andrea Rommele [Ed.]; David M. Farrell [Ed.]; Piero Ignazi [Ed.]. Westport CT: Praeger Publishing, 2005. x, 181p. *ISBN: 0275981053. Includes bibliographical references and index.*

1945 Political parties and the study of political development: new insights from the postcommunist democracies. Marcus Kreuzer; Vello Pettai. **World Pol.** 56:4 7:2004 pp.608-633.

1946 Political parties in Bulgaria: organizational trends in comparative perspective. Maria Spirova. **Party Pol.** 11:5 2005 pp.601-622.

1947 Political parties in Madagascar: neopatrimonial tools or democratic instruments? Richard R. Marcus; Adrien M. Ratsimbaharison. **Party Pol.** 11:4 7:2005 pp.495-512.

1948 Political parties in the regions of Russia: democracy unclaimed. Grigorii Golosov. Boulder CO: Lynne Rienner Publishers, 2004. xvii, 305p. *ISBN: 1588262170. Includes bibliographical references (p. 285-298) and index.*

1949 The political support system for American primacy. Richard K. Betts. **Int. Aff. [London]** 81:1 1:2005 pp.1-14.

1950 Problems of modernizing an ethno-religious party: the case of the Ulster Unionist Party in Northern Ireland. Jocelyn A.J. Evans; Jonathan Tonge. **Party Pol.** 11:3 5:2005 pp.319-338.

1951 Programmatic adaptation and organizational centralization in the AP-PP. Luis Ramiro-Fernández. **Sth. Euro. Soc. Pol.** 10:2 7:2005 pp.207-223.

1952 Il puzzle dei partiti: più forti e più aperti ma meno attraenti e meno legittimi. *[In Italian]*; (The puzzle of contemporary political parties: more open and stronger but less attractive and less legitimate.) Piero Ignazi. **Riv. It. Sci. Pol.** XXXIV:3 12:2004 pp.325-346.

1953 Que y a quienes representan hoy los partidos politicos. *[In Spanish]*; [What and who is represented by today's political parties?] *[Summary]*. Maria Holgado Gonzalez. **Sistema** 188 9:2005 pp.33-43.

1954 Rebels, reds, radicals: rethinking Canada's left history. Ian McKay. Toronto: Between the Lines, 2005. 254p. *ISBN: 1896357970. Includes bibliographical references and index.*

1955 A reconceptualisation of the antecedents of party activism: a multidisciplinary approach. Sue Granik. **Pol. S.** 53:3 10:2005 pp.598-620.

1956 The reform of party funding in Britain. Alan Grant. **Pol. Q.** 76:3 7-9:2005 pp.381-392.

1957 Searching for party effects in post-communist Ukraine. Frank C. Thames. **Comm. Post-Comm. S.** 38:1 3:2005 pp.89-108.

1958 Le Shas : une révolution culturelle et politique. *[In French]*; [The Shas: a cultural and political revolution]. Richard Zrehen. **Outre-terre** 9 2004 pp.241-261.

1959 Soft money and hard choices: why political parties might legislate against soft money donations. D. Gill; C.S. Lipsmeyer. **Publ. Choice** 123:3-4 6:2005 pp.411-438.

1960 'The stupid party': intellectual repute as a category of ideological analysis. Mark F. Proudman. **J. Pol. Ideol.** 10:2 6:2005 pp.199-217.

1961 Third parties: An exchange. Duane Campbell; John Halle; Scott McLarty; Morris Slavin; Thomas Harrison. **New Pol.** X:3 Summer:2005 pp.59-70. *Collection of 5 articles.*

1962 Towards a chequebook democracy? Business, parties and the funding of politics in Italy and the United States. Jonathan Hopkin. **J. Mod. Ital. S.** 10:1 3:2005 pp.43-58.

1963 Uncovering evidence of conditional party government: reassessing majority party influence in congress and state legislatures. William T. Bianco; Itai Sened. **Am. Pol. Sci. R.** 99:3 8:2005 pp.361-372.

1964 A unified theory of party competition: a cross-national analysis integrating spatial and behavioral factors. James Adams; Samuel Merrill; Bernard Grofman. Cambridge, New York: Cambridge University Press, 2005. xviii, 311p. *ISBN: 0521836441, 0521544939. Includes bibliographical references (p. 293-306) and index.*

1965 Vihreä liitto Suomen puoluekarttapallolla periaateohjelmien näkökulmasta tarkasteltuna. *[In Finnish]*; [Green goals and narratives in the Green League party manifestos.] *[Summary].* Rauli Mickelsson. **Politiikka** 46:2 2004 pp.65-93.

1966 Who should govern political parties? Organizational values in Norwegian and Danish political parties. Bernhard Hansen; Jo Saglie. **Scand. Pol. S.** 28:1 2005 pp.1-23.

Left-wing parties
Partis de gauche

1967 70 anos da aliança nacional libertadora (ANL). *[In Portuguese]*; [Seventy years of the National Alliance for Freedom (ANL)] *[Summary].* Anita Leocadia Prestes. **Est. Ib-Am.** XXXI:1 6:2005 pp.101-120.

1968 Accounting for the electoral success of the Liberal Party in Canada: presidential address to the Canadian Political Science Association. André Blais. **Can. J. Pol.** 38:4 12:2005 pp.821-840.

1969 Coalition management in the face of ideological and institutional constraint: the case of France's 'gauche plurielle'. John P. Willerton; Martin Carrier. **Fre. Pol.** 3:1 4:2005 pp.4-27.

1970 The crisis of the German left: the PDS, Stalinism and the global economy. Peter Thompson. New York: Berghahn Books, 2005. v, 136p. *ISBN: 1571815430. Includes bibliographical references (p. 126-132) and index. (Series:* Monographs in German history - 13).

1971 The downfall of the labour party in Israel. Faiza R. Rais. **Strat. S.** XXV:1 Spring:2005 pp.129-150.

1972 Előre a harmadik úton. *[In Hungarian]*; (Go ahead on the Third Way — Tony Blair and New Labour.) Csaba Loppert. **Valóság** 47:10 2004 pp.31-43.

1973 Die "Enkel" Willy Brandts: Aufstieg und Politikstil einer SPD-Generation. *[In German]*; [Willy Brandt's 'grandchildren': rise and style of a generation of SPD politicians]. Matthias Micus. Frankfurt am Main: Campus, 2005. 236p. *ISBN: 3593377446.*

1974 L'épreuve du blairisme. *[In French]*; [The test of Blairism]. Cahiers marxistes. **Cah. Marx.** 228 8-9:2004 pp.3-134.

1975 L'état des gauches centre-européennes. *[In French]*; [The state of the European centre-left]. Nouvelle alternative. **Nouv. Alter.** 19:60-61 3-6:2004 pp.13-137.

1976 Explaining Labour's landslip. Robert M. Worcester; Roger Mortimore; Paul Baines. London: Politico's Publishing, 2005. xiii, 377p. *ISBN: 1842751468, 9781842751466. Includes index.*

1977 The future of unions and labour relations: round table discussion. Billy Hayes; Jim McAuslan; Martin McIvor; Heather Wakefield. **Renewal** 13:1 2005 pp.7-19.

1978 La gauche à l'épreuve de la crise et de l'opposition. *[In French]*; [The Left, political crisis and the opposition]. Gérard Le Gall. **Etat Opin.** 2004 pp.45-70.

1979 Histoire du parti socialiste (1905-2005). *[In French]*; [History of the socialist party (1905-2005)]. Louis. Mexandeau. Paris: Tallandier, 2005. 443p. *ISBN: 2847342052.*

1980 The impact of sector employment on party choice: a comparative study of eight West European countries. Oddbjorn Knutsen. **Euro. J. Pol. Res.** 44:4 6:2005 pp.593-621.

1981 The Latin American left: the difficult relationship between electoral ambition and popular empowerment. Geraldine Lievesley. **Cont. Pol.** 11:1 3:2005 pp.3-18.

1982 The left, elections, and the political party system in the Philippines. Nathan Gilbert Quimpo. **J. Baltic S.** 37:1 3:2005 pp.3-28.

1983   Mark Latham and the ideology of the ALP. Carol Johnson. **Aust. J. Pol. Sci.** 39:3 11:2004 pp.535-551.

1984   Mitregieren in Berlin: die PDS auf dem Prüfstand. *[In German]*; [Governing in Berlin: the PDS put to test]. Rolf Reissig; Rosa-Luxemburg-Stiftung. Berlin: Dietz Vlg Bln, 2005. 89p. *ISBN: 3320020676.*

1985   The mobilisation of the European Left in the early 21st century; *[Summary in French]*; *[Summary in German]*. Albena Azmanova. **Euro. J. Sociol.** XLV:2 2004 pp.273-306.

1986   Money, property and the demise of the CPSU. Atsushi Ogushi. **J. Comm. S. Transit. Pol.** 21:2 6:2005 pp.268-295.

1987   The new bipartisanship within the Chinese communist party. Cheng Li. **Orbis** 49:3 Summer:2005 pp.387-400.

1988   New labour and post-fordist ideology: inherent contradictions. Gavin Lewis. **Arena J.** 23 2005 pp.19-28.

1989   New Labour's approach to the voluntary sector: independence and the meaning of partnership. Jane Lewis. **Soc. Policy Soc.** 4:2 4:2005 pp.121-131.

1990   The northern league: winning arguments, losing influence. Carlo Ruzza. **Cur. Pol. Econ. Euro.** 13:4 2004 pp.309-334.

1991   Un peu de courage. *[In French]*; [A bit of courage.]. Marie-George Buffet; et al; Michel Cool [Discussant]. Paris: Cherche midi, 2004. 171p. *ISBN: 2749102464.*

1992   Policy transfer and programmatic change in the communist successor parties of Eastern and Central Europe. Dan Hough; Marcin Zaborowski; William E. Paterson; James Sloam; Michael Dauderstädt; Piotr Buras; Vladimír Handl; Vladimír Leška. **J. Comm. S. Transit. Pol.** 21:1 3:2005 pp.1-168. *Collection of 10 articles.*

1993   Reformers and revolutionaries in modern Iran: new perspectives on the Iranian left. Stephanie Cronin [Ed.]. New York, London: RoutledgeCurzon, 2004. 288p. *ISBN: 0415331285. Includes bibliographical references and index. (Series:* RoutledgeCurzon/BIPS Persian studies).

1994   Signaling credibility: electoral strategy and New Labour in Britain. Mark Wickham-Jones. **Pol. Sci. Q.** 120:4 Winter:2005-2006 pp.653-673.

1995   Social democrats and neo-liberalism: a case study of the Australian Labor Party. Ashley Lavelle. **Pol. S.** 53:4 12:2005 pp.753-771.

1996   Les socialistes aux portes du pouvoir. *[In French]*; [The socialists at the doorstep of power]. Françoise Seligmann; Pierre Joxe [Foreword]. Paris: Michalon, 2005. 208p. *ISBN: 284186264X.*

1997   Soğuk savaş sonrası avrupa solunda yeni yaklaşımlar: birey, sivil toplum, demokrasi ve sosyalizm. *[In Turkish]*; (New approaches in the European Left: Individual, civil society, democracy and socialism.) Mete Kaan Kaynar. **Akdeniz** 5:9 5:2005 pp.177-201.

1998   Third ways or new ways? The post-communist left in Central Europe. Dan Hough. **Pol. Q.** 76:2 4-6:2005 pp.253-263.

1999   Trade unions, new labour and new labour. Neal Lawson [Ed.]; Paul Thompson [Ed.]; Billy Hayes; Jim McAuslan; Martin McIvor; Heather Wakefield; Edmund Heery; David Coats; Adrian Askew; Nigel Stanley; Colin Crouch; Rajiv Prabhakar; Billy Bragg; Peter Facey; Alan Finlayson; Stan Rosenthal. **Renewal** 13:1 2005 p. *Collection of 10 articles.*

2000   Tradiciones y estrategias de movilización social en los partidos opositores durante el peronismo: el caso del partido comunista y la unión de mujeres de la Argentina. *[In Spanish]*; [Traditions and social mobilization strategies in opposition parties during Peronism: the case of the communist party and the women's union in Argentina]; *[Summary in English]*. Adriana María Valobra. **Canadian J. Lat. Am. Caribbean S.** 30:60 2005 pp.155-182.

2001   Unarmed utopia revisited: the resurgence of left-of-centre politics in Latin America. Francisco Panizza. **Pol. S.** 53:4 12:2005 pp.716-734.

2002   What's left of the radical left? The European radical left after 1989: decline and mutation. Luke March; Cas Mudde. **Comp. Euro. Pol.** 3:1 4:2005 pp.23-49.

2003   Wishful re-thinking. Andrew Pearmain. **Soundings** 29 Spring:2005 pp.179-192.

Party systems
Systèmes de parti

2004 Cartel parties in Western Europe? Klaus Detterbeck. **Party Pol.** 11:2 3:2005 pp.173-191.

2005 The changing party system: stable democracy, contested 'modernisation'. Christos Lyrintzis. **West Euro. Pol.** 28:2 3:2005 pp.242-259.

2006 Changing patterns of party competition in Austria: from multipolar to bipolar system. Wolfgang C. Müller; Franz Fallend. **West Euro. Pol.** 27:5 11:2004 pp.801-835.

2007 Coalition strategies and the BJP's expansion, 1989-2004. E. Sridharan. **Commonwealth Comp. Pol.** 43:2 7:2005 pp.194-221.

2008 Context and coalition-bargaining: comparing portfolio allocation in Eastern and Western Europe. James N. Druckman; Andrew Roberts. **Party Pol.** 11:5 2005 pp.535-555.

2009 'Continuidade na renovação?' Ten years of multiparty politics in Mozambique: roots, evolution and stabilisation of the Frelimo-Renamo party system. Giovanni M. Carbone. **J. Mod. Afr. S.** 43:3 9:2005 pp.417-442.

2010 La crisis del sistema de partidos políticos en Bolivia: causas y consecuencias. *[In Spanish]*; [The crisis of the system of political parties in Bolivia: causes and consequences] *[Summary]*. René Antonio Mayorga. **Canadian J. Lat. Am. Caribbean S.** 30:59 2005 pp.55-92.

2011 Le débat politique entre partis depuis les années 1990. *[In French]*; [The political debate between parties since 1990]. David Fell. **Persp. Chinoises** 85 9-10:2004 pp.5-16.

2012 De-thawing democracy: the decline of political party collaboration in Spain (1977 to 2004). Bonnie N. Field. **Comp. Pol. S.** 38:9 11:2005 pp.1079-1103.

2013 Duverger's law, Penrose's power index and the unity of the UK. Iain McLean; Alistair McMillan; Dennis Leech. **Pol. S.** 53:3 10:2005 pp.457-476.

2014 Electoral competition in heterogeneous districts. Steven Callander. **J. Pol. Econ.** 113:5 10:2005 pp.1116-1145.

2015 Estimating party policy positions: Japan in comparative context. Michael Laver; Kenneth Benoit. **Japanese J. Pol. Sci.** 6:2 8:2005 pp.187-210.

2016 Explaining the demise of the national-New Zealand first coalition. Jonathan Boston; Stephen Church; Hilary Pearse. **Aust. J. Pol. Sci.** 39:3 11:2004 pp.585-603.

2017 Factions of interest in Japan and Italy: the organizational and motivational dimensions of factionalism. Kim Eric Bettcher. **Party Pol.** 11:3 5:2005 pp.339-358.

2018 A house divided: party strength and the mandate divide in Hungary, Russia, and Ukraine. Frank C. Thames. **Comp. Pol. S.** 38:3 4:2005 pp.282-303.

2019 How unstable? Volatility and the genuinely new parties in Eastern Europe. A. Sikk. **Euro. J. Pol. Res.** 44:3 5:2005 pp.391-412.

2020 The ideological organization of Latin American legislative parties an empirical analysis of elite policy preferences. Guillermo Rosas. **Comp. Pol. S.** 38:7 9:2005 pp.824-849.

2021 Indigenous voters and party system fragmentation in Latin America. Raúl L. Madrid. **Electoral S.** 24:4 12:2005 pp.689-707.

2022 The Italian party system between parties and coalitions. Stefano Bartolini; Alessandro Chiaramonte; Roberto D'Alimonte. **West Euro. Pol.** 27:1 1:2004 pp.1-19.

2023 Leasehold or freehold? Leader-eviction rules in the British Conservative and Labour parties. Thomas Quinn. **Pol. S.** 53:4 12:2005 pp.793-815.

2024 O other, where art thou? Support for multiparty politics in the United States. Todd Donovan; Janine A. Parry; Shaun Bowler. **Soc. Sci. Q.** 86:1 3:2005 pp.147-159.

2025 Parties and party systems: a framework for analysis. Giovanni Sartori; Peter Mair [Intro.]. Colchester: ECPR Press, 2005. xxiv, 342p. *ISBN: 0954796616.*

2026 Parties as procedural coalitions in congress: an examination of differing career tracks. Jeffery A. Jenkins; Michael H. Crespin; Jamie L. Carson. **Legis. Stud. Q.** XXX:3 8:2005 pp.365-389.

2027 Parties as programmatic agents: a test of institutional theory in Brazil. Mona M. Lyne. **Party Pol.** 11:2 3:2005 pp.193-216.

2028   Parties over: the demise of Egypt's opposition parties. Joshua A. Stacher. **Br. J. Mid. East. S.** 31:2 11:2004 pp.215-233.

2029   Party cohesion and policy-making in Russia. Paul Chaisty. **Party Pol.** 11:3 5:2005 pp.299-318.

2030   Party competition in emerging democracies: representation and effectiveness in post-communism and beyond. Jack Bielasiak. **Democratization** 12:3 6:2005 pp.331-356.

2031   Party systems and democratic consolidation in Africa's electoral regimes. Michelle Kuenzi; Gina Lambright. **Party Pol.** 11:4 7:2005 pp.423-446.

2032   Patterns of stability: party competition and strategy in Central Europe since 1989. Elisabeth Bakke; Nick Sitter. **Party Pol.** 11:2 3:2005 pp.243-263.

2033   Policy and the dynamics of political competition. Michael Laver. **Am. Pol. Sci. R.** 99:2 5:2005 pp.263-281.

2034   Pre-parliamentary backgrounds of Australian major party MPs: effects on representation. Peter Van Onselen. **J. Legis. St.** 10:4 Winter:2004 pp.84-106.

2035   Public venture capital and party institutionalization. Jóhanna Kristín Birnir. **Comp. Pol. S.** 38:8 10:2005 pp.915-938.

2036   The puzzle of African party systems. Shaheen Mozaffar; James R. Scarritt. **Party Pol.** 11:4 7:2005 pp.399-421.

2037   Regionální stranické soustavy, teritoriální pluralismus a výzkum stranických systémů. *[In Czech]*; (Regional party arrangements, territorial pluralism, and party systems research.) *[Summary]*. Maxmilián Strmiska. **Pol. Čas.** 2 2004 pp.123-133.

2038   The role of parliamentary committees in coalition governments: keeping tabs on coalition partners in the German Bundestag. Dong-hun Kim; Gerhard Loewenberg. **Comp. Pol. S.** 38:9 11:2005 pp.1104-1129.

2039   Runaway state building: how political parties shape states in postcommunist Eastern Europe. Conor O'Dwyer. **World Pol.** 56:4 7:2004 pp.520-553.

2040   So now who do we vote for? John Harris. London: Faber and Faber, 2005. 172p. *ISBN: 0571224229.*

2041   Stanley Baldwin, heresthetics and the realignment of British politics. Andrew J. Taylor. **Br. J. Pol. Sci.** 35:3 7:2005 pp.429-463.

2042   Transformation of political parties in Africa today. Raymond Suttner. **Transformation** 55 2004 pp.1-27.

2043   Whither the Colombian two-party system? An assessment of political reforms and their limits. Erika Moreno. **Electoral S.** 24:3 9:2005 pp.485-509.

Right-wing parties
Partis de droite

2044   Against the system: radical right-wing populism's challenge to liberal democracy. Hans-Georg Betz. **Cur. Pol. Econ. Euro.** 13:3 2004 pp.187-207.

2045   Aux sources idéologiques du Front National : le mariage du traditionalisme et du populisme. *[In French]*; [At the ideological sources of the Front National: the wedding of traditionalism and populism] *[Summary]*. Frédéric Boily. **Pol. et Soc.** 24:1 2005 pp.23-47.

2046   Blue velvet: the rise and decline of the new Czech right. Seán Hanley. **J. Comm. S. Transit. Pol.** 20:3 9:2004 pp.28-54.

2047   Le British National Party et le rejet de l'autre : un paradigme évolutif. *[In French]*; [The British National Party and the rejection of otherness: an evolutionary paradigm] *[Summary]*. Lucienne Germain. **R. Fran. Civil. Brit.** 12:4 Spring:2004 pp.117-131.

2048   Do individual factors explain the different success of the two Belgian extreme right parties. Hilde Coffé. **Acta Pol.** 40:1 4:2005 pp.74-93.

2049   La droite contre la société. *[In French]*; [The Right against society]. Mouvements. **Mouvements** 35 9-10:2004 pp.5-79.

2050   The dynamics of social change in radical right-wing populist party support. Jocelyn A.J. Evans. **Comp. Euro. Pol.** 3:1 4:2005 pp.76-101.

2051   Explaining the emergence of radical right-wing populist parties: the case of Denmark. Jens Rydgren. **West Euro. Pol.** 27:3 5:2004 pp.474-502.

2052   Explaining the gender gap in support for the new right: the case of Canada. Elisabeth Gidengil; Matthew Hennigar; André Blais; Neil Nevitte. **Comp. Pol. S.** 38:10 12:2005 pp.1171-1195.

2053   L'extreme droite et la Ve Republique. *[In French]*; [The extrem right and the 5ᵗʰ Republic]. Jerome Onno. Paris: Connaissances et savoirs, 2005. 737p. *ISBN: 2753900132. Includes bibliographical references (p. [707]-728) and index.*

2054   An extremist autarky: the systemic separation of the French extreme right. Jocelyn A.J. Evans; Gilles Ivaldi. **Sth. Euro. Soc. Pol.** 10:2 7:2005 pp.351-366.

2055   From Vlaams Blok to Vlaams Belang: the Belgian far-right renames itself. Jan Erk. **West Euro. Pol.** 28:3 5:2005 pp.493-502.

2056   Holland and Pim Fortuyn: a deviant case or the beginning of something new? Jens Rydgren; Joop van Holsteyn. **Cur. Pol. Econ. Euro.** 13:3 2004 pp.209-238.

2057   Identitarian politics and populism in Canada and the antipodes. Carol Johnson; Steve Patten; Hans-Georg Betz. **Cur. Pol. Econ. Euro.** 13:4 2004 pp.335-355.

2058   Is extreme right-wing populism contagious? Explaining the emergence of a new party family. J. Rydgren. **Euro. J. Pol. Res.** 44:3 5:2005 pp.413-437.

2059   Legitimation and evolution on the Italian right wing: social and ideological repositioning of Alleanza Nazionale and the Lega Nord. Piero Ignazi. **Sth. Euro. Soc. Pol.** 10:2 7:2005 pp.333-350.

2060   A new right? Moral issues and partisan change in Canada. Michael Lusztig; J. Matthew Wilson. **Soc. Sci. Q.** 86:1 3:2005 pp.109-128.

2061   Die NPD — eine rechtsextreme Partei nach dem gescheiterten Verbotsantrag im Höhenflug? *[In German]*; [The NPD –an extreme right wing party]. Eckhard Jesse. **Politische S.** 56:400 3-4:2005 pp.69-81.

2062   The popular party and European integration: re-elaborating the European programme of Spanish conservatism. Iván Llamazares. **Sth. Euro. Soc. Pol.** 10:2 7:2005 pp.315-332.

2063   Populist parties of the right. Meindert Fennema. **Cur. Pol. Econ. Euro.** 13:2 2004 pp.155-186.

2064   Racial resentment and the changing partisanship of southern whites. Jonathan Knuckey. **Party Pol.** 11:1 1:2005 pp.5-28.

2065   Les racines de la droite américaine. *[In French]*; [The roots of the American right]. Histoire. **Histoire** 284 2:2004 pp.33-59.

2066   The radical right in the Alps: evolution of support for the Swiss SVP and Austrian FPÖ. Anthony J. McGann; Herbert Kitschelt. **Party Pol.** 11:2 3:2005 pp.147-171.

2067   The right and Europe in Italy: an ambivalent relationship. Lucia Quaglia. **Sth. Euro. Soc. Pol.** 10:2 7:2005 pp.281-295.

2068   Russian conservatism in the Putin presidency: the dispersion of a hegemonic discourse. Sergei Prozorov. **J. Pol. Ideol.** 10:2 6:2005 pp.121-143.

2069   A tese da "nova clivagem" e a base social do apoio à direita radical. *[In Portuguese]*; (The 'new cleavage' thesis and the social basis of radical right support.) *[Summary]*. Pippa Norris. **Opin. Pub.** XI:1 3:2005 pp.1-32.

2070   Unity and plurality in the French right. Jim Cordell. **Sth. Euro. Soc. Pol.** 10:2 7:2005 pp.191-206.

2071   The vulnerable populist right parties: no economic realignment fuelling their electoral success. E. Ivarsflaten. **Euro. J. Pol. Res.** 44:3 5:2005 pp.465-492.

D.1.2.2:   **Political movements**
              Mouvements politiques

2072   L'Amérique latine rebelle: contre l'ordre impérial. *[In French]*; [Rebel Latin America: against imperial order]. Contretemps. **Contretemps** 10 5:2004 pp.7-178.

2073   The anti-tobacco movement in the Progressive Era: a case study of direct democracy in Oregon. John Dinan; Jac C. Heckelman. **Expl. Econ. Hist.** 42:4 10:2005 pp.529-546.

2074   Aparición, auge y declinación de un movimiento social: las asambleas vecinales y populares de Buenos Aires, 2001-2003. *[In Spanish]*; (Appearence, peak and decline of a social movement. The popular neighbourhood assemblies of Buenos Aires, 2001-2003.) Federico Matías Rossi. **Euro. R. Lat. Am. Carib. S.** 78 4:2005 pp.67-88.

2075   Backward castes and mobilization process in A.P. E. Venkatesu. **Indian J. Pol. Sci.** LXVI:2 4-6:2005 pp.367-394.

2076   Caught in the crossfire: revolutions, repression, and the rational peasant. T. David Mason. Lanham MD: Rowman & Littlefield, 2004. x, 317p. *ISBN: 0742525384, 0742525392. Includes bibliographical references (p. 285-305) and index.*

2077   Civil society and the democracy movement in Hong Kong: mass mobilization with limited organizational capacity. Kin-man Chan. **Kor. Obs.** 36:1 Spring:2005 pp.167-182.

2078   Les coalitions pacifistes palestiniennes et israéliennes. *[In French]*; [Coalitions of Palestinian and Israelian pacifists]. Denisse M. Roca Servat; Kissy Agyeman. **R. Ét. Palest.** 95 Spring:2005 pp.22-32.

2079   Co-opting the counter culture: Troy Southgate and the National Revolutionary Faction. Graham D. Macklin. **Patt. Prej.** 39:3 9:2005 pp.301-326.

2080   Dalit policies, politics, and parliament. Narender Kumar. Delhi: Shipra Publications, 2004. 216p. *ISBN: 817541152X. Includes bibliographical references (p. [209]-216).*

2081   La dynamique militante à l'extrême gauche : le cas de la Ligue communiste révolutionnaire. *[In French]*; [Militancy dynamics in the extreme left: the case of the Revolutionary Communist League]. Florence Johsua. **Cah. CEVIPOF** 37 4:2004 pp.3-211.

2082   Fascism, anti-fascism, and the resistance in Italy: 1919 to the present. Stanislao G. Pugliese. Lanham MD: Rowman & Littlefield, 2004. xviii, 330p. *ISBN: 0742531228, 0742531236. Includes bibliographical references and index.*

2083   From collective action to institutionalized labor rights: parallel and diverging logics of collective action in Germany and South Africa. Andrew Lawrence. **New Pol. Sci.** 26:2 6:2004 pp.189-204.

2084   Grounding local peace organisations: a case study of southern Sudan. Dorothea Hilhorst; Mathijs van Leeuwen. **J. Mod. Afr. S.** 43:4 12:2005 pp.537-563.

2085   Inside the crusader fortress. Ken Coates [Ed.]; Bertrand Russell Peace Foundation. Nottingham: Bertrand Russell Peace Foundation, 2005. 96p. *ISBN: 0851247164. Includes bibliographical references.* (*Series:* The spokesman - 88).

2086   Iraq and the antiwar movement. Anthony Arnove; Barry Finger; Wadood Hamad; Peter Hudis; Staughton Lynd; Glenn Perusek; Stephen R. Shalom. **New Pol.** X:3 Summer:2005 pp.21-41. *Collection of 8 Articles.*

2087   Justice, sustainability, and the fair trade movement: a case study of coffee production in Chiapas. Mark Hudson; Ian Hudson. **Soc. Just.** 31:3 2004 pp.130-146.

2088   Klaus, Havel and the debate over civil society in the Czech Republic. Martin Myant. **J. Comm. S. Transit. Pol.** 21:2 6:2005 pp.248-267.

2089   Latin America: democracy, globalization, and protest culture. Jon Shefner; Claudio A. Holzner; Takeshi Wada; Julie Stewart; Diane E. Davis; Christina A. Rosan; Victoria Carty; Javier Auyero; Elizabeth Borland. **Mobilization** 9:3 10:2004 pp.219-339. *Collection of 8 articles.*

2090   Memory, youth, hope features of youth activism in the last years of apartheid. Jonathan Grossman. **Socialist Hist.** 26 2004 pp.59-99.

2091   Peacebuilding and engaged citizenship: the role of the diocese of Bacolod. Antonio F. Moreno. **Philip. S.** 52:2 2004 pp.225-254.

2092   Post-Zionism and the Sephardi question some Jews from Arab countries have second thoughts. Meyrav Wurmser. **Mid. East Q.** XII:2 Spring:2005 pp.21-30.

2093   The predicament of Chukotka's indigenous movement: post-Soviet activism in the Russian Far North. Patty A. Gray. Cambridge, New York: Cambridge University Press, 2005. xxiv, 276p. *ISBN: 0521823463. Includes bibliographical references (p. 247-265) and index.*

2094   La révolution orange : un défi pour l'Ukraine, la Russie et l'Europe. *[In French]*; [The Orange Revolution: a challenge for Ukraine, Russia and Europe]. James Sherr. **Pol. Étran.** 70:1 Spring:2005 pp.9-20.

2095   Revolutionary and non-revolutionary paths of radical populism: directions of the Chavista movement in Venezuela. Steve Ellner. **Sci. Soc.** 69:2 4:2005 pp.160-190.

2096   A rewarding engagement? The treatment action campaign and the politics of HIV/AIDS. Steven Friedman; Shauna Mottiar. **Pol. Soc.** 33:4 12:2005 pp.511-565.

2097   The rise and fall of the labour league of youth. Michelle Webb. **Socialist Hist.** 26 2004 pp.45-58.

2098   La seduccion de Marcos a la prensa: versiones sobre el levantamiento zapatista. *[In Spanish]*; [Marcos's seduction to the press: versions on the Zapatista uprising]. Genoveva Flores. Mexico City: Miguel Angel Porrua, 2004. 276p. *ISBN: 9707015152.*

2099   Le sionisme est-il mort ? *[In French]*; [Is Zionism dead?] Mouvements. **Mouvements** 33-34 5-8:2004 pp.5-124.

2100   Social movements and judicial empowerment: courts, public policy, and lesbian and gay organizing in Canada. Miriam Smith. **Pol. Soc.** 33:2 6:2005 pp.327-353.

2101   Understanding the Chiapas rebellion: modernist visions and the invisible Indian. Nicholas P. Higgins. Austin TX: University of Texas Press, 2004. xiii, 259p. *ISBN: 0292702949, 0292705654. Includes bibliographical references (p. 227-250) and index.*

2102   'Whatever it takes': poor people's organizing, OCAP, and social struggle. Jonathan Greene. **S. Pol. Econ.** 75 Spring:2005 pp.5-28.

2103   Who demonstrates? Antistate rebels, conventional participants, or everyone? Pippa Norris; Stefaan Walgrave; Peter Van Aelst. **Comp. Pol.** 37:2 1:2005 pp.189-205.

2104   With a little help from my friends: Partisan politics, transnational alliances, and labor rights in Latin America. M. Victoria Murillo; Andrew Schrank. **Comp. Pol. S.** 38:8 10:2005 pp.971-999.

Anti-capitalist movements
Mouvements anticapitalistes

2105   Africa and globalization: critical perspectives. Nigel C. Gibson; Guy Massamba; Samuel M. Kariuki; Stephen N. Ndegwa; Silvia Federici; Leigh S. Brownhill; Terisa E. Turner; Meredeth Turshen. **J. Asian Afr. S.** 39:1-2 1-3:2004 pp.1-152. *Collection of 6 articles.*

2106   Anti-globalization movements: the developments in Asia. Annamaria Artner. **Cont. Pol.** 10:3-4 9-12:2004 pp.243-256.

2107   Class and protest in Africa: new waves. David Seddon; Leo Zeilig. **R. Afr. Pol. Econ.** 32:103 3:2005 pp.9-27.

2108   Fighting for revolution? The life and death of Greece's revolutionary organization 17 November, 1975-2002. George Kassimeris. **J. Sth. Euro. Balk.** 6:3 12:2004 pp.259-273.

2109   How do organizations matter? Mobilization and support for participants at five globalization protests. Dana R. Fisher; Kevin Stanley; David Berman; Gina Neff. **Soc. Prob.** 52:1 2:2005 pp.102-121.

2110   [L'altermondialisation]. *[In French]*; [Antiglobalization]. Commentaire. **Commentaire** 107 Fall:2004 pp.691-707.

2111   Left docudrama 2004. Joseph G. Ramsey. **Soc. Dem.** 19:1 3:2005 pp.169-180.

2112   Lo nuevo del movimiento social internacional por otra globalización. *[In Spanish]*; ('What's new' in the international social movement for another kind of globalization.) *[Summary]*. José María Aranda. **Cienc. Ergo Sum** 12:2 7-10:2005 pp.133-143.

2113   Mexico: popular mobilization versus neoliberal "democracy". John Stolle-McAllister; Dag MacLeod; Raúl Delgado Wise; Rubén Del Pozo Mendoza; Marie France Labrecque; Georg Gugelberger; Michael Soldatenko; Kara Ann Zugman. **Lat. Am. Persp.** 32:4(143) 7:2005 pp.15-147. *Collection of 7 articles.*

2114   Mobilising against globalisation: Attac and the French intellectuals. Sarah Waters. **West Euro. Pol.** 27:5 11:2004 pp.854-874.

2115 Le mouvement altermondialiste. *[In French]*; [The anti-globalization movement]. Eddy Fougier [Ed.]. **Prob. Pol. Soc.** 897 2:2004 pp.5-108.
2116 Movement of movements: toward a more democratic globalization. Benjamin Shepard. **New Pol. Sci.** 26:4 12:2004 pp.593-605.
2117 Nostalgie ou alter-mondialisme? *[In French]*; [Nostalgia or 'anti-globalization'?] Thierry Pouch. **Temps Mod.** 60:630-631 3-6:2005 pp.310-325.
2118 Reaction and resistance to neo-liberalism in Zambia. Miles Larmer. **R. Afr. Pol. Econ.** 32:103 3:2005 pp.29-45.
2119 La société civile turque dans le défi de l'altermondialisation. *[In French]*; [The Turkish civil society and the challenge of anti-globalization]. Gülçin Erdi Lelandais. **CEMOTI** 37 1-6:2004 pp.209-227.

Environmental movements
Mouvements écologiques

2120 A case of contested ecological modernisation: the governance of genetically modified crops in Brazil. Wendy E. Jepson; Christian Brannstrom; Renato Stancato de Souza. **Env. Plan. C.** 23:2 4:2005 pp.295-310.
2121 Community engagement or community action: choosing not to play the game. James Whelan; Kristen Lyons. **Env. Pol.** 14:5 11:2005 pp.596-610.
2122 Community-based ecological resistance: the Bergama movement in Turkey. Aykut Çoban. **Env. Pol.** 13:2 Summer:2004 pp.438-460.
2123 The death of environmentalism. Michael Shellenberger; Ted Nordhaus; Ludovic Blain; Steve Kretzmann; John Sellers; Michael Brune. **Soc. Policy** 35:3 Spring:2005 pp.19-41. *Collection of 4 articles.*
2124 Economic dependency and environmental attitudes in Turkey. Gabriel Ignatow. **Env. Pol.** 14:5 11:2005 pp.648-666.
2125 Eco-terrorism or justified resistance? Radical environmentalism and the 'war on terror'. Steve Vanderheiden. **Pol. Soc.** 33:3 9:2005 pp.425-447.
2126 Enough is enough: emerging 'self-help' environmentalism in a petrochemical town. Achim Schlüter; Peter Phillimore; Suzanne Moffatt. **Env. Pol.** 13:4 Winter:2004 pp.715-733.
2127 Environmental justice for whom? Class, new social movements, and the environment: a case study of Greenpeace Canada, 1971-2000. John-Henry Harter. **Labour [Canada]** 54 Fall:2004 pp.83-120.
2128 The greening of the globe? Cross-national levels of environmental group membership. Russell J. Dalton. **Env. Pol.** 14:4 7:2005 pp.441-459.
2129 Local environmentalism and the internet. Dave Horton. **Env. Pol.** 13:4 Winter:2004 pp.734-753.
2130 Multi-level networks as a threat to democracy? The case of Portugal's Vasco da Gama bridge. Jeanie Bukowski. **J. Sth. Euro. Balk.** 6:3 12:2004 pp.275-297.
2131 Networking local environmental groups in Germany: the rise and fall of the federal alliance of citizens' initiatives for environmental protection (BBU). William T. Markham. **Env. Pol.** 14:5 11:2005 pp.667-685.
2132 'Obstruction galore': a case study of non-violent resistance against nuclear waste disposal in Germany. Corinna Fischer; Klaus Boehnke. **Env. Pol.** 13:2 Summer:2004 pp.393-413.
2133 Politics of nature: how to bring the sciences into democracy. Bruno Latour; Catherine Porter [Tr.]. Cambridge MA, London: Harvard University Press, 2004. x, 307p. *ISBN: 0674012895, 0674013476. Includes bibliographical references and index.*
2134 Protecting the rain barrel: discourses and the roles of science in a suburban environmental controversy. Stephen Bocking. **Env. Pol.** 14:5 11:2005 pp.611-628.
2135 Reconceiving environmental justice: global movements and political theories. David Schlosberg. **Env. Pol.** 13:3 Autumn:2004 pp.517-540.
2136 Ruining and restoring rivers: the state and civil society in Japan. Paul Waley. **Pac. Aff.** 78:2 Summer:2005 pp.195-215.

2137   The value shift of the Russian greens. Oleg Yanitsky. **Int. R. Sociol.** 15:2 7:2005 pp.363-380.

2138   We want our land back: gendered class analysis, the second contradiction of capitalism and social movement theory. Terisa E. Turner; Leigh S. Brownhill. **Cap. Nat. Social.** 15(4):60 12:2004 pp.21-40.

Nationalist and independence movements
Mouvements d'indépendance et nationalistes

2139   Between war and peace: the role of intellectuals and their ethical dilemmas in the nationalist movements in Taiwan. Zhidong Hao. **Pac. Aff.** 78:2 Summer:2005 pp.237-256.

2140   Histories of Namibia: living through the liberation struggle. Life histories told to Colin Leys and Susan Brown. Colin Leys [Comp.]; Susan Brown [Comp.]. London: Merlin Press, 2005. 165p. *ISBN: 085036499X*.

2141   Imagining the 'mongrel nation': political uses of history in the recent Scottish nationalist movement. Antonia Kearton. **Nat. Ident.** 7:1 3:2005 pp.23-50.

2142   L'imbroglio basque : affrontement des logiques et multiplicité des acteurs. *[In French]*; [The Basque imbroglio: confrontation of logics and multiplicity of actors]. Jérôme Montès. **Banquet** 19-20 1:2004 pp.307-322.

2143   Minorities, peoples, and self-determination: essays in honour of Patrick Thornberry. Nazila Ghanea-Hercock [Ed.]; Alexandra Xanthaki [Ed.]; Patrick Thornberry [Dedicatee]. Leiden MA, Boston MA: Martinus Nijhoff, 2005. xviii, 352p. *ISBN: 9004143017. Includes bibliographical references (p. [337]-352).*

2144   Nationalism and nostalgia: the case of radical Basque nationalism. Diego Muro. **Nat. Nationalism** 11:4 10:2005 pp.571-590.

2145   Nationalism, feminism and autonomy: the ANC in exile and the question of women. Shireen Hassim. **J. Sth. Afr. S.** 30:3 9:2004 pp.433-455.

2146   Other modernities: national autobiography and globalization. Philip Holden. **Biography** 28:1 Winter:2005 pp.89-103.

2147   Palestine, apartheid, and the rights discourse. Raef Zreik. **J. Palestine S.** XXXIV:1(133) Autumn:2004 pp.68-80.

2148   The Palestinian national movement: politics of contention, 1967-2005. Amal Jamal. Bloomington IN: Indiana University Press, 2005. xviii, 229p. *ISBN: 0253345901, 0253217733. Includes bibliographical references (p. [207]-219) and index. (Series:* Indiana series in Middle East studies).

2149   La paradiplomatie identitaire : le Québec, la Catalogne et la Flandre en relations internationales. *[In French]*; [Identity paradiplomacy: Quebec, Catalonia and Flanders in international relations] *[Summary]*; *[Summary in French]*. Stéphane Paquin. **Pol. et Soc.** 23:2-3 2004 pp.203-237.

2150   Le Québec otage de ses alliés. *[In French]*; [Quebec as a hostage to its allies]. Anne Legaré. **R. Pol. Parl.** 106:1032-1033 10-12:2004 pp.103-113.

2151   La radicalisation des nationalistes azéris en Iran. *[In French]*; [Radicalization of the Azeri nationalists in Iran]. Gilles Riaux. **CEMOTI** 37 1-6:2004 pp.15-42.

2152   Realities of resistance: Hizballah, the Palestinian rejectionists, and al-Qa'ida compared. Anders Strindberg; Mats Wärn. **J. Palestine S.** XXXIV:3(135) Spring:2005 pp.23-41.

2153   Reinterpreting the Berber spring: from rite of reversal to site of convergence. Jane Goodman. **J. Nth. Afr. S.** 9:3 Autumn:2004 pp.60-82.

2154   The road not taken: Daghestan and Chechen independence. Moshe Gammer. **Loc. Govt. S.** 24:2 6:2005 pp.97-108.

2155   Sami self-determination in the making? Anne Julie Semb. **Nat. Nationalism** 11:4 10:2005 pp.531-550.

2156   Sovereignty matters: locations of contestation and possibility in indigenous struggles for self-determination. Joanne Barker [Ed.]. Lincoln NE: University of Nebraska Press, 2005. ix, 235p. *ISBN: 0803262515. Conference papers on* Sovereignty 2000: Locations of

Contestation and Possibility, *University of California, 2000. Includes bibliographical references and index. (Series:* Contemporary indigenous issues).

2157 Stratégies et politiques du mouvement nationaliste — révolutionnaire français : départs, desseins et destin d'Unité radicale (1989-2002). *[In French]*; [Strategies and policies of the French revolutionary nationalist movement (1989-2002)]. Nicolas Lebourg. **Banquet** 19-20 1:2004 pp.381-400.

2158 Student political consciousness: lessons from a Namibian mission school. Christian A. Williams. **J. Sth. Afr. S.** 30:3 9:2004 pp.539-557.

2159 Who killed Clemens Kapuuo? Jan-Bart Gewald. **J. Sth. Afr. S.** 30:3 9:2004 pp.559-576.

Women's movements
Mouvements féministes

2160 Befreiung durch Krieg? Frauenrechte in Afghanistan zwischen Weltordnungspolitik und Identitätspolitik. *[In German]*; (Liberation through war? Women's rights in Afghanistan between global order and identity politics.) *[Summary]*; *[Summary in German]*. Renate Kreile. **Int. Pol. Gesell.** 1 2005 pp.102-120.

2161 Black feminist theory: charting a course for black women's studies in political science. Evelyn M. Simien. **Wom. Pol.** 26:2 2004 pp.81-93.

2162 La comisión interamericana de mujeres en el desenvolvimiento público femenino. *[In Spanish]*; [Inter-American Commission of Women]. Karla J. Milla. **Cuad. Am.** XIX:1(109) 1-2:2005 pp.59-74.

2163 Governing NOW: grassroots activism in the National Organization for Women. Maryann Barakso. Ithaca NY: Cornell University Press, 2004. xvi, 192p. *ISBN: 080144280X, 0801489105. Includes bibliographical references and index.*

2164 The NAC's organizational practices and the politics of assisted reproductive technologies in Canada; *[Summary in French]*. Francesca Scala; Éric Montpetit; Isabelle Fortier. **Can. J. Pol.** 38:3 9:2005 pp.581-604.

2165 The other "awakening" in Iraq: the women's movement in the first half of the twentieth century. Noga Efrati. **Br. J. Mid. East. S.** 31:2 11:2004 pp.153-173.

2166 The revolution question: feminisms in El Salvador, Chile, and Cuba. Julie D. Shayne. New Brunswick NJ: Rutgers University Press, 2004. xii, 210p. *ISBN: 0813534836, 0813534844. Includes bibliographical references (p. 187-202) and index.*

2167 The road to Seneca Falls: Elizabeth Cady Stanton and the First Woman's Rights Convention. Judith Wellman. Urbana IL: University of Illinois Press, 2004. xii, 297p. *ISBN: 0252029046, 0252071735. Includes bibliographical references and index. (Series:* Women in American history).

2168 'So few of us and so many of them': US women resisting Desert Storm. Robin L. Riley. **Int. Femin. J. Pol.** 7:3 2005 pp.341-357.

D.1.2.3: **Interest groups**
Groupes d'intérêt

2169 Análisis de organizaciones no gubernamentales y política pública en Venezuela. El caso de CEPOREJUN. *[In Spanish]*; (The analysis of non-governmental organizations and public policy in Venezuela: the CEPOREJUN case.) Carlos E. López C.; Jennifer Fuenmayor. **Cuest. Pol.** 32 1-6:2004 pp.103-128.

2170 Arguments for voluntary action. Tim O'Sullivan. **Administration [Dublin]** 53:1 2005 pp.38-53.

2171 Black voluntary and community sector funding: its impact on civic engagement and capacity building. Karen Chouhan; Clarence Lusane. York: Joseph Rowntree Foundation, 2004. 64p. *ISBN: 1859351700.*

2172 Building civil society through partnership: lessons from a case study of the Christian reformed world relief committee. Roland Hoksbergen. **Dev. Pract.** 15:1 2:2005 pp.16-27.

2173 Diasporas as non-central government actors in foreign policy: the trajectory of Basque paradiplomacy. Gloria Totoricagüena. **Nat. Ethn. Pol.** 11:2 Summer:2005 pp.265-287.

2174 Emerging trends in NGO sector: a study of Tamil Nadu. R. Srinivasan. **Indian J. Pol. Sci.** LXVI:2 4-6:2005 pp.273-288.

2175 Future of civil society: making Central European nonprofit-organizations work. Annette Zimmer [Ed.]; Eckhard Priller [Ed.]; Matthias Freise [Contrib.]. Wiesbaden: VS Verlag fur Sozialwissenschaften, 2004. 736p. *ISBN: 3810040886. Includes bibliographical references.*

2176 Green clubs and voluntary governance: ISO 14001 and firms' regulatory compliance. Matthew Potoski; Aseem Prakash. **Am. J. Pol. Sci.** 49:2 4:2005 pp.235-248.

2177 Greenpeace. Sally Eden. **New Pol. Econ.** 9:4 12:2004 pp.595-610.

2178 Les groupes pro-israéliens en France: une typologie. *[In French]*; (Pro-Israeli interest groups in France: a typology.); *[Summary in French]*. Marc Hecker. **Pol. Étran.** 70:2 Summer:2005 pp.401-410.

2179 Horizontal diffusion, vertical diffusion, and internal pressure in state environmental policymaking, 1989-1998. Dorothy M. Daley; James C. Garand. **Am. Pol. Res.** 33:5 9:2005 pp.615-644.

2180 How to lobby at intergovernmental meetings: mine is a caffe latte. Felix Dodds; Michael Strauss. London, Sterling VA: Earthscan, 2004. xxii, 169p. *ISBN: 1844070743.*

2181 Incongruity between objectives, programmes and beneficiaries: the case of NGOs in Kerala. R. Sooryamoorthy. **Indian J. Pol. Sci.** LXVI:2 4-6:2005 pp.253-272.

2182 Interest group participation in rule making: a decade of change. Scott R. Furlong; Cornelius M. Kerwin. **J. Publ. Admin. Res. Theory** 15:3 7:2005 pp.353-370.

2183 Interest group strategies: navigating between privileged access and strategies of pressure. Anne Binderkrantz. **Pol. S.** 53:4 12:2005 pp.694-715.

2184 Interest groups and health system reform in Greece. Elias Mossialos; Sara Allin. **West Euro. Pol.** 28:2 3:2005 pp.420-444.

2185 Liban: le poids du Hezbollah. *[In French]*; [Lebanon: Hezbollah's weight] *[Summary]*; *[Summary in Spanish]*. Alain Chevalérias [Interviewer]; Karhani [Interviewer]; Mohammed Hussein Fadlallah. **Polit. Int.** 107 Spring:2005 pp.269-280.

2186 Nicht-Regierungsorganisationen des Südens in der Entwicklungspolitik. *[In German]*; (Southern NGOs in development policy and cooperation.) *[Summary]*. Berthold Kuhn. **Welt Trends** 45 Winter:2004 pp.110-123.

2187 Nonprofit development in Hong Kong: the case of a statist-corporatist regime. Eliza W.Y. Lee. **Voluntas** 16:1 3:2005 pp.51-68.

2188 Organisationerne og indflydelsen: hvordan interesseorganisationer søger indflydelse på offentlig politik. *[In Danish]*; (Organizations and influence: how interest organizations seek influence on public policy.) *[Summary]*. Anne Binderkrantz. **Politica** 37:1 2:2005 pp.76-94.

2189 Le pouvoir des ONG en question. *[In French]*; [NGOs and power]. Samy Cohen. **Débat** 128 1-2:2004 pp.57-76.

2190 Pressures on the UK voluntary sport sector. G. Nichols; P. Taylor; M. James; K. Holmes; L. King; R. Garrett. **Voluntas** 16:1 3:2005 pp.33-50.

2191 Quantifying influence in complex decision making by means of paired comparisons. Piet Verschuren; Bas Arts. **Qual. Quan.** 38:5 10:2004 pp.495-516.

2192 Structural isomorphism in Australian nonprofit organizations. Jeffrey Leiter. **Voluntas** 16:1 3:2005 pp.1-32.

2193 Tripartism and other actors in social dialogue. Tayo Fashoyin. **Int. J. Comp. Lab. Law** 21:1 Spring:2005 pp.37-58.

2194 Undermining development: the absence of power among local NGOs in Africa. Sarah Michael. Oxford; Bloomington IN: James Currey; Indiana University Press, 2004. xi, 206p. *ISBN: 0852554389, 0852554397, 0253217725. Includes bibliographical references (p. 178-200) and index. (Series: African issues).*

2195 Volunteer involvement in local government after September 11: the continuing question of capacity. Beth Gazley; Jeffrey L. Brudney. **Publ. Admin. R.** 65:2 3-4:2005 pp.131-142.

2196 Von Verbänden zu Parteien. Elitenwechsel in der Sozialpolitik. *[In German]*; (From associations and interest groups to parties. Elite change in the making of social policy.) *[Summary]*. Christine Trampusch. **Z. Parlament.** 35:4 12:2004 pp.646-666.

2197 What do nonprofit organizations seek? (And why should policymakers care?) Arthur C. Brooks. **J. Policy Anal. Manag.** 24:3 Summer:2005 pp.543-558.

2198 Why Japan signed the mine ban treaty: the political dynamics behind the decision. Kenki Adachi. **Asian Sur.** XLV:3 5-6:2005 pp.397-413.

2199 Zwischen Eigennutz und Gemeinwohl: Verbandsfunktionen in Theorie und Praxis. *[In German]*; [Functions of interest groups in theory and practice]. Alexander Straßner. **Gesell. Wirt. Pol.** 54:2 2005 pp.233-253.

D.1.3: **Social forces**
Forces sociales

D.1.3.1: **Social system**
Système social

2200 After unification: conversations with East Germans. Frederic Pryor. **Orbis** 49:3 Summer:2005 pp.491-502.

2201 Ambivalent consequences of social exclusion for real-existing democracy in Latin America: the example of the Argentine crisis. Jonas Wolff. **J. Int. Rel. Dev.** 8:1 3:2005 pp.58-87.

2202 Capitalists without a class: political diversity among private entrepreneurs in China. Kellee S. Tsai. **Comp. Pol. S.** 38:9 11:2005 pp.1130-1158.

2203 Chinese intellectuals between state and market. Edward X. Gu [Ed.]; Merle Goldman [Ed.]. New York, London: RoutledgeCurzon, 2004. 298p. *ISBN: 0415325978. Includes bibliographical references and index.* (*Series:* RoutledgeCurzon studies on China in transition).

2204 Civil society: a reader in history, theory and global politics. John A. Hall [Ed.]; Frank Trentmann [Ed.]. Basingstoke: Palgrave Macmillan, 2005. ix, 308p. *ISBN: 1403915423, 1403915431. Includes bibliographical references and index.*

2205 'Civil society' and the limits of democratic assistance. Ivelin Sardamov. **Gov. Oppos.** 40:3 Summer:2005 pp.379-402.

2206 Classes, multitudes and the politics of community movements in post-apartheid South Africa. Franco Barchiesi. Durban: University of KwaZulu-Natal Press, 2004. 41p. *ISBN: 1868405559.* (*Series:* CCS research report - 20).

2207 Dalit politics in India and new meaning of caste. Anne Waldrop. **Forum Dev. S.** 31:2 2004 pp.275-305.

2208 Un effet inattendu du régime socialiste. La conversion de l'ancienne organisation des pionniers tchèques. *[In French]*; (An unexpected consequence of the socialist regime: the conversion of the former Czech 'pioneer' organization.) *[Summary]*. Sandrine Devaux. **Politix** 17:67 2004 pp.159-184.

2209 En quête de notabilité. Vivre et survivre en politique dans la Bulgarie post-communiste. *[In French]*; (In search of notability: surviving in Bulgarian post-communist politics.) *[Summary]*. Nadège Ragaru. **Politix** 17:67 2004 pp.71-99.

2210 Entre l'intermédiaire et « l'homme d'honneur ». Savoir-faire et dilemmes notabiliaires en Turquie. *[In French]*; (Between brokers and 'men of honour'. Practices and dilemmas of Turkish notables.) *[Summary]*. Elise Massicard. **Politix** 17:67 2004 pp.101-127.

2211 Les grandes transformations de la société russe. *[In French]*; (The major transformations of Russian society.) *[Summary]*. Kathy Rousselet. **Pouvoirs** 112 2004 pp.23-34.

2212 Incivility: the politics of 'people on the margins' in Jamaica. Hume N. Johnson. **Pol. S.** 53:3 10:2005 pp.579-597.

2213   Income inequality and the taste for revolution. Robert MacCulloch. **J. Law Econ.** XLVIII:1 4:2005 pp.93-123.

2214   Petites sociétes et minorités nationales : enjeux politiques et perspectives comparées. *[In French]*; [Small enterprises and national minorities: political stake and comparative views]. Jacques L. Boucher [Ed.]; Anne Gilbert [Contrib.]; Daniel Tremblay [Contrib.]; Svetla Koleva [Contrib.]; J. Yvon Theriault [Ed.]. Sainte-Foy: Presses de l'Universite du Quebec, 2005. xx, 398p. *ISBN: 2760513599. Includes bibliographical references.*

2215   The quality of terror. Ethan Bueno de Mesquita. **Am. J. Pol. Sci.** 49:3 7:2005 pp.515-530.

2216   Le renouvellement démocratique des pratiques d'intervention sociale. *[In French]*; [The democratic renewal of the practices of social intervention]. Michel Parazelli. **Nouv. Prat. Soc.** 17:1 Autumn:2004 pp.9-32.

2217   Resource dependency and its consequences: the costs of Botswana's shining gems. Kenneth Good. **J. Contemp. Afr. S.** 23:1 1:2005 pp.27-50.

2218   Die Rolle des Staates unter den Bedingungen des zivilisatorischen Umbruchs. *[In German]*; [The role of the state under the conditions imposed by societal change] *[Summary]*. Elżbieta Mączyńska. **Osteuro. Wirt.** 49:4 12:2004 pp.353-367.

2219   Rossiia, sobstvennost', ideia. *[In Russian]*; [Russia, ownership, idea]. Sergei Chernyshev. Moscow: Rosspen, 2004. 448p. *ISBN: 582430551X.*

2220   The rules are different here: an institutional comparison of cities and homeowners associations. Barbara Coyle McCabe. **Admin. Soc.** 37:4 9:2005 pp.404-425.

2221   Select papers from the 2004 annual meeting of the APSA conference group on Taiwan studies (CGOTS). Wei-chin Lee; Cal Clark; T.Y. Wang; Yu-shan Wu. **Iss. Stud.** 41:1 3:2005 pp.1-111. *Collection of 4 articles.*

2222   Social capital in ten Asian societies. Takashi Inoguchi. **Japanese J. Pol. Sci.** 5:1 5:2004 pp.197-211.

2223   Social, economic and civil vulnerability in the United States, France and Brazil. Lúcio Kowarick. **Int. J. Urb. Reg. Res.** 29:2 6:2005 pp.268-282.

2224   La société contre elle-même. *[In French]*; [Society against itself]. Roger Sue. Paris: Fayard, 2005. 159p. *ISBN: 2213622353.*

2225   The transformation of civil society in Turkey: from quantity to quality. Sefa Şimşek. **Turkish S.** 5:3 Autumn:2004 pp.46-74.

D.1.3.2:   **Geographic influences**
              Influences géographiques

2226   The Balkans and the West: constructing the European other, 1945-2003. Andrew Hammond [Ed.]. Aldershot: Ashgate, 2004. xxiii, 236p. *ISBN: 0754632342. Includes bibliographical references and index.*

2227   Central-local relations in an era of multi-level governance: the case of public participation policy in England, 1997-2001. Helen Sullivan; Andrew Knops; Marian Barnes; Janet Newman. **Loc. Govt. S.** 30:2 Summer:2004 pp.245-265.

2228   Changing pattern of centre-periphery relations in Italy: Sidney Tarrow revisited. Paola Mattei. **Reg. Fed. S.** 14:4 Winter:2004 pp.538-553.

2229   Community involvement in rural regeneration partnerships: exploring the rural dimension. Stephen P. Osborne; Arthur Williamson; Rona Beattie. **Loc. Govt. S.** 30:2 Summer:2004 pp.156-181.

2230   Constructing authority alternatives on the periphery: vignettes from Colombia; *[Summary in French]*. Ann C. Mason. **Int. Pol. Sci. R.** 26:1 1:2005 pp.37-54.

2231   Explaining the geometry of desert. Neil Feit; Steven Kershnar. **Publ. Aff. Q.** 18:4 10:2004 pp.273-298.

2232   For space. Doreen B. Massey. London: Sage Publications, 2004. 222p. *ISBN: 1412903610, 1412903629.*

2233   Identità etnica e competizione politica: un'analisi del voto ai partiti etnoregionalisti in Europa occidentale. *[In Italian]*; (Ethnic identity and party competition: an analysis of ethnoregionalist vote in Western Europe.) Filippo Tronconi. **Riv. It. Sci. Pol.** XXXV:1 4:2005 pp.77-106.

2234 Indian freedom movement and ideas on regionalism. Suman Sharma. **India Q.** LX:3 7-9:2004 pp.41-61.

2235 Mapping the Irish policy space: voter and party spaces in preferential elections. Kenneth Benoit; Michael Laver. **Econ. Soc. R.** 36:2 Summer-Autumn:2005 pp.83-108.

2236 The Mediterranean region: reality, delusion, or Euro-Mediterranean project? Athanasios Moulakis. **Mediterr. Q.** 16:2 Spring:2005 pp.11-38.

2237 Temi di ricerca sulle culture di governo locali e le politiche per lo sviluppo. *[In Italian]*; [Research themes on local government cultures and local development policies]. Patrizia Messina. **Riv. It. Sci. Pol.** XXXV:1 4:2005 pp.107-134.

2238 Transformatsiia eksklavnosti v usloviiakh politicheskoi globalizatsii. *[In Russian]*; (Transformation of exclave territoriality under political globalization.) *[Summary]*. A.P. Klemeshev. **Polis [Moscow]** 4(87) 2005 pp.143-157.

D.1.3.3: **Race and ethnicity**
Race et ethnicité

2239 The conceptualization and measurement of symbolic racism. Christopher Tarman; David O. Sears. **J. Pol.** 67:3 8:2005 pp.731-761.

2240 Education and the development of Turkish and Yugoslav immigrants' political attitudes in Germany. Peter Doerschler. **Ger. Pol.** 13:3 9:2004 pp.449-480.

2241 Ethnic competition and the forging of the nation-state of Fiji. John E. Davies. **Round Tab.** 378 1:2005 pp.47-76.

2242 Ethnically privileged migrants in their new homeland. Jasna Čapo Žmegač. **J. Refug. S.** 18:2 6:2005 pp.199-215.

2243 Failures of the discourse of ethnicity: Turkey, Kurds, and the emerging Iraq. Murat Somer. **Secur. Dial.** 36:1 3:2005 pp.109-128.

2244 Der gegenwärtige Antisemitismus. Tendenzen und Interpretationen. *[In German]*; [The contemporary anti-Semitism. Tendencies and interpretations]. Ulrich Bielefeld. **Mittelweg 36** 14:2 4-5:2005 pp.36-52.

2245 The impact of the indigenous movement on democratization: elections in Chiapas (1988-2004); *[Summary in Spanish]*. Silvia Gomez Tagle. **Canadian J. Lat. Am. Caribbean S.** 30:60 2005 pp.183-220.

2246 The indigenous in the plural in Bolivian oppositional politics. Robert Albro. **B. Lat. Am. Res.** 24:4 10:2005 pp.433-453.

2247 A neo-Downsian model of the alternative vote as a mechanism for mitigating ethnic conflict in plural societies. Jon Fraenkel; Bernard Grofman. **Publ. Choice** 121:3-4 10:2004 pp.487-506.

2248 Neuer Antisemitismus? Wandel und Kontinuität der Judenfeindschaft. *[In German]*; [A new anti-Semitism? Change and continuity of the hostility toward Jews]. Klaus Holz. **Mittelweg 36** 14:2 4-5:2005 pp.3-23.

2249 The political economy of hatred. Edward L. Glaeser. **Q. J. Econ.** CXX:1 2:2005 pp.45-86.

2250 Reexamining racial attitudes: the conditional relationship between diversity and socioeconomic environment. Regina P. Branton; Bradford S. Jones. **Am. J. Pol. Sci.** 49:2 4:2005 pp.359-372.

2251 Repetitive and troubling discourses of nationalism in the local politics of mosque development in Sydney, Australia. Kevin M. Dunn. **Env. Plan. D.** 23:1 2:2005 pp.29-50.

2252 Resurgence and remaking of identity: civil beliefs, domestic and external dynamics, and the Turkish mainstream discourse on Kurds. Murat Somer. **Comp. Pol. S.** 38:6 8:2005 pp.591-622.

2253 The struggle for Soviet Jewry in American politics: Israel versus the American Jewish establishment. Frederick A. Lazin. Lanham MD: Lexington Books, 2005. xii, 356p. *ISBN:*

0739108425. *Includes bibliographical references (p. 323-336) and index. (Series:* Studies in public policy).

2254   Trojan horses of race. Jerry Kang. **Harv. Law R.** 118:5 3:2005 pp.1489-1593.

Africa
Afrique

2255   Addressing ethnicity in sub-Saharan Africa: institutions and agency. Omotunde E.G. Johnson. **Constit. Pol. Econ.** 16:1 3:2005 pp.49-69.

2256   Breakdown and reconstitution: democracy, the nation-state, and ethnicity in Nigeria. Abu Bakarr Bah. Lanham MD: Lexington Books, 2005. x, 199p. *ISBN: 0739109545. Includes bibliographical references (p. 181-187) and index.*

2257   The carpenter's revolt: youth, violence and the reinvention of culture in Nigeria. Wale Adebanwi. **J. Mod. Afr. S.** 43:3 9:2005 pp.339-365.

2258   Ethnicity and democracy in Africa. Bruce Berman [Ed.]; Dickson Eyoh [Ed.]; Will Kymlicka [Ed.]. Oxford; Athens OH: James Currey; Ohio State University Press, 2004. xv, 336p. *ISBN: 0821415697, 0821415700. Includes bibliographical references and index.*

2259   Institutions and ethnic politics in Africa. Daniel N. Posner. New York: Cambridge University Press, 2004. xv, 337p. *ISBN: 0521833981, 0521541794. Includes bibliographical references (p. 313-327) and index. (Series:* Political economy of institutions and decisions).

2260   Measuring multi-ethnic spatial segregation in South African cities. A. Horn. **Sth. Afr. Geog. J.** 87:1 2005 pp.58-72.

2261   Overcoming apartheid: can truth reconcile a divided nation? James L. Gibson. **Politikon** 31:2 11:2004 pp.129-155.

2262   Rethinking the rise and fall of apartheid: South Africa and world politics. Adrian Guelke. Basingstoke, New York: Palgrave Macmillan, 2005. xvii, 248p. *ISBN: 0333981227, 0333981235. Includes bibliographical references (p. 236-237) and index. (Series:* Rethinking world politics).

Americas
Amérique

2263   Atonement and forgiveness: a new model for black reparations. Roy L. Brooks. Berkeley CA: University of California Press, 2004. xvii, 325p. *ISBN: 0520239415. Includes bibliographical references (p. 273-302) and index.*

2264   Before Brown: civil rights and white backlash in the modern South. Glenn Feldman [Ed.]. Tuscaloosa AL: University of Alabama Press, 2004. xiii,430p. *ISBN: 0817314318, 0817351345. Includes bibliographical references and index. (Series:* The modern South).

2265   Black cosmopolitanism: racial consciousness and transnational ideology in the nineteenth-century Americas. Ifeoma Kiddoe Nwankwo. Philadelphia PA: University of Pennsylvania Press, 2005. viii, 291p. *ISBN: 0812238788. Includes bibliographical references (p. 257-275) and index. (Series:* Rethinking the Americas).

2266   Black leaders and ideologies in the South: resistance and nonviolence. Preston T. King [Ed.]; Walter E. Fluker [Ed.]. Abingdon: Routledge, 2005. 311p. *ISBN: 0415367875.*

2267   Bloc voting, polarization, and the panethnic hypothesis: the case of little Saigon. Christian Collet. **J. Pol.** 67:3 8:2005 pp.907-943.

2268   The Caribbean postcolonial: social equality, post-nationalism, and cultural hybridity. Shalini Puri. New York, Basingstoke: Palgrave Macmillan, 2004. xii, 300p. *ISBN: 1403961816, 1403961824.*

2269   Critical perspectives on human rights and multiculturalism in neoliberal Latin America. Charles R. Hale; Shannon Speed; María Teresa Sierra; Nancy Postero; José Almeida Vinueza; Milka Castro Lucic; Lynn Stephen. **PoLAR** 28:1 5:2005 pp.1-171. *Collection of 12 articles.*

2270 Ethnicity, class, and nationalism: Caribbean and extra-Caribbean dimensions. Anton Allahar [Ed.]. Lanham MD: Lexington Books, 2005. xix, 281p. *ISBN: 0739108875, 073910893X. Includes bibliographical references (p. 259-278) and index. (Series:* Caribbean studies).

2271 Explaining the great racial divide: perceptions of fairness in the U.S. criminal justice system. Jon Hurwitz; Mark Peffley. **J. Pol.** 67:3 8:2005 pp.762-783.

2272 Groundwork: local black freedom movements in America. Jeanne Theoharis [Ed.]; Komozi Woodard [Ed.]; Charles Payne [Foreword]. New York: New York University Press, 2005. xv, 328p. *ISBN: 0814782841, 081478285X. Includes bibliographical references and index.*

2273 The head Negro in charge syndrome: the dead end of black politics. Norman Kelley. New York: Nation Books, 2004. 246p. *ISBN: 1560255846. Includes bibliographical references (p. 227-233) and index.*

2274 Immigration, African Americans, and race discourse. Stephen Steinberg. **New Pol.** X:3 Summer:2005 pp.42-54.

2275 Inventing vernacular speech-acts: articulating Filipino self-determination in the United States. E. San Juan, Jr. **Soc. Dem.** 19:1 3:2005 pp.136-154.

2276 Latino political power. Kim Geron. Boulder CO: Lynne Rienner Publishers, 2005. vii, 247p. *ISBN: 1588260003, 1588263215. Includes bibliographical references (p. 215-235) and index. (Series:* Latinos, exploring diversity and change).

2277 Macrodynamics of black political participation in the post-civil rights era. Fredrick C. Harris; Valeria Sinclair-Chapman; Brian D. McKenzie. **J. Pol.** 67:4 11:2005 pp.1143-1163.

2278 Multikulturelle Autonomie in Lateinamerika. *[In German]*; [Multicultural autonomy in Latin America]. René Paul Amry; Leo Gabriel; René Kuppe; Gilberto López Rivas; Robert Lessmann; Nicole Schabus. **J. Entwick.pol.** XX:4 2004 pp.8-102. *Collection of 6 articles.*

2279 Old times there are not forgotten: race and partisan realignment in the contemporary south. Nicholas A. Valentino; David O. Sears. **Am. J. Pol. Sci.** 49:3 7:2005 pp.672-688.

2280 Les Palestiniens du Chili. *[In French]*; [Palestinians in Chile]. Cecilia Baeza. **R. Ét. Palest.** 95 Spring:2005 pp.51-87.

2281 The politics of Asian Americans: diversity and community. Pei-te Lien; M. Margaret Conway; Janelle Wong. New York, London: Routledge, 2004. 266p. *ISBN: 0415934648, 0415934656. Includes bibliographical references and index.*

2282 The predicament of difference. Ien Ang [Ed.]; Brett St Louis [Ed.]; Denise Ferreira da Silva; Jo Haynes; Greg Gow; Ellen Rooney; Lisa Lowe; Christine Helliwell; Barry Hindess; Beng-huat Chua. **Ethnicities** 5:3 9:2005 pp.291-421. *Collection of 5 articles.*

2283 Reparations after identity politics. Lawrie Balfour. **Pol. Theory** 33:6 12:2005 pp.786-811.

2284 The two reconstructions: the struggle for black enfranchisement. Richard M. Valelly. Chicago IL: University of Chicago Press, 2004. xvii, 330p. *ISBN: 0226845281, 0226845303. Includes bibliographical references and index. (Series:* American politics and political economy).

2285 The urban voter: group conflict and mayoral voting behavior in American cities. Karen M. Kaufmann. Ann Arbor MI: University of Michigan Press, 2004. viii, 248p. *ISBN: 0472098578, 0472068571. Includes bibliographical references (p. 215-234) and index. (Series:* The politics of race and ethnicity).

2286 Valahol otthon lenni. Tanulmány az amerikai magyar emigránsok százhúsz évéből — New Brunswick példáján keresztül. *[In Hungarian]*; (To be at home. Study of 120 years of Hungarian life in America: the case of New Brunswick.) Csaba Ferenc Smik. **Regio** 15:1 2004 pp.65-88.

2287   Democracy and civil society in the Himalayas: problems of implementation and participation in multi-ethnic societies. Karl-Heinz Kramer. **Pakis. Horiz.** 57:4 10:2004 pp.69-80.

2288   Diaspora involvement in insurgencies: insights from the Khalistan and Tamil Eelam movements. C. Christine Fair. **Nat. Ethn. Pol.** 11:1 Spring:2005 pp.125-156.

2289   Ethnicity and civil society in contemporary Afghanistan. Carol J. Riphenburg. **Mid. East J.** 59:1 Winter:2005 pp.31-51.

2290   Ethnicity and politics in Tajikistan: process and trends. Suneel Kumar. **India Q.** LXI:1 1-3:2005 pp.201-219.

2291   Ethnoscapes, national territorialisation, and the Afghan war. Conrad Schetter. **Geopolitics** 10:1 Spring:2005 pp.50-75.

2292   From ethnic outbidding to ethnic conflict: the institutional bases for Sri Lanka's separatist war. Neil Devotta. **Nat. Nationalism** 11:1 1:2005 pp.141-159.

2293   Prostranstvo ideologicheskogo diskursa postsovetskoi Buriatii. *[In Russian]*; (The space of ideological discourse in post-Soviet Buriatia.) *[Summary]*. D.D. Amogolonova; T.D. Skrynnikova. **Polis [Moscow]** 2(85) 2005 pp.53-63.

2294   Role of ethnicity in the conflict spectrum of South Asia. Huma Baqai. **Pakis. Horiz.** 57:4 10:2004 pp.57-68.

2295   Between minority rights and civil liberties: Russia's discourse over 'nationality' registration and the internal passport. Sven Gunnar Simonsen. **Nat. P.** 33:2 6:2005 pp.211-229.

2296   'Chuzhie' zdes' ne khodiat: radikal'naia ksenofobiia i politicheskii ekstremizm v sotsiokul'turnom prostranstve sovremennoi Rossii. *[In Russian]*; ['Outsiders' do not go out here: radical xenophobia and political extremism in contemporary Russia's sociocultural environment]. T.V. Evgen'eva [Ed.]; G.I. Saprokhina [Ed.]; V.V. Usacheva [Ed.]. Moscow: In-t Afriki RAN, 2004. 306p. *ISBN: 5201047548. Includes bibliographical references.*

2297   Chuzhoi, no loial'nyi: prichiny 'nestabil'noi stabil'nosti' v Dagestane. *[In Russian]*; (Alien, but loyal: reasons for 'unstable stability' in Dagestan.) M.R. Ibragimov; K. Matsuzato. **Polis [Moscow]** 3(86) 2005 pp.102-115.

2298   Cypriots in Britain: diaspora(s) committed to peace? Gilles Bertrand. **Turkish S.** 5:2 Summer:2004 pp.93-110.

2299   De l'exception à la diversité culturelle. *[In French]*; [From exception to cultural diversity]. Serge Regourd [Ed.]. **Prob. Pol. Soc.** 904 11:2004 pp.5-118.

2300   L'egemonia e i suoi limiti. *[In Italian]*; (Hegemony and its limits.) Marco Clementi. **Riv. It. Sci. Pol.** XXXV:1 4:2005 pp.29-56.

2301   Esther Benbassa : les juifs en France et l'antisémitisme. *[In French]*; [Esther Benbassa: Jews in France and anti-Semitism]. Esther Benbassa [Discussant]; Yoram Mouchenik [Interviewer]. **Autre** 6:2 2005 pp.173-189.

2302   Ethnic agenda: relevance of political attitudes to party choice. Maria Sobolewska. **Jnl. Ele. Pub. Op. Par.** 15:2 9:2005 pp.197-214.

2303   Ethnic Germans in Poland and the Czech Republic: a comparative evaluation. Karl Cordell; Stefan Wolff. **Nat. P.** 33:2 6:2005 pp.255-276.

2304   Etnicheskaia gruppa i gosudarstvo kak sub"ekty sotsial'nogo vzaimodeistviia: sotsiopsikhologicheskii i biopoliticheskii aspekty. *[In Russian]*; (Ethnic group and the state as subjects of social interaction.) O. Borisova; A. Oleskin. **Obshch. Nauki Sovrem.** 3 2004 pp.132-142.

2305   Etnichnost' i kul'turnyi pliuralizm v kontekste gosudarstvennoi politiki. *[In Russian]*; (Ethnicity and cultural pluralism in the context of the state policy.) *[Summary]*. A.N. Smirnov. **Polis [Moscow]** 4(87) 2005 pp.30-52.

2306   Europe's angry Muslims. Robert S. Leiken. **Foreign Aff.** 84:4 7-8:2005 pp.120-135.

2307   Les Gypsy studies et le droit européen des minorités. *[In French]*; [Gypsy studies and European law of minorities]. Henriette Asséo. **R. Hist. Mod. Contemp.** 51:4(supp.) 2004 pp.71-86.

2308   The integration of ethnic minorities into political culture: the Netherlands, Germany and Great Britain compared. Thom Duyvené de Wit; Ruud Koopmans. **Acta Pol.** 40:1 4:2005 pp.50-73.

2309   Job discrimination in Northern Ireland and the law in relation to the theory of ethnic nationalism. James Dingley; Jo Morgan. **Nat. Ident.** 7:1 3:2005 pp.51-77.

2310   Ksenofobiia v SMI : strategii preodoleniia. *[In Russian]*; [Xenophobia in the mass-media and strategies for its defeat]. Vasilii Filippov. **Svobod. Mysl'** 6 2005 pp.106-120.

2311   Minority rights in Hungary and the situation of the Roma. Balázs Majtényi. **Acta Jur. Hun.** 45:1-2 2004 pp.131-148.

2312   Nationalist legacies and European trajectories in the Balkans: post-communist liberalization and Turkish minority politics in Bulgaria. Dia Anagnostou. **J. Sth.East Euro. Black Sea S.** 5:1 1:2005 pp.89-111.

2313   On the fate of the Russian ethnic group. Mikhail Rutkevich. **Rus. Pol. Law** 43:2 3-4:2005 pp.70-82.

2314   Political participation strategies of the Circassian diaspora in Turkey. Ayhan Kaya. **Med. Pol.** 9:2 Summer:2004 pp.221-239.

2315   Racist extremism in Central and Eastern Europe. Cas Mudde. **East Euro. Pol. Soc.** 19:2 Spring:2005 pp.161-184.

2316   Recent developments to British multicultural theory, policy and practice: the case of British Muslims. Tahir Abbas. **Citiz. S.** 9:2 5:2005 pp.153-166.

2317   Reconceptualizing clans: kinship networks and statehood in Kazakhstan. Edward Schatz. **Nat. P.** 33:2 6:2005 pp.231-254.

2318   Secret agents: anarchists, Islamists and responses to politically active refugees in London. Michael Collyer. **Ethn. Racial S.** 28:2 3:2005 pp.278-303.

2319   The theory and practice of group representation: reflections on the governance of race equality in Birmingham. Graham Smith; Susan Stephenson. **Publ. Admin.** 83:2 2005 pp.323-344.

2320   Uregulirovanie etnopoliticheskikh konfliktov v Rossii: istoricheskii opyt i sovremennost'. *[In Russian]*; [Historical and contemporary experiences of managing ethno-political conflicts in Russia]. A.Kh.A. Sultygov. **Vest. Mosk. Univ. 12 Pol.** 3 5-6:2005 pp.69-94.

2321   'We are not asking you to hug each other, but we ask you to co-exist': the Kosovo assembly and the politics of co-existence. Andrew J. Taylor. **J. Legis. St.** 11:1 Spring:2005 pp.105-137.

D.1.3.4:   **Religion**
               Religion

2322   Asian philosophies and authoritarian press practice: a remarkable contradiction. Shelton A. Gunaratne. **Javnost** XII:2 6:2005 pp.23-38.

2323   The Babi and Baha'i community of Iran: a case of 'suspended genocide'? Moojan Momen. **J. Genocide Res.** 7:2 6:2005 pp.221-241.

2324   Can secular liberal politics be reincarnated in India? Mehnaaz Momen. **J. Asian Afr. S.** 40:4 8:2005 pp.243-260.

2325   Cent ans de laïcité française. *[In French]*; [A hundred years of French secularism]. René Rémond. **Etudes** 400:1 2004 pp.55-66.

2326   China's religious freedom policy: the art of managing religious activity. Beatrice Leung. **Chi. Q.** 184 12:2005 pp.894-913.

2327   Coalition politics and Hindu nationalism. Katharine Adeney [Ed.]; Lawrence Saez [Ed.]. London, New York: Routledge, 2005. 294p. *ISBN: 0415359813. Includes bibliographical references and index.* (*Series:* RoutledgeCurzon advances in South Asian studies).

2328   La crise de l'état laïque et les nouvelles formes de religiosité. *[In French]*; [The crisis of the secular state and new forms of religiousness]. Olivier Roy. **Esprit** 312 2:2005 pp.27-44.

2329   Dérives sectaires. *[In French]*; [Sectarian drifts]. Vassilis Saroglou; Coralie Buxant; Stefania Casalfiore; Louis-Léon Christians; Jean-Marie Jaspard; Nicolas Guillet. **Ann. Droit Louvain** 64:4 2004 pp.529-645. *Collection of 5 articles.*

2330   Dissonances dans la laïcité. *[In French]*; [Discords in secularism]. Etienne Balibar. **Mouvements** 33-34 5-8:2004 pp.148-161.

2331   Etat et religion. *[In French]*; [State and religion]. Administration. **Administration [Dublin]** 203 9:2004 pp.21-86.

2332   Ethnoreligious politics in France: Jews and Muslims. William Safran. **West Euro. Pol.** 27:3 5:2004 pp.423-451.

2333   L'Europe et le fait religieux : sources, patrimoine, valeurs. *[In French]*; [Europe and the religious fact: sources, patrimony, values]. Vincent Aucante [Ed.]; Olivier Abel [Ed.]; et al; Paul Poupard [Intro.]; Rene Remond [Intro.]; Pierre Morel [Intro.]. Paris: Parole et silence, 2004. 280p. *ISBN: 2845732392. Includes bibliographical references.*

2334   Evangélicos no Brasil. Perfil socioeconômico, afinidades ideológicas e determinantes do comportamento eleitoral. *[In Portuguese]*; (Evangelics in Brazil. Socioeconomic aspects, ideological similarities and the determinants of electoral behavior.) *[Summary]*. Simone R. Bohn. **Opin. Pub.** X:2 10:2004 pp.288-338.

2335   La fin de la laïcité ? *[In French]*; [The end of secularism?] Jacques Robert. Paris: Editions Odile Jacob, 2004. 254p. *ISBN: 2738115306. Includes bibliographical references (p. [243]-246).*

2336   God's things and Caesar's: Jehovah's witnesses and political neutrality. Jolene Chu. **J. Genocide Res.** 6:3 9:2004 pp.319-342.

2337   Heretics and colonizers: forging Russia's empire in the south Caucasus. Nicholas B. Breyfogle. Ithaca NY: Cornell University Press, 2005. xvii, 347p. *ISBN: 0801442427. Includes bibliographical references (p. 319-338) and index.*

2338   Inde : quelle laïcité. *[In French]*; [India: what secularism]. Michael Amaladoss. **Etudes** 401:5 11:2004 pp.441-452.

2339   Islam, Judaism, and the political role of religions in the Middle East. John Bunzl [Ed.]. Gainesville FL: University Press of Florida, 2004. xii, 202p. *ISBN: 0813027004. Includes bibliographical references and index.*

2340   Korporierte Bekenntnisgemeinschaften im bekenntnisneutralen Staat. *[In German]*; [Religious communities in a religiously neutral state]. Ludwig Renck. **Relig. Staat Gesell.** 6:1 2005 pp.97-122.

2341   La laicité : ciment de la République, valeur universelle. *[In French]*; [Secularism: cement of the Republic, universal value]. Gerard Delfau [Ed.]; Marc Halpern [Ed.]. Paris: Edimaf, 2004. 168p. *ISBN: 2847210598.*

2342   Laïcité : il faut poursuivre le débat. *[In French]*; [Secularism: the need to deepen the debate]. André Viola. **R. Rech. Jurid. Droit Prosp.** 29:2 2004 pp.1453-1464.

2343   Laicité : la croix et la bannière. *[In French]*; [Secularism: difficulties]. Jean-Michel Reynaud; Alain Simon. Paris: Bruno Leprince, 2005. 207p. *ISBN: 2909634957. Includes bibliographical references (p. 199-202).*

2344   Laïcité 1905-2005, entre passion et raison. *[In French]*; [Secularism 1905-2005, between passion and reason]. Jean Bauberot. Paris: Editions du Seuil, 2004. 286p. *ISBN: 2020637413. Includes bibliographical references (p. 273-[281]).*

2345   Laïcité et égalité des droits. *[In French]*; [Secularism and the equality of rights]. Antoine Casanova; Michel Vovelle; Jacqueline Lalouette; Pierre Hayat; Pierre Ognier; Émile Poulat; René Mouriaux; Guy Coq; Bernard Descouleurs; Théo Klein; Didier Billion; Jacques Couland; Yves Vargas [Comments by]; Pierre-François Moreau; Samir Amin; André Tosel. **Pensée** 342 4-6:2005 pp.5-164. *Collection of 17 articles.*

2346   Make me a man! Masculinity, Hinduism, and nationalism in India. Sikata Banerjee. Albany NY: State University of New York Press, 2005. ix, 181p. *ISBN: 0791463672, 0791463680. Includes bibliographical references (p. 163-173) and index. (Series: Religious studies).*

2347   Official religious representation in a democratic legislature: lessons from the Manx Tynwald. Peter W. Edge; C.C. Augur Pearce. **J. Chur. State** 46:3 Summer:2004 pp.575-616.

2348   On noncoercive establishment. Daniel Brudney. **Pol. Theory** 33:6 12:2005 pp.812-839.

2349   Politices of Dalit identity. P. Muthaiah. **Indian J. Pol. Sci.** 65:3 7-9:2004 pp.385-402.

2350   Pouvoir religieux et pouvoir politique. *[In French]*; (Religious power and political power.) *[Summary].* Agnieszka Moniak-Azzopardi. **Pouvoirs** 112 2004 pp.93-110.

2351   Le prince et le marabout. *[In French]*; [The prince and the marabout]. Babacar Ndiaye. **Défense Nat.** 60:4 4:2004 pp.169-180.

2352   Public religion and political change in Wales. Paul Chambers; Andrew Thompson. **Sociology** 39:1 2:2005 pp.29-46.

2353   Recognizing religion in a secular society: essays in pluarism, religion, and public policy. Douglas Farrow [Ed.]. Montreal: McGill-Queens University Press, 2004. xx, 201p. *ISBN: 0773528121, 0773528342. Includes bibliographical references (p. 191-196) and index.*

2354   Réflexions sur la laïcité. *[In French]*; [Reflections on secularism]. Migrations société. **Migrat. Soc.** 16:96 12:2004 pp.17-216.

2355   The reinvention of civil society in Eastern Europe: through the looking glass of democracy; *[Summary in German]*; *[Summary in French].* Tomas Mastnak. **Euro. J. Sociol.** XLVI:2 2005 pp.323-355.

2356   Religion and the rise of nationalism: a profile of an East-Central European city. Robert E. Alvis. Syracuse NY: Syracuse University Press, 2005. xxvi, 227p. *ISBN: 0815630816. Includes bibliographical references and index. (Series:* Religion and politics).

2357   Religious parties and democracy: a comparative assessment of Israel and Turkey. Sultan Tepe. **Democratization** 12:3 6:2005 pp.283-307.

2358   Secular philosophy and Muslim headscarves in schools. Cécile Laborde. **J. Pol. Philos.** 13:3 9:2005 pp.305-329.

2359   Separation of religion and state in the twenty-first century: comparing the Middle East and western democracies. Jonathan Fox; Shmuel Sandler. **Comp. Pol.** 37:3 4:2005 pp.317-336.

2360   Strategic extremism: why republicans and democrats divide on religious values. Edward L. Glaeser; Giacomo A.M. Ponzetto; Jesse M. Shapiro. **Q. J. Econ.** CXX:4 11:2005 pp.1283-1330.

2361   Waaqeffannaa : une association religieuse d'Éthiopie entre nationalisme ethnique et idéologie afrocentriste. *[In French]*; (Waaqeffannaa: a religious association between ethnic nationalism and ideology in Ethiopia.) *[Summary].* Thomas Osmond. **Pol. Afr.** 94 6:2004 pp.166-180.

2362   Which countries have state religions? Robert J. Barro; Rachel M. McCleary. **Q. J. Econ.** CXX:4 11:2005 pp.1331-1370.

2363   The Yasukuni shrine dispute and the politics of identity in Japan: why all the fuss? Daiki Shibuichi. **Asian Sur.** XLV:2 3-4:2005 pp.197-215.

2364   You don't understand, we are at war! Refashioning Durga in the service of Hindu nationalism. Anja Kovacs. **Contemp. Sth. Asia** 13:4 12:2004 pp.373-388.

Christianity
Christianisme

2365   An angel directs the storm: apocalyptic religion and American empire. Michael S. Northcott. London: I.B. Tauris, 2004. viii, 220p. *ISBN: 1850434786. Includes bibliographical references and index.*

2366   The apparitions of the Virgin Mary of Medjugorje: the convergence of Croatian nationalism and her apparitions. Zlatko Skrbiš. **Nat. Nationalism** 11:3 7:2005 pp.443-461.

2367   The Catholic Church in state politics: negotiating prophetic demands and political realities. David Yamane. Lanham MD: Rowman & Littlefield, 2005. x, 189p. *ISBN: 0742532305, 0742532291. Includes bibliographical references and index.*

2368   Catholics, democracy, and governing the Church. Gerald J. Russello. **R. Pol.** 67:3 Summer:2005 pp.539-550.

2369   The cube and the cathedral: Europe, America, and politics without God. George Weigel. New York: Basic Books, 2005. 202p. *ISBN: 0465092667. Includes bibliographical references and index.*

2370   The early days of Johane Masowe: self-doubt, uncertainty, and religious transformation. Matthew Engelke. **Comp. S. Soc. Hist.** 47:4 10:2005 pp.781-808.

2371   Imperial presidency revisited — George W. Bushs republikanisches Gottesgnadentum. *[In German]*; (Imperial presidency revisited — George W. Bush's republican divine right.); *[Summary in German].* Claus Leggewie. **Int. Pol. Gesell.** 1 2005 pp.9-24.

2372   'In the beginning was the land': the appropriation of religious themes in political discourses in Zimbabwe. Ezra Chitando. **Africa** 75:2 2005 pp.220-239.

2373   Jimmy Carter: the re-emergence of faith-based politics and the abortion rights issue. Andrew R. Flint; Joy Porter. **Pres. Stud. Q.** 35:1 3:2005 pp.28-51.

2374   John Locke, 'matters indifferent', and the restoration of the Church of England. Jacqueline Rose. **Hist. J.** 48:3 9:2005 pp.601-621.

2375   Media, ethnicity and patriotism — the Balkans 'unholy war' for the appropriation of Mother Teresa. Gëzim Alpion. **J. Sth. Euro. Balk.** 6:3 12:2004 pp.227-243.

2376   Of little faith: the politics of George W. Bush's faith-based initiatives. Amy E. Black; Douglas L. Koopman; David K. Ryden. Washington DC: Georgetown University Press, 2004. xi, 356p. *ISBN: 1589010124, 1589010132. Includes bibliographical references (p. 335-348) and index. (Series:* Religion and politics).

2377   Politics as a Christian vocation: faith and democracy today. Franklin I. Gamwell. Cambridge: Cambridge University Press, 2005. x, 185p. *ISBN: 0521838762, 0521547520. Includes bibliographical references (p. 173-176) and index.*

2378   Religion, politics and sexuality in Romania. Lucian Turcescu; Lavinia Stan. **Euro.-Asia S.** 57:2 3:2005 pp.291-310.

2379   Religions, pouvoir et société : Europe centrale, Balkans, CEI. *[In French]*; [Religions, power and society: Central Europe, the Balkans and the CIS]. Courrier des pays de l'Est. **Cour. Pays Est** 1045 9-10:2004 pp.3-61.

2380   Religious activity and political participation: the Brazilian and Chilean cases. Eric Patterson. **Lat. Am. Pol. Soc.** 47:1 Spring:2005 pp.1-30.

2381   Religious education in the Spanish school system. Àlex Seglers Gómez-Quintero. **J. Chur. State** 46:3 Summer:2004 pp.561-574.

2382   Russkaia teokratiia: mechty i real'nost'. *[In Russian]*; [Russian theocracy: dreams and reality]. E.M. Amelina. **Sots.Gum. Znan.** 2 2004 pp.261-276.

2383   The uses of failure: Christian socialism as a nomadic city of the gift economy. Trevor Hogan. **Thes. Elev.** 80 2:2005 pp.74-93.

2384   The Vatican, the American bishops, and the church-state ramifications of clerical sexual abuse. Jo Renee Formicola. **J. Chur. State** 46:3 Summer:2004 pp.479-502.

Islam
Islam

2385   Al Qaeda and the house of Saud: eternal enemies or secret bedfellows? John R. Bradley. **Washington Q.** 28:4 Autumn:2005 pp.139-152.

2386   Asessing English translations of the Qur'an sectarian bias and political agendas mar most publications. Khaleel Mohammed. **Mid. East Q.** XII:2 Spring:2005 pp.59-71.

2387   Believing in God at your own risk: religion and terrorisms in Uzbekistan. Russell Zanca. **Relig. State Soc.** 33:1 3:2005 pp.71-82.

2388   Between a rock and a hard place: the Islamisation of the Chechen separatist movement. Julie Wilhelmsen. **Euro.-Asia S.** 57:1 1:2005 pp.35-59.

2389   Comment les musulmans renouvellent l'Islam. *[In French]*; [How Muslims are renewing Islam]. Alternatives internationales [Interviewer]; Nasr Abou Zeid. **Alt. Int.** 13 3-4:2004 pp.32-49.

2390   De l'Irak au Liban, un printemps fragile. *[In French]*; [From Iraq to Lebanon, a fragile spring]. Olivier Mongin; Samir Frangieh; Henry Laurens; Philippe Droz-Vincent; Clémence Mayol. **Esprit** 314 5:2005 pp.114-178. *Collection of 5 articles.*

2391   Democracy, Islam and dialogue: the case of Turkey. Bora Kanra. **Gov. Oppos.** 40:4 Autumn:2005 pp.515-539.

2392   Fatwās in Indonesia. Jajat Burhanudin; Syamsul Anwar; Moch. Nur Ichwan; Noorhaidi Hasan; Michael Laffan. **Islam. Law Soc.** 12:1 2005 pp.9-121. *Collection of 5 articles.*

2393   Feminisms, islamophobia and identities. Haleh Afshar; Rob Aitken; Myfanwy Franks. **Pol. S.** 53:2 6:2005 pp.262-283.

2394   The future of political Islam: the importance of external variables. Mohammed Ayoob. **Int. Aff. [London]** 81:5 10:2005 pp.951-962.

2395   The inconvenient rationality of Islamism: Harakah during the Pergau Dam episode. Roger Kershaw. **Indo. Malay. World** 32:94 11:2004 pp.345-365.

2396   The irony of Islah (reform). Gwenn Okruhlik. **Washington Q.** 28:4 Autumn:2005 pp.153-170.

2397   Islam and democracy. Imad-Ad-Dean Ahmad; Lawrence Pintak; Nikki R. Keddie; Nader A. Hashemi; M.A. Muqtedar Khan; Mohammad M. Shabestari; Azza M. Karam; Mahmood Monshipouri; Abdulaziz Sachedina; Marcus Noland; Howard Pack; Naomi Sakr; Gary R. Bunt. **Glo. Dial.** 6:1-2 Winter-Spring:2004 pp.1-117. *Collection of 12 articles.*

2398   Islam and the challenge of democracy. Khaled Abou El Fadl; Joshua Cohen [Ed.]; Deborah Chasman [Ed.]. Princeton NJ: Princeton University Press, 2004. 139p. *ISBN: 0691118418, 0691119384. Includes bibliographical references and index.*

2399   L'Islam aux États-Unis : une nouvelle religion publique? *[In French]*; [Islam in the United States: a new public religion?] Malika Zeghal. **Pol. Étran.** 70:1 Spring:2005 pp.49-59.

2400   Islam et activisme politique. Le cas ouzbek. *[In French]*; (Islam and political activism: the Uzbek case.) *[Summary]*. Bakhtiyar Babadjanov. **Annales** 59:5-6 9-12:2004 pp.1139-1156.

2401   Islam in America: separate but unequal. Geneive Abdo. **Washington Q.** 28:4 Autumn:2005 pp.7-17.

2402   Islam in Indonesia: modernism, radicalism, and the Middle East dimension. Giora Eliraz. Brighton, Portland OR: Sussex Academic Press, 2004. xi, 142p. *ISBN: 1845190408. Includes bibliographical references (p. 120-133) and index.*

2403   Islam is not the solution (or the problem). Daniel Brumberg. **Washington Q.** 29:1 Winter:2005-2006 pp.97-116.

2404   L'Islam politique en Iran. *[In French]*; [Political Islam in Iran]. Yann Richard. **Pol. Étran.** 70:1 Spring:2005 pp.61-72.

2405   Islam turc, Islams de Turquie : acteurs et réseaux en Europe. *[In French]*; [Turkish Islam, Islams of Turkey: actors and networks in Europe]. Samim Akgönül. **Pol. Étran.** 70:1 Spring:2005 pp.35-47.

2406   Islamic identity and political mobilization in Russia: Chechnya and Dagestan compared. Elise Giuliano. **Nat. Ethn. Pol.** 11:2 Summer:2005 pp.195-220.

2407   The Islamic paradox: Shiite clerics, Sunni fundamentalists, and coming of Arab democracy. Reuel Marc Gerecht. Washington DC: AEI Press, 2004. iii, 65p. *ISBN: 0844771791. Includes bibliographical references and index.*

2408   Islamic politics at the sub-regional level in Dagestan: Tariqa brotherhoods, ethnicities, localism and the spiritual board. Kimitaka Matsuzato; Magomed-Rasul Ibragimov. **Euro.-Asia S.** 57:5 7:2005 pp.753-779.

2409   Islamism in the diaspora: Palestinian refugees in Lebanon. Are Knudsen. **J. Refug. S.** 18:2 6:2005 pp.216-234.

2410 Maroc : l'émergence de l'islamisme sur la scène politique. *[In French]*; [Morocco: the emergence of islamism on the political arena]. Khadija Mohsen-Finan. **Pol. Étran.** 70:1 Spring:2005 pp.73-84.

2411 Modern Islamic political thought: the response of the Shi'i and Sunni Muslims to the twentieth century. Hamid Enayat. London: I.B. Tauris, 2005. xiv, 225p. *ISBN: 1850434662. Includes bibliographical references (p. [195]-212) and index.*

2412 Modernity, Islam, and secularism in Turkey: bodies, places, and time. Alev Cinar. Minneapolis MN: University of Minnesota Press, 2005. viii, 199p. *ISBN: 0816644101, 081664411X. Includes bibliographical references (p. 193-195) and index. (Series:* Public worlds - 14).

2413 Modernization, democracy, and Islam. Shireen Hunter [Ed.]; Huma Malik [Ed.]; Ahmedou Ould-Abdallah [Foreword]. Westport CT: Praeger Publishing, 2005. xiii, 361p. *ISBN: 0275985113, 027598530X. Includes bibliographical references and index. Center for Strategic and International Studies.*

2414 Mohamed VI, commandeur des croyants au secours de la laïcité ? *[In French]*; [Mohammed VI, Muslim believers and secularism]. Bernard Cubertafond. **Conf. Médit.** 51 Fall:2004 pp.163-180.

2415 Morocco's Islamists and the legislative elections of 2002: the strange case of the party that did not want to win. Michael J. Willis. **Med. Pol.** 9:1 Spring:2004 pp.53-81.

2416 Mubarak and the Islamists: why did the 'honeymoon' end? Hesham Al-Awadi. **Mid. East J.** 59:1 Winter:2005 pp.62-80.

2417 Muslims and the state in Britain, France, and Germany. Joel S. Fetzer; J. Christopher Soper. Cambridge: Cambridge University Press, 2005. xv, 208p. *ISBN: 0521828309, 0521535395. Includes bibliographical references (p. 169-198) and index. (Series:* Cambridge studies in social theory, religion, and politics).

2418 Nouveaux regards sur l'Islam en France. *[In French]*; [New looks on Islam in France]. Cahiers de l'Orient. **Cah. Orient** 76 10-12:2004 pp.3-164.

2419 The Orient within: Muslim minorities and the negotiation of nationhood in modern Bulgaria. Mary Neuburger. Ithaca NY: Cornell University Press, 2004. xv, 223p. *ISBN: 0801441323. Includes bibliographical references (p. 203-215) and index.*

2420 Pakistans drift into extremism: Allah, the army, and Americas war on terror. Hassan Abbas. Armonk NY: M.E. Sharpe, 2005. xvii, 275p. *ISBN: 0765614960, 0765614979. Includes bibliographical references and index.*

2421 Perception of Islamisation in the Serbian national discourse. Bojan Aleksov. **J. Sth.East Euro. Black Sea S.** 5:1 1:2005 pp.113-127.

2422 Political Islam in Indonesia: present and future trajectory. Anies Rasyid Baswedan. **Asian Sur.** XLIV:5 9-10:2004 pp.669-690.

2423 Political Islam in Turkey: a state of controlled secularity. Pınar Tank. **Turkish S.** 6:1 3:2005 pp.3-19.

2424 The political participation and engagement of Muslim Americans: mosque involvement and group consciousness. Amaney Jamal. **Am. Pol. Res.** 33:4 7:2005 pp.521-544.

2425 La politique morale ou bien gouverner à l'islamique. *[In French]*; [Moral policy or good Islamic governance]. Gudrun Krämer. **Vingt. Sièc.** 82 4-6:2004 pp.131-143.

2426 Public Islam and the common good. Armando Salvatore [Ed.]; Dale F. Eickelman [Ed.]. Leiden MA: Brill, 2004. xxv, 254p. *ISBN: 9004136215. Includes bibliographical references and index. (Series:* Social, economic, and political studies of the Middle East and Asia - 95).

2427 Radical Islam: the death of an ideology? Ray Takeyh; Nikolas K. Gvosdev. **Mid. East Policy** XI:4 Winter:2004 pp.86-95.

2428 Radicalization as a reaction to failure: an economic model of Islamic extremism. M. Ferrero. **Publ. Choice** 122:1-2 1:2005 pp.199-220.

2429 Radikalizatsiia islama v Dagestane: vozmozhnosti i predely dzhikhadizma. *[In Russian]*; (Radicalization of Islam in Dagestan: possibilities and limitations of Jihad.) D. Makarov. **Obshch. Nauki Sovrem.** 6 2004 pp.147-161.

2430 Religion and politics in Turkey. Şerif Mardin; Binnaz Toprak; Fulya Atacan; Gamze Avcı; Metin Heper; Ersin Kalaycıoğlu; Hülya Canbakal; Ali Çarkoğlu; William Hale. **Turkish S.** 6:2 6:2005 pp.145-310. *Collection of 9 articles.*

2431 Religions at war, religions at peace: the case of Sudan. Yehudit Ronen. **Z. Pol.** 52:1 3:2005 pp.80-96.

2432 Remaking Muslim politics: pluralism, contestation, democratization. Robert W. Hefner [Ed.]. Princeton NJ: Princeton University Press, 2005. xii, 358p. *ISBN: 0691120927, 0691120935. Includes bibliographical references and index.* (*Series:* Princeton studies in Muslim politics).

2433 La République, les religions, l'espérance. *[In French]*; [The republic, religions and hope]. Nicolas Sarkozy [Discussant]; Thibaud Collin [Interviewer]; Philippe Verdin [Interviewer]. Paris: Cerf, 2004. 173p. *ISBN: 2204072834.*

2434 Rethinking Islam and liberal democracy: Islamist women in Turkish politics. Yesim Arat. Albany NY: State University of New York Press, 2005. x, 150p. *ISBN: 0791464652. Includes bibliographical references (p. 135-144) and index.*

2435 Revelation or revolution: a Gramscian approach to the rise of political Islam. Thomas J. Butko. **Br. J. Mid. East. S.** 31:1 5:2005 pp.41-62.

2436 Saddam's war of words: politics, religion, and the Iraqi invasion of Kuwait. Jerry M. Long. Austin TX: University of Texas Press, 2004. xiii, 272p. *ISBN: 0292701608, 0292702647. Includes bibliographical references (p. [239]-253) and index.*

2437 Shia political thought. Markaz al-Islami fi Injiltira; Ahmad Vaezi. London: Islamic Centre of England, 2004. 216p. *ISBN: 1904934013. Includes bibliographical references.*

2438 Traditional institutions as tools of political Islam in Bangladesh. Ali Riaz. **J. Asian Afr. S.** 40:3 6:2005 pp.171-196.

2439 Transformation of Islamic political identity in Turkey: rethinking the west and westernization. İhsan D. Dağı. **Turkish S.** 6:1 3:2005 pp.21-38.

2440 Turkey's AKP: a model 'Muslim-democratic' party? Sultan Tepe. **J. Democ.** 16:3 7:2005 pp.69-82.

2441 Unholy alliance: radical Islam and the American left. David Horowitz. Washington DC: Regnery Publishers, 2004. 296p. *ISBN: 089526076X. Includes bibliographical references and index.*

2442 When Islam and democracy meet: Muslims in Europe and in the United States. Jocelyne Cesari. Basingstoke: Palgrave Macmillan, 2004. x, 267p. *ISBN: 0312294018. Includes bibliographical references (p. [247]-261) and index.*

2443 Zentralasiens Regime und der Islam. *[In German]*; (The Central Asian regimes and Islam.) *[Summary]*. Alexander Warkotsch. **Osteuropa** 54:11 11:2004 pp.3-14.

D.1.3.5: Gender
Genre

2444 Activist faith: grassroots women in democratic Brazil and Chile. Carol Ann Drogus; Hannah W. Stewart-Gambino. University Park PA: Pennsylvania State University Press, 2005. xi, 212p. *ISBN: 0271025492. Includes bibliographical references (p. 197-205) and index.*

2445 Boy talk/girl talk: gender differences in campaign communications strategies. Costas Panagopoulos. **Wom. Pol.** 26:3-4 2004 pp.131-155.

2446 Connecting descriptive and substantive representation: an analysis of sex differences in cosponsorship activity. Michele L. Swers. **Legis. Stud. Q.** XXX:3 8:2005 pp.407-433.

2447 Developing power: how women transformed international development. Arvonne S. Fraser [Ed.]; Irene. Tinker [Ed.]. New York: Feminist Press, 2004. xxx, 372p. *ISBN: 1558614842, 1558614850. Includes bibliographical references (p. 349-358) and index. City University of New York.*

2448 Diversity and identity in the non-profit sector: lessons from LGBT organizing in Toronto. Miriam Smith. **Soc. Policy Admin.** 39:5 10:2005 pp.463-480.

2449   The double-edged sword of women's organizing: poverty and the emergence of racial and class differences in women's policy priorities. Erin O'Brien. **Wom. Pol.** 26:3-4 2004 pp.25-56.

2450   Egypt as a woman: nationalism, gender, and politics. Beth Baron. Berkeley CA: University of California Press, 2005. xv, 287p. *ISBN: 0520238575. Includes bibliographical references (p. 261-276) and index.*

2451   The establishment of the Hong Kong women's commission: an advocacy coalition framework analysis. Glenn Kwok-hung Hui. **Publ. Admin. Policy** 13:2 9:2004 pp.123-147.

2452   Femmes et politiques : l'État en mutation. *[In French]*; [Women and politics: the changing State]. Dominique Masson [Ed.]. Ottawa: Presses de l'Université d'Ottawa, 2005. vi, 295p. *ISBN: 2760305902. Includes bibliographical references.*

2453   Foucault and the Iranian Revolution: gender and the seductions of Islamism. Janet Afary; Kevin Anderson. Chicago IL: University of Chicago Press, 2005. xii, 346p. *ISBN: 0226007855, 0226007863. Translated from the French. Includes bibliographical references (p. 303-319) and index.*

2454   Gender & Peacebuilding. Frauen und Geschlechterverhältnisse in Post-Conflict Situationen. *[In German]*; [Gender and peace building. Women and gender relations in post-conflict situations]. Petra Purkarthofer; Annette Lyth; Ilja Luciak. **J. Entwick.pol.** XX:2 2004 pp.6-73. *Collection of 3 articles.*

2455   Gender and post-conflict civil society: Eritrea. Patricia J. Campbell. **Int. Femin. J. Pol.** 7:3 2005 pp.377-399.

2456   Gender and presidential judicial selection. Elaine Martin. **Wom. Pol.** 26:3-4 2004 pp.109-129.

2457   Gender and security. Mary Caprioli; Lori Handrahan; Miranda Alison; Mary-Jane Fox; Paul Higate; Marsha Henry; Pinar Bilgin. **Secur. Dial.** 35:4 12:2004 pp.411-508. *Collection of 7 articles.*

2458   Gender and the state: from differences between to differences within. Johanna Kantola; Hanne Marlene Dahl. **Int. Femin. J. Pol.** 7:1 2005 pp.49-70.

2459   Gender ghosts in McGarry and O'Leary and representations of the conflict in Northern Ireland. Marysia Zalewski. **Pol. S.** 53:1 3:2005 pp.201-221.

2460   Gender, governance and globalization. Georgina Waylen; Shirin M. Rai; Ruth Pearson; Diane Elson; Eleonore Kofman; Angela Hale; Rosa Fernandez; Cassandra Balchin; Simone Browne. **Int. Femin. J. Pol.** 6:4 2004 pp.557-693. *Collection of 9 articles.*

2461   Gendered paradoxes: women's movements, state restructuring, and global development in Ecuador. Amy Lind. University Park PA: Pennsylvania State University Press, 2005. xvi, 182p. *ISBN: 0271025441. Includes bibliographical references (p. 155-177) and index.*

2462   Gendered practices in institutions of hegemonic masculinity: reflections from feminist standpoint theory. Annica Kronsell. **Int. Femin. J. Pol.** 7:2 2005 pp.280-298.

2463   Good girls go to the polling booth, bad boys go everywhere: gender differences in anticipated political participation among American fourteen-year-olds. Marc Hooghe; Dietlind Stolle. **Wom. Pol.** 26:3-4 2004 pp.1-23.

2464   If Bill Clinton were a woman: the effectiveness of male and female politicians' account strategies following alleged transgressions. Elizabeth S. Smith; Ashleigh Smith Powers; Gustavo A. Suarez. **Pol. Psychol.** 26:1 2:2005 pp.115-134.

2465   The impact of feminist scholarship on Australian political science. Marian Sawer. **Aust. J. Pol. Sci.** 39:3 11:2004 pp.553-566.

2466   In het belang van vrouwen. Vertegenwoordigers (m/v) en de constructie van de vertegenwoordigde (v). *[In Dutch]*; (In the interest of women. Representatives (m/f) constructing the Represented (f).) *[Summary]*. Karen Celis. **Res Publica [Bruss.]** XLVI:4 2004 pp.486-511.

2467   Increasing women's political representation: the limits of constitutional reform. Jane Freedman. **West Euro. Pol.** 27:1 1:2004 pp.104-123.

2468   Is same-sex marriage an equal rights issue? Richard McDonough. **Publ. Aff. Q.** 19:1 1:2005 pp.51-63.

2469   "Le mystere de la chambre basse" : comparaison des processus d'entrée des femmes au Parlement, France-Allemagne, 1945-2000:. *[In French]*; ['The mystery of the Lower Chamber': a comparison of the women's entry into parliament, France-Germany, 1945-2000]. Catherine Achin; Frederique Matonti [Foreword]. Paris: Editions Dalloz, 2005. xiv, 637p. *ISBN: 2247060900. Includes bibliographical references (p. [545]-594).*

2470   Literature of the women's suffrage campaign in England. Carolyn Christensen Nelson [Ed.]. Peterborough: Broadview Press, 2004. xli, 353p. *ISBN: 1551115115. Includes bibliographical references (p. 351-353).*

2471   Men, women and the dynamics of presidential approval. Harold D. Clarke; Marianne C. Stewart; Mike Ault; Euel Elliott. **Br. J. Pol. Sci.** 35:1 1:2005 pp.31-51.

2472   Minority representation of a political majority group. Rashmi Shrivastava. **Indian J. Pol. Sci.** LXVI:2 4-6:2005 pp.233-252.

2473   Moving beyond G.I. Jane: women and the U.S. military. Sara L. Zeigler; Gregory G. Gunderson. Lanham MD: University Press of America, 2005. vii, 194p. *ISBN: 0761830936. Includes bibliographical references (p. [173]-185) and index.*

2474   Nanny politics: the dilemmas of working women's empowerment in Santiago, Chile. Kristen Hill Maher; Silke Staab. **Int. Femin. J. Pol.** 7:1 2005 pp.71-89.

2475   Of what is that glass ceiling made? A study of attitudes about women and the oval office. Kate Kenski; Erika Falk. **Wom. Pol.** 26:2 2004 pp.57-80.

2476   Opposing currents: the politics of water and gender in Latin America. Vivienne Bennett [Ed.]; Sonia Davila-Poblete [Ed.]; Nieves Rico [Ed.]. Pittsburgh PA: University of Pittsburgh Press, 2005. xii, 250p. *ISBN: 0822958546. Includes bibliographical references (p. 219-237) and index. (Series: Pitt Latin America).*

2477   Origin stories in political thought: discourses on gender, power, and citizenship. Joanne H. Wright. Toronto: University of Toronto Press, 2004. x, 230p. *ISBN: 0802088120. Includes bibliographical references (p. [205]-219) and index.*

2478   Paradoxes, protests and the mujeres de negro of northern Mexico. Melissa W. Wright. **Gend. Place Cult.** 12:3 9:2005 pp.277-292.

2479   Participation of marginal women in decision making process. Manas Chakrabarty; Padam Nepal; Namrata Pariyar. **Indian J. Pol. Sci.** 65:3 7-9:2004 pp.333-344.

2480   A plea for engendering human security. Anuradha M. Chenoy. **Int. S.** 42:2 4-6:2005 pp.167-179.

2481   Political cares: gendered reporting of work and family issues in relation to Australian politicians. Kathie Muir. **Aust. Femin. S.** 20:46 3:2005 pp.77-90.

2482   Political empowerement of women in Indian legislature: a study. D. Syamala Devi; G. Lakshmi. **Indian J. Pol. Sci.** LXVI:1 1-3:2005 pp.75-92.

2483   Political empowerement of women. Yogendra Narain; S.N. Sahu; L. Lakshmi. **Indian J. Publ. Admin.** LI:1 1-3:2005 pp.34-54.

2484   Political empowerment of women in Soviet Union and Russia: ideology and implementation. K.B. Usha. **Int. S.** 42:2 4-6:2005 pp.141-165.

2485   Political gender equality and state human rights abuse. Erik Melander. **J. Peace Res.** 42:2 3:2005 pp.149-166.

2486   Political participation and attitudinal transformation of rural women. Poonam Vats. Delhi: Abhijeet Publishers, 2004. vi, 304p. *ISBN: 8188683302. Includes bibliographical references (p. [285]-299) and index.*

2487   A politics of accommodation: women and the people's action party in Singapore. Lenore Lyons. **Int. Femin. J. Pol.** 7:2 2005 pp.233-257.

2488   The politics of inclusion and empowerment: gender, class, and citizenship. John Andersen [Ed.]; Birte Siim [Ed.]. Basingstoke: Palgrave Macmillan, 2004. viii, 252p. *ISBN: 1403932387. Includes bibliographical references and index.*

2489   Premières dames en Afrique. *[In French]*; [First ladies of Africa]. Christine Messiant; Roland Marchal; Damien Glez; Catherine Coquery-Vidrovitch; Moussa Touré; Sandrine Perrot; Sadri Khiari; Émile A. Tozo; Fred Eboko; Hervé Maupeu. **Pol. Afr.** 95 10:2004 pp.5-124. *Collection of 9 articles.*

2490   Qatari women: a new generation of leaders? Louay Bahry; Phebe Marr. **Mid. East Policy** XII:2 Summer:2005 pp.104-119.

2491   Quotas as a 'fast track' to equal representation for women: why Scandinavia is no longer the model. Drude Dahlerup; Lenita Freidenvall. **Int. Femin. J. Pol.** 7:1 2005 pp.26-48.

2492   Quotas: changing the way things look without changing the way things are. Louise Vincent. **J. Legis. St.** 10:1 Spring:2004 pp.71-96.

2493   Race and public policy: toward creating race-sensitive measures of public policy fairness. Kenya L. Covington; William E. Spriggs; Susan Tinsley Gooden; Cheryl Hill Lee. **R. Black Pol. Econ.** 32:2 Fall:2004 pp.7-59. *Collection of 3 articles.*

2494   Race, poverty, and domestic policy. C. Michael Henry; James Tobin [Foreword]. New Haven CT: Yale University Press, 2004. xiv, 804p. *ISBN: 0300095414. Includes bibliographical references and index. (Series:* Yale ISPS).

2495   Renegotiating gender and power. Women's organizations and networks in politics: the China Women Mayors' Association. Qi Wang. Lund: Lund University, 2004. 48p. *ISBN: 9197509310. Includes bibliographical references. (Series:* Working papers in contemporary Asian studies - 2).

2496   (The role of women in war and peace: the Palestinian case.); *[Text in Arabic].* Bari'ah Naqshabandi. **Dirasat Hum. Soc. Sci.** 32:1 2:2005 pp.128-139.

2497   Theorizing knowledge from women's political practices: the case of the women's reproductive rights movement. Bice Maiguashca. **Int. Femin. J. Pol.** 7:2 2005 pp.207-232.

2498   (Un)thinking citizenship: feminist debates in contemporary South Africa. Amanda Gouws [Ed.]. Aldershot, Burlington VT: Ashgate, 2005. xii, 281p. *ISBN: 0754638782. Includes bibliographical references and index. (Series:* Gender in a global/local world).

2499   Why women don't run: explaining women's underrepresentation in America's political institutions. Laurel Elder. **Wom. Pol.** 26:2 2004 pp.27-56.

2500   Women and political participation: cultural change in the political arena. M. Margaret Conway; Gertrude A. Steuernagel; David W. Ahern. Washington DC: CQ Press, 2005. xiii, 162p. *ISBN: 156802925X. Includes bibliographical references and index.*

2501   Women and terrorism. Cindy D. Ness [Intro.]; David Cook; Susan McKay; Carolyn Nordstrom; Anne Nivat; Kathleen M. Blee; Brigitte L. Nacos. **S. Confl. Terror.** 28:5 9-10:2005 pp.349-451. *Collection of 8 articles.*

2502   Women and the Nobel Prize for peace. Judith Hicks Stiehm. **Int. Femin. J. Pol.** 7:2 2005 pp.258-279.

2503   Women in Iran from 1800 to the Islamic Republic. Lois Beck [Ed.]; Guity Nashat [Ed.]. Urbana IL: University of Illinois Press, 2004. xiii, 288p. *ISBN: 0252029372, 0252071891. Includes bibliographical references and index.*

2504   Women in Israel: a state of their own. Ruth Halperin-Kaddari. Philadelphia PA: University of Pennsylvania Press, 2004. 363p. *ISBN: 0812237528. Includes bibliographical references (p. [327]-346) and index. (Series:* Pennsylvania studies in human rights).

2505   Women in post-communist politics: explaining under-representation in the Hungarian and Romanian parliaments. Cristina Chiva. **Euro.-Asia S.** 57:7 11:2005 pp.969-994.

2506   Women in the South African Parliament: from resistance to governance. Hannah Evelyn Britton. Urbana IL: University of Illinois Press, 2005. xxii, 198p. *ISBN: 0252030133. Includes bibliographical references and index.*

2507   Women on the sidelines: women's representation on committees in Latin American legislatures. Roseanna Michelle Heath; Leslie A. Schwindt-Bayer; Michelle M. Taylor-Robinson. **Am. J. Pol. Sci.** 49:2 4:2005 pp.420-436.

2508   Women political leaders: past and present. Farida Jalalzai. **Wom. Pol.** 26:3-4 2004 pp.85-108.

2509   Women, urbanization and regional development in Southeast Anatolia: a case study for Turkey. Gülen Elmas. **Turkish S.** 5:3 Autumn:2004 pp.1-24.

2510   Women's political lives in Latin America: reconfiguring terrains of theory, history, and practice. Janise Hurtig; Rosario Montoya. **Lat. Am. Res. R.** 40:1 2005 pp.187-201.

2511   Women's suffrage in Asia: gender, nationalism and democracy. Louise P. Edwards [Ed.]; Mina Roces [Ed.]. New York, London: RoutledgeCurzon, 2004. 240p. *ISBN: 0415332516*. (*Series:* RoutledgeCurzon studies in the modern history of Asia).

D.1.4:   Economic forces
          Forces économiques

D.1.4.1:   Business influences
            Influences commerciales

2512   L'affaire Khodorkovski : ou l'économie politique de la nouvelle Russie. *[In French]*; [The Khodorkovski affair or Russia's new political economy] *[Summary]*. Christophe Cordonnier. **Cour. Pays Est** 1042 3-4:2004 pp.60-71.

2513   Antibiotics, big business, and consumers: the context of government investigations into the postwar American drug industry. Robert Bud. **Ann. Am. Acad. Pol. Soc. Sci.** 46:2 4:2005 pp.329-349.

2514   Big business and the state in Russia. Philip Hanson; Elizabeth Teague. **Euro.-Asia S.** 57:5 7:2005 pp.657-680.

2515   'Business populism' in Thailand. Pasuk Phongpaichit; Chris Baker. **J. Democ.** 16:2 4:2005 pp.58-72.

2516   Business versus business? Grupos and organized business in Colombia. Angelika Rettberg. **Lat. Am. Pol. Soc.** 47:1 Spring:2005 pp.31-54.

2517   Captains or pirates? State-business relations in post-socialist Poland. Roger Schoenman. **East Euro. Pol. Soc.** 19:1 Winter:2005 pp.40-75.

2518   Changing the bases of political support in Mexico: pro-business networks and the market reform agenda. Alejandra Salas-Porras. **R. Int. Pol. Econ.** 12:1 2:2005 pp.129-154.

2519   Corporate campaign contributions, repeat giving, and the rewards to legislator reputation. Randall S. Kroszner; Thomas Stratmann. **J. Law Econ.** XLVIII:1 4:2005 pp.41-71.

2520   Corporatism from the firm perspective: employers and social policy in Denmark and Britain. Cathie Jo Martin. **Br. J. Pol. Sci.** 35:1 1:2005 pp.127-148.

2521   Delaware's politics. Mark J. Roe. **Harv. Law R.** 118:8 6:2005 pp.2491-2543.

2522   Engaging the base and delivering the goods! Wade Rathke. **Soc. Policy** 35:3 Spring:2005 pp.59-61.

2523   Fat cats and self-made men: globalization and the paradoxes of collective action. Melani Cammett. **Comp. Pol.** 37:4 7:2005 pp.379-400.

2524   Flexing muscle: corporate political expenditures as signals to the bureaucracy. Sanford C. Gordon; Catherine Hafer. **Am. Pol. Sci. R.** 99:2 5:2005 pp.245-261.

2525   Government discourses on entrepreneurship: issues of legitimization, subjugation, and power. Lew Perren; Peter L. Jennings. **Entrepren. Theor. Prac.** 29:2 3:2005 pp.173-184.

2526   Interest groups in disjointed corporatism: social dialogue in Greece and European 'competitive corporatism'. Kostas A. Lavdas. **West Euro. Pol.** 28:2 3:2005 pp.297-316.

2527   The invisible enemy: representing labour in a corporate media order; *[Summary in Slovene]*. Jon Bekken. **Javnost** XII:1 4:2005 pp.71-84.

2528   Lobbying and regulation in a political economy: evidence from the U.S. cellular industry. Tomaso Duso. **Publ. Choice** 122:3-4 3:2005 pp.251-276.

2529   No representation without taxation? Rents, development, and democracy. Michael Herb. **Comp. Pol.** 37:3 4:2005 pp.297-316.

2530   Les oligarques et le pouvoir : la redistribution des cartes. *[In French]*; (The oligarchs and power: the redistribution of the cards.) *[Summary]*. Natalie Nougayrède. **Pouvoirs** 112 2004 pp.35-48.

2531   Organizacja pracodawców i przedsiębiorców na szczeblu wspólnotowym. *[In Polish]*; (Organisations of employers and entrepreneurs on community level.) *[Summary]*. Cezary Piątkowski. **Prz. Euro.** 1(8) 2004 pp.125-138.

2532   Party polarization and the business cycle in the United States. Edward J. López; Carlos D. Ramírez. **Publ. Choice** 121:3-4 10:2004 pp.413-430.

2533   Public agencies as lobbyists. J.R. DeShazo; Jody Freeman. **Columb. Law R.** 105:8 12:2005 pp.2217-2309.

2534   Putting Yukos in perspective. William Tompson. **Post-Sov. Aff.** 21:2 4-6:2005 pp.159-181.

2535   Remaking Italian capitalism? The politics of corporate governance reform. Richard Deeg. **West Euro. Pol.** 28:3 5:2005 pp.521-548.

2536   The rise of the Russian business elite. Olga Kryshtanovskaya; Stephen White. **Comm. Post-Comm. S.** 38:3 9:2005 pp.293-307.

2537   Der rot-grüne Einstieg in den Abschied vom „Modell Deutschland". *[In German]*; (Explaining red-green's fare-well to the Modell Deutschland.) *[Summary]*. Stefan Beck; Christoph Scherrer. **Prokla** 35:1 3:2005 pp.111-130.

2538   Shareholder primacy and the distribution of wealth. Paddy Ireland. **Mod. Law R.** 68:1 1:2005 pp.49-81.

2539   Sisyphus meets the Borg: economic scale and inequalities in interest representation. David Lowery; Virginia Gray; Matthew Fellowes. **J. Theor. Pol.** 17:1 1:2005 pp.41-74.

2540   Structural power and public policy: a signalling model of business lobbying in democratic capitalism. Patrick Bernhagen; Thomas Bräuninger. **Pol. S.** 53:1 3:2005 pp.43-64.

2541   Sub-state nationalism and the left-right divide; critical junctures in the formation of nationalist labour movements in Belgium. Jan Erk. **Nat. Nationalism** 11:4 10:2005 pp.551-570.

2542   Trust and political economy: institutions and the sources of interfirm cooperation. Henry Farrell. **Comp. Pol. S.** 38:5 6:2005 pp.459-483.

2543   Vom Korporatismus zum Lobbyismus. Paradigmenwechsel in Theorie und Analyse der Interessenvermittlung. *[In German]*; (From corporatism to lobbyism. A change of paradigm in the theory and analysis of advocacy.) *[Summary]*. Thomas von Winter. **Z. Parlament.** 35:4 12:2004 pp.761-776.

2544   Women and work. Gertrude Ezorsky [Ed.]; Dorothy Sue Cobble; Julia Wrigley; Lynn Chancer; Betty Reid Mandell. **New Pol.** X:3 Summer:2005 pp.124-159. *Collection of 4 articles.*

D.2:   **Political behaviour**
        Comportement politique

D.2.1: **Values**
        Valeurs

2545   The 2004 presidential election, 'moral values', and the democrats' dilemma. Edward Ashbee. **Pol. Q.** 76:2 4-6:2005 pp.209-217.

2546   Antisemitismus und Moral. Einige Überlegungen. *[In German]*; [Anti-Semitism and morals. Some considerations]. Werner Konitzer. **Mittelweg 36** 14:2 4-5:2005 pp.24-35.

2547   Biobanks and bioethics: the politics of legitimation. Brian Salter; Mavis Jones. **J. Euro. Publ. Policy** 12:4 2005 pp.710-732.

2548   Conflicts and commitment obligations. D.W. Haslett. **Publ. Aff. Q.** 18:4 10:2004 pp.345-362.

2549   A new front in the culture war? Moral traditionalism and voting behavior in U.S. house elections. Jonathan Knuckey. **Am. Pol. Res.** 33:5 9:2005 pp.645-671.

2550   Patriotism as bad faith. Simon Keller. **Ethics** 115:3 4:2005 pp.563-592.

2551   Postmaterialism v. egalitarianism as predictors of energy-related attitudes. Juliet Carlisle; Eric R.A.N. Smith. **Env. Pol.** 14:4 7:2005 pp.527-540.

2552   The structure and effects of moral predispositions in contemporary American politics. Herbert F. Weisberg. **J. Pol.** 67:3 8:2005 pp.646-668.

2553   The torture show: reflections on Iraq and the West. Allan Antliff; Sureyyya Evren; Sharif Gemie; Marcus Milwright. **Anarch. S.** 13:1 2005 pp.61-82.

D.2.2:   **Psychological factors**
         Facteurs psychologiques

2554   The American enemy: a story of French anti-Americanism. Philippe Roger; Sharon Bowman [Tr.]. Chicago IL: University of Chicago Press, 2005. xviii, 518p. *ISBN: 0226723682. Translated from the French.*

2555   Before the emergence of critical citizens: economic development and political trust in China. Zhengxu Wang. **Int. R. Sociol.** 15:1 3:2005 pp.155-171.

2556   L'immagine pubblica dei partiti politici: un male necessario? *[In Italian]*; (Public image of political parties: a necessary evil?) Russell J. Dalton; Steven Weldon. **Riv. It. Sci. Pol.** XXXIV:3 12:2004 pp.379-404.

2557   Managing citizen fears: public attitudes toward urban terrorism. Darrell M. West; Marion Orr. **Urb. Aff. R.** 41:1 9:2005 pp.93-105.

2558   National attachment and patriotism in a European nation: a British study. Despina M. Rothì; Evanthia Lyons; Xenia Chryssochoou. **Pol. Psychol.** 26:1 2:2005 pp.135-156.

2559   Participation in voluntary associations: relations with resources, personality, and political values. René Bekkers. **Pol. Psychol.** 26:3 6:2005 pp.439-454.

2560   Policy frames, metaphorical reasoning, and support for public policies. Richard R. Lau; Mark Schlesinger. **Pol. Psychol.** 26:1 2:2005 pp.77-114.

2561   Prenegotiation public commitment in domestic and international bargaining. Bahar Leventoğlu; Ahmer Tarar. **Am. Pol. Sci. R.** 99:3 8:2005 pp.419-434.

2562   Presidential rhetoric and the economy. B. Dan Wood; Chris T. Owens; Brandy M. Durham. **J. Pol.** 67:3 8:2005 pp.627-645.

2563   Psikhologiia politicheskogo sotrudnichestva v Rossii. *[In Russian]*; [The psychology of political cooperation in Russia]. T.P. Elokhina. St. Petersburg: Izdatel'stvo Sankt Peterburgskogo universiteta, 2004. 258p. *ISBN: 5288034826.*

2564   Psychology and the political. Paul Stenner; Fernando Alvarez-Uria; Anna Stetsenko; Igor Arievitch; Jill Morawski; Kimberly Nelson; Ghassan Hage; Dimitris Papadopoulos; Ben Bradley; Angel J. Gordo López; Joan Pujol Tarrés; Niamh Stephenson. **Int. J. Crit. Psychol.** 12 2004 pp.14-186. *Collection of 8 articles.*

2565   The social transformation of trust in government. Russell J. Dalton. **Int. R. Sociol.** 15:1 3:2005 pp.133-154.

2566   Social trust and e-commerce: experimental evidence for the effects of social trust on individuals' economic behavior. Diana C. Mutz. **Publ. Opin. Q.** 69:3 Fall:2005 pp.393-416.

2567   Striking a responsive chord: how political ads motivate and persuade voters by appealing to emotions. Ted Brader. **Am. J. Pol. Sci.** 49:2 4:2005 pp.388-405.

2568   Values-based political messages and persuasion: relationships among speaker, recipient, and evoked values. Thomas E. Nelson; Jennifer Garst. **Pol. Psychol.** 26:4 8:2005 pp.489-515.

2569   Voltooid verleden tijd? Het verband tussen kennis over de nazi-genocide en democratische attitudes bij adolescenten in Brussel. *[In Dutch]*; (Past perfect tense? The link between knowledge of Nazi-genocide and democratic attitudes of adolescents in Brussels.) *[Summary]*. Dimo Kavadias. **Res Publica [Bruss.]** XLVI:4 2004 pp.535-554.

2570   What's in a name? Preference for 'black' versus 'African-American' among Americans of African descent. Lee Sigelman; Steven A. Tuch; Jack K. Martin. **Publ. Opin. Q.** 69:3 Fall:2005 pp.429-438.

D.2.3: Opinion
Opinion

2571 American public opinion toward the military: differences by race, gender, and class? David L. Leal. **Arm. Forces Soc.** 32:1 10:2005 pp.123-138.

2572 Anyone for higher speed limits? Self-interested and adaptive political preferences. Olof Johansson-Stenman; Peter Martinsson. **Publ. Choice** 122:3-4 3:2005 pp.319-331.

2573 The authorities really do matter: party control and trust in government. Luke Keele. **J. Pol.** 67:3 8:2005 pp.873-886.

2574 Biotechnology and media effects. Martin W. Bauer; Jan M. Gutteling; Heinz Bonfadelli. **Int. J. Publ. Opin. Res.** 17:1 Spring:2005 pp.5-89. *Collection of 4 articles.*

2575 China's new nationalism: pride, politics, and diplomacy. Peter Hays Gries. Berkeley CA: University of California Press, 2004. ix, 215p. *ISBN: 0520232976. Includes bibliographical references (p. 181-200) and index.*

2576 Citizen satisfaction with municipal amalgamations; *[Summary in French].* J. Kushner; D. Siegel. **Can. Publ. Admin.** 48:1 Spring:2005 pp.73-95.

2577 Comparing the quality of data obtained by minimally balanced and fully balanced attitude questions. Eric M. Shaeffer; Jon A. Krosnick; Gary E. Langer; Daniel M. Merkle. **Publ. Opin. Q.** 69:3 Fall:2005 pp.417-428.

2578 A different take on the deliberative poll: information, deliberation, and attitude constraint. Patrick Sturgis; Caroline Roberts; Nick Allum. **Publ. Opin. Q.** 69:1 Spring:2005 pp.30-65.

2579 Does presidential rhetoric matter? Priming and presidential approval. James N. Druckman; Justin W. Holmes. **Pres. Stud. Q.** 34:4 12:2004 pp.755-778.

2580 Framing public discussion of gay civil unions. Vincent Price; Lilach Nir; Joseph N. Cappella. **Publ. Opin. Q.** 69:2 Summer:2005 pp.179-212.

2581 Government popularity and public attitudes to social security reform in Brazil. Rachel Meneguello. **Int. J. Publ. Opin. Res.** 17:2 Summer:2005 pp.173-189.

2582 The graying of America and support for funding the nation's schools. Eric Plutzer; Michael Berkman. **Publ. Opin. Q.** 69:1 Spring:2005 pp.66-86.

2583 Interes k politike po-rossiski: motivy iavnye i skrytye. *[In Russian];* (Interest for politics, Russian variety: motives manifest and ulterior.) *[Summary].* G.L. Kertman. **Polis [Moscow]** 1(84) 2005 pp.94-107.

2584 Misstating the State of the Union. David Brock. New York: Akashic Books, 2004. 158p. *ISBN: 1888451807. Mediamatters.*

2585 Newsgroup participants as opinion leaders and seekers in online and offline communication environments. Alex S.L. Tsang; Nan Zhou. **J. Bus. Res.** 58:9 9:2005 pp.1186-1193.

2586 Opinion — policy dynamics: public preferences and public expenditure in the United Kingdom. Stuart N. Soroka; Christopher Wlezien. **Br. J. Pol. Sci.** 35:4 10:2005 pp.665-689.

2587 Osvoenie institutov i tsennostei demokratii ukrainskim i rossiskim massovym soznaniem (predvaritel'nye itogi). *[In Russian];* (Assimilation of institutions and values of democracy by Ukrainian and Russian mass consciousness (preliminary conclusions).) *[Summary].* V.V. Lapkin; V.I. Pantin. **Polis [Moscow]** 1(84) 2005 pp.50-62.

2588 Perceptions of political corruption in Latin American democracies. Damarys Canache; Michael E. Allison. **Lat. Am. Pol. Soc.** 47:3 Fall:2005 pp.91-112.

2589 Political trust, ideology, and public support for government spending. Thomas J. Rudolph; Jillian Evans. **Am. J. Pol. Sci.** 49:3 7:2005 pp.660-671.

2590 Politika Rossii v otnoshenii SNG i obshchestvennoe mnenie. *[In Russian];* (Russia's policy in the CIS and public opinion.) Dmitrii V. Polikanov. **Mon. Obshch. Mnen.** 3(71) 7-9:2004 pp.14-25.

2591 Politisk smag som klassemarkør: en Bourdieu-approach til studiet af politiske holdninger. *[In Danish];* (Political taste as a marker of class: a Bourdieu approach to the study of political opinion formation.) *[Summary].* Rune Slothuus. **Politica** 36:3 9:2004 pp.311-332.

2592　Prioritety vneshnei politiki: evoliutsiia massovykh ustanovok. *[In Russian]*; (Priorities of foreign policy: evolution of the public views.) Vladimir V. Petukhov. **Mon. Obshch. Mnen.** 1(69) 1-3:2004 pp.34-45.

2593　Propaganda and public opinion in Zimbabwe. Michael Bratton; Annie Chikwana; Tulani Sithole. **J. Contemp. Afr. S.** 23:1 1:2005 pp.77-108.

2594　Public attitudes to local government in Turkey: research on knowledge, satisfaction and complaints. Muhammet Kosecik; Isa Sagbas. **Loc. Govt. S.** 30:3 Autumn:2004 pp.360-383.

2595　Public opinion. Daniel Bar-Tal [Discussant]; Mina Zemach [Discussant]; Yaacov Shamir [Discussant]. **Palestine-Israel J. Pol. Econ. Cult.** 11:3-4 2004-2005 pp.125-142.

2596　Public opinion and dynamic representation in the American states: the case of environmental attitudes. Martin Johnson; Paul Brace; Kevin Arceneaux. **Soc. Sci. Q.** 86:1 3:2005 pp.87-108.

2597　Public opinion, democracy, and market reform in Africa. Michael Bratton; Robert B. Mattes; Emmanuel Gyimah-Boadi. Cambridge: Cambridge University Press, 2005. xvii, 466p. *ISBN: 0521841917, 0521602912. Includes bibliographical references and index.* (Series: Cambridge studies in comparative politics).

2598　Public opinion on alcohol service at licensed premises: a population survey in Stockholm, Sweden 1999-2000. E. Wallin; S. Andréasson. **Health Policy** 72:3 6:2005 pp.265-278.

2599　Public opinion on federalism and federal political culture in Canada, Mexico, and the United States, 2004. Richard L. Cole; John Kincaid; Alejandro Rodriguez. **Publius** 34:3 Summer:2004 pp.201-221.

2600　Public opinion, risk perceptions, and genetically modified food regulatory policy: reassessing the calculus of dissent among European citizens. Robert F. Durant; Jerome S. Legge, Jr. **Euro. Uni. Pol.** 6:2 6:2005 pp.181-200.

2601　Public support for democracy in Hong Kong. Ming Sing. **Democratization** 12:2 4:2005 pp.244-261.

2602　The rational public? A Canadian test of the Page and Shapiro argument. Éric Bélanger; François Pétry. **Int. J. Publ. Opin. Res.** 17:2 Summer:2005 pp.190-212.

2603　Reflexiones en torno a una propuesta metodológica para abordar el estudio de la opinión pública como un proceso comunicativo desde una perspectiva multinivel. *[In Spanish]*; [Reflections around a methodological proposal for the study of public opinion as a communicative process from a multilevel perspective]. Maricela Portillo. **R. Mexicana Cien. Pol.** XLVI:190 1-4:2004 pp.71-93.

2604　A review and proposal for a new measure of poll accuracy. Elizabeth A. Martin; Michael W. Traugott; Courtney Kennedy. **Publ. Opin. Q.** 69:3 Fall:2005 pp.342-369.

2605　Sentencing young offenders: public opinion in England and Wales. Julian Roberts; Mike Hough. **Crim. Just.** 5:3 8:2005 pp.211-232.

2606　Silent voices: public opinion and political representation in America. Adam J. Berinsky. Princeton NJ: Princeton University Press, 2004. xiv, 200p. *ISBN: 0691115877. Includes bibliographical references (p. 185-194) and index.*

2607　The 'social gap' in wind farm siting decisions: explanations and policy responses. Derek Bell; Tim Gray; Claire Haggett. **Env. Pol.** 14:4 7:2005 pp.460-477.

2608　Sociopolitical attitudes of the masses and leaders in the Chinese village: attitude congruence and constraint. Jie Chen. **J. Cont. China** 14:44 8:2005 pp.445-464.

2609　Sotsial'no-politicheskaia situatsiia v Iuzhnom federal'nom okruge. *[In Russian]*; (The sociopolitical situation in the Southern federal district.) *[Summary]*. Elena N. Kofanova; Ekaterina A. Kulagina. **Mon. Obshch. Mnen.** 2(74) 4-6:2005 pp.88-99.

2610　Support for extreme right-wing parties in Western Europe: individual attributes, political attitudes, and national context. Alan E. Kessler; Gary P. Freeman. **Comp. Euro. Pol.** 3:3 9:2005 pp.261-288.

2611　A szlovákok magyarságképének alakulása. *[In Hungarian]*; (How Slovaks' image of Hungarians is changing.) *[Summary]*. Judit Hamberger. **Euro. Tükör** 9:3 2004 pp.78-88.

2612   Tides of consent: how public opinion shapes American politics. James A. Stimson. Cambridge, New York: Cambridge University Press, 2004. xxii, 181p. *ISBN: 0521601177, 0521841348. Includes bibliographical references (p. 173-175) and index.*

2613   Tolerancia e intolerancia: estudios contemporáneos. *[In Spanish]*; [Tolerance and intolerance: contemporary studies]. Guillermo M. Almeyra Casares; José Luis Tejeda González; Sebastián Escámez Navas; Alfredo Falero Cirigliano; Vicente Cabedo Mallol; Gilda Waldman Mitnick; Josefina Leonor Brown; Alfredo a Embajada de México en Malasia Pérez Bravo; Iván Roberto Sierra Medel; Gisela Landázuri Benítez; Liliana López Levi; Takao Fujimoto; Fumiko Ekuni; Mónica Beltrán Gaos; Mónica Tarducci; Bárbara Tagliaferro. **Pol. Cult.** 21 Spring:2004 pp.7-200. *Collection of 12 articles.*

2614   Trends: same-sex marriage and civil unions. Paul R. Brewer; Clyde Wilcox. **Publ. Opin. Q.** 69:4 Winter:2005 pp.599-616.

2615   Trends: the war in Iraq. Philip Everts; Pierangelo Isernia. **Publ. Opin. Q.** 69:2 Summer:2005 pp.264-323.

2616   Trust in public institutions in South Africa. Steinar Askvik [Ed.]; Nelleke Bak [Ed.]. Aldershot, Burlington VT: Ashgate, 2005. xii, 268p. *ISBN: 0754643530.*

2617   Understanding public support for British membership of the single currency. Matthew Gabel; Simon Hix. **Pol. S.** 53:1 3:2005 pp.65-81.

2618   Values and interests in attitudes toward trade and globalization: the continuing compromise of embedded liberalism; *[Summary in French]*. Robert Wolfe; Matthew Mendelsohn. **Can. J. Pol.** 38:1 3:2005 pp.45-68.

2619   Veřejné mínění a zahraničněpolitický diskurz ve Velké Británii a ve Francii během irácké krize (září 2002-březen 2003). *[In Czech]*; (Public opinion and foreign political discourse in France and the United Kingdom during the Iraq crisis (September 2002-March 2003).) *[Summary]*. Jan Stuchlík. **Mez. Vzt.** 39:4 2004 pp.23-49.

2620   Victory has many friends: U.S. public opinion and the use of military force, 1981-2005. Richard C. Eichenberg. **Int. Secur.** 30:1 Summer:2005 pp.140-177.

2621   Who cares about human rights? Sam McFarland; Melissa Mathews. **Pol. Psychol.** 26:3 6:2005 pp.365-385.

2622   Why are Latin Americans so unhappy about reforms? Ugo Panizza; Mónica Yañez. **J. Appl. Econ.** VIII:1 5:2005 pp.1-29.

D.2.4:   Political culture
**   Culture politique**

2623   All right now? Explaining the successes and failures of the Slovak centre-right. Tim Haughton; Marek Rybář. **J. Comm. S. Transit. Pol.** 20:3 9:2004 pp.115-132.

2624   Authority orientations and democratic attitudes: a test of the "Asian values" hypothesis. Russell J. Dalton; Nhu-Ngoc T. Ong. **Japanese J. Pol. Sci.** 6:2 8:2005 pp.211-232.

2625   Belarus: Politische Kultur und Systemwechsel. *[In German]*; (Belarus — political culture and systemic change.) Astrid Lorenz. **Welt Trends** 47 Summer:2005 pp.141-153.

2626   Die Berliner Topographie des Terrors in der NS-Gedenkstättenlandschaft. *[In German]*; [Berlin's Topography of Terror and other Nazism memorials]. Reinhard Rürup. **Vorgänge** 44:1(169) 3:2005 pp.75-92.

2627   The British public and political attitude expression: the emergence of a self-expressive political culture? James Stanyer. **Cont. Pol.** 11:1 3:2005 pp.19-32.

2628   Community, identity and the state: comparing Africa, Eurasia, Latin America and the Middle East. Moshe Gammer [Ed.]. New York, London: Routledge, 2004. 188p. *ISBN: 071465664X, 0714685682. Includes index.*

2629   The conservative assault on America: cultural politics, education and the new authoritarianism. Henry A. Giroux. **Cult. Pol.** 1:2 7:2005 pp.139-163.

2630   A consistência democrática na Venezuela em tempos de mudança política. *[In Portuguese]*; (The democratic consistency of Venezuela in a political changing period.) *[Summary]*. Valia Pereira Almao. **Opin. Pub.** XI:1 3:2005 pp.128-146.

2631   Crossnational survey research and subnational pluralism. Kathleen M. Dowley; Brian D. Silver. **Int. J. Publ. Opin. Res.** 17:2 Summer:2005 pp.226-238.

2632   Cultura política en el escenario de la globalización. *[In Spanish]*; [Political culture in the globalization scenario] *[Summary]*. José Guadalupe Vargas Hernández. **Convergencia** 11:36 9-12:2004 pp.159-187.

2633   Cultura política, ideologia e comportamento eleitoral: alguns apontamentos teóricos e reflexões sobre o caso brasileiro. *[In Portuguese]*; (Political culture, ideology, and electoral behavior: some theoretical remarks and reflections about the Brazilian case.) *[Summary]*. Julian Borba. **Opin. Pub.** XI:1 3:2005 pp.147-168.

2634   Culture, capitalism, and democracy in the New America. Richard Harvey Brown. New Haven CT: Yale University Press, 2005. viii, 355p. *ISBN: 0300100256. Includes bibliographical references (p. 299-342) and index.*

2635   Democracy and its friendly critics: Tocqueville and political life today. Peter Augustine Lawler [Ed.]. Lanham MD: Lexington Books, 2004. xi, 191p. *ISBN: 0739107615, 0739107623. Includes bibliographical references and index.*

2636   Democracy off balance: freedom of expression and hate propaganda law in Canada. Stefan Braun. Toronto: University of Toronto Press, 2004. ix, 384p. *ISBN: 0802089593, 0802086365. Includes bibliographical references and index.*

2637   Democratic attitudes and practices in Iraq. Adeed Dawisha. **Mid. East J.** 59:1 Winter:2005 pp.11-30.

2638   Desconfiança política na América Latina. *[In Portuguese]*; (Political mistrust in Latin America.) *[Summary]*. Timothy J. Power; Giselle D. Jamison. **Opin. Pub.** XI:1 3:2005 pp.64-93.

2639   The enduring place of hierarchy in world politics: tracing the social logics of hierarchy and political change. John M. Hobson; J.C. Sharman. **Euro. J. Int. Rel.** 11:1 3:2005 pp.63-98.

2640   Generation X: rids af en ny politisk kultur. *[In Danish]*; (Generation X: sketches of a new political culture.) *[Summary]*. Thomas Palner. **Politica** 36:3 9:2004 pp.254-270.

2641   Global governance, dam conflicts, and participation. Denis Goulet. **Hum. Rights Q.** 27:3 8:2005 pp.881-907.

2642   Happy days and wonder years: the fifties and the sixties in contemporary cultural politics. Daniel Marcus. New Brunswick NJ: Rutgers University Press, 2004. viii, 264p. *ISBN: 0813533902, 0813533910. Includes bibliographical references and index.*

2643   Industrial location and voter participation in Europe. Marc L. Busch; Eric Reinhardt. **Br. J. Pol. Sci.** 35:4 10:2005 pp.713-730.

2644   The miseducation of the West: how schools and the media distort our understanding of the Islamic world. Joe L. Kincheloe [Ed.]; Shirley R. Steinberg [Ed.]. Westport CT: Praeger, 2004. viii, 208p. *ISBN: 0275981606. Includes bibliographical references and index. (Series:* Reverberations: cultural studies and education).

2645   National identity and public support for political and economic reform in Ukraine. Stephen Shulman. **Slavic R.** 64:1 Spring:2005 pp.59-87.

2646   Research note: libertarian-authoritarian value change in Britain, 1974-2001. James Tilley. **Pol. S.** 53:2 6:2005 pp.442-453.

2647   Responsivität und Responsivitätswahrnehmung — Thesen zu einem undurchsichtigen Verhältnis. *[In German]*; (External and internal political efficacy. Theses on an obscure relationship.) Brigitte Geißel. **Z. Pol.wissen.** 14:4 2004 pp.1235-1255.

2648   The role of ideology. Ladan Boroumand. **J. Democ.** 16:4 10:2005 pp.52-63.

2649   Russkii neomarksizm. *[In Russian]*; (Russian Neomarxism.) V. Pastukhov. **Obshch. Nauki Sovrem.** 4 2004 pp.97-107.

2650   Small nations but great differences: political orientations and cultures of the Crimean Tatars and the Gagauz. Ivan Katchanovski. **Euro.-Asia S.** 57:6 9:2005 pp.877-894.

2651   State political culture, primary frontloading, and democratic voice in presidential nominations: 1972-2000. Christopher J. Carman; David C. Barker. **Electoral S.** 24:4 12:2005 pp.665-687.

2652   Transformatsiia ideologicheskikh tsennostei i politicheskikh predpochtenii rossiian. *[In Russian]*; (Transformation of the ideological values and political preferences of Russians.)

[Summary]. Vladimir V. Petukhov; Valery V. Fedorov. **Mon. Obshch. Mnen.** 2(74) 4-6:2005 pp.4-18.

2653 The uses of historical memory. Eric Davis. **J. Democ.** 16:3 7:2005 pp.54-68.

2654 What do they know and how do they know it? Citizen awareness of context. Brady Baybeck; Scott D. McClurg. **Am. Pol. Res.** 33:4 7:2005 pp.492-520.

2655 What is right in Italy? Gianfranco Pasquino. **Sth. Euro. Soc. Pol.** 10:2 7:2005 pp.177-190.

Political socialization
Socialisation politique

2656 L'adoption du projet de loi 112 au Québec : le produit d'une mobilisation ou une simple question de conjoncture politique? *[In French]*; [Adoption of the bill 112 in Quebec: a product of mobilization or a simple question of political circumstances?] *[Summary]*; *[Summary in French]*. Pascale Dufour. **Pol. et Soc.** 23:2-3 2004 pp.159-182.

2657 Aile siyasi etkilerini kaybetmekte midir? Siyasi parti tercihinde nesiller arası değişim. *[In Turkish]*; (Do family lose their political efficacy or not? Revisiting intergenerational transmission of party identification.) *[Summary]*. Mehtap Yeşilorman. **Bilig** 32 Winter:2005 pp.109-124.

2658 Are political orientations genetically transmitted? John R. Alford; Carolyn L. Funk; John R. Hibbing. **Am. Pol. Sci. R.** 99:2 5:2005 pp.153-167.

2659 'Bowling together' isn't a cure-all: the relationship between social capital and political trust in South Korea; *[Summary in French]*. Ji-young Kim. **Int. Pol. Sci. R.** 26:2 4:2005 pp.193-213.

2660 Ciudadanía multicultural: las organizaciones vecinales indígenas de Sinamaica. *[In Spanish]*; (Multicultural citizenships: neighborhood indigenous organizations in Sinamaica.) Nila Leal González; Maia Gutiérrez García. **Cuest. Pol.** 33 7-12:2004 pp.53-76.

2661 Civic engagement and sustainable cities in the United States. Kent Portney. **Publ. Admin. R.** 65:5 9-10:2005 pp.579-591.

2662 Community planning: fostering participation in the congested state? Richard Cowell. **Loc. Govt. S.** 30:4 Winter:2004 pp.497-518.

2663 Democratic disobedience. Daniel Markovits. **Yale Law J.** 114:8 6:2005 pp.1897-1952.

2664 La démocratie en métropoles: gouvernance, participation et citoyenneté. *[In French]*; (Democracy in the metropolis: governance, participation and citizenship.) *[Summary]*. Bernard Jouve. **R. Fran. Sci. Pol.** 55:2 4:2005 pp.317-337.

2665 The development of stable party support: electoral dynamics in post-communist Europe. Margit Tavits. **Am. J. Pol. Sci.** 49:2 4:2005 pp.283-298.

2666 Direct democracy works. John G. Matsusaka. **J. Econ. Persp.** 19:2 Spring:2005 pp.185-206.

2667 Dynamics of interpersonal political environment and party identification: longitudinal studies of voting in Japan and New Zealand. Ken'ichi Ikeda; James H. Liu; Masahiko Aida; Marc Wilson. **Pol. Psychol.** 26:4 8:2005 pp.517-542.

2668 El ejercicio de pensar: the rise and fall of Pensamiento Crítico. Kepa Artaraz. **B. Lat. Am. Res.** 24:3 7:2005 pp.348-366.

2669 Elites, social movements, and the law: the case of affirmative action. Tomiko Brown-Nagin. **Columb. Law R.** 105:5 6:2005 pp.1436-1528.

2670 E-political empowerment: age effects or attitudinal barriers? Lisa E. Thrane; Mack C. Shelley, II; Stuart W. Shulman; Sally R. Beisser; Teresa B. Larson. **J. E-Gov.** 1:4 2004 pp.21-38.

2671 Les Français et la politique : entre désenchantement et colère. *[In French]*; [French people and politics: between disenchantment and anger]. Brice Teinturier. **Etat Opin.** 2004 pp.11-33.

2672   Gondoljuk újra a polgári radikálisokat. *[In Hungarian]*; (Reconsider civil radicalism.) Gábor G. Fodor. Budapest: L'Harmattan, 2004. 167p. *ISBN: 9639457736. Includes bibliographical references (p. 153-167).*

2673   Group-based resources and political participation among Asian Americans. Janelle S. Wong; Pei-te Lien; M. Margaret Conway. **Am. Pol. Res.** 33:4 7:2005 pp.545-576.

2674   Imperial subjects, national citizenship, and corporate subjects: cycles of political participation/exclusion in the modern world-system. Satoshi Ikeda. **Citiz. S.** 8:4 12:2004 pp.333-347.

2675   Indonesia: the politics of inclusion. Andrew Rosser; Kurnya Roesad; Donni Edwin. **J. Contemp. Asia** 35:1 2005 pp.53-77.

2676   'Just because we are amateurs doesn't mean we aren't professional': the importance of expert activists in tenant participation. Liz Millward. **Publ. Admin.** 83:3 2005 pp.735-752.

2677   The limits of civic activism: cautionary tales on the use of politics. Robert Weissberg. New Brunswick NJ: Transaction Publishers, 2005. xi, 349p. *ISBN: 0765802619. Includes bibliographical references (p. 325-341) and index.*

2678   The micro-politics of deliberation: case studies in public participation. Marian Barnes; Andrew Knops; Janet Newman; Helen Sullivan. **Cont. Pol.** 10:2 6:2004 pp.93-110.

2679   Les nouveaux visages de l'engagement. *[In French]*; [The new faces of participation]. Cadres CFDT. **Cadres CFDT** 409 4:2004 pp.7-87.

2680   Novye tendentsii vospriiatiia vlasti v Rossii. *[In Russian]*; (New tendencies in the perception of the power in Russia.) *[Summary]*. E.B. Shestopal. **Polis [Moscow]** 3(86) 2005 pp.137-151.

2681   One size does not fit all: matching breadth of stakeholder participation to watershed group accomplishments. Tomas M. Koontz; Elizabeth Moore Johnson. **Policy Sci.** 37:2 6:2004 pp.185-204.

2682   Osallistuako vai ei? Poliittisen osallistumisen lähtökohtia monimutkaistuvassa demokratiassa. *[In Finnish]*; [To participate or not? Basis for political participation in a more and more complicated democracy] *[Summary]*. Tiina Rättilä. **Kunnall. Aikak.** 32:4 2004 pp.308-322.

2683   Parents, power and public participation: sure start, an experiment in new labour governance. Ulla Gustafsson; Stephen Driver. **Soc. Policy Admin.** 39:5 10:2005 pp.528-543.

2684   La participación ciudadana en el marco de la educación vial. *[In Spanish]*; (Citizen participation within the framework of the terrestrial education.) Alix Aguirre A.; Nelly Manasía F.; Luz María de Martínez de C. **Cuest. Pol.** 33 7-12:2004 pp.27-52.

2685   Participatory governance: planning, conflict mediation and public decision making in civil society. W. Robert Lovan [Ed.]; Michael Murray [Ed.]; Ron Shaffer [Ed.]. Aldershot: Ashgate, 2004. xvi, 263p. *ISBN: 0754618528. Includes bibliographical references and index.*

2686   Party e-newsletters in the UK: a return to direct political communication? Nigel Jackson. **J. E-Gov.** 1:4 2004 pp.39-62.

2687   Party identification and core political values. Paul Goren. **Am. J. Pol. Sci.** 49:4 10:2005 pp.881-896.

2688   Peasant 'participation', rural property and the state in Western Mexico. Monique Nuijten. **J. Peasant S.** 31:2 1:2004 pp.181-209.

2689   "People's houses" as a nationwide project for ideological mobilization in early republican Turkey. Sefa Şimşek. **Turkish S.** 6:1 3:2005 pp.71-91.

2690   Perspektivy transformatsii. *[In Russian]*; (Prospects for transformation.) Vladimir Petukhov. **Svobod. Mysl'** 6 2005 pp.60-74.

2691   Political participation and civic self-organization in Russia. Vladimir Petukhov. **Rus. Pol. Law** 43:3 5-6:2005 pp.6-24.

2692   Political participation as an engine of social solidarity: a sceptical view. Shlomi Segall. **Pol. S.** 53:2 6:2005 pp.362-378.

2693   Political participation on the local level: the role of the city districts in Slovenia. Marjan Brezovsek; Miro Hacek. **Cent. Euro. Pol. Sci. R.** 5:15 Spring:2004 pp.74-94.

133

2694   Politics in the supermarket: political consumerism as a form of political participation. Dietlind Stolle; Marc Hooghe; Michele Micheletti. **Int. Pol. Sci. R.** 26:3 7:2005 pp.245-269.

2695   Popular political support in urban China. Jie Chen. Washington DC; Stanford CA: Woodrow Wilson Center Press; Stanford University Press, 2004. xvi, 230p. *ISBN: 0804749590, 0804750572. Includes bibliographical references (p. 205-223) and index.*

2696   Poverty alleviation and participatory development in the Philippines. Ben Reid. **J. Contemp. Asia** 35:1 2005 pp.29-52.

2697   Priming partisan evaluations of congress. David C. Kimball. **Legis. Stud. Q.** XXX:1 2:2005 pp.63-84.

2698   Progressive activism in a neoliberal context: the case of efforts to retain public housing in the United States. Jason Hackworth. **S. Pol. Econ.** 75 Spring:2005 pp.29-51.

2699   The public spheres of unprotected workers. Matt Davies. **Glo. Soc.** 19:2 4:2005 pp.131-154.

2700   Rationalität, Vernunft und erweiterte Denkungsart. *[In German]*; [Rationality, reason and the enhanced way of thinking]. Ingo Juchler. **Z. Pol.** 52:1 3:2005 pp.97-121.

2701   Réalité économique et liberté d'action politique. *[In French]*; [Economic reality and freedom of political action]. Dominique Strauss-Kahn. **Banquet** 19-20 1:2004 pp.269-280.

2702   Reassessing popular participation in Uganda. F. Golooba-Mutebi. **Publ. Admin. Dev.** 24:4 10:2004 pp.289-304.

2703   Revendications démocratiques en Kabylie. *[In French]*; [Democratic claims in Kabyl region]. Bruno Callies de Salies. **Défense Nat.** 60:8-9 8-9:2004 pp.169-181.

2704   The role of nonformal education in promoting democratic attitudes: findings from Senegal. Michelle Kuenzi. **Democratization** 12:2 4:2005 pp.223-243.

2705   Spolne razlike i školsko iskustvo u razvoju svijesti i prakse građanstva mladih. *[In Croatian]*; (Gender differences and educational experience in the development of the sense and the practice of citizenship of young people.) Vladimir Vujčić. **Pol. Misao** 41:3 2004 pp.143-155.

2706   Strength in numbers: group size and political mobilization. Felix Oberholzer-Gee; Joel Waldfogel. **J. Law Econ.** XLVIII:1 4:2005 pp.73-91.

2707   Support for democracy in Eastern and Western Germany: an attempt to explain the differences; *[Summary in French]*; *[Summary in German]*. Detlef Pollack. **Euro. J. Sociol.** XLV:2 2004 pp.257-272.

2708   Theorizing the authentic: identity, engagement, and public space. Kelly B. Campbell. **Admin. Soc.** 36:6 1:2005 pp.688-705.

2709   Les transformations de l'action collective. *[In French]*; [The transformations of collective action]. Revue nouvelle. **R. Nouvelle** 118:3 13:2004 pp.20-71.

2710   Understanding the political culture of Hong Kong: the paradox of activism and depoliticization. Wai-man Lam; Ming K. Chan [Foreword]. Armonk NY: M.E. Sharpe, 2004. xxvi, 292p. *ISBN: 0765613131, 076561314X. Includes bibliographical references (p. 265-280) and index.* (Series: Hong Kong becoming China. Asia and the Pacific).

2711   Uninterested youth? Young people's attitudes towards party politics in Britain. Matt Henn; Mark Weinstein; Sarah Forrest. **Pol. S.** 53:3 10:2005 pp.556-578.

2712   Virtuous circle or cul de sac? Social capital and political participation in New Zealand. Andrew McVey; Jack Vowles. **Pol. Sci.** 57:1 6:2005 pp.5-20.

2713   What's left of citizenship? Peter Nyers. **Citiz. S.** 8:3 9:2004 pp.203-216.

2714   When popular participation won't improve service provision: primary health care in Uganda. Frederick Golooba-Mutebi. **Dev. Policy R.** 23:2 3:2005 pp.165-182.

2715   Youth, politics and socialization. Marc Hooghe; M. Kent Jennings; Laura Stoker; Judith Torney-Purta; Carolyn Henry Barber; Wendy Klandl Richardson; Daniel Rubenson; André Blais; Patrick Fournier; Elisabeth Gidengil; Neil Nevitte; Dietlind Stolle. **Acta Pol.** 39:4 12:2004 pp.331-441. *Collection of 5 articles.*

D.2.5:   Elections
                Élections

Electoral behaviour
Comportement électoral

2716   Abstention in daylight: strategic calculus of voting in the European Parliament. A.G. Noury. **Publ. Choice** 121:1-2 10:2004 pp.179-211.

2717   L'abstention, symptôme des mutations démocratiques européennes. *[In French]*; [Abstentionism, symptom of European democratic transformations]. Christine Bout De l'An; Fabienne Greffet. **R. Pol. Parl.** 106:1031 7-9:2004 pp.55-66.

2718   All things considered: systematic cognitive processing and electoral decision-making. David C. Barker; Susan B. Hansen. **J. Pol.** 67:2 5:2005 pp.319-344.

2719   Amas de casa, televisión y participación política. México, elecciones 2003. *[In Spanish]*; [Housewives, television and political participation. Mexico, elections 2003]. Aimée Vega Montiel. **R. Mexicana Cien. Pol.** XLVI:190 1-4:2004 pp.97-112.

2720   Ambivalence, information, and electoral choice. Scott J. Basinger; Howard Lavine. **Am. Pol. Sci. R.** 99:2 5:2005 pp.169-184.

2721   Approval voting and parochialism. Jonathan Baron; Nicole Y. Altman; Stephan Kroll. **J. Confl. Resol.** 49:6 12:2005 pp.895-907.

2722   Are politics local? An analysis of voting patterns in 23 democracies. Scott Morgenstern; Stephen M. Swindle. **Comp. Pol. S.** 38:2 3:2005 pp.143-170.

2723   The components of elections: district heterogeneity, district-time effects, and volatility. Scott Morgenstern; Richard F. Potthoff. **Electoral S.** 24:1 3:2005 pp.17-40.

2724   Decomposition of regional voting in South Korea: ideological conflicts and regional interests. Woojin Moon. **Party Pol.** 11:5 2005 pp.579-599.

2725   Direct or indirect? Assessing two approaches to the measurement of strategic voting. André Blais; Robert Young; Martin Turcotte. **Electoral S.** 24:2 6:2005 pp.163-176.

2726   Disengaged or disenchanted? The vote 'against all' in post-communist Russia. Derek S. Hutcheson. **J. Comm. S. Transit. Pol.** 20:1 3:2004 pp.98-121.

2727   Economic voting and electoral behavior: how do individual, local, and national factors affect the partisan choice? Andrew Leigh. **Econ. Pol.** 17:2 7:2005 pp.265-296.

2728   Economics, ideology and vote: Southern Europe, 1985-2000. A. Freire; M.C. Lobo. **Euro. J. Pol. Res.** 44:4 6:2005 pp.493-518.

2729   The effect of socioeconomic factors on voter turnout in Finland: a register-based study of 2.9 million voters. P. Martikainen; T. Martikainen; H. Wass. **Écon. Sociét.** 44:5 8:2005 pp.645-669.

2730   Election forecasting: principles and practice. Michael S. Lewis-Beck. **Br. J. Pol. Int. Rel.** 7:2 5:2005 pp.145-164.

2731   Elections and voters, 1974-2004: old cleavages and new issues. Ilias Nicolacopoulos. **West Euro. Pol.** 28:2 3:2005 pp.260-278.

2732   The electoral success of multi-racial parties in Trinidad and Tobago and Guyana; *[Summary in French]*. Sara Abraham. **Canadian J. Lat. Am. Caribbean S.** 30:60 2005 pp.117-154.

2733   Elektoral'noe uchastie i absenteizm v rossiiskikh regionakh: zakonomernosti i tendentsii. *[In Russian]*; (Electoral participation and absenteeism in the Russian regions: regulation and trends.) A.S. Akhremenko. **Vest. Mosk. Univ. 12 Pol.** 3 5-6:2005 pp.95-113.

2734   Explaining vote switching across first and second-order elections: evidence from Europe. Cliff Carrubba; Richard J. Timpone. **Comp. Pol. S.** 38:3 4:2005 pp.260-281.

2735   Exploring voter alignments in Africa: core and swing voters in Ghana. Staffan I. Lindberg; Minion K.C. Morrison. **J. Mod. Afr. S.** 43:4 12:2005 pp.565-586.

2736 Forecasting the 2005 general election: a neural network approach. Roman Borisyuk; Galina Borisyuk; Colin Rallings; Michael Thrasher. **Br. J. Pol. Int. Rel.** 7:2 5:2005 pp.199-209.

2737 'Going bipartisan': politics by other means. Peter Trubowitz; Nicole Mellow. **Pol. Sci. Q.** 120:3 Fall:2005 pp.433-453.

2738 How postregistration laws affect the turnout of citizens registered to vote. Raymond E. Wolfinger; Benjamin Highton; Megan Mullin. **State Pol. Policy Q.** 5:1 Spring:2005 pp.1-23.

2739 Identidade, oposição e pragmatismo: o conteúdo estratégico da decisão eleitoral em 13 anos de eleições. *[In Portuguese]*; (Identity, oposition and pragmatism: strategic content of electoral decision in 13 election years.) *[Summary]*. Elizabeth Balbachevsky; Denilde Oliveira Holzhacker. **Opin. Pub.** X:2 10:2004 pp.242-253.

2740 The impact of employment status on voting behavior. Robert Grafstein. **J. Pol.** 67:3 8:2005 pp.804-824.

2741 Income tax and elections in Britain, 1950-2001. Paul Johnson; Frances Lynch; John Geoffrey Walker. **Electoral S.** 24:3 9:2005 pp.393-408.

2742 O índice de participação e a importância da educação. *[In Portuguese]*; (The index of participation and the role of education.) *[Summary]*. José Paulo Martins Júnior; Humberto Dantas. **Opin. Pub.** X:2 10:2004 pp.268-287.

2743 The indirect effects of discredited stereotypes in judgments of Jewish leaders. Adam J. Berinsky; Tali Mendelberg. **Am. J. Pol. Sci.** 49:4 10:2005 pp.845-864.

2744 Monotonicity and its cognates in the theory of choice. H. Nurmi. **Publ. Choice** 121:1-2 10:2004 pp.25-49.

2745 Parties and electoral behavior in southern Europe. Richard Gunther. **Comp. Pol.** 37:3 4:2005 pp.253-276.

2746 The phenomenon of Puerto Rican voting. Luis Raul Camara Fuertes. Gainesville FL: University Press of Florida, 2004. xvi, 144p. *ISBN: 0813027195. Includes bibliographical references (p. 129-138) and index. (Series:* New directions in Puerto Rican studies).

2747 Political cynicism, public interest blackballing and voter turnout: the case of South Korea's 2000 national assembly elections. Sunwoong Kim; Kisuk Cho. **Japanese J. Pol. Sci.** 5:1 5:2004 pp.91-112.

2748 The political economy of UK party support, 1997-2004: forecasts for the 2005 general election. David Sanders. **Jnl. Ele. Pub. Op. Par.** 15:1 4:2005 pp.47-71.

2749 Political knowledge and enlightened preferences: party choice through the electoral cycle. Robert Andersen; James Tilley; Anthony F. Heath. **Br. J. Pol. Sci.** 35:2 4:2005 pp.285-302.

2750 Popularity function forecasts for the 2005 UK general election. David Sanders. **Br. J. Pol. Int. Rel.** 7:2 5:2005 pp.174-190.

2751 Protest voting in Austria, Denmark, and Norway. Johannes Bergh. **Scand. Pol. S.** 27:4 2004 pp.367-389.

2752 Redibujando el mapa electoral chileno: incidencia de factores socioeconómicos y género en las urnas. *[In Spanish]*; [Redrawing Chile's electoral map: the incidence of socio-economic and gender factors in the ballot box] *[Summary]*. David Altman. **R. Cien. Pol.** XXIV:2 2004 pp.49-66.

2753 Social norms and the paradox of elections' turnout. J. Amaro de Matos; P.P. Barros. **Publ. Choice** 121:1-2 10:2004 pp.239-255.

2754 Spatial scale and the neighbourhood effect: multinomial models of voting at two recent British general elections. Ron Johnston; Carol Propper; Simon Burgess; Rebecca Sarker; Anne Bolster; Kelvyn Jones. **Br. J. Pol. Sci.** 35:3 7:2005 pp.487-514.

2755 Strategic ticket splitting and the personal vote in mixed-member electoral systems. Robert G. Moser; Ethan Scheiner. **Legis. Stud. Q.** XXX:2 5:2005 pp.259-276.

2756 Teorías del comportamiento electoral y algunas de sus aplicaciones. *[In Spanish]*; [Theories of electoral behavior and some of their applications]. Murilo Kuschik. **R. Mexicana Cien. Pol.** XLVI:190 1-4:2004 pp.47-70.

2757 Theoretic aspects of electoral behaviour. Man Mohan Singh Negi. **Indian J. Pol. Sci.** LXVI:1 1-3:2005 pp.95-104.

2758   The trail of votes in Ukraine's 1998, 1999, and 2002 elections. Mikhail Myagkov; Peter C. Ordeshook. **Post-Sov. Aff.** 21:1 1-3:2005 pp.56-71.

2759   Voting behavior and the electoral context of government formation. Garrett Glasgow; R. Michael Alvarez. **Electoral S.** 24:2 6:2005 pp.245-264.

2760   Why some anti-immigrant parties fail and others succeed: a two-step model of aggregate electoral support. Wouter van der Brug; Meindert Fennema; Jean Tillie. **Comp. Pol. S.** 38:5 6:2005 pp.537-573.

Electoral campaigning
Campagne électorale

2761   American-style of campaigning in Western Europe. Hortenzia Hosszú. **Cent. Euro. Pol. Sci. R.** 5:15 Spring:2004 pp.136-177.

2762   Análisis de contenido del noticiario CNI Canal 40 (durante la tercera semana del mes de mayo) referente a las campañas electorales para diputados federales. *[In Spanish]*; [Content analysis of the CNI newscast Canal 40 (during the third week of May) regarding the federal deputies electoral campaigning]. Rafael Espinoza. **R. Mexicana Cien. Pol.** XLVI:190 1-4:2004 pp.179-206.

2763   The boundaries of campaign finance reform: should the bipartisan campaign reform act regulate redistricting? Anna Wagner. **Columb. Law R.** 105:5 6:2005 pp.1597-1634.

2764   Brand leaders: Clinton, Blair and the limitations of the permanent campaign. Catherine Needham. **Pol. S.** 53:2 6:2005 pp.343-361.

2765   Campaigns, political preferences and turnout: an empirical study of the 1997 French legislative elections. Christine Fauvelle-Aymar; Abel François. **Fre. Pol.** 3:1 4:2005 pp.49-72.

2766   Candidate qualities through a partisan lens: a theory of trait ownership. Danny Hayes. **Am. J. Pol. Sci.** 49:4 10:2005 pp.908-923.

2767   Content and effects of media in the 2004 US presidential campaign. Mitchell S. McKinney; Mary C. Banwart; Lynda Lee Kaid; Daniela V. Dimitrova; Andrew Paul Williams; Kaye D. Trammell; Monica Postelnicu; Kristen D. Landreville; Justin D. Martin; John C. Tedesco; Margaret Scammell; Wojciech Cwalina; Andrzej Falkowski; Walter R. Mears; Candy Crowley; Deborah Potter; Merrie Spaeth; Steve Davis; Roland Schroeder; Moritz Kralemann. **Journalism S.** 6:2 5:2005 pp.151-247. *Collection of 10 articles.*

2768   Débats télévisés et évaluations des candidats: la représentation visuelle des politiciens canadiens agit-elle dans la formation des préférences des électeurs québécois? *[In French]*; [Television debates and candidate evaluation in Quebec]. Thierry Giasson; Richard Nadeau; Éric Bélanger. **Can. J. Pol.** 38:4 12:2005 pp.867-896.

2769   Elecciones 2003: spots políticos y cultura política. *[In Spanish]*; [Elections 2003: political spots and political culture]. Concepción Virriel López. **R. Mexicana Cien. Pol.** XLVI:190 1-4:2004 pp.141-162.

2770   Electores persuadidos. Democracia de masas y televisión. *[In Spanish]*; [Persuaded voters. Mass democracy and television]. Florence Toussaint. **R. Mexicana Cien. Pol.** XLVI:190 1-4:2004 pp.15-29.

2771   Expression v. equality: the politics of campaign finance reform. J. Tobin. Grant; Thomas J. Rudolph. Columbus OH: Ohio State University Press, 2004. x, 144p. *ISBN: 0814209653, 0814251277, 0814290515. Includes bibliographical references (p. 129-137) and index.*

2772   The impact of campaign reform on political discourse. Darrell M. West; L. Sandy Maisel; Brett M. Clifton. **Pol. Sci. Q.** 120:4 Winter:2005-2006 pp.637-651.

2773   The impact of media bias: how editorial slant affects voters. James N. Druckman; Michael Parkin. **J. Pol.** 67:4 11:2005 pp.1030-1049.

2774   Internet en las elecciones del 2003. *[In Spanish]*; [Internet and the 2003 elections]. Delia Crovi. **R. Mexicana Cien. Pol.** XLVI:190 1-4:2004 pp.113-128.

2775 Issue-related learning in a gubernatorial campaign: a panel study. Stephen C. Craig; James G. Kane; Jason Gainous. **Pol. Communic.** 22:4 10-12:2005 pp.483-503.

2776 Keeping the other candidate guessing: electoral competition when preferences are private information. Adam Meirowitz. **Publ. Choice** 122:3-4 3:2005 pp.299-318.

2777 Media and momentum: strategic contributing in a big-city mayoral election. Timothy B. Krebs; David B. Holian. **Urb. Aff. R.** 40:5 5:2005 pp.614-633.

2778 Media matter: how newspapers and television news cover campaigns and influence voters. James N. Druckman. **Pol. Communic.** 22:4 10-12:2005 pp.463-481.

2779 A meta-analysis of campaign contributions' impact on roll call voting. Douglas D. Roscoe; Shannon Jenkins. **Soc. Sci. Q.** 86:1 3:2005 pp.52-68.

2780 The mobilization of core supporters: campaigns, turnout, and electoral composition in United States presidential elections. Thomas M. Holbrook; Scott D. McClurg. **Am. J. Pol. Sci.** 49:4 10:2005 pp.689-703.

2781 A model of political competition in the underlying space of ideology. C.A. Bonilla. **Publ. Choice** 121:1-2 10:2004 pp.51-67.

2782 Money matters in party-centered politics: campaign spending in Korean congressional elections. Myungsoon Shin; Youngjae Jin; Donald A. Gross; Kihong Eom. **Electoral S.** 24:1 3:2005 pp.85-101.

2783 Negative campaigning: an analysis of U.S. Senate elections. Richard R. Lau; Gerald M. Pomper. Lanham MD: Rowman & Littlefield, 2004. xi, 177p. *ISBN: 074252731X, 0742527328. Includes bibliographical references (p. 155-167) and index. (Series:* Campaigning American style).

2784 La neutralidad como forma de encuadre en una campaña electoral. *[In Spanish]*; (The neutrality as form of framing in an electoral campaign.) *[Summary]*. Patricio Dussaillant. **Communic. y. Soc.** XVII:2 12:2004 pp.45-71.

2785 Obilježja pakiranja politike u izbornoj kampanji HDZ-a i SDP-a 2003. godine. *[In Croatian]*; (Features of packaging politics in the electoral campaigns of HDZ and SDP in 2003.) *[Summary]*. Dražen Lalić. **Pol. Misao** 41:1 2004 pp.55-73.

2786 Party control: electoral campaigning in Vietnam in the run-up to the May 2002 national assembly elections. Martin Gainsborough. **Pac. Aff.** 78:1 Spring:2005 pp.57-76.

2787 Pathways to power: the role of political parties in women's national political representation. Sheri Kunovich; Pamela Paxton. **Am. J. Sociol.** 111:2 9:2005 pp.505-552.

2788 Perverse accountability: a formal model of machine politics with evidence from Argentina. Susan C. Stokes. **Am. Pol. Sci. R.** 99:3 8:2005 pp.315-326.

2789 Physische Attraktivität und Wahlerfolg. Eine empirische Analyse am Beispiel der Wahlkreiskandidaten bei der Bundestagswahl 2002. *[In German]*; (Physical attractiveness and electoral success. An empirical investigation on candidates in constituencies at the German federal election 2002.) Markus Klein; Ulrich Rosar. **Polit. Viertel.** 46:2 6:2005 pp.263-287.

2790 Polling politics, media, and election campaigns. Lawrence R. Jacobs; Robert Y. Shapiro; Michael W. Traugott; Mark M. Blumenthal; Robert P. Daves; Frank Newport; Kathleen A. Frankovic; Tom Rosenstiel; Thomas E. Patterson; Bruce W. Hardy; Kathleen Hall Jamieson; Gary Langer; Jon Cohen; Daniel E. Bergan; Alan S. Gerber; Donald P. Green; Costas Panagopoulos; Martin Gilens. **Publ. Opin. Q.** 69:5 2005 pp.635-796. *Collection of 11 articles.*

2791 Pre-electoral coalitions in comparative perspective: a test of existing hypotheses. Sona N. Golder. **Electoral S.** 24:4 12:2005 pp.643-663.

2792 Prensa y elecciones 2003. *[In Spanish]*; [Press and elections in 2003]. Ilya Adler. **R. Mexicana Cien. Pol.** XLVI:190 1-4:2004 pp.129-139.

2793 Priming gender: campaigning on women's issues in U.S. senate elections. Brian F. Schaffner. **Am. J. Pol. Sci.** 49:4 10:2005 pp.803-817.

2794 La producción de noticias. Un acercamiento a la percepción, conocimiento y visión de la política mexicana de los periodistas y el proceso electoral federal del 2003. *[In Spanish]*; [News production. An approach to journalists' perception, knowledge and vision of

Mexican politics and the 2003 electoral process]. Karla A. Planter Pérez. **R. Mexicana Cien. Pol.** XLVI:190 1-4:2004 pp.207-219.

2795 Ralph Nader's campaign strategy in the 2000 U.S. presidential election. Barry C. Burden. **Am. Pol. Res.** 33:5 9:2005 pp.672-699.

2796 Reform in a cold climate: change in US campaign finance law. Dean McSweeney. **Gov. Oppos.** 40:4 Autumn:2005 pp.492-514.

2797 Simbolismo y ritual en la politica mexicana. *[In Spanish]*; [Symbolism and ritual in Mexican politics]. Larissa Adler-Lomnitz; Rodrigo Salazar Elena; Ilya Adler. Mexico City: Universidad Nacional Autonoma de Mexico; Siglo XXI, 2004. 311p. *ISBN: 9682325420, 9703218334.*

2798 Sneaking into the flying circus: how the media turn our presidential campaigns into freak shows. Alexandra Pelosi. New York: Free Press, 2005. xiv, 299p. *ISBN: 0743263049. Includes index.*

2799 State campaign finance laws and interest group electioneering activities. Robert E. Hogan. **J. Pol.** 67:3 8:2005 pp.887-906.

2800 Talking the vote: why presidential candidates hit the talk show circuit. Matthew A. Baum. **Am. J. Pol. Sci.** 49:2 4:2005 pp.213-234.

2801 Television and neopopulism in Latin America: media effects in Brazil and Peru; *[Summary in Spanish]*. Taylor C. Boas. **Lat. Am. Res. R.** 40:2 2005 pp.27-49.

2802 Television news, Mexico's 2000 elections and media effects in emerging democracies. Chappell Lawson; James A. McCann. **Br. J. Pol. Sci.** 35:1 1:2005 pp.1-30.

2803 Televisión y tratamiento de la información político-electoral. *[In Spanish]*; [Television and political-electoral data processing]. Martha Alicia Márquez Rodríguez. **R. Mexicana Cien. Pol.** XLVI:190 1-4:2004 pp.163-178.

2804 Unrepresentative information: the case of newspaper reporting on campaign finance. Stephen Ansolabehere; Erik C. Snowberg; James M. Snyder, Jr. **Publ. Opin. Q.** 69:2 Summer:2005 pp.213-231.

2805 When stereotypes collide: race/ethnicity, gender, and videostyle in congressional campaigns. Ann Gordon; Jerry Miller. New York: Peter Lang, 2005. x, 150p. *ISBN: 0820461253. Includes bibliographical references and index.* (*Series:* Frontiers in political communication - 4).

2806 Zhirinovskii enters politics: a chronology of the emergence of the liberal-democratic party of the Soviet Union, 1990-1991. Andreas Umland. **J. Slav. Mil. S.** 18:1 3:2005 pp.15-30.

Electoral systems
Systèmes électoraux

2807 1902 and the origins of preferential electoral systems in Australia. David M. Farrell; Ian McAllister. **Aust. J. Pol. Hist.** 51:2 6:2005 pp.155-167.

2808 ¿A quién representan nuestros representantes? *[In Spanish]*; [Representing who?] Bernard Manin; Adam Przeworski; Susan C. Stokes; María de los Ángeles Mascott Sánchez; Alejandro Moreno; Israel Arroyo; María Luna Argudín; Teresa González Luna Corvera. **Metapolítica** 8:37 9-10:2004 pp.14-92. *Collection of 6 articles.*

2809 Análisis comparativo del mecanismo empleado para el conteo de votos en los procesos comiciales de Venezuela y Colombia en 1998. *[In Spanish]*; (A comparative analysis of vote counting mechanisms in electoral processes in Venezuela and Colombia in 1998.) Janeth Hernández Márquez; Macuira Montiel González. **Cuest. Pol.** 32 1-6:2004 pp.13-30.

2810 Are voters better represented? John D. Griffin; Brian Newman. **J. Pol.** 67:4 11:2005 pp.1206-1227.

2811 Ballot access restrictions and candidate entry in elections. Thomas Stratmann. **Euro. J. Pol. Econ.** 21:1 3:2005 pp.59-72.

2812 Ballot design and unrecorded votes on paper-based ballots. David C. Kimball; Martha Kropf. **Publ. Opin. Q.** 69:4 Winter:2005 pp.508-529.

2813   Careless with our democracy: group think and voting reform. Ed Randall. **Pol. Q.** 76:3 7-9:2005 pp.402-413.

2814   Channelling ethnicity through electoral reform in Sri Lanka. Amita Shastri. **Commonwealth Comp. Pol.** 43:1 3:2005 pp.34-60.

2815   The citizen candidate model: an experimental analysis. J. Cadigan. **Publ. Choice** 123:1-2 4:2005 pp.197-216.

2816   Comparisons among electoral systems: distinguishing between localism and candidate-centered politics. Bernard Grofman. **Electoral S.** 24:4 12:2005 pp.735-740.

2817   Consequences of electoral systems in Africa: a preliminary inquiry. Staffan I. Lindberg. **Electoral S.** 24:1 3:2005 pp.41-64.

2818   Democracy for all: restoring immigrant voting rights in the US. Ronald Hayduk. **New Pol. Sci.** 26:4 12:2004 pp.499-523.

2819   Democratic electoral systems around the world, 1946-2000. Matt Golder. **Electoral S.** 24:1 3:2005 pp.103-121.

2820   Das demokratische Prinzip und der demographische Wandel. Brauchen wir ein Familienwahlrecht? *[In German]*; [The democratic principle and demographic change. Do we need a family voting legislation?] Rainer Wernsmann. **Der Staat** 44:1 2005 pp.43-66.

2821   Die Einführung des amtlichen Einheitsstimmzettels und seine Bedeutung für ein freies und faires Wahlrecht. *[In German]*; [The introduction of uniform ballot papers: impact on voting rights]. Heiko Holste. **Der Staat** 44:1 2005 pp.99-111.

2822   Ekvilibrium Diuverzhe v usloviiakh ogranichennoi konkurentsii: dumskie vybory 2003 g. *[In Russian]*; (The Duverger equilibrium as checked under the conditions of limited competition: the 2003 Duma elections.) *[Summary]*. A.V. Likhtenshtein; N.B. Iargomskaia. **Polis [Moscow]** 1(84) 2005 pp.135-155.

2823   Elections, parties and democracy in Croatia. Ivan Šiber; Goran Čular; Marijana Grbeša; Aleksandar Štulhofer. **Pol. Misao** 41:5 2004 pp.3-86. *Collection of 4 articles.*

2824   Elections under the French double-ballot system. James Adams; Samuel Merrill, III; Bernard Grofman; Bernard Dolez; Annie Laurent; Bruno Jérôme; Véronique Jérôme-Speziari; Christine Fauvelle-Aymar; Michael S. Lewis-Beck; Libia Billordo. **Fre. Pol.** 3:2 8:2005 pp.98-178. *Collection of 5 articles.*

2825   Electoral redistricting. Michael P. McDonald; Brian F. Schaffner; Michael W. Wagner; Jonathan Winburn; Jason Barabas; Jennifer Jerit; Robert G. Boatright; Jamie L. Carson; Michael H. Crespin; Colin Rallings; Michael Thrasher; Ron Johnston; James Downe. **State Pol. Policy Q.** 4:4 Winter:2004 pp.369-490. *Collection of 7 articles.*

2826   Electoral rules and constitutional structures as constraints on corruption. Jana Kunicová; Susan Rose-Ackerman. **Br. J. Pol. Sci.** 35:4 10:2005 pp.573-606.

2827   Electoral system, coalitional disintegration, and the future of Chile's Concertación; *[Summary in Spanish]*. Peter M. Siavelis. **Lat. Am. Res. R.** 40:1 2005 pp.56-82.

2828   Electoral systems and democratic quality: do mixed systems combine the best or the worst of both worlds? An explorative quantitative cross-national study. Renske Doorenspleet. **Acta Pol.** 40:1 4:2005 pp.28-49.

2829   Electoral systems and the promotion of 'consociationalism' in a multi-ethnic society. The Kosovo assembly elections of November 2001. Andrew Taylor. **Electoral S.** 24:3 9:2005 pp.435-463.

2830   Endogenous institutional change in the Mexican senate. Alberto Diaz-Cayeros. **Comp. Pol. S.** 38:10 12:2005 pp.1196-1218.

2831   Er der virkelig ingen argumenter for at ændre det kommunale valgsystem? *[In Danish]*; (Are there really no arguments for changing from d'Hondt to Hare (LR)?) *[Summary]*. Jørgen Elklit. **Politica** 36:3 9:2004 pp.333-351.

2832   Expert opinion on electoral systems: so which electoral system is 'best'? Shaun Bowler; David M. Farrell; Robin T. Pettitt. **Jnl. Ele. Pub. Op. Par.** 15:1 4:2005 pp.3-19.

2833   Fit for annexation but unfit to vote? Debating Hawaiian suffrage qualifications at the turn of the twentieth century. Lauren L. Basson. **Soc. Sci. Hist.** 29:4 Winter:2005 pp.575-598.

2834   Genèse du mode de scrutin : de la France une et indivisible à la France octogonale. *[In French]*; [Genesis of the voting system: from an indivisible France to an octagonal France]. Nicolas Grigny. **R. Pol. Parl.** 106:1031 7-9:2004 pp.139-152.

2835   Geographical representation under proportional representation: the cases of Israel and the Netherlands. Michael Latner; Anthony McGann. **Electoral S.** 24:4 12:2005 pp.709-734.

2836   The governor's backyard: a seat-vote model of electoral reform for subnational multiparty races. Ernesto Calvo; Juan Pablo Micozzi. **J. Pol.** 67:4 11:2005 pp.1050-1074.

2837   The impact of the electoral system on government formation: the case of post-communist Hungary. Csaba Nikolenyi. **Japanese J. Pol. Sci.** 5:1 5:2004 pp.159-178.

2838   The incumbency disadvantage and women's election to legislative office. Leslie A. Schwindt-Bayer. **Electoral S.** 24:2 6:2005 pp.227-244.

2839   Investigating the dynamics of political compromise. Alan E. Wiseman. **J. Theor. Pol.** 17:4 10:2005 pp.497-514.

2840   It's parties that choose electoral systems (or, Duverger's laws upside down). Josep M. Colomer. **Pol. S.** 53:1 3:2005 pp.1-21.

2841   Izmenenie elektoral'nykh institutov v Rossii (krossregional'nyi sravnitel'nyi analiz). *[In Russian]*; (Alteration of electoral institutions in Russia (cross-regional analysis).) *[Summary]*. P.V. Panov. **Polis [Moscow]** 6(83) 2004 pp.16-28.

2842   Judging partisan Gerrymanders under the elections clause. Jamal Greene. **Yale Law J.** 114:5 3:2005 pp.1021-1062.

2843   Legal aspects of ensuring openness, publicity and transparency in organizing and carrying out of the elections. Aman Agarwal. **Fin. India** XVIII:3 9:2004 pp.1233-1250.

2844   Looking for locals: voter information demands and personal vote-earning attributes of legislators under proportional representation. Matthew Søberg Shugart; Melody Ellis Valdini; Kati Suominen. **Am. J. Pol. Sci.** 49:2 4:2005 pp.437-449.

2845   'Make sure they count nicely this time': the politics of elections and election observing in Zimbabwe. Sara Rich Dorman. **Commonwealth Comp. Pol.** 43:2 7:2005 pp.155-177.

2846   Minor parties in plurality electoral systems. John Gerring. **Party Pol.** 11:1 1:2005 pp.79-107.

2847   Os persistentes problemas estruturais das eleições Americanas: lições de 2004. *[In Portuguese]*; (The looming structural problems in America elections: lessons from 2004.) *[Summary]*. Jeremy D. Mayer. **Relações Int.** 5 3:2005 pp.85-94.

2848   The perverse consequences of electoral reform in the United States. Adam J. Berinsky. **Am. Pol. Res.** 33:4 7:2005 pp.471-491.

2849   Policy-making, local factions and candidate coordination in single non-transferable voting: a case study of Taiwan. Chia-hung Tsai. **Party Pol.** 11:1 1:2005 pp.59-77.

2850   Political culture, representation and electoral systems in the Pacific Islands. Jon Fraenkel; Bernard Grofman; Stephen Levine; Nigel S. Roberts; Howard Van Trease; Asofou So'o; Henry Okole; Robert F. Stockwell; Nic MacLellan. **Commonwealth Comp. Pol.** 43:3 11:2005 pp.261-393. *Collection of 7 articles.*

2851   Political participation and electoral change in nineteenth-century New Zealand. John E. Martin. **Pol. Sci.** 57:1 6:2005 pp.39-58.

2852   Recent Russian federal elections in Dagestan: implications for proposed electoral reform. Robert Bruce Ware. **Euro.-Asia S.** 57:4 6:2005 pp.583-600.

2853   Reforming the Algerian electoral system. Youcef Bouandel. **J. Mod. Afr. S.** 43:3 9:2005 pp.393-415.

2854   Rethinking the vote: the politics and prospects of American election reform. Ann N. Crigler [Ed.]; Marion R. Just [Ed.]; Edward J. McCaffery [Ed.]. New York: Oxford University Press, 2004. xviii, 265p. *ISBN: 0195159845, 0195159853. Includes bibliographical references (p. 235-251) and index.*

2855   The rules matter: an experimental study of the effects of electoral systems on shifts in voters' attention. Michelle L. Chin; Michelle M. Taylor-Robinson. **Electoral S.** 24:3 9:2005 pp.465-483.

2856   Selling a vote. Antonio Quesada. **Euro. J. Pol. Econ.** 21:1 3:2005 pp.73-82.

2857 Sfabrikovannoe bol'shinstvo: konversiia golosov v mesta na dumskikh vyborakh 2003 g. *[In Russian]*; (A manufactured majority: vote-seat conversion in the 2003 Duma elections.) *[Summary]*. G.V. Golosov. **Polis [Moscow]** 1(84) 2005 pp.108-119.

2858 Single transferable vote with borda elimination: proportional representation, moderation, quasi-chaos and stability. Chris Geller. **Electoral S.** 24:2 6:2005 pp.265-280.

2859 Steps toward making every vote count: electoral system reform in Canada and its provinces. Henry Milner [Ed.]. Peterborough: Broadview Press, 2004. 319p. *ISBN: 1551116480. Includes bibliographical references.*

2860 Strategic fools: electoral rule choice under extreme uncertainty. Josephine T. Andrews; Robert W. Jackman. **Electoral S.** 24:1 3:2005 pp.65-84.

2861 Stuck in transition: electoral processes in Zambia 1991-2001. Lise Rakner; Lars Svåsand. **Democratization** 12:1 2:2005 pp.85-105.

2862 Le suffrage universel inacheve. *[In French]*; [Universal suffrage unfinished]. Michel Balinski. Paris: Belin, 2004. 335p. *ISBN: 2701137748. Includes bibliographical references (p. 325-331) and index.*

2863 The contemporary presidency: do Nebraska and Maine have the right idea? The political and partisan implications of the district system. Robert C. Turner. **Pres. Stud. Q.** 35:1 3:2005 pp.116-137.

2864 Wahlrechtsentwicklung im internationalen Vergleich. *[In German]*; (The development of electoral systems in comparative perspective.) Dieter Nohlen; Florian Grotz; Günther Pallaver; John Hulsey; Rudolf Götz; Gerda Neyer. **Öster. Z. Pol.wissen.** 34:1 2005 pp.7-72. *Collection of 4 articles.*

2865 Women's political representation: does the electoral system matter? Manon Tremblay. **Pol. Sci.** 57:1 6:2005 pp.59-75.

Parliamentary elections
Élections parlementaires

2866 The 2003-2004 Russian elections and prospects for democracy. Richard Sakwa. **Euro.-Asia S.** 57:3 5:2005 pp.369-398.

2867 The 2004 general election in India and its aftermath. Krishna K. Tummala. **Asian J. Pol. Sci.** 12:2 12:2004 pp.31-58.

2868 The 2004 Philippine elections: political change in an illiberal democracy. John L. Linantud. **Contemp. Sth.East Asia** 27:1 4:2005 pp.80-101.

2869 After the election. Peter Riddell; Peter Kellner; David Marquand; Shirley Williams. **Pol. Q.** 76:3 7-9:2005 pp.319-340. *Collection of 4 articles.*

2870 Analysis of 17th National Assembly election outcomes in Korea. Hyung Joon Kim; Dohjong Kim. **Kor. Obs.** 35:4 Winter:2004 pp.617-638.

2871 As eleições Espanholas de 14 de Março. *[In Portuguese]*; (The Spanish election of March 14.) *[Summary]*. Belén Barreiro. **Relações Int.** 5 3:2005 pp.111-131.

2872 Der Bundestagswahlkampf von 2002 unter strategisch-personellen Gesichtspunkten. Mit einem Ausblick auf den Bundestagswahlkampf 2005. *[In German]*; [The general elections in 2002 from a strategic and personal perspective]. Florian Hartleb; Eckhard Jesse. **Politische S.** 56:402 7-8:2005 pp.86-97.

2873 Competition, representation and redistricting: the case against competitive congressional districts. Justin Buchler. **J. Theor. Pol.** 17:4 10:2005 pp.431-463.

2874 Conservative party rationality: learning the lessons from the last election for the next. Jane Green. **Jnl. Ele. Pub. Op. Par.** 15:1 4:2005 pp.111-127.

2875 Election 2004: a profile of Indian parliamentary elections since 1952. Tariq Ashraf. New Delhi: Bookwell, 2004. xv, 781p. *ISBN: 8185040842.*

2876 Elections in India: behind the Congress comeback. Steven I. Wilkinson. **J. Democ.** 16:1 1:2005 pp.153-167.

2877   The elections in Israel, 2003. Alan Arian [Ed.]; Michal Shamir [Ed.]. New Brunswick NJ: Transaction Publishers, 2005. vii, 267p. *ISBN: 0765802686. Includes bibliographical references and index.*

2878   The great state Hural election in Mongolia, June 2004. Christian Schafferer. **Electoral S.** 24:4 12:2005 pp.741-747.

2879   Hong Kong's democrats stumble. Joseph Y.S. Cheng. **J. Democ.** 16:1 1:2005 pp.138-152.

2880   The Indonesian general elections 2004. Jusuf Wanandi. **Asia Pac. R.** 11:2 11:2004 pp.115-131.

2881   Die kanadische Unterhauswahl vom 28. Juni 2004: Das Parteiensystem auf dem Weg vom Mehrheits – zum Minderheitsregime? *[In German]*; (The Canadian general election of June 28, 2004: party system transformation from majority to minority regime?) *[Summary]*. Rainer-Olaf Schultze; Jörg Broschek. **Z. Parlament.** 36:2 6:2005 pp.280-300.

2882   Krupnyi gorod – region – Rossiia: dinamika elektoral'nogo povedeniia na parlamentskikh vyborakh. *[In Russian]*; (City, region, Russia: the dynamics of electoral behaviour at parliamentary elections.) *[Summary]*. K.E. Aksenov; A.S. Zinov'ev; D.V. Pleshchenko. **Polis [Moscow]** 2(85) 2005 pp.41-52.

2883   Machterhalt und Zukunftsgestaltung: Elemente erfolgreicher politischer Steuerung in Großbritannien. *[In German]*; (Holding power and shaping the future: elements of successful strategic policy formation and communication in Britain.) *[Summary]*. Bernd-Werner Becker. **Z. Parlament.** 36:2 6:2005 pp.301-310.

2884   Political change and prospects for peace in Jammu and Kashmir: the 2002 state election and recent electoral trends in India. Matthew J. Webb. **Sth. Asia** XXVIII:1 4:2005 pp.87-111.

2885   The politics of locality and temporality in the 2004 Malaysian parliamentary elections. Vejai Balasubramaniam. **Contemp. Sth.East Asia** 27:1 4:2005 pp.44-63.

2886   Presidential coattails, incumbency advantage, and open seats: a district-level analysis of the 1976-2000 U.S. house elections. Franco Mattei; Joshua Glasgow. **Electoral S.** 24:4 12:2005 pp.619-641.

2887   Strukturirovanie elektoral'nogo prostranstva v rossiiskikh regionakh (faktornyi analiz parlamentskikh vyborov 1995-2003 gg.) *[In Russian]*; (The structuring of the electoral space in Russia's regions. (Factor analysis of the 1995-2003 parliamentary elections).) *[Summary]*. A.S. Akhremenko. **Polis [Moscow]** 2(85) 2005 pp.26-40.

2888   The third Blair victory: how and why? Pippa Norris; Christopher Wlezien; Ivor Crewe; John Bartle; Dominic Wring; Anthony Seldon; Peter Snowdon; Andrew Russell; Paul Webb; John Curtice; Ron Johnston; Charles Pattie; David Rossiter; Paul Whiteley; Marianne C. Stewart; David Sanders; Harold D. Clarke; Geoffrey Evans; Robert Andersen; Rosie Campbell; Joni Lovenduski; Patrick Dunleavy; Helen Margetts. **Parl. Aff.** 58:4 10:2005 pp.657-888. *Collection of 14 articles.*

2889   Tonartwechsel in der Schweiz: Der Dreiklang von Volksrechten, Konkordanz und erneuerter „Zauberformel" nach den National – und Ständeratswahlen 2003. *[In German]*; (Change of key in Switzerland: the triad of people's rights, concordance and renewed "magic formula" after the parliamentary elections 2003.) *[Summary]*. Burkard Steppacher. **Z. Parlament.** 36:2 6:2005 pp.311-325.

2890   Unintended consequences: anticipation of general election outcomes and primary election divisiveness. Jeffrey Lazarus. **Legis. Stud. Q.** XXX:3 8:2005 pp.435-461.

2891   Die vierten Parlamente in Estland, Lettland und Litauen: Ähnliche Voraussetzungen, verschiedene Pfade. *[In German]*; (The fourth parliaments in Estonia, Latvia and Lithuania: similar prerequisites, different paths.) *[Summary]*. Axel Reetz. **Z. Parlament.** 36:2 6:2005 pp.326-347.

2892   Die Wahlen zum US-Kongress vom 2. November 2004: Post-Electoral Politics oder Plutokratie? *[In German]*; (Congressional elections in the United States 2004: post-electoral politics or plutocracy?) *[Summary]*. Peter Filzmaier; Fritz Plasser. **Z. Parlament.** 36:2 6:2005 pp.243-258.

2893   When moderate voters prefer extreme parties: policy balancing in parliamentary elections. Orit Kedar. **Am. Pol. Sci. R.** 99:2 5:2005 pp.185-199.

2894   ZANU(PF) strategies in general elections, 1980-2000: discourse and coercion. Norma Kriger. **Afr. Affairs** 104:414 1:2005 pp.1-34.

Presidential elections
Élections présidentielles

2895   2004, année électorale : bilans et perspectives. *[In French]*; [2004, electoral year: reviews and perspectives]. Raluca Grosescu [Ed.]. **Nouv. Alter.** 19:63 12:2004 pp.99-118.

2896   The 2004 presidential election: the emergence of a permanent majority? Paul R. Abramson; John H. Aldrich; David W. Rohde. **Pol. Sci. Q.** 120:1 Spring:2005 pp.33-57.

2897   American presidential election 2004: post election analysis. Chandrakant Yatanoor. **Indian J. Pol. Sci.** LXVI:1 1-3:2005 pp.135-152.

2898   Argentina's landmark 2003 presidential election: renewal and continuity. Omar Sanchez. **B. Lat. Am. Res.** 24:4 10:2005 pp.454-475.

2899   Campaign 2004: constructing the new American ideals/idols in democracy. Robert E. Denton, Jr.; Craig Allen Smith; Michael Pfau; J. Brian Houston; Shane M. Semmler; Kenneth J. Levine; Robert E. Brown; John C. Tedesco; Kenneth Winneg; Kate Kenski; Kathleen Hall Jamieson; Judith S. Trent; Cady Short-Thompson; Paul A. Mongeau; Maribeth S. Metzler; Jimmie D. Trent; Kathleen E. Kendall. **Am. Behav. Sci.** 49:1 9:2005 pp.11-172. *Volume 1. Collection of 9 articles.*

2900   Campaign 2004: the political celebrity spectacle: de/constructing image meaning/mongering (volume 3). W. Lance Bennett; Matthew D. Matsaganis; J. Gregory Payne; Timothy C. Weiskel; G. Thomas Goodnight; R. Lance Holbert; Babak Elahi; Grant Cos; Janis L. Edwards; Laura Ware; Joan L. Conners; Jennifer Willyard; Kurt Ritter. **Am. Behav. Sci.** 49:3 11:2005 pp.361-509. *Collection of 10 articles.*

2901   Chen Shui-bian et le triangle Taipei-Pékin-Washington. *[In French]*; [Chen Shui-bian and the Taipei-Pekin-Washington triangle]. Jean-Pierre Cabestan. **Crit. Int.** 24 7:2004 pp.51-65.

2902   Claiming the mantle: how presidential nominations are won and lost before the votes are cast. Roger Lawrence Butler. Boulder CO: Westview Press, 2004. x, 195p. *ISBN: 0813342082. (Series: Dilemmas in American politics).*

2903   Comparing competing theories on the causes of mandate perceptions. Lawrence J. Grossback; David A.M. Peterson; James A. Stimson. **Am. J. Pol. Sci.** 49:2 4:2005 pp.406-419.

2904   Databases, felons, and voting: bias and partisanship of the Florida felons list in the 2000 elections. Guy Stuart. **Pol. Sci. Q.** 119:3 Fall:2004 pp.453-475.

2905   D'Eltsine à Poutine les élections présidentielles en Russie de 1991 à 2004. *[In French]*; (From Yeltsin to Putin the presidential elections in Russia (1991-2004).) *[Summary]*. Youri Levada. **Pouvoirs** 112 2004 pp.141-152.

2906   The effects of turnout on partisan outcomes in U.S. presidential elections 1960-2000. Michael D. Martinez; Jeff Gill. **J. Pol.** 67:4 11:2005 pp.1248-1274.

2907   Elections and the normalization of politics in Indonesia. Edward Aspinall. **Sth. East Asia Res.** 13:2 7:2005 pp.117-156.

2908   Elections: tax cut versus lockbox: did the voters grasp the tradeoff in 2000? Martin P. Wattenberg. **Pres. Stud. Q.** 34:4 12:2004 pp.838-848.

2909   The electoral college, mobilization, and turnout in the 2000 presidential election. David Hill; Seth C. McKee. **Am. Pol. Res.** 33:5 9:2005 pp.700-725.

2910   Electoral reform and partisan jugglery. Peter H. Argersinger. **Pol. Sci. Q.** 119:3 Fall:2004 pp.499-520.

2911   Enduring controversies in presidential nominating politics. Emmett H. Buell [Ed.]; William G. Mayer [Ed.]. Pittsburgh PA: University of Pittsburgh Press, 2004. ix, 320p. *ISBN: 082294233X, 082295849X. Includes bibliographical references and index.*

2912 O fio da navalha no tempo das eleições norte-americanas. *[In Portuguese]*; [On the razor's edge at the time of the North American elections] *[Summary]*. Enéas de Souza. **Ind. Econ. FEE** 32:3 2004 pp.127-150.

2913 Fraud or fairytales: Russia and Ukraine's electoral experience. Mikhail Myagkov; Peter C. Ordeshook; Dimitry Shakin. **Post-Sov. Aff.** 21:2 4-6:2005 pp.91-131.

2914 From Fujimori to Toledo: the 2001 elections and the vicissitudes of democratic government in Peru. Lewis Taylor. **Gov. Oppos.** 40:4 Autumn:2005 pp.565-596.

2915 The fundamentals in US presidential elections: public opinion, the economy and incumbency in the 2004 presidential election. James E. Campbell. **Jnl. Ele. Pub. Op. Par.** 15:1 4:2005 pp.73-83.

2916 Guinée : le prix d'une stabilité à court terme. *[In French]*; (Guinea: the price of short-term stability.) *[Summary]*. Paul Chambers. **Pol. Afr.** 94 6:2004 pp.128-148.

2917 In play: a commentary on strategies in the 2004 U.S. presidential election. J. Merolla; M. Munger; M. Tofias. **Publ. Choice** 123:1-2 4:2005 pp.19-38.

2918 Informational party primaries and strategic ambiguity. Adam Meirowitz. **J. Theor. Pol.** 17:1 1:2005 pp.107-136.

2919 [L'élection présidentielle de 2004 à Taiwan]. *[In French]*; [The 2004 presidential election in Taiwan]. Perspectives chinoises. **Persp. Chinoises** 82 3-4:2004 pp.33-66.

2920 Minor parties and strategic voting in recent U.S. presidential elections. Barry C. Burden. **Electoral S.** 24:4 12:2005 pp.603-618.

2921 Oligarchie et élection présidentielle. *[In French]*; [Oligarchy and presidential elections]. Arnaud Kalika. **Défense Nat.** 60:1 1:2004 pp.43-54.

2922 Polarized politics and the 2004 congressional and presidential elections. Gary C. Jacobson. **Pol. Sci. Q.** 120:2 Summer:2005 pp.199-218.

2923 Die Präsidentschaftswahl in den USA vom 2. November 2004: Ein knapper Sieg Bushs, aber auch ein Mandat? *[In German]*; (The U.S. presidential election of November 2, 2004: a tight victory for Bush — but also a mandate?) *[Summary]*. Michael Kolkmann. **Z. Parlament.** 36:2 6:2005 pp.259-279.

2924 The strategic importance of state-level factors in presidential elections. Richard J. Powell. **Publius** 34:3 Summer:2004 pp.115-130.

2925 The polls. Religion and the 2000 presidential election: public attitudes toward Joseph Lieberman. Jeffrey E. Cohen. **Pres. Stud. Q.** 35:2 6:2005 pp.389-402.

2926 Thinking about the political impacts of the electoral college. B. Grofman; S.L. Feld. **Publ. Choice** 123:1-2 4:2005 pp.1-18.

2927 Why Bush won the presidential election of 2004: incumbency, ideology, terrorism, and turnout. James E. Campbell. **Pol. Sci. Q.** 120:2 Summer:2005 pp.219-241.

2928 Why the electoral college is bad for America. George C. Edwards. New Haven CT: Yale University Press, 2004. xvii, 198p. *ISBN: 0300100604. Includes bibliographical references and index.*

Regional and local elections
Élections locales et régionales

2929 The 2003 District Council elections in Hong Kong. Joseph Y.S. Cheng. **Asian Sur.** XLIV:5 9-10:2004 pp.734-754.

2930 The 2004 Ba' Kelalan by-election in Sarawak, East Malaysia: the Lun Bawang factor and whither representative democracy in Malaysia. Arnold Puyok. **Contemp. Sth.East Asia** 27:1 4:2005 pp.64-79.

2931 Die brandenburgische Landtagswahl vom 19. September 2004: Reaktionen der Wähler auf Hartz IV. *[In German]*; (The election of the Brandenburg state parliament of September 19, 2004: the voters' reaction to Hartz IV.) Oskar Niedermayer. **Z. Parlament.** 36:1 3:2005 pp.64-80.

2932 Carry on campaigning: the case for 'dumbing down' in the fight against local electoral apathy. Mick Temple. **Loc. Govt. S.** 31:4 8:2005 pp.415-431.

2933   The demise of one-party politics in Mexican municipal elections. Jonathan Hiskey; Damarys Canache. **Br. J. Pol. Sci.** 35:2 4:2005 pp.257-284.

2934   Determinanten van voorkeurstemproporties bij (sub-)lokale verkiezingen. De Antwerpse districtsraadsverkiezingen van 8 oktober 2000. *[In Dutch]*; (Determinants of preferential vote-shares in local elections. The district council elections in Antwerp of October 2000.) *[Summary]*. Peter Thijssen; Kristof Jacobs. **Res Publica [Bruss.]** XLVI:4 2004 pp.460-485.

2935   Does the economy matter? An empirical analysis of the causal chain connecting the economy and the vote in Galicia. Ignacio Lago-Peñas; Santiago Lago-Peñas. **Econ. Pol.** 17:2 7:2005 pp.215-243.

2936   Economic development and the implementation of village elections in rural China. Rong Hu. **J. Cont. China** 14:44 8:2005 pp.427-444.

2937   Elected mayors I: political innovation, electoral systems and revitalising democracy. Mark Sandford. **Loc. Govt. S.** 30:1 Spring:2004 pp.1-21.

2938   Les élections françaises. *[In French]*; [The French elections].   Commentaire. **Commentaire** 27:106 Summer:2004 pp.433-451.

2939   Les élections régionales et cantonales des 21 et 28 mars 2004. *[In French]*; [Regional and local elections of the 21 and 28 March 2004]. Pierre Martin. **Regar. Actual.** 302 6-7:2004 pp.77-89.

2940   Die Landtagswahlen in den neuen Bundesländern 1990 bis 2004. *[In German]*; [Regional elections in new federal states, 1990-2004]. Eckhard Jesse. **Deutsch. Arch.** 37:6 11-12:2004 pp.952-962.

2941   Local elections in Britain. Chris Game. **Loc. Govt. S.** 30:2 Summer:2004 pp.276-280.

2942   Local monotonicity of power: axiom or just a property? Manfred J. Holler; Stefan Napel. **Qual. Quan.** 38:5 10:2004 pp.637-647.

2943   Money and machine politics: an analysis of corporate and labor contributions in Chicago city council elections. Timothy B. Krebs. **Urb. Aff. R.** 41:1 9:2005 pp.47-64.

2944   Nevskii, Lubianka, Kreml': Proekt- 2008. *[In Russian]*; [Nevskii, Lubianka, Kremlin: the 2008 project]. A.A. Mukhin. Moscow: TsPI, 2005. 256p. *ISBN: 5947500361.*

2945   Party politicisation reversed? Non-partisan alternatives in Norwegian local politics. Jacob Aars; Hans-Erik Ringkjøb. **Scand. Pol. S.** 28:2 2005 pp.161-181.

2946   Reihenfolgeeffekte bei der bayerischen Landtagswahl 2003: Die Ersten werden die Ersten sein. *[In German]*; (List order effects at the election of the Bavarian state parliament in 2003: the first shall be the first.) Harald Schoen; Thorsten Faas. **Z. Parlament.** 36:1 3:2005 pp.100-116.

2947   The role of elections in the peace-building and reconstruction of Afghanistan. Kinichi Komano. **Asia Pac. R.** 12:1 5:2005 pp.1-16.

2948   Die saarländische Landtagswahl vom 5. September 2004: Vom Zwei – zum Vierparteiensystem mit einer dominanten CDU. *[In German]*; (The election of the Saarland state parliament of September 5, 2004: from a two party system to a four party system with a dominating CDU.) Jürgen R. Winkler. **Z. Parlament.** 36:1 3:2005 pp.19-34.

2949   Die sächsische Landtagswahl vom 19. September 2004: Debakel für CDU und SPD gleichermaßen. *[In German]*; (The election of the Saxony state parliament of September 19, 2004: disaster for both CDU and SPD.) Eckhard Jesse. **Z. Parlament.** 36:1 3:2005 pp.80-100.

2950   Trends in local elections in Britain, 1975-2003. Colin Rallings; Michael Thrasher; David Denver. **Loc. Govt. S.** 31:4 8:2005 pp.393-413.

2951   When 'no' means 'yes to revolution': electoral politics in Bolivarian Venezuela. Daniel Hellinger. **Lat. Am. Persp.** 32:3(142) 5:2005 pp.8-32.

D.2.6: **Information and media**
Information et médias

2952 'Bridging the differences': political communication experts in Germany. Jens Tenscher. **Ger. Pol.** 13:3 9:2004 pp.516-540.

2953 The CNN effect: the search for a communication theory of international relations. Eytan Gilboa. **Pol. Communic.** 22:1 1-3:2005 pp.27-44.

2954 Communication et citoyenneté. *[In French]*; [Communication and citizenship]. Bernard Wallon [Ed.]. **Après-demain** 467 8-9:2004 pp.5-38.

2955 La communication politique française après le tournant de 2002. *[In French]*; [French political communication after the 2002 event]. Philippe J. Maarek [Ed.]. Paris: L'Harmattan, 2004. 230p. *ISBN: 2747568652. Includes bibliographical references.*

2956 Comparing political communication: theories, cases, and challenges. Frank Esser [Ed.]; Barbara Pfetsch [Ed.]. Cambridge, New York: Cambridge University Press, 2004. xvi, 418p. *ISBN: 0521535409, 0521828317. Includes bibliographical references and index.* (*Series:* Communication, society, and politics).

2957 Comunicación gubernamental: ¿encanto o desencanto? *[In Spanish]*; [Governmental communication: enchantment or disillusion?] Silvia Molina Vedia. **R. Mexicana Cien. Pol.** XLVI:190 1-4:2004 pp.31-45.

2958 Coverage of the endangered species act in four major newspapers. Laura J. Hendrickson. **Natur. Res. J.** 45:1 Winter:2005 pp.135-168.

2959 The Cuban propaganda war: the story of Elián González; *[Summary in Slovene]*. Juan Orlando Pérez. **Javnost** XII:1 4:2005 pp.85-102.

2960 The Iraq dossier and the meaning of spin. James Humphreys. **Parl. Aff.** 58:1 1:2005 pp.156-170.

2961 Jumping out of ordinary time: sacred rhetoric in American political discourse. Eldon J. Eisenach. **Tocqueville R.** XXV:2 2004 pp.57-79.

2962 Just public relations or an attempt at interaction? British MPs in the press, on the web and 'in your face'. Nigel A. Jackson; Darren G. Lilleker. **Euro. J. Communic.** 19:4 12:2004 pp.507-533.

2963 A kommunikáció útjai. *[In Hungarian]*; (The ways of communication.) Lívia Ivaskó [Ed.]; Szimonetta Gál; Özséb Horányi; Lívia Ivaskó; Attila László Nemesi; T. Enikő Németh; Klára Sándor; István Siklaki; Tamás Terestyéni; Benedek Tóth; Borbála Tóth; Péter I. Tóth. Budapest: Gondolat Kiadó, 2004. 195p. *ISBN: 9639567027. Includes bibliographical references.*

2964 Die Kommunikation des politischen Systems: Zur Differenz von Herstellung und Darstellung im politischen System. *[In German]*; (The communication of the political system: on the distinction between production and presentation within the political system.) *[Summary]*. Klaus P. Japp; Isabel Kusche. **Z. Soziol.** 33:6 12:2004 pp.511-531.

2965 Meltdown: the predictable distortion of global warming by scientists, politicians, and the media. Patrick J. Michaels. Washington DC: Cato Institute, 2004. vii, 271p. *ISBN: 1930865597. Includes bibliographical references and index.*

2966 New government, new language? The Third Way discourse in Taiwan. Yu-kang Lee. **Mod. Asian S.** 39:03 7:2005 pp.631-660.

2967 Odnosi s javnošću kao doprinos demokratizaciji i profesionalizaciji procesa javnoga komuniciranja. *[In Croatian]*; (Public relations as a contribution to democratization and professionalization of the process of public communication.) *[Summary]*. Božo Skoko. **Pol. Misao** 41:1 2004 pp.92-101.

2968 Orchestrating party talk: a party-based view of one-minute speeches in the house of representatives. Douglas B. Harris. **Legis. Stud. Q.** XXX:1 2:2005 pp.127-141.

2969 Presidential rhetoric, the public agenda, and the end of presidential television's 'golden age'. Gary Young; William B. Perkins. **J. Pol.** 67:4 11:2005 pp.1190-1205.

2970 Ready … ready … drop! A content analysis of coalition leaflets used in the Iraq war. Andrew M. Clark; Thomas B. Christie. **Gazette** 67:2 4:2005 pp.141-154.

2971   Spin control and freedom of information: lessons for the United Kingdom from Canada. Alasdair S. Roberts. **Publ. Admin.** 83:1 2005 pp.1-23.
2972   Strategic political communciation: rethinking social influence, persuasion, and propaganda. Karen S. Johnson-Cartee; Gary Copeland. Lanham MD: Rowman & Littlefield, 2004. ix, 229p. *ISBN: 0742528812, 0742528820. Includes bibliographical references (p. 203-226) and index.* (*Series:* Communication, media, and politics).
2973   Stratégie d'influence américaine. *[In French]*; [United States' influence strategy]. Harold Hyman. **Défense Nat.** 60:4 4:2004 pp.120-131.
2974   Understanding the relationship between communication and political knowledge: a model comparison approach using panel data. William P. Eveland, Jr.; Andrew F. Hayes; Dhavan V. Shah; Nojin Kwak. **Pol. Communic.** 22:4 10-12:2005 pp.423-446.
2975   Usporedba informativnih programa BBC-ja i HRT-a. *[In Croatian]*; (Comparison of BBC's and HRT's news programmes.) *[Summary]*. Ilija Jandrić. **Pol. Misao** 41:2 2004 pp.72-84.
2976   Valeurs et éthique dans les médias : approches internationales. *[In French]*; [Values and ethics in the media: international approaches]. Patrick J. Brunet [Ed.]; Martin David-Blais [Ed.]. Quebec: Presses de l'Université Laval, 2004. xv, 393p. *ISBN: 2763780903. Includes bibliographical references.*

Communications technology
Technologie des communications

2977   Agenda-setting and the internet: the intermedia influence of internet bulletin boards on newspaper coverage of the 2000 general election in South Korea. Byoungkwan Lee; Karen M. Lancendorfer; Ki Jung Lee. **Asian J. Communic.** 15:1 3:2005 pp.57-71.
2978   Analyzing processes for e-government application development: the emergence of process definition languages. Leon J. Osterweil; Charles M. Schweik; Norman K. Sondheimer; Craig W. Thomas. **J. E-Gov.** 1:4 2004 pp.63-88.
2979   The communication of communication. An illustration: the South African rhetorical promotion of ICTs. Nicolas Péjout. **Politikon** 31:2 11:2004 pp.185-199.
2980   Communication technology. Darin David Barney. Vancouver: UBC Press, 2005. xiii, 208p. *ISBN: 0774811013, 077481182X. Includes bibliographical references and index.* (*Series:* Canadian democratic audit - 8).
2981   The content of U.S. house member web sites. Erica Contini; Mark Dundon; Hana Fullenbaum; Miriam Grill-Abramowitz; Karen Raupp; Jennifer Richter; Richard G. Niemi. **J. E-Gov.** 1:3 2004 pp.55-71.
2982   Coping with globalisation through a collaborative federate mode of governance: the case of China in transition. Xin Zhang. **Policy S.** 26:2 6:2005 pp.199-209.
2983   The cultural politics of information and communications technologies. Jodi Dean; Richard Kahn; Douglas Kellner; Mark Poster. **Cult. Pol.** 1:1 3:2005 pp.51-117. *Collection of 3 articles.*
2984   Digital communication between local authorities and citizens in Denmark. Lars Torpe; Jeppe Nielsen. **Loc. Govt. S.** 30:2 Summer:2004 pp.230-244.
2985   Digital diasporas and conflict prevention: the case of Somalinet.com. Jennifer M. Brinkerhoff. **R. Int. S.** 32:1 1:2005 pp.25-47.
2986   Distribution and media flows. Sean Cubitt. **Cult. Pol.** 1:2 7:2005 pp.193-213.
2987   E-governance and good governance: the Indian context. Anupama Saxena. **Indian J. Pol. Sci.** LXVI:2 4-6:2005 pp.313-328.
2988   E-government, a citizens' perspective. Rowena Cullen. **J. E-Gov.** 1:3 2004 pp.5-28.
2989   E-government in Singapore: demographics, usage patterns, and perceptions. Hairong Li; Benjamin H. Detenber; Wai Peng Lee; Stella Chia. **J. E-Gov.** 1:3 2004 pp.29-54.
2990   Electronic local government and the modernisation agenda: progress and prospects for public service improvement. Paul Beynon-Davies; Steve Martin. **Loc. Govt. S.** 30:2 Summer:2004 pp.214-229.

2991   European Union and e-voting (electronic voting). Alexander H. Trechsel [Ed.]; Fernando Mendez [Ed.]. London: Routledge, 2004. 256p. *ISBN: 0415328799.* *(Series: Routledge advances in European politics).*

2992   Global media: the television revolution in Asia. James D. White. New York, London: Routledge, 2005. 286p. *ISBN: 0415973066. Includes bibliographical references and index. (Series:* East Asia: history, politics, sociology, culture).

2993   Global'noe informatsionnoe obshchestvo i Rossiia. *[In Russian];* (Global information society and Russia.) N. Zagladin. **Mir. Ekon. Mezh. Ot.** 7 7:2005 pp.15-31.

2994   Incentives in e-government. Christian Bock. **J. E-Gov.** 1:4 2004 pp.89-100.

2995   Information technology, public space, and collective action in China. Yongnian Zheng; Guoguang Wu. **Comp. Pol. S.** 38:5 6:2005 pp.507-536.

2996   Informed nationalism: military websites in Chinese cyberspace. Zhou Yongming. **J. Cont. China** 14:44 8:2005 pp.543-562.

2997   Informing and interacting: the use of e-government for citizen participation in planning. Maria Manta Conroy; Jennifer Evans-Cowley. **J. E-Gov.** 1:3 2004 pp.73-92.

2998   Innovations in e-government: the thoughts of governors and mayors. Erwin A. Blackstone [Ed.]; Michael Bognanno [Ed.]; Simon Hakim [Ed.]. Lanham MD: Rowman & Littlefield, 2005. ix, 298p. *ISBN: 0742549127, 0742549135. Includes bibliographical references and index.*

2999   Integrating information technology into public administration: conceptual and practical considerations. K. Kernaghan; J. Gunraj. **Can. Publ. Admin.** 47:4 Winter:2004 pp.525-546.

3000   The internet, alternative public sphere and political dynamism: Korea's non-gaek (polemist?) websites. Woo-young Chang. **Pac. R.** 18:3 9:2005 pp.393-415.

3001   The internet and governance in a global context. Richard Rose; Ernest J. Wilson, III; Richard Heeks; Randolph Kluver; Hilmar Westholm; Arre Zuurmond; László Bruszt; Balázs Vedres; David Stark; Donatella della Porta; Lorenzo Mosca. **J. Publ. Policy** 25:1 1-4:2005 pp.5-190. *Collection of 8 articles.*

3002   The internet and the public sphere. Kees Brants; Peter Dahlgren; Peter Muhlberger; Bart Cammaerts; Leo van Audenhove; Stephen Coleman; Eric W. Welch; Shelley Fulla; Kenneth Rogerson. **Pol. Communic.** 22:2 4-6:2005 pp.143-214. *Collection of 4 articles.*

3003   Internet Macht Politik. *[In German];* (Internet and politics.) Alexander Siedschlag; Simone Abendschön; Norbert Kersting; Eun-jung Lee; Christoph Busch; Arne Rogg-Pietz. **Welt Trends** 48 Autumn:2005 pp.11-91. *Collection of 6 articles.*

3004   Keeping unwanted donkeys and elephants out of your inbox: the case for regulating political spam. Seth Grossman. **Berkeley Techno. Law J.** 19:4 Fall:2004 pp.1533-1575.

3005   The making of Arab news. Noha Mellor. Lanham MD: Rowman & Littlefield, 2005. xii, 161p. *ISBN: 0742538184, 0742538192. Includes bibliographical references (p. 147-158) and index.*

3006   Massornas politiska torgmöten eller de motiverades klubbar? En studie av medborgardiskussioner på Internet. *[In Swedish];* [Political mass discussion or closed societies for the motivated? A study of citizens' discussion on the Internet] *[Summary].* Kim Strandberg. **Politiikka** 46:1 2004 pp.17-29.

3007   New labour's information age policy programme: an ideology analysis. Giles Moss; Ben O'Loughlin. **J. Pol. Ideol.** 10:2 6:2005 pp.165-183.

3008   New technology in ageing parties: internet use in Danish and Norwegian parties. Karina Pedersen; Jo Saglie. **Party Pol.** 11:3 5:2005 pp.359-377.

3009   Perspectives on e-voting and campaigning in the UK and the US. Alexandros Xenakis; Ann MacIntosh; Tim Storer; Ishbel Duncan; Kaye D. Trammell; Andrew Paul Williams. **J. E-Gov.** 2004 pp.53-122. *Collection of 3 articles.*

3010   Political culture, regulation, and democratization: the internet in nine Asian nations. Randolph Kluver; Indrajit Banerjee. **Info. Communic. Soc.** 8:1 2005 pp.30-46.

3011   Politicheskii runet: chto est chto. *[In Russian];* [The Russian political internet: who is who]. Ia.I. Zdorovets. Moscow: Tsentr politicheskoi informatsii, 2004. 97p. *Includes bibliographical references.*

3012   The politics of Internet communication. Robert J. Klotz. Lanham MD: Rowman & Littlefield, 2004. xvi, 257p. *ISBN: 0742529258, 0742529266. Includes bibliographical references and index.*

3013   The politics of the internet in Third World development: challenges in contrasting regimes with case studies of Costa Rica and Cuba. Bert Hoffmann. London, New York: Routledge, 2004. *ISBN: 0415949599. Includes bibliographical references and index. (Series:* Latin American studies: social sciences and law).

3014   A proximity indicator for e-government: the smallest number of clicks. Olivier François Glassey. **J. E-Gov.** 1:4 2004 pp.5-20.

3015   Remodeling the transnational political realm: partnerships, best-practice schemes, and the digitalization of governance. Hans Krause Hansen; Dorte Salskov-Iversen. **Alternatives** 30:2 4-6:2005 pp.141-164.

3016   Some thoughts on e-democracy as an evolving concept. Evan Hill. **J. E-Gov.** 2004 pp.23-39.

3017   Stanovlenie informatsionnogo obshchestva vo Frantsii. *[In Russian]*; (Formation of information society in France.) E.V. Talapina. **Gos. Pravo** 7 7:2004 pp.68-78.

3018   Telecommunications in Africa. J. Hodge [Ed.]; A. Gillwald; J. Hodge; B. Oyelaran-Oyeyinka; K. Lal; P.K. McCormick; G. Marcelle. **Telecom. Policy** 29:7 8:2005 pp.467-572. *Collection of 6 articles.*

3019   Views from inside the net: how websites affect young adults' political interest. Arthur Lupia; Tasha S. Philpot. **J. Pol.** 67:4 11:2005 pp.1122-1142.

Media and politics
Médias et politique

3020   L'affaire Kelly : politique, sémantique et manipulation. *[In French]*; [The Kelly affair: politics, semantics and manipulation]. Jean-Claude Sergeant. **R. Deux Mondes** 1 1:2004 pp.29-41.

3021   All the president's spin: George W. Bush, the media, and the truth. Ben Fritz; Bryan Keefer; Brendan Nyhan. New York: Simon & Schuster, 2004. xi, 336p. *ISBN: 0743262514. Includes bibliographical references and index.*

3022   Analiza procesa dodjele koncesije za treću mrežu hrvatske televizije. *[In Croatian]*; (Analyzing the process of granting concession for the Croatian television third network.) *[Summary]*. Darko Tomorad; Marina Mučalo. **Pol. Misao** 41:2 2004 pp.47-63.

3023   Bring 'em on: media and politics in the Iraq war. Lee Artz [Ed.]; Yahya R. Kamalipour [Ed.]. Lanham MD: Rowman & Littlefield, 2005. xix, 269p. *ISBN: 0742536882, 0742536890. Includes bibliographical references and index. (Series:* Communication, media, and politics).

3024   Celebrity-in-chief: how show business took over the White House. Alan Schroeder. Boulder CO: Westview Press, 2004. viii, 354p. *ISBN: 081334137X. Includes bibliographical references (p. 325-331) and index.*

3025   Citizenship and mediated society. Mojca Pajnik. **Citiz. S.** 9:4 9:2005 pp.349-368.

3026   Communicating threat: the Canadian state and terrorism. Erin E. Gibbs Van Brunschot; Alison J. Sherley. **Sociol. Q.** 46:4 Fall:2005 pp.645-669.

3027   Comparing media systems: three models of media and politics. Daniel C. Hallin; Paolo Mancini. Cambridge: Cambridge University Press, 2004. xv, 342p. *ISBN: 0521835356, 0521543088. Includes bibliographical references and index. (Series:* Communication, society, and politics).

3028   A constructed peace: narrative of suture in the news media; *[Summary in French]*. Jody Lyneé Madeira. **Can. J. Law Soc.** 19:2 2004 pp.93-125.

3029   Defending communicative spaces the remits and limits of the European parliament. Katharine Sarikakis. **Gazette** 67:2 4:2005 pp.155-172.

3030   Dienstleister oder Aufklärer? Nivellierung, Inszenierung und PR als Gefahren für die „Vierte Gewalt". *[In German]*; [Service provider or enlighteners? Levelling, staging and public relations threatening the 'fourth power']. Thomas Leif. **Vorgänge** 44:1(169) 3:2005 pp.34-48.

3031 Entertaining politics: new political television and civic culture. Jeffrey P. Jones. Lanham MD: Rowman & Littlefield, 2005. xiv, 243p. *ISBN: 0742530876, 0742530884. Includes bibliographical references and index. (Series:* Communication, media, and politics).

3032 Epic encounters: culture, media, and U.S. interests in the Middle East since 1945. Melani McAlister. Berkeley CA: University of California Press, 2005. xix, 407p. *ISBN: 0520244990. Includes bibliographical references (p. 363-392) and index. (Series:* American crossroads - 6).

3033 Evaluation of media and understanding of politics: the role of education among Hong Kong citizens. Francis L.F. Lee; Joseph M. Chan; Clement Y.K. So. **Asian J. Communic.** 15:1 3:2005 pp.37-56.

3034 Framing peace policies: the competition for resonant themes. David Levin. **Pol. Communic.** 22:1 1-3:2005 pp.83-108.

3035 Hindi press in the post-SAARC 2004 period. Shahbaz Saeed. **Strat. S.** XXIV:4 Winter:2004 pp.166-185.

3036 HTV — javna televizija? Programsko vijeće HRT-a — institucija javnog nadzora ili političke kontrole? *[In Croatian]*; (HTV: public television? HRT's programme council: institution of public scrutiny or political control?) *[Summary]*. Viktorija Popović. **Pol. Misao** 41:2 2004 pp.17-29.

3037 L'implication des journalistes dans le phénomène Le Pen. *[In French]*; [The involvment of journalists in the Le Pen phenomenon]. Jacques Le Bohec. Paris: L'Harmattan, 2004. *ISBN: 2747570207, 2747570215. Two volumes. Includes bibliographical references.*

3038 The influence of events and (mis)information on Israeli Jewish public opinion: the case of the camp David Summit and the second intifada. Daniel Bar-Tal. **Palestine-Israel J. Pol. Econ. Cult.** 11:3-4 2004-2005 pp.112-124.

3039 International media régime and news management: implications for African states. Meenal Shrivastava; Nathalie Hyde-Clarke. **Politikon** 31:2 11:2004 pp.201-218.

3040 Intramedia mediation: the cumulative and complementary effects of news media use. R. Lance Holbert. **Pol. Communic.** 22:4 10-12:2005 pp.447-461.

3041 Inventing black-on-black violence: discourse, space, and representation. David Wilson. Syracuse NY: Syracuse University Press, 2005. xiv, 193p. *ISBN: 0815630808. Includes bibliographical references (p. 163-179) and index. (Series:* Space, place, and society).

3042 L'Humanité de Jaurès a nos jours. *[In French]*; [L'Humanité from Jaurès to nowadays]. Christian Delporte [Ed.]; et al. : Nouveau Monde Editions, 2004. 419p. *ISBN: 2847360816. Conference papers, Bibliothèque Nationale de France, April 2004.*

3043 Manipulating media content: public sector advertising in the press in Botswana — a comment on media publishing v attorney general of Botswana. Badala Tachilisa Balule. **S. Afr. J. Human Rights** 20:4 2004 pp.653-663.

3044 A measure of media bias. Tim Groseclose; Jeffrey Milyo. **Q. J. Econ.** CXX:4 11:2005 pp.1191-1238.

3045 Media diversity and the contested character of the post-apartheid state. Devan Pillay. **Politikon** 31:2 11:2004 pp.167-184.

3046 Media effects and Russian elections, 1999-2000. Stephen White; Sarah Oates; Ian McAllister. **Br. J. Pol. Sci.** 35:2 4:2005 pp.191-208.

3047 Media i vlast' v sovremennoi Rossii (I). *[In Russian]*; [Media and power in contemporary Russia (Part I)]. M.M. Nazarov. **Sots.Gum. Znan.** 1 2004 pp.20-32.

3048 Media i vlast' v sovremennoi Rossii (II). *[In Russian]*; [Media and power in contemporary Russia (part II)]. M.M. Nazarov. **Sots.Gum. Znan.** 2 2004 pp.16-29.

3049 Media, war and terrorism: responses from the Middle East and Asia. Peter van der Veer [Ed.]; Shoma Munshi [Ed.]. New York, London: RoutledgeCurzon, 2004. 260p. *ISBN: 0415331404. Includes index. (Series:* Politics in Asia).

3050 Medialisierte Kriege und Kriegsberichterstattung. *[In German]*; [Wars in media and war reporting]. Christiane Eilders; Lutz M. Hagen; Andrea Szukala; Oliver Hahn; Adrian Pohr; Helmut Scherer; Romy Fröhlich; Bertram Scheufele; Simone Dammert; Natascha Thomas;

Wolfgang Donsbach; Olaf Jandura; Diana Müller; Frank Esser; Christine Schwabe; Jürgen Wilke; Evelyn Bytzek. **Medien Kommun.wissen.** 53:2-3 2005 pp.205-388. *Collection of 10 articles.*

3051 News incorporated: corporate media ownership and its threat to democracy. Elliot D. Cohen [Ed.]; Arthur Kent [Foreword]. Amherst NY: Prometheus Books, 2005. 319p. *ISBN: 1591022320. Includes bibliographical references and index.*

3052 News media coverage influence on Japan's foreign aid allocations. David M. Potter; Douglas Van Belle. **Japanese J. Pol. Sci.** 5:1 5:2004 pp.113-136.

3053 Nowy stary klientelizm. System obsadzania stanowisk w postkomunistycznej Polsce (na przykładzie nominacji do rad nadzorczych publicznych mediów). *[In Polish]*; (New old clientelism. The appointment system in the Polish post-communist public media.) *[Summary]*. Maciej Tymiński; Piotr Koryś. **Kult. Społ.** XLVIII:2 2004 pp.97-120.

3054 Photojournalism and foreign affairs. David D. Perlmutter. **Orbis** 49:1 Winter:2005 pp.109-122.

3055 Predstavljenost nacionalnih manjina u hrvatskim dnevnim novinama — komparativni pregled 2001.-2003. *[In Croatian]*; (Representation of national minorities in Croatian dailies — a comparative review 2001-2003.) *[Summary]*. Igor Kanižaj. **Pol. Misao** 41:2 2004 pp.30-46.

3056 Presidential press conferences: the importance and evolution of an enduring forum. Martha Joynt Kumar. **Pres. Stud. Q.** 35:1 3:2005 pp.166-192.

3057 Reporting from the front: the media and the military. Judith L. Sylvester; Suzanne Huffman. Lanham MD: Rowman & Littlefield, 2005. xi, 266p. *ISBN: 0742530590, 0742530604. Includes bibliographical references and index.*

3058 Reporting on labour: class consciousness and the uncertain ideological boundaries of Canadian journalism; *[Summary in Slovene]*. Gene Costain. **Javnost** XII:1 4:2005 pp.49-69.

3059 The role of the UK local press in the local constituency campaign. Ralph Negrine. **Journalism S.** 6:1 2:2005 pp.103-115.

3060 The rough and rosy road: sites of contestation in Malaysia's shackled media industry. Graham Brown. **Pac. Aff.** 78:1 Spring:2005 pp.39-56.

3061 Schwarzenegger syndrome: politics and celebrity in the Age of Contempt. Gary Indiana. New York: W.W. Norton & Company, 2005. xviii, 140p. *ISBN: 1565849515.*

3062 Selling intervention and war: the presidency, the media, and the American public. Jon W. Western. Baltimore MD: Johns Hopkins University Press, 2005. xi, 305p. *ISBN: 0801881080, 0801881099. Includes bibliographical references (p. 277-294) and index.*

3063 Silvio Berlusconi: television, power and patrimony. Paul Ginsborg. London, New York: Verso, 2004. xvi, 189p. *ISBN: 1844670007. Includes bibliographical references and index.*

3064 La télévision, média du pouvoir. *[In French]*; (Television as the power's medium.) *[Summary]*. Floriana Fossato. **Pouvoirs** 112 2004 pp.49-61.

3065 Terror, televisão, telemóvel: o papel dos media no 11 de Março. *[In Portuguese]*; (Terror, television and mobile phones: March 11 and the role of the media.) *[Summary]*. Miguel Gaspar. **Relações Int.** 5 3:2005 pp.133-146.

3066 Ugrozy obyvatel'skoi zhurnalistiki. *[In Russian]*; (The menace of narrow-minded journalism.) Elena Khabenskaia. **Svobod. Mysl'** 6 2005 pp.93-105.

3067 Utjecaj pluralizma medija na demokratski proces u Bosni i Hercegovini. *[In Croatian]*; (Influence of media pluralism on the democratic process in Bosnia and Herzegovina.) *[Summary]*. Marko Sapunar; Zoran Tomić. **Pol. Misao** 41:2 2004 pp.3-16.

3068 War, media, and propaganda: a global perspective. Yahya R. Kamalipour [Ed.]; Nancy Snow [Ed.]. Lanham MD: Rowman & Littlefield, 2004. xv, 261p. *ISBN: 0742535622, 0742535630. Includes bibliographical references and index.*

3069 'What do the papers say?' How press reviews link national media arenas in Europe. Jessica Erbe. **Javnost** XII:2 6:2005 pp.75-91.

3070 Your past and the press! Controversial presidential appointments: a study focusing on the impact of interest groups and media activity on the appointment process. Joseph Michael

Green. Dallas TX: University Press of America, 2004. x, 167p. *ISBN: 0761828028. Includes bibliographical references (p. 159-166).*

3071 "Zdes' bylo NTV", TB-6, TBC i drugie istorii. *[In Russian]*; ['Here lies NTV', TV-6, TVS and other stories]. Viktor Shenderovich. Moscow: Zakharov, 2004. 199p. *ISBN: 5815903477.*

E.1: Public policy
Politique publique

3072   Comparaisons internationales en politiques publiques : stratégies de recherche, méthodes et interprétation. *[In French]*; [International comparisons of public policy: research strategies, methods and interpretation]. Monika Steffen. **R. Int. Pol. Comp.** 11:3 2004 pp.339-455.

3073   El control de las ayudas públicas en España: un contexto a cambiar. *[In Spanish]*; [The control of public subsidies in Spain: a context to change]. José Eugenio Soriano García; M. Mathilde Sánchez Gutiérrez. **R. Admin. Públ.** 166 1-4:2005 pp.231-256.

3074   Cross-national policy convergence: causes, concepts and empirical findings. Katharina Holzinger; Christoph Knill; Andrea Lenschow; Duncan Liefferink; Sietske Veenman; Stephan Heichel; Jessica Pape; Thomas Sommerer; Daniel W. Drezner; Per-Olof Busch; Helge Jörgens; Johan Albrecht; Bas Arts; Martin Marcussen; Claudio M. Radaelli; Andrew Jordan; David Levi-Faur. **J. Euro. Publ. Policy** 12:5 2005 pp.76-953. *Collection of 11 articles.*

3075   Décider, gérer, réformer : les voies de la gouvernance. *[In French]*; [Deciding, managing and reforming: processes of governance]. Sciences humaines. **Sci. Hum.** 44 3-5:2004 pp.3-87.

3076   Deliberative democracy in theory and practice: Connecticut's medicaid managed care council. Colleen M. Grogan; Michael K. Gusmano. **State Pol. Policy Q.** 5:2 Summer:2005 pp.126-146.

3077   Democracia y sector publico. *[In Spanish]*; [Democracy and public sector]. Juan Hernandez Bravo De Laguna; Jose M. Dominguez Martinez; Juan Torres Lopez; Alberto Montero Soler; Carles Ramio Matas; Jacint Jordana; Blanca Olias De Lima Gete; Laura Roman Masedo; Rosa Maria Rodriguez Rodriguez; Fernando Harto De Vera; Jose Manuel Canales Aliende; Juan Maldonado Gago; Manuel Mella Marquez; Elena Roldan Garcia; Luis Ortega; Manuel Villoria Mendieta. **Sistema** 184-185 1:2005 pp.13-295. *Collection of 15 articles.*

3078   Dictionnaire des politiques publiques. *[In French]*; [Dictionary of public policies]. Laurie Boussaguet [Ed.]; Sophie Jacquot [Ed.]; Pauline Ravinet [Ed.]; Pierre Muller [Foreword]. Paris: Presses de Sciences Po, 2004. 518p. *ISBN: 2724609484. Includes bibliographical references (p. [461]-506).*

3079   Financing services of general interest in the EU: how do public procurement and state aids interact to demarcate between market forces and protection? Christopher H. Bovis. **Euro. Law J.** 11:1 1:2005 pp.79-109.

3080   Funktsii sovremennogo gosudarstva: vyzovy dlia Rossii. *[In Russian]*; (Functions of the modern state: challenges for Russia.) Sergei Rogov. **Svobod. Mysl'** 8 2005 pp.82-94.

3081   Governance, rurality, and nature: exploring emerging discourses of state forestry in Britain. Kieron G. Stanley; Terry K. Marsden; Paul Milbourne. **Env. Plan. C.** 23:5 10:2005 pp.679-695.

3082   Government size and economic growth: an investigation of causality in India. Ramesh Chandra. **Indian Econ. R.** XXXIX:2 7-12:2004 pp.295-314.

3083   The limits of engineering collective escape: the 2000 reform of the Greek labour market. Dimitris Papadimitriou. **West Euro. Pol.** 28:2 3:2005 pp.381-401.

3084   Meeting the new foreign direct investment challenge in East and Central Europe: place-marketing strategies in Hungary. Craig Young. **Env. Plan. C.** 23:5 10:2005 pp.733-757.

3085   A model of choice for public policy. Bryan D. Jones; Frank R. Baumgartner. **J. Publ. Admin. Res. Theory** 15:3 7:2005 pp.325-351.

3086   Nationalisations et dénationalisations. *[In French]*; (The international experience of nationalisation and denationalisation.) Dominique Barjot; Judith Clifton; Daniel Díaz Fuentes; Pier Angelo Toninelli; Pedro Pablo Ortúñez; Lina Gálvez Muñoz; Francisco Comín; Ana Bela Nunes; Carlos Bastien; Nuno Valério; Vassilis Patronis; Panagiotis Liargovas; Michel Bon [Discussant]; Ian Byatt [Discussant]; Éric Godelier [Discussant]; Stephen C. Littlechild [Discussant]; Robert Millward [Discussant]; Pierre Lanthier [Interviewer]; Martin Chick [Interviewer]; Alexandre Giandou [Interviewer]. **Entr. Hist.** 37 12:2004 pp.9-171. *Collection of 9 articles.*

3087   Nauka i obrazovanie v opasnosti. *[In Russian]*; (Science and education are in danger.) Anatolii Kul'kin. **Svobod. Mysl'** 8 2005 pp.129-146.

3088   The perfect is the enemy of the best: adaptive versus optimal organizational reliability. Jonathan Bendor; Sunil Kumar. **J. Theor. Pol.** 17:1 1:2005 pp.5-39.

3089   Policy, theory and pragmatism: implementing the UK's energy efficiency best practice programme; *[Summary in Spanish]*; *[Summary in French]*. John Rigby. **Policy Pol.** 33:2 4:2005 pp.277-295.

3090   Political institutions, policymaking processes and policy outcomes in Paraguay, 1954-2003; *[Summary in Spanish]*. José Molinas; Aníbal Pérez Liñán; Sebastián Saiegh. **R. Cien. Pol.** XXIV:2 2004 pp.67-93.

3091   La prévention du crime : perspectives canadiennes et internationales. *[In French]*; (Crime prevention: Canadian and international perspectives.) Ross Hastings; Lucie Léonard; Giselle Rosario; Carolyn Scott; Jessica Bressan; Rick Linden; Renuka Chaturvedi; Patricia L. Brantingham; Paul J. Brantingham; Wendy Taylor; Margaret Shaw; Caroline Andrew; Sophie Paquin; Brandon C. Welsh; David P. Farrington; Peter Homel; Tim Hope; Kauko Aromaa; Jukka-Pekka Takala; Sebastian Roché; Anton du Plessis; Antoinette Louw; Amie M. Schuck; Daniel Sansfaçon. **Can. J. Crimin.** 47:2 4:2005 pp.209-479. *Collection of 14 articles.*

3092   The public governance of collaborative spaces: discourse, design and democracy. Chris Skelcher; Navdeep Mathur; Mike Smith. **Publ. Admin.** 83:3 2005 pp.573-596.

3093   Reconsidering risk: adapting public policies to intergenerational determinants and biosocial interactions in health-related needs. Kate W. Strully; Dalton Conley. **J. Health Pol. Policy Law** 29:6 12:2004 pp.1073-1107.

3094   La regolazione: il concetto, le teorie, le modalità. Verso una tipologia unificante. *[In Italian]*; [Regulation: concept, theories, modalities. Towards a unified typology] *[Summary]*. Giorgio Giraudi. **Riv. It. Pol. Pub.** 1 4:2004 pp.57-86.

3095   Responsive government? Public opinion and government policy preferences in Britain and Denmark. Sara Binzer Hobolt; Robert Klemmensen. **Pol. S.** 53:2 6:2005 pp.379-402.

3096   Setting the stage: a dramaturgy of policy deliberation. Maarten A. Hajer. **Admin. Soc.** 36:6 1:2005 pp.624-647.

3097   Understanding tourism policy-making in urban areas, with particular reference to small firms; *[Summary in French]*; *[Summary in German]*. Rhodri Thomas; Huw Thomas. **Tour. Geog.** 7:2 5:2005 pp.121-137.

3098   Usages et effets du savoir : articuler sciences sociales et politiques publiques. *[In French]*; [Uses and effects of knowledge: articulating social sciences and public policies]. Revue internationale des sciences sociales. **R. Inter. Sc. Soc.** 179 3:2004 pp.3-169.

3099   Using geographic information systems to study interstate competition. William D. Berry; Brady Baybeck. **Am. Pol. Sci. R.** 99:4 11:2005 pp.505-519.

3100   The war at home: the domestic causes of Bush's militarism. Frances Fox Piven. New York: New Press, 2004. 165p. *ISBN: 1565849353. Includes bibliographical references.*

3101   Why and how do state governments adopt and implement 'managing for results' reforms? Donald P. Moynihan. **J. Publ. Admin. Res. Theory** 15:2 4:2005 pp.219-243.

3102   Zur Umsetzung der Rechte des UNO-Pakts über wirtschaftliche, soziale und kulturelle Rechte aus schweizer Sicht — Das Projekt eines Fakultativprotokolls zum UNO-Pakt I. *[In German]*; [The implementation of the UN law on economic, social and cultural rights from Swiss perspective] *[Summary]*. C.A. Spenlé; N. Schrepfer. **Z. Öffent. Recht** 59:4 2004 pp.375-414.

Policy evaluation
Évaluation des politiques

3103   L'analyse politique de l'action publique : confrontation des approches, des concepts et des méthodes. *[In French]*; [The political analysis of public action: approaches, concepts and methods]. Bruno Palier; Yves Surel; Richard Balme; Sylvain Brouard; Christine Musselin; Philippe Bongrand; Pascale Laborier; Patrick Hassenteufel; Renaud Payre; Gilles Pollet; Pierre Muller; Pierre Favre; Gil Delannoi. **R. Fran. Sci. Pol.** 55:1 2:2005 pp.7-187. *Collection of 7 articles.*

3104   A critique of the use of path dependency in policy studies. Adrian Kay. **Publ. Admin.** 83:3 2005 pp.553-572.

3105   Developing and testing an integrative framework of public sector leadership: evidence from the public education arena. Sergio Fernandez. **J. Publ. Admin. Res. Theory** 15:2 4:2005 pp.197-217.

3106   Le développement des agences en Grance-Bretagne et en France — l'exemple d'ÉduFrance, transfert d'outre-Manche ou création indigène ? *[In French]*; (The growth of agencies in Britain and France: EduFrance-transferred from Britain or indigenous creation?) *[Summary]*. Anneliese Dodds. **R. Fran. Admin. Publ.** 111 2004 pp.483-500.

3107   The diffusion of innovations: how cognitive heuristics shaped Bolivia's pension reform. Kurt Weyland. **Comp. Pol.** 38:1 10:2005 pp.21-42.

3108   External constraints on local service standards: the case of comprehensive performance assessment in English local government. Rhys Andrews; George A. Boyne; Jennifer Law; Richard M. Walker. **Publ. Admin.** 83:3 2005 pp.639-656.

3109   From policy lessons to policy actions: motivation to take evaluation seriously. G. Gordillo; K. Andersson. **Publ. Admin. Dev.** 24:4 10:2004 pp.305-320.

3110   A funny thing happened on the way to the forum? Reforming patient and public involvement in the NHS in England. Rob Baggott. **Publ. Admin.** 83:3 2005 pp.533-551.

3111   Les grands équipements en sciences de la vie : quelle politique publique? *[In French]*; (High-tech facilities in the life sciences: what should public policy be?) *[Summary]*. Vincent Mangematin; Ashveen Perbaye. **R. Fran. Admin. Publ.** 112 2004 pp.705-718.

3112   How will we know the Millennium Development Goal results when we see them? Building a results-based monitoring and evaluation system to give us the answers. Jody Z. Kusek; Ray C. Rist; Elizabeth M. White. **Evaluation** 11:1 1:2005 pp.7-26.

3113   The importance of being modern: international benchmarking and national regulatory innovation. Martin Lodge. **J. Euro. Publ. Policy** 12:4 2005 pp.649-667.

3114   L'institutionnalisation de l'évaluation des politiques publiques en Belgique : entre balbutiements et incantations. *[In French]*; (The institutionalisation of policy evaluation in Belgium: groping in the dark and black magic.) *[Summary]*. Steve Jacob. **Res Publica [Bruss.]** XLVI:4 2004 pp.512-534.

3115   Interactive policy development: undermining or sustaining democracy? Igor Mayer; Jurian Edelenbos; René Monnikhof. **Publ. Admin.** 83:1 2005 pp.179-199.

3116   L'administration et les politiques de recherche : quelles spécificités? *[In French]*; (Specificities of research policies and their administration.) *[Summary]*. Jean-Richard Cytermann. **R. Fran. Admin. Publ.** 112 2004 pp.625-635.

3117   Investigating the potential of key sectors using multisectoral qualitative analysis: a Welsh case study. Jane Bryan; Calvin Jones; Max Munday. **Env. Plan. C.** 23:5 10:2005 pp.633-656.

3118   Konsequenzen von Staatsreformen für die demokratische Steuerungsfähigkeit. Vergleichende Analyse zu vier Schweizer Kantonen. *[In German]*; (The consequences of political reforms on democratic governance. A comparative analysis of four Swiss cantons.) *[Summary]*. Thomas Widmer; Erwin Rüegg. **Polit. Viertel.** 46:1 3:2005 pp.86-109.

3119   Large-scale social experimentation in Britain: what can and cannot be learnt from the employment retention and advancement demonstration? David H. Greenberg; Stephen Morris. **Evaluation** 11:2 4:2005 pp.223-242.

3120 Maintaining the coalition: class coalitions and policy trajectories. Bill Winders. **Pol. Soc.** 33:3 9:2005 pp.387-423.

3121 On the relationship between political science and administrative science in Germany. Jörg Bogumil. **Publ. Admin.** 83:3 2005 pp.669-684.

3122 Pension reform in Greece: 'reform by instalments' — a blocked process? Platon Tinios. **West Euro. Pol.** 28:2 3:2005 pp.402-419.

3123 Political choice, public policy, and distributional outcomes. Nathan J. Kelly. **Am. J. Pol. Sci.** 49:4 10:2005 pp.865-880.

3124 The political economy of expertise: information and efficiency in American national politics. Kevin M. Esterling. Ann Arbor MI: University of Michigan Press, 2004. xiv, 286p. *ISBN: 0472113984, 0472030647. Includes bibliographical references (p. 259-275) and index.*

3125 The politics of evaluation: participation and policy implementation. David Taylor [Ed.]; Susan Balloch. Bristol: Policy Press, 2005. 261p. *ISBN: 1861346069, 1861346050.*

3126 Public administration, science, and risk assessment: a case study of the U.K. bovine spongiform encephalopathy crisis. Matthias Beck; Darinka Asenova; Gordon Dickson. **Publ. Admin. R.** 65:4 7-8:2005 pp.396-408.

3127 Public service improvement: policies, progress and prospects. Tom Entwistle; Steve J. Martin; Gareth Enticott; Helen Sullivan; Gillian Gillanders; Clive Grace; Liz Millward; Barry Quirk; David Turner; Philip Whiteman; Steven P. Jones; Lucy de Groot; Lyndsay Rashman; James Downe; Jean Hartley. **Loc. Govt. S.** 31:5 11:2005 pp.531-700. *Collection of 10 articles.*

3128 A realist evaluation approach to understanding the best value review process. Paul Davis; Paul Wright. **Loc. Govt. S.** 30:3 Autumn:2004 pp.423-440.

3129 Recently introduced policy instruments and intervention theories. Petrus Kautto; Jukka Similä. **Evaluation** 11:1 1:2005 pp.55-68.

3130 The regulation of political financing in Portugal. Luís de Sousa. **West Euro. Pol.** 27:1 1:2004 pp.124-145.

3131 Regulatory impact assessment and regulatory governance in developing countries. C. Kirkpatrick; D. Parker. **Publ. Admin. Dev.** 24:4 10:2004 pp.333-344.

3132 Results evaluation and impact assessment in development co-operation. Rob D. Van Den Berg. **Evaluation** 11:1 1:2005 pp.27-36.

3133 Social policymaking and inequality in the era of globalization: cross-regional comparisons. Meredith Weiss; Michael J. Bosia; Krista Johnson; Isabella Alcañiz; Galya Benarieh Ruffer; Sheila D. Collins; Michael Parenti; Carl Boggs. **New Pol. Sci.** 27:3 9:2005 pp.261-421. *Collection of 8 articles.*

3134 Targeting, residual welfare and related concepts: modes of operation in public policy. Paul Spicker. **Publ. Admin.** 83:2 2005 pp.345-366.

Public sector
Secteur public

3135 Administración pública y tercer sector. Propuesta analítica y estudio del caso de Andalucía. *[In Spanish]*; (Public administration and non-profit sector. Analitical proposal and study of the Andalusia case.) *[Summary]*. Clemente J. Navaro Yáñez; María Jesús Rodríguez García. **Papers** 73 2004 pp.105-125.

3136 The Barbados Protocols and social dialogue in the Caribbean. Andrew S. Downes; Lawrence Nurse; Tayo Fashoyin; Evelyn Greaves; Lloyd E. Sandiford; John S. Goddard; Leroy Trotman. **J. East Carib. S.** 29:4 12:2004 pp.1-111. *Collection of 6 articles.*

3137 'Best practices' research: a methodological guide for the perplexed. Stuart Bretschneider; Frederick J. Marc-Aurele, Jr.; Jiannan Wu. **J. Publ. Admin. Res. Theory** 15:2 4:2005 pp.307-323.

3138 Buying out the state a comparative perspective on the privatization of infrastructures. Volker Schneider; Simon Fink; Marc Tenbücken. **Comp. Pol. S.** 38:6 8:2005 pp.704-727.

3139   Citizen redress in public contracting for human services. Peter Vincent-Jones. **Mod. Law R.** 68:6 11:2005 pp.887-924.

3140   Contractual uncertainty, power and public contracting. Chris Lonsdale. **J. Publ. Policy** 25:2 5-8:2005 pp.219-240.

3141   Developing infrastructure as a learning process in Greece. Christos J. Paraskevopoulos. **West Euro. Pol.** 28:2 3:2005 pp.445-470.

3142   Données sur le rendement public et décisions des entreprises privées. *[In French]*; [Data on public profit and private enterprises decisions]. Arie Halachmi [Ed.]. **R. Int. Sci. Admin.** 70:1 3:2004 pp.3-178.

3143   Eminent domain for private sports stadiums: fair ball or foul? Philip Weinberg. **Env. Law** 35:2 Spring:2005 pp.311-322.

3144   The evolution of Dyadic interorganizational relationships in a network of publicly funded nonprofit agencies. Kimberley Roussin Isett; Keith G. Provan. **J. Publ. Admin. Res. Theory** 15:1 1:2005 pp.149-165.

3145   The formation of public-private partnerships: lessons from nine transport infrastructure projects in the Netherlands. J. Joop F.M. Koppenjan. **Publ. Admin.** 83:1 2005 pp.135-157.

3146   Interdependent and domestic foundations of policy change: the diffusion of pension privatization around the world. Sarah M. Brooks. **Int. S. Q.** 49:2 6:2005 pp.273-294.

3147   Konkurrenz der öffentlichen Hand für privatwirtschaftliche Unternehmen aus der Perspektive des Vergaberechts. *[In German]*; (Public procurement law and competition of public authorities with business companies.) *[Summary]*. Hans-Peter Schwintowski. **Z. Öffent. Gemein. Unternehm.** 27:4 2004 pp.360-376.

3148   Közpénzek — magánpénzek avagy a számvevőszéki ellenőrzés alkotmányjogi problémái. *[In Hungarian]*; (Public money — private money or the constitutional problems of the control of the state audit office.) Kinga Pétervári. Budapest: Gondolat Kiadó, 2004. 185p. *ISBN: 963950081X. Includes bibliographical references (p. 173-179).*

3149   Les liens entre le CNRS et l'université. *[In French]*; (Relations between the CNRS and the university.) *[Summary]*. Girolamo Ramunni. **R. Fran. Admin. Publ.** 112 2004 pp.637-646.

3150   Où le partenariat public-privé devient l'instrument privilégié du développement économique local. L'exemple de Durban, Afrique du Sud. *[In French]*; (Where the public-private partnership becomes a privileged tool for local economic development. The example of Durban, South Africa.) *[Summary]*. Bill Freund; Benoît Lootvoet. **Tiers Monde** XLVI:181 1-3:2005 pp.45-70.

3151   Performance-based partnership agreements for the reconstruction of the health system in Afghanistan. Valéry Ridde. **Dev. Pract.** 15:1 2:2005 pp.4-15.

3152   Playing by the rules: restricted endowment assets in colleges and universities. Lelia Helms; Alan B. Henkin; Kyle Murray. **Nonprof. Manag. Leader.** 15:3 Spring:2005 pp.341-356.

3153   The politics of privatisation: redrawing the public-private boundary. George Pagoulatos. **West Euro. Pol.** 28:2 3:2005 pp.358-380.

3154   The politics of public-private partnerships. Matthew Flinders. **Br. J. Pol. Int. Rel.** 7:2 5:2005 pp.215-239.

3155   Privatisations, sous-traitance et partenariats public-privé : charity.com ou business.org? *[In French]*; (Privatization, outsourcing and public-private partnerships: charity.com or business.org?) *[Summary]*. Gilles Carbonnier. **Int. R. Red Cross** 86:856 12:2004 pp.725-743.

3156   Die Privatisierungsprüfpflicht als Einstieg in die Verwaltungsprivatisierung. *[In German]*; [Compulsory checks for possible privatization measures as a first step towards the privatization of public administration]. Joachim Sanden. **Verwalt.** 38:3 2005 pp.367-398.

3157   Providing enterprise support for offenders: realising new opportunities or reinforcing old inequalities? Del Roy Fletcher. **Env. Plan. C.** 23:5 10:2005 pp.715-731.

3158   Public sector efficiency: an international comparison. A. Afonso; L. Schuknecht; V. Tanzi. **Publ. Choice** 123:3-4 6:2005 pp.321-348.

3159   Reconstituting the public-private divide under global conditions: the case of Dutch and British water management. Willemijn Dicke; Martin Albrow. **Glo. Soc. Policy** 5:2 8:2005 pp.227-248.

3160   Regulation and public sector development: a post-transition perspective. László Csaba. **Post-Comm. Econ.** 17:2 6:2005 pp.137-152.

3161   Risks in public-private partnerships: shifting, sharing or shirking? Graeme A. Hodge. **Asian J. Publ. Admin.** 26:2 12:2004 pp.155-179.

3162   The state is rolling back: essays in persuasion. Arthur Seldon; Colin Robinson [Ed.]. Indianapolis IN: Liberty Fund, 2004. xxxix, 302p. *ISBN: 0865975434, 0865975515. (Series:* The collected works of Arthur Seldon - 2).

3163   State social services contracting: exploring the determinants of effective contract accountability. Barbara S. Romzek; Jocelyn M. Johnston. **Publ. Admin. R.** 65:4 7-8:2005 pp.436-449.

3164   Valuing the benefits of public libraries. S. Aabø. **Info. Econ. Policy** 17:2 3:2005 pp.175-198.

3165   Veränderung öffentlicher Beschäftigung im Prozess der Liberalisierung und Privatisierung. *[In German]*; (Transformation of public employment in the process of liberalisation and privatization — recommodification of work and emergence of a neoliberal employment regime.); *[Summary in English]*. Roland Atzmüller; Christoph Hermann. **Öster. Z. Soziol.** 29:4 2004 pp.30-48.

3166   Victoria's partly-privatised prison system: an accountability report card. Valarie Sands. **Asian J. Publ. Admin.** 26:2 12:2004 pp.135-154.

3167   Win-win or new imperialism? Public-private partnerships in Africa mining. Suzanne Dansereau. **R. Afr. Pol. Econ.** 32:103 3:2005 pp.47-62.

E.2:   **Economic policy**
            Politique économique

3168   2003 — a fekete év. *[In Hungarian]*; (2003 — the black year.) Magdolna Csath. Budapest: Kairosz Kiadó, 2004. 227p. *ISBN: 9639568155.*

3169   The age of commodity: water privatization in Southern Africa. David A. McDonald [Ed.]; Greg Ruiters [Ed.]. London: Earthscan, 2005. xv, 303p. *ISBN: 1844071359, 1844071340. Includes bibliographical references and index.*

3170   Agenda 2010: German social democracy and the market state. Peter Thompson. **Debatte** 12:1 11:2004 pp.9-24.

3171   The business of governing business in China: institutions and norms of the emerging regulatory state. Margaret M. Pearson. **World Pol.** 57:2 1:2005 pp.296-322.

3172   El ciclo político-económico en Estados Unidos (1991-2004). De la nueva economía de Clinton a la economía de guerra de Bush (segunda parte). *[In Spanish]*; [United States political-economic cycle (1991-2004). From Clinton's new economy to Bush's military economy (second part)]. José García Menéndez. **Est. Inter.** XXXVII:147 10-12:2004 pp.51-96.

3173   Dispossessing H2O: the contested terrain of water privatization. Erik Swyngedouw. **Cap. Nat. Social.** 16:1 3:2005 pp.81-98.

3174   Dois anos de Governo Lula: resultados e alternativas às políticas econômicas adotadas. *[In Portuguese]*; [Two years of Lula's Government: results and alternatives to the adopted economic policies] *[Summary]*. Ricardo Dathein. **Ind. Econ. FEE** 33:1 2005 pp.253-268.

3175   Economic notes: when policies collide. Jeremy Leaman. **Debatte** 12:2 11:2004 pp.154-166.

3176   L'économie israélienne, 1990-2003. *[In French]*; [Israelian economy, 1990-2003]. Mohamed El-Battiui. **R. Ét. Palest.** 95 Spring:2005 pp.33-50.

3177   Ekonomicheskaia nauka v obosnovanii natsional'noi strategii Rossii. *[In Russian]*; (Economics and Russia's national strategy.) E.N. Veduta. **Vest. Mosk. Univ. 12 Pol.** 1 1-2:2005 pp.80-102.

3178   España: un modelo estatista de liberalización económica. *[In Spanish]*; [Spain: a state model of economic liberalization] *[Summary]*. Sebastián Etchemendy. **Desar. Econ.** 44:175 10-12:2004 pp.339-364.

3179   Europeanisation, public goals and group interests: convergence policy in Greece, 1990-2003. Panos Kazakos. **West Euro. Pol.** 27:5 11:2004 pp.901-918.

3180   Az eurorégiók szerepének változása Magyarország uniós csatlakozása után. *[In Hungarian]*; (The changing role of the euroregions following Hungary's accession to the European Union.) *[Summary]*. Barbara Baller. **Euro. Tükör** 9:1 2004 pp.145-171.

3181   Felzárkózás és versenyképesség. Stratégiai dilemmák az EU Lisszaboni programjának megvalósításával kapcsolatban — kísérlet egy vitaindítóra. *[In Hungarian]*; (Reform and competitiveness. Strategic dilemma concerning the realisation of the European Union's Lisbon programme — opening a debate.) *[Summary]*. Ádám Török. **Euro. Tükör** 9:3 2004 pp.60-77.

3182   Globalization, alternative modernities and the political economy of Turkey. E. Fuat Keyman; Berrin Koyuncu. **R. Int. Pol. Econ.** 12:1 2:2005 pp.105-128.

3183   Governmentalities of local partnerships: the rise of a 'partnering state' in New Zealand. Wendy Larner; Maria Butler. **S. Pol. Econ.** 75 Spring:2005 pp.79-101.

3184   Neoconomy: George Bush's revolutionary gamble with Americas future. Daniel Altman. New York: Public Affairs, 2004. xii, 290p. *ISBN: 1586482297. Includes bibliographical references and index.*

3185   New approaches to volatility: dealing with the 'resource curse' in sub-Saharan Africa. Nicolas Shaxson. **Int. Aff. [London]** 81:2 3:2005 pp.311-324.

3186   Políticas de reconversión en contextos de cambio estructural. *[In Spanish]*; [Reconversion policies of contexts of structural change] *[Summary]*. Marcela Meléndez A.; Ricardo Paredes M. **Coy. Econ.** XXXV:1 2005 pp.105-151.

3187   The politics of India's next generation of economic reforms. Montek Singh Ahluwalia; Rahul Mukherji; John Echeverri-Gent; Rob Jenkins; Devesh Kapur; Sanjaya Baru; E. Sridharan. **India R.** 3:4 10:2004 pp.269-428. *Collection of 7 articles.*

3188   Les politiques économiques américaine et européenne face aux attentats terroristes et aux conflits militaires. *[In French]*; [American and European economic policies confronted with terrorist attacks and military conflicts]. Eric Lahille. **ACCOMEX** 56 3-4:2004 pp.42-56.

3189   Postwar reconstruction: some insights from public choice and institutional economics. Tyler Cowen; Christopher J. Coyne. **Constit. Pol. Econ.** 16:1 3:2005 pp.31-48.

3190   Wenn Angst die Hoffnung besiegt. Eine Bilanz der Wirtschaftspolitik der Regierung Lula. *[In German]*; (When fear overcomes hope. A balance sheet of the economic policy of the first year of Lula's government.) *[Summary]*. Leda Paulani. **Prokla** 35:1 3:2005 pp.149-162.

Agricultural and fisheries policy
Politique agricole et de la pêche

3191   Access to land through rental markets: a (counter-) evolution in the World Bank's policy? *[Summary in Spanish]*; *[Summary in French]*. U. Pica Ciamarra. **Land Ref. Land Sett. Coop.** 2 2004 pp.8-20.

3192   Achieving policy objectives to increase the value of the seafood industry in the United States: the technical feasibility and associated constraints. C.E. Nash. **Food Policy** 29:6 12:2004 pp.621-641.

3193   Barreiras técnicas comerciais aos transgênicos no Brasil: a regulação nos estados do sul. *[In Portuguese]*; [Technical barriers to genetically modified products in Brazil: regulation in southern states] *[Summary]*. Victor Pelaez; Leide Albergoni. **Ind. Econ. FEE** 32:3 2004 pp.201-229.

3194   Bolivia: el anandono de la reforma agragaria en zonas de los valles y el altiplano. *[In Spanish]*; (Bolivia: discarded land reform in the valleys and altiplano.) *[Summary]*;

[Summary in French]. M. Urioste Fernández de Córdova. **Land Ref. Land Sett. Coop.** 2 2004 pp.22-38.

3195   Can negotiated land reforms deliver? The case of Kenya, South Africa and Zimbabwe. Samuel Kariuki. **Sth. Afr. J. Int. Aff.** 11:2 Winter-Spring:2004 pp.117-128.

3196   Centralized planning and economic reforms in a mountainous region of Vietnam. Jean-Christophe Castella; Vincent Gevraise; Paul Novosad. **J. Contemp. Asia** 35:2 2005 pp.166-182.

3197   Les conséquences économiques et sociales des crises agricoles. *[In French]*; [Economic and social consequences of agricultural crises]. Joseph Guimet [Ed.]. **J. Off. Repub. Fran.** 27 11:2004 pp.3-161.

3198   Discards in North Sea fisheries: causes, consequences and solutions. T.L. Catchpole; C.L.J. Frid; T.S. Gray. **Marine Policy** 29:5 9:2005 pp.421-430.

3199   Disrupting enclosure in New England fisheries. Kevin St. Martin. **Cap. Nat. Social.** 16:1 3:2005 pp.63-80.

3200   The downsizing of Russian agriculture. Grigory Ioffe. **Euro.-Asia S.** 57:2 3:2005 pp.179-208.

3201   Evaluating agri-environmental policies: design, practice and results. OECD. Paris: OECD, 2005. 410p. *ISBN: 9264010106. Includes bibliographical references.*

3202   Fisheries management in post-Soviet Russia: legislation, principles, and structure. Geir Hønneland. **Ocean Dev. Int.** 36:2 4-6:2005 pp.179-194.

3203   Fishery management under multiple uncertainty. Gautam Sethi; Christopher Costello; Anthony Fisher; Michael Hanemann; Larry Karp. **J. Env. Econ. Manag.** 50:2 9:2005 pp.300-318.

3204   Framings of science and ideology: organic food labelling in the US and Sweden. Mikael Klintman; Magnus Boström. **Env. Pol.** 13:3 Autumn:2004 pp.612-634.

3205   Gestion des conflits fonciers dans le nord ivoirien : droits, autorités et procédures de règlement des conflits. *[In French]*; (Rights, responsibilities and procedures for the settlement of land disputes in northern Côte d'Ivoire.) *[Summary]*; *[Summary in French]*; *[Summary in Spanish].* A. Coulibaly. **Land Ref. Land Sett. Coop.** 2 2004 pp.68-82.

3206   Growing innovation policy: the case of organic agriculture in Ontario, Canada. Alison Blay-Palmer. **Env. Plan. C.** 23:4 8:2005 pp.557-581.

3207   The hau of other peoples' gifts: land owning and taking in turn-of-the-millennium Fiji. Martha Kaplan. **Ethnohistory** 52:1 Winter:2005 pp.29-46.

3208   Household responses, regional diversity and contemporary agrarian reform in Russia. Stephen K. Wegren; David J. O'Brien; Valeri V. Patsiorkovski. **J. Peasant S.** 31:3-4 4-7:2004 pp.552-587.

3209   Issue redefinition, venue change and radical agricultural policy reforms in Sweden and New Zealand. Carsten Daugbjerg; Jacob Studsgaard. **Scand. Pol. S.** 28:2 2005 pp.103-124.

3210   Japan's interventionist state: bringing agriculture back in. Aurelia George Mulgan. **Japanese J. Pol. Sci.** 6:1 4:2005 pp.29-62.

3211   Land reform and the social origins of private farmers in Russia and Ukraine. Jessica Allina-Pisano. **J. Peasant S.** 31:3-4 4-7:2004 pp.489-514.

3212   Land reform in Namibia: economic versus socio-political rationale; *[Summary in Spanish]*; *[Summary in French].* C. Tapia Garcia. **Land Ref. Land Sett. Coop.** 2 2004 pp.40-53.

3213   Moral hazard, inspection policy, and food safety. S. Andrew Starbird. **Am. J. Agr. Econ.** 87:1 2:2005 pp.15-27.

3214   The Newfoundland fishery: ten years after the moratorium. William E. Schrank. **Marine Policy** 29:5 9:2005 pp.407-420.

3215   On the use of targeting to reduce moral hazard in agri-environmental schemes. Rob Fraser. **J. Agr. Econ.** 55:3 11:2004 pp.525-540.

3216   Policy change and network termination: the role of farm groups in agricultural policy making in Australia. Linda Courtenay Botterill. **Aust. J. Pol. Sci.** 40:2 6:2005 pp.207-219.

3217　Politique agricole et agriculture aux États-Unis : évolution et enjeux actuels. *[In French]*; (Agriculture and agricultural policy in the United States: evolution and issues.) *[Summary]*. S. Devienne; G. Bazin; J.P. Charvet. **Ann. Géog.** 114:641 1-2:2005 pp.3-26.

3218　Seeds of deception: exposing corporate and government lies about the safety of genetically engineered food. Jeffrey M. Smith; Michael Meacher [Foreword]. Totnes: Green, 2004. 254p. *ISBN: 1903998417. Includes bibliographical references and index.*

3219　Socio-economic driving forces of arable land conversion: a case study of Wuxian city, China. Yichun Xie; Yu Mei; Tian Guangjin; Xing Xuerong. **Glo. Env. Chan.** 15:3 10:2005 pp.238-252.

3220　Some outstanding issues in the debate on external promotion of land privatisation. Diana Hunt. **Dev. Policy R.** 23:2 3:2005 pp.199-231.

3221　Die Spätgeburt eines Politikfeldes. Verbraucherschutzpolitik in Deutschland. *[In German]*; [Consumer protection policy in Germany] *[Summary]*. Frank Janning. **Z. Pol.** 51:4 12:2004 pp.401-433.

3222　Sub Rosa resistance and the politics of economic reform: land redistribution in post-Soviet Ukraine. Jessica Allina-Pisano. **World Pol.** 56:4 7:2004 pp.554-581.

3223　Sustainable coastal fishery development indicator system: a case of Gungliau, Taiwan. Wen Hong Liu; Ching Hsiewn Ou; Kuo Huan Ting. **Marine Policy** 29:3 5:2005 pp.199-210.

3224　UPA government and agricultural strategy: the need for an integrated policy. G. Sudarshanam; Ch. Bala Ramulu. **Indian J. Publ. Admin.** LI:1 1-3:2005 pp.1-14.

3225　The US farm bill of 2002: implications for CARICOM'S agricultural export trade. Vincent J. Atkins. **Soc. Econ. S.** 53:3 9:2004 pp.61-80.

3226　Ustawa o kształtowaniu ustroju rolnego — zasadność prawnej regulacji obrotu gruntami. *[In Polish]*; (Agricultural structure bill — advisability of legal regulation of land turnover.) *[Summary]*. Andrzej Kołodziej. **Prz. Euro.** 1(8) 2004 pp.147-158.

3227　What restoration schemes can do? Or, getting it right without fisheries transferable quotas. Peter Orebech. **Ocean Dev. Int.** 36:2 4-6:2005 pp.159-178.

3228　When fisheries influence national policy-making: an analysis of the national development strategies of major fish-producing nations in the developing world. Andy Thorpe; Chris Reid; Raymon van Anrooy; Cecile Brugere. **Marine Policy** 29:3 5:2005 pp.211-222.

3229　Who shaped South Africa's land reform policy? Marinda Weideman. **Politikon** 31:2 11:2004 pp.219-238.

Commercial policy
Politique commerciale

3230　Indian textile industry: liberalisation and world market. Jayanta Bagchi. New Delhi: Samskriti, 2004. xv, 306p. *ISBN: 8187374284. Includes bibliographical references (p. [293]-295) and index.*

3231　A national pattern of policy transfer: the regulation of insider trading in France. Nicole de Montricher. **Fre. Pol.** 3:1 4:2005 pp.28-48.

3232　Parallel trade, price discrimination, investment and price caps. Stefan Szymanski; Tommaso Valletti; Gabrielle Demange [Discussant]. **Econ. Policy** 44 10:2005 pp.705-749.

3233　Participatory democracy and chaebol regulation in Korea: state-market relations under the MDP governments, 1997-2003. Yeonho Lee. **Asian Sur.** XLV:2 3-4:2005 pp.279-301.

3234　Political foundations of market-enhancing federalism: theoretical lessons from India and China. Aseema Sinha. **Comp. Pol.** 37:3 4:2005 pp.337-356.

3235　Politics and markets in the Irish 'celtic tiger'. Niamh Hardiman. **Pol. Q.** 76:1 1-3:2005 pp.37-47.

3236　La politique commerciale de Singapour et son intégration régionale. *[In French]*; [Commercial policy in Singapore and its regional integration]. Hank Lim. **Monde Chin.** 2 Summer-Fall:2004 pp.59-68.

3237   Tradeable permits: policy evaluation, design and reform. Organisation for Economic Co-operation and Development. Paris: OECD, 2004. 189p. *ISBN: 9264015027. Includes bibliographical references.*

Development policy
Politique du développement

3238   'Big deal' or big disappointment? The continuing evolution of the South Korean developmental state. Judith Cherry. **Pac. R.** 18:3 9:2005 pp.327-354.
3239   Creative industries: the regional dimension? Mark Jayne. **Env. Plan. C.** 23:4 8:2005 pp.537-556.
3240   Distribution and poverty impacts of tax structure reform in developing countries: how little we know. Norman Gemmell; Oliver Morrissey. **Dev. Policy R.** 23:2 3:2005 pp.131-144.
3241   Entwicklungspolitik. *[In German]*; [Development policy]. Ernst-Otto Czempiel; Christian Hacke; Jackson Janes; Eberhard Sandschneider; Harald Müller; Thomas Weihe; Jeffrey D. Sachs; Stefan Brüne; Franziska Donner; Peter Nunnenkamp; Stephan Klingebiel; Katja Roehder; Catherina Hinz; Stefan Elbe; Georg Koopmann; Helmut Strizek; Rainer Tetzlaff; Marie-Janine Calic; Siegmar Schmidt; Soli Özel; F. Stephen Larrabee; Fraser Cameron; William Richard Smyser; Martin Koopmann; Heinz Kluss; Tim B. Müller; Peter Thiery. **Int. Politik** 59:11-12 11-12:2004 pp.1-171. *Collection of 23 articles.*
3242   Even the 'rich' are vulnerable: multiple shocks and downward mobility in rural Uganda. Kate Bird; Isaac Shinyekwa. **Dev. Policy R.** 23:1 1:2005 pp.55-85.
3243   Falling through the cracks: limits to an instrumental rational role for environmental information in planning. Sarah Hills. **Env. Plan. A** 37:7 7:2005 pp.1263-1276.
3244   A fenntartható fejlődés: mítosz vagy valóság? *[In Hungarian]*; (Sustainable development: myth or reality?) Guy Turchany; László Beranek; György Füleky; Beck István Magyari; Károly Turcsányi. **Valóság** 47:6 2004 pp.1-18.
3245   Impact of Iraqi developments on intra-regional reforms. Kashif Mumtaz. **Strat. S.** XXV:2 Summer:2005 pp.115-125.
3246   Implementing structural funds in Polish and Czech regions: convergence, variation, empowerment? Martin Ferry; Irene McMaster. **Reg. Fed. S.** 15:1 Spring:2005 pp.19-39.
3247   Ownership and incentives in joint forest management: a survey. Tuukka Castrén. **Dev. Policy R.** 23:1 1:2005 pp.87-104.
3248   Policy interventions and administrative instruments for sustainable livestock development in watersheds: some suggestions based on the lead study of five watersheds. Rakshai Hooja; Ranjitha Puskur. **Indian J. Publ. Admin.** LI:1 1-3:2005 pp.70-93.
3249   Re-making the developmental state in Taiwan: the challenges of biotechnology; *[Summary in French]*. Joseph Wong. **Int. Pol. Sci. R.** 26:2 4:2005 pp.169-191.
3250   Solving the problems of economic development incentives. Timothy J. Bartik. **Grow. Chan.** 36:2 Spring:2005 pp.139-166.
3251   State-directed development: political power and industrialization in the global periphery. Atul Kohli. Cambridge, New York: Cambridge University Press, 2004. xii, 466p. *ISBN: 0521545250, 0521836700. Includes bibliographical references (p. 427-445) and index.*
3252   The Third Way and the Third World: poverty reduction and social inclusion strategies in the rise of "inclusive" liberalism. David Craig; Doug Porter. **R. Int. Pol. Econ.** 12:2 5:2005 pp.226-263.
3253   Transformatsiia gosudarstvennoi sotsial'no-ekonomicheskoi politiki na Severe. *[In Russian]*; (Transformation of the state policy in the North.) *[Summary]*. V.N. Kharitonova; I.A. Vizhina. **Region** 2 2004 pp.164-176.
3254   Zu den Rahmenbedingungen entwicklungsbezogener Forschung. *[In German]*; [On the condition of developmental research] *[Summary]*. Gerald Faschingeder; Atiye Zauner. **J. Entwick.pol.** XX:1 2004 pp.4-20.

Energy policy
Politique énergétique

3255   Are green electricity certificates the way forward for renewable energy? An evaluation of the United Kingdom's renewables obligation in the context of international comparisons. Dave Toke. **Env. Plan. C.** 23:3 6:2005 pp.361-374.

3256   Assessing of energy policies based on Turkish agriculture: current status and some implications. C. Sayin; M.N. Mencet; B. Ozkan. **Energy Policy** 33:18 12:2005 pp.2361-2373.

3257   A bargain born of a paradox: the oil industry's role in American domestic and foreign policy. Ran Goel. **New Pol. Econ.** 9:4 12:2004 pp.467-492.

3258   Business opportunities and dynamic competition through distributed generation in primary electricity distribution networks. R. Raineri; S. Ríos; R. Vásquez. **Energy Policy** 33:17 11:2005 pp.2191-2201.

3259   Diversification and energy security risks: the Japanese case. S. Hayden Lesbirel. **Japanese J. Pol. Sci.** 5:1 5:2004 pp.1-22.

3260   Electricity reform in China, India and Russia: the World Bank template and the politics of power. Yi-chong Xu. Cheltenham, Northampton MA: Edward Elgar Publishing, 2004. xiv, 359p. *ISBN: 1843765004. Includes bibliographical references (p. 329-350) and index.*

3261   Electrifying rural Guatemala: central policy and rural reality. Matthew J. Taylor. **Env. Plan. C.** 23:2 4:2005 pp.173-189.

3262   Energy Star product specification development framework: using data and analysis to make program decisions. M. McWhinney; A. Fanara; R. Clark; C. Hershberg; R. Schmeltz; J. Roberson. **Energy Policy** 33:12 8:2005 pp.1613-1625.

3263   A federação Russa: desenvolvimentos recentes no sector energético. *[In Portuguese];* (The energy sector in the Russian Federation.) *[Summary].* Rui C. Nunes. **Relações Int.** 6 6:2005 pp.57-72.

3264   India's energy security of supply and the Gulf. Akhilesh Chandra Prabhakar. **India Q.** LX:3 7-9:2004 pp.120-171.

3265   Liberalisation and the security of gas supply in the UK. P. Wright. **Energy Policy** 33:17 11:2005 pp.2272-2290.

3266   Managing post-privatisation political and regulatory risks in Nigeria — a law and policy perspective. Abba Kolo. **J. Ener. Nat. Resou. Law** 22:4 11:2004 pp.473-506.

3267   Oil consumption and CO2 emissions in China's road transport: current status, future trends, and policy implications. K. He; H. Huo; Q. Zhang; D. He; F. An; M. Wang; M.P. Walsh. **Energy Policy** 33:12 8:2005 pp.1499-1507.

3268   The political economy of electricity reform in Asia. James H. Williams; Navroz K. Dubash; Emily T. Yeh; Joanna I. Lewis; Sunila S. Kale; John Byrne; Leigh Glover; Hoesung Lee; Young-doo Wang; Jung-min Yu; Chris Greacen. **Pac. Aff.** 77:3 Fall:2004 pp.403-451. *Collection of 6 articles.*

3269   Promotional policy and perspectives of usage renewable energy in Lithuania. V. Katinas; A. Markevicius. **Energy Policy** 34:7 5:2005 pp.771-780.

3270   Public and private attitudes towards "green" electricity: the case of Swedish wind power. Kristina Ek. **Energy Policy** 33:13 9:2005 pp.1677-1689.

3271   Reducing subsidies on household fuels in India: how will it affect the poor? S. Gangopadhyay; B. Ramaswami; W. Wadhwa. **Energy Policy** 33:18 12:2005 pp.2326-2336.

3272   Regulatory reforms in the Norwegian gas industry. W.J.N. van Uchelen; M.M. Roggenkamp. **J. Ener. Nat. Resou. Law** 22:4 11:2004 pp.450-464.

3273   Renewables and energy for rural development in Sub-Saharan Africa. Semere Habtetsion [Contrib.]; M.C. Mapako [Ed.]; A. Mbewe [Ed.]; et al. London: Zed Books, 2004. xx, 395p. *ISBN: 1842775189. Includes bibliographical references and index. African Energy Policy Research Network. (Series: African energy policy research).*

3274   The welfare effects and the distributive impact of carbon taxation on Italian households. S. Tiezzi. **Energy Policy** 33:12 8:2005 pp.1597-1612.

Transport policy
Politique des transports

3275   Assessing policies towards sustainable transport in Europe: an integrated model. T. Zachariadis. **Energy Policy** 33:12 8:2005 pp.1509-1525.

3276   Delayer pays principle: examining congestion pricing with compensation. David Levinson; Peter Rafferty. **Int. J. Trans. Econ.** XXXI:3 10:2004 pp.295-312.

3277   L'expertise dans le diagnostic des problèmes publics. Ingénieurs et statistiques des politiques de transport en France. *[In French]*; (The role of expertise in defining public issues. Transports engineers and statistics in France.) *[Summary]*. Fabrice Bardet. **R. Fran. Sci. Pol.** 54:6 12:2004 pp.1005-1023.

3278   From projects to strategies: a transaction cost approach to politicians' problems with strategic transport planning. Tore Sager; Inger-Anne Ravlum. **Plan. Theory Pract.** 6:2 6:2005 pp.213-232.

3279   Die Grenzen der (De-)Regulierung im Verkehr. *[In German]*; [Limits of traffic (de)regulations]. Günter Knieps. **Z. Verkehr.** 75:3 2004 pp.133-158.

3280   Managing Indian railways: the future ahead. V.K. Agarwal; Nitish Kumar [Foreword]. New Delhi: Manas Publications, 2004. 463p. *ISBN: 8170491703.*

3281   Metropolitan institutions and policy coordination: the integration of land use and transport policies in Swiss urban areas. Fritz Sager. **Governance** 18:2 4:2005 pp.227-256.

3282   The new transport charging powers: the (real) issues for business — credibility, fairness and red tape? Timothy B. Whitehead. **Loc. Govt. S.** 31:4 8:2005 pp.491-510.

3283   The Panama canal: operations and traffic. Francisco J. Montero Llacer. **Marine Policy** 29:3 5:2005 pp.223-234.

3284   Polish gminas' attitudes to government motorway and road plans. E.J. Judge; K. Werpachowski; M. Wishardt. **Prz. Geog.** 76:2 2004 pp.125-142.

3285   Transport, demand management and social inclusion: the need for ethnic perspectives. Fiona Raje; Margaret Grieco [Contrib.]; Julian Hine [Contrib.]; John Preston [Contrib.]. Aldershot: Ashgate, 2004. viii, 174p. *ISBN: 0754640450. Includes bibliographical references (p. 159-167) and index. (Series:* Transport and society*)*.

3286   Transport policy — new thinking. Marcus Enoch; Stephen Potter; Stephen Ison; George Williams; Jim Steer; Graham Parkhurst; Stuart Cole; Peter Hendy. **Publ. Mon. Manag.** 25:3 6:2005 pp.147-200. *Collection of 7 articles.*

E.3:   **Financial policy**
       Politique financière

3287   Afrique au Sud du Sahara : quelle stratégie de transition fiscale ? *[In French]*; (Sub-Saharan Africa: in search of a fiscal transition strategy.) *[Summary]*. Gérard Chambas. **Afr. Contemp.** 213 Winter:2005 pp.133-164.

3288   Analysis of US economic development administration expenditure patterns over 30 years; *[Summary in German]*; *[Summary in French]*; *[Summary in Spanish]*. Amy Glasmeier; Lawrence Wood. **Reg. S.** 39:9 12:2005 pp.1261-1274.

3289   Asymmetries in transatlantic monetary policy-making: does the ECB follow the Fed? Ansgar Belke; Daniel Gros. **J. Com. Mkt. S.** 43:5 12:2005 pp.921-946.

3290   Born under a bad sign? The politics of the 2001 Mexican tax reform. Jean F. Mayer; Kenneth Woodside. **Lat.Am. Anal.** 11 6:2005 pp.33-58.

3291   Coalition governments versus minority governments: bargaining power, cohesion and budgeting outcomes. G. Pech. **Publ. Choice** 121:1-2 10:2004 pp.1-24.

3292   Elections and exchange rate policy cycles. Marco Bonomo; Cristina Terra. **Econ. Pol.** 17:2 7:2005 pp.151-176.

3293   Epistemic communities and the diffusion of ideas: Central Bank reform in the United Kingdom. Michael R. King. **West Euro. Pol.** 28:1 1:2005 pp.94-123.

3294   Evolving federations and regional public deficits: testing the bailout hypothesis in the Spanish case. Santiago Lago-Peñas. **Env. Plan. C.** 23:3 6:2005 pp.437-453.

3295   Exchange rates, monetary policy and interest rates in the Dominican Republic during the 1990s boom and new millennium crisis. José R. Sánchez-Fung. **J. Lat. Am. S.** 37:4 11:2005 pp.727-738.

3296   Fair division or fair dinkum? Australian lessons for intergovernmental fiscal relations in the United Kingdom. Adrian Kay; Gillian Bristow; Mark McGovern; David Pickernell. **Env. Plan. C.** 23:2 4:2005 pp.247-261.

3297   Fiscal policy and capital mobility: the construction of economic policy rectitude in Britain and France. Ben Clift; Jim Tomlinson. **New Pol. Econ.** 9:4 12:2004 pp.515-537.

3298   Független, pártsemleges költségvetési rendszer amerikai tapasztalatainak magyar alkalmazása. *[In Hungarian]*; (The Hungarian application of the American experiences on an independent, party-indifferent budgetary system.) Balázs Romhányi. **Pénz. Sz.** IL:9 9:2004 pp.957-975.

3299   Globalisation and the dilemmas of income taxation in Australia. Steffen Ganghof; Richard Eccleston. **Aust. J. Pol. Sci.** 39:3 11:2004 pp.519-534.

3300   Integrating gender into government budgets: a new perspective. Marilyn Marks Rubin; John R. Bartle. **Publ. Admin. R.** 65:5-6:2005 pp.259-272.

3301   An integrative approach to the politics of Central Bank independence: lessons from Britain, Germany and Italy. Lucia Quaglia. **West Euro. Pol.** 28:3 5:2005 pp.549-568.

3302   Intergovernmental transfers and the flypaper effect in Turkey. İsa Sağbaş; Naci Tolga Saruç. **Turkish S.** 5:2 Summer:2004 pp.79-92.

3303   A "magyar modell" — a változó pénzügyi és társadalmi erőtérben. *[In Hungarian]*; (The 'Hungarian model' — in a changing financial and social field of forces.) Csaba Lentner. **Valóság** 47:8 2004 pp.74-89.

3304   Modelo de valorizacion financiera (Argentina, 1976-2001). *[In Spanish]*; [Financial valorization model (Argentina, 1976-2001)] *[Summary]*. Ignasi Brunet; Fernanda Schilman. **Sistema** 188 9:2005 pp.97-112.

3305   Partisanship and the path to financial openness. Scott L. Kastner; Chad Rector. **Comp. Pol. S.** 38:5 6:2005 pp.484-506.

3306   The politics of local income tax in Sweden: reform and continuity. John Loughlin; Anders Lidstrom; Chris Hudson. **Loc. Govt. S.** 31:3 6:2005 pp.349-366.

3307   Quelle fiscalité demain pour les communes et les intercommunalités ? *[In French]*; [What kind of taxation for towns and counties?] Alain Guengant. **Cah. Econ. Bret.** 49:2 6:2004 pp.33-46.

3308   Recent tax policy trends and reforms in OECD countries. Organisation for Economic Co-operation and Development. Paris: OECD, 2004. 170p. *ISBN: 9264016570. Includes bibliographical references (p. 169-170). (Series: OECD tax policy studies - 9).*

3309   Le recul du fédéralisme en Russie : l'exemple du budget. *[In French]*; (A retreat from federalism in Russia: the case of the budget.) *[Summary]*. Alexei Novikov. **Pouvoirs** 112 2004 pp.111-125.

3310   Regulating more effectively: the relationship between procedural justice, legitimacy, and tax non-compliance. Kristina Murphy. **J. Law Soc.** 32:4 12:2005 pp.562-589.

3311   Rethinking fiscal federalism. David A. Super. **Harv. Law R.** 118:8 6:2005 pp.2544-2652.

3312   The Russian "flat tax" reform. Anna Ivanova; Michael Keen; Alexander Klemm; Pierre Pestieau [Discussant]; Andrés Velasco [Discussant]. **Econ. Policy** 43 7:2005 pp.397-444.

3313   State, capital, and the politics of banking reform in sub-Saharan Africa. Catherine Boone. **Comp. Pol.** 37:4 7:2005 pp.401-420.

3314   The statutory tax burden and its avoidance in transitional Russia. Vlad Ivanenko. **Euro.-Asia S.** 57:7 11:2005 pp.1021-1045.

3315   A theoretical basis for the consideration of spending thresholds in the analysis of fiscal referendums. Marc-Jean Martin. **Constit. Pol. Econ.** 15:4 12:2004 pp.359-370.

E.4: **Social policy**
Politique sociale

3316 Analyse des mythes et des réalités dans la politique sociale de l'Etat : le cas de l'Amérique latine. *[In French]*; [An analysis of the myths and realities of the state's social policy: the case of Latin America]. Bernardo Kliksberg. **R. Int. Sci. Admin.** 70:4 12:2004 pp.697-714.

3317 Central Asia. Jane Falkingham; Kathryn H. Anderson; Stephen P. Heyneman; Maria E. Bonilla-Chacin; Edmundo Murrugarra; Moukim Temourov; Sabine Bernabè; Alexandre Kolev; John Micklewright; Sheila Marnie; Babken V. Babajanian. **Soc. Policy Admin.** 39:4 8:2005 pp.337-462. *Collection of 6 articles.*

3318 Children's participation in social policy: inclusion, chimera or authenticity? Tom Cockburn. **Soc. Policy Soc.** 4:2 4:2005 pp.109-120.

3319 Civilizing the margins: Southeast Asian government policies for the development of minorities. Christopher R. Duncan [Ed.]. Ithaca NY: Cornell University Press, 2004. 278p. *ISBN: 0801441757, 080148930X. Includes bibliographical references and index.*

3320 Discrimination positive et déségrégation : les catégories opératoires des politiques d'intégration aux Etats-Unis. *[In French]*; [Positive discrimination and 'disegregation': the operating categories of integration policies in the United States]. Daniel Sabbagh. **Soc. Contemp.** 53 2004 pp.85-99.

3321 Electoral politics, ideology and American social policy. Gillian Peele. **Soc. Policy Admin.** 39:2 4:2005 pp.150-165.

3322 Ethnic data and social policy in Ireland. Bryan Fanning; Maria Pierce. **Administration [Dublin]** 52:3 Autumn:2004 pp.3-20.

3323 Experimenting with a 'whole of government' approach : indigenous capacity building in New Zealand and Australia. Louise Humpage. **Policy S.** 26:1 3:2005 pp.47-66.

3324 Extending entitlement and missed opportunities in Wales. John Holmes. **Youth & Policy** 86 Winter:2005 pp.5-17.

3325 From interest groups to parties: the change in the career patterns of the legislative elite in German social policy. Christine Trampusch. **Ger. Pol.** 14:1 3:2005 pp.14-32.

3326 Future fitness and reform gridlock: towards social inequality and post-democratic politics? Ingolfur Blühdorn. **Debatte** 12:2 11:2004 pp.114-136.

3327 Gender roles and sex equality: European solutions to social security disputes. Ingeborg Heide. Geneva: International Labour Organization, 2004. xi, 117p. *ISBN: 9221157717. Includes bibliographical references.*

3328 International class conflict and social policy. Kevin Farnsworth. **Soc. Policy Soc.** 4:2 4:2005 pp.217-226.

3329 Labour institutions in rural areas: emerging patterns in semi-arid South India. M. Krishnaiah. Delhi: Gagandeep Publications, 2004. xv, 231p. *ISBN: 8188865001. Includes bibliographical references and index.*

3330 The new pension reform as global policy; *[Summary in Spanish]*; *[Summary in French]*. Mitchell A. Orenstein. **Glo. Soc. Policy** 5:2 8:2005 pp.175-202.

3331 Le politiche sociali di fronte alla sfida della giustizia fra le generazioni: un approccio relazionale. *[In Italian]*; [Social policies facing the challenge of intergenerational justice: a relational approach]. Federica Bertocchi. **Sociologia [Rome]** XXXVIII:3 2004 pp.87-99.

3332 The politics of territorial solidarity: nationalism and social policy reform in Canada, the United Kingdom, and Belgium. Daniel Béland; André Lecours. **Comp. Pol. S.** 38:6 8:2005 pp.676-703.

3333 Predpristupni ekonomski program 2005.-2007. Socijalna politika. *[In Croatian]*; (The government of the Republic of Croatia: pre-accession economic program 2005-2007. Social policy.) *[Summary]*. R.H. Vlada. **Revija Soc. Pol.** 12:1 1-3:2005 pp.67-87.

3334 The private sector and privatization in social services: is the Washington consensus 'dead'? *[Summary in Spanish]*; *[Summary in French]*. Santosh Mehrotra; Enrique Delamonica. **Glo. Soc. Policy** 5:2 8:2005 pp.141-174.

3335   Rural poor relief in colonial South Carolina. Tim Lockley. **Hist. J.** 48:4 12:2005 pp.955-976.

3336   Shaping race policy: the United States in comparative perspective. Robert C. Lieberman. Princeton NJ: Princeton University Press, 2005. xviii, 311p. *ISBN: 0691118175. Includes bibliographical references and index.* (*Series:* Princeton studies in American politics).

3337   The social exclusion debate: strategies, controversies and dilemmas. Jonathan S. Davies. **Policy S.** 26:1 3:2005 pp.3-27.

3338   Social policy, freedom and individuality. Anna Yeatman. **Aust. J. Publ. Admin.** 63:4 12:2004 pp.80-89.

3339   Sozialpolitik in Deutschland: Eine systematische Einführung. *[In German]*; [Social policy in Germany: a systematic introduction]. Jürgen Boeckh; Ernst-Ulrich Huster; Benjamin Benz. Wiesbaden: VS Verlag für Sozialwissenschaften, 2004. 464p. *ISBN: 3810040649.*

3340   Teškoće socijalnog partnerstva: europska i hrvatska iskustva. *[In Croatian]*; (Difficulties of social partnership: the European and Croatian experience.) *[Summary]*. Siniša Zrinščak. **Revija Soc. Pol.** 12:2 4-6:2005 pp.175-188.

3341   Vieillesse et dépendance. *[In French]*; [Old age and dependency]. Alain Grand [Ed.]; Hélène Bocquet [Ed.]; Sandrine Andrieu [Ed.]. **Prob. Pol. Soc.** 903 8:2004 pp.5-116.

Health policy
Politique de la santé

3342   Ageism in health policy. Margaret Hodgins; Jutta Greve. **Administration [Dublin]** 52:2 Summer:2004 pp.78-98.

3343   Anti-depressants, suicide, and drug regulation. Jens Ludwig; Dave E. Marcotte. **J. Policy Anal. Manag.** 24:2 Spring:2005 pp.249-272.

3344   Apologiia obschestvennoi meditsini. *[In Russian]*; (An apology for social medicine.) Viacheslav Krasavin. **Svobod. Mysl'** 6 2005 pp.41-59.

3345   L'avortement au tournant du siècle : le dernier tabou. *[In French]*; [Abortion at the turn of the century: the last taboo] *[Summary]*. Françoise Camus-Bader. **R. Fran. Civil. Brit.** 12:4 Spring:2004 pp.75-88.

3346   Cancer and health policy: the postcode lottery of care. Hilary Bungay. **Soc. Policy Admin.** 39:1 2:2005 pp.35-48.

3347   [Changes in health policies]; *[Text in French]*. Patrick Hassenteufel; Bruno Palier; Jean de Kervasdoué; Gérard Vincent; Jean-François Chadelat; Michel Régereau; Alain Parant; Edouard Couty; Marc Dupont; Anne Laude; Didier Sicard; Gilles Brücker; François Bourdillon; Fernand Sauer. **R. Fran. Admin. Publ.** 113 2005 pp.13-158. *Collection of 12 articles.*

3348   Clarifying efficiency-equity tradeoffs through explicit criteria, with a focus on developing countries. Chris James; Guy Carrin; William Savedoff; Piya Hanvoravongchai. **Health Care Anal.** 13:1 3:2005 pp.33-51.

3349   Continuity through change: the rhetoric and reality of health reform in New Zealand. Toni Ashton; Nicholas Mays; Nancy Devlin. **Soc. Sci. Med.** 61:2 7:2005 pp.253-262.

3350   The corporate transformation of health care: can the public interest still be served. John P. Geyman. New York: Springer-Verlag, 2004. xvi, 306p. *ISBN: 0826124666. Includes bibliographical references and index.*

3351   The death of managed care: a regulatory autopsy. Mark A. Hall. **J. Health Pol. Policy Law** 30:3 6:2005 pp.427-452.

3352   The decline in 'free' general practitioner care in Australia: reasons and repercussions. S. Hopkins; N. Speed. **Health Policy** 73:3 9:2005 pp.316-329.

3353   The devil may be in the details: how the characteristics of SCHIP programs affect take-up. Barbara Wolfe; Scott Scrivner. **J. Policy Anal. Manag.** 24:3 Summer:2005 pp.499-522.

3354   Evidence for population health. Richard F. Heller. Oxford, New York: Oxford University Press, 2005. xii, 126p. *ISBN: 0198529740. Includes bibliographical references and index.*

3355   Explicit rationing of elective services: implementing the New Zealand reforms. Kevin Dew; Jacqueline Cumming; Deborah McLeod; Sonya Morgan; Eileen McKinlay; Anthony Dowell; Tom Love. **Health Policy** 74:1 9:2005 pp.1-12.

3356   Fighting with Goliath: the reform of the public health care insurance scheme in Germany, its potential to increase employment and alternative models of reform. Karsten Grabow. **Ger. Pol.** 14:1 3:2005 pp.51-73.

3357   Flattening the National Health Service hierarchy: the case of public health. Stephen Abbott; Jenifer Chapman; Sara Shaw; Yvonne H. Carter; Roland Petchey; Stephanie Taylor. **Policy S.** 26:2 6:2005 pp.133-148.

3358   The future of European health policies. Meri Tuulikki Koivusalo. **Int. J. Health Serv.** 35:2 2005 pp.325-342.

3359   Global trade, public health, and health services: stakeholders' constructions of the key issues. Howard Waitzkin; Rebeca Jasso-Aguilar; Angela Landwehr; Carolyn Mountain. **Soc. Sci. Med.** 61:5 9:2005 pp.893-906.

3360   The global-local dilemma of a Ministry of Health. Experiences from Uganda. A. Jeppsson; H. Birungi; P.O. Östergren; B. Hagström. **Health Policy** 72:3 6:2005 pp.311-320.

3361   The Health and Social Care Professionals Bill (2004) — implications and opportunities for the social professions in Ireland. Tom Farrelly; Colm O'Doherty. **Administration [Dublin]** 53:1 2005 pp.80-92.

3362   The health business under neo-liberalism: the Israeli case. Dani Filc. **Crit. Soc. Policy** 25:2(83) 5:2005 pp.180-197.

3363   Health care transition in urban China. Gerald Bloom [Ed.]; Sheng-lan Tang [Ed.]. Aldershot: Ashgate, 2004. xxii, 228p. *ISBN: 0754639665. Includes bibliographical references and index.*

3364   Health policy and the politics of evidence. Timothy Milewa; Christine Barry. **Soc. Policy Admin.** 39:5 10:2005 pp.498-512.

3365   Health policy in Britain: the politics and organisation of the National Health Service. Christopher Ham. Basingstoke, New York: Palgrave Macmillan, 2004. xv, 288p. *ISBN: 0333961757, 0333961765. (Series:* Public policy and politics*).*

3366   Healthcare reform implementation: stakeholders and their roles-the Israeli experience. T. Horev; Y.M. Babad. **Health Policy** 71:1 1:2005 pp.1-21.

3367   The HIV epidemic in four African countries seen through the demographic and health surveys. Mark Gersovitz. **J. Afr. Econ.** 14:2 6:2005 pp.191-246.

3368   HIV/AIDS in Russia: alarming signs. Pravozashchitnik. **Rus. Pol. Law** 43:1 1-2:2005 pp.5-50.

3369   Human rights audit of mental health legislation — results of an Australian pilot. Helen Watchirs. **Int. J. Law Psych.** 28:2 3-4:2005 pp.99-125.

3370   The impact of China's retail drug price control policy on hospital expenditures: a case study in two Shandong hospitals. Qingyue Meng; Gang Cheng; Lynn Silver; Xiaojie Sun; Clas Rehnberg; Göran Tomson. **Health Policy Plan.** 20:3 5:2005 pp.185-196.

3371   Improving child nutrition? The integrated child development services in India. Michael Lokshin; Monica Das Gupta; Michele Gragnolati; Oleksiy Ivaschenko. **Dev. Change** 36:4 7:2005 pp.613-640.

3372   India's HIV/AIDS crisis: securitising disease. Happymon Jacob. **Pol. Econ. J. India** 12:1 1-6:2005 pp.119-141.

3373   Inequity in the price of physician activity across surgical procedures. Kenshi Hayashida; Yuichi Imanaka. **Health Policy** 74:1 9:2005 pp.24-38.

3374   Institutional vulnerability to social constructions: federalism, target populations, and policy designs for assisted reproductive technology in six democracies. Éric Montpetit; Christine Rothmayr; Frédéric Varone. **Comp. Pol. S.** 38:2 3:2005 pp.119-142.

3375   Is universal coverage a solution for disparities in health care? Findings from three low-income provinces of Thailand. C. Suraratdecha; S. Saithanu; V. Tangcharoensathien. **Health Policy** 73:3 9:2005 pp.272-284.

3376   Kingdon à Bamako: conceptualiser l'implantation d'une politique publique de santé en Afrique. *[In French]*; [From Kingdon to Bamako: conceptualize the public health policy implementation in Africa] *[Summary]*; *[Summary in French]*. Valéry Ridde. **Pol. et Soc.** 23:2-3 2004 pp.183-202.

3377 The Korean economic crisis and coping strategies in the health sector: pro-welfarism or neoliberalism? Chang-yup Kim. **Int. J. Health Serv.** 35:3 2005 pp.561-578.

3378 Measuring health status: information for primary care decision making. P. Kind; G. Hardman; B. Leese. **Health Policy** 71:3 3:2005 pp.303-313.

3379 The negative and positive impacts of HIV/AIDS on democracy in South Africa. Anthony Butler. **J. Contemp. Afr. S.** 23:1 1:2005 pp.3-26.

3380 The new politics of medicine. Brian Salter. Basingstoke, New York: Palgrave Macmillan, 2004. xv, 236p. *ISBN: 0333801121. Includes bibliographical references (p. 208-228) and index.*

3381 Outils et méthodes statistiques pour les politiques de santé et de protection sociale. *[In French]*; [Statistical tools and methods for health policies and social security]. Dossiers solidarité et santé. **Doss. Solid. Santé** 1 1-3:2004 pp.5-72.

3382 Policy swings over thirty-five years of mental health social work in England and Wales 1969-2004. Joan Rapaport. **Practice** 17:1 3:2005 pp.43-56.

3383 The political and social contexts of health. Carme Borrell [Ed.]; Vicente Navarro [Ed.]; et al. Amityville NY: Baywood Publishing, 2004. 241p. *ISBN: 0895032961, 0895032996. Includes bibliographical references and index.*

3384 The political dynamics of tobacco control in Australia and New Zealand: explaining policy problems, instruments, and patterns of adoption. Donley T. Studlar. **Aust. J. Pol. Sci.** 40:2 6:2005 pp.255-274.

3385 The politics of indeterminancy and the right to health. Monica Greco. **Theory Cult. Soc.** 21:6 12:2004 pp.1-22.

3386 Private and public cross-subsidization: financing Beijing's health-insurance reform. M. Wu; Y. Xin; H. Wang; W. Yu. **Health Policy** 72:1 4:2005 pp.41-52.

3387 The promotion of investment alliances by the World Bank: implications for national health policy; *[Summary in Spanish]*; *[Summary in French]*. Jane Lethbridge. **Glo. Soc. Policy** 5:2 8:2005 pp.203-226.

3388 Providing integrated health and social care for older persons: a European overview of issues at stake. Kai Leichsenring [Ed.]; Andy Alaszewski [Ed.]. Aldershot, Burlington VT: Ashgate, 2004. 499p. *ISBN: 0754641961. Includes bibliographical references. European Centre for Social Welfare Policy and Research. (Series: Public policy and social welfare - 28).*

3389 Public participation in regional health policy: a theoretical framework. W.E. Thurston; G. MacKean; A. Vollman; A. Casebeer; M. Weber; B. Maloff; J. Bader. **Health Policy** 73:3 9:2005 pp.237-252.

3390 Reducing health disparities through primary care reform: the New Zealand experiment. M. Hefford; P. Crampton; J. Foley. **Health Policy** 72:1 4:2005 pp.9-23.

3391 Réforme de la Sécu : le dossier. *[In French]*; [Health care system reform]. Pierre Volovitch. **Alter. Econ.** 224 4:2004 pp.49-59.

3392 Réformes des systèmes d'assurance maladie et débats sociaux. *[In French]*; [Sickness insurance reforms and social debates]. Pierre Volovitch [Ed.]. **Chron. Int. IRES** 91 11:2004 pp.1-160.

3393 Relating health policy to women's health outcomes. Jennifer P. Wisdom; Michelle Berlin; Jodi A. Lapidus. **Soc. Sci. Med.** 61:8 10:2005 pp.1776-1784.

3394 SARS in Singapore: surveillance strategies in a globalising city. P. Teo; B.S.A. Yeoh; S.N. Ong. **Health Policy** 72:3 6:2005 pp.279-291.

3395 South Africa's HIV/AIDS policy, 1994-2004: how can it be explained? Anthony Butler. **Afr. Affairs** 104:417 10:2005 pp.591-614.

3396 State health policy making determinants, theory, and methods: a synthesis. Edward Alan Miller. **Soc. Sci. Med.** 61:12 12:2005 pp.2639-2657.

3397 Sub-optimality in NHS sourcing in the UK: demand-side constraints on supply-side improvement. Andrew Cox; Dan Chicksand; Paul Ireland. **Publ. Admin.** 83:2 2005 pp.367-392.

3398 Toward establishing a universal basic health norm. Arnab K. Acharya. **Ethics Int. Aff.** 18:3 2004 pp.65-78.

3399 Variabilitá nei servizi sanitari in Italia. *[In Italian]*; [Variability in Italian health services]. Pierluigi Morosini [Ed.]; Gabriella Palumbo [Ed.]. Turin: Centro Scientifico, 2004. xx, 308p. *ISBN: 887640709X. Includes bibliographical references.*

3400 Welfare reform and health. Marianne P. Bitler; Jonah B. Gelbach; Hilary W. Hoynes. **J. Hum. Res.** 40:2 Spring:2005 pp.309-334.

3401 When health policy is the problem: a report from the field. Bruce Spitz; John Abramson. **J. Health Pol. Policy Law** 30:3 6:2005 pp.327-365.

3402 The who, what, and why of risk adjustment: a technology on the cusp of adoption. David Blumenthal; Joel S. Weissman; Melissa Wachterman; Evette Weil; Randall S. Stafford; James M. Perrin; Timothy G. Ferris; Karen Kuhlthau; Rainu Kaushal; Lisa I. Iezzoni. **J. Health Pol. Policy Law** 30:3 6:2005 pp.453-473.

3403 Why neoliberal health reforms have failed in Latin America. N. Homedes; A. Ugalde. **Health Policy** 71:1 1:2005 pp.83-96.

3404 Wohlfahrtskulturen in Frankreich und Deutschland: gesundheitspolitische Reformdebatten im Ländervergleich. *[In German]*; [Welfare culture in France and Germany: comparing the debates on health policy reforms]. Julia Lepperhoff. Wiesbaden: VS Verlag für Sozialwissenschaften, 2004. 248p. *ISBN: 3531144316.*

Labour policy
Politique du travail

3405 Active labour market programmes in Norway: are they helpful for social assistance recipients? Thomas Lorentzen; Espen Dahl. **J. Euro. Soc. Policy** 15:1 2:2005 pp.27-46.

3406 Breaking out of the pink-collar ghetto: policy solutions for non-college women. Sharon H. Mastracci; Ray Marshall [Foreword]. Armonk NY: M.E. Sharpe, 2004. xvii, 221p. *ISBN: 0765613557, 0765613565. Includes bibliographical references (p. 203-218) and index.*

3407 Business and social policy: a case study of the adoption of workers' compensation in Israel. John Gal. **Soc. Serv. R.** 79:1 3:2005 pp.29-59.

3408 The challenge of child labour. Frans Röselaers. **Bull. Comp. Lab. Rel.** 55 2005 pp.117-129.

3409 Challenging the market: the struggle to regulate work and income. Jim Stanford [Ed.]; Leah F. Vosko [Ed.]. Montreal: McGill-Queens University Press, 2004. ix, 387p. *ISBN: 0773527273. Includes bibliographical references.*

3410 Changes and continuity: labour policy in Mexico after the 2000 regime transition. Jean François Mayer. **Indian J. Publ. Admin.** LI:1 1-3:2005 pp.55-69.

3411 Employability and problem drug users. Peter A. Kemp; Joanne Neale. **Crit. Soc. Policy** 25:1(82-85) 2:2005 pp.28-46.

3412 Evaluation des réformes des systèmes de pensions latino-américains. *[In French]*; [Evaluation of reforms in Latin American pension systems]. Carlos Ochando Claramunt. **R. Int. Sécur. Soc.** 57:2 4-6:2004 pp.33-59.

3413 France. Anne Sonnet. Paris: OECD, 2005. 165p. *ISBN: 9264008462. Includes bibliographical references (p. 159-165).*

3414 Global governance and labor rights: codes of conduct and anti-sweatshop struggles in global apparel factories in Mexico and Guatemala. César A. Rodríguez-Garavito. **Pol. Soc.** 33:2 6:2005 pp.203-233.

3415 In defence of affirmative action in South Africa. Ockert Dupper. **Sth. Afr. Law. J.** 121:1 2004 pp.187-215.

3416 Income mobility in old age in Britain and Germany. Asghar Zaidi; Joachim R. Frick; Felix Büchel. **Age. Soc.** 25:4 7:2005 pp.543-565.

3417 Labour and neo-liberal globalization in South Korea and Taiwan. Tat Yan Kong. **Mod. Asian S.** 39:1 2:2005 pp.155-188.

3418   Labour markets and social policy in Central and Eastern Europe: the accession and beyond. N.A. Barr [Ed.]. Washington DC: World Bank, 2005. xiii, 267p. *ISBN: 0821361198. Includes bibliographical references and index.*

3419   Labour reform in a neo-liberal 'protected' democracy: Chile 1990-2001. Fernando Durán-Palma; Adrian Wilkinson; Marek Korczynski. **Int. J. Hum. Res. Manag.** 16:1 1:2005 pp.65-89.

3420   The mechanism for establishing and changing terms and conditions of employment. Joo-cheong Tham; Pascal Lokiec; Rolf Wank; Maurizio Del Conte; Michele Tiraboschi; Takashi Araki; Mia Rönnmar; Catherine Barnard; Kenneth G. Dau-Schmidt; Carmen L. Brun. **Bull. Comp. Lab. Rel.** 53 2005 pp.73-202. *Collection of 8 articles.*

3421   Migrant sex workers and state regulation in North Cyprus. Fatma Güven-Lisaniler; Leopoldo Rodríguez; Sevin Uğural. **Wom. S. Int. For.** 28:1 1-2:2005 pp.79-91.

3422   Mise en œuvre des politiques pour l'emploi et pouvoir régional: le poids des réseaux sociaux et politiques. *[In French]*; (Labour market policy implementation and regional power structure: the impact of political and social networks.) *[Summary]*; *[Summary in German]*. Monica Battaglini; Olivier Giraud. **Schweiz. Z. Soziol.** 30:3 2004 pp.363-379.

3423   Niedriglöhne? Mindestlöhne! Verbreitung von Niedriglöhnen und Möglichkeiten ihrer Bekämpfung. *[In German]*; [Low pay? Minimum wages!] *[Summary]*. Reinhard Bispinck; Claus Schäfer. **Soz. Fort.** 54:1-2 1-2:2005 pp.20-31.

3424   Occupational rights and new employment regimes in emergent economies. Louise Haagh; Maria Lorena Cook. **Policy S.** 26:2 6:2005 pp.171-197.

3425   'Only looking after the weans'? The Scottish nursery nurses' strike, 2004. Gerry Mooney; Tricia McCafferty. **Crit. Soc. Policy** 25:2(83) 5:2005 pp.223-239.

3426   Opravdanost workfare programa u svijetu i Hrvatskoj. *[In Croatian]*; (The justification of workfare programmes in the world and in the Republic of Croatia.) *[Summary]*. Predrag Bejaković. **Revija Soc. Pol.** 11:3-4 7-12:2004 pp.343-362.

3427   Partisanship amidst convergence: the politics of labor reform in Latin America. María Victoria Murillo. **Comp. Pol.** 37:4 7:2005 pp.441-458.

3428   Perspectives on children's work in the Algarve (Portugal) and their implications for social policy. Antonella Invernizzi. **Crit. Soc. Policy** 25:2(83) 5:2005 pp.198-222.

3429   Le politiche per l'emersione del lavoro non regolare sono davvero fallite? *[In Italian]*; [Have the regularization policies for irregular employment failed?] *[Summary]*. Massimiliano Pacifico. **Riv. It. Pol. Pub.** 1 4:2004 pp.87-118.

3430   The politics of foreign labor policy in Korea and Japan. Yong Wook Lee; Hyemee Park. **J. Contemp. Asia** 35:2 2005 pp.143-165.

3431   Politiques d'activation pour des jeunes chômeurs de longue durée sans expérience de travail : une évaluation. *[In French]*; [Policies for long-term unemployed young people without work experience: an evaluation] *[Summary]*. Bart Cockx; Christian Gobel; Bruno van der Linden. **R. Belge Sécur. Soc.** 46:3 7-9:2004 pp.497-510.

3432   Positive action and the problem of merit: employment policies in the National Health Service. Nick Johns. **Crit. Soc. Policy** 25:2(83) 5:2005 pp.139-163.

3433   Power resources, institutions and policy learning: the origins of workers' compensation in Quebec; *[Summary in French]*. Andrew Stritch. **Can. J. Pol.** 38:3 9:2005 pp.549-579.

3434   Quelles politiques pour l'emploi et le travail décent des jeunes ? *[In French]*; [What policies for decent employment for young people?] Éducation ouvrière. **Edu. Ouvrière** 3:136 2004 pp.1-95.

3435   Redressing gender inequality in employment: the national and sub-regional policy 'fit'. Sally-Anne Barnes; Anne Green; Michael Orton; Jenny Bimrose. **Loc. Econ.** 20:2 5:2005 pp.154-167.

3436   La reforma laboral de 2002: ¿funcionó o no? *[In Spanish]*; [The labour reform of 2002: did it work?] *[Summary]*. Alejandro Gaviria U. **Coy. Econ.** XXXV:1 2005 pp.73-104.

3437   Les réinventions du social dans le Maroc "ajusté". *[In French]*; (Reinventing "social issue" in liberalized Morocco.) *[Summary]*. Myriam Catusse. **R. Mon. Musul. Med.** 105-106 2005 pp.221-246.

3438 Remedying the past or reshaping the future? Justifying race-based affirmative action in South Africa and the United States. Ockert Dupper. **Int. J. Comp. Lab. Law** 21:1 Spring:2005 pp.89-130.

3439 Die „schlichte Notwendigkeit" privater Altersvorsorge. Zur Wissenssoziologie der deutschen Rentenpolitik. *[In German]*; (The imperative of private pensions. Debating German pension policy.) Christian Marschallek. **Z. Soziol.** 33:4 8:2004 pp.285-302.

3440 La stratégie européenne de l'emploi: entre lutte contre la précarité des jeunes et production d'un habitus flexible. *[In French]*; (The European strategy of employment : between fighting against precariousness among the youth and producing more flexibility.) *[Summary]*; *[Summary in German]*. Franz Schultheis. **Schweiz. Z. Soziol.** 30:3 2004 pp.303-318.

3441 Swiss unemployment policy: an evaluation of the public employment service; *[Summary in French]*; *[Summary in German]*. Giovanni Ferro Luzzi; Yves Flückiger; José V. Ramirez; Anatoli Vassiliev. **Schweiz. Z. Soziol.** 30:3 2004 pp.319-337.

3442 Up from the bottom rung. Marvin H. Kosters. **Publ. Inter.** 158 Winter:2005 pp.83-95.

3443 Vive la cotisation sociale! *[In French]*; [Long live social contributions!] Lilian Brissaud; Raphaël Thaller. **Pensée** 340 10-12:2004 pp.109-120.

3444 Zur Situation der Haushaltsarbeiterinnen in Lateinamerika — Eine Bestandsaufnahme nach 25 Jahren Demokratie. *[In German]*; (The situation of household workers in Latin America after 25 years of democracy.) *[Summary]*. Eva Karnofsky. **Lat.Am. Anal.** 10 2:2005 pp.179-202.

Migration policy
Politique migratoire

3445 Africa ad portas? Italiens Migrationspolitik. *[In German]*; (Africa ad portas? Italy's migration policy.). Paolo Cuttitta. **Welt Trends** 45 Winter:2004 pp.124-134.

3446 Albanian refugees seeking political asylum in the United States: process and problems. Bernd J. Fischer. **J. Ethn. Migr. S.** 31:1 1:2005 pp.193-208.

3447 American gulag: inside U.S. immigration prisons. Mark Dow. Berkeley CA: University of California Press, 2004. xiii, 413p. *ISBN: 0520239423. Includes bibliographical references (p. 373-381) and index.*

3448 Are 'nondiscriminatory' immigration policies reversible? Evidence from the United States and Australia. Christian Joppke. **Comp. Pol. S.** 38:1 2:2005 pp.3-25.

3449 Best practices to manage migration: Morocco-Spain. Joaquin Arango; Philip Martin. **Int. Migr. R.** 39:1 Spring:2005 pp.258-269.

3450 Best practices to manage migration: the Philippines. Philip Martin; Manolo Abella; Elizabeth Midgley. **Int. Migr. R.** 38:4 Winter:2004 pp.1544-1560.

3451 Coercive capacity and the politics of implementation: deportation in Germany and the United States. Antje Ellermann. **Comp. Pol. S.** 38:10 12:2005 pp.1219-1244.

3452 The construction of the geography of immigration as a policy problem: the United States and Canada compared. Yasmeen Abu-Laban; Judith A. Garber. **Urb. Aff. R.** 40:4 3:2005 pp.520-561.

3453 The decline and decay of European refugee policy. Satvinder S. Juss. **Oxf. J. Leg. S.** 25:4 Winter:2005 pp.749-792.

3454 Discrimination positive : pourquoi la France ne peut y échapper. *[In French]*; [Positive discrimination: why France cannot escape it]. Yazid Sabeg; Yacine Sabeg. Paris: Calmann-Levy, 2004. 247p. *ISBN: 2702135110.*

3455 Exclusion in the liberal state: the case of immigration and citizenship policy. Christian Joppke. **Euro. J. Soc. Theory** 8:1 2:2005 pp.43-61.

3456 Gefährlich fremd: Deutschland und seine Einwanderung. *[In German]*; [Dangerously alien: Germany and its immigrants]. Bernd Winter. Freiburg: Lambertus, 2004. 162p. *ISBN: 3784115438.*

3457   The grassroots reconfiguration of U.S. immigration policy. Miriam J. Wells. **Int. Migr. R.** 38:4 Winter:2004 pp.1308-1347.

3458   Guestworkers and exploitation. Robert Mayer. **R. Pol.** 67:2 Spring:2005 pp.311-334.

3459   Homeland wanted: interdisciplinary perspective on refugee resettlement in the West. Peter Waxman [Ed.]; Val Colic-Peisker [Ed.]. New York: Nova Science Publishers, 2005. xxii, 247p. *ISBN: 159454266X. Includes bibliographical references and index.*

3460   Homosexualité et migration, droit au séjour et couple homosexuel. *[In French]*; [Homosexuality and migration, right of asylum and homosexual couples]. Christel Cournil. **R. Rech. Jurid. Droit Prosp.** 29:2 2004 pp.1039-1052.

3461   Immigrants at the margins: law, race, and exclusion in Southern Europe. Kitty Calavita. Cambridge: Cambridge University Press, 2005. xx, 257p. *ISBN: 0521846633, 0521609127. Includes bibliographical references and index. (Series:* Cambridge studies in law and society).

3462   Immigrazione, politica e politiche. I casi di Milano, Bologna e Napoli. *[In Italian]*; [Immigration, politics and policy. The cases of Milan, Bologna and Naples] *[Summary]*. Tiziana Caponio. **Riv. It. Pol. Pub.** 1 4:2004 pp.23-56.

3463   'Integration with diversity in modern Britain': New Labour on nationality, immigration and asylum. Vicki Squire. **J. Pol. Ideol.** 10:1 2:2005 pp.51-74.

3464   International labor migration: foreign workers and public policy. David Bartram. Basingstoke, New York: Palgrave Macmillan, 2005. ix, 199p. *ISBN: 1403946744. Includes bibliographical references (p. 177-191) and index.*

3465   The Israeli law of return & its impact on the struggle in Palestine. Daud Abdullah. London: Palestinian Return Centre, 2004. ix, 343p. *ISBN: 1901924505.*

3466   Issue definition, political discourse and the politics of nationality reform in France and Germany. R. Hansen; J. Koehler. **Écon. Sociét.** 44:5 8:2005 pp.623-644.

3467   Migrant resettlement in the Russian Federation: reconstructing "homes" and "homelands". Moya Flynn. London: Anthem Press, 2004. viii, 245p. *ISBN: 1843311178, 184331116X. Includes bibliographical references and index.*

3468   Migration and development: new strategic outlooks and practical ways forward, the cases of Angola and Zambia. Savina Ammassari. Geneva: International Organization for Migration, 2005. 95p. *ISBN: 9211036410.*

3469   Migration, immigration and social policy. Savitri Taylor; Channe Lindstrøm; Liza Schuster; Peter Dwyer; D. Dunkerley; J. Scourfield; T. Maegusuku-Hewett; N. Smalley; Alexandre Afonso; Anniken Hagelund; Bjørg Colding; Hans Hummelgaard; Leif Husted; Lucinda Platt. **Soc. Policy Admin.** 39:6 12:2005 pp.559-721. *Collection of 9 articles.*

3470   Migration in the new Europe: East-West revisited. Agata Gorny [Ed.]; Paolo Ruspini [Ed.]. Basingstoke, New York: Palgrave Macmillan, 2004. xix, 283p. *ISBN: 1403935505. Includes bibliographical references and index. (Series:* Migration, minorities, and citizenship).

3471   The Muslims in France and the French model of integration. Dominique Maillard. **Mediterr. Q.** 16:1 Winter:2005 pp.62-78.

3472   Nationality and migration in modern Mexico. David Fitzgerald. **J. Ethn. Migr. S.** 31:1 1:2005 pp.171-191.

3473   A need to reinvent the wheel? Peter J. van Krieken. **AWR B.** 42(51):3 2004 pp.60-73.

3474   A nemzetközi vándorlás folyamatának irányítása. *[In Hungarian]*; (Management of international migration.) *[Summary]*. Mária Rédei. **Stat. Szem.** 83:7 7:2005 pp.662-680.

3475   Les nouvelles conventions Franco-Africaines relatives à la circulation des personnes : évolution ou statu quo ? *[In French]*; [New Franco-African conventions relating to the movement of people: evolution or status quo?] Léandre Serge Moyen. **Penant** 849 10-12:2004 pp.501-534.

3476   The politics of immigration and public health. James Hampshire. **Pol. Q.** 76:2 4-6:2005 pp.190-198.

3477   Poverty, international migration and asylum. George J. Borjas [Ed.]; Jeff Crisp [Ed.]. Basingstoke, New York: Palgrave Macmillan, 2005. xix, 445p. *ISBN: 1403943656. Papers presented at the UNU-WIDER sponsored conference, Helsinki, September 2002.*

Includes bibliographical references and index. World Institute for Development Economics Research. (Series: Studies in development economics and policy).

3478 Refugees, institutional invisibility, and self-help strategies: evaluating Kurdish experience in Rome. Raffaela Puggioni. **J. Refug. S.** 18:3 9:2005 pp.319-339.

3479 La réglementation de l'immigration algérienne en France : de la règle au calcul, du calcul a la règle. *[In French]*; [The regulation of Algerian immigration in France: from the rule to the count, from the count to the rule]. Sylvestre Tchibindat. Paris: L'Harmattan, 2004. 204p. *ISBN: 2747568873. Includes bibliographical references (p. [193]-202).*

3480 Return policy and legislation in Austria (Part II). Iris Golden. **AWR B.** 42(51):3 2004 pp.3-18.

3481 Secure borders, safe haven, domopolitics. William Walters. **Citiz. S.** 8:3 9:2004 pp.237-260.

3482 Selecting by origin: ethnic migration in the liberal state. Christian Joppke. Cambridge MA: Harvard University Press, 2005. xi, 330p. *ISBN: 0674015592. Includes bibliographical references (p. 297-320) and index.*

3483 El tema migratorio en la agenda del Ministerio de Relaciones Exteriores. *[In Spanish]*; [The issue of migration in the Ministry of Foreign Affairs' agenda]. Martha Ligia González. **Colom. Int.** 59 2004 pp.192-208.

3484 Threatened by diversity: why restrictive asylum and immigration policies appeal to Western Europeans. Elisabeth Ivarsflaten. **Jnl. Ele. Pub. Op. Par.** 15:1 4:2005 pp.21-45.

3485 The transnational politics of U.S. immigration policy. Marc Rosenblum. La Jolla CA: San Diego Centre for Comparative Immigration Studies; University of California Press, 2004. viii, 127p. *ISBN: 0970283849. Includes bibliographical references (p. 114-127). (Series:* CCIS monographs - 3).

3486 UK asylum law and policy: historical and contemporary perspectives. Dallal Stevens. London: Sweet & Maxwell, 2004. xxxv, 466p. *ISBN: 0421763507. Includes bibliographical references (p. [441]-452) and index.*

3487 US visa policy: securing borders and opening doors. Maura Harty. **Washington Q.** 28:2 Spring:2005 pp.23-34.

3488 We have a choice. Rosemary Bechler [Intro.]. **Mediactive** 4 2005 pp.5-20.

3489 Zapori za revne, taborišča za imigrante? *[In Slovak]*; (Prisons for the poor, camps for immigrants?) *[Summary]*. Ana Kralj. **Soc. Del.** 44:3 6:2005 pp.173-186.

Population and family policies
Politique démographique et politique familiale

3490 Abortion: unanticipated consequences and endless debates. James Taranto; Phillip B. Levine; Eileen McDonagh; Elizabeth Fox-Genovese; Jonathan B. Imber. **Society** 42:5 7-8:2005 pp.13-33. *Collection of 5 articles.*

3491 L'accompagnement des personnes handicapées en Belgique : un concept au cœur des nouvelles pratiques sociales. *[In French]*; [Social policy and the disabled persons in Belgium: a concept in the heart of the new social practices] *[Summary]*. Didier Vrancken; Christophe Bartholomé. **Nouv. Prat. Soc.** 17:1 Autumn:2004 pp.98-111.

3492 'Child panic', risk and child protection: an examination of policies from New South Wales and Queensland. Judyth Sachs; Lise Mellor. **J. Edu. Policy** 20:2 3:2005 pp.125-140.

3493 Childhood lost: how American culture is failing our kids. Sharna Olfman. Westport CT: Praeger, 2005. xiv, 226p. *ISBN: 0275981398. Includes bibliographical references and index. (Series:* Childhood in America).

3494 Choice and coercion: birth control, sterilization, and abortion in public health and welfare. Johanna Schoen. Chapel Hill NC: University of North Carolina Press, 2005. xiv, 331p. *ISBN: 0807829196, 0807855855. Includes bibliographical references (p. 303-314) and index. (Series:* Gender and American culture).

3495 Configurations et relations familiales. *[In French]*; [Family configurations and relations]. Cécile Lefèvre; Linda Hantrais; Marie-Thérèse Letablier; Olivier Büttner; Tine Rostgaard;

Julien Damon; Philippe Steck; Kathy Rousselet; Jean-François Tchernia; Pascale Melani; Dagmar Kutsar; Mathilde Darley; Elena Mashkova; Lilia Crudu; Detelina Tocheva; Monika Wator. **Info. Soc.** 124 6:2005 pp.6-133. *Collection of 13 articles.*

3496 Contemplating choice: attitudes towards intervening in human reproduction in Sri Lanka. B. Simpson; V.H.W. Dissanayake. **New Gen. Soc.** 24:1 4:2005 pp.99-117.

3497 Državni predujam za uzdržavanje djece. *[In Croatian]*; (State advance for the support of children.) *[Summary]*. Branka Rešetar. **Revija Soc. Pol.** 12:2 4-6:2005 pp.157-173.

3498 Dynamics and consequences of population ageing: a comparative inter regional perspective of Asian economies. K. Muraleedharan. **Asian Econ. R.** 47:1 4:2005 pp.1-17.

3499 Einstellungen zur Alterspolitik. Ergebnisse des Population Policy Acceptance Survey in Österreich. *[In German]*; (Attitudes to policy on ageing. Results of the population policy acceptance survey in Austria.); *[Summary in English]*. Peter Schimany. **Öster. Z. Soziol.** 29:4 2004 pp.49-70.

3500 Family care, independent living and ethnicity. Sarah Harpeer; Sonya Levin. **Soc. Policy Soc.** 4:2 4:2005 pp.157-169.

3501 Family planning policy in Latin America: rights, development and values. Maureen Rand Oakley; Emilio A. Rodriguez. **Policy S.** 26:2 6:2005 pp.211-227.

3502 Institutional fragmentation and Scandinavian childcare variations. Dietmar Rauch. **J. Publ. Policy** 25:3 9-12:2005 pp.367-394.

3503 Integration in Zeiten des Wandels — Zuwanderung und demographische Krise als gesellschaftspolitische Herausforderungen. *[In German]*; [Integration in changing times –immigration and demographic crisis as socio-political challenge] *[Summary]*. Volker Kronenberg. **Z. Pol.** 52:2 6:2005 pp.169-178.

3504 Jugendpolitik — wider ihren Ruf verteidigt Walter Hornstein. *[In German]*; (Defending youth policy despite its reputation.) *[Summary]*. Werner Schefold [Interviewer]; Wolfgang Schröer [Interviewer]. **Disk.** 2 2004 pp.45-55.

3505 Lone parents, the new deal and the opportunities and barriers to retail employment. Eli Dutton; Chris Warhurst; Dennis Nickson; Cliff Lockyer. **Policy S.** 26:1 3:2005 pp.85-101.

3506 The man in the partnering state: regendering the social through partnership. Gerda Roelvink; David Craig. **S. Pol. Econ.** 75 Spring:2005 pp.103-126.

3507 Marriage, motherhood and welfare reform. Jill Duerr Berrick. **Soc. Policy Soc.** 4:2 4:2005 pp.133-145.

3508 Maternity at work: a review of national legislation, findings from the ILO's Conditions of Work and Employment Database. Ida Oun; Pardo Trujillo. Geneva: International Labour Office, 2005. xi, 76p. *ISBN: 9221175014.*

3509 Meeting parents' needs? Discourses of 'support' and 'inclusion' in family policy. Val Gillies. **Crit. Soc. Policy** 25:1(82-85) 2:2005 pp.70-90.

3510 Old-age benefits and decentralisation: the Spanish case in comparative perspective; (Old-age benefits and decentralisation: the Spanish case in comparative perspective.) *[Summary]*. Jesús Ruiz-Huerta Carbonell; José M. Díaz Pulido. **Euro. J. Soc. Sec.** 6:4 12:2004 pp.299-334.

3511 Pobreza, política social, capital social y familia: una perspectiva necesaria para los proyectos de desarrollo. *[In Spanish]*; (Poverty, social policy, social capital and family: a necessary perspective in development projects.) Cynthia Martínez; Yousett López; Marié González; Ligibther Rojas. **Cuest. Pol.** 33 7-12:2004 pp.11-26.

3512 The politics of childbirth in the context of conflict: policies or de facto practices? R. Giacaman; H. Abdul-Rahim; L. Wick. **Health Policy** 72:2 5:2005 pp.129-139.

3513 Prävention von Gewalt — Initiativen und Programme des Staatsministeriums für Arbeit und Sozialordnung, Familie und Frauen. *[In German]*; [Preventing violence –initiatives and programs of the Staatsministeriums für Arbeit und Sozialordnung, Familie und Frauen]. Christa Stewens. **Politische S.** 55:1(Supp.) 8:2004 pp.73-86.

3514 Public policies and low fertility: rationales for public intervention and a diagnosis for the Spanish case. Fabrizio Bernardi. **J. Euro. Soc. Policy** 15:2 5:2005 pp.123-138.

3515   Rééquilibrer les structures d'âge en France : natalité, fécondité, quelle politique de long terme. *[In French]*; [Re-stabilising age structures in France: natality, fertility, what long-term policy]. Jean Billet. **J. Off. Repub. Fran.** 7 3:2004 pp.1-147.

3516   Rescaling Russia's geography: the challenges of depopulating the northern periphery. John Round. **Euro.-Asia S.** 57:5 7:2005 pp.705-727.

3517   The role of nonprofit organizations in the delivery of family services in 11 EU member and applicant states; *[Summary in French]*; *[Summary in Spanish]*; *[Summary in Chinese]*; *[Summary in Arabic]*. Louise Appleton. **Int. Soc. Work** 48:3 5:2005 pp.251-262.

3518   Street-level bureaucrats and intrastate variation in the implementation of temporary assistance for needy families policies. Norma M. Riccucci. **J. Publ. Admin. Res. Theory** 15:1 1:2005 pp.89-111.

3519   Using repertory grid technique with participants in parenting programmes-a piloting study. Nick Gould; Hilary Gould; Mike Brewin. **Practice** 16:3 9:2004 pp.197-210.

3520   What do women really want? Neil Gilbert. **Publ. Inter.** 158 Winter:2005 pp.21-38.

3521   Women's citizenship in the time of activation: the case of lone mothers in 'needs-based' welfare states. Anne Skevik. **Soc. Pol.** 12:1 Spring:2005 pp.42-66.

Rural and urban policies
Politiques urbaine et rurale

3522   Accès au logement : droits et réalités. *[In French]*; [Access to housing: rights and reality]. Nicole Prud'homme. **J. Off. Repub. Fran.** 1 1:2004 pp.1-196.

3523   Are planning appeal rights necessary? A comparative study of Australia, England and Vancouver BC. Stephen Willey. **Prog. Plan.** 63:3 2005 pp.263-320. *Collection of 9 articles.*

3524   Beyond federal urban policy. William R. Barnes. **Urb. Aff. R.** 40:5 5:2005 pp.575-589.

3525   Building citizens: participatory planning practice and a transformative politics of difference. Jenny Cameron; Deanna Grant-Smith. **Urb. Policy Res.** 23:1 3:2005 pp.21-36.

3526   Chinese housing reform in state-owned enterprises and its impacts on different social groups. Ya Ping Wang; Yanglin Wang; Glen Bramley. **Urb. S.** 92:10 9:2005 pp.1859-1878.

3527   Community, neighbourhood, responsibility. Dave Cowan; Alex Marsh; Morag McDermont; Rowland Atkinson; John Flint; Alan Deacon; Jacqui Croft; Jenny Muir. **Housing S.** 19:6 11:2004 pp.845-966. *Collection of 7 articles.*

3528   Droit au logement : qu'en avons nous fait. *[In French]*; [The right to housing: what have we done with it?] Gilles Desrumaux [Ed.]; Claude Royon [Ed.]. **Econ. Hum.** 368 3-4:2004 pp.8-80.

3529   Europäische Metropolen im Vergleich — Institutionenentwicklung zwischen Konvergenz und Divergenz. *[In German]*; [Comparing European metropolises –institutional development among convergence and divergence]. Manfred Röber; Eckhard Schröter. **Deutsche Z. Kommunalwissenschaften** 43:2 2004 pp.129-158.

3530   From cultural regeneration to discursive governance: constructing the flagship of the 'museumsquartier vienna' as a plural symbol of change. Monika de Frantz. **Int. J. Urb. Reg. Res.** 29:1 3:2005 pp.50-66.

3531   La gestión territorial. *[In Spanish]*; [Territorial management]. Santiago González-Varas Ibáñez. **R. Admin. Públ.** 166 1-4:2005 pp.257-279.

3532   Governance and urban development programmes in Europe. Claude Jacquier; Roger Andersson; Sako Musterd; Iván Tosics; Thea Dukes; Maurice Blanc; Justin Beaumont. **J. Econ. Soc. Geog.** 96:4 2005 pp.363-420. *Collection of 4 articles.*

3533   Housing allowance. Bengt Turner; Marja Elsinga; Mark Stephens; Viggo Nordvik; Per Åhrén; Kath Hulse; Bill Randolph; Sien Winters; J. Hegedüs; N. Teller; Pinar Türker-Devecigil. **Euro. J. Hous. Policy** 5:2 8:2005 pp.103-229. *Collection of 7 articles.*

3534   Housing policy analysis: British housing in cultural and comparative context. Stuart Lowe. Basingstoke: Palgrave Macmillan, 2004. xi, 327p. *ISBN: 0333801784, 0333801792. Includes bibliographical references and index.*

3535   Housing segregation in suburban America since 1960: presidental and judicial politics. Charles M. Lamb. Cambridge, New York: Cambridge University Press, 2005. xiii, 302p. *ISBN: 0521839440, 0521548276. Includes bibliographical references (p. 275-281) and index.*

3536   In search of the city in spatial strategies: past legacies, future imaginings. Geoff Vigar; Stephen Graham; Patsy Healey. **Urb. S.** 42:8 7:2005 pp.1391-1410.

3537   Innovations in urban governance. Jonathan S. Davies [Ed.]; Clarence N. Stone; Kristin Good; Vivien Lowndes; Jonathan S. Davies; Patrick Bond; Mike Geddes. **Policy S.** 26:3-4 9-12:2005 pp.235-358. *Collection of 7 articles.*

3538   Logement, des responsabilités accrues pour les partenaires sociaux. *[In French]*; [Housing, increased responsibilities for social partners]. Revue de la Confédération française démocratique du travail. **R. Confédération française démocratique du travail** 63 1-2:2004 pp.3-32.

3539   Market provision of affordable rental housing: lessons from recent trends in Australia. Judith Yates; Maryann Wulff. **Urb. Policy Res.** 23:1 3:2005 pp.5-20.

3540   Moving to Opportunity: the demonstration's design and its effects on mobility. Judith D. Feins; Mark D. Shroder. **Urb. S.** 42:8 7:2005 pp.1275-1299.

3541   Neoliberalist planning? Re-thinking and re-casting Sydney's metropolitan planning. Pauline M. McGuirk. **Aust. Geog. S.** 43:1 3:2005 pp.59-70.

3542   Paradise planned: community formation and the master planned estate. Gabrielle Gwyther. **Urb. Policy Res.** 23:1 3:2005 pp.57-72.

3543   Pluralism in housing provision in developing countries: lessons from Brazil. Alex Kenya Abiko; Edmundo Werna; et al. New York: Nova Science Publishers, 2004. 254p. *ISBN: 159033857X. Includes bibliographical references (p. 241-248) and index.*

3544   Policy performance and Brownfield redevelopment in Milwaukee, Wisconsin. Christopher A. De Sousa. **Prof. Geog.** 57:2 5:2005 pp.312-327.

3545   Les politiques de protection de l'eau souterraine dans quatre municipalités. *[In French]*; [Protection of ground water in four cities] *[Summary]*. Michèle Boulanger. **Rech. Sociogr.** XLV:3 9-12:2004 pp.549-567.

3546   Private markets, contracts, and government provision: what explains the organization of local waste and recycling markets? Margaret Walls; Molly MacAuley; Soren Anderson. **Urb. Aff. R.** 40:5 5:2005 pp.590-613.

3547   The privatization of council housing. Norman Ginsburg. **Crit. Soc. Policy** 25:1(82-85) 2:2005 pp.115-135.

3548   Quartiers sensibles et cohésion sociale. *[In French]*; [Difficult districts and social cohesion]. Julien Damon [Ed.]. **Prob. Pol. Soc.** 905 11:2004 pp.5-119.

3549   Religion and urban regeneration: a place for faith? *[Summary in French]*; *[Summary in Spanish]*. Robert Furbey; Marie Macey. **Policy Pol.** 33:1 1:2005 pp.95-116.

3550   Revitalizing the city in an anti-urban context: extreme right of urban policies in Flanders, Belgium. Pascal De Decker; Christian Kesteloot; Filip De Maesschalck; Jan Vranken. **Int. J. Urb. Reg. Res.** 29:1 3:2005 pp.152-171.

3551   The role of state-developed housing and housing poverty in Korea. Seong-kyu Ha. **Int. Dev. Plan. R.** 27:2 2005 pp.227-244.

3552   Scalar dialectics in green: urban private property and the contradictions of the neoliberalization of nature. Nik Heynen; Harold A. Perkins. **Cap. Nat. Social.** 16:1 3:2005 pp.99-113.

3553   The search for community cohesion: key themes and dominant concepts of the public policy agenda. David Robinson. **Urb. S.** 42:8 7:2005 pp.1411-1427.

3554   'Someone to watch over me': making supported housing work. Helen Carr. **Soc. Legal S.** 14:3 9:2005 pp.387-408.

3555   Spillovers and local growth controls: an alternative perspective on suburbanization. Pillsung Byun; Brigitte S. Waldorf; Adrian X. Esparza. **Grow. Chan.** 36:2 Spring:2005 pp.196-219.

3556   A step change or a step back? The Thames Gateway and the re-birth of the urban development corporations. Mike Raco. **Loc. Econ.** 20:2 5:2005 pp.141-153.

3557   Sustainable urban livelihoods and marketplace social capital: crisis and strategy in petty trade. Michal Lyons; Simon Snoxell. **Urb. S.** 42:8 7:2005 pp.1301-1320.

3558   'The land that time forgot': reforming access to social housing in England; *[Summary in French]; [Summary in Spanish]*. David Mullins; Hal Pawson. **Policy Pol.** 33:2 4:2005 pp.205-230.

3559   The urban housing manual: making regulatory frameworks work for the poor. Geoffrey K. Payne; Michael Majale. London: Earthscan, 2004. xvi, 134p. *ISBN: 1844071480. Includes bibliographical references and index.*

3560   Urban policy in the New Scotland: the role of social inclusion partnerships. Chris McWilliams; Charlie Johnstone; Gerry Mooney. **Space & Polity** 8:3 12:2004 pp.309-319.

3561   Urban politics, crime rates, and police strength. Thomas Dain Stucky. New York: LFB Scholarly Publishing, 2005. ix, 169p. *ISBN: 1593320906. Includes bibliographical references (p. 129-157) and index. (Series:* Criminal justice).

3562   Urban sprawl and public health: designing, planning, and building for healthy communities. Howard Frumkin; Lawrence D. Frank; Richard Jackson. Washington DC: Island Press, 2004. xxi, 338p. *ISBN: 1559639121, 1559633050. Includes bibliographical references (p. 279-323) and index.*

3563   Urbanism, cities and local self-government; *[Summary in French]*. W. Magnusson. **Can. Publ. Admin.** 48:1 Spring:2005 pp.96-123.

3564   Urban-rural linkages: issue of technology transfer for rural housing. Nirmal Kumar; Rajendra Prasad; Ravi Shankar; K.C. Iyer. **Indian J. Publ. Admin.** 4:4 10-12:2004 pp.1092-1103.

3565   The use of discretion in a rule-bound service: housing benefit administration and the introduction of discretionary housing payments in Great Britain. Bruce Walker; Pat Niner. **Publ. Admin.** 83:1 2005 pp.47-66.

3566   What drives infrastructure spending in cities of developing countries? Ben C. Arimah. **Urb. S.** 42:8 7:2005 pp.1345-1368.

Welfare state
État providence

3567   Agency, actors and change in a child-focused future: 'path dependency' problematised. Alexandra Dobrowolsky; Denis Saint-Martin. **Commonwealth Comp. Pol.** 43:1 3:2005 pp.1-33.

3568   La articulación entre familia y estado de bienestar en los países de la Europa del sur. *[In Spanish]*; [Family-welfare state relation in Southern European countries] *[Summary]*. Lluís Flaquer. **Papers** 73 2004 pp.27-58.

3569   Assessing the impact of Indonesian social safety net programmes on household welfare and poverty dynamics; *[Summary in French]*. Sudarno Sumarto; Asep Suryahadi; Wenefrida Widyanti. **Euro. J. Dev. Res.** 17:1 3:2005 pp.155-177.

3570   The battle of future pensions: global accounting tools, international organizations and pension reforms; *[Summary in French]; [Summary in Spanish]*. Rune Ervik. **Glo. Soc. Policy** 5:1 4:2005 pp.29-54.

3571   Child poverty in Northern Ireland: the limits of welfare-to-work policies. Goretti Horgan. **Soc. Policy Admin.** 39:1 2:2005 pp.49-64.

3572   La clarification des missions de l'état, de la société civile, du secteur privé dans la gouvernance économique et la lutte contre la pauvreté en Afrique. *[In French]*; [The clarification of the missions of the state, of civil society and of the private sector in economic governance and the fight against poverty in Africa]. Donatien Muryando; Irie Dje Bi; Pornon Sanogo; Aziz El Khazzar; Rachid El Houdaïgui; Mohamed Kairouani; Mustafa El Magrhabi. **Cah. Afr. Admin. Publ.** 63 2004 pp.51-95. *Collection of 7 articles.*

3573   Declining employment among young black less-educated men: the role of incarceration and child support. Harry J. Holzer; Paul Offner; Elaine Sorensen. **J. Policy Anal. Manag.** 24:2 Spring:2005 pp.329-350.

3574   Discovering child poverty: the creation of a policy agenda from 1800 to the present. Lucinda Platt. Bristol: Policy Press, 2005. 143p. *ISBN: 1861345836*. (*Series:* Studies in poverty, inequality and social exclusion).

3575   Does the minimum wage affect welfare caseloads? Marianne E. Page; Joanne Spetz; Jane Millar. **J. Policy Anal. Manag.** 24:2 Spring:2005 pp.273-295.

3576   Does 'welfare-to-work' work? A systematic review of the effectiveness of the UK's welfare-to-work programmes for people with a disability or chronic illness. Clare Bambra; Margaret Whitehead; Val Hamilton. **Soc. Sci. Med.** 60:9 5:2005 pp.1905-1918.

3577   Economic crisis, domestic politics and welfare state changes. Shinyoung Kim. **Pac. R.** 18:3 9:2005 pp.375-392.

3578   Eight years of New Labour. Pete Alcock; Paul Dornan; Dan Finn; Marilyn Howard; Kirk Mann; Tom Sefton; Alice Bloch; Robert M. Page. **Benefits** 13:2(43) 6:2005 pp.83-122. *Collection of 7 articles.*

3579   External habit formation and dependency in the welfare state. Keith Jakee; Guang-zhen Sun. **Euro. J. Pol. Econ.** 21:1 3:2005 pp.83-98.

3580   Federalism and the politics of old-age care in Germany and the United States. Andrea Louise Campbell; Kimberly J. Morgan. **Comp. Pol. S.** 38:8 10:2005 pp.887-914.

3581   The fourth attempt to construct a politics of welfare obligations; *[Summary in French]*; *[Summary in Spanish]*. Tony Fitzpatrick. **Policy Pol.** 33:1 1:2005 pp.15-32.

3582   Globalisation, domestic politics, and welfare state retrenchment in capitalist democracies. Duane Swank. **Soc. Policy Soc.** 4:2 4:2005 pp.183-195.

3583   Globalization and its effects on pluralism in welfare states. Liljana Rihter. **Soc. Dev. Iss.** 27:1 Spring:2005 pp.25-34.

3584   Handicaps historiques, blocages corporatistes et institutionnels, résistances des mentalités aux réformes de l'Etat social. *[In French]*; [Welfare reform and resistance to change]. Serge Gouazé. **Alle. Aujourd.** 167 1-3:2004 pp.3-21.

3585   Healthy democracies: welfare politics in Taiwan and South Korea. Joseph Wong. Ithaca NY: Cornell University Press, 2004. xii, 209p. *ISBN: 0801443008. Includes bibliographical references and index.*

3586   A historical review of the South African social welfare system and social work practitioners' views on its current status; *[Summary in Spanish]*; *[Summary in French]*; *[Summary in Chinese]*; *[Summary in Arabic]*. Marquessa Brown; R.J. Neku. **Int. Soc. Work** 48:3 5:2005 pp.301-312.

3587   How to rescue a failing pension regime: the British case. Robin Blackburn. **New Pol. Econ.** 9:4 12:2004 pp.559-579.

3588   Ideas and social policy: an institutionalist perspective. Daniel Béland. **Soc. Policy Admin.** 39:1 2:2005 pp.1-18.

3589   Illegal labour migrants and access to social protection. Paul Schoukens; Danny Pieters. **Euro. J. Soc. Sec.** 6:3 9:2004 pp.229-254.

3590   I'm OK, you're (not) OK: the private welfare state in the United States. B. Guy Peters. **Soc. Policy Admin.** 39:2 4:2005 pp.166-180.

3591   Inter vivos transfers and bequests in three OECD countries. Ernesto Villanueva; Gabrielle Demange [Discussant]; Stefan Hochguertel [Discussant]. **Econ. Policy** 43 7:2005 pp.505-566.

3592   Legal changes in social security in the Nordic countries in the period 1950-2000 from the perspective of subsidiarity and solidarity. Lotta Vahlne Westerhäll. **Euro. J. Soc. Sec.** 6:4 12:2004 pp.335-361.

3593   Local government and welfare generosity: municipality spending on social welfare. Sandra Lien; Per Arnt Pettersen. **Scand. Pol. S.** 27:4 2004 pp.343-365.

3594   A more equal society? New Labour, poverty, inequality and exclusion. John Hills [Ed.]; Kitty Stewart [Ed.]. Bristol: Policy Press, 2005. xv, 391p. *ISBN: 186134578X, 1861345771.*

3595   Mutation des valeurs et transformation du système social en Allemagne. *[In French]*; [The transformation of the social system and values in Germany]. Jérôme Vaillant. **Alle. Aujourd.** 168 4-6:2004 pp.3-115.

3596   The Mutual Obligation policy in Australia: the rhetoric and reasoning of recent social security policy. Stephen Parker; Rodney Fopp. **Cont. Pol.** 10:3-4 9-12:2004 pp.257-270.

3597   Nationalism, public policy, and institutional development: social security in Belgium. Daniel Béland; André Lecours. **J. Publ. Policy** 25:2 5-8:2005 pp.265-285.

3598   The new pensions procedure. David Salter. **Fam. Law** 35 12:2005 pp.977-990.

3599   Old-age income support in the 21st century: an international perspective on pension systems and reform. Robert Holzman; Richard P. Hinz; Hermann von Gersdorff [Contrib.]; et al. Washington DC: World Bank, 2005. ix, 232p. *ISBN: 082136040X. Includes bibliographical references (p. 195-214) and index.*

3600   One hundred years of poverty and policy. Howard Glennerster. York: Joseph Rowntree Foundation, 2004. 188p. *ISBN: 1859352219. Includes bibliographical references.*

3601   One village group unit and one product movement: an alternative strategy for decentralised rural development and poverty alleviation. Hemlata Rao. **Indian Soc. Sci. R.** 6:1 1-6:2004 pp.55-77.

3602   Pension design and gender. Ann-Charlotte Ståhlberg; Agneta Kruse; Annika Sundén. **Euro. J. Soc. Sec.** 7:1 3:2005 pp.57-102.

3603   Pension reform in Germany and Austria: system change v. quantitative retrenchment. Marius R. Busemeyer. **West Euro. Pol.** 28:3 5:2005 pp.569-591.

3604   Políticas sociales para el crecimiento con equidad en Chile, 1990-2002. *[In Spanish]*; [Social policies for equality growth in Chile, 1990-2002] *[Summary]*. José Pablo Arellano M. **Trim. Econ.** LXXII(2):286 4-6:2005 pp.409-449.

3605   Population, prophets, pensions, and politics. Pavel Kohout. **Orbis** 49:4 Fall:2005 pp.731-742.

3606   Population rurale et sécurité sociale au Brésil : une analyse dans le contexte des changements constitutionnels. *[In French]*; [Rural population and social security in Brazil: analysis in the context of constitutional changes]. Kaizô Iwakami Beltrão; Sonoe Sugahara Pinheiro; Francisco Eduardo Barreto de Oliveira. **R. Int. Sécur. Soc.** 57:4 10-12:2004 pp.23-58.

3607   The production of last resort support: a comparison of social assistance schemes in Europe using the notion of welfare production and the concept of social rights. Susan Kuivalainen. **Euro. J. Soc. Sec.** 7:1 3:2005 pp.35-56.

3608   Reforma da previdência: o ajuste no serviço público. *[In Portuguese]*; [Welfare reform: an adjustment in the public services] *[Summary]*. Calino Pacheco Filho; Carlos Roberto Winckler. **Ind. Econ. FEE** 32:4 2005 pp.221-247.

3609   Reinventing welfare regimes: employers and the implementation of active social policy. Cathie Jo Martin. **World Pol.** 57:1 10:2004 pp.39-69.

3610   Second-generation poverty reduction strategies: new opportunities and emerging issues. Ruth Driscoll; Alison Evans. **Dev. Policy R.** 23:1 1:2005 pp.5-25.

3611   Shocking Mother Russia: democratization, social rights, and pension reform in Russia, 1990-2001. Andrea Chandler. Toronto: University of Toronto Press, 2004. xii, 246p. *ISBN: 0802089305. Includes bibliographical references (p. 225-238) and index.*

3612   The social capital of European welfare states: the crowding out hypotheses revisited. Wim van Oorschot; Wil Arts. **J. Euro. Soc. Policy** 15:1 2:2005 pp.5-26.

3613   Social grants as safety net for HIV/AIDS-affected households in South Africa. F. Booysen. **SAHARA J** 1:1 5:2004 pp.45-56.

3614   Social protection around the world: external insecurity, state capacity, and domestic political cleavages. Isabela Mares. **Comp. Pol. S.** 38:6 8:2005 pp.623-651.

3615   Sozialpolitik in Post-Hartz Germany. *[In German]*; (Social politics in post-Hartz Germany.) Christine Trampusch. **Welt Trends** 47 Summer:2005 pp.77-90.

3616   Swiss worlds of welfare. Klaus Armingeon; Fabio Bertozzi; Giuliano Bonoli. **West Euro. Pol.** 27:1 1:2004 pp.20-44.

3617   Le système de revenu minimum pour les chômeurs : étude de cas à Dalian (Chine). *[In French]*; [The minimum income system for the unemployed: case study in Dalian, China]. Daoshun Ge; Yang Tuan. **R. Inter. Sc. Soc.** 179 3:2004 pp.53-63.

3618   Taming the beast: categorizing state welfare policies: a typology of welfare policies affecting recipient job entry. Signe-Mary McKernan; Jen Bernstein; Lynne Fender; Mattew Auer [Ed.]. **J. Policy Anal. Manag.** 24:2 Spring:2005 pp.443-460.

3619   Trust in UK pensions policy: a different approach? *[Summary in French]*; *[Summary in Spanish]*. Patrick John Ring. **Policy Pol.** 33:1 1:2005 pp.55-74.

3620   Uganda: no more pro-poor growth? Robert Kappel; Jann Lay; Susan Steiner. **Dev. Policy R.** 23:1 1:2005 pp.27-53.

3621   Ungleichheit als Schicksal? *[In German]*; [Inequality as fate?] Wolfgang Engler; Wolfgang Kersting; Hanno Scholtz; Matthias Bohlender; Lars Castellucci; Gesa Reisz; Alexander Cammann. **Vorgänge** 43:4(168) 12:2004 pp.4-76. *Collection of 7 articles.*

3622   Useful and priceless children in contemporary welfare states. Pavla Miller. **Soc. Pol.** 12:1 Spring:2005 pp.3-41.

3623   Velfærdsstatsregimer og arbejdsmarkedspolitik — grupperer velfærdsstaterne sig som forventet? *[In Danish]*; (Welfare state regimes and labor market policy — do the welfare states group according to expectations?) *[Summary]*. Søren Hartmann Hede. **Politica** 36:3 9:2004 pp.289-310.

3624   Where's the outrage? Mike Miller [Ed.]. **Soc. Policy** 35:3 Spring:2005 pp.5-8.

3625   Women, family, welfare and work. Betty Reid Mandell. **New Pol.** X:3 Summer:2005 pp.142-159.

E.5:   **Cultural, media and telecommunications policies**
        Politiques de la culture, des médias et des télécommunications

3626   Art for the masses? Justification for the public support of the arts in developing countries — two arts festivals in South Africa. J.D. Snowball. **J. Cult. Econ.** 29:2 5:2005 pp.107-125.

3627   Art for the people? Christo and Jeanne-Claude's 'the gates'. Jesse Lemisch. **New Pol.** X:3 Summer:2005 pp.82-95.

3628   As bibliotecas no liberalismo: uma definição de uma política cultural de regime. *[In Portuguese]*; (Libraries under the liberal order: a definition of a regime's cultural policy.) *[Summary]*. Paulo J.S. Barata. **Anál. Soc.** XL:174 Spring:2005 pp.37-64.

3629   Biculturalism and cultural diversity: how far does state policy in New Zealand and the UK seek to reflect, enable or idealise the development of minority culture? Linda Moss. **Int. J. Cult. Policy** 11:2 7:2005 pp.187-198.

3630   Das brasilianische Ministério de Cultura unter Gilberto Gil: Kulturpolitik und soziales Gewissen. *[In German]*; (The ministry of culture in Brazil under Gilberto Gil: politics of culture and social conscience.) *[Summary]*. Regina Aggio. **Lat.Am. Anal.** 10 2:2005 pp.25-46.

3631   Brave new world: understanding China's creative vision. Michael Keane. **Int. J. Cult. Policy** 10:3 11:2004 pp.265-279.

3632   Consumer perceptions of sponsorship in the arts: a Canadian perspective. François Colbert; Alain d'Astous; Marie-Agnès Parmentier. **Int. J. Cult. Policy** 11:2 7:2005 pp.215-227.

3633   Creative shifts and directions: cultural policy in Singapore. Terence Lee. **Int. J. Cult. Policy** 10:3 11:2004 pp.281-299.

3634   The cultural industries and cultural policy. David Hesmondhalgh; Andy C. Pratt; Nicholas Garnham; Justin O'Connor; Lily Kong; Susan Christopherson; Danielle van Jaarsveld. **Int. J. Cult. Policy** 11:1 3:2005 pp.1-109. *Collection of 7 articles.*

3635   Cultural policy and cultural production: MacLean's magazine and foreign news. David Hutchison. **Br. J. Can. S.** 17:1 2004 pp.44-60.

3636   Down to the wire. Thomas Bleha. **Foreign Aff.** 84:3 5-6:2005 pp.111-124.

3637   Drawing lessons from across the pond: the fungibility of US and British telephone regulation; *[Summary in French]*; *[Summary in Spanish]*. Michael J. Zarkin. **Policy Pol.** 33:2 4:2005 pp.191-204.

3638   E-governance: the case of Andaman and Nicobar Islands. S.S. Sreekumar. **Indian J. Pol. Sci.** LXVI:2 4-6:2005 pp.329-340.

3639   Entertaining the citizen: when politics and popular culture converge. Liesbet van Zoonen. Lanham MD: Rowman & Littlefield, 2005. viii, 181p. *ISBN: 0742529061, 074252907X. Includes bibliographical references (p. 153-171) and index. (Series:* Critical media studies*).*

3640   Globalisation, ICTs, and the new imperialism: perspectives on Africa in the global electronic village (GEV). Yunusa Z. Ya'u. **Afr. Dev.** XXX:1-2 2005 pp.98-124.

3641   Government credible commitment in Korea's information and telecommunications sector development. Jaekwon Cha. **Kor. Obs.** 35:4 Winter:2004 pp.639-663.

3642   International networks and arts policy research. Christopher Madden. **Int. J. Cult. Policy** 11:2 7:2005 pp.129-144.

3643   Japan's telecommunications policy: issues in regulatory reform for interconnection. Yuko Suda. **Asian Sur.** XLV:2 3-4:2005 pp.241-257.

3644   Javni servisi ili komercijalni sadržaji? *[In Croatian]*; (Public services or commercial programming?) *[Summary]*. Marina Mučalo. **Pol. Misao** 41:1 2004 pp.42-54.

3645   Market or party controls? Chinese media in transition. Betty Houchin Winfield; Zengjun Peng. **Gazette** 67:3 6:2005 pp.255-270.

3646   Market valorization in broadcasting policy in Ghana: abandoning the quest for media democratization. Amin Alhassan. **Media Cult. Soc.** 27:2 3:2005 pp.211-228.

3647   Media policy out of the box: content abundance, attention scarcity, and the failures of digital markets. Ellen P. Goodman. **Berkeley Techno. Law J.** 19:4 Fall:2004 pp.1389-1472.

3648   Mobile message services and communications policy. Gerard Goggin; Christina Spurgeon. **Prometheus** 23:2 6:2005 pp.181-194.

3649   Modern blackness: nationalism, globalization and the politics of culture in Jamaica. Deborah A. Thomas. Durham NC: Duke University Press, 2004. xiv, 357p. *ISBN: 0822334089, 0822334194. Includes bibliographical references (p. 311-340) and index. (Series:* Latin America otherwise*).*

3650   Multiculturalism in Taiwan: contradictions and challenges in cultural policy. Li-jung Wang. **Int. J. Cult. Policy** 10:3 11:2004 pp.301-318.

3651   Nemzetek fölötti nyelv és nemzeti fennmaradás. *[In Hungarian]*; (Supranational language and national survival: prospects of cultural policies in East-Central-Europe.) Tibor Frank. **Mag. Tud.** 49:8 2004 pp.808-823.

3652   Network security, survivability and surveillance. T.H. Grubesic; A.T. Murray; J.A. Lewis; V. Mayer-Schönberger; D. Phillips; E.A. Whitley; I. Hosein; S. Bronitt; J. Stellios. **Telecom. Policy** 29:11 12:2005 pp.801-888. Collection of 6 articles.

3653   The Pan-African nation: oil and the spectacle of culture in Nigeria. Andrew H. Apter. Chicago IL: University of Chicago Press, 2005. x, 334p. *ISBN: 0226023540, 0226023559. Includes bibliographical references (p. [309]-321) and index.*

3654   The party and the arty in China: the new politics of culture. Richard Curt Kraus. Lanham MD: Rowman & Littlefield, 2004. xi, 249p. *ISBN: 0742527190, 0742527204. Includes bibliographical references and index. (Series:* State and society in East Asia*).*

3655   The pattern and externality effect of diffusion of mobile telecommunications: the case of the OECD and Taiwan. S.L. Jang; S.C. Dai; S. Sung. **Info. Econ. Policy** 17:2 3:2005 pp.133-148.

3656   Policy networks and market opening: telecommunications liberalization in Spain. J. Jordana; D. Sancho. **Euro. J. Pol. Res.** 44:4 6:2005 pp.519-546.

3657   La politica cultural del estado en los gobiernos populares (1996-2004): entre el ¿liberalismo? y el continuismo socialista. *[In Spanish]*; [Popular governments' cultural policy (1996-2004): between liberalism and socialist continuity? *[Summary]*. Juan Arturo Rubio Arostegui. **Sistema** 187 7:2005 pp.111-124.

3658   Political censorship and the democratic state: the Irish broadcasting ban. Mary P. Corcoran [Ed.]; Mark. O'Brien [Ed.]. Dublin: Four Courts Press, 2005. 151p. *ISBN: 185182846X, 1851828699.*

3659 Pour un débat éclairé sur la politique canadienne du multiculturalisme : une analyse de la nature des organismes et des projets subventionnés (1983-2002). *[In French]*; [For an enlightened debate on Canadian policy of multiculturalism: organisms and subsidized projects analysis] *[Summary]*. Marie McAndrew; Denise Helly; Caroline Tessier. **Pol. et Soc.** 24:1 2005 pp.49-71.

3660 Public aid mechanisms in feature film production: the EU MEDIA Plus Programme. Victor Henning; Andre Alpar. **Media Cult. Soc.** 27:2 3:2005 pp.229-250.

3661 Public funding for film and audiovisual works in Europe: a comparative approach. André Lange; Tim Westcott; European Audiovisual Observatory; European Investment Bank. Strasbourg: European Investment Bank; European Audiovisual Observatory, 2004. 176p. *ISBN: 9287154392.*

3662 Public service broadcasting. Mark Armstrong. **Fis. Stud.** 26:3 9:2005 pp.281-299.

3663 Public television and empowerment in Taiwan. Gary Rawnsley; Ming-yeh Rawnsley. **Pac. Aff.** 78:1 Spring:2005 pp.23-38.

3664 Red net over China: China's new online media order and its implications. Xu Wu. **Asian J. Communic.** 15:2 7:2005 pp.215-227.

3665 Sport in the 'city of culture': the cultural policy connection. John Hughson. **Int. J. Cult. Policy** 10:3 11:2004 pp.319-330.

3666 The telecom crisis and beyond. Restructuring of the global telecommunications system. Dal Yong Jin. **Gazette** 67:3 6:2005 pp.289-304.

3667 Trade and cultural diversity: an Australian perspective. Franco Papandrea. **Prometheus** 23:2 6:2005 pp.227-238.

3668 What's it got to do with morality? Moral rights: an historic and contemporary perspective. Maree Sainsbury. **Media Int. Aust.** 114 2:2005 pp.61-70.

3669 When the 'information revolution' and the US security state collide: money laundering and the proliferation of surveillance. Peter Shields. **New Media Soc.** 7:4 8:2005 pp.483-512.

3670 Who said politicians cannot be conservative? Comparing reform capacity in the Czech and Hungarian telecom administrations. Ole Nørgaard; Luise Pape Møller. **Comm. Post-Comm. S.** 38:3 9:2005 pp.403-419.

3671 Will businesses ever become legitimate partners in the financing of the arts in France? Catherine Morel. **Int. J. Cult. Policy** 11:2 7:2005 pp.199-214.

E.6: **Education policy**
Politique de l'éducation

3672 Academic freedom under fire. Jonathan R. Cole. **Dædalus** 134:2 Spring:2005 pp.5-17.

3673 Affirmative action and desert. J.M. Dieterle. **Publ. Aff. Q.** 19:2 4:2005 pp.81-94.

3674 Boy's education: why governments delayed. Peter West. **Peop. Place** 13:1 2005 pp.41-52.

3675 'Brutal and stinking' and 'difficult to handle': the historical and contemporary manifestations of racialisation, institutional racism, and schooling in Britain. Mike Cole. **Race Ethnic. Edu.** 7:1 3:2004 pp.35-56.

3676 Can redistributing teachers across schools raise educational attainment? Evidence from operation blackboard in India. A. Chin. **J. Dev. Econ.** 78:2 12:2005 pp.384-405.

3677 Celebrating the Universities Service Centre for China Studies. Ezra F. Vogel [Intro.]; Martin King Whyte; Yu-shan Wu; Tse-kang Leng; Scott Rozelle; Jikun Huang; Keijiro Otsuka; Jean C. Oi. **Chi. J.** 53 1:2005 pp.1-144. *Collection of 6 articles.*

3678 The central role of noise in evaluating interventions that use test scores to rank schools. Kenneth Y. Chay; Patrick J. McEwan; Miguel Urquiola. **Am. Econ. R.** 95:4 9:2005 pp.1237-1258.

3679 Children on the margins: comparing the role of school in England and France. Carol Hayden; Catherine Blaya. **Policy S.** 26:1 3:2005 pp.67-83.

3680 Civic education in post-apartheid South Africa: alternative paths to the development of political knowledge and democratic values. Steven E. Finkel; Howard R. Ernst. **Pol. Psychol.** 26:3 6:2005 pp.333-364.

3681   'Clarity bordering on stupidity': where's the quality in systematic review? Maggie MacLure. **J. Edu. Policy** 20:4 7:2005 pp.393-416.

3682   Collaboration: the big new idea for school improvement? Jennifer Evans; Frances Castle; Deborah Cooper; Ron Glatter; Philip A. Woods. **J. Edu. Policy** 20:2 3:2005 pp.223-235.

3683   Comparing state hegemonies: Chinese universities in postwar Singapore and Hong Kong. Ting-hong Wong. **Br. J. Sociol. Edu.** 26:2 4:2005 pp.199-218.

3684   Contribution à la préparation de la loi d'orientation sur l'avenir de l'école. *[In French]*; [Contribution to the preparation of the law on orientation on the future of the school]. Claude Azéma [Ed.]. **J. Off. Repub. Fran.** 16 6:2004 pp.7-97.

3685   Decentralisation and privatisation in education — the role of the state. M.V. Mukundan; Mark Bray; Christopher Bjork; Adam Davidson-Harden; Suzanne Majhanovich; David T. Gamage; Pacharapimon Sooksomchitra; MacLeans A. Geo-Jaja; Holger Daun; David Turner; Ernesto Schiefelbein; Alberto Arenas; Carlos Ornelas. **Int. R. Edu.** 50:3-4 7:2004 pp.223-418. *Collection of 10 articles.*

3686   Democracy and education spending in Africa. David Stasavage. **Am. J. Pol. Sci.** 49:2 4:2005 pp.343-358.

3687   Denmark: lessons from PISA 2000. OECD. Paris: OECD, 2004. 187p. *ISBN: 9264017925. Includes bibliographical references.*

3688   Despite the odds: the contentious politics of education reform. Merilee Serrill Grindle. Princeton NJ: Princeton University Press, 2004. xvi, 257p. *ISBN: 0691117993, 0691118000. Includes bibliographical references (p. 233-248) and index.*

3689   Does school accountability lead to improved student performance? Eric A. Hanushek; Margaret E. Raymond. **J. Policy Anal. Manag.** 24:2 Spring:2005 pp.297-327.

3690   L'école juive et la République. *[In French]*; [Jewish schools and the Republic]. Arche. **Arche** 555 5:2004 pp.44-72.

3691   Education. Stephen Machin; Paul Johnson; Joshua D. Angrist; Leon Feinstein; Eric Eide; Jo Blanden; Nicholas Barr; Robert Dur; Ewart Keep; Alison Wolf. **Oxf. R. Econ. Policy** 20:2 Summer:2004 pp.157-333. *Collection of 10 articles.*

3692   Education policy as an act of white supremacy: whiteness, critical race theory and education reform. David Gillborn. **J. Edu. Policy** 20:4 7:2005 pp.485-505.

3693   Education policy in Britain. Clyde Chitty. Basingstoke: Palgrave Macmillan, 2004. xviii, 231p. *ISBN: 1403902216, 1403902224. (Series:* Contemporary political studies).

3694   Educational policies on migrants and minorities in the Netherlands: success or failure? Rally Rijkschroeff; Geert ten Dam; Jan Willem Duyvendak; Marjan de Gruijter; Trees Pels. **J. Edu. Policy** 20:4 7:2005 pp.417-435.

3695   The effects of user-fee policy on attendance rates among Kenyan elementary schoolchildren; *[Summary in German]*; *[Summary in French]*; *[Summary in Spanish]*; *[Summary in Russian]*. Edith Mukudi. **Int. R. Edu.** 50:5-6 11:2004 pp.447-461.

3696   Egyetemek irányítása — a középkori egyetemtől a Bologna-folyamatig. *[In Hungarian]*; (University management — from medieval university to the Bologna process.) Károly Barakonyi. **Mag. Tud.** 49:4 2004 pp.513-529.

3697   Empowerment and state education: rights of choice and participation. Neville Harris. **Mod. Law R.** 68:6 11:2005 pp.925-957.

3698   L'enseignement des disciplines artistiques à l'école. *[In French]*; [Art education in school]. Jean-Michel Bichat [Ed.]. **J. Off. Repub. Fran.** 4 2:2004 pp.1-197.

3699   The ethnic minority achievement grant: a critical analysis. Leon Tikly; Audrey Osler; John Hill. **J. Edu. Policy** 20:3 5:2005 pp.283-312.

3700   Európa oktatásáról — Maastricht után tíz évvel. Pillanatképek, mindennapok, tendenciák. *[In Hungarian]*; (Education in Europe ten years after Maastricht.) *[Summary]*. János Koncz. **Euro. Tükör** 9:1 2004 pp.47-82.

3701   Europäische Schulen auf dem Prüfstand — PISA und die regionale Mehrsprachigkeit. *[In German]*; [European schools on the test –PISA and regional multilingualism]. Peter J. Weber; Peter H. Nelde. **Euro. Ethn.** 62:1-2 2005 pp.12-22.

3702   An evaluation of the 'new deal' in further education colleges in England. Sai Loo; Norman Lucas. **J. Edu. Work** 17:3 9:2004 pp.301-314.

3703 A felsőoktatás akkreditációja Franciaországban. *[In Hungarian]*; (The accreditation of higher education in France.) Kinga Mandel. **Mag. Tud.** 49:1 2004 pp.81-95.

3704 Financement des universités : le non-dit. *[In French]*; [University funding: what is left unspoken]. Frédéric Lacroix; Patrick Sabourin. **Action Nat.** 94:8 10:2004 pp.86-105.

3705 Globalization and education. Katarina Tomasevski; Robert F. Arnove; Margaret Sutton; Risa L. Lieberwitz; Kathleen D. Hall; Bonnie Urciuoli; Amy Stambach; Heidi Ross; Jingjing Lou; Bradley A.U. Levinson; Denis Meuret. **Indiana J. Glob. Legal S.** 12:1 Winter:2005 pp.1-312. *Collection of 10 articles.*

3706 Henry Giroux and the politics of higher education under George W. Bush: an interview. Mike Alexander Pozo. **R. Edu. Pedagogy Cult. S.** 27:1 1-3:2005 pp.95-107.

3707 Hogy hasznosultak a magyarországi támogatások a környező országok magyar felsőoktatásában és kutatásában? *[In Hungarian]*; (The cost and benefit of Hungary's aid programs for Hungarian higher education and research in Hungary's neighboring countries.) Pál Péter Tóth; Dénes Berényi. **Mag. Tud.** 49:7 2004 pp.770-779.

3708 La inserción social de la Universidade Estadual de Campinas (Unicamp). *[In Spanish]*; (The social involvement of the Universidade Estadual de Campinas (Unicamp).) *[Summary]*. Sandra Brisolla. **R. Iberoamer. Cienc. Tech. Soc.** 2:4 1:2005 pp.97-123.

3709 Is equality of opportunity politically feasible? Stefan Zink. **Econ. Pol.** 17:1 3:2005 pp.111-127.

3710 Iskola és közösség. Felekezeti középiskolások az ezredfordulón. *[In Hungarian]*; (School and community. Pupils in the denominational secondary schools at the turn of the millenium.) Gabriella Pusztai. Budapest: Gondolat Kiadó, 2004. 353p. *ISBN: 9639500984. Includes bibliographical references (p. 340-353).*

3711 Longitudinal gains in civic development through school-based required service. Edward C. Metz; James Youniss. **Pol. Psychol.** 26:3 6:2005 pp.413-437.

3712 National policy and a regional response in South African higher education. Nico Cloete; et al. Oxford: James Currey, 2004. xvi, 144p. *ISBN: 0852554354. Includes bibliographical references. Partnership for Higher Education in Africa.* (*Series:* Higher education in Africa).

3713 Participation in a national, means-tested school voucher program. David E. Campbell; Martin R. West; Paul E. Peterson. **J. Policy Anal. Manag.** 24:3 Summer:2005 pp.523-541.

3714 Pedagógiai realizmus. *[In Hungarian]*; (Educational realism.) István Magyari Beck. **Valóság** 47:1 2004 pp.1-14.

3715 Policy and practice: a twenty year retrospective on gifted education in the Australian state of New South Wales. Jill Forster. **Gifted Edu. Int.** 19:2 2005 pp.182-196.

3716 Policy discourses and changing practice: diversity and the university-college. Adrienne S. Chan. **High. Edu.** 50:1 7:2005 pp.129-157.

3717 Politiques et discours éducatifs : comparaisons internationales. *[In French]*; [Educational policies and discourse: international comparisons]. Revue française de pédagogie. **R. Fran. Ped.** 146 1-3:2004 pp.5-63.

3718 Public education and multicultural policy in Canada: the special case of Quebec; *[Summary in German]*; *[Summary in Spanish]*; *[Summary in French]*; *[Summary in Russian]*. Ratna Ghosh. **Int. R. Edu.** 50:5-6 11:2004 pp.543-566.

3719 Public school music: notes on the public provision of a quasi-private good. L. Langbein. **Publ. Choice** 121:1-2 10:2004 pp.83-98.

3720 Quotas in Brazilian public universities: good or bad idea? Eduardo C. Andrade. **R. Bras. Econ.** 58:4 10-12:2004 pp.453-484.

3721 Raising standards in American schools: the case of no child left behind. Emma Smith. **J. Edu. Policy** 20:4 7:2005 pp.507-524.

3722 La relation entre recherche sociologique et politiques de réforme de l'éducation en Ouzbékistan. *[In French]*; [The relation between sociological research and educational reform policies in Uzbekistan]. Rano Ubaidullayeva. **R. Inter. Sc. Soc.** 179 3:2004 pp.99-111.

3723 Renovating educational identities: policy, space and urban renewal. Kalervo N. Gulson. **J. Edu. Policy** 20:2 3:2005 pp.141-158.

3724   The role of democracy in Uganda's move to universal primary education. David Stasavage. **J. Mod. Afr. S.** 43:1 3:2005 pp.53-73.

3725   Student achievement in charter schools: a complex picture. Richard Buddin; Ronald Zimmer. **J. Policy Anal. Manag.** 24:2 Spring:2005 pp.351-371.

3726   Translating globalization and democratization into local policy: educational reform in Hong Kong and Taiwan; *[Summary in German]; [Summary in French]; [Summary in Spanish]; [Summary in Russian].* Wing-wah Law. **Int. R. Edu.** 50:5-6 11:2004 pp.497-524.

3727   Using evaluation to create "provisional stabilities": bridging innovation in higher education change processes. Murray Saunders; Bernadette Charlier; Joel Bonamy. **Evaluation** 11:1 1:2005 pp.37-54.

3728   Voter support for privatizing education: evidence on self-interest and ideology. Wolfram Merzyn; Heinrich W. Ursprung. **Euro. J. Pol. Econ.** 21:1 3:2005 pp.33-58.

E.7:   **Science policy**
       Politique scientifique

3729   Alcances y limitaciones de la noción de impacto social de la ciencia y la tecnología. *[In Spanish];* (Scopes and limitations of the notion of social impact of science and technology.) *[Summary].* Mario Albornoz; María Elina Estébanez; Claudio Alfaraz. **R. Iberoamer. Cienc. Tech. Soc.** 2:4 1:2005 pp.73-95.

3730   Boundary work in contemporary science policy: a review. Merle Jacob. **Prometheus** 23:2 6:2005 pp.195-208.

3731   Bringing science and technology human resources back in: the Spanish Ramón y Cajal programme. Laura Cruz-Castro; Luis Sanz-Menéndez. **Sci. Publ. Policy** 32:1 2:2005 pp.39-53.

3732   China's government R&D institutes: changes and associated issues; *[Summary in French]; [Summary in Spanish].* Wang Yuan. **Sci. Techno. Soc.** 10:1 1-6:2005 pp.11-29.

3733   Collective benchmarking of policies: an instrument for policy learning in adaptive research and innovation policy. Marianne Paasi. **Sci. Publ. Policy** 32:1 2:2005 pp.17-27.

3734   Committing to vaccine R&D: a global science policy priority. Daniele Archibugi; Kim Bizzarri. **Res. Policy** 33:10 12:2004 pp.1657-1671.

3735   Cómo medir el "impacto" de las políticas de ciencia y tecnología. *[In Spanish];* (How to measure the 'impact' of science and technology policies?) *[Summary].* José Luis Villaveces; Luis Antonio Orozco; Doris Lucía Olaya; Diego Chavarro; Elizabeth Suárez. **R. Iberoamer. Cienc. Tech. Soc.** 2:4 1:2005 pp.125-146.

3736   A comparative study of development strategies and government-industry-university linkages of science and technology parks in Finland and South Korea. Sang-chul Park; Seong-keun Lee; Kwan-ryul Lee. **Kor. Obs.** 35:4 Winter:2004 pp.709-735.

3737   Condicionantes políticos y problemas metodológicos en la evaluación de impacto social de las políticas de I+D e innovación. *[In Spanish];* (Political constraints and methodological problems for the evaluation of R&D and innovation policies' social impact.) Diego Moñux Chércoles; Belén Miranda Escolar; Guillermo Aleixandre Mendizábal; Francisco Javier Gómez González. **R. Iberoamer. Cienc. Tech. Soc.** 2:4 1:2005 pp.173-200.

3738   Controlling mobile phone health risks in the UK: a fragile discourse of compliance. Jack Stilgoe. **Sci. Publ. Policy** 32:1 2:2005 pp.55-64.

3739   Distributional effects of science and technology-based economic development strategies at state level in the United States. Susan E. Cozzens; Kamau Bobb; Kendall Deas; Sonia Gatchair; Albert George; Gonzalo Ordonez. **Sci. Publ. Policy** 32:1 2:2005 pp.29-38.

3740   A dynamic analytic approach to national innovation systems: the IC industry in Taiwan. Ting-Lin Lee; Nick von Tunzelmann. **Res. Policy** 34:4 5:2005 pp.425-440.

3741   The evolutionary responses of Korean government research institutes in a changing national innovation system; *[Summary in French]; [Summary in Spanish].* Deok Soon Yim; Wang Dong Kim. **Sci. Techno. Soc.** 10:1 1-6:2005 pp.31-55.

3742 Evolving a national system of biotechnology innovation: some evidence from Singapore. Sachin Chaturvedi. **Sci. Techno. Soc.** 10:1 1-6:2005 pp.105-127.

3743 Explaining the science and technology policies of regional governments. Luis Sanz-Menéndez; Laura Cruz-Castro; Stephen Roper [Ed.]. **Reg. S.** 39:7 10:2005 pp.939-954.

3744 Fostering entrepreneurship: changing role of government and higher education governance in Hong Kong. Ka Ho Mok. **Res. Policy** 34:4 5:2005 pp.537-554.

3745 Government mediation and transformation of Thailand's national innovation system; *[Summary in French]*; *[Summary in Spanish]*. Patarapong Intarakumnerd. **Sci. Techno. Soc.** 10:1 1-6:2005 pp.87-104.

3746 Higher education-industry research partnerships and innovation in South Africa. Jo Lorentzen; Michael Kahn; William Blankley; Glenda Kruss; David Cooper; Mlungisi Gabriel Cele; Moeketsi Letseka; Gilton Klerck; Andrew Paterson; Shane Godfrey. **Ind. High. Edu.** 19:2 4:2005 pp.109-197. *Collection of 9 articles.*

3747 History, technology, and the capitalist state: the comparative political economy of biotechnology and genomics. Rodney Loeppky. **R. Int. Pol. Econ.** 12:2 5:2005 pp.264-286.

3748 Human rights in the digital age. Mathias Klang [Ed.]; Andrew Murray [Ed.]. London: GlassHouse, 2005. 243p. *ISBN: 1904385311.*

3749 Impacto social de la ciencia y la tecnología en Cuba: una experiencia de medición a nivel macro. *[In Spanish]*; (Social impact of science and technology in Cuba: an experience of measurement at the macro level.) *[Summary]*. Armando Rodríguez Batista. **R. Iberoamer. Cienc. Tech. Soc.** 2:4 1:2005 pp.147-171.

3750 Implementing R&D policies: an analysis of Spain's pharmaceutical research program. Klaus Desmet; Praveen Kujal; Félix Lobo. **Res. Policy** 33:10 12:2004 pp.1493-1507.

3751 The importance of co-ordination in national technology policy: evidence from the Galileo project. Vasilis Zervos; Donald S. Siegel. **Prometheus** 23:2 6:2005 pp.167-180.

3752 Innovation policies for biotechnology in Europe. Paraskevas Caracostas [Intro.]; Marie-Christine Brichard [Intro.]; Thomas Reiss; Sibylle Hinze; Iciar Dominguez Lacasa; Jane Calvert; Jacqueline Senker; Christien Enzing; Annelieke van der Giessen; Sander Kern; Vincent Mangematin. **Sci. Publ. Policy** 31:5 10:2004 pp.342-406. *Collection of 6 articles.*

3753 Institutions and intellectual property: the influence of institutional forces on university patenting. Yixin Dai; David Popp; Stuart Bretschneider. **J. Policy Anal. Manag.** 24:3 Summer:2005 pp.579-598.

3754 Klónozás és génmódosítás: szép új világ? *[In Hungarian]*; (Cloning and transgenesis: a brave new world?) László Solti. **Mag. Tud.** 49:2 2004 pp.198-231.

3755 A magyarországi innováció helyzete az új Európában. *[In Hungarian]*; (Innovation in Hungary in the new Europe.) *[Summary]*. Tamás Balogh. **Euro. Tükör** 9:2 2004 pp.45-60.

3756 National innovation systems in the Asian context. Deok Soon Yim [Intro.]; Pradosh Nath [Intro.]; Wang Yuan; Deok Soon Yim; Wang Dong Kim; Avvari V. Mohan; Isshammudn Ismail; Patarapong Intarakumnerd; Sachin Chaturvedi; Richard T. Mahoney. **Sci. Techno. Soc.** 10:1 1-6:2005 pp.11-139. *Collection of 7 articles.*

3757 Path dependence and value-driven issues: the comparative politics of stem cell research. Thomas Banchoff. **World Pol.** 57:2 1:2005 pp.200-230.

3758 A policy network explanation of biotechnology policy differences between the United States and Canada. Éric Montpetit. **J. Publ. Policy** 25:3 9-12:2005 pp.339-366.

3759 Une politique pour la recherche ? *[In French]*; [A policy for research?] Banquet. **Banquet** 19-20 1:2004 pp.5-260.

3760 Public subsidies to business R&D: do they stimulate private expenditures? María Callejón; José García-Quevedo. **Env. Plan. C.** 23:2 4:2005 pp.279-293.

3761 Public-private partnership in the development of the hepatitis B vaccine in Korea: implications for developing countries; *[Summary in French]*; *[Summary in Spanish]*. Richard T. Mahoney. **Sci. Techno. Soc.** 10:1 1-6:2005 pp.129-140.

3762 La recherche en France aujoud'hui. *[In French]*; [Research in France today]. Débat. **Débat** 134 3-4:2005 pp.76-104.

3763   La recherche, l'heure des choix. *[In French]*; [Research, time to choose]. Dominique Pestre; Jean-Pierre Alix; Marie de Lattre Gasquet; Pierre Martinot-Lagarde; Christophe Laux; Florence Deprest; Jacques Lesourne. **Projet** 285 3:2005 pp.50-90. *Collection of 8 articles.*

3764   S&T institutions in Latin America and the Caribbean: an overview. Léa Velho. **Sci. Publ. Policy** 32:2 4:2005 pp.95-108.

3765   Science for climate change policy-making: applying theory to practice to enhance effectiveness. Anne Arquit Niederberger. **Sci. Publ. Policy** 32:1 2:2005 pp.2-16.

3766   Support institutions and R&D activities in an ICT cluster: the multimedia development corporation in Malaysia's multimedia super corridor cluster; *[Summary in French]*; *[Summary in Spanish]*. Avvari V. Mohan; Isshammudn Ismail. **Sci. Techno. Soc.** 10:1 1-6:2005 pp.57-85.

3767   Tensions of Europe: the role of technology in the making of Europe. Thomas J. Misa; Johan Schot; Erik van der Vleuten; Arne Kaijser; Helmuth Trischler; Hans Weinberger; David Arnold; Ruth Oldenziel; Adri Albert de la Bruhèze; Onno de Wit. **Hist. Techno.** 21:1 3:2005 pp.1-139. *Collection of 5 articles.*

3768   Towards a knowledge-based economy: does the Cyprus R&D capability meet the challenge? Bernard Musyck; Athanasios Hadjimanolis. **Sci. Publ. Policy** 32:1 2:2005 pp.65-77.

3769   Transformations des politiques de recherche en Europe: les cas de la Suisse, de l'Allemagne et de la France. *[In French]*; (Transformations in European research policies: Switzerland, Germany, and France.) Martin Benninghoff; Raphaël Ramuz; Jean-Philippe Leresche. **R. Fran. Admin. Publ.** 112 2004 pp.777-789.

3770   Who participates in R&D subsidy programs? The case of Spanish manufacturing firms. J. Vicente Blanes; Isabel Busom. **Res. Policy** 33:10 12:2004 pp.1459-1476.

3771   Will small be beautiful? Making policies for our nanotech future. W. Patrick McCray. **Hist. Techno.** 21:2 6:2005 pp.177-203.

E.8:   **Environmental policy**
         Politique environnementale

3772   Assessing evidence of environmental inequities: a meta-analysis. Evan J. Ringquist. **J. Policy Anal. Manag.** 24:2 Spring:2005 pp.223-247.

3773   The Canada-US environmental relationship: calm waters but slow sailing. Alan M. Schwartz. **Int. J.** LX:2 Spring:2005 pp.437-448.

3774   Capitalism and ecological sustainability: the shaping of environmental policies. Andriana Vlachou. **R. Int. Pol. Econ.** 11:5 12:2004 pp.926-952.

3775   China's new EIA law — is it just a toothless tiger. Sarah Hayes. **Asia Pac. J. Env. Law** 8:1-2 2004 pp.177-192.

3776   Confronting environmental change in East and Southeast Asia: eco-politics, foreign policy and sustainable development. Paul G. Harris [Ed.]. London, Sterling VA: Earthscan, 2005. xviii, 269p. *ISBN: 9280811134, 1853839728, 185383971X. Includes bibliographical references (p. [241]-260) and index.*

3777   Constitutional environmental rights. Tim Hayward. Oxford, New York: Oxford University Press, 2005. xii, 236p. *ISBN: 0199278679, 0199278687. Includes bibliographical references (p. [217]-228) and index.*

3778   Corruption, political competition and environmental policy. John K. Wilson; Richard Damania. **J. Env. Econ. Manag.** 49:3 5:2005 pp.516-535.

3779   Deliberation in the wilderness: displacing symbolic politics. Simon Niemeyer. **Env. Pol.** 13:2 Summer:2004 pp.347-372.

3780   Development of the Finnish agri-environmental policy as a learning process. L. Kröger. **Euro. Env.** 15:1 1-2:2005 pp.13-26.

3781   Eco-politics and ideology –relocating green themes in modern ideological thinking. Padam Nepal. **Indian J. Pol. Sci.** LXV:4 10-12:2004 pp.603-619.

3782   EIA as regulation: does it work? Per Christensen; Lone Kørnøv; Eskild Holm Nielsen. **J. Env. Plan. Manag.** 48:3 5:2005 pp.393-412.

3783   Environment and sustainable regional development. K. Clement; S. Kidd; F. Bertrand; C. Larrue; C. MacLeod. **Euro. Env.** 15:5 9-10:2005 p. *Collection of 5 articles.*

3784   Environmental compliance in Italy and Greece: the role of the non-state actors. Charalampos Koutalakis. **Env. Pol.** 13:4 Winter:2004 pp.754-774.

3785   Environmental consciousness: the roots of a new political agenda. Stephen Hussey [Ed.]; Paul Richard Thompson [Ed.]. New Brunswick NJ: Transaction Publishers, 2004. viii, 226p. *ISBN: 0765808145. Includes bibliographical references and index. (Series: Memory and narrative).*

3786   Environmental justice in the UK. Helen Chalmers; John Colvin; Gordon Walker; Gordon Mitchell; John Fairburn; Graham Smith; Jane Fielding; Kate Burningham; Judith Petts; Matt Watson; Harriet Bulkeley; Susan Buckingham; Dory Reeves; Anna Batchelor; Simon Dietz; Giles Atkinson. **Loc. Env.** 10:4 8:2005 pp.333-459. *Collection of 7 articles.*

3787   Environmental performance reviews: Chile. OECD. Paris: Organisation for Economic Co-operation and Development, 2005. 218p. *ISBN: 9264009671. (Series: OECD Environmental performance reviews).*

3788   Environmental performance reviews: Spain. OECD. Paris: Organisation for Economic Co-operation and Development, 2004. 211p. *ISBN: 9264108629. (Series: OECD environmental performance reviews).*

3789   Federalism and environmental policy: trust and the politics of implementation. Denise Scheberle. Washington DC: Georgetown University Press, 2004. xix, 219p. *ISBN: 1589011007. Includes bibliographical references and index. (Series: American governance and public policy).*

3790   Global environmental issues: responses from Japan. Lydia N. Yu-Jose. **Japanese J. Pol. Sci.** 5:1 5:2004 pp.23-50.

3791   La gouvernance environnementale au miroir des politiques : les cas des aires marines protégées ouest-africaines. *[In French]*; (Environmental governance as reflected in public policy: the case of West African marine protected areas.) *[Summary].* Tarik Dahou; Jean-Yves Weigel. **Afr. Contemp.** 213 Winter:2005 pp.217-232.

3792   How Cuba is going ecological. Richard Levins. **Cap. Nat. Social.** 16:3 9:2005 pp.7-25.

3793   The impact of environmental regulation on competitiveness in the German manufacturing industry: a comparison with other countries of the European Union. Ursula Triebswetter. Frankfurt am Main, New York: Peter Lang, 2004. 433p. *ISBN: 0820473537. Includes bibliographical references. (Series:* European university studies. Series V, Economics and management – Europaische Hochschulschriften. Reihe V, Volks – und Betriebswirtschaft - 3090).

3794   Integrating environmental policies into local practices: the politics of agri-environmental and energy policies in rural Finland. Maria Åkerman; Minna Kaljonen; Taru Peltola. **Loc. Env.** 10:6 12:2005 pp.595-611.

3795   Measuring progress: program evaluation of environmental policies. Lori Snyder Bennear; Cary Coglianese. **Environment** 47:2 3:2005 pp.22-39.

3796   Nature's experts: science, politics, and the environment. Stephen Bocking. New Brunswick NJ: Rutgers University Press, 2004. x, 298p. *ISBN: 081353397X, 0813533988. Includes bibliographical references (p. 265-287) and index.*

3797   New approaches on energy and the environment: policy advice for the president. Richard D. Morgenstern [Ed.]; Paul R. Portney [Ed.]. Washington DC: Resources for the Future, 2004. xiv, 154p. *ISBN: 1933115009, 1933115017. Includes bibliographical references and index.*

3798   Der Non-Violation Complaint im System der WTO: Neue Perspektiven im Konflikt um Handel und Umwelt. *[In German]*; [The non-violation complaint in the WTO system: new perspectives in the conflict over trade and environment] *[Summary].* Markus Böckenförde. **A. Völk.** 43:1 3:2005 pp.43-89.

3799   Of europeanization and domestication: the implementation of the environmental information directive in Ireland, Great Britain and Germany. Sonja Bugdahn. **J. Euro. Publ. Policy** 12:1 2005 pp.177-199.

3800   Petroleum, fiscal federalism and environmental justice in Nigeria. Chris O. Ikporukpo. **Space & Polity** 8:3 12:2004 pp.321-354.

3801   Planning environmental sanitation programmes in emergencies. Peter A. Harvey; Robert A. Reed. **Disasters** 29:2 6:2005 pp.129-151.

3802   Las politicas de la tierra. *[In Spanish]*; [Earth policies] *[Summary]*. Jose Felix Tezanos. **Sistema** 188 9:2005 pp.3-13.

3803   Protection of human rights and the environment in Russia. Mikhail M. Brinchuk. **Acta Jur. Hun.** 45:3-4 2004 pp.261-279.

3804   Public provision of environmental goods: neutrality or sustainability? A reply to David Miller. Michael Hannis. **Env. Pol.** 14:5 11:2005 pp.577-595.

3805   'Recruitment', 'composition', and 'mandate' issues in deliberative processes: should we focus on arguments rather than individuals? Ben B. Davies; Kirsty Blackstock; Felix Rauschmayer. **Env. Plan. C.** 23:4 8:2005 pp.599-615.

3806   'Respect for nature' in the Earth Charter: the value of species and the value of individuals. Clare Palmer. **Ethics Place Env.** 7:1-2 3-6:2004 pp.97-107.

3807   Responsibility and environmental governance. Luigi Pellizzoni. **Env. Pol.** 13:3 Autumn:2004 pp.541-565.

3808   (Responsibility on environmental damages.) *[Summary]*; *[Text in Arabic]*. M. Khalil Al-Bahr. **Dirasat Sha. Law** 31:2 11:2004 pp.301-321.

3809   Riflessioni metodologiche sull'integrazione tra i processi di azione locale per la sostenibilità e la certificazione ambientale alla scala territoriale. *[In Italian]*; [Methodological reflexions on the integration of local processes for sustainability and environmental certification] *[Summary]*. A. Crimella; S. Pareglio. **Riv. Int. Sci. Soc.** CXII:2 4-6:2004 pp.137-154.

3810   Science and politics in the international environment. Neil E. Harrison [Ed.]; Gary C. Bryner [Ed.]. Lanham MD: Rowman & Littlefield, 2004. xiv, 379p. *ISBN: 0742520196, 074252020X. Includes bibliographical references and index.*

3811   Scientisation v. civic expertise in environmental governance: eco-feminist, eco-modern and post-modern response. Karin Bäckstrand. **Env. Pol.** 13:4 Winter:2004 pp.695-714.

3812   Social and environmental justice in South African cities: including 'invisible stakeholders' in environmental assessment procedures. Dianne Scott; Catherine Oelofse. **J. Env. Plan. Manag.** 48:3 5:2005 pp.445-467.

3813   Sustainability through good advice? Assessing the governance of Swedish forest biodiversity. Erik Hysing; Jan Olsson. **Env. Pol.** 14:4 7:2005 pp.510-526.

3814   The UK approach to delivering sustainable development in government: a case study in joined-up working. Andrea Ross. **J. Env. Law.** 17:1 2005 pp.27-49.

3815   Verantwortung und das Problem der Kuppelproduktion: Reflexionen über die Grundlagen der Umweltpolitik. *[In German]*; (Responsibility and the problem of joint production: reflections on the fundamentals of environmental politics.) Thomas Petersen; Malte Faber. **Z. Pol.wissen.** 15:1 2005 pp.35-58.

3816   Waiting for Godot: sustainable development, international trade and governance in environmental policies. Roberto P. Guimarães. **Cont. Pol.** 10:3-4 9-12:2004 pp.203-226.

3817   Die Zukunftsanleihe — Ein Gesamtkonzept für eine nachhaltige Umweltpolitik. *[In German]*; [A concept for sustainable environmental policy]. Maximilian Gege. **Politische S.** 56:400 3-4:2005 pp.53-68.

Climate change
Changement climatique

3818   Changement climatique : agir avant la catastrophe annoncée. *[In French]*; [Climate change: acting before it's too late]. Mouvements. **Mouvements** 36 11-12:2004 pp.90-109.

3819   Climate policy, ecological modernization and the UK emission trading scheme. F. von Malmborg; P.A. Strachan. **Euro. Env.** 15:3 5-6:2005 pp.143-160.

3820   Environmental change and its implications for population migration. Jon Darrel Unruh [Ed.]; Maarten S. Krol [Ed.]; Nurit Kliot [Ed.]. Dordrecht, London: Kluwer Academic Publishers, 2004. xi, 313p. *ISBN: 1402028687. Includes bibliographical references. (Series:* Advances in global change research - 20).

3821   An exploration of the technical feasibility of achieving CO2 emission reductions in excess of 60% within the UK housing stock by the year 2050. D. Johnston; R. Lowe; M. Bell. **Energy Policy** 33:13 9:2005 pp.1643-1659.

3822   Fair weather friend? Ethics and Australia's approach to global climate change. Matt McDonald. **Aust. J. Pol. Hist.** 51:2 6:2005 pp.216-234.

3823   Icelandic nationalism and the Kyoto protocol: an analysis of the discourse on global environmental change in Iceland. Ingólfur Ásgeir Jóhannesson. **Env. Pol.** 14:4 7:2005 pp.495-509.

3824   Instrument design and choice in environmental regulation. A.Denny Ellerman; Richard Newell; William Pizer; Jiangfeng Zhang; Matti Liski; Juan-Pablo Montero; Till Requate; Rolf Golombek; Michael Hoel; Larry Karp. **Env. Resour. Econ.** 31:2 6:2005 pp.121-251. *Collection of 6 articles.*

3825   Klimawandel, internationale Umweltpolitik und indigene Völker. *[In German]*; [Climate change, international environmental policy and indigenous populations] *[Summary]*. Lioba Rossbach de Olmos. **Anthropos [St. Augustin]** 99:2 2004 pp.551-564.

3826   La lutte contre le changement climatique. *[In French]*; [The fight against climate change]. Pierre-Noël Giraud. **Etudes** 401:4 10:2004 pp.321-332.

3827   Nachhaltige Umwelt – und Klimaschutzpolitik. *[In German]*; [Sustainable environmental and climate protection policy]. Lutz Wicke. **Politische S.** 56:400 3-4:2005 pp.28-44.

3828   Perspektiven der nationalen Politik zum Klimaschutz – Herausforderungen und Langfristszenarien für Deutschland. *[In German]*; [Perspectives of national environmental policy]. Hans-Joachim Ziesing; Jochen Diekmann. **Vier. Wirt.forsch.** 74:2 2005 pp.270-285.

3829   Regionale Klimaschutzprogramme – Zur integrierten Analyse von Kosten des Klimawandels und des Klimaschutzes auf regionaler Ebene. *[In German]*; [Regional climate protection programmes]. Ulrich Fahl; Henrike Koschel; Andreas Löschel; Bastian Rühle; Helmut Wolf. **Vier. Wirt.forsch.** 74:2 2005 pp.286-309.

3830   Standing and global warming: is injury to all injury to none? Bradford C. Mank. **Env. Law** 35:1 Winter:2005 pp.1-84.

Natural resources
Ressources naturelles

3831   Administrative rulemaking and public lands conflict: the forest service's roadless rule. Martin Nie. **Natur. Res. J.** 44:3 Summer:2004 pp.687-742.

3832   African environment and development: rhetoric, programs, realities. B. Ikubolajeh Logan [Ed.]; William G. Moseley [Ed.]. Aldershot, Burlington VT: Ashgate, 2004. xii, 244p. *ISBN: 0754639045. Includes bibliographical references and index. (Series:* King's SOAS studies in development geography).

3833   The Botswana defence force and the war against poachers in Southern Africa. Dan Henk. **Sm. Wars Insurg.** 16:2 6:2005 pp.170-191.

3834   Chine : une apocalypse hydraulique? *[In French]*; [China: an hydrolic apocalyspe?] *[Summary]*; *[Summary in Spanish]*. Pierre Bailet. **Polit. Int.** 107 Spring:2005 pp.361-377.

3835   Closing the groundwater protection implementation gap. R.C. de Loë; R.D. Kreutzwiser. **Geoforum** 36:2 3:2005 pp.241-256.

3836   Comments on Canada's national diamond strategy. Roger Taplin; Thomas Isaac. **J. Ener. Nat. Resou. Law** 22:4 11:2004 pp.429-449.

3837 Conceptualizing desertification in Southern Europe: stakeholder interpretations and multiple policy agendas. M. Juntti; Geoff A. Wilson. **Euro. Env.** 15:4 7-8:2005 pp.228-249.

3838 The cost of natura 2000 in Spain. R. Barberán; P. Egea; L. Pérez Pérez. **Euro. Env.** 15:3 5-6:2005 pp.161-174.

3839 Current arrangements for the control of deforestation and the conservation of terrestrial biological diversity in Thailand. Tom Holden. **Asia Pac. J. Env. Law** 8:1-2 2004 pp.69-102.

3840 Décentralisation constitutionnelle et environnement. *[In French]*; [Constitutional decentralization and environment]. Marie-Laure Lambert-Habib. **R. Jurid. Envir.** 1 3:2004 pp.17-32.

3841 The global/local politics of the Great Bear Rainforest. Karena Shaw. **Env. Pol.** 13:2 Summer:2004 pp.373-392.

3842 The healthy forests initiative: unhealthy policy choices in forest and fire management. Jesse B. Davis. **Env. Law** 34:4 Fall:2004 pp.1209-1245.

3843 Kazakhstan's economy since independence: does the oil boom offer a second chance for sustainable development? Richard Pomfret. **Euro.-Asia S.** 57:6 9:2005 pp.859-876.

3844 Kestävät ohjauskeinot metsäpolitiikassa : lainsäädäntö ja metsäohjelmat metsien kestävän käytön edistämisessä. *[In Finnish]*; [Sustainable steering instruments in Finnish forest policy: implementing sustainable forest use by legislation and forest programmes] *[Summary]*. Katinka Lybäck; Marjukka Laakso. **Hall. Tut.** 23:4 2004 pp.17-28.

3845 The last enclosure: resisting privatization of wildlife in the Western United States. Paul Robbins; April Luginbuhl. **Cap. Nat. Social.** 16:1 3:2005 pp.45-61.

3846 Learning, frames, and environmental policy integration: the case of Swedish energy policy. Måns Nilsson. **Env. Plan. C.** 23:2 4:2005 pp.207-226.

3847 The political geography of national parks. Lary M. Dilsaver; William Wyckoff. **Pac. Hist. R.** 74:2 5:2005 pp.237-266.

3848 A public choice analysis of endangered species listings. R. Patrick Rawls; David N. Laband. **Publ. Choice** 121:3-4 10:2004 pp.263-278.

3849 Recreation wars for our natural resources. Jan G. Laitos; Rachael B. Reiss. **Env. Law** 34:4 Fall:2004 pp.1091-1122.

3850 Regulatory failure in the management of South Korea's national parks. Jungho Suh. **Asia Pac. J. Env. Law** 8:1-2 2004 pp.133-151.

3851 Ride 'em cowboy: a critical look at BLM's proposed new grazing regulations. Joseph M. Feller. **Env. Law** 34:4 Fall:2004 pp.1123-1142.

3852 'Something else to burn': forest squatters, conservationists and the state in modern Tanzania. Thaddeus Sunseri. **J. Mod. Afr. S.** 43:4 12:2005 pp.609-640.

3853 State actors' livelihoods, acts of translation, and forest sector reforms in Northwest Pakistan. Urs Geiser; Bernd Steimann. **Contemp. Sth. Asia** 13:4 12:2004 pp.437-448.

3854 Stealing from the poor? Game theory and the politics of water markets in Chile. Victor Galaz. **Env. Pol.** 13:2 Summer:2004 pp.414-437.

3855 'The supreme court of science' speaks on water rights: the national academy of sciences Columbia river report and its water policy implications. Reed D. Benson. **Env. Law** 35:1 Winter:2005 pp.85-134.

3856 Traveling in opposite directions: roadless area management under the Clinton and Bush administrations. Robert L. Glicksman. **Env. Law** 34:4 Fall:2004 pp.1143-1208.

3857 Unnatural monopoly: the endless wait for gas sector reform in Russia. Rudiger Ahrend; William Tompson. **Euro.-Asia S.** 57:6 9:2005 pp.801-821.

Pollution control
Contrôle de la pollution

3858 The 'domestic politics' bias in analyses of CO_2 taxation in the Nordic countries. Sjur Kasa. **Scand. Pol. S.** 28:1 2005 pp.91-102.

3859   Environmental protection in Taiwan: is it too much too fast? David Lyons. **J. Contemp. Asia** 35:2 2005 pp.183-194.

3860   Environmentalism, democracy, and pollution control. Per G. Fredriksson; Eric Neumayer; Richard Damania; Scott Gates. **J. Env. Econ. Manag.** 49:2 3:2005 pp.343-365.

3861   Equity and information: information regulation, environmental justice, and risks from toxic chemicals. Marc D. Shapiro. **J. Policy Anal. Manag.** 24:2 Spring:2005 pp.373-398.

3862   From a nonpollutant into a pollutant: revising EPA's interpretation of the phrase 'discharge of any pollutant' in the context of NPDES permits. Alison M. Dornsife. **Env. Law** 35:1 Winter:2005 pp.175-208.

3863   Globalising environmental liability: the interplay of national and international law. A.E. Boyle. **J. Env. Law.** 17:1 2005 pp.3-26.

3864   How can domestic households become part of the solution to England's recycling problems? T. SmallBone. **Bus. Strat. Env.** 14:2 3-4:2005 pp.110-122.

3865   Implementing chemicals policy: leaders or laggards? J.P. Richards; G.A. Glegg; S. Cullinane. **Bus. Strat. Env.** 13:6 11-12:2004 pp.388-402.

3866   Incineration politics and the geographies of waste governance: a burning issue for Ireland? Anna R. Davies. **Env. Plan. C.** 23:3 6:2005 pp.375-397.

3867   Low-level radioactive waste management: the U.S. and South Korea. Yearn Hong Choi. **Kor. Obs.** 36:2 Summer:2005 pp.207-227.

3868   OECD environmental performance reviews: France. OECD. Paris: Organisation for Economic Co-operation and Development, 2005. 248p. *ISBN: 9264009124. (Series: OECD environmental performance reviews).*

3869   On the role of cost-benefit analysis in environmental law. Shi-ling Hsu. **Env. Law** 35:1 Winter:2005 pp.135-174.

3870   Partnerships for sustainable mobility: the pilot region of Basel. Stephan F. Lienin; Bernd Kasemir; Roland Stulz; Alexander Wokaun. **Environment** 47:3 4:2005 pp.23-35.

3871   Policy instrument choice and diffuse source pollution. Neil Gunningham; Darren Sinclair. **J. Env. Law.** 17:1 2005 pp.51-81.

3872   The politics of air pollution: urban growth, ecological modernization, and symbolic inclusion. George A. Gonzalez. Albany NY: State University of New York Press, 2005. viii, 144p. *ISBN: 0791463354. Includes bibliographical references (p. 117-139) and index. (Series:* SUNY series in global environmental policy).

3873   The politics of interim radioactive waste storage: the United States. Kenneth A. Rogers; Marvin G. Kingsley. **Env. Pol.** 13:3 Autumn:2004 pp.590-611.

3874   Public participation in environmental impact assessment — implementing the Aarhus convention. Nicola Hartley; Christopher Wood. **Env. Imp. Assess. R.** 25:4 5:2005 pp.319-340.

3875   The regulatory enforcement of pollution control laws: the Australian experience. Carolyn Abbot. **J. Env. Law.** 17:2 2005 pp.161-180.

3876   Strategic environmental assessment can help solve environmental impact assessment failures in developing countries. Habib M. Alshuwaikhat. **Env. Imp. Assess. R.** 25:4 5:2005 pp.307-317.

F:	INTERNATIONAL LIFE
	VIE INTERNATIONALE

F.1:   International law
            Droit international

3877   The 2004 judicial activity of the International Court of Justice. David D. Caron [Ed.]; John R. Crook. **Am. J. Int. Law** 99:2 4:2005 pp.450-459.

3878   Actualité de la pensée de Charles Chaumont et perspectives du droit international. *[In French]*; [News on the thought of Charles Chaumont and international law perpectives]. M. Chemillier-Gendreau. **Belg. R. Int. Law** XXXVII:1 2004 pp.290-308.

3879   Attempts to define 'terrorism' in international law. B. Saul. **Neth. Int. Law R.** LII:1 2005 pp.57-83.

3880   Brandeis's happy incident revisited: U.S. cities as the new laboratories of international law. Shanna Singh. **George Washington Int. Law R.** 37:2 2005 pp.537-557.

3881   Can you put on your red light? Lawrence's sexual citizenship rights in terms of international law. Lisa Limor Rabie. **Columb. J. Tr. Law** 43:2 2005 pp.613-636.

3882   The changing character of sovereignty in international law and international relations. Winston P. Nagan; Craig Hammer. **Columb. J. Tr. Law** 43:1 2004 pp.141-187.

3883   The Chinese universal jurisdiction clause: how far can it go? Zhu Lijiang. **Neth. Int. Law R.** LII:1 2005 pp.85-107.

3884   Closing an International Criminal Tribunal while maintaining international human rights standards and excluding impunity. Larry D. Johnson. **Am. J. Int. Law** 99:1 1:2005 pp.158-174.

3885   Comment juger les crimes d'état ? *[In French]*; [How to judge state crimes?] Philippe Moreau Defarges. **Polit. Int.** 105 Autumn:2004 pp.369-382.

3886   The common law choice of law rules for resulting and constructive trusts. Adeline Chong. **Int. Comp. Law Q.** 54:4 10:2005 pp.855-883.

3887   Compétence universelle. *[In French]*; [Universal competence]. Philippe Coppens; Olivier Corten; Eric David; Philippe Gautier; Pierre d'Argent; Olivier De Schutter; Henri D. Bosly; Michaël Singleton; Philippe Meire. **Ann. Droit Louvain** 64:1-2 2004 pp.15-348. *Collection of 10 articles.*

3888   The conduct of hostilities under the law of international armed conflict. Yoram Dinstein. Cambridge, New York: Cambridge University Press, 2004. xx, 275p. *ISBN: 0521834368, 0521542278. Includes bibliographical references and index.*

3889   Construction site for more justice: the International Criminal Court after two years. Hans-Peter Kaul. **Am. J. Int. Law** 99:2 4:2005 pp.370-384.

3890   Contemporary practice of the United States relating to international law. John R. Crook [Ed.]. **Am. J. Int. Law** 99:1 1:2005 pp.253-273.

3891   The customary international law game. George Norman; Joel P. Trachtman. **Am. J. Int. Law** 99:3 7:2005 pp.541-580.

3892   Declarations accepting the compulsory jurisdiction of the International Court of Justice. Vanda Lamm. **Acta Jur. Hun.** 45:1-2 2004 pp.25-48.

3893   Derecho internacional y desarrollo sustentable. *[In Spanish]*; [International law and sustainable development]. Alan Boyle. **Est. Inter.** XXXVII:147 10-12:2004 pp.5-29.

3894   Direct v. indirect obligations of corporations under international law. Carlos M. Vázquez. **Columb. J. Tr. Law** 43:3 2005 pp.927-959.

3895   The draft Hague judgments convention: some perspectives from arbitration. T.T. Arvind. **Neth. Int. Law R.** LI:3 2004 pp.337-362.

3896   Dred Scott and international law. Mark W. Janis. **Columb. J. Tr. Law** 43:3 2005 pp.763-810.

3897   Die einzelstaatliche Durchsetzung völkerrechtlicher Mindeststandards gegenüber transnationalen Unternehmen. *[In German]*; [The enforcement of international minimum standards with regards to multinational enterprises] *[Summary]*. Anja Seibert-Fohr; Rüdiger Wolfrum. **A. Völk.** 43:2 6:2005 pp.153-186.

3898 The emergence of global administrative law. Benedict Kingsbury; Richard B. Stewart; Jonathan B. Wiener; Nico Krisch; Sabino Cassese; David Dyzenhaus; Janet McLean; James Salzman; Walter Mattli; Tim Büthe; Kalypso Nicolaidis; Gregory Shaffer; Eyal Benvenisti; Martin Shapiro. **Law Contemp. Prob.** 68:3-4 Summer-Autumn:2005 pp.1-356. *Collection of 9 articles.*

3899 Enforcing international law norms against terrorism. Andrea Bianchi [Ed.]; Yasmin Naqvi [Contrib.]. Oxford: Hart Publishing, 2004. 549p. *ISBN: 1841134309. (Series: Studies in international law).*

3900 The evolution of the international law of alienability: the 1997 land law of Mozambique as a case study. Kendall Burr. **Columb. J. Tr. Law** 43:3 2005 pp.961-997.

3901 Les évolutions du secret de la correspondance. *[In French]*; [The evolutions of the secret of correspondence]. Clotilde Morlot-Dehan. **R. Droit Publ.** 2 3-4:2005 pp.357-393.

3902 Executive plans and authorizations to violate international law. Jordan J. Paust. **Columb. J. Tr. Law** 43:3 2005 pp.811-863.

3903 False and reluctant friends? National money laundering regulation, international compliance and non-cooperative countries. Donato Masciandaro. **Euro. J. Law Econ.** 20:1 7:2005 pp.17-30.

3904 From "9-11" to the "Iraq War 2003": international law in an age of complexity. Dominic McGoldrick. Oxford: Hart Publishing, 2004. xv, 380p. *ISBN: 1841134961. Includes index.*

3905 From international law to law and globalization. Paul Schiff Berman. **Columb. J. Tr. Law** 43:2 2005 pp.485-556.

3906 The future of war crimes prosecutions in the former Yugoslavia: accountability or junk justice? Katie Zoglin. **Hum. Rights Q.** 27:1 2:2005 pp.41-77.

3907 Gerichtliche Kontrolle extraterritorialer Hoheitsakte. Zum Guantanamo-Urteil des US Supreme Court. *[In German]*; [On the US Supreme Court's Guantanamo verdict] *[Summary]*. Christian J. Tams. **A. Völk.** 42:4 12:2004 pp.445-466.

3908 Guantanamo, le droit entre parenthèses. *[In French]*; [Guantanamo, law in parentheses]. Patrick Troude-Chastenet. **Etudes** 400:1 2004 pp.11-21.

3909 IGH-Gutachten über "Rechtliche Konsequenzen des Baus einer Mauer in den besetzten palästinensischen Gebieten". *[In German]*; [The ICJ advisory opinion on the 'legal consequences of the construction of a wall in the occupied Palestinian territory'] *[Summary]*. Florian Becker. **A. Völk.** 43:2 6:2005 pp.218-239.

3910 The International Criminal Court's ad hoc jurisdiction revisited. Carsten Stahn; Mohamed M. El Zeidy; Héctor Olásolo. **Am. J. Int. Law** 99:2 4:2005 pp.421-431.

3911 The International Criminal Tribunal for the Former Yugoslavia: an exercise in law, politics, and diplomacy. Rachel Kerr. Oxford: Oxford University Press, 2004. vi, 239p. *ISBN: 0199263051. Includes bibliographical references (p. [220]-236) and index.*

3912 International law and the war on terrorism. William S. Shepard. **Mediterr. Q.** 16:1 Winter:2005 pp.79-93.

3913 International law related to precautionary approaches to national regulation of plant imports. Peter T. Jenkins. **J. World Tr.** 39:5 10:2005 pp.895-906.

3914 International law, U.S. war powers, and the global war on terrorism. Ryan Goodman; Derek Jinks. **Harv. Law R.** 118:8 6:2005 pp.2653-2662.

3915 Is the war on terror just? Alex J. Bellamy. **Int. Rel.** 19:3 9:2005 pp.275-296.

3916 Is there a 'new' law of intervention and occupation? Leslie C. Green. **Isr. Ybk Hum. Rig.** 35 2005 pp.33-69.

3917 Israel's security barrier: an international comparative analysis and legal evaluation. Barry A. Feinstein; Justus Reid Weiner. **George Washington Int. Law R.** 37:2 2005 pp.309-467.

3918 The judicial effects of the 'completion strategies' on the ad hoc International Criminal Tribunals. Daryl A. Mundis. **Am. J. Int. Law** 99:1 1:2005 pp.142-157.

3919 Justice beyond borders: a global political theory. Simon Caney. Oxford: Oxford University Press, 2005. 319p. *ISBN: 019829350X. Includes bibliographical references (p. [282]-308) and index.*

3920   The Lord's Resistance Army case: Uganda's submission of the first state referral to the International Criminal Court. Payam Akhavan. **Am. J. Int. Law** 99:2 4:2005 pp.403-420.

3921   La maxime "qui habet commoda, ferre debet onera et contra" (celui qui jouit des avantages doit supporter aussi les charges et vice versa) en droit international public. *[In French]*; [The maxim "qui habet commoda, ferre debet onera et contra" (who enjoys the advantages must also bear the burden and vice versa) in international public law]. R. Kolb. **Belg. R. Int. Law** XXXVII:1 2004 pp.12-36.

3922   La nature juridique des conventions de coopération transfrontalière entre autorités régionales ou locales relevant d'etats différents. *[In French]*; [The juridical nature of trans-frontier agreements between regional or local authorities from different states]. Philippe Gautier. **Ann. Droit Louvain** 64:3 2004 pp.397-418.

3923   Nemzetközi tárgyilagosság és méltányosság. *[In Hungarian]*; (International objectivity and fairness.) Géza Ankerl. **Valóság** 47:7 2004 pp.1-51.

3924   Orientalism and international law: a matter of contemporary urgency. Richard Falk. **Arab World Geog.** 7:1-2 Spring-Summer:2004 pp.103-116.

3925   People trafficking, human security and development. Pamela Thomas; Anne Gallagher; Burkhard Dammann; Paul Williams; Sharon Bessell; Kathy Richards; Caroline Millar; Toni Makkai; Shane Wright; Rob McCusker; Brian Iselin; Kerry Carrington; Georgina Costello; Hui Zhou; Richard Fairbrother; Felicia Johnston; Margaret Joseph; Murray Proctor; Sallie Yea; Swagata Raha; Iwu Dwisetyani Utomo; Sri Moertiningsih Adioetomo; Ma Khin Mar Mar Kyi; Aida F. Santos; Judith Dixon; Vijay Naidu; Pierre Huetter; Edward Vrkic; Mukole Kongolo. **Dev. B.** 66 12:2004 pp.4-116. *Collection of 25 articles.*

3926   Perspectives on transnationalism, trafficking, and prostitution. Laura Agustín; Gail Kligman; Stephanie Limoncelli; Joyce Outshoorn. **Soc. Pol.** 12:1 Spring:2005 pp.96-155. *Collection of 3 articles.*

3927   Piercing the veil on trafficking in women. D. Singh. **Comp. Int. Law J. Sth. Afr.** XXXVII:3 11:2004 pp.340-363.

3928   The plea of 'necessity' in international legal discourse: humanitarian intervention and counter-terrorism. Ian Johnstone. **Columb. J. Tr. Law** 43:2 2005 pp.337-388.

3929   Prawo międzynarodowe wobec problemu "państwa upadłego". *[In Polish]*; (A 'failed state' in the eyes of international law.) Jerzy Zajadło. **Pań. Prawo** LX:2(708) 2:2005 pp.3-20.

3930   Privatizing the duties of the central authority: should international service of process be up for bid? Emily Fishbein Johnson. **George Washington Int. Law R.** 37:3 2005 pp.769-794.

3931   Rebus revisited: changed circumstances in treaty law. Detlev F. Vagts. **Columb. J. Tr. Law** 43:2 2005 pp.459-484.

3932   Recent developments in international criminal law: trying to stay afloat between Scylla and Charybdis. Olivia Swaak-Goldman. **Int. Comp. Law Q.** 54:3 7:2005 pp.691-704.

3933   Regulatory competition and the location of international arbitration proceedings. Christopher R. Drahozal. **Int. R. Law Econ.** 24:3 9:2004 pp.371-384.

3934   Resolving treaty conflicts. Christopher J. Borgen. **George Washington Int. Law R.** 37:3 2005 pp.573-648.

3935   Retour sur la qualification lege causae en droit international privé. *[In French]*; [Return on the lege causae qualification in private international law] *[Summary]*. Jean-Luc Elhoueiss. **J. Droit Int.** 132:2 4-6:2005 pp.281-313.

3936   Rule, practice, and pragmatism in transnational commercial law. Roy Goode. **Int. Comp. Law Q.** 54:3 7:2005 pp.539-562.

3937   Shelter from the storm: rethinking diplomatic protection of dual nationals in modern international law. Craig Forcese. **George Washington Int. Law R.** 37:2 2005 pp.469-500.

3938   Slouching towards new 'just' wars: international law and the use of force after September 11th. J. Brunnée; S.J. Toope. **Neth. Int. Law R.** LI:3 2004 pp.363-392.

3939   Stateless national groups, international justice and asymmetrical warfare. Anna Moltchanova. **J. Pol. Philos.** 13:2 6:2005 pp.194-215.

3940   Le traitement spécial et préférentiel. Plaidoyer contre les systèmes de préférences généralisées. *[In French]*; [Special and preferential treatment. Pleading against the generalized systems of preferences] *[Summary]*. Corinne Vadcar. **J. Droit Int.** 132:2 4-6:2005 pp.315-339.

3941 Using force lawfully in the twenty-first century. David B. Rivkin, Jr.; Lee A. Casey. **Isr. Ybk Hum. Rig.** 35 2005 pp.15-32.

3942 War crimes law. Gerry J. Simpson [Ed.]. Aldershot: Ashgate, 2004. *ISBN: 0754623203. Two volumes. Includes bibliographical references. (Series:* International library of essays in law and legal theory).

3943 Was heißt eigentlich Völkermord. Überlegungen zu einem problematischen Begriff. *[In German]*; [What's the definition of 'genocide'? Thoughts on a problematic term]. Gerd Hankel. **Mittelweg 36** 14:4 7-9:2005 pp.70-81.

3944 Die Zulässigkeit von Wahrheitskommissionen im Lichte des neuen Internationalen Strafgerichtshofes. *[In German]*; [The validity of truth commissions in light of the International Criminal Court] *[Summary]*. Sandra Bartelt. **A. Völk.** 43:2 6:2005 pp.187-217.

F.1.1:   **International jurisdiction**
               Juridiction internationale

3945 Aggression, international law, and the ICC: an argument for withdrawal of aggression from the Rome Statute. James Nicholas Boeving. **Columb. J. Tr. Law** 43:2 2005 pp.557-611.

3946 Agora: ICJ advisory opinion on construction of a wall in the occupied Palestinian territory. Lori Fisler Damrosch; Bernard H. Oxman; Geoffrey R. Watson; Michla Pomerance; Richard A. Falk; Ruth Wedgwood; Sean D. Murphy; Iain Scobbie; David Kretzmer; Ardi Imseis; Michael J. Dennis. **Am. J. Int. Law** 99:1 1:2005 pp.1-141. *Collection of 10 articles.*

3947 Arab states and the role of Islam in the International Criminal Court. Steven C. Roach. **Pol. S.** 53:1 3:2005 pp.143-161.

3948 Het arrest Sharon van het Hof van Cassatie: bouwstenen voor de verdere rol van universele jurisdictie, internationale immuniteiten en de doorwerking van het internationaal gewoonterecht. *[In Dutch]*; [The judgement of Sharon in cassation: the construction of a role for universal jurisdiction, international immunity and the far-reaching impact of international law]. H. Panken; C. Ryngaert; D. Van Eeck-Houtte. **Belg. R. Int. Law** XXXVII:1 2004 pp.211-254.

3949 The British military in Iraq — the applicability of the espace juridique doctrine under the European convention on human rights. Philip Leach. **Publ. Law** Autumn:2005 pp.448-458.

3950 The continuing debate on a UN convention on state responsibility. James Crawford; Simon Olleson. **Int. Comp. Law Q.** 54:4 10:2005 pp.959-971.

3951 Donor-driven justice and its discontents: the case of Rwanda. Barbara Oomen. **Dev. Change** 36:5 9:2005 pp.887-910.

3952 International society, the International Criminal Court and American foreign policy. Jason Ralph. **R. Int. S.** 31:1 1:2005 pp.27-44.

3953 The Iraqi Special Tribunal for Crimes Against Humanity. Ilias Bantekas. **Int. Comp. Law Q.** 54:1 1:2005 pp.237-253.

3954 Is the International Court of Justice biased? Eric A. Posner; Miguel F.P. de Figueiredo. **J. Legal S.** 34:2 6:2005 pp.599-630.

3955 Judging history: the historical record of the International Criminal Tribunal for the former Yugoslavia. Richard Ashby Wilson. **Hum. Rights Q.** 27:3 8:2005 pp.908-942.

3956 Judicial independence and impartiality in international criminal tribunals. Theodor Meron. **Am. J. Int. Law** 99:2 4:2005 pp.359-369.

3957 Jurisdiction over cross-border wrongs on the internet. Oren Bigos. **Int. Comp. Law Q.** 54:3 7:2005 pp.585-620.

3958   Justice and peace? How the international criminal tribunal affects societal peace in Bosnia. James Meernik. **J. Peace Res.** 42:3 5:2005 pp.271-289.

3959   Justice on the grass: three Rwandan journalists, their trial for war crimes, and a nation's quest for redemption. Dina Temple-Raston. New York: Free Press, 2005. xii, 302p. *ISBN: 0743251105. Includes bibliographical references (p. 283-285) and index.*

3960   The law-in-action of the International Criminal Court. Mahnoush H. Arsanjani; W. Michael Reisman. **Am. J. Int. Law** 99:2 4:2005 pp.385-403.

3961   La mise en place de la Cour pénale internationale. *[In French]*; [The setting up of the International Court of Justice]. Véronique Huet. **R. Rech. Jurid. Droit Prosp.** 29:2 2004 pp.1305-0324.

3962   The offences clause after. Sosa v. Alvarez-Machain. **Harv. Law R.** 118:7 5:2005 pp.2378-2399.

3963   Prestupleniia, podpadaiushchie pod iurisdiktsiiu mezhdunarodnogo ugolovnogo suda i ugolovnoe zakonodatel'stvo stran sodruzhestva nezavisimykh gosudarstv (sravnitel'nyi analiz). *[In Russian]*; (Crimes, coming under jurisdiction of the International Criminal Court and criminal legislation of states of the Commonwealth of Independent States (comparative analysis).) N.A. Safarov. **Gos. Pravo** 7 7:2004 pp.48-59.

3964   Recognition and enforcement of foreign judgments: still a Hobson's choice among competing theories? Christa Roodt. **Comp. Int. Law J. Sth. Afr.** XXXVIII:1 3:2005 pp.15-31.

3965   A reductio ad absurdum of restricted, tribal criminal jurisdiction. Clifton Perry. **Int. J. Appl. Philos.** 18:2 Fall:2004 pp.253-262.

3966   Resolving interpretive conflicts in international human rights law. Kristen Hessler. **J. Pol. Philos.** 13:1 3:2005 pp.29-52.

3967   The right of the accused to self-representation before international criminal tribunals: further developments. Nina H.B. Jørgensen. **Am. J. Int. Law** 99:3 7:2005 pp.663-690.

3968   The Security Council as world legislature. Stefan Talmon. **Am. J. Int. Law** 99:1 1:2005 pp.175-193.

3969   Some notable developments in the practice of the UN secretary-general as depositary of multilateral treaties: reservations and declarations. Palitha T.B. Kohona. **Am. J. Int. Law** 99:2 4:2005 pp.433-449.

3970   The South African litigant and European Union rules of civil procedure. Thalia Kruger. **Comp. Int. Law J. Sth. Afr.** XXXVIII:1 3:2005 pp.75-98.

3971   Stays of proceedings and the Brussels convention. Jonathan Harris. **Int. Comp. Law Q.** 54:4 10:2005 pp.933-950.

3972   Les travaux de la commission du droit international relatifs aux actes unilatéraux des états. *[In French]*; [International Law Commission's works on the states' unilateral acts]. Jean D'Aspremont Lynden. **R. Gén. Droit Int. Publ.** 109:1 2005 pp.163-189.

3973   Uluslararası adalet divanı'nın İsrail'in işgal altındaki filistin topraklarında inşa etmekte olduğu duvar konusundaki kararı. *[In Turkish]*; (Resolution of the International Court of Justice concerning the wall constructed by Israel in the occupied territories.) Erdem Denk. **Uluslararasi İlişkiler** 1:3 Autumn:2004 pp.151-173.

3974   Universal jurisdiction after the creation of the International Criminal Court. Gabriel Bottini. **New York Univ. J. Int. Law Pol.** 36:2-3 Winter-Spring:2004 pp.503-562.

3975   The uses of putativity and negativity in the conflict of laws. Elizabeth B. Crawford. **Int. Comp. Law Q.** 54:4 10:2005 pp.829-853.

3976   Victims' justice: legitimizing the sentencing regime of the International Criminal Court. Steven Glickman. **Columb. J. Tr. Law** 43:1 2004 pp.229-267.

F.1.2:   International sovereignty
          Souveraineté internationale

3977   1993-2003 : dix ans de souveraineté andorrane. *[In French]*; [1993-2003 : ten years of Andorran sovereignty]. José Sanchez. **R. Gén. Droit Int. Publ.** 109:1 2005 pp.123-146.

3978   Autonomous but not sovereign? A review of island sub-nationalism. Godfrey Baldacchino. **Can. R. S. Nation.** XXXI:1-2 2004 pp.77-89.

3979   The case for sovereignty: why the world should welcome American independence. Jeremy A. Rabkin. Washington DC: AEI Press, 2004. xv, 257p. *ISBN: 0844741833. Includes bibliographical references and index.*

3980   Deficienţele cadrului juridic al ONU privind situaţiile de autodeterminare naţională. *[In Romanian]*; [Weaknesses of the UN's position on self-determination] *[Summary]*. Ionuţ Apahideanu. **S. UBB: Pol.** XLIX:1 2004 pp.53-68.

3981   A greater Chinese union. Linda Jakobson. **Washington Q.** 28:3 Summer:2005 pp.27-39.

3982   Inside and outside the EU's 'area of freedom, security and justice': reflexive identity and the unity of legal space. Hans Lindahl. **Arch. Recht. Soz.Philos.** 90:4 2004 pp.478-497.

3983   Iraq: case of 'coercive' democratisation. Shashi Shukla. **India Q.** LXI:1 1-3:2005 pp.142-160.

3984   Legitimacy in international society. Ian Clark. Oxford: Oxford University Press, 2005. viii, 278p. *ISBN: 0199258422. Includes bibliographical references and index.*

3985   Luftverkehr mit nicht anerkannten Staaten: Der Fall Nordzypern. *[In German]*; [Air traffic and non-recognized states: the case of North Cyprus] *[Summary]*. Stefan Talmon. **A. Völk.** 43:1 3:2005 pp.1-42.

3986   L'occupation de l'Iraq. Le Conseil de Sécurité, le droit de la guerre et le droit des peuples à disposer d'eux-mêmes. *[In French]*; [Occupation of Iraq. The Security Council, the law of war and the right to self-determination] *[Summary]*; *[Summary in Spanish]*. Massimo Starita. **R. Gén. Droit Int. Publ.** 108:4 2004 pp.883-916.

3987   Precarious positions: native Hawaiians and US federal recognition. J. Kēhaulani Kauanui. **Contemp. Pac.** 17:1 2005 pp.1-27.

3988   The Romani voice in world politics: the United Nations and non-state actors. Ilona Klimova-Alexander. Aldershot: Ashgate, 2005. xiv, 195p. *ISBN: 0754641732. Includes bibliographical references and index. (Series:* Non-state actors in international law, politics, and governance).

3989   Sovereignty and the global community: the quest for order in the international system. Howard M. Hensel [Ed.]. Aldershot: Ashgate, 2004. xiii, 266p. *ISBN: 0754641996. Includes bibliographical references and index. (Series:* Global interdisciplinary studies).

3990   Sovereignty, international law, and the triumph of Anglo-American cunning. Joseph R. Stromberg. **J. Libertarian S.** 18:4 Fall:2004 pp.29-93.

3991   The sovereignty revolution. Alan MacGregor Cranston; Kim Cranston [Ed.]; Mikhail Sergeevich Gorbachev [Ed.]. Stanford CA: Stanford University Press, 2004. xvii, 102p. *ISBN: 080474761X. Includes bibliographical references (p. [95]-97).*

3992   Uma questão crucial no futuro geopolítico do Golfo pérsico: a sucessão na Casa Real Saudita. *[In Portuguese]*; (The key to the Gulf: the Saudi succession.) *[Summary]*. José Félix Ribeiro. **Relações Int.** 6 6:2005 pp.19-36.

F.1.3:   **International borders**
           Frontières internationales

3993   The Bengal borderland: beyond state and nation in South Asia. Willem van Schendel. London: Anthem Press, 2005. viii, 429p. *ISBN: 1843311445, 1843311453. Includes bibliographical references (p. 400-418) and index. (Series:* Anthem South Asian studies).

3994   Boundary and territorial trends in 2004. John W. Donaldson; Martin Pratt. **Geopolitics** 10:2 2005 pp.398-427.

3995   The invention of the Caribbean in the 20th century. Antonio Gaztambide-Géigel. **Soc. Econ. S.** 53:3 9:2004 pp.127-157.

3996   K uchetu mezhdunarodno-pravovogo opyta v rabote po kodifikatsii morskogo zakonodatel'stva Rossii. *[In Russian]*; (Codification of the Russian legislation of the law of the sea (harmonizing with international law).) A.N. Vylegzhanin; R.A. Kalamkarian. **Gos. Pravo** 3 3:2005 pp.49-61.

3997   Die Notwendigkeit einer Grenze für die Zukunft Europas. *[In German]*; [The necessity of a border for the future of Europe]. Bernd Schilcher. **Politische S.** 56:402 7-8:2005 pp.59-70.

3998   The proliferation security initiative –security v. freedom of navigation? Wolff Heintschel von Heinegg. **Isr. Ybk Hum. Rig.** 35 2005 pp.181-204.

3999   A proposed international legal regime for the era of private commercial utilization of space. John S. Lewis; Christopher F. Lewis. **George Washington Int. Law R.** 37:3 2005 pp.745-768.

4000   Republika Srpska and its boundaries in Bosnian Serb geographical narratives in the post-Dayton period. Denisa Kostovicova. **Space & Polity** 8:3 12:2004 pp.267-287.

4001   Rossiia i Iaponiia: v tupike territorial'nogo spora. *[In Russian]*; [Russia and Japan: stalement over a territorial dispute]. Igor A. Latyshev. Moscow: Algoritm, 2004. 301p. *ISBN: 592650130X. Includes bibliographical references.*

4002   Rossiia: territoriia v prostranstvakh globaliziruiushchegosia mira. *[In Russian]*; (Russia: territory in spaces of globalizing world.) N. Kosolapov. **Mir. Ekon. Mezh. Ot.** 7 7:2005 pp.3-14.

4003   Rules over real estate: trade, territorial conflict, and international borders as institution. Beth A. Simmons. **J. Confl. Resol.** 49:6 12:2005 pp.823-848.

4004   The territorial dispute over the Tiaoyu/Senkaku islands: an update. Steven Wei Su. **Ocean Dev. Int.** 36:1 1-3:2005 pp.45-61.

Seas and waterways
Mers et voies navigables

4005   An analysis of the Aegean disputes under international law. Jon M. Van Dyke. **Ocean Dev. Int.** 36:1 1-3:2005 pp.63-117.

4006   Coastal and port environments: international legal and policy responses to reduce ballast water introductions of potentially invasive species. Jeremy Firestone; James J. Corbett. **Ocean Dev. Int.** 36:3 2005 pp.291-316.

4007   Controlling flags of convenience: one measure to stop overfishing of collapsing fish stocks. Jessica K. Ferrell. **Env. Law** 35:2 Spring:2005 pp.323-390.

4008   Cross-strait interactions on the South China Sea issues: a need for CBMs. Yann-huei Song. **Marine Policy** 29:3 5:2005 pp.265-280.

4009   Declaration and statements with respect to the 1982 UNCLOS: potential legal disputes between the United States and China after U.S. accession to the convention. Yann-huei Song. **Ocean Dev. Int.** 36:3 2005 pp.261-289.

4010   The deep seabed: customary law codified. Ian Bezpalko. **Natur. Res. J.** 44:3 Summer:2004 pp.867-906.

4011   Dividing up the spoils: Australia, East Timor and the Timor Sea. David Mercer. **Space & Polity** 8:3 12:2004 pp.289-308.

4012   The Dugong action plan for the South Pacific: an evaluation based on the need for international and regional conservation of sirenians. Alexander Gillespie. **Ocean Dev. Int.** 36:2 4-6:2005 pp.135-158.

4013   Freier Hafenzugang für Flüchtlingsschiffe? Friedliche Durchfahrt und Nothafenrecht im Kontext von Fluchtbemühungen über See. *[In German]*; [Open port access for refugee ships? Peaceful passage and port of refuge rights in the context of flight attempts over sea] *[Summary]*. Malte Jaguttis. **A. Völk.** 43:1 3:2005 pp.90-128.

4014   Further development of the law of the sea convention: mechanisms for change. Alan Boyle. **Int. Comp. Law Q.** 54:3 7:2005 pp.563-584.

4015   La "guerre" du Kosovo et la liberté de navigation sur le Danube. *[In French]*; [The 'war' in Kosovo and the freedom of circulation on the Danube]. Jens Baldtschun. **R. Droit Int. Sci. Dip. Pol.** 82:2 5-8:2004 pp.135-163.

4016   Implementing integrated oceans management: Australia's south east regional marine plan (SERMP) and Canada's eastern Scotian shelf integrated management (ESSIM) initiative.

Elizabeth Foster; Marcus Haward; Scott Coffen-Smout. **Marine Policy** 29:5 9:2005 pp.391-405.

4017 India, Indian Ocean and regional maritime cooperation. K.R. Singh. **Int. S.** 41:2 4-6:2004 pp.195-218.

4018 International law of the sea/seed: public domain versus private commodity. Carol B. Thompson. **Natur. Res. J.** 44:3 Summer:2004 pp.841-866.

4019 The legal regime of the continental shelf, its economic importance and the vast natural resources of a coastal state. Barry B. Omo Ikirodah. **J. Ener. Nat. Resou. Law** 23:1 2:2005 pp.15-35.

4020 Legal spaces of empire: piracy and the origins of ocean regionalism. Lauren Benton. **Comp. S. Soc. Hist.** 47:4 10:2005 pp.700-724.

4021 Maritime delimitation and fishery cooperation in the Tonkin Gulf. Nguyen Hong Thao. **Ocean Dev. Int.** 36:1 1-3:2005 pp.25-44.

4022 La mer Rouge, enjeu stratégique. *[In French]*; [The Red Sea, strategical stake]. Henri Labrousse. **Défense Nat.** 60:1 1:2004 pp.119-131.

4023 The northwest passage: is Canada's sovereignty floating away? Andrea Charron. **Int. J.** LX:3 Summer:2005 pp.831-848.

4024 Policies of five Caspian coastal states: do concerns about relative gains play any role? Yusin Lee. **Glo. Econ. R.** 33:3 2004 pp.97-111.

4025 The politics of the sea regulating stateless space. John Norton Moore; William L. Schachte, Jr.; Doug Bandow; Katherine Hill [Interviewer]; Zachary Wales [Interviewer]; Gudmundur Eiriksson [Discussant]; Caitlyn L. Antrim; Hurst Groves; J. Ashley Roach; Zou Keyuan; John Donaldson; Alison Williams; John R. Harrald; Alfred M. Duda; Jon Barnett; Meryl J. Williams; Justin P. Leous; Neil B. Parry; Ross B. MacDonald; Francesco Mancini; John G. Dale; Alisa Newman Hood; Daniel Doktori. **J. Int. Aff.** 59:1 Fall-Winter:2005 pp.1-303. *Collection of 19 articles.*

4026 La première décennie de l'autorité internationale des fonds marins. *[In French]*; [The first decade of the International Seabed Authority]. Jean-Pierre Levy. **R. Gén. Droit Int. Publ.** 109:1 2005 pp.101-122.

4027 Prompt release in the United Nations convention on the law of the sea: some reflections on the ITLOS jurisprudence. Yoshifumi Tanaka. **Neth. Int. Law R.** LI:2 2004 pp.237-306.

4028 Rigs-to-reef programs in the Gulf of Mexico. Mark J. Kaiser; Allan G. Pulsipher. **Ocean Dev. Int.** 36:2 4-6:2005 pp.119-134.

4029 The security of merchant shipping. John King. **Marine Policy** 29:3 5:2005 pp.235-245.

4030 The Sino-Vietnamese agreement on maritime boundary delimitation in the Gulf of Tonkin. Zou Keyuan. **Ocean Dev. Int.** 36:1 1-3:2005 pp.13-24.

4031 Towards certainty of seabed jurisdiction beyond 200 nautical miles from territorial sea baseline: Australia's submission to the commission on the limits of the continental shelf. Andrew Serdy. **Ocean Dev. Int.** 36:3 2005 pp.201-217.

4032 The Western European PSSA proposal: a 'politically sensitive sea area'. Julian Roberts; Martin Tsamenyi; Tim Workman; Lindy Johnson. **Marine Policy** 29:5 9:2005 pp.431-440.

F.1.4: **International agreements and conferences**
Accords et conférences internationaux

4033 Le 16ᵉ Sommet de la Ligue des États arabes (Tunis, 22 et 23 mai 2004). *[In French]*; [The 16ᵗʰ Summit of the League of Arab States]. Rafaâ Ben Achour. **R. Gén. Droit Int. Publ.** 108:4 2004 pp.949-962.

4034 The AsiaBarometer: its aim, its scope, its strength. Takashi Inoguchi. **Japanese J. Pol. Sci.** 5:1 5:2004 pp.179-196.

4035 Le cadre international et européen des politiques de lutte contre les changements climatiques. *[In French]*; [International and European framework for environmental policies for tackling climate change]. Marc Pallemaerts. **Cour. Hebdo.** 1858-1859 2004 pp.5-60.

4036   La convention-cadre de l'OMS pour la lutte antitabac. *[In French]*; [Framework Convention WHO on Tobacco Control] *[Summary]*. Gian Luca Burci. **J. Droit Int.** 132:1 1-3:2005 pp.77-100.

4037   Energy and the World Summit on sustainable development: what next? Randall Spalding-Fecher; Harald Winkler; Stanford Mwakasonda. **Energy Policy** 33:1 1:2005 pp.99-112.

4038   The European Union and the World Summit on sustainable development: normative power Europe in action? Simon Lightfoot; Jon Burchell. **J. Com. Mkt. S.** 43:1 3:2005 pp.75-95.

4039   EU-USA trade relations in the Doha development round: market access versus a post-modern trade policy agenda. Andreas Falke. **Euro. For. Aff. R.** 10:3 Autumn:2005 pp.339-358.

4040   Form and substance in international agreements. Kal Raustiala. **Am. J. Int. Law** 99:3 7:2005 pp.581-614.

4041   From intergovernmental negotiations to (sub)national change: a transnational perspective on the impact of CEDAW. Susanne Zwingel. **Int. Femin. J. Pol.** 7:3 2005 pp.400-424.

4042   Implementing ILO child labour convention 182: lessons from the gold mining sector in Burkina Faso. Leslie Groves. **Dev. Pract.** 15:1 2:2005 pp.49-59.

4043   Innovation in international negotiation: content and style. Jan Ulijn; Dean Tjosvold; Andreas Lincke; Finn Wynstra; Gaylen D. Paulson; Charles E. Naquin; Jeanne Duvallet; Alexis Garapin; Daniel Llerena; Stephane Robin; Alice Le Flanchec; Alfred S.H. Wong; Roger J. Volkema; Denise Fleck; Agnes Hofmeister-Toth. **Int. Negot.** 9:2 2004 pp.195-339. *Collection of 7 articles.*

4044   International regimes and Norway's environmental policy: crossfire and coherence. Jon Birger Skjrseth [Ed.]. Aldershot, Burlington VT: Ashgate, 2004. xiv, 240p. *ISBN: 0754642267. Includes bibliographical references and index.* (Series: Ashgate studies in environmental policy and practice).

4045   IUCN as catalyst for a law of the biosphere: acting globally and locally. Nicholas A. Robinson. **Env. Law** 35:2 Spring:2005 pp.249-310.

4046   Japan and the development of Africa: a preliminary evaluation of the Tokyo International Conference on African Development. Kweku Ampiah. **Afr. Affairs** 104:414 1:2005 pp.97-116.

4047   Japan's conciliation with the United States in climate change negotiations. Isao Miyaoka. **Int. Rel. Asia Pacific** 4:1 2004 pp.73-96.

4048   Le mécanisme pour un développement propre : une nouvelle voie de coopération et de transferts nord/sud ? *[In French]*; [Sustainable development: cooperation between the North and the South]. Marianne Moliner-Dubost. **R. Gén. Droit Int. Publ.** 108:4 2004 pp.963-986.

4049   Negotiating cultural space in the global economy: the United States, UNESCO, and the convention on cultural diversity. Stephen Azzi. **Int. J.** LX:3 Summer:2005 pp.765-784.

4050   The new accountability: environmental responsibility across borders. Michael Mason. London: Earthscan, 2005. xvi, 205p. *ISBN: 1844070670, 1844070662. Includes bibliographical references and index.*

4051   North-South climate change negotiations: a sequential game with asymmetric information. A. Caparrós; J.C. Péreau; T. Tazdaït. **Publ. Choice** 121:3-4 10:2004 pp.455-480.

4052   The prospects for a transatlantic climate policy. Dennis Tänzler; Alexander Carius. **J. Transatlan. S.** 2:2 Autumn:2004 pp.209-226.

4053   Ships passing in the night: the current state of the human rights and development debate seen through the lens of the Millennium Development Goals. Philip Alston. **Hum. Rights Q.** 27:3 8:2005 pp.755-829.

4054   The UN decade on indigenous peoples. Jens Dahl. **IWGIA New.** 3 9:2004 pp.8-19.

4055   The United States' imposition of religious freedom: the international religious freedom act and India. Laurie Cozad. **India R.** 4:1 1:2005 pp.59-83.

F.1.5: Refugees and international human rights
Réfugiés et droits de l'homme

4056 Anatomy of an ambush: security risks facing international humanitarian assistance. Frederick M. Burkle, Jr. **Disasters** 29:1 3:2005 pp.26-37.

4057 Anti-democratic associations: content and consequences in Article 11 adjudication. Stefan Sottiaux. **Neth. Q. Hum. Rights** 22:4 12:2004 pp.585-599.

4058 Asymmetrical warfare from the perspective of humanitarian law and humanitarian action. Toni Pfanner. **Int. R. Red Cross** 87:857 3:2005 pp.149-174.

4059 Casting light on the legal black hole: international law and detentions abroad in the 'war on terror'. Silvia Borelli. **Int. R. Red Cross** 87:857 3:2005 pp.39-68.

4060 Las cláusulas de seguridad nacional en el sistema interamericano de protección de los derechos humanos. *[In Spanish]*; [National security clauses in the Inter-American System of Human Rights]. Vanessa Peidro. **Est. Inter.** XXXVII:147 10-12:2004 pp.97-115.

4061 Conseil constitutionnel, Cour européenne des Droits de l'Homme et protection des droits et libertés : sur la prétendue rivalité de systèmes complémentaires. *[In French]*; [Constitutional council, European Court of Human Rights and the protection of rights and liberties: on the so-called rivalry of complementary systems]. Elodie Saillant. **R. Droit Publ.** 6 10-12:2004 pp.1497-1546.

4062 Customary international humanitarian law. Jean-Marie Henckaerts [Ed.]; Louise Doswald-Beck [Ed.]. Cambridge, New York: Cambridge University Press, 2005. *ISBN: 0521539250, 052180888X.*

4063 Dangerous sanctuaries: refugee camps, civil war, and the dilemmas of humanitarian aid. Sarah Kenyon Lischer. Ithaca NY: Cornell University Press, 2005. xii, 204p. *ISBN: 0801442850. Includes bibliographical references and index. (Series:* Cornell studies in security affairs).

4064 The dark side of human rights. Onora O'Neill. **Int. Aff. [London]** 81:2 3:2005 pp.427-440.

4065 Le désastre du Darfour. *[In French]*; [The Darfur disaster]. Robert Oakley Collins. **Géopol. Afr.** 15-16 Summer-Fall:2004 pp.51-73.

4066 Dignità umana e integrità genetica nella Carta dei Diritti Fondamentali dell'Unione Europea. *[In Italian]*; [Human dignity and genetic integrity within the European Union Charter of Fundamental Rights]. Raffaele Bifulco. **Rass. Parl.** XLVII:1 1-3:2005 pp.63-116.

4067 La diplomatie humanitaire du Comité International de la Croix-Rouge. *[In French]*; (The ICRC's humanitarian diplomacy.) Marion Harroff-Tavel. **Relations Int.** 121 1-3:2005 pp.73-90.

4068 Diskriminierung in Bosnien und Herzegowina. *[In German]*; [Discrimination in Bosnia and Herzegovina] *[Summary]*. M. Pöschl. **Z. Öffent. Recht** 60:2 2005 pp.217-236.

4069 Distinguishing means and ends: the counterintuitive effects of UNHCR's community development approach in Nepal. Robert Muggah. **J. Refug. S.** 18:2 6:2005 pp.151-164.

4070 Le droit de la guerre humanitaire. *[In French]*; [Humanitarian law in war]. **Liberté politique. Liberté Pol.** 6 6:2004 pp.49-72.

4071 Le droit des réfugiés à l'épreuve des droits de l'homme : bilan de la jurisprudence de la Cour Européenne des Droits de l'Homme sur l'interdiction du renvoi des étrangers menacés de torture et de traitements inhumains ou dégradants. *[In French]*; [Refugee law against human rights: a review of the European Court on Human Rights' jurisprudence on the prohibition to expel foreigners threatened by torture and inhuman or humiliating treatment]. V. Chetail. **Belg. R. Int. Law** XXXVII:1 2004 pp.155-210.

4072 Les droits de l'homme et la guerre en Tchétchénie. *[In French]*; (Human rights and the war in Chechnya.) *[Summary]*. Theodore P. Gerber; Sarah E. Mendelson. **Pouvoirs** 112 2004 pp.79-92.

4073 Explaining costly international institutions: persuasion and enforceable human rights norms. Darren Hawkins. **Int. S. Q.** 48:4 12:2004 pp.779-804.

4074 From peacekeeping violence in Somalia to prisoner abuse at Abu Ghraib: the centrality of racism. Sherene H. Razack. **Glo. Dial.** 7:1-2 Winter-Spring:2005 pp.134-141.

4075   The future of the UN High Commissioner for human rights. B.G. Ramcharan. **Round Tab.** 378 1:2005 pp.97-112.

4076   Geneva under siege. S. Bosch. **Comp. Int. Law J. Sth. Afr.** XXXVII:3 11:2004 pp.294-311.

4077   La globalisation : approche du phénomène et ses incidences sur l'action humanitaire. *[In French]*; (Globalization: introduction to the phenomenon and its implications for humanitarian action.) *[Summary]*. Jean-Luc Blondel. **Int. R. Red Cross** 86:855 9:2004 pp.493-503.

4078   Hate speech in Rwanda as a test case for international human rights law. Frans Viljoen. **Comp. Int. Law J. Sth. Afr.** XXXVIII:1 3:2005 pp.1-14.

4079   Hinduism and international humanitarian law. Manoj Kumar Sinha. **Int. R. Red Cross** 87:858 6:2005 pp.285-294.

4080   Human rights: above politics or a creature of politics? Francesca Klug. **Policy Pol.** 33:1 1:2005 pp.3-14.

4081   Human rights and indefinite detention. Alfred de Zayas. **Int. R. Red Cross** 87:857 3:2005 pp.15-38.

4082   Human rights conflicts: China and the United States. Qi Zhou. **Hum. Rights Q.** 27:1 2:2005 pp.105-124.

4083   Human rights, the concept and perspectives: a third world view. J.K. Patnaik. **Indian J. Pol. Sci.** LXV:4 10-12:2004 pp.499-514.

4084   Humanitarian and other interventions. Thomas M. Franck. **Columb. J. Tr. Law** 43:2 2005 pp.321-336.

4085   Humanitarian intervention after 9/11. Tom J. Farer; Daniele Archibugi; Chris Brown; Neta C. Crawford; Thomas G. Weiss; Nicholas J. Wheeler. **Int. Rel.** 19:2 6:2005 pp.211-250.

4086   Humanitarian intervention and international relations. Jennifer M. Welsh [Ed.]. Oxford: Oxford University Press, 2004. viii, 229p. *ISBN: 0199267219. Includes bibliographical references and index.*

4087   Humanitarian intervention: elite and critical perspectives. Richard Falk. **Glo. Dial.** 7:1-2 Winter-Spring:2005 pp.37-49.

4088   L'immunité des états en cas de violations graves des droits de l'homme. *[In French]*; [States' immunity in case of severe human rights violations]; *[Summary in English]*; *[Summary in Spanish]*. Christian Tomuschat. **R. Gén. Droit Int. Publ.** 109:1 2005 pp.51-74.

4089   Iraq and the responsibility to protect. Ramesh Thakur. **Glo. Dial.** 7:1-2 Winter-Spring:2005 pp.16-26.

4090   Journalism worthy of the name: an affirmative reading of Article 10 of the ECHR. Herdís Thorgeirsdóttir. **Neth. Q. Hum. Rights** 22:4 12:2004 pp.601-622.

4091   Law, force, and human rights: the search for a sufficiently principled legal basis for humanitarian intervention. Eric A. Heinze. **J. Confl. S.** XXIV:2 Winter:2004 pp.5-32.

4092   Legal regulation of humanitarian assistance in armed conflict: achievements and gaps; *[Summary in French]*. Ruth Abril Stoffels. **Int. R. Red Cross** 86:855 9:2004 pp.515-546.

4093   Living in denial: the application of human rights in the occupied territories. Orna ben-Naftali; Yuval Shany. **Isr. Law R.** 37:1 Spring:2003-2004 pp.17-118.

4094   Mehr als humanitäre Intervention –Menschenrechte in der globalen Gesellschaft. *[In German]*; [More than humanitarian intervention –human rights in global society]. Michael Walzer. **Int. Politik** 60:2 2:2005 pp.8-20.

4095   La muchacha respondona: reflections on the razor's edge between crime and human rights. Angela Snodgrass Godoy. **Hum. Rights Q.** 27:2 5:2005 pp.597-624.

4096   On recognizing children's universal rights: what needs to change in the Convention on the Rights of the Child. Sonja Grover. **Int. J. Child. Rights** 12:3 2004 pp.259-271.

4097   On the relationship between human rights law protection and international humanitarian law; *[Summary in French]*. Hans-Joachim Heintze. **Int. R. Red Cross** 86:856 12:2004 pp.789-814.

4098   El orden europeo e interno de los derechos fundamentales y su protección jurisdiccional. *[In Spanish]*; [European and internal order of fundamental rights and its jurisdictional protection]. Lorenzo Martín-Retortillo Baquer. **R. Admin. Públ.** 165 9-12:2004 pp.7-27.

4099   'Past' violations under international human rights law: the indigenous 'stolen generation' in Australia. Maria O'Sullivan. **Neth. Q. Hum. Rights** 23:2 6:2005 pp.243-302.

4100   The political science of human rights. Todd Landman. **Br. J. Pol. Sci.** 35:3 7:2005 pp.549-572.

4101   Power, capture, and conflict: a call for human rights accountability in development cooperation. Mac Darrow; Amparo Tomas. **Hum. Rights Q.** 27:2 5:2005 pp.471-538.

4102   Private use of prisoners' labor: paradoxes of international human rights law. Colin Fenwick. **Hum. Rights Q.** 27:1 2:2005 pp.249-293.

4103   Putting national interest last: the utopianism of intervention. Michael Radu. **Glo. Dial.** 7:1-2 Winter-Spring:2005 pp.76-85.

4104   The responsibility to protect and the crisis in Darfur. Paul D. Williams; Alex J. Bellamy. **Secur. Dial.** 36:1 3:2005 pp.27-47.

4105   Rights and responsibilities: the dilemma of humanitarian intervention. Chris Abbott. **Glo. Dial.** 7:1-2 Winter-Spring:2005 pp.1-15.

4106   The role of human rights in foreign policy. P. R. Baehr; Monique Castermans-Holleman. Basingstoke, New York: Palgrave Macmillan, 2004. xii, 165p. *ISBN: 1403904634, 1403904642. Includes bibliographical references and index.*

4107   Social rights as human rights: globalizing social protection; *[Summary in French]*; *[Summary in Spanish]*; *[Summary in Arabic]*. Ramesh Mishra. **Int. Soc. Work** 48:1 1:2005 pp.9-20.

4108   Study on customary international humanitarian law: a contribution to the understanding and respect for the rule of law in armed conflict. Jean-Marie Henckaerts. **Int. R. Red Cross** 87:857 3:2005 pp.175-212.

4109   Die symbolische Kraft der Menschenrechte. *[In German]*; [The symbolic force of human rights] *[Summary]*. Marcelo Neves. **Arch. Recht. Soz.Philos.** 91:2 2005 pp.159-187.

4110   Trading human rights: how preferential trade agreements influence government repression. Emilie M. Hafner-Burton. **Int. Org.** 59:3 Summer:2005 pp.593-629.

4111   Trafficking and prostitution reconsidered: new perspectives on migration, sex work, and human rights. Kamala Kempadoo [Ed.]; Jyoti Sanghera [Ed.]; Bandana Pattanaik [Ed.]. Boulder CO: Paradigm Publishers, 2005. xxxiv, 247p. *ISBN: 1594510962, 1594510970. Includes bibliographical references and index.*

4112   Unpeople: Britain's secret human rights abuses. Mark Curtis. London: Vintage, 2004. 377p. *ISBN: 0099469723. Includes bibliographical references and index.*

4113   Visits by human rights mechanisms as a means of greater protection for persons deprived of their liberty. Edouard Delaplace; Matt Pollard. **Int. R. Red Cross** 87:857 3:2005 pp.69-82.

4114   A world without torture. Harold Hongju Koh. **Columb. J. Tr. Law** 43:3 2005 pp.641-661.

Human rights conventions
Conventions sur les droits de l'homme

4115   Conflicting human rights: an exploration in the context of the right to a fair trial in the European Convention on Human Rights. Eva Brems. **Hum. Rights Q.** 27:1 2:2005 pp.294-326.

4116   Do international human rights treaties improve respect for human rights? Eric Neumayer. **J. Confl. Resol.** 49:6 12:2005 pp.925-953.

4117   The interpretation of UK domestic legislation in the light of European convention on human rights jurisprudence. Arden. **Stat. Law R.** 25:3 2004 pp.165-179.

4118   Legality of amnesties in international humanitarian law. The Lomé amnesty decision of the special court for Sierra Leone. Simon M. Meisenberg. **Int. R. Red Cross** 86:856 12:2004 pp.837-851.

4119   Neighbours as human shields? The Israel defense forces' "early warning procedure" and international humanitarian law; *[Summary in French]*. Roland Otto. **Int. R. Red Cross** 86:856 12:2004 pp.771-787.

4120   Sovereignty relinquished? Explaining commitment to the international human rights covenants, 1966-1999. Wade M. Cole. **Am. Sociol. R.** 70:3 6:2005 pp.472-495.

4121   Standing back from the Human Rights Act: how effective is it five years on? Francesca Klug; Kier Starmer. **Publ. Law** Winter:2005 pp.716-728.

4122   Taking the Strasbourg jurisprudence into account: developing a 'municipal law of human rights' under the Human Rights Act. Roger Masterman. **Int. Comp. Law Q.** 54:4 10:2005 pp.907-931.

4123   Why people are committed to human rights and still tolerate their violation: a contextual analysis of the principle-application gap. Christian Staerklé; Alain Clémence. **Soc. Just. Res.** 17:4 12:2004 pp.389-406.

4124   The World Bank and the internalization of indigenous rights norms. Galit A. Sarfaty. **Yale Law J.** 114:7 5:2005 pp.1791-1818.

Refugees
Réfugiés

4125   Agents of change or passive victims: the impact of welfare states (the case of the Netherlands) on refugees. Halleh Ghorashi. **J. Refug. S.** 18:2 6:2005 pp.181-198.

4126   Asylum recognition rates in Western Europe: their determinants, variation, and lack of convergence. Eric Neumayer. **J. Confl. Resol.** 49:1 2:2005 pp.43-66.

4127   Entre droit au retour et réinstallation définitive : la question des réfugiés palestiniens. *[In French]*; [Between the right to return and the final re-settlement: the question of Palestinian refugees]. Jalal Al-Husseini. **Cah. Orient** 75 7-9:2004 pp.31-50.

4128   The guiding principles on internal displacement: an innovation in international standard setting. Roberta Cohen. **Glo. Gov.** 10:4 10-12:2004 pp.459-480.

4129   Has welfare reform created 'chilling effects' for refugees in the United States? Miriam Potocky-Tripodi. **Int. Migr. R.** 38:4 Winter:2004 pp.1534-1543.

4130   Human security and asylum-seeking. Nira Yuval-Davis. **Mediactive** 4 2005 pp.38-55.

4131   Internal displacement in South Asia: the relevance of the UN's guiding principles. Paula Banerjee [Ed.]; Sabyasachi Basu Ray Chaudhury [Ed.]; Samir Kumar Das [Ed.]. Thousand Oaks CA: Sage Publications, 2005. 370p. *ISBN: 0761933131, 0761933298. Includes bibliographical references and index.*

4132   Internally displaced peoples in Bosnia-Herzegovina: impacts of long-term displacement on health and well-being. Maria Kett. **Med. Confl. Surv.** 21:3 7-9:2005 pp.199-215.

4133   The long "last step"? Reintegration of repatriates in Eritrea. Johnathan Bascom. **J. Refug. S.** 18:2 6:2005 pp.165-180.

4134   The long road home: protracted refugee situations in Africa. Gil Loescher; James Milner. **Survival** 47:2 Summer:2005 pp.153-173.

4135   Non-voluntary return? The politics of return to Afghanistan. Brad K. Blitz; Rosemary Sales; Lisa Marzano. **Pol. S.** 53:1 3:2005 pp.182-200.

4136   Pakistan an immigrant country: Afghan migration and its impact on Balochistan. Mansoor Akbar Kundi. **Strat. S.** XXV:2 Summer:2005 pp.55-74.

4137   Rights in exile: Janus-faced humanitarianism. Guglielmo Verdirame; Barbara E. Harrell-Bond. New York, Oxford: Berghahn Books, 2005. xxix, 385p. *ISBN: 1571815260, 1845451031. Includes bibliographical references (p. [340]-371) and index. (Series: Studies in forced migration - 17).*

4138   Though the dog is dead - the pig must be killed: finishing with property restitution to Bosnia-Herzegovina's IDPs and refugees. Charles Philpott. **J. Refug. S.** 18:1 3:2005 pp.1-24.

4139   Transnationalization of human rights norms and its impact on internally displaced kurds. Ayşe Betûl Çelik. **Hum. Rights Q.** 27:3 8:2005 pp.969-997.

4140   The turbulent decade: confronting the refugee crises of the 1990s. Sadako N. Ogata; Kofi Annan [Foreword]. New York: W.W. Norton & Company, 2005. xiv, 402p. *ISBN: 0393057739. Includes bibliographical references and index.*

4141   Unwelcome guests: relations between internally displaced persons and their hosts in North Sulawesi, Indonesia. Christopher R. Duncan. **J. Refug. S.** 18:1 3:2005 pp.25-46.

F.2:   International society
**   Société internationale**

F.2.1:   International and regional integration
**   Intégration internationale et régionale**

4142   Les Amériques à l'heure de l'intégration. *[In French]*; [The Americas at the time of integration]. Sylvain F. Turcotte; Christian Deblock; Marie-Josée Massicotte; Gilbert Gagné; Delphine Nakache; André Marenco dos Santos. **Pol. et Soc.** 23:2-3 2004 pp.3-133. *Collection of 5 articles.*

4143   ASEAN cooperation: the legacy of the economic crisis. Etel Solingen. **Int. Rel. Asia Pacific** 5:1 2005 pp.1-29.

4144   The ASEAN free trade area and the construction of a Southeast Asian economic community in East Asia. Alfredo C. Robles, Jr. **Asian J. Pol. Sci.** 12:2 12:2004 pp.78-108.

4145   ASEAN initiatives to combat haze pollution: an assessment of regional cooperation in public policy-making. David Seth Jones. **Asian J. Pol. Sci.** 12:2 12:2004 pp.59-77.

4146   ASEAN's ninth summit: what did it achieve? Anthony L. Smith. **India Q.** LX:3 7-9:2004 pp.1-25.

4147   Asian monetary and financial cooperations in response to the currency crisis: issues and policy implications. Seung-Cheol Jeon. **J. East Asian Aff.** XVIII:2 Fall-Winter:2004 pp.251-280.

4148   Asian regional governance: crisis and change. Kanishka Jayasuriya [Ed.]. New York, London: RoutledgeCurzon, 2004. 288p. *ISBN: 0415321913. (Series: RoutledgeCurzon/City University of Hong Kong South East Asia).*

4149   Canadian federalism and the challenge of North American integration. G.E. Hale. **Can. Publ. Admin.** 47:4 Winter:2004 pp.497-524.

4150   China engages Asia: reshaping the regional order. David Shambaugh. **Int. Secur.** 29:3 Winter:2004-2005 pp.64-99.

4151   Cooperation culture — notions on the significance of cultural norms and principles in regional and interregional cooperation-processes. Howard Loewen. **S. UBB: Stu. Eur.** XLIX: 1-2 2004 pp.91-102.

4152   Dar al Islam. The Mediterranean, the world system and the wider Europe: the "cultural enlargement" of the EU and Europe's identity. Peter Herrmann [Ed.]; Arno Tausch [Ed.]. New York: Nova Science Publishers, 2004. xi, 314p. *ISBN: 1594542864. Includes bibliographical references (p. 273-305) and index.*

4153   Democracy from above: regional organizations and democratization. Jon C. Pevehouse. Cambridge, New York: Cambridge University Press, 2005. xiv, 248p. *ISBN: 0521844827, 0521606586. Includes bibliographical references (p. 219-242) and index.*

4154   Euro-Mediterranean dialogue. Nadia Mushtaq Abbasi. **Strat. S.** XXV:1 Spring:2005 pp.106-128.

4155   Fast-tracking African unity or making haste slowly? A note on the Amendments to the Constitutive Act of the African Union. Tiyanjana Maluwa. **Neth. Int. Law R.** LI:2 2004 pp.195-236.

4156   The Five Power Defence Arrangements: Southeast Asia's unknown regional security organization. Damon Bristow. **Contemp. Sth.East Asia** 27:1 4:2005 pp.1-20.

4157   Fusion of horizons or confusion of horizons? Intercultural dialogue and its risks. Ken Tsutsumibayashi. **Glo. Gov.** 11:1 1-3:2005 pp.103-114.

4158   The future of North America: seeking a roadmap. John Manley. **Int. J.** LX:2 Spring:2005 pp.497-508.

4159   A globális és a regionális folyamatok politikai hatása. *[In Hungarian]*; (The political effect of global and regional processes.) *[Summary]*. Kálmán Kulcsár. **Társadalomkutatás** 22:1 2004 pp.5-40.

4160   The impact of China-ASEAN free trade agreement on regional trade. Xiangshuo Yin. **J. East Asian Aff.** XVIII:2 Fall-Winter:2004 pp.311-339.

4161   The impact of norms in international society: the Latin American experience, 1881-2001. Arie Marcelo Kacowicz. Notre Dame IN: University of Notre Dame Press, 2005. xiv, 228p. *ISBN: 0268033064, 0268033072. Includes bibliographical references (p. 201-219) and index.*

4162   Issues in regional integration of East Asia: conflicting priorities and perceptions. Matsuo Watanabe. **Asia Pac. R.** 11:2 11:2004 pp.1-17.

4163   The meaning of regional integration: introducing positioning theory in regional integration studies. Nikki Slocum; Luk Van Langehove. **J. Euro. Integ.** 26:3 9:2004 pp.227-252.

4164   Modes of regional governance in Africa: neoliberalism, sovereignty boosting, and shadow networks. Fredrik Söderbaum. **Glo. Gov.** 10:4 10-12:2004 pp.419-436.

4165   Multilateralism in China's ASEAN policy: its evolution, characteristics, and aspiration. Kuik Cheng-Chwee. **Contemp. Sth.East Asia** 27:1 4:2005 pp.102-122.

4166   NAFTA and its discontents. Peter Karl Kresl. **Int. J.** LX:2 Spring:2005 pp.417-428.

4167   Pakistan and the ASEAN Regional Forum.   Fazal-ur-Rahman. **Strat. S.** XXIV:4 Winter:2004 pp.29-51.

4168   Political economy, civil society and the deep integration debate in Canada. Jeffrey M. Ayres. **Am. R. Can. S.** 34:4 Winter:2004 pp.621-647.

4169   The political economy of regionalism: the case of Southern Africa. Fredrik Soderbaum. Basingstoke, New York: Palgrave Macmillan, 2004. xx, 251p. *ISBN: 1403920834. Includes bibliographical references and index.*

4170   Proyectos políticos en nuestra América. *[In Spanish]*; [Political projects in our America]. Sergio Guerra Vilaboy; Cesia Hirshbein; Tomás Straka; Ana Buriano Castro; Pablo Yankelevich; Marcos Cueva Perus. **Cuad. Am.** XIX:3(111) 5-6:2005 pp.85-208. *Collection of 6 articles.*

4171   Regional community building and the transformation of international relations: the case of the Euro-Mediterranean Partnership. Frédéric Volpi. **Med. Pol.** 9:2 Summer:2004 pp.145-164.

4172   Regionalism, economic integration and legalisation in ASEAN: what space for environmental sustainability? Kala K. Mulqueeny. **Asia Pac. J. Env. Law** 8:1-2 2004 pp.5-68.

4173   Reinvigorating the parliamentary dimension of the Barcelona process: the establishment of the Euro-Mediterranean parliamentary assembly. Ioannis Seimenis; Miltiadis Makriyannis. **Mediterr. Q.** 16:2 Spring:2005 pp.85-105.

4174   Rethinking pan-Africanism in the search for social progress. Tukumbi Lumumba-Kasongo. **Glo. Dial.** 6:3-4 Summer-Autumn:2004 pp.62-72.

4175   Security, community, and democracy in Southeast Asia: analyzing ASEAN. Donald K. Emmerson. **Japanese J. Pol. Sci.** 6:2 8:2005 pp.165-186.

4176   Severo-Vostochnaiia i Tsentral'naiia Aziia: dinamika mezhdunarodnykh i mezhregional'nykh vzaimodeistvii. *[In Russian]*; [North-East and Central Asia: international dynamics and inter-regional cooperation]. A.D. Voskresenskii [Ed.]. Moscow: ROSSPEN, 2004. 470p. *ISBN: 5824304491. Includes bibliographical references.*

4177   South Africa and the political economy of regional cooperation in Southern Africa. James J. Hentz. **J. Mod. Afr. S.** 43:1 3:2005 pp.21-52.

4178   L'union africaine comme réponse africaine au défi de la mondialisation. *[In French]*; [The African Union as an African response to the challenge of globalization] *[Summary]*. Reine Djuidje Kouam. **Afr. Dev.** XXX:1-2 2005 pp.125-151.

F.2.2:   **European Union**
              Union européenne

4179   Une certaine idée de l'Europe. *[In French]*; [A certain concept of Europe]. Laurent Fabius. Paris: Plon, 2004. 125p. *ISBN: 225920113X.*

4180   Conceptualizing the EU model of governance in world politics. Ben Rosamond. **Euro. For. Aff. R.** 10:4 Winter:2005 pp.463-478.

4181   Counter-public spheres and the revival of the European public sphere. Jeffrey Wimmer. **Javnost** XII:2 6:2005 pp.93-109.

4182   De l'identité de l'Europe aux frontières de l'Union. *[In French]*; [From European identity to European borders]. Jean-Louis Bourlanges. **Etudes** 400:6 6:2004 pp.729-741.

4183   The disparity of European integration: revisiting neofunctionalism in honour of Ernst Haas. Tanja A. Börzel; Ben Rosamond; Philippe C. Schmitter; Henry Farrell; Adrienne Héritier; Thomas Risse; Gráinne de Búrca; Walter Mattli; Andrew Moravcsik; Mark Rhinard; Beatrice Vaccari. **J. Euro. Publ. Policy** 12:2 2005 pp.216-394. *Collection of 9 articles.*

4184   An emerging European public sphere. Erik Oddvar Eriksen. **Euro. J. Soc. Theory** 8:3 8:2005 pp.341-363.

4185   EU integration, europeanization and administrative convergence: the Greek case. Konstantinos J. Papadoulis. **J. Com. Mkt. S.** 43:2 6:2005 pp.349-370.

4186   Europa med egne øjne. *[In Danish]*; (Europe in its own eyes. European integration in daily life.) Lisa Rosén Rasmussen; Karen Dannesboe. **Nord Ny.** 95 7:2005 pp.21-34.

4187   Europe 1945 to the present. Robin W. Winks; John E. Talbott. New York: Oxford University Press, 2005. xv, 176p. *ISBN: 9780195156911, 0195156919, 0195156927. Includes bibliographical references and index.*

4188   L'Europe face à la mondialisation : entre maîtrise et opportunisme. *[In French]*; [Europe facing globalization: between mastership and opportunism]. Leendert de Voogd. **Européens** 2004 pp.95-109.

4189   The European consociational model: an exportable institutional design? Olivier Costa; François Foret. **Euro. For. Aff. R.** 10:4 Winter:2005 pp.501-516.

4190   The European dream: how Europe's vision of the future is quietly eclipsing the American dream. Jeremy Rifkin. Cambridge: Polity, 2004. xiii, 434p. *ISBN: 0745634249, 0745634257. Includes bibliographical references and index.*

4191   European identity building from the perspective of efficiency. Sylvia Kritzinger. **Comp. Euro. Pol.** 3:1 4:2005 pp.50-75.

4192   European integration and political conflict. Gary Marks [Ed.]; Marco R. Steenbergen [Ed.]. Cambridge: Cambridge University Press, 2004. xiv, 280p. *ISBN: 0521535050, 0521827795. Includes bibliographical references and index. (Series:* Themes in European governance).

4193   European integration, public opinion and immigration policy: testing the impact of national identity. Adam Luedtke. **Euro. Uni. Pol.** 6:1 3:2005 pp.83-112.

4194   European political identity and democratic solidarity after 9/11: the Spanish case. Emmanuel-Pierre Guittet. **Alternatives** 29:4 8-10:2004 pp.441-464.

4195   Europeanization and the unravelling European nation state: dynamics and feedback effects. Stephan Leibfried; Dieter Wolf. **Euro. For. Aff. R.** 10:4 Winter:2005 pp.479-499.

4196   The europeanization of citizenship: between the ideology of nationality, immigration and European identity. Fiorella Dell'Olio. Aldershot, Burlington VT: Ashgate, 2005. xii, 170p. *ISBN: 0754635953. Includes bibliographical references (p. [151]-166) and index.*

4197   Europeizzazione come istituzionalizzazione: questioni definitorie e di metodo. *[In Italian]*; [Europeanization as institutionalization: definitions and methods]. Marco Giuliani. **Riv. It. Pol. Pub.** 1 4:2004 pp.141-161.

4198   The federalization of the EU, the US and 'compound republic' theory: the convention's debate. Sergio Fabbrini; Daniela Sicurelli. **Reg. Fed. S.** 14:2 Summer:2004 pp.232-254.

4199   Festvortrag: Die Europäische Union als Wertegemeinschaft — Eine verfassungsrechtliche Betrachtung. *[In German]*; [The European Union: a union of values –the perspective of constitutional law]. Markus Möstl. **Politische S.** 56:402 7-8:2005 pp.22-33.

4200   The fragility of the EU as a 'community of values': lessons from the Haider affair. Cécile Leconte. **West Euro. Pol.** 28:3 5:2005 pp.620-649.

4201   Die kommunale Selbstverwaltung: Opfer der europäischen Integration? *[In German]*; [Municipal self-management: victims of European integration?] Heinrich Pehle. **Gesell. Wirt. Pol.** 54:1 2005 pp.9-20.

4202   Kompetenzverteilung und Legitimation in der Europäischen Mehrebenenverwaltung. *[In German]*; [Distribution of authority and legitimacy in European multi-level governance]. Gerd Winter. **Europarecht** 40:3 5-6:2005 pp.255-276.

4203   Limits of European citizenship: European integration and domestic immigration policies. Maarten Peter Vink. Basingstoke, New York: Palgrave Macmillan, 2005. xiii, 209p. *ISBN: 1403939365.   Includes bibliographical references and index.* (*Series:* Migration, minorities, and citizenship).

4204   Mind the gap! European integration between level and scope. Tanja A. Börzel. **J. Euro. Publ. Policy** 12:2 2005 pp.217-236.

4205   Neofunctionalism, European identity, and the puzzles of European integration. Thomas Risse. **J. Euro. Publ. Policy** 12:2 2005 pp.291-309.

4206   Per una strategia alternativa. Un nucleo federale in un'Europa a cerchi concentrici. *[In Italian]*; [In favour of an alternative strategy. A federal nucleus in a Europe of concentric circles]. Paolo Vacca. **Federalist** XLVI:2 2004 pp.112-125.

4207   Policy change and discourse in Europe. Vivien A. Schmidt; Claudio M. Radaelli; Jolyon Howorth; Eve Fouilleux; Adrian van den Hoven; Mark Thatcher; Andreas Busch; Andrew Geddes; Virginie Guiraudon; Daniel Wincott. **West Euro. Pol.** 27:2 3:2004 pp.183-379. *Collection of 7 articles.*

4208   Policy change and discourse in Europe: conceptual and methodological issues. Vivien A. Schmidt; Claudio M. Radaelli. **West Euro. Pol.** 27:2 3:2004 pp.183-210.

4209   Political versus instrumental euro-scepticism: mapping scepticism in European countries and regions. Marcel Lubbers; Peer Scheepers. **Euro. Uni. Pol.** 6:2 6:2005 pp.223-242.

4210   Politisk identitet i EU. *[In Danish]*; (Political identity in the EU.) Jørgen Staun. **Nord Ny.** 91 12:2004 pp.27-41.

4211   Quale domani per quest'Europa? *[In Italian]*; [What future for Europe?] Maria Grazia Melchionni. **Riv. S. Pol. Int.** LXXII:2 4-6:2005 pp.201-221.

4212   Quality oriented formation of the European Union from the European Community: political analysis. Govind Krishana Sharma; Bhawna Sharma. **Indian J. Pol. Sci.** LXVI:1 1-3:2005 pp.177-202.

4213   Le rôle des partenaires sociaux dans la construction d'une citoyenneté européenne. *[In French]*; [The role of social partners in the construction of European citizenship]. Jacques Moreau [Ed.]. **Cah. Fondation** 57-58 10:2004 pp.5-107.

4214   The role of language skills and foreign country experiences in the development of European identity. Daniel Fuss; Gema García-Albacete; Miryam Rodríguez-Monter. **Sociologia [Brat.]** 36:3 Spring:2004 pp.273-292.

4215   Le sentiment d'insécurité dans l'Union. *[In French]*; [The feeling of insecurity within the Union]. Bruno Jeanbart. **Européens** 2004 pp.75-86.

4216   Towards a federal Europe? Alexander H. Trechsel; Andreas Auer; Klaus von Beyme; Yannis Papadopoulos; Lori Thorlakson; Thomas Christin; Simon Hug; Tobias Schulz; Fernando Mendez; David McKay; Herbert Obinger; Stephan Leibfried; Francis G. Castles; Andreas Follesdal; Berthold Rittberger; Björn Hörl; Andreas Warntjen; Arndt Wonka. **J. Euro. Publ. Policy** 12:3 2005 pp.401-606. *Collection of 11 articles.*

4217   Les transformations du système Européen de la construction identitaire aux nouvelles formes de gouvernance. *[In French]*; [The transformations of the European system: from identity building to news forms of governance]. Olivier Paye; Nathalie Tousignant; Carole Lager; Arnaud Thysen. **Ét. Int.** XXXVI:1 3:2005 pp.13-99. *Collection of 4 articles.*

4218   La victoire de l'euroscepticisme ? *[In French]*; [The victory of Euroscepticism?] Céline Belot; Kristoff Talin. **R. Pol. Parl.** 106:1031 7-9:2004 pp.41-54.

4219   Was hält Europa zusammen? *[In German]*; [What holds Europe together?] Kurt Biedenkopf; Bronislaw Geremek; Krzysztof Michalski; Michel Rocard. **Transit** 28 Winter:2004-2005 pp.82-93.

4220   Winning the peace: 'lost treasure' of European integration? Catherine Guisan. **Riv. S. Pol. Int.** LXXII:3 7-9:2005 pp.453-470.

Enlargement and accession
Élargissement et adhésion

4221   Accession and reform of the European Union: a game-theoretical analysis of Eastern enlargement and the constitutional reform. Thomas König; Thomas Bräuninger. **Euro. Uni. Pol.** 5:4 12:2004 pp.419-439.

4222   Accession to the EU through the eyes of the Baltic states: addressing the enlargement, the convention on the future of Europe and the constitution. Mykolas Černiauskas. **Slovo** 17:1 Spring:2005 pp.49-63.

4223   L'adhésion de la Turquie à l'Union européenne. *[In French]*; [Turkey's integration into the European Union]. Jean-Raphaël Chaponnière. **Futuribles** 303 12:2004 pp.23-43.

4224   Adhésion turque : la fuite en avant continue. *[In French]*; (Turkish agreement: the relentless pursuit is on.); *[Summary in French]*. Sylvie Goulard. **Pol. Étran.** 70:2 Summer:2005 pp.425-437.

4225   Die Angst der Deutschen vor den Türken und ihrem Beitritt zur EU. *[In German]*; [Germans' fear of Turkey joining the EU]. Baha Gungor. Munich: Diederichs, 2004. 192p. *ISBN: 3720525368.*

4226   Ankara et l'Union européenne : les raisons du " non ". *[In French]*; [Ankara and the European Union: reasons to say 'no']. Jean-Louis Bourlanges. **Polit. Int.** 105 Autumn:2004 pp.39-64.

4227   Assessing the conflict resolution potential of the EU: the Cyprus conflict and accession negotiations. Doga Ulas Eralp; Nimet Beriker. **Secur. Dial.** 36:2 6:2005 pp.175-192.

4228   Attention Europe ! *[In French]*; [EU enlargement]. Outre-terre. **Outre-terre** 7 2004 pp.9-423.

4229   La campagne polonaise pour l'adhésion. *[In French]*; [The Polish campaign for EU membership]. Dominika Tomaszewska. **Européens** 2004 pp.181-193.

4230   CEFTA: between the CMEA and the European Union. Martin Dangerfield. **J. Euro. Integ.** 26:3 9:2004 pp.309-338.

4231   Choosing union: the 2003 EU accession referendum. Aleks Szczerbiak; Paul Taggart; Michelle Cini; Alenka Krašovec; Damjan Lajh; Brigid Fowler; Karen Henderson; Seán Hanley; Evald Mikkel; Geoffrey Pridham. **West Euro. Pol.** 27:4 9:2004 pp.557-777. *Collection of 9 articles.*

4232   La Commission européenne et la gouvernance de l'Europe élargie. *[In French]*; [The European Commission and the governance of an enlarged Europe]. Renaud Dehousse. **Quest. Int.** 5-6:2004 pp.23-37.

4233   Complying with transposition commitments in Poland: collective dilemmas, core executive and legislative outcomes. Radoslaw Zubek. **West Euro. Pol.** 28:3 5:2005 pp.592-619.

4234   The constellations of Europe: how enlargement will transform the EU. Heather Grabbe; Centre for European Reform. London: Centre for European Reform, 2004. 83p. *ISBN: 190122953X.*

4235   Developments in the new member states and applicant countries. Karen Henderson. **J. Com. Mkt. S.** 43:Annual Review 2005 pp.163-180.

4236   Driven to change: the European Union's enlargement viewed from the East. Antoaneta L. Dimitrova [Ed.]. Manchester: Manchester University Press, 2004. xi, 212p. *ISBN: 0719068088, 0719068096. Includes bibliographical references and index.*

4237   "Ein freudloses Ja der EU zur Türkei": Die Entscheidung der Europäischen Union über Beitrittsverhandlungen mit der Türkei. *[In German]*; [The European Union and negotiations with Turkey]. Martin Große Hüttmann. **Gesell. Wirt. Pol.** 54:2 2005 pp.149-162.

4238   Elargissement de l'Union européenne. *[In French]*; [EU enlargement]. Positions et médias. **Posit. Méd.** 50:27 9:2004 pp.35-61.

4239   L'élargissement de l'Union européenne aux pays baltes : coopération, identité et label balte. *[In French]*; [The European enlargement to the Baltic States: cooperation, identity and Baltic label] *[Summary]*. Matthieu Chillaud. **Nordiques** 5 Fall-Summer:2004 pp.69-81.

4240   The enlargement of the European Union and NATO: ordering from the 'menu' in Central Europe. Wade Jacoby. Cambridge, New York: Cambridge University Press, 2004. xiv, 287p. *ISBN: 0521833590. Includes bibliographical references (p. 249-281) and index.*

4241   Enlarging EU environments: Central and Eastern Europe from transition to accession. JoAnn Carmin [Ed.]; Stacy D. VanDeveer [Ed.]; Miranda Schreurs; Ingmar von Homeyer; Petr Jehlička; Andrew Tickle; Eva Kružíková; Zsuzsa Gille; Andreas Beckmann; Henrik Dissing; Regina Axelrod; Lars K. Hallstrom; Ruth Greenspan Bell; Barbara Hicks; Petr Pavlínek; John Pickles; Sandra O. Archibald; Luana E. Banu; Zbigniew Bochniarz; John M. Kramer; Stacy D. VanDeveer; JoAnn Carmin. **Env. Pol.** 13:1 Spring:2004 pp.3-331. *Collection of 14 articles.*

4242   The EU and 'wider Europe': toward an alternative geopolitics of regional cooperation? James Wesley Scott. **Geopolitics** 10:3 2005 pp.429-454.

4243   EU enlargement and immigration policy in Poland and Slovakia. Peter Vermeersch. **Comm. Post-Comm. S.** 38:1 3:2005 pp.71-88.

4244   EU enlargement and party systems in Central Europe. Paul G. Lewis. **J. Comm. S. Transit. Pol.** 21:2 6:2005 pp.171-199.

4245   EU-enlargement and beyond: a simulation study on EU and Russia integration. Pekka Sulamaa; Mika Widgrén. **Empirica** 31:4 2004 pp.307-323.

4246   L'Europe à 25. *[In French]*; [Europe with 25 members]. Questions internationales. **Quest. Int.** 7 5-6:2004 pp.1-95.

4247   Europe centrale et orientale 2003-2004 : retrouvailles européennes. *[In French]*; [Central and Eastern Europe 2003-2004: European reunion]. Courrier des pays de l'Est. **Cour. Pays Est** 1044 7-8:2004 pp.3-254.

4248   The European Union and enlargement: the case of Cyprus. George Christou. Basingstoke, New York: Palgrave Macmillan, 2004. xv, 228p. *ISBN: 1403916322. Includes bibliographical references (p. 212-223) and index.*

4249   European Union enlargement: a comparative history. Wolfram Kaiser [Ed.]; Jürgen Elvert [Ed.]. London: Routledge, 2004. 240p. *ISBN: 0415331374. (Series:* Routledge advances in European politics).

4250   The European Union in the wake of Eastern enlargement: institutional and policy-making challenges. Amy Verdun [Ed.]; Osvaldo Croci [Ed.]. Manchester: Manchester University Press, 2005. xi, 246p. *ISBN: 0719065127. Includes bibliographical references and index.*

4251   Fragen an die politökonomische Sozialforschung im Prozess der Osterweiterung der EU. *[In German]*; [Questions to the political economy social science research in the process of the EU enlargement]. Wolfgang Teckenberg. **Polit. Viertel.** 46:2 6:2005 pp.326-338.

4252   A geopolítica da Turquia: um desafio às sociedades abertas da União Europeia. *[In Portuguese]*; (The geopolitics of Turkey: a challenge to the EU's open societies.) *[Summary]*. José Pedro Teixeira Fernandes. **Relações Int.** 5 3:2005 pp.47-60.

4253   Germany and East-Central Europe: political, economic and socio-cultural relations in the era of EU enlargement. Stephen Wood. Aldershot: Ashgate, 2004. 245p. *ISBN: 0754643093. Includes bibliographical references and index.*

4254   Grenzen der Flexibilität einer erweiterten Europäischen Union. *[In German]*; [Borders of flexibility of an enlarged European Union]. Armin Hatje. **Europarecht** 40:2 3-4:2005 pp.148-161.

4255   The impacts of EU accession on post-communist constitutionalism. András Sajó. **Acta Jur. Hun.** 45:3-4 2004 pp.193-212.

4256 Les instruments de l'élargissement de l'Union européenne. *[In French]*; [Instruments of EU enlargement]. François Bafoil [Ed.]. **Crit. Int.** 25 10:2004 pp.119-185.

4257 Kosovo and Serbia after the French Non. Elizabeth Pond. **Washington Q.** 28:4 Autumn:2005 pp.19-36.

4258 NATO, the EU and Central Europe: differing symbolic shapes in newspaper accounts of enlargement. Jason Dittmer. **Geopolitics** 10:1 Spring:2005 pp.76-98.

4259 Negotiating Turkey's accession: the limitations of the current EU strategy. Andrea Gates. **Euro. For. Aff. R.** 10:3 Autumn:2005 pp.381-397.

4260 New divisions in Europe? East-East divergence and the influence of European Union enlargement. Verena Fritz. **J. Int. Rel. Dev.** 8:2 6:2005 pp.192-217.

4261 Une nouveauté dans l'Acte d'adhésion des dix nouveaux Etats membres de l'Union européenne : la clause de sauvegarde "Marché intérieur". *[In French]*; [An innovation in the accession Act of the ten new member states of the European Union: the safeguard clause "domestic market"]. Pascal Leardini. **R. Droit Union Euro.** 1 2004 pp.53-68.

4262 Les nouveaux voisins orientaux de l'Europe élargie. *[In French]*; [EU enlargement and new Eastern neighbours]. Courrier des pays de l'Est. **Cour. Pays Est** 1042 3-4:2004 pp.3-58.

4263 Observatoire de l'élargissement européen. *[In French]*; [EU enlargement observatory]. Européens. **Européens** 2004 pp.167-193.

4264 Poland's road to the European Union; *[Summary in French]*; *[Summary in German]*. Ania Krok-Paszkowska; Jan Zielonka. **J. Euro. Integ. Hist.** 10:2 2004 pp.7-24.

4265 Politik oder Religion? Die islamische Türkei und die europäische Integration. *[In German]*; [Politics or religion? Islam in Turkey and European integration]. Dietrich Jung. **Neue Pol. Liter.** XLIX:3 2004 pp.365-384.

4266 Postkommunistischer Kapitalismus: Ökonomie, Politik und Gesellschaft im neuen Europa. *[In German]*; (Postcommunist capitalism: economy, politics, and society in the New Europe.) *[Summary]*; *[Summary in German]*. Michael Ehrke. **Int. Pol. Gesell.** 1 2005 pp.142-163.

4267 Quelles convergences régionales au sein des PECO avant l'adhésion? — Mise en évidence des déterminants macro-économiques et géographiques. *[In French]*; (Regional convergence among CEEC before joining the EU. Highlighting the decisive macroeconomic and geographical factors.) *[Summary]*. Frédéric Carluer. **R. Mar. Comm.** 488 5:2005 pp.305-316.

4268 Rasshirenie i uglublenie evropeiskoi integratsii. *[In Russian]*; (Expansion and deepening of European integration.) Iu. Borko. **Mir. Ekon. Mezh. Ot.** 7 7:2004 pp.15-29.

4269 Reconnaissance de la république de Chypre par la Turquie : une nécessité pour l'adhésion de celle-ci à l'union européenne, mais il faudra du temps. *[In French]*; (The recognition of the Republic of Cyprus by Turkey: a necessity if Turkey is to join the European Union, even if time is required.) Ercüment Tezcan. **R. Mar. Comm.** 489 6:2005 pp.376-381.

4270 Les référendums d'adhésion en Europe centrale et orientale : une expérience européenne unique. *[In French]*; [EU membership referendums in Central and Eastern Europe: a unique European experience]. Corinne Déloy. **Européens** 2004 pp.169-179.

4271 Rumyniia: nepodvedennye itogi. *[In Russian]*; (Romania and EU membership.) Angara Samorukova; Nadezhda Feit. **Svobod. Mysl'** 8 2005 pp.179-190.

4272 Les secteurs économiques en difficulté et la clause de sauvegarde prévue par l'Acte d'adhésion des dix nouveaux membres à l'Union européenne. *[In French]*; [Economic sectors in difficulty and the safeguard clause envisaged by the Act accession of the ten new members of the European Union]. Alfonso Mattera. **R. Droit Union Euro.** 1 2004 pp.39-51.

4273 The Slovak economy and EU membership. Bruno S. Sergi [Ed.]; William T. Bagatelas [Ed.]. Bratislava: Iura edition, 2004. 482p. *ISBN: 8080780064. Includes bibliographical references.*

4274 Südosteuropa und die EU-Erweiterung: Aussichten, Probleme, Rückwirkungen aus soziologischer Sicht. *[In German]*; [Southeast Europe and EU enlargement: prospects, problems and consequences from a sociological perspective] *[Summary]*. Anton Sterbling. **Südosteuro. Mitteil.** 44:5 2004 pp.46-60.

4275 Türkei. *[In German]*; [Turkey]. Abdullah Gül; Günter Seufert; Murat Güvenç; Hubert Faustmann. **Südosteuro. Mitteil.** 44:6 2004 pp.6-112. *Collection of 6 articles.*

4276 Turkey, the European Union and security complexes revisited. Thomas Diez. **Med. Pol.** 10:2 7:2005 pp.167-180.

4277 Turkey's road to the EU: political dynamics, strategic context and implications for Europe. Steve Wood; Wolfgang Quaisser. **Euro. For. Aff. R.** 10:2 Summer:2005 pp.147-173.

4278 A Turquia de regresso à Europa? *[In Portuguese]*; [Turkey's return to Europe?] Teresa de Sousa; Manuela Franco. **Relações Int.** 5 3:2005 pp.27-39.

4279 Turquie : un "désir d'Europe" qui dérange. *[In French]*; [Turkey: an upsetting 'desire for Europe']. Nilüfer Göle. **R. Deux Mondes** 10-11 10-11:2004 pp.135-146.

4280 La Turquie et l'Europe. *[In French]*; [Turkey and Europe]. Outre-terre. **Outre-terre** 7 2004 pp.341-374.

4281 La Turquie et l'Europe : une relation embrouillée. *[In French]*; [Turkey and Europe: a confused relation] *[Summary]*. Garip Turunç. **Mon. Dévelop.** 32:4-128 2004 pp.89-113.

4282 La Turquie, une candidate ordinaire. *[In French]*; [Turkey, an ordinary candidate]. Jean-François Bayart. **Polit. Int.** 105 Autumn:2004 pp.81-102.

4283 Wer sind die wahren Europäer? Ostmitteleuropa und die EU-Krise. *[In German]*; (Who are the real Europeans? East Central Europe and the EU crisis.) *[Summary]*. Reinhold Vetter. **Osteuropa** 55:7 7:2005 pp.103-116.

4284 When culture determines politics: Wie der Deutsche Bundestag die Türkei von der EU fernhält. *[In German]*; (When culture determines politics. How the German Bundestag keeps Turkey away from the EU.); *[Summary in English]*. Rainer Hülsse. **Welt Trends** 45 Winter:2004 pp.135-146.

4285 Will the Czech Republic still be a sovereign country? Lasse Kristensen. **Nord Ny.** 91 12:2004 pp.43-61.

EU-member state relations
Relations U.E.-états membres

4286 Beistandsgarantie und Solidaritätsklausel. Völker – und verfassungsrechtliche Herausforderungen für Österreich durch den neuen EU-Verfassungsvertrag. *[In German]*; [Support guarantee and solidarity clause. Constitutional challenges for Austria]. J. Rehrl. **Z. Öffent. Recht** 60:1 2005 pp.31-53.

4287 Bevölkerungsmeinung und Elitendiskurs: Die deutsche und französische Debatte. *[In German]*; (Public opinion and elites in the German and French debate on the European Constitutional Treaty.) *[Summary]*. Carina Sprungk; Sabine von Oppeln. **Welt Trends** 48 Autumn:2005 pp.121-131.

4288 Britain and Europe: continuity and change. Richard Whitman; Vernon Bogdanor; Julie Smith; Andrew Geddes; Paola Subacchi; Karen E. Smith; Hanns W. Maull; Paul Cornish; Geoffrey Edwards; Josef Janning; John Vogler. **Int. Aff. [London]** 81:4 7:2005 pp.373-850. *Collection of 10 articles.*

4289 Britain and Europe since 1945: historiographic perspectives on integration. Oliver J. Daddow. Manchester, New York: Manchester University Press, 2004. xii, 252p. *ISBN: 0719061377. Includes bibliographical references (p. 210-252) and index.*

4290 Britain, France, and EU anti-discrimination policy: the emergence of an EU paradigm. Andrew Geddes; Virginie Guiraudon. **West Euro. Pol.** 27:2 3:2004 pp.334-353.

4291 Britain in the European Union: law, policy, and Parliament. Philip James Giddings [Ed.]; Gavin Drewry [Ed.]. Basingstoke, New York: Palgrave Macmillan, 2004. xi, 277p. *ISBN: 1403904510, 1403904529. Includes bibliographical references (p. 264-267) and index.*

4292 Britain in the European Union today. Duncan Watts; Colin Pilkington. Manchester: Manchester University Press, 2005. xxi, 295p. *ISBN: 0719071798. Includes bibliographical references and index. (Series: Politics today).*

4293   The challenge of public sector reform in EC accession countries: reflections from the Baltics, especially Latvia. C. Jacobs. **Publ. Admin. Dev.** 24:4 10:2004 pp.321-331.

4294   Challenging identities — EU expansion and cultural distinctiveness: the case of Slovakia. Nicolette Makovicky. **Nord Ny.** 91 12:2004 pp.63-79.

4295   Comment la France définit ses intérêts dans l'union européenne. *[In French]*; (The French interests within the European Union.) *[Summary]*. Nicolas Jabko. **R. Fran. Sci. Pol.** 55:2 4:2005 pp.221-242.

4296   Critical junctures and social identity theory: explaining the gap between Danish mass and elite attitudes to europeanization. Trine Flockhart. **J. Com. Mkt. S.** 43:2 6:2005 pp.251-272.

4297   Czechoslovakia/the Czech Republic and European integration: during and after the Cold War; *[Summary in French]*; *[Summary in German]*. Jan Karlas; Petr Kratochvíl. **J. Euro. Integ. Hist.** 10:2 2004 pp.25-42.

4298   Die deutschen Länder und der Konvent zur Zukunft der Europäischen Union: zwischen subnationaler Interessendivergenz und supranationalem Sozialisationsdruck. *[In German]*; (The German Länder and the European convention on the future of the EU: between divergence of sub-national interests and pressure of supranational socialisation.) Michael W. Bauer. **Z. Parlament.** 36:1 3:2005 pp.188-207.

4299   The developing place of Portugal in the European Union. Jose M. Magone. New Brunswick NJ: Transaction Publishers, 2004. xv, 297p. *ISBN: 0765802066.*

4300   Developments in the economies of the new member states and the candidate countries. Debra Johnson. **J. Com. Mkt. S.** 43:Annual Review 2005 pp.199-214.

4301   Developments in the 'old' member states. Michael Bruter. **J. Com. Mkt. S.** 43:Annual Review 2005 pp.147-162.

4302   Droits exclusifs ou spéciaux et aides d'Etat: questions ouvertes. *[In French]*; [Exclusive or special rights and state aid: open questions]. Alain Alexis. **R. Droit Union Euro.** 2 2004 pp.185-200.

4303   Les élections dans l'Union européenne et dans les pays candidats en 2003. *[In French]*; [Elections in the EU and in the countries candidate for membership]. Corinne Déloy. **Européens** 2004 pp.209-273.

4304   Espagne, Grèce et Portugal : une campagne en demi-teinte, mais des impacts retentissants. *[In French]*; [Spain, Greece, Portugal and European elections]. Laurence Loison; Véronique Pujas. **R. Pol. Parl.** 106:1031 7-9:2004 pp.95-104.

4305   L'Europa in Italia: elite, opinione pubblica e decisioni. *[In Italian]*; [Europe in Italy: elite, public opinion and decisions]. Maurizio Cotta [Ed.]; Pierangelo Isernia [Ed.]; Luca Verzichelli [Ed.]. Bologna: Il Mulino, 2005. 407p. *ISBN: 8815102698.*

4306   Europa und die "soziale Malaise" der Franzosen. *[In German]*; [Europe and French social uneasiness]. Henrik Uterwedde. **Dokumente** 61:3 6:2005 pp.19-28.

4307   Az Európai Unió tagországai állampolgárainak a Magyar köztarsaság területére történő beutazásuk, tartózkodásuk és továbbutazásuk 1990-2001 között. *[In Hungarian]*; (Entry, stay and transit of EU-citizens regarding the Hungarian republic in years the 1990-2001.) György Nagy. **Mag. Köz.** 54:1 2004 pp.48-64.

4308   Europäischer Konvent, Europäische Verfassung, nationale Parlamente. *[In German]*; [European Convent, European constitution and national parliaments]. Sven Hölscheidt. **Jahr. Öffent. Gegen.** 53 2005 pp.429-456.

4309   "Europäisierung" der Bundesstaatsreform? Zur Übertragung des EU-Konventsmodells in Deutschland und Österreich. *[In German]*; ('Europeanising' federal state reforms? The translation of the EU-Convention model in Germany and Austria.) *[Summary]*. Florian Grotz. **Polit. Viertel.** 46:1 3:2005 pp.110-131.

4310   Europe from the bottom: assessing personal gains and losses and its effects on EU support. Steffan Mau. **J. Publ. Policy** 25:3 9-12:2005 pp.289-311.

4311   European integration and the French parliament: from ineffectual watchdog to constitutional rehabilitation and an enhanced political role. Francesco Rizzuto. **J. Legis. St.** 10:1 Spring:2004 pp.123-149.

4312   The European Union and British politics. Andrew Geddes. Basingstoke: Palgrave Macmillan, 2004. xv, 252p. *ISBN: 0333981200, 0333981219. Includes bibliographical references and index.* (*Series:* Contemporary political studies).

4313   Europeanization and changing patterns of governance in Ireland. Maura Adshead. **Publ. Admin.** 83:1 2005 pp.159-178.

4314   Europeizacija socijalnih politika: nacionalne prilagodbe u jugoistočnoj Europi. *[In Croatian]*; (Europeanisation of social policies: national adaptations in South East Europe.) *[Summary]*. Maja Gerovska Mitev. **Revija Soc. Pol.** 11:3-4 7-12:2004 pp.321-342.

4315   French relations with the European Union. Helen Drake [Ed.]. London: Routledge, 2004. 240p. *ISBN: 0415305764.* (*Series:* Europe and the nation state).

4316   "If you have a grandpa, send him to Europe". Attitudes of young Austrians towards the EU elections. Reingard Spannring; Claire Wallace; Georg Datler. **Sociologia [Brat.]** 36:3 Spring:2004 pp.253-272.

4317   Implementing the EU's structural policy and subnational mobilisation in Slovenia. Damjan Lajh. **Cent. Euro. Pol. Sci. R.** 5:15 Spring:2004 pp.95-114.

4318   Die Kooperation zwischen europäischen Agenturen und nationalen Behörden. *[In German]*; [The cooperation between European agencies and national authorities]. Thomas Groß. **Europarecht** 40:1 1-2:2005 pp.54-68.

4319   Lessons from managing conflict situations in the EU accession negotiations: the case of Slovenia. Danica Fink-Hafner; Damjan Lajh. **Cent. Euro. Pol. Sci. R.** 5:15 Spring:2004 pp.52-73.

4320   Lessons learned, lessons forgotten: the Swedish referendum on EMU of September 2003. Nicholas Aylott. **Gov. Oppos.** 40:4 Autumn:2005 pp.540-564.

4321   Location, location, location: national contextual factors and public support for European integration. Adam P. Brinegar; Seth K. Jolly. **Euro. Uni. Pol.** 6:2 6:2005 pp.155-180.

4322   The member states of the European Union. Simon Bulmer [Ed.]; Christian Lequesne [Ed.]. Oxford, New York: Oxford University Press, 2005. xviii, 399p. *ISBN: 0199252815. Includes bibliographical references and index.* (*Series:* The new European Union).

4323   The national coordination of EU policy: organisational efficiency and European outcomes. Angelos Sepos. **J. Euro. Integ.** 27:2 6:2005 pp.169-190.

4324   National parliaments in the European Union: are there any benefits to integration? Francesco Duina; Michael J. Oliver. **Euro. Law J.** 11:2 2005 pp.173-195.

4325   Oficiálna rozvojová pomoc Európskej únie a Slovensko. *[In Slovak]*; (Official development assistance of the European Union and Slovakia.) *[Summary]*. Attila Szép. **Medz. Otázky** XIII:4 2004 pp.3-22.

4326   L'opinion européenne. *[In French]*; [European opinion]. Européens. **Européens** 2004 pp.53-109.

4327   Path-dependent institutions and strategic veto players: national parliaments in the European Union. Arthur Benz. **West Euro. Pol.** 27:5 11:2004 pp.875-900.

4328   Un PECO face à l'intégration dans l'Union européenne : quelle place pour la Pologne laitière. *[In French]*; [A Central Eastern European country facing integration in the European Union: a space for a dairy Poland] *[Summary]*. Eugène Calvez; Isabelle Lesage. **Acta Geo.** 175:1514 9:2004 pp.38-63.

4329   Pocketbooks, politics, and parties: the 2003 Polish referendum on EU membership. Radoslaw Markowski; Joshua A. Tucker. **Electoral S.** 24:3 9:2005 pp.409-433.

4330   El proceso de integración europea y sus efectos en las administraciones públicas nacionales: ¿hacia la convergencia administrativa? *[In Spanish]*; (The impact of European integration on national public administrations: towards administrative confluence?) *[Summary]*. Mauricio I. Dussauge Laguna. **Foro Int.** XLV:2 4-6:2005 pp.293-314.

4331   Projecting EU referendums: fear of immigration and support for European integration. Claes H. de Vreese; Hajo G. Boomgaarden. **Euro. Uni. Pol.** 6:1 3:2005 pp.59-82.

4332   Rethinking Britain and Europe: plurality elections, party management and British policy on European integration. Mark Aspinwall. Manchester: Manchester University Press, 2004. xiii, 200p. *ISBN: 0719069661. Includes bibliographical references and index.*

4333   Le rôle des Parlements nationaux dans l'architecture européenne. *[In French]*; [National Parliaments' role in the Euopean architecture]. Stefano Martinelli. **R. Droit Union Euro.** 4 2004 pp.753-769.

4334   Shared hesitance, joint success: Denmark, Finland, and Sweden in the European Union policy process. Torsten J. Selck; Sanneke Kuipers. **J. Euro. Publ. Policy** 12:1 2005 pp.157-176.

4335   Should we stay or should we go? Two views on Britain and the EU. Malcolm Everard MacLaren Pearson; Stephen Pollard. London: Civitas, 2005. ix, 33p. *ISBN: 1903386403. Includes bibliographical references.*

4336   Southern European public bureaucracies in comparative perspective. Dimitri A. Sotiropoulos. **West Euro. Pol.** 27:3 5:2004 pp.405-422.

4337   Spain and the European Union. Carlos Closa; Paul Heywood. Basingstoke: Palgrave Macmillan, 2004. xvi, 274p. *ISBN: 0333753380, 0333753399. Includes bibliographical references and index.* (*Series:* The European Union).

4338   Taking a second look at Germany's motivation to establish Economic and Monetary Union: a critique of 'economic interests' claims. Dorothee Heisenberg. **Ger. Pol.** 14:1 3:2005 pp.95-109.

4339   We Europeans? Mass-observation, 'race' and British identity in the twentieth century. Tony Kushner. Aldershot, Burlington VT: Ashgate, 2004. xi, 281p. *ISBN: 0754602060. Includes bibliographical references and index.* (*Series:* Studies in European cultural transition - 25).

4340   Wer kommt auf uns zu? Zu einigen Problemen der im Jahr 2004 der EU beigetretenen Länder. *[In German]*; [On some problems of the countries that have joined the European Union in 2004] *[Summary]*. Johannes Neumann. **Relig. Staat Gesell.** 6:1 2005 pp.63-95.

4341   What if the British vote no? Charles Grant. **Foreign Aff.** 84:3 5-6:2005 pp.86-97.

4342   When Europe matters: the impact of political information on voting behaviour in EU referendums. Sara Binzer Hobolt. **Jnl. Ele. Pub. Op. Par.** 15:1 4:2005 pp.85-109.

4343   Zum Plebiszit in Frankreich — wie weiter mit der Verfassung? *[In German]*; (The EU-plebiscite in France: whither the constitution?) *[Summary]*. Heinz Kleger. **Welt Trends** 48 Autumn:2005 pp.93-107.

External policies
Politique extérieure

4344   " Politique de voisinage " de l'union européenne, quelles transformations sur le régime commercial régional en Europe? *[In French]*; (European policy's "neighbourhood policy", what transformations for the regional trade regime in Europe?) *[Summary]*. Vitaliy Denysyuk. **R. Mar. Comm.** 485 2:2005 pp.101-114.

4345   The 2003 European Union security strategy: a critical appraisal. Asle Toje. **Euro. For. Aff. R.** 10:1 Spring:2005 pp.117-133.

4346   L'apport de la constitution européenne à la politique commerciale de l'union. *[In French]*; (The contribution of the European constitution to the union's trade policy.) *[Summary]*. Olivier Blin. **R. Mar. Comm.** 485 2:2005 pp.89-100.

4347   As fragilidades da União Europeia face ao terrorismo. *[In Portuguese]*; (The European Union fragilities towards terrorism.) *[Summary]*. Helena Carrapiço. **Relações Int.** 6 6:2005 pp.127-142.

4348   Beyond enlargement. The European neighbourhood policy and its tools. Rosa Balfour; Alessandro Rotta. **Int. Spect.** XL:1 1-3:2005 pp.7-20.

4349   The borders of the polity: migration and security across the EU and the Balkans. Luisa Chiodi [Ed.]. Ravenna: Longo Editore, 2005. 249p. *ISBN: 888063478X.* (*Series:* Balkan and East-European Studies - 24).

4350   Can the EU anchor policy reform in third countries? An analysis of the euro-med partnership. Alfred Tovias; Mehmet Ugur. **Euro. Uni. Pol.** 5:4 12:2004 pp.395-418.

4351   Causes and consequences of the EU's military intervention in the Democratic Republic of Congo: a realist explanation. Catherine Gegout. **Euro. For. Aff. R.** 10:3 Autumn:2005 pp.427-444.

4352   Civilian power or soft imperialism? The EU as a global actor and the role of interregionalism. Björn Hettne; Fredrik Söderbaum. **Euro. For. Aff. R.** 10:4 Winter:2005 pp.535-552.

4353   Coherence and conditionality in European foreign policy: negotiating the EU-Mexico Global Agreement. Marcela Szymanski; Michael E. Smith. **J. Com. Mkt. S.** 43:1 3:2005 pp.171-192.

4354   Constituting the Common Foreign and Security Policy: the European Union's pursuit of being a coherent and effective foreign and security policy actor in global politics. Taylan Özgür Kaya. **Akdeniz** 5:9 5:2005 pp.123-153.

4355   La contribution de la Pologne à la construction politique et stratégique de l'Union européenne. *[In French]*; [Poland's contribution to the political and strategical building of the European Union]. Jan Tombinski. **Défense Nat.** 60:11 11:2004 pp.25-36.

4356   Discourse, ideas, and epistemic communities in European security and defence policy. Jolyon Howorth. **West Euro. Pol.** 27:2 3:2004 pp.211-234.

4357   Does the ENP respond to the EU's post-enlargement challenges? Nathalie Tocci. **Int. Spect.** XL:1 1-3:2005 pp.21-32.

4358   Dotons l'Union européenne d'un budget de PESD. *[In French]*; [Give the European Union a ESPD budget]. Patrice Cardot. **Défense Nat.** 60:7 7:2004 pp.13-26.

4359   The EC and WTO dispute settlement: the initiation of trade disputes by the EC. Stijn Billiet. **Euro. For. Aff. R.** 10:2 Summer:2005 pp.197-214.

4360   ESDP police missions: meaning, context and operational challenges. Michael Merlingen; Rasa Ostrauskaite. **Euro. For. Aff. R.** 10:2 Summer:2005 pp.215-235.

4361   The ESDP-building process and conflict prevention: intergovernmental policy-making and institutional expertise. Jan Karlas. **J. Int. Rel. Dev.** 8:2 6:2005 pp.164-191.

4362   Espace européen. *[In French]*; [European space]. Défense nationale. **Défense Nat.** 60:3 3:2004 pp.5-88.

4363   The EU as a global actor and the role of interregionalism. Mary Farrell; Sebastian Santander; Julie Gilson; Vinod K. Aggarwal; Edward A. Fogarty; Karen E. Smith; Fredrik Söderbaum; Patrik Stålgren; Luk van Langenhove. **J. Euro. Integ.** 27:3 9:2005 pp.249-380. *Collection of 7 articles.*

4364   The EU as a security regime. Frédéric Charillon. **Euro. For. Aff. R.** 10:4 Winter:2005 pp.517-533.

4365   EU defence policy and relations with NATO: some competition may be welcome. Hanna Ojanen. **Y. Finnish For. Pol.** 2004 pp.31-46.

4366   EU external relations: exporting the EU model of governance? Mary Farrell. **Euro. For. Aff. R.** 10:4 Winter:2005 pp.451-462.

4367   The EU, human rights, and the Russo-Chechen conflict. Tuomas Forsberg; Graeme P. Herd. **Pol. Sci. Q.** 120:3 Fall:2005 pp.455-478.

4368   Euro-Mediterranean cultural cooperation in the field of heritage conservation and management. Evangelia Psychogiopoulou. **Euro. For. Aff. R.** 10:2 Summer:2005 pp.237-255.

4369   Europe : élargissement, défense et sécurité. *[In French]*; [Europe: enlargement, defence and security]. **Défense Nat.** 60:5 5:2004 pp.5-134.

4370   Europe : sortir de l'impuissance sécuritaire. *[In French]*; [Europe: leaving security powerlessness behind]. Revue nouvelle. **R. Nouvelle** 118:5 5:2004 pp.26-71.

4371   L'Europe et la défense. *[In French]*; [Europe and defence]. Michel Sevrin [Ed.]. **Cah. Mars** 180 2004 pp.17-121.

4372   The European Union and conflict prevention: policy and legal aspects. Vincent Kronenberger [Ed.]; Jan Wouters [Ed.]. The Hague: T.M.C. Asser Press, 2004. xxix, 614p. *ISBN: 9067041718. Includes bibliographical references and index.*

4373   L'évolution du partenariat UE-ACP de Lomé à Cotonou : de l'exception à la normalisation. *[In French]*; [Evolution of the EU-ACP partnership from Lomé to Cotonou: from exception to normalization] *[Summary]*. Catherine Haguenau; Thierry Montalieu. **Mon. Dévelop.** 32:4-128 2004 pp.65-88.

4374 The external dimension of europeanization: the case of immigration policies. Sandra Lavenex; Emek M. Uçarer. **Coop. Confl.** 39:4 12:2004 pp.417-443.

4375 External policy developments. David Allen; Michael Smith. **J. Com. Mkt. S.** 43:Annual Review 2005 pp.109-126.

4376 Five years of Stability Pact: regional cooperation in Southeast Europe. Joschka Fischer; Gernot Erler; Erhard Busek; Bodo Hombach; Michael Schaefer; Reinhard Priebe; Rainer Stinner. **Südosteuro. Mitteil.** 44:4 2004 pp.6-52. *Collection of 7 articles.*

4377 For the sake of 'peace and security'? The role of security in the European Union enlargement eastwards. Atsuko Higashino. **Coop. Confl.** 39:4 12:2004 pp.347-368.

4378 From EMP to ENP: what's at stake with the European neighbourhood policy towards the Southern Mediterranean? Raffaella A. Del Sarto; Tobias Schumacher. **Euro. For. Aff. R.** 10:1 Spring:2005 pp.17-38.

4379 The future of the European Security and Defence Policy. Anthony King. **Contemp. Sec. Policy** 26:1 4:2005 pp.44-61.

4380 GCC-EU political cooperation: myth or reality? Henner Fürtig. **Br. J. Mid. East. S.** 31:1 5:2004 pp.25-39.

4381 Die Gemeinsame Handelspolitik der Europäischen Union im EU-Verfassungsvertrag: Fortschritte mit einigen neuen Fragezeichen. *[In German]*; [The European Union Common Trade Policy and the constitutional treaty: progress and some new questions]. Jörg Monar. **Aussenwirtschaft** 60:1 3:2005 pp.99-117.

4382 The geopolitical implications of the European Neighbourhood Policy. Roberto Aliboni. **Euro. For. Aff. R.** 10:1 Spring:2005 pp.1-16.

4383 Interinstitutional agreements in the CFSP: parliamentarization through the back door? Andreas Maurer; Daniela Kietz; Christian Völkel. **Euro. For. Aff. R.** 10:2 Summer:2005 pp.175-195.

4384 Maintaining security within borders: toward a permanent state of emergency in the EU? Joanna Apap; Sergio Carrera. **Alternatives** 29:4 8-10:2004 pp.399-416.

4385 La Méditerranée au prisme du nouveau panorama stratégique. *[In French]*; [The Mediterranean Region in the new strategic situation]. Jean-François Daguzan. **Défense Nat.** 60:5 5:2004 pp.101-113.

4386 Les modes d'action extérieure de l'Union européenne : le cas du Caucase du Sud. *[In French]*; [The European system of external action: the case of Southern Caucasus] *[Summary]*. Damien Helly. **R. Fran. Sci. Pol.** 55:2 4:2005 pp.243-268.

4387 Norm-maker and norm-taker: exploring the normative influence of the EU in Macedonia. Annika Björkdahl. **Euro. For. Aff. R.** 10:2 Summer:2005 pp.257-278.

4388 Un partenariat entre l'union et les NEIO : transition en vue de l'intégration ou intégration pour la transition? Quelques données propres à l'Ukraine. *[In French]*; (A partnership between the European Union and the NWIS: transition for integration or integration for transition? A few facts about Ukraine.) Vitaliy Denysyuk. **R. Mar. Comm.** 487 4:2005 pp.220-231.

4389 Préfets d'Europe : le rôle des délégations de la commission dans les pays ACP (1964-2004). *[In French]*; [European prefects: the role of commission delegations in ACP countries (1964-2004).] Véronique Dimier. **R. Fran. Admin. Publ.** 111 2004 pp.433-445.

4390 Quelle politique européenne pour les Balkans de l'Ouest ? *[In French]*; [What European policy for the western Balkans?] Nadège Ragaru. **Polit. Int.** 105 Autumn:2004 pp.195-213.

4391 Reflections from the new near outside: an Israeli perspective on the economic and legal impact of EU enlargement. Alfred Tovias; Amichai Magen. **Euro. For. Aff. R.** 10:3 Autumn:2005 pp.399-425.

4392 Rethinking European Union foreign policy. Thomas Christiansen [Ed.]; Ben Tonra [Ed.]. Manchester: Manchester University Press, 2004. 175p. *ISBN: 071906001X, 0719060028.* (*Series:* Europe in change).

4393   A riddle inside an enigma: unwrapping the EU-Russia strategic partnership. Fabrizio Tassinari. **Int. Spect.** XL:1 1-3:2005 pp.45-57.

4394   The security challenge of small EU member states: interests, identity and the development of the EU as a security actor. Anders Wivel. **J. Com. Mkt. S.** 43:2 6:2005 pp.393-412.

4395   The security dimension of the European Neighbourhood Policy. Dov Lynch. **Int. Spect.** XL:1 1-3:2005 pp.33-43.

4396   Security, immigration and development assistance: an integrated approach. Renato Brunetta; Giovanni Tria; Antonio Preto. **R. Econ. Cond. It.** 3 9-12:2004 pp.337-361.

4397   Struktura społeczno-gospodarcza obszarów problemowych w Unii Europejskiej i Polsce w świetle unijnej polityki regionalnej. *[In Polish]*; (Socio-economic structure of problem areas in the European Union and Poland in the light of EU regional policy.) *[Summary]*. P. Churski. **Prz. Geog.** 76:2 2004 pp.189-208.

4398   A three-phase plan for the European external action service. Andreas Maurer; Sarah Reichel. **Int. Spect.** XL:1 1-3:2005 pp.77-89.

4399   Trading voices: the European Union in international commercial negotiations. Sophie Meunier. Princeton NJ: Princeton University Press, 2005. xiii, 223p. *ISBN: 069112115X. Includes bibliographical references (p. 201-213) and index.*

4400   A transnational political culture? The Alpine region and its relationship to European integration. Daniele Caramani; Claudius Wagemann. **Ger. Pol.** 14:1 3:2005 pp.74-94.

4401   L'Ukraine et l'Europe: l'histoire reprend. *[In French]*; [Ukraine and Europe: history begins again]. Grygoriy Nemyria. **Esprit** 312 2:2005 pp.52-64.

4402   L'Union dans les relations internationales : du "soft power" à la puissance. *[In French]*; [The Union in internaitonal relations: from 'soft power' to power]. Franck Petiteville. **Quest. Int.** 7 5-6:2004 pp.63-72.

4403   Where is the analysis of European foreign policy going? Walter Carlsnaes. **Euro. Uni. Pol.** 5:4 12:2004 pp.495-512.

4404   Wspólnotowość polityki zagranicznej Unii Europejskiej. *[In Polish]*; (The communal character of EU foreign policy.) *[Summary]*. Teresa Łoś-Nowak. **Prz. Euro.** 1(8) 2004 pp.7-25.

4405   The WTO and the regulation of international trade: recent trade disputes between the European Union and the United States. Nicholas Perdikis [Ed.]; Robert Read [Ed.]. Cheltenham: Edward Elgar Publishing, 2005. xvii, 295p. *ISBN: 1843762005. Includes bibliographical references and index.*

Institutions and governance
Institutions et gouvernance

4406   Banca centrale e sviluppi della governance europea. *[In Italian]*; [Central Bank and the developments of European governance]. Lorenzo Chieffi. **Rass. Parl.** XLVII:1 1-3:2005 pp.117-151.

4407   'Charardius alexandrinus', experts and the European Union. Tomaz Boh. **Cent. Euro. Pol. Sci. R.** 5:15 Spring:2004 pp.115-135.

4408   Claims to legitimacy: the European Commission between continuity and change. Myrto Tsakatika. **J. Com. Mkt. S.** 43:1 3:2005 pp.193-220.

4409   Comité des régions, vers une troisième chambre? *[In French]*; [Committee of the Regions, towards a third chamber?]; *[Summary in English]*. Radu Barna. **S. UBB: Stu. Eur.** XLIX: 1-2 2004 pp.143-158.

4410   The Committee of the Regions and subnational representation to the European Union. Tony Cole. **Maastricht J. Euro. Comp. Law** 12:1 2005 pp.49-72.

4411   Compliance, competition and communication. Christoph Knill; Andrea Lenschow. **J. Com. Mkt. S.** 43:3 9:2005 pp.583-606.

4412   Conclusions. Claudio M. Radaelli; Vivien A. Schmidt. **West Euro. Pol.** 27:2 3:2004 pp.364-379.

4413   The contested Council: conflict dimensions of an intergovernmental EU institution. Christina Zimmer; Gerald Schneider; Michael Dobbins. **Pol. S.** 53:2 6:2005 pp.403-422.

4414   Coordinated European governance: self-organizing or centrally steered? Adriaan Schout; Andrew Jordan. **Publ. Admin.** 83:1 2005 pp.201-220.

4415   A critical juncture? The 2004 European elections and the making of a supranational elite. Luca Verzichelli; Michael Edinger. **J. Legis. St.** 11:2 Summer:2005 pp.254-274.

4416   Domesticated eurocrats: bureaucratic discretion in the legislative pre-negotiations of the European Union. Gerald Schneider; Konstantin Baltz. **Acta Pol.** 40:1 4:2005 pp.1-27.

4417   Electing the European Parliament: how uniform are 'uniform' electoral systems? David M. Farrell; Roger Scully. **J. Com. Mkt. S.** 43:5 12:2005 pp.969-984.

4418   Az EU alkotmányozó kormányközi konferenciájának első szakasza. *[In Hungarian]*; (The European Union's intergovernmental conference on the future EU constitution.) *[Summary]*. Árpád Gordos; Bálint Ódor. **Euro. Tükör** 9:1 2004 pp.3-17.

4419   The EU foreign minister: beyond double-hatting. Giovanni Grevi; Daniela Manca; Gerrard Quille. **Int. Spect.** XL:1 1-3:2005 pp.59-75.

4420   EU institutions and the transformation of European-level politics: how to understand profound change (if it occurs). Morten Egeberg. **Comp. Euro. Pol.** 3:1 4:2005 pp.102-117.

4421   Az Európai Parlament. *[In Hungarian]*; (The European Parliament.) Zoltán Horváth; Gábor Tar. Budapest: Magyar Országgyűlés, 2004. 210p. *ISBN: 9632160142. Includes bibliographical references (p. 203-206).*

4422   Európai Parlament – egy különleges transznacionális szervezet. *[In Hungarian]*; (European Parliament – a unique transnational organisation.) *[Summary]*. Ágnes Laczkóné Tuka. **Politik. Szem.** 13:1-2 2004 pp.49-66.

4423   Európai parlamenti választások – Magyarország debütál. *[In Hungarian]*; (European parliamentary elections – Hungary makes its debut.) *[Summary]*. Márta Dezső. **Euro. Tükör** 9:3 2004 pp.106-116.

4424   Az Európai Unió 2004. évi költségvetése és a költségvetés elfogadásához vezető eljárás fontosabb lépései. *[In Hungarian]*; (The European Union's budget for 2004 and the major steps leading to its adoption.) *[Summary]*. Krisztián Kovács. **Euro. Tükör** 9:1 2004 pp.190-201.

4425   Der Europäische Rechnungshof: Institution, Funktion und politische Wirkung. *[In German]*; [The European Court of Auditors: institution, function and political impact]. Michael Freytag. Baden-Baden: Nomos, 2005. 291p. *ISBN: 3832907688.*

4426   Europe inside out. Robin Niblett. **Washington Q.** 29:1 Winter:2005-2006 pp.41-59.

4427   The European central bank: between growth and stability. L.S. Talani. **Comp. Euro. Pol.** 3:2 7:2005 pp.204-231.

4428   The European Parliament elections of June 2004: still second-order? Hermann Schmitt. **West Euro. Pol.** 28:3 5:2005 pp.650-679.

4429   Evropské politické strany a návrh evropské ústavy komparace postojů Evropské lidové strany a strany evropských socialistů a jejich vlivu na proces přípravy návrhu ústavní smlouvy Evropské unie. *[In Czech]*; (European political parties and project of European constitution comparison of attitudes of the European People's Party and the Party of European Socialists and their effect on the process of preparation of European constitution.) *[Summary]*. Petr Fiala; Petr Kaniok; Markéta Pitrová. **Mez. Vzt.** 39:4 2004 pp.5-22.

4430   Explaining the absence of inertia in European Union legislative decision-making. Torsten J. Selck. **J. Com. Mkt. S.** 43:5 12:2005 pp.1055-1070.

4431   Il fondo sociale Europeo e la programmazione delle politiche formative in Italia. *[In Italian]*; [European Social Fund and formative policies in Italy] *[Summary]*. Alessandra De Lellis; Paolo Severati; Stefano Volpi. **Riv. It. Pol. Pub.** 1 4:2004 pp.119-139.

4432   'Governance': agreement and divergence in responses to the EU white paper. Adrian Reilly. **Reg. Fed. S.** 14:1 Spring:2004 pp.136-156.

4433   Governance and institutions: a new constitution and a new commission. Desmond Dinan. **J. Com. Mkt. S.** 43:Annual Review 2005 pp.37-54.

4434 Government-opposition dynamics in the European Union: the Santer commission resignation crisis. N. Ringe. **Écon. Sociét.** 44:5 8:2005 pp.671-696.

4435 Green political theory and the European Union: the case for a non-integrated civil society. Christian Hunold. **Env. Pol.** 14:3 6:2005 pp.324-343.

4436 Größer, weiter, schwächer: Warum die EU einen "harten Kern" braucht. *[In German]*; [Bigger, further, weaker: why the EU needs a 'hard core']. Winfried Veit. **Int. Pol. Gesell.** 2 2005 pp.130-149.

4437 How costs and benefits shape the policy influence of the EP. Charlotte Burns. **J. Com. Mkt. S.** 43:3 9:2005 pp.485-506.

4438 How nation states 'hit' Europe: ambiguity and representation in the European Union. Jan Beyers; Jarle Trondal. **West Euro. Pol.** 27:5 11:2004 pp.919-942.

4439 How the EU constructs the European public sphere: seven strategies of information policy. Michael Brüggemann. **Javnost** XII:2 6:2005 pp.57-73.

4440 Institutionalisierung und Professionalisierung des europäischen Lobbyismus. *[In German]*; (Institutionalization and professionalization of European lobbyism.) *[Summary]*. Christian Lahusen. **Z. Parlament.** 35:4 12:2004 pp.777-794.

4441 Kontinuität oder Pfadsprung? Das institutionelle Dreieck in Europa nach dem Verfassungsvertrag. *[In German]*; (Continuity or path-leap? The institutional triangle in Europe after the constitutional treaty.) Marcus Höreth. **Z. Pol.wissen.** 14:4 2004 pp.1257-1296.

4442 Kooperation oder Konfrontation? Das Verhältnis zwischen Bundesverfassungsgericht und Europäischem Gerichtshof für Menschenrechte. *[In German]*; [The relationship between the Federal Constitutional Court and the European Court of Human Rights]. Stefan Mückl. **Der Staat** 44:3 2005 pp.403-432.

4443 Learning from abroad: regionalization and local institutional infrastructure in cohesion and accession countries. Christos J. Paraskevopoulos; Robert Leonardi; Panayiotis Getimis; Leeda Demetropoulou; Nicholas Rees; Brid Quinn; Bernadette Connaughton; Raffaella Y. Nanetti; Helena Rato; Miguel Rodrigues; Pálné Kovács Ilona; Gyula Horváth; Malgorzata Czernielewska; Jacek Szlachta. **Reg. Fed. S.** 14:3 Autumn:2004 pp.315-495. *Collection of 6 articles.*

4444 Linearität oder Komplexität? Zur Problematik der Theorie von Mehrebenensystemen am Beispiel der Europäischen Union. *[In German]*; [Linearity or complexity? On the theory of multi-level governance in the European Union] *[Summary]*. P. Bußjäger. **Z. Öffent. Recht** 60:2 2005 pp.237-262.

4445 Mapping out political Europe: coalition patterns in EU decision-making. Michael Kaeding; Torsten J. Selck. **Int. Pol. Sci. R.** 26:3 7:2005 pp.271-290.

4446 Modes de scrutin et circonscription unique européenne. *[In French]*; [Electoral system and unique European electoral ward]. Christophe Broquet. **Européens** 2004 pp.197-208.

4447 Monomaniacs or schizophrenics? Responsible governance and the EU's independent agencies. Garrath Williams. **Pol. S.** 53:1 3:2005 pp.82-99.

4448 National parties in the European Parliament: an influence in the committee system? Richard Whitaker. **Euro. Uni. Pol.** 6:1 3:2005 pp.5-28.

4449 Neither a preference-outlier nor a unitary actor: institutional reform preferences of the European Parliament. Simon Hix. **Comp. Euro. Pol.** 3:2 7:2005 pp.131-154.

4450 El nuevo marco institucional de la UE ampliada. *[In Spanish]*; [New institutional framework of the EU enlarged] *[Summary]*. Jean-Victor Louis. **Pap. Econ. Esp.** 103 2005 pp.53-66.

4451 Policy transfer in the European Union: an institutionalist perspective. Simon Bulmer; Stephen Padgett. **Br. J. Pol. Sci.** 35:1 1:2005 pp.103-126.

4452 Power analysis of the Nice treaty on the future of European integration. Y. Kandogan. **Appl. Econ.** 37:10 6:2005 pp.1147-1156.

4453 The power of institutions: state and interest group activity in the European Union. Christine Mahoney. **Euro. Uni. Pol.** 5:4 12:2004 pp.441-466.

4454 Power to the parties: cohesion and competition in the European Parliament, 1979-2001. Simon Hix; Abdul Noury; Gérard Roland. **Br. J. Pol. Sci.** 35:2 4:2005 pp.209-234.

4455   Regards croisés dans les vingt-cinq pays de l'Union Européenne. *[In French]*; [The twenty-five countries of the European Union]. Christine Pina; Sonia Tebbakh. **R. Pol. Parl.** 106:1031 7-9:2004 pp.29-40.

4456   Regulating europarties: cross-party coalitions capitalizing on incomplete contracts. Karl Magnus Johansson; Tapio Raunio. **Party Pol.** 11:5 2005 pp.515-534.

4457   The role of the institutions in the struggle for Europe. Francesco Rossolillo. **Federalist** XLVII:1 2005 pp.45-57.

4458   Spór o Niceę. Podejmowanie decyzji w radzie Unii Europejskiej. *[In Polish]*; (Controversy over Nice. Decision-making in the European Union's Council.) *[Summary]*. Kazimierz Jóskowiak. **Prz. Euro.** 1(8) 2004 pp.55-74.

4459   Technical or political? The working groups of the EU Council of Ministers. Eves Fouilleux; Jacques de Maillard; Andy Smith. **J. Euro. Publ. Policy** 12:4 2005 pp.609-623.

4460   The theory and practice of global and regional governance: accommodating American exceptionalism and European pluralism. Richard Higgott. **Euro. For. Aff. R.** 10:4 Winter:2005 pp.575-594.

4461   Transparency and the EU legislator. Pierpaolo Settembri. **J. Com. Mkt. S.** 43:3 9:2005 pp.637-654.

4462   Voting against spending cuts: the electoral costs of fiscal adjustments in Europe. Carlos Mulas-Granados. **Euro. Uni. Pol.** 5:4 12:2004 pp.467-493.

4463   The wall and Maastricht: exogenous shocks and the initiation of the EMU and EPU IGCs. Paul D. Poast. **J. Euro. Integ.** 26:3 9:2004 pp.281-307.

4464   What does the European Union do? A. Alesina; I. Angeloni; L. Schuknecht. **Publ. Choice** 123:3-4 6:2005 pp.275-320.

4465   The world of committee reports: rapporteurship assignment in the European Parliament. Michael Kaeding. **J. Legis. St.** 11:1 Spring:2005 pp.82-104.

4466   Der Zugang von Interessengruppen zu den Organen der Europäischen Union: eine organisationstheoretische Analyse. *[In German]*; (The access of interest groups to EU institutions.) *[Summary]*. Rainer Eising. **Polit. Viertel.** 45:4 12:2004 pp.494-518.

Internal policies
Politique intérieure

4467   Agir par mimétisme : la Commission européenne et sa politique d'éducation. *[In French]*; [To act through mimicry: the European Commission and its education policy] *[Summary]*. Isabelle Petit. **Can. J. Pol.** 38:3 9:2005 pp.627-652.

4468   L'agriculture, pomme de discorde entre l'Union européenne et les Etats-Unis. *[In French]*; [Agriculture as a source of conflict between the EU and the US]; *[Summary in French]*. Yves Petit. **R. Trim. Droit Euro.** 40:4 10-12:2004 pp.599-620.

4469   Assuming leadership in multilateral economic institutions: the EU's 'development round' discourse and strategy. Adrian van den Hoven. **West Euro. Pol.** 27:2 3:2004 pp.256-283.

4470   Between facts, norms and a post-national constellation: Habermas, law and European social policy. Mark Murphy. **J. Euro. Publ. Policy** 12:1 2005 pp.143-156.

4471   Cohesion policy in the European Union: the building of Europe. Robert Leonardi. New York: Palgrave Macmillan, 2005. xii, 211p. *ISBN: 1403949557. Includes bibliographical references and index.*

4472   Competence allocation in the EU competition policy system as an interest-driven process. Oliver Budzinski; Andt Christiansen. **J. Publ. Policy** 25:3 9-12:2005 pp.313-337.

4473   Constitutional asymmetry and pharmaceutical policy-making in the European Union. Govin Permanand; Elias Mossialos. **J. Euro. Publ. Policy** 12:4 2005 pp.687-709.

4474   Converging divergence: how competitive advantages condition institutional change under EMU. Andrea Herrmann. **J. Com. Mkt. S.** 43:2 6:2005 pp.287-310.

4475   "Detention" von Flüchtlingen, Asylbewerbern und Migranten in Europa. Überlegungen aus ethischer Sicht. *[In German]*; [The detention of refugees, asylum seekers and migrants in

Europe. Considerations from an ethical perspective]. Markus Babo. **AWR B.** 42(51):4 2004 pp.47-57.

4476   The development of rights-based social policy in the European Union: the example of disability rights. Deborah Mabbett. **J. Com. Mkt. S.** 43:1 3:2005 pp.97-120.

4477   Economic policy in the European Union. Sixten Korkman. Basingstoke, New York: Palgrave Macmillan, 2005. xvi, 214p. *ISBN: 1403943443. Includes bibliographical references and index.*

4478   EU homeland security: citizens or suspects? Juliet Lodge. **J. Euro. Integ.** 26:3 9:2004 pp.253-280.

4479   L'euro : ambitions et défis. *[In French]*; [The euro: ambitions and challenges]. Christian de Boissieu. **Quest. Int.** 7 5-6:2004 pp.47-58.

4480   Az Európai Unió fejlesztési forrásai. *[In Hungarian]*; (The development sources of the European Union.) Gábor Iván. Budapest: Magyar Közigazgatási Intézet, 2004. 112p. *ISBN: 9639395137.*

4481   Az Európai Unió környezetvédelmi szabályozása. *[In Hungarian]*; (The Environment Protection Regulation of the European Union.) Zsuzsanna Horváth; Gyula Bándi; György Erdey; István Pomázi. Budapest: KJK-Kerszöv Kft, 2004. 691p. *ISBN: 9632247906. Includes bibliographical references.*

4482   Europäische Regionalpolitik — Gift für rückständige Regionen? *[In German]*; [European regional policy –poison for less developed regions?] Norbert Berthold; Michael Neumann. **Vier. Wirt.forsch.** 74:1 2005 pp.47-65.

4483   Europäische Regionalpolitik nach der EU-Osterweiterung: Neue Ausrichtung erforderlich? *[In German]*; [European regional policy after the enlargement: adjustment necessary?] Martin T.W. Rosenfeld. **Vier. Wirt.forsch.** 74:1 2005 pp.111-125.

4484   Europäischer Grundrechtsschutz nach dem Verfassungsvertrag. *[In German]*; [Protection of fundamental rights in Europe after the constitutional contract] *[Summary]*. Rolf Schwartmann. **A. Völk.** 43:1 3:2005 pp.129-152.

4485   European asylum policy. Timothy J. Hatton. **National Inst. Econ. R.** 194 10:2005 pp.106-119.

4486   The European employment strategy: which way forward? Saskia Klosse. **Int. J. Comp. Lab. Law** 21:1 Spring:2005 pp.5-36.

4487   European immigration policies in comparative perspective: issue salience, partisanship and immigrant rights. Terri Givens; Adam Luedtke. **Comp. Euro. Pol.** 3:1 4:2005 pp.1-22.

4488   Europe's area of freedom, security, and justice. Neil C. Walker [Ed.]. Oxford: Oxford University Press, 2004. xl, 289p. *ISBN: 0199274649, 0199274657. Includes bibliographical references and index. (Series: Collected courses of the Academy of European Law).*

4489   Evaluation et avenir des programmes communautaires. *[In French]*; [Evaluation and future of EU programmes]. Marc Dusautoy. **Cah. Euro. Sorbonne Nouv.** 4 12:2004 pp.11-139.

4490   Evropeiskii Ekonomicheskii i valiutnyi soiuz: predvaritel'nye itogi i perspektiviy razvitiia. *[In Russian]*; (European Economic and Monetary Union: preliminary results and prospects.) V. Gutnik. **Mir. Ekon. Mezh. Ot.** 5 5:2005 pp.3-15.

4491   Explaining EMU reform. Shawn Donnelly. **J. Com. Mkt. S.** 43:5 12:2005 pp.947-968.

4492   Faut-il revoir la politique européenne de l'immigration ? *[In French]*; [Does the European immigration policy need reviewing?] *[Summary]*. Catherine Wihtol de Wenden. **Historiens Géographes** 96:385 1:2004 pp.113-126.

4493   Fisheries science and sustainability in international policy: a study of failure in the European Union's common fisheries policy. Tim Daw; Tim Gray. **Marine Policy** 29:3 5:2005 pp.189-197.

4494   Globalization and European integration: the changing role of farmers in the Common Agricultural Policy. Marjoleine Hennis. Lanham MD: Rowman & Littlefield, 2005. xiii, 223p. *ISBN: 0742518892. Includes bibliographical references (p. 199-216) and index.*

4495   Grundlagen der EU-Regionalpolitik und Ansätze zu ihrer Weiterentwicklung. *[In German]*; [Basis for the EU regional policy and approaches for its development]. Christian Weise. **Vier. Wirt.forsch.** 74:1 2005 pp.74-90.

4496   Hard and soft law in the construction of social Europe: the role of the open method of co-ordination. David M. Trubek; Louise G. Trubek. **Euro. Law J.** 11:3 5:2005 pp.343-364.

4497   Immigration und nationale Sicherheit in der EU und den USA: Die Demontage des Flüchtlingsrechts. *[In German]*; [Immigration and national security in the EU and the USA: the deconstruction of the rights of refugees]. Barbara Franz. **AWR B.** 42(51):4 2004 pp.58-71.

4498   Innovation through the European Social Fund. European Commission. Luxembourg: Office for Official Publications of the European Communities, 2004. 107p. *ISBN: 9289461101*. (*Series:* Employment & social affairs).

4499   Internal policy developments. David Howarth. **J. Com. Mkt. S.** 43:Annual Review 2005 pp.63-84.

4500   Liberal, conservative, social democratic, or … European? The European Union as equal employment regime. Angelika von Wahl. **Soc. Pol.** 12:1 Spring:2005 pp.67-95.

4501   The limited modesty of subsidiarity. N.W. Barber. **Euro. Law J.** 11:3 5:2005 pp.308-325.

4502   Migrations en Europe: les frontières de la liberté. *[In French]*; [Migration in Europe: borders of freedom]. Multitudes. **Multitudes** 19 12:2004 pp.9-118.

4503   Missing the Lisbon target? Multi-level innovation and EU policy coordination. Robert Kaiser; Heiko Prange. **J. Publ. Policy** 25:2 5-8:2005 pp.241-263.

4504   Model otvorene koordinacije protiv siromaštva: Novi "proces socijalnog uključivanja" Europske unije. *[In Croatian]*; (Open co-ordination against poverty: the new 'social inclusion process' of the European Union.) Maurizio Ferrera; Manos Matsaganis; Stefano Sacchi. **Revija Soc. Pol.** 11:3-4 7-12:2004 pp.395-409.

4505   National filters: europeanisation, institutions, and discourse in the case of banking regulation. Andreas Busch. **West Euro. Pol.** 27:2 3:2004 pp.310-333.

4506   Die Neue Ökonomische Geographie und Effizienzgründe für Regionalpolitik. *[In German]*; [The new economic geography and efficiency reasons for regional policy]. Michael Pflüger; Jens Südekum. **Vier. Wirt.forsch.** 74:1 2005 pp.26-46.

4507   La nouvelle politique régionale européenne — mécanismes, acteurs et objectifs d'une réforme complexe. *[In French]*; (New European regional policy: mechanisms, actors, and objectives of a complex reform.) Francesco Gaeta. **R. Fran. Admin. Publ.** 111 2004 pp.447-459.

4508   Peer review of labour market programmes in the European Union: what can countries really learn from one another? Bernard H. Casey; Michael Gold. **J. Euro. Publ. Policy** 12:1 2005 pp.23-43.

4509   Policy benchmarking in the European Union: indicators and ambiguities. Graham Room. **Policy S.** 26:2 6:2005 pp.117-132.

4510   La Politique Agricole Commune dans le commerce mondial des produits agro-alimentaires. *[In French]*; [The Common Agricultural Policy in the world trade of agrofood products]. Gabrielle Rochdi. **R. Trim. Droit Euro.** 41:1 1-3:2005 pp.37-59.

4511   Principals, agents, and the implementation of EU cohesion policy. Jens Blom-Hansen. **J. Euro. Publ. Policy** 12:4 2005 pp.624-648.

4512   Promoting core labour standards and improving social governance in the context of globalization. EU Commission. **Bull. Comp. Lab. Rel.** 55 2005 pp.55-78.

4513   Die rechtliche Stellung des Katalanischen in der EU. *[In German]*; [The legal status of the Catalan language in the EU]. Klaus Ebner. **Euro. Ethn.** 62:1-2 2005 pp.23-32.

4514   Regulating the European labour market: prospects and limitations of a reflexive governance approach. Richard Hobbs; Wanjiru Njoya. **Br. J. Ind. Rel.** 43:2 6:2005 pp.297-319.

4515   A stabilitási és növekedési paktum kérdőjelei. *[In Hungarian]*; (Question marks surrounding the Stability and Growth Pact.) *[Summary]*. Miklós Losoncz. **Euro. Tükör** 9:2 2004 pp.61-78.

4516   The Stability and Growth Pact — theorizing a case in European integration. Martin Heipertz; Amy Verdun. **J. Com. Mkt. S.** 43:5 12:2005 pp.985-1008.

4517   Standortwettbewerb, Einkommenskonvergenz und Reformdruck in der erweiterten Europäischen Union. *[In German]*; (Location competition, convergence of income and pressure for reforms in the enlarged EU.) *[Summary]*. Ognian N. Hishow. **Osteuro. Wirt.** 49:3 9:2004 pp.247-264.

4518   La stratégie européenne pour l'emploi : genèse, coordination communautaire et diversité nationale. *[In French]*; [European employment strategy: genesis, community coordination and national diversity]. Jean-Claude Barbier; Sylla Ndongo Samba. **Rapp. Rech. Centre d'études de l'emploi** 16 10:2004 pp.7-104.

4519   The study of EU public policy: results of a survey. Fabio Franchino. **Euro. Uni. Pol.** 6:2 6:2005 pp.243-252.

4520   Trente ans d'un régime temporaire. Les quotas laitiers dans la PAC : 1984-2014. *[In French]*; (Thirty years of a temporary regim: milk quotas in the CAP: 1984-2014.) Daniel Bianchi. **R. Mar. Comm.** 483 12:2004 pp.655-673.

4521   La Unión y la política monetarias en la "nueva Europa". *[In Spanish]*; (The Union and monetary policy in the 'New Europe'.) *[Summary]*. Ma. Carmen López Martín; Adolfo Rodero Franganillo. **R. Foment. Soc.** 59:236 10-12:2004 pp.773-799.

4522   Variation in dual citizenship policies in the countries of the EU. Marc Morjé Howard. **Int. Migr. R.** 39:3 Fall:2005 pp.697-720.

4523   Why are Europeans so tough on migrants? Tito Boeri; Herbert Brücker; Pierre-Olivier Gourinchas [Discussant]; Pierre Cahuc [Discussant]. **Econ. Policy** 44 10:2005 pp.629-704.

4524   Winners and losers in europeanisation: reforming the national regulation of telecommunications. Mark Thatcher. **West Euro. Pol.** 27:2 3:2004 pp.284-309.

4525   Zur Reform der EU-Agrarpolitik: Umbau statt Abbau von Subventionen. *[In German]*; [On the EU agricultural policy reform: modifications instead of cutbacks in subsidies]. Jörg Volker Schrader. **Z. Wirt.pol.** 54:1 2005 pp.115-132.

Law and jurisdiction
Droit et juridiction

4526   The acquis of the European Union and international organisations. Loïc Azoulai. **Euro. Law J.** 11:2 2005 pp.196-231.

4527   L'application du droit communautaire par les juridictions britanniques (2003-2004). *[In French]*; [Community law implementation by the British jurisdictions (2003-2004)]. Emmanuelle Saulnier-Cassia; d'Angela Ward. **R. Trim. Droit Euro.** 41:1 1-3:2005 pp.105-129.

4528   Avrupa anayasallaşma sürecinde primer hukukta normlar hiyerarşisi. *[In Turkish]*; (Hierarchy of norms in the Primary Law during the European contitutionalisation process.) Füsun Arsava. **Uluslararasi Ilişkiler** 1:2 Spring:2004 pp.1-24.

4529   Bezpośredni skutek dyrektywy w postępowaniu przed sądem krajowym (uwagi na tle najnowszego orzecznictwa). *[In Polish]*; (Direct effects of directives in proceedings before a national court.) Maciej Szpunar. **Pań. Prawo** LIX:9(703) 9:2004 pp.56-69.

4530   Civil jurisdiction and enforcement of judgments in Europe. P. Vlas; M. Zilinsky; F. Ibili. **Neth. Int. Law R.** LII:1 2005 pp.109-129.

4531   Conflit de lois et conflit de juridictions en matière de coopération transfrontalière. *[In French]*; [Law and jurisdiction conflicts in trans-frontier cooperation]. Mathias Audit. **Ann. Droit Louvain** 64:3 2004 pp.481-515.

4532   Le Conseil constitutionnel aux prises avec la Constitution européenne. *[In French]*; [The Constitutional Council and the European constitution]. Anne Levade. **R. Droit Publ.** 1 1-2:2005 pp.19-50.

4533   Le Conseil constitutionnel français et les directives communautaires : l'incompétence du juge suprême comme garantie de l'inopposabilité de la Constitution au droit communautaire. *[In French]*; [The French constitutional council and community directives: incompetence of the supreme judge as guarantor of the inopposability of the constitution to the community legislation]. Pierre-Yves Monjal. **R. Droit Union Euro.** 3 2004 pp.509-522.

4534   Constitutional debates on parliamentary inviolability in Turkey. Ergun Özbudun. **Euro. Constitutional Law R.** 1:2 2005 pp.272-326.

4535   Constitutional questions concerning the European integration, with special regard to Hungary's accession. Olga Borbála Molnár. **Acta Jur. Hun.** 45:1-2 2004 pp.171-192.

4536   Constitutionalizing government in the European Union: Europe's new institutional quartet under the treaty establishing a constitution for Europe. Markus G. Puder. **Columbia J. Euro. Law** 11:1 Winter:2004-2005 pp.77-111.

4537   Culture and European Union law. Rachael Craufurd Smith [Ed.]. Oxford, New York: Oxford University Press, 2004. xlii, 414p. *ISBN: 0199275475. Includes bibliographical references and index. (Series:* Oxford studies in European law).

4538   Deliberative constitutional politics. Carlos Closa; John Erik Fossum; Agustín José Menéndez; Paul Magnette; Ben Crum. **Euro. Law J.** 11:4 7:2005 pp.379-467. *Collection of 5 articles.*

4539   La dimensione autoritativa del diritto amministrativo europeo: i poteri ispettivi in materia di tutela della concorrenza. *[In Italian]*; [Jurisdiction of the European Administrative Law: the protection of the competition]. Alessandro Tonetti. **Riv. Trim. Pubbl.** 1 2005 pp.83-129.

4540   The effect of human rights on criminal evidentiary processes: towards convergence, divergence or realignment? John D. Jackson. **Mod. Law R.** 68:5 9:2005 pp.737-764.

4541   Effektiver Individualrechtsschutz im Gemeinschaftsrecht. *[In German]*; [Effective legal protection of individuals in community law]. Peter Baumeister. **Europarecht** 40:1 1-2:2005 pp.1-35.

4542   L'émergence des instruments juridiques de la coopération transfrontière au sein du Conseil de l'Europe. *[In French]*; [Emerging juridical instruments for trans-frontier cooperation within the Council of Europe]. Nicolas Levrat. **Ann. Droit Louvain** 64:3 2004 pp.365-382.

4543   Europäisches Sprachenverfassungsrecht. *[In German]*; [European constitutional law on language]. Franz C. Mayer. **Der Staat** 44:3 2005 pp.367-402.

4544   The European Convention and mental health law in England and Wales: moving beyond process? G. Richardson. **Int. J. Law Psych.** 28:2 3-4:2005 pp.127-139.

4545   European criminal law. André Klip; Joachim Vogel; Anne Weyembergh; Kai Ambos. **Maastricht J. Euro. Comp. Law** 12:2 2005 p. *Collection of 4 articles.*

4546   The European Union and the systematic dismantling of the common law of conflict of laws. Trevor C. Hartley. **Int. Comp. Law Q.** 54:4 10:2005 pp.813-828.

4547   L'européanisation des administrations : nouvelles missions, nouveaux partenaires. *[In French]*; [Europeanization of administrations: new mandates, new partners]. Jacques Ziller; Valérie Michel; Eva Storskrubb; Nicole Belloubet-Frier; Lene Holm Pedersen; Eva Moll Sørensen; Stefanie Tragl; Károly Mike; Edward Warrington; Ben Morris; Hans Lühmann. **R. Fran. Admin. Publ.** 114 2005 pp.213-334. *Collection of 10 articles.*

4548   Evropa soudců a Evropa politiků vliv ESD na vývoj evropské integrace. *[In Czech]*; (Europe of judges and Europe of statesmans impact of ECJ on development of the European integration.) *[Summary]*. Ivo Šlosarčík. **Mez. Vzt.** 40:1 2005 pp.22-47.

4549   A formal model of delegation in the European Union. Fabio Franchino. **J. Theor. Pol.** 17:2 4:2005 pp.217-247.

4550   Free movement, equal treatment, and citizenship of the Union. Robin C.A. White. **Int. Comp. Law Q.** 54:4 10:2005 pp.885-905.

4551   The future of Europe: judicial interference and preferences. Marie-Pierre Granger. **Comp. Euro. Pol.** 3:2 7:2005 pp.155-179.

4552   The genesis of European rights. Willem Maas. **J. Com. Mkt. S.** 43:5 12:2005 pp.1009-1026.

4553   Governing the body: examining EU regulatory developments in relation to substances of human origin. Joanne Hunt [Ed.]; Chloë J. Wallace [Ed.]. **J. Soc. Welf. Fam. Law** 27:3-4 12:2005 pp.427-437.

4554   Is the single European market an illusion? Obstacles to reform of EU takeover regulation. Jette Steen Knudsen. **Euro. Law J.** 11:4 7:2005 pp.507-524.

4555 The jurisprudence of constitutional conflict: constitutional supremacy in Europe before and after the constitutional treaty. Mattias Kumm. **Euro. Law J.** 11:3 5:2005 pp.262-307.

4556 Legal integration and use of the preliminary ruling process in the European Union. Clifford J. Carrubbo; Lacey Murrah. **Int. Org.** 59:2 Spring:2005 pp.399-418.

4557 Le livre vert de la Commission européenne. *[In French]*; [The green book of the European Commission]. Delphine Derobugny. **R. Trim. Droit Euro.** 41:1 1-3:2005 pp.81-104.

4558 Looking for coherence within the European community. Stefano Bertea. **Euro. Law J.** 11:2 2005 pp.154-172.

4559 Merger control in the European Union: law, economics and practice. Edurne Navarro Varona; et al. Oxford, New York: Oxford University Press, 2005. lix, 682p. *ISBN: 0199276056. Includes bibliographical references and index.*

4560 National constitutional concepts in the new constitution for Europe (part one). Jacques Ziller. **Euro. Constitutional Law R.** 1:2 2005 pp.247-271.

4561 La nature juridique des organismes de coopération transfrontalière entre autorités régionales ou locales. *[In French]*; [The juridical nature of trans-frontier cooperation bodies between regional or local authorities]. Yves Lejeune. **Ann. Droit Louvain** 64:3 2004 pp.435-479.

4562 La nature juridique des partenaires à la coopération transfrontalière. *[In French]*; [The juridical nature of cross-border cooperation partners]. Pierre d'Argent. **Ann. Droit Louvain** 64:3 2004 pp.419-434.

4563 Non-compliance with EU directives in the member states: opposition through the backdoor? Gerda Falkner; Miriam Hartlapp; Simone Leiber; Oliver Treib. **West Euro. Pol.** 27:3 5:2004 pp.452-473.

4564 La nouvelle politique de concurrence de l'Union européenne. *[In French]*; [The new competitiveness policy of the European Union]. Mario Monti. **R. Droit Union Euro.** 2 2004 pp.137-153.

4565 Österreichische Rechtsprechung zur Europäischen Menschenrechtskonvention im Jahr 2003. *[In German]*; [Austrian jurisdiction on the European Convention on Human Rights in 2003]. W. Karl. **Z. Öffent. Recht** 59:4 2004 pp.431-466.

4566 Quelle justice pénale pour l'Europe ? *[In French]*; [What kind of criminal justice for Europe?] David Siritzky. **Européens** 2004 pp.29-45.

4567 Das rechtliche Verhältnis zwischen dem Streitbeilegungsgremium der Welthandelsorganisation und dem Gerichtshof der Europäischen Gemeinschaften. *[In German]*; [The legal relations between the Dispute Settlement Body of the WTO and the European Court of Justice]. Juliane S. Rapp-Lucke. Baden-Baden: Nomos, 2004. 335p. *ISBN: 383290753X.*

4568 Rethinking law in neofunctionalist theory. Gráinne de Búrca. **J. Euro. Publ. Policy** 12:2 2005 pp.310-326.

4569 La société européenne en question. *[In French]*; [European society in question]. Véronique Magnier. **R. Crit. Droit Int. Privé** 93:3 7-9:2004 pp.555-587.

4570 Soziale Daseinsvorsorge im Lichte der neueren EU-Rechts – und EU-Politikentwicklungen. *[In German]*; (New developments in law and politics regarding social services of general interest in the European Union.) *[Summary]*. Frank Schulz-Nieswandt. **Z. Öffent. Gemein. Unternehm.** 28:1 2005 pp.19-34.

4571 Stato di diritto e principio di legalità nell'evoluzione della forma di stato europea. *[In Italian]*; [Rule of law and the principle of legality in the evolution of the European state]. Sergio Stammati. **Rass. Parl.** XLVII:1 1-3:2005 pp.39-61.

4572 Le traité de bayonne et l'accord de Bruxelles sur la coopération transfrontalière entre collectivités territoriales. *[In French]*; [The Bayonne treaty and the Brussels agreement on trans-frontier cooperation within territorial collectivities]. Carlos Fernandez de Casadevante Romani. **Ann. Droit Louvain** 64:3 2004 pp.383-395.

4573 Union européenne : comment rédiger une législation de qualité dans 20 langues et pour 25 états membres. *[In French]*; [European Union: how to read a constitution of quality in twenty languages and for twenty-five members]. Jean-Claude Piris. **R. Droit Publ.** 2 3-4:2005 pp.475-491.

4574   Vers un droit européen de la coopération transfrontalière. *[In French]*; [Towards a European law for trans-frontier cooperation]. Yves Lejeune. **Ann. Droit Louvain** 64:3 2004 pp.353-364.

4575   When is a group not a political group? The dissolution of the TDI group in the European Parliament. Pierpaolo Settembri. **J. Legis. St.** 10:1 Spring:2004 pp.150-174.

4576   Zur Kooperation von EuGH und nationalem Verfassungsgericht. *[In German]*; [On the cooperation between the European Court of Justice and national constitutional courts]. Z. Chojnacka. **Z. Öffent. Recht** 59:4 2004 pp.415-429.

Treaties
Traités

4577   After the constitutional treaty. The question of a political Europe. Ugo Draetta. **Federalist** XLVII:1 2005 pp.18-30.

4578   Austritt, Ausschluss oder institutionelle Anpassung: Optionen nach dem Scheitern des EU-Verfassungsvertrages. *[In German]*; (Exit, exclusion or institutional adaptation: options after the failure of the EU constitutional treaty.) *[Summary]*; *[Summary in German]*. Andreas Maurer. **Int. Pol. Gesell.** 1 2005 pp.165-184.

4579   La Constitución Europea como respuesta a la ampliación. *[In Spanish]*; [European constitution as an extension answer] *[Summary]*. Francisco Aldecoa Luzarraga. **Pap. Econ. Esp.** 103 2005 pp.67-79.

4580   La Constitution de l'Union européenne. *[In French]*; [The EU constitution]. Valéry Giscard d'Estaing. **R. Hist. Dipl.** 4 2004 pp.321-331.

4581   La Constitution européenne. *[In French]*; [The European constitution]. Commentaire. **Commentaire** 108 Winter:2004-2005 pp.957-969.

4582   Constitution européenne : redistribution du pouvoir des Etats au Conseil de l'UE. *[In French]*; [European constitution: state power redistribution in the European Council]. Frédéric Bobay. **Econ. Prévis.** 163 2004 pp.101-115.

4583   Constitution européenne et « modèle social » européen. Analyse juridique d'une imposture politique. *[In French]*; [European constitution and European 'social model'] *[Summary]*. Serge Regourd. **Pensée** 341 1-3:2005 pp.125-137.

4584   Constitution européenne et nations dans le capitalisme contemporain. *[In French]*; [European constitution and nations in contemporary capitalism]. Jean-Claude Delaunay. **Pensée** 341 1-3:2005 pp.97-110.

4585   A constitution for the European Union. Charles B. Blankart [Ed.]; Dennis C. Mueller [Ed.]. Cambridge MA: MIT Press, 2004. xvi, 266p. *ISBN: 0262025663*. (*Series:* CESifo seminar).

4586   The constitution of EU territory. Luiza Bialasiewicz; Stuart Elden; Joe Painter. **Comp. Euro. Pol.** 3:3 9:2005 pp.333-363.

4587   Constitutional legitimacy and credible commitments in the European Union. Antonio Estella. **Euro. Law J.** 11:1 1:2005 pp.22-42.

4588   The constitutional treaty: three readings from a fusion perspective. Wolfgang Wessels. **J. Com. Mkt. S.** 43:Annual Review 2005 pp.11-36.

4589   La constitutionnalisation de l'Union européenne. *[In French]*; [The constitutionalization of the European Union]. Jean Rossetto [Ed.]. **TDP** 8:16 2:2004 pp.111-364.

4590   Continental tremors. Susan Watkins. **New Left R.** 33 5-6:2005 pp.5-21.

4591   Les coopérations renforcées et les nouvelles formes de flexibilité en matière de défense dans la Constitution européenne. *[In French]*; [Reinforced co-operations and new forms of flexibility with regards to defence in the European constitution]. Hervé Bribosia. **R. Droit Union Euro.** 4 2004 pp.647-708.

4592   El debate constitucional sobre la constitución Europea. *[In Spanish]*; (The constitutional debate on the European constitution.) *[Summary]*. Antonio Porras Nadales. **R. Foment. Soc.** 59:236 10-12:2004 pp.751-772.

4593 En cas de non-ratification... Le destin périlleux du " traité-constitution ". *[In French]*; [In the case of non-ratification... the critical future of the 'constitution-treaty']; *[Summary in French]*. Lucia Serena Rossi. **R. Trim. Droit Euro.** 40:4 10-12:2004 pp.621-637.

4594 En forfatning for Europa. *[In Danish]*; (A constitution for Europe. The EU poised between culture and politics.) Sara Priskorn; Iben B. Rørbye; Stine Schulze. **Nord Ny.** 95 7:2005 pp.35-54.

4595 The end of Europe? Laurent Cohen-Tanugi. **Foreign Aff.** 84:6 11-12:2005 pp.55-67.

4596 The EU constitutional treaty: how to deal with the ratification bottleneck. Gian Luigi Tosato; Ettore Greco. **Int. Spect.** XXXIX:4 10-12:2004 pp.7-24.

4597 Europäische Identitätspolitik in der EU-Verfassungspräambel. Zur ursprungsmythischen Begründung eines universalistischen europäischen Selbstverständnisses. *[In German]*; [European identity politics in the European Union constitution preamble. On the myth of origin of a universalistic European self understanding] *[Summary]*. Helmut Heit. **Arch. Recht. Soz.Philos.** 90:4 2004 pp.461-477.

4598 Die europäische Verfassung auf dem Weg zum Europäischen Verfassungsrecht. *[In German]*; [The European constitution on its way to a European constitutional right]. Francisco Balaguer Callejón. **Jahr. Öffent. Gegen.** 53 2005 pp.401-410.

4599 The European constitution, parts I and III: some critical reflections. Jan Wouters [Ed.]. **Maastricht J. Euro. Comp. Law** 12:1 2005 pp.3-9.

4600 The European constitution project from the perspective of constitutional political economy. Lars P. Feld. **Publ. Choice** 122:3-4 3:2005 pp.417-448.

4601 The European convention: bargaining in the shadow of rhetoric. Paul Magnette; Kalypso Nicolaïdis. **West Euro. Pol.** 27:3 5:2004 pp.381-404.

4602 European Union constitution-making, political identity and Central European reflections. Jiří Přibáň. **Euro. Law J.** 11:2 2005 pp.135-153.

4603 Europe's constitutional future. Jo Shaw. **Publ. Law** Spring:2005 pp.132-151.

4604 Europe's constitutional future: federal lessons for the European Union. Erin Delaney; Julie Smith; Angelika Hable; Clive Church; Paolo Dardanelli; Wilfried Swenden; Gerald Baier; Tanja A. Börzel. **Reg. Fed. S.** 15:2 6:2005 pp.131-269. *Collection of 8 articles.*

4605 Europe's constitutional monstrosity. Nico Krisch. **Oxf. J. Leg. S.** 25:2 Summer:2005 pp.321-334.

4606 Examining the aesthetic dimensions of the constitutional treaty. Nathan Gibbs. **Euro. Law J.** 11:3 5:2005 pp.326-342.

4607 La face cachée de la Convention européenne. *[In French]*; [The hidden face of the European Convention]. François-Xavier Priollaud. **Européens** 2004 pp.15-27.

4608 Inside the European Commission: preference formation and the convention on the future of Europe. Dionyssis G. Dimitrakopoulos; Hussein Kassim. **Comp. Euro. Pol.** 3:2 7:2005 pp.180-203.

4609 Le jour où la France a dit non: comprendre le referendum du 29 mai 2005. *[In French]*; [The day France said no: understanding the May 29 2005 referendum]. Dominique Strauss-Kahn [Contrib.]; Jean-Christophe Cambadelis [Contrib.]; Alain Bergounioux [Contrib.]; et al; Fondation Jean-Jaures. Paris: Plon, 2005. 153p. *ISBN: 2259203353.*

4610 Justice and home affairs in the EU constitutional treaty. What added value for the 'area of freedom, security and justice'? Jörg Monar. **Euro. Constitutional Law R.** 1:2 2005 pp.226-246.

4611 Die Konstitutionalisierung Europas zwischen Konvent, Regierungskonferenz und Verfassungsvertrag. *[In German]*; [Constitutionalization of Europe between convention, intergovernmental conference and constitutional treaty]. Andreas Maurer; Daniela Kietz. **Polit. Viertel.** 45:4 12:2004 pp.568-582.

4612 [Le projet de constitution européenne]. *[In French]*; [The European constitution project]. Mouvements. **Mouvements** 32 3-4:2004 pp.148-160.

4613 The new European constitution: themes and questions. W.T. Eijsbouts; Olivier Duhamel; Peter G. Xuereb; Leonard F.M. Besselink; Rick Lawson; András Sajó; Dominique Rousseau; John W. Sap; Paul Craig; Koen Lenaerts; Jiri Zemanek; Jit Peters; Jörg Gerkrath; W.H. Roobol; Gráinne de Búrca; Ingolf Pernice; Jan Herman Reestman;

Spyridon Flogaitis; Andreas Pottakis; Tim Koopmans; P.J.G. Kapteyn; Andreas Auer; Bruno de Witte; Hjalte Rasmussen. **Euro. Constitutional Law R.** 1:1 2005 pp.5-147. *Collection of 25 articles.*

4614 Non a la constitution : pour une certaine idee de l'Europe. *[In French]*; [No to the constitution: a certain idea a Europe]. Alain Griotteray; Etienne Tarride; Pierre Messmer [Foreword]. Monaco: Editions du Rocher, 2005. 152p. *ISBN: 2268054667.*

4615 Une nouvelle phase européenne ? Lecture du projet de constitution européenne. *[In French]*; [A new stage for Europe? The draft of the European constitution]. Christophe Leonzi; Fabien Raynaud. **Esprit** 310 12:2004 pp.129-147.

4616 Il n'y aura pas encore de constitution européenne ! *[In French]*; [There will be no European constitution yet!] André Viola. **R. Rech. Jurid. Droit Prosp.** 29:4 2004 pp.2569-2579.

4617 Oui : plaidoyer pour la constitution européenne. *[In French]*; [Yes: pleading for the European constitution]. François Bayrou. Paris: Plon, 2005. 180p. *ISBN: 2259201830.*

4618 Le pari risqué de Tony Blair. *[In French]*; [Tony Blair's risky gamble]. Jean-Claude Sergeant. **R. Deux Mondes** 9 9:2004 pp.40-52.

4619 Podział kompetencji między Unią Europejską a państwami członkowskimi według konstytucji Europejskiej. *[In Polish]*; (The division of powers between the European Union and the member states under the constitution for Europe.) Katarzyna Kłaczyńska. **Pań. Prawo** LX:3(709) 3:2005 pp.53-66.

4620 La politica economica nella costituzione europea. *[In Italian]*; [Political economy in the European constitution]. Alberto Majocchi. **Federalist** XLVI:2 2004 pp.70-93.

4621 Pour l'Europe votez non ! *[In French]*; [For the sake of Europe, vote no!] Jean-Pierre Chevènement. Paris: Fayard, 2005. 193p. *ISBN: 2213624763.*

4622 Preference formation and EU treaty reform. Dionyssis G. Dimitrakopoulos; Hussein Kassim; Nicolas Jabko; David Hine; Carlos Closa; Peter Bursens; Eiko R. Thielemann. **Comp. Euro. Pol.** 2:3 12:2004 pp.241-374. *Collection of 7 articles.*

4623 Le projet de constitution européenne et le retrait volontaire de l'Union. *[In French]*; [The European constitution project and the voluntary withdrawal from the Union]. Christine Guillard. **TDP** 8:15 1:2004 pp.47-64.

4624 Ratification, the EU constitution, and EU legal scholarship. Francis Snyder [Ed.]. **Euro. Law J.** 11:3 5:2005 pp.259-261.

4625 La réforme des institutions de l'Union européenne dans le cadre de la constitution. *[In French]*; [European Union institutions reform in the framework of the constitution]. Paolo Ponzano. **R. Droit Union Euro.** 1 2004 pp.25-38.

4626 The representative quality of EU treaty reform: a comparison between the IGC and the convention. Johannes Pollak; Peter Slominski. **J. Euro. Integ.** 26:3 9:2004 pp.201-226.

4627 Saving the pound or voting for Europe? Expectations for referendums on the constitution and the euro. Larry LeDuc. **Jnl. Ele. Pub. Op. Par.** 15:2 9:2005 pp.169-196.

4628 Sens et consequences du " non " français : manuel critique du parfait Europeen, la suite. *[In French]*; [Meaning and consequences of the French 'non': critical manual of the perfect European...]. Jacques Genereux. Paris: Editions du Seuil, 2005. 77p. *ISBN: 202083765X.*

4629 Spezifische Bauelemente der europäischen Verfassung. *[In German]*; [Specific elements of the European constitution]. Franz Cromme. **Europarecht** 40:1 1-2:2005 pp.36-53.

4630 Die Staatswerdung Europas — Kaum eine Spur von Stern und Stunde. Der Entwurf einer Verfassung für Europa in seinen tragenden Teilen kritisch abgeklopft und bewertet. *[In German]*; [The becoming of a European state –critical remarks on the constitutional draft]. Jörn Sack. **Der Staat** 44:1 2005 pp.67-98.

4631 Symposium on the proposed European constitution. J.H.H. Weiler; Dieter Grimm; Neil Walker; Philip Pettit; András Sajó; Mark Tushnet; Ran Hirschl; Armin von Bogdandy; Michel Rosenfeld; Miguel Poiares Maduro; Gianluigi Palombella; Otto Pfersmann; Paul Craig; George A. Bermann; Damian Chalmers; Mattias Kumm; Victor Ferreres Comella; Franz C. Mayer. **Int. J. Const. Law** 3:2-3 5:2005 pp.163-515. *Collection of 18 articles.*

4632 Szerződés Európa alkotmányáról — alapvetés a jövőnek. *[In Hungarian]*; (A treaty on Europe's constitution — laying the foundations for the future.) Árpád Gordos; Bálint Ódor. **Euro. Tükör** 9:6 2004 pp.103-121.

4633 Union Européene : l'aventure constitutionnelle. *[In French]*; [European Union: the constitutional adventure]. Jean-Louis Quermonne; André Brigot; Bruno Jeanbart; Elvire Fabry; Colomban Lebas. **Pol. Étran.** 70:2 Summer:2005 pp.245-295. *Collection of 4 articles.*

4634 Union Européenne, projet de traité constitutionnel : éléments d'analyse. *[In French]*; [European Union, constitutional treaty project: elements of analysis]. Béatrice Buguet. **R. Droit Publ.** 2 3-4:2005 pp.463-474.

4635 Út az Európai Unió alkotmánya felé. *[In Hungarian]*; (The path to the constitution for Europe.) *[Summary]*. Krisztina Gál. **Euro. Tükör** 9:7 2004 pp.6-16.

4636 Was für eine Europäische Verfassung? *[In German]*; (Which European constitution?) Carla Krüger [Tr.]; Dorothee Schmidt [Contrib.]; Étienne Balibar. **Prokla** 35:2 6:2005 pp.287-300.

4637 We, the peoples? Constitutionalizing the European Union. Cindy Skach. **J. Com. Mkt. S.** 43:1 3:2005 pp.149-170.

4638 Zur föderalen Struktur der Europäischen Union im Entwurf des Europäischen Verfassungsvertrags. *[In German]*; [Federal structure of the European Union in the European constitutional draft treaty]. Albrecht Weber. **Europarecht** 39:6 11-12:2004 pp.841-856.

F.2.3: **International governmental organizations**
Organisations gouvernementales internationales

4639 American politicization of the International Monetary Fund. Bessma Momani. **R. Int. Pol. Econ.** 11:5 12:2004 pp.880-904.

4640 China and the WTO: the theory and practice of compliance. Gerald Chan. **Int. Rel. Asia Pacific** 4:1 2004 pp.47-72.

4641 Le Commonwealth sans le Zimbabwe. *[In French]*; [The Commonwealth without Zimbabwe]. Charles Zorgbibe. **Géopol. Afr.** 13 Winter:2004 pp.227-237.

4642 The Commonwealth(s) and global governance. Timothy M. Shaw. **Glo. Gov.** 10:4 10-12:2004 pp.499-516.

4643 Le Conseil de paix et de sécurité de l'Union africaine, clé d'une nouvelle architecture de stabilité en Afrique ? *[In French]*; [The Council of Peace and Security of the African Union, key of a new architecture of stability in Africa?] Delphine Lecoutre. **Afr. Contemp.** 212 Autumn:2004 pp.131-162.

4644 Coup d'oeil sur la Commission de l'océan Indien à l'occasion de son vingtième anniversaire (Radioscopie d'une organisation internationale francophone créée dans la zone sud-ouest de l'océan Indien par l'Accord de Victoria du 10 janvier 1984). *[In French]*; [A glance at the Indian Ocean Commission on its twentieth birthday (radioscopy of a french-speaking international organization created in the south-west of the Indian Ocean by the Victoria Agreement, 10 january 1984)]. André Oraison. **R. Jurid. Pol. Ind. Coop.** 58:1 1-3:2004 pp.43-58.

4645 Democracy beyond borders: justice and representation in global institutions. Andrew Kuper. Oxford: Oxford University Press, 2004. 228p. *ISBN: 0199274908. Includes bibliographical references.*

4646 The democratic legitimacy of public-private rule making: what can we learn from the World Commission on Dams? Klaus Dingwerth. **Glo. Gov.** 11:1 1-3:2005 pp.65-83.

4647 Demokratie als Leitbild der afrikanischen Staatengemeinschaft? Zur Theorie und Praxis demokratischer Schutzklauseln in der Afrikanischen Union. *[In German]*; (Democracy as guiding principle of the African state system? Theory and practice of democratic guarantee-clauses in the African Union.) *[Summary]*. Christof Hartmann. **Verf. Recht Übersee** 38:2 2005 pp.201-220.

4648   Do intergovernmental organizations promote peace? Charles Boehmer; Erik Gartzke; Timothy Nordstrom. **World Pol.** 57:1 10:2004 pp.1-38.

4649   Groupthink im West Wing: Der "Vorkrieg" zum Irakkrieg. *[In German]*; [Decision making leading up to the war in Iraq]. Stephan Böckenförde. **Int. Pol. Gesell.** 1 2005 pp.185-205.

4650   The IMF and democratic governance. Devesh Kapur; Moisés Naím. **J. Democ.** 16:1 1:2005 pp.89-102.

4651   International institutions and socialization in Europe. Jeffrey T. Checkel; Frank Schimmelfennig; Liesbet Hooghe; Jan Beyers; Jeffrey Lewis; Alexandra Gheciu; Alastair Iain Johnston; Michael Zürn. **Int. Org.** 59:4 Fall:2005 pp.801-1079. *Collection of 8 articles.*

4652   Limits on streamlining fund conditionality: the International Monetary Fund's organizational culture. Bessma Momani. **J. Int. Rel. Dev.** 8:2 6:2005 pp.142-163.

4653   Maailmanpankin hyvä hallinta. *[In Finnish]*; [Good governance in the World Bank] *[Summary]*. Seppo Tiihonen. **Hall. Tut.** 23:1 2004 pp.15-29.

4654   'Malice to none, goodwill to all?' The legitimacy of Commonwealth enforcement. Chi-kan Lawrence Chau. **Japanese J. Pol. Sci.** 6:2 8:2005 pp.259-280.

4655   Mini-symposium on the consultative board's report on the future of the WTO. Gary Clyde Hufbauer [Comments by]; Patrick A. Messerlin; Steve Charnovitz; William J. Davey; Joost Pauwelyn. **J. Int. Econ. Law** 8:2 6:2005 pp.287-346. *Collection of 5 articles.*

4656   Minority rights in Europe: a review of the work and standards of the Council of Europe. Patrick Thornberry; Maria Amor Martin Estebanez. Strasbourg: Council of Europe Publishing, 2004. 682p. *ISBN: 9287153663. Includes bibliographical references.*

4657   Norm diffusion within international organizations: a case study of the World Bank. Susan Park. **J. Int. Rel. Dev.** 8:2 6:2005 pp.111-141.

4658   The Organization of the Islamic conference: sharing an illusion. Shahram Akbarzadeh; Kylie Connor. **Mid. East Policy** XII:2 Summer:2005 pp.79-92.

4659   The OSCE's post-September 11 agenda, and Central Asia. Maria Raquel Freire. **Glo. Soc.** 19:2 4:2005 pp.189-209.

4660   Le recours à la constitution de l'OIT dans l'acquisition de son autonomie institutionnelle. *[In French]*; [The appeal to the constitution of the ILO within the course of institutional autonomy acquisition]. I. Duplessis. **Belg. R. Int. Law** XXXVII:1 2004 pp.37-70.

4661   Re-discovering international executive institutions. Jarle Trondal; Martin Marcussen; Frode Veggeland. **Comp. Euro. Pol.** 3:2 7:2005 pp.232-258.

4662   Reflections on the Commonwealth at 40. Don McKinnon; Derek Ingram; Stephen Chan; Derek McDougall; David O'Reilly; Timothy M. Shaw; Ian Taylor; Paul D. Williams. **Round Tab.** 380 7:2005 pp.293-391. *Collection of 8 articles.*

4663   Rules for the world: international organizations in global politics. Michael N. Barnett; Martha Finnemore. Ithaca NY: Cornell University Press, 2004. xi, 226p. *ISBN: 0801440904, 0801488230. Includes bibliographical references (p. 207-222) and index.*

4664   Saving the World Bank. Sebastian Mallaby. **Foreign Aff.** 84:3 5-6:2005 pp.75-85.

4665   La Tchétchénie : un défi au sein du Conseil de l'Europe. *[In French]*; [Chechnya: a challenge within the Council of Europe]. Raisons politiques. **R. Droit Int. Comp.** 81 4-6:2004 pp.123-168.

United Nations
Nations unies

4666   Are the health Millennium Development Goals appropriate for Eastern Europe and Central Asia? B. Rechel; L. Shapo; M. McKee. **Health Policy** 73:3 9:2005 pp.339-351.

4667   Compromise and credibility: Security Council reform? Thomas G. Weiss; Karen E. Young. **Secur. Dial.** 36:2 6:2005 pp.131-154.

4668   Fostering human rights accountability: an ombudsperson for the United Nations? Florian Hoffmann; Frédéric Mégret. **Glo. Gov.** 11:1 1-3:2005 pp.43-63.

4669   From keeping peace to building peace: a proposal for a revitalized United Nations Trusteeship Council. Saira Mohamed. **Columb. Law R.** 105:3 4:2005 pp.809-840.

4670   Handlinger eller holdninger? Norges Midtøstenpolitikk i Sikkerhetsrådet 2001-02. *[In Norwegian]*; (Norwegian voting on the Middle East in the UN Security Council.) *[Summary]*. Alexander Wiken Lange. **Internasjonal Pol.** 63:2-3 2005 pp.255-278.

4671   How the United Nations began. V. Israelian. **Int. Aff. [Moscow]** 51:5 2005 pp.26-40.

4672   'In larger freedom': decision time at the UN. Kofi Annan. **Foreign Aff.** 84:3 5-6:2005 pp.63-74.

4673   Informal groups of states and the UN Security Council. Jochen Prantl. **Int. Org.** 59:3 Summer:2005 pp.559-592.

4674   The International Labour Organisation. Steve Hughes. **New Pol. Econ.** 10:3 9:2005 pp.413-425.

4675   International norms, power and the politics of international administration: the Kosovo case. Alexandra Gheciu. **Geopolitics** 10:1 Spring:2005 pp.121-146.

4676   An international relations debacle: the UN secretary-general's mission of good offices in Cyprus 1999-2004. Claire Palley. Oxford: Hart Publishing, 2005. xiii, 395p. *ISBN: 184113578X. Includes bibliographical references and index.*

4677   A intervenção das Nações Unidas e a crise do estado Africano. *[In Portuguese]*; (United Nations intervention and the crisis of the African state.) *[Summary]*. Norrie MacQueen. **Relações Int.** 4 12:2004 pp.127-145.

4678   Irrelevant or malevolent? UN arms embargoes in civil wars. Dominic Tierney. **R. Int. S.** 31:4 10:2005 pp.645-664.

4679   Judge and executioner: the politics of responding to ethnic cleansing in the Balkans. Vaughn P. Shannon. **J. Genocide Res.** 7:1 3:2005 pp.47-66.

4680   Lord Castlereagh's return: the significance of Kofi Annan's high level panel on threats, challenges and change. Gwyn Prins. **Int. Aff. [London]** 81:2 3:2005 pp.373-392.

4681   Mapping the UN-league of nations analogy: are there still lessons to be learned from the league? Alexandru Grigorescu. **Glo. Gov.** 11:1 1-3:2005 pp.25-42.

4682   Les Nations Unies et l'humanitaire : un bilan mitigé. *[In French]*; (The United Nations and humanitarianism: a contrasting statement.); *[Summary in French]*. Sylvie Brunel. **Pol. Étran.** 70:2 Summer:2005 pp.313-325.

4683   Les Nations-Unies et la "nation indispensable" dans l'ombre de l'Irak. *[In French]*; [The United Nations, the United States and the Iraq war]. Simon Chesterman; Heiko Nitzschke. **Banquet** 21 10:2004 pp.217-237.

4684   A ONU e o processo da resolução de conflitos: potencialidades e limitações. *[In Portuguese]*; (The United Nations and conflict management.) *[Summary]*. Carlos Martins Branco. **Relações Int.** 4 12:2004 pp.105-125.

4685   L'ONU entre nécessité et minimalisme. *[In French]*; (UN between necessity and minimalism.); *[Summary in French]*. Lakhdar Brahimi. **Pol. Étran.** 70:2 Summer:2005 pp.299-311.

4686   The political origins of the UN Security Council's ability to legitimize the use of force. Erik Voeten. **Int. Org.** 59:3 Summer:2005 pp.527-558.

4687   Proposals for UN Security Council reform. Yehuda Z. Blum [Comments by]. **Am. J. Int. Law** 99:3 7:2005 pp.632-649.

4688   Revitalizing the United Nations: reform through weighted voting. Joseph E. Schwartzberg. New York: Institute for Global Policy, World Federalist Movement, 2004. xviii, 77p. *ISBN: 0971072744.*

4689   Rien ne change, tout bouge, ou le dilemme des Nations Unies. Propos sur le rapport du groupe de personnalités de haut niveau sur les menaces, les défis et le changement. *[In French]*; [Nothing changes, everything is on the move or the UN dilemma. Comments on the high ranking personalities' report on threats, challenges and change]. Laurence Boisson de Chazournes. **R. Gén. Droit Int. Publ.** 109:1 2005 pp.147-161.

4690   Security, solidarity, and sovereignty: the grand themes of UN reform. Anne-Marie Slaughter [Comments by]. **Am. J. Int. Law** 99:3 7:2005 pp.619-631.

4691   Terrorism and the UN: before and after September 11. Jane Boulden [Ed.]; Thomas George Weiss [Ed.]. Bloomington IN: Indiana University Press, 2004. xvi, 256p. *ISBN: 0253343844, 0253216621. Includes bibliographical references and index.*

4692   UN and international electoral standards. A. Veshnyakov. **Int. Aff. [Moscow]** 51:5 2005 pp.13-25.

4693   UN reform and the United States isolation and impotence. Jeffrey Laurenti. **World Today** 61:8-9 8-9:2005 pp.4-7.

4694   UN summit: the need for change. V. Zaemsky. **Int. Aff. [Moscow]** 51:5 2005 pp.1-12.

4695   UN voices: the struggle for development and social justice. Thomas George Weiss; et al. Bloomington IN: Indiana University Press, 2005. xx, 520p. *ISBN: 0253346428, 0253217881. Includes bibliographical references and index. (Series: United Nations intellectual history project).*

4696   The United Nations and economic and social development. Louis Emmerij; Richard Jolly; Torild Skard; Yves Berthelot; John Toye; Richard Toye; Michael Ward; Bjørn K. Wold; Thomas G. Weiss; Tatiana Carayannis; Helge Hveem; Gunnar M. Sørbø; Ingrid Eide. **Forum Dev. S.** 32:1 2005 pp.9-294. *Collection of 13 articles.*

4697   The United Nations' celebrity diplomacy. Mark Alleyne. **SAIS R.** XXV:1 Winter-Spring:2005 pp.175-185.

4698   United Nations' dedications: a world culture in the making? Gili S. Drori. **Int. Sociol.** 20:2 6:2005 pp.175-200.

4699   The UN's unnecessary crisis. Mats Berdal. **Survival** 47:3 Autumn:2005 pp.7-32.

4700   Yhdistyneet kansakunnat organisaationa. *[In Finnish]*; [The United Nations as an organization] *[Summary]*. Risto Wallin. **Politiikka** 46:1 2004 pp.30-40.

F.2.4:   **International non-governmental organizations**
             Organisations non-gouvernementales internationales

4701   Autonomy or dependence? Case studies of North-South NGO partnerships. Vicky Mancuso Brehm; et al. Oxford: INTRAC, 2004. 207p. *ISBN: 1897748744. Includes bibliographical references.*

4702   Civil society organizations in failing states: the Red Cross in Bosnia and Albania. Catherine Götze. **Int. Peace.** 11:4 Winter:2004 pp.664-682.

4703   Contemporary challenges in the civil-military relationship: complementarity or incompatibility? *[Summary in French]*. Raj Rana. **Int. R. Red Cross** 86:855 9:2004 pp.565-591.

4704   Cracking the code: the genesis, use and future of the code of conduct. Peter Walker. **Disasters** 29:4 12:2005 pp.323-336.

4705   Dead letter or living document? Ten years of the code of conduct for disaster relief. Dorothea Hilhorst. **Disasters** 29:4 12:2005 pp.351-369.

4706   Development NGOs and labor unions: terms of engagement. Deborah Eade [Ed.]; Alan Leather [Ed.]. Bloomfield CT: Kumarian Press, 2005. xxiv, 406p. *ISBN: 1565491963. Includes bibliographical references (p. 371-383) and index. (Series: Development in practice readers).*

4707   Encountering perceptions in parts of the Muslim world and their impact on the ICRC's ability to be effective. Andreas Wigger. **Int. R. Red Cross** 87:858 6:2005 pp.343-365.

4708   Faith-based and secular humanitarian organizations. Elizabeth Ferris. **Int. R. Red Cross** 87:858 6:2005 pp.311-325.

4709   The governance of non-governmental organizations in Uganda. A. Barr; M. Fafchamps; T. Owens. **World Dev.** 33:4 4:2005 pp.657-679.

4710   The influence of the Muslim religion in humanitarian aid. Jamal Krafess. **Int. R. Red Cross** 87:858 6:2005 pp.327-342.

4711   Interview with Ahmad Ali Noorbala. Ahmad Ali Noorbala [Discussant]. **Int. R. Red Cross** 87:858 6:2005 pp.243-251.

4712   Making humanitarian relief networks more effective: operational coordination, trust and sense making. Max Stephenson, Jr. **Disasters** 29:4 12:2005 pp.337-350.

4713   Mouvement citoyen international et développement social. De nouveaux espaces de dialogue interculturel. *[In French]*; [The international social movement and social development. New areas of cross-cultural dialogue] *[Summary]*. Louis Favreau. **Nouv. Prat. Soc.** 17:2 Spring:2005 pp.126-143.

4714   NGOs and conflict prevention in Burundi: a case study. Lennart Wohlgemuth. **Afr. Dev.** XXX:1-2 2005 pp.183-209.

4715   Non-governmental organisations and humanitarian action: the need for a viable change of praxis and ethos. Christos A. Frangonikolopoulos. **Glo. Soc.** 19:1 1:2005 pp.49-72.

4716   Palestinian NGOs in Israel: the politics of civil society. Shany Payes. London, New York: Tauris Academic Studies, 2005. 331p. *ISBN: 1850436304. Includes bibliographical references (p. [277]-315) and index. (Series:* Library of modern Middle East studies - 45).

4717   Patterns of governance: the rise of transnational coalitions of NGOs. Helen Yanacopulos. **Glo. Soc.** 19:3 7:2005 pp.247-266.

4718   Representing transnational environmental interests: new opportunities for non-governmental organisation access within the World Trade Organization? Michael Mason. **Env. Pol.** 13:3 Autumn:2004 pp.566-589.

4719   Ukraine's election: the role of one international NGO. Celeste A. Wallander. **Int. Aff. [Moscow]** 51:3 2005 pp.92-103.

F.3:   **International relations**
            Relations internationales

F.3.1:   **International relations theory**
              Théorie des relations internationales

4720   Abuse and westernization: reflections on strategies of power. Stéphane La Branche. **J. Peace Res.** 42:2 3:2005 pp.219-235.

4721   Africa and international relations: a comment on IR theory, anarchy and statehood. William Brown. **R. Int. S.** 32:1 1:2005 pp.119-143.

4722   The age of absolutism: capitalism, the modern states-system and international relations. Adam David Morton. **R. Int. S.** 31:3 7:2005 pp.495-517.

4723   Allies as rivals: the U.S., Europe, and Japan in a changing world-system. Faruk Tabak [Ed.]. Boulder CO: Paradigm Publishers, 2005. vii, 214p. *ISBN: 1594511225. Includes bibliographical references and index. (Series:* Political economy of the world-system annuals – volume 2).

4724   Approaching perpetual peace: Kant's defence of a league of states and his ideal of a world federation. Pauline Kleingeld. **Euro. J. Philos.** 12:3 12:2004 pp.304-325.

4725   Arms and rights. Perry Anderson. **New Left R.** 31 1-2:2005 pp.5-42.

4726   Assassination and preventive killing. Asa Kasher; Amos Yadlin. **SAIS R.** XXV:1 Winter-Spring:2005 pp.41-57.

4727   Avtoritarizm razvitiia: genezis, funktsii, perspektivy. *[In Russian]*; (Authoritarianism of development: genesis, functions and prospects.) A.V. Riabov; V.A. Krasil'shchikov; V.V. Mikheev; K.L. Maidanik; A.V. Malashenko; V.V. Sumskii; T.E. Vorozheikina; L.S. Okuneva. **Mir. Ekon. Mezh. Ot.** 5 5:2005 pp.41-53.

4728   The battle rages on John J. Mearsheimer versus Paul Rogers. Richard Little; Christopher Hill; Chris Brown; Ken Booth. **Int. Rel.** 19:3 9:2005 pp.337-360.

4729   Bilgi sosyolojisi açısından "doğu ve "batı". *[In Turkish]*; ('East' and 'West' from the sociology of knowledge perspective.) Şennur Özdemir. **Uluslararasi Ilişkiler** 1:1 Spring:2004 pp.61-92.

4730   'Civilizing' missions, past & present. Kenneth Pomeranz. **Dædalus** 134:2 Spring:2005 pp.34-45.

4731   Constituencies and preferences in international bargaining. Ahmer Tarar. **J. Confl. Resol.** 49:3 6:2005 pp.383-407.
4732   The construction and cumulation of knowledge in international relations. Daniel S. Geller; John A. Vasquez; Karena Shaw; Anna M. Agathangelou; L.H.M. Ling; Russell J. Leng; Jack S. Levy; William F. Mabe, Jr.; Hemda Ben-Yehuda; Zeev Maoz; Robert T. Batcher; Jacek Kugler; Ronald L. Tammen; Brian Efird. **Int. S. R.** 6:4 12:2004 pp.1-179. *Collection of 9 articles.*
4733   The construction of an edifice: the story of a first great debate. Joel Quirk; Darshan Vigneswaran. **R. Int. S.** 31:1 1:2005 pp.89-107.
4734   Contingent borders, ambiguous ethics: migrants in (international) political theory. Owen Parker; James Brassett. **Int. S. Q.** 49:2 6:2005 pp.233-253.
4735   Corporate social responsibility — the failing discipline and why it matters for international relations. Michael Blowfield. **Int. Rel.** 19:2 6:2005 pp.173-191.
4736   Democracy and diversionary military intervention: reassessing regime type and the diversionary hypothesis. Jeffrey Pickering; Emizet F. Kisangani. **Int. S. Q.** 49:1 3:2005 pp.23-43.
4737   Do treaties constrain or screen? Selection bias and treaty compliance. Jana von Stein. **Am. Pol. Sci. R.** 99:4 11:2005 pp.611-622.
4738   E.H. Carr v. idealism: the battle rages on. John J. Mearsheimer. **Int. Rel.** 19:2 6:2005 pp.139-152.
4739   Emperyalizmin yapısal teorisi. *[In Turkish]*; (A structural theory of imperialism.) Johan Galtung. **Uluslararası İlişkiler** 1:2 Spring:2004 pp.25-46.
4740   Emperyalizmin yapısal teorisi — kısım 2. *[In Turkish]*; (A structural theory of imperialism — part II.) Johan Galtung. **Uluslararası İlişkiler** 1:3 Autumn:2004 pp.37-66.
4741   Empire, Rifondazione Comunista, and the politics of spontaneity. Emanuele Saccarelli. **New Pol. Sci.** 26:4 12:2004 pp.569-591.
4742   Ethical theory in the study of international politics. Mark Evans [Ed.]. New York: Nova Science Publishers, 2004. x, 169p. *ISBN: 1590339711. Includes bibliographical references and index.*
4743   Ethics and the use of force after Iraq. Terry Nardin; Fernando R. Tesón; Alex J. Bellamy; Michael Wesley; Anthony Burke; Jean Bethke Elshtain; Steven Lee; Allen Buchanan; Robert O. Keohane. **Ethics Int. Aff.** 19:2 2005 pp.1-111. *Collection of 10 articles.*
4744   Ethics of engagement: intellectuals in world politics. Jenny Edkins; Vivienne Jabri; Richard Falk; Maja Zehfuss; Siba N. Grovogui; Larry N. George; David Campbell. **Int. Rel.** 19:1 3:2005 pp.64-134. *Collection of 7 articles.*
4745   Explanatory typologies in qualitative studies of international politics. Colin Elman. **Int. Org.** 59:2 Spring:2005 pp.293-326.
4746   Fighting violence: a critique of the war on terrorism. Tamir Bar-On; Howard Goldstein. **Int. Pol.** 12:2 6:2005 pp.225-245.
4747   Forget 'post-positivist' IR! The legacy of IR theory as the locus for a pragmatist turn. Helena Rytövuori-Apunen. **Coop. Confl.** 40:2 6:2005 pp.147-177.
4748   Géopolitique de l'imperialisme contemporain. *[In French]*; [Geopolitics of modern imperialism]. Samir Amin. **Int. R. Sociol.** 15:1 3:2005 pp.5-34.
4749   Global governance: critical concepts in political science. Timothy J. Sinclair [Ed.]. London, New York: Routledge, 2004. *ISBN: 0415276616. Includes bibliographical references and index.*
4750   The global governance reader. Rorden Wilkinson [Ed.]. London: Routledge, 2004. 320p. *ISBN: 0415332060, 0415332079.*
4751   The impact of leadership turnover and domestic institutions on international cooperation. Fiona McGillivray; Alastair Smith. **J. Confl. Resol.** 49:5 10:2005 pp.639-660.
4752   Imperial liberalism. Robert Cooper. **Nat. Interest** 79 Spring:2005 pp.25-34.
4753   Incomplete agreements and the limits of persuasion in international politics. Jens Steffek. **J. Int. Rel. Dev.** 8:3 9:2005 pp.229-256.

4754 International relations and communitarianism. James M. Goldgeier; James J. Hentz; Richard Falk; Nikolas K. Gvosdev; Colin S. Gray; Rein Müllerson; Max M. Kampelman. **Am. Behav. Sci.** 48:12 8:2005 pp.1545-1682. *Collection of 7 articles.*

4755 Moral evil and international relations. Nicholas Rengger; Renee Jeffrey. **SAIS R.** XXV:1 Winter-Spring:2005 pp.3-16.

4756 A new approach to the analysis of geo-political risk. Paul Ormerod; Shaun Riordan. **Dipl. State.** 15:4 12:2004 pp.643-654.

4757 Occidentalism: the West in the eyes of its enemies. Ian Buruma; Avishai Margalit. New York: Penguin Books, 2004. 165p. *ISBN: 1594200084. Includes bibliographical references and index.*

4758 Political issues for the twenty-first century. David Morland [Ed.]; Mark Cowling [Ed.]. Aldershot: Ashgate, 2004. x, 270p. *ISBN: 0754619036. Includes bibliographical references and index.*

4759 The political morality of the neo-conservatives: an analysis. John Guelke. **Int. Pol.** 42:1 3:2005 pp.97-115.

4760 O politicheskoi nauke, ee sootnoshenii s drugimi otrasliami znaniia i ob izuchenii politicheskogo prostranstva. *[In Russian]*; (Political science, its correlation with other spheres of knowledge, and the study of political space.) *[Summary]*. R. Chellen; M.V. Il'in [Foreword]. **Polis [Moscow]** 2(85) 2005 pp.115-126.

4761 Povorot k sotsiologicheskomu analizu o teorii mezhdunarodnykh otnoshenii. *[In Russian]*; [Sociological analysis of international relations theory]. Iu.M. Prakhova. **Sots.Gum. Znan.** 1 2004 pp.291-304.

4762 Power, morality, and foreign policy. Owen Harries. **Orbis** 49:4 Fall:2005 pp.599-612.

4763 Reading Habermas in anarchy: multilateral diplomacy and global public spheres. Jennifer Mitzen. **Am. Pol. Sci. R.** 99:3 8:2005 pp.401-418.

4764 Regards philosophiques sur la mondialisation. *[In French]*; [Philosophical glance on globalization]. Stephane Courtois [Ed.]; Jocelyne Couture [Ed.]. Sainte-Foy: Presses de l'Universite du Quebec, 2005. ix, 230p. *ISBN: 2760513467. Includes bibliographical references.*

4765 Regime change and its limits. Richard N. Haass. **Foreign Aff.** 84:4 7-8:2005 pp.66-78.

4766 Remembering the future: utopia, empire, and harmony in 21st century international theory. William A. Callahan. **Euro. J. Int. Rel.** 10:4 12:2004 pp.569-601.

4767 Soft power in global politics? Diplomatic partners as transversal actors. Tania Domett. **Aust. J. Pol. Sci.** 40:2 6:2005 pp.289-306.

4768 The state, international competitiveness and neoliberal globalisation: is there a future beyond 'the competition state'? Tore Fougner. **R. Int. S.** 32:1 1:2005 pp.165-185.

4769 Stepping into the fray: when do mediators mediate? J. Michael Greig. **Am. J. Pol. Sci.** 49:2 4:2005 pp.249-266.

4770 System and process in international politics. Morton A. Kaplan. Colchester: ECPR Press, 2005. 252p. *ISBN: 0954796624. Includes index.*

4771 A systemic theory of the security environment. Shiping Tang. **J. Strategic S.** 27:1 3:2004 pp.1-34.

4772 Taoism and the concept of global security. Ralph Pettman. **Int. Rel. Asia Pacific** 5:1 2005 pp.59-83.

4773 Tendentsii klassicheskikh paradigm v zapadnoi teorii mezhdunarodnykh otnoshenii. *[In Russian]*; (Tendencies of classic paradigms of Western theories of international relations.) P. Tsigankov. **Obshch. Nauki Sovrem.** 2 2004 pp.119-130.

4774 Theory as a factor and the theorist as an actor: the 'pragmatist constructivist' lessons of John Dewey and John Kenneth Galbraith. Wesley W. Widmaier. **Int. S. R.** 6:3 9:2004 pp.427-445.

4775 The three faces of securitization: political agency, audience and context. Thierry Balzacq. **Euro. J. Int. Rel.** 11:2 6:2005 pp.171-201.

4776 Uluslararası ilişkilerde klasik jeopolitik teoriler ve çağdaş yansımaları. *[In Turkish]*; (Classical geopolitical theories in international relations and their contemporary interpretations.) İsmail Hakkı İşcan. **Uluslararasi Ilişkiler** 1:2 Spring:2004 pp.47-79.

4777   Understanding international relations. Chris Brown; Kirsten Ainley. Basingstoke: Palgrave Macmillan, 2005. xvii, 294p. *ISBN: 9781403946638, 1403946639, 1403946647. Includes bibliographical references and index.*

4778   Understanding national IR disciplines outside the United States: political culture and the construction of international relations in Denmark. Henrik Ø. Breitenbauch; Anders Wivel. **J. Int. Rel. Dev.** 7:4 12:2004 pp.414-443.

4779   The use of force: military power and international politics. Robert J. Art [Ed.]; Kenneth Neal Waltz [Ed.]. Lanham Md: Rowman & Littlefield, 2004. xi, 483p. *ISBN: 0742525562, 0742525570. Includes bibliographical references.*

4780   Visa diplomacy. Kevin D. Stringer. **Dipl. State.** 15:4 12:2004 pp.655-682.

4781   What difference does difference make? Reflections on neo-conservatism as a liberal cosmopolitan project. Ray Kiely. **Cont. Pol.** 10:3-4 9-12:2004 pp.185-202.

4782   What is your research program? Some feminist answers to international relations methodological questions. J. Ann Tickner. **Int. S. Q.** 49:1 3:2005 pp.1-21.

4783   You still don't understand: why troubled engagements continue between feminists and (critical) IPE. Georgina Waylen. **R. Int. S.** 32:1 1:2005 pp.145-164.

Conflict theory
Théorie des conflits

4784   Assessing the steps to war. Paul D. Senese; John Vasquez. **Br. J. Pol. Sci.** 35:4 10:2005 pp.607-633.

4785   A bargaining theory of minority demands: explaining the dog that did not bite in 1990's Yugoslavia. Erin Jenne. **Int. S. Q.** 48:4 12:2004 pp.729-754.

4786   The behavioral origins of war. D. Scott Bennett; Allan C Stam. Ann Arbor MI: University of Michigan Press, 2004. xii, 289p. *ISBN: 0472098446, 047206844X. Includes bibliographical references (p. 257-276) and index.*

4787   Clausewitz and low-intensity conflict. Stuart Kinross. **J. Strategic S.** 27:1 3:2004 pp.35-58.

4788   The concept and practice of conflict prevention: a critical reappraisal. Moolakkattu Stephen John. **Int. S.** 42:1 2005 pp.1-19.

4789   The concept of logistics derived from Clausewitz: all that is required so that the fighting force can be taken as a given. Domício Proença, Júnior; E.E. Duarte. **J. Strategic S.** 28:4 8:2005 pp.645-677.

4790   Easy targets and the timing of conflict. Helmut Bester; Kai A. Konrad. **J. Theor. Pol.** 17:2 4:2005 pp.199-215.

4791   Ethnic and national conflicts in the age of globalisation: withering away, persisting, or domesticated? Anatoly M. Khazanov. **Total. Mov. Pol. Relig.** 6:2 9:2005 pp.271-286.

4792   Ethnic conflict and international politics: explaining diffusion and escalation. Steven E. Lobell [Ed.]; Philip Mauceri [Ed.]. New York, Basingstoke: Palgrave Macmillan, 2004. 213p. *ISBN: 140396355X, 1403963568. Includes bibliographical references (p. [181]-197) and index.*

4793   European integration as a solution to war. Mette Eilstrup-Sangiovanni; Daniel Verdier. **Euro. J. Int. Rel.** 11:1 3:2005 pp.99-135.

4794   'Evil and international affairs'. Jutta Brunnée; Stephen J. Toope; Farid Abdel-Nour; William D. Casebeer; Scott Kline; Sandra Rafman; P.E. Digeser; Catherine Lu. **Int. Rel.** 18:4 12:2004 pp.405-509. *Collection of 7 articles.*

4795   Filosofiia voiny. *[In Russian]*; [Philosophy of war]. Aleksandr Dugin. Moscow: Iauza, 2004. 253p. *ISBN: 5699070265.*

4796   The future of insurgency. Ian Beckett. **Sm. Wars Insurg.** 16:1 3:2005 pp.22-36.

4797   İlkçağlardan günümüze haklı savaş kavramı. *[In Turkish]*; (Just war concept from the early ages up to present.) Fulya A. Ereker. **Uluslararasi Ilişkiler** 1:3 Autumn:2004 pp.1-36.

4798   International resource conflict and mitigation. Mark F. Giordano; Meredith A. Giordano; Aaron T. Wolf. **J. Peace Res.** 42:1 1:2005 pp.47-65.

4799 Interstate rivalry and the recurrence of crises: a comparison of rival and nonrival crisis behavior, 1918-1994. Brandon C. Prins. **Arm. Forces Soc.** 31:3 Spring:2005 pp.323-352.

4800 Just war in the 21st century: reconceptualizing just war theory after September 11. Eric Patterson. **Int. Pol.** 42:1 3:2005 pp.116-134.

4801 Kapitalistisen maailmantalouden pitkä laskukausi ja tulevaisuuden kriisit ja sodat. Osa 1: Kasvun. *[In Finnish]*; [The long downward phase of the capitalist world economy and future crises and wars. Pt. 1: The growth stops] *[Summary]*. Heikki Patomäki. **Kosmopolis** 34:1 2004 pp.7-23.

4802 Kapitalistisen maailmantalouden pitkä laskukausi ja tulevaisuuden kriisit ja sodat. Osa 2: Kolme skenaariota globaalin hallinnan muutoksista. *[In Finnish]*; [The long downward phase of the capitalist world economy and future crises and wars. Pt. 2: Three scenarios of change of global economic governance] *[Summary]*. Heikki Patomäki. **Kosmopolis** 34:1 2004 pp.90-106.

4803 Keeping the peace after secession: territorial conflicts between rump and secessionist states. Jaroslav Tir. **J. Confl. Resol.** 49:5 10:2005 pp.713-741.

4804 Leader age, regime type, and violent international relations. Michael Horowitz; Rose McDermott; Allan C. Stam. **J. Confl. Resol.** 49:5 10:2005 pp.661-685.

4805 Leadership style, regime type, and foreign policy crisis behavior: a contingent monadic peace? Jonathan W. Keller. **Int. S. Q.** 49:2 6:2005 pp.205-231.

4806 Legitimating the use of force in international politics: a communicative action perspective. Corneliu Bjola. **Euro. J. Int. Rel.** 11:2 6:2005 pp.266-303.

4807 The limits of the war convention. Lionel K. McPherson. **Philos. Soc. Crit.** 31:2 3:2005 pp.147-163.

4808 Machiavelli's legacy: domestic politics and international conflict. David Sobek. **Int. S. Q.** 49:2 6:2005 pp.179-204.

4809 Maintenance processes in international rivalries. Gary Goertz; Bradford Jones; Paul F. Diehl. **J. Confl. Resol.** 49:5 10:2005 pp.742-769.

4810 Making and keeping peace. Suzanne Werner; Amy Yuen. **Int. Org.** 59:2 Spring:2005 pp.261-292.

4811 One step forward, one step back? The development of peace-building as concept and strategy. Andrea Kathryn Talentino. **J. Confl. S.** XXIV:2 Winter:2004 pp.33-60.

4812 Out of evil: new international politics and old doctrines of war. Stephen Chan. London: I.B. Tauris, 2005. xi, 164p. *ISBN: 1850434204. Includes bibliographical references (p. 151-157) and index.*

4813 Preventing ethnic conflict: successful cross-national strategies. Irwin Deutscher; Linda Lindsey [Contrib.]. Lanham MD: Lexington Books, 2005. xv, 211p. *ISBN: 0739109936. Includes bibliographical references and index.*

4814 Putting the numbers to work: implications for violence prevention. Karl R. DeRouen, Jr.; Shaun Goldfinch. **J. Peace Res.** 42:1 1:2005 pp.27-45.

4815 'Small wars' and the law: options for prosecuting the insurgents in Iraq. Nathan A. Canestaro. **Columb. J. Tr. Law** 43:1 2004 pp.73-140.

4816 Teorija nadmoći i rat na teritoriju bivše Jugoslavije (1991.-1995.) *[In Croatian]*; (Power preponderance theory and the war on the territory of former Yugoslavia (1991-1995).) *[Summary]*. Miljenko Antić. **Pol. Misao** 41:2 2004 pp.117-134.

4817 Turvallistaminen, sota ja järjestys muuttuvassa kansainvälisessä järjestyksessä. *[In Finnish]*; [Securitization, war and order in a changing international system] *[Summary]*. Kari Laitinen; Vilho Harle; Anu Pulkkinen; Helle Palu; Matti Keppo; Pauliina Jaakkola; Aki-Mauri Huhtinen; Jari Rantapelkonen. **Kosmopolis** 34:2 2004 pp.4-107. *Collection of 6 articles.*

4818 Understanding international conflicts: an introduction to theory and history. Joseph S. Nye. New York, London: Pearson Addison Wesley, 2005. xii, 276p. *ISBN: 0321300696. Includes bibliographical references and index. (Series: Longman classics in political science).*

4819 Violent adolescence: state development and the propensity for militarized interstate conflict. Charles R. Boehmer; David Sobek. **J. Peace Res.** 42:1 1:2005 pp.5-26.

4820   War in (another) new context: post modernism. Keith D. Dickson. **J. Confl. S.** XXIV:2 Winter:2004 pp.78-91.
4821   War is peace: on post-national war. Ulrich Beck. **Secur. Dial.** 36:1 3:2005 pp.5-26.
4822   War is too important to be left to ideological amateurs. Robert Gilpin. **Int. Rel.** 19:1 3:2005 pp.5-18.
4823   War, trade, and the mediation of systemic leadership. Karen Rasler; William R. Thompson. **J. Peace Res.** 42:3 5:2005 pp.251-269.
4824   'Women, children and other vulnerable groups': gender, strategic frames and the protection of civilians as a transnational issue. R. Charli Carpenter. **Int. S. Q.** 49:2 6:2005 pp.295-334.

Globalization
Mondialisation

4825   Capitalist expansion and the imperialism-globalization debate: contemporary Marxist explanations. Ray Kiely. **J. Int. Rel. Dev.** 8:1 3:2005 pp.27-57.
4826   Civil society and the problem of global democracy. Michael Goodhart. **Democratization** 12:1 2:2005 pp.1-21.
4827   Cosmopolitan global politics. Patrick Hayden. Aldershot: Ashgate, 2005. 174p. *ISBN: 0754642763. Includes bibliographical references and index. (Series:* Ethics and global politics).
4828   The counter-empire to come: an attempted decoding of Hardt's and Negri's empire. Ugo D. Rossi; Hélène Desbrousses [Ed.]; Ugo Pouli [Ed.]. **Sci. Soc.** 69:2 4:2005 pp.191-217.
4829   Critical cosmology: on nations and globalization. A philosophical essay. Gerard Raulet. Lanham MD: Lexington Books, 2005. xix, 99p. *ISBN: 073910859X, 0739108603. Includes bibliographical references and index. (Series:* Out sources).
4830   The endgame of globalization. Neil Smith. New York, London: Routledge, 2005. 176p. *ISBN: 0415950120. Includes bibliographical references and index.*
4831   Entre o 11 de Setembro e o 11 de Março: os limites de um mundo globalizado. *[In Portuguese]*; (Between September 11 and March 11: the limits of a globalized world.) *[Summary]*. Luís Lobo-Fernandes. **Relações Int.** 4 12:2004 pp.77-87.
4832   Epoch and conjuncture in Marxist political economy. Alex Callinicos. **Int. Pol.** 42:3 9:2005 pp.353-363.
4833   Globalisation, cosmopolitanism and the environment. Andrew Dobson. **Int. Rel.** 19:3 9:2005 pp.259-274.
4834   Globalization and inequality: neoliberalisms downward spiral. John Rapley. Boulder CO: Lynne Rienner Publishers, 2004. viii, 193p. *ISBN: 1588262456, 1588262200. Includes bibliographical references (p. 175-187) and index.*
4835   Globalization and the strengthening of democracy in the developing world. Nita Rudra. **Am. J. Pol. Sci.** 49:4 10:2005 pp.704-730.
4836   Globalization, liberalization, and prospects for the state. James Putzel. **Int. Pol. Sci. R.** 26:1 1:2005 pp.5-16.
4837   Globalization theory: a post mortem. Justin Rosenberg. **Int. Pol.** 42:1 3:2005 pp.2-74.
4838   Globalization: towards a new perspective on political economy. Nisar-ul-Haq. **Indian J. Pol. Sci.** 65:3 7-9:2004 pp.317-330.
4839   Globalization: who governs? Robert Gilpin; Reimund Seidelmann; Mario Telò; Pierre Vercauteren; Jacobus Delwaide; Gustaaf Geeraerts; Yves Palau; Jean-Jacques Roche; Éric Remacle; A.J.R. Groom; Thierry Braspenning. **Stud. Dipl.** LVII:1 2004 pp.7-168. *Collection of 10 articles.*
4840   Globalizatsiia i politicheskie potriaseniia XXI veka. *[In Russian]*; (Globalization and political shocks of the 21st century.) *[Summary]*. A.A. Galkin. **Polis [Moscow]** 4(87) 2005 pp.53-70.

4841   Globalizatsiia i Rossiia: paradigma, sotsial'no-politicheskii aspekt, strategiia levykh sil. *[In Russian]*; [Globalization and Russia: paradigms, socio-political aspects and left-wing strategies]. N. G. Bindiukov. Moscow: ITRK, 2004. 368p. *ISBN: 5880101940.*

4842   Good governance, democratic societies and globalisation. Surendra Munshi [Ed.]; Biju Paul Abraham [Ed.]. Thousand Oaks CA: Sage Publications, 2004. 424p. *ISBN: 0761998489. Includes bibliographical references and index.*

4843   Horses for courses? The political discourse of globalisation and European integration in the UK and Ireland. Colin Hay; Nicola J. Smith. **West Euro. Pol.** 28:1 1:2005 pp.124-158.

4844   In praise of empires: globalization and order. Deepak Lal. New York: Palgrave Macmillan, 2004. xxvi, 270p. *ISBN: 1403936390. Includes bibliographical references (p. [217]-262) and index.*

4845   Ipostasi globalizatsii i imperativy vyzhivaniia. *[In Russian]*; (Aspects of globalization and essentials for survival.) Vsevolod Zubakov. **Svobod. Mysl'** 8 2005 pp.44-62.

4846   Küreselleşme ve uluslararası ilişkiler'in geleceği. *[In Turkish]*; (Globalization and the future of international relations.) Gökhan Koçer. **Uluslararasi Ilişkiler** 1:3 Autumn:2004 pp.101-122.

4847   Making sense of the globalisation debate when engaging in political economy analysis. Ian Bruff. **Br. J. Pol. Int. Rel.** 7:2 5:2005 pp.261-280.

4848   Mul'tikul'turizm i prava cheloveka v usloviiakh globalizatsii. *[In Russian]*; [Multiculturalism and human rights in the context of globalization]. S.V. Polenina. **Gos. Pravo** 5 5:2005 pp.66-77.

4849   Nation and empire: hierarchies of citizenship in the new global order. Stephen Castles. **Int. Pol.** 12:2 6:2005 pp.203-224.

4850   National model over globalization: the Japanese model and its internationalization. Hyeong-ki Kwon. **Pol. Soc.** 33:2 6:2005 pp.234-252.

4851   A new world order. Anne-Marie Slaughter. Princeton NJ: Princeton University Press, 2004. xviii, 341p. *ISBN: 0691116989. Includes bibliographical references (p. 319-332) and index.*

4852   Persistent permeability? Regionalism, localism, and globalization in the Middle East. Rex Brynen [Ed.]; Bassel F. Salloukh [Ed.]. Aldershot, Burlington VT: Ashgate, 2004. xii, 187p. *ISBN: 0754636623. Includes bibliographical references and index. (Series:* The international political economy of new regionalisms).

4853   Pluralism, solidarism and the emergence of world society in English school theory. John Williams. **Int. Rel.** 19:1 3:2005 pp.19-38.

4854   Political globalization: state, power and social forces. Morten Ougaard. Basingstoke: Palgrave Macmillan, 2004. xii, 236p. *ISBN: 0333963156. Includes bibliographical references and index. (Series:* International political economy).

4855   Politics of empire: globalisation in crisis. Alan Freeman [Ed.]; Boris Kagarlitsky [Ed.]. London: Pluto Press, 2004. vii, 290p. *ISBN: 0745321836, 0745321844. Includes bibliographical references and index. Transnational Institute.*

4856   Power and politics in globalization: the indispensible state. Howard H. Lentner. New York, London: Routledge, 2004. xii, 227p. *ISBN: 0415948843, 0415948851. Includes bibliographical references and index.*

4857   Reconstituting the global public domain: issues, actors, and practices. John Gerard Ruggie. **Euro. J. Int. Rel.** 10:4 12:2004 pp.499-531.

4858   Reframing global justice. Nancy Fraser. **New Left R.** 36 11-12:2005 pp.69-88.

4859   La régulation globale du capitalisme. *[In French]*; [Global regulation of capitalism]. Philip S. Golub; Otto Holman; Hélène Pellerin; Ismail Erturk; Julie Froud; Sukhdev Johal; Karel Williams; Michèle Rioux; Aykut Çoban; Robert W. Cox. **A Contrario** 2:2 2004 pp.9-188. *Collection of 7 articles.*

4860   September 11 and the Middle East failure of US 'soft power': globalisation contra Americanisation in the 'new' US century. Emad El-Din Aysha. **Int. Rel.** 19:2 6:2005 pp.193-210.

4861   Southeastern Europe in the age of globalism. Matthew Nimetz. **Mediterr. Q.** 16:1 Winter:2005 pp.16-32.

4862   The state, democracy and globalization. Roger King; Gavin Kendall. Basingstoke: Palgrave Macmillan, 2004. ix, 262p. *ISBN: 0333969111, 033396912X. Includes bibliographical references and index.*

4863   Theorizing globalization in a time of war. Mary Hawkesworth. **S. Pol. Econ.** 75 Spring:2005 pp.127-138.

4864   World politics and social movements: the janus face of the global democratic structure. Thomas Olesen. **Glo. Soc.** 19:2 4:2005 pp.109-129.

Realism, idealism and discourse
Réalisme, idéalisme et débats

4865   American realism versus American imperialism. Campbell Craig. **World Pol.** 57:1 10:2004 pp.143-171.

4866   Classical realism and the tension between sovereignty and intervention: constructions of expediency from Machiavelli, Hobbes and Bodin. Alan Chong. **J. Int. Rel. Dev.** 8:3 9:2005 pp.257-286.

4867   Contracting around international uncertainty. Barbara Koremenos. **Am. Pol. Sci. R.** 99:4 11:2005 pp.549-565.

4868   Conversations in international relations. Robert Gilpin [Interviewer]. **Int. Rel.** 19:3 9:2005 pp.361-372.

4869   The dynamics of the democratic peace. Wolfgang Wagner; John MacMillan; Harald Müller; Ewan Harrison; Matthias Dembinski; Andreas Hasenclever; Mark Peceny; Christopher K. Butler; Matthew Rendall; John M. Owen. **Int. Pol.** 41:4 12:2004 pp.465-617. *Collection of 8 articles.*

4870   The emergence of a shared identity: an agent-based computer simulation of idea diffusion. David Rousseau; A. Maurits Veen. **J. Confl. Resol.** 49:5 10:2005 pp.686-712.

4871   Empire, liberalism & the quest for perpetual peace. Anthony Pagden. **Dædalus** 134:2 Spring:2005 pp.46-57.

4872   The enduring dilemmas of realism in international relations. Stefano Guzzini. **Euro. J. Int. Rel.** 10:4 12:2004 pp.533-568.

4873   Les états face aux " nouveaux acteurs ". *[In French]*; [The states facing "new actors"] *[Summary]*; *[Summary in Spanish]*. Samy Cohen. **Polit. Int.** 107 Spring:2005 pp.409-424.

4874   Forum on Habermas. Thomas Diez; Jill Steans; Andrew Linklater; Kimberly Hutchings; Nicole Deitelhoff; Harald Müller; Jürgen Haacke; Martin Weber. **R. Int. S.** 31:1 1:2005 pp.127-209. *Collection of 6 articles.*

4875   Generalising the international. Jenny Edkins; Maja Zehfuss. **R. Int. S.** 31:3 7:2005 pp.451-471.

4876   Global governance. Bernd von Hoffmann [Ed.]. Frankfurt am Main, New York: Peter Lang, 2004. 199p. *ISBN: 3631527705, 0820473251. (Series:* Rechtspolitisches Symposium =. Legal Policy Symposium - Bd. 2).

4877   Globalización, rol del estado y relaciones internacionales en el realismo de Robert Gilpin. *[In Spanish]*; [Globalization, the role of the state and international relations in Robert Gilpin's realism]. Raúl Allard Neuman. **Est. Inter.** XXXVII:146 7-9:2004 pp.5-39.

4878   The good state: in praise of 'classical' internationalism. Peter Lawler. **R. Int. S.** 31:3 7:2005 pp.427-449.

4879   Hard times for soft balancing. Stephen G. Brooks; William C. Wohlforth. **Int. Secur.** 30:1 Summer:2005 pp.72-108.

4880   Hegemony and autonomy. Howard H. Lentner. **Pol. S.** 53:4 12:2005 pp.735-752.

4881   Identiteetistä mielenmaisemaan : kansallisten tarinoiden paluu maailmanpolitiikan tutkimukseen. *[In Finnish]*; [From identities to mindscapes: return of national narratives to international studies] *[Summary]*. Marko Lehti. **Kosmopolis** 34:3 2004 pp.51-71.

4882   Misreading in international relations theory. Ideologiekritische Anmerkungen zum Realismus und Neo-Realismus. *[In German]*; (Misreading in international relations theory.

Critical remarks on realism and neo-realism.) Hartmut Behr. **Z. Pol.wissen.** 15:1 2005 pp.61-90.

4883   On Huntington's civilizational paradigm: a reappraisal. Myongsob Kim; Horace Jeffery Hodges. **Iss. Stud.** 41:2 6:2005 pp.217-248.

4884   Paradigm lost: reassessing theory of international politics. Stacie E. Goddard; Daniel H. Nexon. **Euro. J. Int. Rel.** 11:1 3:2005 pp.9-61.

4885   The realist tradition and the limits of international relations. Michael C. Williams. Cambridge, New York: Cambridge University Press, 2005. ix, 236p. *ISBN: 0521827523, 0521534755. Includes bibliographical references (p. 211-225) and index. (Series:* Cambridge studies in international relations - 100).

4886   Realistic realism? American political realism, Clausewitz and Raymond Aron on the problem of means and ends in international politics. Murielle Cozette. **J. Strategic S.** 27:3 9:2004 pp.428-453.

4887   Tragedy, realism, and postmodernity: kulturpessimismus in the theories of Max Weber, E.H. Carr, Hans J. Morgenthau, and Henry Kissinger. Mark Gismondi. **Dipl. State.** 15:3 9:2004 pp.435-463.

4888   Truth, power, theory: Hans Morgenthau's formulation of realism. Sean Molloy. **Dipl. State.** 15:1 3:2004 pp.1-34.

4889   Uluslararası ilişkilerin "gerçekçi" teorisi: kökeni, kapsamı, kritiği. *[In Turkish]*; (The realist theory of the international relations: origin, scope, critique.) Mustafa Aydin. **Uluslararasi Ilişkiler** 1:1 Spring:2004 pp.33-60.

4890   Waiting for balancing: why the world is not pushing back. Keir A. Lieber; Gerard Alexander. **Int. Secur.** 30:1 Summer:2005 pp.109-139.

4891   What moves man: the realist theory of international relations and its judgment of human nature. Annette Freyberg-Inan. Albany NY: State University of New York Press, 2004. vi, 266p. *ISBN: 079145827X, 0791458288. Includes bibliographical references (p. 231-255) and index. (Series:* SUNY series in global politics).

F.3.2:   **Foreign policy**
             Politique étrangère

4892   Australian foreign policy and the RAMSI intervention in Solomon Islands. Tarcisius Tara Kabutaulaka. **Contemp. Pac.** 17:2 2005 pp.283-308.

4893   Bringing 'comparative' back to foreign policy analysis. Marijke Breuning. **Int. Pol.** 41:4 12:2004 pp.618-628.

4894   Contested terrains. Howard Campbell; Tim Anderson; Katherine E. McCoy; Mario E. Carranza; Angelo Rivero-Santos. **Lat. Am. Persp.** 32:6(145) 11:2005 pp.8-89. *Collection of 4 articles.*

4895   Foreign policy priorities for the Howard government's fourth term. Richard Woolcott. **Aust. J. Int. Aff.** 59:2 6:2005 pp.141-152.

4896   Giving justice its due. George Perkovich. **Foreign Aff.** 84:4 7-8:2005 pp.79-93.

4897   Health, security and foreign policy. Colin McInnes; Kelley Lee. **R. Int. S.** 32:1 1:2005 pp.5-24.

4898   How Europe views America. Fraser Cameron. **Int. Aff. [Moscow]** 51:2 2005 pp.83-95.

4899   The impact of Iran's nuclearization on Israel. Ehsaneh I. Sadr. **Mid. East Policy** XII:2 Summer:2005 pp.58-72.

4900   İran İslam cumhuriyeti'nin Orta Asya ve Azerbaycan politikaları. *[In Turkish]*; (Foreign policy of Islamic republic of Iran towards Central Asia and Azerbaijan.) Atay Akdevelioğlu. **Uluslararasi Ilişkiler** 1:2 Spring:2004 pp.129-160.

4901   Iran's developing military capabilities. Anthony H. Cordesman. Washington DC: CSIS Press, 2005. xii, 147p. *ISBN: 0892064692. Includes bibliographical references. (Series:* Significant issues).

4902   Issues in Australian foreign policy. Tom Conley. **Aust. J. Pol. Hist.** 51:2 6:2005 pp.257-273.

4903   The liberal tradition in Australian foreign policy. Malcolm Fraser; David Reynolds; Neville Meaney; Carl Bridge; Christopher Waters; David Lowe; Frank Bongiorno; Gwenda Tavan; David Lee; Roderic Pitty; Peter Edwards; Gary Smith; Rae Wear. **Aust. J. Pol. Hist.** 51:3 9:2005 pp.332-480. *Collection of 12 articles.*

4904   New Zealand foreign policy under the Clark government: high tide of liberal internationalism? David McCraw. **Pac. Aff.** 78:2 Summer:2005 pp.217-235.

4905   Perspectives on Australian foreign policy, 2004. Matt McDonald. **Aust. J. Int. Aff.** 59:2 6:2005 pp.153-168.

4906   Political myth, or foreign policy and the fantasy of Israel. Roland Boer. **Arena J.** 23 2005 pp.77-95.

4907   Syria and the doctrine of Arab neutralism: from independence to dependence. Rami Ginat. Brighton, Portland OR: Sussex Academic Press, 2005. xix, 310p. *ISBN: 1845190084. Includes bibliographical references and index.*

4908   Syrian motives for its WMD program and what to do. Murhaf Jouejati. **Mid. East J.** 59:1 Winter:2005 pp.52-61.

Africa
Afrique

4909   Consistency and inconsistencies in South African foreign policy. Laurie Nathan. **Int. Aff. [London]** 81:2 3:2005 pp.361-372.

4910   Democratizing foreign policy? Lessons from South Africa. Philip Nel [Ed.]; Janis Van der Westhuizen [Ed.]. Lanham MD: Lexington Books, 2004. viii, 225p. *ISBN: 073910585X. Includes bibliographical references (p. 183-201) and index.*

4911   Dilemme de décision en politique étrangère des états Africains lors de la guerre d'Irak 2003. *[In French]*; [Dilemmas of foreign policy decision-making in African states during Iraq War of 2003]. Geoffrey Likanda Oloba. **Penant** 849 10-12:2004 pp.488-500.

4912   La Grande-Bretagne de Tony Blair et l'Afrique. *[In French]*; (Tony Blair's Britain and Africa.) *[Summary]*. Paul Williams. **Pol. Afr.** 94 6:2004 pp.105-127.

4913   The new South Africa's foreign policy: principles and practice. James Barber. **Int. Aff. [London]** 81:5 10:2005 pp.1079-1096.

4914   Nigeria's new foreign policy thrust: essays in honour of Ambassador Oluyemi Adeniji, CON, at 70. Bola A. Akinterinwa [Ed.]; Kofi Annan [Foreword]; Olu Adeniji [Ed.]. Ibadan: Vantage Publishers, 2004. xxxv, 517p. *ISBN: 9783692550, 9783692569. Includes bibliographical references and index.*

4915   La politique étrangère de la République démocratique du Congo: structures, fonctionnement et manifestations. *[In French]*; [The foreign policy of the Democratic Republic of Congo: structure, functioning and manifestations]. Labana Lasay'Abar; Lofembe Benkenya. Kinshasa: Maison d'editions Sirius, 2004. 96p. *Includes bibliographical references (p. 75-80).*

4916   South Africa's Zimbabwe policy: unravelling the contradictions. Linda Freeman. **J. Contemp. Afr. S.** 23:2 5:2005 pp.147-172.

4917   Unveiling South Africa's nuclear past. Verne Harris; Sello Hatang; Peter Liberman. **J. Sth. Afr. S.** 30:3 9:2004 pp.457-475.

Americas
Amérique

4918   Afghanistan: when counternarcotics undermines counterterrorism. Vanda Felbab-Brown. **Washington Q.** 28:4 Autumn:2005 pp.55-72.

4919   American foreign policy and global opinion: who supported the war in Afghanistan? Benjamin E. Goldsmith; Yusaku Horiuchi; Takashi Inoguchi. **J. Confl. Resol.** 49:3 6:2005 pp.408-429.

4920   American grand strategy in a world at risk. Walter Russell Mead. **Orbis** 49:4 Fall:2005 pp.589-598.

4921   American maximalism. Stephen Sestanovich. **Nat. Interest** 79 Spring:2005 pp.13-23.

4922   American role in the Near East and South Asia. Karamatullah K. Ghori. **Pakis. Horiz.** 57:4 10:2004 pp.45-55.

4923   Amerikanskie konservatory i Evropa. *[In Russian]*; (American conservatives and Europe.) P. Rakhshmir. **Mir. Ekon. Mezh. Ot.** 7 7:2004 pp.30-41.

4924   Arms control, proliferation and terrorism: the Bush administration's post September 11 security strategy. Andrew Newman. **J. Strategic S.** 27:1 3:2004 pp.59-88.

4925   Auto-estima in Brazil: the logic of Lula's south-south foreign policy. Sean W. Burges. **Int. J.** LX:4 Autumn:2005 pp.1133-1151.

4926   Between restoration and liberation: theopolitical contributions and responses to U.S. foreign policy in Israel/Palestine. Robert O. Smith. **J. Chur. State** 46:4 Autumn:2004 pp.833-860.

4927   Bill Graham, Pierre Pettigrew, Jim Peterson. Douglas Goold. **Int. J.** LIX:4 Autumn:2004 pp.929-942.

4928   The birth of ANZUS: America's attempt to create a defense linkage between Northest Asia and the Southwest Pacific. Hiroyuki Umetsu. **Int. Rel. Asia Pacific** 4:1 2004 pp.171-196.

4929   The Bush administration and the nuclear challenges by North Korea. Juergen Kleiner. **Dipl. State.** 16:2 6:2005 pp.203-226.

4930   The Bush administration's foreign policy in historical perspective. Melvyn P. Leffler; Robert Kagan; Walter L. Hixson; Carolyn Eisenberg; Daniel W. Drezner; Arnold A. Offner; Anna Kasten Nelson. **Dipl. Hist.** 29:3 6:2005 pp.395-444. *Collection of 8 articles.*

4931   Bush and the world, take 2. John Lewis Gaddis; James Dobbins; Edward N. Luttwak; Jeffrey E. Garten; John Deutch; Dennis Ross; Francis Fukuyama; William Drozdiak; Selig S. Harrison; Edward P. Joseph; Scott Straus; Stuart Eizenstat; John Edward Porter; Jeremy Weinstein. **Foreign Aff.** 84:1 1-2:2005 pp.2-146. *Collection of 12 articles.*

4932   The Bush doctrine is dead; long live the Bush doctrine? Donald C.F. Daniel; Peter Dombrowski; Rodger A. Payne. **Orbis** 49:2 Spring:2005 pp.199-212.

4933   Bush's Middle East: second-term blues? Nicholas A. Veliotes. **Mediterr. Q.** 16:2 Spring:2005 pp.1-10.

4934   Canada's human security agenda: walking the talk? Elizabeth Riddell-Dixon. **Int. J.** LX:4 Autumn:2005 pp.1067-1092.

4935   Chain of command: the road from 9/11 to Abu Ghraib. Seymour M. Hersh. New York: HarperCollins, 2004. xix, 394p. *ISBN: 0060195916.*

4936   Cheap hawks, cheap doves, and the pursuit of strategy. Harvey Sicherman. **Orbis** 49:4 Fall:2005 pp.613-630.

4937   Coercive diplomacy and an 'irrational' regime: understanding the American confrontation with the Taliban. Shah M. Tarzi. **Int. S.** 42:1 2005 pp.21-41.

4938   Comprendre le soutien des Etats-Unis envers Israël. *[In French]*; [Understanding US support for Israel]. Dana H. Allin; Steven Simon. **Ann. Fran. Rel. Int.** 5 2004 pp.616-637.

4939   Continuidades e descontinuidades no modo Americano de entrar em guerra. *[In Portuguese]*; (Continuity and discontinuity in the American way of going to war.) *[Summary]*. John L. Harper; Rui Tavares [Tr.]. **Relações Int.** 4 12:2004 pp.5-30.

4940   Crude awakenings: global oil security and American foreign policy. Steven A. Yetiv. Ithaca NY: Cornell University Press, 2004. 239p. *ISBN: 0801442680. Includes bibliographical references and index.*

4941   Demilitarising demographics: US policy options for strengthening Georgian internal security. Benjamin Jensen. **Low Int. Confl. Law Enf.** 12:1 Spring:2004 pp.51-90.

4942   Deterring a nuclear Iran. Jason Zaborski. **Washington Q.** 28:3 Summer:2005 pp.153-168.

4943   Deterring terrorists: thoughts on a framework. Daniel Whiteneck. **Washington Q.** 28:3 Summer:2005 pp.187-199.

4944   A dubious template for US foreign policy. Chester A. Crocker. **Survival** 47:1 Spring:2005 pp.51-70.

4945   Empire by denial: the strange case of the United States. Michael Cox. **Int. Aff. [London]** 81:1 1:2005 pp.15-30.
4946   Evaluating the Bush menu for change in the Middle East. Augustus Richard Norton; Louis J. Cantori; Carrie Rosefsky Wickham; Judith S. Yaphe; Michael C. Hudson; Eric Davis. **Mid. East Policy** XII:1 Spring:2005 pp.97-121.
4947   Un fantasme américain : la démocratie au Grand Moyen-Orient. *[In French]*; [An American fantasy: democracy in the Middle East]. Jean-Jacques Salomon. **Futuribles** 302 11:2004 pp.5-27.
4948   The first annual John W. Holmes issue on Canadian foreign policy. Kim Richard Nossal; Thomas S. Axworthy; Paul Heinbecker; Jane Boulden; Alexander Lofthouse; Will Kymlicka; Amitav Rath. **Int. J.** LIX:4 Autumn:2004 pp.747-871. *Collection of 8 articles.*
4949   Foreign policy polemics in the U.S. E. Ananieva. **Int. Aff. [Moscow]** 51:2 2005 pp.23-33.
4950   From containment to n-gagement: Atlanticism in a network-centric world. Henrikki Heikka. **Y. Finnish For. Pol.** 2004 pp.107-119.
4951   The grammar of life — in dialogue with Don Watson's Death Sentence. Annabelle Lukin. **Arena J.** 23 2005 pp.111-127.
4952   La guerre américaine, guerre sans fin ? *[In French]*; [The American war, war with no end?] Bruno Tertrais. **Etudes** 400:4 4:2004 pp.453-463.
4953   The Howard doctrine: an irritant to China. Hou Minyue. **J. East Asian Aff.** XIX:1 Spring-Summer:2005 pp.113-142.
4954   Implications of the U.S. reaction to the world court ruling against Israel's 'separation barrier'. Stephen Zunes. **Mid. East Policy** XI:4 Winter:2004 pp.72-85.
4955   Isolationism revisited: seven persistent myths in the contemporary American foreign policy debate. David Hastings Dunn. **R. Int. S.** 31:2 4:2005 pp.237-261.
4956   Leo Strauss, neoconservatism and US foreign policy: esoteric nihilism and the Bush doctrine. Jim George. **Int. Pol.** 12:2 6:2005 pp.174-202.
4957   Missed opportunities: the 9/11 commission report and US foreign policy. Ted Galen Carpenter. **Mediterr. Q.** 16:1 Winter:2005 pp.52-61.
4958   "More of the same", in der zweiten Amtszeit? *[In German]*; (More of the same? The foreign policy of George W. Bush in the second term.) Heinrich Kreft. **Welt Trends** 46 Spring:2005 pp.109-123.
4959   Myths of neoconservatism: George W. Bush's 'neo-conservative' foreign policy revisited. Steven Hurst. **Int. Pol.** 42:1 3:2005 pp.75-96.
4960   Národní bezpečnostní strategie USA. *[In Czech]*; (US national security strategy.) *[Summary]*. Radek Khol. **Mez. Vzt.** 40:1 2005 pp.71-85.
4961   The new age of assassination. Ward Thomas. **SAIS R.** XXV:1 Winter-Spring:2005 pp.27-39.
4962   New approaches to deterrence in Britain, France, and the United States. David S. Yost. **Int. Aff. [London]** 81:1 1:2005 pp.83-114.
4963   The new imperialism? On continuity and change in US foreign policy. Jim Glassman. **Env. Plan. A** 37:9 9:2005 pp.1527-1544.
4964   New regionalism and modes of governance: comparing US and EU strategies in Latin America. Jean B. Grugel. **Euro. J. Int. Rel.** 10:4 12:2004 pp.603-626.
4965   A new U.S. global defence posture and the future of Korea-U.S. alliance. Sang-hyun Lee. **Kor. World Aff.** 28:2 Summer:2004 pp.117-130.
4966   Not without my sister(s): imagining a moral America in Kandahar. Cynthia Weber. **Int. Femin. J. Pol.** 7:3 2005 pp.358-376.
4967   Nuclear diplomacy up close: Strobe Talbott on the Clinton administration and India. Bill Finan. **India R.** 4:1 1:2005 pp.84-97.
4968   Nuclear superiority or mutually assured deterrence: the development of the US nuclear deterrent. David S. McDonough. **Int. J.** LX:3 Summer:2005 pp.811-823.
4969   Partition versus union: competing traditions in American foreign policy. James Kurth. **Dipl. State.** 15:4 12:2004 pp.809-831.
4970   Permanent war? The domestic hegemony of the new American militarism. Ken Cunningham. **New Pol. Sci.** 26:4 12:2004 pp.551-567.

4971   The political use of military force in US foreign policy. James David Meernik. Aldershot: Ashgate, 2004. 269p. *ISBN: 0754642887. Includes bibliographical references (p. [245]-256) and index.*

4972   La politique nord-coréenne des Etats-Unis. *[In French]*; [US foreign policy for North Korea]. Robert Dujarric. **Ann. Fran. Rel. Int.** 5 2004 pp.591-604.

4973   Readjusting the role of U.S. forces in Korea in a changing world. Yong-sup Han. **Kor. World Aff.** 28:1 Spring:2004 pp.31-45.

4974   Reality bites: the impending logic of withdrawal from Iraq. Barry Rubin. **Washington Q.** 28:2 Spring:2005 pp.67-80.

4975   The rise and fall of conservative reform in the United States: George W. Bush and the transformation of the Reagan legacy. John Samples. **Asia Pac. R.** 11:2 11:2004 pp.96-114.

4976   Securitising the unconscious: the Bush doctrine of preemption and minority report. Cynthia Weber. **Geopolitics** 10:3 2005 pp.482-499.

4977   The strategic sources of foreign policy substitution. David H. Clark; William Reed. **Am. J. Pol. Sci.** 49:3 7:2005 pp.609-624.

4978   The superpower myth: the use and misuse of American might. Nancy E. Soderberg. Hoboken NJ: John Wiley & Sons Ltd, 2005. xii, 404p. *ISBN: 0471656836. Includes index.*

4979   Taking on the world: the international activities of American state legislatures. Timothy J. Conlan; Robert L. Dudley; Joel F. Clark. **Publius** 34:3 Summer:2004 pp.183-199.

4980   Threats all way down: US strategic initiatives in a unipolar world. Wade Huntley. **R. Int. S.** 32:1 1:2005 pp.49-67.

4981   Trading places: America and Europe in the Middle East. Philip H. Gordon. **Survival** 47:2 Summer:2005 pp.87-99.

4982   A transatlantic strategy to promote democratic development in the broader Middle East. Ronald D. Asmus; Larry Diamond; Mark Leonard; Michael McFaul. **Washington Q.** 28:2 Spring:2005 pp.7-22.

4983   The twilight of democracy: the Bush plan for America. Jennifer Van Bergen. Monroe ME: Common Courage Press, 2005. 228p. *ISBN: 1567512933, 1567512925.*

4984   The United States and Asia in 2004: unfinished business. Jonathan D. Pollack. **Asian Sur.** XLV:1 1-2:2005 pp.1-13.

4985   The United States and the North African imbroglio: balancing interests in Algeria, Morocco, and the Western Sahara. Yahia H. Zoubir; Karima Benabdallah-Gambier. **Med. Pol.** 10:2 7:2005 pp.181-202.

4986   US democracy promotion in the Arab Middle East since 11 September 2001: a critique. Katerina Dalacoura. **Int. Aff. [London]** 81:5 10:2005 pp.963-980.

4987   U.S. foreign policy and the future of democracy in Iran. Abbas Milani. **Washington Q.** 28:3 Summer:2005 pp.41-56.

4988   US foreign policy and the Persian Gulf: safeguarding American interests through selective multilateralism. Robert J. Pauly. Aldershot, Burlington VT: Ashgate, 2005. vi, 158p. *ISBN: 0754635333. Includes bibliographical references and index. (Series: US foreign policy and conflict in the Islamic world).*

4989   US policy in Iraq during President Bush's second term: the possibility of international involvement. Ranjit Gupta. **India Q.** LX:4 10-12:2004 pp.85-109.

4990   U.S. policy toward a weak Assad. Dennis Ross. **Washington Q.** 28:3 Summer:2005 pp.87-98.

4991   US strategy in the Middle East and the 2004 presidential election 9/11: towards a redefinition of America's role in the world. Kenneth R. Weinstein. **Asia Pac. R.** 11:2 11:2004 pp.81-95.

4992   Visiones globales y opciones transnacionales en la agenda exterior chilena con Estados Unidos. Aproximación a un estudio de caso. *[In Spanish]*; [Global visions and transnational options in Chile's foreign agenda with the United States. A case study]. José A. Morandé Lavín. **Est. Inter.** XXXVII:147 10-12:2004 pp.117-132.

4993   War and the American presidency. Arthur Meier Schlesinger. Waterville ME: Thorndike Press, 2005. 199p. *ISBN: 0786273445.*

4994   Why not invade North Korea? Threats, language games, and U.S. foreign policy. Peter Howard. **Int. S. Q.** 48:4 12:2004 pp.805-828.

4995   Why the Bush doctrine cannot be sustained. Robert Jervis. **Pol. Sci. Q.** 120:3 Fall:2005 pp.351-377.

Asia
Asie

4996   An assessment of China's Taiwan policy under the third generation leadership. Chen-yuan Tung. **Asian Sur.** XLV:3 5-6:2005 pp.343-361.

4997   China und die Welt. Prämissen, Interessen und Maximen chinesischer Außen – und Sicherheitspolitik. *[In German]*; [China and the world. Premises, interests and maxims of Chinese foreign and security policy]. Sven Bernhard Gareis. **Gesell. Wirt. Pol.** 53:4 2004 pp.449-462.

4998   China's good neighbor policy and its implications for Taiwan. Robert Sutter. **J. Cont. China** 13:41 12:2004 pp.717-731.

4999   China's "new thinking" on Japan. Peter Hays Gries. **Chi. Q.** 184 12:2005 pp.831-850.

5000   China's quest for oil security: oil (wars) in the pipeline? Pak K. Lee. **Pac. R.** 18:2 6:2005 pp.265-301.

5001   Chinese foreign policy in transition: understanding China's 'peaceful development'. Xiaoxiong Yi. **J. East Asian Aff.** XIX:1 Spring-Summer:2005 pp.74-112.

5002   Cold peace: Russia's new imperialism. Janusz Bugajski. Westport CT, Washington DC: Praeger, 2004. 302p. *ISBN: 0275983625.*

5003   Command of the sea with Chinese characteristics. Toshi Yoshihara; James Holmes. **Orbis** 49:4 Fall:2005 pp.677-694.

5004   Defense reform in Taiwan: problems and prospects. Michael S. Chase. **Asian Sur.** XLV:3 5-6:2005 pp.362-382.

5005   Ethnic minority issues in China's foreign policy: perspectives and implications. Yuchao Zhu; Dongyan Blachford. **Pac. R.** 18:2 6:2005 pp.243-264.

5006   First year of the Roh Moo-hyun administration: evaluation and prospects of North Korea policy. Hyeong Jung Park. **Kor. World Aff.** 28:1 Spring:2004 pp.9-22.

5007   Foucault's pendulum: Turkey in Central Asia and the Caucasus. Mustafa Aydın. **Turkish S.** 5:2 Summer:2004 pp.1-22.

5008   The global politics of the Iraq crisis and India's options. Hari S. Vasudevan [Ed.]; Shri Prakash [Ed.]; Mujib Alam [Ed.]. Delhi: Aakar Books, 2004. viii, 336p. *ISBN: 8187879319. Includes bibliographical references. Academy of Third World Studies. Jamia Millia Islamia.*

5009   How Japan can contribute to a peaceful world. Carolina G. Hernandez. **Asia Pac. R.** 12:1 5:2005 pp.87-102.

5010   India's commitment to peaceful coexistence and the settlement of the Indochina war. Gilles Boquérat. **Cold War Hist.** 5:2 5:2005 pp.211-234.

5011   International pressure and North Korea's current options: will inter-Korean relations improve? Gillian Goh. **Asian J. Pol. Sci.** 12:1 6:2004 pp.117-133.

5012   Iraq, terror, and the Philippines' will to war. James A. Tyner. Lanham MD: Rowman & Littlefield, 2005. x, 145p. *ISBN: 0742538605, 0742538613. Includes bibliographical references (p. 135-138) and index.*

5013   The Islamic world and Russia's foreign policy. S. Mironov; B. Piadyshev; V. Popov; A. Poliakov; V. Khrulev; S. Rogov; N. Simonia; M. Titarenko; I. Kudriashova; A. Shumilin. **Int. Aff. [Moscow]** 51:4 2005 pp.88-100.

5014   Iuzhnyi Kavkaz v politike Turtsii i Rossii v postsovetskii period. *[In Russian]*; [The South Caucasus in the politics of Turkey and Russia in the post-Soviet period]. Omer Kodzhaman. Moscow: Russkaiia panorama, 2004. v, 294p. *ISBN: 5931651225. Includes bibliographical references (p. 278-[290]) and index.*

5015   Japan: U.S. partner or focused on abductees? David C. Kang. **Washington Q.** 28:4 Autumn:2005 pp.107-117.

5016   Japanese anti-piracy initiatives in Southeast Asia: policy formulation and the coastal state responses. John F. Bradford. **Contemp. Sth.East Asia** 26:3 12:2004 pp.480-505.

5017   Japanese security policy in transition: the rise of international and human security. Yoshihide Soeya. **Asia Pac. R.** 12:1 5:2005 pp.103-116.

5018   Japan's 'coalition of the willing' on security policies. Robert Pekkanen; Ellis S. Krauss. **Orbis** 49:3 Summer:2005 pp.429-444.

5019   Japon/Afrique. *[In French]*; [Japan and Africa]. Makoto Sato; Chris Alden; Scarlett Cornelissen; Shozo Kamo; Minoru Ogasawara; Minoru Obayashi; Kweku Ampiah; Anne Androuais. **Afr. Contemp.** 212 Autumn:2004 pp.9-129. *Collection of 7 articles.*

5020   Learning to live with the hegemon: evolution of China's policy toward the US since the end of the Cold War. Jia Qingguo. **J. Cont. China** 14:44 8:2005 pp.395-407.

5021   Mapping North East on India's foreign policy: looking past, present and beyond. Manoj Kumar Nath. **Indian J. Pol. Sci.** LXV:4 10-12:2004 pp.636-652.

5022   Miroljubivi uspon — nova kineska vanjskopolitička teorija. *[In Croatian]*; (Peaceful rise — new Chinese foreign-policy theory.) *[Summary]*. Ozren Baković. **Pol. Misao** 41:1 2004 pp.126-137.

5023   Nationalism, internationalism and Chinese foreign policy. Chen Zhimin. **J. Cont. China** 14:42 2:2005 pp.35-53.

5024   Pakistan, Islamisation, army and foreign policy. Bidanda M. Chengappa. New Delhi: A.P.H. Publishing Corporation, 2004. ix, 301p. *ISBN: 8176485489. Includes index.*

5025   Philippine defence policy in the 21st century: autonomous defence or back to the alliance? Renato Cruz De Castro. **Pac. Aff.** 78:3 Fall:2005 pp.403-422.

5026   La politique extérieure : pragmatisme et intérêts nationaux. *[In French]*; [Foreign policy: pragmatism and national interests]. François Godement. **Quest. Int.** 6 3-4:2004 pp.39-49.

5027   Quiet power: Japan's China policy in regard to the Pinnacle islands. Linus Hagström. **Pac. R.** 18:2 6:2005 pp.159-188.

5028   Les relations sino-américaines depuis la fin de la guerre froide. *[In French]*; [Sino-American relations since the end of the Cold War]. Daniel Sabbagh. **Quest. Int.** 6 3-4:2004 pp.59-65.

5029   Russian security policy. Amina Afzal. **Strat. S.** XXV:1 Spring:2005 pp.66-82.

5030   South Korea's squeeze play. Scott Snyder. **Washington Q.** 28:4 Autumn:2005 pp.93-106.

5031   Ubiquity of "power" and the advantage of terminological pluralism: Japan's foreign policy discourse. Linus Hagström. **Japanese J. Pol. Sci.** 6:2 8:2005 pp.145-164.

5032   Uneasy neighbors: India, Pakistan, and US foreign policy. Kanishkan Sathasivam. Aldershot, Burlington VT: Ashgate, 2005. xi, 195p. *ISBN: 075463762X. Includes bibliographical references (p. [181]-190) and index. (Series: US foreign policy and conflict in the Islamic world).*

Europe
Europe

5033   The 'Americanization' of Italian foreign policy? Osvaldo Croci. **J. Mod. Ital. S.** 10:1 3:2005 pp.10-26.

5034   Analysing the foreign policy of small states in the EU: the case of Denmark. Henrik Larsen. Basingstoke, New York: Palgrave Macmillan, 2005. xiv, 242p. *ISBN: 033396473X. Includes bibliographical references (p. 221-233) and index.*

5035   The art of caution: the Iraq crisis and Finnish foreign policy continua. Henri Vogt. **Y. Finnish For. Pol.** 2004 pp.63-76.

5036   La Belgique et sa politique étrangère : 2002-2004. *[In French]*; België en zjin buitenlandse politiek. *[In Dutch]*; [Belgium and its foreign policy: 2002-2004]. Claude Roosens; Christian Franck; Paul Magnette; Hendrik Vos; René Schwok; Bart Kerremans; Philippe

Suinen; Simon Petermann; Leo Michel; Tanguy de Wilde d'Estmaele; Rik Coolsaet. **Integ. Lat.am.** LVII:3 2004 pp.5-146. *Collection of 11 articles.*

5037 British government policy in sub-Saharan Africa under New Labour. Tom Porteous. **Int. Aff. [London]** 81:2 3:2005 pp.281-298.

5038 The collapse of British foreign policy. William Wallace. **Int. Aff. [London]** 81:1 1:2005 pp.53-68.

5039 Les confins dans la politique internationale du Vatican. *[In French]*; [The limits of the Vatican's international policy] *[Summary]*. François Mabille. **R. Ét. Comp. Est-Ouest** 35:4 12:2004 pp.127-147.

5040 Democracy and defence in Latvia: thirteen years of development: 1991-2004. Jan Arveds Trapans. **Euro. Sec.** 14:1 3:2005 pp.51-70.

5041 Enhancing African peace and security capacity: a useful role for the UK and the G8? Alex Ramsbotham; Alhaji M.S. Bah; Fanny Calder. **Int. Aff. [London]** 81:2 3:2005 pp.325-340.

5042 Entre empire et nations : penser la politique étrangère. *[In French]*; [Between Empire and nation: on foreign policy]. Gabriel Robin. Paris: Editions Odile Jacob, 2004. 334p. *ISBN: 2738115195.*

5043 L'Espagne et la guerre en Irak. *[In French]*; [Spain and the Iraq war]. Isaias Barreñada; Ivan Martin; José Antonio Sanahuja. **Crit. Int.** 23 4:2004 pp.9-21.

5044 L'Europe gère les Balkans. La responsabilité finale reste au concert des puissances. *[In French]*; (Europe runs the Balkans. The final responsibility remains to the concert of powers.) Francine Boidevaix. **Relations Int.** 121 1-3:2005 pp.91-112.

5045 The European policy of the German Social Democrats: interpreting a changing world. James Sloam. Basingstoke, New York: Palgrave Macmillan, 2005. xi, 267p. *ISBN: 1403935815. Includes bibliographical references (p. 257-264) and index. (Series:* New perspectives in German studies).

5046 The europeanisation of Greek foreign policy. Spyros Economides. **West Euro. Pol.** 28:2 3:2005 pp.471-491.

5047 The europeanisation of Greek foreign policy: a critical appraisal. Charalambos Tsardanidis; Stelios Stavridis. **J. Euro. Integ.** 27:2 6:2005 pp.217-239.

5048 Ex occidente Lux … Warum der deutsche Anspruch auf einen ständigen Sitz im UN-Sicherheitsrat schlecht begründet ist und wie Deutschland auf anderem Wege „dauerhaft mehr Verantwortung übernehmen" kann. *[In German]*; (Ex occidente Lux …: Germany's ambition for a permanent seat at the UN Security Council is ill-conceived.) Gunther Hellmann. **Polit. Viertel.** 45:4 12:2004 pp.479-493.

5049 La France, l'OTAN et l'Union Européenne : entre logique atlantique et logique européenne. *[In French]*; [France, NATO and the European Union: between the atlantic logic and the European strategy] *[Summary]*. Michèle Bacot-Décriaud. **Arès** 20:3(52) 2:2004 pp.11-19.

5050 France's evolving nuclear strategy. David S. Yost. **Survival** 47:3 Autumn:2005 pp.117-146.

5051 Gás natural: o impacto do gasoduto do Magrebe e do terminal GNL na economia e política externa de Portugal. *[In Portuguese]*; (Natural gas: the impact of the Maghreb pipeline on Portuguese foreign policy.) *[Summary]*. Luís Ferreira Lopes. **Relações Int.** 6 6:2005 pp.91-106.

5052 Geopoliticheskaia strategiia Rossii: vybor optimal'nogo varianta. *[In Russian]*; [Choosing Russia's optimum geopolitical strategy]. A.S. Semchenkov. **Vest. Mosk. Univ. 12 Pol.** 3 5-6:2005 pp.48-68.

5053 German foreign policy and the war on Iraq: anti-Americanism, pacifism or emancipation? Tuomas Forsberg. **Secur. Dial.** 36:2 6:2005 pp.213-232.

5054 Hvor gammel or norsk utenrikspolitikk? *[In Norwegian]*; (How old is Norwegian foreign policy?) *[Summary]*. Iver B. Neumann. **Internasjonal Pol.** 63:2-3 2005 pp.162-182.

5055 Idées, politiques de défense et stratégie. *[In French]*; [Ideas, defence policies and strategy]. Pascal Vennesson; Claude d'Abzac-Epezy; Philippe Garraud; Jean Joana; Thomas Lindemann. **R. Fran. Sci. Pol.** 54:5 10:2004 pp.749-848. *Collection of 5 articles.*

5056   Identita a štátny záujem v slovenskej zahraničnej politike. *[In Slovak]*; (Identity and state interest in the foreign policy of Slovakia.) *[Summary]*. Jozef Bátora. **Medz. Otázky** XIII:2 2004 pp.39-54.

5057   'I'm proud of the British empire': why Tony Blair backs George W. Bush. Inderjeet Parmar. **Pol. Q.** 76:2 4-6:2005 pp.218-231.

5058   The impact of 'democratization in the context of the EU accession process' on Turkish foreign policy. Tarik Oguzlu. **Med. Pol.** 9:1 Spring:2004 pp.94-113.

5059   La implicación de España en el conflicto de Iraq desde la tesis del espacio tridimensional en la práctica del derecho en los asuntos internacionales. *[In Spanish]*; (Spain involvement in the Iraqi conflict from the perspective of tridimensional space in the practice of international law.) Luis V. Pérez Gil. **Foro Int.** XLIV:4 10-12:2004 pp.726-745.

5060   The Ivanov doctrine and military reform: reasserting stability in Russia. Matthew Bouldin. **J. Slav. Mil. S.** 17:4 10-12:2004 pp.619-641.

5061   Just defending national interests? Understanding French policy towards Iraq since the end of the Gulf War. Alex MacLeod. **J. Int. Rel. Dev.** 7:4 12:2004 pp.356-387.

5062   "Mere drops in the Ocean": the politics and planning of the contribution of the British commonwealth to the final defeat of Japan, 1944-45. Thomas Hall. **Dipl. State.** 16:1 3:2005 pp.93-115.

5063   Mudança de regime e política externa: Portugal, a Indonésia e o destino de Timor Leste. *[In Portuguese]*; (Regime change and foreign policy: Portugal, Indonesia and the fate of East Timor.) *[Summary]*. Paulo Gorjão. **Anál. Soc.** XL:174 Spring:2005 pp.7-36.

5064   Multilateralism, multipolarity, and regionalism: the French foreign policy discourse. Norman Bowen. **Mediterr. Q.** 16:1 Winter:2005 pp.94-116.

5065   The myth of the 'German way': German foreign policy and transatlantic relations. Peter Rudolf. **Survival** 47:1 Spring:2005 pp.133-152.

5066   The new German foreign policy consensus. Regina Karp. **Washington Q.** 29:1 Winter:2005-2006 pp.61-82.

5067   Norsk utenrikspolitikk 100 år etter — tilbake til start? *[In Norwegian]*; (Norwegian foreign policy 100 years later: back to start?) *[Summary]*. Torgeir Larsen. **Internasjonal Pol.** 63:2-3 2005 pp.241-254.

5068   La nouvelle politique étrangère italienne. *[In French]*; [Italy's new foreign policy] *[Summary]*. Fabio Liberti. **R. Int. Stratég.** 56 Winter:2004-2005 pp.37-46.

5069   Obshchee prostrantstvo vneshnei bezopasnosti Rossii i ES: ambitsii i real'nost'. *[In Russian]*; (Common space of external security of Russia and EU: ambitions and reality.) D. Danilov. **Mir. Ekon. Mezh. Ot.** 2 2:2005 pp.35-47.

5070   Oljepolitikk og utenrikspolitikk. *[In Norwegian]*; (Petroleum policy and foreign policy.) *[Summary]*. Øystein Noreng. **Internasjonal Pol.** 63:2-3 2005 pp.183-216.

5071   L'opération Licorne en Côte d'Ivoire : banc d'essai de la nouvelle politique française de sécurité en Afrique. *[In French]*; [The Licorne operation in Côte d'Ivoire: new French security policies in Africa]. Pierre Weiss. **Ann. Fran. Rel. Int.** 5 2004 pp.313-326.

5072   Plus jamais la guerre ? Les partis et la normalisation de la politique étrangère de l'Allemagne. *[In French]*; [The war, never again? Political parties and foreign policy normalization in Germany] *[Summary]*. Brian C. Rathbun. **Crit. Int.** 25 10:2004 pp.65-91.

5073   Política externa Portuguesa. O futuro do passado. *[In Portuguese]*; (Portuguese foreign policy. The future of the past.) Nuno Filipe Brito. **Relações Int.** 5 3:2005 pp.147-161.

5074   La politique africaine de la France : ruptures et continuités. *[In French]*; [The French African policy: breaks and continuities]. Magelan Omballa. **Quest. Int.** 5 1-2:2004 pp.54-65.

5075   Le retour de la Grande-Bretagne en Sierra Leone. *[In French]*; [The return of Great Britain in Sierra Leone]. Paul Richards. **Géopol. Afr.** 15-16 Summer-Fall:2004 pp.141-154.

5076   Role theory and foreign policy change: the transformation of Russian foreign policy in the 1990s. Michael Grossman. **Int. Pol.** 42:3 9:2005 pp.334-351.

5077   La Russie et l'Islam. *[In French]*; [Russia and Islam] *[Summary]*; *[Summary in Spanish]*. Viatcheslav Avioutskii. **Polit. Int.** 107 Spring:2005 pp.73-93.

5078   The shift in Italy's euro-Atlantic policy. Partisan or bipartisan? James Walston. **Int. Spect.** XXXIX:4 10-12:2004 pp.115-125.
5079   Les stratégies britanniques en Afrique. *[In French]*; [British strategies in Africa]. Géopolitique africaine. **Géopol. Afr.** 15-16 Summer-Fall:2004 pp.105-211.
5080   Swedish geopolitics: from Rudolf Kjellén to a Swedish 'dual state'. Ola Tunander. **Geopolitics** 10:3 2005 pp.546-566.
5081   'The enemy is at the gate': Russia after Beslan. Dov Lynch. **Int. Aff. [London]** 81:1 1:2005 pp.141-161.
5082   Turkish foreign policy in post Cold War era. Idris Bal [Ed.]. Boca Raton FL: BrownWalker Press, 2004. ix,464p. *ISBN: 1581124236. Includes bibliographical references and index.*
5083   Ukraine: beyond postcommunism. Marko Bojcun. **Debatte** 13:1 4:2005 pp.9-20.
5084   The United Kingdom's 'war against terrorism'. Bradley W.C. Bamford. **Terror. Pol. Viol.** 16:4 Winter:2004 pp.737-756.
5085   Venäjän EU-politiikka ja toimijuuden ongelma. *[In Finnish]*; [Russia's EU policy and the problem of agency] *[Summary]*. Pami Aalto. **Kosmopolis** 34:4 2004 pp.47-66.
5086   Vladimir Putin's vision of Russia as a normal great power. Andrei P. Tsygankov. **Post-Sov. Aff.** 21:2 4-6:2005 pp.132-158.
5087   Vneshnepoliticheskie prioritety liberal'noi Rossii. *[In Russian]*; (Foreign policy priorities of the liberal Russia.) *[Summary]*. E.G. Solov'ev. **Polis [Moscow]** 2(85) 2005 pp.89-101.
5088   Vneshniaia politika Berlinskoi Respubliki: novyi "germanskii put'?" *[In Russian]*; (Foreign policy of the Berlin republic: new 'German way'?) N. Pavlov. **Mir. Ekon. Mezh. Ot.** 2 2:2005 pp.63-75.
5089   Was ging schief? Auslandswissenschaft nach der Postmoderne. *[In German]*; [What went wrong? Foreign policy research after postmodernism]. Thomas Hauschild. **Int. Politik** 60:1 1:2005 pp.23-33.
5090   Die Welt hinter Warschau. Die polnische Außenpolitik gegenüber den Auslandspolen. *[In German]*; (Beyond Warsaw: Polish policy towards Polish communities abroad.) Sebastian Gerhardt. **Osteuropa** 55:2 2:2005 pp.40-57.

F.3.3:   **National and international security**
              Sécurité nationale et internationale

5091   Addressing state failure. Stephen D. Krasner; Carlos Pascual. **Foreign Aff.** 84:4 7-8:2005 pp.153-163.
5092   The Afghan War and its geopolitical implications for India. Salman Haidar [Ed.]. New Delhi: Academy of Third World Studies, 2004. 197p. *ISBN: 8173045585. Includes bibliographical references.*
5093   American dominion: how global interventionism jeopardises US security. Charles V. Peña. **Glo. Dial.** 7:1-2 Winter-Spring:2005 pp.86-96.
5094   China views the revised US-Japan defense guidelines: popping the cork? Paul Midford. **Int. Rel. Asia Pacific** 4:1 2004 pp.113-145.
5095   China y la seguridad energética. *[In Spanish]*; [China and energy security]. Martín Pérez Le-Fort. **Est. Inter.** XXXVII:146 7-9:2004 pp.41-58.
5096   Constructing insecurity: Australian security discourse and policy post-2001. Matt McDonald. **Int. Rel.** 19:3 9:2005 pp.297-320.
5097   Diamond in the rough: is there a genuine environmental threat to security? J.R. McNeill. **Int. Secur.** 30:1 Summer:2005 pp.178-195.
5098   'Doing' security as though humans matter: a feminist perspective on gender and the politics of human security. Heidi Hudson. **Secur. Dial.** 36:2 6:2005 pp.155-174.
5099   European and German security policy, especially border controls, with regard to international terrorism. Torsten Stein. **Isr. Ybk Hum. Rig.** 35 2005 pp.231-250.
5100   Grazhdanskii kontrol' natsional'noi politiki bezopasnosti: opyt stran SNG. *[In Russian]*; [Civil control of national security policy: experiences of CIS countries]. Rafal'

Domisievich [Comp.]; Iu.K. Nazarkin [Comp.]. Moscow: FRPT, 2004. 344p. *ISBN: 5985360016.*

5101 Greetings from the cybercaliphate: some notes on homeland insecurity. David Martin Jones; M.L.R. Smith. **Int. Aff. [London]** 81:5 10:2005 pp.925-950.

5102 Immigration, civil liberties, and national/homeland security. Edna Keeble. **Int. J.** LX:2 Spring:2005 pp.359-372.

5103 Innere Sicherheit durch die Bundeswehr? *[In German]*; [Internal security through the federal army?] *[Summary]*. Tobias Linke. **Arc. Öffen. Recht** 129:4 12:2004 pp.489-541.

5104 Intellectual property and security: a preliminary exploration. Robin Ramcharan. **Contemp. Sec. Policy** 26:1 4:2005 pp.126-159.

5105 Interkulturalität als Sicherheitsstrategie in einer globalisierten Welt. *[In German]*; (Intercultural competence as security strategy.) Andreas Berns; Roland Wöhrle-Chon. **Welt Trends** 46 Spring:2005 pp.130-141.

5106 Kazakhstan's national security: conceptual and operational aspects. Nargis Kassenova. **Loc. Govt. S.** 24:2 6:2005 pp.151-164.

5107 Korea's challenges and opportunities: future and options. Kyong-suk Yi; Kyungsook Lee [Intro.]. Seoul: Seoul Selection, 2004. 246p. *ISBN: 8995376015. Includes bibliographical references.*

5108 The maze of fear: security and migration after 9/11. John Tirman [Ed.]. New York: New Press, 2004. viii, 322p. *ISBN: 1565849167, 156584906X. Includes bibliographical references and index.*

5109 Mezhdunarodnyi terrorizm i natsional'naia bezopasnost' Rossii. *[In Russian]*; [International terrorism and national security in Russia]. A.V. Vakhrameev. **Sots.Gum. Znan.** 1 2004 pp.33-48.

5110 Middle power leadership on the human security agenda. Ronald M. Behringer. **Coop. Confl.** 40:3 9:2005 pp.305-342.

5111 National threat and political culture: authoritarianism, antiauthoritarianism, and the September 11 attacks. Andrew J. Perrin. **Pol. Psychol.** 26:2 4:2005 pp.167-194.

5112 Natsionalnye interesy i osnovnye politicheskie sily sovremennoi Rossii. *[In Russian]*; [National interests and political forces in modern Russia]. E.G. Solov'ev. Moscow: Nauka Publications, 2004. 195p. *ISBN: 5020063169. Includes bibliographical references.*

5113 The new geopolitics of disease: between global health and global security. Alan Ingram. **Geopolitics** 10:3 2005 pp.522-545.

5114 Nordic strategic culture. Iver B. Neumann; Henrikki Heikka; Gunnar Åselius; Nina Græger; Halvard Leira; Mikkel Vedby Rasmussen; Darryl Howlett; John Glenn. **Coop. Confl.** 40:1 3:2005 pp.5-140. *Collection of 6 articles.*

5115 Renormalizing citizenship and life in fortress North America. Davina Bhandar. **Citiz. S.** 8:3 9:2004 pp.261-278.

5116 The roots of the Bush doctrine: power, nationalism, and democracy promotion in U.S. strategy. Jonathan Monten. **Int. Secur.** 29:4 Spring:2005 pp.112-156.

5117 La sécurité internationale en 2002 et 2003 : vers l'insécurité internationale. *[In French]*; [International security in 2002 and 2003: towards international insecurity] *[Summary]*. Louis Balmond; Ilène Choukri. **Arès** 20:3(52) 2:2004 pp.67-95.

5118 Terrifying thoughts: power, order, and terror after 9/11. Steven E. Miller. **Glo. Gov.** 11:2 4-6:2005 pp.247-271.

5119 Ugrozy bezopasnosti Rossii na Severnom Kavkaze. *[In Russian]*; [Threats to Russia's security in the Northern Caucasus]. N.P. Medvedev; P.V. Akinin. Stavropol: Stavropolskoe knizhnoe izdatelstvo, 2004. 336p. *ISBN: 5764409829.*

5120 Ukraine: reform in the context of flawed democracy and geopolitical anxiety. James Sherr. **Euro. Sec.** 14:1 3:2005 pp.157-173.

5121 The violence of security: Hindu nationalism and the politics of representing 'the Muslim' as a danger. Dibyesh Anand. **Round Tab.** 379 4:2005 pp.203-215.

5122 World risk society and war against terror. Keith Spence. **Pol. S.** 53:2 6:2005 pp.284-302.

Armaments industry and military expenditure
Industrie de l'armement et dépenses militaires

5123   L'armement terrestre : secteur en profondes évolutions. *[In French]*; [Terrestrial armament: a sector in deep evolutions]. François Lureau. **Défense Nat.** 60:6 6:2004 pp.11-25.

5124   Arms sales and technology transfer in Indo-Israeli relations. Stephen Blank. **J. East Asian Aff.** XIX:1 Spring-Summer:2005 pp.200-241.

5125   Congressional control over defense and delegation of authority in the case of the defense emergency response fund. Philip J. Candreva; L.R. Jones. **Arm. Forces Soc.** 32:1 10:2005 pp.105-122.

5126   Defense industry developments in the U.S. and Europe: transatlantic or bipolar? Terrence R. Guay. **J. Transatlan. S.** 3:1 Spring:2005 pp.139-157.

5127   The demand for arms imports. Ron P. Smith; Ali Tasiran. **J. Peace Res.** 42:2 3:2005 pp.167-181.

5128   Does defence spending matter to employment in Taiwan? Jr-tsung Huang; An-pang Kao. **Def. Peace Econ.** 16:2 4:2005 pp.101-115.

5129   Evasion costs and the theory of conscription. John T. Warner; Sebastian Negrusa. **Def. Peace Econ.** 16:2 4:2005 pp.83-100.

5130   El gasto en defensa y seguridad en Colombia: barreras analíticas, tendencias y avances recientes. *[In Spanish]*; [Defence spending and security in Colombia: analytic barriers, trends and recent progress]. Nicolás Urrutia Iriarte. **Plan. Desarr.** XXXV:2 7-12:2004 pp.355-387.

5131   Governance and incentive regulation in defence industry enterprises: a case study. Carlos Pestana Barros. **Euro. J. Law Econ.** 20:1 7:2005 pp.87-97.

5132   'I have seen the future and it works': the US defence industry transformation — lessons for the UK defence industrial base. Keith Hayward. **Def. Peace Econ.** 16:2 4:2005 pp.127-141.

5133   Last post for "the greatest generation": the policy implications of the decline of military experience in the U.S. Congress. William T. Bianco. **Legis. Stud. Q.** XXX:1 2:2005 pp.85-102.

5134   Pakistan's defence production: prospects for defence export. Malik Qasim Mustafa. **Strat. S.** XXIV:4 Winter:2004 pp.111-143.

5135   Paying for security: the security-prosperity dilemma in the United States. Uk Heo; Robert J. Eger, III. **J. Confl. Resol.** 49:5 10:2005 pp.792-817.

5136   The real price of war: how you pay for the war on terror. Joshua S. Goldstein. New York: New York University Press, 2004. ix, 228p. *ISBN: 0814731619. Includes bibliographical references and index.*

5137   Regulating private military companies: what role for the EU? Elke Krahmann. **Contemp. Sec. Policy** 26:1 4:2005 pp.103-125.

5138   Toward Pokhran II: explaining India's nuclearisation process. Bhumitra Chakma. **Mod. Asian S.** 39:1 2:2005 pp.189-236.

Armaments
Armements

5139   L'arme nucléaire : totem et tabou. *[In French]*; [Nuclear weapon: totem and taboo]. Alternatives non violentes. **Alter. Non Viol.** 130 2004 pp.1-51.

5140   Armes biologiques : du 20ème au 21ème siècle. *[In French]*; [Biological weapons: from the 20th to the 21st century]. Thérèse Delpech; Brad Roberts; Chandré Gould; Johnathan B. Tucker; Patrick Berche. **Pol. Étran.** 70:1 Spring:2005 pp.87-146. *Collection of 5 articles.*

5141   Battlefield nuclear weapons in South Asia: the case for restraint. Gaurav Rajen; Michael G. Vannoni. **Pol. Econ. J. India** 12:1 1-6:2005 pp.91-104.

5142   Beyond the axis of evil: ballistic missiles in Iran's military thinking. Kamran Taremi. **Secur. Dial.** 36:1 3:2005 pp.93-108.

5143   The Biological Weapons Convention: a failed revolution. Jez Littlewood. Aldershot, Burlington VT: Ashgate, 2004. 250p. *ISBN: 0754638545. Includes index.*

5144   British weapons acquisition policy and the futility of reform. Warren Chin. Aldershot: Ashgate, 2004. x, 300p. *ISBN: 0754631214. Includes bibliographical references and index.*

5145   The checkbook and the cruise missile: conversations with Arundhati Roy. David. Barsamian; Arundhati. Roy. Cambridge MA: South End Press, 2004. xii, 178p. *ISBN: 0896087115, 0896087107. Includes bibliographical references and index.*

5146   Corvette projects of the South African navy and the printed media: different government, different debate. T. Potgieter. **Strat. R. Sth. Afr.** XXVI:2 10:2004 pp.94-126.

5147   Disseminative systems and global governance. Jim Whitman. **Glo. Gov.** 11:1 1-3:2005 pp.85-102.

5148   Extended deterrence: the U.S. credibility gap in the Middle East. Kathleen J. McInnis. **Washington Q.** 28:3 Summer:2005 pp.169-186.

5149   The folly of the U.S. and NATO nuclear weapons politics. Robert S. McNamara. **Int. Aff. [Moscow]** 51:3 2005 pp.104-124.

5150   Les forces nucléaires russes: évolution et perspectives. *[In French]*; (Russian nuclear forces: evolution and perspectives.); *[Summary in French]*. Yuri Fedorov. **Pol. Étran.** 70:2 Summer:2005 pp.357-372.

5151   How to cope with North Korea and nuclear weapons: what Bush could have learned from Lenin, Osgood, and Clinton. Walter C. Celmens, Jr. **J. East Asian Aff.** XVIII:2 Fall-Winter:2004 pp.221-250.

5152   Iadernoe sderzhivanie i rasprostranenie: dialektika "oruzhiia sudnogo dnia". *[In Russian]*; (Nuclear deterrence and proliferation: dialectics of doomsday's weapons.) Aleksei Georgievich Arbatov. **Mir. Ekon. Mezh. Ot.** 1 1:2005 pp.3-15.

5153   Iran, the proliferation magnet. Maria Sultan. **SAIS R.** XXV:1 Winter-Spring:2005 pp.123-142.

5154   Iraq's chemical weapons legacy: what others might learn from Saddam. Richard L. Russell. **Mid. East J.** 59:2 Spring:2005 pp.187-208.

5155   Is missile defence moral? Frederic Labarre. **Int. J.** LX:2 Spring:2005 pp.553-573.

5156   Kuzey Kore'nin nükleer silah programı: sebepler ve sonuçlar. *[In Turkish]*; (North Korea's nuclear ambition: causes and consequences.) Mustafa Kibaroğlu. **Uluslararası İlişkiler** 1:1 Spring:2004 pp.154-172.

5157   A la recherche d'un "secret d'Etat". *[In French]*; [In the search for an 'official secret']. Marcel Duval. **Défense Nat.** 60 8-9:2004 pp.84-96.

5158   Learning to think the unthinkable: lessons from India's nuclear tests. C. Christine Fair. **India R.** 4:1 1:2005 pp.23-58.

5159   North Korea's new cash crop. Andrew J. Coe. **Washington Q.** 28:3 Summer:2005 pp.73-84.

5160   The nuclear posture review: setting the record straight. Keith B. Payne. **Washington Q.** 28:3 Summer:2005 pp.135-151.

5161   Nuclear proliferation in the Middle East: Iran and Israel. Gawdat Bahgat. **Contemp. Sec. Policy** 26:1 4:2005 pp.25-43.

5162   Proliferation of small arms and light weapons: case study — South Asia. Malik Qasim Mustafa. **Strat. S.** XXV:2 Summer:2005 pp.27-54.

5163   The proliferation security initiative and North Korea: legality and limitations of a coalition strategy. James Cotton. **Secur. Dial.** 36:2 6:2005 pp.193-212.

5164   Reflections on nuclear testing in the South Pacific. David Chappell [Ed.]; Jean-Marc Regnault; Stewart Firth; Nic MacLellan; Bruno Barrillot; John Taroanui Doom; Gabriel Tetiarahi. **Contemp. Pac.** 17:2 2005 pp.336-383. *Collection of 7 articles.*

5165   Rudiments of CBMs in South Asia and a comparison of their viability in North Korea and Northeast Asia. Mohammed Badrul Alam. **J. East Asian Aff.** XIX:1 Spring-Summer:2005 pp.165-199.

5166   Russian scientists and rogue states: does Western assistance reduce the proliferation threat? Deborah Yarsike Ball; Theodore P. Gerber. **Int. Secur.** 29:4 Spring:2005 pp.50-77.

5167   The search for Iraq's weapons of mass destruction: inspection, verification and non-proliferation. Graham S. Pearson. Basingstoke, New York: Palgrave Macmillan, 2005. xxxiv, 338p. *ISBN: 1403942579. Includes bibliographical references and index. (Series:* Global issues).

5168   South Africa's weapons of mass destruction. Helen E. Purkitt; Stephen Franklin Burgess. Bloomington IN: Indiana University Press, 2005. 322p. *ISBN: 0253345065, 025321730X. Includes bibliographical references (p. 295-312) and index.*

5169   Stigmatizing the bomb: origins of the nuclear taboo. Nina Tannenwald. **Int. Secur.** 29:4 Spring:2005 pp.5-49.

Armed forces
Forces armées

5170   Air power in the Six-Day War. Kenneth M. Pollack. **J. Strategic S.** 28:3 6:2005 pp.471-503.

5171   Anglo-Canadian defence ties and the changing nature of Canadian military identity. Paul Robinson. **Br. J. Can. S.** 17:1 2004 pp.15-29.

5172   As bases militares Norte-Americanas: uma nova postura global. *[In Portuguese]*; (US military bases: a new global posture.) *[Summary]*. Luís Nuno Rodrigues. **Relações Int.** 5 3:2005 pp.69-83.

5173   Change and transformation in military affairs. Eliot A. Cohen. **J. Strategic S.** 27:3 9:2004 pp.395-407.

5174   Cultural foundations of military diffusion. Emily O. Goldman. **R. Int. S.** 32:1 1:2005 pp.69-91.

5175   La doctrine militaire russe. *[In French]*; [Russian military doctrine]. Viktor Litovkin. **Défense Nat.** 60:1 1:2004 pp.55-71.

5176   Les élites en uniforme. *[In French]*; (Elites in uniform.) *[Summary]*. Barbara Vernon. **Pouvoirs** 112 2004 pp.63-77.

5177   Evolution or revolution? Michael Horowitz; Stephen Rosen. **J. Strategic S.** 28:3 6:2005 pp.437-448.

5178   An evolving view of warfare: war and peace and the American military profession. Matthew J. Morgan. **Sm. Wars Insurg.** 16:2 6:2005 pp.147-169.

5179   Force size for the post-Westphalian world. Keith W. Mines. **Orbis** 49:4 Fall:2005 pp.649-662.

5180   The half-hearted transformation of the Hungarian military. Pál Dunay. **Euro. Sec.** 14:1 3:2005 pp.17-32.

5181   The historical mind and military strategy. Eliot A. Cohen. **Orbis** 49:4 Fall:2005 pp.575-588.

5182   Lessons from Iraq and Bosnia on the theory and practice of no-fly zones. Alexander Benard. **J. Strategic S.** 27:3 9:2004 pp.454-478.

5183   Liberation and occupation: a commander's perspective. Fabio Mini. **Isr. Ybk Hum. Rig.** 35 2005 pp.71-100.

5184   Military coercion in interstate crises. Branislav L. Slantchev. **Am. Pol. Sci. R.** 99:4 11:2005 pp.533-547.

5185   The "myth" of British seapower. Arthur Herman. **Orbis** 49:2 Spring:2005 pp.337-352.

5186   Old wine in new bottles: China-Taiwan computer-based 'information warfare' and propaganda. Gary D. Rawnsley. **Int. Aff. [London]** 81:5 10:2005 pp.1061-1078.

5187   The politics of air power: from confrontation to cooperation in army aviation civil-military relations. Rondall Ravon Rice. Lincoln NE: University of Nebraska Press, 2004. xxii, 283p. *ISBN: 0803239602. Includes bibliographical references (p. 259-270) and index.* (*Series:* Studies in war, society, and the military).

5188   Politics, technology and the revolution in military affairs. John Stone. **J. Strategic S.** 27:3 9:2004 pp.408-427.

5189　A post-imperial power? Britain and the royal navy. Jeremy Black. **Orbis** 49:2 Spring:2005 pp.353-365.

5190　Pour un devoir d'expression des militaires. *[In French]*; [For a 'duty to speak' for the military]. Pascal Courtade. **Défense Nat.** 60:7 7:2004 pp.131-144.

5191　Pourquoi les forces armées américaines rencontrent-elles des difficultés récurrentes à conduire des "opérations militaires autres que la guerre" ? *[In French]*; [Why American armed forces meet recurring difficulties in conducting 'military operations other than war'?] Pierre-Joseph Givre. **Cah. Mars** 182 10-12:2004 pp.87-119.

5192　Die Privatisierung der Sicherheit. Private Sicherheits – und Militärunternehmen in den internationalen Beziehungen. *[In German]*; (The privatization of security. Private military and security companies in international relations.) Gerhard Kümmel. **Z. Int. Beziehung.** 12:1 6:2005 pp.141-169.

5193　Shouldering the soldiering: democracy, conscription, and military casualties. Joseph Paul Vasquez, III. **J. Confl. Resol.** 49:6 12:2005 pp.849-873.

5194　Small wars revisited: the United States and nontraditional wars. Frank G. Hoffman. **J. Strategic S.** 28:6 12:2005 pp.913-940.

5195　Sovremennye politicheskie realii i osobennosti formirovaniia mentaliteta rossiiskikh voennosluzhashchikh. *[In Russian]*; [Current political conditions and mentality of Russian military in the making]. N.A. Baranov. **Sots.Gum. Znan.** 3 2004 pp.182-196.

5196　Strategy & small wars. Frank G. Hoffman; Peter R. Neumann; Alexander Statiev; John Gooch; Martin Thomas. **J. Strategic S.** 28:6 12:2005 pp.913-1060. *Collection of 5 articles.*

5197　A theory of battle or a theory of war? Lawrence Freedman. **J. Strategic S.** 28:3 6:2005 pp.425-436.

5198　Vladimir Putin and military reform in Russia. Dale R. Herspring. **Euro. Sec.** 14:1 3:2005 pp.137-155.

Arms limitation
Limitation des armements

5199　Australia and the South Pacific nuclear free zone treaty: a reinterpretation. Andrew O'Neil. **Aust. J. Pol. Sci.** 39:3 11:2004 pp.567-583.

5200　Combating light weapons proliferation in West Africa. Alex Vines. **Int. Aff. [London]** 81:2 3:2005 pp.341-360.

5201　Conventionalizing US and Russian strategic nuclear forces. Stephen J. Cimbala. **J. Slav. Mil. S.** 17:4 10-12:2004 pp.599-617.

5202　Les désarrois de la lutte contre la prolifération nucléaire. *[In French]*; [The disarray of the fight against nuclear proliferation]. Thérèse Delpech. **Crit. Int.** 23 4:2004 pp.43-52.

5203　Examen critique des mesures préventives contre les armes légères en Afrique. *[In French]*; [Critical review of the preventive measures against light weapons in Africa]. Etienne Rusamira. **Défense Nat.** 60:11 11:2004 pp.129-142.

5204　Fighting the illicit trafficking of small arms. Rachel Stohl. **SAIS R.** XXV:1 Winter-Spring:2005 pp.59-73.

5205　La France et le désarmement. *[In French]*; [France and disarmament] *[Summary]*. Daniel Colard. **Arès** 21:1(53) 7:2004 pp.109-120.

5206　L'Initiative américaine de sécurité contre la prolifération (PSI). *[In French]*; [The American security initiative against proliferation (PSI)]. Bertrand Grégoire. **Défense Nat.** 60:10 10:2004 pp.112-123.

5207　Lutter contre la prolifération des armes de destruction massive et de leurs vecteurs ? *[In French]*; [Fighting against weapons of mass destruction proliferation and its mediums]. Laurent Labaye. **Défense Nat.** 60:10 10:2004 pp.99-111.

5208　No magic bullet: a critical perspective on disarmament, demobilization and reintegration (DDR) and weapons reduction in post-conflict contexts. Robert Muggah. **Round Tab.** 379 4:2005 pp.239-252.

5209 Non-proliferation of nuclear weapons: the European Union and Iran. Eileen Denza. **Euro. For. Aff. R.** 10:3 Autumn:2005 pp.289-311.

5210 La politique chinoise de non prolifération. *[In French]*; [The Chinese non-proliferation policy] *[Summary]*. Karina Polukhina. **Monde Chin.** 1 Spring:2004 pp.103-118.

5211 Prohibitions, weapons and controversy: managing the problems of ordering. Brian Rappert. **Soc. S. Sci.** 35:2 4:2005 pp.211-240.

5212 La prolifération dans une économie en voie de mondialisation. *[In French]*; [Proliferation in a globalizing economy] *[Summary]*. Georges Le Guelte. **Pol. Étran.** 69:3 Fall:2004 pp.625-636.

5213 Prospects of inter-Korean military tension reduction and the ROK approach. Man-kwon Nam. **Kor. World Aff.** 28:3 Fall:2004 pp.249-263.

5214 Quel avenir pour la contre-prolifération nucléaire ? *[In French]*; [What future for the fight against nuclear proliferation?] Marcel Duval. **Défense Nat.** 60:10 10:2004 pp.76-98.

5215 The rise and fall of the NPT: an opportunity for Britain. Michael McCgwire. **Int. Aff. [London]** 81:1 1:2005 pp.115-140.

5216 Six party talks: the way forward. John Barry Kotch. **Kor. Obs.** 36:1 Spring:2005 pp.183-197.

5217 Snikende tiger, skjult drage. Ikke-spredning i en ny tid. *[In Norwegian]*; (Crouching tiger, hidden dragon. Non-proliferation in a new era.) *[Summary]*. Sverre Lodgaard; Helene Revhaug. **Internasjonal Pol.** 63:1 2005 pp.35-58.

5218 South Asia's arms control process: cricket diplomacy and the composite dialogue. Stuart Croft. **Int. Aff. [London]** 81:5 10:2005 pp.1039-1060.

5219 Space weapons: the need for arms control. Ghazala Yasmin. **Strat. S.** XXV:1 Spring:2005 pp.83-105.

5220 Strategic forces U.S. and Russian strategic nuclear forces under cooperative security: Moscow and after. Stephen J. Cimbala. **J. Slav. Mil. S.** 18:2 6:2005 pp.169-187.

5221 The United States and the nuclear dimension of European integration. Gunnar Skogmar. Basingstoke, New York: Palgrave Macmillan, 2004. xi, 331p. *ISBN: 1403938997. Includes bibliographical references (p. 297-313) and index.*

5222 Verhandeln, drohen, belohnen –Wie der Iran vom Atomwaffenkurs abgebracht werden kann. *[In German]*; [How Iran can be persuaded into giving up nuclear weapons]. Joseph Cirincione. **Int. Politik** 60:2 2:2005 pp.65-75.

Intelligence services
Services d'espionnage

5223 Defeating the sixth column: intelligence and strategy in the war on Islamist terrorism. John R. Schindler. **Orbis** 49:4 Fall:2005 pp.695-712.

5224 Du réseau Echelon à la "révolution des affaires du renseignement" aux Etats-Unis. *[In French]*; [From the Echelon network to the 'intelligence services revolution' in the United States]. Claude Delesse. **Ann. Fran. Rel. Int.** 5 2004 pp.945-967.

5225 Executive secrets: covert action and the presidency. William J. Daugherty. Lexington KY: University Press of Kentucky, 2004. xxvii, 298p. *ISBN: 0813123348. Includes bibliographical references (p. [257]-275) and index.*

5226 Intelligence and statecraft: the use and limits of intelligence in international society. P. J. Jackson [Ed.]; Jennifer Siegel [Ed.]. Westport CT: Praeger, 2005. xiii, 288p. *ISBN: 027597295X. Includes bibliographical references and index.*

5227 The Liddell diaries and British intelligence history. Eunan O'Halpin. **Intel. Nat. Sec.** 20:4 12:2005 pp.670-686.

5228 The limits of intelligence reform. Helen Fessenden. **Foreign Aff.** 84:6 11-12:2005 pp.106-120.

5229 The logistics of actionable intelligence leading to 9/11. Kevin Michael Derksen. **S. Confl. Terror.** 28:3 5-6:2005 pp.253-268.

5230   Military and intelligence gathering activities in the exclusive economic zones: consensus and disagreement II. Mark J. Valencia; Kazumine Akimoto; Jon M. Van Dyke; Moritaka Hayashi; Ren Xiaofeng; Cheng Xizhong; O.P. Sharma; Alexander S. Skaridov; Duk-ki Kim; Sam Bateman; Hasjim Djalal; Alexander Yankov; Anthony Bergin. **Marine Policy** 29:2 3:2005 pp.97-187. *Collection of 11 articles.*

5231   Okhrana: vospominaniia rukovoditelei okhrannykh otdelenii. *[In Russian]*; [Intelligence: recollections of the chiefs of intelligence services]. Z. I. Peregudova. Moscow: Novoe Literaturnoe Obozrenie, 2004. 512p. *ISBN: 5824300631.*

5232   The role and effectiveness of intelligence in Northern Ireland. Bradley W.C. Bamford. **Intel. Nat. Sec.** 20:4 12:2005 pp.581-607.

5233   September 11 and the adaptation failure of U.S. intelligence agencies. Amy B. Zegart. **Int. Secur.** 29:4 Spring:2005 pp.78-111.

5234   Spies and bureaucrats: getting intel right. Thomas G. Mahnken. **Publ. Inter.** 159 Spring:2005 pp.22-42.

5235   The contemporary presidency: presidents, lawmakers, and spies: intelligence accountability in the United States. Loch K. Johnson. **Pres. Stud. Q.** 34:4 12:2004 pp.828-837.

5236   Transforming the US intelligence community. Najam Rafique. **Strat. S.** XXV:1 Spring:2005 pp.49-65.

5237   Warning intelligence and early warning with specific reference to the African context. M. Hough. **Strat. R. Sth. Afr.** XXVI:2 10:2004 pp.23-38.

NATO
OTAN

5238   'A train collision in the making'? The proliferation of weapons of mass destruction and the transatlantic alliance. Terry Terriff. **J. Transatlan. S.** 3:1 Spring:2005 pp.105-122.

5239   The Atlantic community in the age of international terrorism. Donald J. Puchala. **J. Transatlan. S.** 3:1 Spring:2005 pp.89-104.

5240   Beyond tradition: new alliance's strategic concepts. Pavel Necas. Rome: NATO Defense College, 2004. 161p. *ISBN: 8887967261.* (*Series:* Monograph - no. 21).

5241   The case of the missing democratic alliance: France, the 'Anglo-Saxons' and NATO's deep origins. David G. Haglund. **Contemp. Sec. Policy** 25:2 8:2004 pp.225-251.

5242   Collision course: NATO, Russia, and Kosovo. Strobe Talbott [Foreword]; John Norris. Westport CT: Praeger Publishing, 2005. xxv, 333p. *ISBN: 0275987531. Includes bibliographical references (p. 323-326) and index.*

5243   Conclusions: where is NATO going? Martin A. Smith [Ed.]. **Contemp. Sec. Policy** 25:3 12:2004 pp.545-555.

5244   The development of the European Security and Defence Policy and its implications for NATO: cooperation and competition. Udo Diedrichs. **J. Transatlan. S.** 3:1 Spring:2005 pp.55-70.

5245   Diaspora geopolitics: Romanian-Americans and NATO expansion. Gabriel Popescu. **Geopolitics** 10:3 2005 pp.455-481.

5246   ESDP and the future of the Atlantic alliance: political and geopolitical considerations. Christopher S. Chivvis. **J. Transatlan. S.** 3:1 Spring:2005 pp.23-38.

5247   EU – és NATO-kapcsolatok — a megegyezések és viták tükrében. *[In Hungarian]*; (EU and NATO relations — agreement and debate.) *[Summary]*. Péter Deák. **Euro. Tükör** 9:1 2004 pp.24-46.

5248   Kaliningradskaia oblast' vo vzaimootnosheniiakh Rossii s ES: medlennyi dreif. *[In Russian]*; (Kaliningrad region issue in Russian-European interrelationships: slow drift.) K. Voronov. **Mir. Ekon. Mezh. Ot.** 3 3:2005 pp.42-53.

5249   Leadership at NATO: Secretary General Manfred Woerner and the crisis in Bosnia. Ryan C. Hendrickson. **J. Strategic S.** 27:3 9:2004 pp.508-527.

5250   NATO: globalization or redundancy? Andrew Cottey. **Contemp. Sec. Policy** 25:3 12:2004 pp.391-408.

5251   The NATO rapid deployment corps: alliance doctrine and force structure. John R. Deni. **Contemp. Sec. Policy** 25:3 12:2004 pp.498-523.

5252   NATO, the EU and ESDP: an emerging division of labour? Richard G. Whitman. **Contemp. Sec. Policy** 25:3 12:2004 pp.430-451.

5253   NATO, the Kosovo war and neoliberal theory. Sean Kay. **Contemp. Sec. Policy** 25:2 8:2004 pp.252-279.

5254   NATO-Russia relations: present and future. Dmitry Polikanov. **Contemp. Sec. Policy** 25:3 12:2004 pp.479-497.

5255   NATO's secret armies: Operation Gladio and terrorism in Western Europe. Daniele Ganser. London, New York: Frank Cass, 2005. 315p. *ISBN: 0714656070, 0714685003. Includes bibliographical references and index.*

5256   A new military ethos? NATO's response force. Sten Rynning. **J. Transatlan. S.** 3:1 Spring:2005 pp.5-21.

5257   Norsk NATO-debatt etter den kalde krigen. *[In Norwegian]*; (Norwegian NATO debate after the Cold War.) *[Summary]*. Nina Græger. **Internasjonal Pol.** 63:2-3 2005 pp.217-240.

5258   Régulations stratégiques occidentales : quelle Alliance voulons-nous. *[In French]*; [Strategic Western regulations: what kind of alliance do we what?] Jean Dufourcq. **Défense Nat.** 60:12 12:2004 pp.137-148.

5259   Russia's relationship with NATO: a qualitative change or old wine in new bottles? Tuomas Forsberg. **J. Comm. S. Transit. Pol.** 21:3 9:2005 pp.332-353.

5260   'The war on terrorism would not be possible without NATO': a critique. David Brown. **Contemp. Sec. Policy** 25:3 12:2004 pp.409-429.

5261   To neither use them nor lose them: NATO and nuclear weapons since the Cold War. Martin A. Smith. **Contemp. Sec. Policy** 25:3 12:2004 pp.524-544.

5262   Transatlantic transformations: equipping NATO for the 21ˢᵗ century. Daniel S. Hamilton [Ed.]; Paul H. Nitze School of Advanced International Studies. Washington DC: Center for Transatlantic Relations, 2004. vi, 196p. *ISBN: 0975332511. Includes bibliographical references.*

5263   US-adriatic charter of partnership: securing the NATO open door policy. Ivan Grdešić. **Pol. Misao** 41:5 2004 pp.104-122.

5264   Where is NATO going? Andrew Cottey; David Brown; Richard G. Whitman; James Sperling; Dmitry Polikanov; John R. Deni; Martin A. Smith. **Contemp. Sec. Policy** 25:3 12:2004 pp.391-555. *Collection of 8 articles.*

Regional security
Securité régionale

5265   ABD-Japonya güvenlik antlaşmaları: oluşumu, evrimi ve sonuçları. *[In Turkish]*; (US-Japan security treaties: formation, evolution and consequences.) Hakan Gönen. **Uluslararasi Ilişkiler** 1:4 Winter:2004 pp.115-139.

5266   ABD'nin orta Asya politikaları ve 11 eylül'ün etkileri. *[In Turkish]*; (US policies toward Central Asia and effects of the September 11.) Çağrı Erhan. **Uluslararasi Ilişkiler** 1:3 Autumn:2004 pp.123-149.

5267   The alienated frontier: why the United States can't get Osama bin Laden. Vanni Cappelli. **Orbis** 49:4 Fall:2005 pp.713-729.

5268   Alliance diversification and the future of the U.S.-Korean security relationship. et al; Charles M. Perry. Herndon VA: Brassey's, 2004. xx, 221p. *ISBN: 1574888951. Includes bibliographical references. Institute for Foreign Policy Analysis. Fletcher School of Law and Diplomacy.*

5269   ASEAN's quest for security: a theoretical explanation. Anindya Batabyal. **Int. S.** 41:4 10-12:2004 pp.349-369.

5270 Beacons of hope? The impact of imposed democracy on regional peace, democracy, and prosperity. Andrew J. Enterline; J. Michael Greig. **J. Pol.** 67:4 11:2005 pp.1075-1098.

5271 La Belgique et le Groupe des Quatre en matière de défense. *[In French]*; [Belgium and the Group of Four in matters of defence]. André Dumoulin [Ed.]. **Cour. Hebdo.** 1862-1863 2004 pp.1-71.

5272 The Black Sea region: cooperation and security building. Oleksandr Pavliuk [Ed.]; Ivanna Klympush-Tsintsadze [Ed.]. Armonk NY: M.E. Sharpe, 2004. xiii, 314p. *ISBN: 0765612259. Includes bibliographical references and index.*

5273 The Black Sea region in an enlarged Europe: changing patterns, changing politics. George Cristian Maior; Mihaela Matei. **Mediterr. Q.** 16:1 Winter:2005 pp.33-51.

5274 Bridging the European divide: middle power politics and regional security dilemmas. Joshua B. Spero. Lanham MD: Rowman & Littlefield, 2004. xiii, 343p. *ISBN: 0742535533. Includes bibliographical references and index.*

5275 Broadening Asia's security discourse and agenda: political, social, and environmental perspectives. Ramesh Chandra Thakur [Ed.]; Edward Newman [Ed.]. New York: United Nations, 2004. *ISBN: 9280810944.*

5276 Canada's emerging role in building "fortress America": implications for sovereignty. William W. Joyce. **Br. J. Can. S.** 17:1 2004 pp.30-43.

5277 The Canadian-American North American defence alliance in 2005. Dwight N. Mason. **Int. J.** LX:2 Spring:2005 pp.385-396.

5278 Central Eurasia in global politics: conflict, security, and development. Mehdi Parvizi Amineh [Ed.]; Henk Houweling [Ed.]. Leiden MA, Boston MA: Brill, 2004. *ISBN: 9004128093. Includes bibliographical references and index. (Series:* International studies in sociology and social anthropology - 92).

5279 The changing incentives for security regionalization: from 11/9 to 9/11. Galia Press-Barnathan. **Coop. Confl.** 40:3 9:2005 pp.281-304.

5280 China and East Asia. Eric Heginbotham; Christopher P. Twomey; Peter Hays Gries; Yan Sun; Barry Eichengreen; Athar Hussain; Amy Hanser; Elizabeth Economy; Joshua Kurlantzick; Andrew Scobell; Michael R. Chambers; Chitra Tiwari. **Curr. Hist.** 104:683 9:2005 pp.243-304. *Collection of 10 articles.*

5281 The Common African Defence and Security Policy. Omar A. Touray. **Afr. Affairs** 104:417 10:2005 pp.635-656.

5282 Confidence - and security - building measures for India and Pakistan. A.Z. Hilali. **Alternatives** 30:2 4-6:2005 pp.191-222.

5283 Corruption and international security. Kim Thachuk. **SAIS R.** XXV:1 Winter-Spring:2005 pp.143-154.

5284 Domestic threats, regional solutions? The challenge of regional security integration in Southern Africa. Anne Hammerstad. **R. Int. S.** 31:1 1:2005 pp.69-88.

5285 Entre el 9/11 y el 11/9: debates y perspectivas sobre el cambio en las relaciones internacionales. *[In Spanish]*; (Between 11/9 and 9/11: debates and perspectives about changes in international relations.) Federico Merke. **Foro Int.** XLIV:4 10-12:2004 pp.690-725.

5286 The Euro-Atlantic security dilemma: France, Britain, and the ESDP. Jolyon Howorth. **J. Transatlan. S.** 3:1 Spring:2005 pp.39-54.

5287 The European Security and Defence Policy: built on rocks or sand? Trevor Salmon. **Euro. For. Aff. R.** 10:3 Autumn:2005 pp.359-379.

5288 European Security and Defence Policy: from Cologne to Sarajevo. Rory Keane. **Glo. Soc.** 19:1 1:2005 pp.89-103.

5289 Europeanization of Nordic security: the European Union and the changing security identities of the Nordic states. Pernille Rieker. **Coop. Confl.** 39:4 12:2004 pp.369-392.

5290 'Fuelling' transatlantic entente in the Caspian basin: energy security and collective action. Adam N. Stulberg. **Contemp. Sec. Policy** 25:2 8:2004 pp.280-311.

5291 La gestion de la cooperacion transfronteriza Mexico-Estados Unidos en un marco de inseguridad global: problemas y desafios. *[In Spanish]*; [Border cooperation between Mexico and United States in the new framework of international insecurity: problems and challenges]. Jose Maria Ramos Garcia. Mexico City: Miguel Angel Porrua, 2004. 235p. *ISBN: 9707014725. Includes bibliographical references (p. 225-235).*

5292 The guard and reserve in America's new missions. Frank G. Hoffman. **Orbis** 49:2 Spring:2005 pp.213-228.

5293 Indian's security concerns: national, regional and global. Baljit Singh. **Indian J. Pol. Sci.** 65:3 7-9:2004 pp.345-364.

5294 Individuals first: a human security strategy for the European Union. Marlies Glasius; Mary Kaldor. **Int. Pol. Gesell.** 1 2005 pp.62-82.

5295 Iraq, Afghanistan and the war on 'terror'. Daniel Byman; Michael Scheuer; Anatol Lieven; W. Patrick Lang. **Mid. East Policy** XII:1 Spring:2005 pp.1-24.

5296 The lack of security cooperation between Southeast Asia and Japan: yen yes, pax nippon no. Sandra R. Leavitt. **Asian Sur.** XLV:2 3-4:2005 pp.216-240.

5297 Missiles and missile defences in South Asia. Jehangir Karamat; Ashok K. Mehta; Khalid Banuri; Rajesh Rajagopalan; Dipankar Banerjee; Ayesha Siddiqa; Pervaiz Iqbal Cheema; Michael Vannoni; Kent Biringer; Syed Rifaat Hussain; Varun Sahni. **Sth. Asian Surv.** 11:2 7-12:2004 pp.169-299. *Collection of 10 articles.*

5298 Morocco, Western Sahara and the future of the Maghreb. Yahia H. Zoubir; Karima Benabdallah-Gambier. **J. Nth. Afr. S.** 9:1 Spring:2004 pp.49-77.

5299 Myanmar's international relations strategy: the search for security. Helen James. **Contemp. Sth.East Asia** 26:3 12:2004 pp.530-553.

5300 Nordisk sikkerheds - og forsvarspolitisk samarbejde i en europæisk kontekst. *[In Norwegian]*; (Nordic security and defence cooperation in a European context.) *[Summary]*. Preben Bonnén. **Internasjonal Pol.** 63:1 2005 pp.59-74.

5301 'Northeast Asian cooperation initiative' and Korea's diplomatic tasks: a strategy for regional cooperation. Geung Chan Bae. **J. East Asian Aff.** XIX:1 Spring-Summer:2005 pp.1-26.

5302 Nuclear security: global directions for the future. Proceedings of an international conference, London, March 2005. IAEA. Vienna: International Atomic Energy Agency, 2005. 326p. *ISBN: 9201059051. Includes bibliographical references and index.*

5303 Old Europe, new Europe and the US: renegotiating transatlantic security in the post 9/11 era. Tom Lansford [Ed.]; Blagovest Tashev [Ed.]. Aldershot, Burlington VT: Ashgate, 2005. xxvi, 322p. *ISBN: 0754641430, 0754641449.*

5304 Ortadogu'da güvenlik algılaması ve dahili risk faktörlerinin etkisi. *[In Turkish]*; (Security perception in the Middle East and the impact of internal risk factors.) Gamze Güngörmuş Kona. **Akdeniz** 4:8 11:2004 pp.113-138.

5305 Pakistan-India relations. Staff Study; Qazi Shakil Ahmad; Farzana Shakoor; B.M. Kutty; Zubeida Mustafa; Nabiha Gul; Nausheen Wasi; Sanam Noor; S.M. Taha; Manjri Sewak. **Pakis. Horiz.** 57:3 7:2004 pp.13-126. *Collection of 9 articles.*

5306 Percepcion de seguridad en Europa. *[In Spanish]*; [Perception of security in Europe] *[Summary]*. Henrique I. Thome. **Sistema** 188 9:2005 pp.63-77.

5307 La política de seguridad fronteriza de Estados Unidos: estrategias e impactos binacionales. *[In Spanish]*; (The U.S. border security policy: strategies and binational impacts.) José María Ramos García. **Foro Int.** XLIV:4 10-12:2004 pp.613-634.

5308 Politics and security in South-East Asia: prospects for India-ASEAN cooperation. Shankari Sundararaman. **Int. S.** 41:4 10-12:2004 pp.371-385.

5309 Pursuing a policy framework for peace and security in Africa: developments, progress and challenges. T.G. Neethling. **Strat. R. Sth. Afr.** XXVI:2 10:2004 pp.71-93.

5310 Redefining transatlantic security relations: the challenge of change. Dieter Mahncke; Wyn Rees; Wayne C. Thompson. Manchester: Manchester University Press, 2004. vii, 242p. *ISBN: 071906211X. Includes bibliographical references and index.*

5311 Şanghay işbirliği örgütü'nün geleceği ve Çin. *[In Turkish]*; (Future of the Shanghai cooperation organization and China.) Selçuk Çolakoğlu. **Uluslararasi Ilişkiler** 1:1 Spring:2004 pp.173-197.

5312 SARS in Asia: crisis, vulnerabilities, and regional responses. Mely Caballero-Anthony. **Asian Sur.** XLV:3 5-6:2005 pp.475-495.

5313   Security and the democratic scene: desecuritization and emancipation. Claudia Aradau. **J. Int. Rel. Dev.** 7:4 12:2004 pp.388-413.
5314   Security perspectives of the Malay Archipelago: security linkages in the second front in the war on terrorism. Andrew T.H. Tan. Cheltenham, Northampton MA: Edward Elgar Publishing, 2004. viii, 309p. *ISBN: 1843769972. Includes bibliographical references (p. 272-291) and index.*
5315   The security situation in Iraq and its political implications. Shri Prakash. **India Q.** LX:4 10-12:2004 pp.16-26.
5316   South Asia's nuclear security dilemma: India, Pakistan, and China. Lowell Dittmer [Ed.]. Armonk NY: M.E. Sharpe, 2005. xxi, 274p. *ISBN: 0765614189. Includes bibliographical references and index.*
5317   Strategic developments in Eurasia after 11 September. Shireen Hunter [Ed.]. Portland OR: Frank Cass, 2004. 174p. *ISBN: 0714655856, 0714684716. Includes bibliographical references and index.*
5318   Taiwan's 2004 presidential election: its impact on inter-strait relations and regional security implications. Jaeho Hwang. **Kor. World Aff.** 28:3 Fall:2004 pp.281-294.
5319   Three futures: global geopolynomic transition and the implications for regional security in Northeast Asia. Brendan Howe. **Mod. Asian S.** 39:4 10:2005 pp.761-792.
5320   Through the looking glass: creeping vulnerabilities and the reordering of security. P.H. Liotta. **Secur. Dial.** 36:1 3:2005 pp.49-70.
5321   Understanding global security. Peter Hough. London: Routledge, 2004. 224p. *ISBN: 041529665X, 0415296668.*
5322   US security strategy in Asia and the prospects for an Asian regional security regime. Ralph A. Cossa. **Asia Pac. R.** 12:1 5:2005 pp.64-86.
5323   The U.S.-Japan security alliance, ASEAN, and the South China sea dispute. Joshua P. Rowan. **Asian Sur.** XLV:3 5-6:2005 pp.414-436.
5324   Weak states as a security threat. Ivan Krastev. **Südosteuro. Mitteil.** 44:4 2004 pp.102-116.
5325   Who's keeping the peace? Regionalization and contemporary peace operations. Alex J. Bellamy; Paul D. Williams. **Int. Secur.** 29:4 Spring:2005 pp.157-195.

Terrorism
Terrorisme

5326   9/11 und die Grenzen des Politischen. *[In German]*; (9/11 and the limits of the political.) Andreas Behnke. **Z. Int. Beziehung.** 12:1 6:2005 pp.117-140.
5327   The Achille Lauro hijacking: lessons in the politics and prejudice of terrorism. Michael K. Bohn. Washington DC: Brassey's, 2004. xix, 235p. *ISBN: 1574887793. Includes bibliographical references (p. 219-222) and index.*
5328   After 9/11: terrorism and crime in a globalised world. David Anderson Charters [Ed.]; Graham F. Walker [Ed.]. Halifax: Dalhousie University, 2005. xxvi, 441p. *ISBN: 1896440460. Includes bibliographical references. Centre for Foreign Policy Studies.*
5329   America and its others: cosmopolitan terror as globalisation? Arvind Rajagopal; Allen Feldman; Randy Martin; Jodi Dean; Paul A. Passavant; Rosalind C. Morris; Jonathan Crary; Nandana Dutta. **Interventions** 6:3 2004 pp.317-450. *Collection of 8 articles.*
5330   Antiterrorism legislation in Australia: a proportionate response to the terrorist threat? Christopher Michaelsen. **S. Confl. Terror.** 28:4 7-8:2005 pp.321-340.
5331   Architettura normativa in materia di terrorismo internazionale. *[In Italian]*; [Legislation and international terrorism]. Umberto Montuoro. **Riv. S. Pol. Int.** LXXII:3 7-9:2005 pp.387-424.
5332   ASEAN counterterrorism cooperation since 9/11. Jonathan T. Chow. **Asian Sur.** XLV:2 3-4:2005 pp.302-321.
5333   Beyond September 11. Amera Saeed. **Strat. S.** XXV:2 Summer:2005 pp.169-187.
5334   Bioterrorism and food safety. Barbara Rasco; Gleyn E. Bledsoe. Boca Raton FL: CRC Press, 2005. xv, 414p. *ISBN: 0849327873. Includes bibliographical references and index.*

5335   Bioterrorisme et risque biologique. *[In French]*; [Bioterrorism and biological risk]. Claude Barès. **Défense Nat.** 60:7 7:2004 pp.93-103.

5336   The challenge of maritime terrorism: threat identification, WMD and regime response. Donna J. Nincic. **J. Strategic S.** 28:4 8:2005 pp.619-644.

5337   The challenges of conceptualizing terrorism. Leonard Weinberg; Ami Pedahzur; Sivan Hirsch-Hoefler. **Terror. Pol. Viol.** 16:4 Winter:2004 pp.777-794.

5338   The changing dimensions of international terrorism and the role of the United States: a comprehensive and multilateral approach to compact global terrorism. Sanjay Gupta. **Indian J. Pol. Sci.** LXV:4 10-12:2004 pp.556-587.

5339   Cities, war, and terrorism: towards an urban geopolitics. Stephen Graham [Ed.]. Oxford: Blackwell Publishing Ltd., 2004. xxiii, 384p. *ISBN: 1405115742, 1405115750. Includes bibliographical references (p. [335]-370) and index. (Series:* Studies in urban and social change).

5340   'Clear and present danger': responses to terrorism. Vaughan Lowe. **Int. Comp. Law Q.** 54:1 1:2005 pp.185-196.

5341   Combating terrorism in East Asia — a framework for regional cooperation. Aldo Borgu. **Asia Pac. R.** 11:2 11:2004 pp.48-59.

5342   Conciliation, counterterrorism, and patterns of terrorist violence. Ethan Bueno de Mesquita. **Int. Org.** 59:1 Winter:2005 pp.145-176.

5343   Confronting Syrian-backed terrorism. Daniel Byman. **Washington Q.** 28:3 Summer:2005 pp.99-113.

5344   'Consider that it is a raid on the path of God': the spiritual manual of the attackers of 9/11. Hans G. Kippenberg. **Numen** LII:1 2005 pp.29-58.

5345   Contending cultures of counterterrorism: transatlantic divergence or convergence? Wyn Rees; Richard J. Aldrich. **Int. Aff. [London]** 81:5 10:2005 pp.905-923.

5346   The cost and impact of international terrorism in the economies of the United States and the European Union: 2001-2004. Inga Grote. **Riv. S. Pol. Int.** LXXII:3 7-9:2005 pp.425-452.

5347   Countering global insurgency. David J. Kilcullen. **J. Strategic S.** 28:4 8:2005 pp.597-617.

5348   Cyberterrorism: the sum of all fears? Gabriel Weimann. **S. Confl. Terror.** 28:2 3-4:2005 pp.129-149.

5349   Democracy against security: the debates about counterterrorism in the European Parliament, September 2001-June 2003. Anastassia Tsoukala. **Alternatives** 29:4 8-10:2004 pp.417-439.

5350   Discourses on the 'war on terrorism' in the U.S. and its views on the Arab, Muslim, and gendered 'other'. Mervat F. Hatem. **Arab S. J.** XI-XII:1-2 Fall-Spring:2003-2004 pp.77-103.

5351   (Dis)qualified bodies: securitization, citizenship and 'identity management'. Benjamin J. Muller. **Citiz. S.** 8:3 9:2004 pp.279-294.

5352   Les djihadistes en Occident : approche comparée des exemples français et américain. *[In French]*; [Jihadists in the West: comparative approach to the French and American cases]. Jean-Luc Marret. **Ann. Fran. Rel. Int.** 5 2004 pp.164-178.

5353   Du terrorisme international en Afrique, de ses manifestations, et de ses conséquences. *[In French]*; [International terrorism in Africa, its manifestations and consequences]. Robert Esposti. **Défense Nat.** 60:1 1:2004 pp.132-145.

5354   Enhancing the status of non-state actors through a global war on terror? Mary Ellen O'Connell. **Columb. J. Tr. Law** 43:2 2005 pp.435-458.

5355   Exploring 'terror/ism': numinosity, killings, horizons. Pierre Mesnard Mendez. **Soc. Dem.** 19:1 3:2005 pp.94-118.

5356   Female suicide bombers — male suicide bombing? Looking for gender in reporting the suicide bombings of the Israeli-Palestinian conflict. Claudia Brunner. **Glo. Soc.** 19:1 1:2005 pp.29-48.

5357   Finanzmärkte und Sicherheit. *[In German]*; (Financial markets and terrorism.) Jan Bittner; Markus Lederer. **Welt Trends** 46 Spring:2005 pp.57-70.

5358   Globalisation and the new terror: the Asia Pacific dimension. David Martin Jones [Ed.]. Cheltenham, Northampton MA: Edward Elgar Publishing, 2004. xv, 316p. *ISBN: 1843764423. Includes bibliographical references (p. 298-308) and index.*

5359   The illicit diamond trade, civil conflicts, and terrorism in Africa. J. Anyu Ndumbe; Babalola Cole. **Mediterr. Q.** 16:2 Spring:2005 pp.52-65.

5360   International terrorism through Polish eyes. Janusz Kochanowski; Jerzy Zajadlo; Bronislaw Wildstein; Wojciech Stankiewicz; Jacek Salij; Krzysztof Indecki; Zdzislaw Galicki; R. Antony Duff; Stefan Bratkowski; Bartosz Bolechów. **Am. Behav. Sci.** 48:6 2:2005 pp.651-794. *Collection of 10 articles.*

5361   The lair and layers of Al-Aqsa uprising terror: some preliminary empirical findings. Richard J. Chasdi. **J. Confl. S.** XXIV:2 Winter:2004 pp.105-134.

5362   The leaderless nexus: when crime and terror converge. Chris Dishman. **S. Confl. Terror.** 28:3 5-6:2005 pp.237-252.

5363   Lockerbie and Libya: a study in international relations. Khalil I. Matar; Robert W. Thabit. Jefferson NC: McFarland & Co, 2004. viii, 327p. *ISBN: 0786416092. Includes bibliographical references (p. 319-320) and index.*

5364   Mapping Jihadist terrorism in Spain. Javier Jordan; Nicola Horsburgh. **S. Confl. Terror.** 28:3 5-6:2005 pp.169-191.

5365   Maritime piracy: defining the problem. Dana Dillon. **SAIS R.** XXV:1 Winter-Spring:2005 pp.155-166.

5366   Measuring success in coping with terrorism: the Israeli case. Nadav Morag. **S. Confl. Terror.** 28:4 7-8:2005 pp.307-320.

5367   The mind of the terrorist: a review and critique of psychological approaches. Jeff Victoroff. **J. Confl. Resol.** 49:1 2:2005 pp.3-42.

5368   Of pirates and terrorists: what experience and history teach. Donald J. Puchala. **Contemp. Sec. Policy** 26:1 4:2005 pp.1-24.

5369   Pathways out of terrorism in Northern Ireland and the Basque country: the misrepresentation of the Irish model. Rogelio Alonso. **Terror. Pol. Viol.** 16:4 Winter:2004 pp.695-713.

5370   Pax Pacifica: terrorism, the Pacific hemisphere, globalisation and peace studies. Johan Galtung. Boulder CO: Paradigm Publishers, 2005. xvi, 170p. *ISBN: 1594511101, 159451111X. Includes bibliographical references (p. 143-163) and index. (Series: Constructive peace studies).*

5371   The political economy of transnational terrorism. B. Peter Rosendorff; Daniel G Arce M.; Geoffrey Heal; Howard Kunreuther; Kevin Siqueira; Ethan Bueno de Mesquita; Walter Enders; Todd Sandler; Quan Li; Carlos Pestana Barros; Isabel Proença. **J. Confl. Resol.** 49:2 4:2005 pp.171-314. *Collection of 8 articles.*

5372   The politics of negotiating the terrorist problem in Indonesia. Anthony L. Smith. **S. Confl. Terror.** 28:1 1-2:2005 pp.33-44.

5373   The role of personal experience in contributing to different patterns of response to rare terrorist attacks. Eldad Yechiam; Greg Barron; Ido Erev. **J. Confl. Resol.** 49:3 6:2005 pp.430-439.

5374   Roots of terrorism: global and local controversies. Pat Lauderdale [Intro.]; Annamarie Oliverio [Intro.]; Charles Tilly; Nachman Ben-Yehuda; Anna Lisa Tota; Asafa Jalata; Irwin M. Cohen; Raymond R. Corrado; Albert J. Bergesen; Yi Han. **Int. J. Comp. Sociol.** 46:1-2 2-4:2005 pp.3-172. *Collection of 8 articles.*

5375   «Sinister nexus»: USA, Norge og Krekar-saken. *[In Norwegian]*; (A sinister nexus: USA, Norway and Mullah Krekar.) *[Summary].* Torkel Brekke. **Internasjonal Pol.** 63:2-3 2005 pp.279-296.

5376   Sovereignty under attack: the international society meets the Al Qaeda network. Barak Mendelsohn. **R. Int. S.** 31:1 1:2005 pp.45-68.

5377   Strategic terrorism: the framework and its fallacies. Peter Neumann; Mike Smith. **J. Strategic S.** 28:4 8:2005 pp.571-595.

5378   Une stratégie contre le "terrorisme international" ? *[In French]*; [A strategy against 'international terrorism'?] Georges le Guelte. **Défense Nat.** 60:2 2:2004 pp.59-73.

5379   Targeting Islamist terrorism in Asia Pacific: an unending war. Barry Desker; Arabinda Acharya. **Asia Pac. R.** 11:2 11:2004 pp.60-80.

5380   Terrorism. Jay Gupta; Luciano Pellicani; Matthias Küntzel; Michael Werz. **Telos** 129 Fall-Winter:2004 pp.14-95. *Collection of 5 articles.*

5381   Terrorism and governance in Kashmir. Sunil Sondhi. **J. Confl. S.** XXIV:2 Winter:2004 pp.92-104.

5382   Terrorism and human rights. Giandomenico Picco; Jayantha Dhanapala; Alex P. Schmid; Kennedy Graham; Laura K. Donohue; Bertil Dunér; Frank Gregory; Edward B. MacMahon, Jr.; Christopher Michaelsen; Gabor Rona; Clive Walker; Andrew Silke; Shri P.R. Chari; Hillel Cohen; Ron Dudai; Sergio Catignani; Rogelio Alonso; Fernando Reinares; Caroline Kennedy-Pipe; Stephen Welch. **Terror. Pol. Viol.** 17:1-2 Winter:2005 pp.11-291. *Collection of 8 articles.*

5383   Terrorism and the Kenyan public. Volker Krause; Eric E. Otenyo. **S. Confl. Terror.** 28:2 3-4:2005 pp.99-112.

5384   Terrorism and violence in Southeast Asia: transnational challenges to states and regional stability. Paul J. Smith [Ed.]. Armonk NY: M.E. Sharpe, 2005. xx,262p. *ISBN: 0765614332. Includes bibliographical references and index.*

5385   Terrorism in Southeast Asia: expert analysis, myopia and fantasy. Natasha Hamilton-Hart. **Pac. R.** 18:3 9:2005 pp.303-326.

5386   Terrorism, social movements, and international security: how Al Qaeda affects Southeast Asia. David Leheny. **Japanese J. Pol. Sci.** 6:1 4:2005 pp.87-110.

5387   Le terrorisme islamiste au Maroc. *[In French]*; [Islam terrorism in Morocco] *[Summary]*. Abdessamad Dialmy. **Soc. Compass** 52:1 3:2005 pp.67-82.

5388   Terrorismus und Generalisierung –Gibt es einen Lebenslauf terroristischer Gruppierungen? *[In German]*; [Terrorism and generalization –is there a trajectory of terrorist organizations?] *[Summary]*. Alexander Straßner. **Z. Pol.** 51:4 12:2004 pp.359-383.

5389   Terrorismus und wehrhafte Demokratie –Impulse für eine Heimatschutz-Strategie der Zukunft. *[In German]*; [Terrorism and democracy –impulse for future security strategies]. Stefan Axel Boës; Andreas Schwegel. **Politische S.** 56:399 1-2:2005 pp.91-102.

5390   Terrorist sanctuaries and Bosnia-Herzegovina: challenging conventional assumptions. Michael A. Innes. **S. Confl. Terror.** 28:4 7-8:2005 pp.295-306.

5391   Terrorists and unconventional weapons: is the threat real? Debra Bennett. **Low Int. Confl. Law Enf.** 12:1 Spring:2004 pp.20-50.

5392   Three circles of threat. Philippe Errera. **Survival** 47:1 Spring:2005 pp.71-88.

5393   Torture and truth: America, Abu Ghraib, and the war on terror. Mark Danner. New York: New York Review Books, 2004. xiv, 580p. *ISBN: 1590171527.*

5394   Transnational dialogue in an age of terror. Marc Lynch. **Glo. Soc.** 19:1 1:2005 pp.5-28.

5395   Transnational terrorism as a spillover of domestic disputes in other countries. Tony Addison; S. Mansoob Murshed. **Def. Peace Econ.** 16:2 4:2005 pp.69-82.

5396   Tsivilizatsionnye istoki mezhdunarodnogo terrorizma. *[In Russian]*; [International terrorism and its roots in civilization]. K.A. Feofanov. **Sots.Gum. Znan.** 5 2004 pp.39-53.

5397   The 'war on terror' in historical perspective. Adam Roberts. **Survival** 47:2 Summer:2005 pp.101-130.

5398   The 'war on terrorism' comes to Southeast Asia. Jim Glassman. **J. Contemp. Asia** 35:1 2005 pp.3-28.

5399   Was ist falsch am Terrorismus? *[In German]*; [What is wrong with terrorist tactics?] *[Summary]*. Michael Walzer. **Mittelweg 36** 13:6 12-1:2004-2005 pp.73-86.

5400   What happened to suicide bombings in Israel? Insights from a terror-stock model. Edward H. Kaplan; Alex Mintz; Shaul Mishal; Claudio Samban. **S. Confl. Terror.** 28:3 5-6:2005 pp.225-235.

5401   When hatred is bred in the bone: psycho-cultural foundations of contemporary terrorism. Jerrold M. Post. **Pol. Psychol.** 26:4 8:2005 pp.615-636.

5402   Who are the Palestinian suicide bombers? Shaul Kimhi; Shemuel Even. **Terror. Pol. Viol.** 16:4 Winter:2004 pp.815-840.

F.3.4: **Foreign relations**
Relations extérieures

5403 The Atlantic alliance under stress: US-European relations after Iraq. David M. Andrews [Ed.]. Cambridge: Cambridge University Press, 2005. x, 293p. *ISBN: 100521614082, 139780521849272, 100521849276, 139780521614085.*

5404 Anglo-American relations. Warren F. Kimball; Klaus Schwabe; John Dumbrell; Lloyd C. Gardner; Jérôme B. Élie. **J. Transatlan. S.** 3:1(Supp.) Spring:2005 pp.1-83. *Collection of 5 articles.*

5405 Beyond the West: terrors in transatlantia. Michael Cox. **Euro. J. Int. Rel.** 11:2 6:2005 pp.203-233.

5406 Bowling by the same rules? EU — United nations relations and the transatlantic partnership. Peter Schmidt. **J. Transatlan. S.** 3:1 Spring:2005 pp.123-138.

5407 Capabilities traps and gaps: symptom or cause of a troubled transatlantic relationship? James Sperling. **Contemp. Sec. Policy** 25:3 12:2004 pp.452-478.

5408 Chirac contre Bush : l'autre guerre. *[In French]*; [Chirac versus Bush: the other war]. Henri Vernet; Thomas Cantaloube. Paris: Editions JC Lattes, 2004. 350p. *ISBN: 270962639X.*

5409 Commonwealth update. Derek Ingram. **Round Tab.** 379 4:2005 pp.177-202.

5410 Culture and international relations. Julie Reeves. London: Routledge, 2004. 240p. *ISBN: 0415318572.* (*Series:* Routledge advances in international relations and global politics).

5411 'Damned high wire', on the special relationship that unites Bush and Blair in Iraq. Lloyd C. Gardner. **J. Transatlan. S.** 3:1(Supp.) Spring:2005 pp.43-62.

5412 Does the European Union transform the institution of diplomacy? Jozef Bátora. **J. Euro. Publ. Policy** 12:1 2005 pp.44-66.

5413 The end of the post-9/11 Sino-U.S. honeymoon. Wu Xinbo; Suisheng Zhao; Evan S. Medeiros; Kurt Campbell; Richard Weitz; Flynt Leverett; Jeffrey Bader. **Washington Q.** 29:1 Winter:2005-2006 pp.119-201. *Collection of 5 articles.*

5414 Etats-Unis / Iran : ennemis ou alliés potentiels. *[In French]*; [United States/Iran: enemies or potential allies]. Azadeh Kian-Thiébaut. **Cah. Orient** 73 1-3:2004 pp.73-87.

5415 Les Etats-Unis vus d'ailleurs. *[In French]*; [The United States seen from abroad]. Banquet. **Banquet** 21 10:2004 pp.5-267.

5416 Europe, Asie, quel rapprochement? Face à l'hégémonisme des États-Unis : les conditions d'un rapprochement euro-asiatique. *[In French]*; (Europe, Asia, which rapprochement? Facing the US hegemony, the conditions of a Euro-Asian rapprochement.) Samir Amin. **Pensée** 341 1-3:2005 pp.83-95.

5417 Europe-États-Unis : quel partenariat transatlantique après la guerre en Irak. *[In French]*; [Europe-United States: what transatlantic relations after the Iraq war]. Gilles Corman. **Etat Opin.** 2004 pp.111-121.

5418 L'évolution récente des relations transatlantiques. *[In French]*; [Recent evolution in transatlantic relations]. Inès Trépant. **Cour. Hebdo.** 1845-1846 2004 pp.1-66.

5419 Foreign perceptions of the USA after the terrorist attacks of 2001. Vladimir Shlapentokh; Joshua Woods. **Int. S.** 41:2 4-6:2004 pp.159-183.

5420 Londres et l'Afrique du Sud : de la tutelle au partenariat. *[In French]*; [London and South Africa: from trusteeship to partnership]. Jean-Claude Sergeant. **Géopol. Afr.** 15-16 Summer-Fall:2004 pp.163-181.

5421 Mexico, Iraq, and the two-party system: studies in white supremacy. Steve Martinot. **Soc. Dem.** 19:1 3:2005 pp.119-135.

5422 Moscow — Seoul: partnership based on trust. V. Denisov. **Int. Aff. [Moscow]** 51:3 2005 pp.125-135.

5423 The new strategic triangle: U.S. and European reactions to China's rise. David Shambaugh. **Washington Q.** 28:3 Summer:2005 pp.7-25.

5424 Occidentalism: a short history of anti-Westernism. Ian Buruma [Ed.]; Avishai Margalit [Ed.]. London: Atlantic, 2005. 165p. *ISBN: 1843542889. Includes bibliographical references and index.*

5425   Putin, Bush i voina v Irake. *[In Russian]*; [Putin, Bush and the war in Iraq]. L.M. Mlechin. Moscow: EKSMO, 2005. 638p. *ISBN: 5699091505.*

5426   Putting an end to the West's double standard in the Israeli-Palestinian conflict. Pascal Boniface. **Int. Spect.** XL:1 1-3:2005 pp.119-121.

5427   Reconstruction of the West. E. Ananieva. **Int. Aff. [Moscow]** 51:3 2005 pp.42-52.

5428   Rossiia-SShA: nevypolnennaia povestka dnia. *[In Russian]*; (Russia-USA: non-fulfilled agenda.) Sergei K. Oznobishchev. **Mir. Ekon. Mezh. Ot.** 1 1:2005 pp.34-44.

5429   Rossiisko-amerikanskie otnosheniia v usloviiakh globalizatsii. *[In Russian]*; [Russian-American relations under the conditions of globalization]. E. Alekseeva. Moscow: Sodeistvie sotrudnichestvu Instituta, 2005. 320p. *ISBN: 5901745078.*

5430   South Africa-North Africa relations: bridging a continent. Iqbal Jhazbhay. **Sth. Afr. J. Int. Aff.** 11:2 Winter-Spring:2004 pp.155-168.

5431   Southern Africa in world politics. Janice Love. Boulder CO: Westview Press, 2005. xx, 235p. *ISBN: 0813343119. Includes bibliographical references and index. (Series: Dilemmas in world politics).*

5432   The transatlantic dimension of security. Julian Lindley-French; Jean-Yves Haine; Jeffrey P. Bialos; Graham Messervy-Whiting; Thanos Veremis; Esther Barbé; Eduad Soler Lecha; Giacomo Luciani. **Int. Spect.** XL:2 4-6:2005 pp.29-98. *Collection of 6 articles.*

5433   Vzaimodeistvie Rossii, Indii i Kitaiia v XXI veke: problemy, perspektivy, napravleniia. *[In Russian]*; [Cooperation between Russia, India and China in the 21st century: problems, prospects and policies]. S.V. Uianaev. Moscow: In-t Dal'nego Vostoka RAN, 2004. *ISBN: 5838100842. Includes bibliographical references.*

5434   What we have discovered about the Cold War is what we already knew: Julius Mader and the Western secret services during the Cold War. Paul Maddrell. **Cold War Hist.** 5:2 5:2005 pp.235-258.

Americas
Amérique

5435   America and the world in the age of terror: a new landscape in international relations. Daniel Benjamin [Ed.]. Washington DC: CSIS Press, 2005. x, 206p. *ISBN: 0892064528. Includes bibliographical references and index. Center for Strategic and International Studies. (Series:* Significant issues - 27:1).

5436   Asymmetry and paradox: social policy and the Canada-U.S. bilateral relationship. Gerard W. Boychuk. **Am. R. Can. S.** 34:4 Winter:2004 pp.689-701.

5437   Base politics. Alexander Cooley. **Foreign Aff.** 84:6 11-12:2005 pp.79-92.

5438   British America in the world. James Kurth; Walter A. McDougall; J.C.D. Clark; David C. Hendrickson; J.G.A. Pocock; Carl Cavanagh Hodge. **Orbis** 49:1 Winter:2005 pp.1-73. *Collection of 6 articles.*

5439   Canada in the world. Pierre Martin; Pierre S. Pettigrew; Adam Chapnick; Julian Lindley-French; Robert W. Cox; Charles F. Doran; Marie Bernard-Meunier; Graham Allison; Marie-Joëlle Zahar; Karsten D. Voigt; Daryl Copeland. **Int. J.** LX:3 Summer:2005 pp.617-762. *Collection of 11 articles.*

5440   Canada-U.S. relations after free trade: lessons learned and unmet challenges. Michael Hart. **Am. R. Can. S.** 34:4 Winter:2004 pp.603-619.

5441   Canadian-American environmental relations: interoperability and politics. Debora L. Vannijnatten. **Am. R. Can. S.** 34:4 Winter:2004 pp.649-664.

5442   Caribbean-European relations and 9/11: continuity or change? Peter L. Clegg. **J. Transatlan. S.** 2:2 Autumn:2004 pp.143-162.

5443   The changing of the guard. Christopher Sands. **Int. J.** LX:2 Spring:2005 pp.483-496.

5444   Confronting Hugo Chávez: United States 'democracy promotion' in Latin America. Christopher I. Clement. **Lat. Am. Persp.** 32:3(142) 5:2005 pp.60-78.

5445   Culture, apology, and international negotiation: the case of the Sino-U.S. 'spy plane' crisis. Kevin Avruch; Zheng Wang. **Int. Negot.** 10:2 2005 pp.337-353.

5446   The democratic-peace thesis and U.S. relations with Colombia and Venezuela. William Avilés. **Lat. Am. Persp.** 32:3(142) 5:2005 pp.33-59.

5447   Do Americans trust other nations? A panel study. Paul R. Brewer; Sean Aday; Kimberly Gross. **Soc. Sci. Q.** 86:1 3:2005 pp.36-51.

5448   Empire and inequality: America and the world since 9/11. Paul Louis Street. Boulder CO: Paradigm Publishers, 2004. xviii, 193p. *ISBN: 1594510598, 159451058X. Includes bibliographical references and index. (Series:* Cultural politics and the promise of democracy).

5449   The end of Atlanticism: America and Europe beyond the U.S. election. Michael Lind. **Int. Pol. Gesell.** 1 2005 pp.25-41.

5450   Les Etats-Unis et la Syrie : le temps des décisions. *[In French]*; [The United States and Syria: decisions' time]. Antoine Sfeir. **Cah. Orient** 73 1-3:2004 pp.95-110.

5451   Les Etats-Unis et le Moyen-Orient. *[In French]*; [The United States and the Middle East]. Cécile Cahour [Ed.]. **Cah. Orient** 73 1-3:2004 pp.3-157.

5452   Europe and America in the age of Bush. Marta Dassù; Roberto Menotti. **Survival** 47:1 Spring:2005 pp.105-122.

5453   The first resort of kings: American cultural diplomacy in the twentieth century. Richard T. Arndt. Dulles VA: Potomac Books, 2005. xxi, 602p. *ISBN: 1574885871. Includes bibliographical references (p. 583-592) and index.*

5454   The hidden diplomatic history of Argentine-Brazilian integration: implications for historiography and theory; *[Summary in French]*. Gian Luca Gardini. **Canadian J. Lat. Am. Caribbean S.** 30:60 2005 pp.63-92.

5455   Inside the mirage: Americas fragile partnership with Saudi Arabia. Thomas W. Lippman. Boulder CO: Westview Press, 2004. ix, 390p. *ISBN: 0813340527. Includes bibliographical references (p. 371-374) and index.*

5456   Inter-American relations in an era of globalization: beyond unilateralism? Harry E. Vanden [Intro.]; Jorge Nef; Ward Stavig; Paul J. Dosal; Martin Needler; Jan Knippers Black; Luis Fernando Ayerbe; Jaime Preciado Coronado; Gaspare M. Genna; Taeko Hiroi; Saul Landau; Gary Prevost; Carlos M. Vilas; Richard L. Harris. **J. Dev. Soc.** 21:3-4 9-12:2005 pp.205-428. *Collection of 13 articles.*

5457   The Korean conundrum: America's troubled relations with North and South Korea. Ted Galen Carpenter; Doug Bandow. New York, Basingstoke: Palgrave Macmillan, 2004. 218p. *ISBN: 1403965455. Includes bibliographical references and index.*

5458   Korea-U.S. relations in the second Bush administration. Changsu Kim. **Kor. World Aff.** 28:4 Winter:2004 pp.361-371.

5459   La maison-blanche face au défi iranien. *[In French]*; [The White House facing the Iranian challenge] *[Summary]*; *[Summary in Spanish]*. Alexis Debat. **Polit. Int.** 107 Spring:2005 pp.169-191.

5460   Peru and Japan: an uneasy relationship. Rubén Berríos. **Canadian J. Lat. Am. Caribbean S.** 30:59 2005 pp.93-129.

5461   Perú, Bolivia y Chile: por una nueva relación trilateral. *[In Spanish]*; [Peru, Bolivia and Chile: a new trilateral relation]. Alejandro Deustua. **R. Cien. Pol.** XXIV:2 2004 pp.212-227.

5462   The relationship: a US perspective. Paul Cellucci. **Int. J.** LX:2 Spring:2005 pp.509-515.

5463   The ROK-U.S. relationship after the U.S. presidential election. Oknim Chung. **Kor. World Aff.** 28:4 Winter:2004 pp.372-390.

5464   Security, reform and peace: the three pillars of U.S. strategy in the Middle East. Washington Institute for Near East Policy. Washington DC: Washington Institute for Near East Policy, 2005. xiii, 82p. *ISBN: 0944029965.*

5465   The troubled relationship. Jean Charest; Norman Hillmer; Rima Berns-McGown; Andrew Cohen; Edna Keeble; Jutta Brunnée; Adrian Di Giovanni; Dwight N. Mason; Daniel Schwanen; James D. Phillips; Peter Karl Kresl; Jerome D. Davis; Alan M. Schwartz; Peter Andreas; Joe Clark; Earl H. Fry; Christopher Sands; John Manley; Paul Cellucci; American Assembly; Jeffrey A. Engel; José M. Magone; Frederic Labarre. **Int. J.** LX:2 Spring:2005 pp.321-573. *Collection of 22 articles.*

5466   «Uma visão intempestiva — um legado intemporal». *[In Portuguese]*; ('An untimely vision, a timeless legacy'. Woodrow Wilson and the irresistible temptation of democratic peace.) *[Summary]*. Mónica Dias. **Relações Int.** 4 12:2004 pp.33-44.

5467   Unfolding Canada-Bangladesh relations. Zaglul Haider. **Asian Sur.** XLV:2 3-4:2005 pp.322-341.

5468   The U.S. Congress and North Korea during the Clinton years: talk tough, carry a small stick. Robert M. Hathaway; Jordan Tama. **Asian Sur.** XLIV:5 9-10:2004 pp.711-733.

5469   US-China relations after 11 September: a long engagement or marriage of convenience? Brendan Taylor. **Aust. J. Int. Aff.** 59:2 6:2005 pp.179-199.

5470   US-Thai relations after 9/11: a new era in cooperation? Paul Chambers. **Contemp. Sth.East Asia** 26:3 12:2004 pp.460-479.

5471   Washington's new European allies: durable or conditional partners? Janusz Bugajski; Ilona Teleki. **Washington Q.** 28:2 Spring:2005 pp.95-108.

5472   Washington's troubling obsession with public diplomacy. David M. Edelstein; Ronald R. Krebs. **Survival** 47:1 Spring:2005 pp.89-104.

Asia
Asie

5473   The Baglihar dam and the Indus water treaty. Shireen M. Mazari. **Strat. S.** XXV:1 Spring:2005 pp.1-13.

5474   Beijing's dilemma with Taiwan: war or peace? Quansheng Zhao. **Pac. R.** 18:2 6:2005 pp.217-242.

5475   China, a unified Korea, and geopolitics. Toshi Yoshihara; James Holmes. **Iss. Stud.** 41:2 6:2005 pp.119-169.

5476   China engages Asia? Caveat lector. Nicholas Khoo; Michael L.R. Smith. **Int. Secur.** 30:1 Summer:2005 pp.196-213.

5477   China eyes the hegemon. Peter Hays Gries. **Orbis** 49:3 Summer:2005 pp.401-412.

5478   China in Africa. Chris Alden. **Survival** 47:3 Autumn:2005 pp.147-164.

5479   China's peaceful rise and Sino-Indian relations. Zhang Guihong. **Chi. Rep.** 41:2 4-6:2005 pp.159-171.

5480   China's strategy in Xinjiang and Central Asia: toward Chinese hegemony in the 'geographical pivot of history'? Michael Clarke. **Iss. Stud.** 41:2 6:2005 pp.75-118.

5481   Chinese images of the United States. Carola McGiffert [Ed.]. Washington DC: Center for Strategic and International Studies, 2005. xx, 156p. *ISBN: 089206465X. Includes bibliographical references and index.* (*Series:* Significant issues - 3).

5482   Chine-USA: choc du XXIe siècle. *[In French]*; [China-USA: clash of the twenty-first century]. Patrick Theuret. **Pensée** 341 1-3:2005 pp.59-71.

5483   A cold peace: the changing security equation in Northeast Asia. Tomohiko Taniguchi. **Orbis** 49:3 Summer:2005 pp.445-457.

5484   Contingent states: greater China and transnational relations. William A. Callahan. Minneapolis MN: University of Minnesota Press, 2004. xxxv,296p. *ISBN: 0816643997, 0816644004. Includes bibliographical references (p. 247-292) and index.* (*Series:* Borderlines - 22).

5485   The future of U.S.-Korea-Japan relations: balancing values and interests. Tae-hyo Kim [Ed.]; Brad Glosserman [Ed.]; Sang-woo Rhee [Foreword]. Washington DC: CSIS Press, 2004. xxii, 218p. *ISBN: 0892064544. Includes bibliographical references and index.* (*Series:* Significant issues).

5486   Getting Asia right. Muthiah Alagappa. **Iss. Stud.** 41:1 3:2005 pp.251-264.

5487   In war we stood united. V. Sokolov. **Int. Aff. [Moscow]** 51:6 2005 pp.173-183.

5488   India in Sri Lanka: between lion and the tigers. Avtar Singh Bhasin. New Delhi: Manas Publications, 2004. 353p. *ISBN: 8170492106. Includes index.*

5489   India-China relations: post conflict phase to post Cold War period. Bidanda M. Chengappa. New Delhi: A.P.H. Publishing Corporation, 2004. vi, 327p. *ISBN: 8176485381. Includes bibliographical references and index.*

5490   The international politics of the Asia-Pacific. Michael B. Yahuda. New York: Routledge, 2004. 355p. *ISBN: 0415207975. Includes bibliographical references.*

5491   Japan and South Korea: the new East Asian core. Michael R. Auslin. **Orbis** 49:3 Summer:2005 pp.459-473.

5492   Japanese-North Korean relations after the 2002 Pyongyang Summit: problems and prospects. Hong Nack Kim. **Kor. World Aff.** 28:2 Summer:2004 pp.163-197.

5493   Le Japon et l'Organisation des Nations-Unies : efforts récompensés et espoirs frustrés. *[In French]*; [Japan and the UN]. Bérénice Jallais. **Ebisu** 33 Fall-Winter:2004 pp.209-237.

5494   Okinawa: women, bases and US-Japan relations. Yumiko Mikanagi. **Int. Rel. Asia Pacific** 4:1 2004 pp.97-112.

5495   Party politics and Taiwan's external relations. Shelley Rigger. **Orbis** 49:3 Summer:2005 pp.413-428.

5496   Prospective developments in Indo-Pakistan trade: impact on Pakistan's economy. Farzana Noshab. **Strat. S.** XXV:2 Summer:2005 pp.75-85.

5497   Pyongyang-Pékin : les maîtres de l'ambiguïté. *[In French]*; [Pyongyang-Peking: masters of ambiguity]. Thérèse Delpech. **Polit. Int.** 105 Autumn:2004 pp.341-352.

5498   Recent writings on India-China relations. Sithara Fernando. **Chi. Rep.** 41:2 4-6:2005 pp.173-182.

5499   Red star ascending, flagging union Jack: Soviet views on the handover of Hong Kong. Michael Share. **Dipl. State.** 15:1 3:2004 pp.57-78.

5500   Les relations sino-américaines : coopération ou confrontation. *[In French]*; [Sino-American relations: cooperation or confrontation]. Bertrand Ateba. **R. Droit Int. Sci. Dip. Pol.** 82:1 1-4:2004 pp.87-107.

5501   Re-orienting Australia-China relations: 1972 to the present. Nicholas Thomas [Ed.]. Aldershot: Ashgate, 2004. xii, 292p. *ISBN: 0754632458.*

5502   Rossiia-Koreia: vzgliad iz proshlogo v nastoiashchee. *[In Russian]*; (Russia-Korea: a look from past into present.) Anatolii V. Torkunov; Valerii I. Denisov. **Mir. Ekon. Mezh. Ot.** 1 1:2005 pp.45-54.

5503   A semblance of cooperation between the two Koreas: why does it occur? Goo Lee. **Kor. World Aff.** 28:2 Summer:2004 pp.142-162.

5504   Sino-Indian security relations: bilateral issues, external factors and regional implications. Zhang Guihong. **Pol. Econ. J. India** 12:1 1-6:2005 pp.61-74.

5505   The sources and limits of Sino-Japanese tensions. Denny Roy. **Survival** 47:2 Summer:2005 pp.191-214.

5506   The sunshine policy and its impact on South Korea's relations with major powers. Choong Nam Kim. **Kor. Obs.** 35:4 Winter:2004 pp.581-616.

5507   Taking the 'taken-for-grantedness' seriously: problematizing Japan's perception of Japan-South Korea relations. Taku Tamaki. **Int. Rel. Asia Pacific** 4:1 2004 pp.147-170.

5508   Tokyo-Paris : des échanges fructueux. *[In French]*; [Tokyo-Paris: some fruitful exchanges]. Cahiers du Japon. **Cah. Japon** 100 Summer:2004 pp.8-21.

5509   Transforming U.S.-Korean relations. John Feffer; Charles K. Armstrong; Katharine H.S. Moon; Jae-jung Suh; Martin Hart-Landsberg; Gi-wook Shin; Paul Yunsik Chang; Samuel S. Kim; Karin Lee; Adam Miles; Alliance of Scholars Concerned about Korea. **Asian Persp. [S. Korea]** 28:4 2004 pp.5-207. *Collection of 7 articles.*

5510   Traumatic legacies in China and Japan: an exchange. Akira Chiba; Lanxin Xiang. **Survival** 47:2 Summer:2005 pp.215-230.

5511   An uncertain future: the politics of U.S.-China military relations — from Nixon, to George W. Bush, and beyond. John Kemmer. **Iss. Stud.** 41:2 6:2005 pp.171-216.

5512   Vers un renouveau japonais ? *[In French]*; [Towards a Japanese renewal?] Jean-Marie Bouissou [Ed.]. **Agir** 17 3:2004 pp.5-152.

5513   Welfare, environment and changing US-Chinese relations: 21st century challenges in China. Maria Weber [Ed.]. Cheltenham, Northampton MA: Edward Elgar Publishing, 2004. xxxi, 181p. *ISBN: 1843768275. Includes bibliographical references and index.*

5514   What China whispers to North Korea. Anne Wu. **Washington Q.** 28:2 Spring:2005 pp.35-48.

Europe
Europe

5515   50 Jahre deutsch-französische Beziehungen: Bilanz und Zukunftsperspektiven. *[In German]*; [50 years French-German relations: balance and prospects]. Jean François-Poncet; Chrystelle Nourry; Gilles Leroux; Daniela Heimerl; Stephan Martens; Andreas Schockenhoff; Jean-Louis Bourlanges. **Dokumente** 61:3 6:2005 pp.29-68. *Collection of 7 articles.*

5516   L'Allemagne, la France et le conflit israélo-palestinien. *[In French]*; (Germany, France and the Israeli-Palestinian conflict.); *[Summary in French]*. Isabel Schäfer; Dorothée Schmid. **Pol. Étran.** 70:2 Summer:2005 pp.411-422.

5517   Anti-Americanism and Americanization in Germany. Mary Nolan. **Pol. Soc.** 33:1 3:2005 pp.88-122.

5518   Belgrade-Moscou : " soft diplomatie " à la française. *[In French]*; [Belgrade-Moscow: "soft diplomacy" French-style]. Isabelle Lasserre; Laure Mandeville. **Polit. Int.** 105 Autumn:2004 pp.147-160.

5519   Berlin-Moskva: strategiia "novogo realizma". *[In Russian]*; (Berlin-Moscow: strategy of 'new realism'.) N. Pavlov. **Mir. Ekon. Mezh. Ot.** 9 9:2004 pp.57-69.

5520   Blair's Africa: the politics of securitization and fear. Rita Abrahamsen. **Alternatives** 30:1 1-3:2005 pp.55-80.

5521   Britain and East Asia. S.R. Ashton; John Boyd; Hugh Davies; K.A. Hamilton; Peter Lowe; Ian Nish. **Dipl. State.** 15:1 3:2004 pp.79-147. *Collection of 6 articles.*

5522   Current Russia –U.S. relationships: challenges and criteria. V. Margelov; V. Krivokhizha. **Int. Aff. [Moscow]** 51:5 2005 pp.41-53.

5523   Decisionmaking process matters: lessons learned from two Turkish foreign policy cases. Esra Çuhadar-Gürkaynak; Binnur Özkeçeci-Taner. **Turkish S.** 5:2 Summer:2004 pp.43-78.

5524   Diplomatie française : le réflexe européen. *[In French]*; [French diplomacy: the European reflex] *[Summary]*; *[Summary in Spanish]*. Isabelle Lasserre [Interviewer]; Michel Barnier. **Polit. Int.** 107 Spring:2005 pp.129-146.

5525   Discord and collaboration between allies: managing external threats and internal cohesion in Franco-British relations during the 9/11 era. Akan Malici. **J. Confl. Resol.** 49:1 2:2005 pp.90-119.

5526   ESDP as a transatlantic issue: problems of mutual ambiguity. Ingo Peters. **Int. S. R.** 6:3 9:2004 pp.381-401.

5527   États Baltes: de la difficulté d'être " petit "... *[In French]*; [Baltic states: on the difficulty of being "small"...] *[Summary]*; *[Summary in Spanish]*. Céline Bayou. **Polit. Int.** 107 Spring:2005 pp.95-112.

5528   Eurabia: the Euro-Arab axis. Bat Yeor. Madison NJ: Fairleigh Dickinson University Press, 2005. 384p. *ISBN: 0838640761, 083864077X. Includes bibliographical references (p. 347-362) and index.*

5529   European choice of Russia. D. Danilov. **Int. Aff. [Moscow]** 51:5 2005 pp.144-158.

5530   The European Union, Turkey and Islam. Erik Jan Zurcher. Amsterdam: Amsterdam University Press, 2004. 174p. *ISBN: 9053567127. Includes bibliographical references.*

5531   Der Fall Abbasi: Wegbereiter eines gemeineuropäischen Anspruchs auf diplomatischen Schutz? *[In German]*; [The Abbasi case: leading the way to a European claim to diplomatic protection?] *[Summary]*. Christian Storost. **A. Völk.** 42:4 12:2004 pp.411-424.

5532   Folket og freden. Utviklingstrekk i norsk fredsdiskurs 1890-2005. *[In Norwegian]*; (The people and the peace.) *[Summary]*. Halvard Leira. **Internasjonal Pol.** 63:2-3 2005 pp.141-161.

5533   The great guessing game: Russia and the Iranian nuclear issue. Vladimir A. Orlov; Alexander Vinnikov. **Washington Q.** 28:2 Spring:2005 pp.49-66.

5534   Greek-Turkish relations in an era of détente. Ahmet O. Evin; Kostas Ifantis; Othon Anastasakis; Ahmet Sözen; Gülay Günlük-Şenesen; Christos Kollias; Ali Çarkoğlu; Kemal Kirişci. **Turkish S.** 5:1 Spring:2004 pp.4-153. *Collection of 7 articles.*

5535   In search of a post-hegemonic order: Germany, NATO and the European Security and Defence Policy. Marco Overhaus. **Ger. Pol.** 13:4 12:2004 pp.551-568.

5536   Israel-Palestine, une passion française : la France dans le miroir du conflit israelo-palestinien. *[In French]*; [Israel-Palestinian Authority, a French passion: France in the mirror of the Arab-Israeli conflict]. Denis Sieffert. Paris: La Découverte, 2004. 270p. *ISBN: 2707143014.*

5537   Many times doomed but still alive: an attempt to understand the continuity of the special relationship. Jérôme B. Élie. **J. Transatlan. S.** 3:1(Supp.) Spring:2005 pp.63-83.

5538   Mitterrand, la fin de la guerre froide et l'unification allemande : de Yalta a Maastricht. *[In French]*; [Mitterrand, the end of the Cold War and German reunification: from Yalta to Maastricht]. Frederic Bozo. Paris: Editions Odile Jacob, 2005. 519p. *ISBN: 2738116426. Includes bibliographical references (p. [485]-494).*

5539   The new transatlantic agenda at ten: reflections on an experiment in international governance. Mark A. Pollack. **J. Com. Mkt. S.** 43:5 12:2005 pp.899-920.

5540   Où vont les Etats-Unis et la Turquie ? *[In French]*; [Where are the United States and Turkey going?] Füsun Türkmen. **Cah. Orient** 73 1-3:2004 pp.59-71.

5541   Para além do Iraque: a crise transatlântica em perspectiva. *[In Portuguese]*; (Beyond Iraq: the transatlantic crisis in perspective.) *[Summary]*. Pierre Hassner; Marta Amaral [Tr.]. **Relações Int.** 4 12:2004 pp.65-76.

5542   The 'poodle theory' and the Anglo-American 'special relationship'. Samuel Azubuike. **Int. S.** 42:2 4-6:2005 pp.123-139.

5543   Power, principles and procedures: reinterpreting French foreign policy towards the USA (2001-2003). Pernille Rieker. **Int. Pol.** 12:2 6:2005 pp.264-280.

5544   Pro - und anti-westliche Diskurse und Identitäten in Südosteuropa. *[In German]*; [Pro and anti Western discourse and identities in Southeast Europe]. Holm Sundhaussen. **Südosteuro. Mitteil.** 45:2 2005 pp.16-29.

5545   Pskov at the crossroads of Russia's trans-border relations with Estonia and Latvia: between provinciality and marginality. Andrey Makarychev. **Euro.-Asia S.** 57:3 5:2005 pp.481-500.

5546   Qu'est-il arrivé à la relation transatlantique ? L'Amérique vue par l'Europe : de la Guerre froide à la guerre contre le terrorisme. *[In French]*; [What happened to transatlantic relations? Europe's perception of America: from the Cold War to the war against terrorism]. Michael Cox. **Banquet** 21 10:2004 pp.81-105.

5547   The state of the union: military success, economic and political failure in the Russia-Belarus union. Ruth Deyermond. **Euro.-Asia S.** 56:8 12:2004 pp.1191-1205.

5548   Terms of estrangement: French-American relations in perspective. Simon Serfaty. **Survival** 47:3 Autumn:2005 pp.73-92.

5549   The Turkish-EU-US triangle in perspective: transformation or continuity? Ziya Önis; Suhnaz Yilmaz. **Mid. East J.** 59:2 Spring:2005 pp.265-284.

5550   Ukraina – ne s Rossiei (prichiny i posledstviia strategicheskikh proschetov rossiiskoi politiki po otnosheniiu k Ukraine). *[In Russian]*; (Ukraine not with Russia (causes and consequences of strategic errors of Russian policy towards Ukraine).) *[Summary]*. V.B. Pastukhov. **Polis [Moscow]** 1(84) 2005 pp.25-35.

5551   Uzbekistan and the United States: authoritarianism, Islamism and Washington's security agenda. Shahram Akbarzadeh. London, New York: Zed Books, 2005. xiv, 166p. *ISBN: 1842774220, 1842774239. Includes bibliographical references (p. [160]-162) and index.*

5552   Vsťahy krajín Visegrádskej štvorky s Čínou. *[In Czech]*; (Relations of Visegrad Four countries with China.) *[Summary]*. Gabriela Gregušová. **Mez. Vzt.** 40:1 2005 pp.7-21.

Middle East
Moyen-Orient

5553   Al-Jazeera: the inside story of the Arab news channel that is challenging the West. Hugh Miles. New York: Grove Press, 2005. 438p. *ISBN: 0802117899. Includes index.*
5554   An Arab spring? Fouad Ajami; Bernard Lewis; David Makovsky. **Foreign Aff.** 84:3 5-6:2005 pp.20-62. *Collection of 3 articles.*
5555   Clash of interest over Northern Iraq drives Turkish-Israeli alliance to a crossroads. Mustafa Kibaroglu. **Mid. East J.** 59:2 Spring:2005 pp.246-264.
5556   La diplomatie saoudienne à l'épreuve de la turbulence. *[In French]*; [Saudi diplomacy in turbulent waters]. Frédéric Charillon. **Etudes** 400:2 2:2004 pp.153-165.
5557   L'Iran entre brouillards et tempêtes. *[In French]*; [Iran, between fogs and storms]. Michel Makinsky. **CEMOTI** 37 1-6:2004 pp.253-274.
5558   Israël-France : l'amour et le ressentiment. *[In French]*; [Israel-France: love and resentment]. Arche. **Arche** 556-557 6-7:2004 pp.42-61.
5559   The Middle East in international relations: power, politics and ideology. Fred Halliday. Cambridge, New York: Cambridge University Press, 2005. xii, 374p. *ISBN: 0521592402, 0521597412. Includes bibliographical references (p. 356-366) and index. (Series: Contemporary Middle East - 4).*
5560   Shia factor in Iran-Iraq relations after Saddam. Kashif Mumtaz. **Strat. S.** XXV:1 Spring:2005 pp.14-32.
5561   The Turkish-Israeli relationship: changing ties of Middle Eastern outsiders. Ofra Bengio. New York, Basingstoke: Palgrave Macmillan, 2004. xi, 236p. *ISBN: 1403965897. Includes bibliographical references (p. [213]-224) and index.*
5562   Washington and Cairo — near the breaking point? Samuel J. Spector. **Mid. East Q.** XII:3 Summer:2005 pp.45-55.

F.3.5:   **International political forces**
    Forces politiques internationales

5563   Ascesa o declino? Gli Stati Uniti nell'era globale. *[In Italian]*; (Rise or fall? The United States in the global era.) Francesco Tuccari. **Riv. It. Sci. Pol.** XXXV:1 4:2005 pp.135-149.
5564   Bashar Al-Assad: in or out of the new world order? Eyal Zisser. **Washington Q.** 28:3 Summer:2005 pp.115-131.
5565   Bridging the gap: ethnicity, legitimacy, and state alignment in the international scene. Cindy R. Jebb. Lanham MD: Lexington Books, 2004. xvi, 341p. *ISBN: 0739105914. Includes bibliographical references (p. 307-324) and index.*
5566   Brotherhood reconsidered: region-building in the Baltics. Mindaugas Jurkynas. **J. Baltic S.** XXXV:1 Spring:2004 pp.1-31.
5567   Il cambiamento di strategia degli USA e le relazioni transatlantiche: implicazioni per il sistema mondiale. *[In Italian]*; (The change of the US strategy and transatlantic relations: implications for the world system.) Fulvio Attinà. **Riv. It. Sci. Pol.** XXXV:1 4:2005 pp.3-28.
5568   China's rise in Southeast Asia: implications for the United States. Elizabeth Economy. **J. Cont. China** 14:44 8:2005 pp.409-425.
5569   La danse des civilisations : l'Orient, l'Occident et Abu Ghraib. *[In French]*; [Dance of the civilizations: East, West and Abu Ghraib]. Susie Linfield. **Esprit** 315 6:2005 pp.66-84.
5570   Destroying world order: U.S. imperialism in the Middle East before and after September 11. Francis Anthony Boyle. Atlanta GA: Clarity Press, 2004. 191p. *ISBN: 093286340X. Includes bibliographical references (p. 177-184) and index.*

5571   Emerging third world powers: China, India and Brazil. Jerry Harris. **Race Class** 46:3 1-3:2005 pp.7-27.

5572   Empire: a blunt tool for democratization. Jack Snyder. **Dædalus** 134:2 Spring:2005 pp.58-71.

5573   Etats-Unis : de l'hégémonisme à la puissance impériale. *[In French]*; [United States: from hegemonism to imperial power]. Pascal Chaigneau. **Défense Nat.** 60:10 10:2004 pp.125-136.

5574   Evoliutsiia global'noi politiki (II). *[In Russian]*; (The evolution of global politics (II).) *[Summary]*. G. Model'ski. **Polis [Moscow]** 4(87) 2005 pp.124-142.

5575   Evoliutsiia mirovoi politiki (I). *[In Russian]*; (The evolution of global politics (I).) *[Summary]*. George Modelski. **Polis [Moscow]** 3(86) 2005 pp.62-82.

5576   Failing states and cumulative causation in the world system; *[Summary in French]*. Robert Hunter Wade. **Int. Pol. Sci. R.** 26:1 1:2005 pp.17-36.

5577   Formirovanie global'nogo mirporiadka i Rossiia. *[In Russian]*; (Formation of global order and Russia.) N. Kosolapov. **Mir. Ekon. Mezh. Ot.** 11 11:2004 pp.3-13.

5578   Forum on the rise of China. William A. Callahan; Arthur Waldron; Shaun Breslin; Chih-yu Shih; Daojiong Zha. **R. Int. S.** 31:4 10:2005 pp.701-785. *Collection of 5 articles.*

5579   Future tense: the coming world order. Gwynne Dyer. Toronto: M&S, 2004. 254p. *ISBN: 0771029780.*

5580   Genèse et enjeux des migrations internationales. *[In French]*; [Origins and stakes of international migration]. Alternatives Sud. **Alt. Sud** 11:1 2004 pp.7-207.

5581   The global view of the United States. Jay Sexton. **Hist. J.** 48:1 3:2005 pp.261-276.

5582   Globalisierung der Ökonomie, Polarisierung der Macht. Dilemmata der US-amerikanischen Hegemonie. *[In German]*; (Globalization of economy and polarization of power. Dilemmas of the US-American hegemony.) *[Summary]*. Carlos Maya-Ambía. **Prokla** 34:4 12:2004 pp.621-634.

5583   The gothic scene of international relations: ghosts, monsters, terror and the sublime after September 11. Richard Devetak. **R. Int. S.** 31:4 10:2005 pp.621-643.

5584   The gravity of imperial politics: some thoughts on power and representation. David Slater. **Arab World Geog.** 7:1-2 Spring-Summer:2004 pp.91-102.

5585   The HBV and HCV pandemics: health, political, and security challenges. Albert B. Knapp. **Pol. Sci. Q.** 120:2 Summer:2005 pp.243-252.

5586   Hegemony: the new shape of global power. John A. Agnew. Philadelphia PA: Temple University Press, 2005. xi, 284p. *ISBN: 1592131530. Includes bibliographical references and index.*

5587   Hegemony unravelling (Part I). Giovanni Arrighi. **New Left R.** 32 3-4:2005 pp.23-80.

5588   Hegemony unravelling (Part II). Giovanni Arrighi. **New Left R.** 33 5-6:2005 pp.83-116.

5589   The human-animal link. William B. Karesh; Robert A. Cook. **Foreign Aff.** 84:4 7-8:2005 pp.38-50.

5590   IBSA forum: the rise of 'new' non-alignment. Abdul Nafey. **India Q.** LXI:1 1-3:2005 pp.1-78.

5591   In America we (used to) trust: U.S. hegemony and global cooperation. Andrew Kydd. **Pol. Sci. Q.** 120:4 Winter:2005-2006 pp.619-636.

5592   Inside multilateralism: the six-party talks. John S. Park. **Washington Q.** 28:4 Autumn:2005 pp.75-91.

5593   'International community' after Iraq. Barry Buzan; Ana Gonzalez-Pelaez. **Int. Aff. [London]** 81:1 1:2005 pp.31-52.

5594   International democracy and the West: the roles of governments, civil society, and multinational business. Richard Youngs. Oxford, New York: Oxford University Press, 2004. viii, 222p. *ISBN: 0199274460. Includes bibliographical references (p. [197]-216) and index. (Series: Oxford studies in democratization).*

5595   International ethics: concepts, theories, and cases in global politics. Mark R. Amstutz. Lanham MD: Rowman & Littlefield, 2005. xiii, 266p. *ISBN: 0742535827, 0742535835. Includes bibliographical references and index.*

5596 Interpreting September 11. Brian Frederking; Michael Artime; Max Sanchez Pagano. **Int. Pol.** 42:1 3:2005 pp.135-151.

5597 Japan's socialization into Janus-faced European international society. Shogo Suzuki. **Euro. J. Int. Rel.** 11:1 3:2005 pp.137-164.

5598 Kriminal'naia globalizatsiia. *[In Russian]*; (Criminal globalization.) V.V. Luneev. **Gos. Pravo** 10 10:2004 pp.26-41.

5599 Legitimnost' v mezhdunarodnykh otnosheniiakh: evoliutsiia i sovremennoe sostoianie problemy. *[In Russian]*; (Legitimacy in international relations: evolution and current state of the problem.) N. Kosolapov. **Mir. Ekon. Mezh. Ot.** 2 2:2005 pp.3-14.

5600 The lessons of HIV/AIDS. Laurie Garrett. **Foreign Aff.** 84:4 7-8:2005 pp.51-65.

5601 The limits and temptations of America's conventional military primacy. Jeffrey Record. **Survival** 47:1 Spring:2005 pp.33-50.

5602 Medzinárodné prostredie Slovenskej republiky v roku 2010. *[In Slovak]*; (International environment of the Slovak Republic in 2010.) *[Summary]*. Alexander Duleba. **Medz. Otázky** XIII:1 2004 pp.103-117.

5603 Miesto a možnosti malých štátov v systéme medzinárodných vzťahov. *[In Slovak]*; (The place and choices of small states in the system of international relations.) *[Summary]*. Urban Rusnák. **Medz. Otázky** XIII:1 2004 pp.92-102.

5604 Miroustroistvo nachala XXI veka: sushchestvuet li al'ternativa "amerikanskoi imperii?" *[In Russian]*; (World architecture of early XXI: is there an alternative to 'American empire'?) A. Terentiev. **Mir. Ekon. Mezh. Ot.** 10 10:2004 pp.35-46.

5605 Mnogomernost' mirovoi politiki (k sovremennym diskussiiam). *[In Russian]*; (World politics' multidimensionality (to current discussions).) *[Summary]*. I.A. Chikharev. **Polis [Moscow]** 1(84) 2005 pp.161-172.

5606 Negotiated revolutions: the prospects for radical change in contemporary world politics. George Lawson. **R. Int. S.** 31:3 7:2005 pp.473-493.

5607 New geopolitics for Russia. N. Arbatova; M. Titarenko; A. Torkunov; A. Bogaturov; B. Piadyshev; M. Kokeev; Ye. Volk; K. Kosachev. **Int. Aff. [Moscow]** 51:2 2005 pp.67-82.

5608 A partnership for Central Asia. S. Frederick Starr. **Foreign Aff.** 84:4 7-8:2005 pp.164-179.

5609 The politics of empire: war, terror and hegemony. David N. Gibbs; Gordon Lafer; Sheila D. Collins; Edward Greer; Gerard Huiskamp; Douglas Kellner; William I. Robinson; Irene Gendzier; Carl Boggs. **New Pol. Sci.** 26:3 9:2004 pp.217-472. *Collection of 10 articles.*

5610 Power in international politics. Michael Barnett; Raymond Duvall. **Int. Org.** 59:1 Winter:2005 pp.39-75.

5611 Rationality and psychology in international politics. Jonathan Mercer. **Int. Org.** 59:1 Winter:2005 pp.77-106.

5612 Renegade regimes: confronting deviant behavior in world politics. Miroslav Nincic. New York: Columbia University Press, 2005. viii, 219p. *ISBN: 0231137028, 0231510292. Includes bibliographical references and index.*

5613 Rhetoric versus reality: rogue states in interstate conflict. Mary Caprioli; Peter F. Trumbore. **J. Confl. Resol.** 49:5 10:2005 pp.770-791.

5614 The right that failed? The ambiguities of conservative thought and the dilemmas of conservative practice in international affairs. Ian Hall; Nicholas Rengger. **Int. Aff. [London]** 81:1 1:2005 pp.69-82.

5615 Ritmy mezhdunarodnogo razvitiia kak faktor politicheskoi modernizatsii Rossii. *[In Russian]*; (International development rhythms as a factor of Russia's political modernization.) *[Summary]*. V.V. Lapkin; V.I. Pantin. **Polis [Moscow]** 3(86) 2005 pp.44-58.

5616 Russian hegemony in Dagestan. Enver Kisriev; Robert Bruce Ware. **Post-Sov. Aff.** 21:1 1-3:2005 pp.26-55.

5617 Sida, un enjeu global de sécurité. *[In French]*; [AIDS and international security]. Stefan Elbe. **Pol. Étran.** 70:1 Spring:2005 pp.163-175.

5618 Social psychology and the identity-conflict debate: is a 'China threat' inevitable? Peter Hays Gries. **Euro. J. Int. Rel.** 11:2 6:2005 pp.235-265.

5619   Soft balancing against the United States. Robert A. Pape. **Int. Secur.** 30:1 Summer:2005 pp.7-45.

5620   Soft balancing in the age of U.S. primacy. T.V. Paul. **Int. Secur.** 30:1 Summer:2005 pp.46-71.

5621   Southeast Asia in the Sino-US strategic balance. Shannon Tow. **Contemp. Sth.East Asia** 26:3 12:2004 pp.434-459.

5622   States of war. Gopal Balakrishnan. **New Left R.** 36 11-12:2005 pp.5-32.

5623   Strategic non-cooperation as soft balancing: why Iraq was not just about Iraq. Judith Kelley. **Int. Pol.** 12:2 6:2005 pp.153-173.

5624   The Taiwan conundrum: heading towards a new war? Chen Qimao. **J. Cont. China** 13:41 12:2004 pp.705-715.

5625   Turkey as regional hegemon — 2014: strategic implications for the United States. Edward J. Erickson. **Turkish S.** 5:3 Autumn:2004 pp.25-45.

5626   The unconscious colossus: limits of (and alternatives to) American empire. Niall Ferguson. **Dædalus** 134:2 Spring:2005 pp.18-33.

5627   United States post-Cold War defence interests: a review of the first decade. K.P. Magyar [Ed.]. Basingstoke: Palgrave Macmillan, 2004. xvi, 264p. *ISBN: 0333772466. Includes index.*

5628   US intervention in Iraq and the future of the normative order. Andrea Kathryn Talentino. **Contemp. Sec. Policy** 25:2 8:2004 pp.312-338.

5629   When — if ever — did empire end? Recent studies of imperialism and decolonization. Stephen Howe. **J. Contemp. Hist.** 40:3 7:2005 pp.585-599.

5630   Whose sovereignty? Empire versus international law. Jean L. Cohen. **Ethics Int. Aff.** 18:3 2004 pp.1-24.

International political economy
Politique économique internationale

5631   'Advice is judged by results, not by intentions': why Gordon Brown is wrong about Africa. Ian Taylor. **Int. Aff. [London]** 81:2 3:2005 pp.299-310.

5632   And the money kept rolling in (and out): Wall Street, the IMF, and the bankrupting of Argentina. Paul Blustein. New York: Public Affairs, 2005. xxii, 278p. *ISBN: 1586482459. Includes bibliographical references and index.*

5633   Antidumping: the third rail of trade policy. N. Gregory Mankiw; Phillip L. Swagel. **Foreign Aff.** 84:4 7-8:2005 pp.107-119.

5634   Brevet du vivant : progrès ou crime? *[In French]*; (Patenting the living: progress or crime?) *[Summary]*. Jean-Pierre Berlan. **Tiers Monde** XLVI:181 1-3:2005 pp.207-221.

5635   The Caribbean economies in an era of free trade. Nikolaos Karagiannis [Ed.]; Michael Witter [Ed.]. Aldershot: Ashgate, 2004. xix, 203p. *ISBN: 0754640701. Includes bibliographical references and index.*

5636   Centre-periphery conflict and institutional development: the significance of North-South relations for the CAP. Christilla Roederer-Rynning. **J. Int. Rel. Dev.** 8:3 9:2005 pp.287-310.

5637   The changing state-market condominium in East Asia: rethinking the political underpinnings of development. Geoffrey R.D. Underhill; Xiaoke Zhang. **New Pol. Econ.** 10:1 3:2005 pp.1-24.

5638   The cocaine war in context: drugs and politics. Lorena Terando [Tr.]; Belen Boville Luca de Tena. New York: Algora Publishing, 2004. 204p. *ISBN: 0875862934, 0875862942, 0875862942. Translated from the spanish Guerra de la cocaina: drogas, geopolitica y medio ambiente. Includes bibliographical references (p. 191-204) and index.*

5639   El comercio exterior de la Rusia poscomunista y los problemas de su adhesión a la organización mundial de comercio. *[In Spanish]*; (Foreign trade in post-communist Russia and some problems related to its adhesion to the World Trade Organization.) Tatiana Sidorenko. **Foro Int.** XLIV:4 10-12:2004 pp.656-689.

5640   Credit where credit is due: open economy industrial policy and export diversification in Latin America and the Caribbean. Andrew Schrank; Marcus J. Kurtz. **Pol. Soc.** 33:4 12:2005 pp.671-702.

5641   Cultural diversity and international economic integration: the global governance of the audio-visual sector. Paolo Guerrieri [Ed.]; Lelio Iapadre [Ed.]; Georg Koopmann [Ed.]. Cheltenham; Northampton MA: Edward Elgar Publishing, 2005. x, 296p. *ISBN: 1843768070. Includes bibliographical references and index.*

5642   Dallas to Doba: oil and Chad, external controls and internal politics. Simon Massey; Roy May. **J. Contemp. Afr. S.** 23:2 5:2005 pp.253-276.

5643   The deep structure of the present moment. David Laibman; William I. Robinson; Jerry Harris; George Liodakis; Robert Went; Anastasia Nesvetailova; Minqi Li; William Minter; Nira Wickramasinghe; Hester Eisenstein. **Sci. Soc.** 69:3 7:2005 pp.277-518. *Collection of 11 articles.*

5644   Economic globalization and civil war. Katherine Barbieri; Rafael Reuveny. **J. Pol.** 67:4 11:2005 pp.1228-1247.

5645   Economic interdependence and international interactions: impact of third-party trade on political cooperation and conflict. Yuan-ching Chang. **Coop. Confl.** 40:2 6:2005 pp.207-232.

5646   Emerging markets — emerging powers: changing parameters for global economic governance. Garth Le Pere. **Int. Pol. Gesell.** 2 2005 pp.36-51.

5647   Empire and beyond. Renaud Damesin; Jean-Michel Denis; Phoebe Moore; Prodromos Ioannou Panayiotopoulos; Paul Thompson; Jim Smyth. **Cap. Class** 86 Summer:2005 pp.17-153. *Collection of 5 articles.*

5648   Exit, vote and sovereignty: migration, states and globalization. Jonathon W. Moses. **R. Int. Pol. Econ.** 12:1 2:2005 pp.53-77.

5649   Free trade with hazardous products? The emergence of transnational governance with eroding state government. Christian Joerges. **Euro. For. Aff. R.** 10:4 Winter:2005 pp.553-574.

5650   From Kyoto to the WTO: evaluating the constitutional legitimacy of the provinces in Canadian foreign trade and environmental policy; *[Summary in French].* Christopher J. Kukucha. **Can. J. Pol.** 38:1 3:2005 pp.129-152.

5651   Global flows: terror, oil and strategic philanthropy. Sandra T. Barnes. **R. Afr. Pol. Econ.** 32:104-105 6-9:2005 pp.235-252.

5652   Globalization, hegemony and power: antisystemic movements and the global system. Thomas Ehrlich Reifer [Ed.]. Boulder CO: Paradigm Publishers, 2004. v, 210p. *ISBN: 159451027X. Includes bibliographical references. (Series:* Political economy of the world-system annuals - 26a).

5653   The governance of global value chains. Gary Gereffi; John Humphrey; Timothy Sturgeon. **R. Int. Pol. Econ.** 12:1 2:2005 pp.78-104.

5654   Government spending and public support for trade in the OECD: an empirical test of the embedded liberalism thesis. Jude C. Hays; Sean D. Ehrlich; Clint Peinhardt. **Int. Org.** 59:2 Spring:2005 pp.473-494.

5655   Hospodárska diplomacia SR v rokoch 1993-2003. *[In Slovak];* (Economic diplomacy of the Slovak Republic in 1993-2003.) Ingrid Brocková. **Medz. Otázky** XIII:1 2004 pp.53-83.

5656   Institutional change in contemporary capitalism: coordinated financial systems since 1990. Pepper D. Culpepper. **World Pol.** 57:2 1:2005 pp.173-199.

5657   Interdependenz und Macht in den Amerikas. *[In German];* [Interdependence and power relations in the Americas]. Hartmut Sangmeister; Andreas Boeckh; Stefan A. Schirm. **Lat.Am. Anal.** 11 6:2005 pp.61-130. *Collection of 3 articles.*

5658   International transformation and the persistence of territoriality: toward a new political geography of capitalism. Hannes Lacher. **R. Int. Pol. Econ.** 12:1 2:2005 pp.26-52.

5659   Kross-kul'turnyi menedzhment i politicheskaia sreda v usloviiakh globalizatsii ekonomiki. *[In Russian];* (The role of globalization in cross-cultural management and the political sphere.) A.I. Kostin; I.A. Kostina. **Vest. Mosk. Univ. 12 Pol.** 1 1-2:2005 pp.103-131.

5660   Markets in transition: conflict, political regimes, and the 'war on terror' in East and Southeast Asia. Kanishka Jayasuriya; Kevin Hewison; Wil Hout; Vedi R. Hadiz; Sally Sargeson; Shaun Breslin. **Crit. Asian S.** 36:4 12:2004 pp.571-675. *Collection of 5 articles.*

5661   Merchants of death revisited: armaments, bankers, and the First World War. T. Hunt Tooley. **J. Libertarian S.** 19:1 Winter:2005 pp.37-78.

5662   Mexico's democracy at work: political and economic dynamics. Russell Crandall [Ed.]; Guadalupe Paz [Ed.]; Riordan Roett [Ed.]. Boulder CO: Lynne Rienner Publishers, 2005. vii, 232p. *ISBN: 1588263002, 1588263258. Includes bibliographical references (p. 201-218) and index.*

5663   Mondialisation du commerce illicite de bois et droit pénal français : un déficit de juridiction. *[In French]*; [Illegal wood trade globalization and French criminal law: a jurisdictional shortcoming]. Julie Vallat. **R. Sci. Crim.** 1 1-3:2005 pp.21-46.

5664   Moving beyond the great game: the geoeconomics of Russia's influence in the Caspian energy bonanza. Adam N. Stulberg. **Geopolitics** 10:1 Spring:2005 pp.1-25.

5665   Multinational enterprises, international relations and international business: reconstituting intellectual boundaries for the new millennium. Darryl S.L. Jarvis. **Aust. J. Int. Aff.** 59:2 6:2005 pp.201-223.

5666   The nation-state and economic globalization: soft geo-politics and increased state autonomy? Maria Gritsch. **R. Int. Pol. Econ.** 12:1 2:2005 pp.1-25.

5667   The new aerospace diplomacy: reconstructing post-Cold War US-Russian economic relations. Geoffrey Allen Pigman. **Dipl. State.** 15:4 12:2004 pp.683-723.

5668   Nový regionalismus ve světové ekonomice: příklad spojených států amerických v podmínkách západní hemisféry. *[In Czech]*; (New regionalism in world politics: example of United States of America in conditions of West hemisphere.) *[Summary]*. Pavel Neumann. **Mez. Vzt.** 39:4 2004 pp.50-60.

5669   Oil and international law: the geopolitical significance of petroleum corporations. Simon Chesterman; Robert Dufresne; Michael T. Klare; Stephen J. Kobrin; Cynthia A. Williams. **New York Univ. J. Int. Law Pol.** 36:2-3 Winter-Spring:2004 pp.307-502. *Collection of 5 articles.*

5670   Order and regulation: global governance as a hegemonic discourse of international politics? Ulrich Brand. **R. Int. Pol. Econ.** 12:1 2:2005 pp.155-176.

5671   Ortadoğu'da ekonomik ilişkilerin siyasi çerçevesi; Türkiye'nin İran, Irak ve Suriye ile bağlantıları. *[In Turkish]*; (Political conditionality of economic interactions in the Middle East; Turkey's relations with Iran, Iraq, and Syria.) Mustafa Aydın; Damla Aras. **Uluslararası İlişkiler** 1:2 Spring:2004 pp.103-128.

5672   La place financière suisse en tant qu'instrument de la politique étrangère helvétique. *[In French]*; (Swiss financial place as an instrument of the Swiss foreign policy.) Marc Perrenoud. **Relations Int.** 121 1-3:2005 pp.25-42.

5673   Political economies and the study of Africa: critical considerations. Gavin Williams. **R. Afr. Pol. Econ.** 31:102 12:2004 pp.571-583.

5674   The political economy of intellectual property protection: the case of software. Kenneth C. Shadlen; Andrew Schrank; Marcus J. Kurtz. **Int. S. Q.** 49:1 3:2005 pp.45-71.

5675   The political economy of liberalization and crisis: 'domestic bank-centered' financial openings and their aftermaths. Shale Horowitz. **Japanese J. Pol. Sci.** 6:1 4:2005 pp.111-136.

5676   Premiers schémas européens et économie internationale durant l'entre-deux-guerres. *[In French]*; (First European projects and international economies during the interwar period.) *[Summary]*. Éric Bussière. **Relations Int.** 123 7-9:2005 pp.51-68.

5677   The Putin thesis and Russian energy policy. Harley Balzer. **Post-Sov. Aff.** 21:3 7-9:2005 pp.210-225.

5678   The rise of regulatory capitalism: the global diffusion of a new order. David Levi-Faur; Zachary Elkins; Beth Simmons; David Lazer; Covadonga Meseguer; Fabrizio Gilardi; Jacint Jordana; David Levi-Faur; Christopher R. Way; Per-Olof Busch; Helge Jörgens; Kerstin Tews; Diahanna L. Post; Jacint Jordana. **Ann. Am. Acad. Pol. Soc. Sci.** 598 3:2005 pp.6-217. *Collection of 12 articles.*

5679   Scarcity, conflicts, and cooperation: essays in the political and institutional economics of development. Pranab K. Bardhan. Cambridge MA: MIT Press, 2005. xi, 306p. *ISBN: 0262025736, 0262524295. Includes bibliographical references (p. 275-294) and index.*

5680   Slavophiles and westernizers redux: contemporary Russian elite perspectives. William Zimmerman. **Post-Sov. Aff.** 21:3 7-9:2005 pp.183-209.

5681   South Africa's economic relations with Africa: hegemony and its discontents. Chris Alden; Mills Soko. **J. Mod. Afr. S.** 43:3 9:2005 pp.367-392.

5682   The terror of neoliberalism. Henry A. Giroux. Aurora; Boulder CO: Garamond Press; Paradigm Publishers, 2004. xxviii, 195p. *ISBN: 1551930544, 1594510113. Includes bibliographical references and index.* (*Series:* Cultural politics and the promise of democracy).

5683   Theories of policy diffusion: lessons from Latin American pension reform. Kurt Weyland. **World Pol.** 57:2 1:2005 pp.262-295.

5684   El tio sam al desnudo. Un paseo por China y el mundo. Visto desde las alturas de la gran muralla a traves de los ojos de un niño inocente. *[In Spanish]*; [Uncle Sam naked. A stroll around China and the world. Seen from the Great Wall highs through the eyes of an innocent child] *[Summary]*. Andre Gunder Frank. **Sistema** 186 5:2005 pp.3-27.

5685   Towards a more coherent oil policy in Russia? Sadek Boussena; Catherine Locatelli. **OPEC R.** XXIX:2 6:2005 pp.85-105.

5686   Trade policy at the crossroads: the Indonesian story. David Vanzetti; Greg McGuire; Prabowo. New York: United Nations, 2005. vi, 32p. *ISBN: 9211126517. Includes bibliographical references.* (*Series:* Policy issues in international trade and commodities. Study - no. 28).

5687   A trade war with China? Neil C. Hughes. **Foreign Aff.** 84:4 7-8:2005 pp.94-106.

5688   Triumph of globalism: American trade politics. Orin Kirshner. **Pol. Sci. Q.** 120:3 Fall:2005 pp.479-504.

5689   Turkey and the East-West gas transportation corridor. Gareth M. Winrow. **Turkish S.** 5:2 Summer:2004 pp.23-42.

5690   Uluslararasılıkta kaos, bir medeniyet dönüşümü ve İslami (f)aktör: Türkiye'de MÜSİAD örneği. *[In Turkish]*; (Chaos in internationality, a civilizational evolution and Islamic (f)actor: the case of MÜSİAD in Turkey.) Şennur Özdemir. **Uluslararasi Ilişkiler** 1:3 Autumn:2004 pp.67-100.

5691   Veto points, veto players, and international trade policy. Robert F. O'Reilly. **Comp. Pol. S.** 38:6 8:2005 pp.652-675.

5692   The World Bank, governance and theories of political action in Africa. Graham Harrison. **Br. J. Pol. Int. Rel.** 7:2 5:2005 pp.240-260.

5693   The WTO medicines decision: world pharmaceutical trade and the protection of public health. Frederick M. Abbott. **Am. J. Int. Law** 99:2 4:2005 pp.317-358.

International religious influences
Influences religieuses internationales

5694   Acteurs internationaux et Islam de France. *[In French]*; [International actors and French Islam]. Samir Amghar. **Pol. Étran.** 70:1 Spring:2005 pp.23-34.

5695   The Al Qaeda 9/11 instructions: a study in the construction of religious martyrdom. Yuval Neria; David Roe; Benjamin Beit-Hallahmi; Hassan Mneimneh; Alana Balaban; Randall Marshall. **Religion** 35:1 1:2005 pp.1-11.

5696   Al Qaeda as a dune organization: toward a typology of Islamic terrorist organizations. Shaul Mishal; Maoz Rosenthal. **S. Confl. Terror.** 28:4 7-8:2005 pp.275-294.

5697   Al Qaida recruitment trends in Kenya and Tanzania. William Rosenau. **S. Confl. Terror.** 28:1 1-2:2005 pp.1-10.

5698   Al-Qaeda and the nature of religious terrorism. Mark Sedgwick. **Terror. Pol. Viol.** 16:4 Winter:2004 pp.795-814.

5699   At the heart of terror: Islam, Jihadists, and Americas war on terrorism. Monte Palmer; Princess Palmer. Lanham MD: Rowman & Littlefield, 2004. vii, 293p. *ISBN: 0742536025. Includes bibliographical references (p. 273-286) and index.*

5700   Brutal truths, fragile myths: power politics and Western adventurism in the Arab world. Mark Huband. Boulder CO: Westview Press, 2004. xvii, 331p. *ISBN: 0813337534. Includes bibliographical references (p. 315-320) and index.*

5701   Can the west win Muslim hearts and minds? Zachary Shore. **Orbis** 49:3 Summer:2005 pp.475-490.

5702   De Jean Paul II à Benoît XVI: la même politique juive? *[In French]*; [From Jean Paul II to Benedict XVI: the same Jewish policy?] Paul Giniewski. **Riv. S. Pol. Int.** LXXII:3 7-9:2005 pp.503-548.

5703   A genealogy of radical Islam. Quintan Wiktorowicz. **S. Confl. Terror.** 28:2 3-4:2005 pp.75-97.

5704   Geopolitika kak religiia. *[In Russian]*; (Geopolitics as religion.) Boris Kagarlitskii. **Svobod. Mysl'** 8 2005 pp.3-15.

5705   Gibt es eine islamische bzw. islamistische Herausforderung an die Identität Europas? Ein Plädoyer für eine euro-islamische "Asabiyya" als Brücke und Leitkultur im Konflikt der Zivilisationen. *[In German]*; [Is there an Islamic challenge to the identity of Europe? An Euro-Islamic "Asabiyya" as bridge and cultural orientation in the clash of civilizations] *[Summary]*. Bassam Tibi. **Relig. Staat Gesell.** 6:1 2005 pp.19-62.

5706   Globalization and diversification of Islamic movements: three Turkish cases. Ahmet T. Kuru. **Pol. Sci. Q.** 120:2 Summer:2005 pp.253-274.

5707   Globalized Islam: the search for a new Ummah. Olivier Roy. New York: Columbia University Press, 2004. xi,349p. *ISBN: 0231134983. Includes bibliographical references and index. (Series:* The CERI series in comparative politics and international studies).

5708   Good Muslim, bad Muslim: America, the Cold War, and the roots of terror. Mahmood Mamdani. New York: Pantheon Books, 2004. xii, 304p. *ISBN: 0375422854. Includes bibliographical references and index.*

5709   Heiliges Recht in moderner Welt: Islamisches Recht zwischen Stabilität und Wandel. *[In German]*; (Sacred law in a modern world: the Sharia between stability and change.) *[Summary]*. Brigitte Weiffen. **Welt Trends** 48 Autumn:2005 pp.133-145.

5710   The intersections of U.S. foreign policy, Islamist militancy, and terrorism. Robert Snyder. **Orbis** 49:4 Fall:2005 pp.743-754.

5711   Islam and international law. Sheikh Wahbeh al-Zuhili. **Int. R. Red Cross** 87:858 6:2005 pp.269-283.

5712   Islam and politics in the contemporary world. Beverley Milton-Edwards. Oxford, Malden MA: Polity, 2004. viii, 240p. *ISBN: 0745627110, 0745627129.*

5713   Islam and the West post 9/11. Ron Geaves [Ed.]. Aldershot, Burlington VT: Ashgate, 2004. xii, 226p. *ISBN: 0754650022, 0754650057. Includes bibliographical references and index.*

5714   L'Islam et les droits de l'homme : l'islamisme, le droit international et le modernisme islamique. *[In French]*; [Islam and human rights: Islamism, international law and Islamic modernism]. Vida Amirmokri. Quebec: Presses de l'Universite Laval, 2004. x, 184p. *ISBN: 2763781764. Includes bibliographical references (p. 167-184).*

5715   Islamist networks: the Afghan-Pakistan connection. Mariam Abou Zahab; John King [Tr.]; Oliver Roy. London: Hurst & Company, 2004. xi, 88p. *ISBN: 1850657041. Translated from the French. Includes bibliographical references (p. 83) and index. (Series:* The CERI series in comparative politics and international studies).

5716   Iszlám és politika. A civilizációk közötti első konfliktus alapjainak elemzése. *[In Hungarian]*; (Islam and politics. The analysis of the grounds of the first conflict between civilizations.) Victor Segesváry. **Valóság** 47:8 2004 pp.1-13.

5717   Jihad: from Quran to bin Laden. Richard Bonney. Basingstoke: Palgrave Macmillan, 2004. xxvi, 594p. *ISBN: 1403933723. Includes bibliographical references and index.*

5718   Jihad in Europe: the wider context. Fidel Sendagorta. **Survival** 47:3 Autumn:2005 pp.63-72.

5719   Küreselleşme batı modernliği ve şiddet: batı' ya karşı siyasal İslam. *[In Turkish]*; (Globalization, Western modernization and terrorism: political Islam against the West.) Rasim Özgür Dönmez. **Uluslararasi Ilişkiler** 1:4 Winter:2004 pp.81-114.

5720   (Means of solving the problem of terrorism from Islamic perspective.) *[Summary]*; *[Text in Arabic]*. Mohammad A.H. Al-Qudah; H.A. Dawoud. **Dirasat Sha. Law** 31:2 11:2004 pp.488-503.

5721   Murder and martyrdom: suicide terror in the third millennium. Julian Madsen. **Arena J.** 23 2005 pp.97-109.

5722   Les musulmans dans la modernité. *[In French]*; [Muslims and modernity]. Hugues Jallon; Nadia Marzouki; Gilbert Wasserman. **Mouvements** 36 11-12:2004 pp.11-87.

5723   Der neue Bin Laden? Zarqawi bekennt sich zu Al-Qaida, besteht aber auf seiner Unabhängigkeit. *[In German]*; [The new Bin Laden? Zarqawi alligns himself with Al-Qaida but insists on staying independent]. Guido Steinberg. **Int. Politik** 60:2 2:2005 pp.78-91.

5724   New religious movements in the 21ˢᵗ century: legal, political, and social challenges in a global perspective. Phillip Charles Lucas [Ed.]; Thomas Robbins [Ed.]. New York, London: Routledge, 2004. 352p. *ISBN: 0415965764, 0415965772. Includes bibliographical references and index.*

5725   Pakistan and the emergence of Islamic militancy in Afghanistan. Rizwan Hussain. Aldershot, Burlington VT: Ashgate, 2005. xiii, 288p. *ISBN: 0754644340. Includes bibliographical references and index.*

5726   The question of religion and world politics. Jonathan Fox; Shmuel Sandler. **Terror. Pol. Viol.** 17:3 Spring-Summer:2005 pp.293-303.

5727   Reconciling approaches to terrorism, militant 'jihad' and human rights. Madeeha Bajwa. **Strat. S.** XXV:2 Summer:2005 pp.142-168.

5728   The Red Sea terror triangle: Sudan, Somalia, Yemen, and Islamic terror. Shaul Shai; Rachel Liberman [Tr.]. New Brunswick NJ: Transaction Publishers, 2005. xi, 223p. *ISBN: 0765802473. Translated from the Hebrew. Includes bibliographical references and index.*

5729   Regulating religion: case studies from around the globe. James T. Richardson [Ed.]. Dordrecht, London: Kluwer Academic/Plenum Publishers, 2004. 578p. *ISBN: 0306478862, 0306478870. Includes bibliographical references and index. (Series: Critical issues in social justice).*

5730   Religion and (inter-)national politics: on the heuristics of identities, structures, and agents. Friedrich Kratochwil. **Alternatives** 30:2 4-6:2005 pp.113-140.

5731   Religion and security: the new nexus in international relations. Robert A. Seiple [Ed.]; Dennis. Hoover [Ed.]. Lanham MD: Rowman & Littlefield, 2004. xi, 198p. *ISBN: 0742532119, 0742532127. Includes bibliographical references and index.*

5732   Religion and world conflict. Jonathan Fox; Shmuel Sandler; Tanja Ellingsen; Susanna Pearce; Stuart A. Cohen; Jonathan Rynhold; Hillel Frisch; Elizabeth A. Oldmixon; Beth Rosenson; Kenneth D. Wald; Gauvav Ghose; Patrick James; Carolyn C. James; Özgür Özdamar; Yehudith Auerbach. **Terror. Pol. Viol.** 17:3 Spring-Summer:2005 pp.293-485. *Collection of 10 articles.*

5733   Religion, violence and 'holy wars'. Hans Küng. **Int. R. Red Cross** 87:858 6:2005 pp.253-268.

5734   Religious terrorism in other faiths. Syed Adnan Ali Shah. **Strat. S.** XXV:2 Summer:2005 pp.126-141.

5735   Rethinking religion: the legacy of the U.S.-Saudi relationship. Rachel Bronson. **Washington Q.** 28:4 Autumn:2005 pp.121-137.

5736   The role of the church in international peacebuilding: lessons from the US-Central America solidarity movement. Sharon Erickson Nepstad. **J. Peacebuilding Dev.** 1:3 2004 pp.20-34.

5737   Sanctionner au nom de la liberté : la dimension religieuse de la politique étrangère américaine. *[In French]*; [Religion and American foreign policy]. Charles Tanenbaum. **Prochoix** 29 Summer:2004 pp.23-56.

5738   Temos papa! Bento XVI, O Vaticano e o mundo. *[In Portuguese]*; (Habemus Papam! Benedict XVI, the Vatican and the world.) *[Summary]*. Bruno Cardoso Reis. **Relações Int.** 6 6:2005 pp.143-154.

5739   Transnational political Islam: religion, ideology and power. Azza M. Karam [Ed.]; John Esposito [Foreword]. London, Sterling VA: Pluto Press, 2004. xiii, 157p. *ISBN: 0745316255. Includes bibliographical references and index. (Series:* Critical studies on Islam).

5740   US v. Islamic militants: invisible balance of power. A dangerous shift in international relations. Sajjad Shaukat. Lahore, Karachi: Ferozsons, 2005. 245p. *ISBN: 9690019589. Includes bibliographical references.*

F.3.6:   International aid
              Aide internationale

5741   Les " mutations impromptues " : état des lieux de l'aide publique au développement. *[In French]*; (Improvized mutations.) *[Summary]*. Jean-Michel Severino; Olivier Charnoz. **Afr. Contemp.** 213 Winter:2005 pp.13-132.

5742   Aid effectiveness in Africa: developing trust between donors and governments. Phyllis R. Pomerantz. Lanham MD: Lexington Books, 2004. ix, 173p. *ISBN: 0739110020, 0739110039. Includes bibliographical references (p. 153-159) and index.*

5743   Aid in the midst of plenty: oil wealth, misery and advocacy in Angola. Philippe Le Billon. **Disasters** 29:1 3:2005 pp.1-25.

5744   La ayuda exterior estadounidense a Israel y Egipto. *[In Spanish]*; (US aid to Israel and Egypt: strategic cooperation.) *[Summary]*. Juan Pablo Prado Lallande. **Com. Ex.** 55:3 3:2005 pp.258-269.

5745   Canada among nations 2004: setting priorities straight. David Carment [Ed.]; Fen Osler Hampson [Ed.]; Norman Hillmer [Ed.]. Montreal: McGill-Queens University Press, 2005. xi, 291p. *ISBN: 0773528369, 0773528377. Includes bibliographical references and index.*

5746   Civil society development versus the peace dividend: international aid in the Wanni. Vance Culbert. **Disasters** 29:1 3:2005 pp.38-57.

5747   Commerce, croissance et réduction de la pauvreté. *[In French]*; (Trade, growth and poverty.); *[Summary in French]*. Philippe Delleur. **Pol. Étran.** 70:2 Summer:2005 pp.373-385.

5748   Community-based development in the Islamic world: proposals for a new US initiative. Jason Ben-Meir. **J. Nth. Afr. S.** 9:4 Winter:2004 pp.111-123.

5749   Conflicting agendas: the politics of development aid in drug-producing areas. Linda Farthing; Benjamin Kohl. **Dev. Policy R.** 23:2 3:2005 pp.183-198.

5750   Corruption and foreign aid in Africa. Herbert H. Werlin. **Orbis** 49:3 Summer:2005 pp.517-527.

5751   Differing perspectives: India, the World Bank and the 1963 aid-India negotiations. Bruce Muirhead. **India R.** 4:1 1:2005 pp.1-22.

5752   Economie solidaire et nouvelles formes de gouvernance au sud, les associations de développement local au Maroc. *[In French]*; (The solidarity economy and new forms of governance in the South: a proposed typography of community development associations in Morocco.) *[Summary]*; *[Summary in French]*. Catherine Baron; Malika Hattab-Christmann. **Recma** 295 2:2005 pp.70-93.

5753   Exploring the politics of poverty reduction: how are the poorest represented? S. Hickey; S. Bracking; M. Green; D. Hulme; B. Harriss-White; F. Cleaver; R. Thorp; F. Stewart; A. Heyer; H. Blair; A. Bebbington; A.G. Lavalle; A. Acharya; P.P. Houtzager; N. Hossain; J. Bastiaensen; T. De Herdt; B. D'Exelle. **World Dev.** 33:6 6:2005 pp.851-1024. *Collection of 12 articles.*

5754   La face cachée de l'aide internationale. *[In French]*; [The hidden face of international aid] *[Summary]*; *[Summary in Spanish]*. Marc-Arntoine Pérouse de Montclos. **Polit. Int.** 107 Spring:2005 pp.425-439.

5755   The faulty premises of the next Marshall Plan. Derek Chollet; James M. Goldgeier. **Washington Q.** 29:1 Winter:2005-2006 pp.7-19.

5756   Foreign aid for a post-euphoric Eastern Europe: the limitations of Western assistance in developing civil society. Tanya Narozhna. **J. Int. Rel. Dev.** 7:3 10:2004 pp.243-266.

5757   Foreign assistance, international norms, and NGO development: lessons from the Russian campaign. Lisa McIntosh Sundstrom. **Int. Org.** 59:2 Spring:2005 pp.419-449.

5758   How to help poor countries. Nancy Birdsall; Dani Rodrik; Arvind Subramanian. **Foreign Aff.** 84:4 7-8:2005 pp.136-152.

5759   Humanitarian organizations in Tajikistan and the coordination of aid to displaced Afghans in no man's land. Indra Øverland. **J. Refug. S.** 18:2 6:2005 pp.133-150.

5760   Inclusive aid: changing power and relationships in international development. Leslie Groves [Ed.]; Rachel Hinton [Ed.]. London: Earthscan, 2004. 212p. *ISBN: 1844070328, 1844070336. Includes index.*

5761   Die internationalen Sozialfonds. *[In German]*; [International social funds]. Johannes Jäger; Hans-Jürgen Burchardt; Andrea Vermehren; Rodrigo Serrano-Berthet; Juliana Ströbele-Gregor; Ana María Isidoro Losada; Tanja Ernst. **Lat.Am. Anal.** 10 2:2005 pp.55-178. *Collection of 6 articles.*

5762   Japan and UN peace operations. Katsumi Ishizuka. **Japanese J. Pol. Sci.** 5:1 5:2004 pp.137-157.

5763   Japan's foreign aid policy to Africa since the Tokyo international conference on African development. Howard Lehman. **Pac. Aff.** 78:3 Fall:2005 pp.423-442.

5764   Learning from Japan's experience. Yoshinori Hiroi; Toshio Murata; Makiko Komasawa. **Techno. Dev.** 18 1:2005 pp.15-39. *Collection of 3 articles.*

5765   Media, bureaucracies, and foreign aid: a comparative analysis of the United States, the United Kingdom, Canada, France, and Japan. Douglas A. van Belle; Jean-Sebastien Rioux; David M. Potter. New York, Basingstoke: Palgrave Macmillan, 2004. ix, 179p. *ISBN: 1403962847. Includes bibliographical references (p. [157]-174) and index. (Series: Advances in foreign policy analysis).*

5766   Peacekeeping's poor cousin: Canada and the challenge of post-conflict policing. Timothy Donais. **Int. J.** LIX:4 Autumn:2004 pp.943-963.

5767   Poverty Reduction Strategy Papers: now who calls the shots? Alastair Fraser. **R. Afr. Pol. Econ.** 32:104-105 6-9:2005 pp.317-340.

5768   Reasons for sub-Saharan Africa's development deficit that the Commission for Africa did not consider. Percy S. Mistry. **Afr. Affairs** 104:417 10:2005 pp.665-678.

5769   Reconsidering geometries of development. Hemant Shah; Karin Gwinn Wilkins. **Pers. Gl. Dev. & Tech.** 3:4 2004 pp.395-415.

5770   Refugee perceptions of the quality of healthcare: findings from a participatory assessment in Ngara, Tanzania. Edmund Rutta; Holly Williams; Andwele Mwansasu; Fredrick Mung'ong'o; Heather Burke; Ramadhani Gongo; Rwegasira Veneranda; Mohamed Qassim. **Disasters** 29:4 12:2005 pp.291-309.

5771   Revisiting foreign aid theories. Ashok Kumar Pankaj. **Int. S.** 42:2 4-6:2005 pp.103-121.

5772   Setting up an early warning system for epidemic-prone diseases in Darfur: a participative approach. Augusto Pinto; Mubarak Saeed; Hammam El Sakka; Adrienne Rashford; Alessandro Colombo; Marta Valenciano; Guido Sabatinelli. **Disasters** 29:4 12:2005 pp.310-322.

5773   The shifting politics of foreign aid. Ngaire Woods. **Int. Aff. [London]** 81:2 3:2005 pp.393-410.

5774   Transformation of donor-assisted income generation activity into a viable enterprise: case study of Lao paper weaving at forest conservation and afforestation project, Laos. Maki Tsumagari. **Techno. Dev.** 18 1:2005 pp.52-62.

5775   Trustees of development from conditionality to governance: Poverty Reduction Strategy Papers in Ghana. Lindsay Whitfield. **J. Mod. Afr. S.** 43:4 12:2005 pp.641-664.

F.3.7: International conflict and conflict resolution
Conflits internationaux et règlement des conflits

5776 Alliances, arms buildups and recurrent conflict: testing a steps-to-war model. Michael P. Colaresi; William R. Thompson. **J. Pol.** 67:2 5:2005 pp.345-364.

5777 ¿Ante la cuarta guerra mundial? *[In Spanish]*; [Before the Fourth World War?] *[Summary]*. Antonio Garcia Santesmases. **Sistema** 186 5:2005 pp.29-43.

5778 Between power and hegemony: business communities in peace processes. Guy Ben-Porat. **R. Int. S.** 31:2 4:2005 pp.325-348.

5779 Between public peacekeepers and private forces: can there be a third way? Christopher Spearin. **Int. Peace.** 12:2 Summer:2005 pp.240-252.

5780 Beyond Rwanda and Kosovo: the interactive dynamics of international peacekeeping and ethnic mobilisation. Alynna J. Lyon. **Glo. Soc.** 19:3 7:2005 pp.267-288.

5781 Conflicts in the Southwest Pacific: the relevance of new security perspectives. Derek McDougall. **Contemp. Sec. Policy** 25:2 8:2004 pp.339-359.

5782 Constitutional features of the UN plan for Cyprus and its antecedents. Clement Dodd. **Turkish S.** 6:1 3:2005 pp.39-51.

5783 Cosmopolitan peacekeeping and the globalization of security. Tom Woodhouse; Oliver Ramsbotham. **Int. Peace.** 12:2 Summer:2005 pp.139-156.

5784 A crisis-density formulation for identifying rivalries. J. Joseph Hewitt. **J. Peace Res.** 42:2 3:2005 pp.183-200.

5785 Defeating transnational insurgencies: the best offense is a good fence. Paul Staniland. **Washington Q.** 29:1 Winter:2005-2006 pp.21-40.

5786 Democracy and ethnic conflict: advancing peace in deeply divided societies. Adrian Guelke [Ed.]. Basingstoke, New York: Palgrave Macmillan, 2004. xii, 254p. *ISBN: 1403912475. Includes bibliographical references and index.*

5787 The demography of conflict and violence. Helge Brunborg; Manus I. Midlarsky; Marie L. Besançon; Henrik Urdal; Helen Ware; John Landers; Quan Li; Ming Wen; Stephen C. Lubkemann. **J. Peace Res.** 42:4 7:2005 pp.371-519. *Collection of 7 articles.*

5788 Des Balkans à l'Afghanistan: les opérations de stabilisation complexes. *[In French]*; (From Balkans to Afghanistan: complex stabilization operations.); *[Summary in French]*. Étienne de Durand. **Pol. Étran.** 70:2 Summer:2005 pp.329-342.

5789 The double democratic deficit: parliamentary accountability and the use of force under international auspices. Hans Born [Ed.]; Geneva Centre for the Democratic Control of Armed Forces; Heiner Hänggi [Ed.]. Aldershot: Ashgate, 2004. xvi, 242p. *ISBN: 0754639525. Includes bibliographical references and index.*

5790 Ending civil war: Rhodesia and Lebanon in perspective. Matthew Preston. London; New York: Tauris Academic Studies; Palgrave Macmillan, 2004. ix, 322p. *ISBN: 1850435790. Includes bibliographical references (p. [283]-315) and index. (Series:* International library of war studies - 2).

5791 The G8, the United Nations and conflict prevention. John J. Kirton [Ed.]; Radoslava Stefanova [Ed.]. Aldershot: Ashgate, 2004. xxv, 334p. *ISBN: 0754608794. Includes bibliographical references and index. (Series:* G8 and global governance).

5792 Gender, conflict, and development. Tsjeard Bouta; Ian Bannon; Georg Frerks. Washington DC: World Bank, 2005. xxviii, 192p. *ISBN: 0821359681. Includes bibliographical references (p. 161-176) and index.*

5793 Gender, conflict and peacekeeping. Dyan E. Mazurana [Ed.]; Angela Raven-Roberts [Ed.]; Jane L. Parpart [Ed.]. Lanham MD: Rowman & Littlefield, 2005. x, 304p. *ISBN: 0742536327, 0742536335. Includes bibliographical references and index. (Series:* War and peace library).

5794 Global regulation: managing crises after the imperial turn. Kees vand der Pijl [Ed.]; Libby Assassi [Ed.]; Duncan Wigan [Ed.]. Basingstoke, New York: Palgrave Macmillan, 2004. x, 253p. *ISBN: 1403939810. Includes bibliographical references (p. 220-237) and index.*

5795 Greed and grievance: the role of economic agendas in the conflict in Solomon Islands. Matthew Allen. **Pac. Econ. B.** 20:2 2005 pp.56-71.

5796   Identity and institutions: conflict reduction in divided societies. Neal G. Jesse; Kristen P. Williams. Albany NY: State University of New York Press, 2005. xiii, 194p. *ISBN: 0791464512. Includes bibliographical references (p. 163-182) and index. (Series: SUNY series in global politics).*

5797   Imperial crusades: Afghanistan, Iraq and Yugoslavia: a diary of three wars. Alexander Cockburn; Jeffrey St. Clair. London, New York: Verso, 2004. 378p. *ISBN: 1844675068. Includes index.*

5798   Interstate peacekeeping: causal mechanisms and empirical effects. Virginia Page Fortna. **World Pol.** 56:4 7:2004 pp.481-519.

5799   The lawful use of force by peacekeeping forces: the tactical imperative. Dale Stephens. **Int. Peace.** 12:2 Summer:2005 pp.157-172.

5800   The legacies of war economies: challenges and options for peacemaking and peacebuilding. Heiko Nitzschke; Kaysie Studdard. **Int. Peace.** 12:2 Summer:2005 pp.222-239.

5801   The legacy of war: conceptualizing a 'culture of violence' to explain violence after peace accords. Chrissie Steenkamp. **Round Tab.** 379 4:2005 pp.253-267.

5802   The lost meaning of strategy. Hew Strachan. **Survival** 47:3 Autumn:2005 pp.33-54.

5803   Managing the global problems created by the conventional arms trade: an assessment of the United Nations register of conventional arms. Edward J. Laurance; Hendrik Wagenmakers; Herbert Wulf. **Glo. Gov.** 11:2 4-6:2005 pp.225-246.

5804   Managing water conflict: Asia, Africa and the Middle East. Ashok Swain. London: Frank Cass, 2004. xii, 234p. *ISBN: 071465566X. Includes bibliographical references.*

5805   Mandates matter: an exploration of impartiality in United Nations operations. Jane Boulden. **Glo. Gov.** 11:2 4-6:2005 pp.147-160.

5806   Mediation: positive conflict management. John M. Haynes; Gretchen L. Haynes; Larry Sun Fong. Albany NY: State University of New York Press, 2004. xvii, 280p. *ISBN: 0791459519, 0791459527. Includes bibliographical references (p. 271-272) and index. (Series:* SUNY series in transpersonal and humanistic psychology).

5807   Moral dilemmas for humanitarianism in the era of "humanitarian" military interventions; *[Summary in French].* Beat Schweizer. **Int. R. Red Cross** 86:855 9:2004 pp.547-564.

5808   Multinational corporations, rentier capitalism, and the war system in Colombia. Nazih Richani. **Lat. Am. Pol. Soc.** 47:3 Fall:2005 pp.113-144.

5809   Multiple paths to knowledge in international relations: methodology in the study of conflict management and conflict resolution. Zeev Maoz [Ed.]; et al. Lanham MD: Lexington Books, 2004. xiii, 373p. *ISBN: 0739106716, 0739106724. Includes bibliographical references and index. (Series:* Innovations in the study of world politics).

5810   The nature of borders and international conflict: revisiting hypotheses on territory. Harvey Starr; G. Dale Thomas. **Int. S. Q.** 49:1 3:2005 pp.123-139.

5811   Neo-humanitarianism: the role of international humanitarian norms and organizations in contemporary conflict. Kurt Mills. **Glo. Gov.** 11:2 4-6:2005 pp.161-183.

5812   Neverending wars: the international community, weak states, and the perpetuation of civil war. Ann Hironaka. Cambridge MA: Harvard University Press, 2005. 191p. *ISBN: 0674015320. Includes bibliographical references (p. 177-187) and index.*

5813   'Not peace but a sword?' Religion, conflict and conflict resolution in the Commonwealth and beyond. Terry A. Barringer; Derek Ingram; Peter Penfold; Jenny Taylor; T. Jack Thompson; Payal Singh Mohanka; Catherine Scott; Neles Tebay; Mehtab Ali Shah; Yeoh Seng Guan; Ida Glaser. **Round Tab.** 382 10:2005 pp.521-651. *Collection of 10 articles.*

5814   Organizations and institutions. Conflict prevention from rhetoric to reality. Albrecht Schnabel [Ed.]; David Carment [Ed.]. Lanham MD: Lexington Books, 2004. xviii, 437p. *ISBN: 0739105493, 0739107380.*

5815   Peacekeeping and legitimacy: lessons from Cambodia and Somalia. Michael Mersiades. **Int. Peace.** 12:2 Summer:2005 pp.205-221.

5816   Political challenge in Latin America: rebellion and collective protest in an era of democratization. Christina Schatzman. **J. Peace Res.** 42:3 5:2005 pp.291-310.

5817   The politics of risking peace: do hawks or doves deliver the olive branch? Kenneth A. Schultz. **Int. Org.** 59:1 Winter:2005 pp.1-38.

5818   Postconflict profit: the political economy of intervention. Michael Bhatia. **Glo. Gov.** 11:2 4-6:2005 pp.205-224.

5819   Proportionality in the morality of war. Thomas Hurka. **Philos. Publ. Aff.** 33:1 Winter:2005 pp.34-66.

5820   Rauhaan tutkien. *[In Finnish]*; [Studying into peace]. R. Väyrynen; O. Borg; O. Apunen; P. Saukkonen; J. Pakkasvirta; D. Lanko; J. Käkönen; J. Galtung; A. Kaski; B. Muthien; F. Möller; G.P. Herd; A. Nokkala; G. von Bonsdorff; H. Hakovirta; H. Patomäki; T. Varis; T. Melasuo; T. Tiilikainen; E. Antola; A. Curticapean; C. Archer; H. Wiberg; H. Rytövuori-Apunen; H.-M. Birckenbach; R. Lintonen; B. Møller. **Kosmopolis** 34:60 2004 pp.1-272. *Collection of 26 articles.*

5821   Roads to reconciliation: conflict and dialogue in the twenty-first century. Amy Benson Brown [Ed.]; Karen Poremski [Ed.]. Armonk NY: M.E. Sharpe, 2005. xiii, 279p. *ISBN: 0765613336. Includes bibliographical references and index.*

5822   Schlock and Blah: counter-insurgency realities in a rapid dominance. Robert R. Tomes. **Sm. Wars Insurg.** 16:1 3:2005 pp.37-56.

5823   Secrets and lies: operation 'Iraqi Freedom' and after. Dilip Hiro. New York: Nation Books, 2004. xxvii, 467p. *ISBN: 1560255560. Includes bibliographical references and index.*

5824   The Solomon Islands: the UN and intervention by coalitions of the willing. Richard Ponzio. **Int. Peace.** 12:2 Summer:2005 pp.173-188.

5825   Special operators: a key ingredient for successful peacekeeping operations management. Joseph L. Homza. **Low Int. Confl. Law Enf.** 12:1 Spring:2004 pp.91-110.

5826   States in armed conflict 2003. Lotta Harbom [Ed.]; Peter Wallensteen; Kristine Eck; Uppsala Universitet, Department of Peace and Conflict Research; Mikael Eriksson. Uppsala: Uppsala University, 2004. 166p. *ISBN: 9150617877. (Series:* Department of Peace and Conflict Research report - 70).

5827   Taking arms against a sea of troubles: conventional arms races during periods of rivalry. Douglas M. Gibler; Toby J. Rider; Marc L. Hutchison. **J. Peace Res.** 42:2 3:2005 pp.131-147.

5828   Taming intractable conflicts: mediation in the hardest cases. Chester A. Crocker; Fen Osler Hampson; Pamela R. Aall. Washington DC: United States Institute of Peace Press, 2004. xii, 240p. *ISBN: 1929223560, 1929223552. Includes bibliographical references (p. 205-224) and index.*

5829   Towards collation and modelling of the global cost of armed violence on civilians. Nathan Taback; Robin Coupland. **Med. Confl. Surv.** 21:1 1-3:2005 pp.19-27.

5830   Trading with the enemy during wartime. Jack S. Levy; Katherine Barbieri. **Security S.** 13:3 Spring:2004 pp.1-47.

5831   Trapped in the dead ground: US counter-insurgency strategy in Iraq. Alastair Finlan. **Sm. Wars Insurg.** 16:1 3:2005 pp.1-21.

5832   Truth-seeking, truth-telling, and postconflict peacebuilding: curb the enthusiasm? David Mendeloff. **Int. S. R.** 6:3 9:2004 pp.355-380.

5833   Twisting arms and flexing muscles: humanitarian intervention and peacebuilding in perspective. Natalie Mychajlyszyn [Ed.]; Timothy M. Shaw [Ed.]. Aldershot, Burlington VT: Ashgate, 2005. x, 151p. *ISBN: 0754616711. Includes bibliographical references (p. [139]-148) and index. (Series:* International political economy of new regionalisms).

5834   United we stand? Divide-and-conquer politics and the logic of international hostility. Aaron Belkin. Albany NY: State University of New York Press, 2005. x, 161p. *ISBN: 0791463435. Includes bibliographical references (p. 131-156) and index. (Series:* SUNY series in global politics).

5835   War evolves into the fourth generation. Thomas X. Hammes; James J. Wirtz; Edward N. Luttwak; Martin van Creveld; Antulio J. Echevarria, II; Michael Evans; John Ferris; Lawrence Freedman; David S. Sorenson; Rod Thornton. **Contemp. Sec. Policy** 26:2 8:2005 pp.189-286.

5836   Winning the peace: an American strategy for post-conflict reconstruction. Robert C. Orr
        [Ed.]; John J. Hamre [Foreword]; Gordon R. Sullivan [Foreword]. Washington DC: CSIS
        Press, 2004. xiii, 353p. *ISBN: 0892064447. Includes bibliographical references and index.*
        (*Series:* Significant issues - 26:4).

Africa
Afrique

5837   Africa: towards durable peace. Ian S. Spears; Elisabeth King; Charles C. Pentland;
        Kristiana Powell; Thomas Kwasi Tieku; John S. Saul; Richard Saunders; Hevina S.
        Dashwood; Rhoda E. Howard-Hassmann; Kim Richard Nossal; Ernie Regehr; Robert O.
        Matthews. **Int. J.** LX:4 Autumn:2005 pp.897-1064. *Collection of 10 articles.*
5838   Le chemin de l'autodestruction : origine et dynamique de la guerre civile en Côte d'Ivoire.
        [In French]; [On the road to self-destruction: origin and dynamics of the civil war in Côte
        d'Ivoire] *[Summary].* Dele Ogunmola; Isiaka Alani Badmus. **Afr. Dev.** XXX:1-2 2005
        pp.210-238.
5839   A comparative perspective of UN peacekeeping in Angola and Namibia. Gwinyayi Albert
        Dzinesa. **Int. Peace.** 11:4 Winter:2004 pp.644-663.
5840   Le conflit au Darfour, point aveugle des négociations Nord-Sud au Soudan. *[In French];*
        (The Darfur conflict: the blind spot in the North-South negotiations in Sudan.) *[Summary].*
        Roland Marchal. **Pol. Afr.** 95 10:2004 pp.125-146.
5841   Conspiracy to murder: the Rwandan genocide. Linda Melvern. London, New York: Verso,
        2004. 358p. *ISBN: 1859845886. Includes bibliographical references and index.*
5842   Dangers of co-deployment: UN co-operative peacekeeping in Africa. David J. Francis; et
        al. Aldershot: Ashgate, 2005. xv, 175p. *ISBN: 0754640272. Includes bibliographical
        references and index.*
5843   Darfur: the fight for peace. Farah Arbab. **Strat. S.** XXIV:4 Winter:2004 pp.144-165.
5844   Decolonizing Africa: colonial boundaries and the crisis of the (non) nation state. Arnold
        Hughes. **Dipl. State.** 15:4 12:2004 pp.833-866.
5845   Environmental conflict between refugee and host communities. Adrian Martin. **J. Peace
        Res.** 42:3 5:2005 pp.329-346.
5846   Erfaringer fra konfliktløsning i Afrika: en vurdering av resultater og virkninger — tilfellet
        Sudan. *[In Norwegian];* [Experiences of conflict resolution in Africa: the case of Sudan].
        Tom E. Vraalsen. **Internasjonal Pol.** 63:1 2005 pp.77-87.
5847   Ethiopie-Erythrée : après la paix, à nouveau la guerre. *[In French];* [Ethiopia-Eritrea: after
        the peace, war again] *[Summary].* Abdou Yéro Ba. **Arès** 20:3(52) 2:2004 pp.51-63.
5848   François Mitterrand, l'armée française et le Rwanda. *[In French];* [François Mitterrand, the
        French army and Rwanda]. Bernard Lugan. Monaco: Editions du Rocher, 2005. 289p.
        ISBN: 2268054152.
5849   Genocide and ethnic cleansing. Cathie Carmichael; T. David Curp; Benjamin Madley;
        Đorđe Stefanović. **Euro. Hist. Q.** 35:3 7:2005 pp.395-492. *Collection of 4 articles.*
5850   Global challenges and Africa: bridging divides, dealing with perceptions, rebuilding
        societies. Richard Cobbold [Ed.]; Greg Mills [Ed.]. London: Royal United Services
        Institute for Defence and Security Studies, 2004. xxiv, 183p. *ISBN: 0855161965. Includes
        bibliographical references. South African Institute of International Affairs.* (*Series:*
        Whitehall paper - 62).
5851   The hidden costs of power-sharing: reproducing insurgent violence in Africa. Denis M.
        Tull; Andreas Mehler. **Afr. Affairs** 104:416 7:2005 pp.375-398.
5852   The international dimensions of the Congo crisis. Georges Nzongola-Ntalaja. **Glo. Dial.**
        6:3-4 Summer-Autumn:2004 pp.116-126.
5853   Is violence inevitable in Africa? Theories of conflict and approaches to conflict prevention.
        Ulf Engel [Ed.]; Annamaria Gentili [Ed.]; Patrick Chabal [Ed.]. Leiden MA: Brill, 2005.
        vi, 245p. *ISBN: 9004144501. Includes bibliographical references and index.* (*Series:*
        African-Europe Group for Interdisciplinary Studies - 1).

5854   Journey into darkness: genocide in Rwanda. Thomas P. Odom; Dennis J. Reimer [Foreword]. College Station TX: University of Texas Press, 2005. xiii, 297p. *ISBN: 1585444278, 158544457X. Includes bibliographical references (p. 285-286) and index. (Series:* Texas A&M University military history - 100).

5855   Liberalization and conflict; *[Summary in French].* David Keen. **Int. Pol. Sci. R.** 26:1 1:2005 pp.73-89.

5856   The missing pillars: a look at the failure of peace in Burundi through the lens of Arend Lijphart's theory of consociational democracy. Daniel P. Sullivan. **J. Mod. Afr. S.** 43:1 3:2005 pp.75-95.

5857   Reintegration of combatants: were the right lessons learned in Mozambique? Jaremey McMullin. **Int. Peace.** 11:4 Winter:2004 pp.625-643.

5858   Social capital building as capacity for postconflict development: the UNDP in Mozambique and Rwanda. Ben K. Fred-Mensah. **Glo. Gov.** 10:4 10-12:2004 pp.437-457.

5859   Stat og konflikt i Afrika. *[In Norwegian]*; (State and conflict in Africa.) Birgitte Kjos Fonn; Stein Sundstøl Eriksen; Ståle Ulriksen; Axel Borchgrevink; Morten Bøås. **Internasjonal Pol.** 62:4 2004 pp.499-601. *Collection of 6 articles.*

5860   Sudan: a flawed peace process leading to a flawed peace. John Young. **R. Afr. Pol. Econ.** 32:103 3:2005 pp.99-113.

5861   Tentatives croisées de déstabilisation dans l'Afrique des Grands Lacs. Le contentieux rwando-ougandais. *[In French]*; (Crossed attempts at destabilization in the Great Lakes region of Africa: Rwanda-Ugandese conflict.) *[Summary].* Bernard Leloup. **Pol. Afr.** 96 12:2004 pp.119-138.

5862   War destroys, peace nurtures: Somali reconciliation and development. Richard Ford [Ed.]; Hussein Mohamed Adam [Ed.]; Edna Adan Ismail [Ed.]. Lawrenceville NJ: Red Sea Press, 2004. xx, 544p. *ISBN: 1569021872. Includes bibliographical references (p. [521]-540) and index.*

5863   Winning the war, but losing the peace? The dilemma of SPLM/a civil administration and the tasks ahead. Adam Branch; Zachariah Cherian Mampilly. **J. Mod. Afr. S.** 43:1 3:2005 pp.1-20.

5864   Západná Sahara — politické a medzinárodno-právne aspekty neukončenej dekolonizácie. *[In Slovak]*; (Western Sahara — political and legal aspects of an unfinished decolonisation.) *[Summary].* Ján Voderadský. **Medz. Otázky** XIII:4 2004 pp.57-79.

Asia
Asie

5865   Afghanistan: winning a three block war. Joseph J. Collins. **J. Confl. S.** XXIV:2 Winter:2004 pp.61-77.

5866   America's miracle man in Vietnam: Ngo Dinh Diem, religion, race, and U.S. intervention in Southeast Asia, 1950-1957. Seth Jacobs. Durham NC: Duke University Press, 2004. x,381p. *ISBN: 0822334291, 0822334402. Includes bibliographical references (p. 339-365) and index.* (*Series:* American encounters/global interactions).

5867   Bons offices, surveillance, médiation : les ratés du processus de paix à Sri Lanka. *[In French]*; [Failures in the peace process in Sri Lanka] *[Summary].* Eric Meyer; Eleanor Pavey. **Crit. Int.** 22 1:2004 pp.35-46.

5868   Changing realities and paradigms in social and political aspects of the Cold War: the Korean conflict. Bruce E. Bechtol, Jr. **Kor. Obs.** 36:2 Summer:2005 pp.265-296.

5869   China's stand on UN peacekeeping operations: changing priorities of foreign policy. Yeshi Choedon. **Chi. Rep.** 41:1 1-3:2005 pp.39-57.

5870   Cooperation, coordination and complementarity in international peacemaking: the Tajikistan experience. Tetsuro Iji. **Int. Peace.** 12:2 Summer:2005 pp.189-204.

5871   Discourses of danger in Central Asia. S. Neil MacFarlane; Stina Torjesen; John Heathershaw; Nicole J. Jackson; Christine Bichsel; Madeleine Reeves; Nick Megoran. **Cent. Asian Sur.** 24:1 3:2005 pp.1-96. *Collection of 7 articles.*

5872   Ethnic conflicts in South Asia: a constructivist reading. Shibashis Chatterjee. **Pol. Econ. J. India** 12:1 1-6:2005 pp.75-89.

5873   India and Pakistan: bargaining in the shadow of nuclear war. Sumit Ganguly; R. Harrison Wagner. **J. Strategic S.** 27:3 9:2004 pp.479-507.

5874   India-Pakistan conflict over Kashmir: peace through development cooperation. Rajen Harshe. **Pol. Econ. J. India** 12:1 1-6:2005 pp.47-60.

5875   India-Pakistan deterrence revisited. Michael Quinlan. **Survival** 47:3 Autumn:2005 pp.103-116.

5876   India's role in Nepal's Maoist insurgency. Rabindra Mishra. **Asian Sur.** XLIV:5 9-10:2004 pp.627-646.

5877   Insurgency in North-East India: the role of Bangladesh. Dipankar Sengupta [Ed.]; Sudhir Kumar Singh [Ed.]. Delhi: Authorspress, 2004. x, 294p. *ISBN: 8172731671. Includes bibliographical references and index. Society for the Promotion of Activities for National Development and Nation Building.*

5878   Koreas in transition to post-Cold War mentality. Yu-hwan Koh. **Kor. World Aff.** 28:2 Summer:2004 pp.131-141.

5879   Local governance after conflict: community development in East Timor. Tanja Hohe. **J. Peacebuilding Dev.** 1:3 2004 pp.45-56.

5880   Long-term effects of peace workshops in protracted conflicts. Deepak Malhotra; Sumanasiri Liyanage. **J. Confl. Resol.** 49:6 12:2005 pp.908-924.

5881   Radiographie du pouvoir chinois. *[In French]*; [Radiography of the Chinese power] *[Summary]*; *[Summary in Spanish]*. Marie Holzman [Interviewer]; Michel Bonnin. **Polit. Int.** 107 Spring:2005 pp.317-339.

5882   Rethinking the greed-grievance nexus: property rights and the political economy of war in Sri Lanka. Benedikt Korf. **J. Peace Res.** 42:2 3:2005 pp.201-217.

5883   Searching for peace in Asia Pacific: an overview of conflict prevention and peacebuilding activities. Annelies Heijmans [Ed.]; Nicola Simmonds [Ed.]; Hans van de Veen [Ed.]. Boulder CO: Lynne Rienner Publishers, 2004. xvi, 848p. *ISBN: 1588262146, 1588262391. Includes bibliographical references (p. 813-824) and index. European Centre for Conflict Prevention.*

5884   UN peace operations and Asian security. Mely Caballero-Anthony; Dipankar Banerjee; Kamarulzaman Askandar; See Seng Tan; Katsumi Ishizuka; Pang Zhongying; Sorpong Peou; Ian Martin; Alexander Mayer-Rieckh; Amitav Acharya. **Int. Peace.** 12:1 Spring:2005 pp.1-125. *Collection of 9 articles.*

5885   Unrest in south Thailand: contours, causes, and consequences since 2001. Aurel Croissant. **Contemp. Sth.East Asia** 27:1 4:2005 pp.21-43.

5886   Untapped power? The status of UN information operations. Dan Lindley. **Int. Peace.** 11:4 Winter:2004 pp.608-624.

5887   Using natural resources management as a peacebuilding tool: observations and lessons from Central Western Mindanao. Darren Evans. **J. Peacebuilding Dev.** 1:3 2004 pp.57-70.

5888   The Vietnam War. Mary Ann Irwin; Dara Orenstein; Carl Abbott; T. Christopher Jespersen; Pierre Asselin; Christopher T. Fisher; John University of Illinois D'Emilio. **Pac. Hist. R.** 74:3 8:2005 pp.410-456. *Collection of 4 articles.*

5889   When governments collide in the Taiwan Strait. Wallace J. Thies; Patrick C. Bratton. **J. Strategic S.** 27:4 12:2004 pp.556-584.

5890   When to withdraw U.S. forces from Korea. Bong Hyon Park. **Kor. World Aff.** 28:1 Spring:2004 pp.46-68.

5891   Would a plebiscite have resolved the Kashmir dispute? Christopher Snedden. **Sth. Asia** XXVIII:1 4:2005 pp.64-86.

Europe
Europe

5892   The Chechen issue: Russia's case and international terrorism. Debidatta Aurobinda Mahapatra. **India Q.** LXI:1 1-3:2005 pp.220-243.

5893   La confrontation Espagne-Maroc sur l'îlot du Persil : des raisons d'une crise et du rôle international de l'Union européenne. *[In French]*; [Spain-Morocco confrontation on the small island of Parsley: reasons of a crisis and international role of the European Union]. Bienvenu Okiemy. **R. Rech. Jurid. Droit Prosp.** 29:2 2004 pp.1281-1301.

5894   EU accession dynamics and conflict resolution: catalysing peace or consolidating partition in Cyprus. Nathalie Tocci. Burlington VT: Ashgate, 2004. viii, 205p. *ISBN: 0754643107. Includes bibliographical references and index.*

5895   A European competitive advantage? Civilian instruments for conflict prevention and crisis management. Antonio Marquina; Xira Ruiz. **J. Transatlan. S.** 3:1 Spring:2005 pp.71-87.

5896   Europeanization and conflict resolution: case studies from the European periphery. Bruno Coppieters. Gent: Academia Press, 2004. ii, 258p. *ISBN: 9038206488. Includes bibliographical references.*

5897   Formes de violences entre Chypriotes turcs et Chypriotes grecs en cohabitation. *[In French]*; [Violence types between cohabiting Turk Cypriots and Greek Cypriots]. Barbara Karatsioli. **CEMOTI** 37 1-6:2004 pp.143-176.

5898   Genesis of the Chechen resistance movement. Syed Adnan Ali Shah. **Strat. S.** XXIV:4 Winter:2004 pp.84-110.

5899   La géopolitique du conflit tchétchène. *[In French]*; [Geopolitics of the Chechen conflict]. Viatcheslav Avioutskii. **Défense Nat.** 60:1 1:2004 pp.77-92.

5900   International crisis management: the approach of European states. Marc Houben. New York, London: Routledge, 2005. 315p. *ISBN: 0415354552. Includes bibliographical references and index.*

5901   Kosovo. *[In German]*; (Kosovo.) Ivan T. Berend; Kurt Faltlhauser; Joachim Rücker; Michael Schaefer; Gjylnaze Syla; Slobodan Samardžić; Rolf Ekéus; Leon Malazogu; Wolf Preuss; Marc Stegherr; Wim van Meurs. **Südosteuro. Mitteil.** 45:3 2005 pp.29-92. *Collection of 10 articles.*

5902   Partisan interventions: European party politics and peace enforcement in the Balkans. Brian C. Rathbun. Ithaca NY: Cornell University Press, 2004. xi, 228p. *ISBN: 0801442559. Includes bibliographical references and index.*

5903   Peace without politics? Ten years of international state-building in Bosnia. Sumantra Bose; David Chandler; Dominik Zaum; Gemma Collantes Celador; Daniela Heimerl; Vanessa Pupavac; Adam Fagan; Florian Bieber; Roberto Belloni; Michael Pugh; Richard Caplan. **Int. Peace.** 12:3 Autumn:2005 pp.322-476. *Collection of 11 articles.*

5904   The quest for viable peace: international intervention and strategies for conflict transformation. Jock Covey [Ed.]; Michael J. Dziedzic [Ed.]; Leonard R. Hawley [Ed.]. Washington DC: United States Institute of Peace Press, 2005. xx, 302p. *ISBN: 1929223676. Includes bibliographical references and index. Association of the United States Army.*

5905   Rally 'round the Union Jack'? Public opinion and the use of force in the United Kingdom, 1948-2001. Brian Lai; Dan Reiter. **Int. S. Q.** 49:2 6:2005 pp.255-272.

5906   Security in Southeast Europe: the war crimes legacy. James Gow. **J. Sth.East Euro. Black Sea S.** 5:1 1:2005 pp.9-20.

5907   Sjeverna Irska izmedu rata i mira. *[In Croatian]*; (Northern Ireland between war and peace.) *[Summary]*. Mirko Bilandžić. **Pol. Misao** 41:2 2004 pp.135-160.

5908   Towards successful peace-keeping: remembering Croatia. Darya Pushkina. **Coop. Confl.** 39:4 12:2004 pp.393-415.

5909   Transforming identities: beyond the politics of non-settlement in North Cyprus. Hannes Lacher; Erol Kaymak. **Med. Pol.** 10:2 7:2005 pp.147-166.

5910   Tsentral'naia Aziia: institutsional'naia struktura mezhdunarodnykh vzaimodeistvii v stanoviashchemsia regione. *[In Russian]*; (Central Asia: the institutional structure of international relations in a region in the making.) *[Summary]*. A.A. Kazantsev. **Polis [Moscow]** 2(85) 2005 pp.78-88.

5911   Turkey and Greece: the Aegean disputes, a unique case in international law. Deniz Bolukbasi. London, Portland OR: Cavendish Publishing, 2004. xx, 992p. *ISBN: 1859419526, 1859419534. Includes bibliographical references and index.*

5912   US mediation in Greek-Turkish disputes since 1954. Theodora Kalaitzaki. **Mediterr. Q.** 16:2 Spring:2005 pp.106-124.

5913   Why the Good Friday agreement in Northern Ireland is not consociational. Paul Dixon. **Pol. Q.** 76:3 7-9:2005 pp.357-367.

Middle East
Moyen-Orient

5914   The abyss in Iraq. Patrick Cockburn. **New Left R.** 36 11-12:2005 pp.35-68.

5915   L'affaire iraquienne. *[In French]*; [The Iraqi case]. Annuaire français de relations internationales. **Ann. Fran. Rel. Int.** 5 2004 pp.180-311.

5916   The ambiguous calm what is Sharon up to, and can he really get away with it? Adam Keller. **New Pol.** X:3 Summer:2005 pp.5-20.

5917   The Arab-Israeli conflict. T. G. Fraser. Basingstoke: Palgrave Macmillan, 2004. 190p. *ISBN: 1403913382, 1403913374. Includes bibliographical references (p. 181-184) and index.* (*Series:* Studies in contemporary history).

5918   Bridges over troubled water: a comparative study of Jews, Arabs, and Palestinians. Dahlia Moore; Salem Aweiss. Westport CT: Praeger, 2004. viii,237p. *ISBN: 027598060X. Includes bibliographical references (p. [201]-222) and indexes.*

5919   Cain's field: faith, fratricide, and fear in the Middle East. Matt Rees. New York: Free Press, 2004. 302p. *ISBN: 0743250478.*

5920   The Cairo dialogue and the Palestinian power struggle. P.R. Kumaraswamy. **Int. S.** 42:1 2005 pp.43-59.

5921   Le choc des civilisations et le conflit israélo-palestinien. *[In French]*; [Clash of civilizations and the Arab-Israeli conflict]. Pascal Boniface. **R. Int. Stratég.** 53 Spring:2004 pp.11-23.

5922   Citizens without sovereignty: transfer and ethnic cleansing in Israel. Robert Blecher. **Comp. S. Soc. Hist.** 47:4 10:2005 pp.725-754.

5923   Commercial pacifism and protracted conflict: models from the Palestinian-Israeli case. Gil Friedman. **J. Confl. Resol.** 49:3 6:2005 pp.360-382.

5924   The conflict in Iraq 2003. Paul Cornish [Ed.]. Basingstoke, New York: Palgrave Macmillan, 2004. xvi, 297p. *ISBN: 1403935254, 1403935262. Includes bibliographical references and index.*

5925   Conflict resolution in the neighbourhood: comparing EU involvement in Turkey's Kurdish question and in the Israeli-Palestinian conflict. Nathalie Tocci. **Med. Pol.** 10:2 7:2005 pp.125-146.

5926   The continuing crisis in Iraqi Kurdistan. Michael M. Gunter; M. Hakan Yavuz. **Mid. East Policy** XII:1 Spring:2005 pp.122-133.

5927   The crisis: the president, the prophet, and the Shah −1979 and the coming of militant Islam. David Harris. New York: Little, Brown & Company, 2004. 470p. *ISBN: 0316323942. Includes bibliographical references (p. 447-461) and index.*

5928   Defeat of terror, not roadmap diplomacy, will bring peace. Newt Gingrich. **Mid. East Q.** XII:3 Summer:2005 pp.3-13.

5929   The end of occupation: Iraq 2004. Adam Roberts. **Int. Comp. Law Q.** 54:1 1:2005 pp.27-48.

5930   Existentialism in Iraq: Security Council resolution 1483 and the law of occupation; *[Summary in French]*. Marten Zwanenburg. **Int. R. Red Cross** 86:856 12:2004 pp.745-769.

5931   The failure of big business: on the socio-economic reality of the Middle East peace process. Markus E. Bouillon. **Med. Pol.** 9:1 Spring:2004 pp.1-28.

5932   Five bad options for Iraq. Daniel Byman. **Survival** 47:1 Spring:2005 pp.7-32.

5933   Forcing choices: testing the transformation of Hamas. Haim Malka. **Washington Q.** 28:4 Autumn:2005 pp.37-53.

5934   From Blitzkrieg to attrition: Israel's attrition strategy and staying power. Avi Kober. **Sm. Wars Insurg.** 16:2 6:2005 pp.216-240.

5935   Grounds for peace: territoriality and conflict resolution. Guy Ben-Porat. **Geopolitics** 10:1 Spring:2005 pp.147-166.

5936   Gulliver unbound: America's imperial temptation and the war in Iraq. Stanley Hoffmann. Lanham MD: Rowman & Littlefield, 2004. viii,153p. *ISBN: 0742536009. Translated from the French. Includes bibliographical references and index.*

5937   How Israelis and Palestinians negotiate: a cross-cultural analysis of the Oslo peace process. Tamara Cofman Wittes [Ed.]. Washington DC: United States Institute of Peace Press, 2005. xiv, 160p. *ISBN: 1929223641, 1929223633. Includes bibliographical references and index.*

5938   Independence, cantons, or bantustans: wither the Palestinian state? Leila Farsakh. **Mid. East J.** 59:2 Spring:2005 pp.230-245.

5939   L'Irak entre transition démocratique et guerre civile. *[In French]*; [Iraq between democratic transition and civil war]. Albert Legault. **Confl. Monde** 2004 pp.13-48.

5940   Iraq: learning the lessons of Vietnam. Melvin R. Laird. **Foreign Aff.** 84:6 11-12:2005 pp.22-43.

5941   The Iraq syndrome. John Mueller. **Foreign Aff.** 84:6 11-12:2005 pp.44-54.

5942   İşgal sonrası Irak'ta olanlar sıradan bir güvenlik sorunu mu? *[In Turkish]*; (Are events in Iraq after the occupation an ordinary security problem?) Nihat Ali Özcan. **Uluslararası İlişkiler** 1:1 Spring:2004 pp.93-118.

5943   Israeli politics as settler politics. Thomas G. Mitchell. **J. Confl. S.** XXIV:2 Winter:2004 pp.135-154.

5944   Israël-Palestine: vers quelle paix juste? *[In French]*; [Israel-Palestine: towards which fair peace?] Alexis Keller. **Esprit** 312 2:2005 pp.6-16.

5945   Killing civilians intentionally: double effect, reprisal, and necessity in the Middle East. Michael L. Gross. **Pol. Sci. Q.** 120:4 Winter:2005-2006 pp.555-579.

5946   Killing with kindness: funding the demise of a Palestinian state. Anne Le More. **Int. Aff. [London]** 81:5 10:2005 pp.981-1000.

5947   Losing Iraq: inside the postwar reconstruction fiasco. David L. Phillips. New York: Westview Press, 2005. ix,292p. *ISBN: 0813343046. Includes bibliographical references and index.*

5948   A new Middle East? Globalization, peace and the "double movement". Guy Ben-Porat. **Int. Rel.** 19:1 3:2005 pp.39-62.

5949   L'observatoire de la colonisation. *[In French]*; [The colonization observatory]. Geoffrey Aronson. **R. Ét. Palest.** 96 Summer:2005 pp.111-122.

5950   The one-state solution: a breakthrough for peace in the Israeli-Palestinian deadlock. Virginia Tilley. Ann Arbor MI: University of Michigan Press, 2005. x, 276p. *ISBN: 0472115138. Includes bibliographical references (p. 261-267) and index.*

5951   Palestine and the Arab-Israeli conflict. Charles D. Smith. Boston MA, New York: Bedford; St. Martin's Press, 2004. xviii, 567p. *ISBN: 1403932360. Includes bibliographical references and index.*

5952   Peace in the Middle East: P2P and the Israeli-Palestinian conflict. et al; Adel Atieh; United Nations Institute for Disarmament. Geneva: UNIDIR, 2005. ix, 44p. *ISBN: 9290451696. Includes bibliographical references.*

5953   Peace-building and democracy promotion in the Middle East. Yezid Sayigh; Peter Sluglett; Maurizio Martellini; Riccardo Redaelli; Giacomo Luciani; Tamara Cofman Wittes; Laura Guazzone; Daniela Pioppi. **Int. Spect.** XXXIX:4 10-12:2004 pp.25-113. *Collection of 7 articles.*

5954 Planning post-conflict reconstruction in Iraq: what can we learn? Andrew Rathmell. **Int. Aff. [London]** 81:5 10:2005 pp.1013-1038.

5955 A political-security analysis of the failed Oslo process. Melissa Boyle Mahle. **Mid. East Policy** XII:1 Spring:2005 pp.79-96.

5956 Problems of belligerent occupation: the scope of powers exercised by the coalition provisional authority in Iraq, April/May 2003-June 2004. Kaiyan Homi Kaikobad. **Int. Comp. Law Q.** 54:1 1:2005 pp.253-264.

5957 Public opinion in the Israeli-Palestinian two-level game. Jacob Shamir; Khalil Shikaki. **J. Peace Res.** 42:3 5:2005 pp.311-328.

5958 Rashomon in the Middle East: clashing narratives, images, and frames in the Israeli-Palestinian conflict. Arie M. Kacowicz. **Coop. Confl.** 40:3 9:2005 pp.343-360.

5959 La reconstruction de l'Irak aura-t-elle lieu? *[In French]*; (Will Iraqi reconstruction take place?); *[Summary in French]*. Gabrielle Lafarge; Alexandra Novosseloff. **Pol. Étran.** 70:2 Summer:2005 pp.343-354.

5960 Rethinking the path to peace: a binational state for Palestinians and Israelis? Holli Thomas. **Arena J.** 23 2005 pp.53-75.

5961 Revisions in need of revising: what went wrong in the Iraq war. David C. Hendrickson; Robert W. Tucker. **Survival** 47:2 Summer:2005 pp.7-31.

5962 Seeking Mandela: peacemaking between Israelis and Palestinians. Heribert Adam; Kogila Moodley. Philadelphia PA: Temple University Press, 2005. xx, 224p. *ISBN: 1592133959, 1592133967. Includes bibliographical references and index.* (*Series:* Politics, history, and social change).

5963 Sharing the land of Canaan: human rights and the Israeli-Palestinian struggle. Mazin B. Qumsiyeh. London, Ann Arbor MI: Pluto Press, University of Michigan Press, 2004. xix, 236p. *ISBN: 0745322492, 0745322484. Includes bibliographical references (p. 220-232) and index.*

5964 Toward an open tomb: the crisis of Israeli society. Michel Warschawski; Peter Drucker [Tr.]. New York: Monthly Review Press, 2004. 124p. *ISBN: 1583671099, 1583671102. Translated from the French. Includes bibliographical references and index.*

5965 The United Nations and Iraq: a role beyond expectations. Thierry Tardy. **Int. Peace.** 11:4 Winter:2004 pp.591-607.

5966 U.S. military fatalities in Iraq: a two-year retrospective. Glenn Kutler. **Orbis** 49:3 Summer:2005 pp.529-544.

5967 Various aspects of US military occupation of Iraq: the struggle against the Iraqi resistance. C. Rajamohan. **India Q.** LX:4 10-12:2004 pp.73-84.

5968 Vers une troisième intifada? *[In French]*; [Towards a third intifada?] *[Summary]*; *[Summary in Spanish]*. Patrick Saint-Paul [Interviewer]; Mohammed Dahlan. **Polit. Int.** 107 Spring:2005 pp.249-268.

5969 What was it all about after all? The causes of the Iraq war. Hakan Tunç. **Contemp. Sec. Policy** 26:2 8:2005 pp.335-356.

5970 What we owe Iraq: war and the ethics of nation building. Noah Feldman. Princeton NJ: Princeton University Press, 2004. 153p. *ISBN: 0691121796. Includes bibliographical references and index.*

5971 Why is there so much conflict in the Middle East? Mirjam E. Sørli; Nils Petter Gleditsch; Håvard Strand. **J. Confl. Resol.** 49:1 2:2005 pp.141-165.

5972 Why war? The cultural logic of Iraq, the Gulf War, and Suez. Philip Smith. Chicago IL: University of Chicago Press, 2005. x, 254p. *ISBN: 0226763889. Includes bibliographical references (p. 237-246) and index.*

5973 A year of opportunity in the Middle East. Aluf Benn. **Washington Q.** 28:2 Spring:2005 pp.81-94.

AUTHOR INDEX

INDEX DES AUTEURS

297

370

PLACE-NAME INDEX

INDEX DES ENDROITS

2163, 2167, 2176, 2179, 2220, 2223,
2253, 2263-2267, 2271-2277, 2279, 2281,
2283-2285, 2359, 2360, 2365, 2367, 2369,
2371, 2373, 2376, 2384, 2390, 2399,
2401, 2424, 2441, 2442, 2445, 2456,
2463, 2464, 2471, 2473, 2475, 2493,
2494, 2499, 2500, 2513, 2519, 2521,
2522, 2524, 2527, 2532, 2533, 2538,
2545, 2549, 2552, 2554, 2557, 2560,
2562, 2565, 2570, 2571, 2575, 2579,
2580, 2582, 2584, 2586, 2589, 2596,
2599, 2604, 2606, 2612, 2615, 2620,
2629, 2634, 2635, 2640, 2642-2644, 2651,
2654, 2658, 2661, 2666, 2670, 2673,
2677, 2681, 2685, 2697, 2698, 2715,
2730, 2737, 2738, 2740, 2746, 2761,
2763, 2764, 2767, 2771, 2772, 2780,
2782, 2783, 2787, 2790, 2793, 2795,
2796, 2798-2800, 2804, 2805, 2810-2812,
2818, 2825, 2833, 2839, 2842, 2847,
2848, 2854, 2862, 2864, 2886, 2892,
2896, 2897, 2899-2902, 2906, 2908, 2909,
2911, 2912, 2915, 2917, 2920, 2922-2928,
2953, 2961, 2964, 2969, 2973, 2981,
2997, 2998, 3003, 3004, 3009, 3012,
3021, 3023, 3024, 3031, 3032, 3041,
3044, 3049-3051, 3054, 3056, 3057, 3061,
3062, 3068, 3070, 3076, 3080, 3085,
3087, 3099, 3100, 3120, 3123, 3124,
3133, 3143, 3152, 3172, 3184, 3188,
3192, 3204, 3217, 3218, 3225, 3241,
3257, 3262, 3288, 3289, 3298, 3300, 3311,
3320, 3321, 3336, 3343, 3347, 3350,
3359, 3393, 3396, 3400, 3406, 3438,
3446-3448, 3451, 3452, 3457, 3485, 3487,
3490, 3493, 3507, 3520, 3524, 3535,
3540, 3561, 3573, 3575, 3580, 3588,
3590, 3591, 3618, 3624, 3625, 3627,
3636, 3637, 3639, 3647, 3669, 3672,
3689, 3691, 3706, 3711, 3721, 3725, 3739,
3747, 3758, 3771, 3773, 3789, 3797,
3824, 3830, 3842, 3845, 3847, 3848,
3851, 3856, 3862, 3867, 3869, 3872,
3873, 3880, 3881, 3890, 3896, 3897,
3902, 3904, 3907, 3908, 3912, 3914,
3915, 3924, 3927, 3930, 3936, 3938,
3945, 3952, 3962, 3979, 3987, 3990,
4009, 4023, 4025, 4028, 4039, 4047,
4049, 4059, 4082, 4109, 4114, 4129, 4148,
4150, 4158, 4159, 4166, 4168, 4190,
4194, 4198, 4257, 4382, 4405, 4460,
4468, 4490, 4497, 4639, 4649, 4659,
4670, 4671, 4683, 4693, 4696, 4699,
4726, 4726, 4730, 4748, 4754, 4765,
4781, 4801, 4802, 4815, 4822, 4830,
4831, 4839, 4844, 4859, 4860, 4865,
4871, 4882, 4886, 4894, 4898, 4900,
4903, 4911, 4918-4924, 4927-4929, 4931,
4932, 4935-4966, 4968-4975, 4977-4980,
4983-4991, 4993-4995, 4997, 5000, 5003,
5008, 5015, 5017, 5020, 5022, 5025,
5028, 5030, 5032, 5033, 5038, 5053,
5061, 5067, 5070, 5080, 5091-5095, 5102,
5108, 5110, 5111, 5115, 5116, 5118, 5126,
5132, 5133, 5135, 5136, 5145, 5148,
5149, 5151, 5155, 5156, 5160, 5165,
5171, 5172, 5178, 5179, 5184, 5185,
5187-5189, 5191, 5194, 5196, 5199, 5201,
5206, 5220-5225, 5228, 5229, 5233, 5235,
5236, 5238, 5241, 5245, 5257, 5262,
5263, 5265, 5266, 5268, 5276, 5277,
5279, 5280, 5290, 5291, 5301, 5303,
5305, 5307, 5310, 5318, 5319, 5322,
5323, 5329, 5333, 5334, 5338, 5343,
5345-5347, 5350, 5352-5354, 5360, 5362,
5363, 5371, 5374, 5375, 5378, 5382,
5385, 5394, 5397, 5398, 5403, 5404,
5408, 5409, 5411, 5413-5415, 5417-5419,
5421, 5425, 5428, 5429, 5432, 5435-5438,
5440, 5441, 5443-5446, 5448-5453, 5455,
5457-5459, 5462-5466, 5468-5472, 5474,
5477, 5481, 5482, 5485, 5487, 5494,
5498, 5500, 5506, 5509, 5511, 5513, 5517,
5521, 5522, 5526, 5534, 5537, 5539-5543,
5546, 5548, 5549, 5551, 5555, 5562,
5563, 5567, 5568, 5570-5573, 5578, 5581,
5582, 5584, 5586, 5588, 5590-5592, 5601,
5604, 5609, 5613, 5614, 5619-5622, 5625-
5628, 5633, 5638, 5642, 5643, 5651,
5652, 5657, 5660, 5667-5669, 5671, 5678,
5687, 5688, 5695, 5704, 5708, 5710,
5713, 5735-5737, 5740, 5744, 5745, 5748,
5749, 5755, 5765, 5769, 5773, 5797,
5802, 5822, 5823, 5831, 5836, 5854,
5866, 5868, 5889, 5890, 5912, 5914,
5915, 5924, 5927-5930, 5933, 5936, 5939,
5941, 5942, 5961, 5967, 5969
see also: Arizona, California, Connecticut,
Florida, Hawaii, Illinois, Louisiana,
Maine, Massachusetts, Michigan,
Nebraska, New Hampshire, New York,
North Carolina, Ohio, Oregon, South
Carolina, Texas, Utah, Washington,
Wisconsin, Wyoming
U.S.S.R. 49, 50, 286, 287, 389, 393, 474, 612,
861, 1613, 1636, 1639, 1737, 1769, 1817,
1835, 1841, 1844, 1918, 1986, 2093,
2253, 2297, 2320, 2484, 3927, 4671,
4845, 5052, 5055, 5156, 5231, 5527,
5704, 5868

SUBJECT INDEX

INDEX DES MATIERES EN ANGLAIS

428

524, 533, 582, 596, 609, 645, 1124, 1189,
1200, 1238, 1402, 1406, 1420, 1436,
1442, 1462, 1473, 1511, 1519, 1542, 1545,
1549, 1559, 1563, 1574, 1583, 1593,
1600, 1604, 1606, 1628, 1652, 1659,
1665, 1666, 1689, 1694, 1710, 1712,
1716, 1722, 1731, 1737, 1748, 1767,
1770, 1781, 1795-1798, 1808, 1809, 1822,
1824, 1827, 1855, 1879, 1881, 1892,
1918, 1933, 1945, 1987, 2039, 2085,
2092, 2094, 2149, 2200, 2201, 2243,
2287, 2294, 2306, 2378, 2385, 2394,
2396, 2401, 2457, 2496, 2505, 2619,
2620, 2625, 2639, 2650, 2750, 2852,
2868, 2885, 2901, 2912, 2930, 2953,
2993, 2996, 3035, 3154, 3171, 3172,
3185, 3200, 3222, 3241, 3245, 3257,
3263, 3289, 3314, 3398, 3430, 3445,
3483, 3605, 3677, 3757, 3773, 3843,
3857, 3875, 3877, 3882, 3884, 3889,
3890, 3893, 3910, 3918-3920, 3922, 3944-
3946, 3951, 3952, 3956, 3958, 3960,
3968, 3969, 3973, 3974, 3979, 3980,
3984, 3988, 3990-3992, 4001-4003, 4010,
4017, 4025, 4036, 4038, 4039, 4041,
4043, 4047, 4052, 4058-4060, 4064, 4067,
4073-4075, 4079, 4081, 4085-4087, 4089,
4091, 4100, 4103-4106, 4108, 4110, 4113,
4116, 4119, 4126, 4128, 4136, 4143, 4146,
4151, 4154-4158, 4161, 4162, 4164-4167,
4171, 4174, 4176, 4180, 4185, 4189,
4195, 4211, 4220, 4227, 4235, 4242, 4252,
4257, 4259, 4260, 4267, 4268, 4277,
4278, 4284, 4288, 4296, 4298, 4300,
4301, 4320, 4325, 4344-4347, 4351-4353,
4359-4361, 4363-4366, 4368, 4374, 4375,
4378, 4382, 4383, 4387, 4388, 4391,
4392, 4394, 4408, 4417, 4430, 4433,
4436, 4460, 4474, 4476, 4490, 4491,
4499, 4516, 4520, 4528, 4542, 4548,
4552, 4561, 4562, 4567, 4572, 4574,
4588, 4637, 4640-4642, 4645, 4652, 4657,
4659, 4667, 4673, 4676, 4678, 4680,
4683, 4686, 4691, 4693, 4697, 4699,
4702, 4707, 4708, 4710, 4711, 4713,
4719-4722, 4724, 4726, 4729-4733, 4735,
4736, 4739, 4740, 4742, 4744, 4746,
4752, 4753, 4755-4757, 4759, 4762, 4765,
4766, 4769, 4770, 4772, 4775-4777, 4779,
4780, 4782, 4785, 4786, 4792-4794, 4796-
4802, 4806, 4811, 4812, 4814, 4817-4821,
4825, 4827, 4832, 4837-4841, 4844, 4846,
4847, 4849, 4852, 4855, 4857, 4858,
4860, 4864, 4866, 4869, 4871, 4872,
4874-4877, 4879, 4881, 4882, 4885, 4886,

4890, 4893, 4895, 4896, 4898, 4900,
4902, 4903, 4905, 4909, 4913, 4918-4923,
4928, 4929, 4931, 4936, 4938, 4944,
4948-4950, 4954-4956, 4959-4962, 4966,
4967, 4969, 4970, 4972, 4976, 4979,
4981, 4982, 4984, 4986, 4988, 4991,
4992, 4994, 4998, 5003, 5005, 5008,
5010, 5011, 5013, 5015, 5022, 5023, 5029,
5030, 5033, 5035, 5037, 5038, 5040,
5041, 5044, 5048, 5050, 5051, 5053,
5054, 5056, 5061, 5065, 5066, 5069,
5072, 5073, 5076, 5080, 5087, 5088,
5090, 5091, 5093, 5094, 5097, 5098,
5101, 5102, 5105, 5113, 5118, 5120, 5121,
5127, 5134, 5142, 5145, 5151-5153, 5155,
5156, 5158, 5162, 5163, 5168, 5172,
5178-5181, 5186, 5192-5194, 5196, 5198-
5201, 5204, 5208, 5209, 5215, 5218,
5219, 5223, 5226, 5227, 5232, 5236,
5237, 5245, 5246, 5248, 5259, 5265-5267,
5277, 5283-5285, 5287, 5289, 5299, 5303,
5305, 5311, 5313, 5317, 5320, 5326, 5330,
5331, 5333, 5342, 5345, 5346, 5361,
5363, 5365-5367, 5370, 5372, 5373, 5376,
5381, 5390, 5392, 5406, 5408-5410, 5419,
5421, 5424, 5427, 5428, 5430-5435, 5438,
5442-5444, 5446, 5447, 5452, 5460-5462,
5465, 5469, 5471-5474, 5476-5479, 5483,
5485, 5487, 5491, 5493-5499, 5502, 5504-
5507, 5510, 5514, 5517-5519, 5521, 5522,
5525, 5526, 5529, 5533, 5539, 5541,
5543, 5546-5548, 5552, 5554, 5557-5560,
5563, 5565, 5566, 5572, 5574, 5578,
5579, 5583, 5589-5596, 5599-5603, 5606-
5608, 5610-5612, 5614, 5615, 5619-5624,
5626, 5630, 5631, 5633, 5636, 5645,
5646, 5649, 5652, 5655, 5656, 5660,
5665, 5667, 5669, 5671, 5672, 5674,
5676, 5683, 5684, 5687, 5690, 5692,
5693, 5696, 5697, 5701, 5702, 5704,
5710, 5711, 5718, 5719, 5727, 5733-5736,
5738, 5740, 5745, 5750, 5756, 5758,
5760, 5763, 5773, 5776, 5778, 5784,
5787, 5794, 5796-5798, 5801-5803, 5805,
5809-5812, 5814, 5817, 5818, 5820, 5822,
5824, 5827, 5830, 5831, 5833-5835, 5839,
5843, 5844, 5852, 5857, 5864, 5865,
5875, 5880, 5882, 5884-5886, 5889, 5895,
5898, 5900, 5908, 5910, 5912, 5914,
5923, 5932-5934, 5942, 5943, 5946, 5953,
5954, 5957, 5961, 5965, 5966, 5971
see also: East-West relations, History of
international relations, North-South
relations, Problems of international
relations, Transatlantic relations

460

SUBJECT INDEX IN FRENCH

INDEX DES MATIERES

2698, 2931, 3125, 3133, 3159, 3175,
3235, 3316-3318, 3318-3325, 3328, 3330-
3334, 3336-3341, 3353, 3361, 3364, 3365,
3377, 3382, 3387, 3388, 3405, 3407,
3416, 3418, 3421, 3426, 3428, 3433,
3437, 3439, 3443, 3469, 3476, 3489,
3491, 3492, 3495, 3497, 3499, 3500,
3502-3504, 3506, 3507, 3510, 3511, 3514,
3521, 3527, 3533, 3537, 3554, 3558,
3560, 3568, 3570, 3571, 3573, 3576-3580,
3582, 3583, 3585, 3587-3592, 3594, 3597-
3599, 3602, 3604, 3607-3609, 3611-3615,
3621, 3622, 3624, 3729, 3926, 4314,
4470, 4471, 4476, 4496, 4498-4500, 4504,
4512, 4570, 5436, 5513, 5660, 5761
voir aussi: Politique d'immigration,
Politique de bien-être, Politique de
l'éducation, Politique de la jeunesse,
Politique de la vieillesse, Politique des
droits de l'homme, Politique du logement
Politique unilatérale 1829, 1949, 3153, 3972,
4085, 4451, 4679, 4812, 4898, 4921,
4931, 4949, 4959, 4980, 4981, 4993,
5065, 5280, 5406, 5416, 5456, 5458,
5563, 5609, 5619, 5628
Politique urbaine 1207, 2557, 3524, 3529-
3532, 3536, 3537, 3548-3551, 3555, 3559,
3560, 3562
Politisation 429, 1620, 1796, 2945, 5258
Politologues 33, 36, 66, 230, 231, 236, 274,
368, 4217, 4760
Pollution 2177, 3808, 3834, 3860, 3861, 3870,
3876, 3897, 4050, 5280
Pollution agricole 3871
Pollution de l'air 3786, 3868, 3872
Pollution de l'eau 3835, 3862, 3871, 4006
Pollution des côtes 4025
Pollution des mers 3791, 4012, 4032
Pollution industrielle 3786, 3824, 3875
Pollution transfrontière 3863
Polygamie 786, 986
Polysémie 4217
Ponts 2130
Popularité 1095, 2581, 2750
Population 1130, 1394, 2547, 3302, 3354,
3496, 3514, 4458, 4666, 5359, 5603
Population indigène 473, 485, 518, 566, 584,
652, 800, 819, 1013, 1041, 1135, 1158,
1429, 1763, 1782, 1791, 1834, 2021,
2093, 2101, 2143, 2155, 2156, 2245,
2269, 2278, 2290, 2461, 2613, 2660,
3319, 3323, 3825, 3965, 3987, 3995,
4054, 4099, 4124, 5374, 5892
Population rurale 2076, 2608, 3208, 3211,
3606

Population urbaine 2557
Populisme 390, 1443, 1481, 1561, 1750, 1952,
1987, 2002, 2021, 2044, 2045, 2051,
2052, 2056-2058, 2063, 2071, 2095, 2403,
2515, 2801, 2884, 2888, 4215, 5280, 5660
Pornographie 743, 844, 1126
Porter, Anthony 749
Ports 1003, 4013
Positivisme 66, 213, 744, 750, 759, 772, 966,
1008, 1064, 3921, 4747, 4783, 4872,
5089, 5269
Possession 99, 179, 363, 387, 800, 809, 1934,
2219, 2538, 2766, 3051, 3138, 3195,
3207, 3255, 3350, 3644, 4011, 4652
Post-colonialisme 430, 1263, 1430, 1431,
1433, 1518, 1530, 1694, 2268, 3475,
4174, 5073, 5329, 5794
Post-fordisme 1988, 3362
Post-Guerre froide 501, 522, 1442, 1491,
1600, 1717, 1808, 1856, 1879, 1910,
1997, 2200, 2290, 2355, 3878, 3924,
4297, 4354, 4356, 4364, 4615, 4654,
4669, 4678, 4787, 4788, 4831, 4839,
4846, 4848, 4922, 4937, 4962, 4963,
4969, 4971, 4988, 5018, 5020, 5028,
5031, 5042, 5045, 5067, 5082, 5089, 5114,
5126, 5160, 5162, 5166, 5179, 5220,
5238, 5241, 5250, 5252, 5253, 5257,
5259, 5261, 5264-5266, 5279, 5289, 5301,
5323, 5407, 5432, 5489, 5490, 5500,
5503, 5522, 5532, 5546, 5590, 5612,
5616, 5620, 5627, 5667, 5735, 5754,
5787, 5870, 5878, 5884, 5892, 5954
Postmodernisme 43, 273, 379, 384, 581, 997,
1210, 1244, 2497, 3811, 4039, 4820, 4873,
4887, 5089
Post-structuralisme 107, 273, 2458
Potentiel de développement 2984, 2990
Pouvoir 1, 22, 40, 83, 86, 150, 177, 213, 355,
415, 497, 581, 595, 763, 901, 985, 1389,
1436, 1446, 1833, 1835, 1913, 2269,
2276, 2300, 2540, 2628, 2683,
2942, 3047, 3254, 3380, 3746, 4101,
4220, 4544, 4720, 4729, 4739, 4740,
4762, 4767, 4779, 4854, 4864, 4880,
4886, 4889, 4951, 5031, 5094, 5116, 5177,
5185, 5388, 5444, 5543, 5559, 5563,
5578, 5609, 5610, 5612, 5622, 5623,
5652, 5679, 5701, 5738, 5739, 5778,
5851, 5886, 5889, 5956
voir aussi: Rapports de pouvoirs,
Répartition des pouvoirs
Pouvoir de l'entreprise 2524
Pouvoir de négociation 970, 2893

573